P9-BAV-675

basic & clinical immunology

basic & clinical immunology

Edited by

H. Hugh Fudenberg, MD

Professor and Chairman
Department of Basic and Clinical Immunology and Microbiology
Medical University of South Carolina, Charleston

Daniel P. Stites, MD

Assistant Professor of Medicine and Laboratory Medicine
Director, Immunology Laboratory
University of California, San Francisco

Joseph L. Caldwell, MD

Assistant Research Immunologist
University of California, San Francisco and
Fort Miley Veterans Administration Hospital, San Francisco

J. Vivian Wells, MD

Senior Staff Specialist in Clinical Immunology
Kolling Institute of Medical Research
Royal North Shore Hospital, Sydney

Los Altos, California 94022 **LANGE Medical Publications**

International Standard Book Number: *0–87041–220–5*
Library of Congress Catalogue Card Number: *76–21030*

A Concise Medical Library for Practitioner and Student

Basic & Clinical Immunology $12.50

Current Medical Diagnosis & Treatment 1976 (annual revision). Edited by M.A. Krupp and M.J. Chatton. 1062 pp. 1976

Current Pediatric Diagnosis & Treatment, 4th ed. Edited by C.H. Kempe, H.K. Silver, and D. O'Brien. 1054 pp, *illus.* 1976

Current Surgical Diagnosis & Treatment, 2nd ed. Edited by J.E. Dunphy and L.W. Way. 1123 pp, *illus.* 1975

Review of Physiological Chemistry, 15th ed. H.A. Harper. 570 pp, *illus.* 1975

Review of Medical Physiology, 7th ed. W.F. Ganong. 587 pp, *illus.* 1975

Review of Medical Microbiology, 12th ed. E. Jawetz, J.L. Melnick, and E.A. Adelberg. 542 pp, *illus.* 1976

Review of Medical Pharmacology, 5th ed. F.H. Meyers, E. Jawetz, and A. Goldfien. 740 pp, *illus.* 1976

Basic Histology. L.C. Junqueira, J. Carneiro, and A.N. Contopoulos. 453 pp, *illus.* 1975

General Urology, 8th ed. D.R. Smith. 492 pp, *illus.* 1975

General Ophthalmology, 7th ed. D. Vaughan and T. Asbury. 334 pp, *illus.* 1974

Correlative Neuroanatomy & Functional Neurology, 16th ed. J.G. Chusid. 448 pp, *illus.* 1976

Principles of Clinical Electrocardiography, 9th ed. M.J. Goldman. 412 pp, *illus.* 1976

Handbook of Psychiatry, 3rd ed. Edited by P. Solomon and V.D. Patch. 706 pp. 1974

Handbook of Surgery, 5th ed. Edited by J.L. Wilson. 877 pp, *illus.* 1973

Handbook of Obstetrics & Gynecology, 5th ed. R.C. Benson. 770 pp, *illus.* 1974

Physician's Handbook, 18th ed. M.A. Krupp, N.J. Sweet, E. Jawetz, E.G. Biglieri, and R.L. Roe. 754 pp, *illus.* 1976

Handbook of Pediatrics, 11th ed. H.K. Silver, C.H. Kempe, and H.B. Bruyn. 705 pp, *illus.* 1975

Handbook of Poisoning: Diagnosis & Treatment, 8th ed. R.H. Dreisbach. 517 pp. 1974

Lithographed in USA

Table of Contents

26. Immunodeficiency Diseases (cont'd)

Ken Fye, MD, Haralampos Moutsopoulos, MD, & Norman Talal, MD

J. Vivian Wells, MD, & Curt A. Ries, MD

34. Infectious Diseases (cont'd)

35. Endocrine Diseases 554

Noel R. Rose, MD, PhD

36. Neurologic Diseases 569

Paul M. Hoffman, MD

37. Eye Diseases 579

G. Richard O'Connor, MD

38. Parasitic Diseases 587

Theodosia M. Welch, PhD

Preface

The past three decades have been marked by rapid advances in all medical and technologic fields pertaining to immunology, so that now this branch of medical science clearly ranks as a special discipline in its own right rather than a subdivision of microbiology or allergy.

With all this interest and activity has come inevitable expansion in the variety and bulk of the supporting literature. There are now a multitude of journals primarily devoted to immunologic topics, and almost all of the medical journals are soliciting or accepting articles on the immunologic features of disease, organ transplants, basic and applied research in immunology, tumor immunology, and immunotherapy.

There are many good books on the subject, and we hope we have not neglected to list any of them in the bibliography pages at the ends of the chapters. Observing that events seemed to have outrun our best competition, the editors decided that another book was justified. *Basic & Clinical Immunology* is already written as we prepare this Preface, and we note that the men and women who make the events happen are still not idle. The result is that as we examine page proof and prepare the Index we are already working on the Second Edition, due in 1978, and will continue to offer new editions biennially. *For these future publications, the reader's comments are urgently solicited.*

The book is divided into four sections, and the sequence of chapters is intended to be logical. The first section describes the fundamentals of immunochemistry and cellular immunology. The second section applies this knowledge to a discussion of immunobiology, an area that bridges basic and clinical immunology. The third section describes the immunologic laboratory tests that are available for evaluation of patients. The fourth section presents the immunologic aspects of a variety of human diseases.

The clinical chapters focus on primary immunologic diseases or on disorders with important immunopathologic characteristics. These discussions are not intended to serve as a manual of clinical treatment; where specific medications or drug dosages are mentioned, the physician should also consult more comprehensive medical texts.

It is hoped that this book will serve as a text for medical students, house officers, graduate students, practicing physicians, and others interested in learning more about the field. Immunologists from both basic and clinical disciplines should find it a comprehensive review.

The support provided by the staff of the publisher—particularly Drs Ransom and Lange—has been invaluable in this venture, and they have our deep appreciation. Much of the art work was done by the expert hand of Ms Laurel Schaubert, who has our thanks. Finally, we wish to express our gratitude to the contributing authors whose knowledge it is that represents whatever value this book may have; and to the institutions that have supported us during the long task of preparing this book.

—The Editors

San Francisco
September 1976

Section I

Basic Immunology

1 . . .
The Historical Background of Immunology

Pierre Grabar, DSc

Immunology is a relatively young branch of medical science. Many observations of importance to immunology were made by microbiologists around the turn of this century, usually in the course of active research in bacteriology and infectious diseases. For many years immunology was studied as part of microbiology, and progress in the field consisted mainly of application of what had been learned about immunologic phenomena to the problems of the diagnosis and control of bacterial infections. Some of the most important advances were made possible by the introduction of chemical technics in the elucidation of the nature of antigens and antibodies.

The explosive increase in fundamental information has made immunology an independent branch of science. *Zeitschrift für Immunitätsforschung* began publication in 1909 and the *Journal of Immunology* in 1916. There are now 25 national member societies in the International Union of Immunological Societies. This chapter will outline some of the contributions by pioneers in immunology which have led to the current state of the art. Where appropriate, reference is made to relevant chapters in this book.

The term *immune* derives from Latin *immunis,* ie, exempt from "charges" (taxes, expenses). However, for nearly a century the term immunity has denoted resistance to possible attack by an infectious agent. Resistance to second attacks of certain diseases had been observed even in ancient times. Attempts to protect against variola (smallpox) were made in ancient China and western Asia by inoculation (variolation) using vesicle fluid from persons with mild forms of smallpox, or by purposely seeking out contact with diseased individuals. Lady Mary Wortley Montagu (1721) introduced into England from Turkey the process of *variolation,* or inoculation with unmodified smallpox virus. It was quite dangerous since disease and death often resulted. Similarly, an ancient Greek king of Pontus, Mithridates VI, tried to protect himself against the effects of poison by administering small amounts of poisonous substances on multiple occasions—a procedure that came to be called *mithridatism.*

Pierre Grabar is a member of the National Academy of Medicine (France), Honorary Chief of Service at the Pasteur Institute (Paris), and Honorary Director of the Institute of Scientific Cancer Research of the National Cancer Research Society (Villejuif).

EARLY IMMUNOLOGY

The first effective—though still empirical—immunization was performed by Edward Jenner, an English physician (1749–1823), who observed that persons who got well after infection with cowpox were protected against smallpox. Jenner introduced vaccination with cowpox in 1796 as a means of protecting against smallpox. The term *vaccination* (L *vacca* cow) was introduced to replace the term variolation.

The scientific approach was not applied to the study of immunologic phenomena until almost a century later as a consequence of work on microbes by Louis Pasteur (1822–1895) and his collaborators. They investigated the possibility of protecting against infection by vaccinations with attenuated strains of microorganisms. Their first observation (1878–1880) was that a culture of *Pasteurella aviseptica* (then called chicken cholera) which had been left in the laboratory during vacation lost its virulence for chickens, and that animals inoculated with this culture were protected against the virulent strain. Pasteur concluded that this culture contained attenuated microbes and, to honor the work of Jenner (nearly 100 years before), extended the term vaccination to denote conferring immunity by injection of attenuated strains of organisms. The idea of using attenuated strains of microorganisms was confirmed by Pasteur when he studied vaccination against anthrax (1881). Research on the mechanisms of protective effects led Richet and Héricourt to the conclusion (1888) that the blood of an animal immunized with staphylococci conferred partial protection against subsequent inoculation with these microorganisms. The next year, Charrin and Roger observed that the serum of an animal immunized with *Pseudomonas aeruginosa* (then called *Bacterium aeruginosum* among other names) agglutinated a suspension of this microbe.

In 1889, Pfeiffer, a pupil of Koch, used cross-immunization of guinea pigs with 2 similar microbes

(*Vibrio cholerae* and *V metchnikovii*) to show that it was possible to distinguish them immunologically, since immunization against one did not protect against the other. The specificity of the protective effects of immunization had already been observed, but this example showed how extremely fine the specificity could be in some cases (Chapters 2 and 3).

"CELLULAR IMMUNITY" THEORY

In 1882 in Messina the Russian zoologist Elie Metchnikoff (1845–1916) studied the role of motile cells of a transparent starfish larva in protection against foreign intruders. He introduced a rose thorn into these larvae and noted that a few hours later the thorn was surrounded by motile cells. This experiment can be considered the starting point of cellular immunology. It had already been established by Koch and Neisser that bacteria can be found in leukocytes, but it was thought that this was the result of bacterial invasion of the leukocytes. Metchnikoff showed that the leukocytes had in fact engulfed the microorganisms. In 1883, Metchnikoff observed that Daphnia, a tiny transparent metazoan animal, can be killed by spores of the fungus *Monospora bicuspidata* and that in some instances these spores are attacked by blood cells and can be destroyed in these cells, thereby protecting the animal against the invaders. In 1884, he extended these observations to the leukocytes of rabbits and humans, using various bacteria. He noted that the engulfment of microorganisms by leukocytes, which he called *phagocytosis*, is greatly enhanced in animals recovering from an infection or after vaccination with a preparation of these microorganisms. He therefore concluded that phagocytosis was the main defense mechanism of an organism. He later showed the existence of 2 types of circulating cells capable of phagocytosis—the polymorphonuclear leukocytes and the macrophages—as well as certain fixed cells capable of phagocytosis, and proposed the general term *phagocytes* for all of these cells (Chapter 7).

The *cellular immunity* theory of Metchnikoff, who worked at the Pasteur Institute in Paris from 1887, was accepted with enthusiasm by some but was criticized by several other pathologists. The inflammatory reaction had been described by Celsus as early as the first century AD, but before Metchnikoff it had been studied only in mammals. Pathologists such as Virchow (1871) agreed that inflammation was due to changes in the connective tissue cells induced by various agents, particularly by abnormal deposits of metabolic products. Cohnheim (1873) and his collaborator Arnold (1875) considered inflammation to be a local vascular lesion due to a noxious agent which allowed blood cells to penetrate into tissues. Metchnikoff, who had observed the same accumulation of motile cells in lower animals with no circulatory vessels, asserted that diapedesis in higher animals was a process of active penetration of these cells through the walls of the vessels (1892). In his opinion, inflammation resulted in an enzymatic digestion process due to ingestion of the noxious agent by the motile phagocytes.

Metchnikoff's theory came under severe criticism somewhat later by those who observed immunity in the absence of cells. Fodor in 1886 was apparently the first to observe a direct action of an immune serum on microbes during the course of his studies on anthrax bacilli. Behring* and Kitasato (1890) demonstrated the neutralizing antitoxic activity of sera from animals immunized with diphtheria or tetanus toxin, which was considered the first proof of humoral immunity. In 1894, Calmette observed the same neutralizing activity of snake venom antiserum. The preparation of large amounts of diphtheria toxin antiserum in horses for human use started almost immediately in the Behring Institute in Marburg (Germany) in 1893; at the Pasteur Institute in Paris (Roux and Martin, 1894); in the USA; and also at the Lister Institute in London (1895). This was the beginning of serum therapy, a form of treatment which developed remarkably over the next 50 years.

"HUMORAL" THEORY

An important humoral defense mechanism described by Pfeiffer and Isaeff (1894) has come to be called the *Pfeiffer phenomenon.* Cholera vibrios injected into the peritoneum of previously immunized guinea pigs lose mobility, are clumped, are no longer stainable, and are later phagocytosed by leukocytes, but they are also lysed in the absence of cells.

A theory of immunity due to humoral factors provoked intense debate between Metchnikoff and the supporters of this new theory, mainly from the laboratory of Robert Koch (1843–1910). At the time of Pfeiffer's discovery, a young Belgian, Jules Bordet (1870–1961), was engaged in the study of agglutination reactions in Metchnikoff's laboratory at the Pasteur Institute. He became interested in the Pfeiffer phenomenon and in 1895 showed that both bacteriolysis and lysis of red cells (which he described in 1898) required 2 factors: one, which he called *sensitizer,* was thermostable and specific; the other, which he called *alexine,* was thermolabile and nonspecific. The factor designated alexine by Bordet came to be called *cytase* by Metchnikoff and *complement* by Ehrlich (Chapter 6). Bordet believed that his "alexine" possessed enzymatic activity and that it consisted of several components.

It is of interest that Bordet's studies of humoral factors were performed in Metchnikoff's laboratory and were in contradiction to the master's theories. Later, both theories gained general acceptance and it

*The particle von was added later to Behring's name after he became famous—about the time he received the Nobel Prize.

was established that humoral factors originated from lymphoid cells.

During this period, the term *antigen* was introduced to designate any substance (then mainly microbes or cells) capable of inducing a reaction against itself and the illogical term *antibody* (both being "anti-") to designate the factor present in the serum possessing this activity. At first, various special names were used to indicate each observed antibody activity, such as *agglutinins, precipitins, sensitizers,* and *opsonins* (Chapters 4 and 16). The first observation of agglutination is described above. The precipitin reaction was described later—in 1897 by Kraus with microbial culture supernates and the serum of immunized animals, and in 1899 by Tchistovitch with serum protein antigens and by Bordet with milk antigens and serum of animals injected with these fluids. The precipitin reaction was introduced by Wassermann and Uhlenhuth into forensic medicine for the identification of blood or meat.

Complement & Immunologic Diagnosis

The term *sensitizer* was used by Bordet to denote the thermostable serum component reacting in the lysis of bacteria. Ehrlich called it *amboceptor.* In 1900, Bordet established the reaction which he designated *alexine (complement) fixation or deviation,* using cholera vibrios, a corresponding immune serum, and complement (fresh normal serum). As a control of fixation of the latter, he added red cells sensitized by the homologous antiserum; the absence of hemolysis proved that the complement had been absorbed by the first reaction (Chapter 6). This system allowed him to make quantitative estimations. In 1901, he described (with Gengou) this general principle, which is still valid and useful and which was first applied by Wassermann, Neisser, and Bruck in 1906 in the diagnosis of syphilis using tissues from syphilitic patients as antigen. Various modifications of this method have been subsequently introduced, eg, the use of an alcoholic extract of guinea pig heart (reagin) as antigen (Landsteiner) and, particularly, the use of lipids (see Chapter 34).

The classical method of diagnosis of typhoid fever by salmonella agglutination reactions was established independently in 1896 by Widal in France and by Durham. The latter worked at that time in Germany in Gruber's laboratory, where agglutination reactions had been under study for several years. A method of diagnosing pneumonia proposed in 1902 by Neufeld consisted of observing the swelling *(Quellung)* of the capsules of pneumococci when the microorganisms were exposed to patient serum containing antipneumococcal antibodies (see Chapter 34).

Resolution of Conflicting Theories

In 1895, Denys and Leclef observed the fixation of antibodies present in an antistreptococcus serum by these organisms and called them *bacteriotropins.* Neufeld and Rimpau had also demonstrated similar in vitro fixation. In 1903, Wright and Douglas, after a careful study of Metchnikoff's observation that phagocytosis of microbes is facilitated by the serum of an immunized animal, used washed cells to demonstrate that the immune serum contained an active factor they called *opsonin.* They proposed the term *opsonization* for the activity, and this phenomenon acted as a "bridge" between the apparently contradictory humoral and cellular theories.

During this same period, Paul Ehrlich (1854–1915) studied the neutralization of toxins by immune serum, using the highly toxic vegetable poisons abrin and ricin, which could be extracted easily in sufficient quantity. These studies enabled him to establish a technic for the evaluation of the antitoxic activity of diphtheria antiserum (1897).

EHRLICH'S "SIDE-CHAIN" THEORY

Ehrlich was interested in the theoretic aspects of immunologic phenomena and in 1896 elaborated his *side-chain theory* to explain the appearance of antibodies in the circulation. He considered it an "enhancement" of a normal mechanism and suggested that cells capable of forming antibodies possessed on their surface membrane specific side chains which were receptors for antigens. He proposed that binding of antigen to the side chains provoked new synthesis of these side chains, which were liberated into serum as antibodies. He expressed the specificity of the reaction of antigens and antibodies as a "key [antigen] in a lock [antibody]" and thought that this reaction was of a chemical nature. During the next few years, he tried to substantiate his theory with various arguments, but the theory was not generally accepted. It was criticized by Bordet, who felt that the antigen-antibody reaction was of colloid nature; by Gruber; and particularly by Arrhenius and Madsen, who insisted on the reversibility of the reaction and on different proportions of reactants in specific precipitates. Nevertheless, Ehrlich's general theory, with modifications and additions, has been taken into consideration by many authors, and his hypothesis on the existence of specific receptors on immunocompetent cells has recently been completely vindicated (Chapter 8).

The transmission of antibodies across the placenta or through the mammary gland in milk from maternal mice to their offspring was observed by Ehrlich in 1892. In 1893, Klemperer demonstrated the existence of antibodies in the eggs of poultry and therefore transmission of antibodies to newborn chicks.

Isoantibody

In 1875, L. Landois published his monograph *Blood Transfusion.* He noted the effects of blood transfusions between members of different species and observed it was preferable to work within a single species. He also stated, however, that there were differences within a single species since a recipient's own cells could be hemolyzed by serum from a nonidentical donor of the same species.

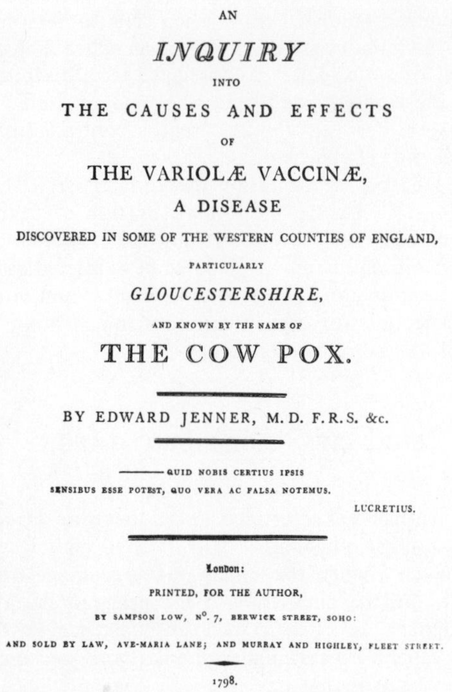

AN

INQUIRY

INTO

THE CAUSES AND EFFECTS

OF

THE VARIOLÆ VACCINÆ,

A DISEASE

DISCOVERED IN SOME OF THE WESTERN COUNTIES OF ENGLAND,

PARTICULARLY

GLOUCESTERSHIRE,

AND KNOWN BY THE NAME OF

THE COW POX.

BY EDWARD JENNER, M. D. F. R. S. &c.

——QUID NOBIS CERTIUS IPSIS
SENSIBUS ESSE POTEST, QUO VERA AC FALSA NOTEMUS.

LUCRETIUS.

London:

PRINTED, FOR THE AUTHOR,

BY SAMPSON LOW, N°. 7, BERWICK STREET, SOHO:

AND SOLD BY LAW, AVE-MARIA LANE; AND MURRAY AND HIGHLEY, FLEET STREET.

1798.

Figure 1–1. Face plate from first edition (1798) of Jenner's *Inquiry Into the Causes and Effects of . . . the Cow Pox.*

Figure 1–2. Louis Pasteur (1822–1895). (Courtesy of the Museum of the Pasteur Institute, Paris.)

Figure 1–3. Robert Koch (1843–1910). (Courtesy of the Museum of the Pasteur Institute, Paris.)

Figure 1–4. Elie Metchnikoff (1845–1916). (Courtesy of the Rare Book Library, the University of Texas Medical Branch, Galveston.)

Figure 1–5. Paul Ehrlich (1854–1915). (Courtesy of the Museum of the Pasteur Institute, Paris.)

Figure 1–6. Emil von Behring (1854–1917). (Courtesy of the Museum of the Pasteur Institute, Paris.)

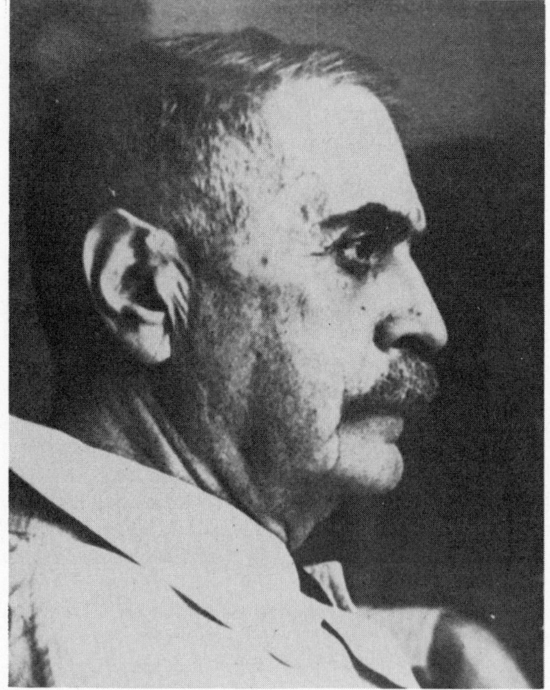

Figure 1–7. Karl Landsteiner (1868–1943). (Courtesy of the Museum of the Pasteur Institute, Paris.)

Figure 1–8. Jules Bordet (1870–1961). (Courtesy of the Museum of the Pasteur Institute, Paris.)

The term *isoantibody* or *isohemagglutinin* was introduced by Bordet, who observed in 1898 that the serum of rabbits injected with red cells of another species agglutinated the red cells whereas rabbit red cells injected into rabbits were not agglutinated. However, in 1902, Landsteiner used the agglutination reaction to demonstrate several different antigenic specificities of red cells in the same species—the blood groups A, B, and O in humans—which became the basis of blood transfusion (Chapter 28). Later, he also discovered Rh specificity, using rhesus monkey blood. The term isoantibody is no longer used for antibodies to antigenic determinants specific for other species. It is now used to indicate antibody in an individual to antigenic determinants in other genetically nonidentical members of the same species, eg, anti-A antibody (isohemagglutinin) in blood group B humans (see Chapter 28).

Ehrlich also observed that the plant toxins abrin and ricin agglutinate red cells. Landsteiner and Raubitchek in 1907 extended these observations, using particularly *Papilionaceae* (a family of beans). These plant-derived hemagglutinins were later termed *lectins* by W.C. Boyd.

Anaphylaxis

At the close of the 19th century, all of the immunologic phenomena observed to that time supported the view that they were defense mechanisms. Apparent contradictions were the observations of Landsteiner and, particularly, the discovery of anaphylaxis by Charles Richet and Portier in 1902. It had already been shown, particularly by Wassermann and von Dugern, that second challenge of a previously immunized organism with the same antigen increased the antibody activity in its serum. Thus, the fact of immunologic memory had to be explained. The discovery of Charles Richet and Portier was absolutely unexpected. They studied the toxic activity of the tentacles of Actinaria by injecting a glycerin extract into dogs. The first injection, in small doses, had no direct observable effect, and they thought the animals were protected. But a second injection resulted in shock—often lethal for the animals. They proposed the term *anaphylaxis* for this phenomenon (Chapters 19 and 29). The next year, Arthus described what is now called the *Arthus phenomenon,* ie, the local necrotic lesion produced by injecting antigen into a previously immunized animal (Chapter 20). This reaction is specific, whereas an analogous but nonspecific reaction was described by Sanarelli and by Shwartzman many years later—the *Shwartzman phenomenon.*

At the beginning of the 20th century, von Pirquet, working in Vienna, studied *serum sickness,* the delayed reaction that occurred following a second injection of a heterologous antistreptococcus serum, and observed that this *hypersensitivity reaction* (von Pirquet and Schick, 1905) sometimes appeared rapidly (Chapter 20). He suggested that this reaction had a direct connection with the presence in the animal of antibodies to the injected serum. In the course of his research on tuberculosis, he observed that a cutaneous reaction appeared more rapidly after a second injection than after the first. He developed the scratch test for tuberculin sensitivity, and in 1906 he proposed the term *allergy* for modified immune reactivity. Since then, this term has been generalized to denote all sensitization phenomena, whereas the better and earlier term *generalized anaphylaxis* is used to denote *anaphylactic shock.*

Another series of investigations on anaphylactic reactions was initiated by Theobald Smith and Otto (1906) and, more successfully, by Rosenau and Anderson in Washington (1909). These investigations showed (1) that the secondary reaction provoked in guinea pigs by the injection of diphtheria toxin and antiserum (this mixture was used at that time for vaccination) was due not to the toxin but rather to antibodies against the antiserum; (2) that the sensitizing time was about 10 days; and (3) that passive sensitization with the serum of a sensitized animal was sufficient to provoke a secondary reaction to the antigen. It was thought that the relatively long time required for sensitization to develop was due to fixation of antibodies to cells. Schultz had demonstrated in 1910 that a contractile reaction occurs in vitro following contact of the antigen with a strip of intestine of a previously sensitized animal. This reaction was also studied by H. Dale with uterine smooth muscle and is now called the *Schultz-Dale reaction* (Chapter 19).

Hay fever was a recognized disease entity for a long time, but until the beginning of this century it was believed to be due to toxic substances in pollen. Experimental "desensitization" was attempted by inoculation of small amounts of pollen to neutralize the supposed toxin (Besredka, 1907; Noon and J. Freeman, 1911). Shortly thereafter, Wolff-Eisner suggested that hay fever might be a hypersensitivity reaction, a concept proved correct in 1921 by Prausnitz and Küstner with different antigens. The term Prausnitz-Küstner (PK) reaction is therefore used to denote the test for passive transfer of reactivity to an allergen (Chapter 19). A similar phenomenon in experimental animals, the *passive cutaneous anaphylaxis (PCA) reaction,* which allows a semiquantitative estimation of antibodies, was described much later—in 1949—by Biozzi, Mene, and Ovary (Chapter 19).

The role of histamine and related substances in inflammatory and anaphylactic reactions is discussed in Chapters 19 and 29, but it is appropriate to cite a few of the more important contributions. Dale and Laidlaw in 1910 showed the similarities between the reactions provoked by histamine and those associated with anaphylaxis. Lewis (1927) explained the "triple response" in skin reactions, and Riley and West (1953) discovered that histamine is present in mast cells and is released by the breakdown of these cells. These observations opened a new field of research into inflammatory and anaphylactic reactions.

ANTITISSUE IMMUNE SERA

Early efforts in the field of transplantation immunology included the production of immune sera against tissue components (Lindemann) and the discovery of tissue and species specificity of antigens. In 1902, Metchnikoff and Besredka prepared antileukocyte antisera and observed that such antisera possessed cytotoxic activity against leukocytes. They also noted that injection of small amounts of antisera induced proliferation of these cells in the injected animal. Metchnikoff envisaged the use of such antisera to enhance the resistance of the organism against infections. Bogomoletz prepared antisera against all lymphoid tissues. The cytotoxic effect of such antisera has been the starting point for the recent use of "antilymphocyte antisera" for inhibition of graft rejection (Woodruff, Starzl). In either case, variable results are obtained because of the multiplicity of antigens on the injected cells and the consequent variety of antibody specificities in the resultant antisera.

It is interesting that nearly all the investigations of that period were performed on mammals. However, Widal and Secard observed that antibodies appear in cold-blooded animals only above certain minimum temperatures, generally 30 C. Some research was also done on invertebrates, but the results were quite variable (Chapter 11). The observed hemagglutinating activity in immunized invertebrates was destroyed at 56 C (Cantacuzene, 1912) and has never been conclusively shown to be due to antibody.

The first 3 decades–until 1910–of active development of immunology as a separate branch of medical science witnessed the discovery and description of most of the fundamental immunologic phenomena, although the mechanisms underlying those phenomena were not elucidated. Although Ehrlich postulated that the immune phenomena must represent an "enhancement" of normal mechanisms, they were considered by most immunologists of the time to be part of the organism's "defense apparatus." This opinion gained force from the general assumption that the organism will react only against foreign ("not self") constituents, and Ehrlich's phrase *horror autotoxicus* emphasized his view that the organism would not react against "self" components, though he admitted the possibility of an autoreaction when the "normal regulatory mechanisms" were disturbed (Chapter 13). Actually, at that time, Metalnikoff, in Metchnikoff's laboratory, had demonstrated autosensitization in guinea pigs to their own spermatozoa, and we know now that autoantibodies exist in small amounts even in "normal" sera (see below).

Development of Vaccines

The next 3 decades–until 1940–were concerned mainly with applications and development of knowledge about immunologic phenomena, particularly in the preparation of immune sera, diagnostic reagents for clinical study of infectious disease, and vaccination programs. A few examples are Haffkine's experiments with cholera vaccination in India in 1892, using himself and his collaborators as control subjects; the use of an attenuated strain of *Mycobacterium tuberculosis,* BCG (bacille Calmette-Guérin, 1908–1921); and vaccination against bacterial toxins using detoxified preparations. Several workers tried to develop a nontoxic but still immunogenic preparation by treating bacterial toxins with various chemicals. Formol was used by Eisler and Löwenstein (1915) for tetanus toxin and by Glenny (1921) for diphtheria toxin, but their preparations were not completely detoxified. Ramon in 1924 developed a method called optimal flocculation for the quantitative measurement of toxins and antitoxins which resulted in a satisfactory method of detoxification. He obtained preparations which he called *anatoxins,* now generally called *toxoids,* as proposed by Ehrlich years before.

In 1916, LeMoignic and Pinoy introduced lipid (as adjuvant) vaccines, and in 1935 Ramon obtained some good results with various other adjuvants to increase the production of antitoxins in horses, although these produced lesions at the site of the injection. These were precursors of the current main adjuvant, Freund's adjuvant (1947), used to augment immune responses (Chapter 22).

IMMUNOCHEMISTRY

Important progress was made during the second period of immunologic studies when the principles of chemistry were applied to immunologic research. Although Ehrlich had suggested years earlier that immunologic reactions must have a chemical basis and although Arrhenius, studying antigen-antibody reactions, introduced the term immunochemistry in 1904, the applications of chemical theory and methodology truly began only during this second period.

Among the most productive applications of chemistry to immunology were the studies of Landsteiner and his collaborators (Prasek, Lampl, van der Scheer, Chase). Space does not permit discussion of their many achievements, and only one will be mentioned. In 1903, Obermayer and Pick suggested that antigens possessed the properties of immunogenicity and a capacity to react with antibodies. Subsequently, Landsteiner and his co-workers, as well as others, observed that these properties could be altered by chemical treatment of antigens (Chapter 3). This initiated in 1914 Landsteiner's studies with artificial conjugated antigens. Various chemical groupings were attached to proteins, and the specificity of these groupings was demonstrated in serologic reactions. In 1921, Landsteiner coined the term *haptens* for those specific groupings which by themselves were incapable of provoking the formation of antibodies but were still responsible for specific reaction with antibodies (Chapter 3). Similar studies were later performed by

Haurowitz and Breinl (1931), who introduced groupings containing arsonate which facilitated their recognition. Landsteiner's book, *The Specificity of Serological Reactions,* published in German in 1933 and in English in 1936, had a great influence on further research, as did Wells's book published in French on *The Chemical Aspects of Immunity* (1927) and Marrack's text *The Chemistry of Antigens and Antibodies* (1935).

IMMUNOLOGIC TOLERANCE

An important observation made by Felton (1942) showed that if mice are injected with very small amounts of pneumococcal polysaccharide they are protected against infection by the corresponding microbe, but if the injection is made with large quantities of polysaccharide the mice can be infected. This *Felton phenomenon* was also called immunologic unresponsiveness and is now known as *immunologic tolerance.* The multiple mechanisms involved in this phenomenon are discussed in Chapter 13.

Identification of Immunoglobulins

Felton was probably also the first to obtain purified preparations of antibodies using horse antisera to pneumococci and precipitating the euglobulin fraction rich in antibodies. The practical isolation of pure antibodies from such sera was achieved by Heidelberger and Kendall (1936) by dissociation of specific precipitates with concentrated salt reagents. As a result of studies by Heidelberger and Pedersen with Svedberg's ultracentrifuge (1937) and by Tiselius and Kabat with electrophoresis in liquid media (1938), it became clear that antibodies belong to that globulin fraction of the serum proteins possessing slow mobility, at that time designated γ-globulins (Chapter 2). In parallel with the development of immunochemistry, studies on the cellular aspects of immunology had been performed mainly by hematologists and pathologists who confirmed the role of white blood cells in the formation of antibodies. Pfeiffer and Marx found that antibodies, which they called sensitizers or fixators, appear earlier in the spleen, lymph nodes, and bone marrow than in the blood. The lymphatic system, which came to be called the reticuloendothelial system, was progressively studied and various cells were described (Chapter 7).

This period of development of the field of immunology also witnessed the isolation of the components of complement, studies on their respective activities, and identification of several specific subgroups among human and animal red cells.

RECENT PERIOD OF IMMUNOLOGY

The period of development of the field of immunology beginning just before World War II was characterized by the emergence of an enormous amount of new data. Most of it comprises the bulk of the individual chapters in this text. A few subjects of fundamental importance will be briefly mentioned here.

Owen observed in 1945 that bovine dizygotic twins possess double serologic specificities. Medawar and his collaborators in London (1935) performed careful experiments on mammals, and Hasek performed similar experiments in Prague using coupled eggs of different species. Their studies on transplantation formed the basis for subsequent research on acquired immunologic tolerance and are of fundamental importance for the problem of tissue grafting (Chapters 13 and 15).

In 1948, Astrid Fagraeus showed that it is through the development of plasma cells (described in 1890 by Cajal) that the actual synthesis of antibodies takes place (Chapter 9). In 1953, Grabar and Williams demonstrated that immunoglobulins are heterogeneous and detected the existence of **IgA** (first called immunoglobulin X and then β_{2A}). The nomenclature of the immunoglobulins was established, and the amino acid sequences of many of them were studied. This rapid progress is due particularly to the work of Porter, Edelman, Hilschmann, Putnam, and others, and the relationships between these structures and genetic information are being studied in many laboratories (Chapter 2).

The central role of the thymus in immunologic processes was first clearly established by experimental studies performed by J.F.A.P. Miller in London in 1961–1962. His studies were performed with neonatal thymectomy in mice. At that time other groups were studying the role of the thymus, including R.A. Good and his group in Minnesota and N.L. Warner in Melbourne. Their initial observations and studies opened up the whole field of the cellular basis for cooperation between cells responsible for cellular and humoral immunity.

The last few decades have seen the emergence of new branches of immunology:

(1) **Immunopathology** has made important contributions to our fund of knowledge and has even offered some therapeutic approaches. Studies of pathologic processes have in many ways helped us to understand normal ones, eg, absence of plasma cells in hypogammaglobulinemic children (see Chapter 26).

(2) **Immunogenetics** has included analysis of amino acid sequences in immunoglobulins (Chapter 2), histocompatibility antigens (Chapter 15), and genetic markers on immunoglobulins (Chapter 5). This contributes to our understanding of the transmission of genetic information and the position on chromosomes of loci controlling histocompatibility antigens.

(3) **Tumor immunology** and the immunochemical analysis of components of various human and animal tumors and leukemic cells have already clarified several important features (Chapter 21). These include the absence of various normal components on tumor cells; the appearance of antigens present normally in fetal life or in tissues other than the one in which the tumor

has developed; and the existence in some tumors of "neoantigens." The latter would imply new genetic information has been acquired by the cells and might depend on introduction of part of a viral genome into the cell. The intensive studies will result, it is hoped, in effective forms of immunotherapy of cancers, including leukemia (Chapters 21 and 28).

(4) Transplantation immunology (Chapter 15) emerged from work on acquired tolerance (mentioned above). Since rejection of grafts is an immunologic phenomenon dependent mainly on the thymus, chemical substances and "antithymocyte" immune sera are being used as immunosuppressive agents. Important information has been obtained in man and in mice from studies on histocompatibility antigens. International centers for human histocompatibility typing have been created to establish compatibility between tissues to be grafted (usually kidney) and the recipient. More recently, provocative associations have emerged between certain HLA phenotypes and susceptibility or resistance to disease, particularly immunologic disease.

(5) Immunologic disorders: The study of immune disorders is emerging as a separate discipline concerned both with "broad-spectrum" and "antigen-selective" immunodeficiency and methods of immunotherapy for these disorders, eg, transfer factor, both broad-spectrum and antigen-selective.

Development of Technics & Instruments

The development of new scientific information is historically related to methodologic advances such as the development of new technics or instruments. The perfection of the microscope by Leeuwenhoek was important for Pasteur's work in bacteriology and Metchnikoff's studies on phagocytosis. The introduction of chemical methods played a major role in Landsteiner's fundamental studies on immunologic specificity. Later, the quantitative precipitation method described by Heidelberger and Kendall (1935) was the most important factor in the development of modern immunochemistry. The establishment of physical or physicochemical methods such as ultracentrifugation (Svedberg and Pedersen, 1939), ultrafiltration through membranes of graded pore sizes (Elford, Grabar, 1930–1935), electrophoresis in liquid medium (Tiselius, 1937), filtration through absorption columns, particularly through Sephadex and similar materials (Porath, 1950), electron microscopy, radioactive labeling, immunofluorescence, and many other advances have made possible the discovery of entire new fields of study (see Chapters 24 and 25).

Immunologic Methods

Among the purely immunologic methods still in original or modified form we may mention complement fixation (Bordet and Gengou, 1901), passive hemagglutination (Boyden 1951), rosette formation (Biozzi and Zaalberg, 1964), plaque formation by immunocompetent cells in agar gel (Jerne, Henry, and Nordin, 1963), and the use of antibodies or antigens labeled by fluorescent compounds (Coons, 1942) or by enzymes (Avrameas and Uriel, 1966). Important contributions were made possible by the use of precipitation in gelled media (Chapters 4 and 24). At the beginning of the century, Bechold facilitated the observation of ring tests (properly called disk tests and first used by Ascoli in the diagnosis of anthrax) by performing them in gels. Oudin (1946–1948) demonstrated later that each antigen-antibody complex formed an independent precipitation band and perfected the simple diffusion method which allows quantitative measurement. The double diffusion method in gels, developed independently by Ouchterlony and by Elek (1948), is particularly useful for qualitative comparisons of antigens and antibodies; immunoelectrophoretic analysis in gels (Grabar and Williams, 1952–1953) and its quantitative modification (Laurell, 1967) have made large contributions to immunology and other branches of science (see Chapter 24).

Other technical advances that have made possible breakthroughs in the investigation of immunologic phenomena include the development of cell or tissue cultures; technics for separation of various populations of cells, including the use of monospecific antisera, purified antibody solutions, or specific immunoabsorbents; and the advantage of working with pure inbred strains of animals raised under germ-free or at least pathogen-free conditions. Various modifications and improvements of these different methods will be presented in appropriate chapters of this book.

FUTURE DEVELOPMENT

Even this brief review of the origins of immunology would lack perspective if we did not urge the reader to consider how much there is yet to be done. Although a considerable body of knowledge has accumulated, many fundamental mechanisms—eg, the induction of antibody formation and the role of immunocompetent cells in cellular immunity—remain to be clarified. Many of the theories proposed to account for these phenomena contain some assumptions or postulates which, in the author's opinion, are either insufficient or superfluous. Since the earliest days of the study of immunologic phenomena, 2 fundamental postulates have persisted: (1) Immunologic phenomena are considered "defense mechanisms." This postulate is historically quite logical because the first observations were of this kind. (2) Under normal conditions, the organism will not react against its own constituents—a concept to which Ehrlich, as we have already noted, applied the term horror autotoxicus.

Two main theories have been proposed to explain the formation of antibodies and their great variability of multiplicity: (1) The *information theory* holds that it is the antigen which dictates the specific structure of the antibody (Haurowitz and Breinl, 1930). Since it has been shown that antibodies differ in their amino acid sequences, this theory as originally stated has been abandoned. However, other hypotheses have been brought forward to explain the specific action of antigens (Haurowitz, 1970). (2) The *genetic theory* holds that the information for synthesis of all possible configurations of antibodies exists in the genome and that specific receptors on immunocompetent cells are normally present, as foreseen by Ehrlich. The existence of immunoglobulins on the surfaces of immunocompetent cells has been proved, but this does not mean that all possible configurations for any possible antigenic specificity are really present under normal conditions. It seems difficult to conceive that the total number of immunocompetent cells would be sufficient to account for great numbers of possible antigenic structures. Nevertheless, it would be difficult to imagine a mechanism that would not depend on genetic information.

The cellular aspects of the same problem of antibody formation as envisaged by Jerne (1955) and Burnet (1957–1959) are encompassed in the *clonal selection theory*. The 2 fundamental postulates mentioned above—ie, the "defense mechanism" concept and the prohibition against reaction to "self" constituents—form the basis of this theory. To explain self-recognition and tolerance for endogenous constituents, it has been suggested that cells capable of reacting against self constituents, which must exist in the developing organism, are eliminated or destroyed as *forbidden clones*. On the other hand, if autoantibodies appear, this can only be an abnormal event, as already asserted by Ehrlich, and must be a consequence of *somatic mutations* of certain cells (Burnet, 1965). Several arguments have been advanced both in support of and in opposition to this theory. The idea that all immunologic phenomena are necessarily a part of the organism's defense apparatus has been abandoned by many authors, whereas somatic mutations and *deletion mechanisms* for certain cells are still often taken into consideration. Because it is the author's opinion that both postulates are unnecessary, he proposes a simpler explanation. Somatic mutations, being a random phenomenon, may modify some items of genetic information, but this cannot explain the appearance of specific autoantibodies. It is now established that certain autoantibodies are present in normal sera. They may also appear in sera from patients with various diseases and can be induced experimentally in animals. At the Microbiology Congress in Rome in 1953, the author suggested that autoantibodies should be regarded as normal physiologic agents which, by their opsonizing activity, serve to help "clean up" the products of dead cells when large numbers of them have been destroyed. Normally, these products can be eliminated after their degradation by the existing autolytic enzymes, and the corresponding immunocompetent cells are therefore not activated to produce antibodies. In cases of massive destruction due to any cause, these enzymes are inhibited by substrate excess, and cells capable of synthesizing autoantibodies, which persist in the normal organism, are induced to form autoantibodies. Thus, for the author, "self-recognition" is at least partially enzymatic, and the formation of antibodies would be a general physiologic mechanism for the elimination of "self" as well as of "not-self" substances. This mechanism would act as a defense system in some cases by eliminating invaders that could not be completely destroyed by the organism's existing enzyme system. The future will show if this line of reasoning explains correctly this fundamental immunologic mechanism.

• • •

CONCLUSION

Immunology started with the work of a few talented scientists using simple methods and instruments and has grown rapidly during the last decades. Thousands of publications, the creation of independent immunology societies with thousands of members in most of the developed countries, the appearance of many special journals or reviews, and the organization of independent International Congresses (the first in Washington in 1971 and the second in Brighton in 1974) are characteristic of this period. Immunology now ranks as an independent branch of science, and we can hope with some justification that the fundamental problems still unsolved will soon yield to the intense investigative efforts now going forward and that new areas of basic and clinical immunology meriting investigation will continue to emerge.

A SHORT CHRONOLOGY OF IMPORTANT ACHIEVEMENTS IN IMMUNOLOGY

1798	Edward Jenner *Cowpox vaccination.*
1880	Louis Pasteur *Attenuated vaccines.*
1883	Elie I.I. Metchnikoff *Phagocytosis, cellular defense theory.*
1888	Pierre P.E. Roux and A.E.J. Yersin *Bacterial toxins.*
1890	Emil A. von Behring and Shibasaburo Kitasato *Antitoxins, foundation of serotherapy.*
1893	Waldemar M.W. Haffkine *First massive vaccinations in India.*
1894	Richard F.J. Pfeiffer and Vasily I. Isaeff *Immunologic lysis of microbes; bacteriolysis.*
1894	Jules J.B.V. Bordet *Complement and antibody activities in bacteriolysis.*
1896	Herbert E. Durham and Max von Gruber *Specific agglutination.*
1896	Georges F.I. Widal and Arthur Sicard *Test for the diagnosis of typhoid (Widal test) on the basis of the Gruber-Durham reaction.*
1900	Karl Landsteiner *A, B, O blood groups.*

1900 Jules J.B.V. Bordet and Octave Gengou
Complement fixation reaction.

1901 Max Neisser and R. Lubowski
Complement deviation. (This was noted independently by Friedrich Wechsberg in the same year and is known as Neisser-Wechsberg phenomenon.)

1902 Charles R. Richet and Paul J. Portier
Anaphylaxis.

1903 Nicholas M. Arthus
Specific necrotic lesions; Arthus phenomenon.

1903 Almroth E. Wright and Stewart R. Douglas
Opsonization reactions.

1905 Clemens P. von Pirquet* and Bela Schick
Serum sickness.

1906 Clemens P. von Pirquet
Introduced term allergie.

1910 Henry H. Dale and George Barger
Isolated histamine from ergot (and from animal intestinal mucosa in 1911).

1910 Henry H. Dale and Patrick Playfair Laidlaw
Demonstrated allergic contraction of muscle by histamine.

1910 William Henry Schultz
Schultz-Dale test for anaphylaxis.

1910 [Francis] Peyton Rous
Experimental viral cancer immunology.

1921 Albert L.C. Calmette and Camille Guérin
BCG vaccination. (The vaccine was developed beginning in 1906; it was used experimentally on newborns from 1921 to 1924 and then in mass vaccinations.)

1921 Carl W. Prausnitz and Heinz Küstner
Cutaneous reactions.

1923 Gaston Ramon
Diphtheria toxin modified with formaldehyde to produce "anatoxin" (toxoid).

1928 Gregory Shwartzman
Necrotic reactions; Shwartzman phenomenon.

1930 Friedrich Breinl and Felix Haurowitz
Template theory of antibody formation.

1935–36 Michael Heidelberger and Forrest E. Kendall
Pure antibodies; quantitative precipitin reactions.

1938 Arne Wilhelm Tiselius and Elvin A. Kabat
Demonstrated that antibodies are γ-globulins.

1942 Albert H. Coons and others
Fluorescein labeling; immunofluorescence.

1942 Jules T. Freund
Adjuvant.

1942 Lloyd D. Felton
Immunologic unresponsiveness.

1942 Karl Landsteiner and Merrill W. Chase
Cellular transfer of sensitivity in guinea pigs. (The investigators had been studying delayed hypersensitivity since the 1930s.)

*Name also appears as Clemens Peter Pirquet von Cesenatico, but common usage is Clemens von Pirquet.

1944 Peter Brian Medawar and Frank Macfarlane Burnet
Theory of acquired immunologic tolerance.

1945 Robin R.A. Coombs, R.R. Race, and A.E. Mourant
Antiglobulin test for incomplete Rh antibodies.

1946 Jacques Oudin
Precipitin reaction in gels.

1948 Örjan Ouchterlony and Stephen D. Elek
Double diffusion (of antigens and antibodies) in gels.

1948 Astrid E. Fagraeus
Antibodies formed in plasma cells.

1948–49 Elvin A. Kabat, W.T.J. Morgan, W.M. Watkins, and others
Structure of ABO blood group antigens.

1952 Ogdon Carr Bruton
Agammaglobulinemia described in humans.

1952 James F. Riley and Geoffry B. West
Histamine in mast cells.

1953 Pierre Grabar and C.A. Williams
Immunoelectrophoretic analysis.

1955–57 Niels K. Jerne and Frank Macfarlane Burnet
Clonal selection theory; discovery of human immunodeficiencies.

1956 Ernest Witebsky and Noel R. Rose
Induction of autoimmunity in animals.

1957 H. Hugh Fudenberg and Henry G. Kunkel
Macroglobulins with antibody activity (eg, cold agglutinins, rheumatoid factor).

1959 R.R. Porter, Gerald M. Edelman, and Alfred Nisonoff
Structure and formation of antibody molecules.

Bloomfield AL: *Bibliography of Internal Medicine: Communicable Diseases.* Univ of Chicago Press, 1958.

Dictionary of Scientific Biography. (Published under the auspices of the American Council of Learned Societies). Scribner's: from 1970.

Foster WD: *History of Medical Bacteriology and Immunology.* Heinemann, 1970.

Humphrey JH, White RG: *Immunology for Students of Medicine,* 2nd ed. Davis, 1964.

Kelly EC: *Encyclopedia of Medical Sources.* Williams & Wilkins, 1948.

Morton LT: *Medical Bibliography: An Annotated Checklist of Texts Illustrating the History of Medicine,* 3rd ed. Lippincott, 1970.

Parish HJ: *History of Immunization.* Livingstone, 1965.

Schmidt JE: *Medical Discoveries: Who and When.* Thomas, 1959.

Who's Who in Science in Europe, 2nd ed. 4 vols. Hodgson, 1972.

Wilson D: *Science of Self: A Report of the New Immunology.* Longman, 1971.

World Who's Who in Science: A Biographical Dictionary of Notable Scientists From Antiquity to the Present. Marquis-Who's Who, 1968.

• • •

References

Achalme P: *L'Immunité dans les Maladies Infectieuses.* Rueff (Paris), 1894.

Besredka A: *Les Immunités Locales.* Masson, 1937.

Bordet J: *Traité de L'Immunité dans les Maladies Infectieuses,* 2nd ed. Masson, 1937.

Burnet FM, Fenner F: *The Production of Antibodies.* Macmillan (Melbourne), 1949.

Delaunay A: *L'Immunologie.* Presse Universitaire (Paris), 1969.

Ehrlich P: *Gesammelte Arbeiten zur Immunitätsforschung.* Hilschwald (Berlin), 1904.

Foster WD: *A History of Medical Bacteriology and Immunology.* Heinemann, 1970.

Landsteiner K: *The Specificity of Serological Reactions.* Thomas, 1936.

Metchnikoff E: *L'Immunité dans les Maladies Infectieuses.* Masson, 1901.

Parish HJ: *A History of Immunization.* Livingstone, 1965.

Pirquet C von, Schick B: *Die Serumkrankheit.* Leipzig, 1905.

Rocha e Silva M, Leme JG: *Chemical Mediators in the Acute Inflammatory Reaction.* Pergamon, 1972.

Wells HG: *The Chemical Aspects of Immunity.* New York, 1925.

Wilson GS: *The Hazards of Immunizations.* Athlone Press, 1967.

Wilson GS, Miles AA (editors): *Topley and Wilson's Principles of Bacteriology and Immunity,* 3rd ed. Arnold, 1946.

2 . . .
The Structure of Immunoglobulins

An-Chuan Wang, PhD

The immune system is made up of 2 major components: *cellular immunity* and *humoral immunity.* These components develop along separate but interrelated pathways of differentiation (see Chapter 11) involving several types of cells and tissues (see Chapter 7). The lymphocyte is the central cell in immunology. Studies of various markers on the membrane of lymphocytes (see Chapter 7) and their functional activities (see Chapter 10) have permitted identification of 2 major populations of lymphocytes, designated *T lymphocytes* and *B lymphocytes.* While they represent separate populations, recent studies have demonstrated several areas of cooperation between T lymphocytes and B lymphocytes (see Chapter 8).

T lymphocytes (T cells) are so named because they are thymus-derived or thymus-influenced during their development (see Chapter 7). T cells are responsible for various functions of cellular immunity, including delayed skin reactivity (see Chapter 10), defense against certain microorganisms such as fungi, intracellular bacterial pathogens, poxviruses, etc (see Chapter 17), immunologic rejection of allografts (see Chapter 15), and antitumor immunity (see Chapter 21).

B lymphocytes (B cells) are so named because they develop in the bursa of Fabricius in birds and in bone marrow in some species, perhaps including man (see Chapter 7). B cells and their progeny, plasma cells, are responsible for the functions of humoral immunity. The latter is expressed through the production of circulating plasma proteins termed *antibodies* or *immunoglobulins.*

The immunoglobulins are the protein molecules that carry antibody activity, ie, the property of specific combination with the substance which elicited their formation *(antigen).* With the possible exception of *natural* antibody, antibodies arise in response to foreign substances introduced into the body. The immunoglobulins comprise a heterogeneous group of proteins which account for approximately 20% of the total plasma proteins. In serum electrophoresis the majority of the immunoglobulins migrate to the zone designated *γ-globulin,* but significant amounts are also found in the β-globulin zone. Different populations of immunoglobulins are also found in varying proportions in extravascular fluids, in exocrine secretions, and on the surface of some lymphocytes. The biologic activities of immunoglobulins can only be understood on the basis of knowledge of their structure, and in this chapter will be described the structure and evolution of immunoglobulin molecules.

An-Chuan Wang is Professor, Department of Basic and Clinical Immunology and Microbiology, Medical University of South Carolina, Charleston.

BASIC STRUCTURE & TERMINOLOGY

Immunoglobulins are glycoproteins composed of 82–96% polypeptide and 4–18% carbohydrate. The polypeptide component possesses almost all of the biologic properties associated with antibody molecules. Antibody molecules are highly heterogeneous, as demonstrated by serologic (ie, antigenic), electrophoretic, and amino acid sequence analysis. This heterogeneity hampered early structural studies. Two major discoveries ushered in the period of detailed structural study of antibodies. The first was the finding that enzymes could be used to digest immunoglobulin molecules into smaller components. The second was the realization that the electrophoretically homogeneous protein found in serum and urine of a patient with multiple myeloma (see Chapter 28) was related to normal immunoglobulins. This *myeloma protein* was found to be structurally homogeneous. It was also called a *monoclonal* protein since it was synthesized by a single *clone* of malignant plasma cells. A clone here refers collectively to the progeny of a single lymphoid cell.

Our present knowledge of immunoglobulin structure is based mainly on studies of monoclonal proteins. The discussion of the details of immunoglobulin structure is introduced with a list of definitions of the relevant terms used here and in Figs 2–1 and 2–2.

List of Definitions

Basic unit (monomer): Each immunoglobulin contains at least one basic unit or monomer comprising 4 polypeptide chains (Fig 2–1).

H and L chains: One pair of identical polypeptide chains contains approximately twice the number of

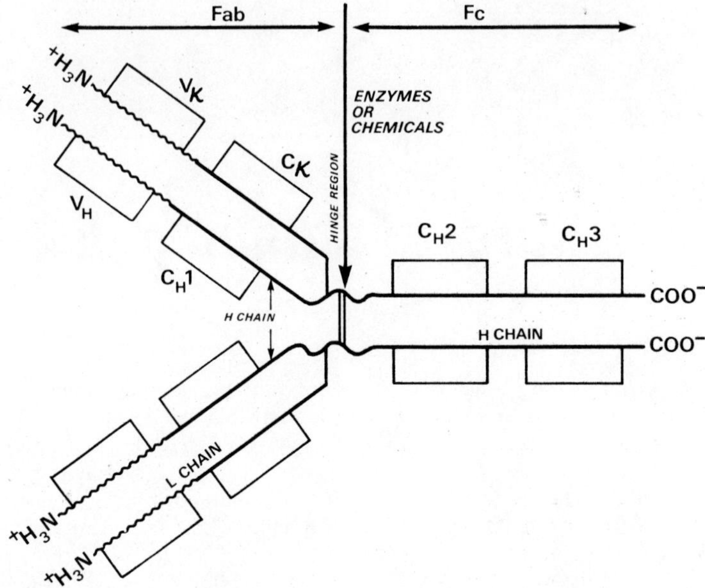

Figure 2–1. A simplified model for an IgG1(κ) human antibody molecule showing the 4-chain basic structure and domains. V indicates variable region; C, the constant region; and the vertical arrow the hinge region. Thick lines represent H and L chains; thin lines represent disulfide bonds.

amino acids, or is approxim~.ely twice the molecular weight of the other pa'. of identical polypeptide chains. The chains of higher molecular weight are designated *heavy (H) chains* (Fig 2–1) and those of lower molecular weight *light (L) chains.*

V and C regions: Each polypeptide chain contains an amino terminal portion, the *variable (V) region;* and a carboxyl terminal portion, the *constant (C) region.* These terms denote the considerable heterogeneity or variability in the amino acid residues in the V region compared to the C region.

Domains: The polypeptide chains do not exist as straight sequences of amino acids but are folded 3-dimensionally with disulfide bonds to form areas called *domains.* The domains in H chains are designated V_H and C_H1, C_H2, C_H3, and C_H4; and those in L chains are designated V_L and C_L.

Antigen-binding site: The part of the antibody molecule which binds antigen is formed by only small numbers of amino acids in the V regions of H and L chains. These amino acids are brought into close relationship by the folding of the V regions.

Fab and Fc fragments: Digestion of an IgG molecule by the enzyme papain produces 2 Fab (antigen-binding) fragments and one Fc (crystallizable) fragment.

Hinge region: The area of the H chains in C region between the first and second C region domains (C_H1 and C_H2) is the hinge region. It is more flexible and is more exposed to enzymes and chemicals. Thus, papain acts here to produce Fab and Fc fragments.

F(ab')$_2$ fragment: Digestion of an IgG molecule by the enzyme pepsin produces one F(ab')$_2$ molecule and small peptides. The F(ab')$_2$ molecule is composed of 2 Fab units and the hinge region, with intact inter-H chain disulfide bonds, since pepsin cleaves the IgG molecule on the carboxyl terminal side of these bonds.

Disulfide bonds: Chemical disulfide (–S–S–) bonds between cysteine residues are essential for the normal 3-dimensional structure of immunoglobulins. These bonds can be interchain (H chain to H chain, H chain to L chain, L chain to L chain) or intrachain.

Classes: There are 5 classes of immunoglobulins designated IgG, IgA, IgM, IgD, and IgE (Table 2–1). They are defined by antigenic differences in the C regions of H chains.

L chain types: L chains are divided into κ and λ types on the basis of antigenic determinants.

S value: The S value refers to the sedimentation coefficient of a protein, measured by the technic of Svedberg. S values of normal immunoglobulins range from 6S to 19S (Table 2–1). In general, the larger the S value of a protein, the higher its molecular weight.

Polymers: Immunoglobulins composed of more than a single basic monomeric unit are termed polymers. The main examples are IgA *dimers* (2 units) and *trimers* (3 units) and IgM *pentamers* (5 units).

J chain: This is a polypeptide chain which is normally found in polymeric immunoglobulins.

Secretory component: IgA molecules in secretions are most commonly composed of 2 IgA units, one J chain, and an additional polypeptide, the secretory component.

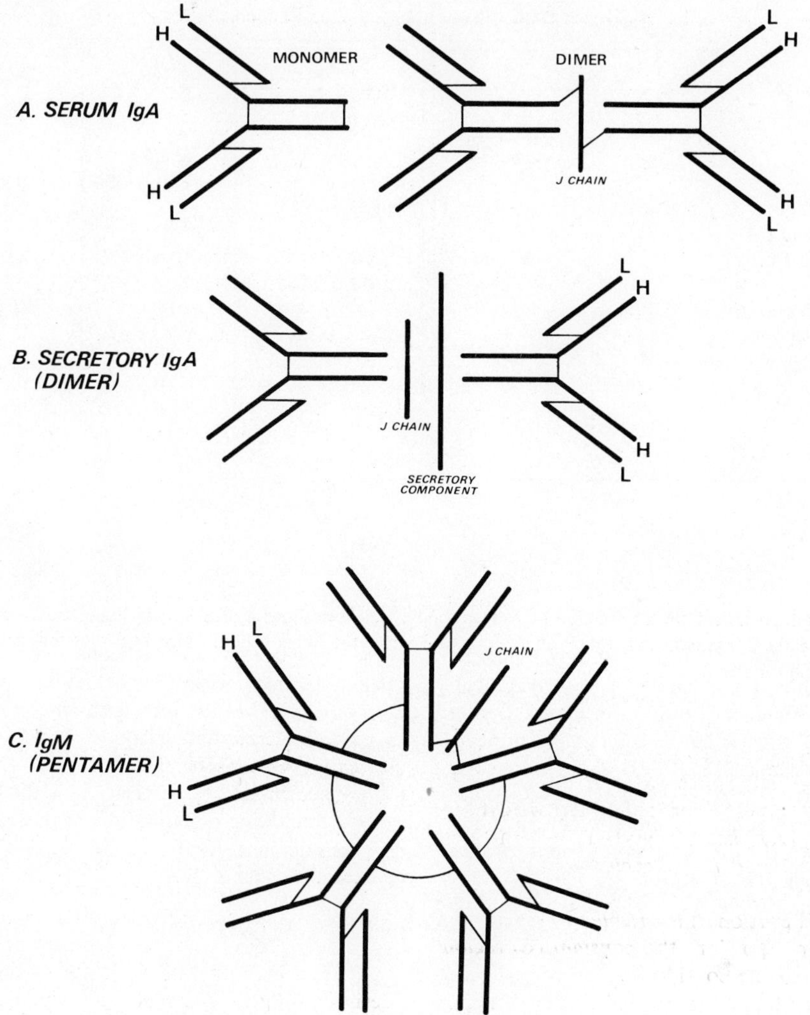

Figure 2–2. Highly schematic illustration of polymeric human immunoglobulins. Polypeptide chains are represented by thick lines; disulfide bonds linking different polypeptide chains are represented by thin lines.

CLASSES & SUBCLASSES OF IMMUNOGLOBULINS

Antigenic determinants of various heavy (H) and light (L) chains of different immunoglobulins can be identified using monospecific antisera against immunoglobulins. Immunoglobulins are classified into classes and subclasses according to the antigenic differences of the constant (C) regions of H chains. Similarly, L chains are classified into kappa (κ) and lambda (λ) types. Subtypes of L chains have been observed occasionally in certain species by serologic or biochemical methods.

Five classes of immunoglobulins have been described in humans (Table 2–1). The antigenically different H chains are designated γ, α, μ, δ, and ϵ, corresponding to the immunoglobulin classes IgG, IgA, IgM, IgD, and IgE, respectively. Most of these classes have been further divided into subclasses. For example, human IgG molecules are divided into 4 subclasses, namely IgG1, IgG2, IgG3, and IgG4, characterized by $\gamma 1$, $\gamma 2$, $\gamma 3$, and $\gamma 4$ H chains, respectively. Similarly, 2 subclasses of IgA (IgA1 and IgA2) have been clearly defined, characterized by $\alpha 1$ and $\alpha 2$ H chains, respectively. Preliminary studies by peptide mapping and complement-fixing activity indicate the existence of at least 2 subclasses of IgM (IgM1 and IgM2), characterized by $\mu 1$ and $\mu 2$ H chains, respectively.

Immunoglobulin G (IgG)

In normal human adults, IgG constitutes approximately 75% of the total serum immunoglobulins. Within the IgG class, the relative concentrations of the 4 subclasses are approximately as follows: IgG1, 60–70%; IgG2, 14–20%; IgG3, 4–8%; and IgG4, 2–6%. These figures vary somewhat from individual to individual and correlate weakly with the presence of

Table 2–1. Properties of human immunoglobulins.

	IgG	IgA	IgM	IgD	IgE
H chain class	γ	α	μ	δ	ϵ
H chain subclass	$\gamma1,\gamma2,\gamma3,\gamma4$	$\alpha1,\alpha2$	$\mu1,\mu2$		
L chain type	κ and λ	κ and λ	κ and λ	κ and λ	κ and λ
Molecular formula	$\gamma_2 L_2$	$\alpha_2 L_2$* or $(\alpha_2 L_2)_2$SC†J‡	$(\alpha_2 L_2)_5$J‡	$\delta_2 L_2$	$\epsilon_2 L_2$
Sedimentation coefficient (S)	6–7	7	19	7–8	8
Molecular weight (approximate)	150,000	160,000* 400,000§	900,000	180,000	190,000
Electrophoretic mobility (average)	γ	Fast γ to β	Fast γ to β	Fast γ	Fast γ
Complement fixation (classical)	+	0	++++	0	0
Serum concentration (approximate; mg/dl)	1000	200	120	3	0.05
Placental transfer	+	0	0	0	0
Reaginic activity	?	0	0	0	++++
Antibacterial lysis	+	+	+++	?	?
Antiviral activity	+	+++	+	?	?

*For monomeric serum IgA.
†Secretory component.
‡J chain.
§For secretory IgA.

certain H chain constant (C) region allotypic markers (see Chapter 5). Thus, the capacity of a given individual to produce antibodies of one or another IgG subclass may be under genetic control. IgG has a molecular weight of approximately 150,000 and a sedimentation coefficient of 6–7S. At alkaline pH (pH 8.6), IgG has the slowest electrophoretic mobility of all major serum proteins except the C1q component of the complement system (see Chapter 6). This property facilitates the isolation of IgG by means of ion exchange chromatography in diethylaminoethyl cellulose columns (see Chapter 24).

Immunoglobulin A (IgA)

IgA is the predominant immunoglobulin class in body secretions. Each secretory IgA molecule consists of two 4-chain basic units and one molecule each of secretory component and J chain (Fig 2–2). The molecular weight of secretory IgA is approximately 400,000. Secretory IgA provides the primary defense mechanism against some local infection owing to its abundance in saliva, tears, bronchial secretions, the nasal mucosa, prostatic fluid, vaginal secretions, and mucous secretions of the small intestine. The predominance of secretory IgA in membrane secretions led to speculation that its principal function may not be to destroy antigen (eg, foreign microbial organisms or cells) but rather to prevent access of these foreign substances to the general immunologic system. IgA normally exists in serum in both monomeric and polymeric forms, constituting approximately 15% of the total serum immunoglobulins.

Immunoglobulin M (IgM)

IgM constitutes approximately 10% of normal serum immunoglobulins and normally exists as a pentamer with a molecular weight of approximately 900,000 (19S). IgM antibody is prominent in early immune responses to most antigens and predominates in certain antibody responses such as natural blood group antibodies. IgM (with IgD) is the major immunoglobulin expressed on the surface of B cells. IgM and IgG antibodies are responsible for most of the specific activities classically associated with antibodies in general, including precipitation, agglutination, hemolysis, complement fixation, and transfusion reactions (see Chapters 4 and 28).

Immunoglobulin D (IgD)

The IgD molecule is a monomer and its molecular weight of approximately 180,000 (7–8S) is slightly higher than that of IgG. This immunoglobulin is normally present in serum in trace amounts (0.2% of total serum immunoglobulins). It is relatively labile to degradation by heat and proteolytic enzymes. There are isolated reports of IgD with antibody activity toward certain antigens, including insulin, penicillin, milk proteins, diphtheria toxoid, nuclear antigens, and thyroid antigens. However, the main function of IgD has not yet been determined. IgD (with IgM) is the predominant immunoglobulin on the surface of human B lymphocytes.

Immunoglobulin E (IgE)

The identification of IgE antibodies as *reagins* and the characterization of this immunoglobulin class marked the major breakthrough in the study of the mechanisms involved in allergic diseases (see Chapter 19). IgE has a molecular weight of approximately 190,000 (8S). It comprises only 0.004% of the total serum immunoglobulins. Upon combination with certain specific antigens called *allergens,* IgE antibodies trigger the release from mast cells of pharmacologic mediators responsible for the characteristic wheal and flare skin reactions evoked by the exposure of the skin of allergic individuals to allergens. IgE antibodies pro-

Table 2–2. Properties of human immunoglobulin chains.

Designation	H Chains					L Chains		Secretory Component	J Chain
	γ	α	μ	δ	ϵ	κ	λ	SC	J
Classes in which chains occur	IgG	IgA	IgM	IgD	IgE	All classes	All classes	IgA	IgA,IgM
Subclasses or subtypes	1,2,3,4	1,2	1,2	. . .	. . .	. . .	1,2,3,4	. . .	. . .
Allotypic variants	Gm(1)–(25)	A2m(1), (2)	. . .	. . .	. . .	Km(1)–(3)†	. . .	. . .	. . .
Molecular weight (approximate)	50,000*	55,000	70,000	62,000	70,000	23,000	23,000	70,000	15,000
V region subgroups			$V_HI–V_HIV$			$V_\kappa I–V_\kappa IV$	$V_\lambda I–V_\lambda VI$		
Carbohydrate (average percentage)	4	10	15	18	18	0	0	16	8
Number of oligosaccharides	1	2 or 3	5	?	5	0	0	?	1

*60,000 for γ3.
†Formerly Inv(1)–(3).

vide a striking example of the bifunctional nature of antibody molecules. Allergen is an alternative name used by allergists for any antigen which stimulates IgE production. IgE antibodies bind allergens through the Fab portion, but the binding of IgE antibodies to tissue cells is a function of the Fc portion. Like IgG and IgD, IgE normally exists only in monomeric form.

FOUR-CHAIN BASIC UNIT

In 1959, Porter used the proteolytic enzyme papain to cleave rabbit IgG into fragments which retained biologic activity. Edelman showed that IgG molecules could be separated into component H and L chains after reduction of the disulfide bonds with mercaptoethanol. These studies established a Y-shaped, 4-chain model for IgG (Fig 2–1). It has subsequently been shown that all normal immunoglobulins have this basic structure. IgG, IgD, and IgE consist of one basic unit each; most of the IgM consists of 5 units; and IgA consists of 1–5 such units.

H chains vary in molecular weight from 50–70 thousand, and the molecular weight of L chains is approximately 23,000 (Table 2–2). The classification and the properties of these polypeptide chains are listed in Table 2–2 and their amino acid compositions in Table 2–3. The molecular weight of the δ chain is lower than that of the μ and ϵ chains but higher than that of the α and most γ chains. The δ chain and γ3 chain are thought to have extended hinge regions.

The two H chains within each basic unit are connected to each other by inter-H chain disulfide bridges. The L chains are connected to the H chains also by disulfide bridges in all immunoglobulins except those of the IgA2 subclass. In A2m(1) molecules of this subclass, the two L chains are linked to each other through the cysteine residue at or near the C termini of these chains (Fig 2–3).

The V regions are quite heterogeneous and have been divided into 3 main groups based on degree of amino acid sequence homology. Homology indicates that a particular amino acid occupies a corresponding

Table 2–3. Approximate amino acid compositions (in percent) of various immunoglobulin polypeptide chains. Values for γ, α, μ, κ, and λ chains were based on data from immunoglobulins isolated from normal human adults. The total of all amino acids measured was taken as unity. Tryptophan was excluded from the calculation.

Amino Acid	Chain					Secretory Component	J Chain
	γ	α	μ	κ	λ		
Lys	7.0	4.7	4.8	6.4	5.4	5.6	4.3
His	2.0	2.2	2.0	1.1	1.7	0.9	0.8
Arg	3.0	3.8	4.0	3.5	2.5	4.9	7.3
Asx	7.9	7.4	8.0	8.2	7.0	10.7	17.0
Thr	7.4	10.0	10.8	8.1	9.3	6.0	9.7
Ser	12.1	10.8	10.5	14.0	14.5	8.6	5.8
Glx	9.6	9.7	10.3	11.2	10.5	10.8	11.2
Pro	8.8	9.1	8.0	5.5	6.3	5.2	6.0
Gly	7.3	7.7	5.7	6.6	7.6	9.9	1.6
Ala	4.8	6.7	6.2	6.4	8.2	5.9	4.4
Cys	2.4	2.8	2.6	2.3	2.4	3.1	5.6
Val	9.6	7.2	9.3	6.7	7.9	8.5	7.6
Met	1.4	0.6	1.3	0.5	0.3	0.0	0.7
Ile	1.8	1.4	3.3	3.2	2.6	3.5	6.5
Leu	6.9	9.9	6.8	8.0	7.0	9.2	6.0
Tyr	4.3	2.7	2.9	4.0	4.5	4.0	4.5
Phe	3.7	3.3	3.5	4.3	2.4	3.2	1.0

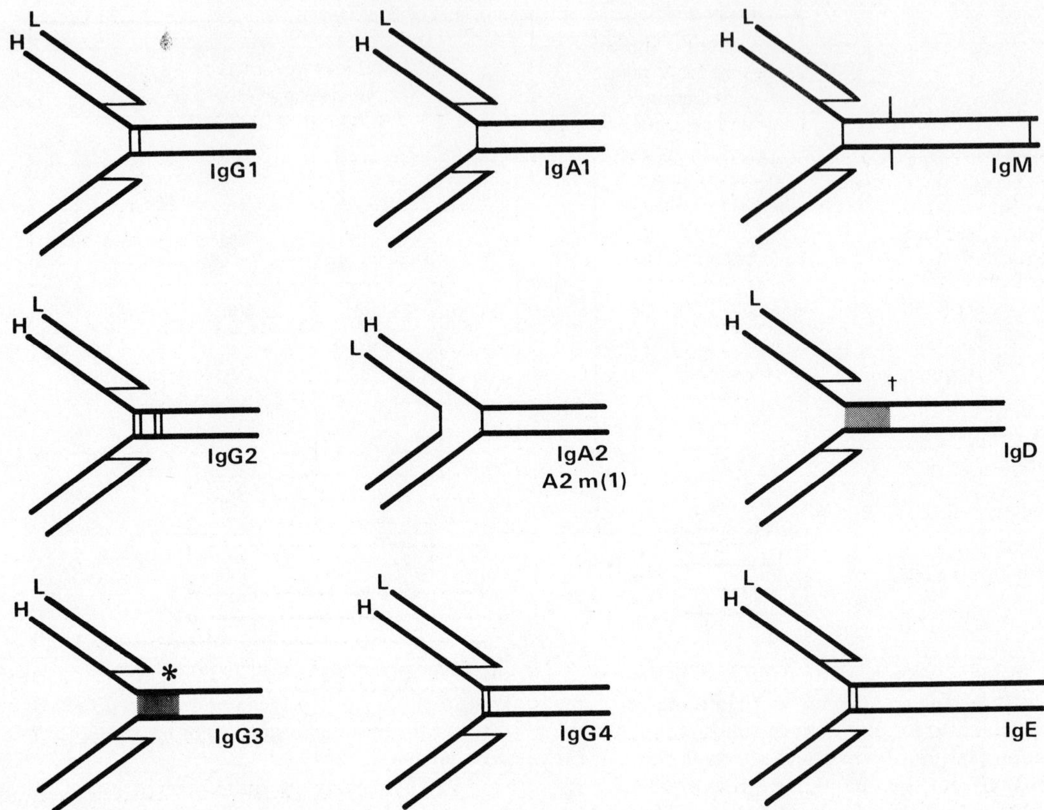

Figure 2–3. Distribution of interchain disulfide bonds in various human immunoglobulin classes and subclasses. H chains are represented by long thick lines and L chains by short thick lines. Disulfide bonds are represented by thin lines.
*5–15; exact number has not been determined.
†Number undetermined.

position in the amino acid sequence of different polypeptides. These are the V_H group for H chains, V_κ group for κ chains, and V_λ group for λ chains. Each group is further divided into several subgroups (Fig 2–4): The term *idiotype* or *idiotypic antigenic determinants* refers to an antigen or set of antigens which, with rare exceptions, are unique to each species of antibody or myeloma protein (see Chapter 12). The idiotype appears to represent mainly the antigenicity of the antigen-binding site of an antibody and is therefore located in the V region. Idiotypic determinants are apparently heritable in several cases (eg, anti-*p*-azophenylarsonate antibodies in A/J mice). In at least one case (antibodies to hemoglobin S in sheep and goat), the idiotype is apparently maintained in evolution in closely related species. This suggests that there are a large number of genes which code for the V regions of immunoglobulin polypeptide chains.

Each basic unit has a hinge region located at the middle of the γ, α, and probably δ chains, and near the middle of the μ and ϵ chains. The 4-chain basic unit is flexible in most H chains at the hinge region, which is rich in proline and is more exposed and vulnerable to cleavage by proteolytic enzymes. Papain digestion of rabbit IgG and human IgG1 produced 2 Fab fragments and one Fc fragment. The Fab fragment retains the antigen-binding activity and is capable of binding one antigenic determinant. On the other hand, the Fc fragment retains most of the other biologic functions, including complement fixation, placental transfer, passive cutaneous anaphylaxis, catabolism, etc. Under appropriate conditions, many other enzymes (eg, pepsin and trypsin) and chemicals (cyanogen bromide) are also capable of splitting immunoglobulins at the hinge region to produce either 2 Fab and one Fc fragment or one $F(ab')_2$ and one Fc fragment. However, the yield of Fc is generally low, and it is therefore difficult to observe the Fc fragment in certain classes and subclasses of immunoglobulins. Following initial cleavage at the hinge region, the enzymes presumably act to further cleave the Fc fragment into smaller pieces.

It is noteworthy that although all normal immunoglobulins possess the characteristic 4-chain basic units, abnormal immunoglobulins deviating from this general structure have occasionally been observed. These abnormal immunoglobulins include Bence Jones proteins consisting only of L chains; H chain disease proteins consisting only of incomplete H chains; and, on rare occasions, incomplete L chains.

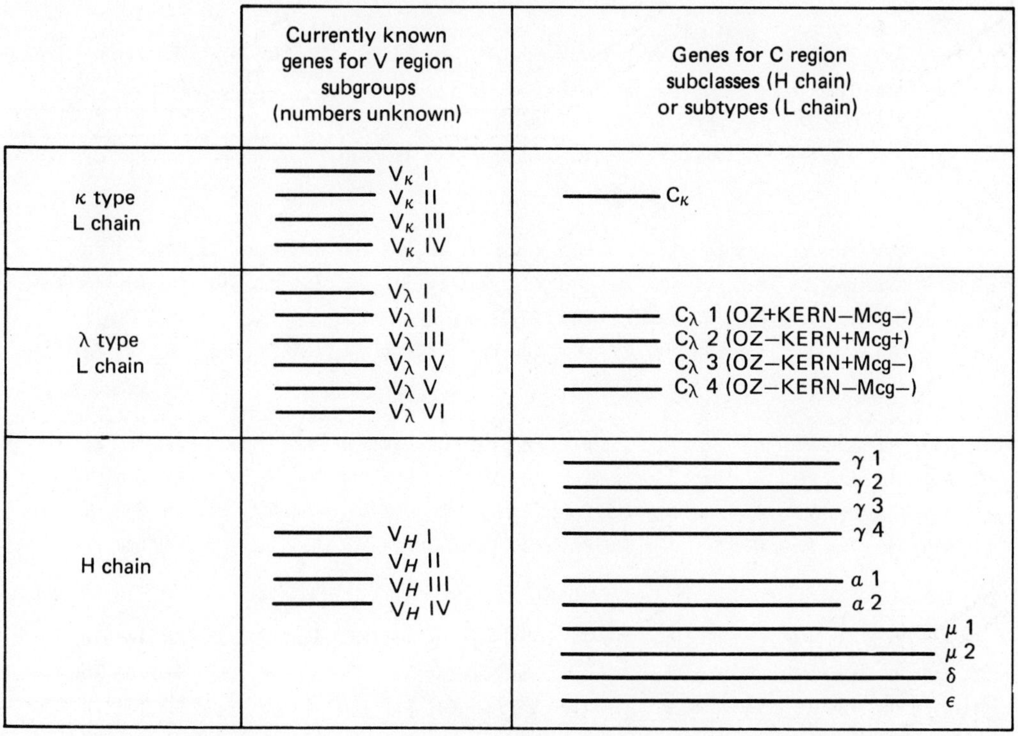

	Currently known genes for V region subgroups (numbers unknown)	Genes for C region subclasses (H chain) or subtypes (L chain)
κ type L chain	Vκ I Vκ II Vκ III Vκ IV	Cκ
λ type L chain	Vλ I Vλ II Vλ III Vλ IV Vλ V Vλ VI	Cλ 1 (OZ+KERN−Mcg−) Cλ 2 (OZ−KERN+Mcg+) Cλ 3 (OZ−KERN+Mcg−) Cλ 4 (OZ−KERN−Mcg−)
H chain	V_H I V_H II V_H III V_H IV	γ 1 γ 2 γ 3 γ 4 a 1 a 2 μ 1 μ 2 δ ε

Figure 2–4. Diagrammatic representation of genes coding for human immunoglobulin polypeptide chains. Each bar represents at least one gene and may represent hundreds. Each gene is labeled with the name of the corresponding protein product or products. One V region gene and one C region gene contribute to each immunoglobulin polypeptide chain. Each box encloses a set of linked genes. The λ subtypes are defined by amino acid substitutions in 3 monoclonal L chains (OZ, KERN, Mcg).

DISULFIDE BONDS

Immunoglobulins have many characteristic interchain and intrachain disulfide bonds. Disulfide bonds are essential to the normal 3-dimensional structure of immunoglobulin molecules. Differences in the location of some disulfide bonds in different immunoglobulin molecules can be reflected in significant differences in biologic activities. Reduction of some disulfide bonds causes a loss of certain biologic activities.

The interchain disulfide bonds are usually weaker than the intrachain bonds. When reduction is carried out in a nondenaturing solvent so that the conformation of the individual chains is largely undisturbed, it is possible in most immunoglobulins to reduce selectively the interchain disulfide bonds and leave the intrachain bonds intact. After selective reduction, the cysteine residues presumably derived from interchain disulfide bonds may be labeled with radioactive iodoacetic acid or iodoacetamide. This procedure greatly facilitates the isolation and amino acid sequence determination of peptides containing the cysteine residues involved in bridging H-H, L-L, or H-L chains.

Fig 2–2 shows the distribution of interchain disulfide bonds in human immunoglobulins. The inter-H chain disulfide bonds are normally located at the hinge region. It is interesting to note that different classes and subclasses of immunoglobulins have different numbers of inter-H chain disulfide bonds. IgM and IgA have one such bond each; IgG1, IgG4, and IgE, 2 bonds; and IgG2, 4 such bonds. IgG3 has the highest number of inter-H chain disulfide bonds. The exact number has not been firmly determined, but different studies have found between 5 and 15. The latter number is probably more reliable, since quantitative analyses suggest that a stretch of amino acid sequence at the hinge region may be repeated 3 times in γ3 chains and that γ3 chains are longer than the other subclasses of γ chains.

Fig 2–5 shows the amino acid sequences around the inter-H chain disulfide bonds and portions of the remaining C regions of various human γ chains. Two unusual features can be observed: (1) the 4 γ chain subclasses have very different amino acid sequences at the hinge region, with less than 60% homology, contrasting with over 90% sequence homology in the remaining portions of their C regions. The marked differences in the hinge region may influence the biologic activity of various IgG subclasses. Thus, different classes and subclasses of immunoglobulins with different biologic properties have widely different disulfide bond patterns at their hinge regions, and, at least in some cases, reduction of disulfide bonds causes a loss

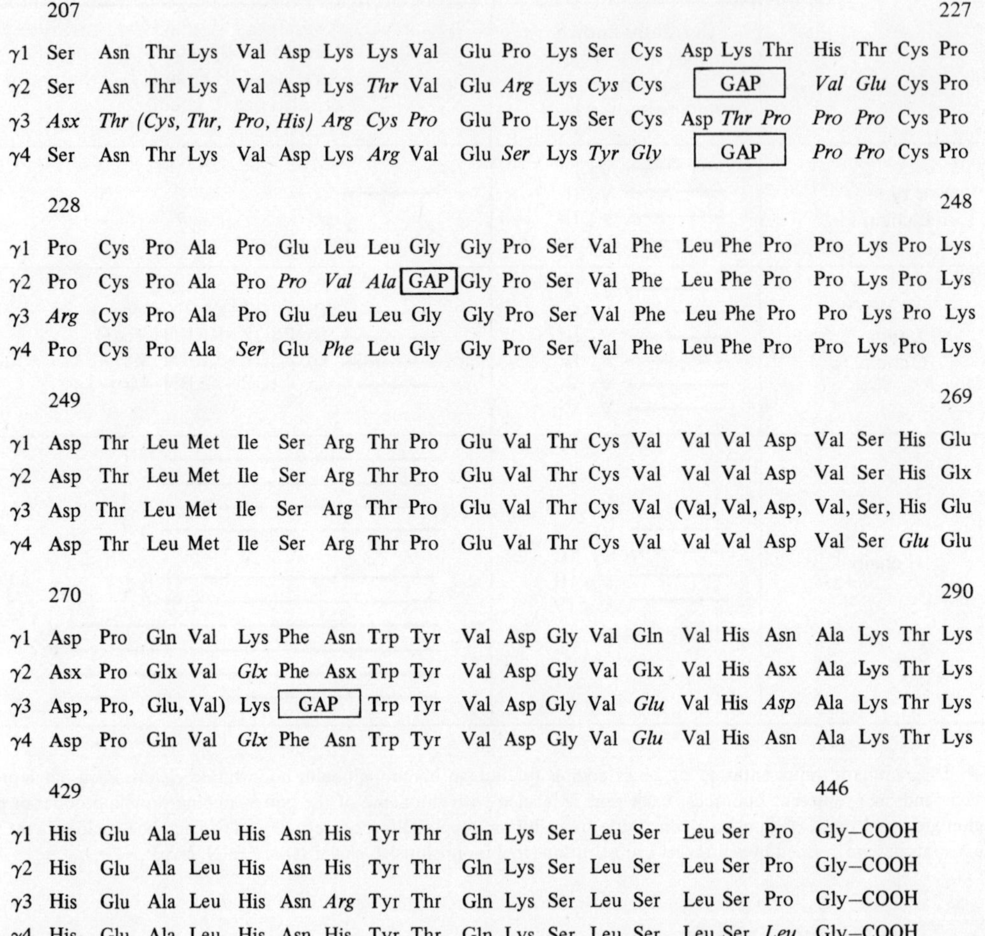

	207				227
γ1	Ser Asn Thr Lys	Val Asp Lys Lys Val	Glu Pro Lys Ser Cys	Asp Lys Thr	His Thr Cys Pro
γ2	Ser Asn Thr Lys	Val Asp Lys *Thr* Val	Glu *Arg* Lys *Cys* Cys	GAP	*Val Glu* Cys Pro
γ3	*Asx Thr (Cys, Thr,*	*Pro, His) Arg Cys Pro*	Glu Pro Lys Ser Cys	Asp *Thr Pro*	*Pro Pro* Cys Pro
γ4	Ser Asn Thr Lys	Val Asp Lys *Arg* Val	Glu *Ser* Lys *Tyr Gly*	GAP	*Pro Pro* Cys Pro
	228				248
γ1	Pro Cys Pro Ala	Pro Glu Leu Leu Gly	Gly Pro Ser Val Phe	Leu Phe Pro	Pro Lys Pro Lys
γ2	Pro Cys Pro Ala	Pro *Pro Val Ala* GAP	Gly Pro Ser Val Phe	Leu Phe Pro	Pro Lys Pro Lys
γ3	*Arg* Cys Pro Ala	Pro Glu Leu Leu Gly	Gly Pro Ser Val Phe	Leu Phe Pro	Pro Lys Pro Lys
γ4	Pro Cys Pro Ala	*Ser* Glu *Phe* Leu Gly	Gly Pro Ser Val Phe	Leu Phe Pro	Pro Lys Pro Lys
	249				269
γ1	Asp Thr Leu Met	Ile Ser Arg Thr Pro	Glu Val Thr Cys Val	Val Val Asp	Val Ser His Glu
γ2	Asp Thr Leu Met	Ile Ser Arg Thr Pro	Glu Val Thr Cys Val	Val Val Asp	Val Ser His Glx
γ3	Asp Thr Leu Met	Ile Ser Arg Thr Pro	Glu Val Thr Cys Val	(Val, Val, Asp,	Val, Ser, His Glu
γ4	Asp Thr Leu Met	Ile Ser Arg Thr Pro	Glu Val Thr Cys Val	Val Val Asp	Val Ser *Glu* Glu
	270				290
γ1	Asp Pro Gln Val	Lys Phe Asn Trp Tyr	Val Asp Gly Val Gln	Val His Asn	Ala Lys Thr Lys
γ2	Asx Pro Glx Val	*Glx* Phe Asx Trp Tyr	Val Asp Gly Val Glx	Val His Asx	Ala Lys Thr Lys
γ3	Asp, Pro, Glu, Val)	Lys GAP Trp Tyr	Val Asp Gly Val *Glu*	Val His *Asp*	Ala Lys Thr Lys
γ4	Asp Pro Gln Val	*Glx* Phe Asn Trp Tyr	Val Asp Gly Val *Glu*	Val His Asn	Ala Lys Thr Lys
	429				446
γ1	His Glu Ala Leu	His Asn His Tyr Thr	Gln Lys Ser Leu Ser	Leu Ser Pro	Gly–COOH
γ2	His Glu Ala Leu	His Asn His Tyr Thr	Gln Lys Ser Leu Ser	Leu Ser Pro	Gly–COOH
γ3	His Glu Ala Leu	His Asn *Arg* Tyr Thr	Gln Lys Ser Leu Ser	Leu Ser Pro	Gly–COOH
γ4	His Glu Ala Leu	His Asn His Tyr Thr	Gln Lys Ser Leu Ser	Leu Ser *Leu*	Gly–COOH

Figure 2–5. Amino acid sequences at the hinge region (residues 207–235), the beginning of the C_H2 domain, and the carboxyl terminus of various human γ chains. Gaps were introduced to achieve maximum homology. The residues are numbered according to the sequence of the human γ1 chain from an IgG1(κ) myeloma protein (Eu). Residues which *differ* from those in γ1 are in italics and those which are disputed are in parentheses.

of certain biologic activities. (2) The area around the inter-H chain disulfide bonds of most H chains is rich in proline residues. These prolines probably form the rigid part of the "hinge" since the rotation of a polypeptide chain around bonds adjacent to a proline residue is relatively hindered. Although the antigen-binding sites are located in the V regions of H and L chains, it is nevertheless not unreasonable to assume that the antibody activity of different antibodies against large or polymeric antigens may be influenced by the degree of flexibility of the hinge region.

In most immunoglobulins, an interchain disulfide bond is present between a cysteine in the H chain and the carboxyl terminal cysteine of a κ chain or the penultimate cysteine of a λ chain. In the H chains, the point of attachment varies from near the center of the chain in human and mouse IgG1 proteins to a position about 100 residues nearer the amino terminus of the chain in most other immunoglobulins (Fig 2–3). In some IgA molecules, the H-L disulfide bond does not exist at all, and a disulfide bond is formed between two L chains, with only noncovalent interactions keeping the H and L chains together. Inter-L chain bonds are also found in Bence Jones proteins, which are commonly secreted as disulfide-bonded dimers.

The intrachain disulfide bonds of immunoglobulin polypeptide chains are spaced regularly along each chain (Fig 2–6A). There are 2 such bonds in an L chain, 4 in γ, α, and δ chains, and 5 in μ and ϵ chains. Each intrachain disulfide bond encloses a loop of about 60 residues. This pattern seems to be invariable except that an additional intrachain bond may sometimes be present in either the C region or the V region or bridging the C and the V regions.

DOMAINS

The polypeptide chains of an immunoglobulin molecule are folded into many domains (Fig 2–6). Each domain has a compact globular structure and is connected to neighboring domains by a narrow but more exposed area. All L chains have 2 domains, designated C_L and V_L. The H chain of IgG or IgA has one V region and three C region domains, while that of IgM and IgE has one V region and four C region domains. These domains are designated as V_H, C_H1, C_H2, C_H3, and C_H4 and can be studied by x-ray crystallography of various immunoglobulins and their fragments (Fig 2–6). There is also close physical approximation between corresponding domains, ie, V_H and V_L, C_H1 and C_L, and the identical H chain domains in the Fc portion. Other evidence in favor of the domain hypothesis has come from experiments on limited proteolysis in which the major products appear to consist of one or more domains (as expected, based on the model, since the areas between the domains are more exposed). It was also found that some of the proteins present in patients with H chain disease (see Chapter 28) had large deletions involving all the C_H1 domain and a portion of the V region. In 3 such H chains, the sequences resume at position number 216 (Eu numbering). This led to the speculation that more than one gene coded for the C region of H chains, with position 216 marking the start of another C region gene.

The domain concept was initially derived from amino acid sequence studies. To date, complete amino acid sequences have been determined for κ, λ, γ, μ, a_1, and ϵ chains of human immunoglobulins. Examination of these sequences indicates that each chain consists of regions, each of approximately 110 amino acid residues, with a high (though variable) degree of amino acid sequence homology between those regions. These regions have been called homology regions, but the term domain is now preferred. Each domain has a char-

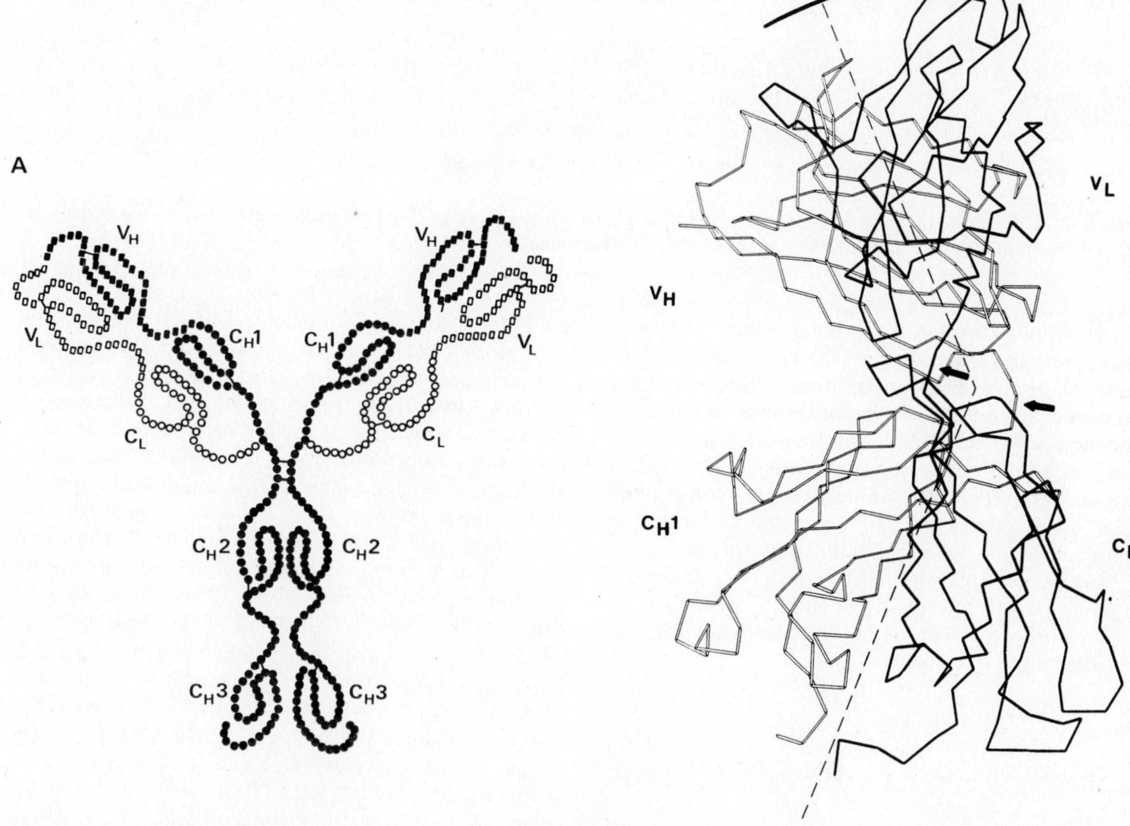

Figure 2–6. Domains of immunoglobulin molecules: *A:* A hypothetical model of an IgG molecule. The V regions of H and L chains (V_H and V_L), the C region of L chains (C_L), and the domains in the C region of H chains (C_H1, C_H2, and C_H3) are folded into compact structures. *B:* A view of the α-carbon backbone of the polypeptide chain of the Fab′ domain of a human IgG1 (λ) protein (New) based on x-ray crystallography. The open line indicates the L chain (V_L and C_L) and the solid line indicates the V_H and C_H1 domains of the H chain. The 2 short arrows indicate the V–C switch region of both chains. The longer arrow indicates a possible relative motion of the V and C_1 domains. (Redrawn and reproduced, with permission, from Proc Natl Acad Sci USA 71:3440, 1974.)

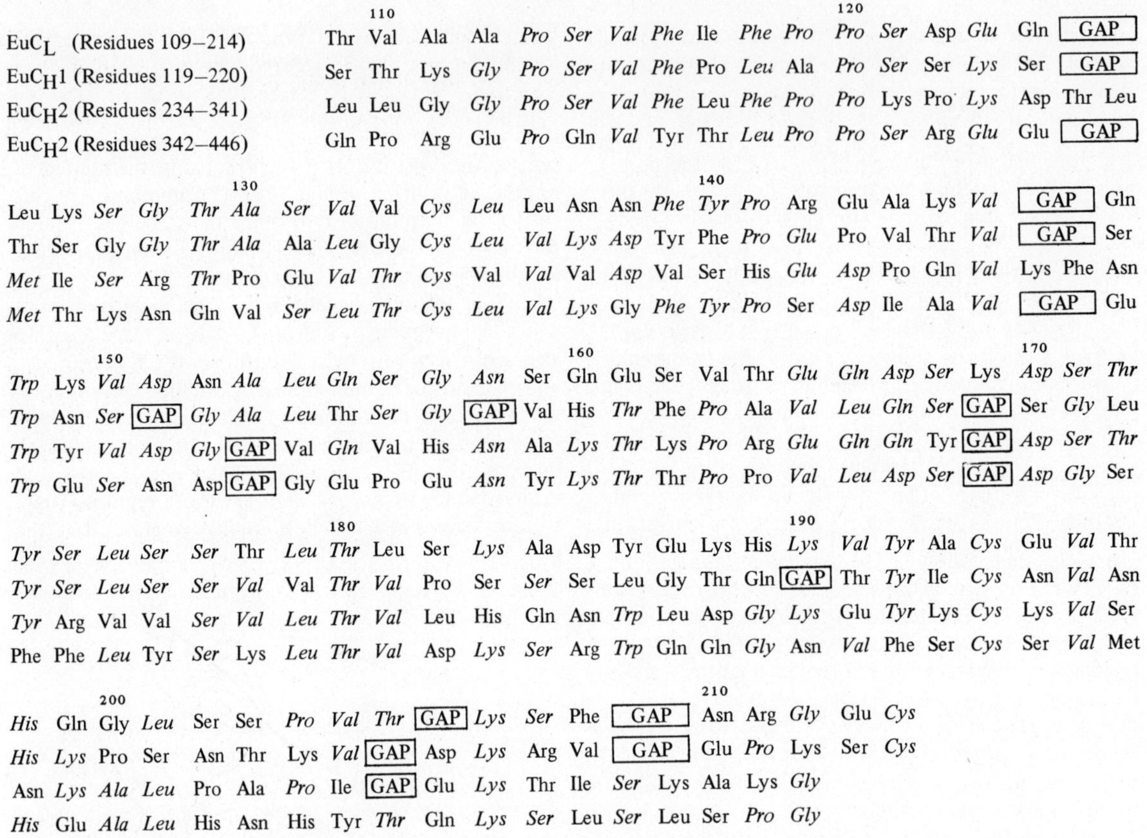

Figure 2–7. Comparison of amino acid sequences of different domains in a single IgG1 (κ) molecule (protein Eu). Residues *homologous* in different domains are in italics. Gaps were introduced to maximize homology.

acteristic intrachain disulfide bond which bridges 2 cysteine residues approximately 60 amino acid residues apart. All domains, including those from the same polypeptide chain, different polypeptide chains, the same molecules, and different molecules show a certain degree of amino acid sequence homology. This led to the conclusion that all immunoglobulin polypeptide chains evolved from a common ancestor which was equivalent to one domain. To illustrate this point, Fig 2–7 compares the amino acid sequences of C regions of an IgG1 (κ) myeloma protein Eu; over 30% of sequence homology can be observed between any 2 of the 4 domains compared.

TWO GENES, ONE POLYPEPTIDE CHAIN

In 1965, Dreyer and Bennett proposed a "2 genes for one polypeptide chain" hypothesis for antibody molecules, suggesting that each antibody polypeptide chain is encoded by 2 separate germ line genes. This proposal was based upon results of amino acid sequencing and peptide mapping of κ Bence Jones proteins and myeloma protein L chains derived from patients with multiple myeloma. At that time, several laboratories independently showed that the carboxyl terminal half of these myeloma κ chains was always identical, except for single amino acid substitutions associated with inherited allotypic markers. In contrast, the amino terminal halves of these κ chains were all different, each having a unique amino acid sequence at its amino terminal half. These findings led to the suggestion that 2 structural genes controlled the synthesis of each immunoglobulin polypeptide chain—one for the carboxyl terminal half of the chain and the other for the amino terminal half of the chain.

The most convincing evidence in support of this hypothesis came from the studies of H chains of 2 monoclonal proteins (IgM [κ] and IgG2 [κ]) from the serum of a single patient. A monoclonal or myeloma protein is the homogeneous product of a single clone of malignant plasma cells. The μ chain and the γ2 chain prepared from monoclonal proteins of the above-mentioned patient had identical amino acid sequences in their V regions. Genetic studies have clearly established that the C regions of the μ chain and the γ2 chain are synthesized by different structural genes. It is believed that the genes coding for the γ and μ chains diverged over 200 million years ago, and there is no precedent wherein 2 different genes remain identical for a stretch coding for over 100 amino acid residues through 200 million years of evolution. Therefore, the identical amino acid sequences at the V regions of a μ chain and a $\gamma 2$ chain indicate that the V region and the C region of an H chain must be synthesized by different structural genes. Subsequent studies in 3 different patients in 3 different laboratories observed in each case the sharing of apparently identical V regions by different classes of H chains. The sharing of identical V regions by a μ chain and a γ chain is consistent with a number of biologic observations. It has long been known that maturation of an immune response is often accompanied by a change in the class of antibody being produced from IgM to IgG. The specificity of the antibody is maintained throughout this change. During the transition period of this change, certain immunocytes are found which synthesize both IgM and IgG molecules. To explain these observations at the level of molecular genetics, the *"genetic switch"* hypothesis proposed that following a primary immunization, a given V region gene is translocated to the C region gene for a μ chain to initiate the synthesis of IgM antibody. Later, in one or more of the immunocytes, this same V region gene is switched to a C region gene for a γ chain to initiate the synthesis of IgG antibody (Fig 2–8). The derepression of a $C\gamma$ gene is accompanied by the simultaneous repression of a $C\mu$ gene in the cells involved in the switch. Genes coding for the V_H, V_L, and C_L regions remain unchanged.

The second line of evidence supporting the "2 genes for one polypeptide chain" hypothesis came from work by many laboratories on the amino acid sequences of H chains from human myeloma proteins. The combined data show that the V regions of human H chains can be classified into at least 4 subgroups designated V_HI, V_HII, V_HIII, and V_HIV, respectively. These subgroups are shared by immunoglobulins of all classes and subclasses, although there are preferential combinations. Thus, approximately 70% of α chains combine with V_HIII regions compared to 20% of γ chains. This sharing of V regions is difficult to reconcile with the concept that the DNA coding for each V region is immediately adjacent on the chromosome to that coding for a C region. It is compatible with the idea that 2 different genes control the synthesis of V and C regions of each H chain, and that V and C region genes are located on different portions of the same chromosome.

The third line of evidence supporting the hypothesis came from the genetic study of rabbit and mouse immunoglobulins. The V region allotypic markers a1, a2, and a3 are on IgG, IgA, and IgM molecules in rabbits. Pedigree analysis of rabbits with both these V region allotypic markers and some C region allotypic markers showed that V region allotypes are linked to the C region allotypes with well-documented genetic recombinations. Therefore, it is unlikely that a single gene codes for both the V region and the C region of rabbit H chain.

SECRETORY COMPONENT & J CHAIN

Immunoglobulins are present not only in serum but also in various body secretions such as saliva, nasal secretions, sweat, breast milk, and colostrum. As mentioned earlier, IgA is the predominant immunoglobulin class in the body secretions of most species. IgA usually exists in human serum as a 4-chain unit of approximately molecular weight 160,000 (7S). This unit may polymerize to give disulfide-bonded polymers with 8-chain, 12-chain, or larger structures. The IgA in se-

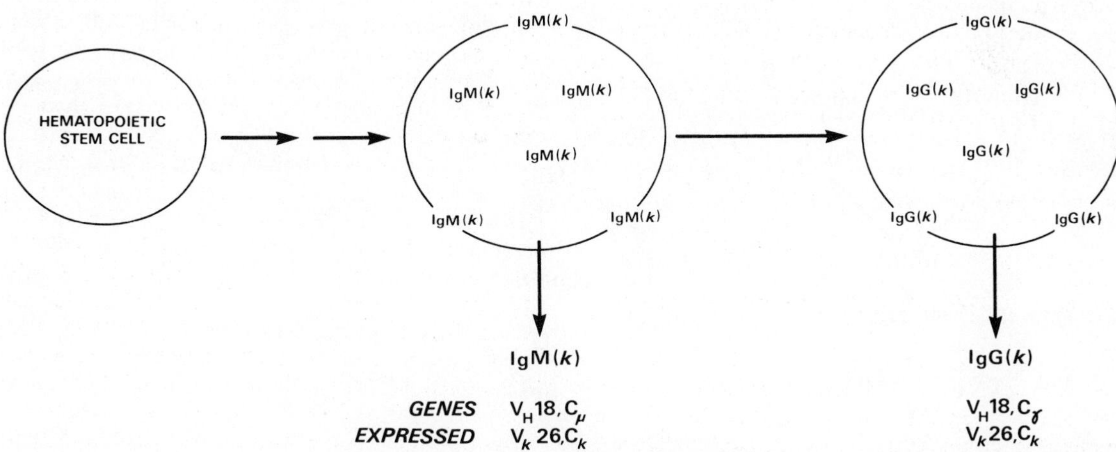

Figure 2–8. Diagrammatic representation of the cytodifferentiation of immunocytes. Simultaneous derepression of $C\gamma$ gene and repression of $C\mu$ gene are postulated as responsible for the switch from IgM-producing cells to IgG-producing cells. The V region is unchanged, and, since it is responsible for the antigen-binding site, antibody specificity (designated 18, 26 in this example) is unchanged.

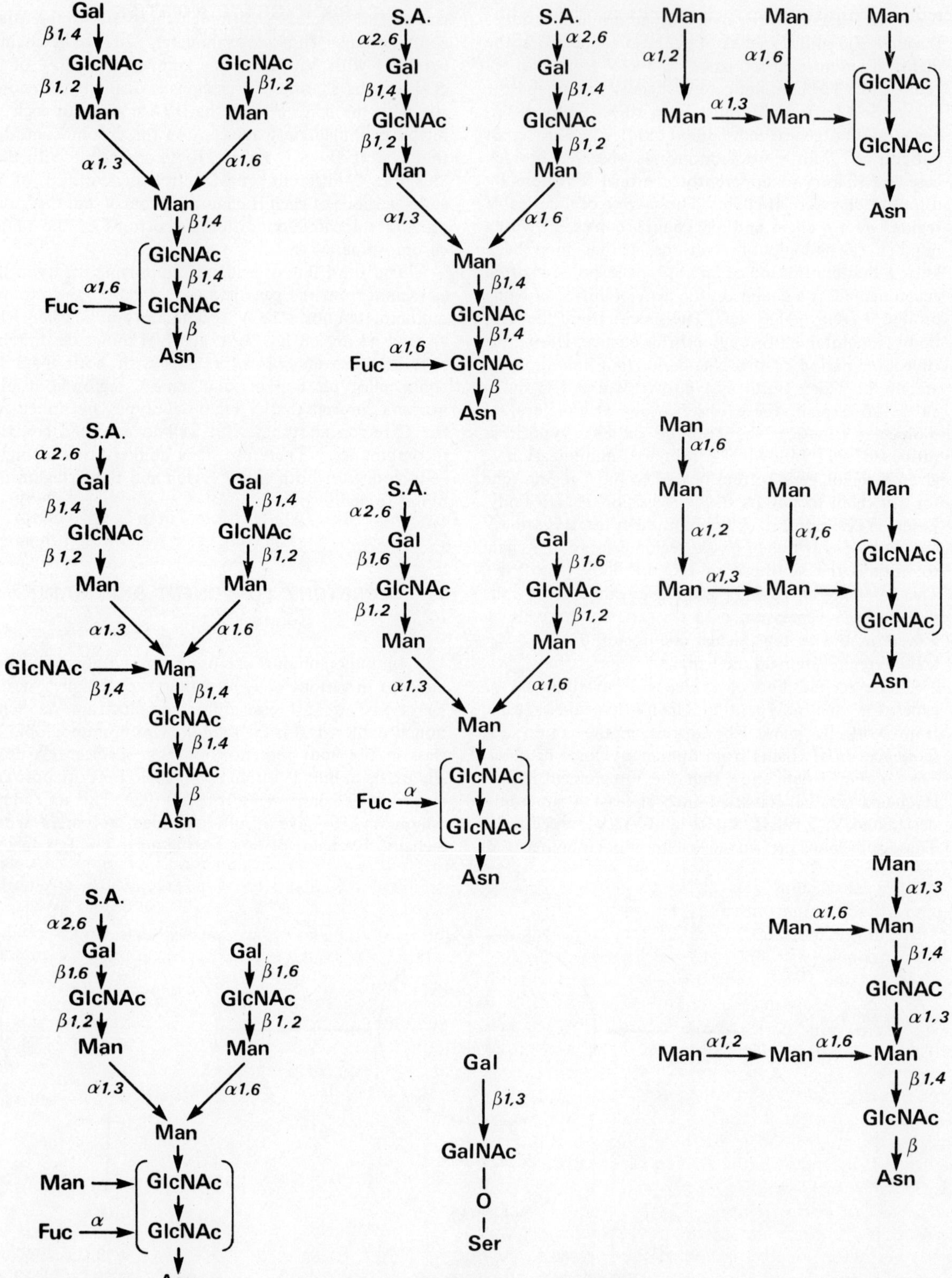

Figure 2–9. Several examples of the structures of the oligosaccharide side chains found in association with immunoglobulin polypeptide chains. S.A., sialic acid; Gal, galactose; GlcNAc, N-acetylglucosamine; Man, mannose; Asn, asparagine; Fuc, fucose; GalNAc, N-acetylgalactosamine; O, oxygen; Ser, serine.

cretions consists of two 4-chain units associated with one of each of 2 additional chain types, the secretory component and the J chain (Tables 2–1 and 2–2). The secretory component is associated only with IgA and is found almost exclusively in body secretions. The J chain is associated with all polymeric forms of immunoglobulins which contain 2 or more basic units. Fig 2–2 shows simplified models of secretory IgA and various polymeric serum immunoglobulins. Evidence suggests that binding of an IgA to secretory component or J chain (or both) may promote the polymerization of additional monomeric 4-chain basic units. The secretory component may exist in free form or bound to IgA molecules by strong noncovalent interactions. The binding does not usually involve covalent bonding, although disulfide bonds have been implicated in a small fraction of human secretory IgA molecules. The secretory component is synthesized by nonmotile epithelial cells near the mucous membrane where secretion occurs. Its function may be to enable IgA antibodies to be transported across mucosal tissues into secretions.

The secretory component is a single polypeptide chain of approximately molecular weight 70,000. The carbohydrate content is high but not precisely known (Table 2–2). Its amino acid composition differs appreciably from that of every other immunoglobulin polypeptide chain, including J chain (Table 2–3). No close structural relationship exists between the secretory component and any immunoglobulin polypeptide chain. Indeed, secretory component can be found free in secretions of individuals who lack measurable IgA in their serum or secretions. The secretory component has an electrophoretic mobility in the fast β range and shows little tendency to form aggregates in phosphate-buffered saline at pH 7.3.

The J chain is a small glycopeptide with an unusually high content of aspartic acid and glutamic acid (Table 2–3). The J chain has a fast electrophoretic mobility on alkaline gels owing to its highly acidic nature. Equilibrium centrifugation in 5.0 M guanidine hydrochloride indicates J chain has a molecular weight of approximately 15,000. Physicochemical studies indicate that the J chain molecule is very elongated with an axial ratio of approximately 18.

Quantitative measurements indicate that there is a single J chain in each IgM pentamer or polymeric IgA molecule. The J chain is covalently bonded to the penultimate cysteine residue of α and μ chains. Whether or not the J chain is required for the proper polymerization of the IgA and IgM basic unit is controversial. Polymeric immunoglobulins of certain lower vertebrates such as nurse shark and paddlefish are apparently devoid of J chain. These observations indicate that J chain is not an absolute requirement for polymerization of the immunoglobulin basic units. Nevertheless, the presence of J chain does facilitate the polymerization of basic units of IgA and IgM molecules into their appropriate polymeric forms.

CARBOHYDRATE MOIETIES OF IMMUNOGLOBULINS

Significant amounts of carbohydrate are present in all immunoglobulins in the form of simple or complex side chains covalently bonded to amino acids in the polypeptide chains (Table 2–2).

The function of the carbohydrate moieties is poorly understood. They probably play important roles in the secretion of immunoglobulins by plasma cells and in the biologic functions associated with the C regions of H chains.

The attachment in most cases is by means of an N-glycosidic linkage between an N-acetylglucosamine residue of the carbohydrate side chain and an asparagine residue of the polypeptide chain. However, other linkages have also been observed, including an O-glycosidic linkage between an amino sugar of an oligosaccharide side chain and a serine residue of the polypeptide chain. Fig 2–9 gives several examples of the oligosaccharide side chains associated with immunoglobulins. In general, carbohydrate is found in only the secretory component, the J chain, and the C regions of H chains; it is not found in L chains or the V regions of H chains. Exceptions to this rule have been found in a small number of myeloma proteins. The secretory component has more carbohydrate than either the α chain or the L chain, which accounts for the higher carbohydrate content in secretory IgA than in serum IgA. Studies on monoclonal immunoglobulins indicated that IgM and IgE generally have an average of 5 oligosaccharides each; IgG one; and IgA, 2 or 3 oligosaccharides. This agrees with the overall carbohydrate content of immunoglobulins, since IgM, IgD, and IgE have the largest amounts of carbohydrate, followed by IgA and then by IgG (Table 2–2). However, these studies were performed on a limited number of monotypic immunoglobulins. In view of the findings that different myeloma proteins of the same class or subclass may differ from one another in carbohydrate content, that an individual myeloma protein occasionally exhibits microheterogeneity with respect to its carbohydrate content, and that V regions of a small number of immunoglobulin polypeptide chains contain carbohydrate, it is incorrect to assume that all immunoglobulins belonging to a given class or subclass have the same number of oligosaccharide side chains.

EVOLUTION OF IMMUNOGLOBULINS

The immune system probably evolved in higher animals in response to the hazards of infection by bacteria, viruses, and other organisms and of the development and spread of aberrant or malignant cells (Chapter 11). The latter function has been called immunologic surveillance (see Chapter 21). As mentioned earlier, all immunoglobulin H and L polypeptide chains consist of domains (Fig 2–6). It is generally accepted that all immunoglobulin structural genes have evolved by gene duplication from a common primordial gene which coded for a single domain. Examination of molecular size reveals that each L chain contains 2 domains; γ and α chains contain 4 each; and μ and ϵ chains contain 5 each.

The protein β_2-microglobulin has been isolated from mammalian serum and urine as a polypeptide of 100 amino acids (MW 11,800). It is present on the surface of lymphocytes and many other body cells. It is also a component of the major histocompatibility antigens (HLA) in man (see Chapter 15). Amino acid sequence analysis shows that β_2-microglobulin has a high degree of homology with the C_H3 domain of human IgG and that both β_2-microglobulin and the δ chain have a methionine residue at the carboxyl terminus. A relationship has been postulated between the gene coding for β_2-microglobulin and the primordial gene coding for C regions of immunoglobulins (Fig 2–10).

The ability to mount an immune response has been examined in several invertebrates including the lobster, horseshoe crab (limulus), starfish, earthworm, and several insect species. The body fluids of many of these species contain substances which agglutinate red

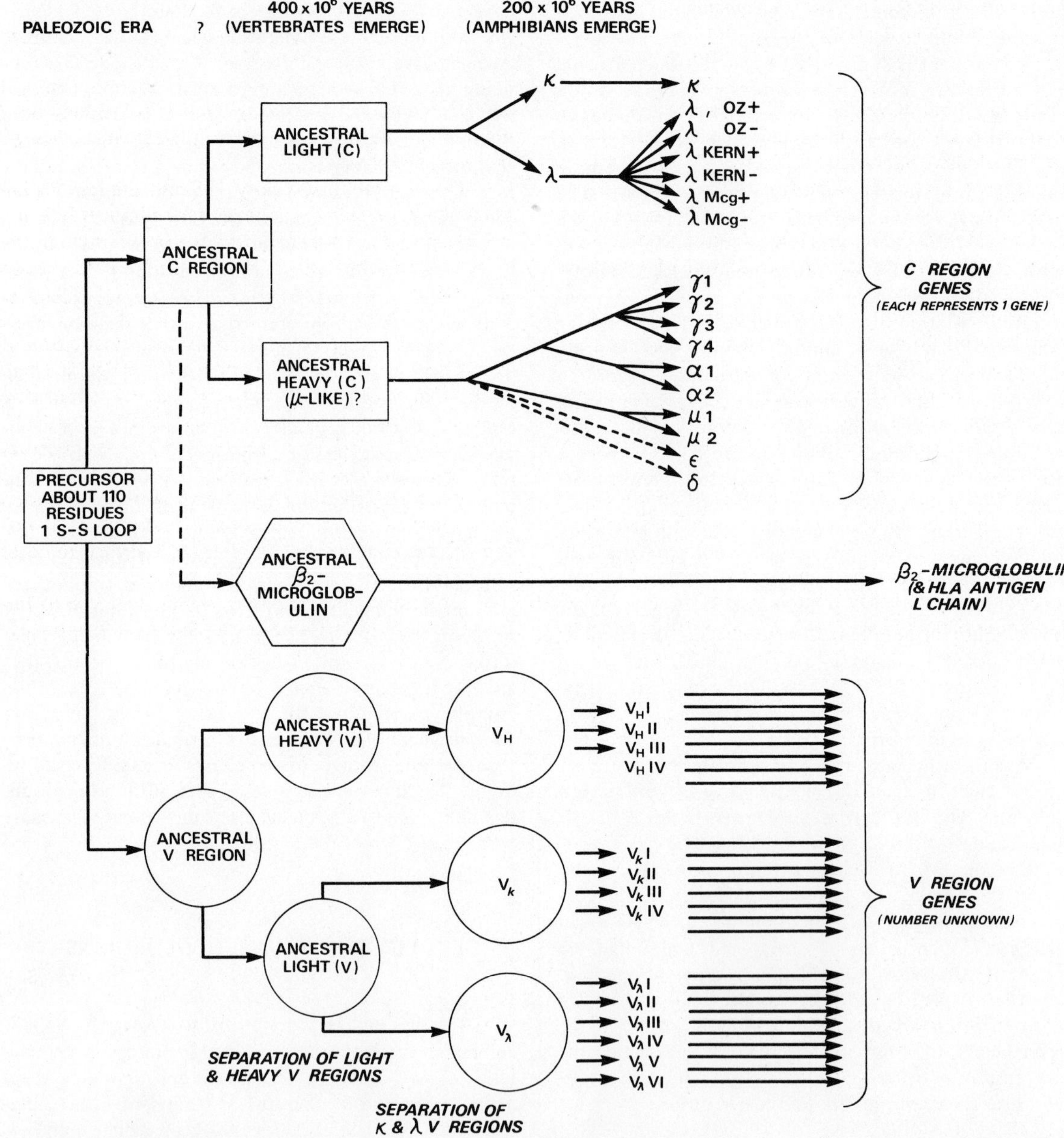

Figure 2–10. A possible scheme for the evolution of genes coding for immunoglobulin polypeptide chains and β_2-microglobulin.

cells of other species, sometimes specifically. However, the molecules responsible for this agglutinating activity do not resemble mammalian immunoglobulins in molecular weight, polypeptide chain structure, or stability.

Molecules with the specificity and inductibility of mammalian antibodies have been described to date only for vertebrates. Humoral antibodies have been demonstrated in all major classes of vertebrates. Antibody formation has been demonstrated in a cyclostome (the lamprey) to antigens such as keyhole limpet hemocyanin and T2 bacteriophage. A more primitive cyclostome, the California hagfish, was found to react to several cellular and soluble antigens with marked antibody production. It appears likely that all vertebrates are capable of producing antibodies.

Chemical analysis of the lamprey antibody indicated that it existed in 2 forms of different sizes: 6.6S and 14S. The 2 forms are antigenically indistinguishable, and both have the basic 4-chain structure (Fig 2–1) with L chains of molecular weight 25,000 and H chains of molecular weight 70,000. The H chains of the lamprey antibody were thought to be homologous to human μ chain. However, other evidence indicates that the lamprey may also have another kind of "antibody" with a unique structure consisting of 4 polypeptide chains of identical size.

Similarly, antibodies isolated from shark, sting ray, bowfin, goldfish, giant grouper, paddlefish, and gar all showed the presence of antigenically indistinguishable 7S (or 8S) and 19S molecules. The H chains of these antibodies were all characterized by a molecular weight of approximately 70,000, high carbohydrate content, and a slower electrophoretic mobility, thus resembling human μ chain. Therefore, it appears likely that μ chain is the most primitive immunoglobulin H chain.

The most primitive animals that possess an immunoglobulin class clearly homologous to human IgG are the amphibians (Table 2–4). Ultracentrifugal analysis of antibodies of frogs and toads demonstrated that a 19S macroglobulin is the early antibody formed after primary immunization with one of a variety of antigens. 7S antibody is formed later in the immune response and is the major immunoglobulin class 2–3 months after immunization. The 19S and 7S antibodies of amphibians are antigenically different. Detailed chemical studies on these molecules indicate that L chains of both forms are similar, with a molecular weight of approximately 23,000, but the H chains differ in molecular weight. The molecular weight of the H chain of the 19S antibody is approximately 72,000 (equivalent to human μ chain). Whether amphibians make an immunoglobulin class resembling IgA is unknown; cells resembling plasma cells have been found in the gut of toads but not of fish.

Immunoglobulins in reptiles resemble those in amphibians. During the course of a humoral immune response, early antibody resembling human 19S IgM and later antibody resembling human 7S IgG have been observed in the tortoise, turtle, tuatara, lizard, alligator, and several other species.

In addition to the early 19S and the late 7S immunoglobulins directly homologous to human IgM and IgG, birds also have IgA. All species investigated in the evolutionary scale higher than birds appear to possess all 3 major classes of immunoglobulins–IgM, IgG, and IgA.

Little information is available on the evolution of IgD. The apparent lack of biologic properties, the high susceptibility to degradation, and the low concentration in serum have made its identification difficult. Nevertheless, a molecule cross-reacting with antiserum to human IgD has been detected in the sera of most primates higher than the New World monkeys. Limited amino acid sequence data on the Fc fragment of IgD showed more sequence homology to IgE than to other immunoglobulin classes.

Molecules with properties similar to those of human IgE have been found in the rabbit, dog, monkey,

Table 2–4. Immunoglobulin classes and subclasses in various vertebrates.

Species	Class and Subclass				
Man	IgG1, IgG2, IgG3, IgG4	IgA1, IgA2	IgM1, IgM2	IgD	IgE
Ape	IgG	IgA	IgM	IgD	IgE
Monkey	IgG	IgA	IgM	IgD	IgE
Mouse	IgG2a, IgG2b, –*, IgG1	IgA1, IgA2	IgM	IgD	IgE
Rat	IgG2a, IgG2b, IgG2c, IgG1	IgA	IgM	?	IgE
Guinea pig	IgG2, –, –, IgG1	IgA	IgM	?	IgE
Rabbit	IgG2, –, –, IgG1	IgA1, IgA2	IgM	?	IgE
Dog	IgG2a, IgG2b, IgG2c, IgG1	IgA	IgM	?	IgE
Cow	IgG2, –, –, IgG1	IgA	IgM	?	?
Horse	IgGa, IgGb, IgGc, IgGT	IgA	IgM	?	?
Fowl	IgG	IgA	IgM	?	?
Reptile	IgG	?	IgM	?	?
Amphibian	IgG	?	IgM	?	?
Fish	?	?	IgM	?	?
Lamprey	?	?	IgM	?	?

*– indicates the absence of an additional subclass corresponding to that in man.

rat, and mouse. Although it is likely that all mammalian species have an immunoglobulin class directly analogous to human IgE, the universal existence of IgE in higher animals has not been firmly established.

A low-molecular-weight immunoglobulin has been observed in lungfish, turtle, and duck. Its H chain has a molecular weight of approximately 38,000. It is likely that this molecule represents a divergent line of immunoglobulin whose H chain has only 2 instead of 3 or 4 C region domains.

Immunoglobulin polypeptide chains corresponding to human κ and λ type L chains have been found in all mammalian and avian species and possibly reptiles, bony fish, and sharks. Both types of L chains can associate with H chains of all classes and subclasses for a given antibody specificity. A clear estimate of when the κ/λ divergence took place is impossible to obtain from the available phylogenetic data. Since the degree of sequence similarity between κ and λ is slightly greater than that between μ and γ, it might be expected that the κ/λ divergence took place after the μ/γ divergence, probably after the divergence of the mammalian line from amphibians (Fig 2–10).

Most or all mammalian species have at least 2 IgG subclasses which differ in biologic properties, electrophoretic mobility, and other properties (Table 2–4). The criteria used to subdivide IgG into subclasses in several species have been (1) clear-cut differences between electrophoretic mobilities of different subclasses; (2) antigenic differences; and (3) differences in biologic properties. Since these are probably insufficient criteria on which to build a completely satisfactory definition of all of the IgG subclasses in any one species, other—as yet undefined—subclasses may well exist in all species except perhaps man, mouse, and rat. Myeloma proteins are available in these 3 species which facilitate the classification of immunoglobulin subclasses.

It is generally accepted that the C regions of H chains belonging to the same subclass are coded for by a single gene. It is noteworthy that subclasses in a species usually do not show immunologic cross-reactions with those of other, even closely related, species. Furthermore, IgG subclasses and their H chain C region allotypes do not always exist in concordance in primates. It has been speculated that more than 10 genes coding for H chain C regions may exist in the genome in all species, with different sets of these genes being expressed in different species. Such mechanisms may also operate in V region genes and may be at least partially responsible for the occurrence of "species-specific" amino acid residues, and allotypes involving multiple amino acid substitutions among polypeptide chains coded for by different alleles.

A general hypothetical scheme for the evolution of immunoglobulins is shown in Fig 2–10. The 4 main stages in this evolution may be summarized as follows: (1) formation of V regions and C regions, and H and L chains, in the production of a functional antibody molecule; (2) formation of the major classes of H chains and major types of L chains; (3) formation of the V region subgroups; and (4) the more recent evolution of C region subclasses of many of these chains. The gene coding for β_2-microglobulin probably evolved from the ancestral C region gene. Gene duplication and point mutation are believed to be fundamental processes leading to diversification at each stage.

• • •

References

Amos B (editor): *Progress in Immunology, I.* Academic Press, 1971.

Brent L, Holborow J (editors): *Progress in Immunology, II.* North-Holland Publishing Co., 1975.

Capra JD, Kehoe JM: Hypervariable regions, idiotypy, and the antibody-combining site. Adv Immunol 20:1, 1975.

Dayhoff MO (editor): *Atlas of Protein Sequence and Structure.* Vol 5. National Biomedical Research Foundation, 1972.

Eisen HN: *Immunology.* Harper & Row, 1974.

Fudenberg HH & others: *Basic Immunogenetics.* Oxford Univ Press, 1972.

Gally JA, Edelman GM: The genetic control of immunoglobulin synthesis. Annu Rev Genet 6:1, 1972.

Gergely J, Medgyesi GA (editors): *Antibody Structure and Molecular Immunology.* North-Holland Publishing Co., 1975.

Hill RL & others: The evolutionary origin of the immunoglobulins. Proc Natl Acad Sci USA 56:1762, 1966.

Hilschmann N, Craig LC: Amino acid sequence studies with Bence Jones proteins. Proc Natl Acad Sci USA 53:1403, 1965.

Hood L, Prahl JW: The immune system: A model for differentiation in higher organisms. Adv Immunol 14:291, 1971.

Ishizaka K, Dayton DH Jr (editors): *The Biological Role of the Immunoglobulin E System.* US Department of Health, Education, & Welfare, 1973.

Kochwa S, Kunkel HG (editors): Immunoglobulins. Ann NY Acad Sci 190:5, 1971. [Entire issue.]

Koshland ME: The structure and function of J chain. Adv Immunol 20:41, 1975.

Mestecky J, Lawton AR (editors): *The Immunoglobulin A System.* Plenum Press, 1974.

Metzger H: Structure and function of γM macroglobulins. Adv Immunol 12:57, 1970.

Milstein C, Pink JRL: Structure and evolution of immunoglobulins. Prog Biophys Mol Biol 21:209, 1970.

Natvig JB, Kunkel HG: Immunoglobulins: Classes, subclasses, genetic against variants and idiotypes. Adv Immunol 16:1, 1973.

Nisonoff A, Hopper JE, Spring SB: *The Antibody Molecule.* Academic Press, 1975.

Porter RR: Structural studies of immunoglobulins. Science 180:713, 1973.

Putnam FW: Immunoglobulin structure: Variability and homology. Science 163:633, 1969.

Singer SJ, Doolittle RF: Antibody active site and immunoglobulin molecules. Science 153:13, 1966.

Smith RT, Miescher PA, Good RA (editors): *Phylogeny of Immunity*. Univ of Florida Press, 1966.

Spiegelberg HL: Biological activities of immunoglobulins of different classes and subclasses. Adv Immunol 19:259, 1974.

Tomasi TB, Grey HM: Structure and function of immunoglobulin A. Prog Allergy 16:81, 1972.

Wang AC, Fudenberg HH: Gene expansion and antibody variability. J Immunogenet 1:303, 1974.

Wang AC, Fudenberg HH: IgA and evolution of immunoglobulins. J Immunogenet 1:3, 1974.

Wu TT, Kabat EA: An analysis of the variable regions of Bence Jones proteins and myeloma light chains and their implications for antibody complementarity. J Exp Med 132:211, 1970.

3 . . .
Immunogenicity & Antigenic Specificity

Joel W. Goodman, PhD

IMMUNOGENS

Immunogenicity

Immunogenicity is a property of substances which can induce a detectable immune response (humoral, cellular, or, most commonly, both) when introduced into an animal. Such substances are called *immunogens* or *antigens.*

Chemical Nature of Immunogens

The most potent immunogens are macromolecular proteins, but polysaccharides, synthetic polypeptides, and other synthetic polymers such as polyvinylpyrrolidone are immunogenic under appropriate conditions (see below). Although pure nucleic acids have not been shown to be immunogenic, antibodies which react with nucleic acids may be induced by immunization with nucleoproteins. Such antibodies appear spontaneously in the serum of patients with systemic lupus erythematosus (see Chapter 27).

Requirements for Immunogenicity

Immunogenicity is not an inherent property of a molecule, as are its physicochemical characteristics, but is operationally dependent on the experimental conditions of the system. These include the antigen, the mode of immunization, the organism being immunized, and the sensitivity of the methods used to detect a response. For example, it was generally agreed that gelatin was nonimmunogenic until the development of more sensitive methods for detecting antibody proved otherwise. The factors that confer immunogenicity are complex and incompletely understood, but it is known that certain conditions must be satisfied in order for a molecule to be immunogenic.

A. Foreignness: The immune system somehow discriminates between "self" and "nonself," so that only molecules that are foreign to the circulation of the animal are normally immunogenic. Thus, albumin isolated from the serum of a rabbit and injected back into the same or another rabbit will not generate the formation of antibody. Yet the same protein injected into any other higher vertebrate animal is likely to evoke substantial amounts of antibody depending on the dose of antigen and the route and frequency of injection.

B. Molecular Size: Extremely small molecules such as amino acids or monosaccharides are not immunogenic, and it is generally accepted that a certain minimum size is necessary for immunogenicity. However, there is no specific threshold below which all substances are inert and above which all are active, but rather a gradient of immunogenicity with molecular size. In a few instances, substances with molecular weights of less than 1000 have proved to be immunogenic, but as a general rule molecules smaller than 10,000 are only weakly immunogenic or not immunogenic at all. The most potent immunogens are macromolecular proteins with molecular weights greater than 100,000.

C. Chemical Complexity: A molecule must possess a certain degree of chemical complexity in order to be immunogenic. The principle has been illustrated very clearly with synthetic polypeptides. Homopolymers consisting of repeating units of a single amino acid are poor immunogens regardless of size, whereas copolymers of 2 or—even better—3 amino acids may be quite active. Once again, it is difficult to establish a definite threshold, and the general rule is that immunogenicity increases with structural complexity. Aromatic amino acids contribute more to immunogenicity than nonaromatic residues since relatively simple random polypeptides containing tyrosine are better antigens than the same polymers without tyrosine and immunogenicity is proportionate to the tyrosine content of the molecule. Also, the attachment of tyrosine chains to the weak immunogen gelatin, which is poor in aromatic amino acids, markedly enhances its immunogenicity.

D. Genetic Constitution of the Animal: The ability to respond to a particular antigen varies with genetic makeup. It has been known for some time that pure polysaccharides are immunogenic when injected into mouse and man but not when injected into the guinea pig. Much additional information has accrued from the use of inbred strains of animals. As one of many examples, strain 2 guinea pigs respond readily in an easily detectable manner to poly-L-lysine, whereas strain 13 guinea pigs do not. The ability to respond is inherited as an autosomal dominant trait. Many

Joel W. Goodman is Professor of Microbiology, University of California School of Medicine, San Francisco.

similar cases have been described, and the genetic control of the immune response is currently one of the most active areas of investigation in biology (see Chapter 12).

E. Method of Antigen Administration: Whether an antigen will induce an immune response depends on the dose and the mode of administration. A quantity of antigen which is ineffective when injected intravenously may evoke a copious antibody response if injected subcutaneously in adjuvant. In general, once the threshold is exceeded, increasing doses lead to increasing—but less than proportionate—responses. However, excessive doses may not only fail to stimulate antibody formation; they can establish a state of specific unresponsiveness.

ANTIGENIC DETERMINANTS

Although strong immunogens are large molecules, only restricted portions of them are involved in actual binding with antibody combining sites. Such areas, which determine the specificity of antigen-antibody reactions, are designated *antigenic determinants.* The number of distinct determinants on an antigen molecule usually varies with its size and chemical complexity. Valence estimates have been made on the basis of the number of antibody molecules bound per molecule of antigen. Such measurements provide minimum values, since steric hindrance may prevent simultaneous occupation of all sites. Furthermore, antibody populations from different animals are likely to vary in specificity, and variations occur also in those of a single individual at different points in time. This means that antibodies specific for all determinants of an antigen molecule may not be present in a particular antiserum. Typical results using this approach give about 5 antigenic determinants for hen egg albumin (MW 42,000) and as many as 40 for thyroglobulin (MW 700,000).

Haptens

Much of our understanding of the specificity of antigen-antibody reactions derives from the pioneering studies of Karl Landsteiner in the early years of the 20th century with small, chemically defined substances which are not immunogenic but can react with antibodies of appropriate specificity. They are called *haptens,* from the Greek word *haptein,* "to fasten." Landsteiner covalently coupled the diazonium derivatives of a wide variety of aromatic amines to the lysine, tyrosine, and histidine residues of immunogenic proteins (Fig 3–1). The conjugated proteins raised antibody specific for the azo substituents, demonstrated by the capacity of the free hapten to bind antibody. The conjugated hapten therefore behaves like a partial or complete antigenic determinant. The total determinant may include amino acids in the protein to which the hapten is linked. The protein, called the *carrier,* has its set of native or integral determinants as well as the new determinants introduced by the conjugated hapten (Fig 3–2).

Although most haptens are small molecules, macromolecules may also function as haptens. The definition is based not on size but on immunogenicity.

The use of hapten-protein conjugates has spotlighted the remarkable diversity of immune mechanisms as well as the exquisite structural specificity of antigen-antibody reactions. Virtually any chemical entity may serve as an antigenic determinant if coupled to a suitably immunogenic carrier. Even antibodies with specificity for metal ions have been produced in this way.

Landsteiner's studies showed that antibody could distinguish between structurally similar haptens. In one series of experiments, antibodies raised to *m*-aminobenzenesulfonate were tested for their ability to bind with other isomers of the homologous hapten and related molecules in which the sulfonate group was replaced by arsonate or carboxylate groups (Table 3–1). As expected, the strongest reaction occurred with the homologous hapten. The compound with the sulfonate group in the *ortho* position was somewhat poorer than

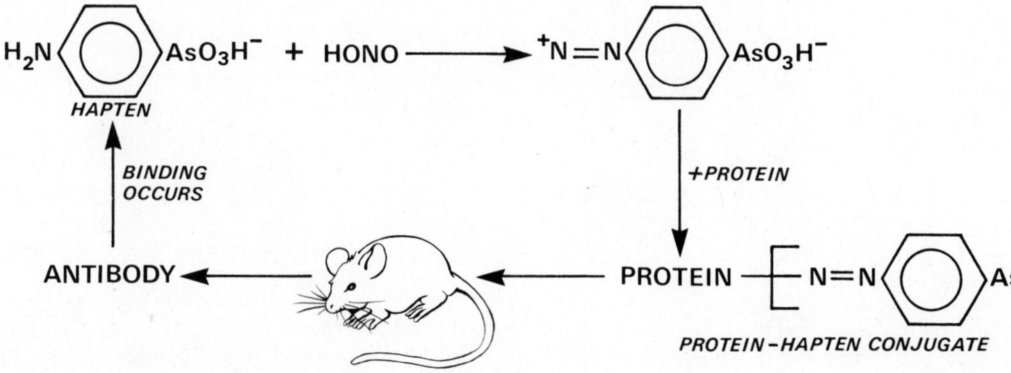

H_2N–C₆H₄–AsO_3H^- + HONO → $^+N{=}N$–C₆H₄–AsO_3H^-

HAPTEN

BINDING OCCURS

+PROTEIN

ANTIBODY ← ← PROTEIN–[N=N–C₆H₄–AsO_3H^-]$_n$

PROTEIN-HAPTEN CONJUGATE

Figure 3–1. The preparation of hapten-protein conjugates and their capacity to induce the formation of antihapten antibody to the azophenylarsonate group in this example.

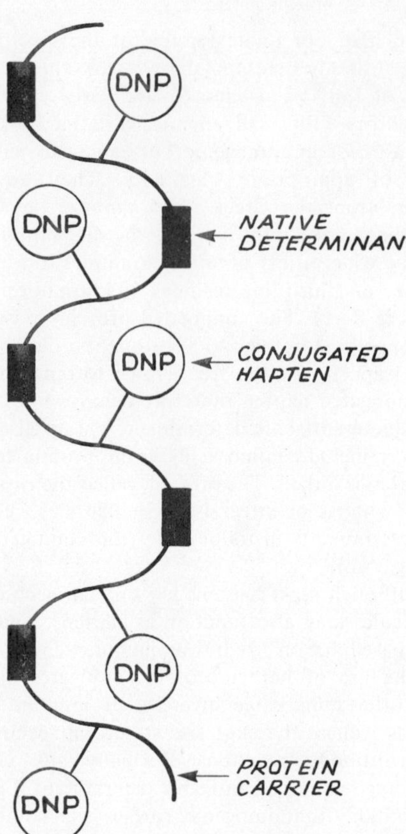

Figure 3–2. Diagrammatic illustration of a hapten-protein conjugate. The protein has several native or integral antigenic determinants denoted by thickened areas. The conjugated dinitrophenyl (DNP) hapten introduces new antigenic determinants.

the *meta* isomer but distinctly better than the *para* isomer. The substitution of arsonate for sulfonate resulted in very weak binding with antibody. Although both substituents are negatively charged and have a tetrahedral structure, the arsonate group is bulkier because of the larger size of the arsenic atom and the additional hydrogen atom. The benzoate derivatives are also negatively charged, but the carboxylate ion has a planar rather than tetrahedral 3-dimensional configuration and shows even less affinity for the antisulfonate antibody.

Another illustration of the exquisite structural specificity of immune reactions is clearly depicted by the work of Avery and Goebel, who prepared antisera against conjugates composed of simple sugars coupled to proteins (Table 3–2). The antisera could readily distinguish between glucose and galactose, which differ only by the orientation of hydrogen and hydroxyl groups on one carbon atom. Similarly, *p*-aminophenol *α*-glucoside and the corresponding *β*-glucoside, which present identical surface configurations but differ stereochemically, could be distinguished despite strong cross-reactivity.

Table 3–1. Effect of variation in hapten structure on strength of binding to *m*-aminobenzenesulfonate antibodies.

NH_2, R (*ortho*)	NH_2, R (*meta*)	NH_2, R (*para*)
ortho	*meta*	*para*

	ortho	*meta*	*para* isomers
R = sulfonate	++	+++	±
R = arsonate	–	+	–
R = carboxylate	–	±	–

Strength of binding is graded from negative (–) to very strong (+++). (From Landsteiner K, van der Scheer J: On cross reactions of immune sera to azoproteins. J Exp Med 63:325, 1936.)

Studies of this kind have shown that antibody recognizes the overall 3-dimensional shape of the antigenic determinant group rather than any specific chemical property such as ionic charge. It is believed that antigenic determinants and antibody combining sites possess a structural complementariness which may be figuratively visualized as a "lock-and-key" arrangement (Fig 3–3). The electron cloud box of the antibody site is contoured to match that of the antigenic determinant, with the affinity of binding directly proportionate to the closeness of fit. The startling diversity of the antibody response is perhaps more comprehensible if antibody specificity is viewed as directed against a molecular shape rather than a particular chemical structure.

Identification of Antigenic Determinants

Much has been learned about the composition, structure, and size of integral (native) determinants of antigen molecules as well as of haptenic determinants from 3 general approaches.

A. Cross-Reaction: This is the reaction of antibody with an antigen other than the one which induced its formation. The former is called a *heterologous* antigen and the latter the *homologous* antigen. The reaction of anti-*m*-aminobenzenesulfonate antibody with any of the other compounds in Table 3–1 is an example of a cross-reaction. Cross-reactions provide a limited amount of information about the composition of antigenic determinants. For example, it was shown that a galactan from the lung thought to be composed only of galactose cross-reacted with horse antiserum against type III pneumococcal polysaccharide, which is composed of glucose and glucuronic acid. A sensitive chemical analysis of this galactan confirmed that it contained a small amount of glucose.

B. Degradation of Complex Antigens: The object is to obtain fragments that represent intact antigenic determinants. It has been applied to a variety of protein and polysaccharide antigens with limited success.

Table 3–2. Reactions of antisera with isomeric glucoside proteins conjugates.*
(+ represents precipitation)

	p-Aminophenol *α*-glucoside	*p*-Aminophenol *β*-glucoside	*p*-Aminophenol *β*-galactoside
Antisera against:			
α-Glucoside	+++	++	0
β-Glucoside	++	+++	0
β-Galactoside	0	0	+++

*Reproduced, with permission, from Humphrey JH, White RG: *Immunology for Students of Medicine.* Davis, 1970.

The obvious disadvantage of this approach is the improbability of obtaining intact determinants without irrelevant portions of the antigen molecule.

C. Synthetic Antigens: This has proved the most productive approach to delineation of antigenic determinants. A variety of studies have employed natural or synthetic homopolymers of a single amino acid or sugar, synthetic polypeptides of defined structure, or synthetic haptens coupled to natural protein carriers. An ordered series of haptens may then be synthesized and binding with antibody assessed by inhibition of the quantitative precipitin reaction between antibody and homologous antigen. In this way, the structure of the antigenic determinant can be precisely defined. Homopolymers must usually be of substantial size in order to be immunogenic, and conformational differences between the integral determinant and the synthetic hapten may complicate interpretation. For this reason, recent efforts have concentrated on conjugating haptens to the side chains of protein carriers. Studies have been performed in great detail on the specificity of antibodies to glycosylated antigens, components of nucleic acids conjugated to proteins or polypeptides, and a myriad of other hapten-protein conjugates. The haptens are not integral parts of the molecular superstructure of the carrier, and conformational considerations are minimized. However, very small haptens are incomplete determinants, which limits their usefulness for determining the extent of antigenic determinants. Perhaps the most reliable estimate of the size of an antigenic determinant was derived from a series of peptides of defined size and structure coupled to a protein carrier.

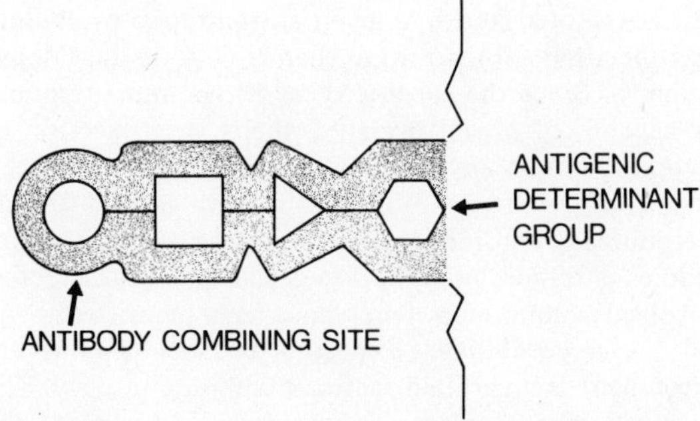

Figure 3–3. A view of the "lock-and-key" complementariness between an antigenic determinant group and an antibody combining site. The determinant can be considered to be composed of discrete subunits, which may be amino acids in a peptide chain or sugars in a saccharide chain. The antibody combining site is then composed of subsites, each of which can accommodate a discrete subunit of the antigenic determinant. (Reproduced, with permission, from Goodman JW: Antigenic determinants and antibody combining sites. In: *The Antigens.* Vol 3. Sela M [editor]. Academic Press, 1975.)

Size of Antigenic Determinants

Antibody complementariness is directed against limited parts of the antigen molecule. Antibodies raised against haptens composed of 2 moieties linked to the same benzene ring, such as glycine and leucine in aminoisophthalylglycylleucine, are specific for one group or the other but not both. Other studies with azoproteins, as well as with dinitrophenylated and penicilloyl proteins, showed that the amino acid in the protein to which the hapten was joined participated in the antigenic determinant.

More precise analysis of determinant group size occurred when it was found that dextrans, which are polysaccharides composed of a single sugar (glucose), are immunogenic. Some dextrans are essentially single chains with very few branch points and provide immunogens for which the size of determinants could be estimated by using an ordered series of oligosaccharides as inhibitors of the dextran-antidextran precipitin reaction. The rationale is based on the premise that each subunit which forms a part of the determinant will contribute binding energy to the reaction with antibody, but enlarging the hapten beyond the size of the determinant will result in no improvement of bind-

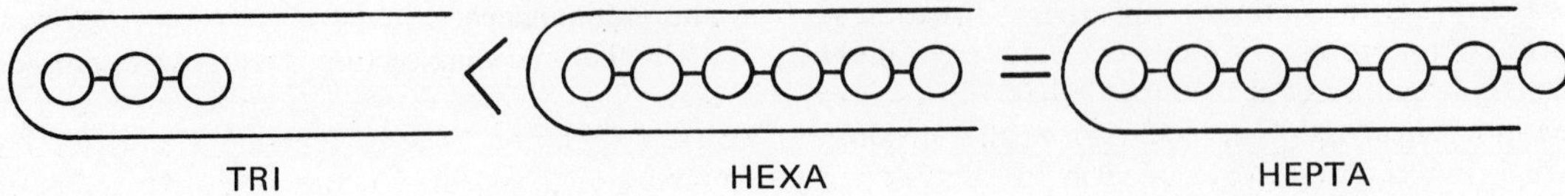

Figure 3–4. Illustration of how hapten binding with antibody permits assessment of the size of antigenic determinants. In the dextran-antidextran system, the hexasaccharide was a better ligand with antibody than smaller oligosaccharides and equal to the heptasaccharide. It was concluded that the hexasaccharide just filled the antibody combining site, providing maximum binding energy. Additional sugar residues lay outside the site, making no contribution to binding.

ing since the additional subunits will lie outside the antibody combining site (see Fig 3–4). Kabat showed that the hexasaccharide was the best ligand with anti-dextran antibody, the heptasaccharide being no better on a molar basis. This was taken to be the size of the antigenic determinant and, by inference, the approximate size of the complementary region of the antibody molecule.

One difficulty that arises in the interpretation of this kind of experiment is that enhanced binding with haptens of increasing size may not necessarily reflect the size of the antigenic determinant but rather the approach to a conformation which is present in the intact antigen and for which the antibody site is complementary. This conformation could involve only a portion of the total hapten in direct binding with antibody, the remainder being essential for the assumption of the required configuration. The results of many studies indicate that antigen conformation is indeed a prominent factor in antibody specificity.

Numerous investigations using homopolymers of amino acids or multichain polymer-protein conjugates as antigens have yielded determinant group sizes in reasonable consonance with the dextran model (Table 3–3). Perhaps the most precise evaluation of determinant size was obtained using immunogens consisting of proteins to which were attached peptides of defined structure. Peptides of the form (D-Ala)$_n$–Gly (where n varied from 1 to 4) were coupled to proteins, and the conjugates induced peptide-specific antibodies in rabbits. Peptides of the general structure (D–Ala)$_n$ (n = 1 to 4) and (D–Ala)$_n$–Gly-ϵ-aminocaproic acid (n = 1 to 3) were used as inhibitors of the homologous precipitin reaction. The antigenic determinant in all instances was a tetrapeptide, the lysine residue of the protein carrier participating in the determinant only when the conjugated hapten was smaller than a tetrapeptide. The consistency of the results and the improbability of conformational complications with such short peptide chains are compelling evidence that the antibody combining site is such as to accommodate 4 amino acid residues. This is in good agreement with other figures in Table 3–3, so we may feel confident that the size of an antigenic determinant has been defined within very narrow limits.

Table 3–3. Estimation of the size of sequentially defined antigenic determinants.

Antigen	Species	Determinant
Dextran	Man	Isomaltohexaose
Dextran	Rabbit	⩾ Isomalto-hexaose
Poly-γ–glutamic acid (killed *B anthracis*)	Rabbit	Hexaglutamic acid
Polyalanyl-bovine serum albumin	Rabbit	Pentaalanine
Polylysyl-rabbit serum albumin	Rabbit	Penta- or hexa-lysine
Polylysyl-phosphoryl-bovine serum albumin	Rabbit	Pentalysine
α-Dinitrophenyl–(lysine)$_{11}$	Guinea pig	α-Dinitrophenyl–heptalysine
α-Dinitrophenyl–polylysine	Guinea pig	α-Dinitrophenyl–trilysine
(D–Ala)$_n$–Gly–RNase	Rabbit	Tetrapeptide
Denatured DNA	Man*	Pentanucleotide

*Sera from patients with systemic lupus erythematosus (see Chapter 27).

Immunopotency

Even large protein antigens possess a limited number of antigenic determinants. An extreme case in point is tobacco mosaic virus protein, which consists of 158 amino acids. A number of rabbit antisera had specificities limited to an eicosapeptide region of the molecule. As noted above, a given antiserum to ovalbumin has specificity for no more than 5 or 6 distinct determinants. Since the specificity of the immune response is capable of great diversity, there is a selection of determinants in any given situation. The capacity of a region of an antigen molecule to serve as an antigenic determinant and induce the formation of specific antibodies is termed *immunopotency*. Some of the factors involved in immunopotency have been identified.

A. Accessibility: Exposure to the aqueous environment is a cardinal factor in immunopotency. The terminal side chains of polysaccharides represent the most immunopotent regions of that class of antigens. A comparison of multichain synthetic polypeptides with sequences of alanine on the outside and tyrosine closer to the backbone, or the reverse (Fig 3–5), showed that antibodies to the former were largely alanine-specific while the latter evoked antibodies with a predominant specificity for tyrosine. The most exposed sequence was the most immunopotent in each instance.

The conformation of macromolecules determines

accessibility to the immune apparatus. Internal sequences within proteins or polysaccharides are not precluded from exposure to the environment. In the case of sperm whale myoglobin, the 3-dimensional structure of which has been elucidated, it was found that peptides from regions which occupied corners of the molecule, and thus were prominently exposed, were important in its immunochemical specificity.

B. Charge: Electrical charge has been considered a dominant factor in specificity since Landsteiner's time, although completely uncharged molecules, such as dextrans, can be immunogenic. As a general rule, charged residues will contribute strongly to the specificity of immunogens in which they are found. This may be a manifestation of the interdependence of charge and accessibility, since charged groups, being hydrophilic, would be in closer contact with the environment than nonpolar groups subject to other conformational restrictions.

C. Genetic Factors: A growing body of evidence attests to genetic control of the ability to produce antibodies of different specificity against a given antigen. Some of the earliest evidence accrued from a comparison of the specificity of anti-insulin antibodies from strain 2 and strain 13 guinea pigs which appear to be directed against opposite ends of the insulin molecule. More recent examples have been found primarily in the responses of mice to synthetic polypeptides (see Chapter 12).

Immunodominance

In the preceding section, factors were considered which may determine why a particular region of an antigen molecule acts as an antigenic determinant, immunopotency being a quantitative expression of the strength of an antigenic determinant. Given a particular determinant, which from earlier consideration may be the size of a tetrapeptide, the subunits of that determinant will contribute unequally to reactivity with antibody. The degree of the influence on reactivity is a measure of the "immunodominance" of the component of the antigenic determinant.

Factors which play crucial roles (on a larger scale) in determining immunopotency are also influential in determining immunodominance. The following are important in immunodominance:

A. Conformation: The immunodominant feature of an antigen may be its conformation rather than a particular subunit of its structure. For example, polymers of the tripeptide L–tyrosyl–L–alanyl–L–glutamic acid form an α-helix under physiologic conditions. The same tripeptide can be attached to a branched synthetic polypeptide (Fig 3–6). The tripeptide itself does not possess an ordered configuration. Antibodies to the 2 polymers did not cross-react, and the tripeptide bound antibodies produced against the branched polymer but not those made against the helical polymer. The immunodominant element of the helical polymer was its conformation. Antiserum

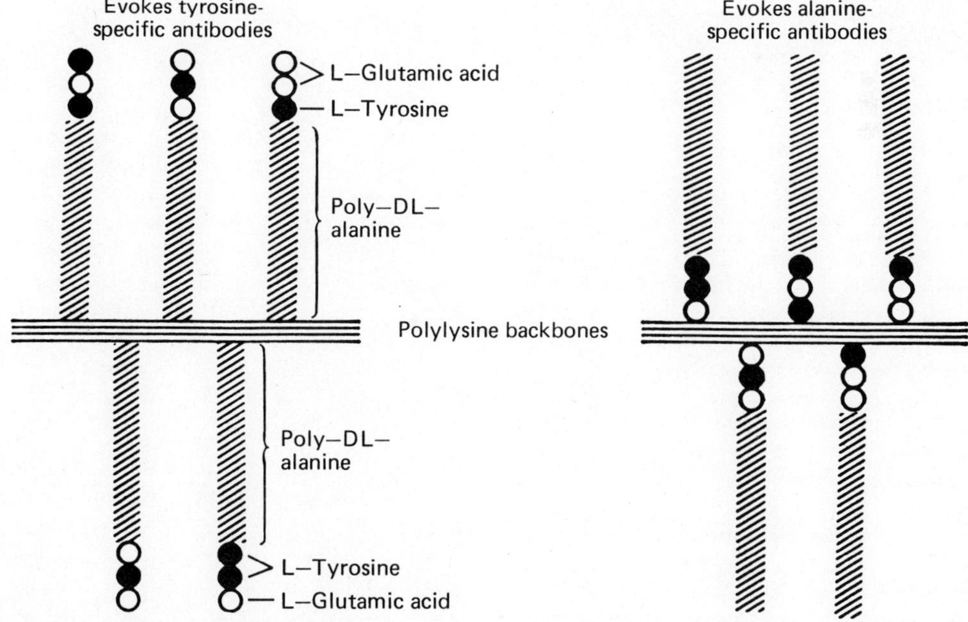

Figure 3–5. *Left:* A multichain copolymer in which L-tyrosine and L-glutamic acid residues are attached to multi-poly–DL–alanyl–poly–L–lysine(poly–[Tyr,Glu]–poly–DL–Ala–poly Lys). *Right:* Copolymer in which tyrosine and glutamic acid are attached directly to the polylysine backbone with alanine peptides on the ends of the side chains. Horizontal lines: poly–L–lysine; diagonal hatching: poly–DL–alanine; closed circles: L-tyrosine; open circles: L-glutamic acid. (From Sela M: Antigenicity: Some molecular aspects. Science 166:1365, 1969.)

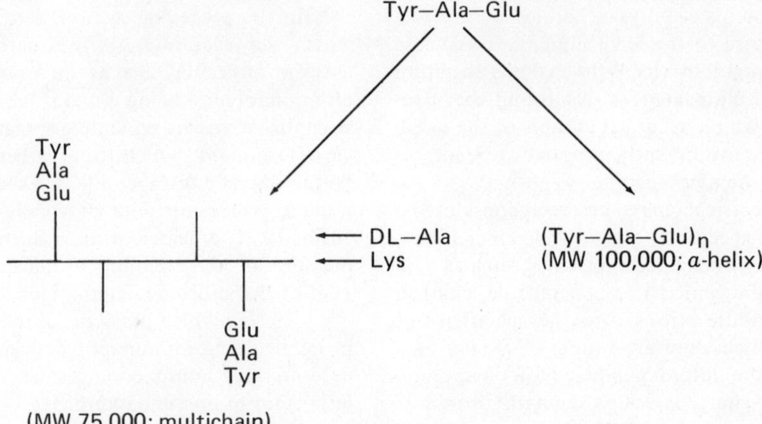

Figure 3–6. A synthetic branched polymer in which peptides of sequence Tyr–Ala–Glu are attached to the amino groups of side chains in multi-poly-DL-alanyl–poly-L-lysine ***(left)*** and a periodic polymer of the tripeptide Tyr–Ala–Glu ***(right)***. (From Sela M: Antigenicity: Some molecular aspects. Science 166:1365, 1969.)

against human hemoglobin A1 combines better with the oxygenated form than the reduced form, and this has been attributed to the difference in quaternary structure between the 2 forms. There are many examples of conformation-dependent antibody specificity.

B. Accessibility: Determinants whose specificity is dictated by the sequence of subunits (amino acids or sugars) within the determinant rather than by the macromolecular superstructure of the antigen molecule are designated *sequential determinants*. In such cases, components of the determinant can act as haptens and bind with antibody, the reaction being demonstrable either directly, by such technics as equilibrium dialysis or fluorescence quenching; or indirectly, by inhibition of the reaction between antigen and antibody. Sequential determinants may either be composed of terminal or internal sequences of macromolecules, or they may be artificially added to carriers, as in the case of the tripeptide Tyr–Ala–Glu.

When the antigenic determinant is a terminal sequence, the terminal residue of the sequence is almost invariably the immunodominant subunit. Again, many examples exist to illustrate this point, which was recognized by Landsteiner when he showed that the terminal amino acid of peptides coupled to a protein carrier exerted a dominant effect on specificity. Goebel made the same observation with glycosides conjugated to protein carriers. In pneumococcal type II polysaccharide, glucuronic acid, which occurs almost exclusively at the terminal nonreducing positions in side chains, is the immunodominant sugar in the specificity of most of the antibodies studied.

Even when specificity is directed toward an internal segment of an antigen, there is a gradient of binding energy for different subunits of the determinant. Dextrans containing very few branch points presumably elicit antibody directed largely or exclusively against interior sequences of glucose. Taking the hexasaccharide as the determinant, the relative contribution to the total binding energy made by each glucose residue was estimated. The results indicated that the first glucose in the determinant contributed 40%, the first 2 glucoses 60%, and the first 3 glucoses 90% of the binding energy of the hexasaccharide. Similar decrements in binding energy were found with other essentially linear polysaccharide and polypeptide antigens.

In general, then, it may be concluded that all determinants exhibit a gradient of immunodominance. When the determinant is comprised of a terminal sequence, the gradient decreases from the most exposed portion inward.

C. Optical Configuration: Antibodies display a pronounced stereospecificity. While amino acid polymers of the D-optical configuration are very weakly immunogenic or nonimmunogenic, D-amino acids can serve as partial or complete determinants when either appended to immunogenic carriers or internally incorporated into synthetic polypeptides. In general, there is little or no cross-reactivity between enantiomorphic determinants. In at least some situations, D-amino acids may be more immunodominant than their stereoisomeric counterparts.

To recapitulate, there is abundant evidence for the existence of antibodies with specificity for conformational features of antigen molecules as well as antibodies whose specificity is directed against sequential determinants. With the latter, antibodies will normally react with small fragments of the antigen, whereas in the former situation disruption of the antigen superstructure results in very weak or negligible activity. Consequently, the determinants of globular proteins, which possess a great deal of ordered structure, have been difficult to delineate in detail, whereas the use of linear or randomly coiled molecules and peptidyl-protein conjugates has met with greater success. Such antigens have provided the most solid information concerning the size and nature of antigenic determinants.

IMMUNOGENIC DETERMINANTS

Immunogens are normally large molecules, and immunogenicity is, within limits, a function of molecular size and complexity. A characteristic of immunogens is their capacity to induce cellular immunity mediated by thymus-derived T lymphocytes (see Chapter 8), which haptens are unable to do. It is believed that an immunogen must possess at least 2 determinants in order to stimulate antibody formation, which is the function of another line of lymphocytes, bursa-derived B cells. At least one determinant must be capable of triggering a T cell response. These relationships and the concept of cell cooperation are discussed in greater detail in Chapter 8. Our concern here is with structural determinants of immunogens which interact with T and B lymphocytes. It has not been possible to identify such determinants on large proteins, but studies with small, well-defined immunogens support the interpretation that specificities of the 2 cell types may be directed against different determinants of the antigen molecule.

The pancreatic hormone glucagon consists of only 29 amino acids but is immunogenic. It has been functionally dissected into component determinants which interact with T cells (immunogenic determinants) and with antibody (haptenic determinants). Using isolated tryptic peptides of the hormone, it was found that antibodies recognized a determinant or determinants in the amino terminal part of the molecule, whereas T lymphocytes responded only to the carboxyl terminal fragment (Fig 3–7). The latter was therefore identified as the immunogenic or "carrier" portion of the molecule and the former as the haptenic region.

Several synthetic molecules about the size of a single antigenic determinant induce an almost purely cellular immune response, with little or no antibody production, but are capable of acting as carriers for conjugated haptens in much the same fashion as macromolecular immunogens. One such unideterminant immunogen is the compound L-tyrosine-*p*-azobenzenearsonate (ABA–Tyr). Despite its molecular weight of only 409, ABA–Tyr induces cellular immunity with little or no antibody production in a variety of animal species. A hapten such as the dinitrophenyl group can be coupled to ABA–Tyr through a spacer group (6-aminocaproic acid) to produce a bideterminant or bifunctional immunogen (Fig 3–8). This antigen induces antibody specific for the dinitrophenyl haptenic determinant and cellular immunity directed against the ABA–Tyr immunogenic determinant.

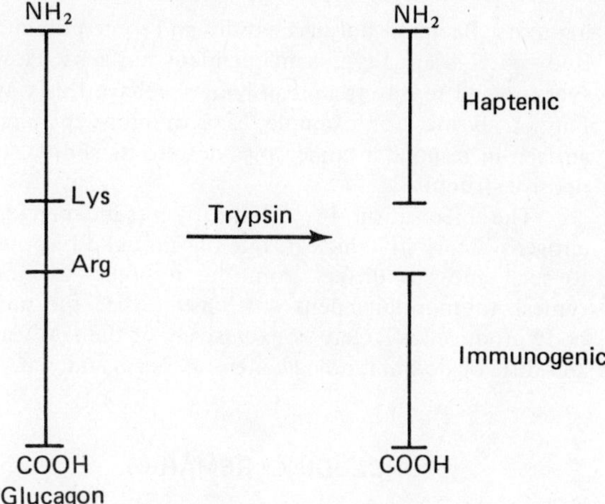

Figure 3–7. The functional dissection of glucagon into immunogenic and haptenic determinants.

Another example is the response of guinea pigs to poly–L–lysine. Responder animals (strain 2 and a fraction of outbred guinea pigs) develop cellular immunity to polymers as small as the heptapeptide. The bifunctional immunogen α-dinitrophenyl–(L–Lys)$_7$ induces antidinitrophenyl antibody responses. Smaller oligomers of lysine do not induce cellular immunity and cannot act as carriers for the dinitrophenyl haptenic determinant.

Experiments with analogues of immunogenic determinants, designed along the lines of Landsteiner's classical studies on the specificity of antihapten antibodies, have shown that cellular (T cell) responses to antigens are as exquisitely specific as antigen-antibody reactions.

THYMUS-INDEPENDENT ANTIGENS

A certain type of molecule may be immunogenic without the apparent participation of T lymphocytes. Such molecules appear to be able to directly trigger B lymphocytes (antibody-producing cells). Their characteristic feature is a structure which consists of repeat-

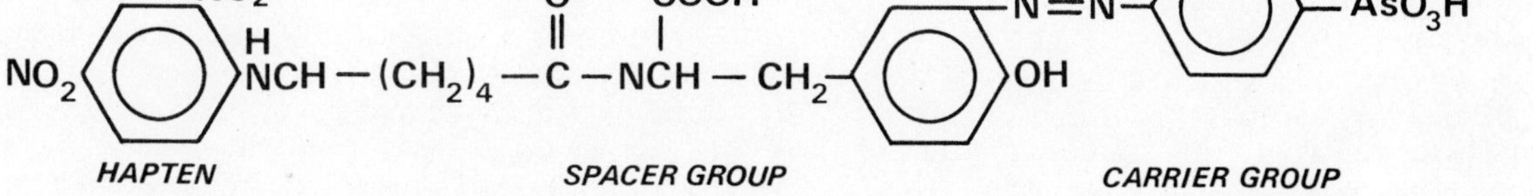

NO_2 NO_2 H NCH — $(CH_2)_4$ — C(=O) — NCH(COOH) — CH_2 — (OH) — N=N — AsO_3H^-

HAPTEN *SPACER GROUP* *CARRIER GROUP*

Figure 3–8. The bifunctional antigen dinitrophenyl-6-aminocaproyl-L-tyrosine-*p*-azobenzenearsonate.

ing units. Bacterial polysaccharides and some polymerized proteins are thymus-independent antigens. However, not all repeating unit polymers behave this way. Poly-L-lysine, for example, is a thymus-dependent antigen in responder guinea pigs despite its simple, repetitive structure.

The mechanism by which thymus-independent antigens act is still unclear, but the immune response to such antigens differs from the response to more typical thymus-dependent antigens in that the antibody produced is largely or exclusively of the IgM class and little or no immunologic memory is engendered.

CONCLUDING REMARKS

The nature and dimensions of haptenic determinants of antigen molecules have received much attention during the past 2 decades, and the problems have now been solved in a reasonably satisfactory way. The use of homopolymers of amino acids or sugars and peptidyl-protein conjugates as antigens has established that a determinant is composed of 4–6 amino acid or sugar residues which contribute unequally to binding with the antibody combining site. The optical configuration and the physical conformation of the determinant weigh heavily in its immunochemical specificity.

These properties bear a strong resemblance to those of the contact regions of enzyme substrates. Six sugar residues entirely fill the combining site of lysozyme. Estimates of the contribution of a given residue in the site to the total free energy of association of a saccharide with the enzyme indicate unequal contribution by the several residues. The proteolytic enzyme papain interacts with a sequence of 7 amino acids in a polypeptide substrate. Here, too, there appears to be an unequal contribution to binding by different subsites in the ligand. The evidence converges toward a coherent image of the dimensions of ligands involved in binding with the active sites of proteins.

In contrast to haptenic determinants, elucidation of the nature and dimensions of immunogenic determinants is still in its infancy. With the exception of thymus-independent antigens, the essential requisite for immunogenicity appears to be recognition by one or more clones of T lymphocytes. A molecule which consists of a single determinant that can trigger a T cell response induces only cellular immunity but can serve as a carrier for a second determinant. The question of why many potent haptenic determinants fail to activate significant T cell responses remains unanswered.

• • •

References

Butler VP Jr, Beiser SM: Antibodies to small molecules: Biological and clinical applications. Adv Immunol 17:255, 1973.

Goodman JW: Antigenic determinants and antibody combining sites. Page 127 in: *The Antigens.* Sela M (editor). Academic Press, 1975.

Kabat EA: The nature of an antigenic determinant. J Immunol 97:1, 1966.

Landsteiner K: *The Specificity of Serological Reactions.* Harvard Univ Press, 1945.

Pressman D, Grossberg AL: *The Structural Basis of Antibody Specificity.* Benjamin, 1968.

Reichlin M: Amino acid substitution and the antigenicity of globular proteins. Adv Immunol 20:71, 1975.

Sela M: Antigenicity: Some molecular aspects. Science 166:1365, 1969.

4 . . .
Antigen-Antibody Reactions

Joseph L. Caldwell, MD

Antibodies in serum and secretions represent a heterogeneous population of molecules capable of noncovalent binding with a large number of extrinsic and intrinsic antigens. The manner in which antibodies react with antigenic determinants, the forces that hold antigen and antibody together, the specificity with which antibody reacts with antigen, and the biologic consequences of antigen-antibody reactions have been the subject of intensive study.

In this chapter we shall consider the forces which promote antigen-antibody reactions and ways of measuring the strength of these interactions. In addition, selected methods of testing for antigen-antibody reactions will be discussed, where they assist our understanding of the basic reactions.

ANTIGEN BINDING

Antigen-Binding Forces

When an antigen and its corresponding antibody physically approach each other, the 2 molecules interact. This interaction does not occur through covalent chemical bonds; instead, the same forces of attraction that act in other protein reactions (such as enzymes and transport proteins) also act to bind antibody to antigen.

Most antigen-antibody interactions involve a summation of the electrostatic charges present on both antigen and antibody molecules, although there is no absolute requirement for charged groups on antigens. There is strong attraction or repulsion between the negatively and positively charged ions present at physiologic pH. In addition, there are weaker forces present including hydrogen bonding, van der Waals forces, and dipole interactions. Since antibody reactions occur in an aqueous environment, hydrophobic and hydrophilic interactions between molecules are important. Water molecules are not electrically neutral; they have a relatively positive pole (the hydrogen end) and a relatively negative pole (the oxygen end). Water molecules are attracted to those regions of the protein molecule that contain polar amino acids, and energy may be required to displace this water and allow antigen to react with antibody. Antibody molecules appear to possess increased numbers of hydrophobic amino acids in their antigen-binding region.

Because noncovalent binding forces are relatively weak and operate over a limited distance, the antigen must closely approach the antibody combining site before the interaction can occur. The strength of the forces holding antigen and antibody together represents a summation of the various forces acting on the molecules, and stronger bonding will result when the 2 sites are complementary to each other in relationship to these interaction points. Since antibody molecules react through a mixture of binding forces, a wide variation in the strength of bonding is possible—from weak bonding, which is present briefly and easily disturbed, to strong bonding, which, once formed, is difficult to dissociate again. Methods have been devised to measure the relative strength or affinity with which antibody binds to antigen. One such method, *equilibrium dialysis,* is discussed below. Since the bonding of these complementary forces is dependent upon the close physical approximation of the 2 molecules, antigen binding can be reduced or prevented by steric obstruction of the combining site even when the noncovalent forces present on each molecule would otherwise result in a strong interaction between the molecules. This fact is used to advantage in detailed chemical studies on the specificity of antigen-antibody reactions. Antibodies prepared against a specific hapten are reacted with chemically similar molecules to determine the relative contribution of molecular configuration or charged ions to the antigenic determinants of the original hapten.

Equilibrium Dialysis

Equilibrium dialysis is an assay seldom employed in the routine clinical evaluation of antigen-antibody interactions, but it demonstrates both the heterogeneity of the typical antibody response and the strength of bonding between antigen and antibody. Essentially, the test involves placing a measured amount of antibody on one side of a semipermeable membrane and a freely diffusible antigen on the other. The antigen is allowed to dialyze across the membrane

Joseph L. Caldwell is Assistant Research Immunologist, University of California School of Medicine and Veterans Administration Hospital, San Francisco.

until it reaches a state of dynamic equilibrium with respect to reaction with the antibody. Haptens are widely used in studies such as these because their small size makes them easily diffusible across the membrane and because good antibody titers can be obtained with haptens as the antigen.

At the start of the assay, the antibody solution is on one side of the membrane and the hapten solution is on the other. The hapten is colored or radioactive or in some other form that can be precisely quantitated. The antibody, because of its larger molecular size, is retained on the original side of the membrane, but the freely diffusible hapten attempts to equilibrate itself by moving across the membrane. As the hapten encounters the antibody, a portion of the hapten molecules becomes bound by the antibody and is effectively removed from the solution. More hapten diffuses into the antibody side, and an equilibrium is finally reached where the *free* hapten is at the same concentration on both sides of the membrane. The degree to which the antigen-binding sites are filled depends on the strength of binding of that particular antibody preparation. The concentration of both free and bound hapten can be determined and the results calculated. The actual assay requires that the antibody be tested at several different dilutions of hapten.

The antibody molecule initially existed as a divalent molecule (using IgG as an example) with all antigen-binding sites empty. As the hapten entered the area, there was a reaction between the 2 molecules and an antigen-antibody complex was formed. (This assay is done with univalent haptens to prevent aggregation or precipitation, although there are special modifications of the assay to measure multivalent antigens.) This reaction can be represented by the following equation:

$$\text{Antibody} + \text{Hapten} \rightarrow \text{Antibody:hapten complex}$$

At the same time, molecules of the complex were simultaneously releasing their hapten and returning to a free state. This reaction, when combined with the first reaction, yields the following expression:

$$\text{Antibody} + \text{Hapten} \rightleftharpoons \text{Antibody:hapten complex}$$

This expression is the familiar law of mass action relationship found in basic chemistry. The mathematics of equilibrium reactions are beyond the scope of this text, and the reader is referred to immunochemistry texts listed in the bibliography (Kabat or Day). Nonetheless, the relationship between free and bound hapten and free and bound antibody is ultimately related to the association constant of the antibody by the following expression:

$$\frac{[AbH]}{[Ab]\ [H]} = \frac{k_1}{k_2} = K_{12}$$

where, [AbH] is the concentration of antibody sites bound with hapten,

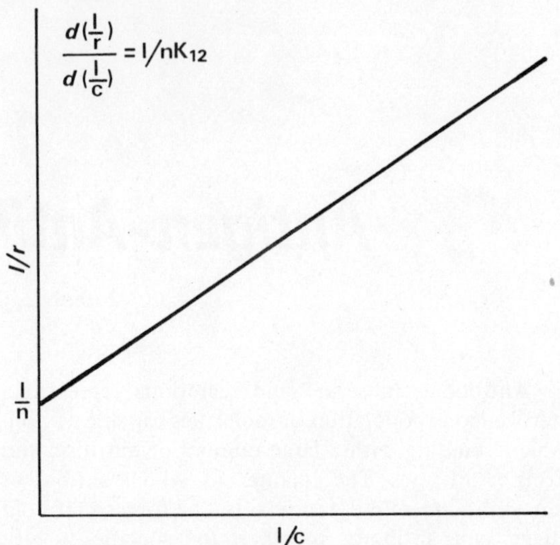

Figure 4–1. Ideal binding in the case of univalent antigen. Langmuir plot. Bound hapten (r) is plotted as the reciprocal against free hapten (c). See text for additional information. (Reproduced, with permission, from Day ED: *Advanced Immunochemistry*. Williams & Wilkins, 1972.)

[Ab] and [H] are the concentrations of free antibody sites or hapten, and

K_{12} is the association constant at equilibrium relating the forward (k_1) and reverse (k_2) reaction constants.

Since we can determine the concentrations of bound and free hapten in the assay system employed, the data can be graphically represented by the plot shown in Fig 4–1. This is a stylized representation of ideal data with the reciprocal of bound hapten (1/r) graphed against the reciprocal of free hapten (1/c). The strength of binding of the antibody population is described by the *intrinsic association constant,* which is determined from the graph as the point where one-half of the antibody combining sites are filled with hapten. This figure is expressed as the reciprocal of the hapten concentration or liters/mole. The intercept of the line is 1/n, where n is the number of antigen-binding sites per molecule of antibody.

The shape of the curve also yields information concerning the heterogeneity of the antibody population being tested. Under conditions of homogeneous binding, the line is straight. When the antibody population is mixed, antibodies of lower affinity will bind larger amounts of hapten at higher hapten concentration and produce a curved line. Actual data from such assays are shown in Figs 4–2 and 4–3. Most antibodies have association constants (K values) in the range of $10^5 - 10^9$ liters/mole. However, very strong binding in the range of $10^{10} - 10^{12}$ liters/mole is possible.

Fig 4–2 shows a top curve which is typical of an antibody population mixed with respect to binding affinities. The lower curve is more homogeneous in

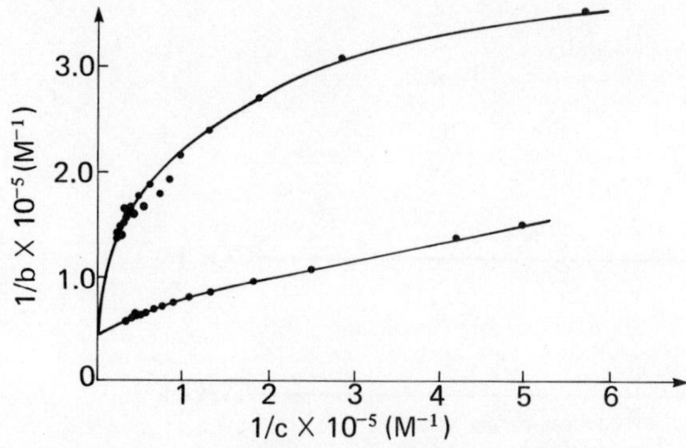

Figure 4–2. Langmuir plot of antidinitrophenyl antibody and radioactive dinitrophenyl ligand. The top curve shows a typical heterogeneous binding curve; the second curve demonstrates almost linear binding. (Reproduced, with permission, from Froese A: Kinetic and equilibrium studies on 2,4-dinitrophenyl hapten-antibody systems. Immunochemistry 5:253, 1968.)

binding, but some curvature is present as the concentration of hapten increases (and the reciprocal of free hapten approaches zero). Fig 4–3 is an antibody population that is demonstrating homogeneous binding. This does not mean that all of the antibodies in this population are identical–only that they have uniform binding affinities in their reaction with this hapten.

At equilibrium, the extent of reaction between antigen and antibody is determined by the rate at which unbound antigen attaches to antibody compared to the rate at which antigen-antibody complexes dissociate. Kinetic studies have shown that these reactions have very high forward rates and low reverse rates. Thus, equilibrium constants are determined more by the stability of the formed complex than by the initial rate at which antigen and antibody combine.

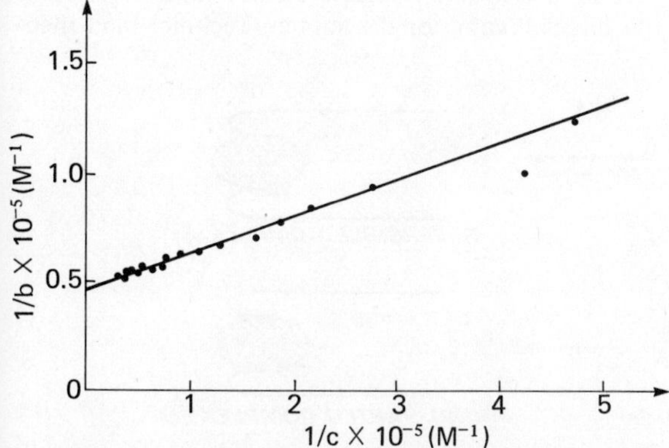

Figure 4–3. A Langmuir plot showing the antigen binding curve of an antibody population with homogeneous binding. (Reproduced, with permission, from Froese A: Kinetic and equilibrium studies on 2,4-dinitrophenyl hapten-antibody systems. Immunochemistry 5:253, 1968.)

LOCATION OF ANTIGEN-BINDING REGIONS

Binding of Antigen by Modified Molecules

Since antibody binding has been compared chemically to the noncovalent binding present between an enzyme and its substrate, information has been sought on the location, size, and specificity of the antigen-binding region of the immunoglobulin molecule. Early theories attempting to explain antibody diversity had attributed antigen specificity to the ability of the antibody molecule to refold its polypeptide chains into many different tertiary configurations. One of these various refolded configurations would then be suitable for reacting with one of the many different antigens in the environment. The antigenic determinant itself was presumed to act as a template for folding of the peptide chains, with the chains of the molecule folding themselves into a conformation that presented amino acids, charge attractions, hydrogen bonding, etc complementary to the particular antigen. This template theory was modified as it became apparent that tertiary structure and antigen-binding ability depended solely on the primary amino acid sequences of the polypeptide chains in the molecule.

Immunoglobulin molecules with known specificities were "unfolded" from their normal conformation with solutions of chemicals such as guanidine hydrochloride, and the peptide chains were allowed to refold spontaneously in the *absence* of antigen. The refolded molecules retained specific antigen-binding capacity, although antigen had not been present during their refolding to act as the template for the redetermination of specificity. These data plus an increased understanding of the importance of specific amino acid sequences in determining biologic properties of proteins caused the "instructional" or "template" theory of antibody diversity to fall into disfavor.

As discussed in Chapter 2, the antibody molecule is composed of both heavy (H) and light (L) polypeptide chains. These chains are classified by their molecular weights and are normally grouped into larger complexes which represent the usual immunoglobulin molecule (Fig 4–4). Enzymatic digestion of rabbit IgG molecules with the enzyme papain results in one Fc and 2 Fab fragments. The Fc fragment can be crystallized, does not bind antigen, and represents the carboxyl terminal portions of the two H chains present in the intact molecule. The Fab fragments are the amino terminal ends of the antibody molecule, possess antigen-binding ability, and do not normally crystallize. The Fab fragment represents a combination of a complete L chain and a portion of the H chain and is usually held together by noncovalent or disulfide bonds. The disulfide bonds of the intact or enzyme-digested protein can be reduced to allow the separation of the chains for additional study.

Binding of Antigen by Isolated Heavy & Light Chains

Separated H and L chains usually demonstrate far less antigen-binding capacity when separated than

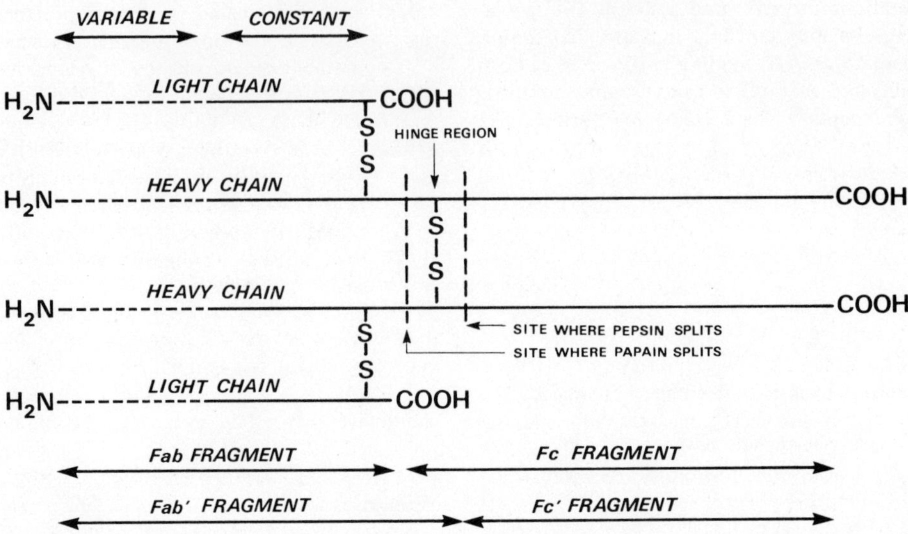

Figure 4–4. Diagrammatic representation of IgG molecule, showing sites of disulfide bonding and enzymatic digestion.

when joined in the intact molecule. Nonetheless, some studies have shown that both H and L chains can have some antigen-binding activity, depending at least partly on the class of antibody and the antigen against which the immunoglobulin is directed. When the separated chains are allowed to recombine, the major portion of the antigen-binding activity of the intact molecule returns. Evidence suggests that H chains have greater binding activity than isolated L chains.

Additional evidence for participation of both H and L chains in antigen binding has come from affinity labeling experiments. Antibodies are prepared against a hapten, eg, azophenylarsonate, and this hapten is then prepared in a chemically modified form with an active diazonium group. This chemical group is a reactive radical which can combine with certain amino acids in the antibody polypeptide chains. When the 2 reagents are mixed, the antibody binds to the azophenylarsonate haptenic determinant and the hapten, in turn, binds covalently by way of the diazonium group to amino acids present in or near the antigen-binding site. The antibody can then be separated into peptide fragments or amino acids and the sites of labeling determined (Fig 4–5). Both L and H chains participate in binding of antigen, with some experiments demonstrating twice as many H chain amino acids labeled as L chain amino acids.

When the active form of the hapten is mixed with the antibody, the chemical can also react with amino acids unrelated to the specific binding of the hapten. To distinguish these unrelated amino acids, the experiment is repeated with the addition of the normal chemical form of the hapten *prior* to the addition of the hapten containing the active chemical group. With the antibody combining site filled with normal hapten, the amino acids labeled in this experiment are those reacting nonspecifically with the reagent. When the results of the 2 experiments are compared, the difference in labeled amino acids should be those involved in the direct binding of the hapten. Technical and theo-

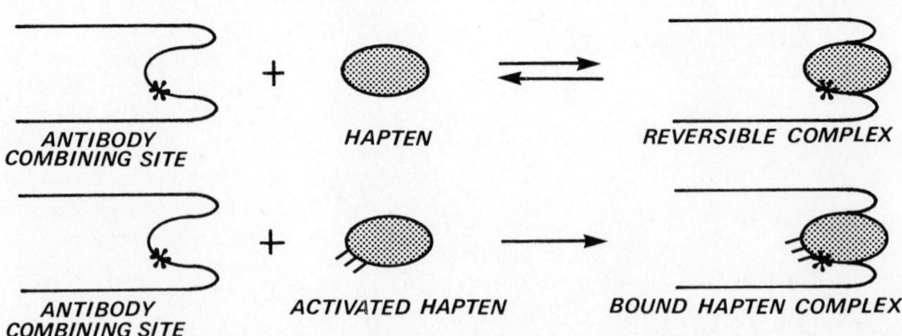

Figure 4–5. Method of affinity labeling. The top figure shows the typical reversible reaction between an antibody molecule and a hapten molecule. The bottom figure shows the hapten molecule with an active chemical group which can react with amino acids present in the polypeptide chain of the antibody. The labeled amino acids should be near the antigen-binding site, but other amino acids are also nonspecifically labeled (see text). (Redrawn and reproduced, with permission, from Singer SJ, Doolittle RF: Antibody active sites and immunoglobulin molecules. Science 153:13, 1966.)

retic considerations prevent such a simple interpretation of the results, but the data indicate that amino acids important to antigen binding are located in both H and L chains and are limited to that amino terminal portion of the peptide chain called the variable (V) region. This type of information agrees closely with data obtained by amino acid sequence studies. If antibodies from the same animal but with specificities for different antigens are compared, the vast majority of amino acid differences between the 2 molecules are seen to be located in the V regions of the H and L chains.

Amino Acids Important in Antigen Binding

If the amino acids that directly participate in the binding of the antigenic determinant are located throughout the V portion of the molecule, denaturation and unfolding of the molecule in a solution of guanidine hydrochloride will spread these amino acids out in a long peptide chain. If the binding amino acids are located in a small patch in the V region, then denaturation will unfold the protein but will not spread out the combining site to any great extent (Fig 4–6). If the binding area is in the form of a patch of closely localized amino acids, the rest of the chain could unfold, leaving a hapten attached to the small area of the V region of the chain. If the binding amino acids are spread through the entire V region, however, then the chain would resist unfolding in the presence of hapten since it would be partially stabilized by the bound hapten. The antibody molecule resists unfolding in the presence of hapten, suggesting that the binding amino acids are located in various portions of the V region and are not lumped together in a small patch.

A similar concept of the V region has been obtained by studying the amino acid sequences of the V regions of different antibodies. About 65% of the human H chain V region is restricted in the variation of amino acids between different antibodies of the same class. At least 4 regions of extreme variability have been identified however, and these *hypervariable regions* are spaced throughout the V region. These hypervariable regions appear to be the antigen attachment sites of the V region (see Chapter 2) and are in close proximity as the antigen-binding site in the V region domain of the intact antibody molecule.

SIZE OF ANTIGEN-BINDING REGION

Many workers have attempted to measure the size of the antigen-binding region of an antibody. The classical experiments of Landsteiner and van der Scheer in the 1930s initially examined this problem. Three haptens were synthesized, and rabbit antibodies were prepared to the largest and most complex of these 3 haptens. This *sym*-aminoisophthalylglycineleucine (hapten A of Fig 4–7) might be too large to be easily encompassed by a single antibody, and the differential reactions with portions of the molecule might give a clue to the determinant size recognized by the antibody. The 2 small determinants of the larger hapten were

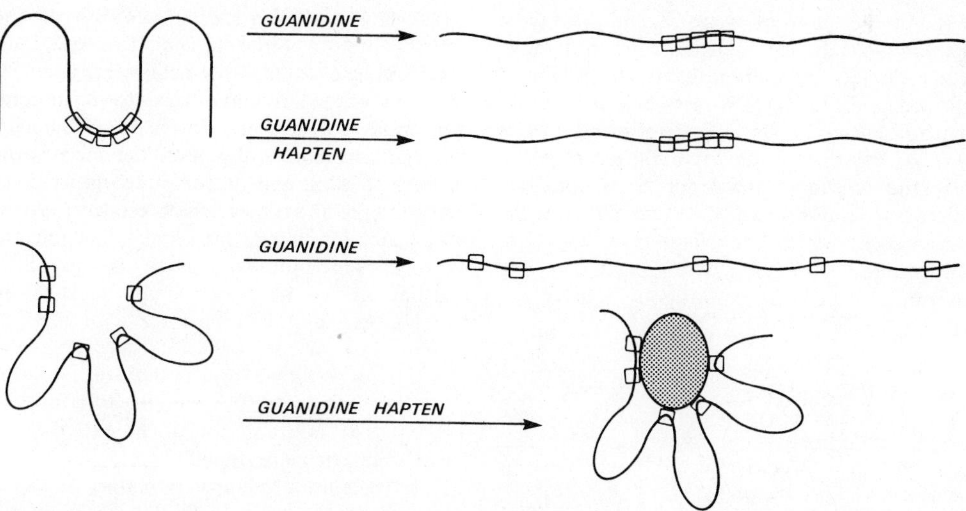

Figure 4–6. Schematic models of 2 possible configurations of the antibody combining site and the effects on each of denaturation with guanidine hydrochloride. The *small* blocks represent contact amino acids. The number and size of these are not to be taken literally. The *large* oval in the lower figure represents hapten. In the *upper* set of figures, the site is composed of several adjacent amino acids along a single polypeptide chain. The presence of hapten has no effect on the course of denaturation. In the *lower* set of figures, the amino acids comprising the binding site are sequentially separated along the length of the polypeptide chains. One or both chains could contribute contact amino acids. The presence of hapten in the site stabilizes this conformation. (Redrawn and reproduced, with permission, from Cathou RE, Werner TC: Hapten stabilization of antibody conformation. Biochemistry 9:3149, 1970.)

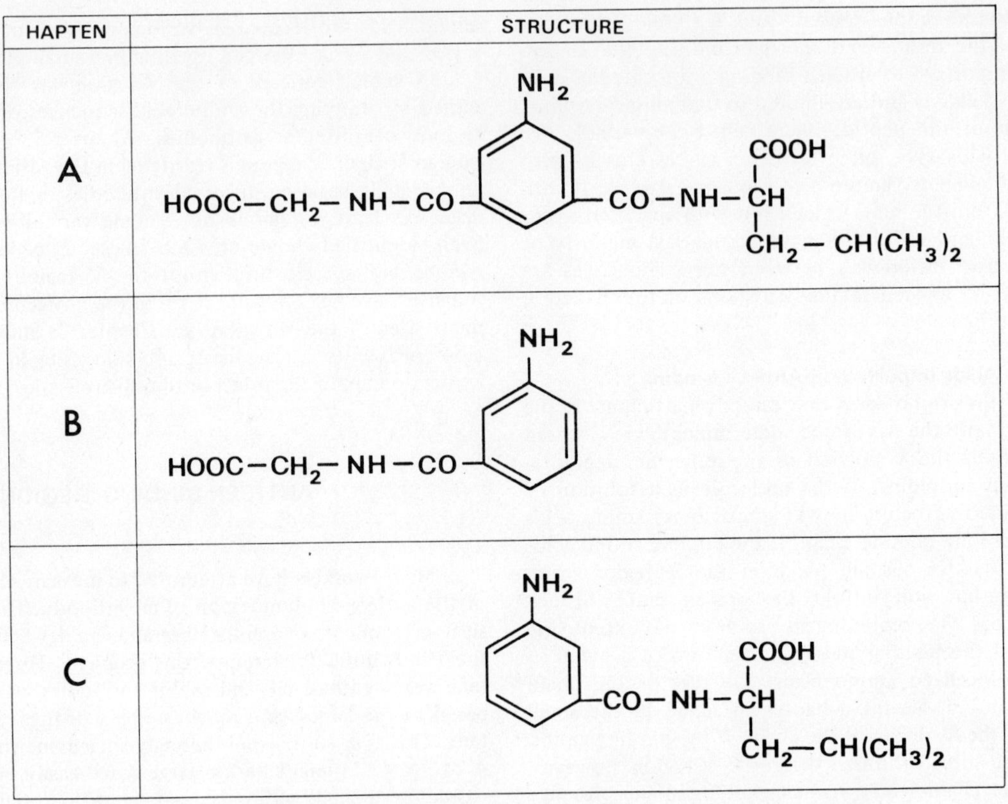

HAPTEN	STRUCTURE
A	NH_2; COOH; $HOOC-CH_2-NH-CO-$ ⟨benzene ring⟩ $-CO-NH-CH$; $CH_2-CH(CH_3)_2$
B	NH_2; $HOOC-CH_2-NH-CO-$ ⟨benzene ring⟩
C	NH_2; COOH; ⟨benzene ring⟩ $-CO-NH-CH$; $CH_2-CH(CH_3)_2$

Figure 4–7. Haptens synthesized by Landsteiner and van der Scheer and used to study the size of the antibody combining region (see text).

prepared (haptens B and C of Fig 4–7), and these were used separately to absorb the antiserum to remove antibody reacting to that determinant. The results of this study are given in Table 4–1. When those antibodies that reacted with hapten B are absorbed out of the serum, the remaining antibodies still reacted with haptens A and C. Analogous results were obtained when the serum was absorbed with hapten C. When the serum was absorbed with both haptens B and C to remove all antibodies reacting with the smaller haptenic determinants, little or no antibody activity was left against the larger hapten A. This strongly suggested that hapten A was too large to result in antibodies directed against the entire determinant.

Table 4–1. Effects of absorption upon reactivity of an antibody against hapten A.

Absorbed With Hapten	Tested on Hapten	Precipitation Results
B	A	4+
	B	0
	C	3+
C	A	2+
	B	1+
	C	0
B + C	A	Tr
	B	0
	C	0

Later experiments were to document haptens which were larger than hapten A and which were able to elicit specific antibodies. Haptenic determinants of similar size but with different charge distribution have resulted in antibodies which recognized not just the haptenic determinants but also the chemical bonds through which the hapten was attached to the protein carrier (as well as several amino acids of the protein itself). Attempts to repeat the experiments of Landsteiner and van der Scheer have also shown that the antibodies resulting from immunization with this hapten series may vary from animal to animal to such an extent that interpretation of the data is far more complex than originally thought.

Dextrans are simple polymers of glucose joined mainly by the α–D(1→6) linkage. Rabbits were injected with the long chain polymers, and the resulting antibodies were tested by inhibition methods to determine the length of polymer that would best react with the antibody. In theory, the polymer length which just matched the length of the antibody combining site and thereby produced the best fit of complementary structures would result in the highest binding activity. The results demonstrated that polymers consisting of 6 glucose units were the best inhibitors of these rabbit antibodies. This could represent an antigen-binding site on the antibody molecule of about 200 nm^2 (compared to a calculated area of about 70 nm^2 for the previously discussed hapten A). Similar experiments are also discussed in Chapter 3. Although early experiments suggested a difference in antibody combining sites depending on the class of antibody (IgM versus IgG), there is no current evidence to suggest that the size of the IgM combining site is smaller than the IgG combining site. The heterogeneity of the typical immune response to even the simplest antigens has greatly complicated attempts to study antigen-binding sites, but data obtained with sugar polymers other than glucose and data from studies with amino acid polymers support a general size equivalent to 6 repeating glucose units.

DETECTION OF ANTIGEN BINDING

In early antibody experiments, many assays consisted of immunizing an animal with an antigen (eg, a rabbit with BSA) and showing that serum taken from the animal several weeks after immunization would precipitate the antigen. Serum taken from the animal prior to immunization or serum from an unimmunized animal would not precipitate the antigen. The reaction could be demonstrated by carefully layering rabbit serum containing antialbumin antibodies over a solution of albumin. A precipitin ring would form in the test tube at the interface between the 2 reagents. The usefulness of this test is limited, however. The liquid interface is easily disturbed by mixing, and the precipitate gradually settles to the bottom of the tube. Individual reactions cannot be distinguished in experiments with several competing antigens, and these results are not quantitative. Later workers improved and modified these methods, and measurement of immunologic reactions can now be extremely sensitive, specific, and quantitative. A few of these reactions will be considered here when they demonstrate a specific property of antigen-antibody reactions. For a more comprehensive discussion of assay methods employed in clinical testing, see Chapter 24.

Precipitation Reactions

When the simple precipitation reaction mentioned above is repeated in a more refined way, much information can be learned concerning the physical characteristics of antibodies and their reactions with antigens. A measured quantity of rabbit antibody is placed in a series of test tubes, and varying amounts of antigen are added, mixed, and allowed to react. A precipitate forms in many of the tubes, and this precipitate can be carefully and quantitatively measured by one of several methods. (The antigen could be labeled with a radioisotope prior to use in the assay, or the washed precipitate could be dissolved and measured spectrophotometrically or in other ways.) A curve similar to that shown in Fig 4–8 is obtained.

Initially, there is no precipitate formation. If the fluid phase of this mixture is tested, there will be no detectable free antigen, but antibody activity will still be present. This is the area of *antibody excess.* With increasing amounts of added antigen, there is an in-

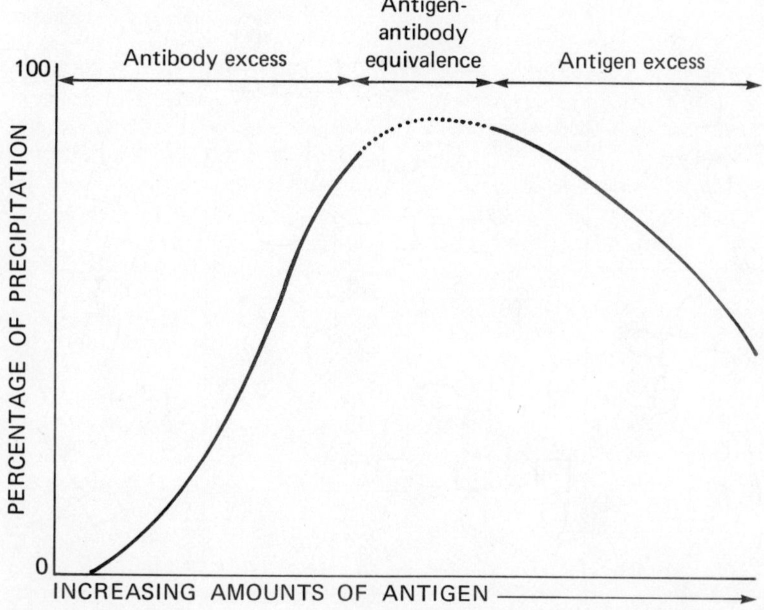

Figure 4–8. A quantitative precipitin curve showing the zones of antibody excess, antigen-antibody equivalence, and antigen excess. With the same antigen preparation, the actual shape of the precipitin curve may vary depending on the affinity of the antibody.

creasing quantity of precipitate formed until a maximum is reached. If the fluid phase of this mixture is tested, it will not show the presence of unbound antigen or antibody. This is the area of *antigen-antibody equivalence.* With additional antigen, testing of the supernate phase will show the presence of unbound antigen. This is the area of *antigen excess.* The reaction between antigen and antibody can occur rapidly, and a precipitate may be noticed in the tubes almost immediately after the addition of antigen. If the reaction is allowed to proceed for several hours, however, the precipitate will seem to increase in amount and a few tubes which were initially clear will develop precipitates.

Why do the antigen-antibody complexes precipitate? The answer is not simple. Conceptually, multivalent antigen and antibody can be considered to form a complex lattice of interlocking aggregates (Fig 4–9). In the region of antibody excess, these complexes are too small to precipitate spontaneously. As more antigen is added, the complexes grow larger and precipitate out of solution. If too much antigen is added, the lattice network of complexes cannot form and again no precipitation occurs.

In actuality, the situation is far more complex. Protein antigens of MW 40–160 thousand can give precipitin curves with sharp peaks in the zone of equivalence. Antigens such as denatured protein, some viruses, and polysaccharides, for example, give broad curves when reacted with specific antibody. Other antigens may have excessive charge on their surface and may be difficult to precipitate at all. Antibodies may also be difficult to precipitate, and immunochemical data suggest that certain animals may produce antibodies or specific subclasses of antibodies that routinely fail to precipitate with antigen when in the zone of antigen-antibody equivalence. This suggests that the amino acid composition of certain immunoglobulins may not contain appropriate concentrations of hydrophobic or hydrophilic amino acids or other characteristics required to produce good precipitation reactions.

Precipitation Inhibition

The quantitative precipitation reaction can be used to examine the ability of an unknown or closely related antigen to interfere with a specific antibody reaction. Assume that you have an antigen with determinants called AA and a rabbit antiserum against this antigen. The antigen to be used in the precipitin assay (frequently called a *ligand*) is labeled with radioactive iodine so that the degree of precipitation can be easily quantitated. We will signify this radioactive ligand by the symbol *AA. When a precipitation assay is done between *AA and the rabbit antibody, we can determine the point when antigen and antibody maximally precipitate each other—the point of equivalence. A series of tubes is prepared and the antibody is dispensed into the tubes with the unknown antigen. This allows the unknown antigenic determinants to potentially react with the rabbit antibody, and the latter would be unavailable to react with the *AA ligand which is added next. The results of such a series of reactions are shown in Fig 4–10, where 3 antigens are used: AA, AB, and BB. The antigen AA can of course inhibit the reaction between *AA and the antibody. The antigen AB can also inhibit, since it contains the A

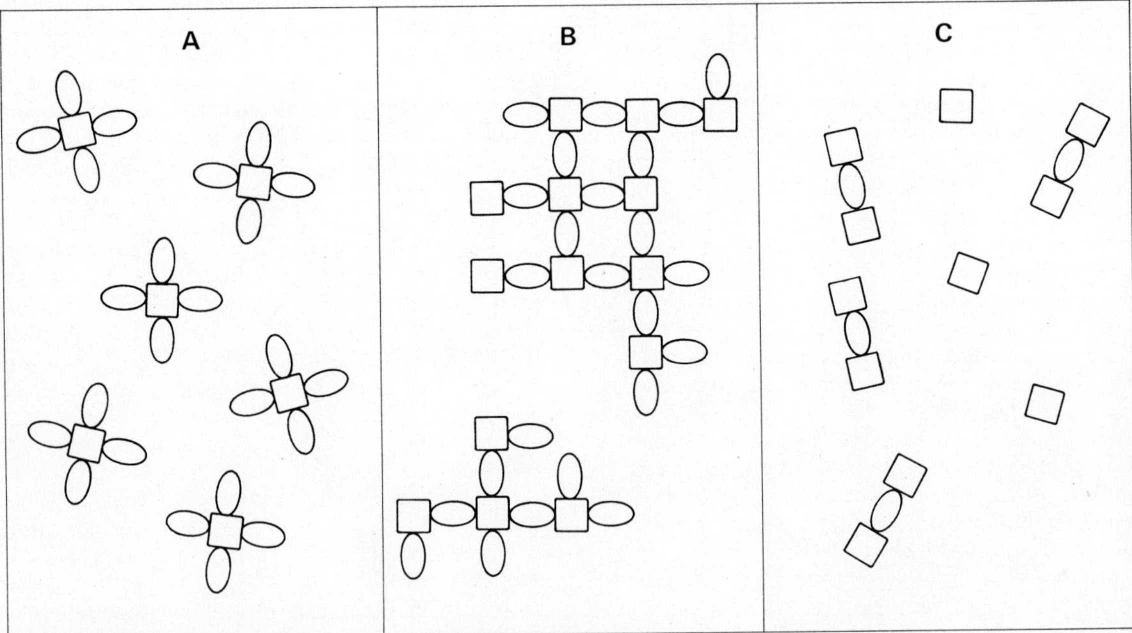

Figure 4–9. Possible arrangement of antigen molecules (squares) and antibody molecules (ovals) under conditions of antibody excess (A), antigen-antibody equivalence (B), or antigen excess (C).

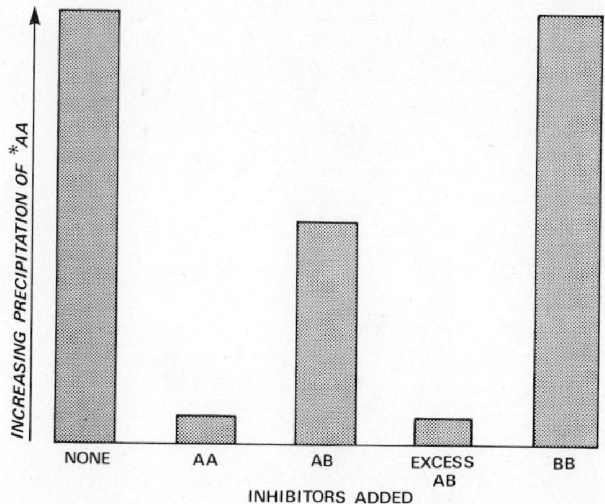

Figure 4–10. Reaction of an antiserum against the determinants AA with radiolabeled *AA. The addition of AA as an inhibitor prevents or greatly decreases the precipitin reaction. The addition of antigen AB, which partially reacts with AA, results in decreased binding, and an excess of AB can produce complete inhibition. The non-cross-reacting antigen BB had no effect on the precipitin reaction.

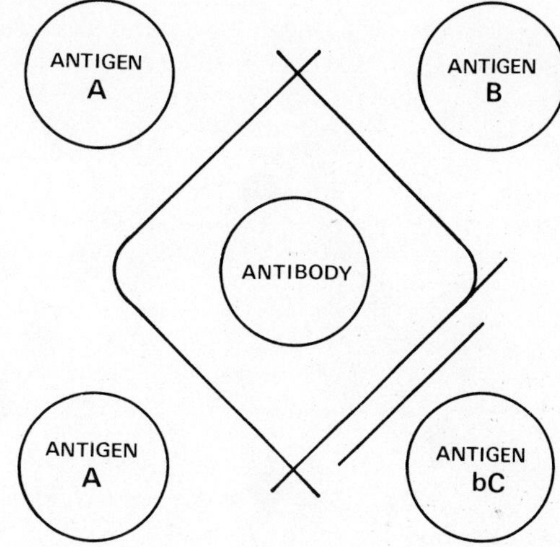

Figure 4–11. Diagrammatic representation of an agar gel diffusion reaction. The antiserum is in the center well, and antigens are in the 4 outside wells. Antigen A is present in 2 wells and produces a line of identity. Antigen B is present in one well and produces a line of partial identity with antigen b. Antigen C is present in only one well.

determinant, but it will be a less effective inhibitor on a weight basis than the antigen AA. The antigen BB will not affect the reaction between *AA and antibody. Greatly modified, it is this antigen-antibody reaction (precipitation inhibition) that forms the basis for very sensitive radioimmunoassays widely used in clinical medicine.

Diffusion in Agar

The easiest modification of the ring precipitation assay described previously was simply to support the reacting proteins in a matrix of agar. The antiserum is mixed in molten agar and placed in a test tube. After all the agar-antiserum mixture in the tube has solidified, antigen is placed in the tube. The proteins diffuse toward each other and form a precipitin layer, but now the ring can be studied in detail without fear of disturbing the interface. In addition, if several antigen-antibody reactions occur simultaneously, they form separate rings that allow estimation of the relative antigen concentrations.

Alternatively, the molten agar can be poured onto flat plates and the antigens and antisera placed in wells cut into the surface of the solidified agar as shown in Fig 4–11. Again, the antigen and antibodies diffuse toward each other, react, and precipitate in the agar. This newer arrangement allows multiple antigen or antibody wells to be arranged to demonstrate antigenic relationships between multiple antigens or antisera. Unrelated antigens show separate precipitin lines. Partial antigenic identity is demonstrated by a series of spurs on the precipitin lines (shown in Fig 4–11). Complete antigenic identity is shown by a fusion of the lines. It must be remembered, however, that complete identity demonstrated by this agar gel diffusion does not mean that the antigens in the separate wells are the same. It means only that the specific antiserum used is detecting the same antigenic determinant on 2 separate molecules. A wide variety of well patterns, sizes, and shapes have been intensively studied for special applications, but a 7-well circle pattern has become the one most commonly used.

The precipitin reaction in agar is not a static reaction but is constantly changing as the reactants continue to diffuse from their wells and through the agar. If the antigen or antibody is present in relative concentrations higher or lower than those required for good precipitation, the lines present in the agar may be altered by blurring or even dissolving after their original formation. This is analogous to the zones of antigen or antibody excess on the precipitin curve (Fig 4–8).

Agglutination

To this point we have considered only reactions between antibody and soluble antigens, but many antigens are particulate in form. Red blood cells, white cells, antigen-coated latex particles, etc are widely employed in clinical and experimental studies of antibody reactions. In these reactions, the antigenic determinants are present on the outside of the particle, and reaction with antibody results in agglutination. Since antibodies are at least bivalent in their activity, this agglutination can take the form suggested in Fig 4–12. The antibody-antigen reactions present in this figure are represented in antibody excess, antigen-antibody equivalence, and antigen excess. A comparison of this diagram with Fig 4–9 shows the similar nature of agglutination and precipitation. As in precipitation, some cells will fail to agglutinate when reacted with antibody, and this failure to agglutinate has been attrib-

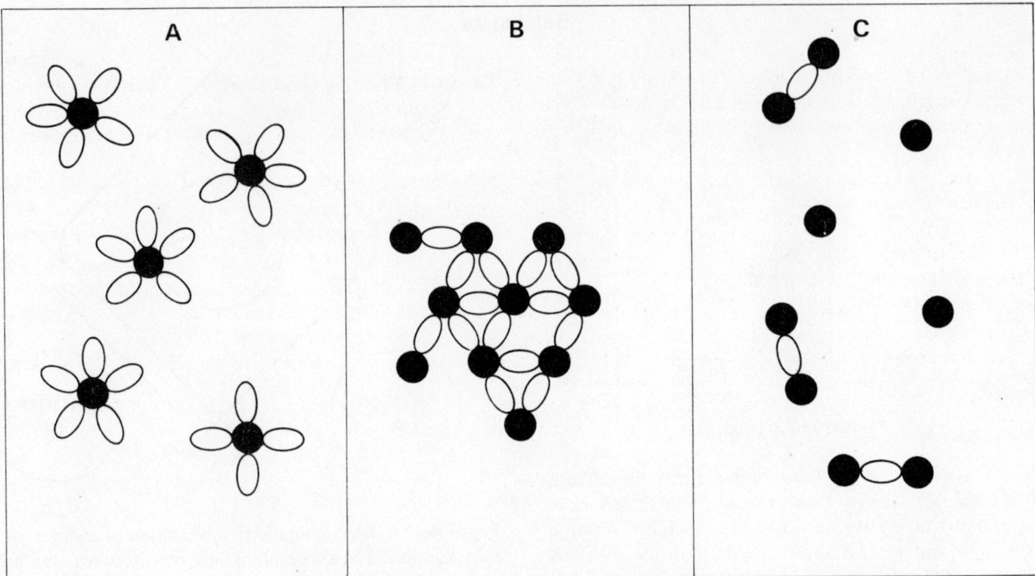

Figure 4–12. Possible arrangement of red blood cells (dark circles) or any other particulate antigen with antibody (ovals) under conditions of antibody excess (A), maximum agglutination (B), and antigen excess (C).

uted to the charge present on the cell. Two major methods are used to overcome the electrostatic forces which are thought to prevent agglutination. An antigenically unrelated protein of appropriate charge may be added to the buffer to neutralize the charged groups on the cell, or the cells may be first treated with an enzyme to remove the undesired charged groups.

The ability to agglutinate a particle depends on the particle having more than one (usually thousands) of reacting antigenic determinants on its surface. A particle with only one antigenic site could not be agglutinated since it could not be cross-linked. The IgM molecule has more antigen-binding sites than the IgG molecule, and IgM antibodies are normally better agglutinators than other immunoglobulins.

CONFORMATIONAL CHANGES RESULTING FROM ANTIGEN BINDING

Antigen-antibody complexes participate in a variety of immune functions, but just how the noncovalent attachment of antigen to the antigen-binding site of the antibody molecule alters the molecule sufficiently to activate these biologic responses is unknown. Several explanations have been suggested. One proposal is that the antibody molecule itself undergoes subtle but definite alterations in structure after binding antigen. This *allosteric* model would require that immune cells, complement molecules, and other functional systems of the immune response be able to detect these minimal changes in the antibody molecule. A second model is that several antigenic determinants react with the antibody molecule in a manner sufficient to distort its shape. This *distortion* of the molecule might uncover or activate normally hidden regions of the polypeptide chains, and these activated regions would act as receptors for subsequent immune activation. Lastly, the *associative* model suggests that the linking of antigens may present an array of active determinants formed by the antibodies themselves or formed from the cross-linking of otherwise mobile antigenic determinants. A recent review of this subject found the exact mechanism still unsettled, but more evidence supported the associative model than the others.

OVERVIEW

Immunoglobulin molecules are present in a vast variety of antigen specificities, and our knowledge of their physicochemical properties has increased dramatically in the last few years. The initial problems of general structure and function have been intensively studied, and a large body of information has accumulated. The more difficult problems of relating specific amino acid composition and tertiary polypeptide configuration to antigenic specificity and biologic activity are now being approached.

• • •

References

Capra JD, Kehoe JM: Hypervariable regions, idiotypy, and the antigen-combining site. Adv Immunol 20:1, 1975.

Day ED: *Advanced Immunochemistry*. Williams & Wilkins, 1972.

Froese A: Kinetic and equilibrium studies on 2,4-dinitrophenyl hapten-antibody systems. Immunochemistry 5:253, 1968.

Goodman JW: Antigenic determinants and antibody combining sites. Page 127 in: *The Antigens.* Vol 3. Sela M (editor). Academic Press, 1975.

Haber E, Poulsen K: The application of antibody to the measurement of substances of physiological and pharmacological interest. Page 250 in: *The Antigens.* Vol 2. Sela M (editor). Academic Press, 1974.

Kabat EA: *Structural Concepts in Immunology and Immunochemistry*, 2nd ed. Holt, Rinehart, & Winston, 1976.

Koshland ME, Reisfeld RA, Dray S: Differences in amino acid composition related to allotypic and antibody specificity of rabbit IgG heavy chains. Immunochemistry 5:471, 1968.

Metzger H: Effect of antigen binding on the binding of antibody. Adv Immunol 18:169, 1974.

Metzger HL, Wofsy L, Singer SJ: Affinity labeling of the active sites of antibodies to the 2,4-dinitrophenyl hapten. Biochemistry 2:979, 1963.

Pinckard RN, Weir DM: Equilibrium dialysis and preparation of hapten conjugates. Page 16.1 in: *Handbook of Experimental Immunology,* 2nd ed. Weir DM (editor). Blackwell, 1973.

5 . . .

Genetic Markers of Human Immunoglobulins

Moses S. Schanfield, PhD

A great deal of information has been obtained in recent years on the structure and function of the antibody molecule and the roles of different cells in the processing of antigens and the production of antibodies. Genetic factors are now thought to play an important part, and, in laboratory animals, much of the emphasis on the genetic control of these immune responses has been on genes associated with histocompatibility antigens and immune response (Ir) genes (see Chapter 12). Some work has been done in animals on the association of genetic markers on immunoglobulin with specific immune responses. Similar studies have been undertaken in man with less striking results. This chapter will introduce the reader to the complex area of the genetic markers present on antibodies and will indicate areas in which these genetic markers are associated with a significant role in antibody function and immune response.

GENETIC MARKERS ON ANTIBODIES

Inherited differences on human immunoglobulins have been referred to as allotypes, allotypic markers, genetic markers, or genetic determinants. Thus far, they have been found on IgG H chains (Gm markers), IgA H chains (Am markers), and κ type L chains (Km markers, formerly called Inv). In addition, each allotypic determinant is restricted to one of the IgG or IgA subclasses. The recommended notation includes the H chain subclasses of the allotypic determinant, so that the genetic markers on IgG1 have the prefix G1m; IgG2, G2m; IgG3, G3m; and IgA2, A2m. There are no confirmed allotypic markers on IgG4 and IgA1 subclasses. The presently accepted allotypic markers on human immunoglobulins are listed in Table 5–1. In addition to the allotypic determinants which are restricted to a single immunoglobulin subclass, there are markers which act as allotypic determinants within a specific subclass and also appear on all members of at least one other subclass. These markers are termed isoallotypic determinants (formerly nonmarkers). They are briefly summarized in Table 5–2.

In humans, allotypic markers have thus far been found only on the C region (constant regions) of the IgG and IgA H chains. Studies on the localization of the H chain allotypic determinant indicate that each determinant is associated with a specific domain of the H chain (see Chapter 2). In some cases the determinants have already been associated with specific amino acid sequences (Table 5–3). It is possible that different biologic properties of immunoglobulins such as the binding of complement, binding to Fc receptors, passive cutaneous anaphylaxis, or interaction with staphylococcal A protein may be associated with allotypic determinants; however, adequate evidence to support this view is not yet available.

Population and family studies in different human populations have demonstrated the existence of large differences both in the frequency and kinds of combinations of allotypic markers. These different combinations are inherited as units, previously called phenogroups, allogroups, or haplotypes. The latter term is the one currently preferred. Analysis of family data also showed that the Gm allotypic markers were genetically linked to the Am allotypic markers, ie, inherited

Table 5–1. Human allotypic markers on immunoglobulin polypeptide chains.*

IgG1		IgG2		IgG3	
Alphameric	Numeric	Alphameric	Numeric	Alphameric	Numeric
G1m a	1	G2mn	23	G3m b0	11
x	2			b1	5
f	3			b3	13
z	17			b4	14
				b5	10
				c3	6
IgA2		**κ Chains**		c5	24
Alphameric	**Numeric**	**Alphameric**	**Numeric**	g	21
				s	15
A2m 1	1	Km 1	1	t	16
2	2	(Inv) 2	2	u	26
		3	3	v	27

*Both the alphameric and numeric notations have been widely used, and both are acceptable.

Moses S. Schanfield is Director of Transfusion Services and Reference Laboratory, Milwaukee Blood Center, Milwaukee.

Table 5–2. Distribution of isoallotypic determinants by immunoglobulin subclass.

Isoallotype	Subclass IgG1	IgG2	IgG3	IgG4
nG1m(a)	+ (a neg only)	+	+	–*
nG3m(b0)	+	+	+ (b0 neg only)	–
nG3m(b1)	+	+	+ (b1 neg only)	–
nG3m(g)	–	+	+ (g neg only)	–
nG4m(4a)	+	–	+	+ (4b neg only)
nG4m(4b)	–	+	–	+ (4a neg only)

*Serologically undetectable, but the amino acid sequence is present.

Table 5–3. Localization of immunoglobulin allotypic markers and associated amino acid substitutions.

Chain	Domain	Allotype	Amino Acid	Position
IgG1	C_H1	G1m(f)=(3)	Arg	214
	C_H1	G1m(z)=(17)	Lys	214
	C_H3	G1m(a)=(1)	Arg, Asp, Glu, Leu	355–358
	C_H3	G1m(x)=(2)		
IgG2	C_H2	G2m(n)=(23)		
IgG3	C_H2	G3m(g)=(21)	Tyr	296
	C_H2	G3m(b1)=(5)		
	C_H2	G3m(u)=(26)	Phe	436
	C_H3	G3m(b0)=(11)		
	C_H3	G3m(b3)=(13)		
	C_H3	G3m(b5)=(10)		
	C_H3	G3m(c3)=(6)		
	C_H3	G3m(c5)=(24)		
	C_H3	G3m(s)=(15)		
	C_H3	G3m(t)=(16)		
	C_H3	G3m(v)=(27)		
IgA2	C_H1	A2m(1)=(1)	Lack of disulfide bridge between H and L chain	
		A2m(2)=(2)	Disulfide bridge between H and L chain	
κ light chain	C_L	Km(1+2+3–)	Ala, Leu	153, 191
	C_L	(1+2–3–)	Val, Leu	153, 191
	C_L	(1–2–3+)	Ala, Val	153, 191

Table 5–4. Approximate haplotype frequencies in several human populations.

G1m	G2m	G3m	A2m	Caucasian	Afro-American	Orient: Chinese	Orient: Japanese	New Guinea: Papuan	New Guinea: Melanesian
f	n	b0,1,3,4,5,u,v	1	0.484	0.107	*	*	*	*
f	. . .	b0,1,3,4,5,u,v	1	0.292	0.018	*	*	*	*
z,a	. . .	g,u,v	1	0.175	0.022	0.121	0.349	0.205	0.108
z,a	. . .	g,u,v	2	*	*	*	0.047	*	0.023
z,a,x	. . .	g,u,v	1	0.045	0.027	0.069	0.160	0.011	*
z,a,x	. . .	g,u,v	2	*	*	*	0.038	*	*
z,a	n	b0,1,3,4,5,u,v	1	*	*	*	*	0.681	0.070
z,a	. . .	b0,1,3,4,5,u,v	1	*	0.134	*	*	0.030	0.012
z,a	. . .	b0,1,3,4,5,u,v	2	*	0.455	*	*	*	*
z,a	. . .	b0,1,c3,5,u	1	*	0.036	*	*	*	*
z,a	. . .	b0,1,c3,5,u	2	*	0.143	*	*	*	*
z,a	. . .	b0,1,5,c3,u,v	1	*	(0.02)	*	*	*	*
z,a	. . .	b0,3,5,s,v	1	*	0.01	*	*	*	*
z,a	. . .	b0,3,5,s,v	2	*	(0.05)	*	*	*	*
f,a	n	b0,1,3,4,5,u,v	1	*	*	0.112	0.028	*	0.190
f,a	n	b0,1,3,4,5,u,v	2	*	*	0.672	0.151	*	0.535
z,a	. . .	b0,3,5,s,t,v	1	*	*	*	(0.05)	*	*
z,a	. . .	b0,3,5,s,t,v	2	*	*	0.026	(0.20)	*	*
			Km^1	0.10	0.30	0.30	0.30	0.05	0.10

*Indicates a frequency of less than 0.01 or not thus far detected in that population.
( )Frequency uncertain because too few specimens have been studied.

as a unit. However, the Gm–Am haplotypes are not genetically linked to the Km allotypic markers. Table 5–4 lists the approximate frequencies of some of the commonly found Gm–Am and Km[1] haplotypes in several human populations.

If a particular antigen is detected in a sample of serum, the serum is designated as, eg, G1m(a). If the antigen is tested for but not found, this is indicated by the term G1m(a-). The gene or genes coding for the synthesis of G1m(a) are indicated by $G1m^a$.

TESTING FOR ALLOTYPES

Allotypic typing is the detection of allotypic markers on immunoglobulins and is usually performed in man by passive hemagglutination inhibition (see Chapter 24). However, direct precipitation has occasionally been used. Each test system consists of an allotype-specific antiserum called an agglutinator, diluted serum or plasma to be tested, and indicator red blood cells coated with the allotype-specific Gm, Am, or Km antigen. The latter are called either coated red blood cells or sensitized red blood cells. The test can be performed in test tubes, on tiles or microflocculation plates, in the wells of microtiter plates, or by autoanalyzer.

Whichever method is used, the results are identical in that, if the serum tested for a specific allotypic marker contains that marker, it inhibits the agglutination of the coated red blood cells by the agglutinator and no agglutination is observed. However, if the serum does not contain that marker, it will not inhibit the agglutination of the coated red blood cells by the agglutinator and agglutination will be observed.

Two methods are currently used to coat red blood cells with Gm, Am, or Km antigens. The older is the coating of red cells with incomplete (non-saline-agglutinating) Rh (Rhesus) antibodies (Chapter 28). However, not all immunoglobulin markers are carried on Rh antibodies. Purified myeloma proteins carrying the desired genetic markers can be chemically coupled to red blood cells to provide a method of coating red cells with antigens not found in incomplete Rh antibodies. Chromic chloride and bis-diazotized benzidine have been used as coupling agents. However, other compounds may work equally well.

Agglutinators for a specific allotypic marker can be found in the sera of normal individuals who are negative for that specific marker and have been immunized against it either in utero or through transfusion. These sera are generally referred to as serum normal agglutinators (SNaggs). Agglutinators have also been found in the sera of individuals with rheumatoid arthritis; however, these antibodies are often mixtures of anti-immunoglobulins with antibodies against nonallotypic determinants and are therefore not useful for immunoglobulin allotyping. These sera are referred to as rheumatoid agglutinators (Raggs). In addition, several specificities have been detected using the absorbed serum of laboratory animals which had been immunized with either purified myeloma proteins or serum. For certain antigens, these are the only source of agglutinators.

Gm ALLOTYPES & SUBCLASS SERUM LEVELS

The total level of IgG in adults is relatively constant while the levels of IgA, IgD, IgE, and IgM tend to vary with age, sex, and race. There are no data on the age differences in levels of IgG subclasses; however, the relationship of subclass levels is known to be IgG1 (60–70%), IgG2 (14–20%), IgG3 (4–8%), and IgG4 (2–6%). Although the total level of IgG appears to be rather constant with regard to Gm phenotypes, the levels of the subclasses, at least in Caucasians, appear to be related to the Gm type of the individual. The most pronounced difference, which has been conclusively verified, is that IgG3 levels are about twice as high in individuals homozygous for G3m(b) as in individuals homozygous for G3m(g), with heterozygotes demonstrating an intermediate or higher level of IgG3. Similar findings have been observed for IgG2 in that individuals homozygous for G2m(n) have higher levels of IgG2 than individuals homozygous for G2m(n-); again the heterozygotes are intermediate. Although allotypic markers have not yet been detected on IgG4, it has been shown that IgG4 levels appear to be associated with the IgG2 allotypic marker G2m(n). Thus, G2m(n) homozygotes have the highest levels of IgG4; individuals negative for G2m(n) have the lowest levels; and heterozygotes have levels intermediate between the two. This association may relate to the isoallotypic markers N4a and N4b in that N4b is found only in association with $Gm^{f;n;b}$, while N4a can be found with $Gm^{za;-;g}$, $Gm^{f;-;b}$ and $Gm^{f;n;b}$. Unlike IgG2, IgG3, and IgG4, the levels of IgG1 do not vary with the presence of G1m(za), G1m(z,a,x), or G1m(f). The levels appear to be about the same. However, there does appear to be an effect of gene dosage, so that an individual homozygous for G1m(za) has about twice as much IgG1 containing G1m(za) as an individual heterozygous for G1m(za); a similar pattern is observed for G1m(f). Individuals homozygous for $Gm^{f;n;b}$ will have, on the average, higher levels of IgG2, IgG3, and IgG4 than an individual homozygous for $Gm^{za;-;g}$. The concentrations of all 4 subclasses of IgG appear to be under genetic control, and to some extent this is related to the Gm phenotype of the individual. The information presented above is for Caucasian populations because it is these people who have been most extensively studied. Data from non-Caucasian populations indicate that the differences observed in IgG3 levels in Caucasians also occur in non-Caucasians who have both G3m(b) and G3m(g).

Gm ALLOTYPES & LEVELS OF OTHER IMMUNOGLOBULINS

Possible associations between Gm allotypes and other immunoglobulin classes have not yet been fully investigated. One interesting example has been discovered involving IgD. Although the biologic role of IgD is still largely unknown, Caucasian individuals homozygous for $Gm^{f;b}$ appear to have lower levels of IgD than do individuals homozygous for $Gm^{za(x);g}$. This is primarily due to an excess of individuals with low serum levels of IgD among individuals homozygous for $Gm^{f;b}$.

ROLE OF ALLOTYPES IN HYPOGAMMAGLOBULINEMIA

Common variable hypogammaglobulinemia is usually detected because patients present in adulthood with a history of recurrent infections (see Chapter 26). The vast majority of these patients have a low serum IgG level, and often the ratios of the residual IgG subclasses are abnormal. In some cases the subclass deficiency is absolute; in other cases it appears to be less marked. Genetic analysis of the patients and their families indicates that in most cases regulatory genes, independent of IgG structural genes, appear to be involved. However, in some cases the disease is associated with rare haplotypes characterized by the lack of a single subclass. In any case, testing for allotypic markers associated with different subclasses is often useful diagnostically when coupled with family studies.

Individuals with IgG1 deficiency (either alone or associated with other deficiencies) have a tremendous compensatory rise in IgG3 levels (if IgG3 is present) such that the total levels of IgG may be nearly normal. Furthermore, if the individual involved is genetically heterozygous for G3m(b) and G3m(g), the rise appears to be exclusively in G3m(b), with G3m(g) usually depressed. This suggests that the regulatory mechanism that attempts to compensate biologically for the lack of IgG1 appears to be associated with the G3m(b) structural gene. In contrast, individuals with IgG2 and IgG4 deficiency who have nearly normal levels of IgG do not show any marked increase of IgG1 or IgG3. This implies that specific subclass deficiencies may lead to specific immune response deficiencies characterized by distinct clinical patterns.

RESTRICTIONS OF SUBCLASS & ALLOTYPE IN SPECIFIC ANTIBODIES

Different IgG subclasses differ in their biologic properties such as complement binding, transfer of reverse passive cutaneous anaphylaxis, and the ability to bind to monocytes. These differences in biologic functions extend also to subclass restrictions in antibodies against specific antigens and in some cases to restrictions in genetic type within a subclass. Thus far, isolated antibodies to dextran, levan, and teichoic acid appear to be almost exclusively IgG2. In addition, some of the antibodies were restricted to a single G2m type, being either positive or negative for G2m(n). In contrast, anti-A-isoagglutinins, antitetanus toxoid, and antidiphtheria toxin consist primarily of IgG1 antibodies. In addition, iso- and autoantibodies to red blood cells appear to be almost exclusively IgG1 or IgG3. There have been reported examples of autoantibodies to red blood cells which were IgG4 subclass. Studies of the IgG1 allotypic determinants in individuals heterozygous for G1m(a) and G1m(f) indicate that the antibody, whether isoimmune or autoimmune, shows some degree of allelic exclusion. Alleles in an individual heterozygous at a gene locus are generally both expressed in the phenotype. Allelic exclusion refers to the situation where one allele is not expressed in the phenotype. In the above example with G1m(a) and G1m(f) heterozygosity, the antibody is almost exclusively G1m(a)-positive. G1m(a)-positive antibodies may also be of higher affinity than G1m(f)-positive antibodies. The few characterized IgG inhibitors of antihemophilic factor VIII have almost always been of the IgG4 subclass.

It is concluded that V (variable) region genes determining antibody specificity are associated with specific subclasses. In some cases they may be associated with specific allotypic determinants within a subclass. It is therefore of interest to know whether an individual's ability to respond to a specific antigen is related to the genetic type of his immunoglobulins.

ALLOTYPES & IMMUNE RESPONSE

There have as yet been very few studies of the relationship between the genetic markers on the immunoglobulins in man and the level of response to a specific antigen. The first report on this subject indicated that high responders to *Salmonella adelaide* flagellar antigens carried the haplotype $Gm^{za;g}$, but this has not been confirmed. Another study indicated that individuals heterozygous for haplotypes found in Caucasians produce higher levels of antibodies against meningococcal C polysaccharide. There are also data from New Guinea which indicate that the response to tetanus toxoid is associated with the presence of G1m(f). Finally, there is some evidence that individuals heterozygous for Caucasian Gm haplotypes can have higher levels of Rh antibodies; however, this was not statistically significant. It therefore appears likely that the level of the immune response to certain antigens is related to the Gm type of the individual. This will be apparent with antigens that are primarily cleared by circulating antibodies rather than by T cell-mediated mechanisms. However, further work is needed to identify the systems in which the response is linked to genes controlling the immunoglobulin allotypic determinants.

ALLOTYPES & DISEASE

We have noted that the response to certain antigens may be associated with the genetic markers on an individual's antibodies. Immunoglobulins play a role in many diseases, their primary role being to provide protection against infection. In some cases, the presence of too much immunoglobulin, abnormal immunoglobulin, or genetically different immunoglobulin may be associated with a specific disease or clinical problem. Do these observations relate to the genetic markers on the antibodies a person carries?

Antibodies to immunoglobulins and their genetic markers have been extensively studied in nonhemolytic transfusion reactions—specifically, the urticarial and anaphylactoid reactions (see Chapter 28). Antibodies against Gm or Km determinants have been reported as responsible for a small proportion of urticarial reactions. The reports that anti-IgA may be responsible for urticarial reactions have not been supported in several studies; however, the role of anti-IgA has been repeatedly confirmed in anaphylactoid reactions. Both class-specific and allotype-specific antibodies may be involved, especially the former. As anaphylactoid reactions can occur in individuals who have had no previous transfusion, they can be unexpected and life-threatening. Unfortunately, routine screening for antibodies to IgA in all prospective transfusion donors and recipients is not currently feasible (see Chapters 26 and 28).

Only a few studies of disease associations with either a specific haplotype or phenotype have yielded consistent results. One problem has been in studying enough markers and haplotypes to detect statistically significant differences. However, there is fairly strong evidence that in Southeast Asia and in Oceania the frequency of the $Gm^{fa;n;b}$ haplotype is associated with the high incidence of malaria. There is also evidence that among families with a high incidence of hay fever, asthma, and eczema (see Chapter 29) there is a markedly higher frequency of individuals heterozygous for Gm haplotypes when compared to unaffected siblings. Observations from the same families also indicate that levels of IgE specific for a particular allergen are similarly related to the Gm phenotype of the individual. The V region genes for IgE are probably the same as those for IgG, and a linkage of the IgE H chains with those of IgG would suggest an association between clinical allergic phenomena and the Gm phenotype of the individual.

Incomplete autoantibodies of the Rh type are predominantly IgG1 and IgG3. Studies on red cell destruction in these patients with hemolytic anemia are consistent with the previously known biologic properties of the subclasses. Thus, patients with IgG3 autoantibodies have the highest levels of red cell destruction. Unfortunately, there is no information on possible differences between different genetic types. In contrast, individuals with IgG1 antibodies show variable patterns of red cell destruction. These differences follow reported differences in the ability of different IgG1 antibodies to bind to monocytes. The variations in IgG1 binding to monocytes possibly reflect genetically determined structural variations in IgG1 molecules and may or may not be related to allotypic differences. In addition, as stated above, among individuals with IgG1 autoantibodies who have both G1m(za) and G1m(f), the autoantibodies are usually IgG1 of type G1m(za), suggesting an association of the V region genes with this haplotype. Finally, patients with only IgG2 and IgG4 antibodies on their red cells tend to have normal values for red cell survival.

Studies in multiple myeloma (see Chapter 28) indicate that the frequencies of the monoclonal proteins produced represent the approximate proportions of the classes and subclasses of immunoglobulins in normal serum. In addition, there do not appear to be any differences in the frequencies of allotypic markers in these patients. However, there are no data on possible differences in survival or severity of the disease relating to IgG genetic type.

Cystic fibrosis (mucoviscidosis) is an inherited disorder characterized by dysfunction of the exocrine glands of the pancreas, respiratory system, and sweat glands. It is not normally associated with immunologic problems. However, studies indicate that the serum of affected individuals (and their unaffected parents) contains an immunoglobulin which stops the beating of oyster cilia and produces asynchrony in rabbit tracheal cilia much more quickly than does serum from individuals with no family history of this disease. Studies of the purified cystic fibrosis factor indicated it was predominantly IgG1. Furthermore, in studies of an individual doubly heterozygous for IgG1 allotypic markers and cystic fibrosis, it was found that the cystic fibrosis factor showed allelic exclusion such that the cystic fibrosis factor was only of the type G1m(za) whereas the serum contained both G1m(za) and G1m(f). Data on the distribution of immunoglobulin phenotypes in these families have not yet yielded information on the role the Gm phenotype of the individual may play in the expression of the disease. It is now known that the active agent is a low-molecular-weight polypeptide chain which binds selectively to IgG1. Further studies may clarify the role of the Gm polymorphism in the binding of this protein and its biologic consequences.

CONCLUSION

It is becoming increasingly evident that antibodies are not infinitely variable; the specific antibody is often restricted to a single subclass and in some cases to one of the 2 alternative genetic types within that subclass. In the future, the use of the genetic markers on antibodies may be a routine tool in the evaluation of patients with abnormal immune responses.

• • •

References

Fudenberg HH & others: *Basic Immunogenetics.* Oxford, 1972.

Grubb R: *The Genetic Markers of Human Immunoglobulins.* Springer, 1970.

Natvig JB, Kunkel HG: Genetic markers of human immunoglobulins. Ser Haematol 1:66, 1968.

Natvig JB, Kunkel HG: Human immunoglobulins: Classes, subclasses, genetic variants, and idiotypes. Adv Immunol 16:1, 1973.

6 . . .
The Complement System

Neil R. Cooper, MD

MECHANISM OF ACTION OF THE COMPLEMENT SYSTEM

The complement (C) system is the primary humoral mediator of antigen-antibody reactions. It consists of at least 15 chemically and immunologically distinct serum proteins which are capable of interacting with each other, with antibody, and with cell membranes. These interactions lead to the generation of biologic activity. The biologic sequelae of activation of this system range from lysis of a spectrum of different kinds of cells, bacteria, and viruses to direct mediation of inflammatory processes. In addition, complement is able to recruit and enlist the participation of other humoral and cellular effector systems and induce histamine release from mast cells, directed migration of leukocytes, phagocytosis, and release of lysosomal constituents from phagocytes.

The individual proteins of this system are normally present in the circulation as functionally inactive precursor molecules. Together they comprise approximately 15% (w/w) of the plasma globulin fraction. The native precursor molecules are designated by numerals–C1, C2, C3, etc–or, in the case of certain of the components, by symbols or trivial names–properdin, factor B, factor D, etc. Each complement component must be activated sequentially under appropriate conditions in order for a complement reaction to progress. Thus, activation is not a single event but rather a dynamic process which enables the proteins to become interacting members of a functionally integrated system. Complement enzymes formed during the activation process are designated by a bar placed over the symbol of the component, eg, $C\overline{1s}$, $C\overline{42}$, factor $\overline{B}$. An activated, biologically active but nonenzymatic state of a component may also be identified by a bar placed over the term for the component, eg, $C\overline{567}$. Fragments of the components arising from enzymatic cleavage are denoted by letters following the term employed for the component, eg, C4a, C4b.

Most of the biologically significant activities of the complement system occur during activation of the last 6 reacting complement components, C3 and C5 through C9 (Fig 6–1). There are 2 parallel but entirely independent mechanisms or pathways leading to activation of the terminal, biologically important portion of the complement sequence. These mechanisms of activation, termed the classical and the alternative or properdin pathways, respectively, are triggered by different substances. Each involves several reaction steps. The 2 activation pathways converge at the midpoint of the complement system, and the remainder of the reaction sequence, involving the reactions of C5 through C9, is common to both pathways. The terminal portion of the complement sequence may also be directly activated by certain noncomplement serum and cellular enzymes without participation of the early reacting factors. Among the trypsinlike enzymes capable of activating at the C3 or C5 stage of the reaction are the fibrinolytic enzyme plasmin and certain lysosomal enzymes (Fig 6–1).

THE CLASSICAL COMPLEMENT PATHWAY

The classical pathway may be activated by antigen-antibody complexes or aggregated immunoglobulins (Table 6–1). Human immunoglobulins belonging to the IgG1, IgG2, and IgG3 subclasses and IgM class are capable of initiating the classical pathway, whereas IgG4 subclass and IgA, IgD, and IgE classes are inactive in this regard. Among the IgG subclasses, IgG3 is most active, followed (in order) by IgG1 and IgG2. Immunologic activation occurs via binding of the first complement component (C1) to a site located in the Fc region of the IgG or IgM molecule.

The classical pathway may also be activated non-

Table 6–1. Activation of the complement (C) system.

	Classical	Alternative
Immunologic	IgG, IgM	IgA, IgG, IgE
Nonimmunologic	Trypsinlike enzymes	Trypsinlike enzymes
	DNA	Lipopolysaccharides
	Staphylococcal protein A	Plant and bacterial polysaccharides
	C-reactive protein	Cobra venom factors

Neil R. Cooper is with the Department of Molecular Immunology, Scripps Clinic and Research Foundation, La Jolla, California.

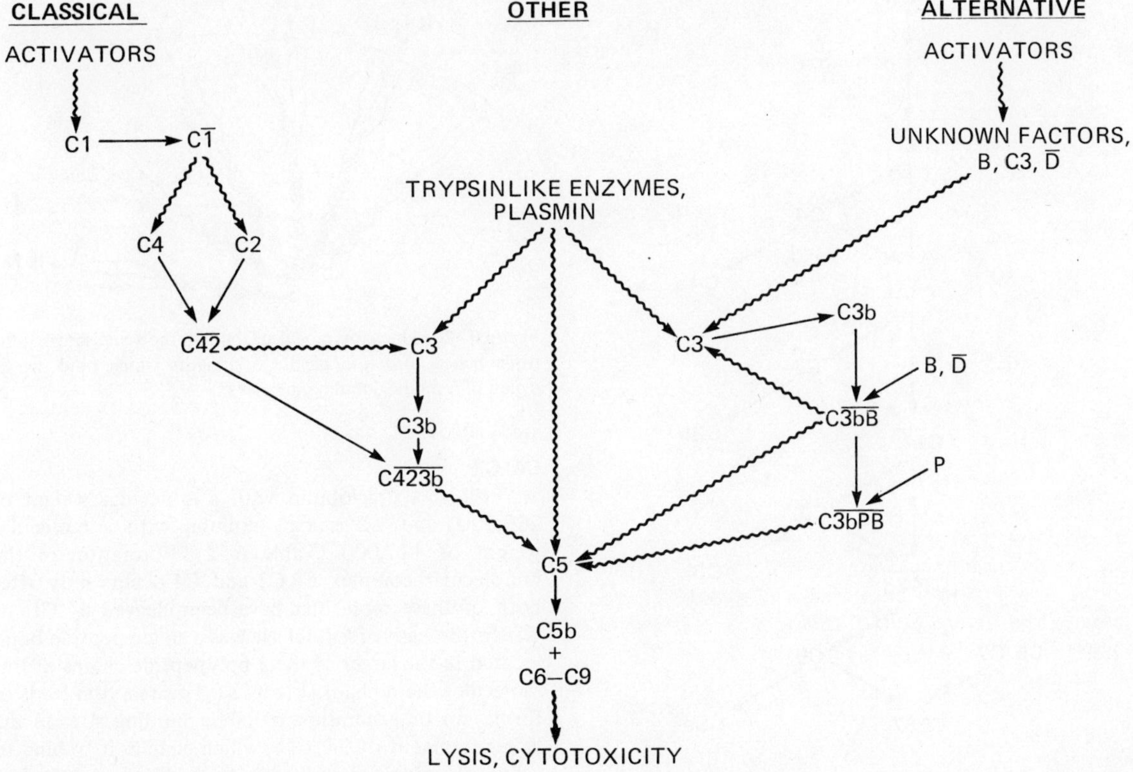

Figure 6–1A. Schematic diagram of the mechanisms of assembly of the complement (C) system on the surface of a complement activator.

immunologically by a number of chemically diverse substances, including DNA, C-reactive protein, and certain cellular membranes and trypsinlike enzymes (Table 6–1). Activation occurs by direct binding of C1 to these substances or, in the case of enzymes such as the fibrinolytic enzyme plasmin, by direct proteolytic attack on the C1 molecule.

The classical pathway comprises the reaction steps of the first (C1), second (C2), third (C3), and fourth (C4) complement components. The pathway may be subdivided into 2 functional units: first, activation of the first component, C1; and second, generation of 2 related complex complement enzymes, C$\overline{42}$ and C$\overline{423}$.

C1

The first functional unit of the classical complement pathway is created by the activation of C1 following attachment to the activating agent or after proteolytic attack. C1 consists of 3 distinct protein molecules–termed C1q, C1r, and C1s–which are held together by a calcium-dependent bond (Table 6–2). C1 is present in the circulation as a firm C1q - C1r - C1s macromolecule, and individual subunits are only found in pathologic conditions. C1 may, however, be readily dissociated and reassociated on removal and restoration of calcium ions. C1q has a molecular weight of 400,000; electrophoretically, it is one of the most cationic proteins of human serum. It is a unique serum protein in that its structure is chemically very similar to that of collagen or basement membrane. Like collagen, it contains large amounts of glycine and the hydroxylated amino acids hydroxylysine and hydroxyproline and a significant carbohydrate content consisting in large part of glucose and galactose residues linked as disaccharide units to the hydroxyl group of hydroxylysine. C1q contains a total of 18 polypeptide chains of 3 distinct types which are organized into a structure, visualized by electron microscopy, consisting of 6 peripheral globular portions connected by fibrillar strands to a central structure. The polypeptide chains of the collagenlike portion of each of the 6 subunits form, in all likelihood, a triple helix. A schematic representation of the C1q molecule is shown in Fig 6–2. The C1q molecule bears the sites which enable the C1 molecule to bind to the Fc region of IgG and IgM molecules and is able to bind approximately 6 IgG molecules. The IgG or IgM binding sites appear to be associated with the peripheral globular subunits of the C1q molecule.

C$\overline{1r}$ is a β-globulin with a molecular weight of 170,000 (Table 6–2). Following attachment of C1 via C1q to immune complexes, C1r acquires the ability to enzymatically activate C1s. Integrity of the C1 macromolecule and calcium ions are required for this process.

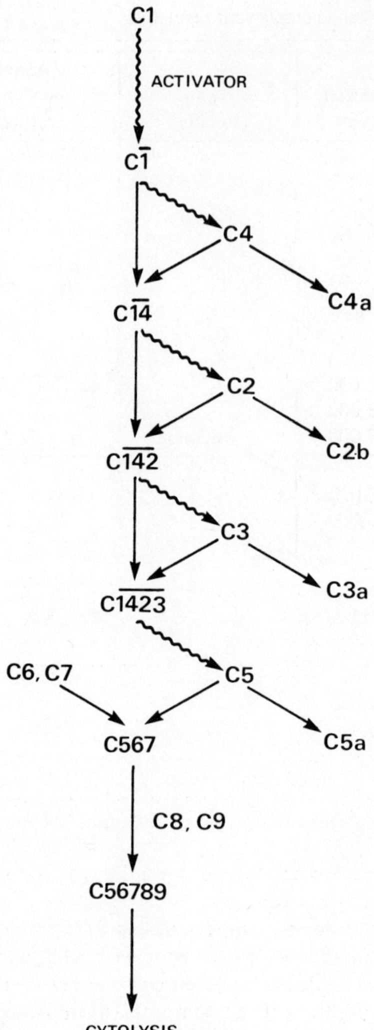

Figure 6–1B. Schematic diagram of the classical pathway of complement activation.

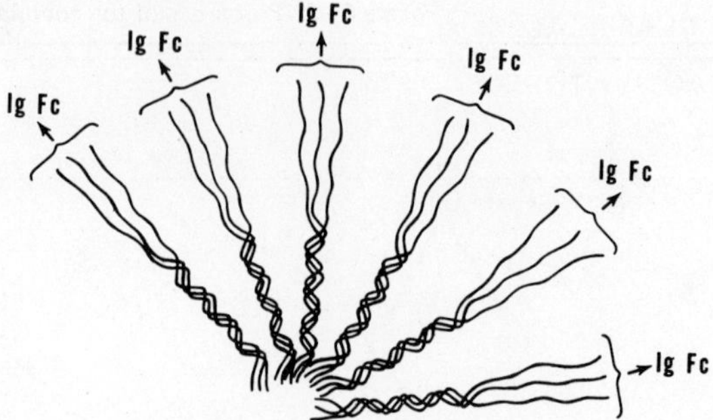

Figure 6–2. Schematic model of the C1q molecule showing the triple helical structure of the 6 subunits which bind the Fc region of immunoglobulin molecules.

C1s is an α-globulin with a molecular weight of approximately 90,000 (Table 6–2). Following cleavage of a single peptide bond in the C1s molecule by $C\overline{1r}$, $C\overline{1s}$ acquires proteolytic enzyme activity. The de novo generated enzyme is of the serine esterase type and thus inhibitable by analogues of diisopropylfluorophosphate. The enzymatic site is located in the smaller of the 2 chains produced on proteolytic activation of the molecules; these chains are linked to each other by disulfide bridges. Upon generation of the $C\overline{1s}$ enzyme, the initial phase of the classical complement pathway is completed, and the earlier reactants, including antigen, antibody, C1q, and $C\overline{1r}$, are not necessary for progression of the complement reaction.

Activated $C\overline{1s}$ mediates the next phase of the complement reaction: formation of the key complement enzyme $C\overline{42}$ (Fig 6–1). $C\overline{42}$ is formed from 2 enzymatically inactive molecules C4 and C2.

C4, C2

C4 is a β_1-globulin with a molecular weight of 206,000, and C2 is a β_1-globulin with a molecular weight of 117,000 (Table 6–2). Formation of the bimolecular complex of C2 and C4 occurs only after both of these molecules have been cleaved by $C\overline{1s}$ or $C\overline{1}$. In the case of C4, $C\overline{1}$ cleaves a single peptide bond located in the larger of the 3 polypeptide chains of this molecule, the α-chain (Fig 6–3). This reaction leads to formation or generation of labile binding sites in the larger fragment of C4, C4b, which enables it to bind to cells or biologic membranes for a brief period after generation. C4a is the small peptide produced by $C\overline{1}$ cleavage of C4. Its biologic role remains to be proved. In a similar manner, cleavage of C2 by $C\overline{1}$ generates a labile binding site in the larger C2 fragment, C2a, which allows it to bind to C4b. The molecular weight of the assembled $C\overline{42}$ is 280,000, and its subunit composition may be described as $C\overline{4b2a}$. $C\overline{42}$ may also be formed free in solution on combination of nascent C2a with C4b which has lost its binding site before becoming bound. Formation of $C\overline{42}$, however, is not an efficient process; the majority of the C2 and C4 molecules entering into this reaction lose their labile binding sites before achieving union with membranes or with each other and diffuse away as inactive reaction products.

$C\overline{42}$ is a proteolytic enzyme which assumes the role of continuing an ongoing complement reaction, and earlier reacting components are no longer required after $C\overline{42}$ has been formed (Fig 6–1). $C\overline{42}$, also termed C3 convertase, cleaves and thereby activates the next reacting component of the sequence, C3. The enzymatic site of $C\overline{42}$ resides in the C2 moiety of the complex.

C3

C3, the substrate of $C\overline{42}$, is a β_1-globulin with a molecular weight of 180,000. C3 is cleaved by $C\overline{42}$ at a single site located near the amino terminus of the larger (α) chain of the molecule (Fig 6–4). The smaller of the 2 resulting fragments, C3a, is a biologically potent peptide which will be discussed later. A labile binding site is uncovered in the larger fragment, C3b, which

Table 6–2. Properties of the complement components and complement regulators.

Name	Synonyms	Molecular Weight	Electrophoretic Mobility	Approximate Serum Concentration (μg/ml)
Classical pathway				
C1q	C′O, 11S protein	400,000	γ_2	180
C1r	. . .	170,000	β	. . .
C1s	C$\overline{1}$ esterase	90,000	α	110
C2	. . .	117,000	β_1	25
C4	β_1E	206,000	β_1	600
C3	β_1C	180,000	β_1	1600
C5	β_1F	180,000	β_1	80
C6	. . .	95,000	β_2	75
C7	. . .	110,000	β_2	55
C8	. . .	163,000	γ_1	80
C9	. . .	80,000	α	200
Alternative pathway				
Properdin	. . .	185,000	γ_2	25
Factor B	C3 proactivator (C3PA) Glycine-rich β glycoprotein (GBG) β_2 glycoprotein II	95,000	β_2	200
Factor D	C3 proactivator convertase (C3PAse) Glycine-rich β glycoproteinase (GBGase)	25,000	α	. . .
C3	Factor A, hydrazine-sensitive factor (HSF)	180,000	β_1	. . .
Complement regulators				
C$\overline{1}$ inactivator	C$\overline{1}$ esterase inhibitor	105,000	α_2	180
C3b inactivator	KAF	100,000	β	. . .
Anaphylatoxin inactivator	AI	300,000	α	. . .

enables this molecule to attach to membranes at sites near to but distinct from those utilized by antibody and C$\overline{42}$. A major proportion of C3 molecules entering this reaction fail to achieve binding and accumulate in the fluid phase as inactive cleavage fragments.

The attachment of C3b to membrane receptors in the vicinity of C$\overline{42}$ molecules leads to generation of the last enzyme of the classical pathway, C$\overline{423}$. This enzyme has C5, a β_1-globulin with a molecular weight of 180,000, as its natural substrate. As the presence of C3b in proximity to C$\overline{42}$ enables the enzyme to cleave C5, C3b is thought to be a modifier of the specificity of the C$\overline{42}$ enzyme.

The classical complement pathway thus consists of a series of enzyme-substrate and protein-protein interactions which lead to the sequential formation of several complement enzymes. It should be emphasized that the reactions involved are highly specific, and other molecules have not been found which can substitute for the required complement components. In addition, as the reactions are enzymatically mediated, there is a considerable turnover of molecules of C2,

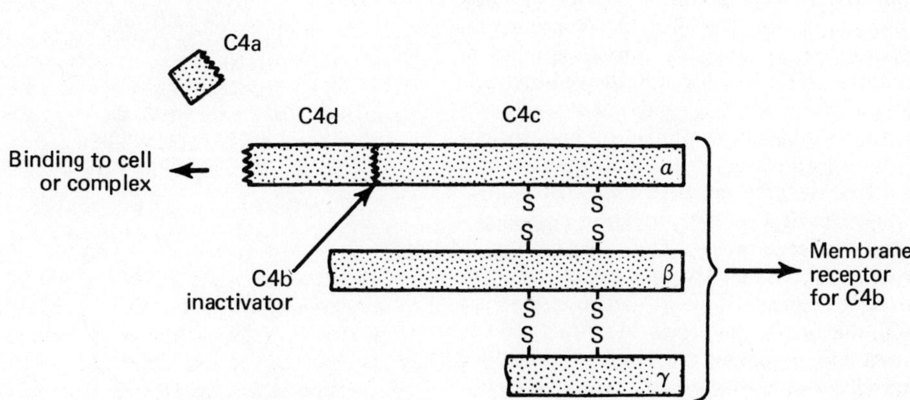

Figure 6–3. Schematic model of the C4 molecule.

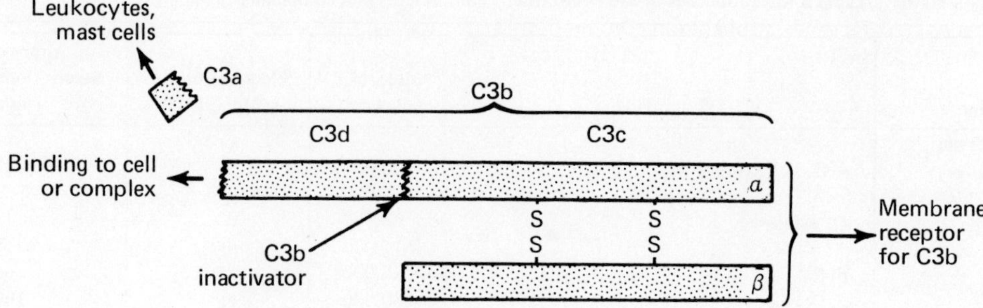

Figure 6–4. Schematic model of the C3 molecule.

C3, C4, and C5 at the respective steps in the reaction and an accumulation of reaction products free in solution. Since some of these reaction products have biologic activity, it is evident that a relatively small stimulus to complement activation may lead to considerable generation of these biologically active products.

THE ALTERNATIVE COMPLEMENT PATHWAY

The alternative complement pathway or properdin pathway may be activated immunologically by human IgA and also by some human IgG and IgE molecules (Table 6–1). The pathway may also be readily initiated nonimmunologically by certain complex polysaccharides, lipopolysaccharides, and trypsinlike enzymes.

The alternative pathway was originally described as the properdin system, a group of proteins involved in resistance to infection, which was similar to, but distinct from, complement. The properdin system was found to be involved in the destruction of certain bacteria, the neutralization of some viruses, and the lysis of erythrocytes from patients with paroxysmal nocturnal hemoglobinuria. The system did not seem to require specific antibody. Several of the factors involved in the system were identified and isolated in a partially purified state. These included properdin, factor A, a high-molecular-weight protein similar in certain properties to C4 which was destroyed by treatment of serum with hydrazine; and a heat-labile substance (factor B) which was similar to but distinct from C2. Investigations indicate that the recently identified alternative pathway of complement activation is in fact identical to the properdin system described earlier. Properdin was isolated and found to be a glycoprotein with a molecular weight of 185,000, having the electrophoretic mobility of a γ_2-globulin (Table 6–2). Factor A has been identified as C3. Factor B has several synonyms as a result of its involvement in several systems subsequently shown to be different activities of the alternative pathway (Table 6–2); it is a β_2-globulin with a molecular weight of 95,000. Factor D, a more recently discovered member of the pathway, is an α-globulin with a molecular weight of 25,000. Other factors not yet isolated are also involved.

Activation of the alternative pathway by particulate activators such as insoluble polysaccharides, cell-bound antibody, or certain cells, triggers a series of reactions which are rapidly being characterized. The activators interact with at least one initiating factor and with factors B, D, and native C3. In this process a proteolytic enzyme is generated which has C3 as its natural substrate. This enzyme cleaves C3 and deposits C3b on the surface of the activating particle.

At this stage of the reaction sequence there is a positive feedback mechanism which amplifies an initial stimulus to the alternative pathway and leads to additional C3 cleavage (Fig 6–5). This cyclic amplifying system enables a relatively minor degree of activation of the complement system to be reflected in considerable activation of the biologically important terminal portion of the complement reaction sequence. The feedback mechanism is initiated and controlled by the major cleavage fragment of C3, C3b. This factor (C3b) formed by the alternative pathway, the classical pathway, or noncomplement enzymes such as plasmin and thrombin interacts with factor B in the presence of

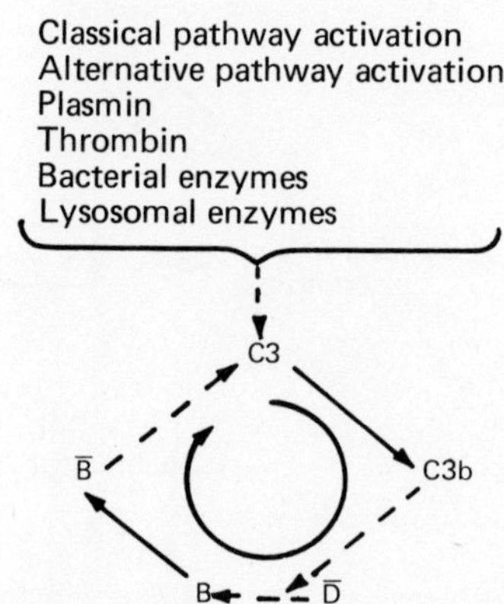

Figure 6–5. The C3b-dependent positive feedback mechanism.

factor $\overline{\text{D}}$ to lead to cleavage and activation of factor B. The newly activated factor B, probably in conjunction with C3b as C$\overline{\text{3b,B}}$, in turn cleaves C3 and produces additional C3b.

The alternative pathway may also be activated by an isolated protein obtained from cobra venom. This substance has been extensively used to deplete complement activity in vivo for the purpose of studying its biologic function. This protein, cobra venom factor, forms a reversible complex with factor B in the presence of magnesium ions. Factor B, altered slightly by incorporation into the complex, is susceptible to cleavage and activation by factor $\overline{\text{D}}$. A C3 cleaving enzyme is thus generated.

The C$\overline{\text{3b,B}}$ enzyme formed on a surface by interaction of C3b with factors B and D cleaves either C3 or C5. These activities are stabilized by properdin (Fig 6–1).

There are numerous analogies in physicochemical properties of the factors of the alternative and classical complement pathways and the mechanisms of activation of these proteins. C$\overline{\text{1s}}$ is similar to factor $\overline{\text{D}}$ in that both are serine esterase enzymes. C$\overline{\text{1s}}$ cleaves C4 and C2, and the larger fragment of each is incorporated into a new enzyme in the presence of magnesium. Factor $\overline{\text{D}}$ cleaves factor B, a molecule very similar in physicochemical properties to C2, in the presence of another protein, C3b, which is physicochemically similar to C4b, and thereby mediates the magnesium-dependent formation of a new proteolytic enzyme. These similar complex enzymes cleave the same single peptide bond in C3. In each instance, the newly generated C3b modulates the activity of the complex enzyme, enabling it to cleave C5.

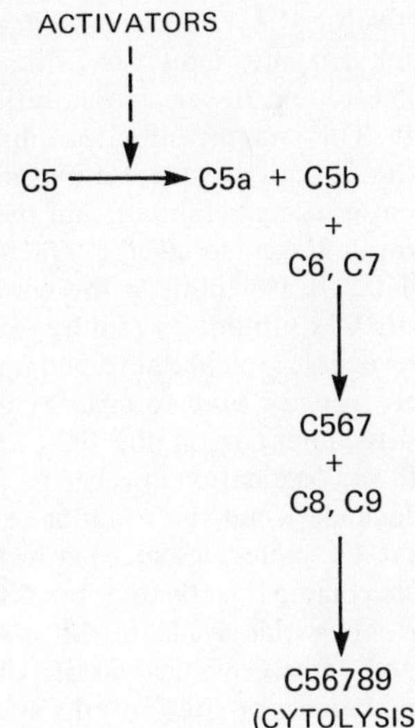

Figure 6–6. Schematic diagram of the membrane attack mechanism.

THE REACTION OF C5–C9: THE MEMBRANE ATTACK MECHANISM

The terminal portion of the complement sequence is termed the membrane attack system since C5–C9 must become membrane-bound in order for membrane changes or damage to occur. Following activation, this portion of the complement sequence may become attached to the surface of a cell bearing the activating enzyme of the classical or alternative pathways, or it may become bound to the membrane of a different cell or membrane not bearing any previously reacted complement components. The latter is an example of bystander lysis of cells.

The complement attack mechanism is initiated on cleavage of C5 by C$\overline{\text{423}}$, C$\overline{\text{3b,B}}$, or certain enzymes such as plasmin (Fig 6–1). The activation reaction results in generation of a small biologically active peptide, C5a (MW 17,000), and a larger fragment C5b (MW 163,000). Two or more labile binding sites are thereby generated in the nascent C5b fragment. One of these enables C5b to bind to cells or biologic membranes for a brief period after activation, while the other sites serve as acceptors for the next 2 reacting factors, C6 and C7. C5b attached to membranes also has the ability to bind C6 and C7 (Fig 6–6). C6 and C7 are β_2-globulins with molecular weights of 95,000 and 110,000, respectively. The firm trimolecular C567 complex provides a binding site for a single molecule of C8, a γ_1-globulin with a molecular weight of 163,000. The tetramolecular C567, 8 complex furnishes binding sites for C9, an α-globulin with a molecular weight of 80,000. The fully assembled complex, which contains one molecule each of C5, C6, C7, and C8 and up to 6 molecules of C9, has a cumulative molecular weight of approximately 1 million. This complex has been isolated after generation in serum, and its subunit composition has been characterized. The complex is able to produce structural membrane damage leading to cytotoxicity and lysis when bound to the surface of cells.

CONTROL MECHANISMS OF THE COMPLEMENT SYSTEM

Uncontrolled activation of the complement system is prevented by the lability of the activated combining sites generated at multiple stages of the complement reaction, including the reaction steps involving C2, C3, C4, and C5, and by time- and temperature-dependent dissociation of some of the active complexes such as the C$\overline{\text{42}}$ and C$\overline{\text{423}}$ complexes. In addition, several serum proteins have been identified which serve to modulate and limit activation of the complement system. These proteins bind to or enzymatically attack only the specifically activated forms of the components.

$C\overline{1}$ inactivator ($C\overline{1}$ esterase inhibitor) is a multispecific serum enzyme inhibitor with a molecular weight of 105,000 and the electrophoretic mobility of an α_2-globulin. This enzyme inhibitor inhibits not only $C\overline{1}$ but also the fibrinolytic enzyme plasmin, the kinin-forming system enzyme kallikrein, and the coagulation system enzymes Hageman factor (factor XII) and factor XI. $C\overline{1}$ inactivator inhibits the enzymatic activity of $C\overline{1}$ or its $C\overline{1s}$ subunit by rapidly forming a firm, essentially irreversible stoichiometric complex with $C\overline{1}$. $C\overline{1}$ inactivator does not bind to proenzyme C1 or C1s. The site of attachment is on the light chain of $C\overline{1s}$. Classical pathway activation proceeds past the $C\overline{1}$ inactivator blockade when the stimulus to activation is so intense that $C\overline{1}$ molecules succeed in forming $C\overline{42}$ sites before becoming inactivated by $C\overline{1}$ inactivator molecules or when the available $C\overline{1}$ inactivator has been consumed. However, activation of the kinin-forming, coagulation, or fibrinolytic systems would also be expected to facilitate activation of the complement system by consuming $C\overline{1}$ inactivator.

Another key control protein of the complement system is C3b inactivator. This serum enzyme attacks C3b free in solution or on the surface of cells and cleaves the molecule into 2 or more fragments (Fig 6–4). The C3b degradation products are unable to function in the $C\overline{423}$ or $C\overline{3b,B}$ enzymes or to participate in the cyclic C3b-dependent feedback mechanism. Serum also contains an enzyme, possibly the same molecule as the C3b inactivator, which similarly cleaves C4b into fragments and abolishes its biologic activity (Fig 6–3).

Human serum also contains an enzyme, the anaphylatoxin inactivator, an α-globulin with a molecular weight of 300,000 which destroys the biologic activities of the C3a and C5a fragments of C3 and C5, respectively. Inactivation is accomplished by cleavage of the carboxyl terminal arginine from each of these molecules.

Among the other inhibitors or inactivators of activated complement components which have been described is an inhibitor of C6. This protein is a β_1-globulin.

METHODS OF DETECTION & QUANTITATION OF COMPLEMENT COMPONENTS

Certain precautions are necessary in the handling of blood specimens for complement studies. The serum should be allowed to separate at room temperature (approximately 25 C). Blood should not be placed in a refrigerator (4 C) nor a water bath (37 C) to achieve separation of serum from the blood clot. The serum should be removed from the blood clot as soon as possible and frozen at –20 C if complement studies are not being performed immediately. The sera should be frozen at –70 C to prevent loss of complement activity in hemolytic tests if the tests are not to be performed within 4 days.

Some laboratory studies require inactivation of complement to avoid hemolysis. This is normally achieved by heating the serum at 56 C for 30 minutes. While hemolytic activity is normally abolished by this procedure, the individual complement components vary in their heat lability. Some components are relatively stable after heating at 56 C for 30 (or even 60) minutes and retain significant functional activity, although the whole serum is negative in a hemolytic complement test.

Complement activity is generally measured by assessing the ability of serum in limiting dilution to lyse sheep red cells sensitized with rabbit antisheep antibody (hemolysin). Complement titrations of this type provide an overall measure of the integrity of the classical complement pathway and of the membrane attack mechanism. The values are expressed as 50% hemolytic complement units per ml (CH_{50}). One CH_{50} unit is defined as the quantity or dilution of serum required to lyse 50% of the cells in the test serum (see Chapter 24).

A similar assay system is employed to measure the hemolytic activity of individual complement components in isolated form or in serum. In this type of assay system, all the components except the one in question are supplied in excess and certain stringent reaction conditions are employed which are known to be optimal for each component. Under such conditions, the number of hemolytic units may be converted on a weight basis to the absolute concentration of the active complement component. This use of hemolytic activity measurements for absolute quantitation of complement components has a firm theoretical and mathematical basis since it has been shown that the individual reaction steps of a number of the components conform to a one-hit process. Hemolytic values obtained by such titrations are expressed as site-forming units or effective molecules.

The pattern of depletion of complement components following treatment of serum with potential complement-activating agents may indicate the pathway of complement activation involved. Classical pathway activation depletes C1, C4, C2, C3, and C5 and, to a lesser extent, late-acting components as indicated in Fig 6–7. Alternative pathway activation, while depleting only small amounts of C1, C4, and C2, leads to significant consumption of C3–C9 (Fig 6–8).

Many of the complement components can be quantitated in serum or other body fluids by single radial diffusion in agar (Chapter 24). This test is based on the fact that the extent of diffusion of an antigen into agar containing specific antibody is proportionate to the absolute antigen concentration. All of the complement components having serum levels above approximately 20 μg/ml, and for which antiserum is available, can be measured by this technic. However, it should be noted that this method of quantitation, although very useful, does not distinguish between active and inactive complement molecules.

Other methods are available which are not quantitative but which furnish evidence of complement acti-

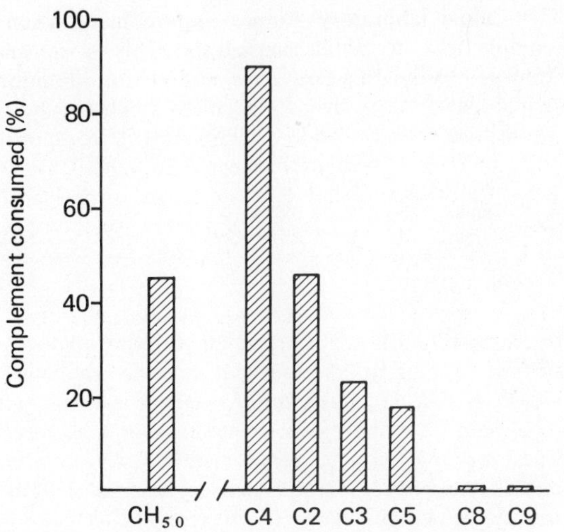

Figure 6–7. Typical component depletion pattern for classical pathway activation.

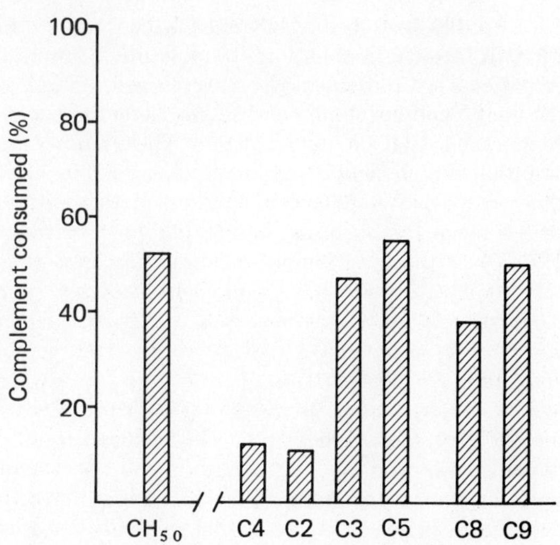

Figure 6–8. Typical component depletion pattern for alternative pathway activation.

vation. One such technic involves measurement of the physicochemical status of individual complement components by the technic of immunoelectrophoresis. In the case of certain of the components such as $C\overline{1s}$, C2, C3, C4, and factor B, the cleaved activated forms of the components are readily distinguished by an altered electrophoretic mobility. The effect of activation on the mobility of factor B is depicted in Fig 6–9. The native precursor molecule migrates as β_2-globulin on immunoelectrophoresis in agar while activated factor B migrates as a γ-globulin. Activated C2 also migrates more cathodally than native C2, while activated $C\overline{1s}$, C3, and C5 migrate more anodally than the respective native proteins.

Evidence of complement activation may also be obtained by showing a decrease in the immune adherence titer of the serum being investigated. Immune adherence is an agglutination reaction between a cell bearing $C\overline{423}$ and an indicator cell, often human erythrocytes, which has a receptor for C3b. The test is generally performed by incubating dilutions of serum with antibody-coated erythrocytes during which time $C\overline{1}$ and $C\overline{423}$ attach to the surface of the cells in proportion to their relative serum concentrations. Subsequently, human erythrocytes are added and the final dilution of serum giving measurable agglutination is taken as the end point.

Complement may also be demonstrated on diseased tissues at the site of tissue damage by employing specific antibody. An example is the nonimmunoglobulin Coombs test, an agglutination reaction performed with erythrocytes from patients with autoimmune hemolytic anemia and dilutions of antisera to C3, C4, or other complement components. As complement is not normally found on cells, the presence of agglutination with anticomplement sera constitutes evidence for complement activation. In a variant of this technic, complement may be localized in diseased tissues by using fluorescent or radiolabeled antisera to individual complement components. The finding of deposited complement components in the site of tissue damage constitutes evidence for activation of the complement system in the tissue.

Direct evidence of activation of the complement system in vivo may be obtained from metabolic studies with purified radiolabeled complement components.

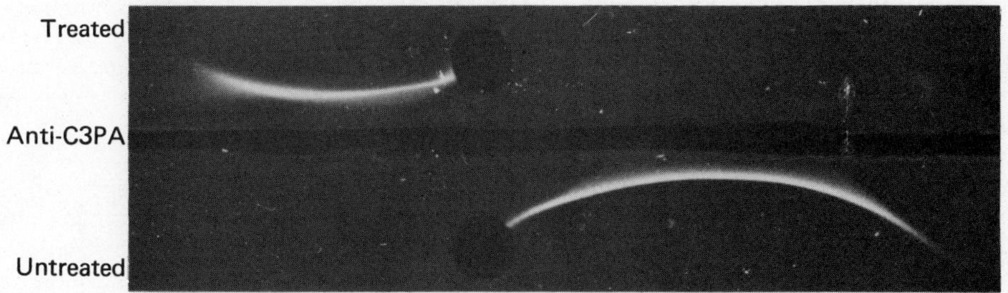

Figure 6–9. Immunoelectrophoretic analysis of factor B (C3PA) in native form ***(bottom)*** and after activation ***(top)***. Anti-factor B (C3PA) is in the slot, and the anode is to the right.

Such studies have been performed with C1q, C3, C4, C5, and factor B in normal individuals and in a number of patients with diseases, including glomerulonephritis, rheumatic and autoimmune diseases, hereditary angioedema, and renal allograft rejection. These studies indicate that complement components are normally among the most rapidly metabolized of all plasma proteins with a mean fractional catabolic rate of approximately 1.4–2% of the plasma pool per hour. Because of the very rapid turnover of complement proteins, static measurements of circulating levels of the complement components often fail to detect in vivo complement activation. Such activation and the pathway involved are, however, readily detected and quantitated by metabolic studies. Hypercatabolism has been found in patients with proliferative glomerulonephritis, systemic lupus erythematosus, seropositive rheumatoid arthritis, hereditary angioedema, and renal allograft rejection. Metabolic studies also reveal reduced synthesis of complement—C3 in some patients with membranoproliferative glomerulonephritis and C4 in some patients with IgG-IgM cryoglobulinemia and Sjögren's syndrome.

BIOLOGIC CONSEQUENCES OF COMPLEMENT ACTIVATION

Cytolytic & Cytotoxic Damage

Complement has been shown to be capable of mediating the lytic destruction of many kinds of cells including erythrocytes, platelets, bacteria, viruses possessing a lipoprotein envelope, and lymphocytes, although with greatly varying degrees of efficiency in each instance. Either complement pathway may produce cytolytic damage. Some species of complement are more efficient in producing lysis of certain cell-antibody combinations. Some cells are quite resistant to destruction by complement even in the presence of marked complement activation on the cell surface. There are many reasons why complement may fail to lyse cells, including the presence of antigenic modulation, a phenomenon whereby antibody alters the distribution of antigen on the cell surface, or a spatial arrangement of antigenic sites which does not facilitate complement activation in a region of the membrane susceptible to lysis. Lack of binding sites for the late-reacting complement components is another possible cause of failure of complement to lyse a cell. Most commonly, however, complement fails to produce lysis because of the nature and structure of the cell wall or membrane or because of a lack of substrate for late complement action. Factors in addition to complement may also be required, as in the lysis of gram-negative bacteria.

As the complement components free in serum become attached to the surfaces of cells and other biologic membranes, changes in membrane ultrastructure occur (Table 6–3). There are alterations in membrane electrical charge and membrane environment owing to the accumulation of complement proteins on the cell surface. Membrane swelling also occurs. Complement action produces circular lesions having a diameter of 8–12 nm in many types of membranes (Fig 6–10). These occur during the reaction of C5–C9. Their significance is not clear since the lesions do not penetrate the cell membrane and the presence of such lesions does not always lead to cell lysis.

Table 6–3. Consequences of attachment of complement proteins to membranes.

Accumulation of bulk of complement proteins
Changes in membrane environment and charge
Modification of membrane properties and functions
Stimulation of cellular functions
Membrane lesions and swelling
Membrane damage or disruption

The mechanism by which late-acting complement components produce destructive changes in cellular membranes is not known. It is conceivable that damage is mediated by enzymatic activity of the C5–C9 complex, although the bulk of available evidence is against this possibility. Alternatively, cell membrane damage may occur through hydrophilic or hydrophobic disruption of basic membrane structure by the C5–C9 complex. Following the action of C9, there appear to be several steps within the cell membrane which occur before a cell undergoes final osmotic lysis. The nature and significance of these steps are not known.

Formation of Complement-Dependent Reactive Sites on Membranes

New sites are generated or uncovered in the b fragments of C3 and C4 as a consequence of proteolytic cleavage of the molecules during complement activation (Figs 6–3 and 6–4). The labile binding sites which were uncovered or generated by proteolytic cleavage and which permit binding to membranes have

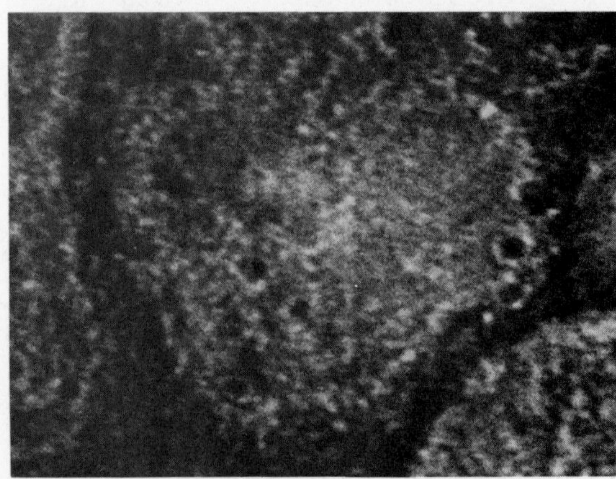

Figure 6–10. Electron micrograph demonstrating the circular lesions produced in the membrane of an enveloped virus by the cytolytic action of complement.

been considered earlier. The biologically active cleavage fragments will be considered below. In addition, however, other reactive sites are generated in C3b and C4b which are recognized by various cells having receptors for C3b or C4b (Figs 6–3 and 6–4). These sites appear to be stable. The secondary or responding cells bind to these sites in C3b or C4b regardless of whether the b fragments are free in solution or attached by the labile binding site to an immune complex or to another cell. In the latter instance, C3b or C4b molecules serve as a bridge between the cell bearing C3b or C4b bound via the labile binding site and the responding cell having a receptor for C3b or C4b. Attachment of the responding or effector cell to C3b or C4b in this manner may trigger any of several responses by the responding cell.

Many kinds of cells possess receptors for C3b and C4b (Table 6–4). These include phagocytic cells, lymphocytes, primate erythrocytes, and certain nonprimate platelets. The consequences of attachment of C3b or C4b depend on the responding cell type. Numerous phagocytic cells, such as macrophages, monocytes, and polymorphonuclear leukocytes, have C3b receptors. When the responding or effector cell is phagocytic, attachment leads to engulfment or attempted engulfment of the cell or membrane bearing C3b. For this reason, bound C3b or C4b may be considered to be opsonins. Although many phagocytic reactions proceed in the absence of complement and a number of phagocytic cells have receptors for the Fc portion of certain antibody molecules, the presence of C3b on the target cell or complex facilitates adherence and ingestion.

C3b receptors are also present on human erythrocytes and platelets from many nonprimate species (Table 6–4). This reaction is termed immune adherence. The biologic significance of attachment of complexes or cells bearing C3b to human erythrocytes is not clear, although it may be an immobilizing mechanism important in dealing with pathogenic agents. Adherence to nonprimate platelets triggers specific release of vasoactive amines and nucleotides from the platelet. Platelet lysis does not ensue.

In addition, human B lymphocytes have receptors for C3b or C4b (Table 6–4). Although the biologic significance of the presence of these receptors is unclear, it is evident that this reaction brings antigens in direct surface contact with potential antibody-forming cells. It is conceivable that bound complement components play a role in this manner in the induction of an immune response.

Table 6–4. Cells possessing C3b and C4b receptors.

B lymphocytes
Neutrophils
Monocytes
Macrophages
Erythrocytes (primates only)
Platelets (rabbit, rodents, cat, dog, but not primates)

Biologic Actions of Complement Cleavage Products

The low-molecular-weight fragments of C3 and C5—C3a and C5a, respectively—stimulate the release of histamine from mast cells (Table 6–5). This property is termed anaphylatoxin activity. Nanomolar amounts of C3a and C5a are adequate for histamine release. The released histamine in turn enhances capillary permeability and produces edema and contraction of smooth muscle. The 2 peptides, however, are chemically distinct from each other. C3a is an extremely basic peptide with a molecular weight of 8900. The primary amino acid sequence of the 77-residue C3a peptide has recently been established. C5a is larger (MW 17,000) and somewhat more acidic. C3a and C5a are also biologically distinct in that they react with different cellular receptors, since tissue rendered unresponsive to C3a will continue to respond to C5a and vice versa. The biologic activity of each peptide is abolished by the action of the serum anaphylatoxin inactivator which removes the carboxyl terminal arginine of each of these molecules.

C3a and C5a also have chemotactic activity, ie, the ability to induce migration of leukocytes into an area of complement activation (Table 6–5). The binding of C3a and C5a to leukocytes—particularly polymorphonuclear leukocytes—initiates a series of changes involving several enzymes within the leukocyte which culminate in migration of the cells toward the area of complement activation. The trimolecular C567 complex also has chemotactic activity.

There are also other biologic consequences of activation of the complement system mediated by complement cleavage products. These include the generation of a kinin, probably a fragment of C2, which increases vascular permeability and contracts smooth muscle (Table 6–5). This kinin does not function through release of histamine. It is thought to be involved in the symptomatology of hereditary angioedema. Functional $C\overline{1}$ inactivator is genetically lacking in this disease, which is characterized by uncontrolled activation of the complement system.

C3a has also been found to possess nonhistamine-dependent kininlike activity. Activation of the alternative pathway of complement in the presence of leukocytes leads to release of leukocyte lysosomal enzymes. This is a specific reaction, as other compartments of this cell are not affected and lysis does not ensue. The active principle is C5a.

Table 6–5. Biologic effects of complement activation peptides.

C3a	Chemotactic activity Histamine release Kininlike activity
C4a C2b	Kinin?
C5a	Chemotactic activity Histamine release Lysosomal enzyme release

BIOLOGIC SIGNIFICANCE OF THE COMPLEMENT SYSTEM

The biologic reactions considered above are individual aspects of an integrated system which is able to produce inflammation and facilitate the localization of an infective agent (Fig 6–11). Thus, the kinin and anaphylatoxin activities lead to contraction of smooth muscle, increased vascular permeability, and edema. The chemotactic agents trigger an influx of leukocytes which remain fixed in the area of complement activation through attachment to specific sites on bound C3b and C4b molecules. Phagocytosis or release of lysosomal and other constituents facilitates the destruction of an infective agent. As is evident from Fig 6–11, there are multiple backup systems which produce similar biologic activities. A minor stimulus to activation of the system produces relatively little of these biologic mediators, while a greater stimulus to activation can be visualized as leading to the generation of additional cleavage products and reactive sites on the components.

Evidence for the biologic importance of this system in host defenses has come from studies of several experimentally induced diseases in animals, from human immunologic disease processes, and from the markedly increased susceptibility to infection which characterizes some congenital or acquired deficiencies of complement components or complement regulators in man. These disease entities bear certain hallmarks which imply the participation of complement. These include a depression in circulating levels of the complement components, the finding of complement components deposited in the site of tissue damage, and infiltration of polymorphonuclear leukocytes. In animals, it has been possible to further define the pathogenic role of complement in certain conditions. One of the most telling examples is the experimental disease nephrotoxic nephritis, which is induced by the injection into an animal of antibody directed against glomerular basement membrane. The injected antibody rapidly fixes to the glomerular basement membrane, and the result is immediate structural and functional injury. Antibody attachment is rapidly followed by activation of complement, which is reflected in a fall in circulating levels and by fixation of complement components to the glomerular basement membrane, where they may be visualized by fluorescence technics. An influx of polymorphonuclear leukocytes rapidly ensues, followed by destruction of the glomerular basement membrane and proteinuria, which are consequences of the release of degradative enzymes from the leukocytes. The essential role of complement in leading to the influx of leukocytes and facilitating their localization is shown by the fact that infiltration and tissue damage are prevented if the antibody is first rendered unable to fix complement or if the animal is depleted in vivo of C3. Similar mechanisms are involved in the inflammatory component of a number of human diseases, including several types of glomerulonephritis, rheumatoid arthritis, autoimmune hemolytic anemias,

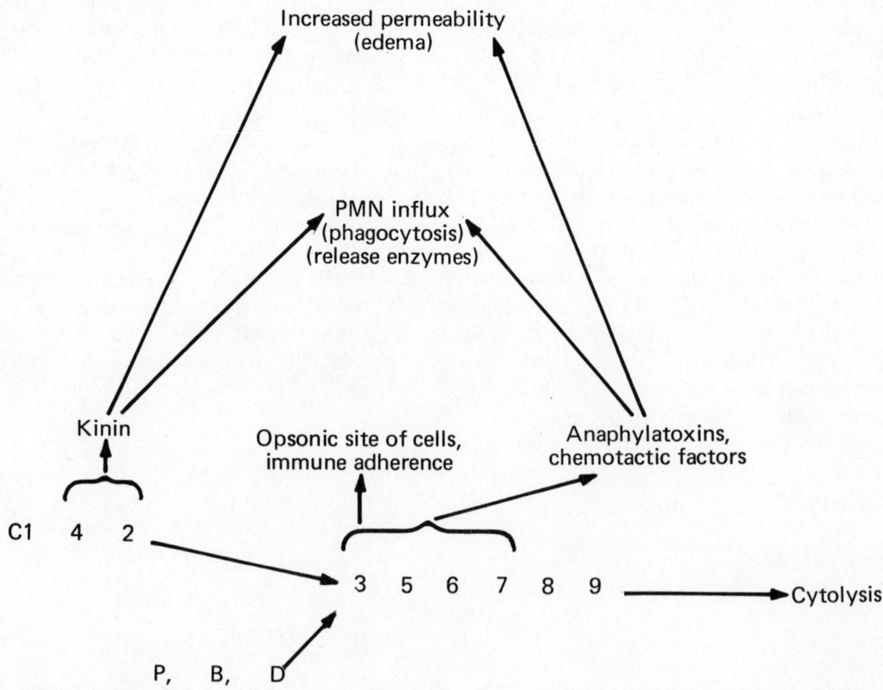

Figure 6–11. Biologic consequences of complement activation. (PMN = polymorphonuclear leukocyte; P = properdin; B = factor B; D = factor D.)

Table 6–6. Human disorders associated with complement deficiencies.

C1q	Systemic lupus erythematosus or similar syndrome, hypogammaglobulinemia
C1r	Renal disease, systemic lupus erythematosus or similar syndrome, recurrent infections, rheumatoid disease
C1s	Systemic lupus erythematosus
C2	Arthralgia, systemic lupus erythematosus or similar syndrome, nephritis, susceptibility to infection
C3	Repeated infections
C4	Systemic lupus erythematosus
C5	Leiner's disease, recurrent infections, systemic lupus erythematosus
C7	Raynaud's phenomenon
$C\overline{1}$ inactivator ($C\overline{1}$ esterase inhibitor)	Hereditary angioedema
C3b inactivator	Recurrent infections

and others. Metabolic studies with purified radiolabeled complement components have documented and quantitated in vivo complement activation in these and other diseases as noted earlier.

The physiologic role of complement in the maintenance of a normal state of health is dramatically illustrated by the predisposition to disease or susceptibility to infection which characterizes congenital deficiency of certain of the complement components or their regulators (Table 6–6). Thus, more than half of the 36 reported individuals with hereditary deficiencies of the components of the classical complement pathway–C1q, C1r, C1s, C4, and C2–are chronically ill and suffer from several diseases, including chronic renal disease, systemic lupus erythematosus, and recurrent infections. All 3 of the reported individuals with C3 deficiency suffer from recurrent life-threatening infections. Congenital deficiency of $C\overline{1}$ inactivator leads to uncontrolled activation of the complement system and hereditary angioedema. The single reported patient with absence of C3b inactivator has very low circulating levels of factor B and C3, indicating constant activation of the alternative complement pathway. This patient also suffers from recurrent severe infections. While it is not clear how the absence of a complement component or a regulator predisposes to disease, these conditions indicate a major physiologic role for the complement system in vivo.

• • •

References

Alper CA, Rosen FS: Genetic aspects of the complement system. Adv Immunol 14:252, 1972.

Austen KF (editor): The immunobiology of complement. Transplant Proc 6:1, 1974.

Cooper NR: Activation of the complement system. Page 155 in: *Contemporary Topics in Molecular Immunology.* Vol 2. Reisfeld R, Mandy W (editors). Plenum Press, 1973.

Cooper NR, Polley ML, Müller-Eberhard HJ: Biology of complement. Page 289 in: *Immunological Diseases,* 2nd ed. Samter M (editor). Little, Brown, 1971.

Götze O, Müller-Eberhard HJ: The C3-activator system: An alternate pathway of complement activation. J Exp Med 134:90, 1971.

Müller-Eberhard HJ: Complement. Annu Rev Biochem 44:697, 1975.

Müller-Eberhard HJ, Götze O, Kolb WP: Activation and function of the alternate complement pathway. Page 251 in: *Advances in the Biosciences.* Vol 12. Raspe G (editor). Pergamon Press, 1973.

Osler AG, Sandberg AL: Alternate complement pathways. Prog Allergy 17:51, 1973.

Rapp HJ, Borsos T: *Molecular Basis of Complement Action.* Appleton-Century-Crofts, 1970.

Ruddy S, Gigli I, Austen F: The complement system of man. (3 parts.) N Engl J Med 287:489, 545, 642, 1972.

Vogt W: Activation, activities and pharmacologically active products of complement. Pharmacol Rev 26:125, 1974.

7 . . .
Cells Involved in Immune Responses

Steven D. Douglas, MD

HISTOLOGIC ORGANIZATION OF THE LYMPHORETICULAR SYSTEM

The lymphoid and reticuloendothelial tissues are composed primarily of a network of interlocking reticular cells and fibers with a supporting framework of reticular cells associated with lymphatic vessels. The main cell type that occupies the interstices of the reticular network is the lymphocyte. The other cell types present in various states of differentiation include lymphoblasts, plasma cells, monocyte-macrophages, endothelial cells, and rare eosinophils and mast cells. In mammals, the aggregate of lymphocytes constitutes about 1% of total body weight; the human body for example, contains about 10^{12} lymphocytes. Lymphocytes in the tissues are in dynamic equilibrium with the circulating blood. Most of the lymphocytes are found in the spleen, lymph nodes, and Peyer's patches of the ileum. For functional purposes, the lymphoid system can be divided into 3 main functional units (Fig 7–1): (1) the stem cells, (2) the primary or central lymphoid organs (thymus and "bursa equivalent"), and (3) the peripheral lymphoid system.

Thymus

The thymus is derived embryologically from the third and fourth branchial pouches and differentiates as ventral out-pocketings from these pouches during the sixth week of fetal life. During vertebrate embryogenesis, the thymus is the first organ to begin the manufacture of lymphocytes (see Chapter 11). The thymus has the highest rate of cell production of any tissue of the body. Available evidence suggests that the vast majority of cells produced in the thymus die there. The thymus is central to the development and function of the immune system; however, it does not directly participate in immune reactions. In the adult, the thymus consists of many lobules, each containing a cortex and medulla (Fig 7–2). Lymphocytes produced by mitosis in the lobules appear to migrate to the medulla, where they further differentiate and then emigrate from the thymus. The medulla also contains thymic (Hassall's) corpuscles, composed of layers of epithelial cells. The function of thymic corpuscles is not known.

The thymus reaches its maximum size (as a percentage of body weight) in most vertebrates either at birth or shortly thereafter. Subsequently, the gland begins a gradual process of involution. In man, the thymus decreases from 0.27% of total body weight to 0.02% between the ages of 5 and 15 years.

Neonatal removal of the thymus has profound effects on the immune system in many species of animals. In certain strains of mice, removal of the thymus leads to "wasting disease" (runting) with marked lymphoid atrophy and death. In other strains of mice, severe lymphopenia may occur with depletion of cells from the paracortical areas of lymph nodes and periarteriolar regions of the spleen. These thymectomized animals have an impaired capacity to mount a humoral antibody response to certain antigens and impaired allograft rejection (see Chapter 15).

Impaired thymic development may be associated with immunologic deficiency disorders (see Chapter 26). The thymus also appears to have an endocrine function and to produce a number of thymic hormones. In the "nude" mouse failure of development of the thymus and marked deficiency of mature T lymphocytes are noted. Histologic abnormalities of the thymus frequently occur in certain autoimmune diseases, particularly systemic lupus erythematosus and myasthenia gravis. These abnormalities include both lymphoid hyperplasia and the development of thymomas. This association between thymomas and autoimmunity suggests a possible relationship between thymic function and disorders of the immune system (see Chapter 14).

Bursa of Fabricius & Mammalian "Bursa Equivalents"

The bursa of Fabricius, which is present in birds, is a lymphoepithelial organ located near the cloaca. Histologically, the bursa is lined with pseudostratified epithelium and contains within it lymphoid follicles divided into cortical and medullary portions (see below). In chickens, removal of the bursa of Fabricius leads to marked deficiency in immunoglobulins, impairment in development of germinal centers, and absence of plasma cells. The "bursa-dependent" lymphoid system has been shown to be independent of the

Steven D. Douglas is Professor of Medicine and Microbiology, University of Minnesota School of Medicine, Minneapolis.

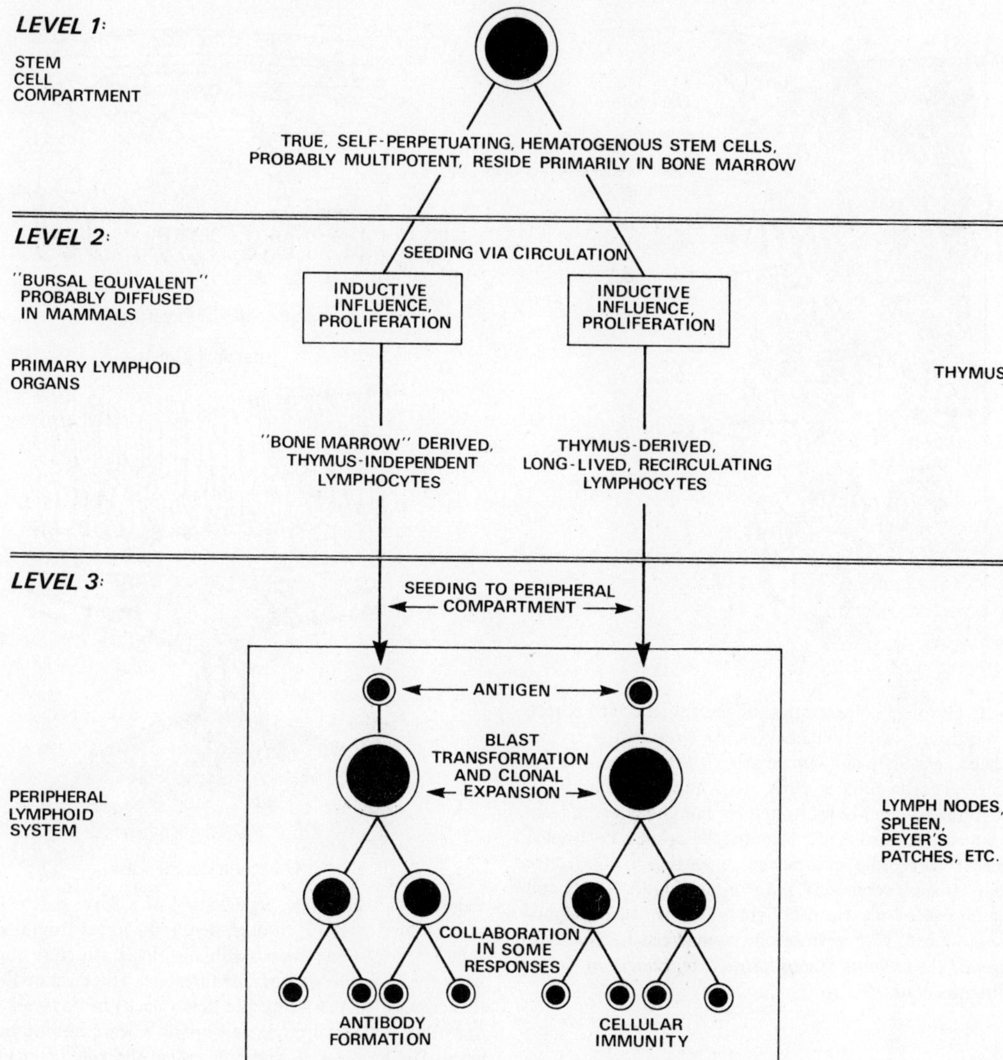

Figure 7–1. Functional compartments of the lymphoid system. (Reproduced, with permission, from Nossal GJV, Ada GL [editors]: The functional anatomy of the lymphoid system. Page 61 in: *Antigens, Lymphoid Cells, and the Immune Response.* Academic Press, 1971.)

thymus. The mammalian equivalent of the bursa of Fabricius has not yet been identified.

The lymphoid system can thus be divided into 2 functional compartments: the thymus-dependent (derived, or processed) T lymphocytes and the "bursa equivalent" (non-thymus-processed, or thymus-independent) B lymphocytes.

Using the term B cell should not be taken to mean that the existence of a bursal organ in nonavian vertebrates is assumed. The "bursa equivalent" may exist in several diffuse sites. Although the term B cell has commonly been interpreted as a reference to a bone marrow lymphocyte, a site of origin in the marrow has not been definitely established. Rodent bone marrow has relatively few B cells.

Lymph Node Architecture

The lymphoid tissues may show varying degrees of histologic complexity. The lamina propria of the trachea, small intestine, and vaginal mucosa usually contains diffuse lymphoid tissue. Solitary lymph nodules may occur in the submucosa or mucosa of these tissues. The Peyer patches of the ileum (Fig 7–3) and the tonsillar ring of Waldeyer consist of collections of lymphoid nodules in the submucosa.

The lymph nodes are usually located at the junction of major lymphatic tracts. Afferent lymphatics enter the nodes at the subcapsular sinus from which there is centripetal flow toward the major efferent lymphatic duct, which drains into the thoracic or right lymphatic duct (Fig 7–4). The histology of the lymph node depends on the state of activity of the node. The "resting" lymph node, which has not been subjected to recent antigenic stimulation, can be morphologically divided into cortex, paracortical areas, and medulla. The margin between the cortex and paracortex may be

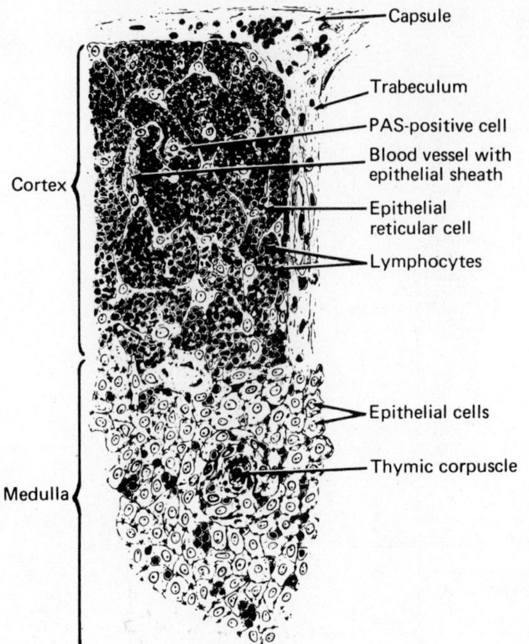

Figure 7–2. Histologic organization of the thymus. The cortex is heavily infiltrated with lymphocytes. As a result, the epithelial cells become stellate and remain attached to one another by desmosomes. The medulla is closer to a pure epithelium, although it too is commonly infiltrated by lymphocytes. A large thymic corpuscle consisting of concentrically arranged epithelial cells is seen. The capsule and trabeculae are rich in connective tissue fibers (mainly collagen) and contain blood vessels and variable numbers of plasma cells, granulocytes, and lymphocytes. (Reproduced, with permission, from Weiss L: *The Cells and Tissues of the Immune System: Structure, Functions, Interactions.* Prentice-Hall, 1972.)

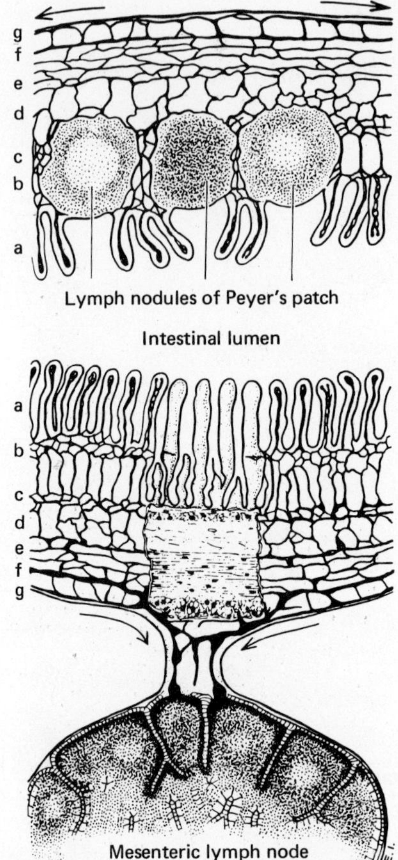

Figure 7–3. Histologic organization of a Peyer patch. Diagram of magnified sections, through ileum; the upper from the area of a Peyer patch, the lower (with histologic structure suggested) from the opposite side of this intestine. The diagram illustrates the disposal of the lymphatic nets (black) in its layers and the direction of flow of chyle and lymph toward mesenteric lymph node. The letters ***a, b,*** and ***c*** designate the villi, lamina propria, and muscularis of tunica mucosa; ***d,*** the tunica submucosa; ***e*** and ***f,*** the circular and longitudinal layers of tunica muscularis; and ***g,*** the tunica serosa. (Reproduced, with permission, from Kampmeier OF: *Evolution and Comparative Morphology of the Lymphatic System.* Thomas, 1969.)

obscure and contain many "resting" lymphocytes. Within the cortex there are a few aggregates of lymphocytes called primary follicles. The paracortical areas contain postcapillary venules lined by cuboid epithelium through which passes the blood supply to the node (Fig 7–5). In the "resting" node, the medulla is composed of connective tissue surrounding the hilus. The antigen-stimulated lymph node (Fig 7–6) shows an increased turnover of lymphocytes. Following antigenic stimulation, the paracortical area is hypertrophied and contains large lymphocytes and blastlike cells and is easily distinguished from the cortex. The cortex contains "germinal" centers composed of metabolically active and mitotic cells. The medulla of the stimulated node contains numerous plasma cells which actively secrete antibody.

Spleen

The histologic organization of the spleen (Fig 7–7) reveals areas composed of lymphocytes which are predominantly adjacent to the proximal portion of the splenic arterioles. The "resting" spleen shows masses of lymphocytes surrounding these arterioles (the white pulp). Following antigenic stimulation, blast cells may be seen throughout the splenic follicles and often near the arteriole. The red pulp and marginal area between red and white pulp contain plasma cells. The splenic periarteriolar unit may be functionally similar to the paracortical area of lymph nodes.

LYMPHOID CELLS

Morphology

The term lymphocyte refers to a cell type which can be defined by certain morphologic features. Visualized by light microscopy, lymphocytes are ovoid cells

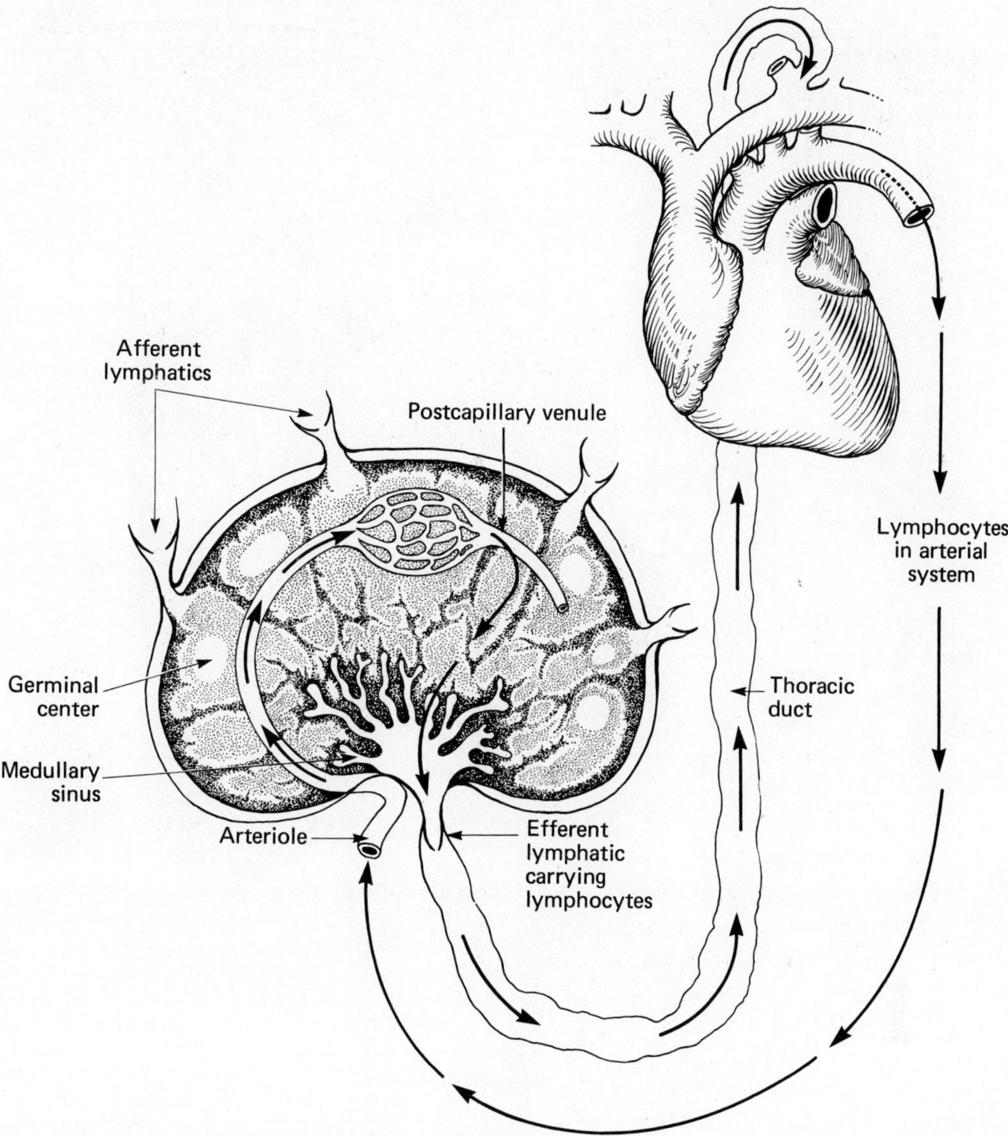

Figure 7–4. Diagrammatic representation of the circulation pathway of lymphoid cells in lymph through lymphatics, vascular system, and lymph nodes.

8–12 μm in diameter. They contain densely packed nuclear chromatin and a small rim of cytoplasm that stains pale blue with Romanovsky stains. The cytoplasm contains a number of azurophilic granules and occasional vacuoles. In the area where most cytoplasmic organelles are present (Golgi zone), the cytoplasmic rim is thickened. Phase contrast microscopy of living lymphocytes reveals a characteristic slow ameboid movement which gives a "hand mirror" contour. Histochemical studies have demonstrated nucleolar and cytoplasmic ribonucleoprotein. The cytoplasm contains some glycogen. The lymphocyte contains a number of lysosomal hydrolases. Mitochondrial enzymes are also present in the lymphocyte cytoplasm. By conventional light microscopy, the 2 main lymphocyte subpopulations (T cells and B cells) are indistinguishable.

Electron microscopic examination of the "resting" circulating lymphocyte (Fig 7–8) reveals a dense heterochromatic nucleus which contains some less electron-dense areas referred to as euchromatin. The nucleolus contains agranular, fibrillar, and granular zones. The nucleus is surrounded by the nuclear membrane complex. The cytoplasm of the resting lymphocyte contains organelle systems characteristic of eukaryotic cells (Golgi zone, mitochondria, ribosomes, lysosomes). Many of these organelle systems, however, are poorly developed. There are many free ribosomes,

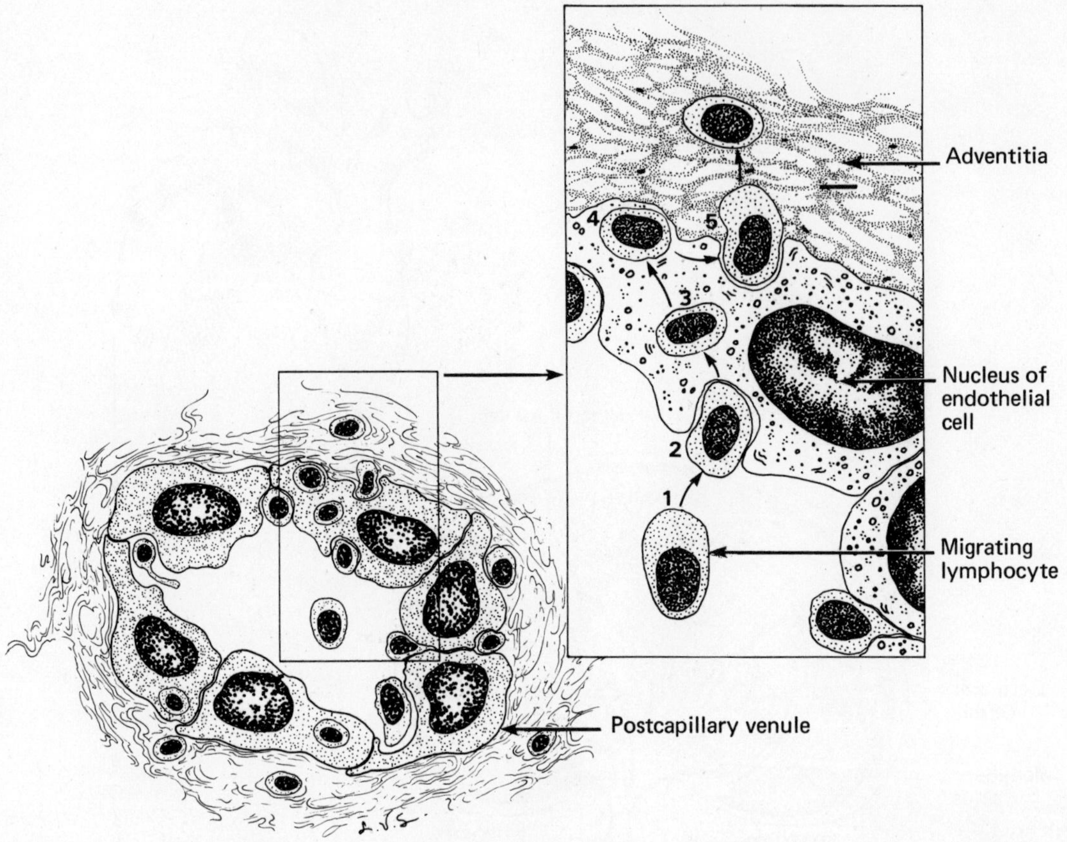

Adventitia
Nucleus of endothelial cell
Migrating lymphocyte
Postcapillary venule

Figure 7–5. Diagrammatic representation of migration of lymphocytes from a postcapillary venule in the paracortical area of a lymph node into the adventitia.

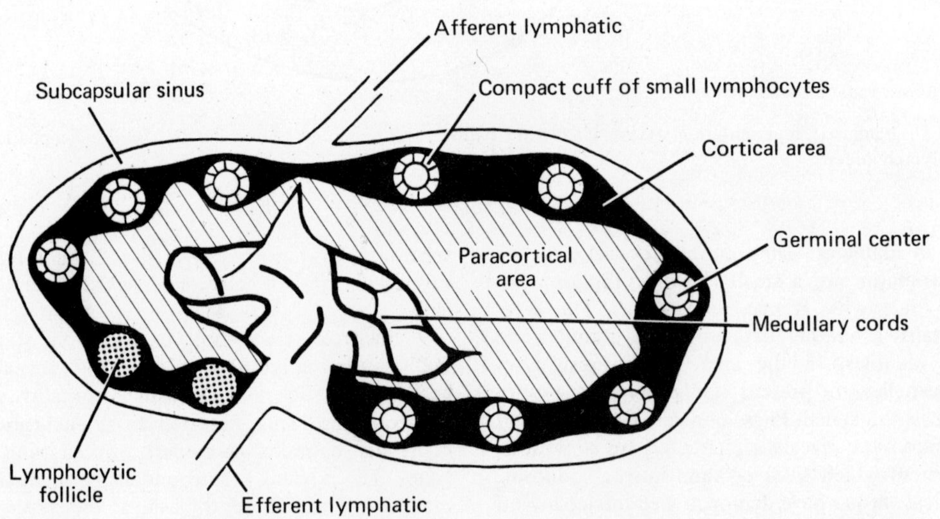

Figure 7–6. Diagram of immunologically active lymph node. (Reproduced, with permission, from Cottier H, Turk J, Sobin L: A proposal for a standardized system of reporting human lymph node morphology in relation to immunological function. Bull WHO 47:377, 1972.)

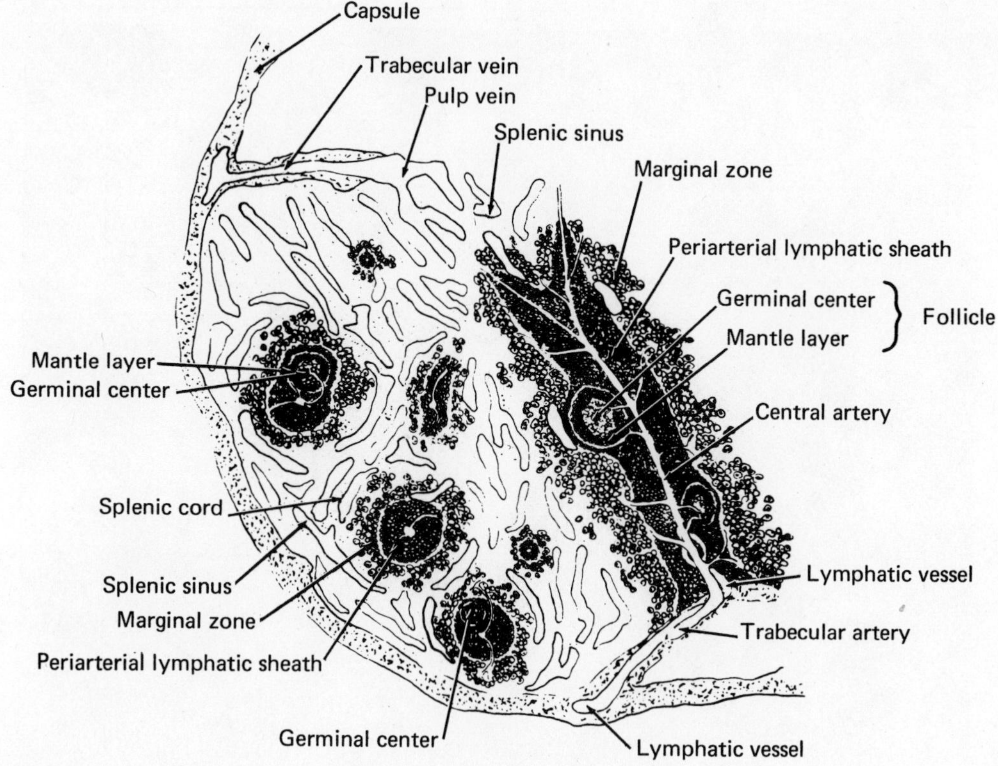

Figure 7–7. Histologic organization of the spleen. (Reproduced, with permission, from Weiss L: *The Cells and Tissues of the Immune System: Structure, Functions, Interactions.* Prentice-Hall, 1972.)

occasional ribosome clusters, and occasional strands of granular endoplasmic reticulum. A small Golgi zone is present which contains vacuoles, vesicles, and occasional lysosomes. Microtubules are often present, and there are frequent typical mitochondria. The cytoplasm usually contains several lysosomes. The plasma membrane of the lymphocyte is a typical unit membrane which may show small projections and, under some circumstances, longer pseudopodia or uropods. Thus, plasma membrane specialization may be related to cell attachment to surfaces or to cell-cell interaction.

In thin sections of cells examined by transmission electron microscopy, the lymphocyte can be distinguished from cells of the plasma cell series by the extensive development and dilatation of granular endoplasmic reticulum and a well-developed Golgi zone in plasma cells (Fig 7–9). The lymphocyte can be distinguished from mononuclear phagocytes (monocyte-macrophages) by the presence of a larger Golgi zone and more numerous lysosomes in the mononuclear phagocyte.

The blast cell, in contrast to the small lymphocyte, has a nucleus characterized by loosely packed euchromatin, a large nucleolus, and a large cytoplasmic volume containing numerous polyribosomes and an extensively developed Golgi zone (Fig 7–10). Blast cells are present in lymph nodes in vivo following antigenic stimulation, or in cultures of lymphocytes stimulated in vitro with phytomitogens. The blast cell is easily distinguished by light microscopy and measures 15–30 μm in diameter. It is possible to study the plasma membranes of these cells by the freeze fracture technic; platinum-carbon replicas reveal the presence of intramembranous particles in all membrane systems examined (Fig 7–11).

The surface topography of cells can be examined using scanning electron microscopy (Fig 7–12). The evidence with this technic, although controversial, suggests that the majority of B lymphocytes have a complex villous surface whereas the majority of T lymphocytes have a relatively smooth surface morphology. In contrast, cells of the monocyte-macrophage series have ruffled plasma membranes.

T Lymphocytes & B Lymphocytes

The general features of these cell types will be considered in order to provide a basic and more detailed understanding of their interactions in immune responses (see Chapter 8), their function (Chapter 10), and their alterations in immunologic deficiency diseases (Chapter 26) and autoimmune diseases (Chapter 27).

A. Surface Markers on B and T Lymphocytes: It has been possible to define characteristic markers for the detection of B and T lymphocytes using immunofluorescence microscopy, radioautography, or rosettes

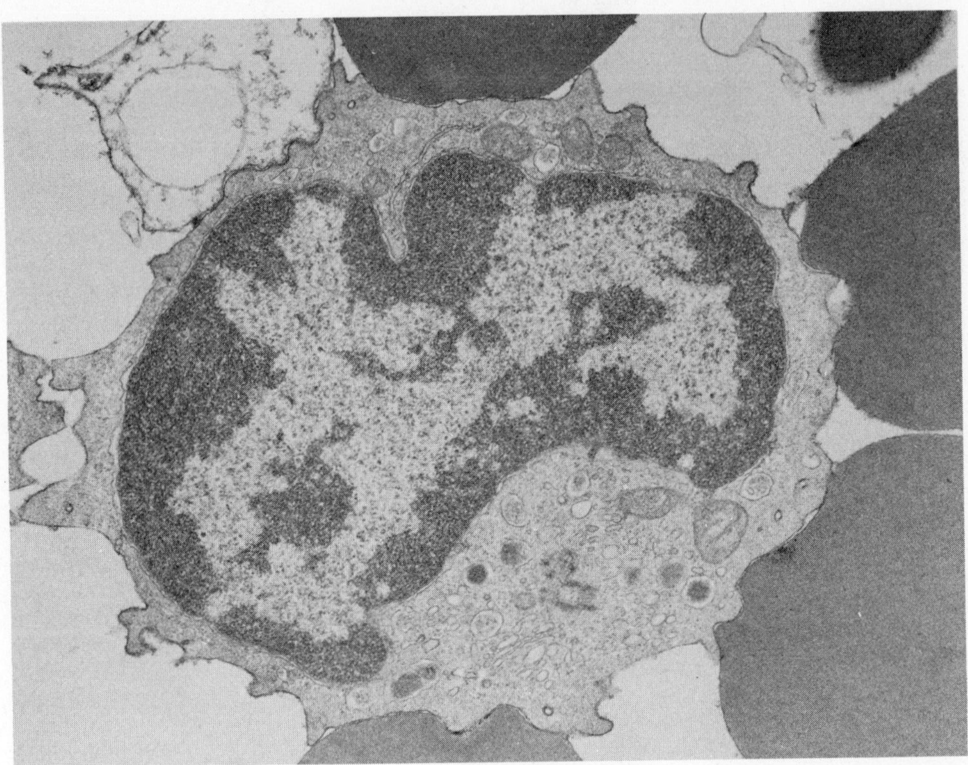

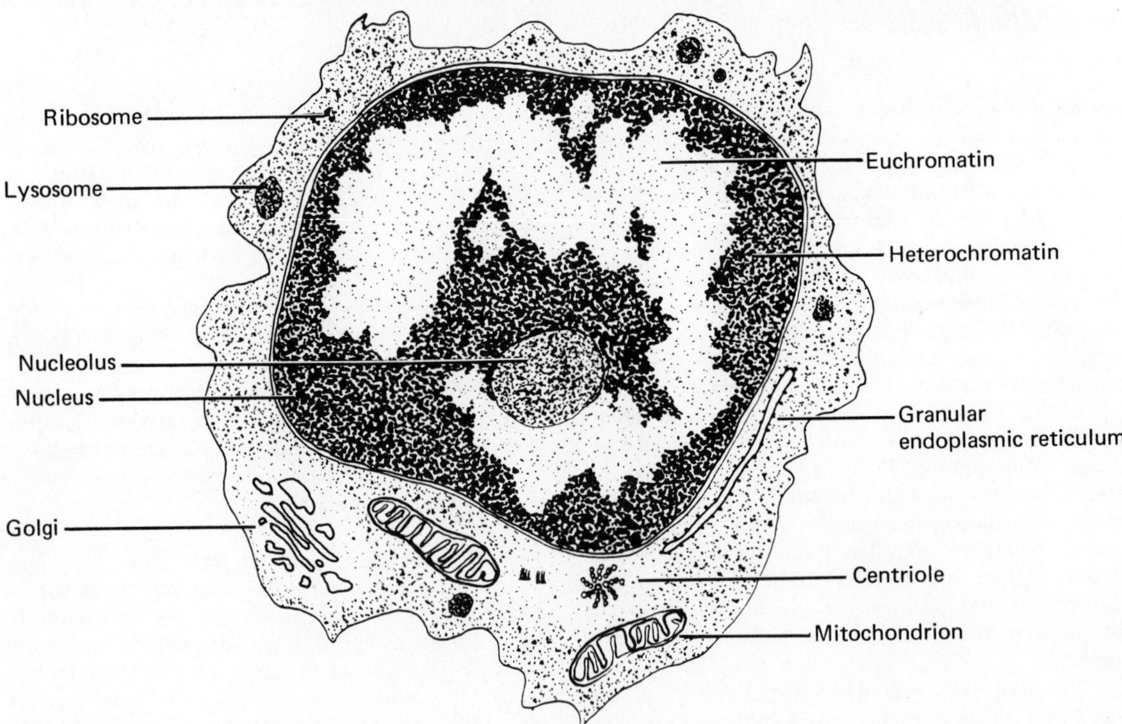

Figure 7–8. ***Top:*** Electron micrograph of normal circulating human lymphocyte. (X 33,000.) ***Bottom:*** Diagrammatic representation of the micrograph.

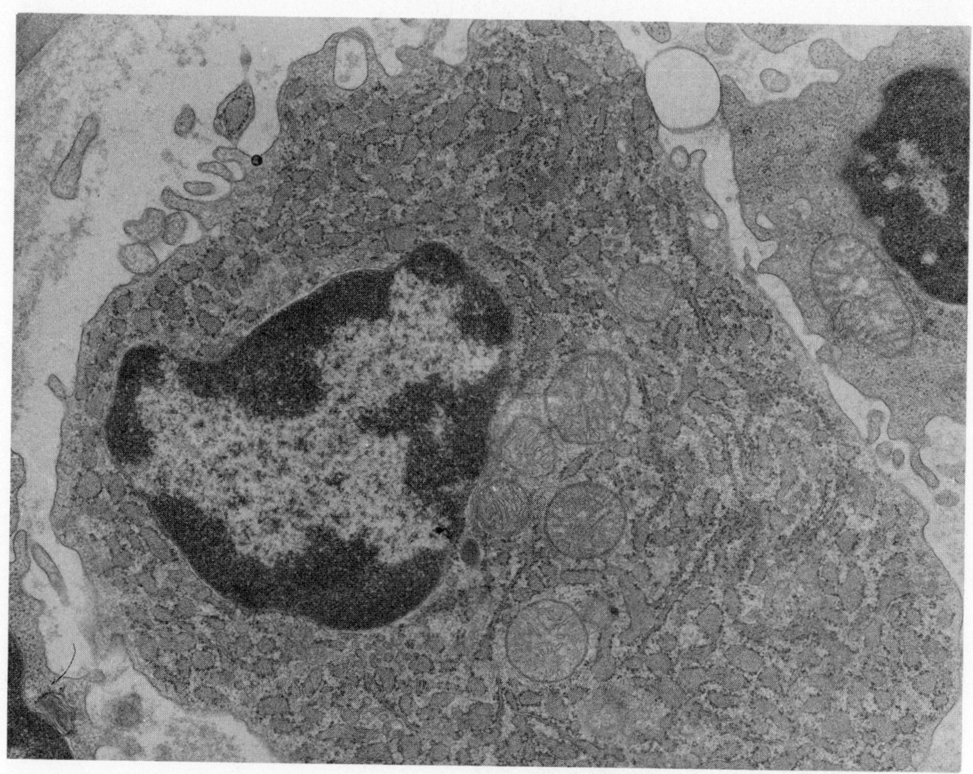

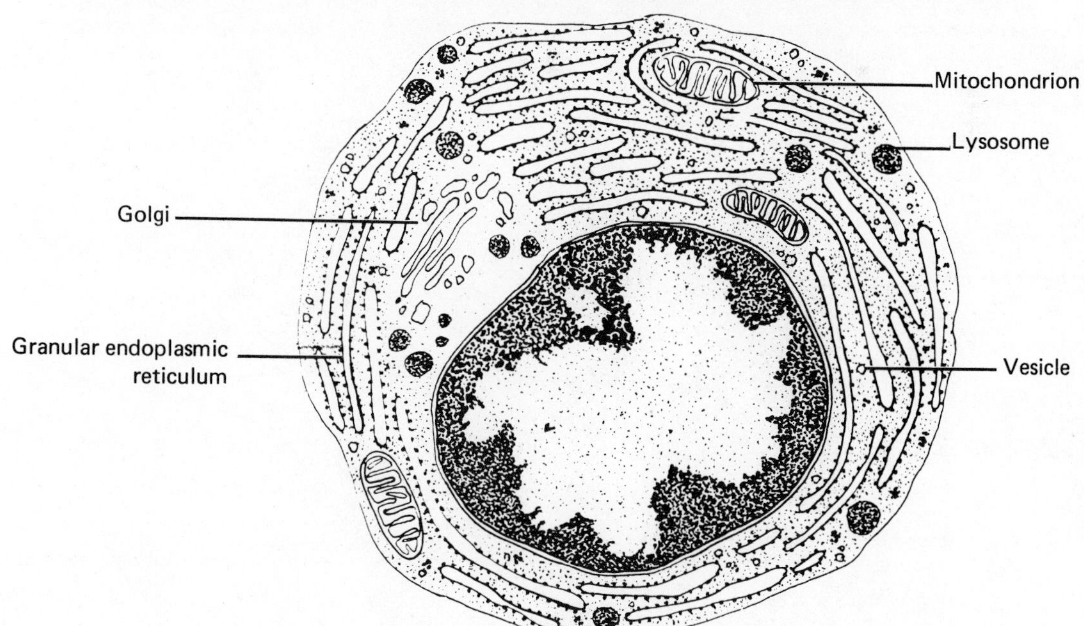

Figure 7–9. ***Top:*** Electron micrograph of human lymph node plasma cell. (X 23,000.) ***Bottom:*** Diagrammatic representation of cell shown at top.

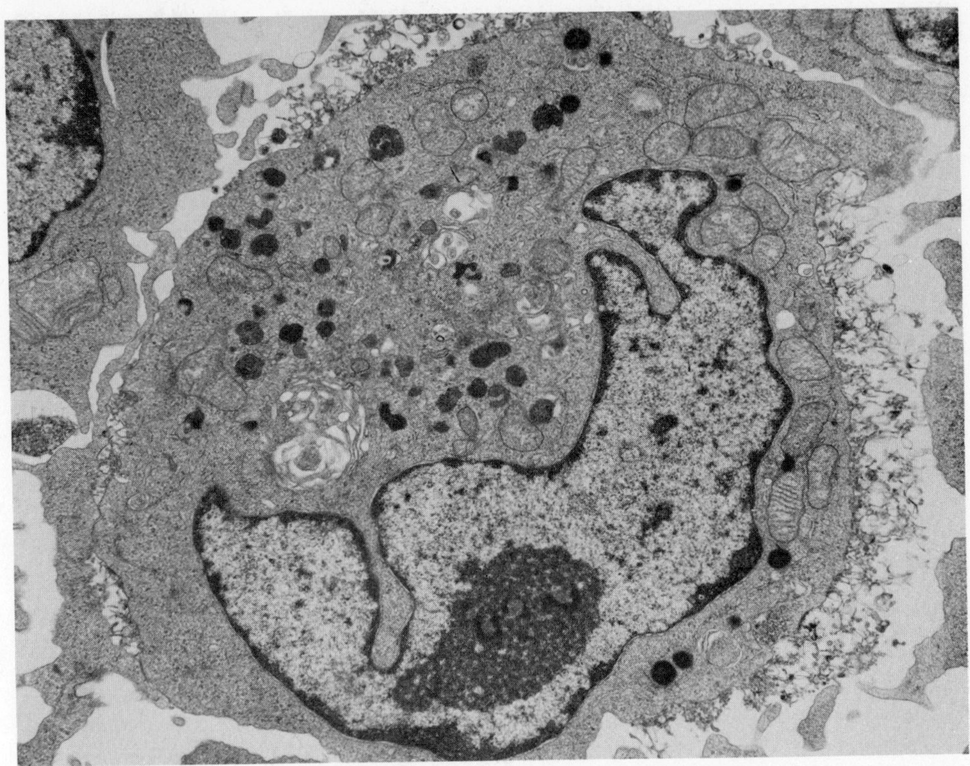

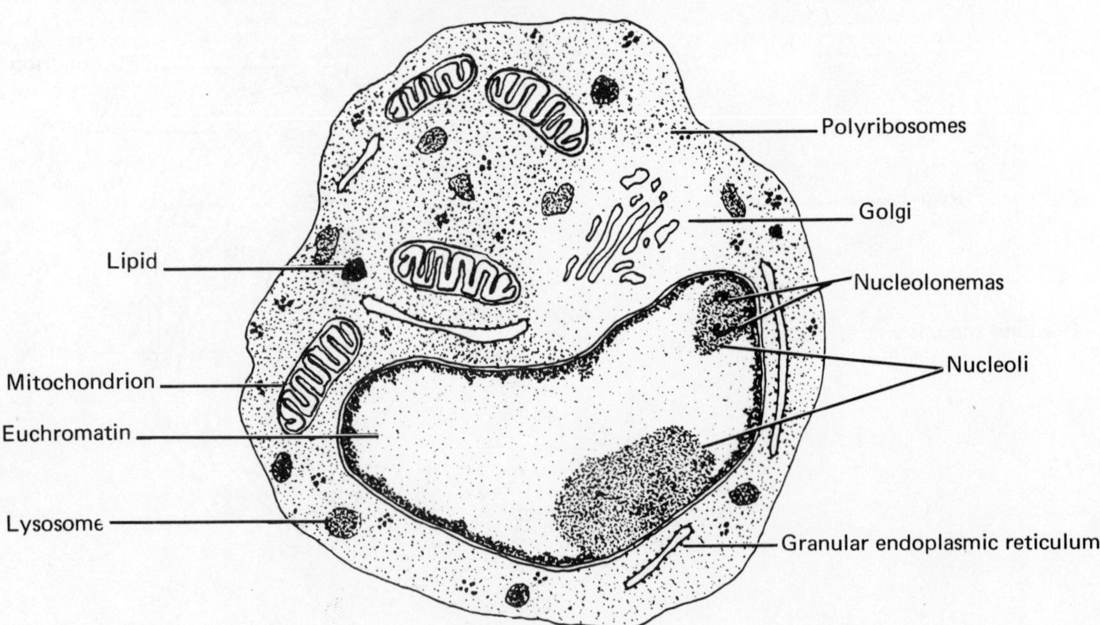

Figure 7–10. ***Top:*** Electron micrograph of a cell from a 3-day culture of human lymphocytes incubated with phytohemagglutinin (lymphoblast). (X 15,500.) ***Bottom:*** Diagrammatic representation of lymphoblast.

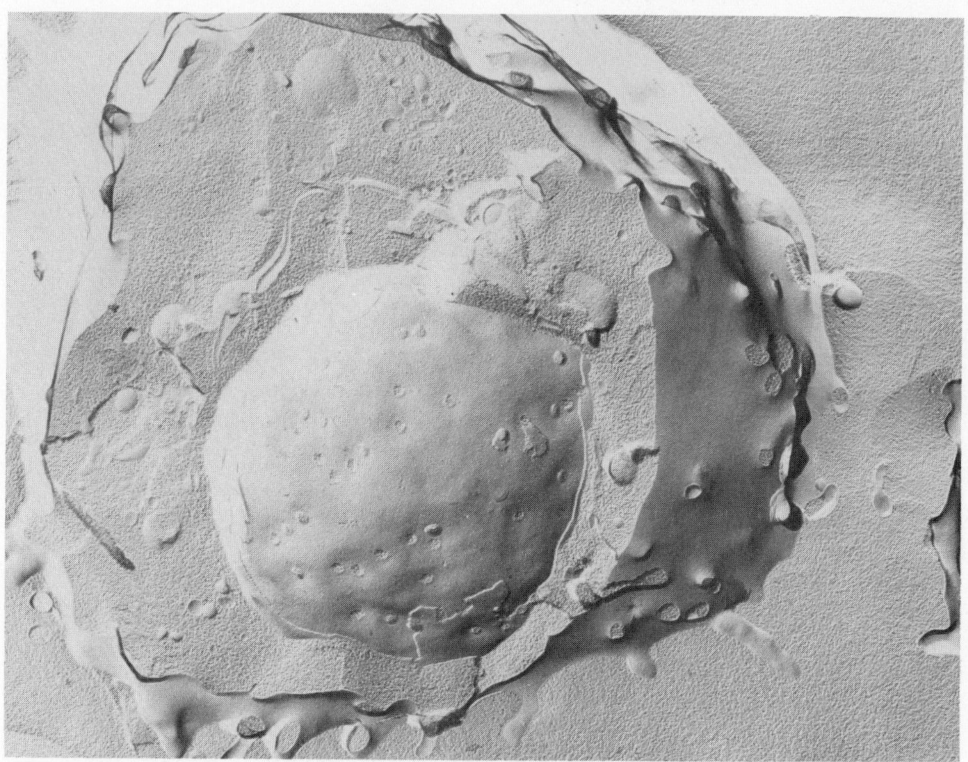

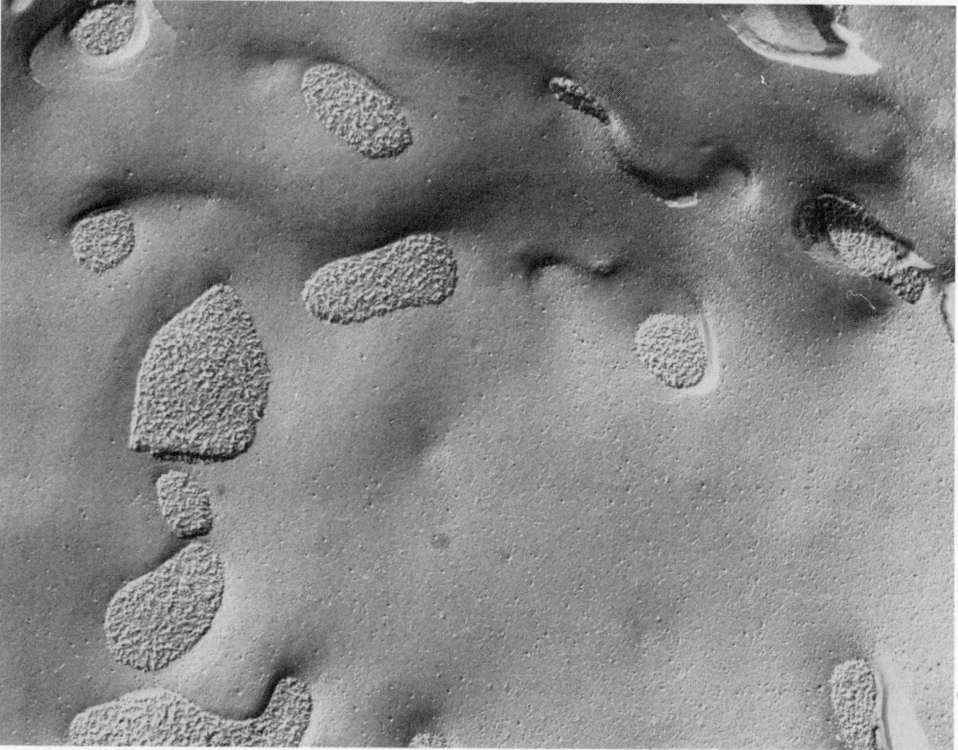

Figure 7–11. *Top:* Platinum-carbon replica of normal human lymphocyte prepared using the freeze fracture technic. The exposed faces reveal the nucleus, nuclear pores, and various cytoplasmic organelles. (X 25,000.) ***Bottom:*** Higher magnification of electron micrograph of the cell shown at top. Intramembranous particles are evident. (X 78,000.)

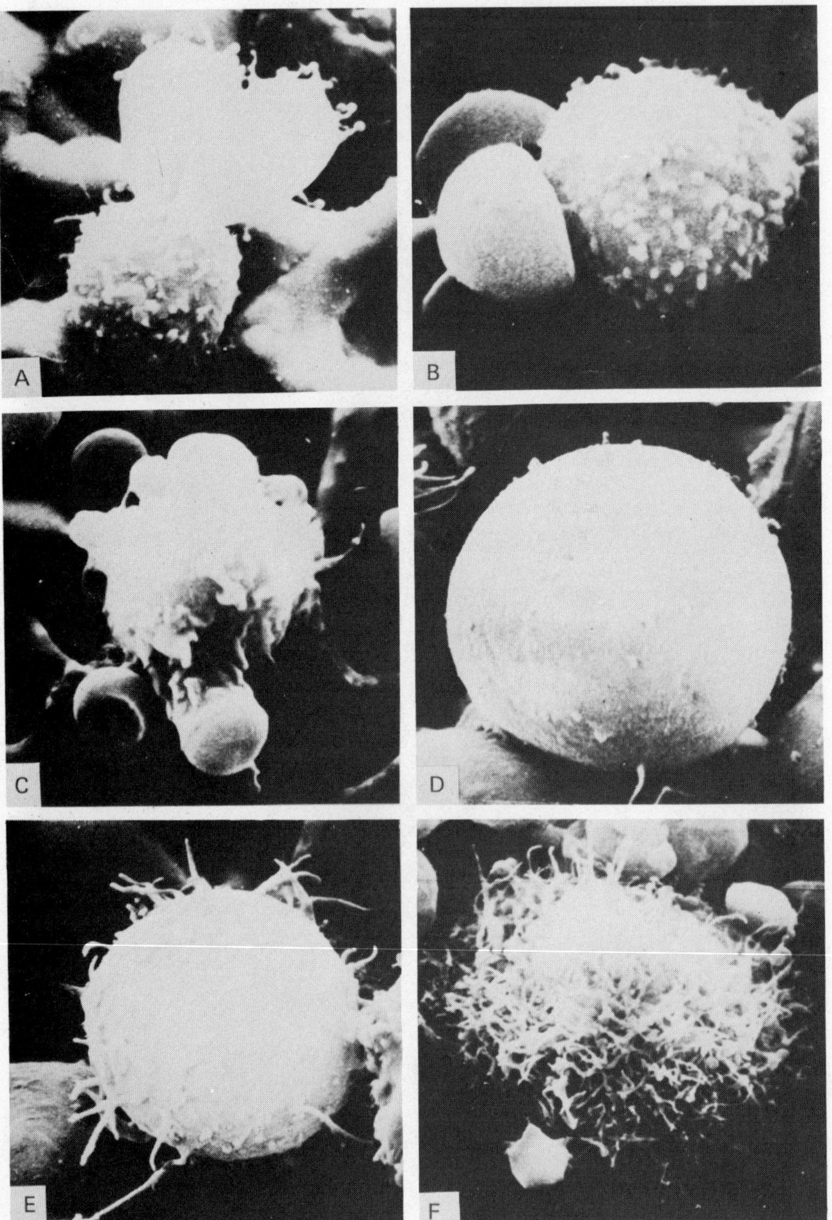

Figure 7–12. *A:* Rosetting T lymphocyte with intermediate type of surface architecture illustrating the narrow zone of attachment of the sheep red blood cell to T cell surface. (X 7000.) *B:* Rosetting B lymphocyte with intermediate type of surface architecture showing broader zone of contact between the sheep red blood cell and B lymphocyte surface. (X 9000.) *C:* Erythrocyte antibody complement-monocyte rosette. The rosetting monocyte has ridgelike ruffled membranes and few microvilli. A sheep red blood cell is in the process of being phagocytosed. (X 6000.) *D:* Smooth cultured T cell (cell line MOLT-4). Most of the cells had surfaces of this type, with very few microvilli. (X 6200.) *E:* Villous cultured T cell (MOLT-4). About 20% of cells had this type of surface, but relatively large areas of exposed surface were frequently visible between the microvilli. (X 6000.) *F:* Rosetting cultured B cell (cell line 8866). Most of these cells had villous surfaces, both before and after rosetting. (X 3100.) (Reproduced, with permission, from Polliack A, Fu SM, Douglas S: Scanning electron microscopy of human lymphocyte-sheep erythrocyte rosettes. J Exp Med 140:152, 1974.)

with erythrocytes coated with immunoproteins (see Chapter 25). Certain generalizations can be made from these studies. It should be pointed out, however, (1) that overlapping cell populations exist; (2) that the specificity of these markers requires further investigation; and (3) that the identification of subpopulations of B and T cells is more complex. There is an important distinction between a plasma membrane determinant, which is an antigen or immunoprotein actually present on the membrane and detected by labeled antibody methods; and a receptor, an immunoprotein or antigen which is recognized by the plasma membrane of the lymphocyte, or macrophage.

The B lymphocyte in man and most mammalian species is characterized by the presence of readily detectable surface immunoglobulin. Surface immunoglobulin can be demonstrated using fluoresceinated polyvalent or monovalent antisera directed against various immunoglobulin classes. In addition, most of the B lymphocytes have a receptor for antigen-antibody complexes, or aggregated immunoglobulin. This receptor appears to be specific for a site on the Fc portion of the immunoglobulin molecule and is known as the *Fc receptor*. It has been possible to demonstrate a receptor for the third component of complement on some B cells, using erythrocytes coated with antibody and complement. Lymphocytes bearing this receptor have been called complement receptor lymphocytes. The complement receptor has been shown to be distinct from the Fc receptor. B cells have also been identified using antisera prepared against lymphocytes from patients with the B cell form of chronic lymphocytic leukemia (see Chapter 28).

In mice, several characteristic antigens have been demonstrated on T lymphocytes. These include the theta (θ) antigen, antigens known as thymus-leukemia (TL) antigens, and antigens known as Ly antigens (lymphocyte alloantigens) (see Chapter 11).

In man, T lymphocytes have the property of forming rosettes with sheep erythrocytes, and this marker is used to identify human T cells (see Chapter 25). In addition, antisera prepared against brain tissue react with T cells, as do antisera prepared in rabbits injected with thymocytes. Various markers have been used to determine the distribution of B and T lymphocytes in various tissues (Table 7–1).

Table 7–1. Lymphocyte distribution in various tissues in man.

Tissue	Approximate % T Cells	Approximate % B Cells
Peripheral blood	55–75	15–30
Bone marrow	<25	>75
Lymph	>75	<25
Lymph node	75	25
Spleen	50	50
Tonsil	50	50
Thymus	>75	<25

Table 7–2. Selectivity of lymphocyte mitogens for T and B cells.

	Human T	Human B	Mouse T	Mouse B
Phytomitogens (lectins)				
Phytohemagglutinin (PHA)	+	?	+	–
Concanavalin A (ConA)	+	–	+	–
Wax bean	+	–	n.s.	
Pokeweed mitogen (PWM)	+	+	+	+
Insoluble PHA, PWM, ConA	+	+	+	+
Bacterial products				
Lipopolysaccharide (LPS)	–	–	–	+
Aggregated tuberculin	n.s.		–	+
Miscellaneous				
Anti-immunoglobulin sera	–	+	–	?
Dextran polyvinylpyrrolidone	n.s.		–	+
Trypsin	n.s.		–	+

n.s. = Not studied.

B. Functional Properties: The function of various subpopulations of lymphocytes is discussed in Chapters 8 and 10. Several reagents stimulate lymphocytes in vitro, including plant lectins, bacterial products, polymeric substances, and enzymes. Morphologic transformation occurs following stimulation with the formation of blast cells or in some instances plasma cells. Lymphocyte transformation may also be assessed biochemically by the measurement of RNA, DNA, or protein synthesis. The specificity of various mitogenic substances for human and murine T and B lymphocytes is illustrated in Table 7–2. The detailed functional aspects of B and T lymphocytes, their interaction, and their alteration in disease are discussed in subsequent chapters (Chapters 8 and 25).

MONONUCLEAR PHAGOCYTES (MONOCYTE-MACROPHAGES)

The mononuclear phagocytes include the circulating peripheral blood monocytes, promonocytes, precursor cells in the bone marrow, and tissue macrophages. The tissue macrophages are present in several tissues, organs, and serous cavities. The organization of the mononuclear phagocyte systems is shown in Table 7–3. There is a wide spectrum of morphologic features in the various types of mononuclear phagocytes, but in general these cells have a well-developed Golgi complex and many lysosomes (Fig 7–13). Their surface membranes are characterized by prominent microvilli and ruffles.

Mononuclear phagocytes originate from precursor cells in the bone marrow. They circulate in the peripheral blood as monocytes. The tissue macrophages are derived both from blood monocytes and also local proliferation of macrophages.

The major functional properties of monocyte-macrophages are adherence to glass, ingestion of parti-

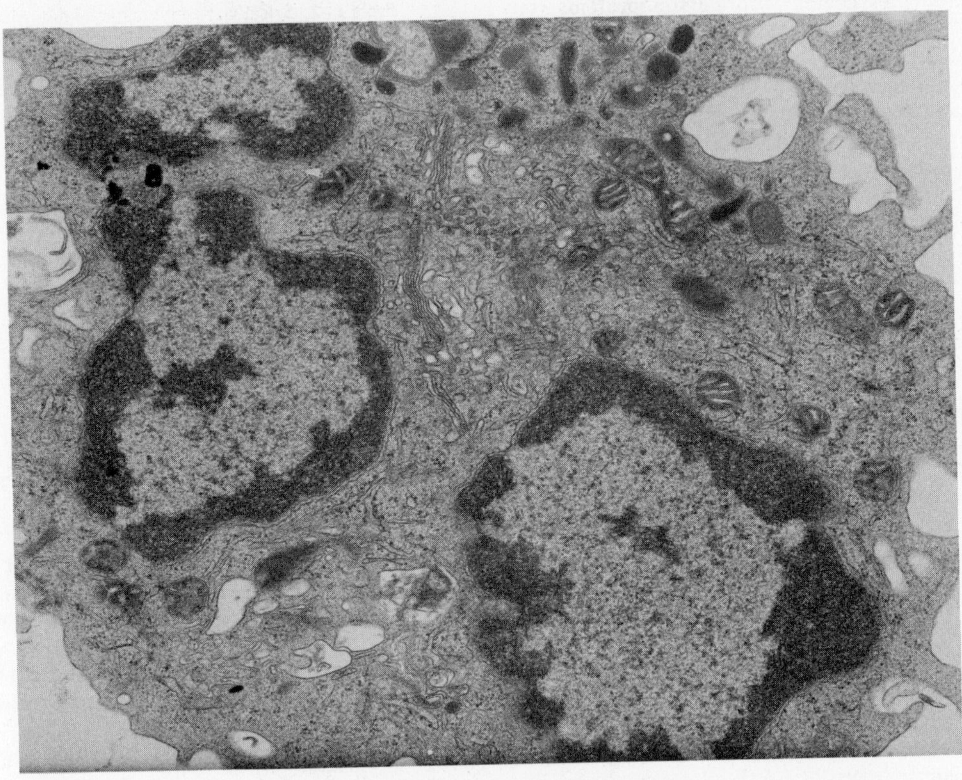

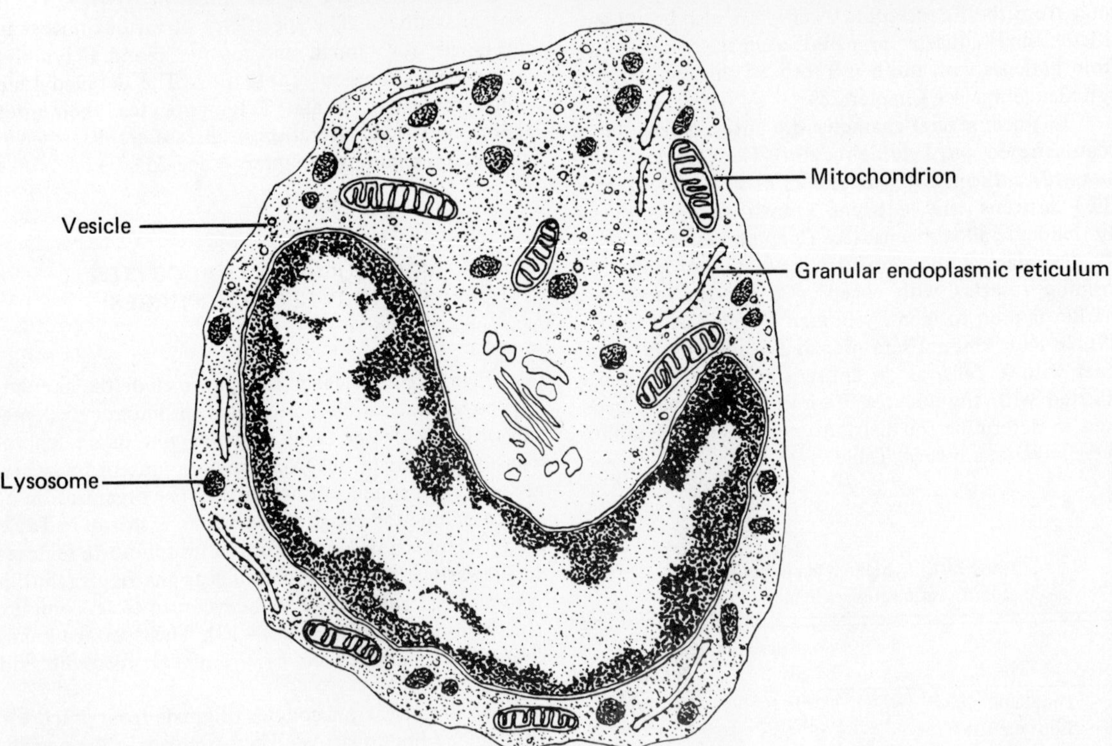

Figure 7–13. *Top:* Electron micrograph of normal human blood monocyte. (X 34,500.) ***Bottom:*** Diagrammatic representation of monocyte.

Table 7–3. The mononuclear phagocyte system.*

Cells	Localization
Precursor cells	Bone marrow
↓	
Promonocytes	Bone marrow
↓	
Monocytes	Bone marrow, blood
↓	
Macrophages	Connective tissue (histiocytes) Liver (Kupffer cells) Lung (alveolar macrophages) Spleen (free and fixed macrophages) Lymph node (free and fixed macrophages) Bone marrow (macrophages) Serous cavity (pleural and peritoneal macrophages) Bone tissue (osteoclasts?) Nervous system (microglial cells?)

*Reproduced, with permission, from Van Furth R & others: Bull WHO 46:849, 1972.

cles smaller than 0.1 μm by pinocytosis, and engulfment of particles larger than 0.1 μm by phagocytosis. During engulfment, the particle first adheres to the plasma membrane of the cell and is then ingested. The monocyte-macrophage is capable of both nonimmunologic and immunologic phagocytosis. Monocyte-macrophages have a plasma membrane receptor which recognizes 2 of the 4 subclasses of human IgG (IgG1 and IgG3); this binding site on the IgG molecule has been localized to the C_H3 domain of the immunoglobulin molecule (see Chapter 2). The monocyte-macrophage also has an independent receptor system which recognizes the activated third component of complement (C3). Cells of the monocyte-macrophage series are active in killing bacteria, fungi, and tumor cells.

Mononuclear phagocytes have the capacity to bind antigen and antigen-antibody complexes. The monocyte macrophage frequently degrades antigen which binds to its surface. There is evidence that small amounts of antigen bound to the macrophage surface are potent in the induction phase of the immune response. The possible role of the mononuclear phagocyte in interaction with B and T lymphocytes during the immune response is discussed elsewhere (see Chapter 8).

OTHER CELL TYPES INVOLVED IN IMMUNOLOGIC PHENOMENA

Neutrophils

The polymorphonuclear neutrophil, or granulocyte, comprises approximately 60% of the circulating leukocytes in man. The neutrophil is 10–12 μm in diameter in smears and 7–9 μm in diameter in sections. The nucleus has 3–5 lobes joined by narrow chromatin threads. The mature neutrophil is primarily a phagocytic cell with 2 distinct types of granules (Fig 7–14). These are known as the primary or azurophilic granules, which contain acid hydrolases, myeloperoxidase, and lysozyme; and the secondary or specific granules, which contain lactoferrin and some lysozyme. Further work is necessary to establish the subcellular localizations of alkaline phosphatase. The primary granules also contain a number of cationic proteins which have antibacterial activity. In the mature neutrophil 80–90% of the granules are specific granules and 10–20% are azurophilic granules. Neutrophils have a half-life of about 6–20 hours in the peripheral blood, and their survival in tissues under steady state conditions is about 4–5 days. Granulocytes are produced at a rate of 1.6×10^9 cells/kg/day. These cells are capable of migrating toward stimuli (chemotaxis) in the presence of a number of chemotactic factors, including bacterial products, tissue proteases, and complement components. Once localized in inflammatory areas, the neutrophil is capable of binding and ingesting appropriately opsonized materials. Following phagocytosis, there ensues a complex sequence of morphologic and biochemical events. The major biochemical concomitants of phagocytosis include an increase in phospholipid metabolism, marked stimulation of the hexose monophosphate shunt, and generation of hydrogen peroxide. A number of clinical disorders related to impaired killing of bacteria by neutrophils have been described (see Chapter 26). Tests of neutrophil function are described in Chapter 25.

Basophils & Mast Cells

The circulating basophil and tissue mast cell are characterized by oval, very electron-dense granules which contain a number of biologically active compounds, including heparin and histamine. These cells are frequently found in connective tissue in the skin surrounding small blood vessels, hair follicles, and adipose tissue. Mast cells are also present in the submucosa of the small intestine and in the sheaths of peripheral nerves and meninges. They are also present in the diffuse connective tissue throughout the reticuloendothelial system. Fig 7–15 shows an electron micrograph of a tissue mast cell. Basophils and mast cells as targets for IgE in anaphylaxis and in allergic phenomena are discussed in Chapters 19 and 20.

Eosinophils

The circulating eosinophils comprise 2–5% of normal peripheral blood leukocytes. They are round cells with a diameter of about 12 μm. Eosinophils are characterized morphologically by a type of granule that stains orange with Romanovsky stains. By electron microscopy, this granule has been shown to contain a characteristic crystalloid (Fig 7–16). Tissue eosinophils are morphologically identical to circulating eosinophils. A second granule type has recently been identified in eosinophils. The eosinophil has been demonstrated to have phagocytic potential, to ingest antigen-antibody complexes, and to have an important role in anaphylactic and allergic phenomena (see Chapters 19 and 20).

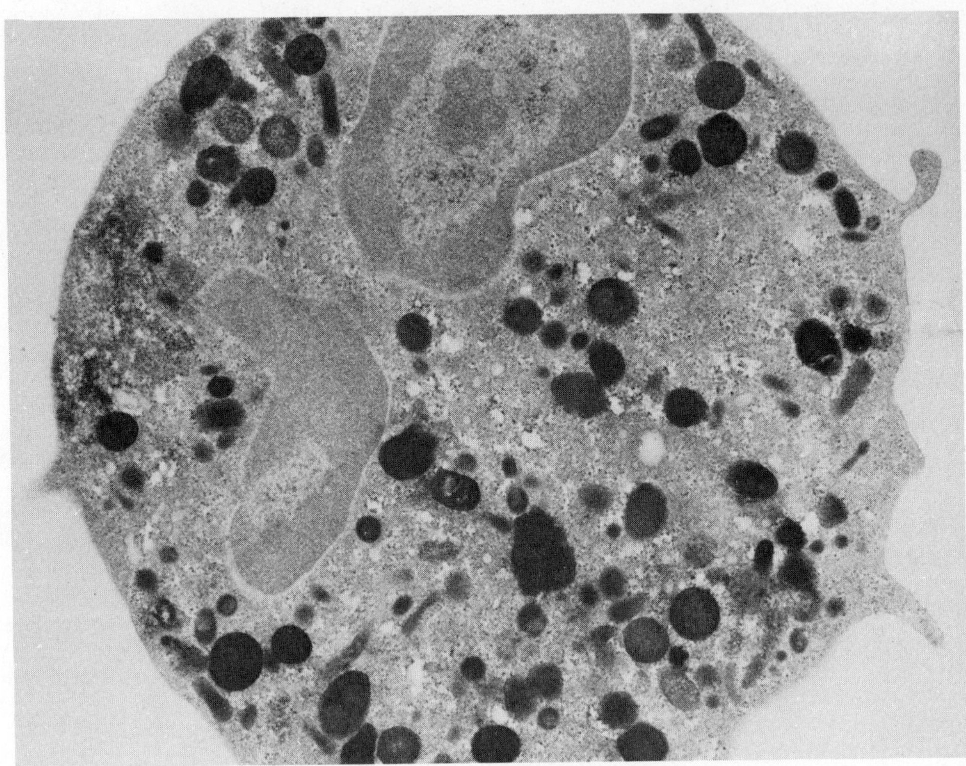

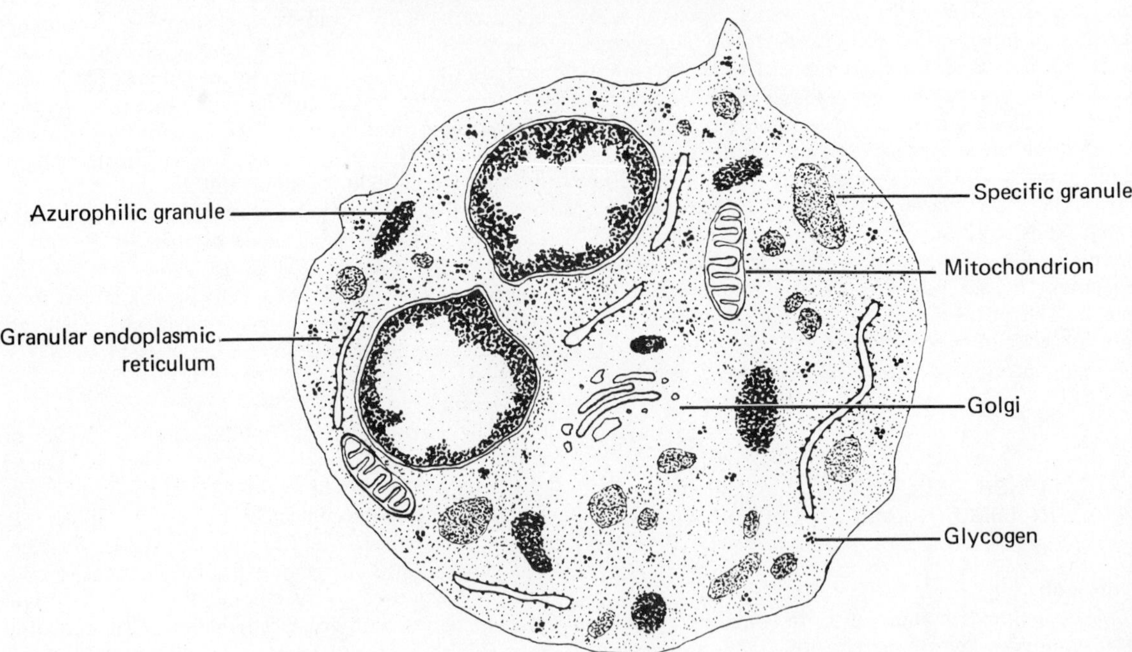

Figure 7–14. ***Top:*** Electron micrograph of human blood polymorphonuclear neutrophil. (× 30,000.) ***Bottom:*** Diagrammatic representation of polymorphonuclear neutrophil.

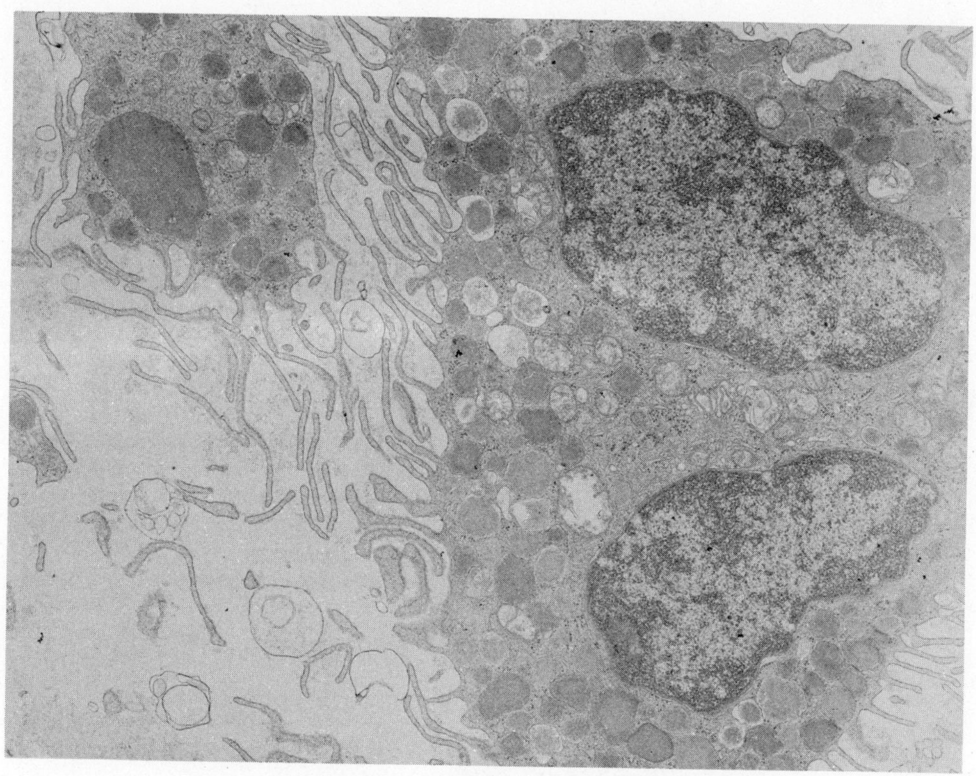

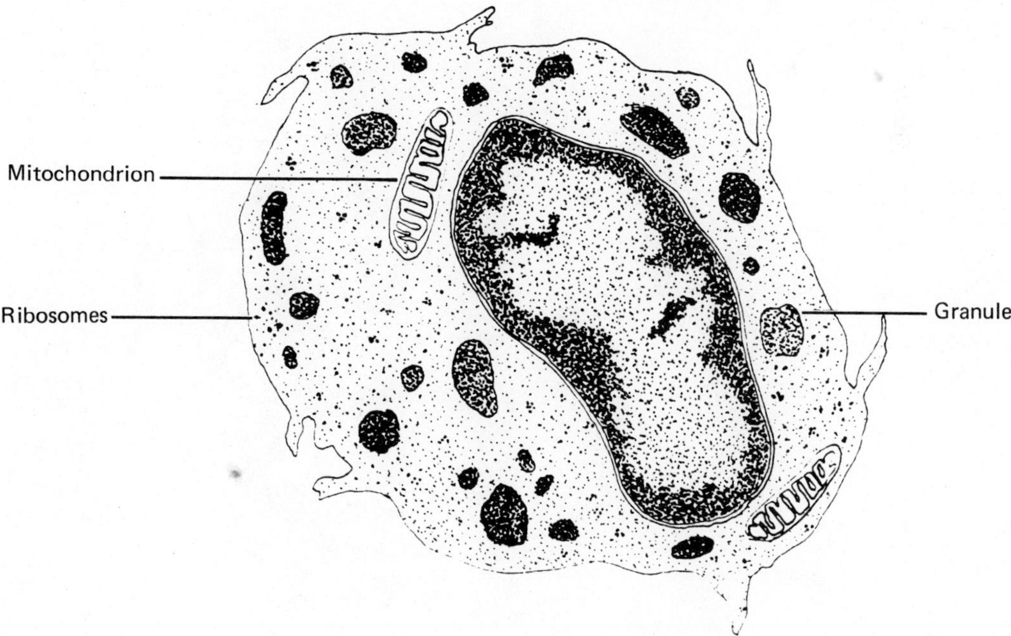

Figure 7–15. *Top:* Electron micrograph of tissue mast cell. (× 17,250.) ***Bottom:*** Diagrammatic representation of tissue mast cell.

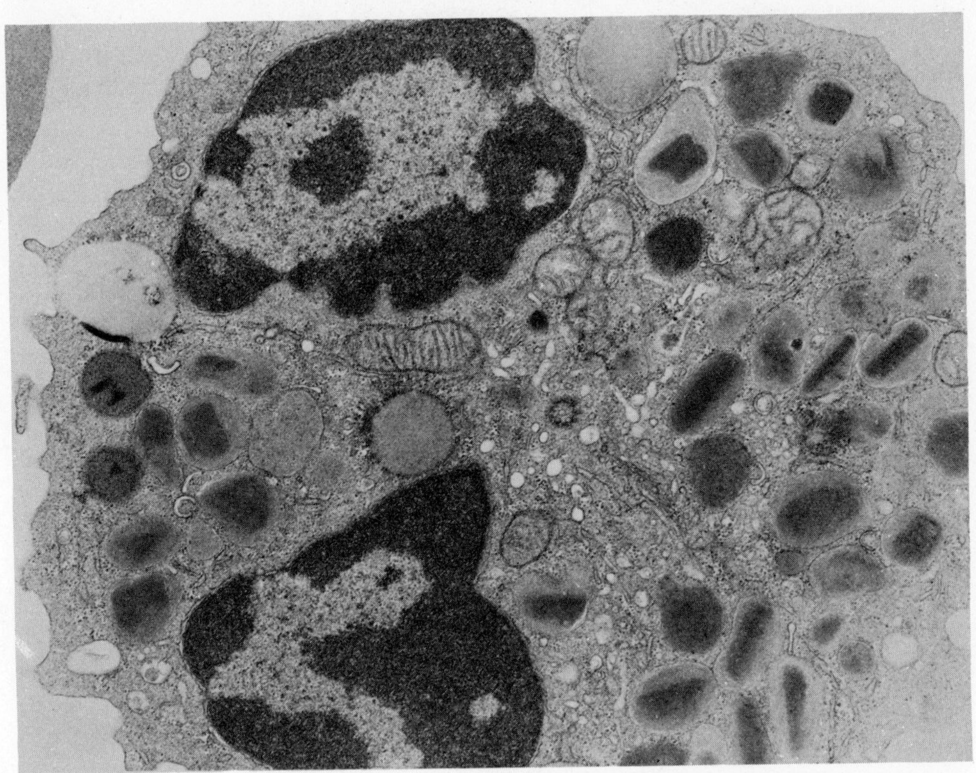

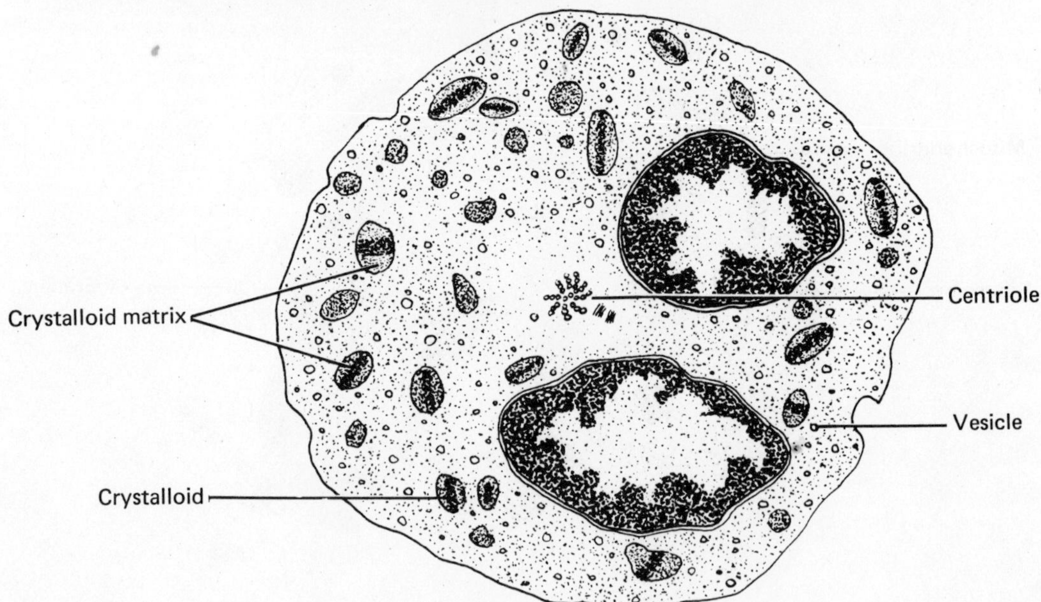

Figure 7–16. *Top:* Electron micrograph of mature human blood eosinophil. (× 12,000.) ***Bottom:*** Diagrammatic representation of eosinophil.

• • •

References

Abramoff P, LaVia MF: *Biology of the Immune Response.* McGraw-Hill, 1970.

Cottier H, Turk J, Sobin L: A proposal for a standardized system of reporting human lymph node morphology in relation to immunological function. Bull WHO 47:375, 1972.

Douglas SD: Electron microscopic and functional aspects of human lymphocyte response to mitogens. Transplant Rev 11:39, 1972.

Douglas SD: Human lymphocyte growth in vitro: Morphologic, biochemical and immunologic significance. Int Rev Exp Pathol 10:41, 1971.

Elves MW: *The Lymphocytes,* 2nd ed. Lloyd-Luke Ltd, 1972.

Gell PGH, Coombs RRA, Lachmann PJ (editors): *Clinical Aspects of Immunology,* 3rd ed. Blackwell, 1974.

Greaves MD, Owen JJT, Raff MC: *T and B Lymphocytes: Origins, Properties and Roles in Immune Responses.* Excerpta Medica, American Elsevier, 1973.

Kampmeier OF: *Evolution and Comparative Morphology of the Lymphatic System.* Thomas, 1969.

Möller G (editor): T and B lymphocytes in humans. Transplant Rev, vol 16, 1975. [Entire issue.]

Nossal GJV, Ada GL (editors): *Antigens, Lymphoid Cells, and the Immune Response.* Academic Press, 1971.

Pearsall N, Weiser R: *The Macrophage.* Lea & Febiger, 1970.

Roitt I: *Essential Immunology,* 2nd ed. Blackwell, 1974.

Taub RN, Douglas SD: Physiologic and immunologic role of lymphocytes. Pages 363–408 in: *Physiologic Pharmacology.* Vol 5. Root WS, Berlin NI (editors). Academic Press, 1974.

Weiss L: *The Cells and Tissues of the Immune System: Structure, Functions, Interactions.* Prentice-Hall, 1972.

Yoffey JM, Courtice FC: *Lymphatics, Lymph and the Lymphomyeloid Complex.* Academic Press, 1970.

8 . . .
Cell Cooperation in Immune Responses

John J. Marchalonis, PhD

T & B CELL COOPERATION

The requirement for cooperation between thymus-derived lymphocytes (T cells) and bone marrow-derived lymphocytes (B cells) was established by studies showing that neither cell population alone could mount an immune response to antigens such as erythrocytes whereas admixture of the cell populations resulted in the production of high levels of antibody. The B cells are the precursors of antibody-forming cells. The T cells do not synthesize readily detectable amounts of immunoglobulin but are needed as "helper" cells which stimulate the B cells to differentiate into producers of antibody. In addition to T and B cells, accessory cells such as macrophages are necessary for an immune response to occur. The area of cell interactions in immune responses is a complex one, and a variety of mechanisms have been proposed. At present it is probably reasonable to regard collaborative immune responses as a series of interrelated processes in which antigen-specific recognition is performed by immunoglobulins and in which nonspecific mediators of various sorts function as modifiers to regulate the intensity and quality of the response.

THYMUS DEPENDENCE OF ANTIGENS & IMMUNOGLOBULINS

Antigens vary in their degree of dependence on T cell interaction for the production of specific antibodies. Some antigens have been designated as *thymus-independent* because athymic mice or B cell suspensions in tissue culture will mount strong antibody responses. Examples of thymus-independent antigens are *Escherichia coli* lipopolysaccharide, polymerized flagellin from *Salmonella adelaide,* pneumococcal polysaccharide S–III, polyvinylpyrrolidone, dextrans, and levans. Such antigens are large polymers generally consisting of identical repeating units. They will interact directly with B cells. At least some of them are B cell mitogens which bind to most, if not all, B cells, and initiate DNA synthesis and immunoglobulin secretion. Antigens such as erythrocytes, serum proteins, and hapten-carrier complexes are strongly *thymus-dependent.* In the latter case it is generally considered that helper T cells recognize the carrier whereas B cells react to the hapten (see Chapter 3).

Production of certain classes of immunoglobulins is also thought to exhibit various degrees of thymus dependence. IgM antibodies are influenced least by the absence of a thymus, and this class of immunoglobulin is usually produced in response to thymus-independent antigens. The synthesis of IgE is strongly dependent upon T cell interaction, and the production of IgG antibodies also requires the mediation of T cells. These distinctions, like the one above, are not absolute. In certain circumstances IgM responses are dependent on T and B cell collaboration, and athymic mice have been observed to synthesize IgG in a primary response.

SPECIFIC RECOGNITION OF ANTIGEN BY T & B CELLS

Both T and B cells bind erythrocyte, protein, and hapten antigens, as shown in studies involving immunocytoadherence, radioautography using radioiodinated antigens, and inhibition of specific lymphocyte functions by radioiodinated antigens ("hot antigen suicide"). The number of binding cells observed for common antigens is generally consistent with the expectations implied in Burnet's clonal selection theory, ie, the frequency of B or T cells from unimmunized mice which bound ^{125}I-labeled serum albumin, flagellin, or hemocyanin ranged from approximately one binding cell per 10^4 lymphocytes to one binding cell per 10^3 lymphocytes. The binding was specific because combination of the cells with labeled antigen was inhibitable by competition with unlabeled homologous antigen. The frequency of specific binding of both T and B lymphocytes to some antigens was higher than this value, possibly because of extensive cross-reactions. For example, approximately 1% of T or B cells was found to bind to the dinitrophenyl hapten. Although

John J. Marchalonis is Head of the Molecular Immunology Laboratory, The Walter and Eliza Hall Institute of Medical Research, Parkville, Victoria 3052, Australia.

there was some initial controversy regarding the existence of antigen-binding T cells, it has now been conclusively shown that lymphocytes bearing the θ (or Thy-1) alloantigen bind antigen. Moreover, antigen receptors on such T cells may migrate to one pole of the cell ("cap"), disappear, and subsequently reappear. These observations indicate that T cells, like B cells, synthesize their surface recognition molecules. The possibility exists that T cells express fewer antigen receptors per cell than do B cells. However, the conclusion reached in some reported studies is that the number of antigen molecules bound per T cell is not markedly different from that bound per B cell.

The nature of the lymphocyte receptor for antigen has provided challenges to immunologists since Ehrlich proposed in 1896 that the "side chains" which allowed cells to recognize antigen were identical to the antibodies that subsequently appeared in the circulation. The antigen-binding technics cited above allowed testing of this hypothesis by using antisera to immunoglobulins to inhibit specific combination of antigen with lymphocytes. Binding of antigen to murine B cells was effectively inhibited by antisera to L chains and μ chains, whereas antisera to γ chains were sometimes effective. Binding of antigen to T cells was inhibited effectively by antisera to L chains. The only antisera to H chains which successfully blocked T cell binding were specific for μ chain, although not all antisera were equally potent. These data are in accord with Ehrlich's receptor hypothesis but do not formally establish it, because the observed blocking might be due to steric hindrance or to some general alteration in the properties of the lymphocyte membrane. Antisera to histocompatibility antigens (see Chapter 15) will inhibit binding by T and B cells, and antiserum to Thy-1 (θ) antigen occasionally blocks antigen binding by T cells The inhibition data thus establish that both T and B cells express immunoglobulin L chain and μ chain determinants on their surfaces. Studies involving direct binding to lymphocytes of labeled antisera specific for immunoglobulins clearly demonstrate the presence of these determinants on B cells. Although a number of workers now report the presence of surface immunoglobulin κ chains and occasionally μ chains on T cells by direct binding assays, this is usually much more difficult to demonstrate than surface immunoglobulin on B cells.

Confirmation that lymphocyte surface immunoglobulin acts as a receptor for antigen required the isolation of surface immunoglobulin and assessment of its capacity to bind antigen. A new radioiodination technic was devised with a reaction catalyzed by the enzyme lactoperoxidase and H_2O_2 such that only accessible surface proteins were labeled. This technic has proved useful in determining the general physicochemical properties and antigen-binding capacities of surface immunoglobulins of normal and neoplastic B and T cells. The major surface immunoglobulin of B cells contains L chains and μ chains and has a molecular weight of approximately 200,000. Recent work suggests that a putative IgD-like molecule is also present on at least some murine B cells. This molecule is similar in size to the IgM molecule but contains an H chain distinct from μ chain. In addition, IgG molecules have occasionally been isolated from B cell surfaces, although their level is low relative to that of 7S IgM. Normal and activated–eg, "helper"–T cell populations possess a surface immunoglobulin (MW 200,000) which contains L chains, and H chains similar to μ chains. A number of functional distinctions suggest, however, that the surface IgM-like immunoglobulin of T cells is not identical to the B cell surface molecule. These molecules might represent IgM subclasses. It has been difficult to establish conclusively the existence of T cell surface immunoglobulin because some workers have stated that they were unable to isolate any immunoglobulin from T cells. Moreover, the possibility had to be excluded that B cells or plasma cells present in the T cell populations were the actual source of detected immunoglobulin. The first problem was essentially a technical one, and a number of groups have isolated immunoglobulin from T cells using radioiodination or other methods. Various solutions have been offered to explain the problem of contaminating immunoglobulin from B cells. Among the most straightforward of these are the following: (1) T cells have been shown to resynthesize receptor immunoglobulin; (2) T cells incorporate labeled amino acids into immunoglobulin at too high a level to be explained by contamination; and (3) monoclonal T lymphoma cells grown in continuous cell culture express and synthesize membrane immunoglobulin similar to that observed on normal and activated T cells. Surface immunoglobulins have been isolated from (1) human peripheral blood lymphocytes, thymus cells, and chronic lymphocytic leukemia cells (monoclonal B cells; see Chapter 28); (2) murine B cells and various murine T cell populations; (3) rat thymus and spleen lymphocytes; and (4) chicken thymus, spleen, and bursa lymphocytes.

The capacity of a subpopulation of surface immunoglobulin from murine B cells to bind antigen was shown by the isolation of complexes of dinitrophenylated mouse hemoglobin and surface immunoglobulin obtained from splenic lymphocytes of congenitally athymic nu/nu mice. The latter are homozygous for the nu ("nude") gene and lack both a detectable thymus gland and body hair. Detection of these complexes was feasible because of the high percentage of normal B cells which bind dinitrophenylated proteins. Cytophilic antibodies apparently did not play an appreciable role in the binding of dinitrophenylated hemoglobin by B cells because the percentage of these cells was not increased by incubation with antisera to dinitrophenyl. Complexes of dinitrophenylated hemoglobin and cell surface immunoglobulin were detected by specific immunologic precipitation using systems specific for dinitrophenyl and for mouse immunoglobulin. Such complexes were released from the cell surface by incubation at 37 C and by limited proteolysis with trypsin. The population of radioiodinated cell surface immunoglobulin was found to mimic the heterogeneous population of antibodies normally found in serum. Affinity chromatography removed cell surface immunoglobulin specifically reactive to the dinitrophenyl group but did not impair the capacity of the surface immunoglobulin to combine with other antigens.

Surface immunoglobulin isolated from specifically activated murine helper T cells was also shown to combine with antigen. T cells which function as helper cells in specific T/B collaboration were prepared by reconstituting heavily irradiated mice with syngeneic thymus lymphocytes plus antigen. Significant fractions of radioiodinated, released 7S IgM-like immunoglobulin of these activated helper T cells exhibited binding specificity toward the antigen used in the respective activation procedure, eg, erythrocytes, hemocyanin, or chicken immunoglobulin. Helper T cells activated to sheep erythrocytes, for example, when mixed in culture with spleen cells of congenitally athymic nu/nu mice (source of B cells and macrophages), supported hemolytic plaque-forming responses more than 10 times larger than those supported by normal thymus cells or T cells activated to a different antigen. The helper response and the ability to detect radioiodinated surface immunoglobulin were eliminated by antisera directed against the Thy-1 (θ) antigen, thereby indicating the T cell nature of the helper cells and the T cell origin of the specific immunoglobulin. Further support for this conclusion derived from the finding that the helper cell population was virtually lacking in plaque-forming B cells for sheep erythrocytes. Helper function in all cases was obvious only when T cells possessing immunoglobulin of the appropriate specificity were present. Helper T cells therefore possess surface IgM-like immunoglobulin (termed IgT by some workers) which apparently performs functions in the recognition of antigen and plays a collaborative role in specific cooperation between T and B cells (see below).

TRANSFORMATION OF T & B CELLS

Although lymphocyte populations are clonally restricted with respect to both antigen recognition and their subsequent responses, a number of polyclonal mitogens exist which can activate large subpopulations of lymphocytes. This phenomenon is worth considering here because certain nonspecific T cell replacing factors (to be considered below) might qualify as B cell mitogens. The lectin of the jack bean, concanavalin A, binds to glycoproteins containing α-mannosyl or α-glucosyl moieties and stimulates all murine T cells to synthesize DNA, divide, and release substances which can nonspecifically replace T cells in some immune responses. This molecule allows a distinction between T and B cells of the mouse, because although both cell types bind more than 10^6 concanavalin A molecules per cell, only T cells are stimulated when the lectin is presented in soluble form. Lipopolysaccharide from gram-negative bacteria such as *E coli,* on the other hand, stimulates murine B cells but not T cells. Many polyanions such as dextran sulfate and polyadenylic acid are mitogens for murine B lymphocytes. T cells might be refractory to stimulation with polyanions because they contain a relatively large number of negatively charged groups such as sialic acid on their surface. B cells activated by lipopolysaccharide synthesize DNA and differentiate into cells secreting IgM. An interesting dose effect applies in mitogenesis by lipopolysaccharide; low doses of the mitogen generate specific antibody formation, but high doses activate the majority of the cells.

Other mitogens such as phytohemagglutinin (PHA) from the red kidney bean *(Phaseolus vulgaris)* stimulate only subpopulations of T or B cells. In the mouse, PHA activates a subpopulation of T cells and does not stimulate B cells. The situation with PHA is not as clear-cut in man, however, because both T and probably B cells are stimulated. The activation of B cells might be indirect in that T cells of a mixed population could be stimulated by the mitogen and subsequently synthesize a factor which initiates the division of B cells. The mitogen from the pokeweed *(Phytolacca americana)* also stimulates B cells and a T cell subset of both man and mouse. This mitogen was discovered in an interesting fashion because it was observed that children who had eaten pokeweed berries possessed peripheral blood cells resembling plasma cells.

Antisera of various specificities have also been reported to initiate DNA synthesis in lymphocytes. The majority of rabbit peripheral blood lymphocytes, a mixture of T and B cells, are activated by antisera to immunoglobulin. Human peripheral blood lymphocytes can be activated by antisera to immunoglobulins. However, murine B cells are not activated by antisera to immunoglobulin, although the cells bind such reagents extremely well. This discrepancy emphasizes a major fact of lymphocyte activation, namely, binding of ligand to its surface receptor is not sufficient to initiate differentiation. In the case of antigen-directed transformation, a "second signal" of a nonspecific nature is probably necessary to allow a cell which has bound antigen to differentiate into an activated T cell or an antibody-secreting B cell. Cyclic nucleotides such as 3′,5′-cyclic guanosine monophosphate (cGMP) and ligands which result in the production of this nucleotide are thought to mediate lymphocyte division. In contrast, the nucleotide 3′,5′-cyclic adenosine monophosphate (cAMP) inhibits division and might induce a refractory or "tolerant" state in lymphocytes. The exact biochemical mechanisms involved in lymphocyte activation by antigens and mitogens remain problematic, but certain of the collaborative interactions among lymphocytes and accessory cells might involve similar mechanisms.

COOPERATION BETWEEN T & B CELLS

Fig 8–1 illustrates schematically the origins of T and B cells, some of their differentiation pathways, and their responses to thymus-dependent and thymus-independent antigens. The cells termed T_2 here represent a T cell subset which responds to certain alloantigens in GVH or mixed leukocyte reactions (see Chapter 15). The T_1 subset responds to foreign antigens or strong histocompatibility antigens. In response to thymus-dependent antigens, the T_1 cells can differentiate into either helper T cells or suppressor T cells. Antigen-specific suppressor T cells may mediate antigenic competition and tolerance by releasing suppressive substances. Positive cooperation between helper T cells and B cells expressing IgM results in a switch to B cells expressing IgG (see Chapter 2). The latter cells may be capable of self-replication. Similarly, production of IgE and probably IgA requires some sort of T cell "help." Helper function can be either antigen-specific or nonspecific in nature. In addition to the requirement for T and B cells in immune cooperation, accessory cells such as macrophages are necessary for activation of B cells. Macrophages are adherent phagocytic cells which are not specific for antigen. Interaction with antigen on macrophages is probably needed also for the stimulation of helper T cells. Models for cooperation are quite complex, involving at least 3 cell types, antigen, and specific and nonspecific factors (Fig 8–2).

A large body of evidence supports the contention that both T cells and B cells possess specific receptors for antigen and cooperate in the elaboration of an antibody-forming response to thymus-dependent antigens. This collaboration could occur either (1) by direct contact and interaction of T and B cells in which the T cell focuses and presents antigen to B cells of the appropriate specificity; or (2) by a mechanism in which the T cells release a product which can stimulate B cells. A strong genetic requirement for compatibility in histocompatibility antigens has been reported for cooperative interactions involving direct contact of activated T cells and specific B cells. In case (2), the T cell factor can be specific for antigen or nonspecific. There is evidence that both antigen-specific and nonspecific factors are involved in the production of antibodies to thymus-dependent antigens. These factors have been

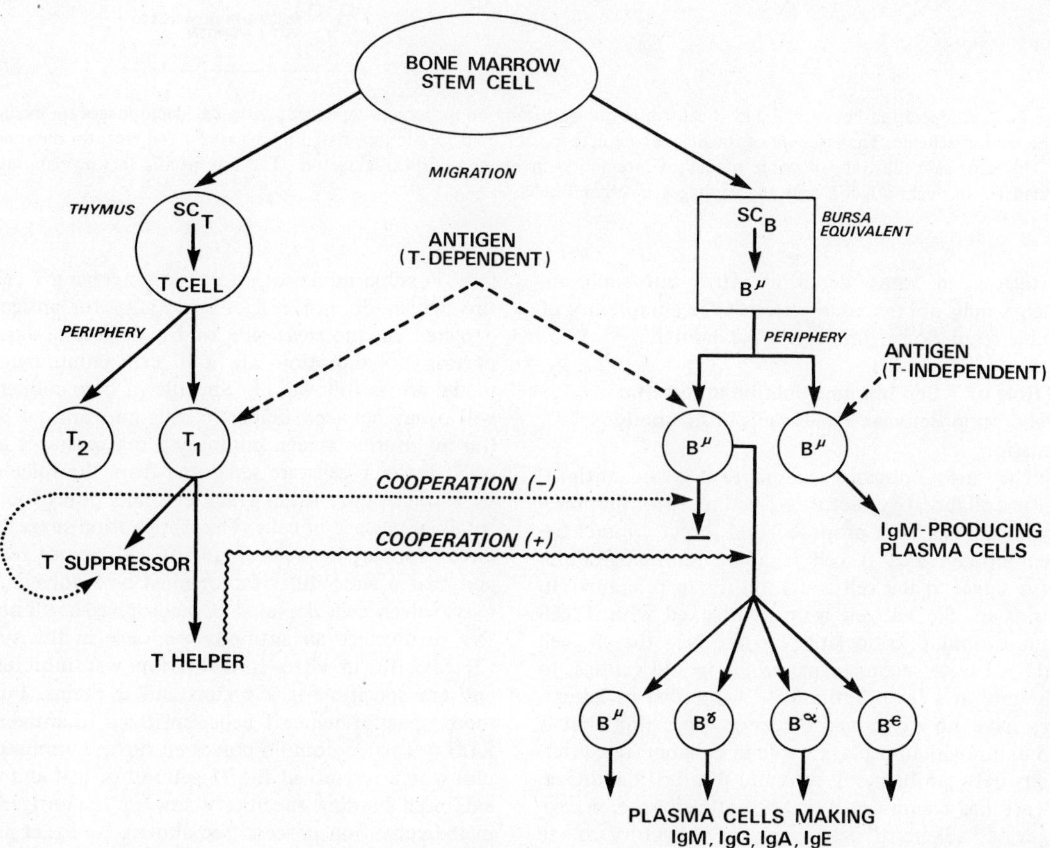

Figure 8–1. Simplified scheme for the origin of T and B cells and their functional interactions. In this text, T_1 designates the T cell subset which responds specifically to usual foreign antigens and mediates specific helper function and delayed hypersensitivity. T_2 designates a separate T cell subset which responds to certain alloantigens and mediates GVH and mixed leukocyte reactions. SC designates a stem cell, SC_T a T stem cell, and SC_B a B stem cell.

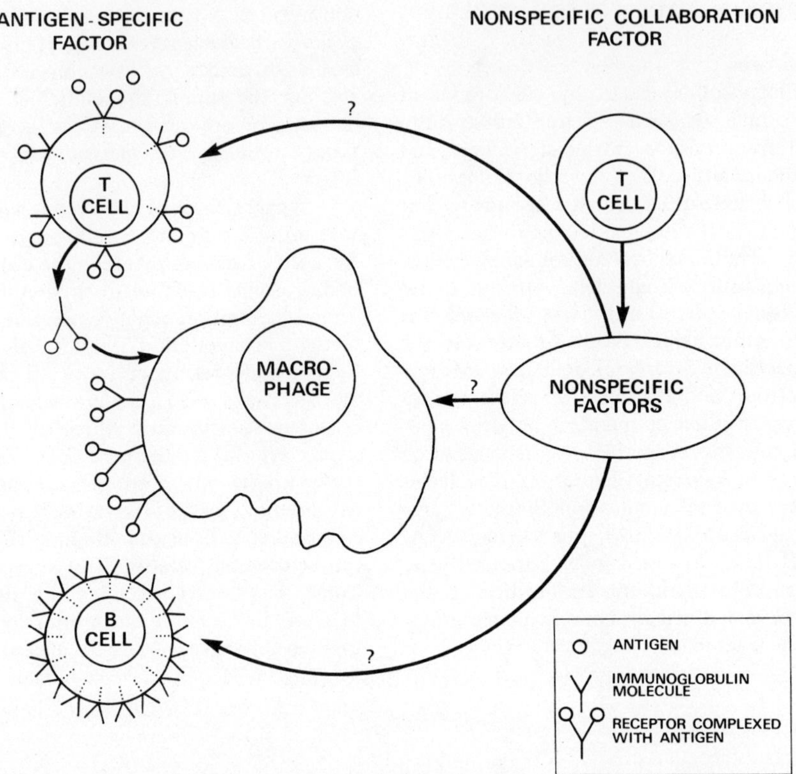

Figure 8–2. Cooperation between T and B cells in antibody formation to thymus-dependent antigens. Macrophages are included in the interaction scheme. The *left side* of the diagram depicts specific collaboration mediated by released T cell receptor immunoglobulin. The *right side* illustrates possible modes of interaction involving nonspecific factors. The nonspecific factors elaborated by activated T cells might affect B cells, macrophages, or other T cells.

investigated in some detail in vitro, but such approaches may not necessarily reflect the complexity of immune regulation within the intact animal.

The Role of T Cell Immunoglobulin in Specific Collaboration Between T & B Cells in Antibody Formation

The most obvious candidate for an antigen-specific collaborative factor is T cell receptor immunoglobulin. It has been proposed that direct contact between antigen and B cell receptor immunoglobulin gives a signal to the cell which results in tolerance. In contrast, if the antigen were complexed with T cell immunoglobulin (associative antibody), the B cell would receive a second signal which would cause it to proliferate and form antibodies. A number of laboratories have now obtained evidence suggesting that T cell immunoglobulin plays a role in collaborative interactions between helper T cells and B cells. In addition, evidence has accumulated that a third cell type, macrophages or "adherent" cells, plays an obligatory role in such collaboration.

Fig 8–2 schematically represents T and B cell cooperation involving macrophages and the presence of an antigen-specific factor (T cell immunoglobulin) which concentrates antigen onto the macrophage surface. Possible modes of interaction involving T cell factors which do not reflect specificity for antigen are depicted on the *right* side of Fig 8–2. The data supporting collaboration via a T cell immunoglobulin model are as follows: (1) Specific in vitro cooperation will occur between helper T cells and normal B cells (nu/nu murine spleen containing macrophages and B cells) if the T cells are separated from the spleen cells by a nucleopore filter which contains pores too small to allow passage of cells. This observation suggests that direct contact between T and B cells is not required and that a subcellular factor must be involved. Moreover, spleen cells depleted of macrophages will not suffice to produce an antibody response in this system. (2) Specific in vitro collaboration was inhibited by antisera specific for κ chains and μ chains. Furthermore, specific helper T cells sensitized to antigens, eg, KLH or fowl γ-globulin possessed surface immunoglobulin which resembled the 7S subunit of IgM and which exhibited binding specificity toward the antigen used in the activation process (see above). An exact parallel was found between the presence of this specific 7S IgM and the capacity of T cells to mediate specific cooperation in vitro. Other workers have also presented evidence supporting the hypothesis that immunoglobulin from helper T cells mediates cooperation with B cells;

some, for example, have inhibited in vitro collaborative responses using antiserum directed against L chains. Others have isolated antigen-specific factors with molecular weights of approximately 180,000, a value consistent with that obtained for T cell IgM surface immunoglobulin. The molecule possesses L chain antigenic determinants. A putative nonimmunoglobulin antigen-specific collaborative factor has been reported (see below).

If the scheme implicating macrophages (or "adherent" cells) in specific T/B cell collaboration is generally correct, T cell immunoglobulin should be cytophilic for macrophages. This possibility was directly tested using preparations of surface proteins of lymphocytes labeled by means of lactoperoxidase-catalyzed radioiodination and solubilized by incubation. Binding to peritoneal exudate macrophages of ^{125}I-labeled T cell immunoglobulin from both normal thymus lymphocytes and activated helper cells was shown by direct assay, depletion assay, and radioautography. Under the conditions used for radioautography, only macrophages bound ^{125}I-labeled T cell immunoglobulin; lymphocytes did not take up the immunoglobulin. Moreover, solubilization of the macrophage and polyacrylamide gel electrophoresis of released ^{125}I-labeled protein indicated that only IgM type immunoglobulin (containing μ and L chains) had attached to the macrophage surface. T cell immunoglobulin did not bind to T cells nor B cells but sometimes showed a slight affinity for macrophages. Solubilization of ^{125}I-labeled B cell immunoglobulin from the macrophage surfaces followed by polyacrylamide gel electrophoresis showed the presence of material migrating like L chain and γ chain. These reports provide support for the hypothesis that specific T/B cell collaboration can occur via the binding of T cell immunoglobulin carrying antigen to the surfaces of macrophages. The fact that a single molecule carries out a recognition function (presumably through the Fab piece) and a collaborative function (presumably through the Fc piece) is a novel—but not unique—event which may have implications for other systems involving recognition and interaction among cells.

The observation that cell surface immunoglobulin of T cells showed no detectable propensity to bind to T cells provides additional evidence militating against the possibility that T cell 7S IgM is a product of plasma cells which is cytophilic for T cells. T cells, particularly activated T cells, possess Fc receptors which bind immunoglobulin. In this case, however, these receptors show a preference for IgG. The divergent cytophilic properties of 7S IgM-like immunoglobulins of T cells and B cells further raise the possibility that these immunoglobulins differ structurally in their Fc regions. It may be that these molecules represent different IgM subclasses, and further chemical studies are required to verify this point.

Two possible models of suppressor T cell action follow from the T cell immunoglobulin cooperation scheme. In the first place, nonspecific suppression (competition) should result if macrophages are saturated by excess amounts of T cell immunoglobulin which has different specificity for antigen but the proper Fc region for macrophage binding. Immunoglobulin of certain monoclonal T lymphoma cells has fulfilled this expectation and blocked T/B cell cooperation in vitro. Specific suppression of B cell responses might result if antigen bound to the antigen-combining regions of T cell immunoglobulin, in the absence of the Fc fragment, impinged directly upon antigen-specific B cells. The signal for tolerance would be given, for example, by a complex of antigen and Fab, but the second signal (see above) for proliferation and differentiation would not be given. Data consistent with this notion have been obtained in rats with an antigen-specific suppressive T cell factor with a molecular weight of 50,000, possibly corresponding to a portion of the Fab region, and IgM with a molecular weight of approximately 100–200 thousand mediating a specific helper effect. However, V region dimers and even portions of Fab regions probably would not react with antisera directed against C region antigenic determinants.

Nonspecific Factors in T/B Cell Cooperation

Different molecules might be involved in nonspecific replacement of T cell function or amplification of function of small numbers of residual T cells in populations supposedly depleted of T cells. Such factors might interact with B cells alone, or T cells alone, or even operate at the level of accessory cells (Fig 8–2). A major source of soluble factors which replace T cells is the supernate obtained from cultures of allogeneic lymphocytes which have participated in an in vitro mixed leukocyte reaction. Effective factors have also been observed in supernates of T cell cultures stimulated to divide by mitogens such as concanavalin A. Allogeneic factors are usually found to be macromolecular components, but some discrepancies in molecular weight have been noted. Some T cell replacing factors have molecular weights of approximately 150,000, whereas others occur with molecular weights of approximately 40,000. Other workers have also reported a nonspecific mediator of in vitro T/B cell cooperation which was sufficiently small to pass through a dialysis membrane. These discrepancies might reflect aggregation and dissociation, or proteolytic degradation, or the presence of distinct nonspecific factors. Moreover, *E coli* lipopolysaccharide and cGMP can replace the requirement for T cells in in vitro thymus-dependent immune responses. The chemically pure complex of polyadenylic acid and polyuridylic acid (poly A • U) can amplify T cell function both in vivo and in vitro to the extent that T cell-depleted populations (< 5% normal numbers of T cells) can respond to antigens such as erythrocytes.

Various factors can substitute for T cells and allow B cells to become antibody producers. These might be considered B cell mitogens of a particular sort because they not only initiate DNA synthesis but also direct the cell to express its genetic programming for immunoglobulin synthesis and secretion.

Genetic Influences on T/B Cell Cooperation

The immune response, like other complex physiologic systems, is under precise genetic control. In principle, this genetic control can be expressed at any level in the response, including antigen recognition (by B or T cells), antigen processing, T/B cell cooperation, and various stages of cell differentiation following contact with antigen. A number of immune response gene systems have been described in mice. Some of these are involved in the determination of immunoglobulin idiotypes; some are implicated in T/B cell cooperation and are closely linked to genes specifying the major histocompatibility antigens; and others are not associated with any known genetic marker.

Immune response genes linked to the genes coding for histocompatibility antigens have been described in greatest detail in mice and guinea pigs. Such genes may also exist in man because certain diseases are correlated with some HLA markers. The genetic region encoding the H-2 antigens of mice has 2 major regions, the K region and the D region, both of which specify histocompatibility antigens (see Chapter 12). These genetic regions are separated by 0.5 map units, which allow space for about 100 genes. Between the K and D markers is the Ss-Slp marker, which controls levels of a serum protein and is also implicated in complement levels. Between the K and Ss-Slp regions lies the I or immune response region. This is a complex area which can be dissected further into at least 3 subregions. Genes localized in the Ir region condition the immune responses to low levels of naturally occurring antigens, including serum proteins, and to synthetic polypeptide antigens such as the copolymer (T,G)-A--L formed from the amino acids tyrosine, glutamic acid, alanine, and lysine. Fig 8–3 illustrates some of the major markers of the H-2 gene complex of mice. The relationships between the H-2 gene complex and Ir genes are discussed in detail in Chapter 12.

Histocompatibility-linked Ir genes control responses to thymus-dependent antigens; no Ir genes linked to histocompatibility antigens have been observed in systems which are thymus-independent. Mice of the responder strain C57Bl/6 (H-2^b) respond to (T,G)-A--L by producing IgM and IgG antibodies in the primary response and by giving a large IgG response after secondary stimulation with the antigen. In contrast, mice of a nonresponder strain DBA/1 (H-2^q) give a normal IgM primary response but do not produce IgG antibodies in a primary or secondary response. Nonresponder mice thus mount a response to (T,G)-A--L which resembles the responses given to thymus-independent antigens, where B cells respond with a minimum (or absence) of T cell help. Neonatal thymectomy converts responder mice to apparent nonresponders, thereby indicating the requirement for helper T cells in this response.

It was initially considered that histocompatibility-linked Ir genes were expressed only on T cells, and, since they were correlated with specific responses to certain antigens, they were thought to encode receptors for those antigens. More recent evidence has established that histocompatibility-linked Ir gene functions are expressed on B cells as well as T cells: (1) Limiting dilution analyses of responders and nonresponders showed that both B cell and T cell function were deficient in nonresponders. (2) T cells of nonresponder mice can bind the antigen to which these mice fail to respond. (3) Effective cooperation occurred between B and T cells only when they both showed identity in their major H-2 regions. Semiallogeneic combinations (eg F_1 cells) can cooperate with parental cells in reactions to antigens where the response to antigens is not genetically restricted in either parent. However, when combinations of responder and nonresponder cells are used, F_1 helper T cells will cooperate with responder B cells but not with nonresponder B cells.

The above results suggest the presence of molecules which are not directly involved in the recognition of antigens but are primarily concerned with interactions between cells of the immune system. These molecules, genetically coded for by genes of the histocompatibility-linked Ir complex, could occur on the surfaces of T and B cells and determine whether cooperative interactions would occur among T cells, B cells, and, possibly, macrophages.

Fig 8–4 illustrates one suggested model for T cell activation and T/B cell cooperation requiring interaction among homologous Ir products and cell interaction factors (both encoded by the H-2 gene complex) in addition to antigen recognition. The specific T

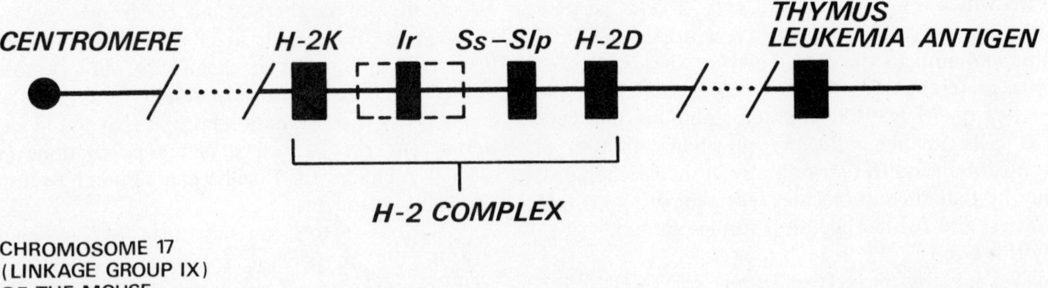

Figure 8–3. Diagram of the H-2 region of linkage group IX of the mouse. A number of genes affecting T/B cell cooperation to certain antigens lie within the Ir region of the H-2 complex.

cell is activated when antigen is presented to it on the surface of a macrophage bearing compatible Ir molecules and cell interaction factors were postulated to undergo a transition to an "activated configuration." When T cells bearing activated Ir and cell interaction molecules impinge upon a B cell, the Ir and cell interaction molecules of the latter become transformed and the B cell differentiates into an antibody-secreting cell. This activation of B cells can be specific for antigen if antigen is held by the T cell receptor (which need not be specified by the histocompatibility gene complex). The T cell receptor in hapten-carrier situations would combine with the carrier position, and the haptenic moiety would be presented to the B cell receptor. Nonspecific induction of B cells would occur when an activated T cell comes in contact with a B cell bearing the proper Ir and cell interaction molecules but receptors for a different antigen.

T/B cell cooperation might also be mediated via soluble complexes. A nonspecific B cell-inducing complex would consist of the cell interaction molecule associated covalently with the Ir product. An antigen-specific complex would comprise these 2 molecules plus the T cell receptor bound to antigen. Recently, an antigen-specific factor was isolated from supernates of T cells activated to (T,G)-A--L which can replace T cells in T/B cell cooperation. This factor reacted with antisera directed against molecules specified by genes lying at the "K end" of the H-2 complex and interacted only with B cells of responder mice. It will be interesting to know whether similar factors can be isolated from T cells activated specifically to other antigens, because (T,G)-A--L has been reported to cross-react antigenically with H-2 antigens. Moreover, since histocompatibility antigens are ubiquitous in cell distribution, similar factors might be obtained from other cell types, including macrophages. Suppression could also occur under the scheme described here either by direct contact or by transfer of surface molecules. In this case, impingement upon a B cell of the cell interaction molecule alone would cause suppression nonspecifically; a complex of cell interaction factor plus receptor plus antigen would focus onto specific B cells and bring about specific suppression.

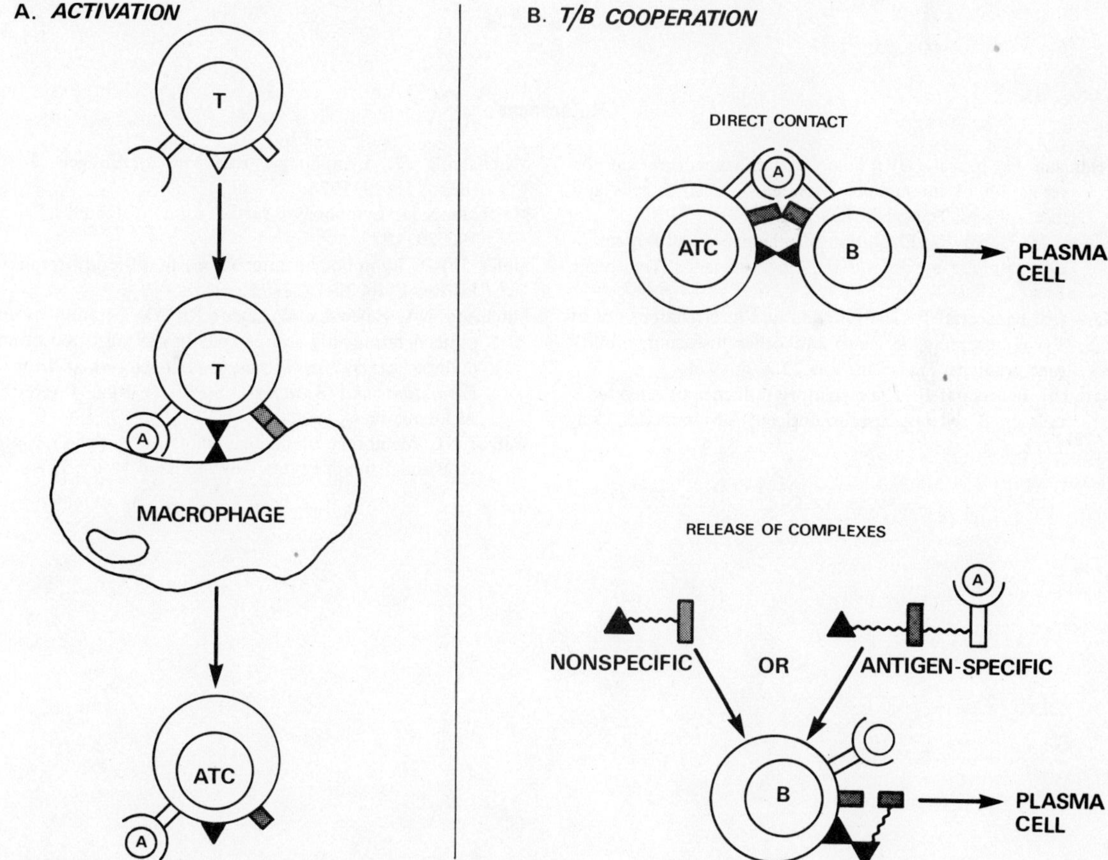

Figure 8–4. One model for T/B cooperation in response to antigens which are regulated by genes linked to genes encoding H-2 antigens. *A:* The T cells are activated by antigen present on the surface of a macrophage bearing the proper response gene product, Ir (Δ), and cell interaction factor (□). These molecules change conformation in the transition to the activated cell state as depicted by color changes. *B:* ATC interact with B cells bearing the proper Ir products and cell interaction factors either by direct contact or by release of antigen-specific complexes or nonspecific complexes. Y, antigen-receptor; A, antigen; ATC, activated T cell.

CONCLUSIONS

It is an undeniable fact that T and B cells, with the assistance of accessory cells, cooperate in the generation and regulation of immune responses to various antigens. The phenomenology of these collaborative interactions is quite complex, and it is clear that no simple model will explain the plethora of in vitro and in vivo results presently in the literature. Collaborative effects occur which involve T cell recognition of specific antigen and interaction with antigen-specific B cells. The recognition molecule on T cells is a special type of IgM-like immunoglobulin which can mediate T/B cell cooperation in vivo and in vitro, with both helper and suppressor T cell effects being noted.

Studies of the genetics of immune responsiveness to certain thymus-dependent antigens indicate that genes present in the complex encoding histocompatibility antigens play an important role in cooperation between T and B cells for those antigens where the response is under this genetic control. Models to account for the histocompatibility restrictions on cooperation postulate the existence of noncovalent cell surface complexes of cell interaction factors, immune response gene products (both encoded by the histocompatibility-Ir gene complex), and receptors for antigen. It is not known whether these products of linked genes exist in a functionally linked array on the lymphocyte membrane. Further information is also required on the biochemical mechanisms of lymphocyte activation and differentiation in order to elucidate the exact roles of nonspecific T cell replacing factors in the generation of antibody-secreting B cells. The immune reaction to thymus-dependent antigens is a dynamic, complex response involving stimulation, suppression, and complicated feedback regulation of several types of cells. Extensive study is still required to analyze fully the various components of this reaction. Although the present phenomena appear quite complex, it is likely that a simpler pattern will emerge in which specific recognition is imparted by immunoglobulin V region and nonspecific factors operate through general mechanisms for cell stimulation.

• • •

References

Feldmann M, Nossal GJV: Tolerance, enhancement and the regulation of interactions between T cells, B cells and macrophages. Transplant Rev 13:3, 1972.

Greaves M, Janossy G: Elicitation of selective T and B lymphocyte response by cell surface binding ligands. Transplant Rev 11:97, 1972.

Katz DH, Benacerraf B: The function and interrelationships of T cell receptors, Ir genes and other histocompatibility gene products. Transplant Rev 22:175, 1974.

Katz DH, Benacerraf B: The regulatory influence of activated T cells on B cell responses to antigen. Adv Immunol 15:1, 1972.

Marchalonis JJ: Lymphocyte receptors for antigen. J Med (Basel) 5:329, 1974.

Marchalonis JJ: Lymphocyte surface immunoglobulins. Science 190:20, 1975.

Miller JFAP: Lymphocyte interactions in antibody responses. Int Rev Cytol 33:77, 1972.

Mitchison NA, Rajewsky K, Taylor RB: Cooperation of antigenic determinants and of cells in the induction of antibodies. Page 547 in: *Developmental Aspects of Antibody Formation and Structure.* Sterzl J, Riha I (editors). Academic Press, 1970.

Warner NL: Membrane immunoglobulins and antigen receptors on B and T lymphocytes. Adv Immunol 19:67, 1974.

9 . . .
Biosynthesis of Antibodies

J. Vivian Wells, MD

The preceding chapters summarized our knowledge of the structure of antibodies, their reactions with antigens, the cells which synthesize these antibodies, and interactions between cells which influence the overall production of antibody. The purpose of this chapter is to examine the mechanisms involved in the intracellular synthesis of antibodies and their secretion into the surrounding environment.

TECHNICS FOR STUDY OF ANTIBODY BIOSYNTHESIS

Sources of Cells

Many different cell sources have been used for the study of immunoglobulin biosynthesis. They include cells in short-term cultures from lymph nodes, spleen, bone marrow, synovial tissue, or peripheral blood of human subjects or animals such as rabbits or mice. More recently, cells have been obtained from athymic "nude" mice since spleens from these animals provide an almost pure population of B cells. Cells have also been used from long-term self-replicating lymphoid cell lines. Once again, these have been obtained either from normal human subjects or from patients with diseases such as rheumatoid arthritis, multiple myeloma, macroglobulinemia, Burkitt's lymphoma, infectious mononucleosis, and hypogammaglobulinemia. In most cases, long-term lymphoid cell lines do not mirror lymphoid cells of the original donor in terms of secreting an antibody of known specificity.

Long-term cell lines have also been established from animal species. These include murine plasma cell tumors maintained in culture or by serial passage in generations of mice. Such plasma cell tumors have been used extensively for the study of antibody biosynthesis. Recently, studies have been performed using cells which represent somatic hybrids between human and murine cells.

Early studies of antibody biosynthesis were performed with intact cells to detect whole immunoglobulin molecules secreted into the surrounding medium. Various factors were then investigated to test their effects on antibody biosynthesis. These included stimulatory agents, metabolic inhibitors, and agents employed in an effort to synchronize the cell cycle. Although these studies provided data on the rates of secretion of whole immunoglobulin and the effects of various factors on these secretion rates, they did not provide data on the means by which immunoglobulins were synthesized and assembled within the cell.

Methods were then developed which permitted intracellular or subcellular studies of biosynthesis. The most important single advance was the use of a "pulse" of radiolabeled amino acid such as ^{14}C- or ^{3}H-leucine. Radioactive amino acid administered to a synchronized culture of cells would be incorporated into newly synthesized immunoglobulin. Aliquots of the culture could then be taken at defined intervals and the subcellular location of the radiolabeled amino acid determined as well as its position in newly synthesized polypeptide chains.

Immunochemical Methods

Immunoglobulins are detected by one or more immunochemical methods (see Chapters 4 and 24), including immunoelectrophoresis, radioimmunoelectrophoresis, sulfate precipitation technics, hemagglutination inhibition, Gm allotyping, radioimmunoassay, immunofluorescence, etc. In addition, specific antibody can be detected in some experiments.

The "pulse" studies with radiolabeled amino acid involve more complicated immunochemical analysis, including gel chromatography after various procedures have been used to disrupt the cells and, in some cases, to break down the polypeptide chains. A common approach is to lyse cells and centrifuge the intracellular contents. The soluble proteins are electrophoresed in polyacrylamide gels containing the detergent sodium dodecyl sulfate. Electrophoresis separates polypeptides according to molecular size, and such gels are then analyzed for optical density, location of radioisotope, and specific precipitation with antisera to polypeptide chains.

Specialized studies are now being performed to analyze the sizes of the ribosomes involved in immunoglobulin biosynthesis, determine the characteristics of the mRNA and tRNA, and estimate the nature of the

J. Vivian Wells is Senior Staff Specialist in Clinical Immunology, Kolling Institute of Medical Research, Royal North Shore Hospital of Sydney, St. Leonards, N.S.W. 2065, Australia.

genes involved in controlling immunoglobulin biosynthesis.

CONTROL OF ANTIBODY BIOSYNTHESIS

Immunoglobulins are synthesized on ribosomes in the cytoplasm. Before this process is described in detail, the factors that influence the overall control of antibody biosynthesis will be briefly discussed.

Cell Cycle

Most antibody is produced in the late G_1 and early S phases of the cell cycle (Fig 9–1). Synthesis may begin earlier in G_1 in plasma cells than in lymphocytes. Similarly, it may persist longer into the S phase in plasma cells. It has been suggested that a mature plasma cell might be genetically arrested in a functional G_1 state with continued immunoglobulin synthesis. Immunoglobulin production in the cell cycle is closely correlated with the stage of differentiation of the cell. Immunoglobulin synthesized by a lymphocyte in cell culture may comprise only 5% of the total protein synthesized by the cell, whereas in a plasma cell it may comprise up to 43% of the proteins synthesized in a short period. This correlation between the amount of immunoglobulin synthesized and cell type is directly related to the histologic demonstration of poorly developed endoplasmic reticulum in lymphocytes and markedly developed granular endoplasmic reticulum in plasma cells (see Chapter 7).

Genetic Factors

Genetic factors operate at many levels in immune responses. These include immune response genes which influence whether or not an animal will respond to a particular antigen (see Chapter 12). Other regulatory genes are undoubtedly involved also in control of biosynthesis. The emphasis in this chapter is on the structural genes which code for the immunoglobulin polypeptide chains. The present view is termed the "two genes, one polypeptide chain" hypothesis (see Chapter 2). Biosynthetic data support the view that an individual H chain or an individual L chain is synthesized as a single polypeptide chain. It would appear, therefore, that fusion of the V region and C region probably occurs at the level of DNA and not at a later stage. There is no evidence to support the hypothesis that different sets of genes code for secreted immunoglobulin versus membrane immunoglobulin.

IMMUNOGLOBULIN BIOSYNTHESIS

The synthesis, assembly, and secretion of an immunoglobulin is presented schematically in Fig 9–2.

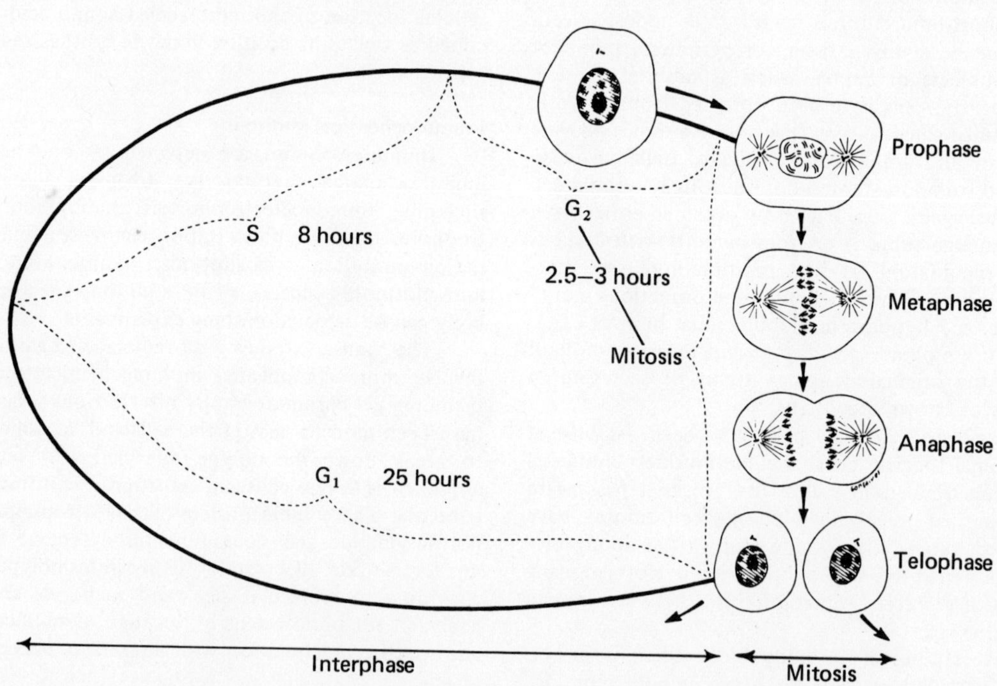

Figure 9–1. Phases of the cell cycle. G_1 (presynthetic) phase is variable and depends on many factors including the rate of cell division in the tissue. The S (DNA synthetic) phase lasts about 8 hours. The G_2 phase lasts 2–3 hours. The times are from Young in J Cell Biol 14:357, 1962. (Reproduced, with permission, from Junqueira LC, Carneiro J, Contopoulos A: *Basic Histology*. Lange, 1975.)

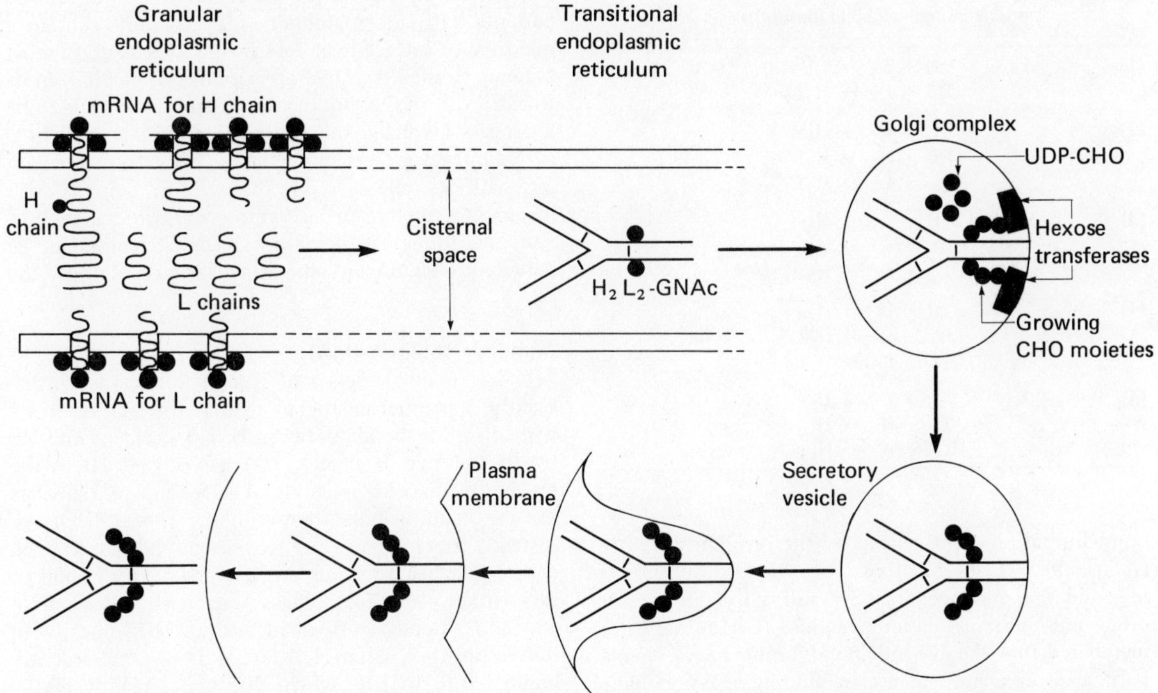

Figure 9–2. Diagrammatic representation of the biosynthesis and assembly of an immunoglobulin molecule. CHO, carbohydrate; mRNA, messenger RNA molecules; GNAc, N-acetylglucosamine; UDP, uridine diphosphate. (Redrawn and reproduced, with permission, from Sherr CJ, Schenkein I, Uhr JW: Synthesis and intracellular transport of immunoglobulin in secretory and nonsecretory cells. Ann NY Acad Sci 190:250, 1971.)

The possibility that different forms are synthesized for secreted immunoglobulin and membrane immunoglobulin will be discussed below. DNA directs the synthesis of the appropriate mRNA. The mRNA for an L chain has been measured as 13S in one experimental system. This is larger than would be expected for the synthesis of a polypeptide chain with a molecular weight of 23,000. It has now been found, however, that most mammalian mRNAs carry a long stretch of polyadenylic acid at one end of the mRNA. The function of this polyadenylic acid is unknown. It is possible to use mRNA in a cell-free system provided that ribosomes, initiation and termination factors, tRNAs, and peptide-synthesizing enzymes are available. This system can synthesize protein, but it is likely that maximal protein synthesis can be accomplished only when mRNA is used with its corresponding homologous synthetic apparatus.

The actual synthesis of immunoglobulin is accomplished by tRNAs which sequentially add amino acids at the growing end of the polypeptide chain, working from the N-terminus to the C-terminus. This synthesis occurs on ribosomes. Different ribosomes are used for the synthesis of the H chain (270–300S) and L chain (190–200S). In plasma cells, protein synthesis is associated with membrane-bound aggregates of ribosomes in the granular endoplasmic reticulum. In lymphocytes, it is more commonly seen in conjunction with smooth or free ribosomes. As with protein synthesis in general, the newly synthesized immunoglobulin is gradually released from the ribosomes commencing with the first part of the polypeptide chain to be synthesized.

ASSEMBLY & SECRETION OF IMMUNOGLOBULINS

The H and L chains are generally synthesized in equimolar amounts or with a small to moderate L chain excess. Initial assembly of the L chain to the H chain may occur while the H chain is still on its polyribosome. However, the bulk of assembly generally occurs after the chains have been released from their ribosomes into the cisternae of the endoplasmic reticulum. Several factors affect immunoglobulin assembly, including the following: (1) the fit between the newly synthesized H and L chains, (2) the relative numbers of chains, (3) the concentration of H and L chains at individual sites in the cisternae, and (4) the rate of disulfide bond formation. Predictably, assembly is more quickly accomplished if equimolar amounts of complementary H and L chains are present in balanced concentration in the cisternae. The rate of disulfide

Table 9–1. Pathway of covalent assembly during immunoglobulin biosynthesis.

(1)	H + L	→ HL
	HL + HL	→ H_2L_2
(2)	H + L	→ HL
	HL + H	→ H_2L
	H_2L + L	→ H_2L_2
(3)	H + L	→ HL
	HL + L	→ HL_2
	HL_2 + H	→ H_2L_2
(4)	H + H	→ H_2
	H_2 + L	→ H_2L
	H_2L + L	→ H_2L_2
(5)	L + L	→ L_2
	L_2 + H	→ HL_2
	HL_2 + H	→ H_2L_2

bond formation is influenced by the proximity of the chains, the availability of enzymes for disulfide bonding, and the presence of active sulfhydryl groups on other nonimmunoglobulin proteins. It should be remembered that the disulfide bond joining heavy chains is of a lower energy than that binding heavy to light chains. Table 9–1 lists the pathways which have been reported for covalent assembly of immunoglobulins. The initial disulfide bond in the first 3 is between the H and L chains; in the fourth it is between the H chains; and in the fifth it is between L chains. The latter is not usually a significant pathway in normal biosynthesis but is important in the pathogenesis of excess secreted monoclonal L chain dimers. There is no single assembly pathway that operates for all cells or all immunoglobulins of any one class. Free L chains may be secreted within 20 minutes of synthesis. Fully assembled IgG may be secreted 30–40 minutes after the onset of synthesis. A variable factor is the rate of disulfide bond formation since this may require 2–20 minutes to occur.

Immunoglobulin M (IgM)

Free μ chains can be detected intracellularly after release from the ribosomes. The new chains combine with L chains to form the 7S monomer subunit (μ_2L_2). This subunit is the main intracellular form of IgM in murine plasma cell tumors. In one case, the pentamer 19S molecule was the main form of intracellular IgM. The IgM synthesis rate in this latter case was approximately 80 molecules of IgM per cell per second. B cells from athymic nude mice can be stimulated by Sepharose-bound concanavalin A to synthesize and secrete antibody. In this situation, an increase in intracellular synthesis of protein, including IgM, can be demonstrated within 10–14 hours and initiation of secretion within 24–30 hours. The main form of IgM in this experiment was the 7S monomer, with small amounts of polymerized 19S IgM. The 7S IgM contains only small amounts of carbohydrate, whereas the 19S IgM contains the full complement of oligosaccharides. In contrast to murine plasma cell tumors, the cells of patients with macroglobulinemia generally contain a majority of intracellular IgM in the 19S form. In most systems studied, the IgM appears in the medium in its final 19S form. Polymerization therefore appears to be a process involving the addition of J chains and final carbohydrate groups immediately prior to or coinciding with its release from the cell. In humans with macroglobulinemia or autoimmune disorders, such as systemic lupus erythematosus, the 7S form can be detected in significant amounts after secretion into the blood.

Immunoglobulin A (IgA)

The major subclass of IgA in humans is synthesized in a manner analogous to that for IgG, ie, H_2L_2 with disulfide bonds between H and L chains and between the two H chains. It appears that HL is the major precursor in assembly. The second IgA subclass has no disulfide bonds between the H and L chains. Instead, the L chains are covalently bound to each other. The heavy chains are also covalently bound to each other. A third subclass has been described in which HL bonds are formed but not HH bonds, with the result that serum IgA exists in a noncovalently bonded form $(HL)_2$, which dissociates readily in the presence of denaturing agents. Adequate studies have not been performed on IgA synthesis and assembly, but the evidence suggests that even when molecular polymerization is noted in the serum the major intracellular form of IgA is the H_2L_2 monomer. It is probable that polymerization and the addition of J chain occur immediately prior to secretion from the cell.

Immunoglobulin Carbohydrate

Carbohydrate is added to immunoglobulin molecules in an orderly sequence beginning with N-acetylglucosamine, which links the oligosaccharide to the appropriate amino acid residue in the polypeptide chain. Hexose transferase enzymes add the appropriate sugars to the carbohydrate chain; the carbohydrates added include mannose, galactose, sialic acid groups, and finally fucose. Although it is generally considered that carbohydrate facilitates the initial secretion of immunoglobulin molecules from the cell (and its subsequent contact with membranes), carbohydrate is not essential for secretion from the cell since L chains, which lack carbohydrate, can be excreted.

Immunoglobulin Variants

Considerable insight into the genetic control of immunoglobulin synthesis has been achieved by studying human tumors which synthesize mutant forms of immunoglobulins. These may be either "heavy chain diseases" (see Chapters 2 and 28) or instances of multiple myeloma in which only fragments of L chains are synthesized.

The study of murine plasma cells undergoing mutations has yielded valuable insights into the mechanisms of immunoglobulin biosynthesis. Such mutations occur spontaneously in vivo, but laboratory studies identified the cells which underwent mutation, measured their frequency, and defined factors which perhaps influenced the mutation rate. The variants are blocked at different stages in the synthesis, assembly, and secretion of immunoglobulins, and these blocks most commonly involve the L chain. In murine plasma cell tumors, the cytotoxic drug melphalan was associated with the highest mutation rates. These studies are now being applied to human myeloma cells, since this drug is routinely used in patients with multiple myeloma. It is possible that the appearance of melphalan-induced variants in immunoglobulin biosynthesis may be reflected clinically in subsequent relapse due to the development of drug resistance.

Rarely, one finds a patient with abnormal plasma cells and other indications of multiple myeloma in whom no abnormal protein is detected in serum or urine. Immunofluorescence studies may detect intracellular immunoglobulin in these plasma cells. It appears that there is a defect in biosynthesis in these cases, resulting in a form of immunoglobulin which is not secreted from the cell.

SECRETED & MEMBRANE IMMUNOGLOBULIN

Conflicting results have been obtained in studies comparing secreted and membrane-bound immunoglobulins. This is partly a consequence of the variety of methods and cell types used for laboratory studies. There is no evidence to support the suggestion that different genes or biosynthetic pathways exist for the synthesis of discrete secreted and membrane immunoglobulins. The turnover of intracellular and membrane immunoglobulin in lymphocytes is slower than in plasma cells. B cells stimulated with mitogen increase newly synthesized IgM production, and these immunoglobulin molecules leave small B cells either very early or very late after synthesis. Under these conditions, it appears that the main cellular pool of IgM is membrane immunoglobulin which is freely exchangeable among all IgM molecules. In plasma cells, however, immunoglobulin is rapidly secreted, usually without a membrane phase. Independent studies have shown that the order of addition of carbohydrate to immunoglobulin molecules is the same for secreted and membrane immunoglobulin. No structural differences have been detected in the 7S form of IgM within the cell and in membrane IgM or IgM secreted into the medium. It is hoped that new methods for the purification of lymphocyte membrane immunoglobulin will clarify the relationship between membrane immunoglobulin and secreted immunoglobulin in cells at different stages of differentiation and stimulation.

• • •

References

Baumal R & others: The regulation of immunoglobulin synthesis and assembly. Ann NY Acad Sci 190:235, 1971.

Buxbaum JN: The biosynthesis, assembly, and secretion of immunoglobulins. Semin Hematol 10:33, 1973.

Fahey JL, Buell DN, Sox HC: Proliferation and differentiation of lymphoid cells: Studies with human lymphoid cell lines and immunoglobulin synthesis. Ann NY Acad Sci 190:221, 1971.

Knopf PM: Pathways leading to expression of immunoglobulins. Transplant Rev 14:145, 1973.

Melchers F, Andersson J: Proliferation and maturation of bone marrow derived lymphocytes. Page 217 in: *Cellular Selection and Regulation in the Immune Response.* Edelman GM (editor). Raven Press, 1974.

Morrison SL & others: The identification of mouse myeloma cells which have undergone mutations in immunoglobulin production. Page 233 in: *Cellular Selection and Regulation in the Immune Response.* Edelman GM (editor). Raven Press, 1974.

Salmon SE: Immunoglobulin synthesis and tumor kinetics of multiple myeloma. Semin Hematol 10:135, 1973.

Sherr CJ, Schenkein I, Uhr JW: Synthesis and intracellular transport of immunoglobulin in secretory and nonsecretory cells. Ann NY Acad Sci 190:250, 1971.

Uhr JW, Vitetta ES, Melcher UK: Regulation of cell surface immunoglobulin and alloantigens on lymphocytes. Page 133 in: *Cellular Selection and Regulation in the Immune Response.* Edelman GM (editor). Raven Press, 1974.

Vitetta ES, Uhr JW: Cell surface immunoglobulin. 9. A new method for the study of synthesis, intracellular transport, and exteriorization in murine splenocytes. J Exp Med 139:1599, 1974.

Williamson AR: Biosynthesis of immunoglobulins. Page 229 in: *Defence and Recognition.* Biochemistry Series One, vol 10. Porter RR (editor). Butterworth, 1973.

10 . . .
Mediators of Cellular Immunity

Ross E. Rocklin, MD

When antigen is injected intradermally into an appropriately sensitized host, a delayed skin reaction may develop over the course of 24–48 hours which is characterized by a mononuclear cell infiltrate. There is ample evidence from experiments involving the transfer of lymphoid cells between laboratory animals (adoptive transfer) that the actual number of antigen-reactive cells present at the site of injection is very small. The great majority of infiltrating cells are apparently immunologically uncommitted, having been attracted to the site by the antigen-responding cells or substances released by these cells. It has been suggested that the initial reaction of antigen with a few specifically sensitized lymphocytes results in the production of soluble mediators, also called lymphokines, which, through their biologic activity, are capable of recruiting host inflammatory cells, activating them, and keeping them at the site. These substances may serve as a means of communication between the cellular reactants which ultimately participate in the cellular hypersensitivity response and may also provide a means by which to amplify this reaction.

A number of in vitro models have been developed which allow investigators to isolate the cells involved in the cell-mediated immune reaction and to study their function and interactions. These experiments basically involve culturing sensitized lymphocytes, activating them with specific stimulants (such as tuberculin PPD, candida) or nonspecific stimulants (such as phytohemagglutinin [PHA] or concanavalin A), and assaying the culture media from these cells for the presence of various biologic activities. A list of some lymphocyte mediators is shown in Table 10–1. These factors affect the behavior of macrophages, polymorphonuclear leukocytes, lymphocytes, and other cell types. By virtue of their biologic effects, one can see how they may play a role in vivo in the expression of cell-mediated immunity in the skin, in resistance to infection by intracellular facultative organisms, and in inflammation.

While these substances exert marked biologic effects on cells in the microenvironment, they are produced in only minute quantities by activated lymphocytes. Few, if any, of the mediators have been purified sufficiently to know their structure so that their detection might be simplified. We do not know, at this writing, how many chemically distinct mediators there are nor how many are actually involved in vivo in cell-mediated immune reactions. However, there is less than total confusion in this field because several lymphocyte mediators have been partially characterized by physicochemical technics and shown to be distinct entities having effects on different indicator cells. During the next few years further progress will no doubt be made in the isolation and purification of lymphocyte mediators, and it is hoped that more will be learned about their function in cell-mediated immune reactions.

This chapter will describe the known characteristics and functions of soluble lymphocyte factors, their assay systems, possible in vivo effects, pharmacologic modulation, and clinical significance.

Ross E. Rocklin is Assistant Professor of Medicine, Department of Medicine, Harvard Medical School, Robert B. Brigham Hospital, Boston.

Table 10–1. Products of activated lymphocytes.

Mediators affecting macrophages
Migration inhibitory factor (MIF)
Macrophage activating factor (indistinguishable from MIF)
Chemotactic factor for macrophages
Mediators affecting polymorphonuclear leukocytes
Chemotactic factors for neutrophils, eosinophils, and basophils
Leukocyte inhibitory factor (LIF)
Mediators affecting lymphocytes
Mitogenic factors
Factors affecting antibody production
Transfer factor
Factors affecting other cell types
Cytotoxic factors–lymphotoxin
Growth inhibitory factors
Clonal inhibitory factor
Proliferation inhibitory factor
Osteoclast-activating factor
Interferon
Tissue factor
Colony stimulating activity

FACTORS AFFECTING MACROPHAGES

Macrophage Migration Inhibitory Factor (MIF)

The first of the lymphocyte mediators to be described was MIF. Many years ago it was shown that cells would not migrate out of spleen fragments taken from tuberculous guinea pigs if old tuberculin was present in the culture medium. The migration of mononuclear cells from explants obtained from normal animals was not inhibited when exposed to the same antigen. Explants of normal cells, in the presence of sera from immune animals, were not inhibited in their migration following exposure to old tuberculin, whereas explants from tuberculous guinea pigs in the presence of normal serum were inhibited by old tuberculin. Thus, cells were shown to be directly or inherently antigen-sensitive and not reactive because of the influence of circulating antibody. More recently, the explant system was replaced by a more quantitative and reproducible method that utilizes peritoneal exudate cells obtained from immune animals and placed in small glass capillary tubes. Peritoneal exudate cells consist primarily of macrophages (70–80%) and some lymphocytes (10–20%). The capillary tubes are sealed at one end, centrifuged, and then cut at the cell-fluid interface. The portion of the capillary containing the cells is placed in a chamber, which is then filled with culture medium that may or may not contain antigen. The chambers are then incubated at 37 C for 18–24 hours. During this period, the cells migrate out of the capillary tube onto the glass surface of the chamber. In the presence of a specific antigen, it can be shown that the sensitized peritoneal exudate cells do not migrate as far as cells which are not exposed to antigen. The areas of cell migration are measured with an instrument called a planimeter, and the ratio of migration inhibition in the presence of antigen to that in the absence of antigen is calculated.

An investigation into the mechanism of migration inhibition of peritoneal exudate cells revealed the involvement of 2 cell types. By separating lymphocytes from macrophages, the role of each cell has been defined in this system. It was shown that the sensitized lymphocyte carried immunologic information and elaborated a soluble factor, MIF, following stimulation by specific antigen. MIF then acted upon the macrophages to inhibit their migration. This latter reaction was immunologically nonspecific in that MIF affected cells from nonimmune as well as immune animals.

Human lymphocytes have also been shown to produce MIF. Human MIF will inhibit the migration of human monocytes or guinea pig macrophages used as indicator cells. The production of antigen-induced MIF by human and animal lymphocytes is closely associated with the presence of in vivo cellular hypersensitivity of the host to that antigen (Fig 10–1). MIF is not found in the culture fluid of lymphocytes cultured either in the absence of antigen or in the presence of an antigen to which the donor is not sensitive. Under some circumstances, however, lymphocytes will release MIF in the absence of a specific immunologic reaction.

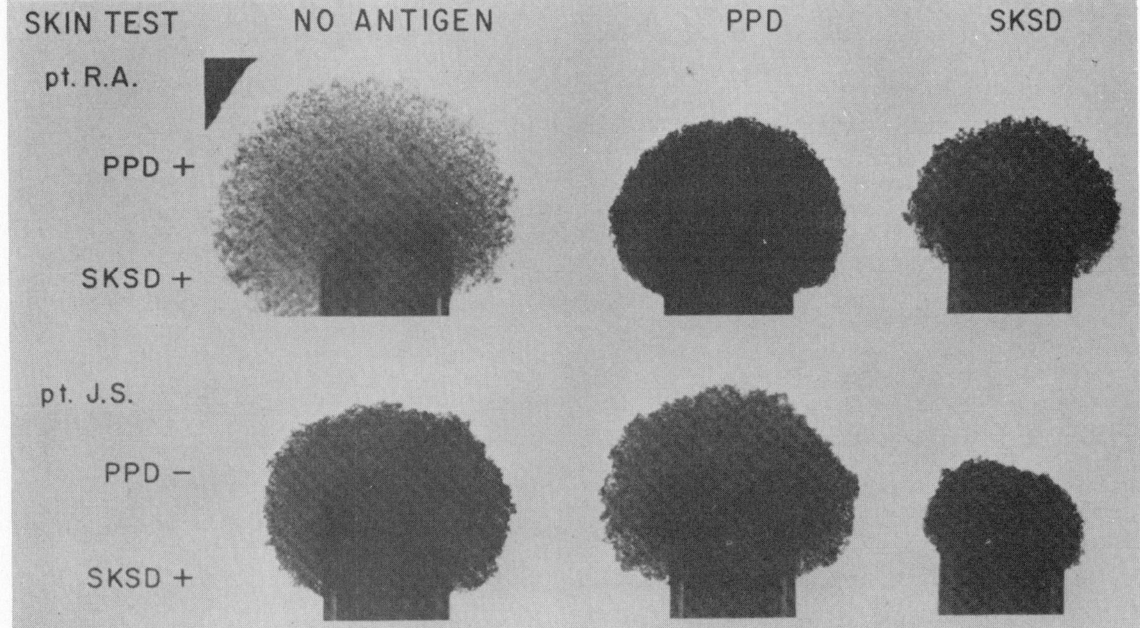

Figure 10–1. The effects of supernates from cultures of lymphocytes from patients RA and JS on normal guinea pig macrophages in capillary tubes. Delayed skin tests in patient RA were positive for both PPD and streptokinase-streptodornase (SK-SD), and MIF was produced in response to both antigens; patient JS was skin test positive for SK-SD but negative for PPD, and MIF was produced only in response to SK-SD. (Reproduced, with permission, from Rocklin RE & others: J Immunol 104:95, 1970.)

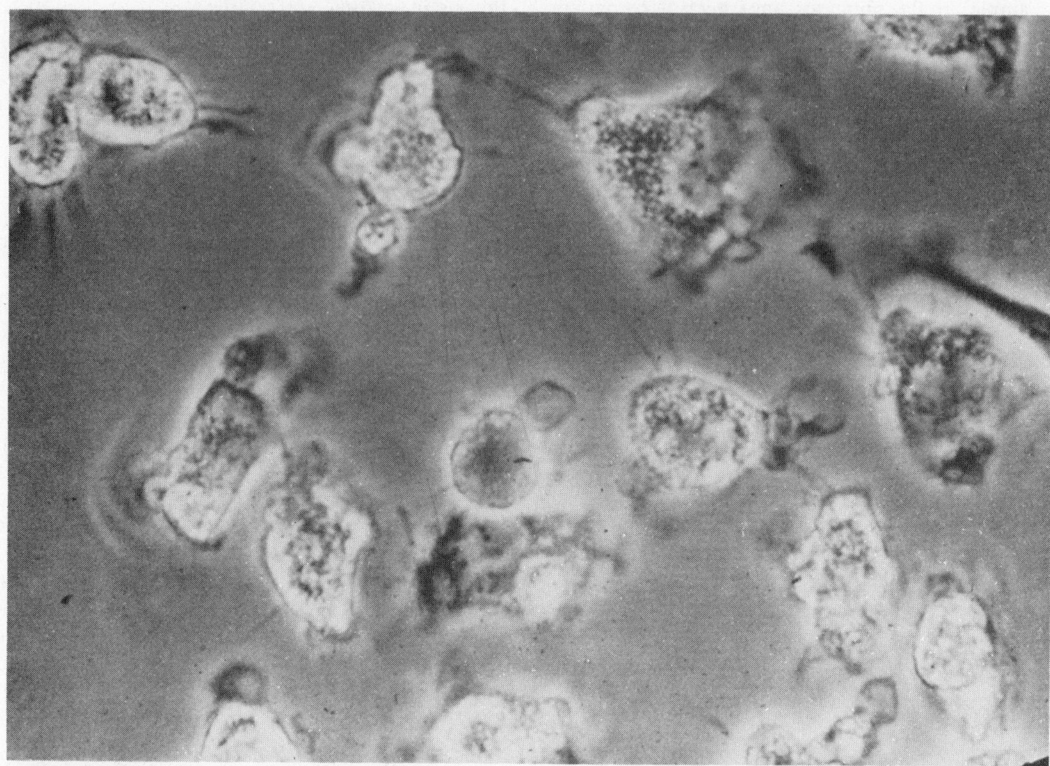

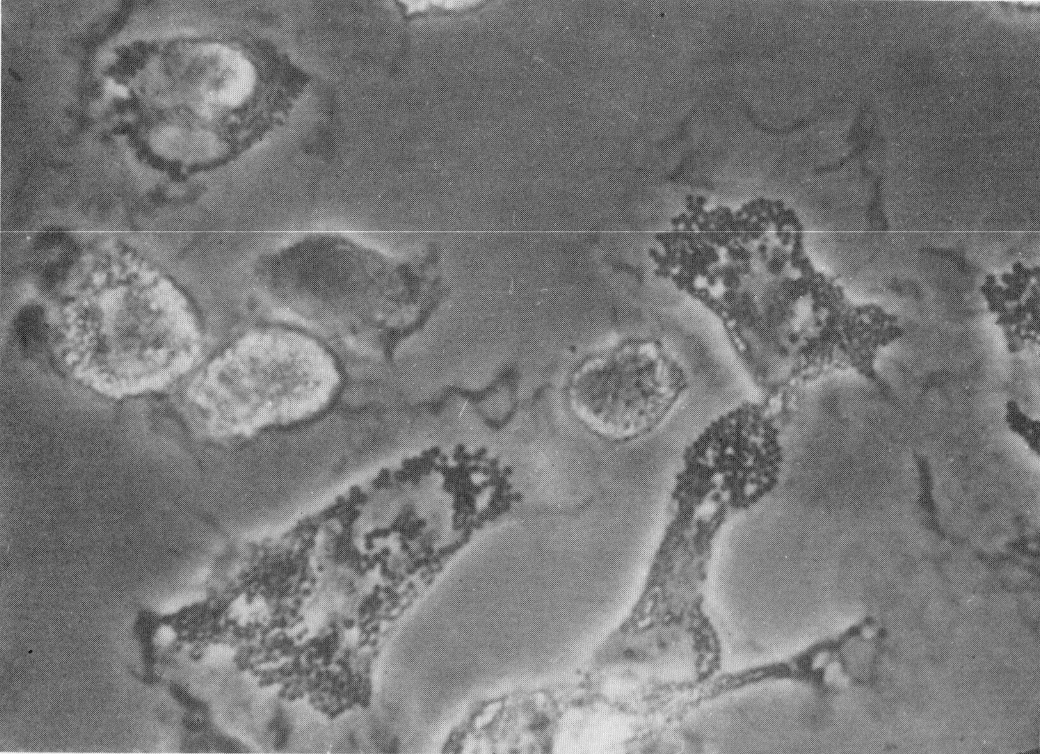

Figure 10–2. The appearance of macrophages after incubation with control supernates ***(top)*** compared with the appearance of macrophages incubated with MIF-rich fractions ***(bottom)***. Note that the latter are more spread out. (Reproduced, with permission, from Nathan CF, David JR, unpublished data.)

For example, if lymphocytes have been activated in vitro by mitogens or other nonspecific stimulants, these cells will produce MIF as well as other mediators.

MIF production can be detected 4–6 hours after lymphocytes have been activated in vitro. The cells will continue to release MIF for as long as 4 days provided that a stimulus persists. MIF is stable at 56 C for 30 minutes and is a nondialyzable macromolecule. MIF activity is not diminished when the material is treated with RNase and DNase but is inactivated following enzymatic treatment with trypsin and chymotrypsin. The active synthesis of MIF by cells following stimulation was confirmed by experiments showing that puromycin blocked MIF production. Puromycin is an inhibitor of de novo protein synthesis. In addition, puromycin also affects macrophages in that they no longer respond to preformed MIF. Dactinomycin (actinomycin D), an inhibitor of DNA-dependent RNA synthesis, also prevents lymphocytes from elaborating MIF. Nontoxic doses of corticosteroids do not prevent the lymphocyte from producing MIF in vitro, although they are effective in obliterating the delayed hypersensitivity skin test. Their effect is probably on the macrophage response to preformed MIF.

The properties of guinea pig and human MIF are shown in Table 10–2. Attempts to estimate the size of MIF by sucrose density centrifugation and gel filtration on Sephadex G-100 indicate that guinea pig MIF has a molecular weight of 35–55 thousand and that human MIF is a slightly smaller macromolecule (MW 25,000). Results employing electrophoresis on acrylamide gels demonstrate that guinea pig MIF migrates anodally to albumin, indicating that it is more acidic. Also, the enzyme neuraminidase, which cleaves terminal sialic residues, destroys its activity, suggesting that sialic acid moieties may be necessary for its biologic activity. These results imply that guinea pig MIF is an acidic glycoprotein. Centrifugation of guinea pig MIF in a cesium chloride gradient to determine its buoyant density verifies the glycoprotein nature of this material. Human MIF, on the other hand, appears to be less acidic in that it migrates with albumin on gel electrophoresis, is not inactivated by neuraminidase treatment, and has a buoyant density similar to that of pure protein.

How MIF affects macrophage migration is not known. It would appear that cells which come out of the capillary first are retarded in their migration because they clump together and may physically impede the migration of cells behind them. This could result from membrane changes which cause the cells to become more sticky.

Table 10–2. Comparison of the properties of human and guinea pig MIF.

	Human MIF	Guinea Pig MIF
Stability at 56 C	Stable	Stable
Approximate molecular weight determined by gel filtration	25,000	35,000–55,000
Disc gel electrophoresis	Albumin	Prealbumin
Isopyknic centrifugation in cesium chloride	Protein	Denser than protein
Neuraminidase	Resistant	Sensitive
Chymotrypsin	Sensitive	Sensitive

Macrophage Activation Factor

Macrophages obtained from animals made immune by infection exhibit enhanced function when these cells are cultured in vitro. They appear more spread out on glass (Fig 10–2), are more adherent and more phagocytic, and show enhanced bactericidal activity even against organisms antigenically unrelated to those that have infected the host. The in vivo state of activation of macrophages obtained from animals undergoing an active infection can be simulated in vitro by exposing macrophages or monocytes from normal individuals to lymphocyte mediators. It was first shown in the guinea pig that normal macrophages could be "activated" after 72 hours of incubation with a macromolecule similar or identical to MIF. The changes observed included increased adherence to their culture vessel, increased rates of phagocytosis, increased oxidation of glucose through the hexose monophosphate shunt pathway, increased ruffled membrane activity, and increased motility. Monocytes isolated from human blood are plated in monolayers and cultivated with MIF for several days.

Activation of the monocyte monolayers can be measured in a number of ways. One can determine the amount of cellular protein or DNA content per culture dish. This is a measure of cell adherence. The metabolism of monocyte monolayers can be assessed by pulsing them with radioactive ^{14}C-labeled glucose. After a brief incubation period, the amount of $^{14}CO_2$ that has been liberated from the cultures is collected in filter paper and the radioactivity determined. Phagocytosis can be assessed by exposing the monocyte-macrophage monolayers to starch particles and then counting the number of particles which have been ingested per cell. Enhanced bactericidal activity of macrophage monolayers can be determined by exposing the MIF-rich or control monolayers to varying numbers of bacteria and then incubating the monolayers for a short time. The cells are then disrupted, the contents plated, and the numbers of surviving bacteria are counted in the MIF-rich monolayers and compared with the counts in the control monolayers.

The tumoricidal capacity of macrophages activated by lymphocyte mediators has been studied in a syngeneic tumor system in strain 2 guinea pigs. Monolayers of normal macrophages were incubated for 3 days in MIF-rich supernates and then co-cultured with radiolabeled hepatoma cells for an additional 24 hours. Cytotoxicity was measured by comparing the number of adherent tumor cells remaining in dishes containing similar numbers of activated and control macrophages. MIF-activated macrophages were cytotoxic for hepatoma and fibrosarcoma cells but not syngeneic fibroblasts or kidney cells. Activation was achieved by supernate preparations devoid of lymphotoxin activity, suggesting that this effect was not due to the adsorption of this mediator on to macrophages.

It is of interest that the activation of macrophages or monocytes takes several days to occur while the inhibition of migration of macrophages may be observed within 24 hours. Just how the inhibition of macrophage migration is related to the later activation of these cells is not known. It has been observed that the inhibition of macrophage migration is a reversible process, ie, that cells initially inhibited in the first 24 hours may again begin to migrate and will actually travel at a faster rate than macrophages in control chambers. It may be that the initial effect of MIF on macrophage function is to change the surface properties of that cell, so that it becomes more sticky. This is observed in one assay as inhibition of migration. Later on, other metabolic changes occur in that cell so that it becomes activated, and in fact its function in general is enhanced. A list of the effects of lymphocyte mediators on macrophage function is shown in Table 10–3.

Table 10–3. Effects of activation of macrophages in vitro by lymphocyte mediators.

Increased adherence to culture vessel
Increased ruffled membrane activity
Increased phagocytosis
Increased pinocytosis
Increased membrane adenylate cyclase
Increased incorporation of glucosamine into membrane components
Decreased electron-dense surface material
Increased glucose oxidation through hexose monophosphate shunt
Increased levels of lactate dehydrogenase in cytoplasm
Decreased levels of certain lysosomal enzymes (acid phosphatase, cathepsin-D, β-glucuronidase)
Increased number of cytoplasmic granules
Enhanced bacteriostasis
Enhanced tumoricidal activity

Macrophage (Monocyte) Chemotactic Factor

As mentioned earlier, the majority of cells infiltrating the site of a delayed hypersensitivity reaction are rapidly dividing, nonsensitive mononuclear cells. This observation has led to the suggestion that the few antigen-activated lymphocytes present might be producing substances which would recruit monocytes. Studies have shown that antigen- or mitogen-activated lymphocytes elaborate a chemotactic substance which selectively attracts macrophages or monocytes. The chemotactic assay is carried out using a chamber which consists of upper and lower compartments separated by a micropore filter of defined pore size. The suspension of macrophages or monocytes is placed in the upper compartment and the chemotactic material in

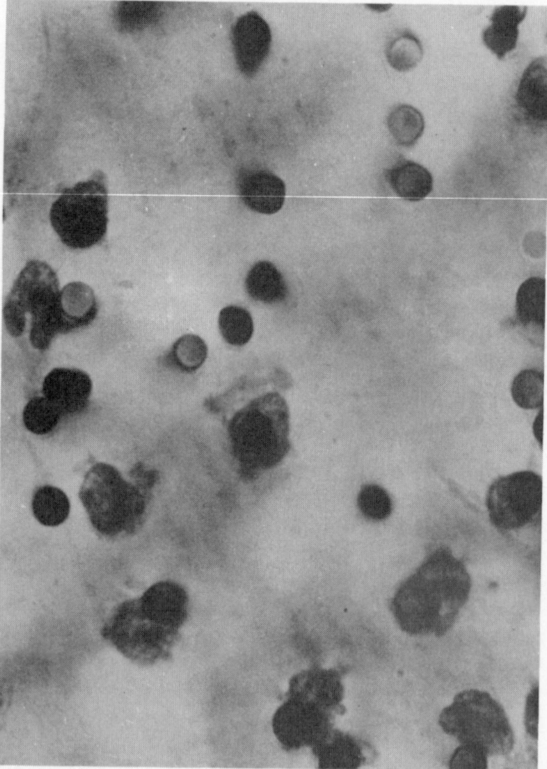

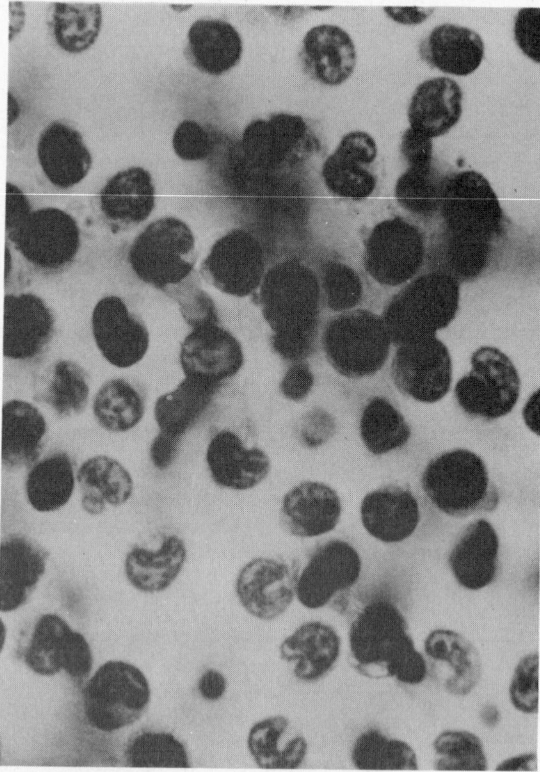

Figure 10–3. The number of cells which have migrated through micropore filters in the absence *(left)* and presence *(right)* of a chemotactic stimulant. (Reproduced, with permission, from Snyderman R & others: J Immunol 108:857, 1972.)

the lower compartment. Usually, one places culture fluid from unstimulated lymphocytes or from antigen- or mitogen-stimulated lymphocytes in the lower compartment to serve as a chemotactic stimulus. The chambers are incubated at 37 C for varying times, and the number of cells which migrate through the micropore filter from the top to the bottom are then counted (Fig 10–3). The chemotactic activity of the culture fluid is assessed morphologically by determining the number of cells that have migrated through the micropore filter. A chemotactic index is calculated by subtracting the number of cells which have migrated through the filter, in the presence of the control fluids, from the number of cells migrating through the filter in the presence of the culture fluid obtained from activated lymphocytes. A variation of this assay is one which labels the indicator macrophages with a radioactive substance such as ^{51}Cr and also uses 2 filters instead of one. After the appropriate incubation time, the amount of radioactivity present in the lower filter is determined. This latter modification correlates very well with the morphologic counting of cells, and is perhaps more objective.

The production of macrophage chemotactic factor is antigen-specific. The factor is heat-stable after incubation at 56 C for 30 minutes (Table 10–4). Its molecular weight in the guinea pig is 35–55 thousand and in man appears to be 12–25 thousand. On acrylamide gel electrophoresis, the chemotactic activity can be found to migrate in that part of the gel associated with albumin. Its buoyant density is similar to that of pure protein, and it is inactivated by treatment with chymotrypsin but not neuraminidase.

The process of chemotaxis or directed migration takes place when the cells are presented with a gradient of the chemotactic material. If the chemotactic material is placed in the upper chamber, as well as being in the lower chamber, then the net result is a loss of directed movement of the cells toward the lower chamber. Furthermore, it has been shown that MIF does not interfere with the activity of chemotactic factor. If MIF is placed in the upper chamber with the cells and the chemotactic factor is placed in the lower chamber, then the net result is an increased movement of the cells toward the lower compartment. When chemotactic factor is placed in the upper chamber with the cells and MIF in the lower chamber, the net result is a loss of directed movement toward the lower chamber.

Table 10–4. Comparison of the properties of human and guinea pig chemotactic factor for macrophages.

	Human	Guinea Pig
Stability at 56 C	Stable	Stable
Approximate molecular weight determined by gel filtration	12,500	35,000–55,000
Disc gel electrophoresis	Albumin	Albumin
Isopyknic centrifugation in cesium chloride	. . .	Like protein
Neuraminidase	. . .	Stable
Chymotrypsin	Sensitive	Sensitive

FACTORS WHICH AFFECT POLYMORPHONUCLEAR LEUKOCYTES

Leukocyte Inhibitory Factor (LIF)

The system of polymorphonuclear leukocyte migration inhibition in man appears to be analogous to that seen in the macrophage system. Polymorphonuclear leukocytes are inhibited in their migration by a soluble material termed leukocyte inhibitory factor or LIF. The effect of LIF is solely on polymorphonuclear leukocyte migration and not upon the migration of macrophages. LIF is produced by sensitized lymphocytes following incubation with specific antigen as well as after stimulation by concanavalin A. LIF can be assayed using human buffy coat cells, as indicated, or by purifying polymorphonuclear leukocytes from the blood and placing them either in capillary tubes, as in the MIF system, or in agar. Cell migration is measured at 18–24 hours, the relative areas of migration are determined, and the amount of inhibition of cell migration is calculated.

Human LIF is nondialyzable, heat-stable at 56 C for 30 minutes, and has an approximate molecular weight on gel filtration of 68,000. Electrophoretically, LIF has a charge similar to that of albumin and a buoyant density similar to that of pure protein. It is inactivated by enzymatic treatment with chymotrypsin but is resistant to the effects of neuraminidase. LIF appears to be a protease because of its sensitivity to the alkylating effects of diisopropyl fluorophosphate. In contrast, human MIF is resistant to this compound. It is not known how LIF affects polymorphonuclear leukocyte function in other respects.

Chemotactic Factors for Neutrophils, Basophils, & Eosinophils

Sensitized lymphocytes elaborate chemotactic factors for all 3 types of polymorphonuclear leukocytes. There appear to be 2 factors which affect the directed movement of eosinophils. One of these factors requires the interaction of the mediator with specific antigen-antibody complexes in order to generate the activity, whereas the other factor is active in the absence of antigen-antibody complexes. The chemotactic factors are similar in molecular weight, ranging from 24–55 thousand. The chemotactic factor for neutrophils has been separated from that for macrophages. Both of these factors have been found to migrate in different parts of a gel during electrophoresis. It is not clear, however, whether these factors are all distinct materials or the same substance with chemotactic activity for multiple cell types. These chemotactic factors may play a role in various chronic inflammatory disorders or in certain types of delayed hypersensitivity reactions such as the Jones-Mote (cutaneous basophil hypersensitivity) reaction.

MEDIATORS AFFECTING LYMPHOCYTES

Lymphocyte Mitogenic Factor

Following stimulation by specific antigen, sensitized lymphocytes release into the culture fluid a substance which has mitogenic activity for nonsensitized lymphocytes. This material induces normal lymphocytes to undergo blast transformation and incorporate increased amounts of ^{3}H-thymidine into cellular DNA. Lymphocyte mitogenic factor may be detected in the culture fluids of antigen-stimulated lymphocytes after 24–48 hours. These culture fluids are then incubated with nonsensitive lymphocytes for about 6 days. Cell division and transformation are monitored, either by counting the numbers of transformed cells on stained slides or by measuring the incorporation of ^{3}H-thymidine into cellular DNA. Cell division in the cultures that have been incubated with culture fluids obtained from antigen-stimulated lymphocytes is significantly greater than that due to culture fluids from unstimulated lymphocytes.

Lymphocyte mitogenic factor is a nondialyzable macromolecule and is heat-stable at 56 C for 30 minutes. It is resistant to treatment with RNase and DNase as well as treatment with proteolytic enzymes such as trypsin. It has a molecular weight of approximately 20–30 thousand. This factor is produced within the first 24 hours of culture, and while it is produced by lymphocytes prior to their cell division, it is not clear whether DNA synthesis is required in order for the cells to be able to generate the material.

Mitogenic factors capable of activating or recruiting nonsensitive lymphocytes could furnish a mechanism for expanding a cellular reaction and producing greater amounts of other mediators. The exact role of lymphocyte mitogenic factor in the proliferative response is not clear. It may be that the first stage of proliferation is initiated after activated lymphocytes have released this factor. The second stage would be the nonspecific activation of other lymphocytes by the material. Alternatively, some sensitized lymphocytes may directly proliferate in the absence of lymphocyte mitogenic factor when stimulated by specific antigen.

Factors Affecting Antibody Production

Following stimulation by a specific antigen, lymphocytes from several species produce soluble factors which modulate antibody production. In the mouse, a material has been described that triggers B cells to make 19S IgM class antibody to sheep red cells. In addition, factors have been reported which also increase IgG and IgE antibody production. In man, a material induces B cells to proliferate, lose their C3 receptors, increase their protein synthesis, and induce production of IgG antibody to specific antigens. On the other hand, there are factors capable of suppressing antibody production.

The factors modulating antibody production have not been well characterized, and it is not known whether they are the same factor acting at a different concentration or several distinct materials. The enhancing factor appears to be a nondialyzable, heat-stable macromolecule. The antibody-suppressing factor appears also to be a nondialyzable material with a molecular weight of 25–55 thousand. This material may provide a mechanism by which T cells and B cells cooperate in the production of antibody to certain antigens (see Chapter 8).

Transfer Factor

The ability to transfer delayed hypersensitivity in man can be accomplished by means of a dialyzable material obtained from sensitized individuals. Sensitized lymphocytes contain a substance of low molecular weight called transfer factor which is released either by disrupting the cells or by stimulating them with a specific antigen. This material has the capability of preparing nonsensitive lymphocytes so that they too are then able to respond to specific antigen by undergoing increased DNA synthesis and mediator production.

Transfer factor has a molecular weight of less than 4000, is resistant to treatment by DNase and RNase, but is orcinol-positive. The mechanism by which transfer factor is able to prepare nonsensitized lymphocytes to respond to specific antigen is unknown. There is some indication that the material may be a single-stranded polynucleotide which either is informational or may provide some part of a receptor for antigen. Transfer factor can specifically transfer delayed hypersensitivity without preparing the host to make antibody against the same antigen. It has recently been used as a therapeutic agent in selected patients with immunodeficiency (see Chapter 26).

MEDIATORS AFFECTING OTHER CELL TYPES

Cytotoxic Factors (Lymphotoxin) & Growth Inhibitory Factors

Immune lymphocytes may bring about the cytolysis of certain susceptible target cells in 2 ways. One involves attachment of the lymphocyte directly to the target cell, bringing about lysis of the cell by unknown mechanisms; this is referred to as direct lymphocyte-mediated cytolysis. A second mechanism involves the release of a factor which, in the absence of the lymphocyte, may also bring about the lysis of certain target cells. This material has been referred to as lymphotoxin. This phenomenon was first described in the rat, where lymph node lymphocytes obtained from sensitized rats produced a soluble factor which killed normal rat embryo fibroblasts. Subsequently, lymphotoxic substances have been described in other species, including man. Sensitized human lymphocytes, in response to specific antigen or in response to mitogens, release a soluble factor or factors which have cytotoxic effects on certain target cells.

There are several assay systems which can detect

the activity of lymphotoxin. Lymphocytes are cultured with and without a stimulant for 1–2 days, and the culture fluids are then collected and incubated with the target cells, one of the most susceptible being the mouse L cell or fibroblast. Cytotoxic activity by lymphotoxin on the mouse L cell can be detected in a number of ways: morphologic counting of the viable remaining cells (Fig 10–4), incorporation of ^{14}C-labeled amino acids into cell protein, or release of ^{51}Cr from labeled target cells.

Guinea pig lymphotoxin is heat-labile, has an estimated molecular weight of 35–55 thousand, migrates with albumin on electrophoresis, has a buoyant density similar to that of protein, and is inactivated by chymotrypsin but not by neuraminidase. Human lymphotoxin is heat-stable, has a molecular weight of 80–90 thousand, migrates past albumin on electrophoresis, and also has a buoyant density similar to that of pure protein (Table 10–5).

The following mechanism has been postulated for the action of lymphotoxin on susceptible target cells: The lymphocyte, having been activated by intimate contact with target cell membranes, is induced to synthesize the mediator. Following its production, lymphotoxin binds to the target cell membrane, where it effects target cell lysis. Target cell membrane disruption, or physical dislodgment, promotes the lymphocyte's release from the target cell and subsequent cessation of lymphotoxin secretion. This mechanism would inhibit an indiscriminate destruction by lymphocytes which produce the factor and would prevent nonspecific cell damage in the host. The significance of in vivo production of lymphotoxin is unclear. Its role might be related to tumor surveillance, ie, the destruction of neoplastic cells, but how it relates to other delayed hypersensitivity reactions is not clear.

Some activities have been described which, rather than causing the lysis of target cells, inhibit their

Table 10–5. Comparison of the properties of human and guinea pig lymphotoxin.

	Human	Guinea Pig
Stability at 56 C	Stable	Labile
Approximate molecular weight determined by gel filtration	90,000	35,000–55,000
Disc gel electrophoresis	Post-albumin	Albumin
Isopyknic centrifugation in cesium chloride	Like protein	Like protein
Neuraminidase	Stable	Stable
Chymotrypsin	Sensitive	Sensitive

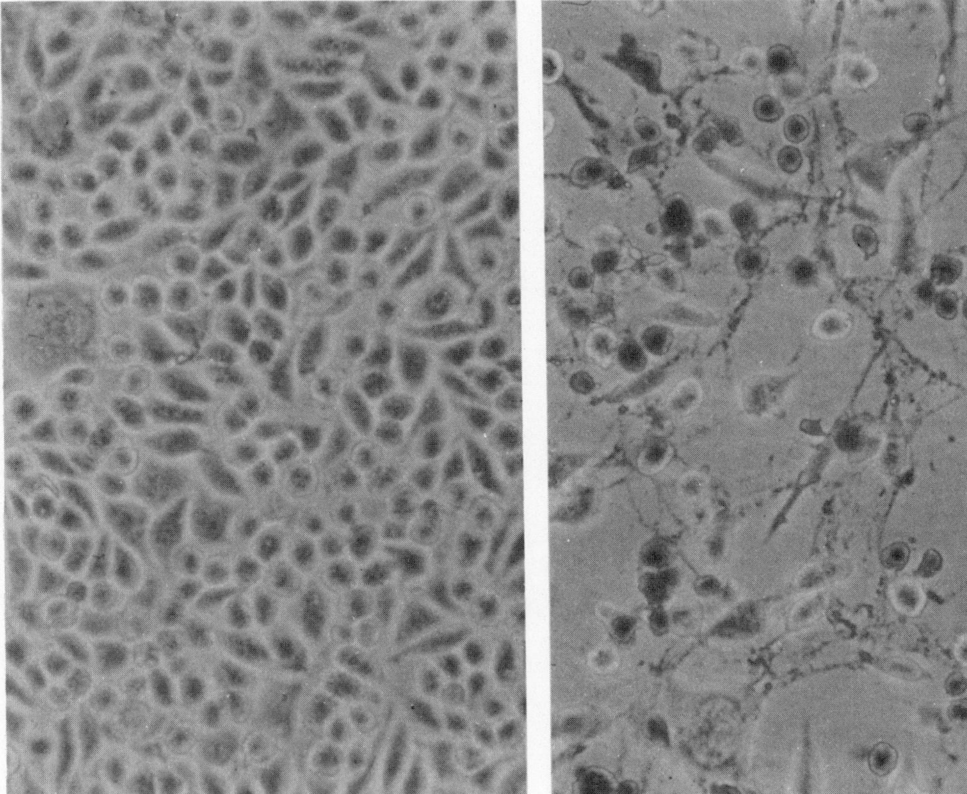

Figure 10–4. Effect on mouse L cell monolayers of incubation for 48 hours with supernates from cultures of lymphocytes. ***Left:*** Control supernates. ***Right:*** Supernates containing lymphotoxin. (Reproduced, with permission, from Rosenberg SA & others: J Immunol 110:1623, 1973.)

growth pattern. Such materials have been referred to as proliferation inhibition factor and cloning inhibition factor. These effects are mainly observed on certain target cells such as human HeLa cells. It has recently been shown that all 3 of these activities may be present in the same culture fluid. When present in high concentration, the effect of lymphotoxin may be seen. At lower levels, a permanent growth inhibition may be observed to occur, and at still lower concentrations of mediator only a temporary inhibition of cell growth is noted. It is still not clear whether the effects of lysis and growth inhibition are the result of 3 separate macromolecules or one molecule which can exert diverse effects on different cells depending upon its concentration in the medium.

Interferon

Viruses can induce interferon production in many cell types. Lymphocytes may also produce interferon-like materials when stimulated by either viral or nonviral inducers. Interferon-like activity can be detected in the culture fluid of both antigen- and mitogen-stimulated normal lymphocytes. Interferon stimulated by mitogen takes 3 days to be produced, whereas that induced with antigen takes 7 days. One way in which interferon can be assayed is by taking the culture fluids from unstimulated or stimulated lymphocytes and incubating them in monolayers of neonatal foreskin fibroblasts for 18–24 hours at 37 C. The monolayers are washed and infected with bovine vesicular stomatitis virus. The number of viral plaques is determined. The interferon titer is defined as that concentration of culture supernate which results in a 50% reduction in the number of viral plaques.

The antigen- or mitogen-induced interferon and the virus-induced interferon material share some similar characteristics. They are stable at pH 4.0–10.0, stable at 4 C for 24 hours, nonsedimentable at 100,000 *g* for 2 hours, and resistant to DNase and RNase but destroyed by trypsin. Their effect is specific for cells of human origin.

Interferon production following or during a specific immunologic reaction is potentially important to the host. Persons who are unable to mount an adequate cellular immune response are plagued by viral infections, and the ability of their lymphocytes to release interferon following stimulation by certain antigens may help determine the level of their resistance to this type of infection.

Osteoclast-Activating Factor

There are several substances which are capable of causing the resorption of bone. These include parathyroid hormone, prostaglandin E_2, and vitamin D metabolites and other sterols. Recently, another mediator of bone resorption has been identified that could be of importance in causing the hypercalcemia seen in neoplastic disease or in the pathogenesis of bone resorption in dental caries. This material is produced by lymphocytes in vitro following stimulation by specific antigen or mitogen and is capable of forming osteoclasts in bone and activating these cells. The technic for measuring bone resorption in organ culture consists of labeling shafts of radius or ulna from 19-day rat fetuses with ^{45}Ca. The culture fluids from lymphocytes are incubated with the organ cultures for 4–6 days. The ratio of ^{45}Ca released into the medium from control and treated bone cultures is used as a measure of bone resorption.

Osteoclast activating factor has a molecular weight of 13–25 thousand, is heat-labile, and is inactivated by proteolytic enzymes. It can be differentiated from other bone-resorbing material, including parathyroid hormone, vitamin D metabolites, and prostaglandin E_2.

Procoagulant Factor Activity (Tissue Factor)

Antigen- or mitogen-stimulated lymphocytes produce a procoagulant material which when incubated with factor VIII-deficient plasma is able to correct the prolonged clotting time. This material is antigenically distinct from factor VIII and has been identified as being tissue factor. It is very labile and has not yet been well characterized. The pathophysiologic importance of lymphocyte tissue factor also has yet to be determined, but it is interesting to consider the various entities characterized by both lymphocytic infiltration and pathologic thrombosis, eg, rejection of a transplanted kidney.

Colony-Stimulating Factor

The differentiation of bone marrow cells into granulocytes and mononuclear cells in vitro can be accomplished by the addition of a colony-stimulating factor. While blood monocytes and tissue macrophages appear to be a major source of this material, recent evidence suggests that lymphocytes may also actively produce the material during an immunologic reaction. Mitogen-activated lymphocytes from thymus and spleen elaborate colony-stimulating factor after 4 days in culture. Analysis reveals a heat-stable glycoprotein with a molecular weight of approximately 40–60 thousand.

IN VIVO SIGNIFICANCE OF MEDIATORS

Skin Reactive Factor

That products of activated lymphocytes may play a role in the expression of delayed hypersensitivity was shown when lymphocyte mediators were injected into the skin of normal animals. A partially purified preparation of lymphocyte mediators derived from antigen-stimulated cells caused the accelerated development of a delayed hypersensitivity reaction in the skin of normal guinea pigs. The reaction was characterized by the development within 3–5 hours of erythema and induration which reached a peak by 8–12 hours and disappeared by 30 hours. Histologically, the lesion simulated a delayed hypersensitivity reaction in that the infiltrate was comprised primarily of mononuclear cells. The factor or factors responsible for this reaction could be destroyed by trypsin and papain but were resistant to the effects of DNase and RNase. Furthermore, drugs such as puromycin, chlorphenesin, and dactinomycin prevented its production. Cortisone, however, had no effect on its production in vitro by lymphocytes, although it could prevent the expression of this reaction in vivo. Since preparations used to elicit this response contain several mediators, including MIF, chemotactic factor, lymphotoxin, and mitogenic factor, it is not clear at present whether one or a combination of these is responsible for the development of the skin reaction. Some preparations of skin reactive factor also possess vasoactive properties. When injected into the skin, this material will induce the extravasation of Evans blue dye between 20 minutes and 4 hours later. The increased permeability induced by skin reactive factor is not blocked by inhibitors of histamine or 5-hydroxytryptamine but is affected by inhibitors of the kinin system.

Macrophage Disappearance Reaction

If one injects mineral oil intraperitoneally into normal guinea pigs, there ensues over the next few days the development of a peritoneal exudate cell population characterized primarily by macrophages. If specific antigen is injected intraperitoneally along with the oil in an appropriately sensitized guinea pig, then the exudate which forms in that animal contains considerably fewer macrophages. This phenomenon has been termed the macrophage disappearance reaction and is associated with a delayed hypersensitivity state. Moreover, it can be shown that culture fluids derived from antigen-stimulated lymphocytes can substitute for intact cells in eliciting this reaction in vivo. This reaction is mediated by a factor similar to if not identical with MIF. The mechanism responsible for this reaction is unknown but may involve the fact that the macrophages have become sticky and adhere to the peritoneum and therefore are not present in the exudate.

Mediator Activity Found in Serum

The usual means for eliciting mediator production is by culturing lymphocytes in vitro, and MIF and interferon activities can be detected in the serum of animals undergoing an immunologic reaction. Serum collected from animals immunized with BCG and then desensitized by administering a large dose of old tuberculin antigen intravenously was found to contain these activities. When serum from the desensitized animal was filtered on a Sephadex column, both activities were found in the same fraction (MW 45,000).

Effect of Mediators on Lymph Node Architecture

A vasoactive material can be recovered from guinea pig lymph node cells which increases vascular permeability within 30 minutes of injection into normal skin. This material, termed lymph node permeability factor, could be extracted from lymph nodes of immunized animals but could also be obtained in equal amounts from nonimmune animals. Extracts of this material are also obtained from other tissues, including spleen, thyroid, lung, kidney, liver, and muscle. This vasoactive material can be differentiated from other known permeability factors, such as histamine, 5-hydroxytryptamine, bradykinin, and kallikrein. Lymph node permeability factor appears to be different in many respects from the other mediators already discussed. It is released without an immunologic stimulus and is found in numerous tissues, suggesting that it may not play a primary role in the delayed hypersensitivity reaction. It may, however, play a secondary role by contributing to the inflammatory process per se through its release subsequent to cell or tissue damage.

If the efferent lymph is collected from animals undergoing an immunologic reaction, one can detect mediator-like activity in this fluid. MIF-like and mitogenic factor activity is present in efferent lymph several days after antigen has been injected into the draining lymph nodes. One also observes other changes during this time, including increased vascular permeability, increased flow rate of lymph, and increased output of lymphocytes into the efferent lymph. If preformed mediators are injected into the afferent lymphatics, then one can show changes similar to those that develop in response to antigenic challenge. These changes include increased tissue weight and increased numbers of cells in the efferent lymph as well as paracortical distention and germinal center enlargement. It is thought that the mediators may in some way cause cellular retention by plugging the efferent vessels, thus regulating the rate of efflux of these cells.

CELL TYPES PRODUCING MEDIATORS

Delayed hypersensitivity reactions are generally assumed to be mediated by T cells. It has been further assumed that antigen-induced production of lymphocyte mediators is also a function of the T cell. The recent availability of technics to separate T and B cells into purified subpopulations has permitted an evaluation of which cell types, in fact, produce these substances. Various studies indicate that both cell types are capable of producing some mediators. For example, both T cells and B cells are capable of producing MIF, chemotactic factor for macrophages, leukocyte inhibitory factor, and interferon. It would appear that lymphocyte mitogenic factor and colony-stimulating factor are produced only by T cells. Several of the lymphocyte mediators from both B and T cells appear to have similar chromatographic patterns. If B cells do produce the same mediators as T cells, then one must reinterpret the role of the B cell in cellular immunity.

PHARMACOLOGIC MODULATION OF MEDIATOR PRODUCTION

Cyclic 3′,5′-adenosine monophosphate (cAMP) plays an important role as a "second messenger" in the regulation of intracellular metabolism. In most normal secretory cells, an increased level of cAMP results in increased production of cell products. In contrast, the immune system is affected differently by cyclic nucleotides. For example, the antigen-induced release of histamine from basophils is abrogated by agents known to raise intracellular levels of cAMP. It has also been shown that immunologic reactions, such as lymphocyte-mediated cytotoxicity and the inhibition of macrophage migration by MIF, are also abrogated by agents which raise cAMP levels. Drugs such as isoproterenol, epinephrine, and prostaglandin E_1, which raise cAMP levels by stimulating adenylate cyclase, and theophylline, which retards its breakdown, interfere with the MIF-induced inhibition of guinea pig macrophages. This effect appears to be on the macrophage response to MIF and not due to inactivation of MIF by the drug. The dibutyryl derivative of cAMP is also effective in blocking MIF activity on macrophages. There is a suggestion that some drugs which elevate levels of cAMP also depress the lymphocyte production of MIF.

The vasoactive amine histamine also appears to play a role in modulating the lymphocyte response to antigen. There is preliminary evidence that histamine affects the lymphocyte production of MIF. Histamine has no effect on the macrophage response to preformed MIF. The effects of histamine on the lymphocyte production of MIF can be blocked by certain types of antihistamines (H_2) but not others (H_1). It is not known whether the inhibitory effect on MIF production by histamine acts via its ability to raise cAMP levels or is due to the activation of certain suppressor lymphocytes which may subsequently act upon the MIF-producing cells.

CLINICAL SIGNIFICANCE

The production of soluble mediators by lymphocytes from normal subjects generally correlates positively with the in vivo state of cellular immunity in that donor. These substances are usually not produced by antigens which fail to elicit a positive delayed skin test. Lymphocytes from some patients with depressed cellular immunity and cutaneous anergy (negative delayed skin tests to multiple antigens) also do not produce these mediators in response to antigenic stimulation. For example, lymphocytes from patients with the DiGeorge syndrome, sarcoidosis, chronic mucocutaneous candidiasis, Wiskott-Aldrich syndrome, Hodgkin's disease, and rheumatoid arthritis do not produce the mediator MIF. In some cases, however, the proliferative response to antigens and mitogens may be normal, even though MIF production is depressed. The cutaneous anergy in these patients may be due to a lack of mediator production (MIF) by their lymphocytes. In other anergic patients, MIF production and proliferative responses are normal, perhaps indicating intact lymphocyte function. Abnormalities in macrophage function or the inflammatory response might explain the anergy observed in these latter patients.

The MIF assay has also been used for the detection of sensitized lymphocytes in patients with certain disease whose pathogenesis may involve an immune mechanism. Lymphocytes from patients with glomerulonephritis produce MIF in response to glomerular basement membrane antigens. Lymphocytes from some of these patients also react to group A streptococci, antigens known to cross-react immunologically with human glomeruli. Although these studies suggest that the lymphocyte may play a significant role in the pathogenesis of certain glomerular lesions, they do not permit one to distinguish whether this involvement is primary to the initiation of tissue damage or secondary, ie, resulting from tissue damage. MIF production has also been found in patients with thyroiditis, pernicious anemia, multiple sclerosis, and Guillain-Barré syndrome when their lymphocytes have been tested with various tissue antigens.

BIOLOGIC SIGNIFICANCE

Lymphocyte mediators might relate to the development of a cellular immune reaction in the following way: Antigen-sensitive lymphocytes, when stimulated by the appropriate antigen, become activated and start synthesizing the various lymphocyte mediators. Chemotactic factors for monocytes and polymorphonuclear leukocytes recruit inflammatory cells to the reaction site. Once there, the macrophages and polymorphonuclear leukocytes might be held at the site by MIF and LIF. Macrophages might be activated to an enhanced state by the action of the activating factor. Other lymphocytes are recruited to participate in the reaction by the mitogenic factor. Lymphocyte mitogenic factor nonspecifically activates other lymphocytes in the area which would perhaps, in turn, start producing lymphocyte mediators. These events have the effect of amplifying an initially small reaction. Once activated, the inflammatory cells become bactericidal or tumoricidal. Furthermore, the vasoactive properties of some of the mediators may account for part of the inflammation. Other protein systems, including the complement system, the kinin system, and the clotting system, are also called into play. If antigen remained at the site, such a reaction would continue, abating as the antigen supply was exhausted. In addition, there may be control systems which inactivate the mediators as they are produced, but these are not well defined at present.

• • •

References

Bloom BR: In vitro approaches to the mechanism of cell-mediated immune reactions. Adv Immunol 13:205, 1971.

Bloom BR, Glade P (editors): *In Vitro Methods in Cell-Mediated Immunity.* Academic Press, 1970.

David JR: Macrophage activation by lymphocyte mediators. Fed Proc 34:1730, 1975.

David JR, David RR: Cellular hypersensitivity and immunity: Inhibition of macrophage migration and the lymphocyte mediators. Prog Allergy 16:300, 1972.

Lawrence HS: Transfer factor. Adv Immunol 11:195, 1969.

Lawrence HS, Landy M (editors): *Mediators of Cellular Immunity.* Academic Press, 1969.

Nelson DS (editor): *Immunobiology of the Macrophage.* Academic Press, 1976.

Rocklin RE: Clinical applications of in vitro lymphocyte tests. Prog Clin Immunol 2:21, 1974.

Spitler LE, Levin AS, Fudenberg HH: Transfer factor. Clin Immunobiol 2:154, 1974.

Section II

Immunobiology

11 . . .
Phylogeny & Ontogeny of the Immune Response

Daniel P. Stites, MD, & Joseph L. Caldwell, MD

PHYLOGENY OF IMMUNITY IN ANIMALS

The immune response originated in organisms with a nucleus (eukaryotic), probably in response to a need to distinguish self from nonself. Unicellular organisms (protozoa) have undergone evolutionary changes that allow them to differentiate food or invading microorganisms from autologous cell components. Multicellular organisms (metazoa) have also evolved highly complex and functionally integrated cells and tissues which exhibit varying degrees of immunologic individuality. Such cell-specific or tissue-specific antigens arise from a restricted phenotypic expression of the genome. In such organisms specialized cells or immunocytes have developed which protect the entire body from microbial invaders, from incursions of foreign tissue, and from diseases that may be caused by altered or neoplastic cells (immune surveillance).

The steps in the evolution of the immune response in animals cannot be retraced with any certainty. Study of the phylogenetic organization of the animal kingdom as it exists today can at best give only a hazy picture of the many evolutionary events that have resulted in the fantastically complex system of immunity possessed by higher vertebrates. Nevertheless, the study of immunity in extant species has justified the concept of an orderly progression in immunologic development as one ascends the phylogenetic tree. Furthermore, a great deal has been learned about many of the individual functional units in the immune response by detailed study of lower species that have a limited capacity for immune responses—eg, in invertebrates, one can examine cellular immunity in the absence of specific antibodies.

From an evolutionary standpoint, cellular immunity and particularly phagocytosis preceded the development of antibody production in animals. Invertebrates characteristically demonstrate primitive forms of graft rejection and phagocytosis, but in no invertebrate species have molecules been identified that have a functional or physicochemical structure analogous to vertebrate immunoglobulins. On the other hand, all vertebrate species synthesize antibody, reject grafts, and exhibit immunologic memory. Thus, there is a relatively sharp delineation between the complexity of immunity in invertebrates and vertebrates; no clearly transitional forms have thus far been identified.

The fully developed immune response is characterized by *specificity* and *anamnesis.* These 2 essential criteria must be borne in mind when distinguishing true immunity from primitive or paraimmunologic phenomena in the phylogenetic analysis which follows.

Daniel P. Stites is Assistant Professor of Medicine and Laboratory Medicine and Director, Immunology Laboratory, University of California, San Francisco. Joseph L. Caldwell is Assistant Research Immunologist, Ft. Miley Veterans Hospital, San Francisco.

IMMUNITY IN INVERTEBRATES

Survival of unicellular invertebrate species has been achieved to a large degree by their remarkable reproductive capacity rather than by development of specific immune responses to deal with environmental challenges. Perhaps the most primitive type of self-recognition mechanism is the ability of certain protozoa to reject transplantation of foreign nuclei. However, this phenomenon is really quasi-immunologic and probably depends on enzymatic rather than specific antigenic differences among various species.

All invertebrate species do exhibit some form of self-versus-nonself recognition (Fig 11–1). However, true cellular immunity with specific graft rejection and anamnesis has been conclusively demonstrated only in certain earthworms (annelids) (Table 11–1). Although invertebrates with coelomic cavities possess a variety of humoral substances such as bacteriolysins, hemolysins, and opsonins, none of these have been specifically induced by immunization nor do these rather ill-defined substances have any known physicochemical similarities with vertebrate antibodies. The study of invertebrate immunology has been impeded by the difficult problems of in vivo laboratory cultivation of many species, the unavailability of safe anesthetics, and the relatively small amounts of humoral or cellular elements recoverable for in vitro study. Nevertheless, a

Table 11–1. Evolution of immunity in invertebrates.*

Phylum or Subphylum	Graft Rejection	Immunologic Specificity of Graft Rejection	Immunologic Memory	Phagocytosis	Encapsulation	Nonspecific Humoral Factors	Phagocytic Ameboid Coelomocytes	Leukocyte Differentiation	Inducible Specific Antibodies
Protozoa	Yes. Enzyme incompatibility.	No	No	Yes; whole organism.	No	No	No	No	No
Porifera (sponges)	Yes. Aggregation inhibition, species-specific glycoprotein.	No	No	No	Yes	No	No	No	No
Coelenterata (corals, jellyfish, sea anemones)	Yes, with graft necrosis.	?	?	No	Hyperplastic growth around graft.	No	No	No	No
Annelida (earthworms)	Yes	Yes. First and second set graft rejection.	Short term, either positive or negative.	Yes	Yes	Yes. Nonspecific hemagglutinins, ciliate lysins, bacteriocidins.	Yes	No	No
Mollusca	Yes	?	?	Yes	Yes	Yes. Hemagglutinins act as opsonins.	Yes	No	No
Arthropoda	Yes	?	?	Yes	Yes	Yes	Yes	No	No
Echinodermata	Yes. Prolonged 4–6 months.	?	?	Yes	Yes	Yes	Yes	Yes. Cellular infiltrate in graft rejection.	No
Protochordata (tunicates)	Yes. Genetically determined alloimmunity.	Probable. Tolerance possible.	?	Yes	Yes	Yes	Yes. Macrophage, lymphocyte, and eosinophil.	Yes. Lymphocytes present.	No

*Modified from Hildemann WH, Reddy AL: Fed Proc 322:2188, 1973.

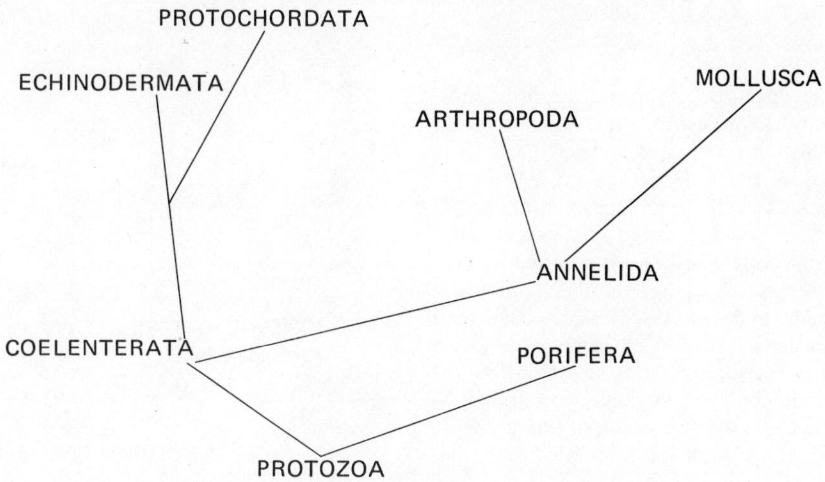

Figure 11–1. Simplified scheme of invertebrate phylogeny.

fascinating array of primitive or quasi-immunologic phenomena have been identified, including the following: (1) self-recognition, (2) phagocytosis, (3) encapsulation, (4) allo- and xenograft rejection, (5) humoral defenses, and (6) leukocyte differentiation.

The most primitive invertebrates, the protozoa, are capable of phagocytosis and rejection of foreign nuclei through enzymatic incompatibilities. Very early experiments (1907) with sponges (Porifera) demonstrated species-specific reaggregation of dispersed colonies which could be clearly identified by different colors in individual parent colony members. Failure of different species of sponges to re-form colonies is regulated by specific surface glycoproteins and requires divalent cations, Ca^{++} and Mg^{++}. This phenomenon is in a sense a primitive type of graft rejection.

Chronic tissue graft rejection with necrosis of engrafted tissue first appears with the coelenterates (corals, jellyfish, and sea anemones), but there is no conclusive evidence for specificity of immunologic memory in coelenterates. However, cellular proliferation in the vicinity of the foreign graft does occur and is very reminiscent of proliferation that occurs both in vivo and in vitro in engrafted vertebrate systems. There is considerable evidence for specific immune responsiveness with memory in annelids that have received skin allografts or xenografts. However, a curious finding of either enhanced survival or rejection in second set grafts remains unexplained. Coelomocytes, the wandering ameboid phagocytes found in all coelomate (those with a coelom) invertebrates (annelids, mollusks, arthropods, and echinoderms) are capable of transferring immunity to tissue grafts. However, a system of cellular receptors or genetically determined histocompatibility antigens remains to be demonstrated. Mollusks and arthropods appear to lack the form of transplantation immunity demonstrable in annelids, but conclusive experiments on this point are lacking. Transplantation immunity in echinoderms is problematic, and most experiments have been inconclusive for technical reasons. The highest form of invertebrate—the tunicates or protochordates—exhibits differentiated leukocytes. An incompletely understood system of genetically determined antigens responsible for the rejection of fusion between various tunicate species has been described.

In addition to acting as effector cells for graft rejection, the coelomocytes are avid phagocytes. Intracoelomic injections of radiolabeled bacteria of aggregated proteins are cleared at rapid rates by these remarkable cells. There is no accelerated rate of clearance (immune elimination) with subsequent injections. When confronted with particles too large to be engulfed, the coelomocytes are capable of walling them off or encapsulating them. This process of encapsulation of foreign debris is reminiscent of abscess formation in vertebrates and can effectively wall off a noxious substance from contact with host tissues.

Coelomate invertebrates all possess a group of poorly characterized nonspecific humoral substances present in the hemolymph bathing the coelomic cavity. Functionally, these substances agglutinate foreign red blood cells, inactivate ciliary movements, kill some bacteria, and, in mollusks, can enhance phagocytosis by coelomocytes, ie, they are opsonins. The action of all of these humoral defense mechanisms is nonspecific, and there is no conclusive evidence for structural or functional homology with vertebrate immunoglobulins.

Leukocyte cellular differentiation appears first with echinoderms and protochordates. Radiosensitive lymphocytes have been identified in tunicates, but their function is unknown. Eosinophilic leukocytes and macrophages are also present. The results of experiments directed at elucidation of the possible diverse immunologic functions of leukocytes in these phyla are awaited with great interest.

IMMUNITY IN VERTEBRATES

The most advanced invertebrates, the protochordates, are probably the ancestors of the true chordates from which all higher vertebrates are descended (Fig 11–2). However, at the level of the most primitive extant vertebrate species, the agnathae, an entirely new component in the immune system is apparent—antibody. Specific antibody synthesis is a property possessed by all vertebrates. Cellular immunity, present in a primitive form in invertebrates, is highly developed and immunologically specific in all vertebrates. Graft rejection is accelerated after primary sensitization, and a true second set rejection phenomenon occurs. However, some difference in the expression of immunologic functions is evident between warm-blooded and cold-blooded animals.

The hallmark of vertebrate immunity is the presence of a truly 2-component immune system, best demonstrated in birds, where 2 independent central lymphoid organs exist—the thymus, which controls cellular immunity, and the bursa, which determines antibody-producing capacity (Table 11–2).

The evolution of immunoglobulins in vertebrates is discussed in detail in Chapter 2. Graft rejection occurs in all vertebrate species. However, in agnathae and cartilaginous fish, skin grafts are rejected at a much slower rate than in higher vertebrates. Nevertheless, these relatively primitive vertebrates exhibit typical accelerated second set graft rejection. Bony fish have a highly complex histocompatibility system and consequently exhibit various types of immunologic tissue rejection. Most amphibians are capable of typical graft rejection, but urodeles and apoda seem to have developed only slow, chronic rejection capacities. Reptiles, birds, and mammals show chronic rejection of first set grafts and accelerated rejection of second set grafts. The evident evolutionary trend in vertebrates from slow to accelerated graft rejection may actually reflect weak expression of histocompatibility antigens rather than any inherent deficiency in the effector mechanism of cellular immunity. A highly polymorphic histocompatibility system with strong antigens such as exists in rodents and primates (Chapter 15) favors accelerated rejection.

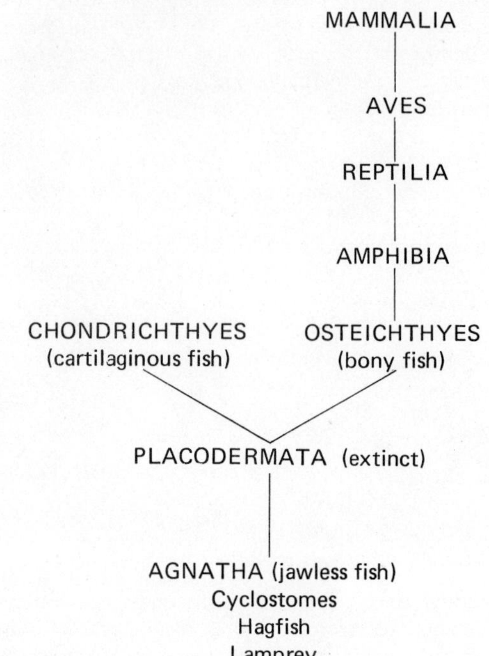

Figure 11–2. Simplified scheme of the vertebrate subphylum. Each major class is represented in capitals.

An interesting and unique feature of vertebrate immunity is the effect of temperature on immune expression in some species. Cold-blooded (ectothermic) classes of fish, amphibians, and reptiles have no internal regulation of temperature, as contrasted to warm-blooded birds and mammals. Ectotherms have accelerated immune responses at warmer temperatures. In amphibians, the inductive or recognition phases of the immune response are independent of temperature,

Table 11–2. Immunologic features exhibited by various vertebrate classes.

Class	Lymphocytes	Plasma Cells	Thymus	Spleen	Lymph Nodes	Bursa	Antibodies	Allograft Rejection
Agnatha (jawless fish)	+	–	PRIM	PRIM	–	–	+	+
Chondrichthyes (cartilaginous fish)								
Primitive	+	–	+	+	–	–	+	+
Advanced	+	+	+	+	–	–	+	+
Osteichthyes (bony fish)	+	+	+	+	–	–	+	+
Reptilia	+	+	+	+	+(?)	+(?)	+	+
Aves	+	+	+	+	+(?)	+	+	+
Mammalia	+	+	+	+	+	+(?)	+	+

PRIM = primitive.
? = Indicates some question regarding the presence of lymphoid structures under consideration, although such structures or their functional counterparts may have been described.

but the productive phase shows marked temperature dependence. Experimentally, this phenomenon has been demonstrated by the failure of graft rejection in engrafted animals maintained at low temperatures but the immediate onset of rejection when an animal engrafted in the cold is placed in a warmer environment.

Several generalizations regarding phylogenetic emergence of immunity are possible. First, primitive and quasi-immunologic phenomena are present in the simplest forms of extant animal species. Second, cellular immunity precedes humoral immunity in evolution. And third, a truly bifunctional immune system with dual central lymphoid organs in a highly differentiated form is the most recent immunologic evolutionary development.

ONTOGENY OF IMMUNITY IN VERTEBRATES

A hallmark of vertebrate immunity is its division into 2 distinct components–the thymus-influenced system and the bursa-influenced system. Lymphocytes influenced by the thymus–T cells–are responsible for a wide variety of cellular immune reactions, including GVH reactions, graft rejection, helper activities for T-dependent antigens, and suppressor functions. Lymphocytes influenced by the bursa–B cells–are responsible for immunoglobulin synthesis and eventually differentiate into antibody-forming plasma cells. Data from many species (man, mouse, rat, sheep, and chicken) suggest that ontogenic development of these 2 components of the immune system proceeds separately during fetal development.

The detailed experimental data available on lymphoid development in the mouse and the potential clinical relevance of ontogenic events in the human single these species out for detailed discussion in this chapter. Relevant data on development of immunity in avian species will also be considered since it is in birds that the distinctions between anatomic and functional compartments of the thymus-influenced and bursa-influenced systems are most evident.

LYMPHOID CELL DEVELOPMENT

Stem cells of the human hematopoietic system appear to arise in the embryonic yolk sac during the second and third weeks of gestation. These proliferating stem cells initiate production of erythrocyte, megakaryocyte, granulocyte, lymphocyte, and monocyte cell series. Stem cells migrate from the yolk sac into the developing hepatic parenchyma at about the sixth week of gestation, and their subsequent proliferation makes the liver the major blood-forming organ of early fetal life. Lymphoid precursors from these sites of stem cell proliferation then undergo morphologic and functional differentiation into T and B cells in peripheral lymphoid organs.

T CELLS

Human Embryonic Development

The thymus is the first lymphoid organ to develop. It arises from tissue in the area of the third branchial pouch, and this tissue forms an epithelial framework for the subsequent migration of prothymic stem cells. Small lymphocytes can be demonstrated in thymic tissue by the eighth to ninth weeks of gestation. The exact origin of these first thymic precursor cells in humans is unknown, but animal studies suggest that they originate from stem cells within the fetal liver. It was at first thought that thymic epithelial cells underwent local transformation to lymphoid precursors, but it is now established that this tissue is populated by cells originating in other regions. Small lymphocytes appear in human fetal peripheral blood at 7–8 weeks of gestation.

Subsequent to this thymic lymphoid infiltration, there is an increase in the lymphoid population of spleen, lymph nodes, and bone marrow during the 12th to 16th weeks. The stromal portions of lymph nodes have formed by the 12th week, but a significant cellular population does not appear in these sites until the fourth month. Plasma cells, considered to be the terminal differentiation cells of antigen-stimulated B lymphocytes, are usually not demonstrable in the lymph nodes of normal full-term infants, but they can be found in some fetuses when intrauterine infections occur during pregnancy.

T Cell Differentiation

The thymus acts on cellular differentiation in at least 2 ways: (1) It modulates the transformation of prethymic cells into functional postthymic cells, and (2) after the postthymic cells have left the thymic environment and migrated to peripheral tissues the thymus continues to affect the quantity and functional activity of T cells.

Histologically, the adult thymus can be divided into cortical and medullary regions (Fig 11–3). Stem cells are carried into the cortical region, and the subcapsular regions of the thymus contain large numbers of rapidly dividing cells. A large percentage of these subcapsular cells apparently lyse or die before they leave the thymus. It is not understood why these cells are so metabolically active. Cells gradually migrate inward from the cortex toward the medullary portion of the gland and morphologically have a greater resemblance to small lymphocytes than to thymic blast cells. From this tissue, the cells migrate to peripheral lymphoid organs and do not appear to return to the thymus.

The large prothymocytes appear to be committed to producing T cells by the time they appear in the

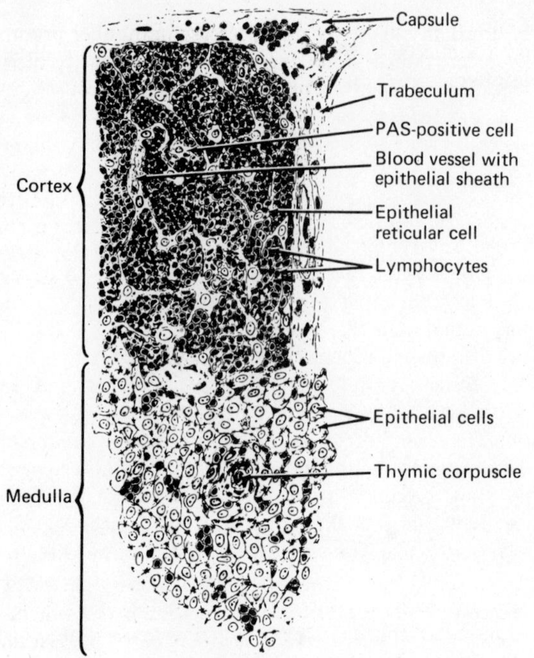

Figure 11–3. Histologic organization of the thymus.

subcapsular regions of the gland. Suspensions of these large cortical thymic cells can be activated in vitro by a number of compounds (tissue extracts, endotoxin, synthetic polynucleotides, and cAMP) to express membrane antigens normally found only on postthymic T cells. In the athymic nude mouse, there is no deficiency of prothymic cells and the bone marrow and spleen cell populations may have as many inducible T cells as normal mice. Currently, the proposed mechanism by which the thymic environment affects the maturing cell includes specific thymic polypeptides which attach to membrane receptors (analogous to hormones and their receptors) and initiate cellular differentiation.

Functions of Human Fetal Lymphocytes

Phytohemagglutinin (PHA) is a plant lectin widely used to evaluate lymphocyte activation in normal as well as diseased humans (Chapter 25). Lymphocyte proliferation that follows culture with soluble PHA is primarily a function of T cells, whereas locally concentrated or insoluble PHA can also stimulate B cell proliferation.

Various workers have studied the response of human fetal lymphocytes to PHA. One study which employed a single stimulatory dose of PHA detected a 4-fold increase in DNA synthesis in 22 fetal thymic cultures in specimens ranging from 16–24 weeks of gestation. Fetal spleen cell cultures responded less uniformly, and little or no response was obtained with bone marrow or liver cell cultures. In another study the response of fetal thymocytes to PHA as early as 14 weeks' gestation was shown, and in this series a number of younger, nonresponsive thymocyte preparations were included. A positive correlation was also noted between the onset of thymic PHA responsiveness, the demarcation of thymus into cortex and medulla, and the rise in peripheral blood lymphocyte counts. A later study correlated the response of PHA stimulation with morphologic changes in 22 thymocyte specimens from fetuses aged 12–22 weeks. Until the 18th week of gestation, there was a progressive increase in degree of lymphocyte transformation. Thereafter, the level declined to that of adult thymic lymphocytes. It was concluded from morphologic study that the thymic medulla was the probable source of PHA-responsive cells.

All of the studies cited above were performed employing a single dose of PHA and analyzing DNA synthesis during a single time period. The time-dose kinetic responses to PHA of lymphocytes from 22 fetuses (5–19 weeks) have been measured. PHA responsiveness was noted first in thymus at 10 weeks and in peripheral blood and spleen 3–4 weeks later. Bone marrow and hepatic lymphoid cells did not respond to this mitogen. PHA-induced DNA synthesis increased in all responsive organs with increasing fetal age. Careful dose-response kinetics, especially when stimulating thymocytes with PHA, is of paramount importance since the dose-response curve is quite sharply demarcated (Chapter 25). The foregoing studies clearly document the early and rather remarkable appearance of at least one functional attribute of fetal thymocytes and peripheral lymphocytes during embryonic development.

Using the unidirectional mixed lymphocyte culture (MLC), investigators can detect histocompatibility differences in nonimmunized allogeneic subjects. PHA and allogeneic cells both stimulate T lymphocytes, but the responding populations are not identical. The MLC has been used both to assess the immunocompetence of fetal lymphocytes and to estimate the presence of histocompatibility antigens at early stages of development. Fetal lymphocytes from thymus, liver, and occasionally spleen can respond in vitro to both normal adult and leukemic lymphocytes. Further studies have emphasized the clear separation between the strong response of lymphoid cells from fetal liver to allogeneic lymphocytes and their failure to respond to PHA. Cells strongly reactive in MLC were also present in fetal spleen and thymus. The fact that MLC-responsive and PHA-nonresponsive cells are present at 10 weeks of gestation suggests that the MLC response is more primitive than PHA reactivity.

In a detailed study of the time-dose response kinetics of MLC-responsive cells in 22 human fetuses ranging from 5–20 weeks' gestation, MLC-responsive cells were found in fetal liver as early as 7½ weeks' gestational age. This, the earliest cellular immune reaction detectable in the fetus, clearly preceded lymphoid development of the thymus; the latter occurs between 9–10 weeks of gestation. The identity of the MLC-responsive fetal hepatic cells remains obscure. Allogeneic cell interactions may represent a unique form of immune reaction distinct from the usual antigenic activation. Thus, the MLC response in liver cells from human fetuses could result from stem cell proliferation. A unique primordial role for hepatic cells in establishing immunocompetence in the mouse has been demonstrated. A few patients with severe combined immunodeficiency disease (Chapter 26) have peripheral blood lymphocytes which react in the MLC but do not respond to PHA. These data suggest that a developmental defect exists in the T cells but not in the so-called hepatic-dependent lymphoid cells.

Recently, partial initial success has resulted from immune reconstitution of a patient with severe combined immunodeficiency disease with an allogeneic fetal hepatic graft. The use of this source of stem cells and immunocompetent lymphoid precursors warrants further trial in patients without histocompatible sibling donors.

Murine T Cell Development

Several theories that have been advanced to explain the development of sublcasses of mature T cells with different functional characteristics are summarized in Fig 11–4. The main differences between the alternative theories relate to the influence of antigen on T cell maturation. The cells could require antigen exposure before they differentiated into functionally different populations, or they could be precommitted to a certain activity prior to antigen exposure.

Several murine membrane antigens have recently been described which allow a more precise and direct delineation of thymic maturational events. These include Thy-1 (theta), TL, Ly-1, Ly-2, and Ly-3 antigens. TL is a membrane antigen present on prothymic cells (in mice carrying the TL-positive gene), and this antigen is lost during thymic maturation of the cell. At the same time the amount of Thy-1 antigen, normally present in large amounts on prothymic cells, is reduced in quantity. The Ly antigens are developed during this maturation response, but some of the cells will undergo additional maturation and lose either the Ly-1 marker or the Ly-2,3 markers. When T cells are released from the thymus to localize in peripheral tissues, they contain roughly 50% cells with Ly-1,2,3; about 30% with Ly-1; and less than 10% with Ly-2,3. By lysing different subpopulations of T cells with specific Ly antisera and complement, it has been possible to assign functional characteristics to these subsets. Ly-1 cells appear to be functional helper cells in the T cell - B cell interaction necessary to produce antibody against thymus-dependent antigens. Allogeneic cells which differ at the Ir gene region activate the Ly-1 subpopulation of T cells in the mixed lymphocyte reaction. Cells positive for Ly-2,3 antigens appear to be responsible for cytolysis of allogeneic lymphocytes or tumor cells by directing their activity against serologically defined histocompatibility antigens. The Ly-1 cells appear to function as helper cells in this process. The Ly-1 and Ly-2,3 cell populations are not greatly reduced by thymectomy in the adult animal. The Ly-1,2,3 - positive cells are very sensitive to the effects of adult thymectomy and decrease in number promptly after the thymus is removed. It is not known whether these cells represent a transitional cell population destined to mature into one of the previous cell types or whether they represent a functionally distinct population with their own separate activity.

Thus it appears that thymic cells are committed within the thymus to their functional characteristics and do not depend on antigen exposure for this differentiation. No series of thymic antigens analogous to the Ly system has been described in man.

B CELLS

The use of specific T cell membrane markers to follow embryonic development is a relatively new technic. B cell development has been somewhat easier to study since these cells possess specific cell surface markers (eg, membrane immunoglobulin) which have been more intensively investigated. The first animal model in which it was possible to distinguish between T and B cells was the chicken, and this model will be discussed in some detail.

Bursa of Fabricius

The avian bursa performs a maturation function for B cells analogous to the function of the thymus in the maturation of T cells. The bursa arises from epithelial tissues in the region of the cloaca and–somewhat like the thymus–is seeded or infiltrated by stem cells migrating from yolk sac and hepatic sources. With rapid proliferation of these stem cells, the bursa becomes a lymphoid organ during the 13th–19th days of the 21-day embryonic development (8 days prior to hatching). Membrane-bound IgM is the first immunoglobulin to be detected on bursal lymphoid cells. Several days later, IgG can be found on a few cells. As the lymphoid cells mature, they leave the bursa and relocate in peripheral tissues; if peripheral lymphocytes are tested for membrane immunoglobulin, the order in which they appear in these distal sites is found to be similar to that in which they developed within the bursa (IgM→IgG→IgA).

If the bursal tissue is surgically removed prior to the migration of postbursal cells to peripheral lymphoid tissue, the hatched chicken will be immunodeficient. It will not have B cells or plasma cells in its spleen or lymph nodes, and the chicken will be hypogammaglobulinemic all of its life. However, if bursectomy is performed after the migration of postbursal cells to peripheral tissue, the peripheral B cells continue to increase in number. The chicken will develop tissue plasma cells and serum immunoglobulins, and it will retain apparently normal immune function for months to years. Bursectomy can also be done during the sequential maturation steps of surface immunoglobulin. Bursectomy after the development of IgM but before the appearance of surface IgG stops

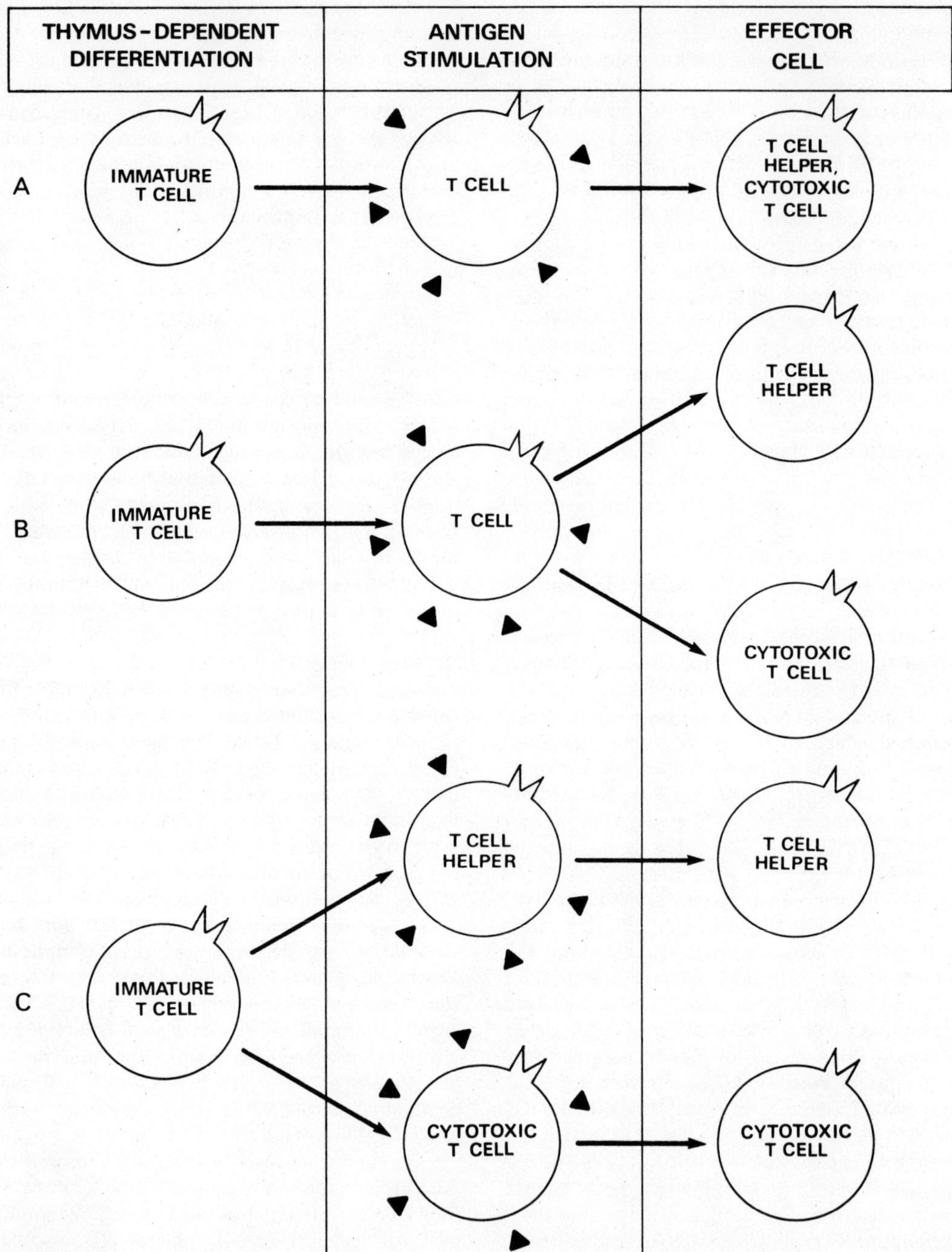

Figure 11–4. Several alternative maturation schemes have been proposed to account for the diversity of T cell functions. *A:* After stimulation by antigen, a single T cell mediates all T cell functions. *B:* After stimulation by antigen, a single T cell precursor generates progeny with different functional capacities. *C:* During differentiation but prior to exposure to antigen, precursor cells produce progeny committed to different functional capacities. (Modified and reproduced, with permission, from Cantor H, Boyse EA: J Exp Med 141:1376, 1975.)

further differentiation. Such chickens demonstrate only IgM lymphocytes in their peripheral lymphoid tissues and will produce only serum IgM in response to vigorous immunization. Bursectomy done at or soon after hatching (when the maturation sequence has further progressed) frequently leaves the bird unable to develop an IgA response but with nearly normal IgM and IgG antibody responses. Such data have been interpreted to indicate 2 important points: (1) the bursa is the only tissue in chickens to produce or influence the differentiation and maturation of B cells; and (2) when a bursal lymphocyte is mature enough to leave that tissue for peripheral sites, it is already committed to the production of a single class of immunoglobulin.

Several theories have been advanced to explain the sequence of events in the bursa which lead to this restricted expression of membrane and functional immunoglobulin production. These theories will be discussed in a later section, but it should be noted here that exposure of the bursal tissue to antigen does not appear to accelerate or otherwise alter the maturation process.

Human B Cell Development

Because the bursa is such an important organ in the differentiation of B lymphocytes, it is not surprising that considerable effort has been expended in an effort to identify the equivalent bursal site in humans. In man—indeed, in all mammals—it has been impossible thus far to clearly identify the anatomic site where B cell maturation occurs. Early investigators tested the appendix, the sacculus, and Peyer's patches as plausible sites, but current evidence favors the bone marrow or fetal liver and spleen as the most likely site of the bursa equivalent in mammals.

In man, the first lymphocytes to demonstrate membrane immunoglobulin are cells bearing IgM or IgG which develop in the fetal liver at about 9½ weeks of gestation. Cells with membrane IgA are noted at about 11½ weeks, and after this time IgM, IgG, and IgA cells become detectable in the liver, spleen, thymus, and peripheral blood. Extensive proliferation of these cells results in an increase of B cells such that by 15 weeks the proportion of immunoglobulin present on B cells is similar to that found in a full-term infant. Plasma cells are rare, however, and normally very few fetal cells actively produce antibodies. In man, as in the chicken, the maturation sequence IgM→IgG→IgA is present.

Two other immunoglobulin classes are present in man (IgD and IgE), but very little is known concerning their expression or maturation during fetal development. When fetal lymphocytes from cord blood are examined for membrane immunoglobulin, about 10% of the cells have IgM, about 8% have IgG, and less than 2% show IgA. Of interest, however, is the finding that many fetal B cells stain for IgD. Cells frequently show dual staining for IgD and IgM, and the temporal expression of IgD raises the possibility that it represents a "fetal" immunoglobulin analogous to fetal hemoglobin. This question is presently unresolved.

Murine B Cell Development

Despite the immense amount of information that has been accumulated on mouse embryology, it has not been possible to clearly identify tissue representing a bursa equivalent. Preliminary evidence implicated gut-associated lymphoid tissue or bone marrow sites as regions involved in B cell induction, but surgical removal of this gut tissue or destruction of bone marrow with radioisotopes during embryonic development fails to block B cell differentiation.

Immunofluorescence studies on the chronologic development of lymphocytes with membrane immunoglobulin would suggest that the fetal liver and spleen are the sites of earliest B cell induction and that these tissues may be the bursa equivalent. Mouse fetal liver and spleen have been surgically removed and small portions of the tissue grown in tissue culture. Cells with surface immunoglobulin were detected in these extracorporeal fetal organ cultures. Initially, cells bearing IgM surface immunoglobulin were detected and followed by IgG-bearing cells a few days later. IgA-positive cells were found after 7 days in culture. This suggested that the fetal liver and spleen promote the in vitro induction of lymphocyte maturation.

Since a specific bursa-like organ has not been identified, it has not been possible to surgically remove the stimulus for B cell differentiation and demonstrate the sequential maturation (IgM → IgG → IgA) of lymphocytes as shown in the chicken. Attempts to halt lymphocyte maturation by other methods have produced interesting results. Heterologous antisera for specific immunoglobulin classes have been injected into fetal mice in an attempt to suppress that specific class of maturing antibody. When anti-IgM was used to suppress cells expressing this heavy chain class on their surface, nearly complete suppression of B cell maturation was demonstrated. Lymph nodes from these mice contained greatly reduced or absent germinal centers, and B cells were absent or greatly reduced in the spleen. Serum immunoglobulin was also depressed. These mice had little or no immunoglobulin production when immunized with potent immunogens even if adjuvant was also used. T cells functioned as expected and did not appear to be reduced in these B cell-suppressed animals.

Experiments to demonstrate selective suppression of IgA or IgG have been more difficult to perform for a variety of technical considerations. Complete IgG blocking was difficult to achieve, but a few such mice have been studied. These mice also lacked IgA lymphocytes. Mice injected with IgA-suppressing antiserum demonstrated variable degrees of suppression, but the function of IgM and IgG did not appear to be affected.

Models of B Cell Differentiation

The three main models that have been advanced to explain the maturation of B cells are summarized in Fig 11–5. In the first model, the probursal stem cells migrate to the bursal tissue and differentiate into B cells. The sequence of maturation follows the IgM→IgA pattern, and lymphocytes that have matured to

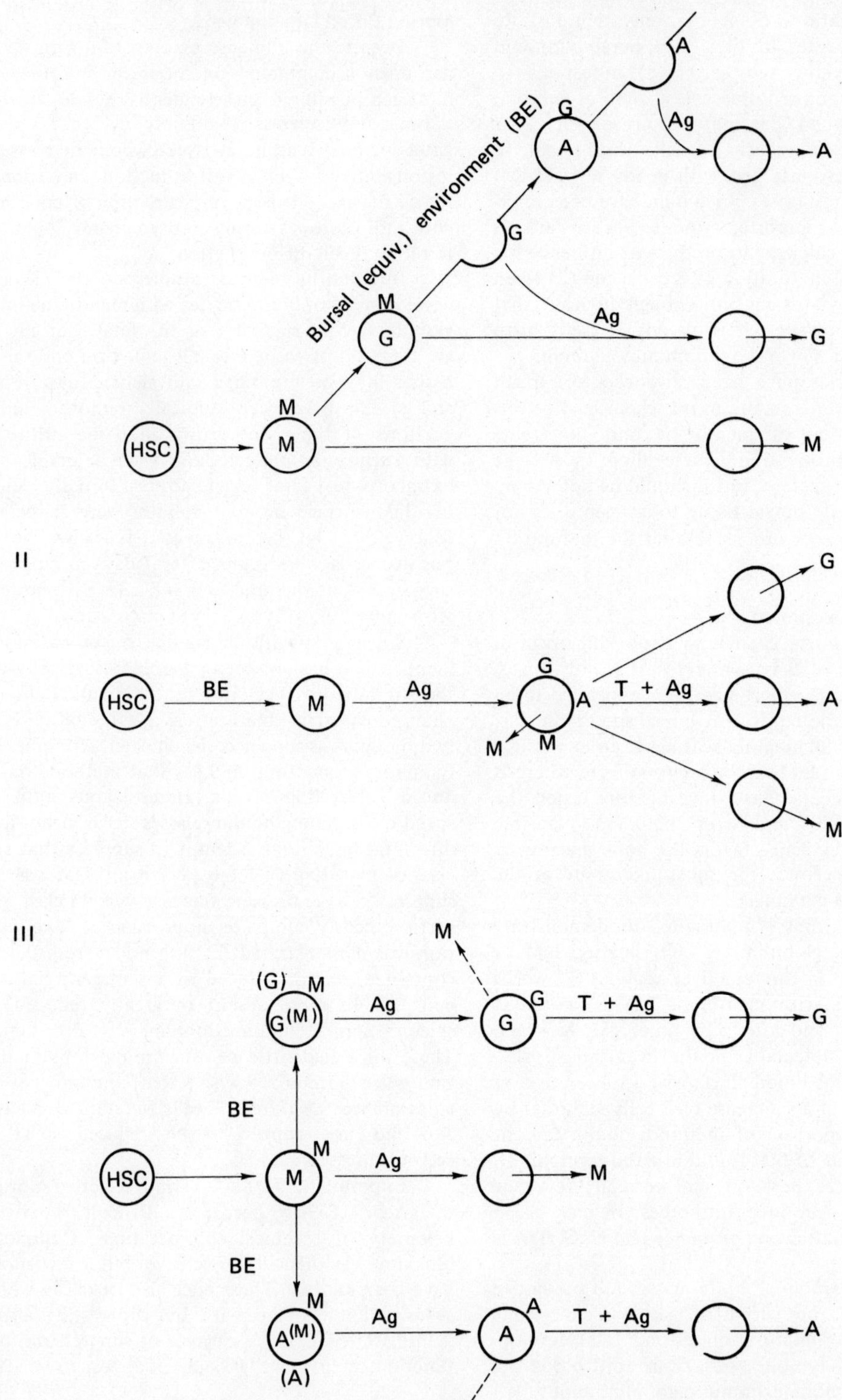

Figure 11–5. Three proposed models of B cell-to-plasma cell differentiation. Hematopoietic stem cells (HSC) under the influence of the bursal environment (BE) or antigen (AG) differentiate to plasma cells producing IgG, IgM, or IgA. Helper T cells are indicated by the letter T. G, A, and M represent IgG, IgA, or IgM molecules present on cell surface or within cell cytoplasm. (See text for additional discussion.) (Reproduced, with permission, from Warner NL: Membrane immunoglobulins and antigen receptors on B and T lymphocytes. Adv Immunol 19:153, 1974.)

one immunoglobulin type may still possess membrane immunoglobulin of the preceding class (ie, an IgG-committed cell may still have some IgM on its surface). This allows for the small percentage of cells known to stain for 2 immunoglobulin classes. These cells are continuously leaving the bursal environment and localizing in peripheral lymphoid tissues. When these cells are exposed to antigen, they respond with production of plasma cells limited to secretion of a single class of antibody.

In the second model of B cell differentiation, the antibody-producing plasma cells originate from a multipotential B cell. In this model, it is antigen that initiates the maturational expression of different heavy chain classes. Thus, cells destined to produce IgG or IgA could result from lymphocytes expressing only IgM on their surface, whereas model I would require the cell to have membrane immunoglobulin of the same heavy class it was destined to produce.

A third model has lymphocytes randomly selected for IgM, IgG, or IgA production, with most of these cells still retaining IgM as their major surface immunoglobulin. Upon exposure to antigen, these cells secrete first IgM and then are further maturated into IgG- or IgA-secreting cells. An enormous quantity of experimental data has been generated in an attempt to clarify the precise maturation sequence of these cells, but no clear preference for one model over the other has emerged.

Maturation of Functional Lymphocytes

Although the development of B and T cells appears to progress rapidly during embryonic growth, one must not conclude that the fetus is able to mount a vigorous immune response to extrinsic antigen. The development of the functional capacity of fetal immune responses is under intensive investigation. For example, newborn mice are unable to produce humoral antibody to ordinary antigenic stimulation during the first few days after birth. All of the morphologic cell types needed for immune responses have been identified, but they lack the ability to function actively as lymphoid cells. This may be secondary to delayed maturation of additional membrane receptors. These additional membrane components may be required for cell-to-cell interaction or reaction with processed antigenic determinants.

Increasing numbers of different membrane markers and receptors are being identified. Some of the latter (Fc receptor, complement receptor, etc) may reach functional maturity at widely variable times compared to the membrane markers and thereby limit functional capacity. In addition, immunization of the immature animal frequently results in antibody production of a more restricted response than is present in immunized adult animals. Since the B cells divide and produce antibody, heterogeneity of antibodies resulting from immunization can be roughly considered to reflect the degree of capacity of mature B lymphocytes. Fetal and newborn mice produce small antibody populations which are quite restricted in terms of heterogeneity. Maturation of the B system to produce a heterogeneous adult type immune response occurs initially at 1–2 weeks of age.

THYMIC HUMORAL FACTORS

Transplantation of syngeneic thymus tissue into neonatally thymectomized mice can restore immunocompetence. Humoral factors derived from the thymus can also partially restore the same type of immunocompetence. This has been demonstrated by subcutaneous implantation of thymus grafts enclosed in a semipermeable chamber. Later experiments have used isolated and purified thymic extracts to achieve similar restorative effects.

In humans, evidence for the existence of thymic humoral factors has only recently been obtained. A single patient with the DiGeorge syndrome received a thymus graft enclosed in a semipermeable chamber and subsequently developed normal cellular immunity. Patients with primary immunodeficiencies have demonstrated enhanced T cell function both in vivo and in vitro following administration of the thymic humoral substance *thymosin.*

A listing and characterization of the major humoral factors present in the thymus is presented in Table 11–3. It is apparent that many of these factors share certain properties which may result from their relative impurity.

Thymosin

A protein with lymphocytopoietic capacity was originally obtained from bovine thymus extracts. Currently, thymosin is obtained from thymic homogenates by acetone and ammonium sulfate precipitation followed by gel filtration. The major biologic activity is present in so-called fraction 5. A wide variety of immunologic properties have been associated with thymosin (Table 11–3). Direct assay procedures for thymosin are not available. However, using a sheep red cell rosette enhancement assay, serum thymosin levels have been shown to decrease with age and following thymectomy. Serum thymosin activity is reduced in severe combined immunodeficiency disease and in the DiGeorge syndrome. Studies of in vitro activity of thymosin in man have shown an increase in number of bone marrow cells reacting with antithymocyte antibody and an increased response of bone marrow cells to PHA and, to a lesser extent, to ConA. In some immunodeficiency disorders, thymosin used in vitro can increase depressed E rosettes, PHA response, and responses to allogeneic cells (MLC). Treatment of some immunodeficient patients with thymosin has enhanced T cell-mediated immunity. It has been postulated that the major effect of thymosin is to enhance maturation of prothymocytes to mature T cells.

Thymopoietin

This substance was originally termed "thymin"

Table 11–3. Properties and biologic activities of thymic humoral factors.

Substance	Molecular Weight	Characteristics	Biologic Activities
Thymosin	12,000	Protein	Restores T cell immunity following thymectomy in mice. Increases number of bone marrow cells with Thy-1 marker. Increases helper T cells, GVH, and MLC activity in mice. Decreases autoantibody in NZB/NZW mice. Increases T cells, PHA, and MLC activity in vivo and in vitro in man.
Thymoprotein I and II	7000	Protein	Impairs neuromuscular transmission. Increases number of bone marrow cells with Thy-1 marker.
Thymic factor	1000	Peptide	Increases Thy-1 antigen and ConA reactivity in mouse marrow cells. Increases intracellular cAMP.
Thymic humoral factor	>700–<5000	Polypeptide	Increases MLC reaction in mice. Increases GVH activity in mice. Increases intracellular cAMP. Increases T and B cell cooperation in antibody production. Decreases wasting disease following neonatal thymectomy. Is lymphocytopoietic. Restores ability to reject tumor and skin graft following thymectomy.
Thymic replacing factor	45,000–60,000	(Unknown)	(Unknown)
Lymphocyte-stimulating hormone			
LSHh	15,000	Protein	Increase plaque-forming cells and antibody responses in mice.
LSHr	60,000	Protein	

and was isolated from animals with autoimmune thymitis and myasthenia. Thymopoietin can result in impaired neuromuscular transmission and is presumably produced by thymic epithelial cells. It can be extracted from normal thymus by saline. Thymopoietin induced bone marrow cells to acquire the Thy-1 antigen and responsiveness to ConA. Its in vitro effects in humans are not well defined.

Thymic Factor

This low-molecular-weight peptide is thought to be secreted by thymic epithelial cells. Humoral biologic activities have been demonstrated using thymic factor in vitro. Thymic factor is capable of enhancing the rejection of Moloney virus-induced sarcomas in thymectomized mice, increasing Thy-1 antigen and ConA responsiveness of bone marrow cells and increasing cAMP levels within cells. Thymic factor levels have been assayed using a mouse rosette assay and found to be reduced in nude mice, systemic lupus erythematosus, T cell immunodeficiency, and aged humans. In vitro studies in man have not been performed.

Thymic Humoral Factor

A polypeptide has been isolated from mouse and calf thymus capable of preventing wasting disease, restoring GVH activity, and enhancing the ability to reject tumor and skin grafts in neonatally thymectomized mice. In the mouse, thymic humoral factor also increases the cooperative effect between T and B cells in antibody production and produces increased intracellular levels of cAMP. Thymic humoral factor has not been studied in vitro in man.

Thymic Replacing Factor

Following stimulation of T cells by histocompatibility factors or mitogens, a substance is produced which will restore the immune responsiveness of T cell-deprived cultures. Thymic replacing factor is not antigen-specific. It is estimated to have a molecular weight between 45,000 and 60,000.

Lymphocyte-Stimulating Hormone

Two substances obtained from calf thymus have been described which have the capacity to cause lymphocytopoiesis. The first, LSHh, has a molecular weight of approximately 15,000. The second, LSHr, has a molecular weight of approximately 80,000. Both LSHh and LSHr enhance the formation of plaque-forming cells and antibody titers and are lymphocytopoietic.

HUMAN FETAL COMPLEMENT DEVELOPMENT

During cellular development, there is a corresponding growth of other components of the immune system. Hemolytic complement is present in human fetal cord serum at birth. Cord serum levels of total complement activity and specific complement proteins (C3, C4, and C5) appear to be lower than maternal levels. Fetal production of specific complement proteins has been demonstrated by a variety of methods. Some complement proteins are genetically polymorphic, and typing of maternal and fetal molecules has shown genetic discordance. Furthermore, C2 has been detected in the cord serum of an infant born to a mother deficient in C2. Production of C3, C5, and C1 inactivator by hepatic cells and of C1 by columnar epithelium of the colon has been demonstrated by autoradiographic technics and functional assays.

DEVELOPMENT OF IMMUNOGLOBULINS IN HUMAN SERUM

The development of membrane immunoglobulin has already been discussed; less information is available on the synthesis of circulating serum antibodies. Spleen cell cultures from fetuses of gestational age 13–31 weeks have demonstrated IgM and IgG synthesis at 20 weeks. The cultures were supplemented with radioactive amino acids, and the labeled proteins were detected by radioimmunoelectrophoresis. No IgA or IgD synthesis was noted. Other workers have noted evidence for serum IgM synthesis as early as 10½ weeks and for serum IgG synthesis as early as 12 weeks. Production of fetal immunoglobulins has also been supported by the demonstration of paternal immunoglobulin allotypic determinants absent in maternal blood but present in the cord serum of newborns. Maternal immunization to fetal allotypic determinants of paternal origin in the seventh month of pregnancy has also been reported.

The pattern of serum immunoglobulin development can be altered considerably by intrauterine infections. Plasma cell maturation, normally absent in the term fetus, can occur as early as the second trimester in spleen and other organs of fetuses infected with Treponema or Toxoplasma organisms. Measles infection in utero also results in production of increased amounts of circulating immunoglobulin. In summary, while fetal immunoglobulin synthesis is normally not very active by term, a small amount of fetal immunoglobulin is present and this amount can be greatly increased under conditions of appropriate in utero stimulation.

• • •

References

Phylogeny

Cooper EL (editor): *Contemporary Topics in Immunobiology.* Vol 4: *Invertebrate Immunology.* Plenum Press, 1974.

Du Pasquier L: Ontogeny of the immune response in cold-blooded vertebrates. Curr Top Microbiol Immunol 61:37, 1973.

Hildemann WH: Some new concepts in immunologic phylogeny. Nature 250:116, 1974.

Hildemann WH, Reddy AL: Phylogeny of immune responsiveness: Marine invertebrates. Fed Proc 32:2188, 1973.

Marchalonis JJ, Cone RE: The phylogenetic emergence of vertebrate immunity. Aust J Exp Biol Med Sci 51:461, 1973.

Smith RT, Miescher PA, Good RA (editors): *Phylogeny of Immunity.* Univ of Florida Press, 1966.

Ontogeny

Boyse EA, Abbott J: Surface reorganization as an initial inductive event in the differentiation of prothymocytes to thymocytes. Fed Proc 34:24, 1975.

Cantor H, Boyse EA: Functional subclasses of T lymphocytes bearing different Ly antigens. 1. The generation of functionally distinct T cell subclasses as a differentiative process independent of antigen. J Exp Med 141:1376, 1975.

Cantor H, Boyse EA: Functional subclasses of T lymphocytes bearing different Ly antigens. 2. Cooperation between subclasses of Ly+ cells in the generation of killer activity. J Exp Med 141:1390, 1975.

Cooper MD, Lawton AR: The development of the immune system. Sci Am 230:58, Dec 1974.

Friedman H (editor): Thymus factors in immunity. Ann NY Acad Sci 249:1–547, 1975. [Entire issue.]

Lawton AR, Kincade PW, Cooper MD: Sequential expression of germ line genes in development of immunoglobulin class diversity. Fed Proc 34:33, 1975.

Miller RG, Phillips RA: Development of B lymphocytes. Fed Proc 34:145, 1975.

Mosier DE, Cohen PL: Ontogeny of mouse T lymphocyte function. Fed Proc 34:137, 1975.

Shiku H & others: Expression of T cell differentiation antigens of effector cells in cell-mediated cytotoxicity in vitro. J Exp Med 141:227, 1975.

Stites DP & others: Ontogeny of immunity in humans. Clin Immunol Immunopathol 4:519, 1975.

Warner NL: Membrane immunoglobulins and antigen receptors on B and T lymphocytes. Adv Immunol 19:67, 1974.

Weissman IL & others: Differentiation of thymus cells. Fed Proc 34:141, 1975.

12 . . . Genetic Regulation of Immune Responses

Joseph L. Caldwell, MD

Animals vary greatly in their individual immune responses to specific antigens. Multiple factors are known to contribute to this variability of responsiveness, including the type of antigen, quantity of antigen, route of immunization, presence of adjuvant, and age and health of recipient. In addition, there is evidence for a series of genetic loci which greatly limit or modify the strength and character of the immune response to a variety of synthetic and natural antigens. Those immune response genes associated with the major histocompatibility complex (MHC) have been the most extensively investigated, but other loci not associated with the MHC are also known to modify immune responses. An increasing number of antigens have been used to demonstrate genetic control of a particular immune response, but in general these antigens can be divided into 3 categories of immunogens: weakly immunogenic alloantigens, minimal immunizing amounts of more complex protein antigens, and defined synthetic antigens usually prepared from polymers of L-amino acids. Variations in antibody responses in the guinea pig to L-amino acid polymers were among the first genetically controlled responses to be studied in detail and we shall consider these data first.

GUINEA PIG IMMUNE RESPONSE GENES LINKED TO THE MAJOR HISTOCOMPATIBILITY COMPLEX

When a group of randomly bred guinea pigs were immunized with a series of synthetic polypeptide antigens, striking variations were noted in the antibody responses of individual animals. Most of the guinea pigs produced vigorous circulating antibody responses, had positive skin tests to the antigens, and responded with acute anaphylactic responses after subsequent intravenous administration of antigen. Some animals failed to produce a response to the antigen, however, and subsequent breeding studies with these animals suggested that the control of the immune response was determined by a single genetic locus.

Joseph L. Caldwell is Assistant Research Immunologist, University of California School of Medicine and Veterans Administration Hospital, San Francisco.

Differences Among Guinea Pig Strains

Immunization experiments with similar antigens in 2 inbred strains of guinea pigs helped clarify the interpretation of these data. The 2 inbred strains (strain 2 and strain 13) were mated and the F_1 (first generation) hybrids as well as the original strains were immunized with dinitrophenyl conjugates of 3 synthetic antigens. The carrier molecules for the haptens were linear polymers of L-lysine (PLL), glutamic acid and alanine (GA), or glutamic acid and tyrosine (GT). The relationship between carrier and hapten in the composition of an antigen has been discussed in Chapter 3. The antihapten antibody responses elicited are summarized in Table 12–1. The results show that immune responsiveness to specific antigens was limited to certain strains of guinea pigs and that the ability to respond to the antigen seemed to be transmitted to the F_1 hybrid as a dominant trait. There was also evidence that more than one genetic locus might control the response to different antigens.

It was not clear if this selective response was the result of certain strains not recognizing either the carrier molecule or the haptenic determinant, so a series of other haptens were conjugated to poly-L-lysine and used to immunize a group of randomly bred guinea pigs. These animals were similar to the ones employed in the original experiments. The differential antibody responses documented that it was the *carrier* and not the haptenic group which determined immune responsiveness. A particular guinea pig would either react to the poly-L-lysine conjugate and produce antibodies against all of the haptens, or no response would occur. This genetic locus was named the PLL locus, and

Table 12–1. Antihapten antibody responses to dinitrophenyl (DNP) polypeptide conjugates in inbred guinea pigs.*

Antigen	Strain 2	Strain 13	F_1 Hybrid
DNP-PLL	+	–	+
DNP-GA	+	–	+
DNP-GT	–	+	+

*Results combined from several experimental sources. +, response; –, no response.

guinea pigs were classified as either responder (strain 2) or nonresponder (strain 13) animals based on their immune responses to this antigen. Responses to other amino acid polymers (poly-L-ornithine and poly-L-arginine) were also found to be under the control of the PLL locus.

Linkage to Histocompatibility Genes

When the strain 2 X strain 13 F_1 hybrids were back-crossed with a parental strain, evidence for linkage of the response gene to the histocompatibility region was obtained (Fig 12–1). The F_1 hybrids were mated to strain 13 animals, and all animals possessing the strain 2 histocompatibility antigens produced a positive response to immunization with poly-L-lysine antigens. None of the animals possessing strain 13 histocompatibility antigens responded to these polypeptides. These results for histocompatibility linkage supported data previously obtained in inbred strains of mice (see later discussion).

There had been previous evidence for several immune response genes—one locus regulating the positive response for glutamic acid-tyrosine polymers in strain 13 animals and one regulating a positive response for poly-L-lysine and glutamic acid-alanine polymers in strain 2 animals. Both of these genes had been shown to be linked to the histocompatibility complex of the guinea pig. A synthetic polymer of L-glutamic acid, L-alanine, and L-tyrosine (GAT) was prepared and tested in both strains. This antigen is more complex in that it contains both GA and GT determinants. Both strain 2 and strain 13 animals made antibodies which reacted with this antigen. A surprising finding, however, was the demonstration that the strain 13 animals (normally unresponsive to the GA determinants) produced anti-GAT antibodies which did not bind the simple GA polymer. Thus, an immune response against the complex GAT antigen had been induced by the immunization procedure, but the immune regulation present in the strain 13 guinea pigs had resulted in antibodies capable of recognizing only GT determinants present on the larger GAT antigen. There is evidence in other species with other antigens to support this concept of selective recognition of determinants present on complex molecules. There is also limited evidence that this carrier gene effect may limit the selection or expression of antibody diversity.

Since immune response genes seemed to be linked to histocompatibility antigens, there was some question concerning their physical association on the membrane surface of cells participating in immune responses. Alloantisera against strain 2 or strain 13 histocompatibility antigens were tested to note their effects on the in vitro responses of lymphocytes to antigens. The alloantisera had been carefully absorbed to remove activity directed against immunoglobulins. Part of the results of such studies are shown in Table 12–2. Although the data in this table are greatly simplified from the actual data, the blocking of in vitro cell responses seemed to relate the particular histocompatibility antigen to the immune response and blocking activity appropriate for that strain. Since the animals were F_1 hybrids previously immunized against both antigens, the expected in vitro response was stimulation with the addition of antigen. With the addition of normal serum, there was no blocking of the stimulation resulting from either antigen. When anti-strain 2 antiserum (strain 2 is a responder to GL—a polymer of glutamic acid and lysine—but not to GT—a polymer of glutamic acid and tyrosine) was added to the culture, it blocked only the response to the GL antigen but not to the GT antigen. When anti-strain 13 alloantiserum was added to the cultures, the opposite results were obtained (strain 13 is a responder to GT but not to GL). Thus, antibodies to specific guinea pig strains were able to block the antigen receptors for antigens controlled by immune response genes, and this suggested that these receptors were physically close to each other on the lymphocyte membrane.

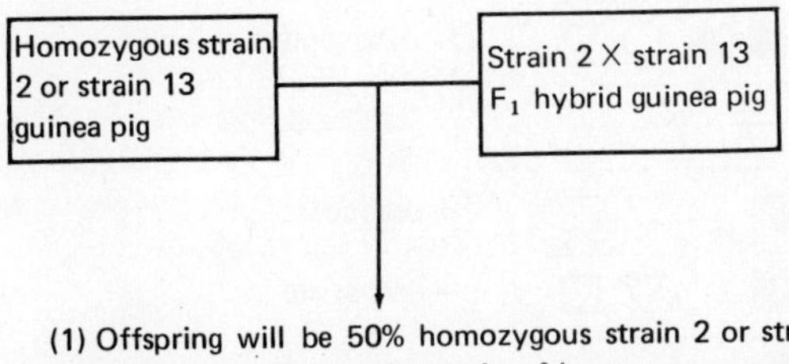

Homozygous strain 2 or strain 13 guinea pig

Strain 2 X strain 13 F_1 hybrid guinea pig

(1) Offspring will be 50% homozygous strain 2 or strain 13 guinea pigs depending on the strain of homozygous parent.

(2) Remaining 50% of offspring will be strain 2 X strain 13 hybrids.

Figure 12–1. Homozygous strain 2 or strain 13 guinea pigs were mated with F_1 hybrids between these 2 strains, and the resulting offspring were tested for immune responsiveness to synthetic antigens. The ability to respond to specific antigens was found to be linked to strain histocompatibility genes, and homozygous offspring could respond only if they carried the appropriate histocompatibility antigens.

Table 12–2. Effect of suppression by alloantisera on in vitro lymphocyte responses in F_1 hybrid (2 X 13) guinea pigs.*

Alloantisera Added to Culture	Lymphocyte Response To	
	DNP-GL	GT
Normal serum	Stimulation	Stimulation
Anti-strain 2	Blocked	Stimulation
Anti-strain 13	Stimulation	Blocked

*Modified and reproduced, with permission, from McDevitt HO, Landy M (editors): *Genetic Control of Immune Responsiveness.* Academic Press, 1972. Lymphocyte stimulation was measured by tritiated thymidine incorporation. The expected response was stimulation in all cultures, but alloantisera blocked some responses. DNP-GL is dinitrophenyl-conjugated glutamic acid-lysine polymer, and GT is glutamic acid-tyrosine polymer.

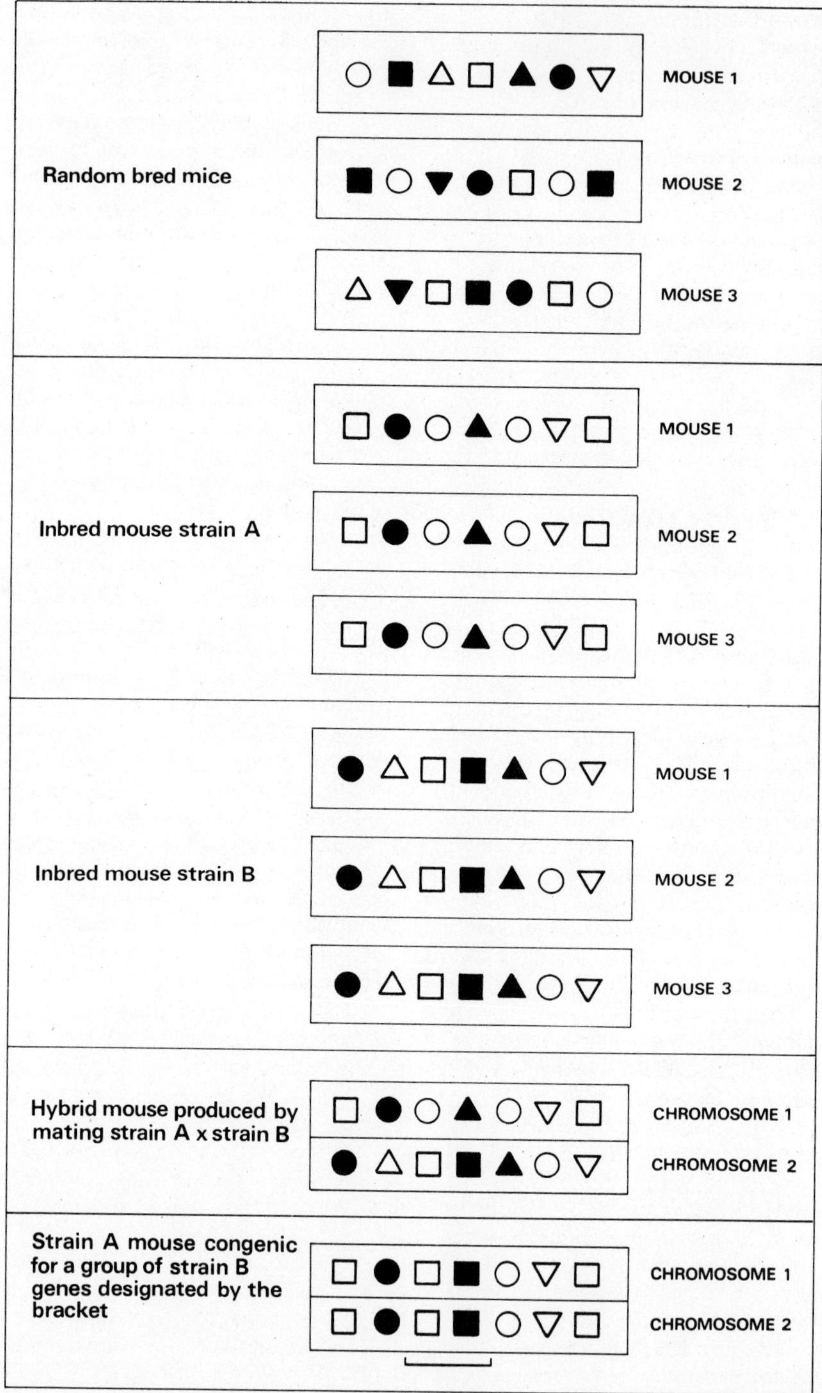

Figure 12–2. Randomly bred mice may vary widely from mouse to mouse when compared for specific genetic loci, represented by symbols within the bars. By extensive inbreeding, it is possible to secure inbred mouse strains which genetically may differ considerably from strain to strain but which are the same within a particular strain. Individual homozygous mice within a specific inbred strain are considered to possess the same genetic composition. Since mice have duplicate chromosomes, when an F_1 hybrid mouse is prepared by mating 2 inbred strains, one chromosome will contain the genes from each inbred strain. Congenic mice are homozygous mice containing all of the genes of one strain except for a specific locus or group of genes derived from a different strain.

MURINE IMMUNE RESPONSE GENES LINKED TO THE MAJOR HISTOCOMPATIBILITY LOCUS

Although considerable information has been obtained from experiments with guinea pigs, the larger number of genetically defined inbred strains of mice has allowed a far more detailed analysis of the location and mechanism of histocompatibility-linked immunoregulatory genes. However, at this point it is necessary to introduce a more detailed explanation of what constitutes an inbred mouse strain and, more importantly, to explain inbreeding and the concepts of congenic and recombinant mice.

Inbred Mice

A randomly bred mouse contains a heterogeneous complement of genes derived from the general gene pool of the breeding population. If one compares 2 such mice, a large number of genetic differences will be apparent between the 2 animals. This condition is represented in Fig 12–1 by the different symbols present in the bar. If such mice are progressively inbred, the variation in genetic composition decreases and the mice become more and more alike in genetic content. In other words, in a highly inbred mouse strain the chances are great that all mice of that strain are genetically identical. There are many such inbred strains and there are marked genetic differences among strains, but there is genetic uniformity within a strain (represented in Fig 12–2 by bars containing similar symbols).

The histocompatibility antigens of these different strains can be determined by assaying with specific antisera directed at histocompatibility antigens. These antisera detect antigenic markers present on cell membranes, and they have been assigned numerical designations or symbols. The transplantation antigens of the mouse are complex and numerous, and over 50 different serologic specificities have been described and assigned numbers. Not all specificities are present in any one strain, but any particular strain of inbred mouse inherits a specific group of antigens. Since the genes controlling these membrane markers are inherited as a group, however, it has become standard to assign a letter symbol to represent the entire H-2 histocompatibility complex. Thus, a series of serologic specificities, inherited as a group within a particular inbred strain of mouse, can be referred to by a simple letter symbol. Some of the antigenic specificities are listed in Table 12–3 along with the letter representing that genetic region. Thus, mice with the H-2^a histocompatibility complex will express the transplantation antigens listed in the first row. In addition, they will possess other genetic loci normally found in this region of the chromosome.

Congenic Mice

Each mouse has 2 chromosomes for each histocompatibility region, one from each parent, and a hybrid mouse from 2 inbred mouse strains will share

Table 12–3. Some antigenic specificities of the principal H-2 types.*

H-2 Symbol	H-2 Specificities
a	1 – 3 4 5 6 8 – 23 – – – – 35 36
b	– 2 – – 5 6 – – – – – – 33 35 36
d	– – 3 4 – 6 8 – – – 31 – – 35 36
k	1 – 3 – 5 – 8 – 23 – – 32 – – –
q	1 – 3 – 5 6 – 17 – 30 – – – – –

*Reproduced, with permission, from McDevitt HO, Landy M (editors): *Genetic Control of Immune Responsiveness*. Academic Press, 1972.

the genetic complement of both strains. This situation is represented in Fig 12–2 by the 2 bars filled with light and dark symbols from each of the 2 parental strains. If a particular genetic region is selected for the preparation of a congenic mouse (the H-2 histocompatibility region, for example), the hybrid mouse is back-crossed many times to the desired background strain and progeny with the desired characteristic are selected after each back-cross. Normal crossing over of chromosomal segments during meiotic division will result in the gradual exchange of undesired segments of the hybrid animal and lead to a mouse that is different from the background strain only in the desired genetic trait or traits. (This is obviously a very simple description of the actual process.) The importance of such mice is that they allow the chromosomal localization of genes which affect the characteristic under study, particularly if a genetic recombination or crossover occurs. Recombinant mice result when there is chromosomal recombination within the specific genetic region of interest. Congenic mice are diagrammatically represented in Fig 12–2.

Description of H-2 Locus

The MHC of the mouse is located on the 17th chromosome and is called the H-2 complex. This complex is diagrammed in Fig 12–3 and has been divided into 4 main regions: K, I, S, and D. These regions will be briefly discussed below.

A. K and D Regions: The K and D regions code for the so-called serologically defined transplantation antigens present on the membranes of all mouse cells. As previously mentioned, these polymorphic antigens are numerous, and each inbred mouse strain possesses a distinctive pattern of antigens. The antigens appear to be glycoproteins with a molecular weight of about 45,000 with one or 2 attached polysaccharides. The antigenic portion of the molecule is apparently determined by the protein structure and not by the sugar groups. Two separate molecules–one carrying specificities determined by the K region and one with specificities determined by the D region–can be isolated from cell membranes by physicochemical means. If the mouse is a hybrid, then 4 different molecules (2 for each chromosome) can be identified. The K and D regions form the boundaries of the H-2 complex.

B. I Region: The I region of the H-2 complex is

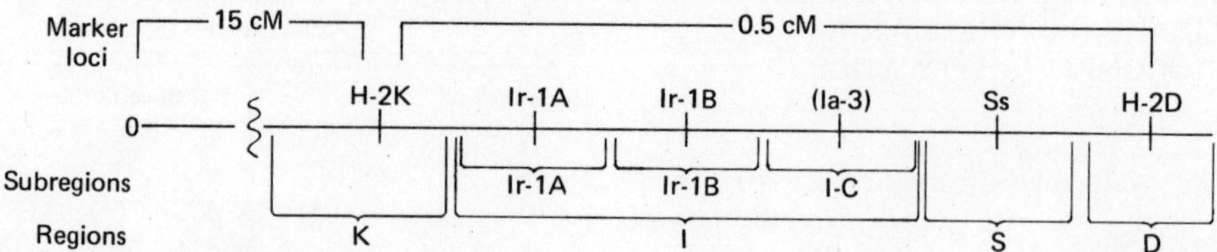

Figure 12–3. Genetic fine structure map of the *H-2* gene complex of mouse chromosome 17, showing marker loci, regions, subregions, and map distances. (cM = centiMorgan.) (Reproduced, with permission, from Shreffler DC, David CS: Adv Immunol 20:125, 1975.)

currently the subject of intensive investigation. Experimental studies using recombinant strains have localized specific immune response genes to this chromosomal region, and the I region has been subdivided into 3 parts (Ir-1A, Ir-1B, and I-C) based both on responses to antigens and responses to reactions with antisera prepared against Ia determinants. The Ia antigens (I region-associated antigens) have been defined by alloantisera prepared in recombinant mice which differ only in certain areas of the I region. The antigens are designated by numerical symbols (Ia.1, Ia.2, etc) in a manner analogous to the designation of the membrane antigens determined by the K and D regions. The Ia antigen present on the cell membrane is associated with a glycoprotein with a molecular weight of about 30,000. As with histocompatibility antigens, the Ia determinants produced by different I region subdivisions appear to be on different molecules. Present evidence indicates that Ia and histocompatibility antigens are on separate molecules. The I region is important in the cooperative response of B and T cells to antigen (see Chapter 8).

C. S Region: The S region of the H-2 complex controls the quantitative and qualitative expression of a serum β-globulin thought to be C4. Several different traits are inherited with the S region, and this region may represent several closely linked genes; however, no recombinant strain has been identified that separates these traits. The Ss trait (serum substance) controls the quantitative level of the serum β-globulin. The Slp (sex-limited protein) trait controls the expression of a testosterone-dependent allotypic marker present on the Ss protein. The Ss trait is expressed as a high or low concentration of the protein, and the Slp trait is expressed as a dominant allele determining the presence of the serologically defined marker under proper hormonal conditions. The Slp trait results in the expression of the marker on some but not all of the Ss proteins, so a mixed population of serum molecules may be present.

The Ss locus also affects the total level of serum hemolytic complement. C1, C2, and C4 activity is low in mice with the low Ss genotype. The Ss protein of the mouse has been identified as immunochemically similar to the human complement protein C4. Antisera prepared against human and mouse C4 give strong cross-reactions in agar gel diffusion assays with purified Ss protein.

H-2 Linkage of Ir Genes

Variations in immune responses to branched synthetic polypeptides have been an important laboratory tool in defining H-2-linked immune response genes. An example of one of these antigens is shown in Fig 12–4. Similar compounds have been prepared in which the poly(Tyr,Glu) or poly-D,L-Ala side chains have been varied. If polymers of tyrosine and glutamic acid are present, the compound is abbreviated (T,G)-A- -L. The terminal polymer may also be histidine and glutamic acid ([H,G]-A- -L) or phenylalanine and glutamic acid ([Phe,G]-A- -L).

When mice of the CBA strain (H-2^k) and C57 strain (H-2^b) were immunized with (T,G)-A- -L and their antibody responses examined, it became apparent that a quantitative difference existed in the immune response of these 2 strains to the same amount of antigen. The C57 response was about 10 times higher than the CBA response. When CBA × C57 hybrid mice were tested, evidence suggested that a single dominant gene controlled this trait. When (H,G)-A- -L was used as the antigen, the CBA mice produced a good immune response while the C57 mice had low antibody production. The differential responses to these 2 antigens plus (Phe,G)-A- -L are listed in Table 12–4 for a number of different H-2 haplotypes. Since the immune responsiveness to different antigens seemed to form patterns related to inheritance of specific histocompatibility complexes, it was possible to predict in different

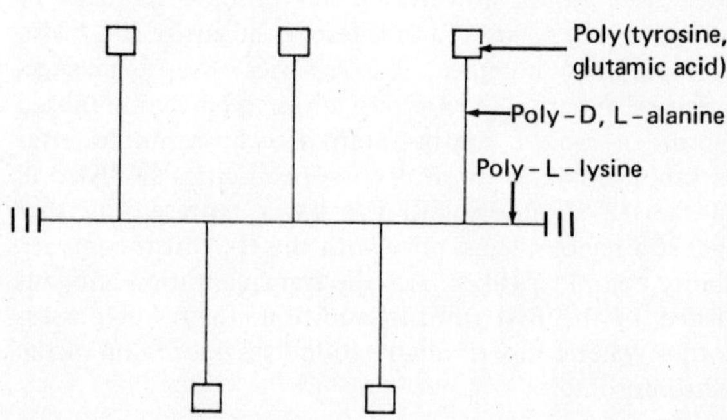

Figure 12–4. A schematic structural diagram of (T,G)-A- -L. (Reproduced, with permission, from McDevitt HO, Landy M [editors]: *Genetic Control of Immune Responsiveness.* Academic Press, 1972.)

Table 12–4. Response of inbred mouse strains, grouped by H-2 type, to a series of synthetic polypeptide antigens.*

	Antibody Response To		
H-2 Type	(T,G)-A- -L	(H,G)-A- -L	(Phe,G)-A- -L
a	Lo	Hi	Hi
b	Hi	Lo	Hi
d	Med-Var	Med-Var	Hi
k	Lo	Hi	Hi
q	Lo	Lo	Hi
s	Lo	Lo	Lo

*Reproduced, with permission, from McDevitt HO, Landy M (editors): *Genetic Control of Immune Responsiveness.* Academic Press, 1972.

inbred strains the immune response to several antigens by knowing their H-2 type and immune response to a single synthetic antigen. Such results are analogous to the variable guinea pig responses previously noted.

Since data from the guinea pig experiments suggested that immune responses to hapten-polypeptide conjugates were limited by the polypeptide carrier molecule, similar experiments were done in many mouse strains using dinitrophenyl conjugates of these peptides. The results supported the concept that an immune response gene (called Ir-1) determined the antibody response to these antigens, and the control of the response was determined by carrier molecules and not by the haptenic determinants. Similar experiments with congenic and recombinant mouse strains restricted the Ir-1 gene to the region between the K region and the S region of the H-2 complex.

Another synthetic antigen—poly-L-(phenylalanine, glutamic acid)-poly-L-proline-poly-L-lysine, or (Phe,G)-Pro-L—has helped demonstrate that genetic control can determine an immune response to a particular antigenic determinant present on a larger, more complex molecule. DBA/1 mice ($H\text{-}2^q$) immunized with this antigen produced antibody predominantly against the (Phe,G) determinant and not against the Pro-L determinant, while SJL mice ($H\text{-}2^s$) mice produced antibody against Pro-L. When the DBA/1 × SJL hybrid was tested, the genetic control of the anti-(Phe,G) response was linked to the H-2 complex while the response to Pro-L was not so linked. Thus, genes which control antibody responses to particular determinants on complex antigens may or may not be linked to H-2 genes. Immune responses to a complex antigen may be partially under H-2-linked control, but the effect of a gene causing low or no response may be masked by antibody responses to other portions of the same molecule.

Similar data in other species support the finding that preferential responses to particular antigenic determinants may be under genetic control. Antibody produced by strain 2 and strain 13 guinea pigs recognizes different antigenic portions of insulin molecules, and rabbits can have differential responses to subunits of the enzyme lactate dehydrogenase. Some rat strains also produce variable responses to subunits of this enzyme, and this regulation has been linked to the same region of the rat histocompatibility locus which controls the response to (T,G)-A- -L.

Immune regulation is not limited to synthetic antigens. A variety of naturally occurring immunogenic proteins have also been shown to elicit antibody responses controlled by genes linked to the H-2 complex. Some of these antigens and the type of response that they produce in selected H-2-defined mice are listed in Table 12–5. Data from recombinant strains have localized all currently known genetic control genes to the Ir-1A and Ir-1B subregions, but there is no reason why the I-C region may not be found to express similar control function.

Ir Control of Cell Function

Cell transfer and in vitro culture experiments have attempted to delineate the site of immune response regulation. Mouse strains which are Ir-1 and nonresponders to the antigen (T,G)-A- -L produce an IgM response that is as good as that produced by responder strains, but they fail to produce an IgG response. Potentially, the I region could affect the switch from IgM to IgG production. The nonresponder strains possess B cells able to produce IgG against the specific antigen, since these same strains can be converted to high responses by complexing the antigen to a second carrier (one which is recognized by the strain as a high-response carrier).

Table 12–5. Immune responses of independent *H-2* haplotypes to 15 antigens.*

H-2 Haplotype	IgA	IgG	Slp	LDH_B	TG	OA	OM	BGG	H-Y
b	l	h	n	h	l	h	l	l	h
d	l	l	–	h	l	h	l	l	m
f	–	h	m	h	l	–	l	–	l
j	l	–	–	l	–	h	–	–	–
k	h	l	m	l	h	l	h	h	m
n, p	m	h	–	h	m	h	–	–	l
q	l	l	h	h	h	h	l	l	m
r	h	h	–	l	–	h	–	–	m
s	h	h	–	h	h	l	l	l	–
u	–	–	–	l	–	–	–	–	–
v	l	h	–	l	–	–	–	–	–

IgA, IgG = immunoglobulin A and G myeloma protein of BALB/c origin
Slp = sex-limited protein
LDH_B = lactate dehydrogenase B isozyme
TG = thyroglobulin
OA = ovalbumin
OM = ovomucoid
BGG = bovine γ-globulin
H-Y = male histocompatibility antigen
h = high response
l = low response
m = moderate response
n = no response

*Modified and reproduced, with permission, from Shreffler DC, David CS: Adv Immunol 20:125, 1975.

Adult thymectomy can block the IgG response of a high-responder mouse, but it does not decrease the IgM response. Such mice thus resemble low-responder mice in their antibody response. Infusion of histocompatible T cells from higher-responder mice can convert a low response to a high response. Histoincompatible cells result in a GVH reaction which can also substitute for the T cell effect in converting low to high responses. Such evidence suggests that Ir gene action is exerted on T cells.

The dual response to (Phe,G) and Pro-L determinants present on the same molecule has been discussed. Only the (Phe,G) response was found to be H-2 controlled, and cell transfer experiments suggest that unresponsiveness to (Phe,G) is a defect of the T cell population while unresponsiveness to Pro-L is a defect of the B cell population.

While most evidence supports a role of Ir genes in the immune regulation of carrier protein recognition, there is also evidence for Ir gene regulation of some B cell populations (and of both T and B cells) in certain animals with specific antigens. Certainly, these genes are important in the T and B cell cooperation needed for most immune responses (see Chapter 8).

Additional Responses Under I Region Control

The antibody response to natural or synthetic antigens is not the only immune response thought to be under control of genes located in the I region. This region also affects the mixed lymphocyte culture reaction, GVH reactivity, and susceptibility to viral oncogenesis.

A. Mixed Lymphocyte Culture (MLC) Responses and GVH Reactions: When lymphocytes from 2 allogeneic strains of mice are grown together in culture, the lymphocytes undergo blastic transformation. If one group of cells is treated with x-rays or mitomycin C to prevent transformation, then the resulting one-way response can be measured by the incorporation of radioisotopes into the transforming cells. Early mouse experiments linked this lymphocyte activation response to differences in the H-2 complex, and it was thought that differences in the serologically defined transplantation antigens (determined by the K and D regions) resulted in stimulation in this assay. This is analogous to the concept that human HLA histocompatibility antigens control the lymphocyte response to foreign tissue grafts. For this reason, donor and recipient tissues in human transplantation work are matched for the serologically defined HLA antigens.

Since recombinant mouse strains are available which differ from each other only in portions of the H-2 locus, the MLC responses of cells from these mice were most informative. A number of these reactions are summarized in Table 12–6. It can be seen that differences in the serologically defined antigens yield only weak to moderate stimulation in this test. Strongest stimulation is present when the entire I region of the responding cell differs from that of the stimulating cell. Thus, it seems that the major stimulus for lymphocyte transformation in the culture assay is located in the I region, although genes controlling lower levels of response are present throughout the complex.

Table 12–6. Mixed lymphocyte culture responses of mouse lymphocytes discordant at varying portions of the H-2 locus.*

Strain Differences	Culture Response
K	Weak
D	Weak to moderate
I + S	Strong
S	Weak
I-A + I-B	Strong
I-C + S	Very weak to moderate
S + D	Very weak

*Reproduced, with permission, from Shreffler DC, David CS: Adv Immunol 20:125, 1975.

When adult lymphocytes are injected into neonatal mice, splenomegaly results which is directly related to the degree of histoincompatibility between the 2 mice. Testing of recombinant strains in the splenomegaly assay for the ability to produce GVH disease suggests that the classical histocompatibility antigens (K and D region membrane antigens) produce only moderate splenomegaly, while I region differences produce strong GVH reactions.

B. Viral Oncogenesis: The susceptibility to viral oncogenesis has been shown to be associated with certain H-2 haplotypes. For example, the ability of Gross leukemia virus to induce leukemia is determined by an H-2-associated gene *Rgv*-1 (resistance to Gross virus-1). This *Rgv*-1 gene confers resistance in mice with the H-2^k haplotype and may represent an Ir gene which influences the immune response to modified cell surface antigens resulting from viral infections. (See Chapters 17 and 21 for discussions of immune responses to infectious agents and for comments on viral antigens present on the membranes of transformed cells.) The *Rgv*-1 gene has been mapped to the K end of the H-2 complex.

An interesting in vitro model for immune responses to modified cell surface determinants has recently been described, and this model could be of use in studying the immune response to chemical- or viral-induced changes in cellular antigens. Mixed lymphocyte cultures established between lymphocytes of the same strain of mice (syngeneic cultures) should not result in blastic transformation, since both cell populations possess the same lymphocyte surface antigens. However, when cells of one population are modified by chemically conjugating the surface proteins with a hapten (dinitrophenyl groups, for example), cellular stimulation ensues with the development of cytotoxic lymphocytes directed against the hapten-modified cells. The cytotoxic lymphocytes will not lyse normal cells of that mouse strain but will kill those syngeneic cells which have been conjugated with the hapten. This cytolytic response was first considered to be hapten-specific, but later data demonstrated that the specificity involved related to the type of chemical reaction used to modify the cell.

What is more important is that repeating these culture experiments with lymphocytes from recombinant mice demonstrated that only cells which shared K or D region transplantation antigens could be lysed by the cytolytic effector cells. Preliminary evidence also suggests that the ability to recognize hapten-modified cells may be under the control of an I region gene. This cytotoxic response could not be blocked by addition to the culture of hapten-conjugated cells which differed at H-2 antigens but could be blocked by the addition of antibody against the hapten. Presumably, this antibody attaches to the hapten groups and protects them from the lytic action of the cytotoxic cells.

Such data suggest a potential model in which viral infection of cells produces antigenic alterations in membrane transplantation antigens. Genes present in the I region could modulate the response of host cells to these new determinants and induce cytotoxic lymphocytes. The cytolytic response could be modified by the presence of antiviral antibodies.

Summary of Major Histocompatibility Complex (MHC) Information

Murine immune responses to a multitude of antigens appear to be under the control of genes within the major histocompatibility complex. The traits determined by these genes are summarized in Fig 12–5. This introduction has attempted to cover the major points of what is known about this genetic region without introducing unnecessary controversial data and without resorting to complicated genetic tables. However, it is apparent that our knowledge in this area is incomplete and there are several alternative interpretations for the available data. Reviews listed in the reference section should be consulted for additional information. Most of the genes in this region control membrane proteins, and the mechanism by which these cell receptors control the response of cells to antigen exposure is unknown. Progress in this area of immunology should be rapid over the next few years.

HUMAN IMMUNE RESPONSE GENES LINKED TO THE MAJOR HISTOCOMPATIBILITY LOCUS

The amount of information available about the major histocompatibility locus of man (HLA) and

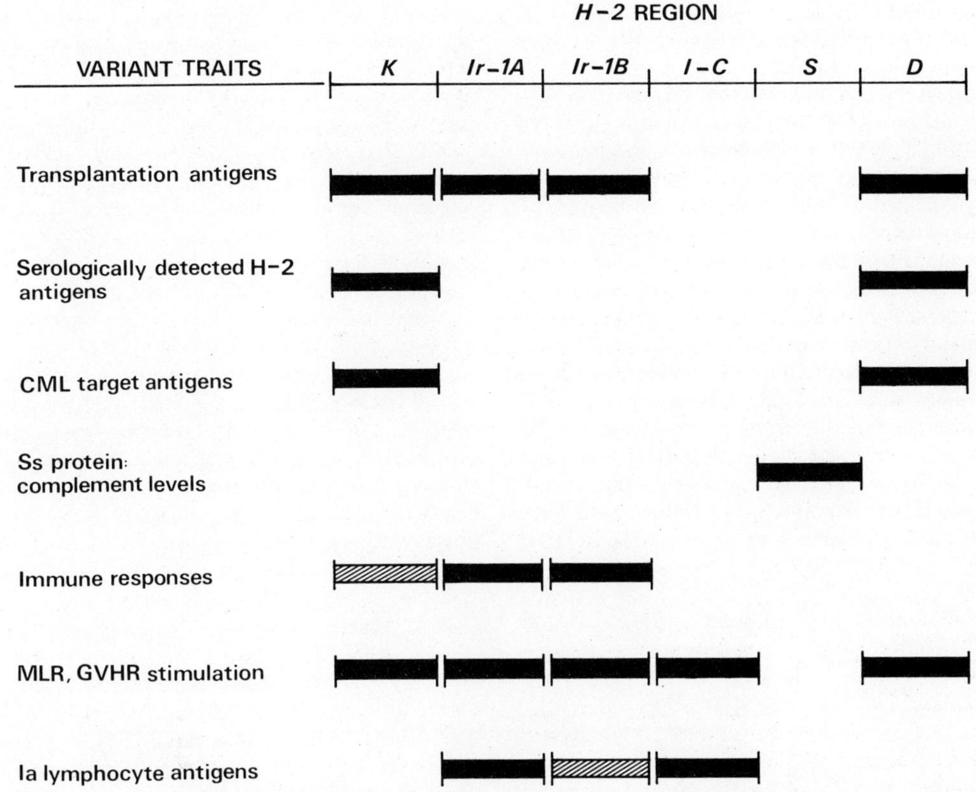

Figure 12–5. Map of the *H-2* complex, showing probable locations of genes controlling variant traits associated with the complex. Hatched areas indicate uncertainty about localization to that region. CML, cell-mediated lympholysis; MLR, mixed leukocyte reaction; GVHR, graft-versus-host reaction. (Reproduced, with permission, from Shreffler DC, David CS: Adv Immunol 20:125, 1975.)

about its possible influence on immune responses is very small compared with the information available on the murine H-2 complex. Current evidence suggests that the HLA complex can be diagrammed as shown in Fig 12–6. The most important difference between the 2 species is that the genetic region controlling the reactivity of cells in mixed lymphocyte cultures (and presumably other immune response genes analogous to the I region of the mouse) maps *outside* the 2 regions controlling the serologically defined transplantation antigens.

The use of synthetic antigens in inbred mouse strains allowed precise investigations of H-2-linked immune responses. Such data are not available for man. Nonetheless, there are suggestions that Ir genes may exist in man. As an example, the antisera used to detect human histocompatibility antigens usually are obtained from women who are sensitized during pregnancy against paternal antigens expressed by the developing fetus. Attempts to induce similar antibodies in volunteers by the injection of selected histocompatible lymphocytes demonstrated an association between the presence of HLA-A3 in the immunized subject and the ability to produce antibodies against the HLA-A2 antigen. Producing anti-HLA-A2 antibodies was very easy in people who possessed the HLA-A3 antigen and difficult in people who lacked this antigen.

More recently, lymphocytes from healthy individuals were cultured with varying concentrations of streptococcal antigens. Lymphocyte activation to these antigens varied from no response to intermediate response to high antigen doses and to high response with low antigen doses. HLA typing of the cells suggested an association between a high response and HLA-B5.

Such data certainly do not prove the existence of Ir genes in man, but human studies are limited by several important restrictions that do not impede mouse studies. First, the antisera detecting human histocompatibility antigens are not as well defined as mouse reagents, and one antiserum may cross-react with several HLA antigens. Such cross-reactions may make it difficult to determine the haplotype of the subjects under study. Second, mouse reagents to Ia antigens have been used to localize I regions in the mouse, but no such reagents exist for man. Third, it is not possible to immunize humans to the wide variety of synthetic and natural antigens which have been employed in animal studies.

HLA & Disease

If HLA-associated immune regulation occurs in man, one can employ the serologically determined transplantation antigens as markers for this genetic region. Certain HLA antigens are more commonly inherited as haplotype groups, and this linkage disequilibrium results in certain haplotypes which are assumed but not proved to possess an associated group of immune response genes. Different disease states and immune disorders have been examined to determine if certain haplotypes or antigens are more common, but a problem in the assessment of such data is the great variation in frequency of different HLA antigens within the populations studied. Tremendous differences exist in the frequency of expression of HLA antigens by different ethnic groups, and it may be difficult to determine whether a particular HLA antigen or haplotype is increased or decreased with respect to a matched control group of persons of similar ethnic background.

A. Hodgkin's Disease: Some of the earliest clinical studies relate Hodgkin's disease to a group of cross-reacting antigens called 4c. This group (known to contain antigens such as HLA-B5, HLA-Bw35, and HLA-Bw15) was found in over 50% of patients with Hodgkin's disease compared with 26% of a control group. Other studies have also reported an increased incidence of HLA-B5, HLA-B7, HLA-Bw35, and HLA-A11 antigens in this disease, but the percentage of increase over the control group has varied greatly. Patients with other types of lymphoreticular disorders (lymphoma, reticulum cell sarcoma) have had increased frequencies of HLA-B12 and HLA-B13.

B. Ragweed Allergy: Some correlation of HLA haplotypes with immune responses to the protein antigen E of ragweed pollen has been reported. Patients with ragweed hay fever and positive skin reactions to antigen E were identified, and they and their family members were HLA-typed. Specific haplotypes which appeared to correlate positively with ragweed sensitivity were identified, and 20 of the 26 persons with this haplotype had clinical ragweed allergy whereas none of the 11 people without the haplotype had allergy to antigen E. An immune response gene was postulated in this haplotype, which controlled both IgE and IgG antibody responses to antigen E.

C. Leukemia: Early studies of HLA types of patients with acute leukemia were done in France and

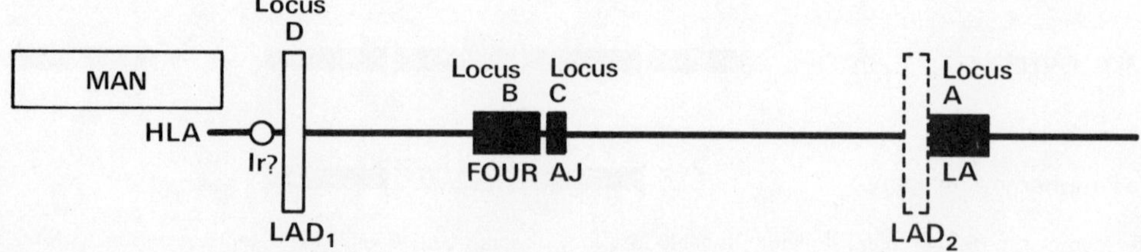

Figure 12–6. Current model of the major histocompatibility locus of man showing the old and newly revised nomenclature for different regions. The new locus designations (A, B, C, and D) are shown above the older names.

included 116 patients in clinical remission. They were tested for the presence of 10 HLA antigens and were found to have a normal distribution. Subsequent workers have reported either a normal distribution, an increased occurrence of the haplotype combination HLA-A2,B12, or a decrease in the frequency of HLA-A1 or HLA-A11. In acute myelogenous leukemia, the patients were reported to have normal distribution, an increased frequency of HLA-A2 or HLA-B12, or a decreased frequency of HLA-A11.

Chronic leukemias have not been well studied. The few reports suggest a normal distribution or an increase in the frequency of HLA-A9, HLA-B27, or HLA-Bw15 in patients with chronic lymphocytic leukemia.

D. Idiopathic Ankylosing Spondylitis: The association between ankylosing spondylitis and Reiter's syndrome and the presence of HLA-B27 is the strongest of any of the diseases studied. Over 90% of patients with spondylitis have the HLA-B27 antigen, and it has been useful as a predictor of those patients likely to develop this disease. In one study, 35 of 40 patients had the antigen compared to under 10% of a control population.

E. Gluten-Sensitive Enteropathy: In a group of 24 unrelated patients with untreated gluten-sensitive enteropathy, over 80% of the patients possessed HLA-B8 compared to a 20% incidence in a control patient population. HLA-A1 was also present in increased frequency, but this may be related to the strong haplotype linkage present between A1 and B8.

F. Other Diseases: Limited data are available for several other diseases. HLA-A2 is reported to be increased in patients with glomerulonephritis. HLA-B5 may be increased in infectious mononucleosis and HLA-Bw15 in systemic lupus erythematosus, although some workers report normal distributions. HLA-B8 shows an increased incidence in patients with myasthenia gravis.

Lymphocyte-Defined Antigens

The problems inherent in defining serologic differences in HLA-related histocompatibility antigens have resulted in another approach to identification of possible immune response genes associated with disease (or in laboratory investigation of normal persons). The HLA-D locus controls the in vitro lymphocyte activation between allogeneic cells. If, as the mouse data suggest, the majority of this response reflects differences at Ir loci, then the strength of the lymphocyte reaction between human lymphocytes may reflect the degree of disparity of human immune response genes. Studies are currently under way to test lymphocytes from many persons with and without known disease to see if a system of culture responses or lymphocyte-defined antigens can be classified. Such studies hold considerable promise for the elucidation of potential human immune response genes.

• • •

References

Benacerraf B, McDevitt HO: The histocompatibility-linked immune response genes. Science 175:273, 1972.

Cerottini J-C, Brunner KT: Cell mediated cytotoxicity, allograft rejection and tumor immunity. Adv Immunol 18:67, 1974.

Dausset J: Correlation between histocompatibility antigens and susceptibility to illness. Prog Clin Immunol 1:183, 1972.

Doherty PC, Zinkernagel RM: T cell mediated immunopathology in viral infections. Transplant Rev 19:89, 1974.

Falchuk ZM, Rogentine GN, Strober W: Predominance of histocompatibility antigen HL-A8 in patients with gluten-sensitive enteropathy. J Clin Invest 51:160, 1972.

Feltkamp TEW & others: Myasthenia gravis, autoantibodies, and HL-A antigens. Br Med J 1:131, 1974.

Glasser DL, Silvers WK: Genetic determinants of immunological responsiveness. Adv Immunol 18:1, 1974.

Haughton G, Whitmore AC: Genetics, the immune response and oncogenesis. Transplant Rev 28:75, 1976.

Katz DH, Benacerraf B: The function and interrelationships of T-cell receptors, Ir genes and other histocompatibility gene products. Transplant Rev 22:175, 1975.

McDevitt HO, Landy M (editors): *Genetic Control of Immune Responsiveness.* Academic Press, 1972.

McDevitt HO, Oldstone MBA, Pincus T: Histocompatibility-linked genetic control of specific immune responses to viral infections. Transplant Rev 19:209, 1974.

Möller G (editor): HLA antigens and disease. Transplant Rev, vol 22, 1975. [Entire issue.]

Sachs DH, Dickler HB: The possible role of I region determined cell surface molecules in the regulation of immune responses. Transplant Rev 23:159, 1975.

Shreffler DC, David CS: The H-2 major histocompatibility complex and the I immune response region: Genetic variation, function and organization. Adv Immunol 20:125, 1975.

13 . . .
Specific Immunologic Unresponsiveness

William D. Linscott, PhD

Inability to detect an immune response in an animal after contact with an antigen may be due to any of a large number of factors, including the following: (1) A generally depressed immune system, due to drug treatment, overwhelming disease, or genetic defects. (2) A hereditary absence of responder cells for that particular antigen. (3) Immunologic immaturity. (4) Inadequate exposure to the antigen (dose, physical form, route of administration). (5) Elimination of the antigen through nonimmunologic pathways. (6) Specific active interference with the immune response by suppressor lymphocytes. (7) Masking of one or more components of the immune response by an excess of free antigen, antibody, or antigen-antibody complexes. (8) Specific depletion or inactivation of responsive lymphocytes as a result of contact with the antigen or with antibody against cell receptors for antigen.

Important recent advances in knowledge have led to a blurring of the distinctions between the *absence* of an immune response and the *masking* of such a response. This has served to further confuse the problems of terminology in this field. "Classical" immunologic tolerance has traditionally denoted that condition in which responsive cell clones have been eliminated or inactivated by prior contact with antigen, with the result that no immune response occurs. "Immunologic paralysis" has often been used to denote a pseudotolerant condition in which an ongoing immune response is masked by the presence of overwhelming amounts of antigen. Where inability to respond to an antigen is secondary to genetic factors rather than the result of prior contact with the antigen, the terms "nonresponder" or "low responder" are most often used.

Tolerance may be recognized by the failure to develop a delayed skin reaction, by absence of cells containing or secreting antibody against the tolerated antigen, by absence of free antibody in the circulation, by failure to eliminate the antigen in an accelerated fashion, by failure of cells to respond to the antigen in vitro by an increase in DNA synthesis, or by numerous other means. Tolerance may exist at the level of antibody production, cellular immunity, or both.

William D. Linscott is Associate Professor of Microbiology, University of California School of Medicine, San Francisco.

IMMUNOLOGIC TOLERANCE

Effect of Age

Because tolerance is induced most readily upon contact of antigen with immunologically immature cells, it is most easily demonstrated by exposing an individual to antigen during the perinatal period. There is no particular age at which an individual suddenly becomes immunologically mature. Rather—as reviewed in Chapter 11—there is a steady increase in the proportion of mature lymphocytes, beginning at a time well before birth and highly variable with different species and different antigens. Mice, rats, and hamsters—among others—are immunologically relatively immature at birth and readily become tolerant to many antigens administered during the perinatal period. Guinea pigs and sheep are more mature at birth, and induction of tolerance in these animals is correspondingly more difficult. Since antigen processing is an important aspect of the immune response, it may well be that the relative immaturity of the reticuloendothelial system at birth is an important factor in the ease of tolerance induction early in life.

Antigen Dose Versus Amount of Lymphoid Tissue

Mature lymphocytes are constantly dying and being replaced by immature ones. In any individual exposed to an antigen, some cells will be rendered tolerant while others will be unaffected and still others may be jolted into an immune response. The total immune response to any particular antigen will depend heavily on how many cells are affected in each of these ways. This response will be determined by a variety of different factors, particularly antigen concentration and the number of mature lymphocytes present. Because of the progressive maturation of the immune system, the dose of antigen needed to induce tolerance increases sharply with age after birth. Whereas 15 million allogeneic bone marrow cells might induce long-lasting chimerism and intolerance in a certain strain of rat at birth, many times this dose might be required in 3-day-old rats, and by 1 week of age the required dose might be uattainably large depending on the strain combination used. Similarly, rabbits given 500 mg of a purified foreign serum protein during the first few days of life remain tolerant to that antigen for many months. On the other hand, normal adult rabbits may have to be injected daily for many weeks with one or more *grams* of such a protein to induce a similar degree of unresponsiveness. In adult animals, tolerance is sometimes preceded by an immune phase which is not seen in neonates. Tolerance induction in mature individuals can be facilitated by first destroying most of their immunologically competent cells—using radiation, cytotoxic drugs, or antilymphocyte antibodies. The preceding statements are not meant to imply that tolerance can only be induced in immature but not in mature cells. It seems quite clear that mature lymphocytes can also be made tolerant, both in vitro and in vivo. However, much more antigen is necessary, particularly in vivo, where a preexisting state of immunity would cause a much faster elimination of injected antigen.

Persistence of Antigen

The tolerant state is dependent on persistence of a threshold amount of antigen somewhere within the immune system. With replicating antigens such as foreign lymphoid cells, persistent antigen is usually easily detectable and often remains for life. Injection of lymphocytes which have been sensitized against a tolerated foreign cell population will usually eliminate these foreign cells rapidly; shortly thereafter, tolerance for their antigens will begin to decrease. In contrast to replicating antigens, a foreign protein such as BSA is catabolized fairly rapidly in an animal such as a mouse or a rabbit; this results in spontaneous termination of tolerance to the protein after many days, weeks, or months, depending on the size of the original dose. This spontaneous loss of the tolerant state is sometimes accompanied by a brief burst of antibody production against the tolerated antigen, thought to be triggered as the amount of antigen in the system falls from a *tolerizing* to an *immunizing* concentration. The location within the immune system of this critical tolerance-maintaining antigen reservoir is unknown, but in most cases it appears to be sequestered so as to be unaffected by passively administered antibody. Much of the antigen may be within lymphocytes themselves, because transfer of tolerant spleen cells to a syngeneic, antigen-free, irradiated host usually does not result in any change in the cells' inability to respond to the tolerated antigen. The duration of tolerance after a single neonatal injection of a nonreplicating antigen is proportionate to the amount injected and inversely proportionate to the rate at which it is catabolized. Tolerance can be maintained indefinitely by periodic supplemental injections of the same material.

Low-Dose Tolerance

Low-dose (low-zone) tolerance is a special case contrasting with classical (high-dose) tolerance. It is usually less complete and less persistent than classical tolerance and is induced with very small (subimmunogenic) doses of soluble antigen, preferably given repeatedly for several days or weeks. An animal so treated will produce no antibody, and when later challenged with a highly immunogenic dose of the same antigen it will make much less antibody than a normal control. For example, newborn rats were injected daily for 2 weeks with a wide range of doses of bacterial flagellin antigen. Control rats received no antigen. All animals, including controls, were then given a stimulatory dose (10 μg) of flagellin twice a week for 4 more weeks, and their antibody responses were then measured. As shown in Fig 13–1, pretreatment with very low and very high doses of antigen resulted in a high degree of tolerance (low-dose and high-dose), while an intermediate amount sensitized the recipients, as shown by a response somewhat higher than that of the controls.

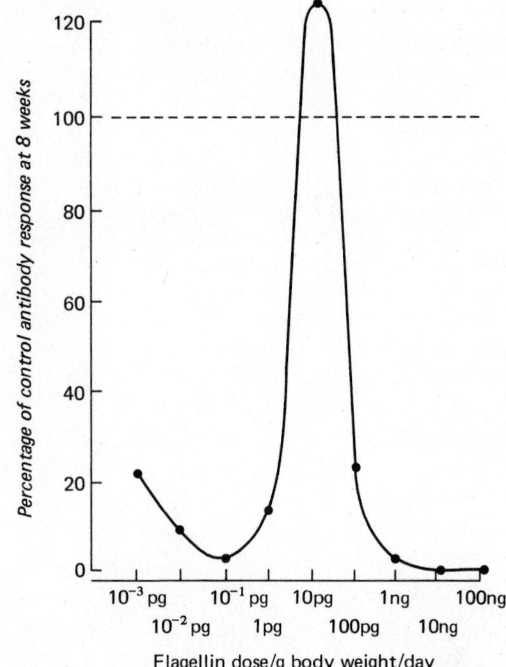

Figure 13–1. Relationship of antigen dose to the induction of tolerance. (See text for details.)

Although a wide variety of antigens can induce low-dose tolerance in newborn mice, only a few antigens seem to be effective in older animals. Adult mice which have been irradiated, thymectomized, or otherwise compromised immunologically are susceptible to low-dose tolerance induction by many antigens which can only induce high-dose tolerance in normal mice. This suggests that a diminished ability to produce antibody facilitates induction of low-dose tolerance.

Recent experiments have shown that low-dose tolerance to foreign proteins occurs primarily in the T cell population, not among B cells. This is presumably a result of the greater susceptibility of T cells to tolerization by small amounts of antigen.

Antigen Clearance & the Possible Role of Macrophagelike Cells

Aqueous solutions of serum proteins such as albumin or γ-globulin contain some aggregated molecules whose numbers can be increased greatly by heating or other treatments. Aggregated and deaggregated fractions can be separated by ultracentrifugation. Numerous experiments have shown that the aggregates are much more rapidly removed from the circulation—and far more immunogenic—than the deaggregated protein. In contrast, the deaggregated proteins are often highly tolerogenic. An immunogenic dose of *aggregated* human γ-globulin can be prevented from immunizing a mouse by the simultaneous injection of a large dose of *deaggregated* globulin. In fact, a mouse so treated will be tolerant to human γ-globulin.

BALB/c mice are much more resistant to the induction of tolerance by heterologous γ-globulins than are most other mouse strains. However, if BALB/c mice are injected with carrageenan (a macrophage-paralyzing compound) before they are given bovine γ-globulin, then a high proportion develop tolerance to this protein.

Other experiments have shown that antigen bound to macrophages is highly immunogenic. Only 0.001 as much macrophage-bound BSA was required to immunize a mouse as compared to unbound albumin. When free and macrophage-bound BSA were administered at the same time, the free albumin markedly inhibited the immune response to the macrophage-bound protein. Comparisons suggest that macrophage-bound and aggregated proteins are about equally immunogenic and that deaggregated proteins can be made almost equally immunogenic by incorporation into suitable adjuvants. Interestingly, previously immunized animals respond about equally well to deaggregated, aggregated, and macrophage-bound forms of an antigen.

These results have led to the suggestion that direct interaction of antigen with a lymphocyte may result in tolerance induction, whereas, if this interaction is modulated by macrophages or dendritic cells, immunization will occur instead. This suggestion is supported by recent evidence obtained in vitro. When primed spleen cells were incubated with the supernate from a thymocyte-antigen culture and then washed, they formed antibody to this antigen. However, if the spleen cells were first depleted of their glass-adherent cells (eg, macrophages and dendritic cells), then exposure to the thymocyte-antigen culture supernate induced tolerance, not antibody formation. Thus, the presence or absence of glass-adherent cells among the sensitized spleen cells determined whether a product of T cell-antigen interaction induced tolerance or an antibody response.

Tolerance at the Cellular Level

The experimental result which has probably contributed most toward understanding the processes of tolerance induction is the demonstration, by Habicht, Chiller, and Weigle, that tolerance occurs separately in T and in B lymphocytes; that it develops faster and lasts longer in T cells; and that it takes up to 25 times more antigen to tolerize a B cell than to tolerize a T cell. These results were obtained in cell transfer experiments, in which thymus or bone marrow cells from normal mice or mice tolerant to human γ-globulin were mixed and transferred into irradiated, syngeneic recipients (which acted as living test tubes) along with aggregated γ-globulin to stimulate antibody production. The number of cells secreting anti-γ-globulin antibodies in the spleens of the irradiated recipients was then determined 15 days later. The results, summarized in Table 13–1, showed that bone marrow (supplying B cells) or thymocytes (supplying T cells) alone were unable to produce antibody against human γ-globulin. A combination of normal bone marrow and normal thymocytes resulted in good antibody formation, whereas equivalent cells from tolerant mice were unable to substitute for either the T cell or the B cell component. Therefore, both the T cells and the B cells of these mice were tolerant.

Table 13–1. Demonstration of tolerance in both bone marrow and thymus cell populations taken from mice tolerant to human γ-globulin (HGG).

Cell Populations Injected Into Irradiated Mice*	Aggregated HGG Also Injected	Number of Cells Secreting Anti-HGG Antibody
Normal BM + Normal T	No	0
Normal BM + Normal T	Yes	2250
Normal BM	Yes	0
Normal T	Yes	0†
Normal BM + Tolerant T	Yes	0
Tolerant BM + Normal T	Yes	0
Tolerant BM + Tolerant T	Yes	0

*BM = bone marrow cells; T = thymus cells.

†Mice did not survive beyond 14 days owing to lack of bone marrow protection against radiation damage; those alive at 11 days had no antibody-secreting cells.

Kinetics of Tolerance Induction & Loss

The speed with which T and B cells acquire and lose tolerance has been studied both in vivo and in vitro. Adult mice had to be exposed continuously to large amounts of BSA for 20–30 days before antibody to this antigen could no longer be detected, and it took about 50 days after the last injection of BSA before the response again approached normal. Such experiments are not very enlightening because of the inability to control different variables independently. More useful information has been obtained from cell transfer experiments, in which mice were injected with deaggregated γ-globulin and then killed at intervals. Their spleen, bone marrow, and thymus cells could be transferred separately to irradiated recipients, often with the addition of normal bone marrow or thymus cells in attempts to reconstitute a lost activity. The recipient mice were challenged with an immunogenic dose of γ-globulin, and their antibody response was measured. These experiments showed that within 24 hours after contact with antigen the T cells in the thymus had begun to show tolerance, which was complete within

48 hours. The B cells in the spleen were tolerant within 3 days, but those in the bone marrow required as long as 1–2 weeks to become tolerant. Since B cells migrate continuously out of the marrow, complete B cell tolerance in peripheral lymphoid tissue presumably would not occur until all the bone marrow B cells had been tolerized. As will be seen later, there is evidence that B cells can be made tolerant within a few hours under conditions where no T cells are capable of recognizing the tolerizing antigen.

In mice made tolerant to deaggregated human γ-globulin, the B cells lost tolerance within 40–50 days after the tolerizing exposure to antigen while the T cells remained tolerant about 3 times longer. Thus, if mice were tested 20–30 days after the induction of tolerance, they were found to have both tolerant B and tolerant T cells, whereas if they were tested at 80 days they had tolerant T cells and reactive B cells. Rabbits made tolerant to BSA at birth often remain so, at least at the T cell level, for 6 months or more.

Suppressor Cells in Tolerance

Classical tolerance has not heretofore been regarded as an inhibitory or suppressive phenomenon because cells from a tolerant animal usually do not exert any inhibitory effect on the immune response of normal lymphocytes to the tolerated antigen. Recently, however, evidence of such a suppressive effect has been obtained in several laboratories but not in all. The reasons for the conflicting results are not yet apparent. These studies indicate that after exposure to a wide range of cellular and purified antigens, under a variety of conditions, 2 different populations of T cells are induced which have more or less conflicting activities. One population functions as helper T cells, which are essential in the cooperative interaction with B cells and antigen, resulting in the initiation of antibody production (Chapter 8). The second population seems to have both antigen-specific and perhaps nonspecific inhibitory effects against B cells, against helper T cells, and against cellular immunity in general. Suppressor cell production is favored by the use of protein antigens in aqueous solution, while helper cells are favored by the use of Freund's complete adjuvant. Suppressor cells seem to be most abundant early in the immune response, and to be effective they must act during the first 1 or 2 days after their target cells have been exposed to antigen.

The fact that suppressor T cells have been found in some tolerant animals but not in others is difficult to evaluate. It may be that the assays were not sufficiently sensitive, or that suppressor cells have nothing to do with tolerance, or that they are involved in the early stages of tolerance induction but are not necessary for maintaining the tolerant state. Further research will help to determine which of these alternatives has most substance.

Tolerance Induction by Nonimmunogens & the Possible Role of T Cells

Certain substances known as haptens, when injected alone into experimental animals, fail to induce an immune response; yet when complexed with an immunogenic carrier these substances elicit antibody formation. For example, polyglutamic acid failed to immunize adult rabbits, yet when rabbits were injected with this antigen complexed with methylated BSA they made a good antibody response both to polyglutamic acid and to BSA. This indicated that the rabbits had B cells capable of making antibody to polyglutamic acid; their inability to respond to this antigen alone might have resulted from a lack of T cells capable of recognizing polyglutamic acid. When polyglutamic acid was coupled to methylated BSA, T cells reactive with the albumin part could cooperate with B cells reactive with the glutamic acid part, and the cooperation allowed antibody to be produced. A further important finding was that when normal rabbits were injected with polyglutamic acid alone they became *tolerant* to this substance, ie, when subsequently immunized with glutamic acid-albumin conjugates they made antibody against BSA but not against glutamic acid. The results suggested that direct contact with polyglutamic acid alone made their B cells tolerant to this material. Similar observations have been made in mice and guinea pigs with a variety of other substances. The only difference is that when the nonimmunogen was quite small, such as dinitrophenyl groups, it had to be coupled to some larger carrier molecule before it could induce tolerance. In such cases, tolerance was best when the carrier itself was also nonimmunogenic, such as autologous γ-globulin or albumin. For example, an injection of autologous γ-globulin coupled with the hapten dinitrophenyl made the animal unable later to respond to the hapten part of a dinitrophenyl-BSA complex.

The above results suggested that B cells could be made tolerant to certain substances in the absence of T cells capable of reacting with the same material. This was confirmed by experiments in guinea pigs with DNP-D-GL (DNP conjugated to a copolymer of D-glutamic acid and D-lysine). Guinea pigs appear to lack T cells capable of recognizing the carrier D-GL, although they have B cells able to respond to DNP if it is coupled, for example, to ovalbumin. It was found that DNP-D-GL induced rapid and profound B cell tolerance to DNP in guinea pigs, even if they had previously been sensitized to DNP-ovalbumin (Table 13–2). Yet if DNP-D-GL was injected into DNP-sensitized guinea pigs undergoing a GVH reaction

Table 13–2. B cell tolerance in guinea pigs.

Animal Injected With Antigen (DNP-D-GL)	Results of Injection
Normal guinea pig	B cell tolerance to DNP.
Guinea pig previously sensitized to DNP-ovalbumin	B cell tolerance to DNP.
Guinea pig previously sensitized to DNP-ovalbumin and currently undergoing GVH reaction	Antibody production to DNP determinants.

(which provides a nonspecific substitute for helper T cell function in the antibody response), these animals made anti-DNP antibody instead of being tolerized to DNP. Thus, B cells exposed to DNP in the absence of functioning T cells became tolerant, while those exposed to DNP in the presence of functioning T cells were stimulated to make antibody.

Similar results were obtained in mice so depleted of T cells that they were unable to make an antibody response to human γ-globulin. The B cells in these mice rapidly developed tolerance to γ-globulin. If T cell activity was replaced by an injection of bacterial lipopolysaccharide, which nonspecifically stimulates B cell mitosis, human γ-globulin did not induce B cell tolerance but rather stimulated a good antibody response.

Treatment of B cells with trypsin within 48 hours after exposure to antigen prevented the development of tolerance in many but not all cases. Whether the trypsin removed antigen or provided a stimulatory signal is not known.

The cumulative evidence strongly suggests that if a B cell is stimulated in an appropriate way by T cell factors or by a mitogen within a short time (1–2 days) after the B cell has interacted with antigen, then antibody formation will be induced. In the absence of an appropriate stimulus, tolerance is likely to ensue. The absence of reactive T cells may accelerate or otherwise facilitate tolerance induction in B cells. Perhaps the reason it takes longer in vivo to induce tolerance in B cells than in T cells is that the antigen-reactive T cells may have to be tolerized before the B cells can be made tolerant.

With regard to the induction of tolerance in T cells, it has already been mentioned that this takes less antigen and occurs more rapidly than is the case with B cells. In contrast to the finding that dinitrophenyl groups induce B cell tolerance most effectively when coupled with a nonimmunogenic carrier, it has been found that dinitrophenyl groups do not induce T cell tolerance when coupled to nonimmunogenic carriers but only when coupled to immunogens. Similar results were obtained with azobenzenearsonate. This could result from insufficiently strong binding of the small hapten to T cell surface receptors—a binding which might be considerably reinforced if it also involved adjacent structures on a highly immunogenic carrier. A similar explanation has been invoked to account for the high degree of carrier specificity which accompanies delayed skin reactions to most small haptens. On the other hand, picryl chloride coupled to autologous cells has been used successfully to induce T cell tolerance to this chemical.

The Effect of Epitope Density

The density of antigenic determinants (epitopes) on a larger structure has an important effect on the induction of tolerance. Dinitrophenyl haptenic groups coupled to a carrier of polymerized bacterial flagellin can induce antihapten antibodies in vitro in normal mouse spleen cells (Fig 13–2). By varying the number of hapten groups substituted on each flagellin molecule, it was possible to induce tolerance rather than an immune response. For example, at an average density of 0.7 dinitrophenyl groups per flagellin molecule, both intermediate and high concentrations of this con-

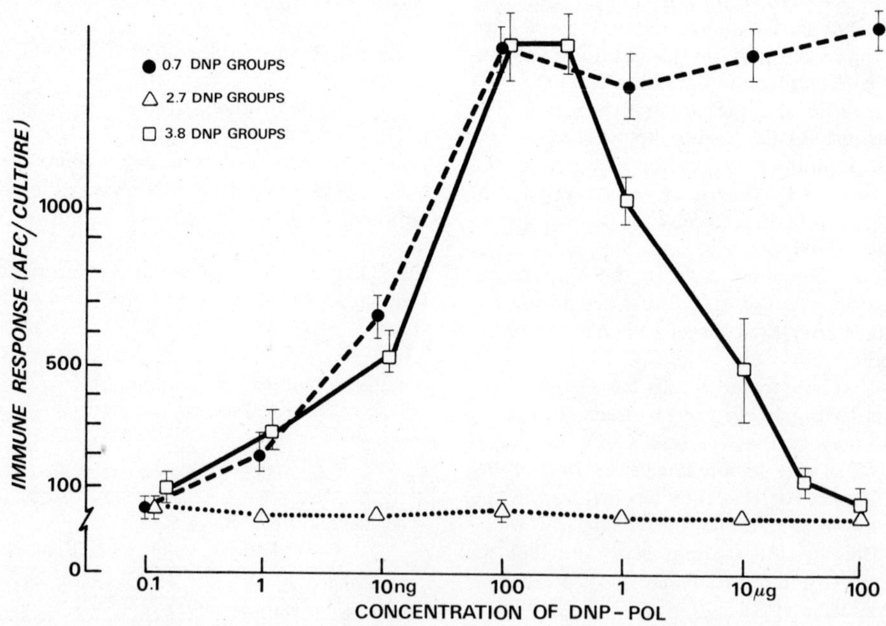

Figure 13–2. The effect of altering the number of DNP groups conjugated to polymerized flagellin (POL) on the primary anti-DNP response elicited by DNP-POL in vitro. A typical experiment is shown, with 4 cultures per point. Similar results were always obtained with these substitution ratios. (Reproduced, with permission, from Feldman M: J Exp Med 135:735, 1972.)

jugate induced a good antihapten antibody response in vitro. At an average density of 2.7 groups per molecule, intermediate concentrations of the conjugate gave good antibody responses, but high concentrations induced tolerance to the dinitrophenyl group. With 3.8 or more haptens per molecule, all concentrations of the conjugate induced tolerance to the hapten. The critical factors were not the absolute amount of dinitrophenyl groups in the culture nor the degree of alteration of flagellin as a result of the coupling process, but only the amount of hapten per molecule of flagellin carrier. Even very large amounts of lightly substituted flagellin (0.7 groups per molecule) did not induce tolerance to the hapten. When polymerized flagellin was conjugated with both dinitrophenyl and a second hapten (one dinitrophenyl group and 4 dansyl groups per molecule), a good antidinitrophenyl response was obtained, again demonstrating that it was not simply the chemical alteration of flagellin by the conjugation process that resulted in tolerance.

Partial (Incomplete) Versus Complete Tolerance

Tolerance is seldom absolute. A small amount of antibody against the tolerated antigen may be produced, or a skin graft may show greatly prolonged, but not indefinite, survival. It seems likely that this is a reflection of the relative proportions of T and B cells made tolerant—as compared to those made immune—by a given contact with antigen. Lymphocytes have surface receptors with a wide range of affinities for a given antigen, and there is evidence, at least in some cases, that those cells with the highest-affinity antigen receptors are the ones made tolerant by the smallest amount of antigen. This suggests that tolerance induction is proportionate to the amount of antigen bound by the cell. Thus, any amount of antigen is likely to induce tolerance in some cells while immunizing others, and what is observed at the whole animal level will depend on the ratio between these 2 cell populations. In turn, this ratio will depend on the physical form and the amount of antigen present, the numbers of T and B cells and their affinities for the antigen, the state of activation of these cells, the rate of antigen processing by macrophagelike cells, and numerous other factors.

Another cause of incomplete tolerance may be related to antigen complexity. Rabbits injected at birth with a mixture of foreign serum proteins might receive a large dose of one protein and a very small dose of another protein present in lower concentration. Thus, they might become tolerant to the former and not to the latter. If they were then challenged at age 3 months with the same mixture of proteins, they might make antibody against one of the proteins in the mixture. If no effort was made to determine the specificities of the antibodies produced, the rabbits might be judged not tolerant or only partially tolerant. As another example, mice injected at birth with allogeneic bone marrow cells may show greatly prolonged but not indefinite survival of skin grafts from the same donor of the bone marrow cells. This could be secondary to the presence in the skin graft of a small amount of unique skin-specific transplantation antigen not present in the original graft of bone marrow cells, though all other antigens are shared. Thus, the skin graft would survive a long time because the host was tolerant to nearly all of its transplantation antigens, but it might finally be rejected by an immune response against the minor unshared antigen.

Specificity of Tolerance

One might assume that the specificity of tolerance would be the same as that for antibody—ie, an antigen which cross-reacts very weakly with another antigen would only induce a low degree of tolerance against that antigen. However, several sets of experimental results have conflicted with these expectations. It appears that these discrepancies may be explained on the basis of a broader antigen cross-reactivity of T cells than of antibody and the greater susceptibility of T cells to tolerance induction by small amounts of antigen. For example, mice made tolerant by injection with deaggregated human γ-globulin were then tested for their ability to make antibody against porcine, equine, or fowl γ-globulin by injecting them with these antigens in aggregated form. This experiment is summarized in Table 13–3. Although equine and porcine γ-globulin cross-reacted only about 1–3% with human γ-globulin, there was a 76–91% reduction in the number of cells producing antibody to equine and porcine proteins in the mice tolerant to human globulin, as compared with normal mice similarly injected with

Table 13–3. Effect of cross-reaction among antigens on antibody production in tolerant mice.

	Type of Aggregated γ-Globulin Injected	Percentage of Globulin Cross-Reactions With Human Immunoglobulin	Antibody-Forming Cells per Million Spleen Cells	Percentage of Reduction in Antibody-Forming Cells
Normal mice	Man	. . .	2253	
	Pig	2–3%	989	
	Horse	1%	4701	
	Fowl	0%	69	
Mice tolerant to human γ-globulin	Man		0	100%
	Pig		241	76
	Horse		428	91
	Fowl		67	3

either porcine or equine globulins. However, fowl γ-globulins which do not cross-react at all with human proteins elicited a normal antibody response. Thus, the mice tolerant to human globulins made far less antibody against porcine and equine globulins than would have been expected on the basis of a 1–3% cross-reaction between the human and the other 2 proteins.

Other experiments showed that, in fact, the B cells of these mice had not been made tolerant but that a high proportion of the T cells which should have interacted with porcine and equine proteins failed to do so. It was concluded that many of the T cells capable of recognizing porcine and equine proteins were also able to bind human γ-globulins firmly enough to be tolerized; in other words, antigen cross-reactivity at the T cell level was considerably broader than at the antibody level, where such comparisons traditionally have been made. Work from another laboratory strongly supports this conclusion: rats tolerized by injections of deaggregated γ-globulin from the goat, pig, cow, horse, or rabbit showed a marked reduction in antitrinitrophenyl antibody-forming cells upon challenge with trinitrophenyl conjugates of sheep γ-globulin, even though sheep γ-globulin cross-reacts undetectably with 3 of the 5 species of γ-globulin used. Since B cells specific for the trinitrophenyl hapten should have been completely unaffected by pretreatment with foreign γ-globulin, the reduced response probably reflects tolerization by the various γ-globulins of appreciable numbers of T cells capable of recognizing the sheep γ-globulin carrier to which the hapten was attached, thus reducing the number of helper T cells available to interact with the trinitrophenyl hapten and its specific B cells.

Termination of Tolerance

Tolerance of a host (strain A) for a replicating antigen such as allogeneic lymphoid cells (strain B) may persist indefinitely or may decrease with time, as a weak but ongoing immune response gradually eliminates the foreign cell population. This process can usually be accelerated by injecting the tolerant host with normal strain A lymphoid cells which, not being tolerant of strain B antigens, will act to reject the colonizing strain B cell population. This rejection will be even more rapid if the newly injected strain A cells have previously been sensitized against strain B transplantation antigens. Occasionally it has been possible to terminate tolerance to a foreign graft by means of antiserum against the graft antigens, but immune lymphoid cells are usually required, and even they sometimes fail to end tolerance for reasons which are not understood.

In tolerance to a nonreplicating antigen such as BSA, normal catabolic processes will reduce the antigen concentration to a sufficiently low level over a period of weeks or months so that it is no longer capable of maintaining tolerance. This process can seldom be accelerated by injecting antibody against the antigen, and even immune lymphoid cells usually fail to modify this spontaneous termination of tolerance. The reasons for this are not clear except that much of the tolerance-maintaining antigen is probably sequestered from the circulation, perhaps within cells.

In 1961, Weigle reported that tolerance in rabbits to neonatally injected BSA could be terminated by injection of other heterologous albumins; soon thereafter, it was found that even BSA substituted with arsanilic and sulfanilic haptens was effective. Subsequently, it was found that in order to terminate tolerance the terminating antigen had to cross-react moderately well, but not too completely, with the tolerated antigen, and that injecting the tolerated antigen at the same time as the cross-reacting antigen prevented the termination of tolerance. When tolerance to BSA in rabbits was terminated by injecting human serum albumin, subsequent injections of BSA usually elicited less and less antibody until tolerance finally returned. It was also found that all of the antibody produced in the above instance could be absorbed by human albumin, which cross-reacts only about 15% with BSA. This indicated that antibody was only being produced against those antigenic determinants which were shared between the 2 proteins, and thus that tolerance to many of the bovine determinants was still in effect (Table 13–4).

The following theory was developed to account

Table 13–4. Termination of tolerance to bovine serum albumin (BSA) by injection of human serum albumin (HSA). (Ab = antibody.)

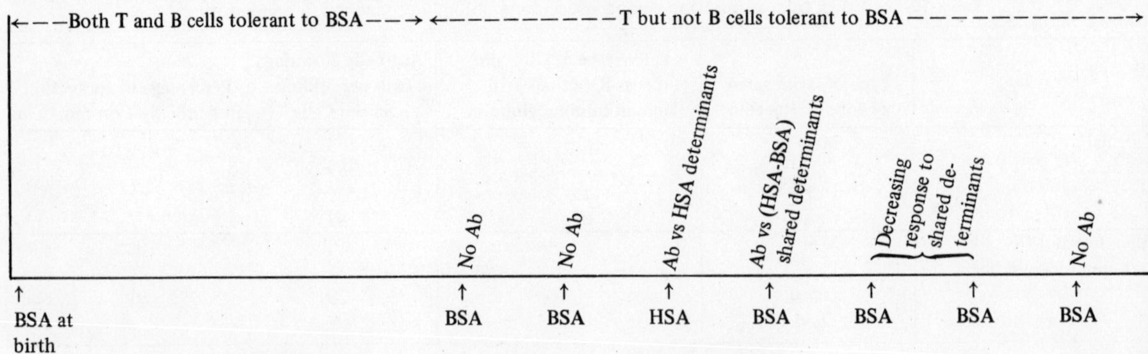

for these observations. It was postulated that at the time tolerance was terminated by human albumin the animal had T cells tolerant to BSA but no tolerant B cells. The injection of human protein generated a pool of sensitized lymphocytes, probably B cells, some of which were capable of interacting with those antigenic determinants shared between bovine and human albumins. Subsequent injection of BSA stimulated these sensitized B cells in the absence of specific T cells. Since the only cells stimulated were those previously sensitized by human albumin, the only antibody produced was against determinants shared by both proteins—which explains why all of the antibody could be absorbed with human albumin. Repeated injections of BSA gradually depleted this pool of sensitized B cells, so that less and less antibody was produced, and when the pool was exhausted the animal was once again tolerant. Antigens which cross-react too completely with the bovine protein fail to terminate tolerance because the T cells which they need in order to stimulate reactive B cells have all been made tolerant by the BSA given at birth. Antigens which cross-react too little with the bovine protein are ineffective because the pool of sensitized lymphocytes which they induce is unable to recognize any of the determinants on the bovine molecule.

One problem with this theory is that it appears to require that sensitized B cells be triggered into antibody production by antigen in the absence of helper T cells, whereas there is much evidence that T cells are important in the secondary immune response. However, there are some indications that B cells can be brought to such a highly reactive state, either through repeated stimulation with antigen or through the use of endotoxin, that they can be triggered into antibody secretion in the absence of T cells.

The ability of a large dose of BSA to prevent termination of tolerance by a simultaneous injection of human albumin is probably due to competition between the human albumin and BSA for the B lymphocyte antigen receptors capable of reacting with both antigens. This would prevent the essential buildup of a pool of sensitized cells reactive to bovine protein. If only a small amount of the tolerated antigen is present, then this competition is not great enough to prevent the termination of tolerance—as has been shown with thyroglobulin antigens.

Another method of terminating tolerance experimentally is also based on the above precepts. In mice whose T cells are tolerant to human γ-globulin but whose B cells are not (ie, 90 days after the induction of tolerance), the simultaneous injection of human γ-globulin and bacterial lipopolysaccharide (a B cell mitogen which can substitute for helper T cell function) will induce antibody formation, whereas lipopolysaccharide or human γ-globulin alone will not. This method fails when attempted 25 days after tolerance induction, when both T and B cells are tolerant.

Mechanisms of Tolerance Induction

The mechanism by which antigen induces tolerance in T and B lymphocytes is unknown. It may be that direct contact between a lymphocyte and a sufficient amount of antigen can either kill the cell or render it unable to differentiate or to replicate. This might occur as a result of the *absence* of a signal for the cell to differentiate, from the presence of *too much* signal to differentiate, or from a *different* signal to become tolerant. Such signals might come from macrophages, from suppressor or other T cells, from the cross-linking of cell surface antigen receptors by polymeric antigens or by antigen-antibody complexes, or from disturbances in the normal process of clearing foreign substances which attach to receptors on the cell membrane.

Another mechanism of tolerance induction might involve inability of the tolerant cell to bind antigen. Several experiments have shown that tolerant animals can have a sharply reduced number of lymphocytes capable of binding the tolerated antigen. Whether this occurs through elimination of antigen receptors, their saturation by antigen, or elimination of the entire cell is not clear.

The role of suppressor cells in tolerance is not clear. They have been found in some cases, but not in others. If tolerance is due only to a lack of cells capable of responding to an antigen and not to any kind of suppression, then it should not be so difficult to terminate tolerance by the injection of normal lymphoid cells. This usually works fairly well with tolerance to transplantation antigens on a foreign cell population, but it seldom succeeds when the tolerated antigen is a foreign serum protein. Whether this is due to persistent antigen ("super-tolerogen") in sufficient quantity to tolerize the newly-injected cells, or to active suppression, or to other factors, is not often clear. Recent evidence suggests that active suppression of immune function by T cells occurs in many tolerant animals.

It is hoped that a more complete understanding of the mechanisms of tolerance induction and maintenance will make it possible to increase the survival times of tissue transplants and to provide new methods of treatment of allergic and autoimmune diseases by making people selectively unresponsive to particular antigens without interfering with their ability to react against infectious agents.

IMMUNOLOGIC ENHANCEMENT

Soon after it was discovered that many infectious diseases could be prevented by vaccines or immune sera, attempts were made to treat cancer by these same technics. However, preimmunization of animals with living or killed tumor cells often had an effect opposite to that desired: survival of tumor cells was enhanced, and the vaccinated animals died of cancer sooner than unvaccinated controls. This unexpected phenomenon was called *immunologic enhancement,* and it is still under intensive investigation.

Transfer by Serum

Early attempts to determine the mechanisms responsible for enhancement showed that it could be passively transferred by serum. Mice could be immunized against a tumor, and their serum, when injected into normal mice, would prolong the survival of the tumor in these mice. Much experimental data indicated that the enhancing factor in immune serum was probably specific antibody against tumor cell antigens, and it seemed to be one or another subclass of IgG, (although IgA and occasionally even IgM have also been implicated). Enhancing sera frequently showed dual response in transfer experiments: A large dose of serum would often accelerate tumor destruction, while a smaller dose enhanced tumor survival. For maximum enhancement, antibody usually had to be present against all or nearly all of the antigens present on the tumor cell surface. There was often a good correlation between low antigen density (and thus low susceptibility to complement-dependent cytolysis) and ease of enhancement. Paradoxically, some antisera which could kill tumor cells in vitro in the presence of complement still enhanced the survival of those same cells in vivo. This may have resulted partly from the low activity of mouse complement in vivo, whereas guinea pig or rabbit complement was usually employed in the in vitro tests; and partly from the ability of some antibodies to be cytotoxic at high concentrations and to exert blocking effects at lower concentrations. Chemical treatments which destroy the ability of antibody to fix complement often increase the enhancing activity of that antibody.

In general, one or 2 doses of antigen or of enhancing serum had a maximal effect which could not be increased by additional injections; also, in some cases it was possible to treat tumor cells with enhancing serum in vitro, wash them, and still observe enhanced growth after injection into a normal host. Washed, antibody-coated tumor cells injected into the skin on one side of a mouse showed more rapid growth and longer survival than similar but untreated tumor cells injected into the opposite side of the same mouse. It was almost universally found that enhancement could not be induced in immune animals, ie, in animals which had already rejected a tumor or a normal tissue graft. Conversely, enhancement was much more easily induced in immunosuppressed animals than in normal controls.

Although the early experiments were done with tumor cells, it was later found that the survival of normal tissues such as kidney or heart grafts can be enhanced by prior treatment of the recipient with graft antigens or immune sera. Timing of the injections seemed to be quite critical, and highly variable results were obtained with different species and different types of grafts. There is a strong possibility that under different circumstances, several different basic mechanisms, acting singly or in combination, may contribute to the enhanced survival of tumor or normal tissue grafts. Classical immunologic tolerance may also play a role in some cases but not in others.

We will now consider a number of different observations relating to enhancement and then examine what is known about the basic mechanisms.

Transplantation

In studies to determine why kidney allografts survive a long time in some patients but not in others, blood lymphocytes from different patients were incubated with fibroblasts or other cells from the kidney donors both with and without the addition of the patient's serum. Patients with long-surviving kidney grafts often had lymphocytes which were cytotoxic for the graft antigens, but their serum frequently contained "blocking factors" which protected cells bearing graft antigens from destruction by these cytotoxic lymphocytes. These results have been confirmed in model systems involving long-term survival of kidney allografts in rats, where pretreatment of rats with tissue antigens from a potential kidney donor sometimes allows the permanent survival of a later kidney allograft from that donor—even in the absence of immunosuppression. Serum from rats carrying a long-surviving transplant can precondition other rats so that they will accept a similar graft on a long-term basis. These experiments are usually most successful when the kidney donor is a first generation hybrid, sharing half of its transplantation antigens with the recipient. This indicates that the concentration of transplantation antigens on the cells of the graft is an important factor in enhancement.

Other studies have shown that lymphoid cells from rats with long-surviving kidney allografts are capable of inducing GVH reactions in animals of the strain from which the graft was derived. This indicates that prolonged graft survival is not solely a consequence of classical immunologic tolerance because tolerant rats usually do not have many cells reactive against tolerated antigens. Other evidence bearing on this question includes the ability of rats with long-surviving kidney allografts to reject skin grafts from the kidney donor, with no effect on the kidney's survival. It would appear that the longer the kidney has been in place the slower the skin graft will be rejected. It is difficult to rule out the possibility that the skin graft might be rejected secondary to some unique antigen not present in the kidney. There is some evidence that antigens of long-surviving grafts may be partially covered, making them unable to take up labeled antibody as readily as a recent graft.

Suppression of Delayed Skin Reactions

When mice are injected with low doses of sheep red blood cells intravenously, they develop good delayed hypersensitivity and no antibody; at high doses, they show high levels of antibody and no delayed hypersensitivity. If the mice are treated with cyclophosphamide up to 2 days before the injection of sheep red blood cells, they make much less antibody to high doses of this antigen and show good delayed hypersensitivity even with very high antigen doses. Inhibition of delayed hypersensitivity is not solely related to antibody production, however, because if sheep red blood cells are injected in Freund's complete adjuvant they induce both high levels of antibody and good delayed hypersensitivity. Also, the injection of mycobacteria in saline several weeks before sheep red blood cell injection allows development of good delayed hypersensitivity and high levels of antibody. There is some evidence that serum taken from mice after an inhibitory injection of sheep red blood cells is able to block both the induction and the expression of delayed hypersensitivity.

Enhancement Versus Tolerance

The discovery that immune serum could block the activity of immune cells in vitro and in vivo led to speculation that similar effects might account for immunologic tolerance. Accordingly, several investigators made mice or rats tolerant by classical methods (injection of foreign lymphoid cells at birth) and later assessed the activity of cells and serum from these tolerant subjects. In some cases it was found that these animals did have some lymphocytes capable of attacking cells from the tolerated donor strain and that their serum could block this attack. On the other hand, lymphoid cells from tolerant animals had much less activity in GVH assays than cells from normal or immune animals. And it has proved impossible to make an animal tolerant of a skin allograft by pretreating it with serum from a classically tolerant donor. It seems reasonable to conclude that in classically tolerant animals a few lymphocytes may survive which can still react against the tolerated antigens, although most of the potentially reactive cells have been eliminated or made tolerant. Serum blocking factors somehow suppress the activity of the residual nontolerant cells.

Tetraparental mice can be produced by scrambling together the fertilized ova of 2 different mouse strains shortly after they begin to divide. The resulting mouse is a mosaic of cells derived from both parent strains and is completely tolerant of tissue grafts from either parent strain. Nevertheless, it has been found that lymphocytes from tetraparental mice are capable of destroying parental strain fibroblasts in vitro and that this destruction is prevented by blocking factors in their serum. These blocking factors can specifically mask the transplantation antigens of lymphocytes from either parent strain, preventing them from being recognized in a mixed lymphocyte culture. Such cell and serum activity is completely absent from first generation hybrid mice, which are a *subcellular* mosaic of all the transplantation antigens of both parent strains.

Possible Mechanisms of Immunologic Enhancement

Several different immunologic phenomena have been discovered which could contribute to immunologic enhancement. One which can strongly affect the afferent arm of the immune response is the ability of preexisting antibody to circumvent immunization entirely. How this occurs is not yet known, but the principle is widely used. Injection of a moderate amount of anti-Rh antibody into an Rh-negative woman at the time she gives birth to an Rh-positive baby will prevent her from becoming immune to the Rh antigen present on any of the baby's red cells which may enter her circulation during birth. Thus, she will not endanger any future Rh-positive children by producing antibodies against this red cell antigen. Pretreatment with antitumor antibodies can delay the development of sensitized lymphocytes in a tumor-grafted host (Chapter 21); in some cases this can markedly reduce the number of cytotoxic lymphocytes which appear. Preexisting antibody may cause the body to eliminate foreign substances via a nonimmunologic pathway. There might also be some type of feedback inhibition of the antibody response. It is well established that in an ongoing antibody response the amount of antibody produced is regulated by the amount of antibody already present in the circulation.

Under some conditions of immunization, as mentioned previously, suppressor T cells appear which can specifically inhibit an immune response against that antigen. Although little is yet known about how these suppressor cells function, it seems likely that they could contribute to enhancement-like phenomena.

One of the most difficult problems concerns the nature of the various "blocking factors" present in immune serum and their mechanism of operation. It seems likely that, under different circumstances, these factors can include soluble tumor (or graft) antigens, antigen-antibody complexes, or antibody alone. It has been possible to obtain tumor-associated blocking factor by absorption of immune serum with specific tumor cells, followed by elution of the factor from the washed cells at low pH and filtration through membranes of different pore sizes. A large (greater than MW 100,000) and a small (less than MW 10,000) component have been separated, and full blocking activity (ie, prevention of cytotoxic destruction of tumor cells in vitro by immune lymphocytes) was restored by recombining these 2 separate components. It may be that the large component is antibody and the small one is an antigen fragment, and that the intact antigen-antibody complex protects tumor cells by combining with, and thus masking, their antigens from attack by cytotoxic lymphocytes or macrophages. It is unclear why antibody alone should not be able to accomplish the same result. Antigen-antibody complexes should be capable of interfering with the activity of cytotoxic lymphocytes or macrophages by binding directly to these cells via their antigen receptor sites. Soluble tumor antigen should also be able to do the same thing. A critical factor—as yet unstudied—may be the survival time of these various blocking factors in the tissue fluids, or on the surface of the appropriate cells. With repeated washing, the white blood cells from some cancer patients become increasingly cytotoxic for the patient's tumor cells in vitro, and the wash fluid can be shown to contain a blocking factor. Also, the ratio of antigen to antibody in blocking antigen-antibody complexes may be important. In one study, immune rat lymph node cells were able to destroy tumor cells in vitro. Serum from immune rats did not affect this killing, but when critical amounts of soluble tumor antigen were added to this serum it strongly blocked the killing reaction. Too much or too little antigen was without effect. Other studies found that soluble tumor antigen alone was able to inhibit the cytotoxic activity of immune lymphocytes against tumor cells.

In summary, the survival of a tumor or normal tissue graft may be shortened or markedly prolonged depending upon complex immunologic processes. Enhanced survival may involve some degree of immunologic tolerance. There may be a delay in the onset of the immune response or decreased vigor of the response due to inhibitory mechanisms. Target cells may be protected from immune attack by blocking antibodies or antigen-antibody complexes. Perhaps the "blindfolding" of cytotoxic cells by saturation of their surface receptors for antigen by excess free antigen or by antigen-antibody complexes may occur. The relative importance of these and other mechanisms, and the final outcome for the host, will depend on a large number of variables, many of which are still unknown.

• • •

References

Baldwin RW, Price MR, Robins RA: Blocking of lymphocyte-mediated cytotoxicity for rat hepatoma cells by tumor-specific antigen-antibody complexes. Nature [New Biol] 238:185, 1972.

Basten A & others: Cell-to-cell interaction in the immune response. 10. T-cell dependent suppression in tolerant mice. J Exp Med 140:199, 1974.

Benjamin DC, Weigle WO: The termination of immunological unresponsiveness to BSA in rabbits. 2. Response to a subsequent injection of BSA. J Immunol 105:1231, 1970.

Brent L: Tolerance and enhancement in organ transplantation. Transplant Proc 4:363, 1972.

Brent L, Holborow J (editors): Mechanisms of immunological unresponsiveness. In: *Progress in Immunology II.* Vol 3. Elsevier, 1974.

Chiller JM, Habicht GS, Weigle WO: Cellular sites of immunologic unresponsiveness. Proc Natl Acad Sci USA 65:551, 1970.

Chiller JM, Habicht GS, Weigle WO: Kinetic differences in unresponsiveness of thymus and bone marrow cells. Science 171:813, 1971.

Feldman JD: Immunological enhancement: A study of blocking antibodies. Adv Immunol 15:167, 1972.

Feldman M: Induction of B cell tolerance by antigen specific T cell factor. Nature [New Biol] 242:82, 1973.

Golub ES, Weigle WO: Studies on the induction of immunologic unresponsiveness. 3. Antigen form and mouse strain variation. J Immunol 102:389, 1969.

Hellström F, Hellström KE, Allison AC: Neonatally induced allograft tolerance may be mediated by serum-borne factors. Nature [New Biol] 230:49, 1971.

Hellström KE, Hellström I: Lymphocyte-mediated cytotoxicity and blocking serum activity to tumor antigens. Adv Immunol 18:209, 1974.

Jones VE, Leskowitz S: Immunochemical studies of antigenic specificity in delayed hypersensitivity. 4. The production of unresponsiveness to delayed hypersensitivity with a single antigenic determinant. J Exp Med 122:505, 1965.

Kapp JA & others: Genetic control of immune responses in vitro. 5. Stimulation of suppressor T cells in nonresponder mice by the terpolymer [L-glutamic acid^{60}-L-alanine^{30}-L-tyrosine^{10}] (GAT). J Exp Med 140:648, 1974.

Katz DH, Benacerraf B (editors): *Immunological Tolerance.* Academic Press, 1974.

Katz DH & others: Carrier function in anti-hapten antibody responses. 4. Experimental conditions for the induction of hapten-specific tolerance or for the stimulation of anti-hapten anamnestic responses by "non-immunogenic" hapten-polypeptide conjugates. J Exp Med 134:201, 1971.

Mackaness GB, Lagrange PH, Ishibashi T: The modifying effect of BCG on the immunological induction of T cells. J Exp Med 139:1540, 1974.

Mitchison NA: The dosage requirements for immunological paralysis by soluble proteins. Immunology 15:509, 1968.

Roelants GE, Goodman JW: Tolerance induction by an apparently non-immunogenic molecule. Nature 227:175, 1970.

Ruben TJ, Chiller JM, Weigle WO: The cellular basis of cross-tolerance. J Immunol 111:805, 1973.

Scott DW: Cellular events in tolerance. 2. Similar specificity of carrier cross-tolerance in vivo and cross-stimulation in vitro. J Immunol 112:1354, 1974.

Shellam GR, Nossal GJV: Mechanism of induction of immunological tolerance. 4. The effects of ultra-low doses of flagellin. Immunology 14:273, 1968.

Sjögren HO & others: Suggestive evidence that the "blocking antibodies" of tumor-bearing individuals may be antigen-antibody complexes. Proc Natl Acad Sci USA 68:1372, 1971.

Wegmann TG, Hellström I, Hellström KE: Immunologic tolerance: "Forbidden clones" allowed in tetraparental mice. Proc Natl Acad Sci USA 68:1644, 1971.

Weigle WO: Immunological unresponsiveness. Adv Immunol 16:61, 1973.

Wright PW & others: Allograft tolerance: Presumptive evidence that serum factors from tolerant animals that block lymphocyte-mediated immunity in vitro are soluble antigen-antibody complexes. Proc Natl Acad Sci USA 70:2539, 1973.

14 . . .
Autoimmunity

Norman Talal, MD, Ken Fye, MD, & Haralampos Moutsopoulos, MD

Autoimmunity is both a major immunologic phenomenon in clinical medicine and an important immunobiologic clue to the workings of the immune system. Autoimmunity plays a role in a wide range of clinical situations, including aging, response to viral and other infections, organ-specific immunologic diseases (eg, thyroiditis), and generalized systemic immunologic diseases (eg, systemic lupus erythematosus). Autoimmunity can be either transient and reversible or persistent and life-threatening. An entire area of clinical medicine, the "autoimmune diseases" (of which rheumatoid arthritis is an important example), is concerned with illnesses in which autoimmunity plays a dominant pathogenetic role.

As a phenomenon in immunobiology, autoimmunity affords an opportunity to study the normal regulation of the immune response through examination of one of its major derangements. The discrimination of self from nonself is an essential and primary function of the immune system, and it is surprising how often and how easily this discriminatory recognition system is disturbed. Immune reactions are mediated by effector cells such as B lymphocytes and their plasma cell progeny, which secrete antibody; by effector T lymphocytes, which produce lymphokines and mediate cellular immunity (Chapter 10); or by monocytes and tissue macrophages. These effector cells are regulated by an intricate network of control mechanisms which include specific immunoglobulin receptors on lymphocyte surface membranes; secreted antibody itself, which can compete for antigen with cell receptors; and specialized subpopulations of T lymphocytes which send "on and off" signals to these effector cells (Chapter 8). Autoimmunity is marked by an abnormal or excessive activity on the part of immune effector cells. This activity can include the production of autoantibodies by B lymphocytes and tissue infiltration or destruction by T lymphocytes and macrophages. These effector cells may not be deranged primarily but may merely be responding to an aberrant set of regulatory signals received from a disordered control system. The word autoimmunity is used to indicate immunologic self-injury and is not intended to imply an etiologic mechanism. For example, the destruction of normal tissue by the host's immune system in its response to a viral immunogen is considered an "autoimmune" phenomenon even though the immune response is triggered by a foreign antigen.

Genetic, immunologic, and viral factors all play an important role in the pathogenesis of autoimmunity. The genetic basis of immunologic regulation is an area of great current interest in immunobiology. A cluster of genes located within the major histocompatibility (H-2) region of the mouse (termed I or immune response region) controls several characteristics of the immune response, eg, the magnitude and immunoglobulin class of antibodies produced in response to specific immunogens, the differences in susceptibility to leukemia viruses, and the intensity of the cellular immune response, such as GVH and mixed lymphocyte reactions. Genetically determined cell surface antigens, termed Ia (I region-associated), are important immunologic factors involved in antigen recognition, cellular interaction, and cellular cooperation. Much evidence suggests that genes associated with the major histocompatibility locus in man (HLA) may also be important in immune regulation and in the pathogenesis of autoimmunity. For example, some human autoimmune diseases such as chronic active hepatitis and chronic thyroiditis are more frequent in patients with HLA-B8. Genetically determined lymphocyte membrane antigens in man (possibly the counterpart of Ia antigens in the mouse) determine the magnitude of response in mixed lymphocyte reactions and may be even more closely related to the development of autoimmunity. The relationship between genetic factors and autoimmunity is most dramatically demonstrated in animal models such as the NZB (New Zealand Black) mouse in which an autoimmune disease resembling systemic lupus erythematosus develops spontaneously. Although the exact mechanism by which genetic factors and autoimmunity are related is unclear, it is likely that immune response genes, lymphocytic surface antigens, and possible receptors for specific viruses are involved.

Norman Talal is Professor of Medicine, Department of Medicine, University of California School of Medicine and Veterans Administration Hospital, San Francisco. Ken Fye and Haralampos Moutsopoulos are Postdoctoral Fellows in Immunology, Department of Medicine, University of California School of Medicine, San Francisco.

IMMUNOLOGIC TOLERANCE

Autoimmunity reflects a loss of immunologic tolerance to tissue and cellular antigens. Immunologic tolerance is the result of an active physiologic process and is not simply the lack of an immune response. Before one can understand the pathogenetic processes that lead to autoimmunity, one must define the mechanisms by which tolerance is induced and maintained.

Mechanisms of Tolerance

It was once thought that lymphocytes which responded to antigenic challenge during ontogeny would be killed. Therefore, all the clones of lymphocytes capable of responding to autoantigens were eliminated before maturation. Only after ontogenetic and immunologic maturation would lymphocytes be capable of generating an immune response without self-destruction. The proponents of this "forbidden clone" theory offered a number of hypothetical pathogenetic mechanisms to explain autoimmunity. Autoimmune phenomena were said to result from (1) somatic mutation of lymphocytes into self-reacting cells; (2) changes in the nature of autoantigens, perhaps due to viral infection; (3) exposure of antigens "hidden" from the immune system during ontogeny; (4) immunization to antigens cross-reactive with autoantigens; or (5) intense stimulation of lymphocyte proliferation, as with the use of adjuvants.

The forbidden clone theory is less popular now. Lymphocytes from experimental animals can be sensitized to syngeneic fibroblasts and thymic reticulum. Lymphocytes capable of sensitization and effector function are present in tolerant animals, suggesting that they were not eliminated as "forbidden clones." Furthermore, normal human B cells possess membrane receptors capable of reacting with antigens such as DNA and thyroglobulin. It appears, therefore, that lymphocytes capable of reacting to self antigens are normally present but are suppressed or inactivated, perhaps by more than one mechanism.

The sensitization of lymphocytes by syngeneic fibroblasts and thymic reticulum can be inhibited by autologous serum (but not by nonsyngeneic serum). This inhibition has been attributed to serum factors that block lymphocyte receptor sites and thereby prevent recognition of and sensitization to autoantigens. These serum factors do not disrupt effector function of sensitized lymphocytes. When lymphocytes are incubated in vitro, these blocking factors are shed from the membranes, allowing sensitization to occur. The exact nature of these blocking factors is unknown, but they may be antigen-antibody complexes. Serum blocking factors are important in certain models of experimental tolerance. Mice inoculated at birth with allogeneic cells will accept skin grafts from donors of the same allogeneic histocompatibility type. Since lymphocytes from these tolerant recipients may be cytotoxic to donor cells in vitro, the in vivo tolerance is thought to be related to serum blocking factors.

Soluble antigens themselves may act as serum blocking factors under some circumstances. Many antigens are T cell-dependent, ie, antibody production depends on T cell as well as B cell sensitization. Tolerance can be induced by inhibition of either T cell or B cell activity. Low concentrations of soluble antigens in the serum may induce and maintain tolerance by interacting directly with B cell receptors, thereby avoiding the normal cooperative interaction involving T cells and macrophages. Exposure of lymphocytes to massive amounts of antigen may also result in tolerance. High-dosage antigenic challenge markedly increases DNA synthesis in thymocytes and leads to a suppressor T cell effect and tolerance. Challenge with intermediate doses of antigen results in moderate increases in thymocyte DNA synthesis and induces helper T cell function and antibody production. It is unclear how suppressor T cells override the helper T cell function.

Autoimmunity may be secondary to a disruption of the normal presentation of autoantigens to the immune system. This may result from genetic abnormalities, as a consequence of viral infection, or from a combination of mechanisms. Manipulation of autoantigens in a way that stimulates helper T cell function (use of adjuvants, immunogenic carriers, cross-reacting antigens, etc) also induces autoimmune phenomena.

Antibodies are themselves powerful immunosuppressive agents. When anti-sheep red blood cell antibodies are administered to mice along with sheep red blood cells, the recipient's primary immunoglobulin response is suppressed. The antibody is thought to prevent interaction of the sensitizing antigens with host lymphocytes. Anti-sheep cell antibody may inhibit the production of antibody-forming cells against sheep red blood cells by combining with small amounts of antigen bound to macrophages and preventing the interaction of carrier macrophages and effector lymphocytes.

Antibody can also suppress cell-mediated immune responses. If rats are pretreated with anti-sheep red blood cell antibody, the cell-mediated immune response usually induced by the administration of sheep red blood cells and adjuvant is suppressed. The ability of antibodies to suppress cellular immunity has also been demonstrated in a transplantation model using Lewis and Brown Norway rats. These 2 strains have major differences in their histocompatibility antigens. If the kidney of a Lewis-Brown Norway F_1 hybrid rat is transplanted into a bilaterally nephrectomized adult Lewis rat, the graft is rejected in 10 days. If the recipient is pretreated with antibody against graft antigens, the rejection reaction is significantly delayed.

Antibodies may act as feedback inhibitors of B cell function, suppressing both effector and memory capabilities. Several possible mechanisms have been suggested: (1) antibody binding to antigen may induce conformational changes in the antigen which interfere with antigen-lymphocyte interaction; (2) the antibody may act as a carrier which presents the antigen to suppressor T cells in the appropriate physical or configurational state to ensure maximum suppressor cell stimulation; (3) antibody may induce tolerance by stimulating massive and exhaustive differentiation of competent cells into short-lived antibody-producing cells; and (4) an antibody may stimulate production of an anti-idiotypic antibody which coats the B cell, rendering it susceptible to antibody-dependent cell-mediated cytotoxicity.

Tolerance to some autoantigens may depend in part on continuous low serum levels of autoantibody against those antigens. If this continuous antibody production is interrupted, autoimmunity might result.

The development of self-tolerance involves early contact between self antigens and receptor sites on the surface of lymphocytes reactive to these antigens. Both T and B lymphocytes can become tolerant. Cells from either the thymus or the bone marrow of mice made tolerant with monomeric human γ-globulin can induce tolerance to aggregated human γ-globulin in adoptive transfer experiments. The kinetics of tolerance in these 2 lymphocyte populations differ greatly. Thymocytes become tolerant to human γ-globulin within 24 hours of exposure, and this tolerance lasts for 100 days. By contrast, bone marrow tolerance requires an induction period of 15–21 days. The long latent period between exposure and tolerance to human γ-globulin may indicate either a relative resistance of bone marrow cells to tolerance or a requirement for thymic cell - bone marrow interaction before tolerance can be induced. The thymus may produce a circulating humoral factor that induces tolerance in bone marrow lymphocytes; alternatively, specific suppressor thymocytes may migrate to the bone marrow and proliferate to induce tolerance in primary bone marrow lymphocytes. Bone marrow tolerance is of short duration, lasting approximately 49 days.

Suppressor lymphocytes are T cells that act as inhibitors of antibody production. Several lines of evidence indicate the presence of suppressor T cells: (1) Thymocytes transplanted from mice made unresponsive to sheep red blood cells block anti - sheep cell antibody formation in recipient animals. (2) Spleen cells from unresponsive mice will inhibit the ability of normal T cells to augment anti - sheep red cell antibody formation. (3) Antilymphocyte serum, which eliminates T cells, increases the antibody response of mice to pneumococcal type III polysaccharide and to other "thymus-independent" antigens. (4) Spleen cells from old NZB mice, when transplanted into young NZB mice depleted of T cells by antilymphocyte serum, will induce a persistent Coombs-positive hemolytic anemia (instead of the temporary anemia seen when old spleen cells are transplanted into normal young NZB mice).

Suppressor cells also inhibit cell-mediated immunity. Picryl chloride is a contact sensitizer in mice, and normal lymph node cells from sensitized mice will transfer the sensitivity to picryl chloride to lethally irradiated recipients. Lymph node cells from animals made unresponsive to picryl chloride can block the ability of normal cells to transfer this reactivity.

The ability to transfer suppressor activity with thymocytes and the loss of suppression following antilymphocyte serum administration support the contention that the active suppressor cell is a T lymphocyte. Intrathymic injection of bovine γ-globulin will suppress the immune response to later administration of bovine γ-globulin in adjuvant. Also, B cell tolerance to sheep red cells cannot be induced, even by high-dosage antigen administration, in the absence of thymocytes. Neonatally thymectomized mice, athymic ("nude") mice, and mice treated with antilymphocyte serum show an enhanced antibody response to thymus-independent antigens. In mice treated with antilymphocyte serum, this enhanced response can be eliminated by thymocyte administration. It appears that thymus-independent antigens stimulate suppressor but not helper T cells. There is still considerable controversy about the exact nature of the suppressor T cell. It is probably produced in the thymus, has a moderate life span, and has a predilection for the spleen and thymus. Helper T cells are probably long-lived peripheral blood lymphocytes with a predilection for lymph nodes.

Suppressor T cells could act in part by recognition of B cell idiotypes. Antigen receptors on B cells may be recognized by T cells, and those B cells with specific receptors for autoantigens may thus be actively suppressed. The major evidence that T cells can recognize and directly affect production of immunoglobulin comes from work with BALB/c mice. It has been shown that hybrid BALB/c x SJL female mice immunized against paternal SJL "b" γ-globulin allotype have permanent suppression of the production of this specific γ-globulin. When normal spleen cells are transplanted with suppressed spleen cells into lethally irradiated BALB/c mice, there is a temporary synthesis of "b" allotype γ-globulin. Treatment with antilymphocyte serum also results in temporary "b" allotype production. Therefore, the suppression of synthesis and release of "b" allotype immunoglobulin in this model is thought to be related to suppressor T cell activity.

Helper T cells generally work through carrier recognition. How is the suppressor T cell effect mediated? Immunization experiments with ascaris protein (carrier) conjugated with dinitrophenyl groups (hapten) have demonstrated that transplanted thymocytes made tolerant to the carrier showed suppression of the B cell response to hapten. However, T cells tolerant to the hapten did not suppress B cell responsiveness to hapten-ascaris conjugates in rats that were depleted of their own thymocytes. These findings suggest that suppressor T cells show the same carrier specificity as helper T cells.

T lymphocytes are capable of nonspecific suppressor effects as well. Future work on suppressor T cells will probably reveal several mechanisms by which they exert their effects.

Autoimmunity & Tolerance

Autoimmunity can be induced by maneuvers that overcome the mechanisms of tolerance or that bypass the normal requirement for helper T cells (Table 14–1). For example, the administration of Freund's complete adjuvant with homologous tissue will result in the formation of autoantibodies against these injected tissue antigens.

Viral infections may stimulate autoimmune phenomena directed against host tissue antigens. In certain viral infections, virus-specific antigens appear on the host cell surface. In addition, host-specific antigens can be detected in the lipid envelopes of viruses such as leukemia viruses. Repeated inoculations of experimental animals with viruses grown in syngeneic tissue cultures will lead to the formation of a variety of autoantibodies. Influenza virus cultured in chorioallantoic cells will induce autoantibodies against antigens common to chorioallantoic and liver cells. In humans, influenza, measles, varicella, coxsackie, and herpes simplex viral infections have all been associated with autoimmune phenomena, including thrombocytopenia and Coombs-positive antibody. Immunity against tumor-specific antigens can be increased by immunizing mice with influenza virus grown in tumor cells. Infection of NZB, NZW (New Zealand White), and NZB/NZW hybrid mice with polyoma or lymphocytic choriomeningitis viruses accelerates the onset of autoimmunity. In virus-induced autoantibody production, the virus may act as a carrier and circumvent the need for helper T cells.

Haptens and drugs may induce autoimmunity. If the host becomes sensitized to a hapten bound to host tissues, this tissue may become an innocent target of an autoimmune reaction. Autoimmunity can be produced in animal models using experimental haptens like oxazolone or dinitrophenyl. Methyldopa binds to human erythrocytes and may result in positive direct and indirect Coombs tests. Antinuclear antibody production in some patients receiving procainamide or hydralazine may be due to binding of these drugs to nuclear materials.

Nonspecific stimulation of the helper T cell effect can result in autoimmunity. The injection of allogeneic cells in a chronic GVH reaction appears to stimulate nonspecific helper T cell activity, which frequently results in antinuclear antibody formation and other evidence of autoimmunity. Infectious agents act either as carriers or as nonspecific adjuvants in those nonviral infectious diseases (such as leprosy, malaria, and syphilis) associated with autoantibody production.

Exposure to cross-reacting antigens will induce loss of tolerance. Animals formerly tolerant to BSA become reactive after administration of dinitrophenylated bovine albumin or other cross-reacting antigens. Cross-reactivity with foreign antigens may be the explanation for organ-specific (antithyroid) or non-organ-specific (antinuclear) autoantibody formation seen in a number of human disease states (Chapter 27).

Table 14–1. Possible methods of induction of autoimmunity.

(1) Injection of homologous tissue with Freund's complete adjuvant
(2) Infection by viruses which contain cross-reacting antigens or alter host antigens, rendering them autoimmunogenic
(3) Binding of foreign haptens (such as drugs) to host tissues
(4) Nonspecific stimulation of helper T cell activity
(5) Exposure to cross-reacting foreign antigens
(6) Loss of suppressor T cell activity

THE ROLE OF VIRUSES IN AUTOIMMUNITY

Several experimental animal models of autoimmunity, as well as certain examples drawn from clinical medicine, leave little doubt that viruses play an important role in the pathogenesis of autoimmunity. Certain viruses in susceptible animals and humans lead to persistent and chronic states of infection. These "slow virus" diseases often show features of autoimmunity and immune complex formation.

Moreover, the nucleic acids of certain viruses (eg, C-type leukemia viruses) may actually become integrated into mammalian genes and be transmitted from parent to progeny as part of the genetic information of the cell. These "virogenes" may become expressed in the host under certain circumstances and these newly formed antigens may become immunogenic, leading to the formation of antiviral antibodies. Such an antiviral immune response may occur quite frequently. Circulating immune complexes of viral antigens and antiviral antibodies may be deposited in blood vessels and along glomerular basement membrane, sometimes causing glomerulonephritis. For example, neonatal infection of mice with lymphocytic choriomeningitis virus can lead to a chronic persistent virus infection and immune complex nephritis. The renal deposits contain viral antigen, antibody, and complement. A similar pathologic disorder develops if lymphocytic choriomeningitis virus is inoculated into adult immunosuppressed mice.

The outcome of the interaction between virus and host is influenced by genetic and immunologic factors which vary from one mouse strain to another. To make matters even more complicated, viruses can themselves interfere with the normal functioning of the host immune system. Therefore, in any given situation, it may be difficult to decide what is most responsible for the autoimmunity and immunopathology. It could be viral interference with normal immune function or an abnormal immune response incapable of adequately responding to the virus.

Polyarteritis nodosa is one human autoimmune disease in which a known virus has been clearly implicated. The hepatitis B virus is found in about one-third of these patients. The serum of such patients contains circulating immune complexes which appear to consist of viral antigen and antiviral antibody. Serum complement levels may be diminished. Deposits of viral antigen-antibody complexes and complement have been detected in the walls of involved blood vessels. Such complexes have also been deposited along glomerular basement membranes in a few patients with the glomerulonephritis of hepatitis virus-associated polyarteritis nodosa.

A number of chronic diseases of the central nervous system are also associated with chronic virus infections. Subacute sclerosing panencephalitis, a degenerative brain disease of children, is related to measles virus infection. The serum and cerebrospinal fluid of patients with subacute sclerosing panencephalitis contain extremely high titers of antimeasles antibodies, and viral inclusion bodies are seen in the brain cells. Scrapie, a degenerative brain disease of sheep, is another example of slow virus disease of the central nervous system. The spongioform encephalopathies (kuru and Jakob-Creutzfeldt disease) may also be caused by viral agents.

The clinical disorders associated with the Epstein-Barr (EB) virus demonstrate the broad variety of immunopathologic responses that can occur to a single viral agent. EB virus is a herpeslike DNA virus that is strongly implicated in the pathogenesis of infectious mononucleosis. Autoantibodies and splenomegaly may occur in this disorder. There is considerable evidence that the abnormal circulating peripheral blood lymphocytes in infectious mononucleosis are T lymphocytes specifically sensitized to EB viral antigens present on the surface of B lymphocytes. Apparently, in infectious mononucleosis the EB virus infects B lymphocytes and causes a profound host T cell response to new cell surface antigens produced as a result of virus expression. Infectious mononucleosis is a self-limited disease, and most patients recover. However, EB virus is also associated with the malignant lymphoproliferative disease known as Burkitt's lymphoma. In this disorder, originally described in African children, infection with EB virus results in a permanent malignant transformation of B lymphocytes. Genetic and immunologic factors may determine whether the host response to EB virus will be one of no disease, a self-limited immunopathologic disorder such as infectious mononucleosis, or a malignant lymphoma.

During the last decade, considerable discussion has focused on a possible role for virus infection in the pathogenesis of systemic lupus erythematosus. Systemic lupus erythematosus is an acute or chronic inflammatory disease in which antibodies to DNA and RNA appear in association with reduced serum complement concentrations and immune complex glomerulonephritis. Patients with systemic lupus erythematosus tend to have elevated serum antibodies to a number of viruses, including measles, myxoviruses, and EB virus. These augmented antibody responses to viral antigens probably reflect a general heightened antibody response rather than an immune response to specific etiologic agents. The antibodies to RNA have greatest specificity for viral nucleic acid—further possible evidence implicating virus infection in this disease. Endothelial cells and lymphocytes from patients with lupus erythematosus contain tubular structures visible with the electron microscope that were originally thought to represent viral inclusions but are now considered to be nonspecific alterations of internal cell membranes. These tubular reticular structures are also seen in other connective tissue diseases such as dermatomyositis and Sjögren's syndrome.

Recent evidence suggests that the kidneys and spleens of patients with lupus erythematosus contain antigens cross-reactive with murine leukemia viral antigens. However, these antigens are also present in tissues of normal individuals. Since the presence of a human leukemia virus has not been adequately demonstrated to date, it is difficult to draw conclusions based on these very recent findings. Nevertheless, possible implication of leukemia virus in systemic lupus erythematosus is particularly interesting because murine leukemia virus is involved in the pathogenesis of the lupus-like syndrome of NZB mice.

ANIMAL MODELS FOR HUMAN AUTOIMMUNE DISEASE: NZB MOUSE DISEASE

Much of our knowledge about genetic, immunologic, and virologic factors in the pathogenesis of autoimmunity comes from studies with animal models, in particular the NZB (New Zealand Black) and the NZW (New Zealand White) mouse. NZB and NZB/NZW F_1 mice spontaneously develop LE cells, antinuclear antibodies, antibodies to nucleic acids such as DNA and RNA, antibodies to murine leukemia viral antigens, autoimmune hemolytic anemia, and immune complex glomerulonephritis. In addition, they have a generalized lymphocytic and plasma cell infiltration of many organs, including the lungs, liver, kidneys, and salivary glands. The autoimmune hemolytic anemia is most severe in NZB mice, whereas the immune complex glomerulonephritis is most marked in NZB/NZW F_1 mice (particularly the females).

These mice are generally considered a model for human systemic lupus erythematosus. As in the human disease, the glomerulonephritis is due to the deposition of immune complexes and complement. The immune complexes contain complement and antibodies to DNA and to a viral antigen characteristic of murine leukemia virus. The anti-nucleic acid antibodies that appear in NZB mice may represent immunization to viral nucleic acids or to host nucleic acids. This important point is unresolved.

Aged NZB and NZB/NZW mice develop malignant lymphomas and monoclonal macroglobulinemia. Thus, in addition to their autoimmune disease, New Zealand mice develop features of another human disorder: Waldenström's macroglobulinemia. This latter condition is considered a malignant proliferation of lymphocytes or lymphocytoid plasma cells, in many ways analogous to chronic lymphocytic leukemia. The association of both autoimmune and malignant lymphocytic disorders in a single inbred mouse strain has several important implications for pathogenesis.

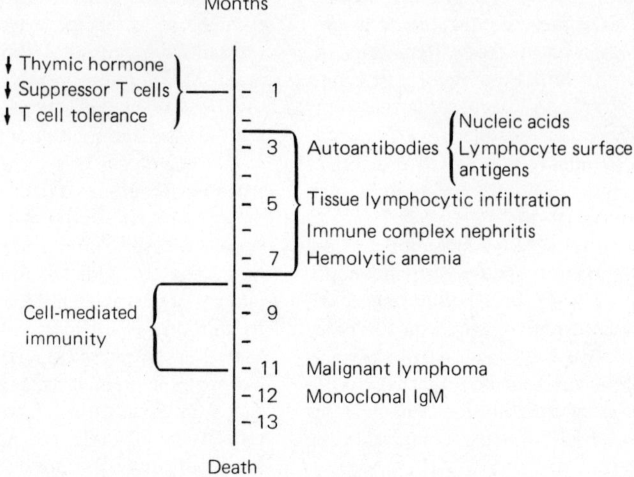

Figure 14–1. Immunologic and immunopathologic events throughout the life span of NZB and NZB/NZW mice.

The immune disorders of New Zealand mice can be seen as a progressive escape of B cells from T cell regulation, manifest first as autoimmunity and later as B cell malignancy. A temporal presentation of this scheme is shown in Fig 14–1. At about 1 month of age, there is a decrease of serum thymic hormone activity (Chapter 11), a decrease of suppressor T cell function, and the development of T cell resistance to immunologic tolerance. At approximately 3 months of age, serum autoantibodies appear and various tissues and organs become infiltrated by lymphocytes and plasma cells. Autoantibodies to nucleic acids, to lymphocyte surface antigens, and to viral antigens are particularly significant subsequent pathogenetic events. From 5 months onward there is a progressive appearance of clinical disease manifest as immune complex glomerulonephritis and autoimmune hemolytic anemia. Gross defects in cell-mediated immunity appear after approximately 8 months. After 11 months, malignant lymphomas and monoclonal IgM may develop. The majority of mice die from the autoimmune disease, from the malignant process, or from intercurrent infection.

The immunologic status of NZB and NZB/NZW F_1 mice is summarized in Table 14–2. The immunologic properties of these animals vary greatly depending upon age and stage of disease. In general, their immune status can best be characterized as an imbalance in which B cell activity and antibody responses are excessive and T cell activity and cell-mediated immunity are depressed. This imbalance could arise because of a defect in T cell regulation of other T or B lymphocytes. This state of disordered immunologic regulation would leave these mice particularly susceptible to unusual forms of virus expression and to the development of autoimmunity and malignancy.

Table 14–2. Immunologic abnormalities in NZB and NZB/NZW mice.

Premature development of competence in B and T cells
B cells produce excessive antibody responses
T cells are unable to develop and maintain tolerance
Loss of suppressor T cell function
Decreased serum thymic hormone activity
Deficient T cell functions later in life
Loss of recirculating T lymphocytes
Spontaneous production of thymocytotoxic antibody

NZB and NZB/NZW mice appear clinically normal for the first 3–4 months of life. However, careful immunologic studies have revealed that New Zealand mice develop immunologic competence prematurely in both B and T cells. In the first days and weeks of life, they have excessive antibody responses to a variety of experimental antigens, including foreign proteins, sheep erythrocytes, and synthetic nucleic acids. At this age, they also show a resistance to the induction and maintenance of immunologic tolerance to soluble foreign proteins and sheep erythrocytes. This resistance to immunologic tolerance is particularly apparent in the T cells of New Zealand mice. Left with primarily B cell tolerance, which is short-lived, New Zealand mice maintain tolerance poorly to a variety of experimental antigens. As a consequence, they are unable to remain tolerant to the leukemia virus, which they harbor from birth, and they form antibodies to viral antigens. Recent experiments also indicate that a deficiency of suppressor T cells appears at 1–2 months of age. This is also the age when thymic hormone activity in the serum of New Zealand mice declines markedly. Treatment of New Zealand mice with thymosin, a thymic hormone preparation (Chapter 11), has resulted in the restoration of suppressor cell activity. However, such treatment has not significantly modified either the serologic or pathologic features of the autoimmune disease.

Older New Zealand mice have markedly deficient T cell effector functions demonstrated by decreased responsiveness to mitogens, impaired ability to induce GVH disease, and impaired capacity to reject malignant tumors. They also have marked alterations in their lymphoid populations with a deficiency of long-lived recirculating T lymphocytes demonstrated in lymph nodes and spleen. These findings are associated with a moderate decrease in T lymphocytes in peripheral lymphoid organs.

The cellular immunologic abnormalities of New Zealand mice are explainable by a progressive loss of thymic function with age. One mechanism to account for this loss may involve a thymocytotoxic autoantibody which appears spontaneously and early in NZB mice. This antibody has specificity for T lymphocytes and is cytotoxic in the presence of complement. It is predominantly an IgM immunoglobulin and is reactive in the cold. A closely similar antilymphocytic antibody is also present in the serum of humans with systemic lupus erythematosus.

OTHER ANIMAL MODELS FOR AUTOIMMUNE DISEASES

In addition to the immune disorders of NZB and NZB/NZW F_1 mice, there are several other animal models of autoimmunity which support the hypothesis that genetic, immunologic, and viral factors are all involved in pathogenesis. These animal models for human disease include Aleutian disease of mink, equine infectious anemia, autoimmune thyroiditis in the obese strain of chickens, and canine systemic lupus erythematosus.

Aleutian disease of mink is characterized by glomerulonephritis, vascular lesions resembling those of polyarteritis nodosa, severe hypergammaglobulinemia, and marked systemic plasma cell proliferation. Ranch-raised mink homozygous for a recessive Aleutian coat-color gene are particularly susceptible to this virus-related illness. Although the virus has not been characterized, this disease can be transmitted by cell-free extracts. Highly susceptible mink die of renal failure 3–5 months after infection, whereas non-Aleutian mink rarely die earlier than 5 months after infection and 50% are alive after 1 year. Chronically infected mink excrete virus in the urine, saliva, and feces. Therefore, horizontal transmission is easy and is a significant economic hazard on mink ranches.

The hypergammaglobulinemia in this disease is generally polyclonal but may at times appear monoclonal. Antibodies to viral antigens appear in high titer, and circulating viral antigen-antibody complexes are present in the serum. These complexes are deposited in blood vessels and can be eluted along with complement from glomerular capillaries. The disorder appears to represent an enormous antibody response to viral antigen leading to immune complex vasculitis and nephritis. Cellular immunity in these animals has not been studied. It is not known why the mink are unable to clear the virus and instead develop a persistent viremia.

Equine infectious anemia is a naturally occurring virus infection of horses characterized by fever, weight loss, anemia, hepatitis, lymphadenopathy, splenomegaly, glomerulonephritis, and hypergammaglobulinemia. The virus resembles, by ultrastructure, the C-type particle of leukemia virus and is similar to the virus of NZB mice. Antibodies to viral antigens and circulating antigen-antibody immune complexes containing viral antigens appear in the blood. The glomerular deposits contain antibody and complement. Erythrocytes from infected horses are coated with complement and show an increased fragility and decreased life span. These findings are analogous to the hemolytic anemia that occurs in various autoimmune states, including the hemolytic anemia in NZB mice and in human systemic lupus erythematosus. Lymphocyte transformation in response to mitogens appears normal in sick animals, as does the number of B and T lymphocytes.

The obese strain of chickens is characterized by the spontaneous development of severe thyroiditis during the first weeks of life, leading eventually to hypothyroidism. The thyroid glands show extensive lymphocytic and plasma cell infiltrates with formation of germinal centers. Antibodies against thyroglobulin are present in the serum. The number of B cells infiltrating the thymus is markedly increased, and bursectomy can suppress the development of the disease. Recent evidence suggests that this is predominantly a B cell disorder, with antibody-dependent cellular cytotoxicity playing a significant role in the destruction of thyroid tissue. This disorder appears analogous to Hashimoto's thyroiditis in humans.

Canine systemic lupus erythematosus was reported in a colony of dogs that developed autoimmune hemolytic anemia, glomerulonephritis, polyarteritis, thyroiditis, thrombocytopenic purpura, positive LE cell preparations, and the formation of antibodies to nuclear antigens. Antibodies to native DNA are also produced by these animals. Breeding experiments suggested a possible infectious agent. Cell-free filtrates prepared from the spleens of these dogs induce antinuclear antibodies when injected into newborn dogs and into (BALB/c x A/J)F_1 mice. Approximately 6% of such injected mice also develop malignant lymphomas. C-type viral particles characteristic of leukemia virus are prominent in the lymphoid tumors. One lymphoid tumor produced in this manner synthesizes a monoclonal immunoglobulin that has strong binding affinity for double-stranded DNA. This monoclonal immunoglobulin, an IgAκ type myeloma protein, has binding characteristics for DNA similar to antibodies that occur in lupus erythematosus and in NZB/NZW F_1 mice. The tumor has been established in tissue culture where the cells produce numerous C-type viral particles. This finding again raises the possibility of a C-type leukemia virus being involved in systemic lupus erythematosus.

CONCLUSION

A reasonable concept of pathogenesis for autoimmunity can be drawn from clinical experience and from the animal models. According to this concept, autoimmunity may arise whenever there exists a state of immunologic imbalance in which B cell activity is excessive and suppressor T cell activity is diminished. This imbalance occurs as a consequence of genetic, viral, and environmental mechanisms acting singly or in combination. A central mechanism in this concept involves a disturbance of the delicate balance between suppressor and helper activity of regulatory T cells. Either an excess of helper T activity or a deficiency of suppressor T activity could lead to the development of autoimmunity. The mechanisms by which such a balance may be upset are complex but may involve both viral factors and the abnormal production of thymic hormones.

A schematic representation of the balance of forces acting on the B cell is presented in Fig 14–2. The B cell is shown diagrammatically with several different membrane receptors present on its cell surface. One receptor (immunoglobulin) is capable of interacting with the antigen itself. This receptor can be identified easily because immunoglobulin (particularly IgM and IgD) and idiotypic determinants of immunoglobulin are prominently displayed on the B cell surface. The figure shows 2 other B cell receptors which respond to signals transmitted from regulatory T lymphocytes. It is not known for certain that helper and suppressor T cells represent different subpopulations (as shown in the diagram), nor is it known how their signals arise or how these signals are transmitted to the B cell surface. The simplest model would be a soluble mediator, perhaps composed of multiple subunits, which serves to transmit these regulatory signals to the B cell. The balance of T regulatory signals arriving at the B cell surface would determine whether the B lymphocyte remains inactive or whether it goes into active synthesis and proliferation. If the B lymphocyte represents a clone with potential for producing an autoantibody, then this balance of signals would determine whether or not autoimmunity appears. In New Zealand mice, for example, these signals appear deranged and the B lymphocytes produce autoantibodies. If the imbalance of regulatory signals results in excessive B cell proliferation, malignant lymphomas might develop as they do in some New Zealand mice.

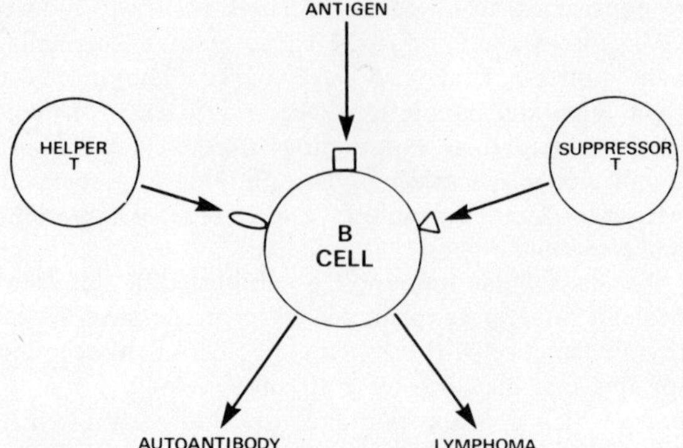

Figure 14–2. A schematic representation of the forces acting on B cells.

If we accept the animal model as valid for the human situation, then we must conclude that a similar imbalance of T cell regulatory signals may be operative in human autoimmune disease and human lymphoid malignancies. This pathogenetic formulation, although still theoretical, may give rise in the future to more rational therapeutic approaches than those currently available. For example, either through hormonal, viral, or other means we might hope to restore the balance between T regulatory signals and thereby reverse autoantibody production and lymphoproliferation by potentially harmful B cell clones.

• • •

References

Allison AC: Unresponsiveness to self antigens. Lancet 2:1401, 1971.

Allison AC, Denman AM, Barnes RD: Cooperating and controlling function of thymus-derived lymphocytes in relation to autoimmunity. Lancet 2:135, 1971.

Altman A, Cohen IR, Feldman M: Normal T cell receptors for alloantigens. Cell Immunol 7:134, 1973.

Bach JF, Dardenne M, Salomon JC: Studies of thymic products. 4. Absence of serum thymic activity in adult NZB and (NZB x NZW)F_1 mice. Clin Exp Immunol 14:247, 1973.

Carnaud C & others: Increased reactivity of mouse spleen cells sensitized in vitro against syngeneic tumor cells in the presence of a thymic humoral factor. J Exp Med 138:1521, 1973.

Cohen IR: The recruitment of specific effector lymphocytes by antigen-reactive lymphocytes in cell-mediated autosensitization and allosensitization reactions. Cell Immunol 8:209, 1973.

Cohen IR, Globerson A, Feldman M: Autosensitization in vitro. J Exp Med 133:834, 1971.

Cohen IR, Wekerle H: Regulation of autosensitization: The immune activation and specific inhibition of self-recognizing thymus-derived lymphocytes. J Exp Med 137:224, 1973.

Gershon RK: T-cell control of antibody production. Chap 1 in: *Contemporary Topics in Immunology*. Vol 3. Cooper MD, Warner NL (editors). Plenum Press, 1974.

Henson JB, McGuire TC: Equine infectious anemia. Prog Med Virol 18:143, 1974.

Howie JB, Helyer BJ: The immunology and pathology of NZB mice. Adv Immunol 9:215, 1968.

Lambert PH, Dixon FS: Pathogenesis of the glomerulonephritis of NZB/W mice. J Exp Med 127:507, 1968.

Levy JA: Autoimmunity and neoplasia: The possible role of C-type viruses. Am J Clin Pathol 62:258, 1974.

Lewis RM, Schwartz RS: Canine systemic lupus erythematosus. J Exp Med 134:417, 1971.

Mellors RC: Autoimmune and immunoproliferative diseases of NZB/Bl and hybrids. Int Rev Exp Pathol 5:217, 1966.

Orgad S, Cohen IR: Autoimmune encephalomyelitis: Activation of thymus lymphocytes against syngeneic brain antigens in vitro. Science 183:1083, 1974.

Porter DD, Larsen AE: Aleutian disease of mink. Prog Med Virol 18:32, 1974.

Rowley DA & others: Specific suppression of immune responses. Science 181:1133, 1973.

Staples PJ, Talal N: Relative inability to induce tolerance in adult NZB and NZB/NZW F_1 mice. J Exp Med 129:123, 1969.

Sugai S, Pillarisetty RJ, Talal N: Monoclonal macroglobulinemia in NZB/NZW F_1 mice. J Exp Med 138:989, 1973.

Talal N: Immunologic and viral factors in the pathogenesis of systemic lupus erythematosus. Arthritis Rheum 13:887, 1970.

Talal N & others: Effect of thymosin on thymocyte proliferation and autoimmunity in NZB mice. Ann NY Acad Sci 249:438, 1975.

Weigle WO: Recent observations and concepts in immunological unresponsiveness and autoimmunity. Clin Exp Immunol 9:437, 1971.

Witebsky E & others: Spontaneous thyroiditis in the obese strain of chickens. 1. Demonstration of circulating autoantibodies. J Immunol 103:708, 1969.

Ziff M: Viruses and the connective tissue diseases. Ann Intern Med 75:951, 1971.

15 . . .
Transplantation Immunology

Herbert A. Perkins, MD

Transplantation of certain organs is now a common clinical procedure, and the technics of procuring and implanting the organs are sufficiently well established so that the only major obstacle to performing the procedure is an insufficient supply of cadaver organs. However, a high percentage of organ grafts are unsuccessful, especially when the donor of the transplanted organ is unrelated to the recipient. These failures are related almost entirely to the immunologic response of the recipient to the foreign histocompatibility antigens of the donor organ. This rejection response can lead to death of tissue, and attempts to suppress the recipient's immune response with high doses of adrenal corticosteroids or cytotoxic agents may result in death of the patient due to complications related to those agents.

Herbert A. Perkins is Clinical Professor of Medicine, University of California School of Medicine, San Francisco, and Director of Research, Irwin Memorial Blood Bank, San Francisco.

The rejection response has both humoral and cellular components. Circulating antibody in the serum of the recipient can react with donor cells. This is associated with immediate (hyperacute) or accelerated graft rejection and is accompanied by deposition of platelets and fibrin in the graft vessels and invasion of neighboring tissues with granulocytes (Fig 15–1). More delayed and slowly progressive rejection is accompanied by infiltration of the graft by host mononuclear cells (Fig 15–2). As will be discussed below, these 2 types of response (humoral and cellular) are directed against determinants on the cell membrane which are products of distinct but closely linked genes.

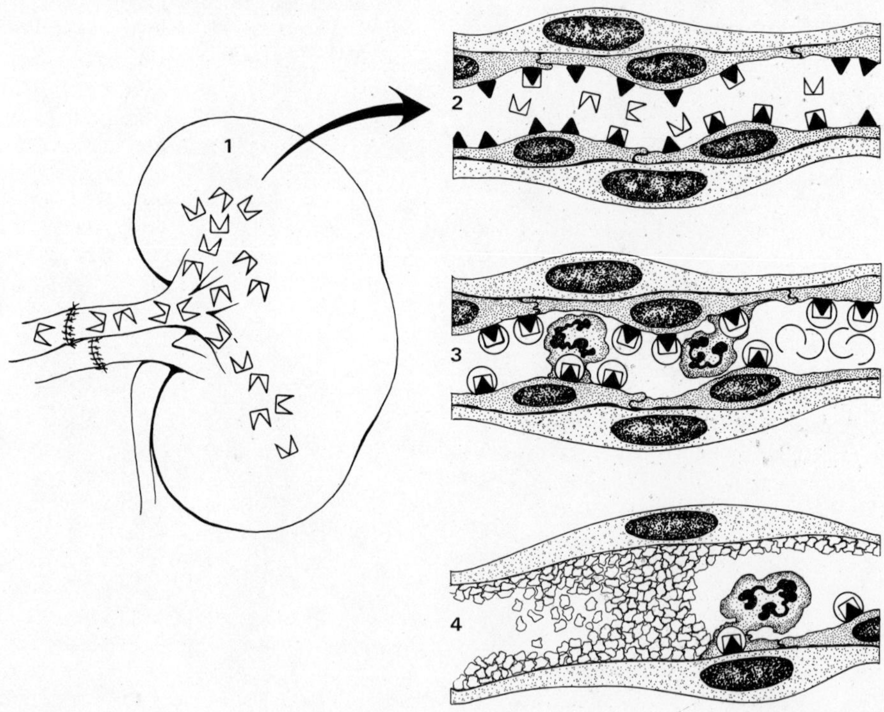

Figure 15–1. Mechanisms of hyperacute rejection. *1:* Preformed antibodies enter the donor kidney. *2:* The antibodies react with the antigenic determinants of endothelial cells of the capillaries of the donor kidney. *3:* Following activation of complement, polymorphonuclear leukocytes are attracted to and destroy endothelial cells. *4:* Platelets attach to denuded areas of the capillaries, forming a platelet plug, activating coagulation, and resulting in obstruction of the vessel. (Redrawn and reproduced, with permission, from Good RA, Fisher DW: *Immunobiology*. Sinauer Associates, Inc., 1971. [Original source: Hospital Practice.])

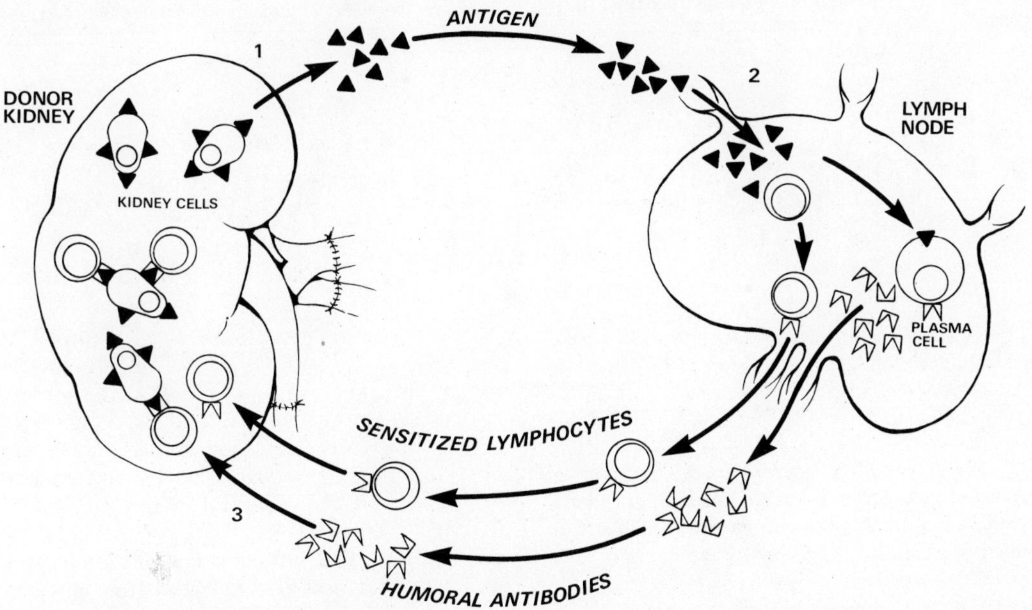

Figure 15–2. Mechanisms of primary acute rejection. *1:* Soluble antigens are released from donor kidney cells. *2:* Soluble antigens enter lymph nodes and stimulate lymphocytes. B lymphocytes proliferate and form plasma cells which produce specific antibodies. Other lymphocytes are sensitized and become cytotoxic. *3:* The humoral antibodies and sensitized lymphocytes return to and destroy the graft. ***Note:*** In more chronic forms of rejection, the damage is believed to result primarily from the sensitized lymphocytes. (Redrawn and reproduced, with permission, from Bellanti JA: *Immunology*. Saunders, 1971.)

The Major Human Histocompatibility Loci

In all animal species thus far studied, including man, the most important determinants responsible for graft rejection are products of a closely linked cluster of genes on a single chromosome. The proof of this statement is the higher graft survival rate observed when the organ donor and the recipient are siblings who can be demonstrated by serologic reactions to possess similar pairs of chromosomes containing these genes. However, there is also clear evidence that matching for these major histocompatibility loci is not in itself enough to ensure prolonged graft survival. Kidneys from sibling donors matched for these major loci survive only if immunosuppressive agents are administered. Marrow grafts from sibling donors matched for these major loci often lead to fatal GVH disease. These problems will be discussed in greater detail below.

Table 15–1. Major human histocompatibility loci, 1967.

	LA Alleles	4 Alleles
LA	HL-A1	HL-A5
4	HL-A2	HL-A7
	HL-A3	HL-A8
	3 alleles	3 alleles
	Total = 6	

The HLA Genes & Their Allelic Products

In man, the major histocompatibility region has been named HLA. This terminology was originally intended to indicate H for human, L for leukocyte, and A for the first defined genetic locus for human leukocyte antigens. Progress in defining HLA antigens and their genetic relationship has been greatly facilitated by a series of International Histocompatibility Workshops. Following each workshop, a nomenclature committee sponsored by the World Health Organization has recommended terminology for newly accepted antigens.

By 1967, it was obvious that there were 2 separate HLA loci (Table 15–1). These loci were close enough together on the same chromosome so that the 2 antigens which were products of a single chromosome were almost always inherited together, but the loci were far enough apart so that crossover occurred in approximately 1% of meiotic divisions. It became common practice to call the first locus the LA locus, since it included the LA-1, LA-2, etc antigens first described by Rose Payne. Similarly, the second locus was commonly referred to as the 4 locus, since its antigens were associated with the 4a (W4) and 4b (W6) antigens first described by Van Rood.*

*Genetic control of 4a and 4b is still not clearly established. It now appears likely that they are products of a locus separate from the established HLA loci but with a high degree of linkage disequilibrium with the 4 locus antigens.

Table 15–2. Major human histocompatibility loci, 1970.

Locus	LA Alleles	4 Alleles
LA	HL-A1	HL-A5
4	HL-A2	HL-A7
	HL-A3	HL-A8
	HL-A9	HL-A12
	HL-A10	HL-A13
	HL-A11	W5
	W28	W10
		W14
		W15
		W17
		W18
		W22
		W27

Number of Alleles	
LA	7
4	13
Total	20

Table 15–3. Major human histocompatibility loci, 1972.

Locus	LA Alleles	4 Alleles
LA	HL-A1	HL-A5
4	HL-A2	HL-A7
MLC	HL-A3	HL-A8
	HL-A9	HL-A12
	W23	HL-A13
	W24	W5
	HL-A10	W10
	W25	W14
	W26	W15
	HL-A11	W16
	W19	W17
	W29	W18
	W30	W21
	W31	W22
	W32	W27
	W28	

Number of Alleles	
LA	16
4	15
Total	31

The 1970 Workshop increased the number of recognized antigens from 6 to 20 and introduced the practice of applying W (Workshop) prefixes for antigens which were only provisionally accepted (Table 15–2).

By 1972, the number of antigens had been increased to 31. Some previously recognized antigens had been split into subtypes (indented in Table 15–3), and it was apparent that mixed lymphocyte culture (MLC) reactions were caused by differences in products of a third gene locus in the HLA region.

MLC reactions occur when lymphocytes from 2 different individuals are cultured together. They respond to differences in cell surface determinants by enlarging, becoming more primitive in appearance, synthesizing DNA at an increased rate, and undergoing cell division. This reaction is conveniently quantitated by measuring the incorporation of tritiated thymidine into DNA. As a rule, one of the lymphocyte preparations is treated with mitomycin or irradiation prior to placement in the culture medium so that this cell cannot itself respond, thus serving only as the stimulator to the other (responder) population. Under some circumstances, a 2-way MLC is done in which neither population is pretreated, and thymidine incorporation summates the response of both populations to each other. The MLC response was first believed to result from differences in HLA antigens, since the lymphocytes of HLA-identical siblings did not stimulate each other in MLC and all other combinations did. However, when cells from HLA-identical *unrelated* individuals are tested, 90% respond. The response of unrelated HLA-identical cells might have been attributed to the limitations of ensuring absolute HLA identity by serologic technics, but studies soon showed that in occasional families there could be MLC stimulation between HLA-identical sibling cells or failure of a response when the siblings were not HLA-identical. These data have been interpreted to mean that the MLC response is not to HLA antigen differences but to determinants which are products of genes closely linked to but separate from HLA. There may be multiple MLC loci controlling lymphocyte responses in mixed lymphocyte cultures, just as there are multiple HLA loci, but the major MLC gene appears to be on the far side of the 4 gene from the LA gene (Table 15–3). The frequency of crossover between the 4 gene and the MLC gene is approximately 0.5%.

MLC differences are believed to be a major factor in rejection of organ transplants. The mechanism of action of MLC genes may be inferred from in vitro studies using the procedure known as cell-mediated lymphocytolysis. In the lymphocytolysis test, a standard MLC is prepared and incubated and, after several days, target lymphocyte cells labeled with ^{51}Cr are added. Injury or death of target cells is indicated by leaking of ^{51}Cr into the supernatant solution. Results with this test indicate that MLC differences are required for target cell killing but that these differences are required only in the first or recognition phase. In the second, or cell injury phase, killing of target cells is dependent not on MLC differences but on differences in HLA antigens or in products of genes closely linked to HLA.

After the 1975 Workshop, the number of HLA loci had increased to 4, and the WHO committee recommended a change in terminology (Table 15–4). The number of antigens now accepted is 51 (Table 15–5). HLA-A is the former LA locus. HLA-B is the former 4 locus. HLA-C is a third locus, with antigens defined by the appropriate serum antibodies in the same way as A and B locus antigens are defined. C locus antigens were distinguished from B locus antigens with great difficulty because of the close approximation of the 2 genes and a high degree of linkage dis-

Table 15–4. HLA terminology, 1975.

HLA	Regional or system designation
A, B, C, D, etc	Locus symbols
1, 2, 3, etc	Number identifying specificities belonging to each locus
w	Prefix to indicate a provisional specificity

Table 15–5. Major human histocompatibility loci, 1975.*

Locus A	Locus B	Locus C	Locus D
HLA-A1	HLA-B5	HLA-Cw1	HLA-Dw1
A2	B7	Cw2	Dw2
A3	B8	Cw3	Dw3
A9	B12	Cw4	Dw4
A10	B13	Cw5	Dw5
A11	B14		Dw6
A28	B18		
A29	B27		
Aw19	Bw15		
Aw23	Bw16		
Aw24	Bw17		
Aw25	Bw21		
Aw26	Bw22		
Aw30	Bw35		
Aw31	Bw37		
Aw32	Bw38		
Aw33	Bw39		
Aw34	Bw40		
Aw36	Bw41		
Aw43	Bw42		

HLA-A
HLA-C
HLA-B
HLA-D

Number of Alleles	
A	20
B	20
C	5
D	6
Total	51

*As explained in the Announcement of the New Nomenclature for the HLA System (J Immunol 116:573, 1976), all of the W (Workshop) designations for provisionally identified specificities are indicated by a lower case w inserted between the locus letters and the allele and specificity number.

equilibrium. Two families have so far been found in which a crossover between B and C locus genes has been identified. In addition, the HLA antigens are freely movable in the fluid phase of the cell membrane. When HLA antibodies are added, the appropriate antigens form clusters (identifiable by fluorescent labeling of the antibody) and eventually aggregate into a cap at one end of the cell. A, B, and C locus antigens can be shown to "cap" independently with the corresponding antibodies and are thus physically distinct molecules.

HLA antigens have been detected on the cells of all organs thus far tested. Although their reactivity varies with the type of cell, it is believed that the HLA antigens are expressed on almost all cells. The major exception is the mature nonnucleated human red blood cell. HLA antigens are expressed on human red cells only to a limited extent if at all. In contrast, leukocytes and platelets react strongly with anti-HLA sera. Soluble HLA antigen preparations have been obtained from a variety of cells. They are primarily protein. It appears likely that HLA antigens are constantly disappearing from the cell surface and being resynthesized. This may explain why the nonnucleated red cell is deficient in such antigens since it is incapable of synthesizing new proteins.

The HLA-D locus is the former MLC locus. It has also been referred to as the LD-1 locus (the first lymphocyte-defined locus). The terminology was changed to HLA-D because of the importance of the products of this locus in histocompatibility and because of preliminary evidence that they can be typed with serum antibodies if the target cells are primarily B lymphocytes. Thus far, however, the recognized HLA-D determinants have been established by typing with an MLC technic. Lymphocytes believed to be homozygous for an HLA-D determinant are used as typing cells. If they fail to stimulate a responder cell, that responder cell is assumed to share that HLA-D determinant.

Although products of the C and D HLA loci are internationally recognized, few laboratories have the capability of identifying them. Further discussions will be largely restricted to products of the A and B loci.

Haplotypes & Their Inheritance

The haplotype is that portion of the phenotype determined by closely linked genes of a *single* chromosome. In the case of the major human histocompatibility gene complex, it includes one HLA-A antigen, one HLA-B antigen, one HLA-C antigen, and one HLA-D determinant. Haplotype analysis is of importance principally in family studies, for if the A antigen and the B antigen of that chromosome can be defined, it can usually be assumed that all HLA antigens and MLC determinants produced by that chromosome will also be present regardless of our current inability to detect them. In a family study, it thus becomes necessary to determine whether 2 members share the same 2 haplotypes, whether they differ by one haplotype, or whether they are different for both haplotypes. Fig 15–3 illustrates inheritance of haplotypes. Since there can be only 2 paternal and 2 maternal haplotypes, there are only 4 possible combinations in the children. It follows that there is a 25% chance that 2 siblings will be HLA-identical (share 2 haplotypes). An additional 50% will share one haplotype, and the final 25% will not share any haplotype. Parents share one haplotype with all children and almost always differ for the other. The degree of haplotype sharing is of fundamental importance in predicting organ graft survival.

When a family donor is considered for a transplant, it is important to type for HLA as completely as possible and then analyze the inheritance of haplotypes. To assume HLA identity because of phenotype identity can be erroneous for a number of reasons. Two similar but not completely identical antigens may be indistinguishable when testing with available anti-

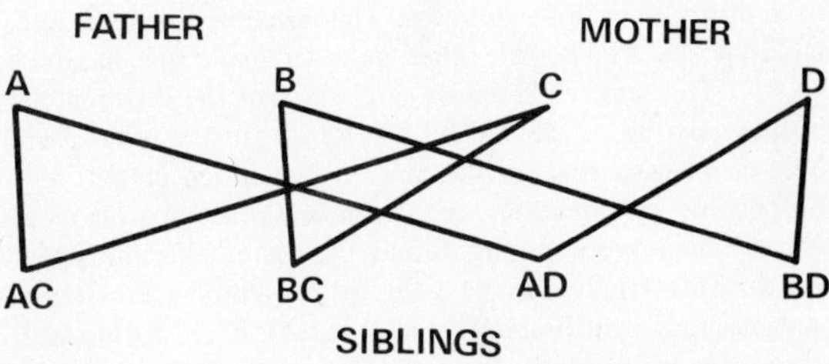

Figure 15–3. Inheritance of haplotypes. A and B represent the paternal haplotypes and C and D the maternal haplotypes. AC, BC, AD, and BD are the only possible combinations in their children.

Table 15–6. Cross-reacting antigen groups.

HLA-A1,Aw36
A2,A28
A3,A11
A9,Aw23,Aw24
A10,Aw25,Aw26,Aw34
Aw19,A29,Aw30,Aw31,Aw32,Aw33

HLA-B5,B18,Bw35
B7,B27,Bw22,Bw42
B8,B14
B13,Bw40,Bw41
Bw15,Bw17
Bw16,Bw38,Bw39

sera. For example, HLA-A3 was originally defined by antibodies which reacted with HLA-A11 also. At that time, a patient with HLA-A3 would have been considered identical to a patient with HLA-A11. Cross-reacting antibodies of this type are common. The most widely accepted antigen groups which react with cross-reacting antibodies are listed in Table 15–6. Furthermore, phenotype identity may be present with only 3 HLA factors defined, and it is possible that each person has a different fourth factor not presently identifiable. Finally, if parents share antigens, siblings may have the same phenotype but on the basis of different haplotypes. They would then be expected to differ in their MLC determinants.

An example of haplotype analysis is presented in Table 15–7. In this example it is easy to see which factors (which haplotype) in the first child have come from the father and which from the mother. This example has been made intentionally easy in that all family members have 4 identifiable factors, there is no homozygosity, and the parents do not share any antigen. Nonetheless, the same principles apply in more complicated circumstances, and haplotypes can be established with confidence in almost all cases (keeping in mind the possibility of gene cross over mentioned above).

Table 15–7. Haplotypes.

Father	A	A1,B8
	B	A2,B12
Mother	C	A3,B5
	D	A9,B7
Children	AC	A1,A3,B5,B8
	AD	A1,A9,B7,B8
	BC	A2,A3,B5,B12
	BD	A2,A9,B7,B12

The first child's A1 and B8 had to come from his father since his mother lacks those antigens. This establishes one paternal haplotype as A1,B8; the other paternal haplotype has to be A2,B12. The same child shows similarly that the maternal haplotypes must be A3,B5 and A9,B7. Results in the other 3 children are consistent with this, and the 4 children present all of the possible combinations. It is common practice to label the paternal haplotypes A and B and the maternal haplotypes C and D. This family can be used to show how a crossover is recognized. If a fifth child typed as A1,A9,B7,B12, the A9,B7 came from his mother. The father must have contributed A1 from his A haplotype and B12 from his B haplotype as a result of crossover between the A and B loci on that pair of chromosomes. Of course, nonpaternity must be excluded in such situations.

Frequency & Distribution of HLA Antigens

With the large number of HLA factors known and the tens of thousands of combinations potentially possible, it is not surprising that the most common HLA phenotype has a frequency of only 1:100 and that in any large series half the patients may have a phenotype not duplicated by any other member of the series (Table 15–8). With the antisera in current use, it should be possible to define 4 HLA factors (a complete set) in 75% of random Caucasian individuals. If the gene frequencies for individual antigens are counted, definable HLA antigens account for approximately 98% of A locus antigens and approximately 95% of locus B antigens. The number of antigens yet to be defined may, however, be very large. If fewer than 4 factors are identified by typing, the explanation may be that an antigen yet to be defined is present, but homozygosity for an antigen becomes more and more probable as sera to define new antigens become available. The frequency of identification of all 4 antigens

Table 15–8. Frequency of repetition of HLA phenotypes in 1141 random blood and organ donors in the San Francisco area.

Phenotype	Number of Different Phenotypes	Total Number of Donors	Percentage of Total
A1,A3,B7,B8	1	11	1.0
A2,A3,B7,B12	1	9	0.8
A1,A2,B8,B12	1	8	0.7
A1,–,B8,–	1	8	0.7
A1,A2,B7,B8	1	6	0.5
A2,A9,B12,Bw35	1	6	0.5
A2,A3,B7,–	1	6	0.5
Repeated 6 or or more times	7	54	4.7
Repeated 5 times	13	65	5.7
Repeated 4 times	15	60	5.3
Repeated 3 times	44	132	11.6
Repeated 2 times	111	222	19.5
Repeated 2 or more times	190	533	46.7
Single example	608	608	53.3

These figures may overestimate the frequency of identical phenotypes since blanks can represent undefined factors as well as homozygosity and since serologic identity may be proved to be inaccurate with better definition of antigens. Moreover, phenotype identity is not synonymous with haplotype identity—eg, an A1,A3,B7,B8 phenotype is most likely to be a result of A1,B8 and A3,B7 haplotypes based on the known frequencies of haplotypes but could be a result of A1,B7 and A3,B8 haplotypes.

is lower when cells from racial groups other than Caucasian are tested because most of the antisera in use have been obtained from Caucasian immunization. Studies at the International Histocompatibility Workshop in 1972 demonstrated the high degree of polymorphism of the HLA system in different groups, making it an extremely useful tool for anthropologic studies. For example, HLA-A1 is rarely present in non-Caucasians, and these same groups obviously have common antigens not yet recognized.

Typing HLA Antigens

Although any cell of the body may theoretically be used for HLA typing, the most readily available and therefore the most useful are the leukocytes and platelets of the peripheral blood. Platelets can be tested for HLA antigens by complement fixation, but the technic is insensitive and it has not been possible to find antisera in sufficient quantities to define all known HLA antigens in this way. Granulocytes or mixed leukocytes from the peripheral blood will react to HLA antibodies by agglutination, and it was by this technic that the HLA factors were originally detected. However, there are 2 reasons why this method is little used for this purpose: (1) the granulocytes must be tested within a few hours after collection; and (2) false-positive results produce poorer reproducibility than in the next approach to be mentioned.

Currently, almost all HLA typing is done by a lymphocyte cytotoxicity procedure. Lymphocytes are incubated with serum containing antibody and then with complement (which must be from rabbits). Injury to the cell membrane is detected by a variety of approaches. The proportion of dead cells can be noted after staining with trypan blue. Alternatively, the cells can be stained with eosin and counted with the aid of an inverted phase microscope. Lymphocytes can be incubated with ^{51}Cr before the test, and radioactivity in the supernatant solution then counted after incubation. This is an excellent research tool but is impractical for routine typing because of the volume of typing serum it requires. The shortage of antisera defining the newer specificities limits most typing to microtechnics using 1 or 2 μl of serum per well in plastic plates. A fourth technic which has limited but increasing acceptance is fluorochromasia. Lymphocytes are labeled with a compound that fluoresces under an ultraviolet microscope. Injured cells lose their fluorescence. Since this method—in contrast to the first 2 mentioned—labels living cells, it avoids the problem of subtracting from each well the number of spontaneously dead cells which are present in wells without antibody. It also avoids the risk that dead cells may lyse completely and thus go unrecognized. Lymphocytes are sturdy cells and can be isolated from blood that has been shipped long distances without refrigeration. They can also be frozen in liquid nitrogen for prolonged storage, and this is an excellent means of preserving them for repeated typing and cross-matching and of providing cells of known phenotypes with which to identify new antibodies. When cadaver donors are typed, lymph nodes provide a superior source of lymphocytes for typing and cross-matching.

Sera with HLA antibodies are easy to find. They are found in as high as 60% of recipients of multiple transfusions, and 20% or more of women have such antibodies following their second and subsequent pregnancies. Most of these sera, however, have multiple antibodies and are useless for typing. Strong monospecific antisera are difficult to find for all but the more common specificities. Typing usually must be done using sera known to contain weak antibodies or containing more than one antibody. Errors in interpretation are minimized by using multiple antisera to define each specificity. HLA typing sera to define all known antigens are not commercially available. Each laboratory must find its own antisera and exchange them with other investigators. The National Institute of Allergy and Infectious Diseases does maintain a bank of typing sera and will supply suitable applicants with reagents to type for organ transplantation. They prefer to do this with preloaded plastic plates in order to prevent waste of antisera.

The most likely source of monospecific antibodies is women immunized by pregnancy, but suitable sera have been found after transfusions or after rejection of an organ transplant. Deliberate immunization is an effective approach but carries the risk of inducing unwanted antibodies (eg, to red cell antigens) and hepatitis.

Indications for Histocompatibility Testing

HLA typing has been useful in anthropologic studies and has proved useful in paternity testing. It has found increasing acceptance as a diagnostic aid based on known high degrees of association between certain HLA factors or MLC determinants and certain diseases (Table 15–9). This association may be explained, at least in part, by evidence that specific immune response genes may be part of the major histocompatibility gene complex. The primary indication for histocompatibility testing, however, is to select donor-recipient pairs for organ transplantation.

Kidney Transplantation

The usefulness of HLA typing to select a donor from the immediate family is unquestioned. Renal allografts from HLA-identical siblings have uniformly

Table 15–9. Examples of association of HLA antigens and disease.

Disease	Antigen	Relative Risk*	*p*
Ankylosing spondylitis	B27	120.9	$<10^{-6}$
Reiter's syndrome	B27	40.3	$<10^{-6}$
Acute anterior uveitis	B27	30.7	$<10^{-6}$
Diabetes mellitus, insulin-dependent	B8	2.1	5×10^{-5}
	Bw15	3.0	$<10^{-6}$
	LD-8a	4.5	10^{-3}
	LD-W15a	3.7	1.4×10^{-3}

*Normal risk = 1.0.

superior long-term survival—in the range of 95 to 100%. A number of centers report better survival if the related donor shares one haplotype than if he shares none.

Graft survival is shortened when an unrelated (cadaver) donor is used, and the usefulness of HLA typing in this situation is more controversial. Correlation between degree of HLA matching and graft survival has been noted in many European centers but has not been significant in most of the material reported from the USA. In some centers a positive correlation is shown only when mismatching at the B locus is one of the criteria or when the recipient has antibodies to random cells. There are several possible explanations for these discrepancies. HLA antibodies which react with the cells of the kidney donor almost always cause early acute rejection. This is true even if the antibody is undetectable prior to transplant. Thus, matching for HLA will limit the likelihood that an antibody reacting with the donor's cells has failed to be detected. The sensitivity of cross-matching technics varies with the procedures used and the experience of the personnel. The possibly greater effect of matching at the B locus as compared with matching at the A locus could be related to the fact that the B locus is closer to the MLC locus, so that matching at the B locus is more likely to include matching at the MLC locus. Matching at the B locus may be more likely to result in matching at the MLC locus in the more inbred populations of Europe than in the ethnically heterogeneous populations of the USA. Direct evidence that matching at the MLC locus correlates positively with kidney graft survival has been reported at several centers. Survival is much better in cases where a low degree of response occurs in an MLC test than with a high response. For unknown reasons, the correlation is better when a 2-way MLC test is done (one in which both donor and recipient cells are able to undergo blastic transformation in the culture). Given the predictive value of the MLC test, it is regrettable that it has not been possible to shorten that test sufficiently to obtain an answer within the time limits imposed by the available technics of storage for cadaver donor kidneys. It is therefore of no use in the one situation in which it would be most valuable. A solution to this problem may arise in one of 4 ways: a shortened MLC, successful longer preservation of the donor kidney, serologic typing for MLC determinants, or typing for MLC determinants with primed responder cells.

Despite the controversy about the correlation between HLA matching and graft survival, most centers continue to type and to match donor and recipients as closely as possible for these antigens. Many regional networks have been established to facilitate exchange of kidneys over long distances in order to achieve a better match. Still other centers try for the best match they can achieve but nevertheless can show that they are justified in transplanting all kidneys regardless of the degree of mismatch as long as the cross-match test is negative and the donor organ is compatible in the ABO red cell system.

One further controversy concerns the effect of previous blood transfusions on renal allograft survival. Patients with end-stage renal failure are often transfused, and HLA antibodies are a common result. The more HLA antibodies formed, the more likely an available kidney will be incompatible on cross-match. Some evidence indicates that patients who have formed antibodies to random lymphocytes have poor graft survival even if the cross-match is negative. For these reasons, attempts have been made to minimize antibody formation by transfusing only leukocyte-poor or frozen red cells into potential graft recipients. These preparations still contain approximately 5% of the original leukocytes of the whole blood, and cytotoxic antibodies still develop, although to a significantly lesser degree. Despite the logic of the above, several centers now claim that graft survival is better in the group of patients who have been transfused with blood containing the buffy coat than in patients never transfused or (in one report) transfused with frozen red cells only. If this is true, it could be hypothesized that transfusions may result in production of antibodies which are enhancing as well as antibodies which are cytotoxic. Unfortunately, the correlation between previous transfusions and graft survival has been conflicting in reports from different centers. Until more data are available, it is impossible to conclude whether transfusions should be avoided or encouraged for potential transplant recipients or whether packed red blood cells or frozen or leukocyte-poor red cells are preferable.

Other Solid Organ Transplants

The statements that have been made about kidney transplants are presumably applicable also to transplants of the heart, liver, etc. However, no center has performed a sufficient number of such transplants to prove that HLA matching is essential. Nonetheless, no organ should be transplanted until it has been shown that the cross-match test (donor lymphocytes versus recipient serum) is negative. The cross-match test should employ not only a recent serum sample from the recipient but also the previously most reactive sample if antibody had been previously detected. To ensure that antibodies are detected to the greatest extent possible, each sample of recipient serum should be tested against a panel of cells containing all known HLA antigens as well as blanks (less than 4 HLA antigens). The blanks may represent antigens not yet defined.

Marrow Transplants

Marrow transplantation is still an experimental procedure but is being employed with increasing frequency in the treatment of aplastic anemia and leukemia (see Chapter 28). Results prior to the development of HLA typing were so disastrous that marrow transplants are currently restricted almost entirely to situations in which an HLA-identical sibling is available as the donor. Marrow transplants pose an additional problem that does not arise in transplanting other organs. Immunocompetent cells introduced into the host can respond to the foreign antigens of the patient, causing serious or even fatal GVH disease. The frequency of this occurrence in HLA-identical sibling marrow transplants indicates that at least one more major genetic locus is involved. These immunologic problems do not occur when the donor is an identical twin. Matching for HLA is particularly important in the marrow recipients because they frequently have received prior platelet transfusions, resulting in antibody formation. Since non-HLA antibodies may play a role, it is strongly recommended that family members not be used as donors of blood components for the patient if a marrow transplant is contemplated. Even with proof of HLA identity, a cross-match test should still be done, using recipient serum against donor cells and donor serum against recipient cells. MLC matching may be of equal or even greater importance, and it is essential that the HLA matched siblings be tested to be sure that they are not responsive to each other in the MLC test. The greater importance of MLC compatibility as compared with that of HLA is suggested by several cases in which MLC-compatible but HLA-incompatible marrows have been successfully transplanted.

Blood Transfusion

Every blood transfusion introduces into the recipient immunocompetent cells with the potential for initiating a graft and inducing GVH disease. This almost never occurs because of the efficiency with which the recipient responds to and eliminates the donor cells. When a patient's immunocompetence is markedly impaired, however, GVH disease may result. This is particularly likely to occur in severe forms of congenital immunodeficiency. While it has not been considered a problem in the immunosuppressive therapy given for a kidney transplant or as therapy for leukemia, it is considered a potential risk after marrow transplantation. When transfusions are necessary in a patient with severe immune deficiency, it is customary to irradiate the blood components in the hope of destroying the viability of immunocompetent cells likely to proliferate. The minimal amount of radiation required to achieve this purpose has not been clearly established, and insufficient evidence is available to determine whether the function of transfused cells (eg, platelets) is compromised at higher radiation levels. In general, between 1500 and 3000 rads are administered to each unit of blood.

Platelet Transfusions

Although platelets per se are not capable of inducing a graft, the transfusion of platelets is of direct interest in this discussion of transplantation immunology. Platelets carry the largest proportion of HLA antigens in whole blood and are highly immunogenic. Even leukemic patients, whose immune response should be depressed by the therapy usually given, respond readily to platelets with formation of HLA antibodies. Antibodies have become detectable as early as 4 days after the first platelet transfusion in patients previously exposed to HLA factors by pregnancy or transfusion and have occurred as early as 10 days after transfusion in patients with no prior exposure. With repeated platelet transfusion, the proportion of patients with detectable antibodies increases up to about 60% or more of such recipients. These antibodies react with the incompatible antigens of transfused platelets, destroying them with a rapidity in proportion to the strength of the antibody. Refractoriness to random platelet transfusions will be noted prior to the appearance of detectable antibody, and strong antibodies can result in violent chill and fever reactions with platelet concentrates alone.

Since these antibodies are directed (for the most part) against HLA antigens, it is not surprising that platelets from a donor of compatible HLA type will continue to survive normally. The technic of plateletpheresis permits collection of an effective dose of platelets from a single selected donor in a few hours. The best donor is, of course, an HLA-identical sibling, but other family members may, by chance, lack the antigens with which the patient's antibodies react. If they share one haplotype with the recipient, they can be incompatible for no more than 2 HLA antigens. If a compatible platelet donor is not available within the family, unrelated platelets may survive as well provided that the HLA match is identical or very close. In a number of centers in this country, the HLA types of volunteer blood donors are being determined, and computer files make these individuals available for retrieval at need. Plateletpheresis is a time-consuming procedure; the veins of the donor may become injured by repeated phlebotomies, so that a free flow of blood becomes difficult to achieve. It thus appears sensible to use platelets from random donors as long as they are effective and to turn to selected family or unrelated donors only as necessary, remembering that family donors should not be used if a marrow transplant is intended.

Granulocyte Transfusions

Transfusion of granulocytes is still an experimental procedure. An effective dose requires a selected donor to remain connected for approximately 4 hours to a continuous flow centrifuge or to a set of nylon fiber filters which remove his granulocytes and release the rest of the blood to be returned to the donor. HLA matching problems are the same as with platelet transfusions, but incompatible granulocytes are much more likely to result in a violent chill and fever reaction than are platelets. It appears prudent to minimize the possibility of this occurrence, whenever possible, by performing a cross-match test with recipient serum and donor leukocytes. In order that antibodies to granulocytes (as well as HLA antibodies) will be detected, an agglutination cross-match is recommended.

Current Research Efforts

The major problem limiting the success of organ transplantation is immunologic rejection. Better methods of immunosuppression would obviously be helpful.

These should be more selective in their effect, so that the patient will retain an ability to respond immunologically to foreign organisms. They should be free from other serious side-effects. Hope for control of the immune response to specific foreign histocompatibility antigens is more likely to come from immunologic manipulations than from cytotoxic agents. The most promising advances in this area have come with the recognition that some antibodies protect the graft instead of destroying it. Experiments in animals indicate that passive transfusion of antibodies to histocompatibility antigens may in some instances result in more prolonged graft survival while in others it causes accelerated rejection. Purified soluble histocompatibility antigens can be injected to induce active antibody formation, but reliable means of ensuring that the resulting antibodies will be protective rather than cytotoxic have not been achieved. Protective antibodies appear analogous to the enhancing or blocking antibodies found in the sera of many patients with cancer. The lymphocytes of these patients are cytotoxic to their tumor cells but are ineffective in the presence of their serum. A possibly oversimplified explanation of this finding would be that protective antibodies react with the antigens without causing obvious harm. They thus block the antigen sites, preventing access of cytotoxic lymphocytes or antibodies.

Of less practical certainty is an approach to inducing true tolerance to specific histocompatibility antigens by eliminating clones of immunoresponsive cells which react with those antigens. This appears to have been accomplished on a limited basis in eliminating donor clones which may cause GVH disease. Donor marrow has been incubated in tissue culture medium with killed recipient cells. At the point of maximum stimulation in this MLC technic, tritiated thymidine labeled with high specific activity (hot pulse) is added to the culture. A lethal dose of radiation is thus incorporated by the responding cells, but the short radius of tritium radioactivity leaves other cells unharmed. Following this procedure, the marrow cells no longer respond to the original antigens to which they were exposed but do respond to other antigens. This suggests that the responding clone has been eliminated. Clinical experience with this approach has been too limited to justify any firm conclusions. The technic can work, of course, only to prevent GVH disease. There is as yet no known way to eliminate the clones of responding cells in the recipient which react only with the donor antigens. It must also be admitted that there is no evidence that the response of donor cells to recipient antigens has been permanently eliminated.

CONCLUSION

All attempts to achieve better control of graft rejection depend on a better understanding of the immunologic mechanisms involved and the genetic products responsible. Better definition of HLA antigens is necessary, and the search for further antigens at the A and B loci will continue. Serologically defined antigens of the third and possibly further loci need to be identified. Better serologic technics are needed for HLA typing and for cross-matching, and current supplies of typing sera are grossly inadequate.

Specific MLC (HLA-D) determinants need to be defined. Work in this area is just beginning. Once they are defined, it is hoped that they can be identified with antibodies by serologic technics that are simpler and much faster than MLC tests.

With improvement of basic knowledge, clinical experience will then demonstrate which antigens and immunologic mechanisms are most important and can evaluate the success of experimental procedures to manipulate them to the advantage of the graft.

• • •

References

Announcement: New nomenclature in the HLA system. J Immunol 116:573, 1976.

Belzer FO & others: Is HL-A typing of clinical significance in cadaver renal transplantation? Lancet 1:774, 1974.

Busch GJ, Galvanek EG, Reynolds ES Jr: Human renal allografts: Analysis of lesions in long-term survivors. Human Pathol 2:253, 1971.

Cochrum KC & others: The correlation of MLC with graft survival. Transplant Proc 5:391, 1973.

Dausset J, Colombani J (editors): *Histocompatibility Testing 1972.* Munksgaard, 1972.

Dausset J & others: Serologically defined HL-A antigens and long-term survival of cadaver kidney transplants: A joint analysis of 918 cases performed by France-Transplant and the London Transplant Group. N Engl J Med 290:979, 1974.

Fefer A & others: Marrow transplants in aplastic anemia and leukemia. Semin Hematol 11:353, 1974.

Möller G: HLA and disease. Transplant Rev, vol 22, 1975. [Entire issue.]

Opelz G, Mickey MR, Terasaki PI: HL-A and kidney transplants: Reexamination. Transplantation 17:371, 1974.

Patel R, Terasaki PI: Significance of the positive cross-match test in kidney transplantation. N Engl J Med 280:735, 1969.

Payne R & others: A new leukocyte isoantigen system in man. Cold Spring Harbor Symp Quant Biol 29:285, 1964.

Perkins HA (editor): *A Seminar on Histocompatibility Testing.* American Association of Blood Banks, 1970.

Perkins HA & others: Nonhemolytic febrile transfusion reactions: Quantitative effects of blood components with emphasis on isoantigenic incompatibility of leukocytes. Vox Sang 11:578, 1966.

Rapaport FT, Dausset J (editors): *Human Transplantation.* Grune & Stratton, 1968.

Ray JG & others: *Manual of Tissue Typing Techniques.* National Institute of Allergy & Infectious Diseases, 1974.

Van Rood JJ, van Leeuwen A: Leukocyte grouping: A method and its application. J Clin Invest 42:1382, 1973.

16 . . .
The Secretory Immune System

Stephen P. Hauptman, DO, & Thomas B. Tomasi, Jr., MD, PhD

The importance of local immunity to pathogens was established in the first part of this century. These early studies demonstrated that the levels of antibodies in nonvascular fluids correlated well in certain cases with resistance to infection at mucous membranes and could be induced independently of systemic immunity (circulating antibodies). However, whether they were locally produced or resulted from transudation from serum was not known until recently. The demonstration that IgA is the predominant immunoglobulin in many secretions–in contrast to its relatively low concentration in serum (compared to IgG)–formed the basis for the hypothesis of a distinct immune system common to external secretions now referred to as the secretory or mucosal immune system. This chapter will review the secretory immune system and its structural and biologic characteristics.

IMMUNOGLOBULINS

Secretions can be conveniently divided into 2 general categories: external and internal (Fig 16–1). External secretions bathe mucous membranes in contact with the external environment and in general are characterized by a predominance of IgA. The IgG/IgA ratio is often less than 1 in these secretions, compared to 4:1 to 5:1 in serum. Internal secretions contain immunoglobulins in proportions similar to those in serum with the exception of IgM, probably because of its larger size and more limited diffusion. The IgM and IgE in external secretions are present in larger amounts than can be explained by simple transudation from serum. The IgM, IgE, IgA, and small amounts of IgG of most external secretions are produced locally in the lamina propria of *normal* mucous membranes. Inflammation (eg, following invasive infections) is associated with increased permeability of capillaries and transudation of serum proteins.

There is a voluminous literature on the secretory immunoglobulir system related to differences between secretory sites and between species. We will limit this discussion to humans as much as possible and consider the various mucous membranes as a unit system. Where appropriate, discrepancies from one tissue or species to the other will be indicated. However, 2 common characteristics of external secretions can be defined. First, the various immunoglobulin classes are present in proportions that are significantly different from those in serum, and the levels are therefore not explicable by simple transudation. Second, there is independent regulation of the serum and secretory antibody, either through selective transport or local synthesis. More recently, the independent regulation of systemic and local cell-mediated immunity has also been reported. It is now known that this dissociation has biologic importance; natural infection or immunization may stimulate one system without necessarily having any effect on the development of immunity in the other.

Structure of Secretory IgA (SIgA)

Early data showing quantitative differences in serum and secretory IgA levels led to structural studies of IgA isolated from these 2 sources. Human serum IgA exists mainly as a monomer, with 10–15% in polymeric form, whereas IgA in external secretions exists mainly as a dimer. Significant amounts of 7S IgA and IgA polymers larger than dimers are also found in some external secretions.

Secretory IgA is composed of an IgA dimer, a molecule of secretory component (SC, MW 70,000), and a molecule of J chain (MW 15,000). Secretory IgA is an 11S molecule of MW 400,000 (Fig 16–2). Secretory component is not found in 7S IgA, either in serum or in secretions. A small amount of dimeric IgA with attached secretory component (SIgA) can be demonstrated in normal serum. This SIgA may be increased in certain diseases, especially those involving mucous membranes, such as gastrointestinal disorders. The IgM present in secretions has also been shown to have secretory component bound to it, but IgG and IgE do not. Secretory component can be found free (unattached to IgA) in normal gastrointestinal and salivary fluids and also, in the absence of IgA, in the secretions of newborns and patients deficient in IgA. Free secretory component can be shown to complex in vitro with both polymeric IgA and IgM by a mechanism of disulfide interchange to form stable covalent bonds. It has been hypothesized that secretory component is coiled around the Fc portion of both IgA molecules of

Stephen P. Hauptman is Assistant Professor of Medicine, Cardeza Foundation, Thomas Jefferson University, Philadelphia. Thomas B. Tomasi, Jr., is Professor of Medicine and Chairman of the Department of Immunology, Mayo Medical School, Rochester.

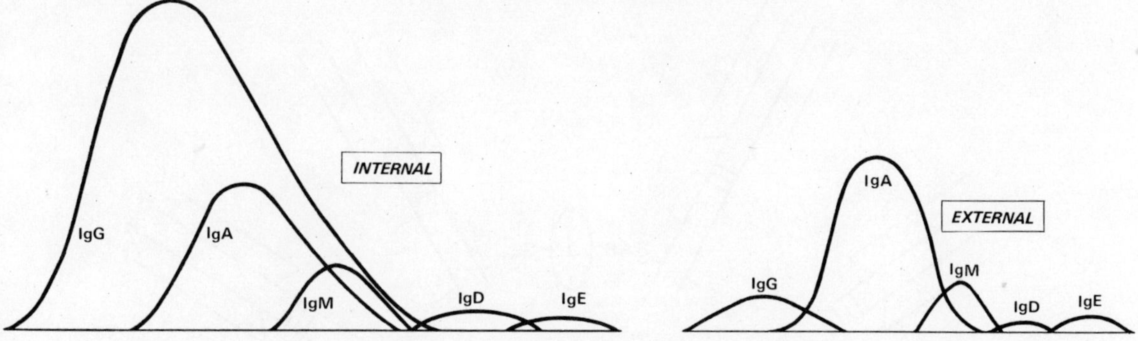

Figure 16–1. Body secretions characterized by immunoglobulin content.

the dimer, extending from one hinge region to the other with secondary forces interacting between the Fc region and secretory component. This interaction may well account for the stabilization of SIgA against proteolytic attack. It has been postulated that this gives a selective advantage to SIgA in secretions.

J Chain

J chain is a polypeptide of MW 15,000 and is disulfide-bonded in polymeric IgA and IgM. It is not present in 7S monomeric IgA and IgM nor in IgG, IgD, and IgE. Because of its association with polymeric immunoglobulins, it is suggested that J chain functions in vivo by inducing polymerization of the subunits of IgA and IgM. Repolymerization of reduced IgM subunits can occur in the presence or absence of J chain. Those polymers re-formed in the presence of J chain resemble the native protein (19S), and the subunits are disulfide-bonded. In the absence of J chain, a more heterogeneous group of polymers is formed. Two polymeric IgA myelomas have been found which lack J chain, illustrating that J chain is not a prerequisite for polymerization. Immunoglobulin synthesis experiments utilizing mouse myeloma cells show that J chain is incorporated into IgA and IgM just prior to secretion of the polymer. In the IgA system, the size of the intracellular pool of J chain may be the limiting factor determining the amount of monomeric versus polymeric IgA secreted by the cell.

Polymeric IgA and IgM are disulfide-bonded to J chain so that only 2 of the monomeric units of IgA or IgM are bound to J chain; the remainder of the subunits are bound directly to each other by disulfide bonds not involving J chain (Fig 16–3). In vitro experiments suggest that the mechanism of polymerization is one in which J chain links two 7S monomers together as a relatively stable dimer. Complexing with J chain alters the conformation of the subunits so that they are then able to interact directly through noncovalent forces with other subunits not containing J chain. These forces are responsible for bringing the subunits into close enough apposition to allow the remaining intersubunit disulfides (not involving J chain) to form. The above findings, together with the

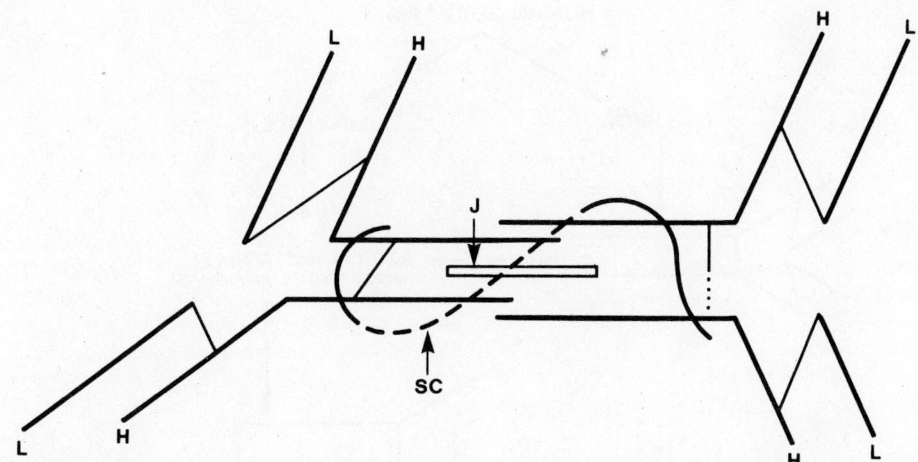

Figure 16–2. Model for SIgA. (SC, secretory component; H, heavy chain; L, light chain; J, J chain.) (Modified from Heremans JS: The IgA system in connection with local and systemic immunity. In: *The IgA System.* Mestecky J, Lawton AR [editors]. Plenum Press, 1974.)

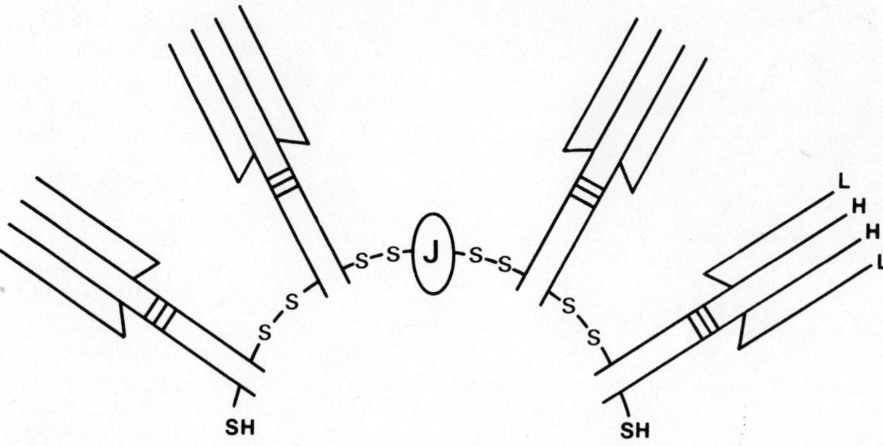

Figure 16–3. Model for polymeric IgA of the tetramer type depicting a linear array. (H, heavy chain; L, light chain; J, J chain.)

fact that J chain is bound to the penultimate cysteine of a chains, suggests the following hypothesis. By virtue of its role in polymerization of immunoglobulin subunits, J chain may be responsible for the ability of polymeric IgA and IgM to bind to secretory piece. The entire process depends on a disulfide exchange reaction between J and a chains with the generation of an SH group on the a chain that would be available to interact with secretory component.

It has been postulated that secretory component on the epithelial cell membrane acts as a receptor for polymeric IgA and IgM. In myeloma sera, a fraction of the polymeric IgA molecules are disulfide-bonded to either albumin or a_1-antitrypsin and not to secretory piece, whereas external secretions contain SIgA and both albumin and a_1-antitrypsin are free. This suggests the possibility that the essential SH group is bonded in sera by albumin and a_1-antitrypsin, and these proteins are displaced by secretory component in the process of secretion. This has not been proved.

Distribution of IgA Subclasses

Two subclasses of IgA (IgA1 and IgA2) can be identified in serum and secretions. IgA1 accounts for approximately 90% of the total *serum* IgA and a similar proportion of bone marrow IgA plasma cells, whereas in *secretions*, the IgA2 comprises as much as 60% of the total IgA (Fig 16–4). The subclasses differ antigenically as well as in their galactosamine content, the length of their hinge region, the number of interchain disulfide bonds, and metabolic properties (Table 16–1).

The IgA2 subclass may be further subdivided by allotypic markers on the heavy chain. The genetic locus which codes for this heavy chain marker occurs in 2 allelic forms, referred to as A2m(1) and A2m(2).

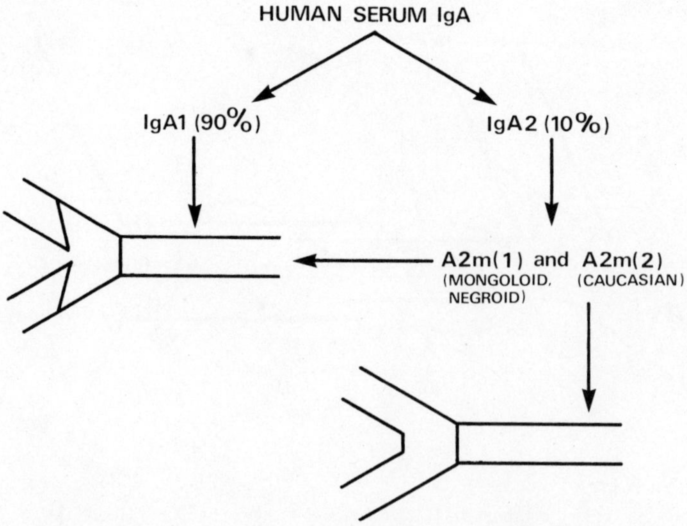

Figure 16–4. Distribution of subclasses of IgA with S–S bonds shown.

Table 16–1. IgA subclass characteristics.

	IgA1	IgA2
Serum (proportion)	90%	10%
Serum (concentration)	1.8 mg/ml	0.22 mg/ml
Milk (proportion)	40%	60%
Electrophoretic mobility (pH 8.6)	Slower	Faster (anode)
Galactosamine amino sugar	Present	Not present
Hinge region	Duplicated	12–13 residue gap
Serum half-time	5.9 days	4.5 days
Fractional catabolic rate	24%	34%
Synthetic rate	24 mg/kg/day	21.3 mg/kg/day
Genetic marker on Fc (allotypic)	Absent	Present A2m(1) Absent A2m(2)
Dissociability in acid, urea, etc	No	Yes A2m(1) No A2m(2)
Noncovalent interaction	Weak	Strong
Monomer of subclass combines with secretory component	No	Yes A2m(1) No A2m(2)

They also have different incidences in various races—eg, the A2m(1) marker is more common in Caucasians. The class and subclass antigens on IgA are responsible for anaphylactic transfusion reactions in IgA-deficient patients. These patients not infrequently develop antibodies against these antigenic determinants following multiple transfusions. Antibodies to allotypic specificity have also been responsible for some urticarial reactions.

A major difference between the subclasses of IgA is related to their dissociability in the presence of nonaqueous solvents (denaturants) such as urea or guanidine. Exposure of the IgA1 subclass to denaturants does not result in dissociation into H and L chains, whereas similar treatment of most (though not all) IgA2 proteins produces disulfide-linked dimer H and dimer L chains. This is due to the lack of the L–H disulfide bond in these IgA2 proteins (Fig 16–4). This characteristic is found only with IgA2 A2m(1) type, whereas the A2m(2) IgA proteins, like the IgA1 subclass do not dissociate in denaturants. The presence or absence of the L–H interchain bridge in human IgA2 is therefore an expression of a particular allotype. Recently, it has been proposed that secretory component stabilized the potentially dissociable IgA A2m(1) protein (Fig 16–5). Colostral IgA of the IgA2 A2m(1) variety did not dissociate in urea as did the serum A2m(1) type IgA. In vitro experiments demonstrated that free secretory piece would bind to and stabilize A2m(1) IgA2 myeloma proteins which on subsequent exposure to denaturants would not form dimer H and L chains. The findings suggest that stabilization with secretory component may occur through its interaction with the α chain, resulting in the formation of an L–H interchain disulfide bridge in the IgA2 protein. This might produce a more stable antibody and represents a selective advantage for antibodies functioning in the hostile environment of external secretions which are enriched in the IgA2 subclass compared to serum.

SYNTHESIS & TRANSPORT OF SIgA

Origin of IgA in Secretions

Evidence for the local production of the major portion of SIgA has been presented from a number of laboratories. Utilizing fluorescent antibody or in vitro culture technics, local synthesis of IgA has been demonstrated in the salivary glands, the gastrointestinal tract, the mammary glands, and a number of other secretory sites in a variety of species. The site of synthesis of IgA is primarily in submucosal plasma cells. For example, in the lamina propria of human gastrointestinal tract, there are approximately 20 IgA cells per IgG cell in close contact with the overlying glandular epithelium. This ratio is in contrast with that of peripheral lymph nodes and spleen, where the ratio is 1:3 (IgA:IgG).

Immunoglobulins in secretions may reach these fluids either by transudation from serum or by local

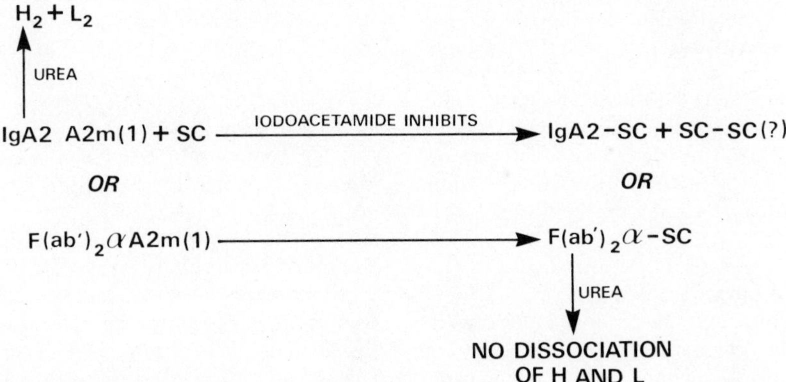

Figure 16–5. Stabilization of IgA2 A2m(1) immunoglobulin molecules by secretory component (SC).

synthesis in the lamina propria. Most studies report that only small amounts of IgA pass from serum into external secretions, and most of this appears to be 7S IgA. A question arising from studies of exocrine secretions is whether the 10S IgA dimer found in these fluids is formed intracellularly or is formed by 2 monomers after secretion from the cell. In this regard, a number of studies indicate that the dimer is assembled intracellularly. IgA and IgM intestinal immunocytes adjacent to the glandular epithelium specifically bind fluorescein-labeled secretory component. This interaction is specifically blocked by human dimeric IgA and 19S IgM. Some cells do not stain with fluorescein-labeled secretory component, suggesting that they contain 7S IgA. In vitro experiments have also demonstrated that secretory component binds to polymeric IgA and IgM in solution while showing little affinity for monomeric subunits. These findings suggest that in cell cytoplasm, affinity for secretory component is mediated by polymers of IgA or IgM. Immunofluorescence microscopy of human bone marrow cells shows intracellular polymeric IgA and IgM in both normal and myeloma cells. The number of positive cells corresponds to the respective serum concentrations of these proteins. In mouse myeloma cells, approximately 20% of the intracellular IgA is in the polymeric form. All of these findings (and others) indicate that polymeric IgA and IgM are synthesized intracellularly and that the monomer-to-polymer transition may occur at the time of secretion. It has been clearly demonstrated that J chain, rather than carbohydrate addition, controls IgA polymerization in the mouse. J chain may be the limiting factor in determining the proportion of monomer to dimer secreted by a given cell. In fact, studies suggest that the human gastrointestinal tract may contain 2 types of cells, one containing J chain and producing polymer IgA and the other lacking J chain and secreting only 7S IgA.

In most external secretions (saliva, colostrum, and gastrointestinal fluids), 7S IgA is present in addition to the predominant 11S IgA. There is an excess of 7S IgA over IgG in certain fluids, suggesting that the monomer IgA is either selectively transported from serum or locally synthesized. 7S IgA may result, at least in part, from locally produced IgA which is not complexed to secretory component and which may be transported into secretions by a route different from that of dimer IgA and similar to that of IgG. Some may also reflect dissociation of polymeric IgA. Some Fc fragments of *a* chains in normal intestinal fluid are polymeric. Unless special studies involving light chain antisera are used, they may be confused with intact 7S IgA. These Fc fragments result from bacterial proteolysis.

Origin of Secretory Component in Secretions

Secretory component is produced locally in glandular epithelium, whereas IgA and J chain are products of submucosal plasma cells. In the early description of SIgA, fluorescent antiserum to colostral 11S IgA was noted to stain the cytoplasm of salivary glandular epithelial cells in addition to the interstitial tissue. When antiserum to SIgA was absorbed with IgA, epithelial cell fluorescence persisted owing to the presence of secretory component in these cells. Further evidence of a separate cell origin for secretory component is the demonstration of this protein in human fetal tissue as early as 8 weeks of age, when immunoglobulins are not yet detected. Free secretory piece is found in the external secretions of patients with hypogammaglobulinemia in the absence of detectable immunoglobulins. In vitro culture studies performed on rabbit mammary tissue also provide evidence suggesting that this protein and IgA are synthesized in different cells.

The Synthesis & Transport of SIgM

The finding of large amounts of IgM in secretions and plasma cells in mucosal tissues of IgA-deficient patients suggests that IgM is also produced locally. Local IgM synthesis occurs in certain secretory tissues, and there is a predominance in mucosal fluids, such as saliva, of IgM relative to IgG. Gut-associated plasma cells that contain cytoplasmic IgM bind secretory component, and this noncovalent interaction can be blocked specifically by 19S IgM. Secretory component combines with IgM in aqueous solution. It can be estimated that 70% of the IgM in secretions contains covalently bound secretory component, while the remainder of IgM is noncovalently complexed to secretory component before isolation. In contrast, native SIgA polymers from secretory fluids are essentially all complexed to secretory component. In the native as well as recombined SIgA and SIgM, both noncovalent and covalent (S–S) forces stabilize the conformation. Two pieces of evidence support the stabilization of IgA and IgM induced by secretory component. First, before free component is incubated with isolated IgA and IgM, an accessible antigenic determinant is present on the free protein. After incubation with either IgM or IgA, this determinant becomes inaccessible and there is stabilization of the secretory molecules so that they are less easily denatured. Second, as mentioned above, the component stabilizes the IgA2 A2m(1) molecule so that it no longer dissociates into dimers of heavy and light chains when exposed to denaturation (Fig 16–5).

IgE in Secretory Fluids

IgE is present in secretory fluids of nasal, salivary, and urinary origin in greater proportions than can be explained by simple transudation from serum. In the tonsils, the bronchial lymph nodes, and the lamina propria of the respiratory and gastrointestinal mucosa, approximately 4% of the plasma cells contain IgE cells. This is in contrast to the spleen and subcutaneous lymph nodes, where rare (< 1%) IgE cells are found. The IgE in external secretions does not possess secretory component and is physicochemically and antigenically similar to serum IgE. In addition to the role of local synthesis in producing IgE in secretions, it appears that like IgA, a major portion of *serum* IgE is derived from submucosal plasma cells. The route of transport of IgE into secretions is unknown. Since it does not complex with secretory component, it may follow the same route as IgG and 7S IgA. Alternatively, an unidentified receptor other than secretory component may be involved in IgE transport.

IgG in Secretory Fluids

IgG in normal external secretions is derived from both local synthesis and transudation from serum. Intestinal lymphatic drainage in the gastrointestinal tract of the dog has shown that the lymph:serum concentration ratio of most proteins is related to the molecular sieving property of intestinal capillaries. The concentration of IgG in lymph draining the intestine is what would be expected based on its molecular size, and this suggests that very little IgG is produced in the dog intestine. IgG reaches the interstitial fluid bathing the lamina propria by permeating the capillary walls, but the route across the epithelium is unknown. Fluorescent antibody studies have demonstrated IgG in the interstitial space with only small numbers of IgG-containing plasma cells (relative to IgA). When inflammation occurs, there may be both an increase in transudation of IgG from serum as well as an invasion of the mucosa by IgG-producing plasma cells.

Route of Transport of SIgA & SIgM

The following hypothesis is consistent with the above data, with observations utilizing fluorescent antibody to secretory component, and with electron microscopy employing horseradish peroxidase-labeled anti-secretory component (Fig 16–6): IgA (mostly dimeric) is secreted from the submucosal plasma cells. The quantity of polymer versus monomer depends on the production of intracellular J chain. Dimeric IgA with attached J chain diffuses through the interstitium and crosses the basement membrane to enter the intercellular space. Since the apical portions of 2 adjacent epithelial cells are in close apposition, macromolecules the size of IgA cannot gain access to the lumen. Secretory component, found on the lateral epithelial cell membrane, may act as a receptor protein, complexing with dimeric IgA and thus allowing its transport into the epithelial cell by an endocytotic process. From the apical cytoplasm it is transported across the epithelial cell's luminal surface, probably by reverse pinocytosis. A similar mechanism of transport seems likely for IgM. It has been suggested that secretory piece may prevent proteolysis of SIgA during its transport through the epithelial cell and may protect its function as antibody while on the surface of the mucosa and in the luminal fluid.

Origin of Serum IgA

Studies on immunoglobulin metabolism have revealed that the synthetic rate for IgA is similar to that of IgG (Table 16–2). Furthermore, studies of the synthetic rates depend upon IgA molecules being in equilibrium with the circulating pool. Since there is considerable transfer of IgA to external secretions, the daily production of IgA may be significantly greater than that of IgG. This discrepancy is not explained on the basis of greater numbers of IgA cells compared to IgG cells in peripheral lymphoid tissue (spleen and lymph nodes) since it has been shown that the ratio of IgG to IgA cells in these tissues is approximately 3:1. Secretory lymphoid tissue, particularly the gut, has been shown to be a major source of circulating IgA in several species. Following the oral ingestion of anti-

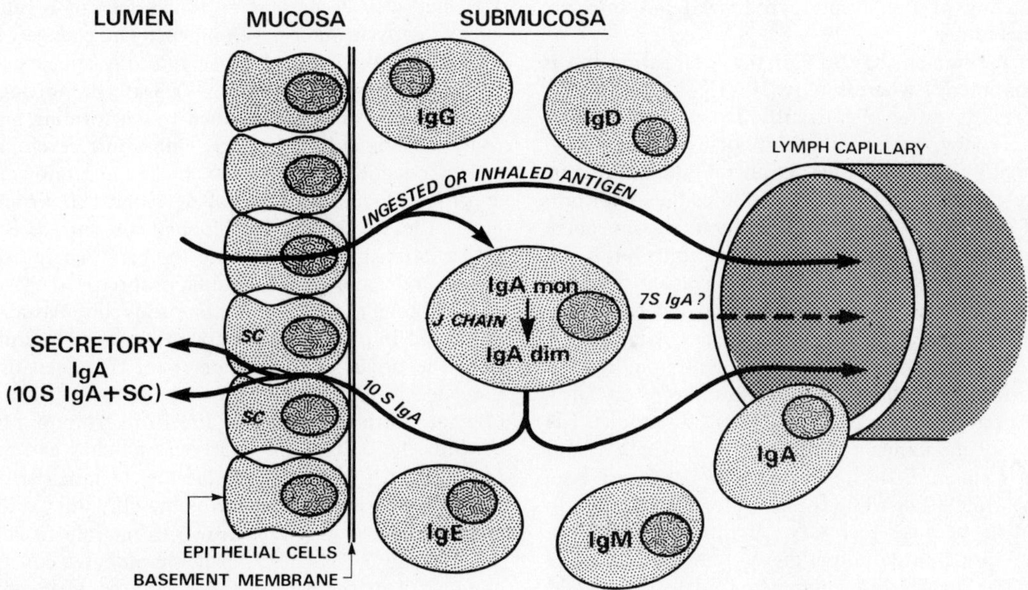

Figure 16–6. Site of synthesis and transport of SIgA. (SC, secretory component; IgA mon, IgA monomer; IgA dim, IgA dimer.)

Table 16–2. Metabolic properties of IgA.

Protein Used in Metabolic Study	% Intra-vascular	Total Circulating Pool (mg/kg)	Half-Time (Days)	Fractional Catabolic Rate*	Synthetic Rate (mg/kg/day)
^{131}I myeloma 7S IgA	42	95	5.8	0.252	24
Whole plasma transfusion	...	...	5.9	...	...
^{14}C glycine in vivo labeling	...	...	6.4	...	...
^{131}I myeloma IgA	...	...	8.7, 9.9, 10.3	...	...
Mouse ^{131}I IgA	...	...	1.0	...	26
Human ^{131}I IgG	45	494	23	0.067	34
Mouse ^{131}I IgG	...	...	4.1	...	84

*Fraction of intravascular pool catabolized per day.

gens, 2 types of responses are seen. As a result of the absorption of small amounts of intact protein, antibodies are formed in peripheral lymphoid tissues and a "parenteral" response of IgM followed by IgG is elicited in the serum. The "enteric" response, a result of direct antigenic stimulation of submucosal lymphoid tissue, produces an IgA antibody which is transported either into external fluids or into the circulation as serum IgA antibody. Oral immunization of mice with ferritin elicits IgA cells containing antiferritin antibodies in the gastrointestinal tract, and the majority of circulating antiferritin antibodies are of the IgA class. In contrast, when ferritin is given in repeated parenteral doses, IgG-containing plasma cells producing specific antibodies are found primarily in lymph nodes and spleen. The serum antiferritin antibody is of the IgG class. Furthermore, when mice are irradiated (either whole body or bowel alone), serum levels of IgA—but not of IgG or IgM—are suppressed, and this diminution in IgA can be prevented by shielding the gastrointestinal tract. This is thought to be due to rechanneling of the locally synthesized IgA into the intestinal lumen.

In the human, 85–90% of the total serum IgA is 7S (monomeric) whereas only 10–15% is polymeric. These results differ significantly from sera of other species, ie, dog, mouse, cow, and horse, in which polymers predominate. Whether peripheral lymphoid tissue or secretory intestinal tissue contributes the major portion of serum IgA in man is presently unknown. There are studies which suggest an intestinal contribution to circulating polymeric IgA. Utilizing isolated perfused loops of intestine, investigators found newly synthesized SIgA in the lumen and polymeric IgA in the perfusion fluid. It is also possible that monomeric and polymeric IgA, synthesized in intestinal secretory sites, diffuse or are transported in 2 different directions. The majority of monomer, produced by cells which do not contain J chain, diffuses into the lymphatics and then into the circulation while the polymer is secreted into the lumen because secretory component acts as a receptor preferentially binding polymeric IgA. The smaller size of 7S IgA compared to 10S IgA would facilitate its diffusion into the lymphatics. On the other hand, fluorescent studies have shown that human bone marrow may also be a major source of both monomeric and polymeric serum IgA. The question of the relative contribution of these sites is still not settled.

Ontogeny of IgA & Gut-Associated Lymphoid Cells

The ontogeny of B and T cells has been best defined in birds, and they have served as a prototype for developmental studies (see Chapter 11). During embryonic development of the chicken, stem cells of yolk sac, fetal liver, and bone marrow origin seed the thymus and bursa of Fabricius (a dorsal evagination of the hindgut), and these cells develop thymic or bursal lymphoid cells, respectively. Bursa-processed lymphoid cells are thought to undergo orderly differentiation as suggested by the "intrabursal switch" hypothesis. According to this theory, the first immunoglobulin-bearing lymphocytes to appear are those carrying IgM on their surfaces, followed sequentially by IgG- and IgA-bearing lymphocytes. Recent studies suggest that IgD may also be present on the surface of B cell precursors early in their development. The change of surface immunoglobulin to IgG and IgA appears to be antigen-independent (Fig 16–7). Data supporting this hypothesis have been obtained by performing bursectomy at various times in early embryonic development and by injecting antibodies to chicken immunoglobulin at different stages of bursal development. From the bursa, these cells seed the bloodstream and, as B cells (bursa-derived cells), populate the germinal centers of lymph nodes, spleen, and lamina propria.

Although immunoglobulin-producing plasma cells are found in the lamina propria after antigenic stimulation, the origin of the precursors of these cells is still unsettled in mammals. It has been proposed that they originate during intrauterine life from lymphoid tissue beneath the epithelium in Peyer's patches and in the appendix. Using a microinjection technic, tritiated thymidine was injected into the thymus and the labeled thymocytes were shown to migrate to Peyer's patches. By 3 days after birth, thymocytes constitute about 90% of the cells in these patches; whereas by 1 week of age, as B cells appear, adult proportions of

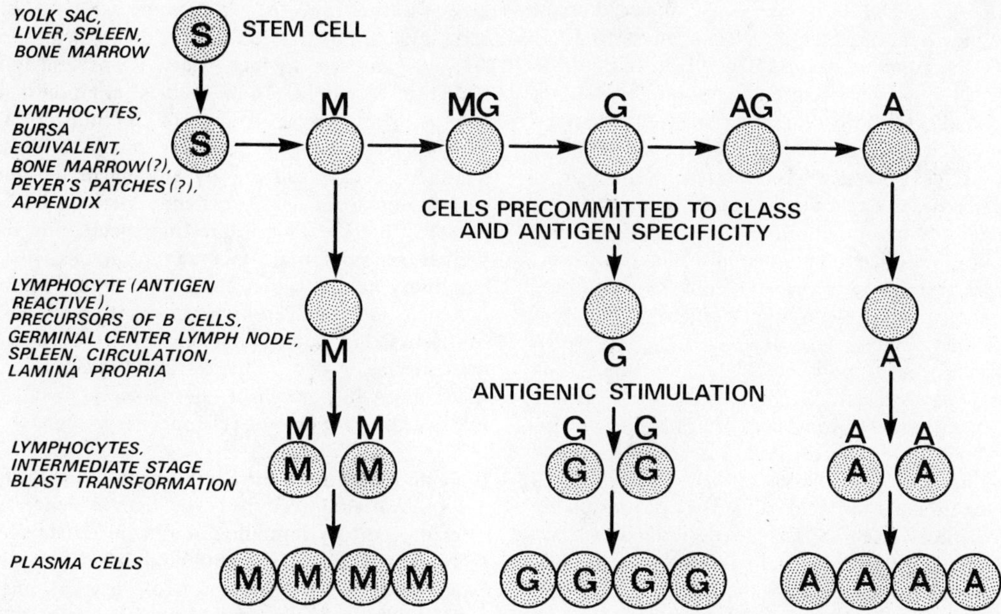

Figure 16–7. Ontogeny of B cells showing intrabursal switch mechanism (antigen-independent) and maturation to plasma cell (antigen-dependent). (See text for details.)

lymphocytes are obtained (70% T, 30% B in adult mouse Peyer's patches). In addition to the influx of T cells, the size of the follicle increases and corticomedullary differentiation takes place. That maturation is induced by exposure to intestinal antigen is evidenced by the undeveloped follicles of Peyer's patches present in the fetus and in germ-free mice. Antigen is thought to be transported to the lymphoid tissue in Peyer's patches through the overlying epithelial cells. The Peyer patch epithelium is different from the surrounding mucosa; it lacks microvilli and has a very attenuated cytoplasm. These special epithelial cells overlying the patches contain many vesicles and have been called "M" cells.

In addition to inducing blast transformation and proliferation in gut-associated lymphoid tissue, antigens also induce B cells to migrate to other sites such as intestinal lamina propria, where they undergo differentiation into immunoglobulin-producing plasma cells of the IgA variety. However, seeding of cells to sites such as the lamina propria of the gut is not entirely dependent on antigen, since homing occurs to antigen-free (fetal) explants of intestine. Lymphoblasts in the thoracic duct lymph of rats have a preference for homing to the intestine. An allogeneic transfer system in the rabbit has shown the preferential homing of Peyer's patch cells to the intestinal lamina propria. There they differentiated into plasma cells containing IgA. These experiments were done by transferring allogeneic donor lymphoid cells (Peyer's patches, peripheral blood lymphocytes, and popliteal lymph nodes) from rabbits of one immunoglobulin allotype into lethally irradiated recipients of another allotype. Fluorescent antisera to donor immunoglobulin allotype and to rabbit immunoglobulin were used to identify cells containing donor immunoglobulin in the recipient. Cells from popliteal lymph nodes homed almost entirely to the spleen and gave rise mostly to IgG cells, whereas Peyer patch cells homed to both the spleen and gut and in both sites gave rise mostly to IgA cells (Table 16–3). These studies suggest that the tissue environment is not important in terminal differentiation of plasma cells to produce IgA as the cells are precommitted to IgA production before they leave the patches.

The characteristics of Peyer's patch cells grown in culture have been examined using fluorescent antisera. Only 1% of the fresh Peyer's patch cell suspension consists of plasma cells staining for cytoplasmic immunoglobulin, and this staining is evenly divided between IgM and IgA cells. After 4 days of cell culture, the proportion of immunoglobulin-containing cells increased to 10%, with 80% of these being IgM cells. If

Table 16–3. Homing properties of Peyer's patch cells.*

Source of Cells	Spleen % of Donor Cells Containing		Gut Lamina Propria Cells Containing	
	IgG	IgA	IgG	IgA
Popliteal lymph nodes	74	8	Few	None
Peyer's patch	13	77	Few	Many

*Data from Craig SW, Cebra JJ: Peyer's patches: An enriched source of precursors for IgA-producing immunocytes in the rabbit. J Exp Med 134:188, 1971.

the culture is done in the presence of pokeweed mitogen, immunoglobulin-containing cells increase to 17%, with a 60% preponderance of IgA over IgM. In contrast to the small numbers of immunoglobulin-containing cells, the studies demonstrated a significant percentage (31%) of patch lymphocytes bearing immunoglobulin on their surfaces (B cells). The surface proteins were κ chains, μ chains, α chains, and secretory component, as determined both by immunofluorescence and by radioiodination of surface membrane proteins. However, when these proteins were stripped from the membrane with Pronase, only μ chains and κ chains were regenerated on the surface, suggesting that the other membrane proteins were nonspecifically absorbed. Craig and Cebra's hypothesis is that lymphocytes bearing IgM in Peyer's patches produce an intermediate precursor cell which eventually differentiates into a plasma cell secreting IgA (probably via an intermediate B cell having α chain determinants). However, using anti-allotype antiserum, α chain surface determinants have been identified, suggesting that α chain-positive cells do exist but that the Fc fragment is buried and therefore unreactive with the usual anti-α chain antisera.

From studies of immunoglobulin levels in nude athymic mice, a relationship between the thymus and IgA B cell differentiation is suggested. Serum IgA levels are markedly decreased to about 20% of normal in these animals, and they do not respond to antigenic challenge with a normal rise in IgA antibody. It is interesting to note that in mouse gut-associated lymphoid tissue the majority of lymphoid blast cells are T cells, with smaller numbers of IgA B cells. All of these cells home to the lamina propria of the intestine, where the B cells differentiate into IgA-producing plasma cells. If Peyer's patch cells are the precursors of the blast cells migrating to the intestinal wall where differentiation to IgA plasma cells occurs, then the failure of development of Peyer's patch germinal centers, because of the lack of T cells, should be associated with a lack of intestinal IgA plasma cells. This is exactly what is seen in nude mice. Peyer's patches have no germinal centers, and, although IgA-bearing lymphocytes are seen, IgA plasma cells in the gut are markedly decreased. The relationship between IgA development and T cells seems to indicate that in the absence of T cells, IgA-bearing lymphocytes in Peyer's patches cannot be stimulated by antigen and, therefore, proliferation and seeding to the intestine to become IgA plasma cells cannot occur. This is consistent with the finding that almost all patients with IgA deficiency have normal numbers of B cells with surface α chains and often have associated T cell defects.

A specialized tissue with many characteristics similar to gut-associated lymphoid tissue has been recently described in the lung. This has been referred to as bronchial-associated lymphoid tissue, and cells isolated from these tissues home to both lung and intestinal lamina propria, giving rise to IgA cells. This suggests a common receptor mechanism on cells from secretory sites. A particularly important example of this may be illustrated in studies on transmissible viral gastroenteritis in swine. In this disease, oral—but not parenteral—immunization of pregnant swine prior to delivery gives rise to high titers of antiviral IgA antibodies in the milk. These studies, along with others employing different routes of immunization with pneumococcal antigens, suggest the possibility that lymphoid cells sensitized by antigen in the gut may seed the breast in later pregnancy, perhaps under hormonal influence. This interesting speculation requires further experimental documentation. Patients with hereditary ataxia-telangiectasia have thymic abnormalities, defects in delayed hypersensitivity, and low or absent serum IgA but normal numbers of B lymphocytes with surface IgA (see Chapter 26). Perhaps they lack a specific IgA helper cell or, alternatively, possess a relative excess of suppressor cells specific for IgA.

Biologic Function of the Secretory Immune System

A. Antiviral Activity: The best evidence for the role of secretory immunoglobulins in resistance to infections is that obtained with viral diseases. It has been established that the induction of virus-specific secretory antibodies is determined by the type of viral antigen (live virulent, attenuated, or inactivated) and the route and dose of immunization (parenteral or local). This is exemplified by the work of Ogra and Karzan on poliovirus. These workers demonstrated similar IgM, IgG, and IgA serum responses after immunization of humans with either oral live attenuated poliovaccine (Sabin) or parenteral inactivated vaccine (Salk). However, a significant secretory antibody response in the alimentary tract and nasopharynx occurred only after oral immunization and persisted for as long as 5 years. In addition, infants with double-barreled colostomies were locally immunized in the distal colon and local immunization produced predominantly IgA antibody. Only the immunized segments were capable of preventing colonization of the poliovirus. These and other experiments demonstrate that secretory immunoglobulins with virus-neutralizing activity produced by natural or vaccine-induced viral infections are largely SIgA antibodies. Antibody titers in secretions are better correlated than serum titers with resistance to reinfection following subsequent rechallenge with live virus. Thus, immunity to many respiratory viruses which produce their disease locally in the respiratory mucosa seems to be mediated by locally produced, largely SIgA antiviral antibodies. A role for cell-mediated reactions in preventing colonization of mucous membranes has not yet been established but may also be of importance. A partial list of viruses for which local synthesis and protection against infection in secretory tissues has been shown is seen in Table 16–4. As an example of the role of the secretory system in preventing viral infections, the data obtained with a "common cold"-producing rhinovirus is shown in Table 16–5. After immunization and rechallenge with the virus, nasal antibody and protection from illness were seen only after the intranasal immunization of volunteers.

Studies on immunity after either natural infection or immunization suggest that there are 2 general types

Table 16–4. Viruses for which local synthesis of antibody in secretory tissues has been reported. On the right are listed viruses in which protection against infection shows a high correlation with the titers of secretory antibody.

Local Synthesis of Secretory Antibody (Primarily IgA)	Protection Against Infection by Secretory Antibody
Poliovirus	Poliovirus
Influenza virus	Influenza virus
Parainfluenza virus	Parainfluenza virus
Measles virus	Rhinovirus
Rubella virus	Rubella virus
Respiratory syncytial virus	
Rhinovirus	
Echovirus	
Adenovirus	
Coxsackievirus	

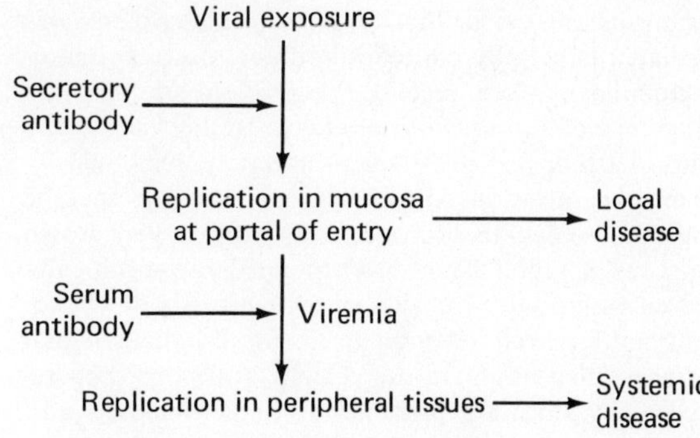

Figure 16–8. Sequence of spread of viral infection.

of virus infections with respect to the importance of serum versus secretory antibody protection (Fig 16–8). Following viral exposure there is replication of the virus in the mucosa at the portal of entry, ie, the respiratory or gastrointestinal tract. Viruses such as rhinovirus, respiratory syncytial virus, myxoviruses, and certain types of adenoviruses remain localized superficially in the mucosa. For example, with the oral Sabin poliovaccine, secretory antibody is induced and is effective in preventing replication and subsequent mucosal penetration by the virus; therefore, it also prevents establishment of the carrier state. The second type of viral infection is exemplified by poliovirus, echovirus, and measles virus, where, following the initial mucous membrane phase, systemic infection occurs. In this group of viruses, circulating antibody is important in preventing viral dissemination and peripheral organ disease. In the latter group, a patient, although immune to systemic infection by virtue of serum antibody, may become a carrier, with the virus persisting at the portal of entry, if there is no secretory antibody response. This may be found after the Salk (subcutaneous) vaccination for polio.

Table 16–5. Neutralizing antibodies in serum and nasal fluids following intramuscular and intranasal immunizations with rhinovirus type 13. Following immunization, volunteers were challenged with the live virus and the development of symptoms recorded. Note that only the group which developed nasal antibody showed significant protection against challenge with the live virus.*

Route of Vaccination	Number in Group	Geometric Mean Titer (Reciprocal)		Illness (%)
		Serum	Nasal	
Intranasal	28	53.8	4.5	36
Intramuscular	11	72.5	1.5	82
Control (no vaccine)	23	4.0	1.3	78

*Data from Perkins JC & others: Evidence for protective effect of an inactivated rhinovirus vaccine administered by the nasal route. Am J Epidemiol 90:319, 1969.

An important example of the possible dissociation between systemic and local immunity is seen following infection with respiratory syncytial virus. This virus is a frequent cause of bronchiolitis in infancy despite significant titers of passively acquired maternal IgG neutralizing antibodies. Obviously, serum antibody is not protective against respiratory syncytial virus since infection occurs at the height of maternally derived antibody titers. If an activated vaccine is given parenterally for immunization, even higher levels of IgG antibodies develop in the serum of the infant, but these afford little protection. In fact, more serious disease frequently occurs in children previously immunized by the parenteral route (killed virus) when exposed to the live virus. It has been suggested that the virus multiplies in the lung in the absence of mucosal immunity, and if high titers of IgG antibody are present in the serum, transudation occurs into the local site and the interaction of serum IgG (complement-fixing) antibody with antigen in the lung produces a hypersensitivity reaction of the Arthus (immune complex) type (see Chapter 31). Similarly, a severe form of measles occurs, often complicated by pneumonia, in children previously immunized parenterally with the inactivated measles vaccine who subsequently become infected with the live virus. In these cases, measles antigen, antibody, and complement have been found in blood vessel walls in the local skin lesion.

B. Antibacterial Activity: Until recently, the function of the secretory system in bacterial infections has been difficult to demonstrate experimentally because of the lack of an effector mechanism of IgA for bacterial killing such as opsonization and complement fixation. The low levels of several complement components and the apparently small numbers of phagocytes on most mucosal surfaces have contributed to this dilemma. The recent discovery of a diminution in bacterial adherence to mucous membranes resulting from specific antibody, including SIgA, has opened up a new area for investigation.

Over a decade ago, studies in human volunteers and in animals orally immunized with killed cholera organisms suggested that immunity to cholera was mediated largely by coproantibodies (intestinal immunoglobulins). More recently, it was shown that the adherence of *Vibrio cholerae* in vivo to the walls of the intestinal loops of rabbits was markedly decreased by prior immunization and by the presence of specific coproantibodies. In addition, when vibrios were grown on slices of rabbit ileum in vitro, antibody specifically prevented growth. This was due to an antibody-dependent antibacterial reaction occurring on the mucosal surface which inhibited the growth of absorbed bacteria and required the presence of viable mucosal cells. Essential to bacterial colonization of mucous membranes is the requirement that bacteria selectively adhere to epithelial surfaces. Selectivity of adherence is exemplified in the pattern of colonization of certain bacterial species, eg, certain strains of streptococci colonize only limited locations within the human oral cavity. It seems that surface antigens of indigenous and pathogenic bacteria influence their adherence to mucosal surfaces and thus affect successful colonization. Opposing the adherence of bacteria to mucous surfaces are factors related to the cleansing action of these membranes, ie, mucous secretions, cilial beating of epithelial cells in the trachea, intestinal motility and peristalsis in the bowel, rapid fluid flow, and epithelial desquamation. SIgA antibodies augment these effects by binding to antigenic components on the surface of bacteria, thereby inhibiting adherence and colonization. Thus, SIgA isolated from parotid fluid specifically inhibited the attachment of certain strains of streptococci to human buccal epithelial cells, although it had no effect on strains to which it did not exhibit antibody activity (Table 16–6).

It is well established that IgA does not fix complement via the classical pathway in a manner similar to that of IgG or IgM. Since lysis and killing of bacteria probably involve complement fixation, it does not seem that the antibacterial effect of IgA is complement-mediated. The recent description of an alternative pathway of complement fixation has revived the effort to implicate complement in IgA antibacterial activity. Aggregates of IgA myeloma proteins fix complement, starting with C3, but not the earlier components. The steps leading to the activation of C3 involve the components of the properdin pathway (see Chapter 6). Although very small amounts of complement and alternative pathway components have been found in pulmonary secretions, it is still not known whether sufficient amounts of these components are present in secretions to be biologically significant. Thus, the question whether complement fixation by the alternative pathway has biologic significance with respect to SIgA antibodies is still unanswered.

The ability of phagocytes to engulf particulate matter has been shown to be enhanced in the presence of specific antibody with or without complement. Although secretory IgA antibodies can combine and coat bacteria in vivo, the evidence that this enhances phagocytosis of bacteria is not conclusive. Some reports claim opsonizing properties for IgA for certain bacteria and red cells. It may be that there is some variation with the type of antigen or phagocytic cell involved. However, most carefully performed studies using highly purified preparations of IgA have failed to show promotion of phagocytosis.

The formation of plaque on teeth appears to be a requirement for caries production. Certain strains of *Streptococcus mutans* are cariogenic and produce dextran polymers from sucrose. These polymers enable *S mutans* to adhere to and colonize smooth surfaces of teeth, and they are necessary for the formation of plaque. Antisera directed against *S mutans* cells inhibit the adherence of these cells to smooth surfaces, independently of bacterial killing. The inhibition of adherence correlates positively with inhibition of the synthesis of cell-associated polysaccharide and with bacterial glucosyltransferase enzyme inhibition. Rats immunized with *S mutans* were orally reinfected with live *S mutans.* These rats developed salivary antibodies of the IgA class which inhibited glucosyltransferase activity and decreased caries production when compared to control rats. These studies suggest that it may someday be possible to immunize against dental caries, although much more work is needed in this important area.

C. Inhibition of Absorption of Nonviable Antigens by Gastrointestinal Mucosa: Contrary to earlier opinion, we now know that adults of many mammalian species absorb small but significant amounts of macromolecular antigens across the epithelial cells of mucous membranes. Recent studies using an inverted gut sac technic have shown that oral immunization with protein antigens specifically inhibits the uptake of the immunizing protein but not that of an unrelated antigen (Table 16–7). In the rat intestine, absorption of BSA or horseradish peroxidase was decreased if there was prior immunization with the corresponding antigen. Thus, local immune reactions may provide a control mechanism for the intestinal absorption of intact macromolecules. It has been postulated, but not proved, that the diminution in absorption is mediated by secretory antibodies. This would protect the organism against harmful antigens by forming nonabsorbable complexes which would be degraded by proteolytic enzymes on the surface of the intestine. Whether

Table 16–6. Inhibition of adherence of *Streptococcus salivarius* to human buccal epithelial cells by parotid fluid SIgA.*

Prior Treatment of Bacteria	Adherence (%of Control)†
Buffer (control)	100
Parotid fluid	56
65 μg of SIgA	24
SIgA + anti-IgA	98

*Data from Williams RC, Gibbons RJ: Inhibition of bacterial adherence by secretory immunoglobulin A: Mechanism of antigen disposal. Science 177:697, 1972.

†(Number of bacteria per epithelial cell in test system ÷ Number of bacteria per epithelial cell in control system) × 100.

Table 16–7. Effect of immunization on the intestinal uptake of antigen in adult rats using the inverted gut sac technic.*

Oral Immunization With:	Protein Absorption Of:	Absorption (% of Control)	
		Jejunum	Ileum
Bovine serum albumin (BSA)	^{125}I HRP	99	97
	^{125}I BSA	50	70
Horseradish peroxidase (HRP)	^{125}I BSA	80	110
	^{125}I HRP	38	33

*Data from Walker WA, Isselbacker KJ, Block KJ: Intestinal uptake of macromolecules: Effect of oral immunization. Science 177:608, 1972.

similar mechanisms operate in the absorption of inhaled antigens across the respiratory mucosa is not yet known.

D. Local Cell-Mediated Immunity on Secretory Surfaces: Cell-mediated immunity is as important in protection against certain viral and bacterial infections as it is for homograft rejection and tumor immunity. T cells and macrophages, both of which participate in cell-mediated reactions, have been found in large numbers in the gastrointestinal lamina propria. Following nasal immunization of guinea pigs with dinitrophenyl-human gamma globulin conjugates or influenza virus, lymphocytes from the respiratory tract of these animals inhibit macrophage migration in the presence of specific antigens. Lymphocytes obtained by bronchial lavage from parenterally immunized animals showed much smaller amounts of activity. Therefore, depending upon the route of immunization, local cell-mediated immunity in the respiratory tract can exist independently from that found systemically. This has been demonstrated for both viruses and bacteria in man. The significance of these findings in relationship to secretory antibodies remains to be established. Lymphocyte-mediated, antibody-dependent cytotoxicity, another important and recently described cell-mediated reaction, has been demonstrated only for IgG antibodies, but studies on IgA are lacking.

From the foregoing discussion, it seems that patrol of the vast area of both respiratory and intestinal absorptive surfaces against offending agents, be they live organisms or nonviable antigens, is a primary responsibility of the secretory system.

• • •

References

Bienenstock J, Johnson N, Perey DYE: Bronchial lymphoid tissue: 1. Morphologic characteristics. Lab Invest 28:686, 1973.

Bockman DE, Cooper MD: Pinocytosis by epithelium associated with lymphoid follicles in the bursa of Fabricius, appendix, and Peyer's patches: An electronmicroscopic study. Am J Anat 136:455, 1973.

Cebra JJ, Craig SW, Jones PP: Cells contributing to the biosynthesis of SIgA. Page 23 in: *The Immunoglobulin A System.* Mastecky J, Lawton AR (editors). Plenum Press, 1974.

Craig SW, Cebra JJ: Peyer's patches: An enriched source of precursors for IgA-producing immunocytes in the rabbit. J Exp Med 134:188, 1971.

Evans RT, Genco RJ: Inhibition of glucosyltransferase activity by antisera to known serotypes of *Streptococcus mutans.* Infect Immun 7:237, 1973.

Freter R: Parameters affecting the association of vibrios with the intestinal surface in experimental cholera. Infect Immun 6:134, 1972.

Grey HM & others: A subclass of human γA-globulins (γA_2) which lacks the disulfide bonds linking heavy and light chains. J Exp Med 128:1223, 1968.

Halpern MS, Koshland M: Novel subunit in secretory IgA. Nature 228:1276, 1970.

Hauptman SP, Tomasi TB Jr: The mechanism of IgA polymerization. J Biol Chem 250:3891, 1975.

Jerry LM, Kunkel HG, Adams L: Stabilization of dissociable IgA_2 proteins by secretory component. J Immunol 109:275, 1972.

Kincade PW, Cooper MD: Immunoglobulin A: Site and sequence of expression in developing chicks. Science 179:398, 1973.

Koshland ME, Wilde CE: Mechanism of immunoglobulin polymer assembly. Page 129 in: *The Immunoglobulin A System.* Mastecky J, Lawton AR (editors). Plenum Press, 1974.

Ogra PL, Karzan DT: Distribution of poliovirus antibody in serum, nasopharynx and alimentary tract following segmental immunization with poliovaccine. J Immunol 102:1423, 1969.

Perkins JC, & others: Evidence for protective effect of an inactivated rhinovirus vaccine administered by the nasal route. Am J Epidemiol 90:319, 1969.

Pollard M, Sharon M: Responses of the Peyer's patches in germ-free mice to antigenic stimulation. Immunity 2:96, 1970.

Tomasi TB Jr, Bienenstock J: Secretory immunoglobulins. Adv Immunol 9:1, 1968.

Tomasi TB Jr, Grey HM: Structure and function of immunoglobulin A. Prog Allergy 16:81, 1972.

Tomasi TB Jr, Hauptman SP: Modulation of the assembly of immunoglobulin subunits by J chain. Page 111 in: *The Immunoglobulin A System.* Mastecky J, Lawton AR (editors). Plenum Press, 1974.

Tomasi TB Jr & others: Characteristics of an immune system common to certain external secretions. J Exp Med 121:101, 1965.

Walker WA, Isselbacker KJ, Block KJ: Intestinal uptake of macromolecules: Effect of oral immunization. Science 177:608, 1972.

Williams RC, Gibbons RJ: Inhibition of bacterial adherence by secretory immunoglobulin A: Mechanism of antigen disposal. Science 177:697, 1972.

17 . . .
Immunity & Infection

David J. Drutz, MD

We live in a world filled with microorganisms; every facet of our existence brings us into contact with bacteria, fungi, viruses, and a diversity of other parasitic or potentially parasitic life forms. We possess a rich natural microflora on all body surfaces, within all orifices, and throughout most of the gastrointestinal tract. Even vital digestive functions are mediated partly by intestinal flora. Considering the continuous nature of our encounters with microorganisms, and notwithstanding the often mutually beneficial relationship, it is surprising that infections are not more common. However, through eons of coexistence, humans have developed a sophisticated mechanism for dealing with potential invading pathogens. Such mechanisms are the essence of *natural resistance,* which can be defined as the combined protective effects of anatomic barriers, baseline cellular phagocytosis, digestion by phagocytic cells, and effector mechanisms (such as complement), all of which are modified by nutritional status, hormonal status, and genetic makeup.

Host defenses against infection are at once local and systemic, nonspecific and specific, and humoral and cellular. It is difficult to identify any infectious agent that fails to stimulate multiple host defense mechanisms; indeed, the concept of overlapping host defenses is crucial to our understanding of susceptibility to infection. Thus, "immunologic redundancy" may account for a reasonable measure of good health even in the face of an apparently significant host immune defect.

HOST DEFENSES AT BODY SURFACES

In order for an invading pathogen to produce an infection, it must somehow slip through an impressive barrier of surface defenses which operate wherever intact body tissues confront the environment. Such defenses are potent even though relatively nonspecific. They are seldom accorded the great significance they deserve.

David J. Drutz is Associate Professor of Medicine and Chief, Division of Infectious Diseases, Department of Medicine, The University of Texas Health Science Center at San Antonio; and Audie L. Murphy Memorial Veterans Hospital, San Antonio.

Discharge of Microorganisms From the Body

A variety of normal functions act to continually reduce the body's bacterial burden. The mucociliary escalator of the respiratory tract brings microorganisms and foreign material to the oropharynx, where they may be coughed out or swallowed and excreted in the bowel contents. Desquamation and other forms of epithelial cell turnover at body surfaces remove large numbers of adherent microbes. Defecation results in the elimination of about 10^{12} bacteria daily, and urination eliminates microorganisms colonizing the urethral epithelium. Salivation, lacrimation, and sneezing also displace potentially infective microorganisms. Patients with Sjögren's syndrome, which is characterized by severe impairment of lacrimation and salivation, are at risk of ocular and oral sepsis resulting from loss of these vital defense mechanisms.

Local Production of Chemical Antimicrobial Factors

Lysozyme (muramidase), a cationic low-molecular-weight enzyme present in tears, saliva, and nasal secretions, reduces the local concentration of susceptible bacteria by attacking the mucopeptides of their cell walls. Salivary glycolipids prevent attachment of potentially cariogenic bacteria to oral epithelial cell surfaces through a process of competitive inhibition. Similar substances present on cell surfaces apparently act as the attachment sites for bacteria. Saliva also contains a lactoperoxidase-SCN-H_2O_2 system that possesses antibacterial activity in vitro. Gastric acidity retards access of Salmonella species and *Vibrio cholerae* to the intestine. Achlorhydria and gastric resection increase susceptibility to salmonellosis, cholera, and possibly giardiasis *(Giardia lamblia).* Neutralization of gastric contents with bicarbonate greatly increases the susceptibility of human volunteers to cholera and shigellosis. Acidity of skin and vaginal secretions retards local colonization by potential pathogens. Spermine, a polyamine present in prostatic secretions, is a potent (and highly pH-dependent) inhibitor of gram-positive microorganisms at concentrations normally encountered in semen. Seminal plasma also possesses potent bactericidal activity related to the presence of zinc.

Bacterial Interference

The normal biota of body surfaces serves an important host defense function. The skin commensal *Propionibacterium acnes* appears to be capable of retarding skin colonization with *Staphylococcus aureus* and *Streptococcus pyogenes* through the production of antibacterial skin lipids. Mechanical removal of the lipids with acetone permits local multiplication of these pathogenic cocci under experimental conditions.

Anaerobic bacteria in the bowel are able to retard the local growth of Salmonella species through the production of fatty acids. Antibiotics which selectively eliminate the responsible anaerobes indirectly predispose to salmonellosis. Resident bowel flora may also prevent acquisition of Shigella species by their effect on local pH as well as by producing volatile fatty acids harmful to shigella. Bile acids are excreted as glycine and taurine conjugates and are deconjugated by gut anaerobes. Deconjugated bile salts are inhibitory for a number of microorganisms, including *Bacteroides fragilis, Clostridium perfringens,* lactobacilli, and enterococci.

Streptococcus viridans in the pharynx appears to prevent the local growth of pneumococci. *Staphylococcus epidermidis* and diphtheroids in the nasal vestibule retard colonization by *S aureus.* The mechanisms of these important microbial interactions are unclear.

Attachment to & Penetration of Epithelial Cells

Intact skin is not easily infected, and most infections of otherwise normal persons begin at mucosal surfaces. For many pathogens, the first step in initiation of infection is attachment to an epithelial cell surface. Ability to attach to epithelial cells may be a prime determinant of virulence. For example, virulent Mycoplasma species appear capable of attaching to tracheal epithelial cells in vitro, whereas avirulent strains are incapable of such attachment. Virulent strains of shigella and enteropathogenic *Escherichia coli* attach better than avirulent strains to small bowel epithelium. In viral illnesses, attachment of viruses to specific membrane receptor sites is a crucial factor in initiating infection.

A. Mechanisms of Epithelial Cell Attachment: Epithelial cell attachment is partially a function of microbial surface factors. Such factors have received great attention in relation to the opsonization step of phagocytosis (see below) and toxicity, but they may be of even greater importance in relation to epithelial adherence. For example, gonococcal pili (fimbriae) appear to be important as stabilizers to prevent detachment of gonococci from urethral epithelium during micturition. Pili may also play a role in the attachment to gut epithelium of Shigella species, vibrios, *E coli,* and other microorganisms. Fimbriae are more likely to be associated with general adhesive properties than with specific pathogenicity. For example, many saprophytic Klebsiella species are fimbriated.

An antiphagocytic surface factor, the M protein of *S pyogenes,* appears also to be important in the attachment of this pathogen to human epithelial cells. The *K88* surface antigen of *E coli* subserves an intestinal attachment function in piglet diarrhea. Attachment of bacteria to surfaces may be enhanced by the synthesis of polymers. For example, *Streptococcus mutans,* a mouth inhabitant believed to be of potential importance in producing dental caries, synthesizes glucans and fructans from dietary sucrose. These materials enhance attachment of the microorganisms to teeth.

B. Significance of Epithelial Cell Penetration: Microbial attachment is not necessarily followed by epithelial cell penetration. Infections with *Mycoplasma pneumoniae, Corynebacterium diphtheriae, Bordetella pertussis,* and *G lamblia* take place entirely at the epithelial surface. Other pathogens penetrate into epithelial cells where they replicate and produce the principal manifestations of disease. This is the mechanism whereby Shigella species infect the colon. Finally, there are pathogens which do not stop at the stage of epithelial cell invasion but proceed to systemic spread. This pattern is typical of salmonellosis.

It has become apparent that epithelial cell invasion is an important mechanism of infection for many other potential pathogens, including protozoa, spirochetes, chlamydiae, enteroviruses, *Listeria monocytogenes,* and *Neisseria gonorrhoeae.* In an intraepithelial cell location, pathogens may be protected from antibiotics and from ingestion and killing by polymorphonuclear leukocytes and mononuclear phagocytes.

Epithelial cell penetration appears to involve a process of endocytosis similar in many ways to phagocytosis. The factors that determine the "hospitality" of epithelial cells for invading pathogens is unclear. Intraepithelial microbes appear to be viable, but this is not surprising since epithelial cells lack the comprehensive antimicrobial armamentarium of phagocytes such as polymorphonuclear leukocytes, monocytes, and macrophages. Some microorganisms, such as *Toxoplasma gondii,* appear capable of actively promoting endocytosis. The mechanism by which this is accomplished is unclear; however, toxoplasmas which are coated with antibody lose this capability even though the antibody is not directly harmful to the protozoon.

C. Host Defenses Against Attachment to Epithelial Cells: It is clearly in the interest of the host to prevent attachment of potential pathogens to epithelial cells. This may be partially accomplished by members of the normal microbial flora which attach to mucosal cells and cover up critical receptor sites. Attachment may also be retarded by local factors such as glycoproteins and pH. Nevertheless, it is now apparent that antibody at the local mucosal level plays a significant role in dictating the outcome of mucosal invasion. The antibody response at mucosal surfaces is mediated principally by secretory IgA. The presence of this immunoglobulin does not represent spillover from systemic sources. Not only is the level of IgA in serum about 3 times lower than in mucosal secretions; the secretory IgA also possesses a different structure. Mucosal immunity appears to be highly localized; elevated antibody titers in salivary secretions, for example, may not be associated with similar activity in the tears.

The mechanisms by which secretory IgA operates

against microorganisms in the complex environment of secretions are not entirely clear. Secretory IgA appears to have major importance in protection from many viral infections. Since antiviral activity does not require the presence of complement, it is likely that secretory IgA prevents mucosal invasion by viruses through a process of neutralization (see below). Secretory IgA is active against Mycoplasma species as well, perhaps by immobilizing, inhibiting the attachment of, or limiting the growth of virulent microorganisms.

There are several potential mechanisms by which secretory IgA could operate against bacteria. Although IgA does not fix complement in the classical manner, secretory IgA can produce lysis of coliform bacteria in vitro in the presence of complement and lysozyme. IgA might act locally in the bowel to augment phagocytosis. There is some suggestion that alveolar macrophages might possess surface receptors for IgA, thus allowing secretory IgA to subserve an opsonic function in respiratory secretions, though this remains speculative. The clearest role for secretory IgA in bacterial disease is in the prevention of bacterial attachment to mucosal cells. Under experimental conditions, IgA can prevent the attachment of oral streptococci and *V cholerae* to mucosal surfaces. The latter observation appears to explain why intraluminal gut antibody (coproantibody) levels are so important in protecting guinea pigs from oral challenge with *V cholerae.* Secretory IgA is believed to be important in retarding the colonization of mucosal surfaces with a variety of other microorganisms as well, including *N gonorrhoeae.* The mechanism by which secretory IgA blocks attachment of bacteria to mucosal cells is uncertain.

Not surprisingly, microorganisms have evolved countermeasures to permit their attachment to mucosal epithelial cells despite the presence of secretory IgA. *Streptococcus sanguis,* group H streptococci, *N gonorrhoeae,* and *N meningitidis* have all been shown to elaborate an IgA protease in vitro which cleaves and inactivates the IgA1 subclass of secretory IgA. If this material is active under clinical circumstances, it may help to explain the apparent paradox of repeated gonococcal infections despite high secretory IgA levels in genital secretions.

SYSTEMIC IMMUNITY TO INFECTION

Cellular Systems of Systemic Immunity

Once microorganisms have breached local defense mechanisms, a number of tightly integrated immunologic events are called into play which are predominantly related to the activity of 2 types of phagocytic cells: polymorphonuclear leukocytes and mononuclear phagocytes. These cells have been termed "professional phagocytes" because their membranes possess specialized receptors for the Fc portion of IgG molecules (IgG1 and IgG3 subclasses) and for activated C3. These receptors augment the process of phagocytosis by assisting in the ingestion of microorganisms with IgG or activated C3 on their surfaces. Nonprofessional or facultative phagocytes, in contrast, include endothelial cells, epithelial cells, fibroblasts, and other cells which will ingest microorganisms under specialized conditions but which do not possess specialized membrane receptors for IgG or C3.

A. Polymorphonuclear Neutrophil Leukocytes: These cells are concerned principally with the destruction of microorganisms which rely upon the evasion of phagocytosis for survival. Once ingested, such microorganisms generally perish. Microorganisms of this type are considered *extracellular pathogens;* their prototype is the pneumococcus.

B. Mononuclear Phagocytes: These cells are concerned principally with the control of microorganisms which are able to survive intracellular residence and against which neutrophils are ineffective. The principal effector cells are monocytes and macrophages. Monocytes are immature circulating forms of mature tissue macrophages. Monocytes may serve as a backup system to neutrophils in acute infections, but they phagocytose less efficiently and lack many of the potent bactericidal systems of the neutrophil. Macrophages are much more important in chronic infections. Sensitized lymphocytes may augment the bactericidal activities of macrophages through direct cell-to-cell contact or by the intervention of soluble mediators or lymphokines. Conversely, macrophages may process ingested or adsorbed microbial antigens preparatory to the sensitization of lymphocytes. Intracellular pathogens such as *Mycobacterium leprae, M tuberculosis, L monocytogenes, Salmonella typhi,* and many viruses appear to be under control of lymphocytes and macrophages.

Humoral Systems of Systemic Immunity

The role of humoral factors in systemic infection is largely related to augmentation of phagocytic function through the processes of chemotaxis and opsonization. However, some mechanisms of antimicrobial activity independent of phagocytosis may be mediated by humoral factors.

A. Complement-Mediated Bacteriolysis: Antibodies to cell wall antigens of gram-negative bacteria may cause bacteriolysis in the presence of complement (whereas antibodies to gram-positive bacteria serve principally as opsonins). Most studies demonstrating lysis by antibody and complement have employed microorganisms passaged in vitro for some time. Few studies have examined the susceptibility to lysis of bacteria fresh from human infections or from animal passage. It is unlikely that direct bacteriolysis of gram-negative microorganisms is a significant host defense mechanism in most diseases.

Bacterial variants which have lost cell wall material (L forms) are susceptible to complement-mediated lysis even when the gram-positive and gram-negative microorganisms from which they are derived are resistant to the effects of antibody and complement.

B. Viral Neutralization: Humoral antibodies probably constitute one of the more important mechanisms of host resistance to viral infections. Antibody molecules act primarily by neutralizing the antigenic receptor constituents on the virion, thereby preventing their attachment to and subsequent penetration of host cells. Although the surface of a viral particle contains numerous repeated sequences of antigen, a single antibody molecule may be sufficient to neutralize infectivity because structural rearrangement of the entire viral surface apparently occurs after the complexing of antibody to even a single antigenic determinant. Neutralization of viruses by antibodies is usually specific since the antibody is synthesized in response to specific antigenic components of the viral capsid or envelope. As a result of this specificity, host resistance mediated by antibodies is somewhat limited in that it will not provide protection against infections with a wide variety of viruses nor even against more than one antigenic type of the same virus. This specificity may be a formidable problem in the production of vaccines for mass immunization.

Secretory IgA appears to be the dominant host defense mechanism against infection with myxoviruses (influenza), paramyxoviruses (parainfluenza), enteroviruses (polio), and probably rhinoviruses. Circulating antibody also plays an important role in measles and mumps. However, termination of established infection for many of these infections is probably related to cell-mediated immune mechanisms.

In some viral infections—notably herpes simplex gingivostomatitis—antibodies are plentiful yet play no clear role in the pattern of recurrences or in the presence of protection. Other antiviral mechanisms such as cell-mediated immunity and interferon (see below) may be of greater importance.

C. Beta-Lysin: Beta-lysin is a highly reactive heat-stable cationic protein which is bactericidal for gram-positive microorganisms (except streptococci). Its release from platelets during coagulation results in serum levels which are far higher than plasma levels. Beta-lysin acts at the cell membrane of gram-positive bacteria to produce a nonenzymatic destructive effect similar to that of histones. Gram-negative microorganisms are resistant to its effects except under experimental conditions or in the presence of antibody, complement, and lysozyme.

D. Lysozyme: Lysozyme is a basic protein which originates from the lysosomes of phagocytic cells and is present in serum in a concentration of 1–2 μg/ml. It is actively secreted by monocytes and macrophages. Its mechanism of action is discussed later.

Microbial Agglutination & Bloodstream Clearance

Bacteria which gain access to the circulation are generally cleared from the blood by the fixed tissue macrophages of the mononuclear phagocyte system—especially the Kupffer cells of the liver. Features of opsonization and phagocytosis are presumably the same as for other mononuclear phagocytes (see below). However, there is evidence that the agglutination of microorganisms by serum factors, perhaps on a nonspecific basis, serves to augment the clearance of microorganisms from the bloodstream as well.

POLYMORPHONUCLEAR NEUTROPHIL LEUKOCYTE FUNCTION

The mature human neutrophil is an end-stage cell which, once released from the bone marrow, circulates with a half-life of 6–7 hours before losing functional capability and leaving the body in a random (non-age-related) fashion. About 10^8 neutrophils are turned over daily. The total blood granulocyte pool is composed of approximately equal numbers of circulating and marginated cells. Only the circulating pool is sampled by standard blood cell counting technics. Both marginated and bone marrow granulocyte pools are called into play during acute infections. Phagocytosis by neutrophils is composed of 4 interrelated phases: chemotaxis, opsonization, ingestion, and killing.

Chemotaxis

Chemotaxis is the process whereby phagocytic cells are attracted to the vicinity of invading pathogens. Chemotaxis represents a change in the direction of leukocyte mobility (ie, polarization) but not its speed. Chemotaxis may reflect actual linear attraction of phagocytic cells or a more subtle process whereby inhibition of random neutrophil migration keeps phagocytes in an area once they have arrived there by chance. The former phenomenon clearly occurs in vitro and is presumed to take place in vivo as well.

Although some bacteria elaborate chemotactic factors in the absence of serum, most chemotactic factors are of host origin. The complement system appears to be the most important source of these leukotactic factors. As shown in Fig 17–1, chemotactic activation may occur in various ways. When specific antibody reacts with the surface of a microorganism, the antigen-antibody complex sequentially activates the hemolytic complement components C1, C4, and C2. The antigen-antibody-C142 complex, or the properdin pathway, or both, attack C3 and C5 in the serum to yield C3a and C5a, which are low-molecular-weight peptides with chemotactic activity. Simultaneously, C3b, the opsonically active fragment of C3, is fixed to the surface of the microorganism. A complex of complement proteins acting later in the hemolytic sequence, $C\overline{567}$, assembles and has chemotactic activity as well. This leukotactic factor can also be generated by the action of trypsin on the native (biologically inactive) $C\overline{567}$ complex. Non-complement-related enzymes such as tissue and bacterial proteases and thrombin can cleave C3 and C5 to yield leukotactic fragments. Other sequentially reacting protein systems (kallikrein system; fibrinolysis system) also contain factors with leukotactic activity. Finally, leukocytes contain factors that are directly or indirectly chemotactically active, and leukotactic factors may arise

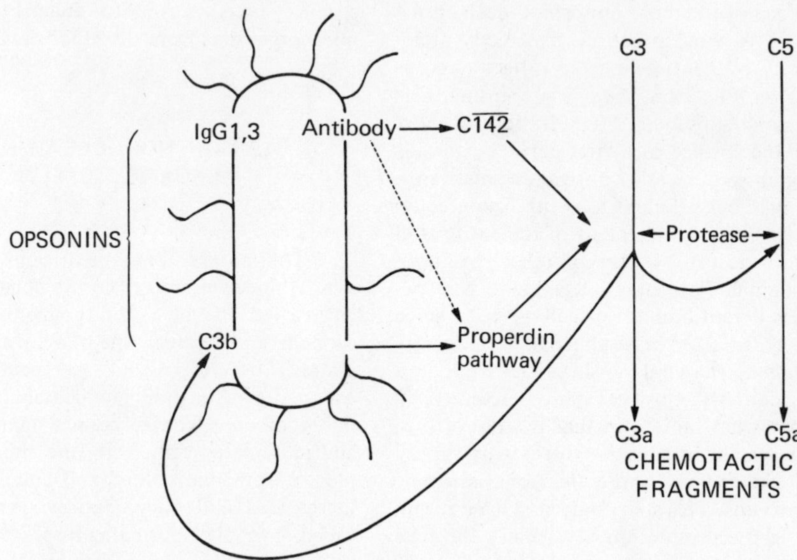

Figure 17–1. Serum-mediated generation of chemotactic factors and opsonization of microorganisms. (Reproduced, with permission, from Stossel TP: Phagocytosis. N Engl J Med 290:719, 1974.)

from sensitized lymphocytes following contact of the cells with antigen (leukotactic lymphokines).

The action of chemotactic substances on phagocytic cells may be likened to that of hormones; presumably, their effect is on the surface of the motile cell. The greater intrinsic motility of neutrophils as compared with monocytes appears to account for their more rapid accumulation at infective foci.

When active factors reach the surface of the neutrophil, an esterase is activated, the hexose monophosphate shunt is activated (see below), calcium fluxes occur in the cells, and microfilaments (composed of actin) and microtubules (composed of tubulin) assemble, providing the motility needed to propel the cell toward the microorganism activating these events. Myosin has also been found in phagocytic cells, and it is likely that the motility of such cells may have a close molecular relationship to muscle contraction.

Opsonization

The function of serum opsonins (Gk *opsonein* to prepare food for) is to react with microorganisms and make them more susceptible to ingestion by phagocytes. The virulence of many pathogens relates in part to their ability to evade phagocytosis by virtue of certain surface antigens. Microorganisms in which antiphagocytic surface factors are of importance include *Streptococcus pneumoniae, Klebsiella pneumoniae, Haemophilus influenzae, N meningitidis,* and *Pseudomonas aeruginosa* (capsular polysaccharides); *Bacillus anthracis* (capsular polypeptide); *N gonorrhoeae* (pili composed of protein); *S pyogenes* (capsular hyaluronic acid and M protein); and *S aureus* (protein A, which has the capacity to bind to the Fc portion of IgG, thereby competing with phagocytes for the Fc sites of opsonins). Opsonization of bacteria may occur by one of 3 mechanisms:

First, *specific antibody alone* (subclasses IgG1 and IgG3) may act as an opsonin as shown in Fig 17–2. This mechanism has been explored most thoroughly in studies employing pneumococci under conditions of abundant antibody. Here, anticapsular antibody combines with the surface polysaccharide antigens of the pneumococci through antibody combining sites located on the Fab portion of the immunoglobulin molecule. The Fc portion of the molecule, which is critical to its function as an opsonin, is then free to attach to Fc receptor sites on the surface of phagocytes, thus completing a bridge between bacteria and phagocytic cell.

Second, *specific antibody acting in concert with complement* via the classical C1, C4, C2 pathway may promote microbial opsonization. Here, a quantity of antibody apparently insufficient to opsonize on its own may react with bacteria and activate sequentially the hemolytic complement sequence. Receptor sites for activated C3 are present on the surface of phagocytes (Fig 17–2). The activated C3 on the bacterial surface apparently serves as a bridge between bacteria and phagocyte, prompting ingestion.

Thirdly, opsonization can be *nonspecific* and involves a heat-labile (ie, inactivated by heating at 56 C) serum opsonin system. Normal 7S immunoglobulin isolated from nonimmune animals has been shown to participate functionally in this system (at least in the case of pneumococcus). The immunoglobulin does not appear to be directed toward the capsule, and its site of binding on the pneumococcus is unknown. The fixation of activated C3 on the surface of microorganisms is critical to opsonization in this system, but the mechanism involves activation of the alternative com-

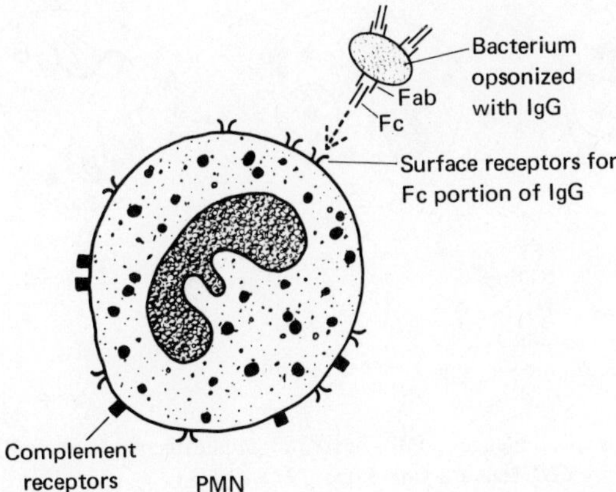

Figure 17–2. Schematic representation of receptors on the surface of a neutrophil (PMN) that interact with complement components and with the Fc portion of IgG molecules. (Reproduced, with permission, from Cline MJ: *The White Cell.* Harvard Univ Press, 1975.)

plement pathway, bypassing C1, C4, and C2. Since the heat-labile opsonin system is present in nonimmune animals (and presumably man) and is not dependent upon the presence of anticapsular antibody for its action, it has been considered to play an important role in the early and critical preimmune stages of infection prior to the production of specific antibody. This is also the stage at which surface phagocytosis is considered most important (see below). The precise role of the heat-labile opsonin system in human infection is not clear, but it has been suggested that the abnormal susceptibility of patients with sickle cell anemia to fulminating pneumococcal infection may be related to their demonstrably low levels of heat-labile pneumococcal opsonins. Such patients may fail to utilize fully the alternative pathway of complement activation, perhaps because some of the necessary components are synthesized in the spleen. Patients with sickle cell anemia undergo early autosplenectomy as a result of repeated infarcts.

There are 3 other factors that may promote phagocytosis of microorganisms in association with the above systems.

A. Surface Phagocytosis: As noted, many microbial pathogens may possess antiphagocytic surface components (such as pneumococcal capsular polysaccharide) which protect them from phagocytosis in the absence of specific antibody. Yet there are often no homologous antibodies in the serum before the fifth or sixth day of illness. Survival of a patient during the preantibody stage of infection may depend not only upon the heat-labile opsonin system but also upon surface phagocytosis. Here, encapsulated bacteria are trapped between leukocytes themselves, between leukocytes and tissue surfaces, or along with leukocytes in the interstices of fibrin clots. Surface phagocytosis may occur with mononuclear phagocytes as well as neutrophils. Heavily encapsulated type 3 pneumococci may resist surface phagocytosis for some time. Surface phagocytosis is much less efficient in areas where leukocytes are not tightly packed (pleural, pericardial, and joint fluids; cerebrospinal fluid).

B. Natural Antibody: Antibodies present in the serum in the absence of apparent specific antigen contact are referred to as natural antibodies. They may in fact reflect contact with microorganisms possessing related antigens. For example, more than 80% of persons over the age of 1 year have antibody to type 7 pneumococci although the carrier rate of this microorganism is only about 1%. The antibody appears following exposure to certain *S viridans* strains which possess a cross-reacting surface antigen.

Presumably, natural antibodies may participate with the heat-labile opsonin system in preventing infection with microorganisms which do not possess surface factors posing a serious challenge to phagocytosis.

C. Tuftsin: Leukokinen, a γ-globulin moiety, is capable of stimulating pinocytosis and phagocytosis by neutrophils under experimental conditions. The biologic activity of leukokinen rests in a single peptide, tuftsin–so called because it was discovered by workers at Tufts University. The peptide (Thr-Lys-Pro-Arg) is apparently produced in the spleen. It has also been prepared synthetically. A membrane enzyme of the neutrophil appears capable of splitting tuftsin from leukokinen. Splenectomy results in a severe deficiency of tuftsin and may be one of several reasons why splenectomized patients are more susceptible to certain infections.

Ingestion

Polymorphonuclear leukocytes are actively phagocytic; energy for this process is derived from glycolysis (Fig 17–3). This form of metabolism is important since neutrophils are often isolated in hypoxic surroundings, such as the interior of abscesses. Upon particle or microbial contact, cell pseudopodia are extended which fuse on the distal side of the material to be ingested; the particle becomes encased within a phagocytic vesicle or *phagosome,* and the lining of the phagosome, therefore, is inverted plasma membrane. The phagosome buds off from the cell periphery and moves centripetally, apparently through the mediation of microtubules.

The destruction of susceptible microorganisms within neutrophils is intimately associated with the process of degranulation, the release of granule contents into phagosomes. Human neutrophils contain 3 types of granules. Primary granules first become apparent at the promyelocyte stage of cell development in the bone marrow. They assume an azure tint with Wright-Giemsa stain (hence they are also known as azurophilic granules). Primary granules contain abundant hydrolytic lysosomal enzymes, large amounts of myeloperoxidase (the green hue of which is largely responsible for the color of pus), lysozyme, elastase, and cationic proteins. Secondary (specific) granules appear as the promyelocyte matures to a myelocyte in the marrow. They are smaller than primary granules, stain poorly (neutrophilic), and later outnumber pri-

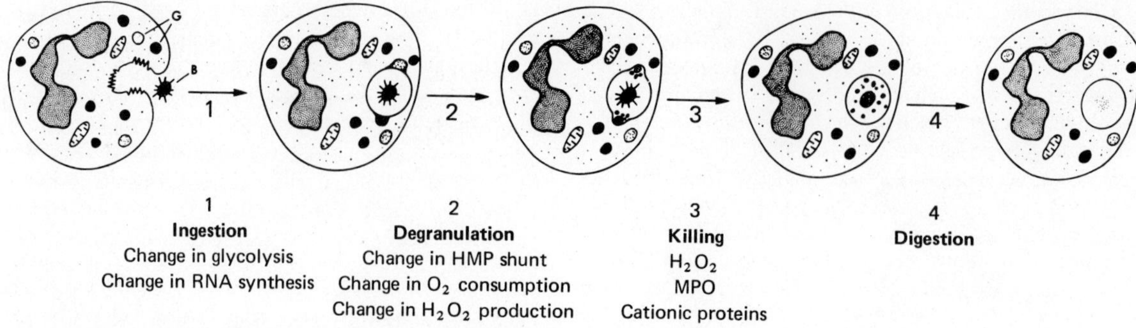

Figure 17–3. Different stages of phagocytosis resulting in major biochemical changes. HMP, hexose monophosphate shunt; MPO, myeloperoxidase. (Reproduced, with permission, from Cline MJ: *The White Cell.* Harvard Univ Press, 1975.)

mary granules in the mature neutrophil. Secondary granules contain lactoferrin and lysozyme.

As the phagosome forms during microbial engulfment, neutrophil granules undergo violent movement in proximity to the phagosome, fuse with the phagocytic vacuole, and disappear from the cytoplasm (degranulate). Secondary granules are the first to fuse with the phagosome. As with chemotaxis and ingestion, microfilaments and microtubules may be important in the fusion of phagosomes and granules.

Whereas phagocyte mobility and ingestion are dependent upon glycolytic metabolism, subsequent cellular events involve oxygen consumption and stimulation of the hexose monophosphate shunt as shown in Fig 17–3. The burst of oxygen consumption is cyanide-independent (and therefore mitochondrial enzyme-independent). The exact mechanism of the respiratory burst is unclear, but it probably involves activation of intracellular phosphopyridine nucleotide oxidases (perhaps NADPH oxidase). Whatever enzymes are involved, the oxidases reduce molecular oxygen to compounds with antimicrobial activity (notably superoxide and hydrogen peroxide) as noted below. The enzymes responsible for peroxide synthesis are presumably located on the external surface of the plasma membrane (which is also, of course, the internal surface of the phagolysosomal membrane). Since hydrogen peroxide can penetrate into the cytoplasm, even if selectively secreted into the phagocytic vacuole, catalase and coupled glutathione are important for peroxide destruction. Superoxide dismutase may protect the cell cytoplasm from superoxide anion.

Killing

The mechanisms by which neutrophils kill microorganisms are not clearly understood. Multiple interlocking phenomena (redundancy) probably exist within the cell some of which are likely to be active against only a specific class of microorganisms. For example, the mechanisms responsible for killing Candida species may be different from those that are operative in the killing of *Serratia marcescens* or streptococci. Microbial killing mechanisms comprise 2 broad categories: nonoxidative and oxidative.

A. Nonoxidative Killing Mechanisms: Systems of microbicidal activity which are independent of hydrogen peroxide include those based upon cationic proteins, lactoferrin, lysozyme, elastase, and production of acid in the phagocytic vacuole. Nonoxidative microbicidal mechanisms are of obvious importance because certain bacteria can clearly be killed by neutrophils under anaerobic conditions.

1. Cationic proteins from azurophilic granules were the first antimicrobial substances defined in the neutrophil. They bind to bacteria within the phagosome and damage microbial membrane barriers.

2. Lactoferrin from specific granules may exert antimicrobial function by binding and withholding required iron from ingested bacteria. Lactoferrin may also protect other antimicrobial functions of neutrophils by binding iron.

3. Lysozyme, present in both primary and specific granules, attacks mucopeptides in the cell walls of various bacteria. Bacteria intrinsically insensitive to lysozyme become sensitive to it in the presence of hemolytic complement or ascorbic acid and hydrogen peroxide. Because bacterial death often precedes temporally the action of lysozyme, this enzyme may serve in a digestive rather than microbicidal capacity.

4. Elastase from primary granules attacks mucopeptides of certain bacterial cell walls and may also be more important in digestion than killing.

5. High acidity (pH 3.5–4.0) in the phagocytic vacuole has been reported by some investigators. This acidity could result from lactic acid production accompanying phagocytosis-related glycolysis, or it might reflect production of carbonic acid in the presence of carbonic anhydrase. Teleologically, an extremely low vacuolar pH would appear to be detrimental to maximal neutrophil microbicidal activity since the highly acid environment would be below the pH optima of many lysosomal enzymes.

B. Oxidative Mechanisms: Oxidative mechanisms of microbial killing appear to be mediated by at least 2 systems:

1. Hydrogen peroxide (H_2O_2)—Many of the proposed bactericidal mechanisms of neutrophils appear to be related to the generation of H_2O_2 in the phagocytic vacuole. Reaction with a halide (such as iodide from membrane-bound thyroxine; or chloride, which might reach the vacuole by diffusion) and myeloperoxidase results in (1) halogenation of the microbial cell wall (the actual mechanism of microbial damage is unclear), (2) generation of bactericidal aldehydes from amino acids, and (3) cleavage of peptide bonds in the exterior portion of the microorganism. Two additional and potentially important H_2O_2-mediated activities are not reliant upon the presence of myeloperoxidase: (1) Bacteria normally unsusceptible to lysozyme may be killed by the synergistic action of H_2O_2, ascorbic acid, and lysozyme; and (2) cellular unsaturated fatty acids derived from membrane lipids may form the bactericidal compound malonyldialdehyde through the action of myeloperoxidase. (The latter mechanism may be more important in mononuclear phagocytes.)

2. Free radicals–Oxidative reactions involving ground state molecular oxygen are believed to proceed frequently by one-electron steps that result in the production of highly reactive free radicals including superoxide anion ($O_2^{-\cdot}$). The enzyme superoxide dismutase appears to be responsible for protecting the cell from its own superoxide anion by catalyzing the reaction

$$O_2^{-\cdot} + O_2^{-\cdot} + 2H^+ \rightarrow H_2O_2 + O_2^{\cdot}$$

Alternatively, it could function to ensure the production of H_2O_2, which some believe to be the actual killing agent. Since superoxide dismutase can also inhibit bacterial killing, however, it appears likely that superoxide anion is itself required for microbicidal activity. Other candidate antimicrobial factors arising from chemical reactions involving molecular oxygen include singlet oxygen and hydroxyl radical. The relaxation of highly excited, unstable singlet oxygen to the ground state is accompanied by an intraphagocytic burst of light (chemiluminescence) which can be detected in a liquid scintillation spectrometer.

An important clue to the significance of oxidative microbicidal events in the human neutrophil (and monocyte) has come from studies of chronic granulomatous disease which is characterized by intact phagocytosis and degranulation but impaired respiratory burst, impaired H_2O_2 and superoxide production, and impaired chemiluminescence. These cells cannot kill adequate numbers of most bacteria but do kill catalase-negative bacteria such as streptococci and pneumococci normally. Catalase-negative microorganisms generate their own H_2O_2, which, in the absence of catalase, apparently compensates for the metabolic deficiency of the cells in chronic granulomatous disease.

THE MONONUCLEAR PHAGOCYTE SYSTEM & ITS FUNCTION

The mononuclear phagocyte system has its origin in the bone marrow monoblast and promonocyte. Only the intermediate stage cell (the monocyte) is ordinarily encountered in the circulation. The ratio of circulating to marginated monocytes in humans is approximately 1:3. Monocytes circulate with a half-life of 8½ hours, leaving the circulation randomly (ie, unrelated to age). There is a daily monocyte turnover of approximately 7×10^6 cells per hour per kg body weight.

Unlike neutrophils, monocytes do not die when they leave the circulation but mature to macrophages (histiocytes) in the tissues: alveolar macrophages (lung), Kupffer cells (liver), and macrophages of spleen sinusoids, lymph nodes, peritoneum, and other areas. There is some evidence that macrophages in the lung and liver may proliferate locally as well. Macrophage maturation is accompanied by an increase in cell size and in numbers of cytoplasmic organelles including mitochondria and lysosomes (containing hydrolytic enzymes) as well as other morphologic, biochemical, and functional changes. These changes vary from tissue to tissue according to the state of the host (normal, infected, or otherwise stimulated). The synthetic activities of macrophages can also be stimulated in culture, the best-known example being the increase in lysosomal hydrolases after exposure in vitro to foreign serum. Functional maturity of these cells is shown by increasing phagocytic capability, increased numbers of Fc receptors for IgG on the cell surface, and increased responsiveness to lymphocyte activation. Mature macrophages in unique environments may achieve distinctive cellular physiology (eg, alveolar macrophages are unique in being dependent predominantly on aerobic metabolism).

Chemotaxis

Although humoral mediators of mononuclear phagocyte chemotaxis are less well elucidated than is the case with neutrophils, C5a appears to be important. Other complement-related mediators are probably involved as well. Recruitment of mononuclear phagocytes is effected to a major degree by chemotactic materials released from sensitized T lymphocytes. Additional lymphocyte-derived substances, such as migration inhibitory factor, encourage the accumulation of chemotactically attracted phagocytes in inflammatory foci.

Opsonization

The membranes of human monocytes and macrophages contain receptors for IgG (subclasses IgG1 and IgG3) and C3. Presumably, therefore, the process of opsonization is similar to that which occurs with neutrophils. Mycoplasma species have the interesting ability (in vitro) to attach to macrophages in the absence of antibody or complement. When so attached, they retard ameboid movement of the phagocytic cell. In the presence of antibody, mycoplasmas are phagocytosed and killed. Such experimental observations permit dissection of the attachment and ingestion phases of mononuclear phagocyte function, but their practical significance is uncertain.

Ingestion

Monocytes and macrophages (except for alveolar macrophages) resemble neutrophils in metabolic events associated with phagocytosis (glycolytic mechanisms for particle ingestion, postphagocytic burst in oxygen consumption with H_2O_2 generation, and hexose monophosphate shunt activation). The phagocytic capability of alveolar macrophages is impaired when the oxygen tension drops below 25 mm Hg; other macrophages may function normally under these conditions. Alveolar macrophages also show little increment in postphagocytic oxygen consumption.

Killing

Monocytes possess 2 lysosomal populations. The first appears early in monocyte maturation and contains myeloperoxidase, arylsulfatase, and acid phosphatase. The contents of the second, later-appearing lysosomes are unknown. As monocytes mature to macrophages in the tissues, additional lysosomal structures develop on a continuing basis reflecting both the prolonged life span of these phagocytic cells and their ability to synthesize new membrane and membrane receptors. Preexisting primary lysosomes may fuse with phagocytic vacuoles or pinocytotic vesicles to produce secondary lysosomes. At least in vitro, their formation and contents are closely related to the extracellular milieu. There is a definite relationship between endocytic activity and the formation of lysosomes; as macrophages mature, there is a progressive rise in lysosomes and their hydrolytic enzyme content.

The mechanisms by which monocytes and macrophages kill microorganisms are largely unknown. Enzymes found in mononuclear phagocytes (including acid phosphatase, β-glucuronidase, lipase, lysozyme, hyaluronidase, and others) appear to serve a digestive rather than a microbicidal function. These cells do not possess the bactericidal cationic proteins of neutrophils; lactoferrin is absent; and myeloperoxidase is not found beyond the monocyte phase of macrophage development. In the presence of oxygen and clofazimine, a phenazine dye used in the treatment of leprosy, H_2O_2 generation in the human macrophage is stimulated and killing is enhanced. Furthermore, monocyte microbicidal activity is impaired in chronic granulomatous disease. These observations strongly suggest that monocytes and macrophages employ an H_2O_2-generating system in microbial killing. Catalase, which is present in macrophages, may substitute for myeloperoxidase, which is not present, and may thus catalyze the oxidation of substrates in the presence of H_2O_2. Under in vitro conditions, catalase can substitute for myeloperoxidase in the myeloperoxidase-H_2O_2-halide microbicidal system. Lipid peroxidation, which occurs in alveolar macrophages and monocytes, may be another mechanism potentiating the antimicrobial action of H_2O_2 because malonyldialdehyde, a catabolite of lipid peroxides, has antibacterial activity.

Fate of Intracellular Microorganisms

Depending upon their ability to survive intracellular conditions, phagocytosed microorganisms may be either killed and digested, killed and poorly degraded, or not killed and merely sequestered within the cells. Some microorganisms have apparently developed mechanisms for ensuring their intracellular survival in macrophages. Thus, *M tuberculosis, Toxoplasma gondii* (unless coated with specific antibody), and *Chlamydia psittaci* may escape intracellular killing by preventing the fusion of phagosomes with lysosomes. Dead microorganisms do not possess this capability. *M lepraemurium,* a pathogen of rodents and an important model for studying intracellular parasitism, appears to be resistant to phagolysosomal contents despite the occurrence of phagolysosomal fusion. *M leprae,* the etiologic agent of human leprosy, appears capable of escaping the phagolysosome, coming to lie free and uninhibited in the cell cytoplasm. Typhus-producing rickettsial species escape from phagolysosomes and multiply freely in the macrophage cytoplasm in the absence of specific antibody. However, antibody-coated rickettsiae are unable to escape the phagolysosome.

Cell-Mediated Immunity (Lymphocyte-Macrophage Interaction)

Acquired resistance to a broad range of intracellular parasites has its origin in a cell-mediated immune response involving both macrophages and lymphocytes. During the induction of immunity, macrophages probably facilitate the engagement of antigen-sensitive T lymphocytes, although the mechanism by which this is accomplished is unclear. Antigen-activated T cells, the specific mediators of cellular resistance to infection, are generated in regionally stimulated lymphoid tissue and then released into the general circulation.

Interactions between mononuclear phagocytes and sensitized lymphocytes occur during expression of cellular resistance to infection. Sensitized lymphocytes produce soluble factors (lymphokines), one of which, MIF, encourages circulating blood monocytes to localize at sites of microbial invasion. In addition, lymphocytes specifically committed to microbial antigens can be stimulated (at least in vitro) to release products which enhance (activate) the endocytic and microbicidal capacity of macrophages (Fig 17–4). The mechanisms by which lymphokines might augment macrophage killing are unclear. Indeed, whether such factors actually function in vivo is also unclear. The principal role of sensitized lymphocytes may be to encourage accumulation of abundant mononuclear phagocytes at foci of microbial invasion.

Although cell-mediated immunity may be induced specifically through the action of sensitized lymphocytes, it is expressed nonspecifically in the sense that macrophages, once stimulated to a state of enhanced microbicidal activity, will perform this function nonspecifically. Thus, animals infected with *T gondii* will more readily limit infection with *L monocytogenes* and other intracellular parasites through the presence of activated macrophages. The practical significance of this observation is unclear, however, since experimental animals appear to eliminate the homologous sensi-

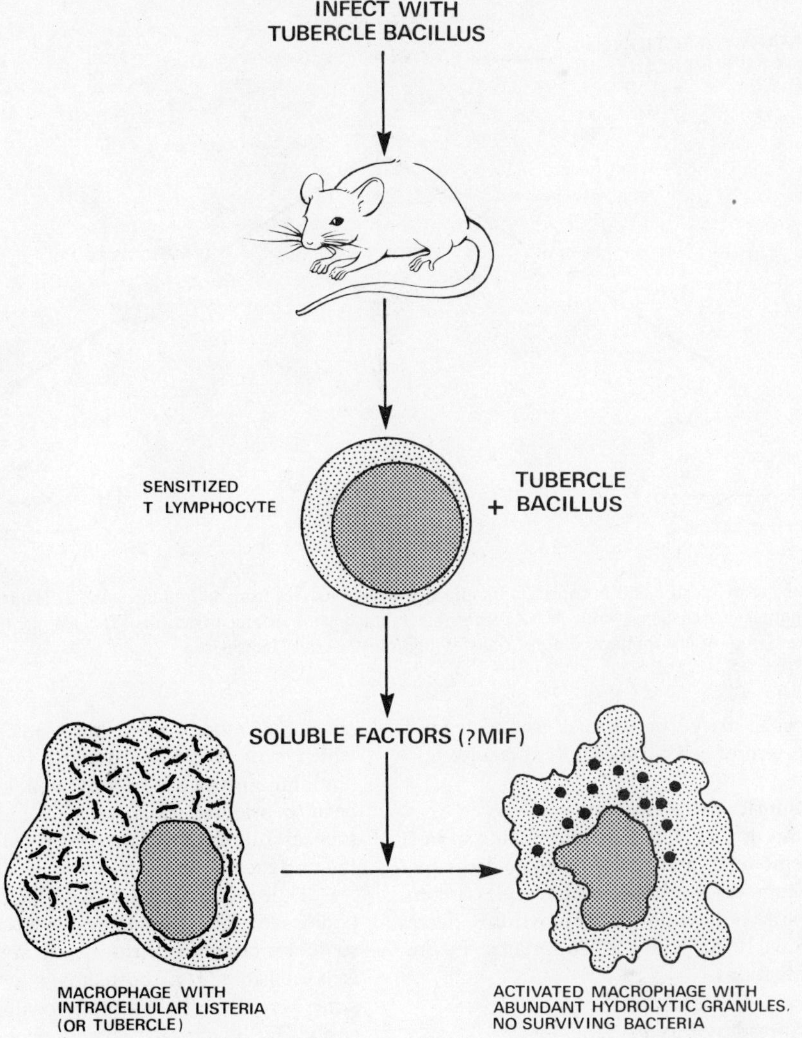

Figure 17–4. Macrophage killing of intracellular bacteria triggered by specific cell-mediated immunity reaction. (The final stage shown is probable but still hypothetical.) (Redrawn and reproduced, with permission, from Roitt IM: *Essential Immunology,* 2nd ed. Blackwell, 1974.)

tizing microorganism much more efficiently than the heterologous challenge microorganism.

The importance of lymphocytes in immunity to intracellular infection is well demonstrated by the phenomenon of adoptive immunity, wherein lymphocytes transferred from an animal with immunity to a given infection (such as tuberculosis) confer immunity to the same pathogen upon a normal animal (Fig 17–5). The animals must be closely related genetically to demonstrate this phenomenon; otherwise, a GVH reaction might ensue. The use of transfer factor (an immunologically active dialyzable lymphocyte extract) in humans is based upon the principles of adoptive immunity. Since whole lymphocytes are not transferred between individuals, a GVH response is not a problem.

There is a close relationship between cell-mediated immunity and delayed hypersensitivity; skin test reactivity to a given pathogen is generally transferred along with adoptive immunity to that pathogen. These processes are not inseparable, however. Thus, RNA extracted from *M tuberculosis* may transfer immunity but not skin test reactivity. Conversely, mycobacterial lipids may be more important in the delayed hypersensitivity skin test response than in immunity.

SPECIAL ASPECTS OF VIRAL IMMUNITY

Viruses represent a structurally and biochemically diverse group of infectious agents, and a variety of defense mechanisms have evolved that serve to protect the host from viral infection. Viruses of pathogenic

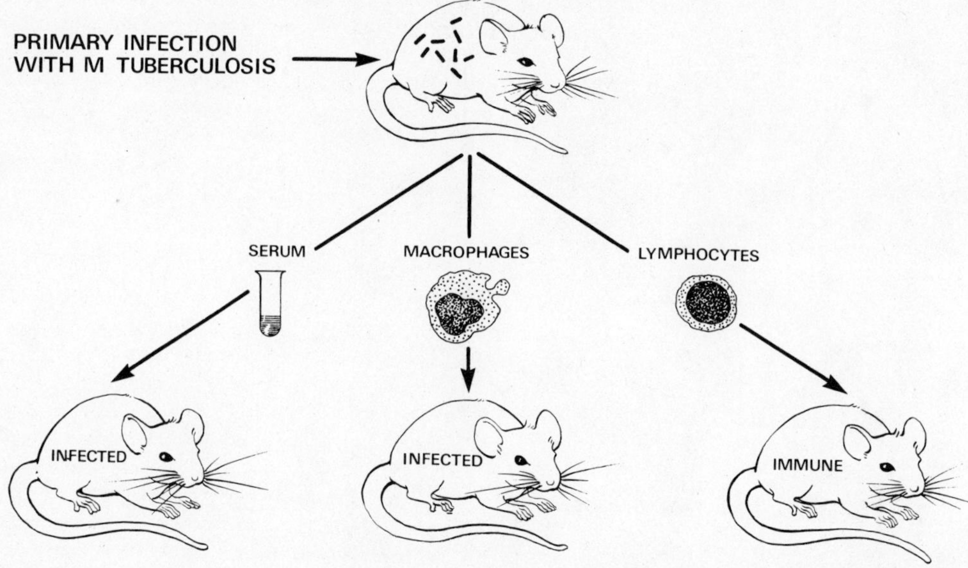

Figure 17–5. Transfer of specific and nonspecific immunity by lymphocytes from an immune animal. The recipient of the lymphocytes resisted simultaneous challenge with *M tuberculosis* combined with listeria organisms. The recipients were not immune to listeria given alone. Serum or macrophages did not transfer immunity. (After Mackaness.)

importance may be placed in 2 broad groups depending upon the pattern of cell pathology that results.

Viruses Which Spread Extracellularly

These viruses do not alter the composition of host cell plasma membranes and are generally adequately controlled by humoral mechanisms. Examples are enteroviruses (such as poliovirus) and rhinoviruses. Secretory IgA is probably of principal importance in preventing these infections.

Viruses Which Spread by Fusion

Viruses which spread by fusion of infected cells with their uninfected neighbors or by direct placement of viral antigens onto the host cell surface are controlled predominantly by cell-mediated immunity. Examples are poxviruses (vaccinia) and herpesviruses (herpes simplex). Myxo- and paramyxoviruses such as influenza, measles, and mumps mature by budding from host cell membrane. Most myxo- and paramyxoviruses elicit both cell-mediated and humoral immune mechanisms; neither system may be indispensable. For example, patients with congenital X-linked hypogammaglobulinemia control infections with these agents in a normal fashion; patients with depressed cell-mediated immunity do not appear to be unduly susceptible to these infections either. In contrast, the latter are at great risk from herpesvirus infections.

Defense Against Viruses

Three principal components contribute to host defense against viral infections: antibody, cell-mediated immunity, and interferon.

A. Antibody: Antibodies are generally considered to function by preventing adsorption and promoting elution of viruses from host cells. The mechanism by which viruses are neutralized by secretory IgA and humoral antibodies is not well understood and has been considered previously. Lipid-containing viruses such as rubella virus may be lysed by complement in the presence of antibody.

Unlike the situation with bacteria and fungi, antibodies are not considered to have an important opsonic function for viruses, nor are these microorganisms considered to be handled by phagocytes in the same way. Rarely, antibody-coated virus may be ingested by macrophages and degraded in phagolysosomes. Host cells infected with surface-maturing viruses (rhabdo-, myxo-, and paramyxoviruses) or with viruses that direct the placement of viral glycoproteins onto the cell membrane are lysed by complement in the presence of antibody. Such cell remnants may then be phagocytosed and destroyed by macrophages.

B. Cell-Mediated Immunity: T lymphocytes can identify viral components present on cell surfaces and undergo blastic transformation. These lymphocytes may then destroy virus-infected cells by direct cytotoxicity or induce macrophages to virucidal activity, perhaps by affecting cytotoxic effector cells.

C. Interferon: Interferons are a family of low-molecular-weight proteins elaborated by infected host cells which protect noninfected cells from viral infection. They may be produced by cultured cells or by intact animals in response to a variety of infecting agents (viruses, rickettsiae, protozoa) as well as to bacterial endotoxin, synthetic anionic polymers, and polynucleotides (especially double-stranded RNA).

Interferon is released from infected cells almost as soon as virus is produced; hence, it is available much sooner than antibody (Fig 17–6). Its mechanism of

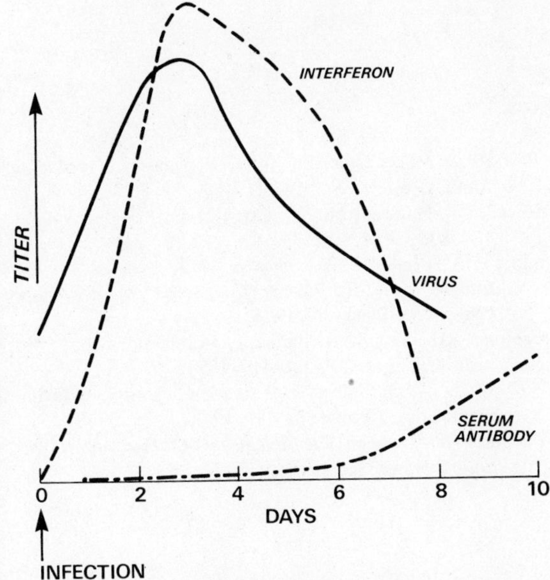

Figure 17–6. Appearance of interferon and serum antibody in relation to recovery from influenza virus infection of the lungs of mice. (From Isaacs A: New Scientist 11:81, 1961.)

action appears to involve production of a translational inhibitory protein which binds to host cell ribosomes and prevents translation of viral (but not host cell) messenger RNA. It does not block viral adsorption or cell penetration (Fig 17–7). Interferon is highly specific in terms of the host (ie, human versus lower animals) but is not virus-specific, having inhibitory activity against a wide variety of viruses.

A limiting factor in studies of interferon has been the difficulty of producing adequate amounts for human use. Synthetic interferon inducers (such as synthetic polyriboinosinic and polyribocytidilic acids; poly I:C) have been employed but are often toxic. Interferon is principally of prophylactic usefulness and has no significant effect once infection is established.

FEVER

The occurrence of fever in infectious diseases is so universal that its presence generally stimulates a search for an invading pathogen. In relatively few infections (eg, gonorrhea, lepromatous leprosy) is fever absent. Despite its nearly universal occurrence and its historical association with infection, the true significance of fever remains uncertain. It appears to be useful as an indicator of infective and other inflammatory responses but not important as a host defense mechanism. Although "fever therapy" has been used with limited success in the attempted treatment of temperature-sensitive microorganisms *(N gonorrhoeae, T pallidum, M leprae),* there is no evidence that fever plays a role in limiting infection under clinical circumstances.

Current concepts of fever production indicate that the common stimulus to body temperature elevation is the response of the hypothalamus to a circulating substance known as endogenous pyrogen or leukocytic pyrogen. Endogenous pyrogen is a protein which is freshly synthesized or cleaved off from an inactive precursor in the phagocyte in response to several stimuli including phagocytosis, endotoxin, or the pyrogenic steroid etiocholanolone. Human neutrophils and monocytes are capable of generating endogenous pyrogen, whereas lymphocytes are not. However, it is possible that lymphocytes may produce soluble factors which enhance pyrogen production by macrophages. Such lymphocyte function is presently unproved.

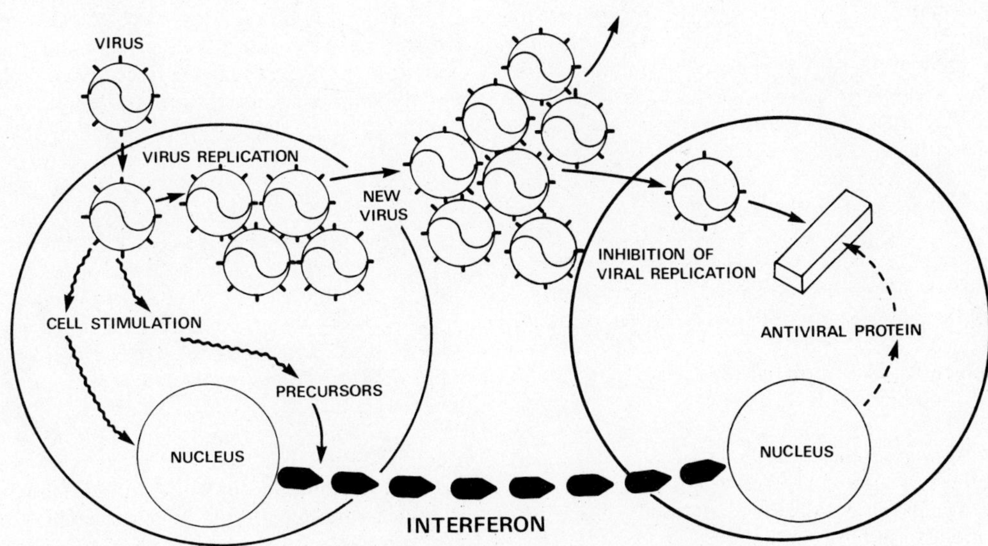

Figure 17–7. Schematic representation of interferon activity.

• • •

References

Cline MJ: *The White Cell.* Harvard Univ Press, 1975.

Davis BD & others: *Microbiology,* 2nd ed. Harper & Row, 1973.

DeChatelet LR: Oxidative bactericidal mechanisms of polymorphonuclear leukocytes. J Infect Dis 131:295, 1975.

Frenkel JK, Caldwell SA: Specific immunity and nonspecific resistance to infection: Listeria, protozoa, and viruses in mice and hamsters. J Infect Dis 131:201, 1975.

Knight V (editor): *Viral and Mycoplasmal Infections of the Respiratory Tract.* Lea & Febiger, 1973.

Moulder JW: Intracellular parasitism: Life in an extreme environment. J Infect Dis 130:300, 1974.

Schlessinger D (editor): *Microbiology, 1975.* American Society for Microbiology, 1975.

Starr RP & others (editors): *Annual Review of Microbiology.* Annual Reviews, Inc, 1975.

Stossel TP: Phagocytosis. (3 parts.) N Engl J Med 290:717, 774, 833, 1974.

Van Furth R (editor): *Mononuclear Phagocytes in Immunity, Infection, and Pathology: Conference on Mononuclear Phagocytes.* Blackwell, 1975.

Waldman RH, Ganguly R: Immunity to infections on secretory surfaces. J Infect Dis 130:419, 1974.

Winkelstein JA: Opsonins: Their function, identity, and clinical significance. J Pediatr 82:747, 1973.

Youmans GP & others: *The Biologic and Clinical Basis of Infectious Diseases.* Saunders, 1975.

18 . . .
Metabolism of Immunoglobulins

J. Vivian Wells, MD

Immunoglobulins are constantly being synthesized and catabolized in the body. The serum immunoglobulin level is a static measurement of the balance of these dynamic processes in equilibrium in a metabolic steady state. Metabolic turnover studies with labeled immunoglobulin permit analysis of its synthesis rate, turnover rate, distribution in the body, and the factors affecting its catabolism.

PRINCIPLES OF METABOLIC TURNOVER STUDIES

An aliquot of the immunoglobulin to be studied is isolated and labeled, reintroduced into the subject as a "tracer," and the fate of the labeled molecules observed. Several requirements are basic to all metabolic turnover studies with tracer-labeled immunoglobulins: (1) the labeled immunoglobulin must be easily and quantitatively detectable; (2) its distribution in the body and its catabolism should be representative of the parent molecule; (3) it should not be denatured during isolation and labeling; (4) the label should be safe and quantitatively excreted in the urine; and (5) mathematical methods must be available to analyze the data.

TECHNICS OF METABOLIC STUDIES

The stages in a study include preparation of the labeled immunoglobulin; injection into the patient; collection of serial samples of plasma and urine; measurement of labeled protein in these samples; plotting of residual plasma concentration or plasma activity as a function of time on semilogarithmic graph paper; and calculation of the various parameters which measure turnover or metabolism. Different types of labels have been used to perform these studies.

Passive Infusion of Antibody

Serologic technics may be used to follow the fate of infused antibodies, eg, antibodies to Rh erythrocyte antigens, poliovirus, tetanus toxoid, and rabies virus. Antibody has been administered to pregnant women at term, and, since IgG is transferred across the placenta, survival of this antibody can be followed in the infant after delivery. Passively infused antibody generally shows a biphasic survival curve when plotted semilogarithmically against time owing to an initial period of rapid catabolism and equilibration of the antibody molecules. The second part of the survival curve is linear and permits estimation of a plasma half-time (T½) of the protein. Antibody infusions frequently contain mixtures of antibodies with different catabolic rates, and interpretation of the curve is difficult. This method is used in animals to study the transfer of antibodies across placenta, yolk sac, and mucosal surfaces.

Survival of Antibody After Immunization

The titer of antibody can be followed after active immunization with antigen. This method unfortunately is not helpful in metabolic studies since continuing synthesis causes a much slower decline of antibody levels than that observed following passive infusion and gives a falsely long estimate of antibody survival. Antibody measurement after immunization with selected antigens is used in subjects with suspected immunodeficiency (see Chapter 26) as a test of their humoral immune function.

Infusion of Immunoglobulin

Survival of IgA and IgM has been measured immunochemically after infusion of purified immunoglobulin or whole plasma into subjects with immunoglobulin deficiency (see Chapter 26). Study of infused IgG is limited, since IgG catabolism is related to the total plasma IgG concentration, and elevation of plasma IgG by passive infusion of IgG will itself increase IgG catabolism. In addition, patients with selective IgA deficiency who receive plasma infusions risk sensitization to IgA with the development of anti-IgA antibodies.

Radioisotope-Labeled Immunoglobulin

Immunoglobulins can be labeled with radioisotopes in vivo or in vitro. In vivo labeling consists of incorporation of radiolabeled amino acids into the immunoglobulin during biosynthesis (see Chapter 9). The most commonly used isotope is ^{14}C; others

J. Vivian Wells is Senior Staff Specialist in Clinical Immunology, Kolling Institute of Medical Research, Royal North Shore Hospital of Sydney, St. Leonards, N.S.W. 2065, Australia.

include ^{3}H, ^{13}C, ^{15}N, ^{35}S, and ^{75}Se. Labeled amino acids can be administered to patients and the rate of incorporation into serum or urinary immunoglobulins or fragments measured. A major restriction of biosynthetic experiments is reutilization of labeled amino acids, which gives erroneously long values for immunoglobulin survival. Major ethical problems arise from the use of these long-acting radioisotopes in vivo, and they are not recommended.

Studies performed with immunoglobulins labeled in vitro with radioiodine (^{125}I or ^{131}I) have proved the most productive and adaptable.

Present technics of isolation, purification, radiolabeling, and storage of immunoglobulins yield preparations whose metabolic behavior is apparently the same as that of the native molecules. The best radiolabeling method for metabolic studies is iodination with iodine monochloride. This can achieve uniform iodination with less than 1 atom of iodine per molecule of immunoglobulin, avoiding denaturation of the protein.

During turnover studies, it is necessary to administer potassium iodide to block the thyroidal uptake of iodine released from catabolism of the immunoglobulin. Prevention of reutilization of the label is an important prerequisite to accurate mathematical analysis.

Analysis of Results

There are 3 main sources of data for the calculation of metabolic parameters: (1) plasma radioactivity at selected times after injection; (2) urinary excretion of radioactivity after catabolism; and (3) total body radioactivity. Several mathematical models and methods have been used to calculate these parameters from the basic data. Some rely only on plasma activity, which can be accurately measured. Total body activity can be measured by either a whole body counter or by serial subtraction of urinary activity. IgG turnover studies may require continuous observations for 4 weeks, and there is therefore a great risk of introducing errors through incomplete urine collections. These errors are cumulative and lead to falsely low values for the catabolic rates. Errors also occur if there is impaired renal function with a delay in the excretion of the free radiolabel. More recent methods for analysis have employed computer models using data on plasma activity and, if available, whole body activity measured with the whole body counter. An additional step is to measure the free iodide pool by injecting into the patient, at the same time as the labeled immunoglobulin, a sample of sodium iodide with a different isotopic label.

For routine purposes, the most practical approach is to analyze the results based on the plasma activity curve (Q_P). The Q_P values are plotted against time on semilogarithmic graph paper, assuming a value of 1 (ie, 100%) for the calculated Q_P value at the start of the study (time = 0). An example of such a curve is shown in Fig 18–1. The Q_P plasma curve has a straight-line slope after equilibration is reached, and the curve can be resolved by standard subtraction methods into its component exponential curves. Data from the graph are used to calculate the various turnover parameters by solving a series of equations derived from the Mat-

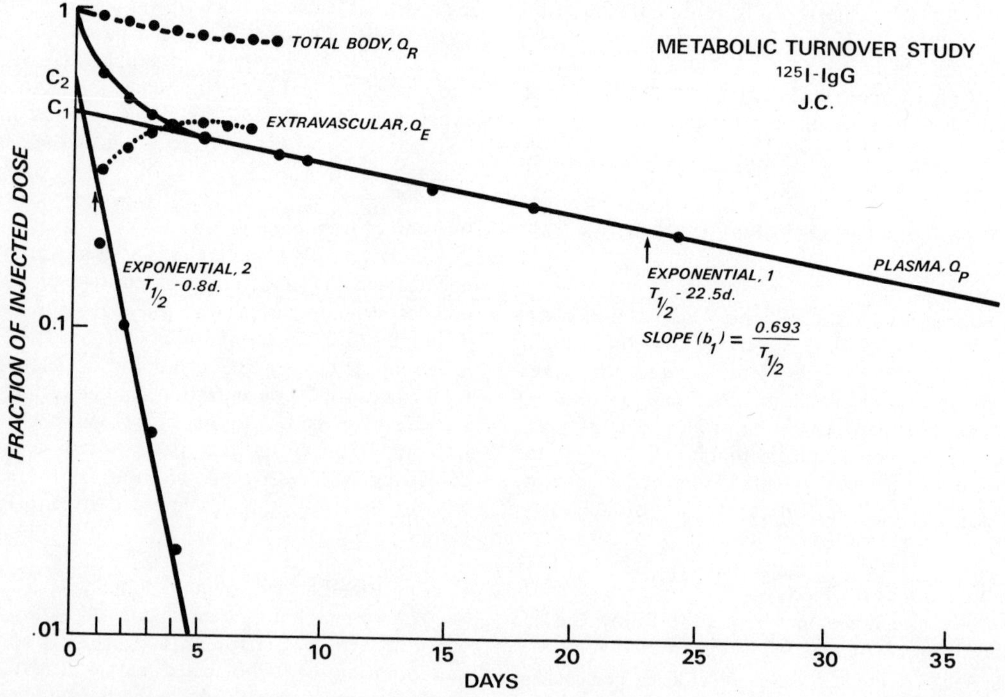

Figure 18–1. Semilogarithmic diagram of the survival of ^{125}I-IgG. Plasma T½ is 22.5 days. The terms are defined in Table 18–1.

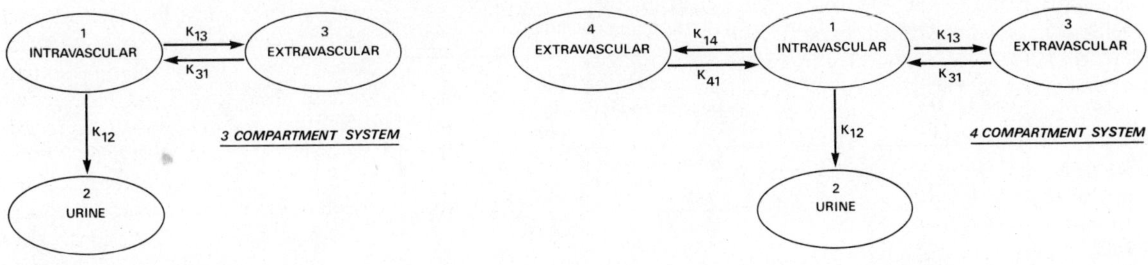

Figure 18–2. Mathematical models for protein metabolism with 3 and 4 compartments. The transfer rate of isotope from one compartment to another per unit time is given by the kinetic rate constant K. The excretion rate from the intravascular pool into urine is therefore K_{12}.

thews mammillary models (Fig 18–2). It is not necessary to know these equations, but it is essential to an understanding of metabolism to note the definitions of the various metabolic parameters (Table 18–1).

Assessment of Denaturation

It is necessary to assess the degree of protein denaturation in the labeled immunoglobulin preparation since significantly denatured protein is rapidly catabolized. The excretion of free isotope in the first 48 hours of study ($Q_{U\,1+2}$) should generally be less than 12%, and the value on the first day should be greater than that on the second day. Occasionally, a value for $Q_{U\,1+2}$ greater than 12% is due not to protein denaturation but to an intrinsically high catabolic rate in that patient. In such cases, the value on the second day is generally higher than that on the first day.

METABOLISM OF IMMUNOGLOBULINS

Data from several laboratories for turnover studies in human subjects with normal immunoglobulin levels are summarized in Table 18–2.

Immunoglobulin G (IgG)

The mean plasma volume in the subjects studied for whole IgG synthesis was 41 ml/kg (range, 33–50 ml/kg). The mean fractional turnover rate was 6.9% of the plasma pool catabolized per day, with a mean plasma half-time of 21 days. With a mean plasma pool of 500 mg/kg and a distribution ratio of 0.52, this indicated a mean IgG synthesis rate of 36 mg/kg/day. These values were obtained with IgG purified from normal human serum by chromatography with diethylaminoethyl cellulose. Studies on the metabolism of the

Table 18–1. Definitions of terms used in metabolic turnover studies.

Term	Unit	Definition
Q_{Pt}	% (or decimal)	Percentage of protein-bound plasma activity at time *t* compared to plasma activity at time 0
Q_U	%	Percentage of total injected activity excreted in free form in the urine in a designated period
Q_{U1+2}	%	Q_U in first 2 days of a turnover study
Plasma half-time (T½)	Days	Graphic half-time of final slope of curve Q_P
Plasma volume (PV)	ml/kg	$\frac{\text{Activity of standard} \times \text{Volume injected} \times 100}{Q_{P0}}$
Plasma IgG pool	mg/kg	$\frac{\text{PV} \times \text{Serum concentration (mg/dl)}}{\text{Body weight (kg)}}$
Distribution ratio (DR)	. . .	Fraction of total body IgG located in plasma $\text{DR} = \frac{\text{Plasma IgG pool}}{\text{Total body IgG pool}} = \frac{b1}{K_{12}}$
Total body IgG pool	mg/kg	$\frac{\text{Plasma IgG pool}}{\text{DR}}$
Fractional turnover rate (FTR)	% per day	Percentage of plasma pool catabolized and cleared into urine per day $\text{FTR} = K_{12} \times 100$
Absolute IgG catabolic rate	g/day mg/kg/day	Mass of protein catabolized per day = FTR × Plasma pool
IgG synthesis rate	g/day mg/kg/day	IgG synthesis rate = IgG catabolic rate in condition of equilibrium with steady serum protein levels and body weight

Table 18–2. Summary of data on immunoglobulin turnover studies in human subjects.

Class or Subclass	Serum Level (mg/dl)	Plasma IgG Pool (mg/kg)	Distribution Ratio	Total Body IgG Pool (mg/kg)	Plasma T½ (days)	Fractional Turnover Rate (% per day)	Synthesis Rate (mg/kg/day)
IgG range (mean)	600–1600 (989)	280–820 (500)	0.32–0.64 (0.52)	570–2050 (1030)	14–28 (21)	4.3–9.8 (6.9)	20–60 (36)
IgG1	690	298	0.51	589	21	8.0	25.4
IgG2	. . .	. . .	0.53	. . .	20	6.9	. . .
IgG3	50	20	0.64	31	7	16.8	3.4
IgG4	. . .	. . .	0.54	. . .	21	6.9	. . .
IgA1	230	101	0.55	185	5.9	24.0	24
IgA2	32	14.0	0.55	24.5	4.5	34.0	4.3
IgM	100	23	0.74	36	5.1	10.6	2.2
IgD	2.3	0.83	0.75	1.1	2.8	37.0	0.4
IgE	0.0076	0.0015	0.51	0.003	2.4	72.0	0.002

individual IgG subclasses were performed in different laboratories using purified myeloma proteins of the different IgG subclasses. Since IgG1 is present in normal serum in greater amounts than the other subclasses, it had appropriately higher levels for serum concentration, plasma IgG pool, total body IgG pool, and synthesis rate. The other metabolic parameters, however, were very similar in IgG1, IgG2, and IgG4 subclasses with a distribution ratio of 0.51–0.54, a plasma half-time of 20 or 21 days, and a fractional turnover rate of 6.9–8% per day. The IgG3 subclass, however, was metabolically very different, with a higher plasma localization (0.64), a much shorter plasma half-time (7 days), and a much faster turnover rate (16.8% per day). These properties of IgG3 molecules are related to structural differences in the $\gamma 3$ chain and the number of disulfide bridges between the H chains.

The various factors that influence immunoglobulin metabolism will be discussed below, including diseases associated with an increased or decreased serum IgG level. Abnormalities in metabolism can be associated with a normal serum IgG level, eg, patients with various connective tissue diseases including systemic lupus erythematosus, rheumatoid arthritis, polymyositis, and vasculitis. Subjects show increased fractional turnover rates and shortened plasma half-times, indicating hypercatabolism of IgG, but a simultaneous increase in IgG synthesis masks this hypercatabolism and even results in *elevated* serum IgG levels. The hypercatabolism in these patients was the result of an unknown defect in the host and was not due to an abnormality in the injected IgG.

IgG turnover studies in various diseases support the concept of the "concentration-catabolism" effect, which states that the catabolic rate of IgG is related directly to its serum concentration. A low functional turnover rate is seen with reduced serum IgG levels and a high fractional turnover rate with high serum IgG levels.

Immunoglobulin M (IgM)

IgM is catabolized at an average rate of 10.6% of the plasma pool per day and has a short half-time (5.1 days). An average of 74% of the total exchangeable IgM is located intravascularly. Unlike IgG, the fractional turnover rate in IgM metabolism is independent of the serum concentration. Labeled monoclonal IgM was found in several studies to be catabolized at the same rate as polyclonal IgM.

IgM metabolism has been measured in several diseases, including rheumatoid arthritis, hepatic cirrhosis, chronic active hepatitis, idiopathic cold agglutinin syndrome, giant hypertrophic gastritis, adult celiac disease, etc. The serum IgM level was elevated in some studies as a result of an increased rate of IgM synthesis. In some of these cases there may be an increase in fractional turnover rate. Several patients with primary biliary cirrhosis and increased serum IgM levels had increased rates of IgM synthesis. In patients with gastrointestinal disease, it is necessary to test for and measure any gastrointestinal loss of intact radiolabeled IgM since this will affect subsequent calculation of the catabolic rate.

It is also possible to study the metabolism of human IgM proteins with antibody activity. Normal IgM and IgM rheumatoid factor generally show similar values for both proteins for fractional turnover rate, plasma half-time, and intravascular localization, even in patients with clinically severe rheumatoid arthritis. One patient had peripheral neuropathy, episcleritis, and active disease, but studies have not been performed on a sufficient number of patients with vasculitis to establish whether increased synthesis and catabolism are present. This possibility exists since the deposition of IgM rheumatoid factor and autologous IgG is thought to be of etiologic significance in the vasculitis.

Monoclonal IgM cold agglutinins have been used in turnover studies. The mean fractional turnover rate was 14.5% per day for autologous IgM and 15.6% per day for the same labeled cold agglutinin in heterologous studies. The cold agglutinins are therefore catabolized more rapidly than normal IgM, but there is no direct correlation between the fractional turnover rate and the presence or the degree of active hemolysis. Untreated patients with chronic idiopathic cold agglutinin syndrome synthesize IgM at approximately 10 times the normal rate. The change in serum IgM levels and cold agglutinin titers following chemotherapy is attributed to a reduction in the increased synthesis rate and not to an increase in catabolic rate. Studies in a different laboratory did not demonstrate an increased fractional turnover rate. The catabolism of the 7S IgM cold agglutinin monomer is increased 50- to 100-fold compared to the intact 19S pentamer.

Markedly increased IgM synthesis is also found in subjects with tropical splenomegaly syndrome. This disease represents an abnormal immune response to repeated malarial infection in inhabitants of certain malarial regions, characterized clinically by massive splenomegaly, and has a poor prognosis. Splenectomy results in a marked reduction in IgM synthesis and clinical improvement.

Immunoglobulin A (IgA)

Table 18–2 lists data on turnover studies with both IgA subclasses. While both subclasses have the same distribution ratio (0.55), IgA2 molecules are catabolized more rapidly with a shorter plasma half-time. However, since IgA2 normally comprises only about 15% of serum IgA, the generally accepted values for IgA metabolism are those of the IgA1 subclass. Mean serum levels of IgG (989 mg/dl) and IgA (230 mg/dl) are markedly different, but this difference is not directly reflected in their respective synthesis rates (36 and 24 mg/kg/day). The disparate levels are explained by the higher fractional turnover rate and shorter plasma half-time for IgA. IgA and IgM metabolism are similar in that the fractional turnover rate is independent of the serum immunoglobulin concentration.

Immunoglobulin D (IgD)

An unusual feature of IgD metabolism is the high turnover rate (37% per day) and short plasma half-time (2.8 days). Patients show a wide range of IgD levels, apparently explained by variations in IgD synthesis rates. However, different studies have yielded conflicting results regarding whether IgD catabolism is inversely related to the serum IgD level or whether it follows the concentration-catabolism effect.

Immunoglobulin E (IgE)

IgE has the lowest serum concentration of the 5 classes of immunoglobulins, and its metabolic pool size is approximately 100,000 times smaller than that of IgG. The low concentration of IgE in serum is the result of the highest turnover rate, the shortest half-time, and the lowest synthesis rate of the immunoglobulins. IgE follows a unique pattern in its metabolism. IgE survival is prolonged in patients with markedly increased serum IgE levels, especially IgE multiple myeloma. This has been ascribed to the normal tendency of IgE to fix to cell surface receptors in various tissues. It is possible that the normal fixation of IgE to cell surface receptors may also be involved in the normal catabolism of IgE. Patients with very high serum IgE levels may have saturated those cell surface receptors involved in IgE catabolism and prolonged survival results for IgE molecules not bound to cell surface receptors.

Markedly decreased rates of IgE synthesis are found in patients with hypogammaglobulinemia. Deficiency of IgE frequently is found in association with selective IgA deficiency. The IgE deficiency present in these patients is due to decreased IgE synthesis.

Immunoglobulin Subunits

Several structural subunits of immunoglobulins have been investigated in metabolic studies. These include Bence Jones proteins, ie, monomer or dimer L chains; H chains and L chains prepared by reduction and alkylation of the parent immunoglobulin molecule; Fab, $F(ab')_2$, and Fc fragments obtained by enzymatic digestion of immunoglobulins; and abnormal myeloma proteins that lack L chains and which are present in the blood and urine of patients with H chain disease (see Chapters 2 and 28).

Initially, it was thought that Bence Jones proteins were the excreted catabolic products of myeloma proteins, but studies demonstrated that Bence Jones L chains were synthesized de novo in the malignant plasma cell. Normal subjects have very small amounts of free L chains in serum and urine, and these levels increase in patients with renal disease or autoimmune disorders without monoclonal gammopathy. Turnover studies of L chains in subjects with normal renal function showed rapid disappearance, and the fractional disappearance rate includes both endogenous catabolism and loss of labeled protein in urine. L chain monomers are frequently catabolized more rapidly than corresponding L chain dimers. Turnover studies in patients with multiple myeloma or renal disease also show high turnover rates, but the rate and the degree of proteinuria correlate positively with the serum creatinine concentration. While fractional turnover rates are lower in patients with impaired renal function (suggesting that normal renal function permits maximal catabolism of L chains), it has not been confirmed that there are intrinsically different rates of catabolism in normal subjects and subjects with multiple myeloma. The turnover rate of L chains is approximately 100 times that of the intact IgG molecule, and the kidney is clearly an important site for L chain catabolism. The infusion of IgG will itself increase the turnover rate and shorten the plasma half-time of the IgG molecules, but L chains do not have this effect on the rate of IgG metabolism. This observation supports the conclusion that structural determinants in the Fc region of the immunoglobulin molecule are responsible for determining catabolism of that immunoglobulin.

Studies with enzymatic fragments of antibody molecules support this view on the role of the Fc region. Fab or $F(ab')_2$ fragments are rapidly metabolized, with half-times in plasma of 3–5 hours. Fc fragments survive approximately 30–50 times longer than purified L chains, Fab, or $F(ab')_2$ fragments. Their survival is only moderately reduced from that of intact IgG. A different pattern is seen in the catabolism of Fc fragments of myeloma protein or of H chain disease proteins. H chain disease proteins have half-times similar to those of intact IgG molecules, but their turnover rate is generally higher (8% vs 4% per day). Owing to its smaller size, only 24% of H chain disease protein equilibrated in the intravascular compartment. H chain disease protein (lacking L chains) may survive longer than Fc fragment (prepared by enzymatic digestion) because the former are synthesized de novo in malignant lymphoid cells.

Therapeutic Immunoglobulin Preparations

The Fc fragment is important in catabolism of various therapeutic preparations of human γ-globulin. Such preparations have traditionally been given by intramuscular or subcutaneous injection, and this limits the volume that can be injected. Furthermore, a significant amount is broken down at the site of injection. Attempts were therefore made to give γ-globulin by the intravenous route since this would be less painful and more efficient and would thus permit the administration of larger volumes at more frequent intervals. Intravenous injection of standard γ-globulin preparations frequently causes serious—even fatal—reactions, associated with the presence of aggregates possessing an anticomplement effect. This anticomplementary activity requires the structural integrity of the Fc fragment and the formation of immunoglobulin aggregates. These aggregates, and the anticomplementary activity, can be removed by prolonged incubation at 37 C, prior ultracentrifugation, or enzymatic digestion with enzymes such as plasmin or pepsin.

Turnover studies with γ-globulin treated in this way revealed that major changes in the Fc fragment by enzyme digestion destroyed the structural requirements in the Fc fragment which determined its rate of catabolism. These preparations were therefore rapidly cleared from the body and were unable to exert any prolonged therapeutic effect. Although incubation or centrifugation removed the aggregates, they reappeared during storage of the preparations. Intravenous preparations were therefore developed using very low concentrations of enzymes for limited digestion of the IgG molecules. Turnover studies with such preparations still generally show a markedly increased value for $Q_{U\,1+2}$, indicating that there is a population of molecules that has been structurally altered during preparation. The other metabolic values in normal subjects injected with these modified γ-globulins generally show an increased turnover rate, a shortened plasma half-time, and normal plasma localization. These preparations are used clinically in patients with hypogammaglobulinemia. Further turnover studies and clinical trials are required before the various intravenous γ-globulin preparations can be recommended for widespread application.

FACTORS CONTROLLING IMMUNOGLOBULIN METABOLISM

Antigenic stimulation from many sources is a key factor in continuing immunoglobulin synthesis in normal subjects. Very low immunoglobulin synthesis rates are found in animals raised in an organism-free environment. At the other extreme, markedly increased immunoglobulin synthesis is found in patients with chronic infections (see below). While it is obvious that antigenic stimulation is associated with increased immunoglobulin synthesis, the manner in which a feedback mechanism controls this synthesis is unknown. As infection subsides, the normal pattern is for immunoglobulin synthesis to diminish gradually. Possible clues to these control mechanisms are provided by recent studies demonstrating low-molecular-weight factors associated with certain types of lymphocytes or malignant plasma cells. These factors appear to suppress the synthesis of normal immunoglobulins.

Neither the controlling factors nor the actual sites of immunoglobulin catabolism have yet been positively established. It is clear that an intact Fc region is essential to its normal catabolism. In transport studies of IgG molecules, the Fc piece could competitively inhibit the transport of whole IgG molecules. It is not known which area of the Fc fragment controls the catabolism of the whole molecule. Removal of sialic acid groups or reduction of the interchain disulfide bonds does not appear to alter the catabolic rate of IgG molecules. Several studies support the view that immunoglobulin molecules are attached to receptors and that this attachment has an important influence in the catabolism of the molecule. The major current view is that attachment to these receptors protects the immunoglobulin from catabolism and constitutes a necessary step for specific cellular uptake or transport of the attached molecule. In this hypothesis, unattached IgG molecules are therefore thought to be susceptible to catabolism. Little is known concerning the details of catabolism of IgA, IgD, and IgM.

Studies have ascribed a major role to the gastrointestinal tract in this catabolic system. Fc receptors for IgG were detected on the microvillous membranes of intestinal mucosal cells. Similar receptors are postulated to occur on other body membranes that require transport of immunoglobulin. IgG is normally transferred across the placenta from mother to fetus, especially in the third trimester of pregnancy. This is an active process since in many cases the serum IgG level in the fetus is greater than that in the mother.

Several unsuccessful attempts have been made to localize catabolism of individual immunoglobulins in specific organs. The only successful one has been the demonstration of catabolism of Bence Jones proteins in the kidney. However, the kidney does not normally play a significant role in the catabolism of whole immunoglobulin molecules. Clarification of the problem awaits isolation of IgG-binding receptors from mucosal cells.

Immunosuppressive drugs have been used for some time to alter the manifestations of abnormal immune function in patients with various diseases. Data are now available on the effects of such drugs on immunoglobulin metabolism. The main drugs studied in this way are corticosteroid drugs and azathioprine. These studies were originally performed in animals and generally showed that high-dose prednisone therapy produced significantly shortened immunoglobulin survival with an increased catabolic rate. Several studies have been performed in human subjects with various diseases, including rheumatoid arthritis, systemic lupus erythematosus, psoriatic arthritis, asthma, sarcoidosis, scleroderma, chronic active hepatitis, renal allotransplantation, etc. The great majority of patients receiving standard therapeutic dosage show the features of hypercatabolism ie, an increased fractional turnover rate, and a shortened plasma half-time. The main variation occurs in IgG synthesis rate and is reflected in the serum IgG levels. Hypercatabolism leads to a reduction of serum IgG levels if the IgG synthesis rate remains unchanged or decreased. Several patients receiving prednisone therapy show no change in their IgG synthesis rate and therefore have lower serum IgG levels. Other patients did show a reduction in IgG synthesis rate; an average of 33.4% reduction in IgG synthesis rate was observed in patients with autoimmune disorders treated with azathioprine. Significant reduction in IgG synthesis rates was also observed in all but one of 12 patients with chronic active hepatitis treated with prednisone. It appears that both prednisone and azathioprine cause hypercatabolism of IgG in almost all subjects and, in addition, cause a reduction in IgG synthesis in a significant number of patients.

Table 18–3. Disorders associated with abnormalities in immunoglobulin metabolism.

Disorders resulting in hypogammaglobulinemia
Decreased immunoglobulin synthesis
Congenital and acquired hypogammaglobulinemia
Selective immunoglobulin deficiency
Chronic lymphocytic leukemia
Ataxia-telangiectasia (IgA)
Wiskott-Aldrich syndrome (IgM)
Excessive loss of immunoglobulins
Nephrotic syndrome
Gastrointestinal loss (lymphatic abnormalities, ulcerating conditions, unknown mechanisms)
Hypercatabolism
Familial idiopathic hypercatabolic hypoproteinemia
Myotonic dystrophy
Cryoglobulinemia
Multiple myeloma
Wiskott-Aldrich syndrome (IgG)
Disorders resulting in hypergammaglobulinemia
Diffuse increase in synthesis (polyclonal gammopathy)
Cirrhosis
Connective tissue diseases
Infection
Increased synthesis of a single class (monoclonal gammopathy)
Multiple myeloma
Waldenström's macroglobulinemia
Benign monoclonal gammopathy
Decreased catabolism: Renal tubular disease (cystinosis, adult Fanconi's syndrome)

IMMUNOGLOBULIN METABOLISM IN VARIOUS DISORDERS

Disorders associated with abnormalities in immunoglobulin metabolism are listed in Table 18–3. They are conventionally divided into those associated with a reduced serum immunoglobulin level and those associated with an increased serum immunoglobulin level. The latter group includes both polyclonal and monoclonal gammopathy. Table 18–4 summarizes turnover data from 18 representative metabolic studies: 7 had a reduced serum level of normal IgG, 6 had polyclonal hypergammaglobulinemia, and 5 had monoclonal hypergammaglobulinemia.

Hypogammaglobulinemia

The 3 main factors to be considered in this group are decreased synthesis, excessive abnormal loss, and hypercatabolism. The mean values listed in Table 18–4 show that all subjects with reduced serum IgG levels had (1) reduced serum IgG level, (2) normal distribution of the intravascular pool, and (3) reduced plasma and total body IgG pools. Wide variations were seen, however, in the plasma half-time (T½), fractional turnover rate, and IgG synthesis rate. The plasma T½ and fractional turnover rate could be reduced, normal, or increased, while the IgG synthesis rate was either markedly reduced or at the lower limit of the normal range. The IgG deficiency in common variable hypogammaglobulinemia and in hypogammaglobulinemia secondary to chronic lymphocytic leukemia is predominantly due to a marked reduction in IgG synthesis rate with a normal or prolonged plasma T½ and a normal or reduced turnover rate. The small amount of IgG synthesized in these patients is catabolized more slowly and thus survives longer. Normal IgG in a patient with IgG multiple myeloma may be synthesized in reduced amounts, but the main feature is its rapid catabolism. This pattern of rapid catabolism was also seen in 2 patients with renal allotransplantation and nephrotic syndrome who were receiving immunosuppressive therapy. It was noted above that immunosuppressive therapy frequently was associated with hypercatabolism with or without a reduction in IgG synthesis rate.

Hypercatabolism of normal nonmyeloma IgG in patients with multiple myeloma has important therapeutic implications. Prophylactic injections of γ-globulin have been given to patients with multiple myeloma to prevent infections, but this does not have a consistent beneficial therapeutic effect. This may be partly

Table 18–4. Summary of data from 18 representative IgG turnover studies in 18 patients.

Subject Diagnosis	Serum IgG Level (mg/dl)	Plasma IgG Pool (mg/kg)	Distribution Ratio	Total Body IgG Pool (mg/kg)	Plasma T½ (days)	FTR* (% per day)	IgG Synthesis Rate (mg/kg/day)
Hypogammaglobulinemia							
1. Nodular lymphoid hyperplasia	140	40	0.49	80	22.5	6.3	2
2. Primary hypogammaglobulinemia	142	70	0.43	170	23.7	6.8	5
3. Primary hypogammaglobulinemia	300	110	0.50	220	35.3	3.9	4
4. Chronic lymphocytic leukemia	195	120	0.43	290	28.8	5.6	7
5. IgG multiple myeloma	250	130	0.56	240	8.8	14.0	19
6. Renal allotransplantation	440	180	0.44	400	13.5	11.8	21
7. Nephrotic syndrome	560	140	0.56	250	9.1	13.5	19
Mean values (1–7)	290	113	0.49	236	20.2	8.8	11
Polyclonal gammopathy							
8. Acute infective hepatitis	1950	650	0.41	1590	9.7	17.2	112
9. Acute infective hepatitis	2200	960	0.47	2050	15.3	9.6	93
10. Hepatic cirrhosis	1680	810	0.49	1650	11.2	13.5	109
11. Hepatic cirrhosis	2380	1280	0.65	1960	11.5	9.2	117
12. Chronic active hepatitis	1700	650	0.37	1750	11.6	16.0	104
13. Chronic active hepatitis	4350	2230	0.65	3440	6.8	15.8	352
Mean values (8–13)	2377	1097	0.51	2073	11.0	13.6	148
Monoclonal gammopathy							
14. Multiple myeloma	2700	1030	0.50	2070	8.9	15.5	160
15. Multiple myeloma	5500	2940	0.63	4670	9.0	12.3	362
16. Multiple myeloma	3720	1460	0.34	4290	10.5	19.4	283
17. Benign monoclonal gammopathy	1640	940	0.36	2600	19.0	12.1	109
18. Biclonal gammopathy	3300	2600	0.54	4810	11.3	11.4	296
Mean values (14–18)	3372	1794	0.47	3688	11.7	14.1	242
Normal controls (mean)	989	500	0.50	1030	21	6.9	36

*FTR = fractional turnover rate (see Table 18–1).

explained if one assumes that the injected immunoglobulin is rapidly catabolized, as is normal IgG, and is therefore unable to exert a prolonged therapeutic effect. More frequent administration of larger doses would be required to achieve satisfactory IgG levels.

Intact radiolabeled immunoglobulin can be excreted in the urine in nephrotic syndrome or in the gastrointestinal secretions owing to abnormalities in the lymphatic vessels, or in generalized or local ulcerating conditions of the bowel.

Three interesting but rare situations characterized by hypercatabolism merit further comment. The first is familial idiopathic hypercatabolic hypoproteinemia in which the hypercatabolism affects several proteins, including albumin and immunoglobulin. An unusual feature is the occurrence of several cases in one family. The mechanism of this hypercatabolism is unknown. Hypercatabolism may be restricted to a single class of protein, as in the hypercatabolism of IgG in patients with myotonic dystrophy; the reason for this selective action is not known. An unusual mechanism has been described in a patient with hypogammaglobulinemia in whom hypercatabolism was noted for IgG subclasses IgG1, IgG2, and IgG4. IgG3 showed normal survival in this patient. The hypercatabolism was secondary to the combination of IgG1, IgG2, and IgG4 with an IgG-binding monoclonal cryogel IgM.

Polyclonal Gammopathy

All 6 patients listed in Table 18–4 with polyclonal gammopathy showed markedly increased plasma and total body IgG pools and IgG synthesis rates, combined with short plasma half-times and increased fractional turnover rates. The marked increase in IgG synthesis is more than sufficient to compensate for the rapid catabolism; therefore, increased serum IgG levels are maintained. The increased turnover rate correlates positively with the high serum IgG level and the concentration-catabolism effect. The use of immunosuppressive drugs in some patients with polyclonal gammopathy may also contribute to hypercatabolism.

Monoclonal Gammopathy

The pattern in monoclonal gammopathy is that of increased plasma and total body IgG pools and markedly increased IgG synthesis rates. The turnover rate was increased in all subjects studied, and plasma half-times were shortened in most patients. High serum levels of monoclonal IgG are due primarily to increased synthesis and not to prolonged survival of IgG with reduced catabolism. IgG synthesis does not correlate with the diagnosis nor the severity of the disease in the individual patient.

• • •

References

Andersen SB: *Metabolism of Human Gamma Globulin (γ_{ss}-Globulin).* Blackwell, 1964.

Jensen K: Metabolism of Bence Jones proteins in non-myeloma patients with normal renal function. Scand J Clin Lab Invest 25:281, 1970.

Jensen K: Metabolism of Bence Jones proteins in multiple myeloma patients and in patients with renal disease. Scand J Clin Lab Invest 26:13, 1970.

Levy AL, Waldmann TA: The effect of hydrocortisone on immunoglobulin metabolism. J Clin Invest 49:1679, 1970.

Levy J & others: The effect of azathioprine on gammaglobulin synthesis in man. J Clin Invest 51:2233, 1972.

Matthews CME: The theory of tracer experiments with ^{131}I labelled plasma proteins. Phys Med Biol 2:36, 1957.

Morell A, Terry WD, Waldmann TA: Metabolic properties of IgG subclasses in man. J Clin Invest 49:673, 1970.

Morell A & others: Metabolic properties of human IgA subclasses. Clin Exp Immunol 13:521, 1973.

Rossing N & others: Immunoglobulin (IgG and IgM) metabolism in patients with rheumatoid arthritis. Scand J Clin Lab Invest 32:15, 1973.

Waldmann TA, Strober W: Metabolism of immunoglobulins. Prog Allergy 13:1, 1969.

Waldmann TA & others: IgE levels and metabolism in immune deficiency diseases. Page 247 in: *The Biological Role of the Immunoglobulin E System.* Ishizaka KI, Dayton DH Jr (editors). United States Government Printing Office, 1973.

Waterhouse C, Abraham G, Vaughan J: The relationship between L-chain synthesis and γ-globulin production. J Clin Invest 52:1067, 1973.

Wells JV, Fudenberg HH: Metabolism of radio-iodinated IgG in patients with abnormal serum IgG levels. 1. Hypergammaglobulinemia. 2. Hypogammaglobulinemia. Clin Exp Immunol 9:761, 775, 1971.

Wells JV, Penny R: Survival studies on a commercial preparation of intravenous human gammaglobulin labeled with ^{131}I. Australas Ann Med 18:271, 1969.

Wochner RD: Hypercatabolism of normal IgG: An unexplained immunoglobulin abnormality in connective tissue diseases. J Clin Invest 49:454, 1970.

Wolstenholme GEW, O'Connor M (editors): *Protein Turnover.* CIBA Foundation Symposium 9 (New Series), 1973.

19 . . .
Immediate Hypersensitivity

Oscar L. Frick, MD, PhD

The term immediate hypersensitivity denotes an immunologic sensitivity to antigens that manifests itself by tissue reactions occurring within minutes after the antigen combines with its appropriate antibody. Such a reaction may occur in any member of a species (anaphylaxis) or only in certain predisposed or hyperreactive members (atopy).

In 1890, von Behring discovered the prophylactic use of antiserum against diphtheria toxin. In the search for other prophylactic antisera, Portier and Richet noted an immediate shocklike reaction in a sensitive dog to a sea anemone toxin; this harmful reaction they called *antiphylaxis* (or anaphylaxis), to distinguish it from the helpful *prophylaxis*. Within the next decade, hay fever and asthma were recognized as human counterparts of animal anaphylactic reactions, and histamine was considered to be the primary pharmacologic mediator of such symptoms. Later it was discovered that skin tests could be used for the specific diagnosis of the troublesome antigen and that a prolonged series of injections of these antigens could help relieve allergic symptoms.

ANAPHYLAXIS

Anaphylaxis is a manifestation of immediate hypersensitivity resulting from the in vivo interaction of cellular sites with antigen and specific antibody.

Generalized anaphylaxis is a shocklike state occurring within minutes following an appropriate antigen-antibody reaction. Upon the first exposure of an animal to an antigen, a cytotropic antibody can form which sensitizes mast cells and basophils in tissues and blood, respectively. After a second exposure to the antigen, the sensitized animal reacts to histamine and other mediators released by mast cells as a result of the antigen-antibody reaction. Histamine causes a marked vasodilatation and leakage of intravascular fluids, resulting in shock. There are smooth muscle spasms, especially in certain smooth muscle-containing organs such as guinea pig bronchi and canine liver. These are the principal specific shock organs in these 2 species. The extreme bronchoconstriction in the guinea pig results in respiratory obstruction, asphyxia, and death. The extreme vasodilatation and leakage of fluids in the dog or in man causes profound shock and death. Epinephrine may be a lifesaving treatment in anaphylaxis.

Local anaphylaxis may occur in specific target organs such as the gastrointestinal tract, nasal mucosa, or skin. Experimentally, the skin or other tissue may be passively sensitized with serum from a sensitized animal; subsequent intravenous or local injection of antigen will result in a local anaphylactic reaction. This method has been used for the passive cutaneous anaphylaxis (PCA) test, in which the skin of an animal (guinea pig, rabbit, man, rat or mouse, etc) is injected with serum from a sensitive animal of the same or another species. After an appropriate latent period, the antigen is given intravenously along with Evans blue dye, and this will react with the skin-fixed antibody, causing the release of histamine. This results in vasodilatation and leakage of albumin, to which the blue dye is attached, producing a blue spot. This blue spot indicates that an anaphylactic reaction has taken place in the skin.

In Vitro Anaphylaxis

Several tissue models of anaphylaxis have been developed for experimental studies. The Schultz-Dale test uses isolated smooth muscle from a sensitized animal. Ileum, uterus, or a tracheal ring is suspended in a physiologic buffered saline solution. Such smooth muscle strips can also be passively sensitized by bathing them in serum from a hypersensitive animal. After addition of antigen to the bath, smooth muscle contractions occur within seconds or minutes. Alternatively, finely chopped lungs or skin fragments from actively sensitized animals (or such fragments passively sensitized with serum from an immunized animal) are suspended in physiologic buffer. Addition of antigen causes release of histamine and slow-reacting substance of anaphylaxis (SRS-A), which is quantitated by bioassay or chemical means. Peritoneal mast cells from actively or passively sensitized rats, upon addition of antigen, show visible degranulation, and histamine and serotonin release may be measured in the supernate.

Any antigen should be able to elicit anaphylaxis in a properly sensitized animal. These may be proteins, chemical haptens such as drugs attached to proteins, carbohydrates, or, occasionally, nucleic acids. These antigens usually must be soluble antigens. Cellular anti-

Oscar L. Frick is Professor of Pediatrics, University of California, San Francisco.

gens such as sheep red cells or bacteria cause weak anaphylaxis, which probably indicates that soluble antigens are eluted from the cell surface to participate in such reactions.

Antibody Classes

Cytotropic antibodies, especially of the IgG and IgE classes, are involved in anaphylactic sensitization. In special circumstances, IgA and IgM may also be involved. Homocytotropic antibodies—antibodies that will sensitize an animal of the same species—are usually considered cardinal in such reactions. These are IgE in all species so far examined (γG_1 or γG_a electrophoretic mobility in guinea pigs and rats, respectively). Heterocytotropic IgG antibodies and occasionally IgM and IgA antibodies can passively sensitize tissues (especially skin) of other species. The classic example is rabbit IgG antibody, which can passively sensitize guinea pig skin for PCA. On the contrary, IgG antibodies of ungulates such as sheep, goats, and horses are unable to sensitize guinea pig skin for PCA. Apparently the former have a specific skin-fixing site on their Fc portions.

Sensitization of Target Tissue for Anaphylaxis

In most cases 10–14 days are required after immunization before IgG antibodies result in active anaphylactic sensitization; IgE sensitization may occur somewhat earlier. Passive sensitization has a latent period (time between injection of antibody and challenge with antigen) of 3–6 hours for IgG antibodies. This latent period allows antibody to "fix" to the target mast cells. However, the IgG passive sensitization is short-lived; the IgG molecules become detached within 12–24 hours. An antigenic challenge at this later time causes no (or minimal) anaphylaxis. There is an inverse squared relationship between the local IgG antibody concentration (c) and time (t) of the latent period: $c = 1/t^2$. In fact, if there is sufficient antibody concentration, the latent period can be reduced to almost zero and the reaction can occur immediately after passive sensitization.

Passive sensitization with IgE antibody may occur within 6 hours but becomes stronger by 24–72 hours, the usual time at which antigenic challenge is made. Anaphylactic reactions occurring after 48–72 hours are almost exclusively due to IgE antibodies (IgG antibodies are already detached and do not participate in such a reaction). IgE antibodies remain fixed to the target mast cells for many weeks, eg, 3 weeks in rats and 6 weeks in man.

Molecular Models of Anaphylaxis

Following the first exposure to antigen, the animal responds with antibody formation (Fig 19–1). Cytotropic antibodies. such as IgG or IgE, fix to the

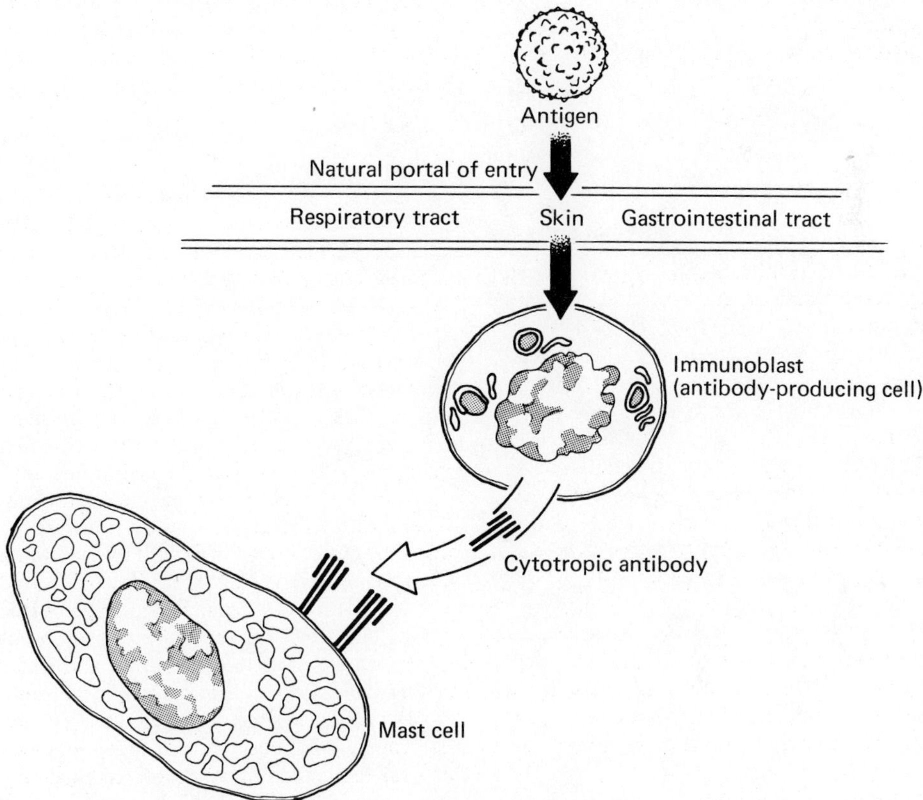

Figure 19–1. Atopic sensitization.

surface of mast cells and the animal is considered sensitized. Such antibodies may also be passively introduced into the general circulation or into local tissues.

With the second exposure, the antigen seeks out these tissue-fixed antibodies and reacts with them at the cell surface (Fig 19–2). An antigen molecule combines with 2 antibody molecules to form a bridge. This bridging causes a physical distortion of the antibody molecules and triggers an enzymatic cascade at the cell surface which causes the dissolution or expulsion of mast cell granules. These granules dissolve and release histamine, serotonin, and heparin, their pharmacologically active agents. Free histamine and serotonin act on adjacent smooth muscle and vascular endothelial cells, causing the clinical symptoms of anaphylaxis (eg, bronchospasm and edema). Other mediators are also released from mast cell granules—SRS-A, eosinophil chemotactic factor of anaphylaxis (ECF-A), and bradykinin. These also exert their pharmacologic effects on neighboring cells. The optimal ratio of antigen to antibody to elicit anaphylaxis is slight to moderate antigen excess. So-called "toxic complexes" of composition Ag_3Ab_2 or Ag_5Ab_3 best trigger such anaphylactic reactions. These are small complexes which best bridge surface receptors in the combining site of sensitizing antibodies. Complexes of Ag_2Ab_1 formed in extreme antigen excess do not trigger anaphylaxis. Such complexes are unable to bridge antibodies because both combining sites on each antibody molecule are attached to 2 different antigen molecules. Large amounts of antibody are complexed by relatively few antigens in zones of antibody excess or at the optimal proportions for precipitation. These are usually insufficient for triggering anaphylactic reactions, but in these zones minimal anaphylaxis can occur.

This molecular model of anaphylaxis can be duplicated (Fig 19–3) with immunoglobulin reacting with antibody molecules fixed to the mast cell. The reaction forms complexes of a composition appropriate to trigger anaphylaxis. Anti-IgE antibodies will complex with the Fc portion of the tissue-fixed IgE molecule, and such bridging will trigger histamine release. Similarly, tissue-fixed antibodies may be aggregated by mild heating or bisdiazotized benzidine. This creates nonantigenic bridges among tissue-fixed cytotropic antibodies and triggers the anaphylactic reaction. IgE or IgG antibody-fixing cell receptors on mast cells may be blocked with normal or myeloma proteins of the same class which compete with antibody molecules for these receptors. Such blocking of receptors by normal or myeloma proteins prevents antibody fixation, and no triggering of anaphylaxis is possible.

Target Cells & Mediator Release

Target cells for anaphylaxis are the tissue-fixed mast cells, especially in shock organs such as lung,

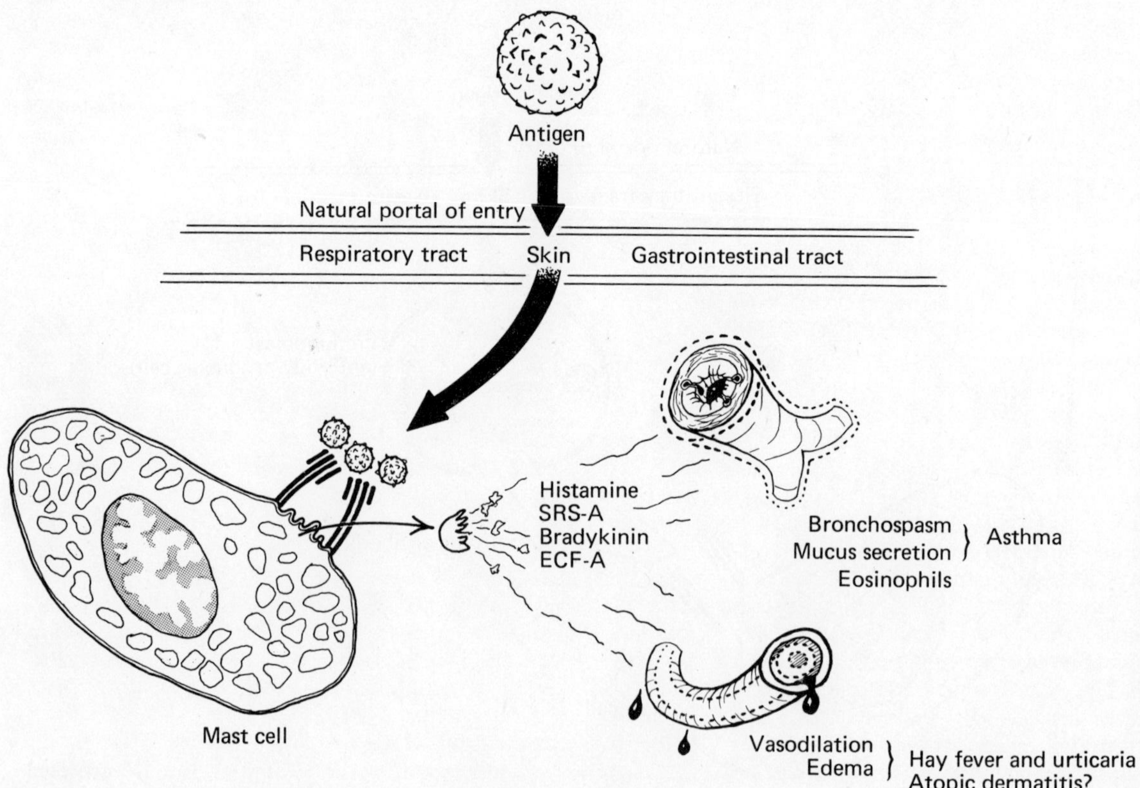

Figure 19–2. Atopic reaction.

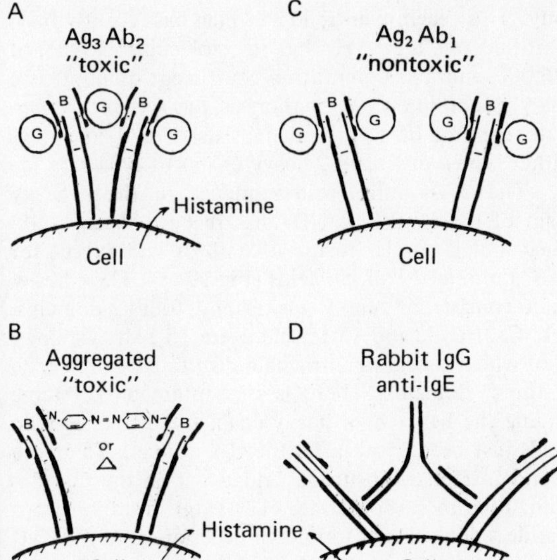

Figure 19–3. Diagrammatic reaction of antigen (G)-antibody (B) complexes in anaphylaxis. ***A:*** "Toxic" complex–Ag_3Ab_2 in moderate antigen excess. ***B:*** "Toxic" complex by aggregation of 2 antibody molecules by bisdiazotized benzidine or heat. ***C:*** "Nontoxic" complex–Ag_2Ab_1 in extreme antigen excess. ***D:*** Rabbit IgG anti-IgE bridging two IgE molecules by Fc_ϵ.

1. Releaser attaches to mast cell membrane

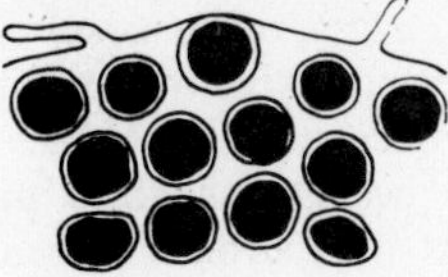

2. Mast cell degranulates

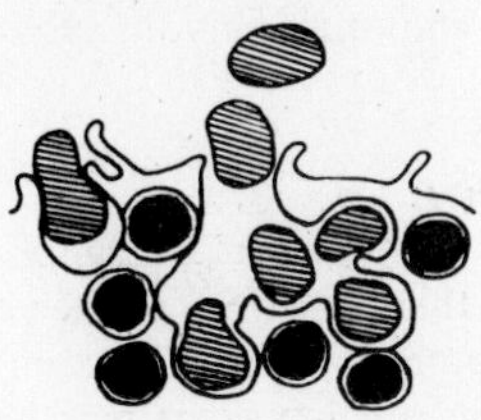

3. Histamine is released from exposed granules by cation exchange

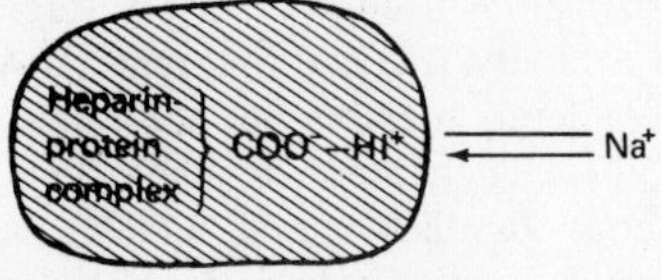

Figure 19–4. Suggested mechanism of histamine (HI^+) release by antigen. (Reproduced, with permission, from Uvnas B: Degranulation of mast cells. Page 286 in: *Allergology*. Yamamura Y & others [editors]. Excerpta Medica, 1974.)

bronchial smooth muscle, and vascular endothelium. Blood basophils may also act as target cells. Antibody molecules fixed to mast cells are physically distorted by antigen, and this activates serine esterases in a pathway similar to the classical complement cascade (Chapter 6). The speed and completeness of activation of this enzyme cascade are modulated by the cAMP-cGMP "second messenger" balance in the cytoplasm of such target cells. This cascade is energy- and calcium-dependent and causes dissolution or expulsion of mast cell granules (Fig 19–4). Positively charged histamine and serotonin are electrostatically complexed with negatively charged heparin and protein. After dissolution of the granule, positively charged sodium ions from extracellular fluid exchange with positively charged histamine and serotonin on heparin and cause their release in a free state. Free histamine and serotonin exert their pharmacologic effects on adjacent smooth muscles and vascular endothelial cells. Similar mechanisms probably exist for the release of other mediators: SRS-A, ECF-A, and bradykinin. Cromolyn sodium apparently can stabilize mast cell membranes or granules and can prevent the release of mediators.

In summary, anaphylaxis is a reaction found in almost all vertebrate animal species (hamster excepted) which results from sensitization of tissue-fixed mast cells by cytotropic antibodies following exposure to antigen. Subsequent exposure to antigen results in complexing of an antigen molecule with 2 antibody molecules in mild to moderate antigen excess. Complexed antibody molecules are physically distorted and initiate an enzyme cascade ending in the release of pharmacologic mediators which exert their effects upon adjacent target tissue.

ALLERGY & ATOPY

Von Pirquet proposed the term *allergie* (Gk *allos* other + *ergon* work) in 1906 to denote an immune deviation from the original state or a "changed reactivity" of an individual. An allergic individual was one who deviated from the expected immunologic response. Von Pirquet included all forms of altered immunologic responsiveness, encompassing reactions to toxins, bacteria, and other infectious agents; patients with pollen hay fever; and urticaria-producing foods. Coca in 1923 coined the word *atopy* (Gk *atopos* uncommon) to denote an abnormal state of hypersensitivity as distinguished from hypersensitive responses in normal individuals, eg, contact dermatitis, serum sickness, anaphylaxis, and tuberculous infection.

Clinical Types of Atopy

Until recently, atopy was thought to be restricted to humans, but such conditions have now been described in dogs, rats, and even a baby walrus. In genetically susceptible individuals, atopy may affect one or more primary shock organ systems. In man, atopy involving the respiratory system (the nasal mucosa, bronchioles, and aural mucosa) can cause hay fever, asthma, and serous otitis. With the skin as shock organ, urticaria, angioneurotic edema, and atopic dermatitis (eczema) occur. Sensitized intestinal and urinary systems react with antigen to cause vomiting, abdominal pain, diarrhea, and urinary frequency and pain on urination. Vascular involvement, especially of the central nervous system, may result in headaches, personality changes, and other nervous system manifestations.

Genetic Basis of Atopy

Hay fever and asthma can be familial. If both parents have atopy, there is a 75% chance of the child having atopic symptoms; with one parent involved, there is a 50% chance. Thirty-eight percent of atopic patients have no parental history of atopy.

With the recent discovery of immune response genes associated with HLA haplotypes, a ragweed hay fever haplotype has been postulated. Ragweed-allergic patients in a family tree had the same HLA haplotype, whereas nonallergic members of the family had different haplotypes. The numerical haplotype designation among allergic families varied widely, but within a family ragweed sensitivity was associated with a single haplotype. It remains to be determined whether allergic responses to many antigens are determined by one haplotype or whether the response to any one antigen is haplotype-determined.

Allergens

Allergens are the antigens that give rise to allergic sensitization of the IgE antibody class. Most natural allergens are somewhat peculiar in that their molecular weight appears to be restricted to the range 15–40 thousand. They are extremely polar compounds, induce sensitization in very small amounts (ng to μg), and have many sulfhydryl groups, indicating much cross-linking. Purified allergens were observed to be brownish in color and to contain an enolized sugar-lysine combination. This is characteristic of the "ripening" or "Mailliard reaction" and was suggested as a requirement for allergenicity. However, more recent purifications and amino acid sequencing of ragweed (RA-5) and of bee venom allergen phospholipase A showed that they do not have the enolized sugar-lysine.

An allergen can result in both IgE and IgG antibodies, but mild formalin or glutaraldehyde treatment to form "allergoids" reduces the allergenicity (IgE formation) without affecting the antigenicity (IgG "blocking" antibody formation).

Antibodies

Prausnitz and Küstner used serum to passively transfer the allergic reactivity from an atopic patient to the skin of a normal individual. These antibodies were subsequently called reaginic or skin-sensitizing antibody. This reaginic antibody in man has recently been identified as IgE. IgE has a molecular weight of 196,000 and a sedimentation coefficient of 8S; it is a fast γ_1-globulin on electrophoresis, has a high carbohydrate content of 12%, and consists of 2 light chains (either type κ or λ) and 2 heavy chains of type ε.

The 550-amino acid sequence of the ε heavy chain of myeloma IgE ND* has recently been established and is similar to the μ chain of IgM except for the C terminal 19 amino acids (Fig 19–5). The ε heavy chain consists of one V region and four C domains, Cε1, Cε2, Cε3, and Cε4. There are 15 half-cysteines, 10 of which form one intrachain disulfide bond in each of the 5 domains. There is one interchain cysteine binding the light and ε heavy chain and 2 inter-ε chain bonds just before and after the Cε2 domain. There is a second intrachain disulfide bridge within the Cε1 domain. Rich in carbohydrate (12%), IgE has 6 oligosaccharide side chains of unknown function: 3 in the Cε1, one in the Cε2, and 2 in the Cε3 domains (A–F in Fig 19–5).

The skin-fixing or mast cell cytotropic activity resides in the Cε3 or Cε4 domains, and the well-known heat lability of reaginic skin fixation involves these 2 regions. Reduction of disulfide bonds also alters cytotropic activity. A working hypothesis is that firm attachment of the IgE molecule to the mast cell membrane involves at least 2 kinds of sites within the Cε3 and Cε4 regions of the ε chain. The primary recognition site for the mast cell surface receptor appears to be located in the Cε4 region. Secondary binding may be located in either Cε3 or Cε4. And, finally, the inter-heavy chain bond assisting half-cysteine 318 may exert an avidity effect which binds the ε chain firmly to the mast cell membrane.

The primary biologic property of IgE is tissue fixation, ie, cytotropism for the mast cell and basophil membranes. Like IgA, IgE does not fix complement by the classical pathway. In very large amounts, IgE can fix C3 by the alternative pathway, but this is probably not biologically relevant. IgE does not cross the placenta. Five patients with IgE myeloma have been discovered and these have provided sufficient material for the above structural and sequencing data.

Animal antisera to human IgE myeloma proteins have been labeled with fluorescein or ^{125}I, and the labeled antisera used to localize the tissue and cellular distribution of IgE. Plasma cells forming IgE have been found extensively in the secretory surfaces inside the body, eg, the bronchi and bronchioles of the respiratory tract, the gastrointestinal mucosa, and the urinary bladder. The tonsils and adenoids were especially rich in IgE-forming plasma cells. This secretory distribution of IgE-forming cells is similar to that of secretory IgA-producing plasma cells. Thus, both can be considered secretory immunoglobulins. The highest concentrations are found in nasal polyps, particularly in polyps of allergic individuals. The systemic lymphoid organs, such as the spleen, liver, and regional lymph

*IgE ND = the IgE myeloma protein from "patient ND."

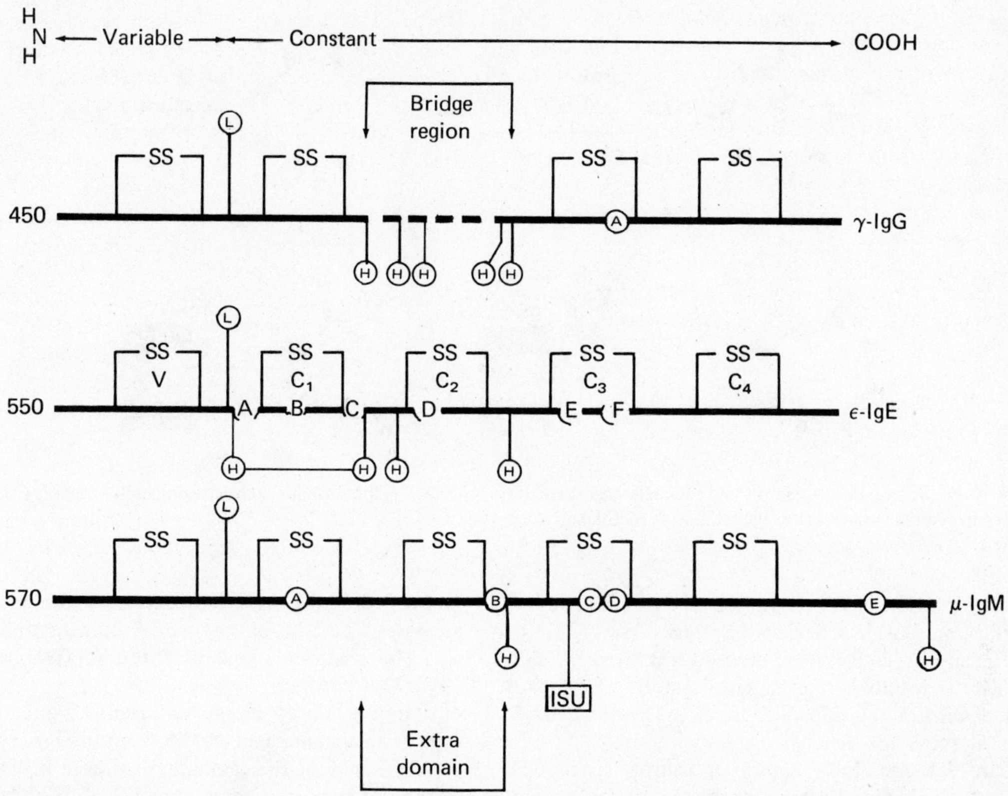

Figure 19–5. Diagrammatic representation of domains, inter-heavy chain bonds (L = light chain, H = heavy chain), and carbohydrate units (A, B, C, etc). Deletion of a counterpart to the $C_\epsilon 2$ and $C_\mu 2$ domains is one possible explanation to the general structure of the bridge region in the γ-chain. (Reproduced, with permission, from Bennich H: Structure of IgE. Prog Immunol 2:49, 1974.)

nodes, have only rare IgE-forming lymphocytes (which is also true for the circulating blood). When radiolabeled IgE was injected into monkeys, IgE was found only on blood basophils and tissue mast cells. No other cells contained surface IgE. On electron microscopy, basophils have IgE in large patches on their surfaces. With high concentrations of antibody, capping occurs, and the cell eventually removes the cap. The number of IgE molecules on a basophil surface has been estimated at 5300–27,000 in nonallergic individuals and at 15,000–41,000 in highly allergic individuals. Passive sensitization with IgE myeloma protein of a normal individual's basophils (containing 5300 IgE molecules) raised the number of IgE molecules to 36,000–the same as in the highly allergic individual.

Measurement of IgE

There is so little IgE in the serum that it escaped detection for many decades because the methods for immunoglobulin detection were not sufficiently sensitive. The normal adult IgE level is about 250 ng/ml. In severely allergic individuals, where IgE concentration is about 700 ng/ml, a specific IgE precipitin band is detectable by Ouchterlony immunodiffusion. However, for most studies such sensitivity is not sufficient, and radioisotopic methods are required for IgE quantitation.

A. Radioimmunodiffusion (Rowe's Method): Dilute rabbit anti-IgE against E-myeloma protein is dissolved in agarose and the mixture poured onto a glass plate. Wells are cut into the agarose and are filled with either diluted standards of serum containing serum IgE or the samples to be tested. IgE diffuses into the agarose and reacts with the anti-IgE to form an invisible circle of precipitate. The agarose is overlayered with sheep anti-rabbit IgG previously radiolabeled with radioactive iodine, and the plate is thoroughly washed. Autoradiography demonstrates circles of precipitate around the wells. This is due to a sandwich of a top layer of ^{131}I sheep anti-rabbit IgG, a middle layer of rabbit anti-IgE, and a bottom layer of IgE from the patient's serum. This method will detect levels of 50 ng or more of IgE and is useful for allergic patients.

B. Radioimmunosorbent Test (RIST) for Total IgE Concentration: This most sensitive of the detection methods detects 1 ng or less of IgE in serum. Rabbit anti-IgE myeloma protein is coupled to cyanogen bromide-activated microcrystalline cellulose or other immunosorbent. Dilutions of an IgE-containing standard serum or an unknown patient's serum are reacted with the anti-IgE-coated particles. After thorough washing, the particles are reacted with ^{125}I rabbit anti-IgE myeloma protein. After additional

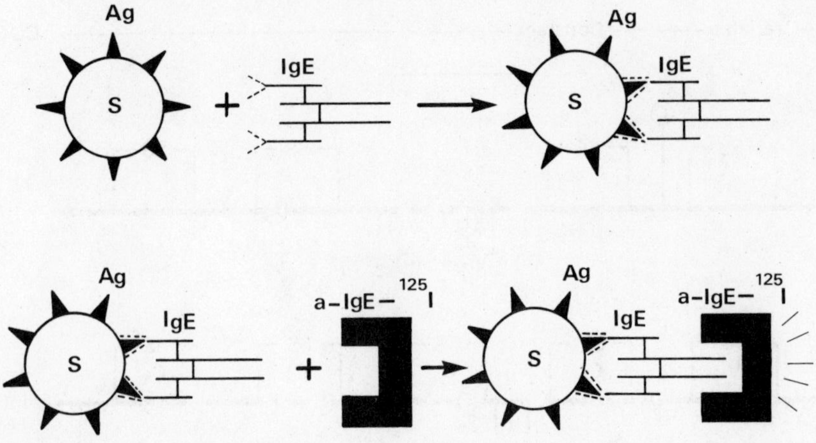

Figure 19–6. Schematic diagram of the radioallergosorbent test (RAST). S is the sorbent, with antigenic determinants (Ag). Human IgE attaches to the antigen and is detected with radiolabeled anti-IgE.

washing, the particles are counted in a gamma counter to determine the amount of bound IgE.

In an alternative assay method, rabbit anti-IgE is coupled to insoluble beads. One aliquot of beads is reacted with radiolabeled IgE myeloma protein, while other aliquots are reacted either with dilutions of a standard IgE-containing serum or dilutions of a patient's serum. The relative inhibition of binding of radiolabeled IgE resulting from IgE in the test sample or standard is determined and graphed. From this plot, the IgE concentration in the sample can be determined with an accuracy of less than 1 ng/ml.

C. Radioallergosorbent Test (RAST) for Specific IgE Concentration: Purified allergen extract is coupled to cellulose particles or paper disks. Patient's serum containing IgE antibody or a standard serum is reacted with the allergen-coupled immunosorbent. After thorough washing, ^{125}I-labeled rabbit anti-IgE is reacted with the immunosorbent (Fig 19–6). After further washing, the radioactivity on the centrifuged sorbent is determined and is a measure of the amount of specific serum IgE antibodies to that allergen. This measures 1 ng of specific IgE antibody.

Specific IgE antibodies in human serum also have been measured by passively sensitizing monkey tissues, such as strips of monkey ileum or finely chopped monkey lung or skin tissues. The passively sensitized monkey smooth muscle preparation is suspended in a buffer bath, and allergen added to the bath will cause contractions of the smooth muscle which can be measured by a kymograph. Passively sensitized monkey lung or skin fragments are reacted with allergen and centrifuged. The supernate is then measured for histamine or SRS-A.

Serum Concentrations of IgE

Serum concentrations of IgE are at times expressed in international units (IU): 2.3 ng IgE = 1 IU. The normal newborn infant has virtually no IgE in its cord serum (± 1–2 IU/ml). By the age of 1½–4½ months, the mean is 9 IU/ml in healthy children. This increases to 32 IU/ml between 9 months to 3 years of age. The adult level is about 90 IU/ml (with a range of 29–800 IU/ml).

In a group of allergic children, 17 out of 21 children with asthma had elevated serum IgE levels (Fig 19–7). Three of the remaining children had IgE levels in the upper normal range. Only 7 of 21 children with allergic rhinitis had increased IgE, while 14 were in the upper normal range. IgE levels present in nasal secretions mirror those in the serum. IgE levels in nasal secretions ranged from 10–150 ng/ml in a group of normal children and adults to 36–850 ng/ml in a group of asthmatic children. A group of Ethiopian children with active ascaris infection were noted to have a

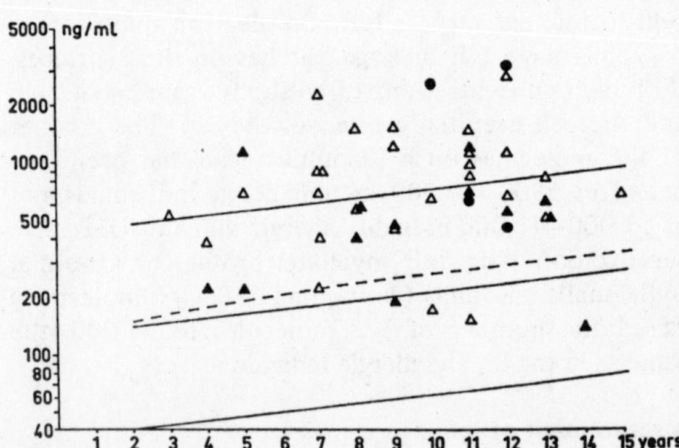

Figure 19–7. Serum IgE concentrations in children with asthma (△), asthma plus eczema (▲), and allergic rhinitis (hay fever) during the pollination season (●). The solid line (–) represents the regression line and 95% confidence limits calculated on the logarithmic IgE values in 132 healthy children; the dotted line (- - -) represents the regression line calculated on the arithmetic IgE values in the same children. (Reproduced, with permission, from Berg T, Johansson SGO: IgE concentrations in children with atopic diseases. Int Arch Allergy Appl Immunol 36:220, 1969.)

mean serum IgE level of 4400 ng/ml (range, 240–14,300 ng/ml), which is 30 times the normal IgE level. Subsequently, patients with other parasitic infections, especially other roundworms, were found to have extremely high serum IgE levels. Patients with atopic dermatitis had an IgE level 9 times the normal mean, whereas patients with urticaria and other dermatoses had normal IgE levels.

Recent findings suggest that measurement of total IgE levels may be useful in the early detection of allergy in infants. A survey of 34 infants from allergic families found 11 to have serum IgE levels greater than 20 IU/ml. Ten of these 11 children had allergic symptoms.

The serum IgE level apparently reflects an excess of IgE antibody in a pathophysiologic sense because allergic reactions occur upon sensitized mast cells in tissues. The amount of IgE in skin tissue can be measured by injecting dilute rabbit anti-IgE serum into the skin. Normal serum IgE concentrations of 65–130 IU/ml gave a threshold skin reaction with a 1:10,000 dilution of rabbit anti-IgE serum. In highly allergic patients, a 1:20 million dilution of rabbit anti-IgE still reacted in the skin. There was a rough correlation between minimal tissue concentration of IgE necessary to give a threshold skin response and the serum concentration of IgE. Measurement of skin IgE in this way is not generally recommended because injecting a foreign animal serum into the skin could sensitize the patient to rabbit proteins.

Specific IgE Antibodies

The most widely used method of measuring specific IgE antibodies to a variety of allergens is the radioallergosorbent test (RAST). This assay is used extensively for the diagnostic quantitation of IgE antibodies to a variety of allergens. It is used to measure IgE antibody titers during the treatment of patients and to standardize allergens in a modified test.

A group of 20 children with ragweed hay fever were followed for 5 years and treated with preseasonal ragweed injections for 4 of those 5 years (Table 19–1). Over the 4 years, IgE antibodies against ragweed fell and reached a low plateau. Concomitantly, the symptom index of hay fever fell and reached a plateau. IgG blocking antibodies rose during the therapy. Because the children were doing so well, with minimal symptoms, the preseasonal therapy was omitted in the fifth year. Subsequently, IgE antibodies rose, the symptoms became more severe, and the IgG blocking antibodies fell. This suggested that treatment had been stopped too soon and should be resumed. The radioallergosorbent test will probably find its greatest usefulness in monitoring the course of allergic therapy.

Using a standard allergen coupled to an immunosorbent and a standard patient's serum containing antibodies to that allergen, this allergen assay can be inhibited by similar unknown allergen solutions for standardization purposes. For example, a known system (such as ragweed antigen E) coupled to an immunosorbent and reacted with a known patient's IgE antiserum to ragweed antigen E gives a certain level binding of radiolabeled anti-IgE. An aliquot of unknown allergen containing the same amount of qualitatively identical antigen E should theoretically inhibit this reaction 100% if added prior to the immunosorbent-bound antigen E. A lesser quantity of antigen E or a partially related antigen would cause less complete inhibition. Therefore, this test can be used to standardize unknown allergen preparations in both quantity and quality. It is anticipated that the FDA will shortly require this method for standardization of all commercial allergens in the USA.

IgE & Cell-Mediated Immunity

A reciprocal relationship between serum IgE antibody levels and cellular immunity has been demonstrated in rats immunized with dinitrophenyl-ascaris extract. Thymus-derived lymphocytes appear to regulate the production of IgE, and immunization with ascaris antigen and *Bordetella pertussis* vaccine stimulated T cells. A second immunization on day 5 with ascaris protein conjugated with the dinitrophenyl hapten caused high titers of IgE antibody. Neonatally thymectomized or lethally irradiated rats could not make anti-dinitrophenyl IgE antibody. IgE antibody

Table 19–1. Changes in symptoms and antibody levels produced by allergy treatment.*

Season	Number of Patients†	Mean Seasonal Symptom Index (SI)	Mean "Postseason" Allergen-Specific IgE Antibody Titer (units)	Mean IgG "Blocking Antibodies" (units)
1967 (control)	8	0.445	2,520	<10
1967 (treated)	9	0.150	1,150	121
1968 (treated)	17	0.183	1,400	272
1969 (treated)	16	0.136	740	. . .
1970 (treated)	15	0.126	940	196
1970 (untreated)	12	0.243	1,715	65

*Reproduced, with permission, from Levy DA. In: *Conference on the Biological Role of the IgE System.* Ishizaka K, Dayton DH Jr (editors). US Department of Health, Education, & Welfare, 1973.

†Includes only those patients for whom all 3 sets of data are available.

Note: SI × IgE Ab: $r_s = 0.94$ ($p = 0.02$). SI × IgG Ab: $r_s = 0.7$ ($p > 0.1$).
IgE Ab × IgG Ab: $r_s = 0.7$ ($p > 0.1$). r_s = symptom index.

production was not restored with B cells alone but was restored with both T and B cells. Thus, T cells helped B cells turn on the IgE antibody mechanism.

Sublethal whole body irradiation, adult thymectomy and splenectomy, T cell immunosuppression with antithymocyte serum, or radiomimetic drugs (5-bromouridine deoxyriboxide and dactinomycin) all enhanced IgE production, which lasted for weeks. It appeared that IgE production persisted in the absence of T cells. IgG and IgM antibodies occurred soon after immunization and did not stop IgE production. Next, thymus (or spleen) cells from hyperimmunized rats were injected into irradiated rats that were producing IgE antibodies. This caused a rapid fall (within 2 days) in IgE. Thus, IgE production by B cells appears to be under regulatory control by T cells.

IgE production in man may also be under T cell regulatory control. A patient with thymic alymphoplasia, with high serum IgE level (16 μg/ml) and allergic symptoms, had severe depletion of small lymphocytes in the thymic-dependent paracortical areas of lymph nodes, but lymphoid and plasma cells were normal. Patients with Wiskott-Aldrich syndrome have high serum IgE, eczema, and impairment of cellular immunity. Similarly, eczema also occurs in patients with ataxia-telangiectasia and impaired cellular immunity. Patients with Hodgkin's disease or sarcoidosis, with acquired impairment of cellular immunity, are being reported with high serum levels of IgE. On the other hand, patients with X-linked hypogammaglobulinemia (often with compensatory hyperreactive cellular immunity) commonly have eczema.

Humoral and cellular immune responses were recently evaluated in 10 patients with active atopic dermatitis. IgE levels were elevated (mean = 6420 IU/ml; normal mean = 90 IU/ml), but complement receptor lymphocytes and surface immunoglobulin-positive B cells were normal. T cell function was diminished in that 6 out of 9 patients were unresponsive to concentrated candida (1:10) and streptokinase-streptodornase (1:1) extracts as delayed skin tests. Spontaneous sheep erythrocyte T cell rosettes were below normal, and 2 of 10 patients had reduced PHA responsiveness. Eighteen patients with moderate to severe atopic dermatitis had a mean of only 13.7% active T cell rosetting lymphocytes compared to 29.6% in 30 normal adults. In both of these studies, all patients were being treated with topical corticosteroids, and these drugs could have caused impaired cellular immunity. In summary, there appears to be an inverse relationship between IgE concentration and cellular immunity.

TARGET CELLS OF IgE-MEDIATED ALLERGIC REACTIONS

Mast Cells

Basophilic cells in connective and subcutaneous tissues were first recognized by Ehrlich, who associated a "feeding" or "mast" function with them. Others described them as "emergency kits" against infection or tissue damage. The primary function of mast cells appears to be storage of granules containing potent inflammatory and repair materials which are released upon injury to the organism. They contain strong pharmacologically active materials such as heparin, histamine, serotonin, bradykinin, and SRS-A; tissue repair materials such as hyaluronic acid; and factors affecting other cells, such as eosinophil chemotactic factor of anaphylaxis (ECF-A) and platelet-aggregating factor. It has been generally accepted that mast cells in all tissues are the same. However, the drug cromolyn sodium prevents the release of mediators from human mast cells in the bronchi and nose but does not affect skin mast cells. Differences in mast cells are currently being sought by electron microscopy.

Basophils

Basophilic cells comprise 0.5–2% of circulating white cells. They were once thought to be identical to mast cells, from which they are indistinguishable by light microscopy, but electron microscopy reveals that the structure of granules is different in the 2 types of cells. Basophils contain histamine and SRS-A; their histamine release is not inhibited by cromolyn sodium. The content of other mediators is under study.

Other Target Cells

Blood platelets contain serotonin and possibly other allergic inflammatory mediators. In some species, like the rabbit, platelets also contain heparin and histamine. Histamine released from rabbit platelets is involved in the deposition of IgG immune complexes in the renal tissue of rabbits with acute glomerulonephritis. Such immune complex deposition can be prevented by prior treatment of the rabbit with antihistamine drugs. Furthermore, it has been suggested that fibroblasts and other connective tissue cells might be sources of secondary mediators in allergic reactions (eg, kinins and prostaglandins).

MEDIATORS OF ALLERGIC REACTIONS

Physiologic Role of Allergic Mediators

The primary role of the mediators of allergic reactions appears to be defense against injury, first by causing inflammation and then by stimulating tissue repair. In the presence of large concentrations of antihistamines, surgical wound healing is considerably impaired. Heparin temporarily suspends blood clotting, which permits inflammatory cells to enter the area of tissue injury. Histamine causes leakage by blood vessel endothelial cells and permits additional inflammatory cells and serum proteins, such as antibody, to enter the area of damaged tissue. There appears to be a role for histamine and perhaps other mediators in normal growth—especially fetal growth. The highest concentrations of histamine are present during the fetal period. In pregnant rats given chronic high doses of antihistamines, fetal growth and maturation were impaired. Histamine appears to have a role in the control of microcirculation at the capillary level, where there appears to be a homeostatic balance between capillary constriction caused by epinephrine and capillary dilatation caused by histamine.

Although diseases such as acute glomerulonephritis are associated with deposition of antigen-IgG-complement complexes in the kidney or lung, these may be harmful overreactions of a normal defense mechanism. In intestinal parasitic nematode infestations in the rat, IgE on mast cells reacts with parasitic antigens. This causes the release of histamine and serotonin, which results in leakage of serum proteins from intestinal blood vessels. Among such proteins are IgG and IgM antibodies against the parasite, and these antibodies are apparently involved in the normal clearing of parasites from the intestine. Therefore, this is a useful defense mechanism. In animals, the acquisition of IgE antibodies to parasites results in permanent protection against subsequent infection by that parasite. This is known as the "self-cure phenomenon."

Facilitation by mediators of other cells entering the field of reaction may augment inflammation or may function in negative feedback control of the inflammation. The release of ECF-A causes the influx of eosinophils into the area of allergic inflammation. Electron micrographs have shown eosinophil phagocytosis of ferritin-antibody complexes. Eosinophil granules contain arylsulfatase, an enzyme that splits SRS-A into 2 inactive fragments. This provides an inactivating control on smooth muscle spasm induced by SRS-A.

Pharmacologic Role of Mediators

Histamine is a bioactive amine (MW 111) which causes smooth muscle contractions of human bronchioles and small blood vessels, increased permeability of capillaries, and increased secretion by nasal and bronchial mucous glands. Histamine is stored in mast cells and in basophil granules and is released upon dissolution of the granules. Its maximal reaction occurs in 1–2 minutes, and its duration of action is about 10 minutes. Therefore, histamine in man could be responsible for the symptoms of hay fever, urticaria, angioedema, and the bronchospasm of acute anaphylaxis.

SRS-A is an acidic lipopeptide (MW ~ 400) which has a prolonged constrictive effect on smooth muscle, at times lasting for hours. Such contraction can occur in the presence of antihistamines, and this is the basis for the bioassay of SRS-A. The muscle contractions can be terminated by epinephrine. SRS-A is not preformed in mast cell granules but is formed as a result of an antigen-antibody reaction and is subsequently released from the granule. SRS-A is probably the principal mediator for the prolonged bronchospasm of human asthma. Diethylcarbamazine, an antifilarial drug, is antagonistic to the function of SRS-A.

Serotonin, or 5-hydroxytryptamine (MW 176), occurs in murine mast cells and human platelets. It has a pharmacologic role in anaphylaxis in mice, rats, and rabbits but apparently not in man. It is antagonized by lysergic acid. Serotonin is preformed, is held in mast cell granules, and, similar to histamine, is released as a result of an antigen-antibody reaction.

ECF-A, an acidic peptide with a molecular weight of about 500, is also released as a result of an antigen-antibody reaction. It is preformed, like histamine and serotonin, and upon release it causes an influx of eosinophils into the area of allergic inflammation. The eosinophils dispose of antigen-antibody complexes and exert a feedback control on SRS-A through their granular enzyme, arylsulfatase.

Platelet-aggregating factor (PAF) is released by rabbit basophils and causes platelets to aggregate. This releases histamine, which is involved in immune complex deposition. Whether this factor has a similar role in man is not certain.

Bradykinin is a 9-amino-acid peptide split by the enzyme kallikrein from a serum α_2-globulin precursor. The release of bradykinin from mast cells has recently been demonstrated. In man, it causes slow, sustained contraction of smooth muscles, including those of the bronchi and vessels; increased vascular permeability; increased secretion of mucous glands, including those in the bronchi; and stimulation of pain fibers. Therefore, bradykinin could be responsible for the symptoms of hay fever, angioedema (associated with painful swelling), and asthma.

Secondary Mediators

Prostaglandins F and A cause increased smooth muscle contraction and increased capillary permeability. They may have a role in asthma and urticaria in man. There is apparently a homeostatic feedback control in that PGE_1 and PGE_2 have opposite effects to maintain homeostasis. Prostaglandins are inhibited by aspirin and indomethacin.

Histamine Release From Sensitized Leukocytes (Basophils)

A practical in vitro miniature allergic reaction is used extensively as an investigative and diagnostic test for allergy. Leukocytes from a heparinized blood sample drawn from an allergic individual are incubated with the allergen for 15 minutes. The leukocyte sample is centrifuged, and the histamine content of the supernate is measured spectrofluorometrically (or by radiolabeled histamine or bioassay). With increasing amounts of antigen, there is increased histamine release. The histamine is expressed as a percentage of the total amount of histamine present in an aliquot of leukocytes. Blood basophils are the only source of histamine in the blood, and although a buffy coat preparation is used one is actually measuring basophil histamine release. The degree of sensitivity in a patient is directly proportionate to the amount of histamine released by antigen (Fig 19–8). The degree of sensitivity in different patients may be compared by the relative amounts of antigen required to release 50% of

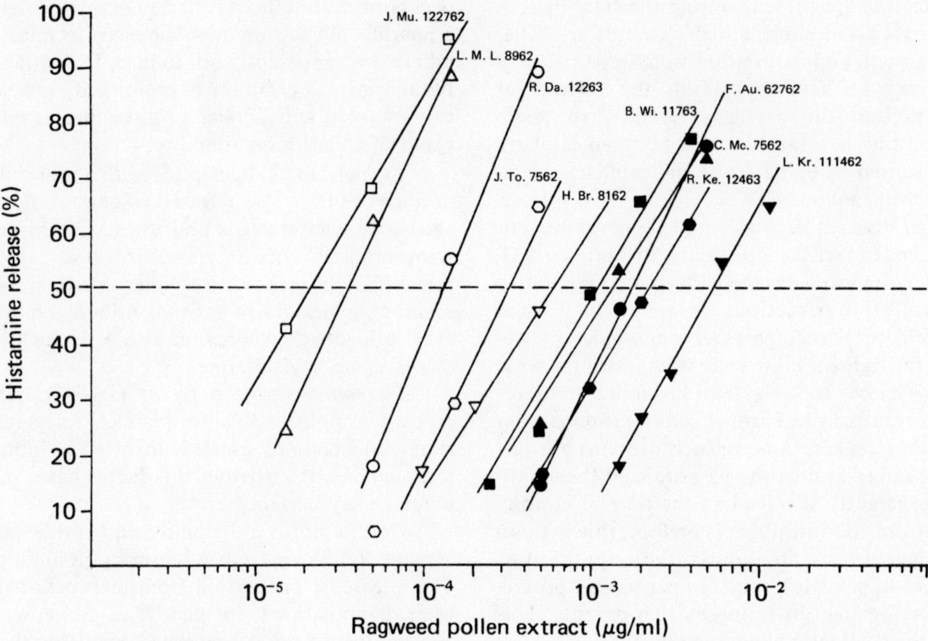

Figure 19–8. Dose-response relationships for histamine release as a function of antigen concentration (cells from 10 ragweed-sensitive donors). (Reproduced, with permission, from Lichtenstein LM, Osler AG: Studies on the mechanism of hypersensitivity phenomena. Histamine release from human leukocytes by ragweed pollen antigen. J Exp Med 120:507, 1964.)

the histamine from their white cells. Fig 19–8 shows that patient J. Mu. is 300 times more sensitive than patient L. Kr. A remarkable correlation between the degree of symptoms and the amount of antigen necessary for 50% release from leukocytes has been noted (Fig 19–9). This test has been useful in following the course of patients during hyposensitization therapy (Fig 19–10). At the start of therapy, this patient required 5 μg of antigen to release 50% of his histamine, whereas after 2½ years of therapy he required 5150 μg of antigen to release the same percentage of histamine. This is a 1000-fold decrease in his cell sensitivity and correlated positively with his clinical improvement.

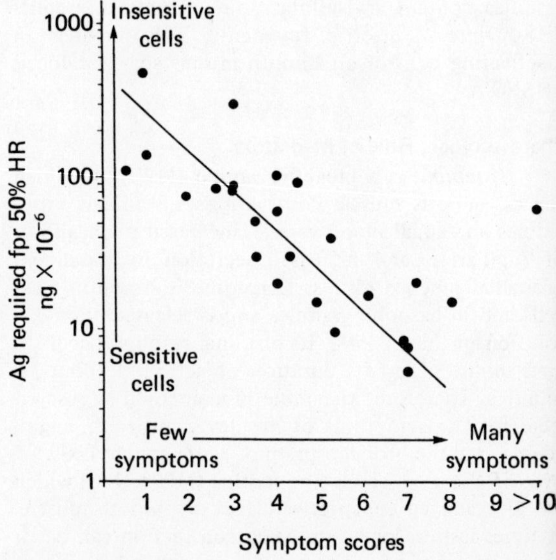

Figure 19–9. Correlation between average seasonal symptom scores of hay fever patients and measurements of cellular sensitivity to antigen E (ng antigen required for 50% histamine release [HR] from a standard suspension of isolated washed leukocytes). (Reproduced, with permission, from Lichtenstein LM, Norman PS: Human allergic reactions. Am J Med 46:169, 1969. Also in: Norman PS: Present status of hyposensitization treatment. Page 46 in: *Proceedings of the Sixth Congress of the International Association of Allergology*. Excerpta Medica Foundation, 1968.)

Autonomic Nervous Controls as "Mediators" of Allergic Reactions

The catecholamines (epinephrine, norepinephrine, dopamine) are agonists of the sympathetic nervous system; acetylcholine is the parasympathetic agonist. These substances modulate the severity of the allergic reaction by regulating the amount of mediator release from target cells and the degree of responsiveness of shock organ cells. Catecholamines contain a catechol nucleus (a benzene ring with 2 adjacent hydroxy groups) and an amine group. Epinephrine acts primarily as a hormone, and norepinephrine is a neurotransmitter at both peripheral and central levels. Both compounds occur naturally in mammals. Another synthetic catecholamine, isoproterenol, has important pharmacologic effects on the allergic reaction.

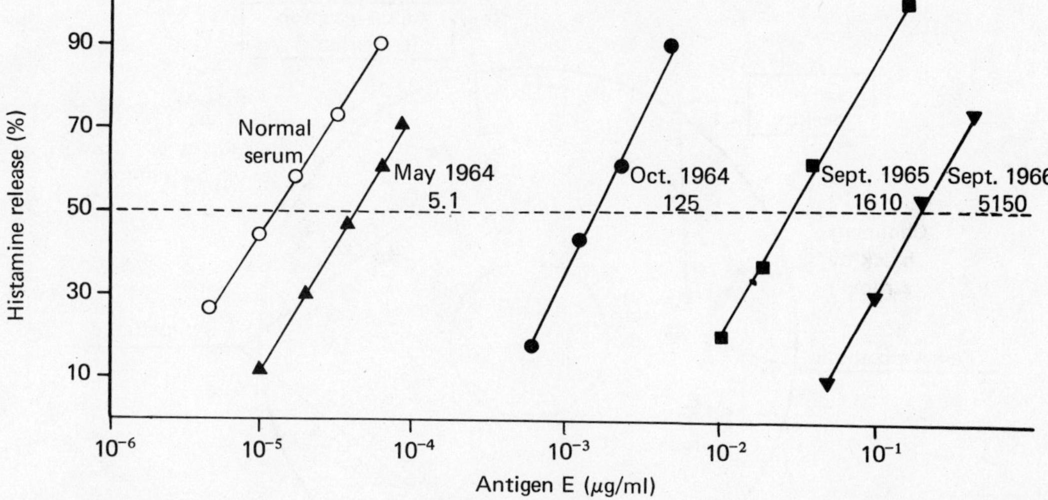

Figure 19–10. Dose-response curves of cells suspended in normal serum or in the patient's own serum obtained before immunotherapy (May 1964) and after approximately 1, 2, and 3 years of immunotherapy. The numbers to the right of the curves in allergic serum indicate the ratio of the antigen concentration required for 50% histamine release in the allergic sera as compared to the normal serum (open symbols). (Reproduced, with permission, from Lichtenstein LM, Norman PS: Human allergic reactions. [Editorial.] Am J Med 46:170, 1969.)

The autonomic nervous system is divided into sympathetic (adrenergic) and parasympathetic (cholinergic) systems, and these exert generally opposing actions on the various organs of the body. These 2 systems maintain homeostasis in bronchial smooth muscle cells; cholinergic stimulation through acetylcholine causes smooth muscle constriction, whereas adrenergic stimulation through epinephrine causes relaxation. Thus, there is constant alternating responsiveness of bronchial smooth muscles to cholinergic and adrenergic stimuli, maintaining smooth muscle tone or homeostasis.

CELL RECEPTORS & ALLERGIC REACTIONS

Target cells have receptors, presumably on their surfaces, for the autonomic agonists acetylcholine and epinephrine. Adrenergic receptors apparently have a receptive substance with a steric configuration complementary to the amine group in the catecholamine. This interaction initiates a chain of biochemical reactions which culminate in the ultimate reaction of that cell. Although receptors have not as yet been biochemically defined, they are usually described in terms of actions induced by agonists and by blockage of such actions by antagonistic agents. On this basis, Ahlquist described adrenergic α and β receptors which often had antagonistic or synergistic effects. α-Adrenergic receptors respond primarily to norepinephrine, with epinephrine or isoproterenol causing a 10- or 100-fold reduced response, respectively. On the other hand, β-adrenergic receptors respond primarily to isoproterenol, with epinephrine and norepinephrine similarly causing a 10- or 100-fold reduced response. Thus, epinephrine is a natural agonist for both α and β receptors, with its ultimate effect probably modulated by other factors. α-Adrenergic receptors are blocked by ergot alkaloids, haloalkylamines (eg, phenoxybenzamine, Dibenamine), benzodioxans, and imidazolines. β-Adrenergic receptors are blocked by propranolol, dichloroisoproterenol, and pronethanol.

β-Adrenergic receptors have been further classified, depending upon their action on certain tissues, into β_1 and β_2 receptors. β_1-Adrenergic stimulation causes an increase in heart rate (chronotropic effect) as well as an increased force of cardiac contraction (inotropic effect). Increased mobilization of free fatty acids from fat cells also occurs, producing a rise in blood lipids. β_2-Adrenergic receptors cause relaxation of smooth muscles, especially in the bronchus, uterus, and bladder. They also cause inhibition of peripheral glucose uptake and increased muscle glycogenolysis, both of which cause a rise in blood glucose. The agonist for both β_1 and β_2 receptors is isoproterenol; both are blocked by propranolol. There are, however, several newly synthesized agonists for β_2 adrenergic receptors, eg, metaproterenol (Alupent, Metaprel), albuterol (Salbutamol), and terbutaline (Bricanyl). These have been developed for treatment of asthma to act primarily as bronchodilators and to avoid the cardiac stimulatory effects of β_1 receptors. The β_2 receptors are blocked specifically by butoxamine, while pronethanol has primarily a β_1 blocking action.

Whether α-adrenergic receptors exist in the human bronchus is a question under current study, and there is some disagreement. In animals such as the guinea pig, α-adrenergic stimulation by norepinephrine

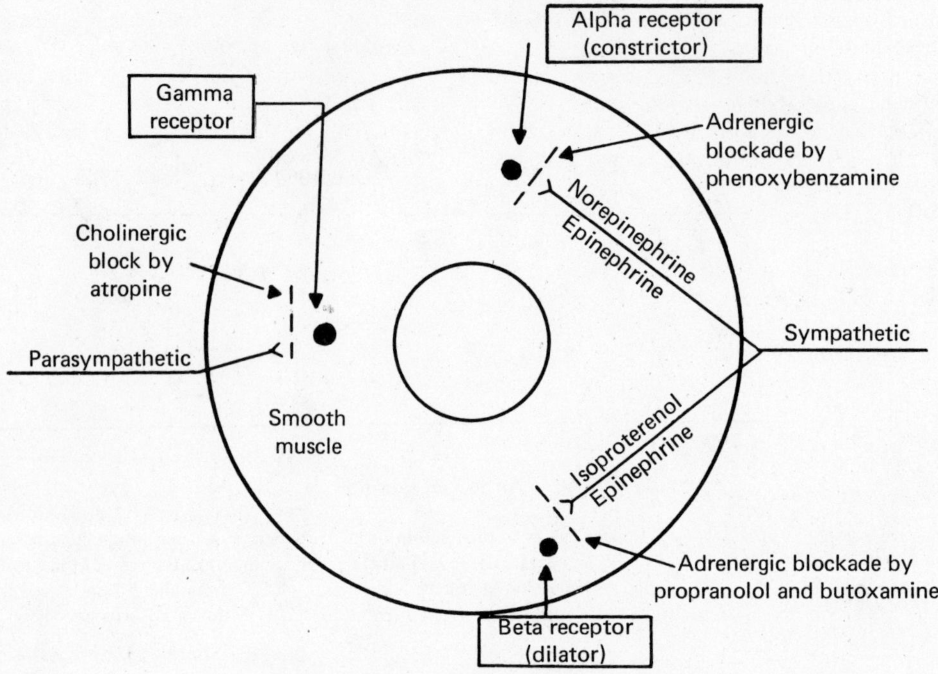

Figure 19–11. Autonomic receptors of smooth muscle of blood vessels and bronchi. (Reproduced, with permission, from Reed CE: The role of the autonomic nervous system in the pathogenesis of bronchial asthma: Is the normal bronchial sensitivity due to beta adrenergic blockade? Page 404 in: *Proceedings of the Sixth Congress of the International Association of Allergology*. Excerpta Medica Foundation, 1968.)

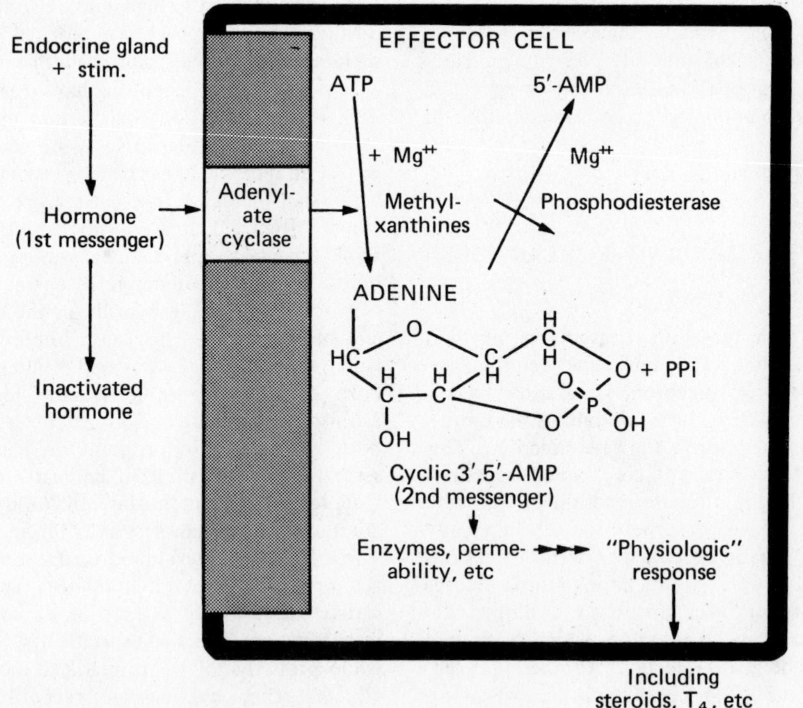

Figure 19–12. Second messenger system involving adenylate cyclase. (Reproduced, with permission, from Sutherland EW: On the biological role of cyclic AMP. JAMA 214:1281, 1970.)

or propranolol blocking of β-adrenergic receptors results in bronchoconstriction. Such an effect has not been conclusively demonstrated in man.

In summary, the allergic shock organ tissues, smooth muscle, and vascular endothelium have responses modulated by the autonomic nervous system (Fig 19–11). Cholinergic stimulation by the action of acetylcholine on a cholinergic or a γ receptor on target cells causes smooth muscle contraction and increased capillary permeability. α-Adrenergic stimulation by norepinephrine acting on the α receptor causes bronchial smooth muscle contraction and vasoconstriction (in the guinea pig). β-Adrenergic stimulation by epinephrine or isoproterenol causes smooth muscle relaxation and decreases capillary permeability. Cholinergic stimulation is blocked by atropine, and α-adrenergic effects are blocked by phenoxybenzamine, while β_2 stimulation is blocked by propranolol. Therefore, the use of appropriate agonists and antagonists to these reactions provides a pharmacologic basis for control of symptoms resulting from allergic reactions.

Considerable evidence is emerging that the β-adrenergic receptor is a cell membrane enzyme, adenylate cyclase. This enzyme is changed from a relatively inactive to an active form by isoproterenol or epinephrine. Activated adenylate cyclase catalyzes the formation of cyclic nucleotide (as shown in Fig 19–12) by acting upon ATP in the cell cytoplasm to form cyclic 3′,5′-adenosine monophosphate (cAMP), which consists of adenylic acid with a diesterified phosphate group at the C3′ and C5′ positions of the attached ribose. cAMP in the presence of dibasic cations (Ca^{++} and Mg^{++}) modulates the activity of cell enzymes and permeability barriers. Furthermore, cAMP is converted to an inactive 5′-AMP by phosphodiesterase.

According to the hypothesis of Sutherlund, hormones such as norepinephrine and epinephrine (catecholamines) act as the first messenger, which reacts with a receptor enzyme (such as adenylate cyclase), which in turn activates a second messenger, cAMP. This second messenger induces the cell to perform its physiologic function, the fat cell to undergo lipolysis; the liver cell to undergo glycogenolysis; the smooth muscle cell to relax; and the mast cell to inhibit its release of mediators.

Intracellular concentration of cAMP rises in the target cell upon external stimulation with prostaglandins PGE_1 and PGE_2 and also increases with histamine itself (Fig 19–13). There appears, therefore, to be a catalytic subunit of adenylate cyclase in the membrane which responds to one of 3 or more independent receptor subunits. Such receptor subunits can be blocked independently by drugs, eg, β-adrenergic receptor is blocked by propranolol; the histamine receptor is of the H_2 type which is blocked by burimamide; and the prostaglandin receptor may possibly be blocked by indomethacin or by aspirin. Basophils, in which the β-adrenergic receptor is blocked by propranolol, will still respond to prostaglandins PGE_1 or PGE_2 with a rise in intracellular cAMP—and also to exogenous histamine in a similar manner—whereas burimamide-treated basophils fail to respond to histamine but will respond with a rise in intracellular cAMP to epinephrine or PGE_1 stimulation. It has been suggested that the release of histamine from mast cells by antigen and antibody will exert a negative feedback control upon other basophils to inhibit further release of histamine. The concept of 3 independent receptors on target cells causing a rise in intracellular cAMP is of possible major therapeutic interest in status asthmaticus, wherein the

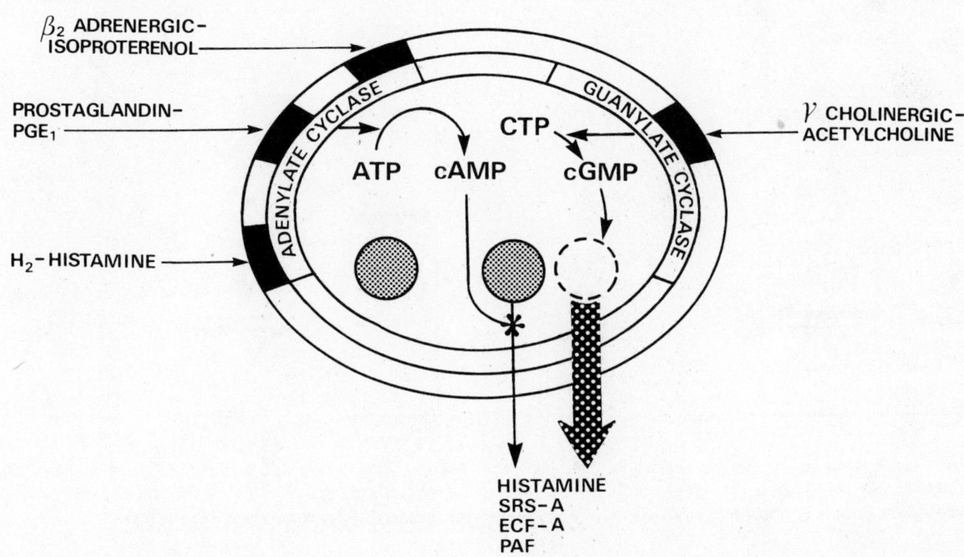

Figure 19–13. Schematic representation of a cell showing the relationships between intracellular cAMP and various independent receptor subunits.

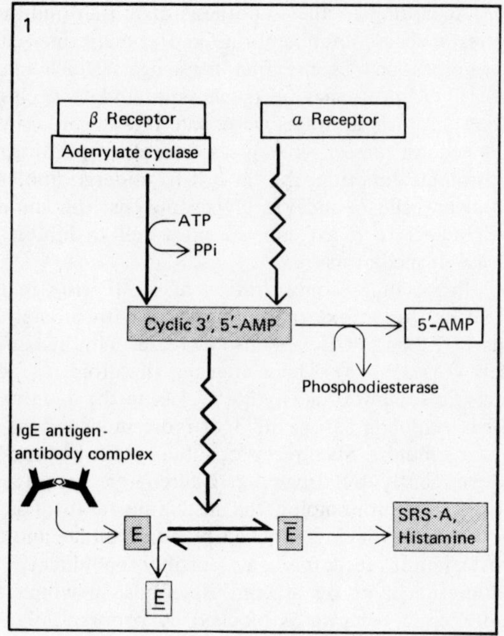

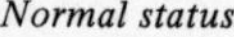

Normal status.

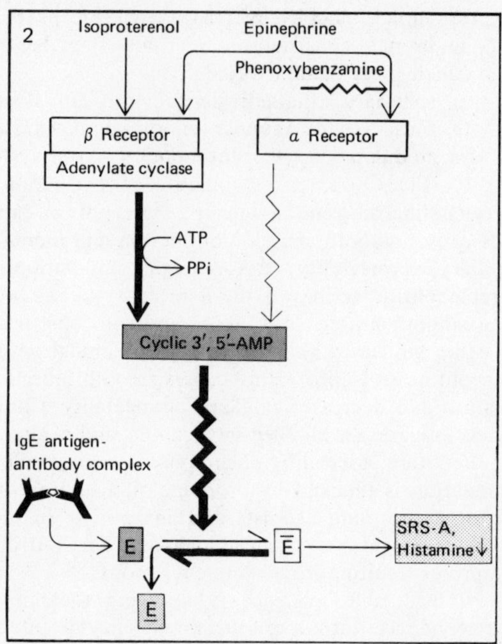

Epinephrine with phenoxybenzamine blocks the α-adrenergic receptors, causing a rise in intracellular cAMP and a decrease in release of both histamine and SRS-A.

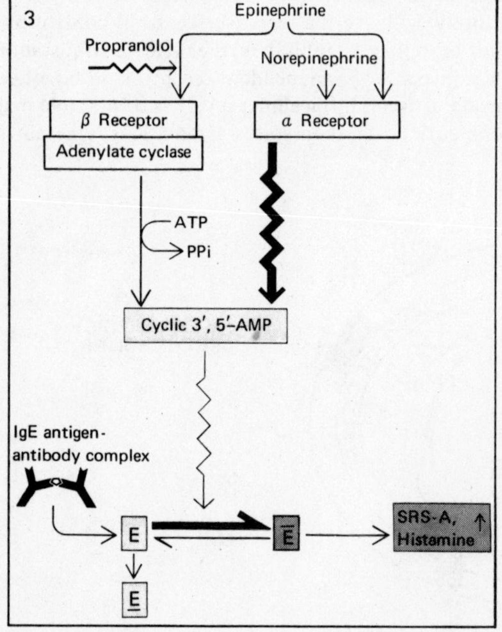

Norepinephrine stimulates α-adrenergic receptors, and propranolol, which blocks the β-adrenergic receptors, causes a fall in cAMP and a rise in histamine and SRS-A release.

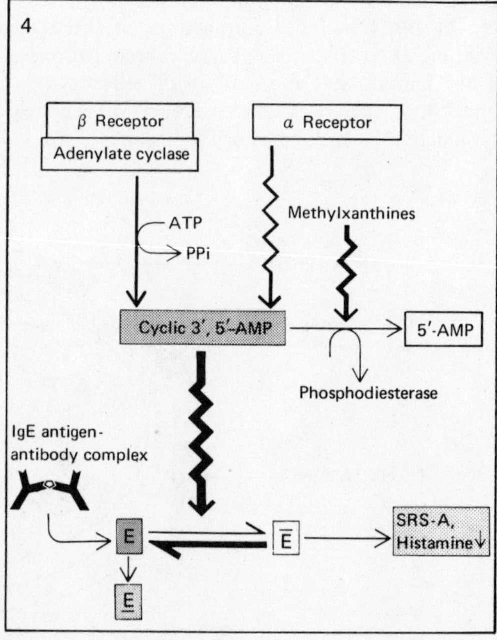

Theophylline, a methylxanthine, blocks phosphodiesterase and thereby the destruction of cAMP; thus, elevated cAMP causes inhibition of histamine and SRS-A release.

Figure 19–14. Biochemical control of mediator release from mast cells. (Modified and reproduced, with permission, from the chapter by Orange RP & Austin KF in *Immunobiology*, edited by Good RA, Fisher DW. Copyright © 1971 by Sinauer Associates, Sunderland, Mass.)

β-adrenergic receptor appears to be unresponsive to epinephrine but is still apparently responsive to prostaglandin PGE_1.

Lymphocytes which form antibodies or which participate in cellular immune responses by undergoing mitogenesis and enlargement in response to antigen or plant lectins are under similar autonomic and biochemical regulatory controls. A rise in intracellular cAMP induced by epinephrine or prostaglandin PGE_1 in such lymphocytes inhibits mitogenesis and aborts further immune responsiveness. Therefore, hormonal influences upon antibody formation and immune response is under intensive current study.

The α-adrenergic receptor is less well understood. Several workers have suggested that ATPase may function as the α receptor. It may compete for ATP with adenylate cyclase in the direct formation of inactive 5′-AMP without the intermediary cAMP formation step. Norepinephine may stimulate ATPase to utilize ATP directly to form inactive 5′-AMP; such a diversion of precursor ATP would cause a lowering of the intracellular cAMP, and this in turn would result in an increased mediator release from such a stimulated basophil.

Phosphodiesterase converts cAMP to inactive 5′-AMP. Methylxanthine drugs such as theophylline, theobromine, and caffeine inhibit phosphodiesterase

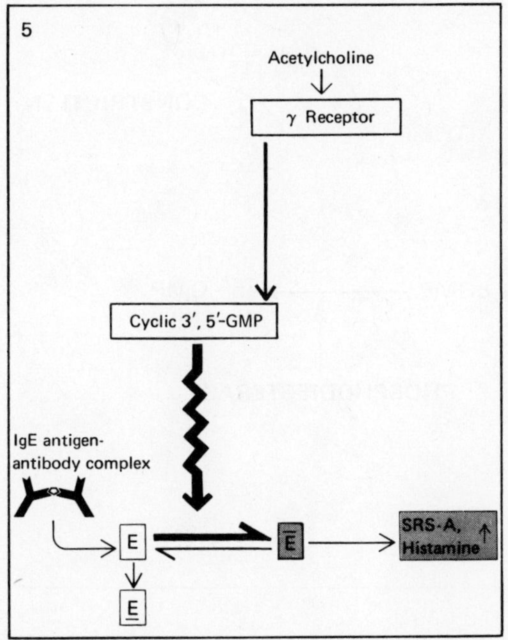

The presence of carbachol (an acetylcholine derivative), produces a rise in intracellular cGMP and a concomitant rise in histamine and SRS-A release. There is no effect on cAMP. (Recently, these observations have been confirmed in a purified, isolated rat mast cell preparation.)

Figure 19–14 (cont'd).

and its destruction of cAMP; therefore, a high cAMP level is maintained. Leukocytes from ragweed-allergic individuals exposed to ragweed antigen E had a dose-dependent release of histamine. This was inhibited by increasing doses of epinephrine and, independently, by increasing doses of theophylline. In fact, the effect of these 2 drugs was synergistic in that an ineffective inhibitory dose either of epinephrine alone or of theophylline alone, when given together, resulted in important inhibition of histamine release. This synergistic effect of catecholamines and theophylline in the treatment of bronchospasm in asthma has been known for many years, and it is currently customary to use combinations of these drugs in single tablets for the major bronchodilator therapy of asthma.

The cholinergic or γ receptor in target cells appears to be guanylate cyclase, which occurs either in the membrane or in the cell cytoplasm. Inactive guanylate cyclase is converted by acetylcholine to active guanylate cyclase, and this converts guanosine triphosphate (GTP) into a cyclic nucleotide called cyclic 3′,5′-guanosine monophosphate (cGMP). In mast cells, the intracellular rise in cGMP is associated with an increase in mediator release. This release can be blocked by atropine. Similarly, in bronchial smooth muscle, a rise in intracellular rise in cGMP is associated with smooth muscle contraction which is blocked by atropine. cGMP is destroyed by phosphodiesterase by conversion to an inactive form, 5′-GMP, or guanyl monophosphate. Although both adenyl phosphodiesterase and guanyl phosphodiesterase are destroyed by the methylxanthines, it has been demonstrated recently that adenyl phosphodiesterase is about 10 times more susceptible to methylxanthine than is guanyl phosphodiesterase. This may explain the preferential action of methylxanthines on the cAMP system over that on the cGMP system and therefore its effectiveness in the treatment of asthma.

In summary, the biochemical modulation of mediator release from mast cells has been demonstrated using a preparation of IgE-sensitized cells prepared from minced human lung. This mediator release is illustrated in Fig 19–14.

THE BALANCE THEORY OF REGULATION CONTROLS

A balance has been proposed between cAMP and cGMP to maintain homeostatic controls of cell activation. This is illustrated in Fig 19–15. In an asthmatic individual, cholinergic stimulation through acetylcholine acting upon guanylate cyclase causes a rise in cGMP. In the mast cell, mediator release is augmented and the bronchial smooth muscle constricts. This mechanism is blocked by atropine. Guanyl phosphodiesterase inactivates the elevated cGMP, converting it to 5′-GMP and turning off the response. Asthmatic symptoms may be further augmented by norepineph-

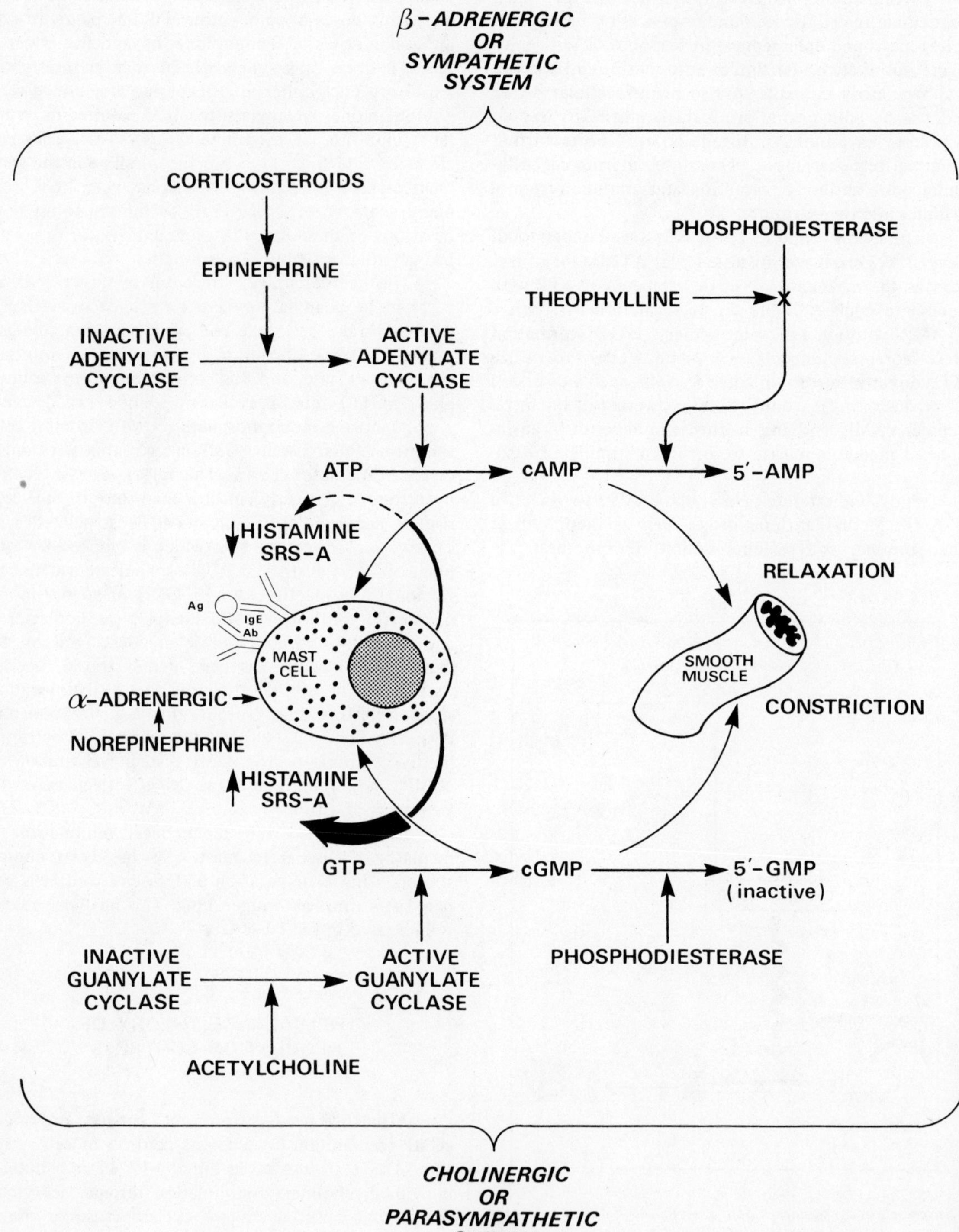

Figure 19–15. The balance theory of sympathetic and parasympathetic regulation.

rine, which stimulates the α-adrenergic receptor to decrease cAMP, and therefore augments the release of mediators from mast cells and possibly increases smooth muscle bronchoconstriction. This mechanism can be blocked by an α-adrenergic blocking agent such as phentolamine. Opposing these mechanisms is the cAMP system, in which epinephrine, isoproterenol, PGE_1 or PGE_2, and even histamine activate adenylate cyclase, which converts ATP to cAMP. This elevated cAMP level inhibits the release of mediators from the sensitized mast cells and results in bronchial smooth muscle relaxation. Methylxanthines such as theophylline further augment the cAMP level by inhibiting adenyl phosphodiesterase to prevent the destruction of cAMP. One action of corticosteroid hormones appears to be the improvement of epinephrine function on the β-adrenergic receptor to augment cAMP levels. This schema of a balance between cGMP and cAMP in asthma suggests that there are points in the mechanism which are likely to respond to pharmacologic control and could thus be of significance in the treatment of asthma.

THE β-ADRENERGIC BLOCKADE THEORY OF ASTHMA

It has been proposed that the basic problem in asthmatic individuals is a partial β-adrenergic blockade. Such a blockade would interfere with the homeostatic control of bronchi and target cells (mast cells and basophils).

The Hypothalamically "Imbalanced" Anaphylactic Guinea Pig

The anterior hypothalamus mediates parasympathetic responses, and the posterior hypothalamus mediates sympathetic responses. Electrolytic removal of one hypothalamic division, or electric stimulation of the antagonistic division, caused an autonomic imbalance in the guinea pig. Such a guinea pig, when sensitized for anaphylaxis, had markedly altered responses to antigen. There was only mild anaphylaxis when the anterior hypothalamus (parasympathetic) was removed, and there was great augmentation of anaphylaxis when the posterior hypothalamus (sympathetic) was removed. Correspondingly, similar effects were noted with electric stimulation of the appropriate hypothalamic area.

The *Bordetella pertussis*-Induced Hypersensitive State of Mice & Rats

The normal mouse or rat is a poor experimental animal in which to demonstrate anaphylaxis because these animals are relatively insensitive to histamine and serotonin. They form, primarily, IgG antibodies to soluble protein antigens. However, they are quite sensitive to catecholamines, with a marked rise in blood glucose following epinephrine injection.

B pertussis inoculation alters the responsiveness of mice and rats to the chemical mediators of anaphylaxis. Five days after *B pertussis* injection, these animals become extremely hypersensitive to histamine, serotonin, bradykinin, and, in one strain, to acetylcholine. They also become quite hypersensitive to cold, barometric pressure changes, and respiratory irritants. They become much less sensitive to catecholamines, responding with no rise in blood glucose after epinephrine injection. There is enhanced antibody formation, especially of the IgE class. *B pertussis* causes reduced functioning of the β-adrenergic receptors and therefore an autonomic imbalance. A similar β-adrenergic defect might account for the symptoms of asthma in humans.

In humans, such an autonomic imbalance would result in a disturbed homeostatic control of bronchi and target cells, resulting in a weak β-adrenergic response and an overactive cholinergic control. Such an imbalance could account for many of the nonimmunologic "triggers" of asthma attacks in man. These triggers include emotional upset, which is vagally mediated and inhibits the sympathetics; hyperirritable airways to cold, smoke, and irritant chemicals, which are cholinergically mediated and reversed by atropine; and nocturnal attacks, when histamine levels in the blood are highest and catecholamine and corticosteroid levels are lowest. The recumbent position also enhances cholinergic responsiveness. Furthermore, β-adrenergic blockade diverts the normal protein antigen-induced antibody formation from IgG and IgM classes to the IgE pathway. These features are all characteristic of human patients with asthma.

Hyperreactivity of the airways to inhaled small doses of methacholine is observed in asthmatic individuals and can be used as a differential diagnostic test for asthma. Although a β-adrenergic defect has been postulated in asthma, the same findings could be explained by a hyperreactive cholinergic receptor system. A defective response to isoproterenol (10 mM) has been demonstrated in mixed leukocytes of asthmatic individuals where there was no rise in cAMP level. On the contrary, in patients with hay fever and in normal control patients, there was a 3- or 4-fold rise in cAMP. Although a genetic defect in β-adrenergic receptors is postulated, most asthmatics have been treated with catecholamines and methylxanthines for long periods of time. This may have caused iatrogenic unresponsiveness of the β-adrenergic receptor. Therefore, the basis of the defect is under continued investigation.

Other investigators have studied patients with another atopic disease, atopic dermatitis (or eczema). Cultured epithelial cells from skin biopsies of normal patients underwent mitosis, which was inhibited by catecholamines in a β-adrenergic pattern—namely, isoproterenol inhibited more than epinephrine and epinephrine inhibited more than norepinephrine. On the other hand, skin biopsy epithelial cells from patients with atopic dermatitis, from both involved and uninvolved areas, underwent mitosis but were not inhibited by catecholamines. This suggested that patients with atopic dermatitis may also have a β-adrenergic

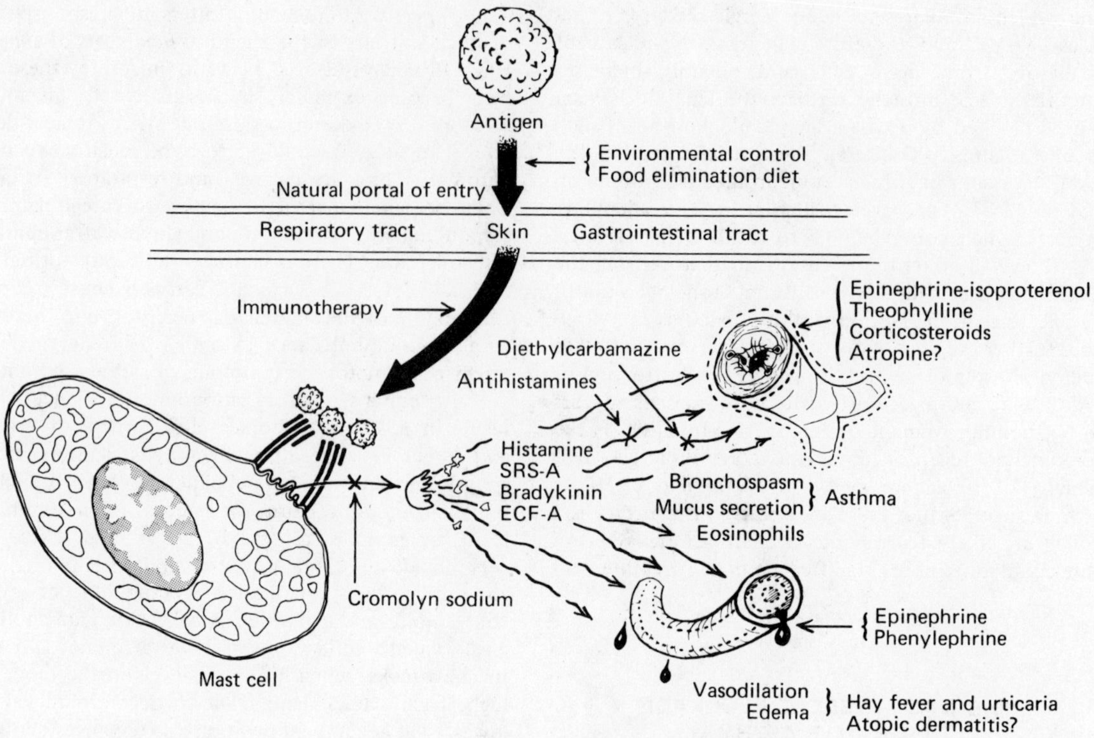

Figure 19–16. Therapeutic approaches to atopic reaction.

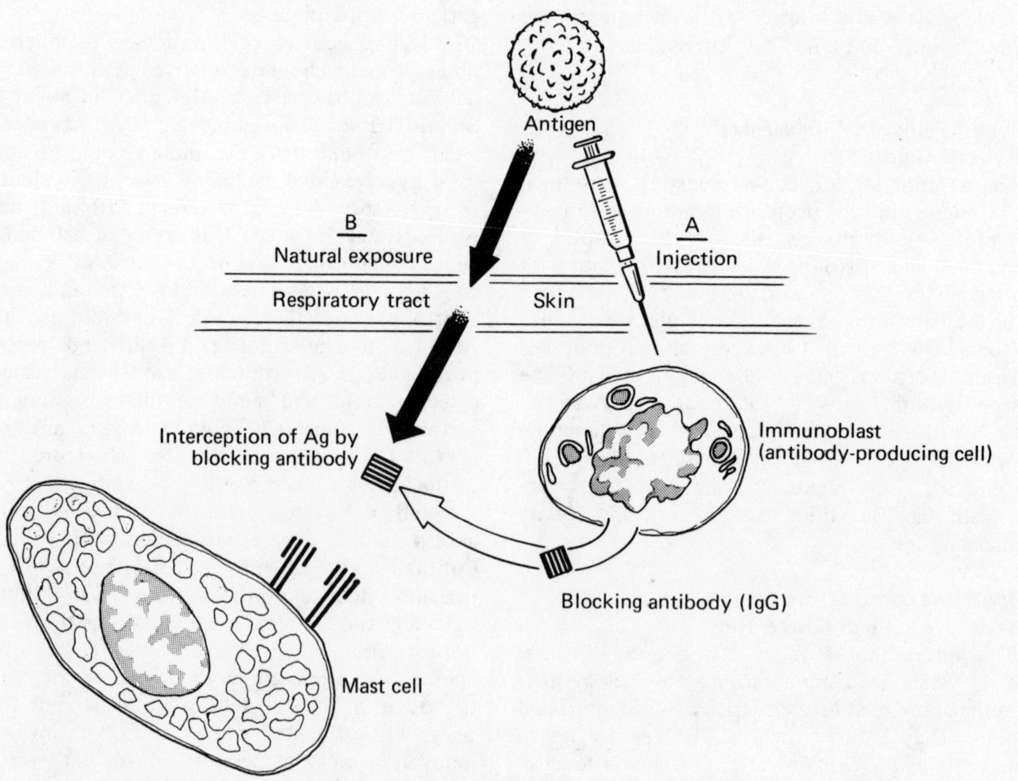

Figure 19–17. Immunization treatment.

abnormality, since cell mitosis is under β-adrenergic control.

Both patients with hay fever and patients with previous asthma (up to 22 years without an attack) show increased airway responsiveness to methacholine. This suggests a basic β-adrenergic defect in such patients.

In summary, either β-adrenergic blockade or cholinergic overreactivity could produce an autonomic imbalance and could account for increased airway irritability, for hypersensitivity to allergic mediators, for reduced sensitivity to catecholamines, and possibly for increased IgE production in certain allergic individuals.

Central Nervous System Reflexes in Patients With Asthma

Central neural control of bronchi is superimposed upon the biochemical sympathetic and parasympathetic agents acting upon target cells and smooth muscle cells. There are superficial irritant receptors in bronchi of animals and of humans. These receptors are stimulated by inhalation of irritating chemicals, such as sulfur dioxide and histamine, and by physical irritants such as cold air. Afferent fibers via the vagus nerve reach the brain stem, where they synapse with efferent vagal fibers returning to the bronchial smooth muscle. Stimulation of irritant receptors leads to a vagal reflex arc via the brain stem that results in reflex bronchial smooth muscle contraction and bronchospasm. In asthmatic individuals, these irritant receptors are hyperreactive, which is apparently the basis for the methacholine test. Asthmatic patients usually respond with bronchoconstriction to inhalations of 0.25 mg methacholine, whereas the nonallergic individual will rarely react to even 25 mg of this compound. A positive methacholine inhalation test is used as a differential diagnostic test for asthma.

In a dog model of asthma, which responds with bronchoconstriction after exposure to inhaled antigen, deposition of antigen into one bronchus via a tube caused bronchospasm in both lungs. This indicates that a reflex arc controlling bronchospasm exists. As a result of an antigen-antibody reaction on the surface of a mast cell in the bronchus, histamine is released which acts upon irritant receptors to initiate the vagal reflex, resulting in bronchospasm. This is an alternative to the direct effect of histamine on bronchial smooth muscles. Parenteral or locally administered atropine blocks the bronchospasm following an antigen inhalation challenge in such asthmatic dogs and in similar allergic humans. Cooling blocks vagus impulses. In an asthmatic dog with the vagi surgically exposed and cooled with ice water, antigen-induced bronchospasm could be stopped within seconds by cooling the vagus. Upon warming the vagus, bronchospasm returned promptly, only to be terminated on recooling the vagus. The relative degree of the importance of the vagal reflex bronchospasm versus direct histamine-induced bronchospasm in asthma is currently under study by several groups.

APPROACHES TO THE TREATMENT OF ALLERGY BASED UPON THE MECHANISM OF THE REACTION

The first point of attack on the allergic mechanism is identification of the specific allergen by a careful history and skin test with subsequent avoidance of the allergen (Fig 19–16). This approach is frequently successful in the treatment of allergy due to animal danders, house dust, molds, or foods. The next point of attack is the antigen-antibody reaction on the surface of the mast cell. Immunotherapy or hyposensitizing injection of the allergen stimulates the formation of an IgG blocking antibody, which remains in the circulation or tissues. Upon exposure to antigen, these IgG blocking antibodies react with the antigen, forming a complex which is then removed by the reticuloendothelial system (Fig 19–17). If the antigen cannot reach the IgE on the target cells, the allergic reaction does not take place. In some patients, the clinical improvement correlates well with the degree of blocking antibodies present; in others, there is no correlation.

A second protective mechanism achieved by immunotherapy is the induction of IgE immune tolerance in which IgE antibody production is suppressed by continued immunotherapy. If little or no IgE is produced, then continued sensitization of the mast cell does not occur. (See Chapter 29 for a discussion of the beneficial effects of allergen injections.)

A third action of immunotherapy is nonspecific target cell desensitization, the mechanism of which is unknown. Children with both ragweed and Alternaria allergies, when treated with ragweed alone, had a decrease in the leukocyte histamine release with both ragweed and Alternaria. In fact, histamine release with anti-IgE antibodies was also dramatically reduced, indicating that the basophils were "desensitized." There are perhaps additional mechanisms by which immunotherapy works as well.

The next area of allergy therapy is the enzyme cascade leading to release of histamine from mast cells, with attempts to stabilize lysosomal membranes in the mast cell. Cromolyn sodium acts by preventing the release of mediators from mast cell granules, probably by stabilizing lysosomal membranes. It does not prevent the antigen-antibody reaction. Previously it had been suggested that glucocorticoids stabilize lysosomal membranes; whether this actually occurs in humans is still under investigation.

Another action of corticosteroids is the inhibition of histidine decarboxylase, an enzyme which converts histidine into histamine. In guinea pigs, repeated treatment with compound 48/80 causes mast cells to lose their histamine content. In the presence of corticosteroids, mast cells fail to reaccumulate histamine until corticosteroids are withdrawn. Huge concentrations of corticosteroids in man (eg, 300 mg prednisone) could conceivably inhibit antibody formation, but this is not an effect found with the usual dosage of corticosteroids given to man.

The next area of therapeutic attack is interference with the action of the mediators of allergy. Prior administration of antihistamines, which resemble histamine in chemical structure, blocks histamine receptors on shock organ cells. When histamine is subsequently released, the receptors are occupied, and histamine is unable to act and is promptly destroyed by monoamine oxidases. Diethylcarbamazine appears to have a similar competitive action for SRS-A. Furthermore, the enzyme arylsulfatase can destroy SRS-A.

Finally, one can attempt to treat allergic diseases by counteracting the effects of the allergic reaction on the shock organ. As outlined above, biochemical control of mediator release and smooth muscle contraction can be counteracted both by appropriate blocking agents (atropine to block the cholinergics, phentolamine to block the α-adrenergics) and by reinforcment the β-adrenergic system with isoproterenol and exogenous epinephrine.

• • •

References

Ahlquist RP: A study of the adrenotropic receptors. Am J Physiol 153:586, 1948.

Bennich H: Structure of IgE. Prog Immunol 2:49, 1974.

Berg TLO, Johansson SGO: Allergy diagnosis with the radioallergosorbent test (RAST). J Allergy Clin Immunol 54:209, 1974.

Berg TLO, Johansson SGO: IgE concentration in children with atopic diseases. Int Arch Allergy Appl Immunol 36:219, 1969.

Berrens L: The chemistry of atopic allergens. Monogr Allergy 7:1, 1971.

Frick OL: The atopic state: A particular kind of immune reaction. Ann Allergy 24:95, 1966.

Gleich GJ & others: Measurement of the potency of allergy extracts by their inhibitory capacities in the radioallergosorbent test. J Allergy Clin Immunol 53:158, 1974.

Gold WM, Kessler GF, Yu DYC: Role of vagus nerves in experimental asthma in allergic dogs. J Appl Physiol 33:719, 1972.

Ishizaka K, Ishizaka T: Physicochemical properties of reaginic antibody. 1. Association of reaginic activity with an immunoglobulin other than γA or γG globulin. J Allergy 37:169, 1966.

Ishizaka T, Soto CS, Ishizaka K: Mechanisms of passive sensitization. 3. Number of IgE molecules and their receptor sites on human basophil granulocytes. J Immunol 111:500, 1973.

Johansson SGO: Raised levels of a new immunoglobulin class (IgND) in asthma. Lancet 2:951, 1967.

Levine BB & others: Ragweed hay fever: Genetic control and linkage to HL-A haplotypes. Science 178:1201, 1972.

Levy DA: Manipulation of the immune response to antigens in the management of atopic disease in man. Page 239 in: *Conference on the Biological Role of the IgE System.* Ishizaka K, Dayton DH Jr (editors). US Department of Health, Education, & Welfare, 1973.

Lichtenstein LM, Norman PS: Human allergic reactions. Am J Med 46:163, 1969.

May CD & others: Significance of concordant fluctuation and loss of leukocyte sensitivity to two allergens during injection therapy with one nonspecific desensitization. J Allergy Clin Immunol 50:99, 1972.

Norman PS: Present status of hyposensitization treatment. Page 460 in: *Allergology.* Rose B (editor). Excerpta Medica Foundation, 1968.

Orange RP, Austen KF: Chemical mediators of immediate hypersensitivity. Page 115 in: *Immunobiology.* Good RA, Fisher DW (editors). Sinauer Associates, 1971.

Orange RP, Murphy RC, Austen KF: Inactivation of slow reacting substance of anaphylaxins (SRS-A) by arylsulfatases. J Immunol 113:316, 1974.

Sutherland EW: On the biological role of cyclic AMP. JAMA 214:1281, 1970.

Szentivanyi A: The beta-adrenergic theory of the atopic abnormality in bronchial allergy. J Allergy 42:201, 1968.

Tada T, Ishizaka K: Distribution of IgE-forming cells in lymphoid tissues of human and monkey. J Immunol 104:377, 1970.

Townley RG, Ryo UY, Kang B: Bronchial sensitivity to methacholine in asthmatic subjects free of symptoms for one to 21 years. J Allergy 47:91, 1971.

Widdicombe JG, Kent DC, Nadel JA: Mechanism of bronchoconstriction during inhalation of dust. J Appl Physiol 17:613, 1962.

20 . . .
Immune Mechanisms in Tissue Damage

J. Vivian Wells, MD

Traditionally, it has been thought that a major stimulus to the development of these immune responses is protection against microorganisms which threaten the welfare of the host (see Chapter 17). It is now clear, however, that these protective immune responses also may prove deleterious to the host, as is the case in autoimmune disorders (see Chapter 14). Thus, immune responses to an infecting organism may eradicate the organism but at the same time produce significant pathologic or even lethal effects in the host. Pathogenetic mechanisms that can produce both beneficial and deleterious effects will be described in this chapter as immune mechanisms that cause tissue damage.

Various immune mechanisms involved in the production of tissue damage were classified in 1963 by Gell and Coombs into 4 basic types:

- **Type I**: Anaphylactic
- **Type II**: Cytotoxic
- **Type III**: Arthus type and antigen-antibody complexes
- **Type IV**: Delayed hypersensitivity

This classification does not depend on the host species nor on the method of antigen exposure. In this chapter the classification of Gell and Coombs will be used as a basis for the discussion of immune mechanisms in tissue damage (Fig 20–1).

TYPE I REACTIONS

Anaphylactic or reagin-dependent reactions are also termed immediate hypersensitivity reactions to distinguish them from reactions associated with delayed hypersensitivity (type IV). Immediate hypersensitivity was discussed in Chapter 19, but certain aspects will be discussed here for comparison with mechanisms involved in type II, III, and IV reactions.

Type I reactions are produced by pharmacologically active substances released from tissue cells, such as basophils and mast cells, following reaction between antigen and specific antibody adsorbed to the tissue cell membrane. Depending on the mode of administration of antigen, the clinical features may be systemic or local. Generalized anaphylaxis includes the following abnormalities in different systems: (1) Respiratory tract: bronchial obstruction and laryngeal edema. (2) Gastrointestinal tract: nausea, vomiting, cramping pain, and diarrhea (occasionally with blood in the stool). (3) Cardiovascular system: hypotension and shock. (4) Skin: very pruritic, circumscribed, discrete wheals with raised, erythematous serpiginous borders and blanched centers. These may coalesce into giant hives resembling angioedema.

The various factors involved in the production of anaphylactic responses will now be summarized briefly.

Components of Type I Reactions

A. Reaginic Antibodies: Reaginic antibodies are also called *homocytotropic antibodies* because of their autologous tissue-binding properties. Most of the antibodies responsible for type I reactions in man belong to the IgE class. Studies in lower species have demonstrated a class of antibodies comparable to human IgE. Many lower species also contain specialized IgG antibodies which can bind to tissues and function as reaginic antibodies producing type I reactions. The binding of reaginic antibodies is accomplished via the Fc region of the molecule.

Guinea pig passive cutaneous anaphylaxis is the passive transfer of guinea pig anaphylactic serum antibody by intradermal injection into an area of shaved skin. This injection is followed 4–24 hours later by an intravenous injection of specific antigen and Evans blue dye. The site of interaction is demarcated by extravasation of blue dye from the dilated blood vessels. The comparable test in man is the classical Prausnitz-Küstner (PK) reaction. In this test, serum from a *sensitized* subject is injected into the skin of a *nonsensitive* recipient, and the recipient is challenged with antigen after a latent period of at least 12 hours. The classical wheal-and-erythema response may be elicited up to 6 weeks after the first injection. This test is no longer routinely used because there is a risk of transfer of serum hepatitis and because methods for the measurement of serum concentrations of total IgE and specific IgE class antibody have become available.

The physicochemical characteristics of IgE are

J. Vivian Wells is Senior Staff Specialist in Clinical Immunology, Kolling Institute of Medical Research, Royal North Shore Hospital of Sydney, St. Leonards, N.S.W. 2065, Australia.

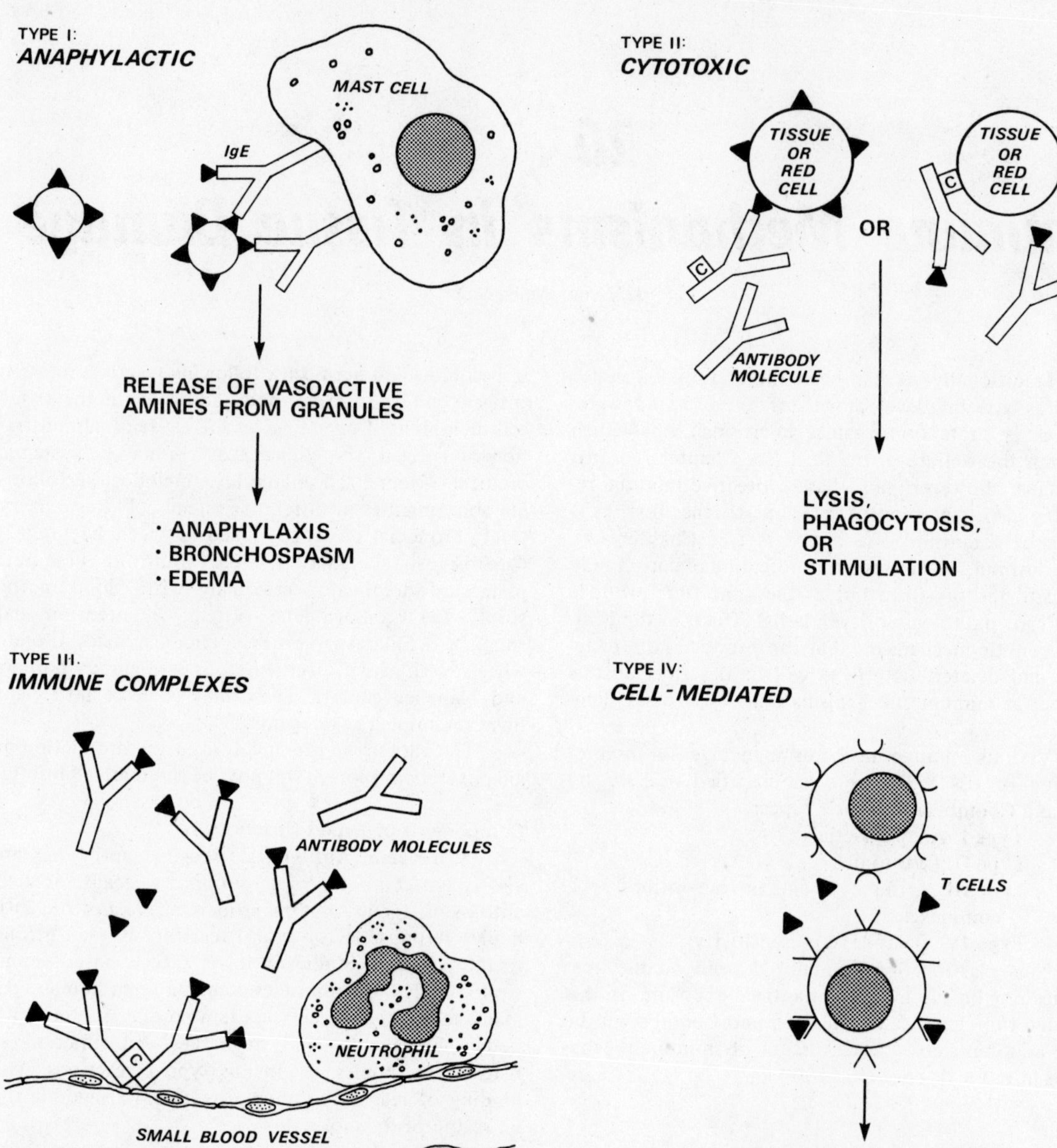

Figure 20–1. Schematic diagrams of the 4 types of immunologic mechanisms which may produce tissue damage. The diagrams are described in the text. C indicates complement; ▲, antigen; U and V, specific receptors for antigens.

summarized in Chapter 2, but it is emphasized that the serum concentration of IgE in normal subjects is approximately 0.004% that of IgG (Chapter 19). The Fc region of the IgE molecule is heat-labile, and heating results in loss of the ability of IgE to passively sensitize tissue cells.

B. Antigen (Allergen): Many antigens are capable of inducing IgE antibody under appropriate conditions. Systemic anaphylaxis is most likely encountered following exposure of a sensitized subject to compounds such as heterologous proteins (antisera, hormones, enzymes, Hymenoptera venom, pollen extract, and food), polysaccharides (iron dextran), diagnostic agents (iodinated contrast materials, sulfobromophthalein), and therapeutic agents (antibiotics, vitamins). The IgE antibody response to an antigen is T-dependent and is under complex genetic control. For example, the IgE and IgG antibody responses to Ra5, an allergen from ragweed pollen, are clinically associated with histocompatibility antigen HLA-B7.

C. Tissue Cells (Basophils and Mast Cells): A basophil or mast cell possesses membrane receptors capable of binding the Fc region of IgE molecules. Bound IgE molecules are in a state of dynamic equilibrium since

Fc fragments of IgE molecules compete with whole IgE molecules for the receptor. Bridging of adjacent membrane IgE molecules by specific antigen initiates a series of biochemical changes resulting in the release of the active substances stored in mast cells and basophils. It is probable that considerably fewer than 100 IgE molecules must be activated to initiate this exquisitely sensitive process. In experimental conditions, it is possible to induce release of vasoactive amines by the addition of aggregated IgE antibodies to mast cells or basophils. Complement is not involved in this reaction. In man, as noted above, IgE is the reaginic antibody classically responsible for binding to target cells and inducing anaphylaxis. Rare instances occur, however, where IgG myeloma proteins are capable of inhibiting the binding of IgE reaginic antibodies to monkey lung tissue and the release of histamine.

Conditions other than the reaction between reaginic antibodies and antigen can result in the release of vasoactive amines from target cells. The chemical detergent 48/80 is frequently used in experimental studies to induce the release of vasoactive amines from target cells. Activation of either the alternative or classical pathways of complement can generate a factor which releases histamine from both nonsensitized and sensitized human basophils in the absence of antibody. Complement-mediated release of vasoactive amines consistently occurs more quickly than allergen-mediated release.

D. Intracellular Biochemical Events: The postulated sequence of biochemical events occurring in the target cell following antigen bridging of IgE molecules on the surface of the target cell and resulting in the release of vasoactive amines is summarized in Fig 20–2. There are several steps in the process with varying requirements for energy, and several factors are known to influence the process at different stages.

(1) Activation of a cellular proesterase requires entry of extracellular Ca^{++} into the cell. This step is inhibited by diisopropyl fluorophosphate and is associated with contraction of microfilaments.

(2) Additional proesterase is activated autocatalytically.

(3) An energy-requiring stage with microfilaments moving granules alongside microtubules or plasma membrane is inhibited by glucose deprivation (eg, 2-deoxyglucose).

(4) A further step requiring Ca^{++} is inhibited by ethylenediaminetetraacetic acid.

(5) A step leading to release of amines (perhaps exchanged for Na^{+}) is inhibited by elevation of the intracellular concentration of cAMP.

Considering the multiple biochemical stages, the multiple levels of inhibition, and, in particular, the importance of intracellular concentrations of cAMP and cGMP, it is not surprising that several pharmacologic agents influence the rate of release of vasoactive amines from target cells. These drugs act at different levels on α-adrenergic, β-adrenergic, and prostaglandin receptors. It was known for almost 40 years that epinephrine could suppress antigen-induced type I reactions. This is now known to be due to its action as a β-adrenergic agent by stimulating adenylate cyclase activity, which leads to an increased intracellular concentration of cAMP. This in turn suppresses the release of vasoactive amines. Conversely, α-adrenergic agents, which produce reductions in intracellular concentrations of cAMP, lead to increased release of vasoactive amines.

The reader is referred to Chapter 19 for a detailed discussion of vasoactive amines and the histochemistry and pharmacology of anaphylactic reactions.

E. Pharmacologically Active Amines:

1. Histamine–Histamine is the most important

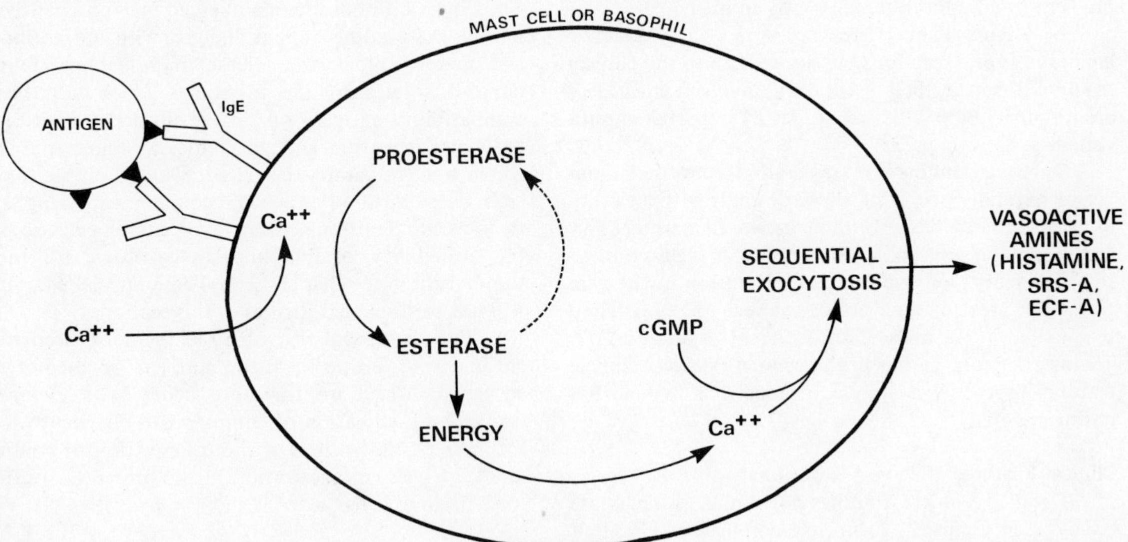

Figure 20–2. Schematic diagram of the major biochemical events in a Type I reaction which follows antigen-bridging of IgE molecules on a target cell and results in release of vasoactive amines.

vasoactive amine, but the observation that antihistamine compounds failed both in experimental situations and in clinical applications to control all the manifestations of type I reactions led to the realization that a mixture of vasoactive amines is generally released from target cells. Histamine exists in a preformed state within granules in mast cells, basophils, platelets, and perhaps other tissue cells. The in vivo effects of histamine in man are mainly of the erythematous and angioedematous type and are attributed to increased capillary permeability secondary to partial interruption of vascular endothelium. Histamine also produces increased respiratory airway resistance.

2. Slow-reacting substance of anaphylaxis (SRS-A)–SRS-A does not exist in a preformed state, but its production is induced during a type I anaphylactic reaction. Its origins and chemical structure are disputed. It appears to be an acidic lipid with a molecular weight of 400–500 and an exquisite capacity for producing both increased vascular permeability and contraction of smooth muscle. It is not inhibited by antihistamines.

3. Eosinophil chemotactic factor of anaphylaxis (ECF-A)–ECF-A was discovered when it was established that neither histamine nor SRS-A was chemotactic for human eosinophils. ECF-A exists in a preformed state in the mast cell granule as an acidic peptide with a molecular weight of 500–600.

4. Serotonin–Serotonin (5-hydroxytryptamine) exists in a preformed state in the granules of mast cells, platelets, and enterochromaffin cells. It causes capillary dilatation, increased permeability, and smooth muscle contraction (in some species). It is probably not an important vasoactive amine in type I reactions in man.

5. Heparin–Heparin is an acidic mucopolysaccharide which accounts for metachromatic staining of mast cell granules by basic dyes. It contributes to anaphylaxis in dogs but not apparently in man.

6. Kinins–Kinins are not primary vasoactive amines in type I reactions but contribute to the clinical features through their secondary involvement. They are discussed with other examples of humoral amplification systems on p 239.

7. Prostaglandins–Prostaglandins comprise a number of naturally occurring aliphatic acids with a variety of biologic activities including increased permeability and dilatation of capillaries, smooth muscle contraction, bronchial constriction, and alteration in the pain threshold. Most of their actions appear to be mediated by changes in the intracellular concentration of cAMP. Their exact role in the production of various clinical features in type I anaphylactic reactions in man has not been defined.

Clinical Features of Type I Reactions

Detailed clinical findings in human subjects are discussed in Chapter 29, but it is emphasized here that the division into general and local type I anaphylactic reactions is artificial. The general reaction is associated with widespread dissemination of the antigen with systemic symptoms of edema, urticaria, and bronchial constriction. The local reaction is manifested most frequently in diagnostic skin tests, but such a patient should be considered sensitized on a systemic basis; the local administration of an excessive amount of antigen or the intravenous administration of a small amount of antigen to such a patient may be accompanied by generalized anaphylaxis.

TYPE II REACTIONS

Type II reactions are classically considered to be cytotoxic in character and involve the combination of IgG or IgM antibodies with antigenic determinants on a cell membrane. Alternatively, a free antigen or hapten may be adsorbed to a tissue component or cell membrane, and antibody subsequently combines with this adsorbed antigen. Complement fixation frequently occurs in this situation and leads to cell damage. There are situations, however, particularly in experimental studies, where the combination of cell-bound antigen and antibody does not result in damage to the cell membrane. The combination may in fact lead to stimulation of the cell, some examples being long-acting thyroid stimulator (LATS) (see Chapter 35), antilymphocyte antisera, and anti-immunoglobulin antisera. The latter 2 examples are documented in experimental studies, but their role in vivo has not been clarified.

Blocking antibody is another example of the second (cell-stimulating) type of type II reaction. Some antibodies to an antigen competitively inhibit the reaction between that antigen and antibodies of a different class or with different biologic properties. Thus, IgG antibodies to an allergen may competitively inhibit the binding of that allergen with IgE antibody and thereby block the release of vasoactive amines. Other examples include antibodies which mask histocompatibility antigens on tissue cells and permit them to escape rejection and antibodies in cancer patients which bind to tumor-associated antigens on the tumor cell. These antibodies are not complement-fixing, and they permit continued growth of tumor cells despite the availability of lymphocytes cytotoxic for those tumor cells (see Chapter 21). These special examples will not be discussed further in this section.

The usual sequelae of attachment of circulating antibody to either a tissue antigen or membrane-adsorbed antigen are, therefore, cell lysis or cell inactivation with activation of complement; phagocytosis of the target cells with or without activation of complement; or lysis or inactivation in the presence of effector lymphoid cells.

COMPLEMENT-DEPENDENT ANTIBODY LYSIS

The target for the cytotoxic reaction may be either a formed blood element or a specific cell type within a particular tissue.

Formed Blood Elements

A. Red Blood Cells: Red cell lysis is the most important clinical instance involving type II cytotoxic reactions. The lysis of red blood cells by antibody and complement has been extensively studied in vitro, and there are numerous examples of similar mechanisms operating in vivo. After transfusion with grossly incompatible blood, red cell lysis may occur intravascularly. If antibodies against relatively minor determinants are present, direct cell lysis may not occur but the binding of antibody to the red cell antigen leads to increased phagocytosis by cells of the monocyte-macrophage system, especially in the spleen. Complement is frequently (not always) involved in this process. Similar phenomena also occur when subjects become sensitized to red blood cell antigens following bacterial or viral infection or after interaction with drugs which alter the red cell membrane. The clinical features of autoimmune hemolytic anemia and drug-induced hemolytic anemia are discussed in Chapter 28.

B. Platelets: Platelets are lysed by a variety of mechanisms which result in the release of biologically active components such as serotonin and factors which operate in the early stages of coagulation. Platelet sensitization may be associated with antibody, as in idiopathic thrombocytopenic purpura, or with antidrug antibodies, as in Sedormid- or quinidine-induced thrombocytopenia (see below and Chapter 28).

C. Polymorphonuclear Leukocytes: Granulocytopenia may result from type II cytotoxic reactions associated with antibodies specific for granulocytes or antibodies to drugs adsorbed onto the granulocyte surface. This is an uncommon mechanism for the production of granulocytopenia, however, compared to bone marrow suppression or direct toxic effects of drugs on granulocytes.

D. Lymphocytes: Interest in this phenomenon was stimulated by the discovery that certain diseases, such as systemic lupus erythematosus, are associated with cold-reactive serum antibodies specific for lymphocytes. In vitro tests indicate that some of these antibodies can specifically lyse T cells. The relevance of these cells to other features of systemic lupus erythematosus is not known.

Kidney

Type II reactions can be produced in almost any tissue by inducing heterologous antibodies to different tissue components and by varying the conditions under which the antibody is introduced into the experimental animal. In practical terms, some tissues or organs have been studied extensively in lower species and are of great importance in man, eg, the kidney.

Nephrotoxic serum nephritis has been experimentally induced in numerous animal species by the injection of heterologous antibody against a renal extract. The antigen may be either a crude homogenate of kidney or highly purified components of glomerular basement membrane. The main effects are seen in glomeruli and occur in 2 stages. The heterologous phase is seen a few hours after the administration of the antibody and is characterized by proteinuria, reduced glomerular filtration, and polymorphonuclear infiltration of the glomeruli. This stage is due to the administered heterologous nephrotoxic antibody and is short-lived. Within 4–6 days, the autologous stage is reached, with further indications of glomerular damage caused by the host antibody response. An increase in the dose of heterologous antibody increases the severity of the inflammatory reaction and may cause the death of the animal from renal failure within 2–3 weeks. The degree of tissue damage and inflammation is directly related to the degree of involvement of various humoral amplification systems which will be discussed later in this chapter. They include activation of the complement system, in particular C3a and C5a (see Chapter 6), the release of lysosomal enzymes from polymorphonuclear leukocytes, the deposition of fibrinogen or fibrin in the glomeruli, and other as yet undetermined factors. If complement depletion is achieved in an animal by treatment with cobra venom factor, the polymorphonuclear leukocyte inflammatory response does not appear and the glomeruli are generally spared damage. Factors other than complement components chemotactic for polymorphonuclear leukocytes are involved, however, since proteinuria can be produced in animals depleted of complement or polymorphonuclear leukocytes if sufficiently large amounts of injected antibody are deposited along the glomerular basement membrane.

An alternative method of inducing nephritis secondary to antibody reacting with glomerular basement membrane is to inject antigens isolated from glomerular basement membrane. This has been confirmed in several species, including rabbits, monkeys, and sheep. In the sensitized animal, antibodies to glomerular basement membrane may be detected in the serum or may be deposited in a linear pattern along the membrane. Antibodies can be eluted from the affected kidney and produce a similar pattern of nephritis when reinjected into another animal of the same species. Circulating antibodies directed against the glomerular basement membrane will persist in the circulation of nephrectomized animals, and these antibodies can be transferred in cross-circulation experiments to a previously healthy animal of the same species.

Deposition of antibodies in a linear pattern along the human glomerular basement membrane occurs in 3 types of disease states:

(1) Subjects who received renal allografts in the earlier years of renal transplantation were generally treated with antilymphocyte antiserum. Most of these early antilymphocyte antisera are now known to have contained antibodies against glomerular basement membrane antigens. These antibodies were apparently

formed in response to lymphocyte membrane antigens which shared antigenic determinants with glomerular basement membrane antigens. The species most often used to prepare the antilymphocyte antiserum were the horse, goat, and sheep. This heterologous antibody was injected into patients and then deposited along the glomerular basement membrane of the transplanted kidney. Its effects in producing renal disease were overshadowed in this situation by the process of graft rejection, but this situation is analogous to classical nephrotoxic serum nephritis.

(2) The classical example of linear deposition of glomerular basement membrane antibodies is Goodpasture's syndrome. The clinical features of this disease are discussed in Chapter 32, and it is mentioned briefly in this section. This deposition denotes the existence of antibodies with specificity for glomerular and pulmonary basement membranes. The deposition of antibodies in these 2 sites accounts for the main symptoms of hematuria, renal failure, and recurrent hemoptysis. The pattern of linear staining in a patient with Goodpasture's syndrome is shown in Fig 20–3.

(3) Immunofluorescent examination of renal biopsy specimens from patients with renal disease shows that linear deposition of antibodies to glomerular basement membrane may occur in several diseases, including scleroderma, diabetic glomerulonephritis, systemic lupus erythematosus, malignant hypertension, polyarteritis nodosa, or toxemia of pregnancy. The primary disease process leads to renal damage, and this in turn sensitizes the patient to glomerular basement membrane. Antibodies to glomerular basement membrane develop as a secondary phenomenon. These patients show only slight to moderate antibody deposition of the linear type with a coincidental granular deposition of preformed immune complexes and complement (see below). Fibrin deposition is frequently heavy in such cases.

Skin

Type II reactions caused by the deposition of circulating antibody along the basement membrane at the dermal-epidermal junction are termed pemphigoid disorders (see Chapter 33).

Other Tissues

Other tissues which have been studied include muscle, thyroid, myocardium, brain, testis, and ovary. Tissue homogenate is used to sensitize a homologous animal by injection in adjuvant, or an antiserum to the

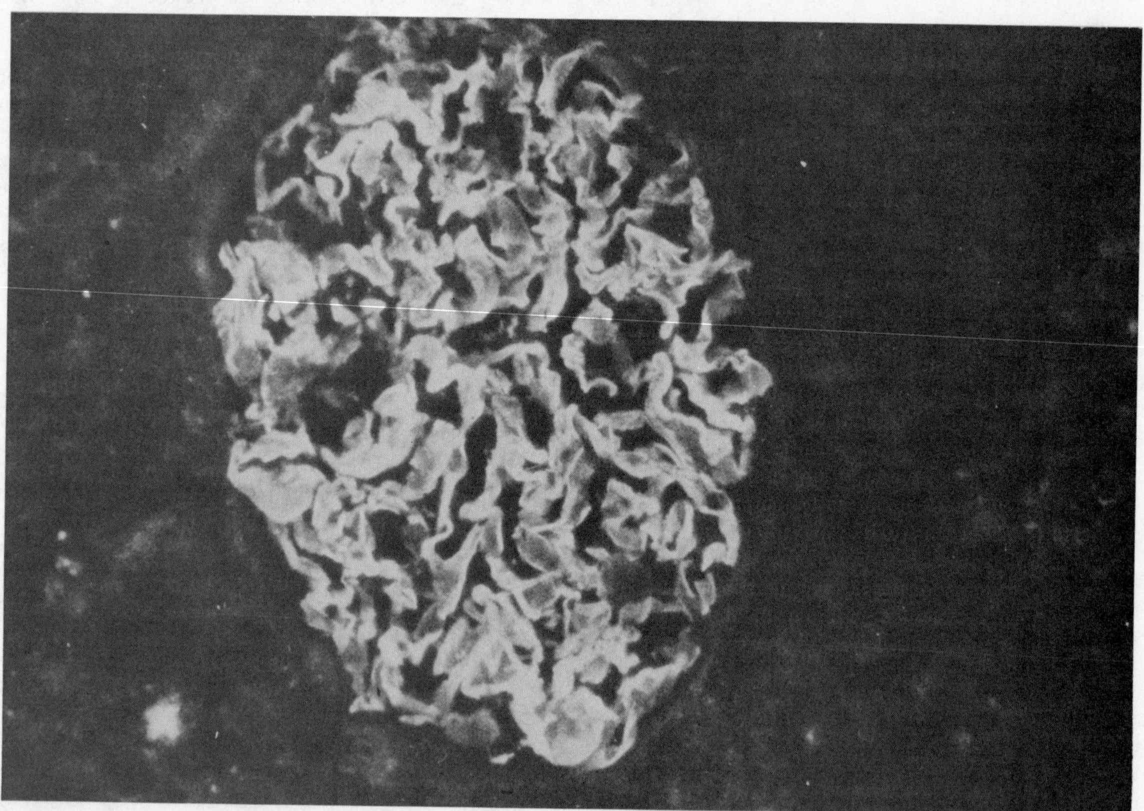

Figure 20–3. Direct immunofluorescence microscopy with fluorescein-labeled anti-IgG antiserum of a renal biopsy specimen demonstrating smooth, linear, ribbonlike deposition of IgG antibodies to glomerular basement membrane. The specimen was taken from a 16-year-old girl with Goodpasture's syndrome.

homogenate is prepared in a heterologous species. In each case, the production of tissue damage is thought to reflect the deposition of circulating heterologous or autologous antibody on target cells with subsequent lysis of the cell or damage to the tissue containing the particular antigen.

ANTIBODY-DEPENDENT CELL-MEDIATED CYTOTOXICITY

Considerable confusion has arisen in the last few years over the terminology, methodology, interpretation, and clinical application of cell lysis studies. In such studies, either circulating cells or tissue cells, such as lymphocytes or monocytes, are tested for their ability to lyse target cells. The test cell is prepared from a subject who may or may not be sensitized to antigens on the target cell, and the target cell may or may not be coated with complement. The roles of antibody and complement vary in different systems. It is appropriate in this section to discuss cell-mediated cytotoxic reactions which are antibody-dependent. These cytotoxicity tests therefore include several variables, including test cells, target cells, source of antibody, source of complement, and the label used to indicate or measure cell damage.

Test cells are most frequently isolated from peripheral blood in human subjects, but in experimental studies with animals they may be isolated from almost any lymphoid tissue. T cells are probably not able to mediate this type of cellular toxicity. The number of macrophages in the test cell population is also important in interpretation of the results.

A wide variety of target cells have been used from syngeneic, allogeneic, and xenogeneic animals. The most frequent target cells used in tests to determine the cytotoxic functions of human cells include chicken red blood cells, normal peripheral blood lymphocytes from other human subjects, human tumor cells, cells from long-term cultures of lymphoblastoid cell lines, and murine mastocytoma cells.

The antibody tested includes specific antibody to antigens on their target cells, antibody to antigens to which the donor of the test cell has been sensitized, and normal IgG. Complement is generally tested in the system by providing fresh serum from a human, rabbit, or guinea pig source.

The 3 main methods used to indicate damage or lysis of the cell are (1) entry of a dye into the cell, (2) loss of the ability of the cell to adhere to surfaces, and (3) loss of cell-bound ^{51}Cr. The measurement of ^{51}Cr released from ^{51}Cr-labeled target cells is now the most common method of measuring cytotoxicity. The mechanism proposed is that antibody or antibody-antigen complexes are attached to the target cell and are bound by their Fc regions to receptors for the Fc region on the membrane of the effector cell; the proximity of the test cell and the target cell then permits lysis of the target cell to occur. It is possible that complement components may be involved in this process, but their role is controversial. Antibody-dependent cell-mediated cytotoxicity requires only very small amounts of antibody to facilitate cell lysis. Much controversy still surrounds the identity of the main cell type responsible for this type of cytotoxicity. It is generally accepted that cells in the monocyte-macrophage series can lyse cells by this mechanism. The disagreement concerns the identity of the type of lymphocyte which can accomplish antibody-dependent cell-mediated cytotoxicity. The general methods used to characterize these populations of lymphocytes do not yield sufficient data to identify this cell. The view that these lymphocytes required a membrane receptor for the Fc region of antibody molecules to accomplish cell lysis led to the conclusion that these cells were B cells. This conclusion was disputed since other B cell markers could not be demonstrated consistently on these cells and it was shown that T cells could acquire an Fc receptor during lymphocyte transformation. Similarly, it could not be confirmed that these cells were T cells. The term killer cell or K cell has therefore been introduced to refer to this type of cell. Null cells, which lack both T and B cell markers, are probably identical to K cells.

Examples of cytotoxicity in the absence of antibody will be discussed in the section on type IV reactions.

TYPE III REACTIONS

These reactions are secondary to localization of antigen-antibody complexes in tissues, and inflamma-

Table 20–1. Pathogenesis of inflammatory lesions in type III reactions.

(1) Formation of antigen-antibody complexes (generally in antigen excess).
(2) Fixation of complement by the complexes.
(3) Release of complement components chemotactic for leukocytes.
(4) Damage to platelets, causing release of vasoactive amines.
(5) Increased vascular permeability.
(6) Localization of antigen-antibody complexes in vessel walls.
(7) Further fixation of complement and release of chemotactic factors.
(8) Infiltration with polymorphonuclear leukocytes.
(9) Ingestion of immune complexes by neutrophils and release of lysosomal enzymes.
(10) Damage to adjacent cells and tissues by lysosomal enzymes.
(11) Deposition of fibrin.
(12) Regression and healing if the lesion is due to a single dose of antigen, or chronic deposition and inflammation if there is continuing formation of immune complexes.

tion is the main feature. Classical reactions of this type are the *Arthus reaction* and *serum sickness.* Similar sequences of events occur in both examples and also in immune complex diseases, now increasingly recognized in clinical medicine. The pathogenesis of the characteristic inflammatory lesions in type III reactions is summarized in Table 20–1.

ARTHUS REACTION

The classical Arthus reaction is produced in experimental animals by the local tissue interaction between antigen and circulating antibody. This results in destructive inflammation of small blood vessels, ie, vasculitis. Following intradermal injection of antigen into an appropriately sensitized animal, the area shows local swelling and erythema in 1–2 hours. This reaction increases to a maximum 3–6 hours after injection and disappears within 10–12 hours. Microscopic examination of the tissue shows neutrophils initially, and these cells are replaced by mononuclear cells and eosinophils with degradation of phagocytosed immune complexes and disappearance of the inflammation. When a limited amount of antibody is available for experimental study, the antibody can be injected intradermally and an Arthus reaction can then be induced by injection of the antigen either into the site where the antibody was previously injected or into the bloodstream.

Probable clinical counterparts of Arthus type reactions with local concentrations of antigen are various examples of *hypersensitivity pneumonitis* or *extrinsic allergic alveolitis* from inhalation of organic dusts. In these cases, the inhaled antigens may be fungal in origin, may be associated with insects, or may be heterologous proteins such as avian proteins in bird handler's pneumonitis. Fungi frequently involved are thermophilic actinomycetes and *Micropolyspora faeni.* The clinical features are described in detail in Chapter 31, but a characteristic feature of the acute disease is the onset of symptoms of chills, cough, dyspnea, and fever 4–6 hours after inhalation of the responsible antigen. The usual pattern is resolution of such an attack within 12–18 hours, although some residual pulmonary findings may persist for several days.

SERUM SICKNESS

The term serum sickness classically refers to the combination of symptoms and signs seen in patients 3 days to 3 weeks after the injection of foreign (heterologous) serum. It includes fever, malaise, urticarial and erythematous skin rashes, arthralgia, lymphadenopathy, and splenomegaly. The abnormal findings usually subside within 1–2 weeks. In the first 4 decades of this century, it was not uncommon for up to 50% of patients to develop this reaction after treatment with horse serum as an antiserum to diphtheria, tetanus, or other organisms. It has almost disappeared in these situations, since alternative methods of active immunization have been developed for these diseases, but it is still seen in developing countries. In developed countries the reaction now occurs as serum sickness reactions to drugs such as penicillin and in patients after renal allotransplantation who receive heterologous antilymphocyte serum to suppress or prevent graft rejection. A key feature in serum sickness is the formation of antigen-antibody complexes in the bloodstream and their subsequent deposition at various sites throughout the body. Many diseases are now known to be associated with formation of intravascular immune complexes, although these complexes are variably involved in the production of symptoms and signs in different diseases. Diseases associated with significant clinical features secondary to formation and deposition of immune complexes are now collectively termed the *immune complex disorders.*

IMMUNE COMPLEX DISORDERS

Immunologic Pathogenesis

Some of these disorders are listed in Table 20–2. It should be emphasized that pathogenetic mechanisms listed in Table 20–1 operate to varying degrees in these disorders and are influenced by many factors. These factors include the nature of the host, antigen, antibody, antigen-antibody complexes, complement, platelets, and polymorphonuclear leukocytes. In many cases, these factors can only be studied in experimental animals.

A. Host: Animal species vary greatly in their propensity to develop the manifestations of immune complex disorders. Rabbits have been studied in detail as experimental animals since they develop a variety of pathologic lesions after single or multiple injections of selected foreign antigens. Several species are known to be affected by certain types of persistent long-term virus infections, including lymphocytic choriomeningitis in mice, equine infectious anemia in horses, and Aleutian mink disease. It also appears that genetic factors are important within a species, since different strains of mice show varying degrees of susceptibility to persistent virus infections. Although it is an accepted clinical observation that some families have a greater than normal susceptibility to certain diseases associated with immune complex deposition (eg, rheumatoid arthritis), the level at which these genetic factors operate has not been clarified. Since the various phenomena associated with immune complexes can only develop in the presence of antibody, there must be some form of genetic control at the level of immune response genes with development of appropriate antibody response to injected antigen (see Chapter 12).

Table 20–2. Examples of human diseases associated with immune complexes detectable in plasma and deposited in tissues.

Microbial infections
Bacterial and spirochetal
Acute poststreptococcal glomerulonephritis
Syphilis
Mycoplasmal pneumonia
Subacute bacterial endocarditis
Shunt nephritis *(Staphylococcus albus)*
Lepromatous leprosy
Viral
Chronic HB_SAg infections
HB_SAg in polyarteritis nodosa
Guillain-Barré syndrome
Infectious mononucleosis glomerulonephritis
Parasitic infections
Malarial nephrotic syndrome
Tropical splenomegaly syndrome
Leishmaniasis
Trypanosomiasis
Schistosomiasis
Disseminated malignancy
Solid tumors
Carcinoma of lung
Carcinoma of breast
Carcinoma of colon
Malignant melanoma
Leukemia
Acute lymphoblastic leukemia
Chronic lymphocytic leukemia
Lymphoma: Hodgkin's disease
Autoimmune disorders
Systemic lupus erythematosus
Hashimoto's thyroiditis
Rheumatoid arthritis
Miscellaneous
Essential mixed cryoglobulinemia
Celiac disease
Dermatitis herpetiformis
Crohn's disease
Ulcerative colitis
Henoch-Schönlein nephritis
Hepatic cirrhosis
Sickle cell anemia
Drug reactions
Serum sickness
Penicillamine nephropathy

B. Antigen: Almost any injected foreign antigen which elicits a detectable antibody response can lead to the development of immune complex deposition. However, the traditional method of producing an immune complex disorder has been injection of serum from a heterologous species. Such a serum contains many different foreign serum proteins, and this was a problem in defining the contributing factors during experimental studies. Accordingly, experiments were done with single foreign serum proteins—eg, BSA—injected into a selected species such as the rabbit. The pathologic effects of injected antigens vary according to the injection protocol. A single injection is likely to be associated with healing, as in serum sickness. However, the intravenous injection of a large dose of antigen to a previously sensitized animal may, if the patient or animal escapes death from immediate type I anaphylactic reaction, exhibit a severe type III reaction with an accelerated onset within 4 days. In this case, the histologic findings are those of an acute Arthus reaction.

Foreign extrinsic antigens other than foreign serum proteins can produce immune complex disorders. These include a variety of bacterial and viral organisms and therapeutic agents such as drugs (see Table 20–2). In many cases, the drugs act as haptens bound to serum proteins to elicit the appropriate antibody responses and thence immune complex deposition.

Persistent or continuous administration of antigen leads to an increased deposition of immune complexes in the renal glomeruli. This may occur with exogenous antigen in experimental animals, with endogenous antigens such as nucleic acid antigens (as in systemic lupus erythematosus), and with infection with persistent replicating viruses. In exogenous antigens, the situation is further complicated by the fact that changes may be observed in the nature of the disease depending on whether the antigen is administered as one injection per day or multiple injections during the day. It is likely that these varying experimental results, in relation to variations in antigen administration, reflect basic differences in antibody responses.

C. Antibody: IgG and IgM are the antibody classes normally involved in the deposition of immune complexes in tissues. There is considerable variation in the affinity or avidity of the antibodies involved in immune complex formation; the genetic makeup of the host and the nature, route, and timing of antigen administration define the nature and affinity of the antibody elicited by that antigen. A general division into precipitating and nonprecipitating antibodies has been suggested in immune complex formation. Precipitating antibodies were thought to be associated with self-limiting forms of disease such as serum sickness, while nonprecipitating antibodies were associated with a longer half-life for circulating immune complexes and with chronic immune complex deposition. Further studies have shown that this division is not strictly correct, and chronic immune complex deposition can be associated with both precipitating and nonprecipitating antibodies.

D. Antigen-Antibody Complexes: Most of our increased understanding of immune complex disorders originated with the realization that they are dynamic processes. There are constantly changing concentrations of antigens, antibodies, and antigen-antibody complexes, and these changes themselves influence the biologic behavior of the complexes. Regional changes in the tissue and serum greatly affect complexes and determine whether they are in antigen excess, equivalence, or antibody excess. These conditions can only be analyzed in detail in experimental animals, and summaries will be given of experimental studies in several laboratories on the relationship between antigen-antibody complexes, their catabolism, and their deposition in different tissues.

One group of experiments showed that small immune complexes formed under conditions of great antigen excess were approximately 11S in size, with the molecular formula Ag_2Ab_2. With low to moderate degrees of antigen excess, small immune complexes were still formed but their size was 8.5S and their molecular formula Ag_1Ab_1. The antigen-antibody ratio varied from 0.85–1.2 for immune complexes formed in the range of 5- to 60-fold antigen excess. If they were formed in higher degrees of antigen excess (eg, up to 500-fold), the antigen-antibody ratio remained in the region of 1.2–1.25. The molecular formulas for such complexes were Ag_2Ab_2, Ag_1Ab_1, and possibly small amounts of Ag_2Ab_1.

Another study compared the results of single or repeated injections of 0.5 g of BSA into rabbits. A single injection of the antigen was generally associated with the formation of low-affinity IgG antibodies. These formed poorly aggregating immune complexes with a molecular weight of 300–500 thousand and with the molecular formula Ag_2Ab_1 or Ag_3Ab_2. Rarely, one observed large immune complexes (MW > 1 million) with low-affinity IgM antibody. The histologic feature in the kidney for both groups was that of acute diffuse glomerulonephritis. Animals given repeated injections could be arbitrarily divided into those producing low levels and those producing intermediate levels of antibody. Those producing low levels of antibody produced antibody of high affinity which formed immune complexes with a molecular weight of 500–700 thousand. The renal histologic picture of these animals was that of diffuse proliferative glomerulonephritis. Those that produced intermediate levels of antibody tended to form immune complexes with molecular weights greater than 1 million.

Another experimental approach was to prepare hapten-protein conjugates of defined size and antigenic valency and to examine their behavior in experimental animals (as models for immune reactions to drugs). Antigen with a valency less than 4 showed restricted activity with antibody in complement fixation or precipitation reactions and formed mainly soluble immune complexes. Thus, complexes with a density less than 19S tended to fix complement poorly and had a prolonged intravascular half-life. Immune complexes with a density greater than 19S generally had a ratio of antigen to antibody of 2:5 or less, fixed complement efficiently, and had a relatively short intravascular half-life. Whereas the antigenic valency appeared to restrict lattice formation and precipitation, in vitro precipitation could be enhanced by the addition of human or rabbit complement, eg, C1q. These observations on the relationship between the composition of the immune complexes and their clearance from plasma have implications in the organ distribution of deposited immune complexes.

Studies of the rate of clearance of radiolabeled immune complexes showed that immune complexes with a molecular size greater than 11S (molecular formula greater than Ag_2Ab_2) were rapidly removed in the liver by the monocyte-macrophage system; less than 1% was deposited in lungs, kidneys, or spleen. This distribution was unchanged in rabbits depleted of complement, but the immune complex had to include 2 or more IgG molecules. If the immune complexes were formed from reduced and alkylated antibodies, then the immune complexes were not cleared by the liver. With the injection of increasing amounts of preformed immune complexes, the monocyte-macrophage system appeared to become saturated and the liver was no longer capable of clearing excess amounts of immune complexes greater than 11S. Increased amounts were therefore found in the circulating plasma, and it was suggested that such complexes were then more likely to lodge in the renal glomeruli. A corollary of this study was that the in vivo interaction of fixed tissue macrophages and IgG antibodies in soluble immune complexes was not mediated by circulating complement components.

Other studies have been done to assess the clearance in experimental animals of complexes between staphylococcal enterotoxin and equine IgA antitoxin. Equine IgA antibodies fix complement poorly and form soluble immune complexes in antibody excess. Three different situations were tested: toxin excess, toxin-antitoxin equivalence, and antibody (antitoxin) excess. In conditions of toxin excess, the clearance of immune complexes from the circulation was slow and was independent of the concentration of antitoxin until there was sufficient antitoxin present in the plasma to bind 80% of enterotoxin. In conditions of equivalence, there was rapid clearance of the immune complexes by the monocyte-macrophage system. In antibody excess, the immune complexes were nonprecipitating complexes of high molecular weight yet their clearance rate was slow and decreased even further with the addition of more antitoxin. It was concluded that the rapid removal of toxin and its catabolism by the monocyte-macrophage system was not an important mechanism for in vivo detoxification by antibody.

The behavior of circulating immune complexes can be influenced by the administration of certain drugs. Analysis of the survival in mice of injected preformed immune complexes with a molecular formula of Ag_2Ab_2 showed no difference in intravascular survival between control and cortisone-treated mice. However, there was significantly prolonged intravascular survival of immune complexes with a molecular formula greater than Ag_2Ab_2 in cortisone-treated mice compared to controls. This was associated with enhanced and prolonged deposition in renal glomeruli. This observation, if confirmed, has important implications for the role of corticosteroid therapy in immune complex disorders such as systemic lupus erythematosus (see Chapter 27).

E. Complement: The important role of the complement system in immune complex disorders has been known for some time in terms of the biologic activities of components such as C3a, C5a, and $C\overline{567}$ in producing changes such as inflammation and chemotaxis.

Recent studies have outlined a further role in terms of the relationship between circulating immune complexes in plasma and the attachment of such complexes to the surfaces of lymphocytes and platelets. The term *complex release activity* refers to the release of immune complexes from the membranes of circulating lymphocytes or platelets and the maintenance of such complexes in a soluble form in the plasma. This activity appears to be mediated by the alternative pathway for complement activation; it relies on the presence of Mg^{++} ions and functions in C4 and C5 deficiency. This complex-releasing activity appears to increase with age in experimental animals with the result that a lower percentage of immune complexes is bound to cell membranes immediately after injection of preformed immune complexes. It has yet to be established whether this means that the higher percentage of immune complexes in the plasma in older animals predisposes them to increased tissue deposition of the circulating complexes.

F. Platelets: Immune complexes bind to the platelet membrane, leading to the release of its stored vasoactive amines. In a type III reaction, vasoactive amines are also released from basophils initially attracted to the area by chemotaxis. As indicated earlier in this chapter, the vasoactive amines lead to increased vascular permeability and to small blood vessel damage, resulting in precipitation of immune complexes at the basement membrane. Binding of immune complexes to platelets appears to be more efficient with preformed immune complexes formed in antibody excess rather than at equivalence. Immune complexes formed in antigen excess are frequently inactive in this regard. Absence of the Fc fragment from the antibody slows the reaction but does not affect the final extent of the reaction.

G. Polymorphonuclear Leukocytes: Infiltration by polymorphonuclear leukocytes is a crucial step in the production of the pathologic sequelae of immune complex deposition in tissues. Various factors affect the release of lysosomal enzymes which produce the tissue damage. The binding of immune complexes to neutrophils can lead to the release of lysosomal hydrolases from neutrophils. Phagocytosis need not occur before these lysosomal enzymes are released. Antigen added to fixed nonphagocytosable antibody attached to an insoluble collagen membrane induced the release of lysosomal enzymes from added polymorphonuclear leukocytes. The cells retained their viability after this selective release of lysosomal enzymes, and non-granule-associated cytoplasmic enzymes remained in significant amounts. Agents which increased the intracellular concentration of cAMP–eg, prostaglandin E_1 and theophylline–inhibited this selective exclusion of lysosomal enzymes without affecting cell viability. The complement component C5a induced the selective release of lysosomal enzymes from intact, viable, cytochalasin B-treated human polymorphonuclear leukocytes without requiring phagocytosis or cellular adherence to surfaces. The extracellular concentration of Ca^{++} is crucial in this situation since the addition of increasing amounts of Ca^{++} enhances the release of enzymes, but a Ca^{++} concentration of greater than 2 mM inhibits secretion of the enzymes.

Detection of Immune Complexes

Tests for the detection of circulating immune complexes in animals or in patients with a suspected immune complex disorder are described in detail in Chapter 24. The fact that several tests are used to detect circulating immune complexes indicates that no single test is sufficient for all situations. This is not surprising in view of the dynamic nature of the processes involved in the formation of immune complexes at different stages of antigen administration. Unfortunately, in man, the identity of the antigen is generally unknown and so specific detection of the antigen is not possible. Exceptions to this rule, where the identity of the antigen is known, include nucleic acid antigens in systemic lupus erythematosus, drugs in drug sensitivity, and HB_sAg in some cases of polyarteritis nodosa. Immune complexes are generally detected by their behavior as cryoglobulins, their propensity to adhere to cell membranes, their physical characteristics, or their property of interaction with complement components such as C1q.

Clinical Features of Immune Complex Disorders

The clinical features of immune complex disorders are discussed in subsequent chapters in relation to the organ systems they most frequently affect. Some general comments will be made here.

The systemic symptoms and signs of classical serum sickness following a single administration of antigen are likely to result from systemic deposition in blood vessels or clearance by the monocyte-macrophage system. Nevertheless, with repeated antigen administration, persistent viral infection, or continuous availability of an endogenous antigen such as DNA, the renal glomeruli remain the chief site of deposition of circulating immune complexes. In some cases, the predominant microscopic finding is the deposition of IgA and complement in the mesangium (Fig 20–4). The antigen deposited in the kidney in these cases of *IgA nephropathy* is unknown. Recent reports have emphasized that chronic deposition of circulating antigen-antibody complexes frequently involves extraglomerular renal structures, including the interstitium, Bowman's capsule, and the walls of peritubular capillaries. This may occur in patients with advanced malignancy with the renal deposition of circulating tumor antigen-antibody complexes. In patients with systemic lupus erythematosus, examination by direct immunofluorescence of skin biopsies from both clinically normal skin and diseased skin frequently shows the deposition of immune complexes and complement at the dermal-epidermal junction. Marked deposition at this skin site is significantly associated with heavy deposition in the renal glomeruli. It has been suggested–but not confirmed–that the deposition of circulating immune complexes in the choroid plexus may be of pathogenetic significance in the development of

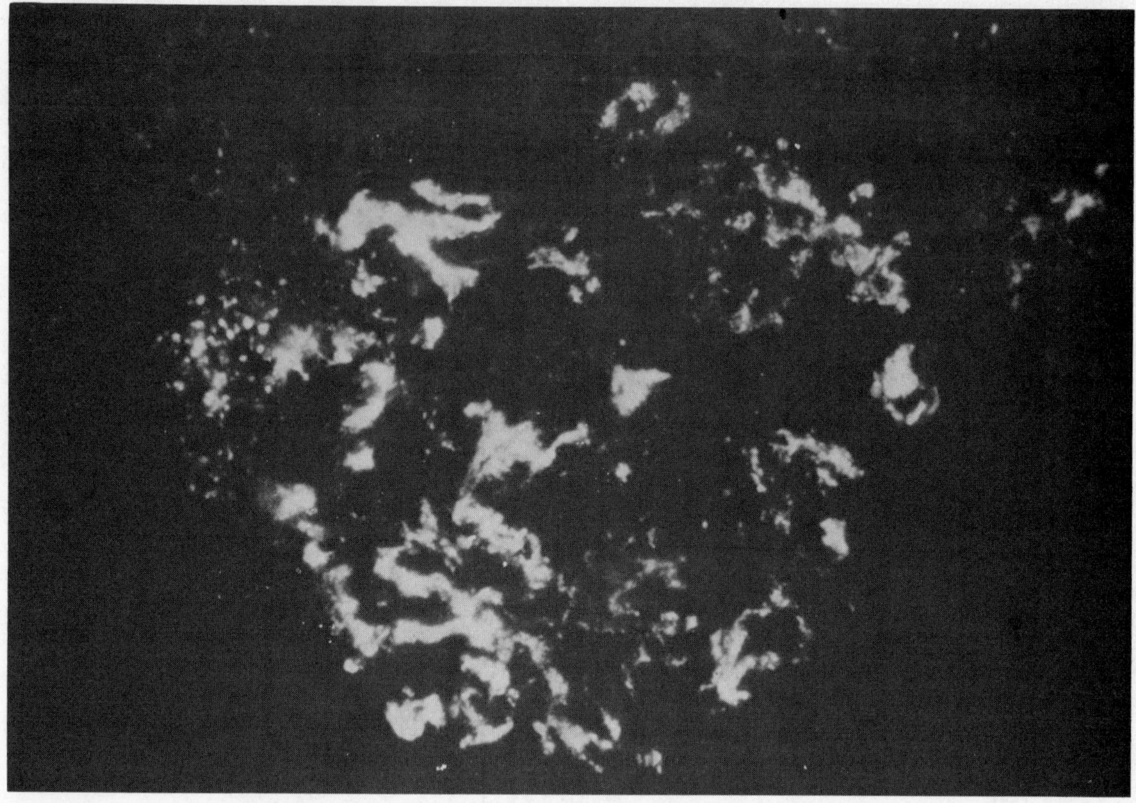

Figure 20–4. Direct immunofluorescence microscopy with fluorescein-labeled anti-IgA serum demonstrating granular deposition of IgA in the mesangium of a glomerulus in a renal biopsy specimen taken from a 30-year-old woman with IgA nephropathy and hematuria.

the cerebral manifestations of systemic lupus erythematosus.

TYPE IV REACTIONS

Cell-mediated immune reactions occur as the result of the interactions between actively sensitized lymphocytes and specific antigens. They are mediated by the release of *lymphokines*, direct cytotoxicity, or both. They occur without the involvement of antibody or complement. The classical lesion of a cell-mediated immune reaction is the delayed skin reaction which develops over a period of 24–48 hours and which has the characteristic mononuclear cell infiltrate (Fig 20–5). The first stage in such a reaction is the binding of antigen by a small number of specific antigen-reactive T lymphocytes. The evidence for and against the role of immunoglobulin in T lymphocyte function as the specific antigen receptor was summarized in Chapter 8. This initial stage is followed by the production and release of soluble mediators with a wide variety of biologic activities. These products of activated lymphocytes, or lymphokines, have various activities on macrophages, polymorphonuclear leukocytes, lymphocytes, and other cell types. Their overall function is to amplify the initial cellular response by recruitment of other lymphocytes (both T and B cells), to induce mitogenesis in these cells, to attract polymorphonuclear leukocytes, and, in particular, to attract, localize, and activate macrophages at the site of the lesion. Although there are distinct lymphocyte mediators for some of the functions that have been described, it is not clear whether there are a small number of molecules with multiple functions at different concentrations or whether a different molecule is specific for each in vitro function. There are normal control mechanisms which lead to resolution of such a lesion, but these have not been clarified. In cases where multiple doses of antigen have been given to a hypersensitive individual, the lesions may progress to the stage of local ulceration and necrosis.

An important corollary to the delayed skin reaction is that activated cells in these lesions can nonspecifically affect cells other than those specific for the initial sensitizing and challenging antigen. Thus, the

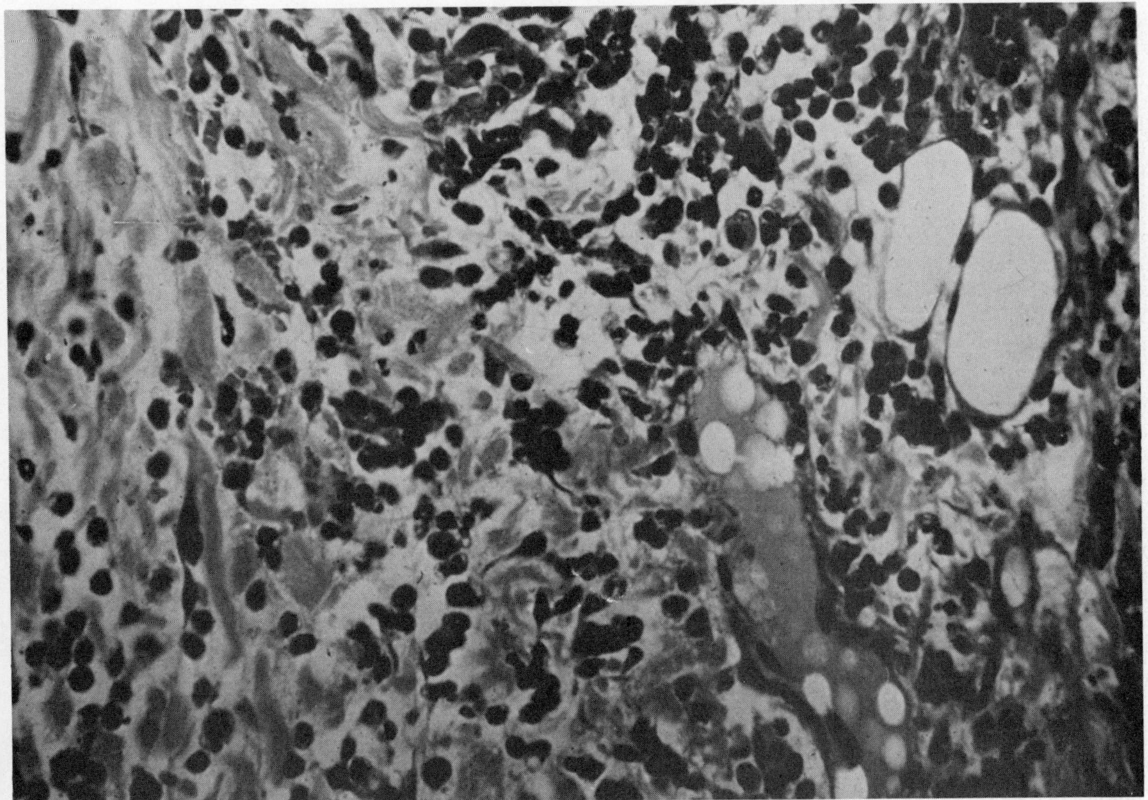

Figure 20–5. Photomicrograph of a skin biopsy of a positive delayed skin test 48 hours after the injection of PPD into a previously sensitized guinea pig. Note the characteristic mononuclear cell infiltrate.

inflammatory cells that arise may be bactericidal or tumoricidal, and this is the basis of the current trials of immunotherapy in the treatment of tumors with agents which nonspecifically induce delayed skin reactions, eg, BCG and levamisole (Table 20–3).

In some cases, the extent and duration of inflammation in the delayed skin reaction are increased by the involvement of other systems, including the complement, clotting, and kinin systems (see below).

Contact sensitivity to a simple defined chemical is probably the only example of a pathologic process which is wholly the result of a delayed skin reaction. Most other examples of allergic reactions include multiple mechanisms. It is generally the rule that cellular and humoral reactions to an antigen proceed at the same time, though in varying degrees. Emphasis is usually placed on the effects of repeated or prolonged delayed skin reactions and their possible role in producing symptoms. However, it is equally true that disease may be due to or associated with *anergy,* ie, the absence of delayed skin reactivity. It is not uncommon in patients with some forms of tumors (see Chapter 21), immunodeficiency (see Chapter 26), and infections (see Chapter 34). This will not be discussed in detail, but several factors may lead to delayed type anergy, including suppressive factors in plasma.

Table 20–3. Summary of the 4 main types of direct cytotoxicity.

Type	Activating Agents	Effector Cells	Specificity	
			Effector Cells	**Target Cells**
(1) Allograft-induced	Alloantigens	T cells	Specific	Specific
(2) Tumor antigen-induced	Cell membrane antigens (including tumor-specific antigens)	T cells and "armed" macrophages	Specific	Specific ↓ Nonspecific
(3) Mitogen-induced	PHA Soluble antigens	T cells (?) B cells	Nonspecific (PHA) Specific (antigens)	Nonspecific
(4) Antibody-dependent	7S antibody specifically bound to cell membrane antigens	K cells and macrophages	Nonspecific	Specific, antibody-dependent

CELL-MEDIATED CYTOTOXICITY

Both T cells and macrophages are capable of direct cytotoxicity (Table 20–3). This cytotoxicity may take the form of actual cytolysis or of cytostasis. Cytolysis is frequently measured by the release of ^{51}Cr from ^{51}Cr-labeled target cells by the sensitized test lymphocytes. Cell-mediated lympholysis is often tested in the MLC reaction, where effector cells develop which are cytotoxic for the stimulator lymphocytes. This T cell-mediated cytotoxicity is specific and rapid and causes death of the target cells within minutes after first exposure. It is influenced by the ratio between lymphocytes and target cells. It requires physical contact between lymphocytes, and supernates do not appear to be cytotoxic in this test. This activity is inactivated by treatment of the cells with trypsin. Studies of cell-mediated lympholysis in patients with primary immunodeficiency syndromes show that there is not always a direct correlation between the T cell functions of MLC reactions, mitogen responses, and cytotoxicity. This has been interpreted as providing support for the hypothesis that there are subpopulations of T cells with different functions. The induction of T cell cytotoxicity by alloantigens such as those expressed on allogeneic leukocytes or on tumor cells requires the presence of a small number of macrophages in the initial stages. Specific cytotoxic cells can be detected after 2–4 days of incubation. No antibody is added to the system, and the short incubation period excludes the possibility of production of specific antibody by B cells in the initial culture system.

Extensive studies have been performed on the generation of cytotoxic cells after stimulation of lymphocytes with mitogens such as PHA or ConA. It is clear that both nonspecific and specific cytotoxicity can be generated in experiments depending on the reaction mixture. Thus, incubation of lymphocytes, ConA, and potential target cells of allogeneic or syngeneic origin leads to the formation of blast cells. Both adherence and nonspecific cytotoxicity can be demonstrated in these blast cells, with the mitogen ConA acting as a polyclonal activator of the lymphocytes. If the mitogen is removed during the cytotoxicity test, then specific cytotoxicity is demonstrated for the allogeneic cells. Nonspecific cytotoxicity is demonstrated if the ConA is present during the cytotoxicity test; however, no cytotoxicity is demonstrated against syngeneic cells if ConA is not maintained in the mixture. Thus we see a mixture of specific and nonspecific direct T cell cytotoxicity in mitogen-induced cytotoxicity.

Although there is now an extensive literature of experimental studies on cytotoxicity, these tests have not reached the stage of application in routine clinical immunology laboratories. It is expected that within a few years assessment of the immune status of a subject will include measurement of antibody-mediated and direct cell cytotoxicity as functions of his or her mononuclear cells.

• • •

HUMORAL AMPLIFICATION SYSTEMS

The 4 types of immune mechanisms have been discussed above as distinct entities. It must be emphasized, however, that in the intact animal a typical immune reaction will involve a mixture of the 4 types of reactions. Thus, we see a combination of type II and type III reactions in virus infections. Both the type of immune reaction (its extent and variety) and the type of associated clinicopathologic phenomena are complicated by the involvement in immune reactions of several body systems collectively termed *humoral amplification systems.* Various interrelationships between these systems often lead to involvement of one or more of them after initial activation of immune processes. Each is composed of a series of proteins, substrates, inhibitors, and enzymes. These systems include the *complement, coagulation, kinin,* and *fibrinolytic* systems (Fig 20–6).

Complement System

This complex system of at least 15 distinct serum proteins is described in detail in Chapter 6. It is reemphasized here that involvement of the complement system can be initiated by a wide variety of stimuli along either the classical or alternative pathways of activation. Recent studies have clearly demonstrated the variety of biologic activities of different complement components apart from the classical observation of the function of cell lysis. Thus, we have the important biologic effects of C3a and C5a which, as anaphylatoxins, induce the release of histamine from the granules of mast cells, producing increased capillary permeability, edema, and smooth muscle contraction. Both C3a and C5a, together with the trimolecular complex $C\overline{567}$, also have chemotactic activity for polymorphonuclear leukocytes. These functions all contribute to the degree of inflammation at the site of an antigen-antibody reaction involving complement activation. Other amplification systems are also involved in the complement system, eg, the fibrinolytic enzyme plasmin can directly attack C1, C3, and C5; the plasma proteolytic enzyme thrombin, which converts fibrinogen to fibrin, can attack C3; and a fragment of C2 has a kininlike activity in causing increased vascular permeability and contraction of smooth muscle.

Coagulation

Studies have not demonstrated a common mode of activation of the coagulation and complement systems, although, as mentioned above, thrombin formed during activation of the later stages of the coagulation system has the ability to act on complement components. It is certainly true, however, that damage to the endothelium of small blood vessels leads to activation of the coagulation pathway by *Hageman factor* (factor XII) and at the same time leads to local changes in-

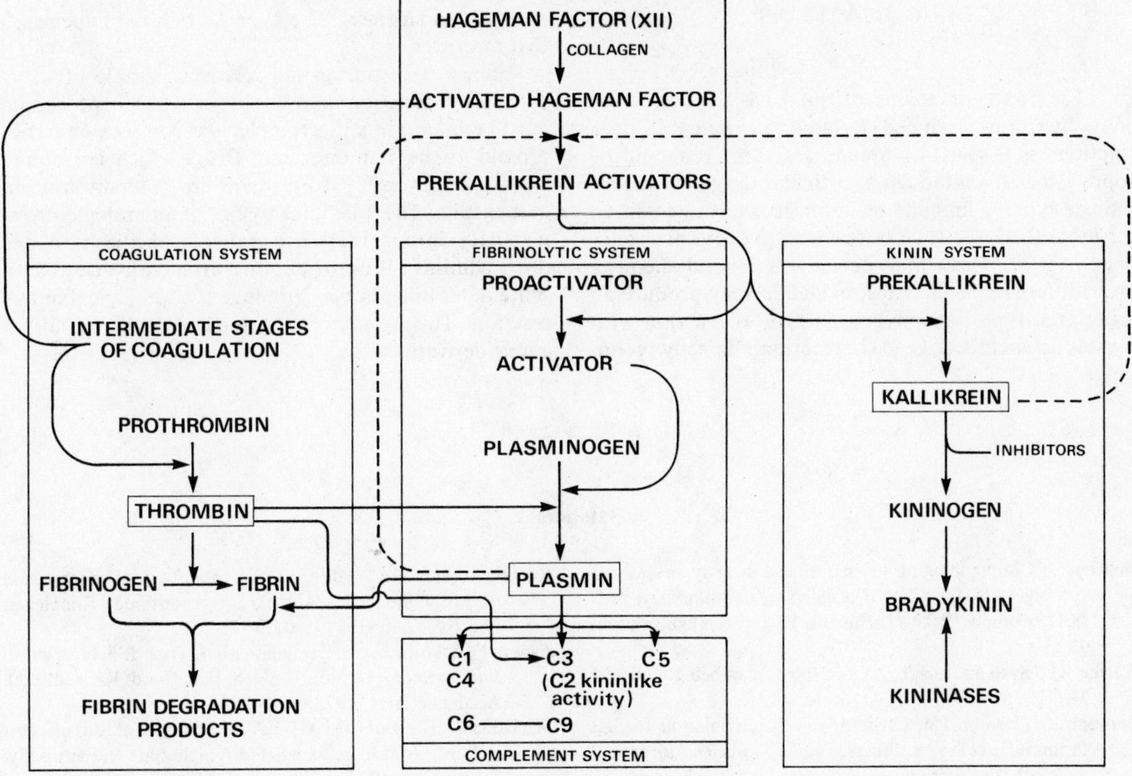

Figure 20–6. Schematic diagram demonstrating the multiple relationships between the coagulation, fibrinolytic, complement, and kinin systems.

cluding the release of tissue enzymes which may then activate the complement system. Obviously, if the damage is produced initially by the deposition of immune complexes or bacteria, then the complement system would be involved.

Factor XII is activated by exposure to collagen, and this leads to the formation of kinins as well as activation of subsequent stages in the coagulation system. In some local immune reactions, histologic examination reveals thrombosed small blood vessels, frequently with associated necrosis.

Kinin System

This system is also known as the *kallikrein system.* It is initiated by activation of factor XII, leading eventually to the formation of kallikrein, which acts on an α-globulin substrate *kininogen* to form *bradykinin.* Bradykinin is a nonapeptide which produces marked and prolonged slow contractions of smooth muscle. Its activity in plasma is inactivated by kininases. The pathway of formation of bradykinin can be inhibited in at least 3 stages by C1 inactivator (C1 esterase inhibitor), which normally inactivates C1. This α_2-globulin is absent in patients with hereditary angioneurotic edema, and this may result in increased activity of the kinin system during an attack of angioneurotic edema. Involvement of the kinin system in immune reactions is further emphasized by the fact that the enzyme kallikrein, which cleaves kininogen to produce bradykinin, is itself directly chemotactic for polymorphonuclear leukocytes.

The kinins possess a variety of activities, including chemotaxis, smooth muscle contraction, dilatation of peripheral arterioles, and increased capillary permeability.

Fibrinolytic System

This system is also initiated by the activation of factor XII, and it then proceeds through intermediate stages to the formation of plasmin from its precursor plasminogen. Plasmin is a proteolytic enzyme of broad specificity which can digest not only fibrin but also fibrinogen, factor XIIa, clotting factors V and VIII, prothrombin, C1 inactivator, C1, C3, and C5. Clearly, both factor XII and plasmin have several actions relevant to different humoral amplification systems.

These 4 systems are involved in several mechanisms which serve to amplify and to control an initial small stimulus. They are particularly suited to modify the vascular and cellular events in immune and nonimmune reactions in terms of hemostasis, inflammation, and tissue repair.

DRUG REACTIONS

The above discussion of the 4 basic types of immune reactions included isolated examples of drug reactions as a specific immune reaction. It should be appreciated that although a particular drug may induce a single type of immune reaction, it is not uncommon for more than one type of reaction to occur in a sensitized subject. These may occur either simultaneously or at different stages. Thus, penicillin may produce an acute fatal type I anaphylaxis, a type II reaction with hemolytic anemia, a type III reaction clinically resembling serum sickness, or a type IV delayed hypersensitivity reaction.

Since many drugs are relatively simple in structure, they function immunologically as haptens and must be bound to a macromolecular complex or carrier protein to be immunogenic. Drugs which are bound loosely or reversibly to proteins are generally not immunogenic. The phenomenon of immunologic cross-reactivity means that in a patient sensitized to one drug, administration of another drug with shared antigenic determinants may produce a pathologic immune reaction. This occurs with various penicillin or sulfonamide derivatives.

• • •

References

Ackroyd JF: Immunological mechanisms in drug hypersensitivity. Page 913 in: *Clinical Aspects of Immunology.* Gell PGH, Coombs RRA, Lachmann PJ (editors). Blackwell, 1975.

Austen KF: Systemic anaphylaxis in the human being. N Engl J Med 291:661, 1974.

Benveniste J, Henson PM, Cochrane CG: A possible role for IgE in immune complex disease. Page 187 in: *The Biological Role of the Immunoglobulin E System.* Ishizaka K, Dayton DH (editors). Department of Health, Education & Welfare Publication No. (NIH) 73-502, 1973.

Brentjens JR & others: Extra-glomerular lesions associated with deposition of circulating antigen-antibody complexes in kidneys of rabbits with chronic serum sickness. Clin Immunol Immunopathol 3:112, 1974.

Calder EA & others: Characterization of human lymphoid cell-mediated antibody-dependent cytotoxicity (LDAC). Clin Exp Immunol 18:579, 1974.

Cerottini J-C, Brunner KT: Cell-mediated cytotoxicity, allograft rejection, and tumor immunity. Adv Immunol 18:67, 1974.

Cochrane CG, Koffler D: Immune complex disease in experimental animals and man. Adv Immunol 16:185, 1973.

Colman RW: Formation of human plasma kinin. N Engl J Med 291:509, 1974.

Coombs RRA, Gell PGH: Classification of allergic reactions responsible for clinical hypersensitivity and disease. Page 761 in: *Clinical Aspects of Immunology.* Gell PGH, Coombs RRA, Lachmann PJ (editors). Blackwell, 1975.

David JR: Lymphocyte mediators and delayed-type hypersensitivity. N Engl J Med 288:143, 1973.

Grant JA & others: Complement-mediated release of histamine from human leukocytes. J Immunol 114:1101, 1975.

Haakenstad AO, Mannik M: Saturation of the reticuloendothelial system with soluble immune complexes. J Immunol 112:1939, 1974.

Henney CS: T cell mediated cytolysis: Consideration of the role of a soluble mediator. J Reticuloendothel Soc 17:231, 1975.

Hunsicker LG, Wintroub BU, Austen KF: Humoral amplification systems in inflammation. Page 179 in: *Clinical Immunobiology.* Vol 1. Bach FH, Good RA (editors). Academic Press, 1972.

Kotkes P, Pick E: Studies on the inhibition of macrophage migration induced by soluble antigen-antibody complexes. Clin Exp Immunol 19:105, 1975.

Lamm E, Stetson CA Jr: Inflammation. Page 139 in: *Clinical Immunobiology.* Vol 1. Bach FH, Good RA (editors). Academic Press, 1972.

MacDonald HR, Bonnard GD: A comparison of the effector cells involved in cell-mediated lympholysis and antibody-dependent cell-mediated cytotoxicity in man. Scand J Immunol 4:129, 1975.

Mawas C & others: Cell-mediated lympholysis in vitro: Independence of mixed lymphocyte reactions and T-cell mitogen responses from the in vitro generation of cytotoxic effectors in primary immunodeficiency diseases. Clin Exp Immunol 20:83, 1975.

Michael AF & others: Immunologic aspects of the nephrotic syndrome. Kidney Int 3:105, 1973.

Miller GW & others: Complement-dependent alterations in the handling of immune complexes by NZB/W mice. J Immunol 114:1166, 1975.

Morrison DC & others: Two distinct mechanisms for the initiation of mast cell degranulation. Int Arch Allergy Appl Immunol 49:172, 1975.

Normann SJ: Clearance of equine antitoxin-toxin complexes by the reticuloendothelial system. J Immunol 108:521, 1972.

Nussenzweig V: Receptors for immune complexes on lymphocytes. Adv Immunol 19:217, 1974.

Orange RP, Austen KF: Immunologic and pharmacologic receptor control of the release of chemical mediators from human lung. Page 151 in: *The Biological Role of the Immunoglobulin E System.* Ishizaka K, Dayton DH (editors). Department of Health, Education & Welfare Publication No. (NIH) 73-502, 1973.

Parker CW: Drug therapy: Drug allergy. (3 parts.) N Engl J Med 292:511, 732, 957, 1975.

Roy LP & others: Etiologic agents of immune deposit disease. Page 1 in: *Progress in Clinical Immunology.* Vol 1. Schwartz RS (editor). Grune & Stratton, 1972.

Simpson IJ & others: Guinea-pig nephrotoxic nephritis. 1. The role of complement and polymorphonuclear leukocytes and the effect of antibody subclass and fragments in the heterologous phase. Clin Exp Immunol 19:499, 1975.

Ward PA: Leukotaxis and leukotactic disorders: A review. Am J Pathol 77:520, 1974.

Weissmann G & others: Mechanisms of lysosomal enzyme release from leukocytes exposed to immune complexes and other particles. J Exp Med 134(Suppl):149, 1971.

Wilson CB, Dixon FJ: Immunopathology and glomerulonephritis. Annu Rev Med 25:83, 1974.

World Health Organization: Cell-mediated immunity and resistance to infection. WHO Technical Report Series No. 519, 1973.

21 . . .
Tumor Immunology

Vera S. Byers, PhD, & Alan S. Levin, MD

HISTORICAL ASPECTS OF TUMOR IMMUNOLOGY

The possibility that spontaneously arising tumors might have "nonself" neoantigens on the surfaces of their tumor cells has been a matter of discussion in biology for many years. The role of host immunologic responses in the protection of patients against tumor growth was recognized by early oncologists who noted that cancer patients with draining abscesses in their tumors lived longer than patients whose tumors appeared uninflamed. In 1959, Berg reported that women with breast carcinoma whose tumors were infiltrated with lymphocytes had a better prognosis than women whose tumors were free of lymphocytes. This implied that host immune cells were capable of reducing the rate of growth and metastasis of primary tumors.

Experimental support for these clinical observations began to appear in the 1920s with the discovery that tumors arising in one animal were rejected when implanted into another animal and that the rejection was more rapid if the recipient animal had been previously immunized with low doses of tumor cells. On the basis of this work, it was concluded that tumor antigens were present on malignant cells and that these antigens mediated the rejection. However, in the 1930s, the use of inbred animals demonstrated that the tumors were rejected because of transplantation antigens. These transplantation antigens reflected genetic differences between outbred animals (see Chapter 12) and not differences between normal and malignant cells. These experiments ultimately gave origin to the field of tissue typing and increased our knowledge of the group transplantation antigens called H-2 in mice and HLA in humans. Both of these transplantation systems are inherited by classical autosomal genetic mechanisms. However, the development of transplantation genetics invalidated most of the previous data on tumor antigens since rejection of an allogeneic tumor in an immunized animal is probably secondary to transplantation antigens and not to "tumor antigens." At this time the actual existence of "tumor antigens" was strongly questioned.

Work in tumor immunology began again in the 1950s with the demonstration that tumor antigens did indeed exist. These experiments were performed with chemically induced tumors in inbred strains of animals. Since then, virally and spontaneously induced animal and human tumors have also been demonstrated to have tumor-associated antigens. This new field was given a conceptual basis and a clear direction for continuing research effort by the theory of immune surveillance developed by Thomas and by Burnet and Medawar. This theory proposes that malignant cells are constantly arising in all individuals and that the cells of the lymphoid system are continuously patrolling the host, seeking out and destroying these cells before they become clinically significant tumors.

These fundamental observations served as a basis for the new burst of interest in tumor immunology.

ETIOLOGIC FACTORS IN TUMORIGENESIS

The search for etiologic factors in human and animal tumors began with the discovery that men who worked as chimney sweeps had a remarkably high incidence of scrotal carcinoma. This was the result of chronic exposure to hydrocarbons present in chimney soot. Since that observation, many other environment-related malignancies have been recognized in humans and animals. These include bronchogenic carcinomas in coal and uranium miners, osteogenic sarcomas in radium painters, and skin cancer in areas chronically exposed to sunlight in farmers. Animal models of chemical carcinogenesis began with Foley, who in 1953 described sarcomas induced by treating mice with 3-methylcholanthrene. The antigens on these chemically induced tumors form one type of tumor-associated antigen which will be discussed later.

Tumor virology began in 1911 when Peyton Rous demonstrated that the filtrate of a chicken tumor would produce undifferentiated sarcomas when inoculated into normal chickens. Since then, many animal

Vera S. Byers is Adjunct Assistant Professor, Department of Dermatology, University of California School of Medicine, San Francisco. Alan S. Levin is Adjunct Assistant Professor, Department of Dermatology, University of California School of Medicine, San Francisco.

viruses have been discovered which produce a broad variety of tumors ranging from leukemias to osteogenic sarcomas. These virus-induced tumors cross-react immunologically within the virus class producing the tumor.

With the exception of Burkitt's lymphoma (and possibly nasopharyngeal carcinoma) in humans in which Epstein-Barr virus (EBV) has been implicated, it has been difficult to establish viral etiology in human malignancies. However, there is biochemical and immunologic evidence for viral etiology in the case of some carcinomas and sarcomas which will be discussed later.

Host Response to Tumor

Any antigen should be capable of stimulating both the B lymphocyte system (antibody production) and the T lymphocyte system (cellular immunity). Functionally, however, the relative proportion of T and B cell immunity evoked against a given antigen seems to be variable. Some factors modifying this variability in response are the mode of presentation of the antigen to the immunocompetent host, the chemical composition of the antigen, and the genetic character of the host animal. Some antigens are known as either "pure T cell" or "pure B cell" antigens. This means that within the range of sensitivity of the test, such antigens stimulate only one arm of the immune system.

Antigens eliciting both humoral and cell-mediated immunity exist on most tumors. In virally induced tumors, tumor antigens on the transformed cells can be detected by serologic methods. Also present on these cells are antigens detected by the ability of a recipient animal to reject the infected cells. These antigens are called tumor-associated transplantation antigens (Fig 21–1). Since tumor rejection is probably mediated by T cells, these tumor antigens are probably T cell stimulatory. It is not clearly understood if B cell antigens can also mediate tissue rejection.

As will be discussed later, this distinction is quite important in cancer immunotherapy. In animal systems, T cell immunity seems to be responsible for graft rejection (and tumor rejection). Therefore, the most protective host response is assumed to be mediated by T cell antigens. Conversely, there is evidence that humoral antitumor immunity may in some cases be harmful. Since it is presently impossible to control the nature of antibodies induced against a specific antigen, any therapy that increases the production of antibodies against tumor antigens should be avoided.

The protection which is afforded the host by tumor antigens is dependent on the ability of these antigens to mediate tumor cell destruction by the immune system, and in large part this depends on the location of the tumor antigen on the tumor cell. Maximum protection is probably afforded by tumor antigens firmly intercalated within the plasma membrane, displaying some portion of the molecule on the cell surface. The current model of the cell membrane is shown in Fig 21–2, and if it is assumed that some of the proteins in the membrane are tumor antigens, it can be seen that these could serve as targets for com-

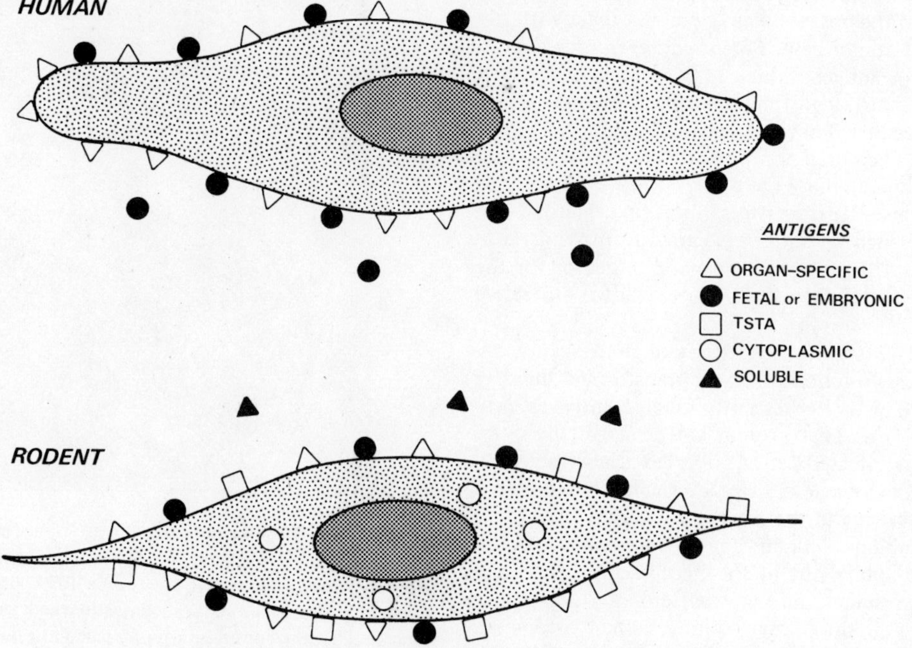

Figure 21–1. Antigens present on tumor cells. ***Top:*** Schematic representation of antigens which have been identified on human tumor cells. ***Bottom:*** Schematic representation of antigens which have been identified on rodent tumor cells. At right is a list of humoral and cellular immune responses which have been reported against these antigens. (TSTA, tumor-specific transplantation antigen.) (Redrawn and reproduced, with permission, from Coggin JH & others: Cancer Res 34:2092, 1974.)

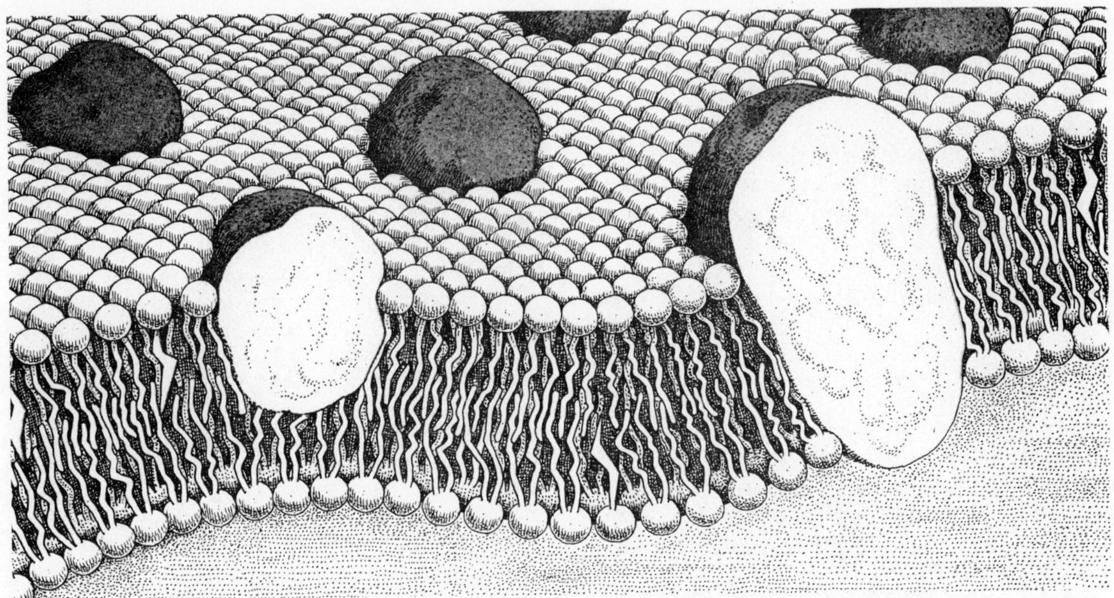

Figure 21–2. Current model of cell membrane visualized as composed primarily of polar lipid molecules arranged in a bilayer, their hydrophilic "heads" outward and their hydrophobic "tails" inward. Embedded in this lipid matrix, and sometimes extending through it, are proteins which make up the membrane's "active sites" and molecules of steroid which are much less numerous in the inner layer. (Reproduced, with permission, from the cover of Hospital Practice 8(1), 1973. Courtesy of Singer SJ.)

plement-fixing antibody or cytotoxic lymphocytes, resulting in eventual tumor cytolysis. However, tumor antigens which are sequestered within the cytoplasm or nuclear portions of the cells will evoke immune responses (upon tumor cell destruction) which are inconsequential to the host since they will not react with the intact viable tumor cells. Potentially even more harmful are tumor antigens which form a thick, easily shed coat on the surfaces of tumor cells. Not only is humoral and cellular immunity against such antigens not protective (since they are probably spaced away from the plasma membrane), but the antigens evoke antibody responses that serve as blocking factors. An example of such an antigen is carcinoembryonic antigen (CEA). Although this is a good indicator for the presence of malignancy, it serves no known protective function.

Fig 21–3 shows the pattern of fluorescence obtained by the reaction of virally transformed hamster cells (SV40) with fluorescently labeled antivirus antibody. The virus coat protein antigen is in the cytoplasm of the infected cell. Antibodies against this antigen would not react with intact viable cells unless it were also present in the plasma membrane. Fig 21–4 shows membrane immunofluorescence produced by the virus budding out of the plasma membrane. Fig 21–5 shows much the same pattern of fluorescence (membrane) produced by staining human osteogenic sarcoma cells with anti-osteogenic sarcoma antibody.

Histocompatibility antigens and tumor antigens are, in most systems, inversely related. Tumor cells that have a high concentration of tumor antigens have a low concentration of histocompatibility antigens.

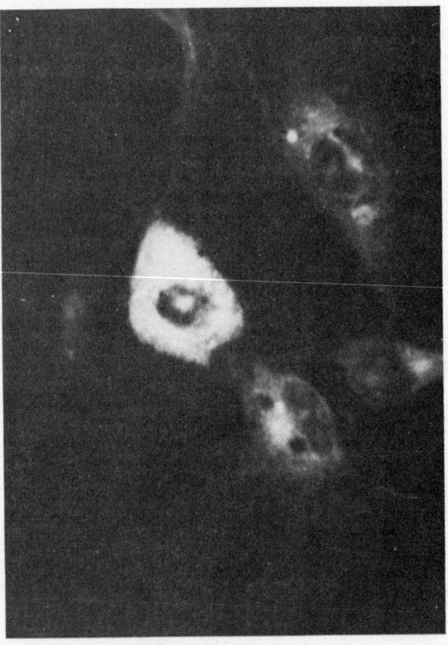

Figure 21–3. Cytoplasmic fluorescence (indirect stain). Dog osteogenic sarcoma-derived cells in culture infected with RD-114 virus, a xenotropic cat C-type RNA virus. Cells were fixed with acetone 6 days postinfection and reacted with an intermediate reactant of antisera prepared in guinea pigs against a purified internal protein component of the virus (P-30). It was reacted with a final reactant of fluorescein-labeled anti-guinea pig gamma globulin. This pattern is typical of cytoplasmic fluorescence of virally infected cells. (Courtesy of John Riggs, PhD.)

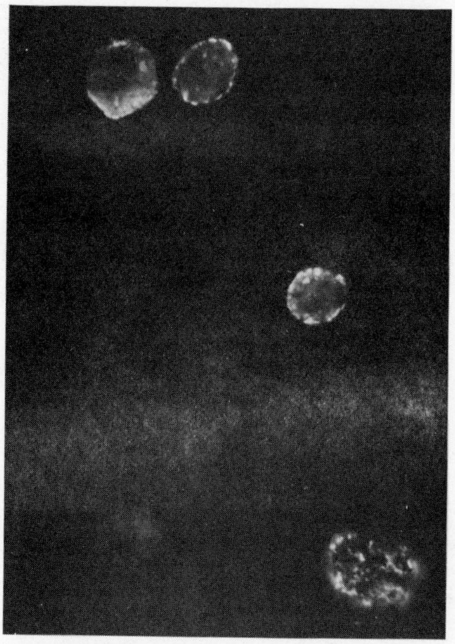

Figure 21–4. Membrane immunofluorescence (indirect). Dog osteogenic sarcoma-derived cells in culture chronically infected with a xenotropic murine C-type virus and stained with an intermediate reactant of rabbit antisera against the purified glycoprotein moiety of the virus coat protein (gp 69/71) and a final reactant of fluorescein-labeled anti-rabbit gamma globulin. The infected cells were viable (unfixed) at the time of staining and observation, and the pattern of fluorescence is typical of membrane type. In focus there is a rim of fluorescence around the cell, and mosaic patterns can be seen if one focuses above the plane of the cell. This antigen is on the membrane of the cell since C-type viruses reproduce by budding from the surface of the cell. (Courtesy of John Riggs, PhD.)

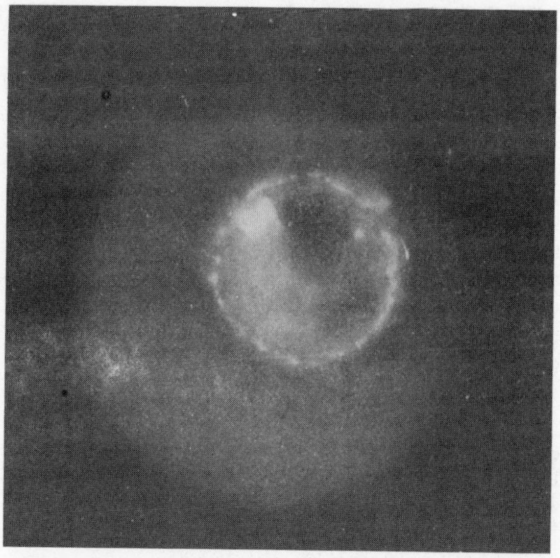

Figure 21–5. A viable osteogenic sarcoma tumor cell stained by indirect immunofluorescence to show the membrane-associated tumor antigens. A single cell suspension is first reacted with human IgG anti-tumor antibodies, then with fluorescein-labeled goat anti-human IgG. The membrane fluorescence, appearing as a white halo in this illustration, is a bright apple green. (Reproduced, with permission, from Byers VS & others: Cancer Res 35:2520, 1975.)

There is also a similarity in the mobility of these antigens on the cell surface. Murine teratoma tumor antigens and H-2 antigens on teratoma cells have been shown to co-cap, ie, the 2 antigen systems move together rather than independently within the membrane. These data, together with data indicating cross-reactivity between normal transplantation antigens and tumor antigens, have led to the suggestion that tumor antigens on the membrane may, at least in some systems, actually be HLA or H-2 antigens which are slightly altered to form neoantigens. This would offer an easy explanation of why histologically similar spontaneous human tumors cross-react.

The nature of tumor antigens is related to their cause. Chemically induced tumors have tumor antigens characteristic of the chemical which caused them, and virally induced tumors have antigens characteristic both of the virus coat proteins and of the tumor antigens induced by the virus. However, both these types of tumors and spontaneously occurring human tumors also have organ-specific antigens as well as embryonic antigens on the surface membrane. Some of these antigens are firmly fixed in the plasma membrane, but others are easily shed into the environment. Embryonic antigens seem to be most easily shed, and the presence of antibody augments this shedding. The antigen-antibody complexes released to the surroundings serve as blocking factors (described later). New antigens are re-formed on the cell membrane after a number of hours.

Fetal Antigens

As mentioned before, fetal antigens are not strictly defined tumor antigens, since they can also be found on normal fetal tissue. The 2 most widely studied fetal antigens, CEA and α-fetoprotein, are in the serum of patients. These can be detected by antibodies.

CEA is found in adenocarcinomas of the human digestive system, particularly carcinoma of the colon. It is not found in normal colon but is present in gut, liver, and pancreas of human fetuses between the second and sixth months of gestation. Highly sensitive radioimmunoassays have been developed to detect this antigen in serum, and about 70% of colon carcinoma patients in the USA produce the antigen. The antigen is found in about 90% of patients with carcinoma of the pancreas, in about 35% of patients with breast carcinoma, and in several other types of tumor patients. Carcinoembryonic antigen has also been found to be slightly elevated in pregnant women, in people who are heavy smokers, and in 5% of normal people without any known disease. It is, however, very useful in the diagnosis and monitoring of patients with elevated CEA levels since surgical removal of tumor results in a fall in CEA levels while recurrence of tumor results in a subsequent elevation of this antigen.

Alpha-fetoprotein is an embryonic α-globulin serologically detected in the blood of most patients with hepatoma and in some patients with embryonal carcinoma. Although it is present in low levels in tissue or blood of normal individuals, it can be found in high concentrations in cord blood. Some transplantable mouse and rat hepatomas also synthesize α-fetoprotein. The antigen secreted by tumor cells is immunologically no different from normal fetal protein found in cord blood and in normal fetal liver. Elevated levels of α-fetoprotein have also been found in patients with cirrhosis of the liver and hepatitis.

Several virus-induced animal tumors have fetal antigens associated with their cell membrane. These include hamster cells transformed by SV40 virus, adenovirus-induced hamster tumors, and Rauscher leukemia virus-infected mouse spleen cells. It will not be surprising if additional membrane-associated fetal antigens are found on human tumors.

Tumor-Associated Antigens on Virus-Induced Tumors

Viruses are composed of RNA or DNA plus a protein coat. Viral infection of cells results in the production of 2 major classes of antigens. V antigens are specific to the virus and can be detected on the isolated virus and on or in infected cells. These antigens are thought to be viral coat proteins. T (for tumor) antigens, the second group, are thought to be protein products of the viral genome and are found only in infected cells. Their specific role in viral oncogenesis is unknown, but they are not found on uninfected cells or on the isolated virus. In general, antibodies against V antigens will react with the isolated virus and with infected cells; they are specific for the particular virus. T antigens cross-react with all cells infected with that virus, but there is no cross-reaction between infected and uninfected cells or with the isolated virus.

The RNA and DNA viruses produce different immunologic patterns after infection of a cell. RNA viruses replicate in the cytoplasm and bud out from the cell. They produce a protein T antigen found usually in the cytoplasm of the cell. V antigen found on the cell membrane is probably the coat protein of the virus. DNA viruses such as adenoviruses and SV40 produce a T antigen (about 9 hours after infection) which is usually in the nucleus but can also be found in the cytoplasm. At about 15 hours, a V antigen located both in the nucleus and in the cytoplasm is seen in lytically infected cells. This antigen is probably the viral coat. Such cells also produce a transplantation antigen on the cell membrane. This antigen can be used to immunize an animal, and this immunization will protect it against later inoculation with similarly infected cells. Viral DNA or RNA is not usually immunogenic; therefore, most V antigens seen in infected or transformed cells are coat protein.

Antigens on Chemically Induced Tumors

Contemporary work in chemically induced tumors in animals began in the early 1950s with 3-methylcholanthrene. Although today many chemicals are known carcinogens, 3-methylcholanthrene is probably the most frequently used.

Three major types of antigens are expressed on the surface of these chemically induced tumors. *Private antigens* are produced by the interaction of the carcinogen with the genome of the target cell. These are antigens specific to that particular tumor. They do not cross-react with a similarly induced tumor in another syngeneic animal, and 2 separate tumors induced in the same organ in the same host by the same carcinogen have their own non-cross-reacting private antigens. This implies that the carcinogen interacts in a different fashion with each genome. The new antigen which results is the product of a stable mutation. It is passed on to future generations of transformed cells in the presence or absence of the carcinogen. These tumors can maintain their tumor antigens through many generations when passaged through a series of immunocompetent hosts. Therefore, private antigens are thought to be a specific representation of the interaction of the carcinogen with the genome of a single cell or clone of cells.

Fetal antigens are a second class of tumor-associated antigen; these are not tumor antigens by strict definition since they are normally present on embryonic tissues (but not present on adult tissues). Fetal antigens on tumor cells from the same organ system in different animals can immunologically cross-react. These tumors can be induced by the same or by different carcinogens. This implies that the carcinogenic agent caused the expression not only of antigens characteristic of the chemical transformation of the cell but also of antigens characteristic of dedifferentiation of that cell type.

Cross-reacting antigens specific to all tumors induced by the same or similar carcinogens are a third type of antigen on these cells. There is frequently also a loss of normal tissue antigens in these chemically transformed cells.

Spontaneous Human Tumors

Most human tumors cross-react immunologically among specific histologic types on both a humoral and a cellular level. A list of some of the cross-reactive tumors is given later. Functionally, this cross-reaction means that investigators can use a few standard cell lines of a given tumor as target cells in immunologic studies. These standard cells must possess the tumor-associated antigens characteristic of that histologic type. These tumors undoubtedly possess additional "private" antigens not shared among the tumors of a given histologic group.

HOST RESPONSE TO TUMORS

Once it was demonstrated that tumors possessed antigens which could stimulate an immune response, i was necessary to determine what role, if any, these immune responses played in host protection. Did they protect against primary tumors in normal individuals? Did they prevent metastases in patients with primary tumors? Could they control a benign neoplastic growth and prevent its malignant transformation? What were the mechanisms by which the immune system exerted its effect, and which arm of the immune system was most beneficial—the thymus-derived lymphocytes (T cells), the antibody-producing cells (B cells), or the monocyte series? Was immunotherapy feasible—ie, could any form of active or passive immunization make the primary tumor regress or prevent metastases in patients in whom the primary tumor had been removed? Most importantly, if tumor immunity was protective and tumor-bearing patients could be shown to have such immunity, how could spontaneous tumors grow at all?

In Vivo Experiments

Animal experiments were devised in an attempt to answer these questions. In most animal tumor systems, the tumor-bearing host was capable of recognizing the growing tumor as foreign and could mount a humoral and cellular immune response against it during some stage of tumorigenesis. This was demonstrated in a large series of in vivo experiments. Normal animals challenged with large doses of a syngeneic tumor died from that tumor. An animal preimmunized with smaller doses of syngeneic tumor was able to specifically reject subsequent large challenging doses of that tumor. Immunized animals could reject much larger doses of tumor than were lethal to nonimmunized littermates.

These experiments have been reproduced with many different animal and tumor combinations. It is important to note, however, that challenge with progressively increasing doses of tumor cells will eventually overwhelm even preimmunized animals regardless of the strength of the immunity.

Other in vivo proof of tumor immunity is the demonstration that a tumor-bearing animal is capable of rejecting a test inoculum of his own tumor administered in a location different from the primary site. This is called concomitant immunity. The lymphocytic infiltrate that forms around this transplanted tumor is quite similar to those infiltrates forming around transplanted allogeneic kidneys undergoing rejection secondary to disparate transplantation antigens.

Passive transfer of immunity can be accomplished by injection of syngeneic immune lymphocytes into tumor-bearing animals. This passive immunization can cause the tumor to be rejected. Immunized lymphocytes, when mixed with tumor cells and injected into a nonimmunized animal, can specifically prevent the tumor cells from growing.

Although much knowledge has been derived from these in vivo experiments, many of the important questions in tumor immunology, especially those related to the protective role of the immune response, can only be answered by dissecting the system and studying separately both the changes in antigens on the cells of a growing tumor and the humoral and cellular responses against the tumor as it grows and metastasizes. Therefore, in vitro systems form a critical aspect of modern tumor immunology.

In Vitro Experiments

Several different in vitro methods have been used to detect humoral and cellular immunity against tumors. Humoral immunity is by far the easiest to study, although its role is still unclear. Indirect immunofluorescence (see Chapter 24) has been one of the principal technics used for such studies. In general, many spontaneous human tumors elicit antibody production by the host. These antibodies can be demonstrated to coat the tumor in vitro and to kill neoplastic cells in the presence of complement. This has been repeatedly documented in human leukemias. Although such antibody coating can be demonstrated in vivo, it is not clear whether humoral immunity plays a similar protective role in vivo. In the case of solid tumors, the cells on the periphery of the tumor are often found to be coated with antibody, but this antibody does not seem to affect tumor growth. SV40 tumors induced in hamsters have a long latent period between infection and the appearance of a palpable tumor. During this time, antibody cytostatic to the tumor cells is present in the infected animals, yet it obviously does not prevent formation of a clinically apparent tumor.

Much attention has been focused on cellular immunity against tumors since a great deal of experimental evidence is available which shows this immunity to be protective in animals. Lymphoid cells from immunized animals capable of rejecting a tumor test graft are cytotoxic to cultured tumor cells of that histologic type. This tumor-specific cytolysis or cytostasis by sensitized leukocytes has formed the basis for most in vitro tests of tumor-specific cell-mediated immunity. In general, leukocytes (or purified lymphocytes) are mixed with radiolabeled tumor cells. Cytolysis is measured by the release of radiolabel from target cells after short-term incubation (Fig 21–6). Cell-mediated immunity can also be measured by plating the target cell-lymphocyte mixture in culture dishes and recording the number of tumor cells adherent to the dish several days later (Fig 21–7). If the original lymphocytes were immune to tumor antigens, a significant reduction in the number of adherent cells will be seen. Blastogenesis, in which lymphocytes undergo DNA synthesis in response to tumor antigens, and macrophage inhibition, in which macrophage migration is inhibited by a factor secreted by immune lymphocytes in response to tumor antigen, are also commonly used tests.

The mechanisms by which lymphocytes kill tumor cells are obviously of fundamental interest. Studies of these mechanisms are complicated by the finding that more than one cell type can be responsible for cell killing. Thymus-derived lymphocytes have been primarily implicated in allograft and tumor rejection. This mode of cytotoxicity is the best studied, and it is clear

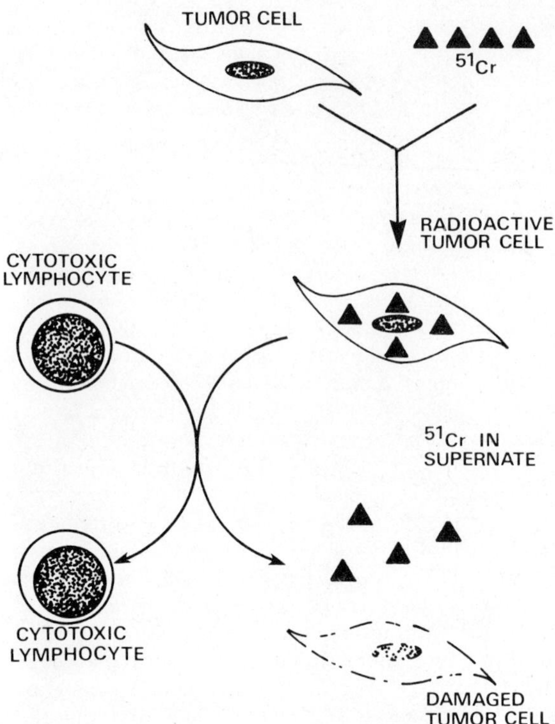

Figure 21–6. Chromium-51 lytic assay. Human peripheral blood lymphocytes are stirred with radiolabeled tumor cells at ratios of about 100 lymphocytes per one target tumor cell. The mixture is circulated for 4–6 hours, and the ^{51}Cr (or other radioisotope) in the supernatant fluid is counted as a measure of lymphocyte-mediated cytolysis.

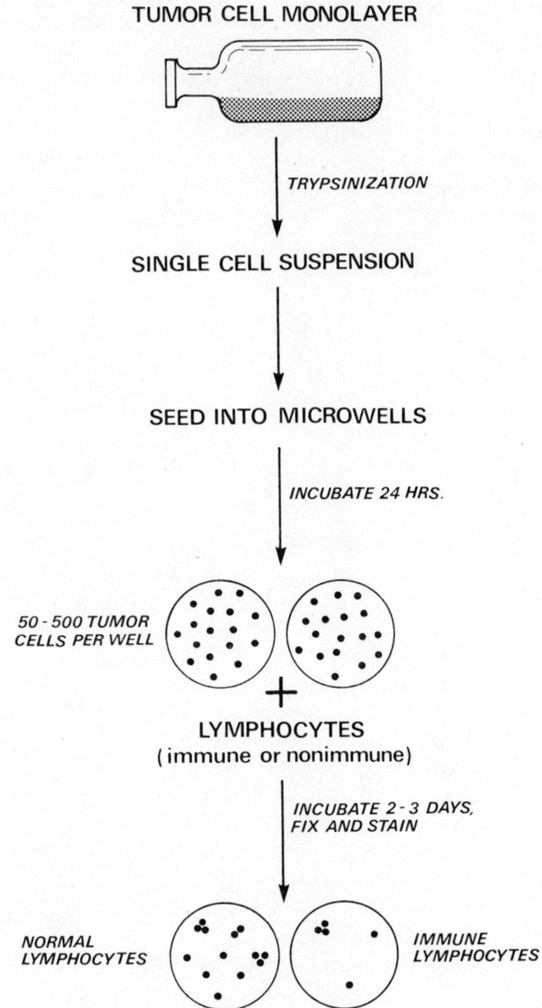

Figure 21–7. Microcytotoxicity assay.

that these cytotoxic lymphocytes can specifically bind to the membranes of tumor cells and cause cytolysis. At least 2 other types of cytotoxic mechanisms are also known. Both antibody-dependent cell-mediated cytotoxicity and cytotoxicity mediated by "armed macrophages" are definitely non-T cell killing of tumor cells, and they are probably very important in vivo.

MECHANISMS OF CELL-MEDIATED CYTOLYSIS

(See Fig 21–8.)

Cytotoxic T Cells

Cytotoxic T lymphocytes play an important role in rejection of tumors and allografts. Mice rendered immunodeficient in T cells by neonatal thymectomy retain skin grafts. Normal skin graft rejection can be restored by infusions of pure syngeneic T cells. Accelerated rejection of autologous tumors of homologous skin grafts can be induced by injection of syngeneic T cells taken from mice preimmunized against appropriate tumor antigens or histocompatibility antigens. T cells "educated" in vitro against histocompatibility or tumor antigens and injected into these immunodeficient animals can also induce accelerated allograft rejection of skin or tumors in vivo. Evidence indicates that mature thymus-derived lymphocytes are the only cells necessary for this type of rejection. This tumor cell destruction is independent of complement, and there is no requirement for antitumor antibodies in this system (although they may play an inhibitory role if they are present). The only requirement is that the T cells be viable.

Cytotoxic T cells are small lymphocytes. Antigenic contact causes these lymphocytes to differentiate into blast cells which later regress into small lymphocytes. These small lymphocytes exhibit immunologic memory; a second antigenic challenge with the same antigen produces a more rapid response than the first challenge.

Cytotoxicity takes place in 2 phases. The first phase is cell contact. This initial contact is mediated through antigen-specific receptors on the surface of the

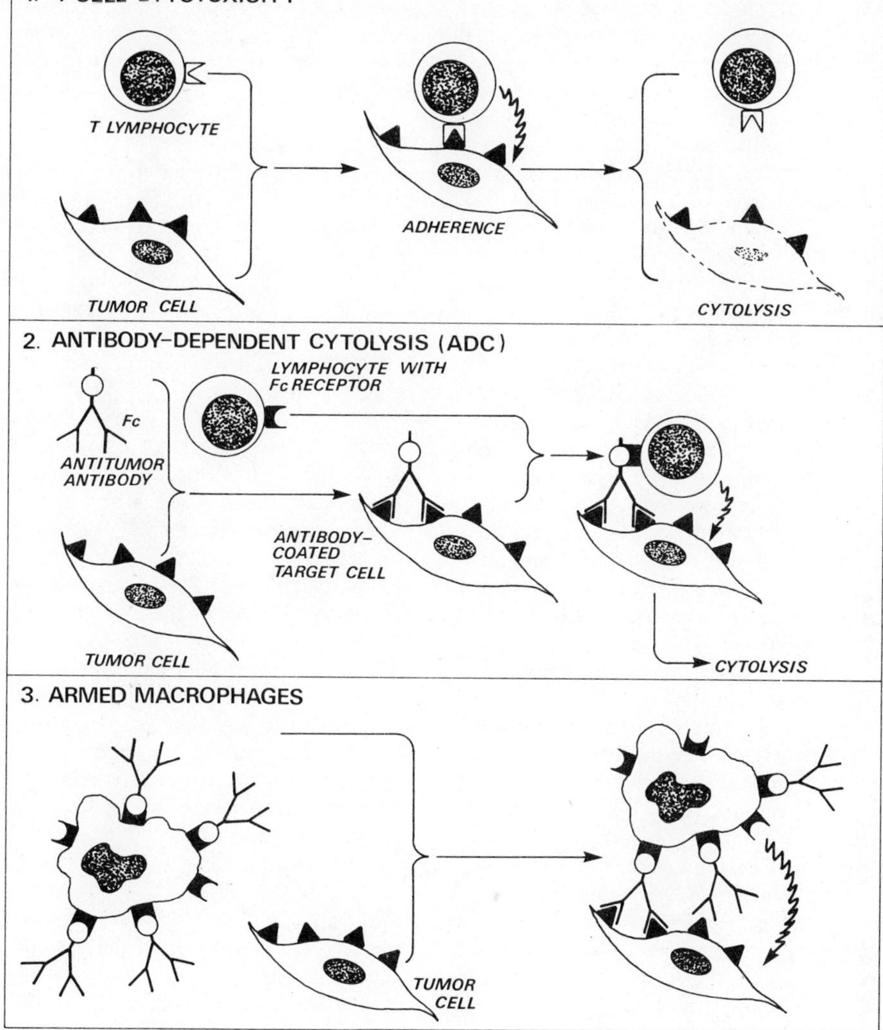

Figure 21–8. Mechanisms of cell-mediated tumor-specific cytolysis.

mature lymphocyte. The nature of these receptors is unclear, but the bond formed is strong enough to allow the cytotoxic lymphocytes to be adsorbed out onto tumor cell monolayers. Adherence is both specific and necessary for later cell lysis. It is rapid, occurring in 5–10 minutes, and energy-dependent, requiring ATP. A large portion of the lymphocyte - target cell surface is involved in this interaction, suggesting that in addition to specific bonds, nonspecific ones may also be formed. This first phase can be inhibited by artificially raising levels of intracellular cAMP in the lymphocyte. The second phase, cell lysis, takes several hours. This can occur in the absence of lymphocytes and culminates in the lysis of the cell membrane. Cell lysis is thought to be a result of progressive membrane permeability changes initiated during the first phase and developing in the second phase. These changes disrupt the osmotic regulation of the cell and cause eventual rupture.

Antibody-Dependent Lymphocyte Cytotoxicity

Target tumor cells coated with antitumor antibody can be specifically lysed by nonimmune lymphocytes from normal animals. The effector cells of this lytic reaction are not clearly defined. They are characterized by having Fc receptors on their membrane. These Fc receptors are protein moieties on the cell membrane which specifically recognize a peptide sequence in the third domain of the constant region (Fc region) of certain immunoglobulin molecules which is exposed *when these antibodies are complexed to antigen.* Monocytes, neutrophils, B cells, and null (K) cells are known to have Fc receptors. Since antigenic particles coated with antibodies would have many Fc sites exposed, this is a logical and well-known method by which phagocytosis of particulate antigens such as bacteria and fungi occurs. Since these Fc receptors are not an exclusive property of lymphocytes, the cytolysis that is seen in these experimental systems may actually be due to a small number of contaminating neutrophils or monocytes. It is therefore unclear at present whether lymphocytes are actually the effector cells. It is clear, however, that T lymphocytes are not involved in this cytotoxicity reaction. It has been speculated that the effector cells are B cell precursors with Fc receptors but no B cell surface markers. These cells also, however, lack surface immunoglobulin, normally considered a characteristic of B lymphocytes. It is safest, therefore, to summarize the available data by stating that effector cells in this reaction are non-T cells, without surface immunoglobulin, and with Fc receptors on their membrane. Whether they truly represent B cell precursors has yet to be determined.

Antibody-dependent cell-mediated cytolysis may involve complement. The amount of surface-bound tumor antibody required for lysis is far less than that necessary for classical complement-mediated cell lysis. IgG probably is the only antibody effective in this system; IgM and IgA do not produce lysis. Target cells must be pretreated with antibody, and pretreatment of lymphocytes does not produce lysis. This is an important distinction, because it indicates that cytophilic antibody—antibody that nonspecifically binds to the surface of lymphocytes—is not an active agent in this system. This is the principal reason that antibody-dependent lymphocyte-mediated cytotoxicity is considered a completely different mechanism from the "armed macrophage" system discussed next.

The many studies suggesting clinical correlates of T cell cytotoxicity are discussed later. Few reports have described the role of antibody-dependent cytotoxicity in human tumor immunity, but this system has been studied in human bladder carcinoma. Effector cells in this in vitro cytotoxicity assay could be removed by passage over glass bead columns coated with antigen(immunoglobulin)/antibody complexes, suggesting that these cells also have Fc receptors on their surfaces.

Armed Macrophages

Macrophages are the third type of cytotoxic cell. Although they are fundamentally nonspecific in their lytic mechanism, macrophages become specific by means of antigen-specific receptors fixed to their surfaces. These antigen-specific molecules can be of 2 types. They can be cytophilic antibodies (IgG or IgM) which bind to macrophages in the usual fashion by Fc receptors, or they can be produced as the result of the interaction between antigen and T cells. This second factor is thought to originate from T cells and may be the T cell receptor. The specificity of the system resides only in the contact between tumor cell and armed macrophage. During contact, the macrophage becomes nonspecifically activated. It is cytotoxic not only for the cell against which it was armed but also for local bystander cells. The activation and cytotoxic effect of macrophages persist for a short time after antigen removal. After several days, they are no longer activated but are still armed. These cells may have a potent role in vivo. If one injects "armed macrophages" mixed with tumor cells into an animal, a strong rejection effect can be demonstrated. This effect is not seen, however, if the tumor cells and the armed macrophages are injected separately at different locations.

Nonspecific Macrophages

The role of the macrophage has been under active study for at least 20 years. It was first thought to process antigen before the processed antigen was "fed" to the antibody-producing B cells. Later, it was demonstrated to be an essential partner in the cooperation between T cells, B cells, and antigen in the induction of antibody formation. The cell is heavily implicated in both induction and effector phases of the T cell response against tumors.

Macrophages from animals chronically infected with protozoa, intracellular bacteria, or metazoa, or from animals immunized with BCG become nonspecifically activated. They are able to exert a strong growth-retarding effect on neoplastic cells. This differs from the "armed macrophage" effect only in that it is completely nonspecific. This mechanism is important, since it may be one of the fundamental mechanisms by which immunotherapy with BCG and DNCB produces its effect. Many studies have indicated that cancer patients have decreased macrophage function, although it is not clear if this is a cause or an effect.

The most interesting question regarding nonspecific killing by macrophages is whether these cells can discriminate between normal and malignant cells. Several studies have suggested that such discrimination may be possible. The mechanism for discrimination may be the recognition by these cells of a general tumor antigen found on the surface of all neoplastic cells or an abnormality in the growth cycle of these malignant cells.

Perhaps the most informative statement that can be made concerning the role of macrophages is that they are always found in close association with lymphoid cells whenever an immunologic reaction is occurring. Although their importance is clear, their exact function is unknown.

ROLE OF THE IMMUNE SYSTEM IN GROWING TUMORS

Almost all animal and human tumors have specific neoantigens on their surface. Both humoral and cellular immunity against these antigens are present in tumor-bearing animals at some phase of their disease. Immunotherapy with agents which increase tumor-specific cell-mediated immunity retards tumor growth. The fact remains, however, that tumors grow and metastasize in animals or humans with intact immune systems (as measured by our present assays). It is essential to determine the role of tumor-specific immunity in animals and humans with growing tumors.

Table 21–1. Proposed mechanism by which autochthonous neoplasms escape immune rejection.*

I. **Special properties of tumor cell antigens:**
Antigen location.
Special covering.
Antigen type weak; autosoluble.
Antigenic transition, immune selection.
II. **Special change in the host:** Immunosuppression: local, regional, carcinogen-induced, age-related, genetic defect–related, stress-related.
III. **Immunologic enhancement**
IV. **Genetic disposition of host:**
Immunologic defect (inborn).
Oncogene-related.

*Reproduced, with permission, from Coggin JH & others: Cancer Res 34:2092, 1974.

The central questions in tumor immunology are the following: Is there some subtle defect in the immune response which allows a malignant cell to grow and produce a clinically evident tumor? Alternatively, is the malignant cell which produces the tumor antigenically deficient? Can the pattern of spontaneous regression followed by later relapse, which is characteristic of some types of tumors such as malignant melanoma, be the result of alterations in the immune response? Can the immune response exert any control over metastatic events? Is it ineffective against them, could it prevent them, or can it actually promote them? (See Table 21–1.)

Several working hypotheses, intended to answer some of these questions, have been suggested. These are now discussed, and they all attempt to present a unified picture of the host-tumor relationship. All have data to support them, but it must be emphasized that these data have come from large numbers of divergent experimental systems. These studies include animal species with chemically induced, virus-induced, and spontaneously arising tumors. The systems include humans with tumors or with other defined disorders, such as immunodeficiencies, that may influence tumor development and growth.

Immune Surveillance

The theory of immune surveillance developed from observations that—teleologically—the cellular immune response against foreign tissue grafts made no sense. The organism was certainly never presented with grafts of foreign cellular antigens during its evolution (except for fetal antigens during pregnancy), yet it was capable of specifically rejecting allografts in a rapid and highly efficient fashion. It was suggested that the actual role of this surveillance system was to enable the organism to reject primary neoplasms. These tumors were identified as "nonself" tissues by their tumor-associated antigens. Later theories suggested that malignant cells are constantly arising in all animals but are normally eliminated by the immune system. In some individuals, however, a subtle defect, either in the ability of the immunologic system to recognize tumor antigens or in the rapidity with which an immune response can be mounted, allows the tumor to grow until it is too large for the cellular immune system to destroy effectively.

This theory has several implications: that normal individuals have certain levels of tumor-specific immunity at all times; that familial tendencies to cancer are secondary to inherited defects in the immune system; and that the immune system is constantly exerting a regulatory effect on both growing primary tumors and metastasizing cells. Only those cells that have a decreased antigenic density subsequently grow and metastasize. Therefore, metastatic tumors should be much less antigenic than primary tumors.

Several lines of evidence support the theory of immune surveillance. Individuals who are genetically immunodeficient have an increased incidence of tumors—so much so that cancer is as frequently the primary cause of death as recurrent infection. The same holds true for individuals who are immunosuppressed (usually for the purpose of renal allografting); the incidence of tumor in these people is much higher than in nonimmunosuppressed cohorts in the population. Additional evidence is the fact that mice that are genetically thymus-deficient (nude mice) will accept tumor transplants, whereas such transplants are rejected by mice possessing normal thymic function.

There are also arguments against the existence of an immune surveillance system. In both immunosuppressed patients and genetically immunodeficient individuals, the tumors that appear are usually lymphoreticular. Since in genetically immunodeficient patients there is already one abnormality in the lymphoid system, these tumors could be simply a manifestation of an additional abnormality. The largest group of immunosuppressed patients are renal allograft recipients, who have a high incidence of reticulum cell sarcomas and lymphomas. Since all patients in this population had rejected at least one kidney graft, the cancers may be explained on the basis of functional demand or overburdening of the system. Both of these factors may predispose individuals to cancer. In controlled experiments, patients with rheumatoid arthritis were immunosuppressed to the same extent as the renal allograft patients. This group of patients demonstrated no increased incidence of cancer. Nude mice accept transplanted tumors; however, these tumors grow locally, do not invade the basement membrane, and seldom metastasize. Thus, it appears that factors other than the immune response are influencing tumor growth.

At present, the evidence indicates that this theory as originally proposed is too broad to be correct. However, in certain cases (especially virally induced tumors in animals), it seems to be correct. As laboratory methods to study tumor immunity are clarified, this theory will probably be modified to apply to a more restricted system.

Immune Stimulation

The effect of cell-mediated immunity on target cells may be 2-fold, so that a strong cellular immune response against the tumor can kill it, or at least prevent its growth, whereas a weak immune response may actually stimulate tumor growth. This theory was suggested by experiments demonstrating that hybrid animals, in which the embryo had a different major histocompatibility antigen from the mother, were significantly larger at birth than animals in which the fetus and mother did not differ at the histocompatibility locus. It was suggested that a mild cellular immune reaction against histocompatibility antigens might aid trophoblastic implantation and then stimulate the embryo up to or beyond the morula stage.

Initial data dealing with immunostimulation came from experiments in which varying amounts of normal or immune syngeneic lymphocytes were mixed with syngeneic tumor cells and injected into irradiated thymectomized animals. Tumor cells mixed with normal lymphocytes in some cases grew faster in the host animal than tumor cells that were not mixed with lymphocytes. Mixtures of tumor cells with low numbers of immune lymphocytes produced the most rapid tumor growth. At higher ratios of immune lymphocytes to tumor cells, an inhibitory effect was evident and the tumor did not grow. It was suggested that this experiment might duplicate the lymphocyte-tumor interaction present in early stages of tumor growth. Tumor cells might be "sneaking through" the immune defense system aided by the immunostimulant effect of feeble immature immune responses in susceptible individuals. Experiments in animal systems confirmed that lymphocytes taken from the host animal in early stages of tumor growth were indeed stimulatory to the tumor, whereas lymphocytes taken later showed the characteristic inhibitory effect found by other investigators.

Other animal systems have shown that low numbers of immune lymphocytes mixed with tumor cells and injected intravenously into recipients promoted the development of metastatic nodules. Injection of very small numbers of tumor cells (which were shown to produce low levels of cell-mediated antitumor immunity) produced more metastases than higher numbers of tumor cells (which resulted in higher levels of cell-mediated immunity against the tumors). The mechanism of action of the immunostimulation seen in these experiments is not known. Immune lymphocytes may specifically bind to tumor cells, forming clumps of cells that would facilitate the establishment of metastatic growths.

The importance of this theory, if it is true, is that therapeutic measures to enhance cellular immunity in patients with tumors could enhance growth of the tumor if the responses were not strong enough. It could also mean that an individual with a weak immune system might more effectively fight his tumor if he were immunosuppressed. To date, there has been no evidence that immunostimulation occurs in humans. Since it is postulated to occur early in the host-tumor interaction, before the tumor is clinically evident, it is a difficult theory to test in spontaneously arising human tumors. For this reason, the most sensible procedure initially is to test all new forms of immunotherapy on a small number of patients and then to evaluate these individuals carefully to determine whether immunotherapy prolongs survival or accelerates the disease process.

Blocking Factors

A surprising finding in tumor immunology was the fact that many animals and humans have strong tumor-specific cell-mediated immunity and yet the tumors continue to grow and to metastasize. The discovery of serum blocking factors has provided one possible explanation for this phenomenon.

Blocking factors are found in the serum of patients with tumors. They appear to be soluble tumor antigen or tumor antigen-antibody complexes circulating in the plasma. They work by blocking the cytotoxic effect of specifically sensitized lymphoid cells by binding to their specific receptors (Fig 21–9). They are detectable in vitro by their ability to inhibit immune lymphocyte killing of tumor cells. Lymphocytes are washed well and then mixed with tumor cells in the micro growth inhibition assay. This assay measures the ability of lymphocytes to inhibit attachment and growth of tumor cells in culture dishes. Immune lymphocytes are far more effective in preventing tumor cell growth than are nonimmune lymphocytes. However, if serum from a patient with "blocking factors" is added to the lymphocyte target cell mixture, it is found to block the inhibition of tumor growth. Tumor cells in the blocked assay grow as well as tumor cells with no immune lymphocytes added to their culture. The blocking effect is tumor-specific, in that sera which will block the reaction between melanoma-sensitized lymphocytes and melanoma tumor cells will not block the reaction between another non-cross-reacting tumor type such as breast carcinoma. At present, blocking factors are thought to be antigen-antibody complexes. They act both on the target tumor cells and on the sensitized lymphocytes. The current tendency is to call the effect on lymphocytes "inhibition" and the effect on tumor cells "blocking." These separate effects are demonstrable by preincubating either the tumor cells or the lymphocytes with blocking factors prior to mixing them together.

The discovery of blocking factors has greatly altered our concept of immunologic tolerance. Some experimental phenomena previously attributed to "central tolerance" have more recently been shown to be secondary to blocking factors. Prior reports regarding the lack of cell-mediated immunity in tumor-bearing animals may not be correct. Inadequately washed lymphocytes may have had blocking factors present on their surface, with the result that lymphocytes from tumor-bearing animals would appear to be centrally unreactive (tolerant) to the tumor.

Blocking factors have been demonstrated in a wide range of in vivo unresponsive states ranging from viral or chemically induced tumors in animals to a large number of spontaneous malignancies in humans. Blocking factor from a patient with cytotoxic lympho-

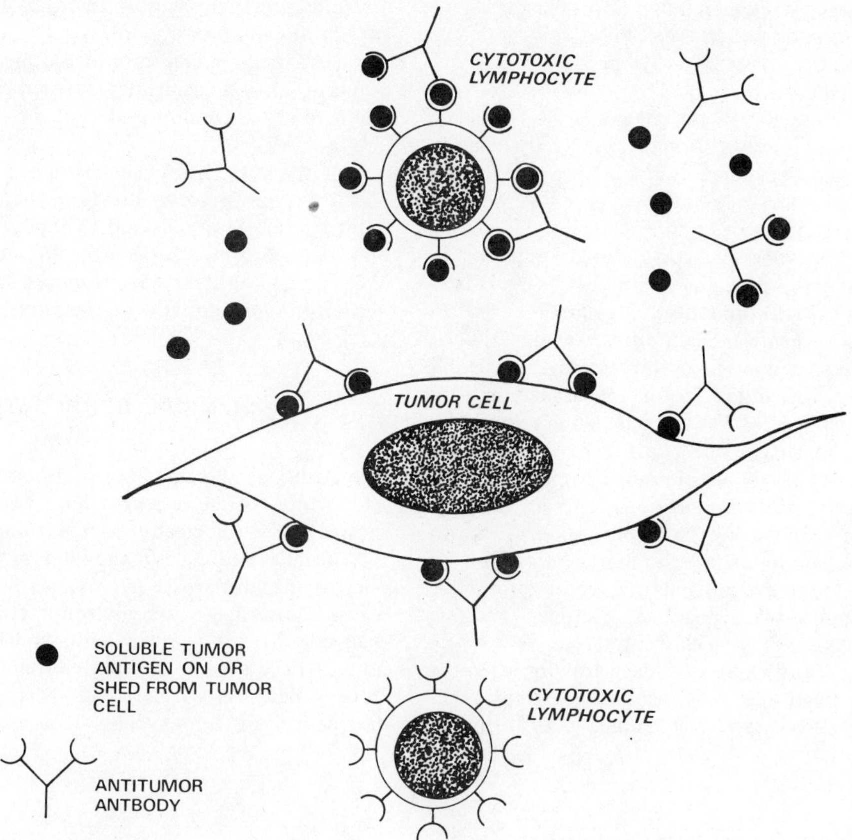

Figure 21–9. Blocking factors. The soluble tumor antigen being shed from the tumor cell serves both to block the receptors of the antigen-specific cytotoxic lymphocytes and to induce tumor-specific antibodies. These in turn bind to the tumor antigen of the tumor cells and coat the tumor cell with "nontumor" antigens so that any antigen-specific cytotoxic lymphocytes still active are unable to recognize the tumor antigens on the surface of the tumor cells.

cytes against breast carcinoma will specifically block the reaction of these cytotoxic lymphocytes against the tumor cell. Blocking factors have been demonstrated in almost all of the standard tests for cell-mediated immunity, including the macrophage migration inhibition test, the lymphocyte activation test, the microcolony inhibition test, and the chromium release test. It is therefore important to wash lymphocytes well before testing them in in vitro assays for tumor-specific immunity.

Serial studies on tumor-bearing hosts, both animals and humans, indicate that the antigen portion of the blocking factor is probably shed from the growing tumor. Surgical removal of the tumor seems to eliminate the blocking factor. This implies that blocking occurs optimally with both antigen and antibody present, possibly complexed. The antibody would persist longer since existent plasma cells continue antibody production even in the absence of antigenic stimulation.

This work has strongly influenced all forms of immunotherapy. Vaccination with tumor cells could either stimulate protective cellular immunity against the tumor or result in humoral immunity. Humoral immunity could either contribute to a cytotoxic reaction or be a component of a blocking factor. This could explain the general lack of success of tumor vaccines in humans. Therefore, emphasis in immunotherapy has been on methods which specifically stimulate only cellular immunity, not humoral immunity. These methods include use of transfer factor, sensitized lymphocytes, and the development of vaccines using tumor cells that have been chemically modified to be strong T cell antigens.

Recently, a deblocking factor has been described. Deblocking factors are antibodies which, when mixed with blocking factors, can neutralize their activity and allow cytotoxic lymphocytes once again to lyse tumor target cells. These deblocking factors have not been well characterized but are suggested to be antibodies directed against the variable region of the blocking antibodies—ie, directed against the antigen combining region of the antibody.

In summary, animals and humans have both humoral and cellular antitumor immunity at some time during the development of their tumor. Several reasons have been offered to explain how tumors can grow and metastasize in the face of an intact immune system and active antitumor immunity (by in vitro measurements):

(1) The immune system may exert no control over the tumor as it grows normally, especially in slow-growing, spontaneous human tumors.

(2) The in vitro tests available may not measure the relevant parameters of immunity.

(3) There may be local or systemic immunosuppression during the time the tumor cells appear and begin to divide. This immunosuppression may be related to viruses, chemical carcinogens, age, genetics, or stress. Suppression may be quite transient, occurring concomitantly with initial tumor appearance, and by the time the suppression has dissipated, the tumor may have grown too large to be controlled (immune surveillance). Alternatively, the immune response against tumors both in normal individuals and in those in whom cancer occurs may be both weak and late in appearing (too late to manage the tumor burden).

(4) The tumor cell antigens may be nonprotective because of their location, because of antigen masking, or because they are only weakly antigenic.

(5) At an early phase of tumor growth, when the tumor is still small, the weak response existing at that time may specifically stimulate tumor growth (immunostimulation), allowing it to reach a size uncontrollable by the immune system.

(6) Blocking factors which appear as the tumor begins to shed antigen may further predispose to accelerated growth and metastases.

A sequence has been postulated (Fig 21–10) in which the tumor grows slowly in the presence of both cytotoxic effector cells and antibody until it can produce enough tumor antigen to block the lymphocytes and enough antibody is produced to mark a new period of rapid growth and metastasis for the tumor.

CLINICAL CORRELATES

Although data in human tumor systems are limited, many different assays have been developed to show that histologically related tumors antigenically cross-react. Immune lymphocytes or antibodies from one patient with breast carcinoma not only specifically react against that patient's tumor cells but also react against cells from other patients with breast carcinomas. In the same fashion, serum blocking factors from patient A, which could specifically inhibit the destruction of tumor cells from patient A by the

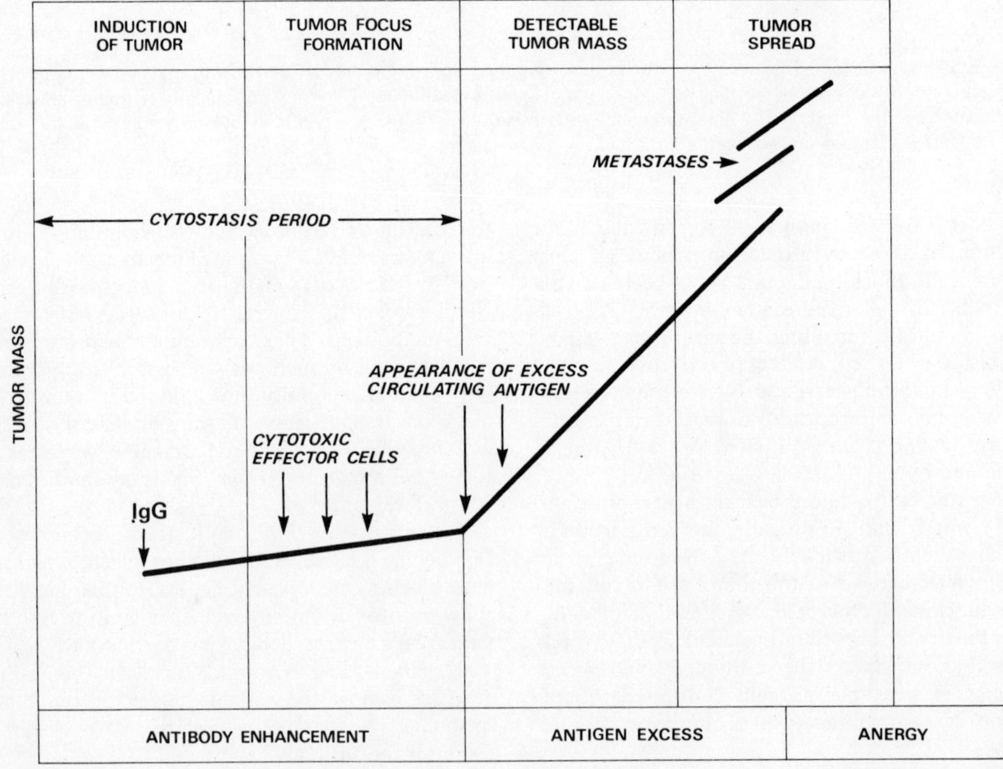

Figure 21–10. Sequence of immunologic events in relation to tumor growth in animals. (Redrawn and reproduced, with permission, from Coggins JH & others: Cancer Res 34:2092, 1974.)

immune lymphocytes from patient A, could also prevent the destruction of tumor cells from patient B by the lymphocytes of patient B. This was true provided that patient B had the same histologic type of tumor as patient A. This type of cross-reactivity has been demonstrated for the following tumors: carcinoma of the colon, breast, kidney, ovary, bladder, endometrium, and uterine cervix; Wilms's tumor, malignant melanoma, malignant gliomas, and sarcomas. These tumors usually cross-react at both the humoral and the cellular level.

This cross-reactivity is important both for testing purposes and for therapy. It means that a standard line of cells derived from the appropriate tumor may be used to test a large series of patients' lymphocytes for immunity to the tumor. Also, lymphocytes from any individual reactive against the tumor line may be used for passive transfer of immunity against the tumor.

A series of patients with different tumors has been followed over several years to monitor the role played by the immune system in the course of the disease. Malignant melanoma was considered to be typical of these neoplasms. Patients were studied whose primary tumors had been surgically removed and who showed no evidence of metastases. Such patients had high cell-mediated immunity against malignant melanoma cells (as measured by colony inhibition) and no serum blocking factor activity. A second group of patients had disseminated disease, and almost all of this group died from the tumor during the period in which they were observed. These patients had levels of cell-mediated immunity higher than normal but not as high as in disease-free patients with surgically removed tumors. All sera from this second group had blocking factor activity. The third group of patients comprised those who developed metastatic disease during the observation period. Blocking factors appeared in their sera several months before metastases became clinically evident and were present in all patients with clinically evident metastases. When metastases were removed, the blocking factors often disappeared, and this correlated positively with a long disease-free interval.

Therefore, the pattern that emerged from these studies was of a disease process in which cellular immunity against the tumor was always intact but in which the development of metastases correlated positively with the presence of blocking factors. Removal of tumor corresponded with the loss of blocking factors. This pattern has been noted with other tumors studied with these same laboratory methods, and this finding suggests that in malignant melanoma it is blocking factor and not cellular immunity that is the key in host-tumor interaction. A patient with malignant melanoma undergoing spontaneous remission did not have blocking factor; instead, his serum *potentiated* the cytotoxic effect of lymphocytes from other malignant melanoma patients against their tumors and counteracted the effect of blocking factor. This suggested an additional serum factor, an antagonist to the first, which was termed "deblocking factor."

Neuroblastomas in young children have been tested by these assays. This tumor is especially interesting from an immunologic point of view because of the high incidence of spontaneous remission. Regardless of whether the neuroblastomas were actively growing or in remission, the patients' lymphocytes still possessed active cellular immunity specifically directed against tumor cells. Mothers of these patients also had cellular immunity specifically directed against neuroblastoma cells. We may conclude that in patients with neuroblastomas, as in patients with malignant melanomas, tumor-specific cell-mediated immunity is present at all phases of the disease. This immunity can persist for many years (longer than 10 years) after patients are tumor-free. Tumor growth was correlated with the presence of blocking factor. Tumor regression was correlated with the occurrence of deblocking factor.

The mechanism of these interactions is suggested to be the following: A growing tumor initially produces cellular immunity but no humoral immunity. The tumor then begins to shed tumor antigens and to stimulate the production of antibodies which coat the tumor with "self" antigens. At this point, the lymphocytes lose access to the tumor "nonself" antigens and their protection becomes ineffective. The tumor then begins to grow in the presence of these blocking factors and ultimately metastasizes. Removal of the tumor mass predisposes to the elimination of blocking factors, both because the tumor antigens are no longer being produced and because the stimulus to the humoral system is eliminated. These observations are noted in animals bearing SV40-induced tumors (Fig 21–10) and in humans with malignant melanoma. In patients with malignant melanoma who are undergoing spontaneous regression of metastatic lesions following removal of the primary tumor, an absence of blocking factors and the presence of strongly positive cellular immunity are noted. The appearance of serum blocking factors precedes recurrent metastasis by several months.

It is important to note that the colony inhibition assay was used for these studies. This assay and the micro growth inhibition test are thought to detect a wider range of cell-mediated immune activities than other tests.

A slightly different picture has been presented by studies on bladder carcinoma and osteogenic sarcoma. In these diseases, the patient with a small primary osteogenic sarcoma or a primary bladder carcinoma has high cell-mediated immunity against the tumor. This immunity decreases following surgical removal of the tumor.

The presence of blocking factors and their role in determining the clinical course of the disease are not firmly established for all tumors. It is probable that each histologic type of tumor will produce a somewhat different pattern depending on its rate of growth and its tendency to shed tumor antigens. In malignant melanoma, therapeutic immunostimulation may be detrimental, and therapy should be directed toward eliminating or inactivating blocking factors. However, immunotherapy aimed at increasing cell-mediated immunity in bladder carcinoma and osteogenic sarcoma should be beneficial; indeed, studies to date show that tumor-specific transfer factor therapy, when initiated immediately after surgical removal of the primary tumor, significantly prolongs the disease-free interval when compared to controls.

IMMUNOTHERAPY

If cancer is regarded as an immunodeficiency disorder, cancer immunotherapy can be considered a method of repairing the immune defect which allowed the tumor to arise initially. Recently accumulated data have called into question the validity of this assumption, which is based on the immune surveillance theory. Nonetheless, experiments in animals and clinical studies in humans using different methods of immunotherapy have suggested that this is a promising approach regardless of its theoretical basis.

Immunotherapy offers a method by which occult tumor cells may be sought out and specifically destroyed. Its chief value is its high degree of sensitivity in tumor cell detection, but immunotherapy does have important limitations. A lesion with a volume of 1 ml—usually the smallest lesion that is clinically detectable—contains about 10^9 tumor cells. If one considers that there are only about 15×10^9 lymphocytes in the body and that, of these, at most only 1% are specifically committed against an antigen, it is evident that on the basis of numbers alone the tumor has an advantage. On the other hand, one lymphocyte can kill more than one tumor cell, and accessory cells (specific or nonspecific) in the form of macrophages are available, so that immunotherapy might be effective in cases with small tumors. At present, the vast majority of tumor immunologists do not see initial cancer treatment as the major role of immunotherapy; primary treatment is reserved for chemotherapy, radiotherapy, or surgery. Immunotherapy is seen as prophylactic therapy to destroy occult metastases remaining after maximal reduction of the tumor mass.

Four types of immunotherapy have been used in animals and man: (1) non-tumor-specific immunization, (2) active immunization with tumor cell vaccines, (3) passive immunization with sensitized and nonsensitized lymphocytes, and (4) tumor-specific transfer factor.

Nonspecific Immunization

One of the first agents used to increase T cell immunity in cancer patients was DNCB. This compound was known to produce contact sensitivity. It had been used for treatment of malignant melanoma and of cutaneous lymphoma in the following manner: The patient was initially sensitized to the compound by topical application of an immunogenic dose. A delayed hypersensitivity reaction resulted from exposure to the chemical. Various dilutions of the chemical were then incorporated into a series of pastes, and these pastes were applied to small areas of skin to determine the lowest concentration of DNCB that would produce a cutaneous reaction. One dilution below this amount—termed a subclinical dose—was then applied to large areas of skin over and around cutaneous tumors. The parts of the skin which contained no tumor were unchanged in appearance, while the skin in the area of tumors became red and inflamed. These areas of inflammation included small tumor lesions not apparent prior to treatment. Eventually, the lesions cleared and regressed, and the tumor cells were destroyed. The cure rate of this therapy in cutaneous lymphoma is high, but its success against malignant melanoma was equivocal.

The mechanism of action of this compound is unknown, but the clinical evidence strongly suggests that it works as a hapten which produces an additive effect. Tumor-specific lymphocytes in the area of the tumor, probably already present at the time the chemical is applied, combine their effect with those of DNCB-specific lymphocytes to increase the concentration of mediators produced in the local immune environment. These mediators have the net effect of stimulating lymphocyte blastogenesis and cytotoxicity. These include lymphocyte transformation factor, macrophage attraction and inhibitory factors, cytotoxic factors, and transfer factor. These factors also attract and retain macrophages in the local area of the tumor and produce the inflammatory responses noted.

Another type of non-tumor-specific immunotherapy widely used at present is immunization by scarification with BCG. This attentuated form of live human tubercle bacillus has been used for many years to immunize against tuberculosis. It was noted that immunized populations had a lower incidence of cancer (especially leukemia) than nonimmunized populations. A protective effect was noted in mice immunized with BCG prior to challenge with leukemia cells. Additional guinea pig studies involved inoculation of animals with solid tumors followed by immunization with attenuated bacilli over the tumor site. The results suggested possible clinical benefit with this agent in patients with other types of cancer. Trials have been reported with leukemia, osteogenic sarcoma, and malignant melanoma. To date this therapy has not been shown to be successful in any disease other than malignant melanoma. Its action in this cancer has been very interesting. The bacillus, administered by scarification over the site of the cutaneous tumor, will cause regression of the treated lesion and will often produce clearing of distal skin lesions. It has no effect on visceral lesions, however. Therefore, if the melanoma is confined to the skin, the patient may remain disease-free for long periods and may even be cured. If the disease is more widespread, immunizations do not enhance longevity. The mechanism of action in this phenomenon is unclear. Perhaps there is a compartment of active cells, possibly in the lymphocyte series, that is restricted to the skin. Alternatively, perhaps the accessory cells needed for amplification of the response are more concentrated in the skin.

Along with the stimulatory effect on lymphocytes produced by immunization with BCG, there seems to be an additional effect of the antigen on macrophages. Macrophages from animals infected with tuberculosis have been shown to be highly activated, and these cells can destroy not only tubercle bacilli but also tumor cells. It is therefore likely that the macrophages are activated by the vaccine in a similar manner, further enhancing the antitumor effect.

The primary concern in the use of BCG in cancer patients is the possibility of the induction of humoral immunity against the tumor. One of the classical methods of producing antibodies to antigens is to emulsify them in Freund's complete adjuvant (a mineral oil suspension of tubercle bacilli). Since a major portion of blocking factors are probably antibodies, the humoral antitumor response is of concern. Vaccine immunization over the site of the tumor may induce blocking factors and thereby enhance the growth of the tumor. Studies of the effect of vaccine on antibody responses are now in progress. It is clear, however, that active immunization in cancer is a 2-edged sword, and each mode of therapy must be carefully monitored to be sure that it does not make the disease worse.

Other nonspecific agents that activate lymphocytes have been proposed for immunotherapy. One of these is MER, a *m*ethanol *e*xtract *r*esidue of the Calmette-Guérin attenuated tubercle bacillus. This extract is claimed to be more active immunologically than the bacillus itself. A methanol-soluble extract of *Mycobacterium butyricum* has also been used, as have extracts of *Bordetella pertussis* and *Corynebacterium parvum*.

Long-term observation of leukemia patients in remission induced by chemotherapy indicates that those patients treated with either attenuated bacillus, *C parvum* vaccine, or irradiated leukemic cells remained tumor-free longer than untreated individuals. Disseminated malignant melanoma patients were treated with intravenous injections of phytohemagglutinin, an agent that nonspecifically causes T cells to go into blastogenesis both in vitro and in vivo. Patients responded to this treatment with inflammation and decreased size of tumor nodules. Biopsies revealed lymphocytic infiltrates, tumor necrosis, and a heavy coat of complement-fixing IgG on the tumor cells.

Active Immunization With Tumor Cell Vaccines

Even before it was definitely established that there were tumor antigens on human tumors, vaccines were prepared from surgically removed primary tumors and were used for immunization. Except in leukemia, where tumor cells are treated with neuraminidase to remove the glycocalyx from the cells, thereby unmasking tumor antigens, these vaccines have been totally unsuccessful. None of the studies included laboratory tests to determine the mechanism of action of these vaccines, but clinical trials demonstrated that survival rates of the vaccinated individuals were either the same as or lower than the rates observed in untreated controls. In the absence of laboratory data, the reason for the lack of success is unclear, but it is quite possible that blocking factors were produced which prevented the cellular immune system from controlling tumor growth.

Modified tumor cells. Despite the notable lack of success in using tumor cells as vaccines, the idea still has strong appeal. Some antigens found in animal studies are pure T cell antigens; these will only stimulate cellular immunity and not humoral immunity. Recently, methods have been devised to chemically modify human tumor cells so that they also become pure T cell antigens. It has been confirmed in animal studies that vaccination with these modified tumor cells does not produce antibodies, and they are currently being evaluated clinically. The advantage of this method would be that it could produce active cellular immunity both against the "public antigens" present on all tumors of that histologic type and against the "private antigens" present only on the tumor of that spécific individual. (Such private antigens do not cross-react with other antigens of the same histologic type.)

Passive Immunization With Sensitized and Nonsensitized Lymphocytes

On the whole, passive immunization of tumor-bearing animals with nonsensitized or sensitized lymphocytes has not been successful. Transfusions of lymphocytes in tumor-bearing animals from either nonimmunized or immunized donors are effective in leukemia only if the number of lymphocytes per tumor cell mass is high enough. Many investigators demonstrated that syngeneic lymphocytes sensitized to tumor antigens could be injected into tumor-bearing animals—or mixed with the tumor cells and then injected into normal animals—and produce tumor killing as measured by the survival of the host animal. In humans, however, syngeneic lymphocytes sensitized against tumors are not available. Allogeneic lymphocytes from immune donors are rapidly destroyed in a host-versus-graft reaction (graft rejection) and often never reach the site of the tumor. These host-versus-graft and graft-versus-host reactions may be used to a slight advantage. Nonimmunized lymphocytes injected into patients with acute leukemia induce remission of short duration, probably because of the rejection of the allogeneic lymphocytes from the nonimmune donor. However, a graft-versus-host reaction can also occur in those patients with leukemia who are not capable of killing the foreign cells; some patients have died of this secondary disease.

Tumor-Specific Transfer Factor

Transfer factor has been tried in several types of tumors, and the preliminary results are encouraging. This molecule is believed to alter host lymphocytes so that they become tumor-specific. Transfer of tumor-specific cell-mediated immunity has been demonstrated with malignant melanoma, breast carcinoma, osteogenic sarcoma, and nasopharyngeal carcinoma.

This transfer has been measured by migration inhibition, blastogenesis, and cytolytic assays. The skin test reactivities of the donors were also transferred to the cancer patients. In some patients with malignant melanoma, osteogenic sarcoma, and breast carcinoma, both clinical and laboratory evidence of increased cell-mediated immunity following transfer factor therapy was obtained. Two of 8 patients with malignant melanoma demonstrated tumor regression concomitant with transfer factor therapy. Patients with metastatic osteogenic sarcoma treated with tumor-specific transfer factor demonstrated lymphocytic infiltrates around the tumor which remained present for variable periods up to 6 months after injection. Preliminary data suggest that the disease-free period and overall survival in osteogenic sarcoma patients are prolonged in people prophylactically treated with transfer factor.

Patients with metastatic breast carcinoma treated with tumor-specific transfer factor also demonstrated transfer of tumor-specific cell-mediated immunity. Inflammation was noted around metastatic lesions in these patients. Patients with nasopharyngeal carcinoma have been treated with transfer factor prepared from individuals who have recovered from infectious mononucleosis, the theory being that since EB virus is implicated in both diseases the same antigens will be expressed on cells from both diseases. Leukemia is also being treated with transfer factor, but the data are still very preliminary.

CONCLUSION

At present it appears that immunotherapy will be used prophylactically in a few types of cancers at certain stages to prevent or inhibit recurrences. The major role of immunotherapy will be in combination with either chemotherapy or radiotherapy following maximal surgical resection. Immunotherapy should be able to eliminate many of the cells remaining after treatment by other modes of therapy since it will destroy tumor cells by a different mechanism than that used by chemotherapy or radiotherapy. At present, immunotherapy has not been combined with the other modalities for 2 reasons: (1) the effect of immunotherapy alone has not been explored in the majority of cancers, and it is therefore difficult to assess the independent contribution of 2 therapies used simultaneously unless one knows the effect of each singly; and (2) very little information is available on the immunosuppressive nature of chemotherapy. It is expected that the white blood cell count will drop sharply during conventional chemotherapy or radiotherapy. The question, however, is whether the white blood cells which reappear after these treatments are of the same composition as those before treatment, or whether one or more of the subpopulations of cells has been eliminated.

Studies are in progress to answer both of these questions. Clinical trials have been established in which patients are randomized between chemotherapy alone and chemotherapy with immunotherapy. Studies of the immune response of animals and humans treated with radiotherapy and immunotherapy are also in progress. Once these treatment methods are adjusted to produce minimal immunosuppression, immunotherapy can be added for maximal benefit. Animal studies indicate that sequential therapy can vastly improve survival rates. In one such report, a syngeneic metastasizing tumor was used, and survival rates were increased from 25% with a regimen of chemotherapy alone to 90–100% using a short nonimmunosuppressive course of chemotherapy followed immediately by immunotherapy.

• • •

References

Baldwin RW: Immunological aspects of chemical carcinogenesis. Adv Cancer Res 18:1, 1973.

Byers VS & others: Quantitative immunofluorescent studies on the tumor antigen-bearing cell in giant cell tumor of bone and osteogenic sarcoma. Cancer Res 35:2520, 1975.

Byers VS & others: Tumor-specific cell-mediated immunity in household contacts of cancer patients. J Clin Invest 55:500, 1975.

Coggin JH Jr, Anderson NG: Cancer, differentiation and embryonic antigens: Some central problems. Adv Cancer Res 19:105, 1974.

Coggin JH Jr & others: Proposed mechanisms by which autochthonous neoplasms escape immune rejection. Cancer Res 34:2092, 1974.

Coligan JE & others: Isolation and characterization of carcinoembryonic antigen. Immunochemistry 9:377, 1972.

Fidler IJ: In vitro studies of cellular mediated immunostimulation of tumor growth. J Natl Cancer Inst 50:1307, 1973.

Gooding LR, Edidin M: Cell surface antigens of a mouse testicular teratoma: Identification of an antigen physically associated with H-2 antigens on tumor cells. J Exp Med 140:61, 1974.

Hellstrom KE, Hellstrom I: Lymphocyte mediated cytotoxicity and blocking serum activity to tumor antigens. Adv Immunol 18:209, 1974.

Immunological control of virus associated tumors in man: Prospects and problems. (Symposium.) Cancer Res 36:559, 1976.

Jeejeebhoy HF: Stimulation of tumor growth by the immune response. Int J Cancer 13:665, 1974.

Levin AS & others: Osteogenic sarcoma: Immunologic parameters before and during therapy with tumor-specific transfer factor. J Clin Invest 55:487, 1975.

Levy MH, Wheelock EF: The role of macrophages in defense against neoplastic disease. Adv Cancer Res 20:131, 1974.

O'Toole C & others: Cellular immunity to human urinary bladder carcinoma: 2. Effect of surgery and preoperative irradiation. Int J Cancer 10:92, 1972.

O'Toole C & others: Lymphoid cells mediating tumor-specific cytotoxicity to carcinoma of the urinary bladder: Separation of the effector population using a surface marker. J Exp Med 139:457, 1974.

Prehn RT: The immune response as a stimulator of tumor growth. Science 176:170, 1972.

Stratton JA & others: A comparison of the acute effects of radiation therapy including or excluding the thymus on the lymphocyte subpopulations of cancer patients. J Clin Invest 56:88, 1975.

Stutman O: Immunodepression and malignancy. Adv Cancer Res 22:261, 1975.

22 . . .
Immunosuppression & Immunopotentiation

David R. Webb, Jr., PhD

Since the time of Ehrlich and Landsteiner, scientists studying immunochemistry and the biology of the immune response have been interested in how such responses might be modified. Although the initial impetus for such interest resulted from studies on the rejection of transplanted tissue, more recent interest in immunosuppression and immunopotentiation has centered on the use of such methods to more clearly define the mechanisms by which the immune system works.

In the broadest sense it could be said that interest in immunopotentiation developed first with the work of Jenner. A more systematic approach resulted from the work of Pasteur and Koch in their attempts to "vaccinate" or otherwise protect both humans and animals from disease. In this sense, any inoculation may be regarded as immunopotentiation.

Suppression or destruction of lymphoid cells had been observed as early as 1899 by Metchnikoff. Shortly thereafter Smith, in 1909, demonstrated that passively administered specific antibody given concomitantly with antigen would lead to a suppression of the immune response. Thus, immunosuppression, like immunopotentiation, was a recognized immunologic phenomenon long before anything was known about the underlying mechanisms.

IMMUNOSUPPRESSION

Given this brief introduction, it is apparent that broad definitions of both immunosuppression and immunopotentiation could include virtually all aspects of the immune response. However, for the purposes of discussion it is possible to delineate more strictly the various aspects of immunosuppression under 3 general headings: (1) natural immunologic unresponsiveness or tolerance, (2) artificially induced unresponsiveness, and (3) pathologically induced unresponsiveness (Table 22–1).

Natural Immunologic Unresponsiveness or Tolerance

Since this subject is considered in Chapter 13,

David R. Webb, Jr. is in the Department of Cell Biology, Roche Institute of Molecular Biology, Nutley, New Jersey.

Table 22–1. Types of immunosuppression.

Class	Mechanism of Induction
Natural immunologic unresponsiveness	Tolerance to self-antigens induced during ontogeny
Artificially induced unresponsiveness	Paralysis by antigen Use of specific antisera (antilymphocyte serum, antithymocyte serum, anti-Ig, Thy-1, etc) Excess of antigen-specific antibody Cytotoxic drugs or hormone therapy Radiation Surgery
Pathologically induced immunosuppression	Immunodeficiency disease, resulting in enhanced tumor growth, and frequent viral, bacterial, and fungal infections

little will be said about it here. Suffice it to say that many of the current concepts of immunology developed from a consideration of the failure of the host to respond to "self" antigens. The existence of a natural mechanism of immunosuppression has lent much impetus to attempts to artificially manipulate the immune response.

Artificially Induced Unresponsiveness

As previously noted, as early as the 1900s experiments suggested that it was possible to artificially alter or suppress the immune response. Parker has suggested that artificially induced immunosuppression be divided into 6 general categories: (1) administration of antigen, (2) administration of specific antisera or antibody, (3) use of other "biologic" reagents such as antilymphocyte antisera, (4) use of cytotoxic drugs, (5) radiation, and (6) surgical ablation of lymphoid tissue. These areas will be considered when we examine how immunosuppression may be induced.

Pathologically Induced Immunosuppression

This subject might at first appear to be an offshoot of natural tolerance. However, the observation that many disease states can alter immunoresponsiveness has led to considerable research into the mechanisms responsible. This warrants, then, separate consideration. It has been known for many years that patients suffering from a variety of infectious diseases are more susceptible to infection with other pathogens. Proliferative disorders involving immunocompetent cells (eg, lymphomas, multiple myeloma, leukemia) as well as chronic infectious diseases such as syphilis, tuberculosis, and leprosy may induce both specific and nonspecific suppression of responsiveness. This immunosuppression results from specific interaction of the host's immune system and the disease, leading to ablation of the "normal" immunologic function of the host. The process may be active or passive; an invading organism may produce a substance which suppresses the host's immune response or, alternatively, the host's normal mechanisms of resistance may be blocked.

Induction of Immunosuppression

A. Immunoparalysis by Antigen: The use of specific antigen as a method of inducing suppression in humans has been employed successfully for many years for allergen desensitization. This method is not infallible, however, as anyone who has ever undergone allergic desensitization will attest.

The ability of a given antigen to induce an immunosuppressive state depends on many factors. These include the antigen's chemical nature and molecular size, the route of injection, the timing of injection, and the nature of the immune response to be affected. Generally speaking, it is easier to induce both responsiveness and nonresponsiveness to moderately large antigens (MW 10^4-10^5). In addition, proteins are by far the most effective antigens and therefore are the most effective in the induction of suppression. Antigen suppression is also critically dependent on the route of injection, the most common routes being subcutaneously or intramuscularly. There are many modifications of these methods, however. Two closely related antigens can be injected together, resulting in antigen competition and subsequent suppression. Antigen fragments or nonmetabolizable antigens (such as some synthetic polypeptides of D-amino acids) can also result in immune suppression. The problems of using antigen-induced suppression relate to our lack of understanding of the mechanism of suppression induced in this way. Thus, it is possible to induce hyperreactivity or sensitivity using a protocol which, theoretically, should induce suppression. This is especially dangerous if such hypersensitization leads to possible anaphylaxis.

B. Induction by Antisera or Specific Antibody: Experimental immunologists have known for some time that the development and control of some immune responses were related to changes in levels of circulating antibody. It is possible to show, for example, that the injection of specific antibody against the immunizing antigen will suppress the immune response to that antigen. The mechanism of such suppression is thought to be related to a homeostatic feedback mechanism, ie, once the immune system has produced sufficient antibody, it can shut itself off. It has been shown that antibody-producing cells will bind antigen-antibody complexes via an Fc receptor on their surface, and this may in part account for the mechanism of this mode of suppression. However, such suppression can be induced using antibody fragments minus their Fc portion. This suggests that simple blocking of the relevant antigenic determinants, thus preventing stimulation of the relevant lymphocyte, may be the more general mechanism of action.

In practical terms, the usefulness of this technic has been dramatically demonstrated in the injection of anti-Rh antibody in potentially sensitized pregnant women to prevent subsequent erythroblastosis. This method of immune suppression offers additional advantages in that it is highly specific and usually suppresses responsiveness to a specific antigen. Whether or not this method can be extended to transplantation antigens to prevent graft or organ rejection remains to be seen. It has proved to be difficult to suppress the response via specific antibody when more complex antigens are used and when exposure to the antigenic stimulus is great.

C. Antilymphocyte Serum: While the administration of specific antibody is directed at suppressing only certain specific antigen-sensitive cells, the use of antibodies directed against the lymphocytes themselves attempts to produce indiscriminate immunosuppression. When thymocytes, spleen cells, lymph node cells, or thoracic duct lymphocytes from one animal species are injected into another animal species, specific antilymphocyte serum may be generated. Such specific antiserum can be subsequently injected into the animal from which the immunizing lymphocytes are derived. This will induce a nonspecific decrease in immunoresponsiveness. For example, following injection of antilymphocyte serum, lymphocytopenia occurs, and there follows a decrease in cellular immunity. The effect on humoral responses is variable. With lymphocytes in culture, the serum can be demonstrated to lyse lymphocytes in the presence of complement or, in its absence, to cause agglutination or blast transformation. Antilymphocyte serum is effective in suppressing cellular immunity against a variety of tissue graft systems (ie, heterografts, xenografts, secondary allograft rejection). This may be related to the fact that antilymphocyte serum can suppress the response to histoincompatible antigens and thereby interfere with the ability of antigen-sensitive cells to respond to these antigens.

Interestingly, it appears that certain thymus-derived or T lymphocytes are resistant to antilymphocyte serum both in vitro and in vivo. This may account for its restricted action on the immune response.

In terms of mode of administration and therapy, the usual regimen calls for treatment with antilymphocyte serum prior to exposure to antigen as well as continued treatment following antigen exposure. Such treatment does not lead to irreversible suppression, since when the serum is discontinued a cellular immune response may be expressed. Choice of a therapeutic regimen is also frustrated by the fact that the mechanism of action of antilymphocyte serum is poorly understood. At this juncture there are no definitive data which explain all of the effects which potent sera are known to produce. A choice of regimen must be dictated by what is known about the efficiency--in terms of titer, cytotoxicity, and effects on the immune response—of a particular batch of serum. Furthermore, since antilymphocyte serum is an antiserum raised in a heterologous species, the question of serum sickness arises; there may be complications due to nephritis resulting from repeated injections of a foreign serum. However, it appears that at least some of the danger can be abated by the concomitant use of corticosteroids.

In addition to specific antibody and antilymphocyte serum, there appears to be an inhibitory serum factor present in the α-globulin fraction of serum. Its usefulness, however, remains to be determined.

D. Cytotoxic Drugs or Hormone-Induced Immunosuppression: A number of drugs and hormones may be used to effect suppression of the immune response. Virtually any drug which affects mammalian cell metabolism can alter immune responses. Such drugs as cyclophosphamide, busulfan, phenylalanine mustard, mercaptopurine, 5-fluorodeoxyuridine (floxuridine, FUDR), methotrexate, and azathioprine will block immune responses depending on when they are given. In general (with the exceptions of cyclophosphamide, busulfan, and phenylalanine mustard), simultaneous administration of the drug with antigen will suffice to induce suppression. The excepted drugs are usually given 48 hours in advance of antigen. Treatment with these agents in advance of antigen probably results in killing antigen-sensitive cells nonspecifically; therefore, these drugs are generally immunosuppressive. On the other hand, drugs administered simultaneously with antigen can be assumed to be primarily active against specific antigen-sensitive cells. This specificity is attributed to the fact that many drugs, such as dactinomycin and chloramphenicol, interfere with DNA, RNA, or protein synthesis, so that only actively metabolizing or dividing (ie, antigen-stimulated) cells are affected. However, as these drugs are administered systemically, there is no question but that they block the growth and development of many cell types. This may be particularly dangerous when they affect hematopoietic cells and lead to anemia or thrombocytopenia. Alkylating agents (cyclophosphamide) pose the additional danger of being carcinogenic as well as teratogenic.

Hormones, particularly the corticosteroids, represent another group of potent immunosuppressive agents which act nonspecifically on lymphocytes. These drugs are normally given in advance (48 hours) of antigen administration and produce stronger and more direct suppression of delayed hypersensitivity (cell-mediated) responses than of humoral immune responses. This effect is temporary and usually disappears after a day or two.

At least part of this immunosuppression is secondary to the ability of corticosteroids to deplete immature thymus-derived T cells from spleen and thymus. This also may account for the stronger effects of these drugs on cell-mediated immunity. Corticosteroids have proved useful in studying cell-mediated tumor immunity and experimental autoimmune disease.

The mechanism of action of the corticosteroids is still poorly understood, although the target cell appears to be an immature T cell. In addition to affecting T cell function, these drugs alter the ability of the reticuloendothelial system (macrophages, etc) to take up and process antigen. The corticosteroids probably have multiple target cells and several mechanisms of action.

The administration of cytotoxic drugs or hormones is most commonly undertaken in combination with other modes of immunosuppression. This therapy has been worked out empirically rather than being based on a rational understanding of drug action and synergy. In retrospect, the rationale relates to the fact that immune responses involve heterogeneous populations of cell types with differing drug or hormone sensitivities and are therefore more apt to be modified by a combination therapeutic approach.

E. Radiation: Suppression of the immune response also occurs when animals or humans are subject to stress following surgical manipulation or x-ray radiation. Immune suppression induced by trauma is a poorly defined area of study which has not been systematically explored; however, some information is available on the suppression following radiation.

In experimental animal models, irradiation with x-rays has long been used to suppress immune responses or to study lymphocytic cells required for developing immune responses. The sum of this evidence indicates that most lymphocytes are sensitive to x-rays. Radiation induces profound lymphocytopenia in lymphoid organs and in the general circulation and suppresses most immunocompetent cell functions. However, there does exist a population of lymphocytes which are radiation-resistant and which have specialized functions in the immune response.

F. Surgery: Surgical removal of lymph nodes, thymus, or spleen can alter the immune response. Removal of the thymus may have serious consequences in terms of loss of immunosurveillance function and increased evidence of neoplasia, but at present this possibility remains largely theoretical. Splenectomy has been shown to be immunosuppressive, particularly in autoimmune diseases and some lymphoproliferative diseases such as Hodgkin's disease. In animals, splenectomy does not alter immune responses since compensatory changes occur in lymphoid cells in lymph nodes.

Naturally Induced Immune Suppression

From time to time the immune system spontaneously suppresses itself. While there is no question that the immune system is capable of fine manipulation of its responses, the type of suppression considered here relates to situations in which an effective immune response is otherwise expected. This pertains particularly to neoplastic disease.

For many years immunologists puzzled over the fact that neoplasms kill their hosts even though the host animal or patient possesses high titers of circulating antibody or cytotoxic cells against the tumor. The reasons for this apparent paradox appear to be complex. A vigorous humoral response may not be unqualifiedly beneficial since antitumor antibody may bind circulating tumor antigen and mask its antigenicity. This may also occur with tumor antigens present on cell surfaces. Under certain circumstances, tumor cells can be stimulated to grow by contact with specific antibody or specific antigen-sensitive cells. This situation represents a condition where a specific immune response is counterproductive or harmful.

IMMUNOPOTENTIATION

The obvious counterpoint to immunosuppression is immunopotentiation or enhancement of the immune response. By enhancement we may mean an increase in the rate at which the immune response develops, an increase in the intensity or level of the response, a prolongation of the response, or the development of a response to an otherwise nonimmunogenic substance.

The agents which enhance immune responses are generally termed adjuvants and may be divided into 2 categories: (1) General potentiation refers to substances which may enhance both cellular and humoral immune responses to a wide variety of antigens. 2) Specific potentiation deals with a special class of molecules which enhance specific responses to certain antigens only (Table 22–2).

In concert with studies on immunosuppression, experiments dealing with potentiation have added significant contributions to our understanding of how the immune system functions. As suggested earlier, everything—including vaccination—which involves a stimulation of a previously nonimmune state could be termed potentiation. For purposes of this discussion, however, we consider immunopotentiation to be limited to those states in which there is an increase in the immune response above that which can be achieved by injection of antigen alone.

Table 22–2. Classification of immunopotentiators.

Class	Compounds	Mechanism
General potentiation (nonspecific)	Water and oil emulsions and inorganic compounds	Not clear. Possibly delayed or slow release of antigen, or enhancement of inflammatory response
	Synthetic polynucleotides	Stimulates antigen processing and helper T cell function; may enhance effector function
	Hormones, cyclic nucleotides, and drugs which affect cyclic nucleotide levels	Affect all cell types and all aspects of the immune response
	Bacterial endotoxins	Seem to stimulate B cells but may also affect T cells and macrophages
	Allogeneic effect	Specific stimulation of T cells to release "factors" active in the immune response
Possible specific potentiation	Transfer factor	Unknown but suspected to be information transfer
	Immunogenic RNAs	Appear to transfer specific genetic information

General Potentiation

A wide variety of compounds are capable of potentiating immune responses, ie, acting as adjuvants. These can be grouped into several categories: (1) water and oil emulsions (Freund's adjuvant); (2) synthetic polynucleotides; (3) hormones, drugs, and cyclic nucleotides; (4) endotoxins; and (5) allogeneic effect. In addition to studying the mechanisms and modes of action of adjuvants, a substantial effort has been directed toward finding immunopotentiating agents which stimulate only a particular kind of response, ie, cellular immunity or humoral immunity. Selective adjuvants would allow tumor immunologists to stimulate the most efficacious arm of the immune response to augment tumor rejection. It should be noted, however, that the mechanism of action of virtually all known adjuvants is poorly understood. This hampers attempts to use adjuvants in patient care.

A. Water and Oil Emulsions and Inorganic Compounds (Freund's Adjuvant): The use of mineral oil preparations to intensify immune responses was introduced by Freund in the 1940s. His particular mixture consisted of mineral oil, lanolin, and killed mycobacteria (Freund's complete adjuvant). This adjuvant, mixed with aqueous antigen, became very popular with experimental immunologists over the years. It is prohibited for human use because it produces severe local granulomatous reactions.

Although Freund's complete adjuvant has been in extensive use for 20 years, its mechanism of action is poorly understood. At least part of its potentiating capacity appears to be due to the slower release of antigen to the appropriate target cells. This is not its sole mechanism of action, however, since Freund's incomplete adjuvant (minus the bacteria) is a poor substitute for the complete form. Recent evidence suggests that certain components of the mycobacterium itself, such as cell wall lipids and mucopolysaccharides as well as mycobacterial RNA, may be potent adjuvants which in themselves provide a possible explanation for the efficiency of Freund's complete adjuvant.

A variety of inorganic compounds such as alum (potassium aluminum sulfate), aluminum hydroxide, and calcium phosphate have been used as adjuvants. Alum-precipitated antigen preparations are frequently employed to aid in desensitization of allergic individuals. Presumably, they induce high titers of circulating antibody and result in antibody-mediated suppression of the allergic response. Once again, the mechanism of action of these compounds is poorly understood. It may relate both to the slow release of antigen by these compounds and to their ability to cause inflammation, thereby intensifying the general reaction to antigen exposure. A combination of these factors probably accounts for their activity.

B. Synthetic Polynucleotides: Nucleic acids can have biologic effects other than those related to their genetic informational role. As synthetic polyribonucleotides in double- and single-stranded form became available, Braun showed these compounds to be potent stimulators of virtually all aspects of immunoresponsiveness. The most studied synthetic polynucleotide is a double-stranded homoribopolymer consisting of one strand of polyadenylate and one strand of polyuridylate, usually abbreviated poly AU. As is not true of the water and oil emulsions, much more is known about the mode of action of this compound. Its primary target is apparently the thymus-derived T cell. The addition of poly AU concomitantly with antigen will stimulate helper T cell function, delayed hypersensitivity, and cell-mediated cytotoxicity. There is evidence that it also acts directly on B cells (antibody-forming cells) to increase production of antibody and possibly to enhance cellular proliferation. The mechanism of action of the polynucleotides appears to be at the level of the cell membrane and to be related in some way to changes in cyclic nucleotide metabolism. The usefulness of synthetic polynucleotides as immune potentiators in humans is still under study, and it remains to be seen whether they will prove useful in a clinical setting.

C. Hormones, Drugs, and Cyclic Nucleotides: As discussed in the section on immunosuppression, lymphocytes are sensitive to a wide variety of drugs. Much of this sensitivity can be attributed to the fact that these cells when stimulated by antigens are very active metabolically. Thus, any drug known to be an effective metabolic inhibitor or stimulator will probably influence immunocompetent cells. Evidence is accumulating that lymphocytes, particularly T cells, are remarkably sensitive to hormonal modification. It is possible to demonstrate direct effects on T lymphocyte activation using biogenic amines, cholinergic agents, growth hormone, insulin, corticosteroids, prostaglandins, progesterone, testosterone, and possibly hormones from the pituitary.

Many of the drugs and hormones—particularly the biogenic amines, cholinergic agents, and prostaglandins—appear to be linked to changes in cyclic nucleotide metabolism in lymphocytes. A voluminous literature has appeared on the effects of both of these agents and cyclic nucleotides on all aspects of immunoresponsiveness. This literature shows that agents that raise intracellular cAMP levels will block or delay antigen- or mitogen-stimulated lymphocyte blast transformation and induce certain immature T lymphocytes to develop into more mature cells. Cyclic GMP, on the other hand, is involved in the stimulation of proliferation and transformation via mitogen or antigen. Alterations in cAMP levels appear to block several efferent functions of immunocompetent cells such as antibody secretion, cell-mediated cytotoxicity, and one stage of IgE-mediated histamine release. Thus, the addition of drugs which raise cyclic nucleotide levels can enhance or suppress various aspects of the immune response. The usefulness of such drugs is already being exploited in the treatment of allergic asthma, general allergic responses, immunodeficiency disease, cancer, and benign proliferative disorders such as psoriasis. The future of such compounds looks quite promising.

D. Endotoxins: Bacterial endotoxins—cell wall components from gram-negative bacteria (eg, *Escherichia coli,* shigella, salmonella)—have long been known to produce a variety of effects on the immune response and immunocompetent cells. For example, they nonspecifically stimulate proliferation of B cells as well as induce the nonspecific appearance of anti-red blood cell antibody (particularly anti-sheep red blood cell antibody). In addition, these compounds serve as potent adjuvants of immune responses. Their principal limitation is that, by themselves, they are immunogenic. This is particularly undesirable in an agent of potential therapeutic use. In addition, these compounds are quite pyrogenic. Their principal usefulness has been in elucidating the mechanism of development of immune responses and the method of control.

The mode of action of these compounds is poorly understood. Their effects appear limited to interactions which occur at the cell membrane level. Evidence suggests that their activity may partly be due to changes in intracellular cyclic nucleotide levels. Whether this can account for all of their effects remains to be seen.

E. Allogeneic Effect: In recent years, several laboratories have reported that T lymphocytes stimulated in an allogeneic system—or supernatants from T cells stimulated by alloantigens—would cause enhancement of immune responses both specifically and nonspecifically. This effect has been regarded as a somewhat novel experimental finding whose relationship to the normal immune response is difficult to perceive. However, it may be related to soluble T cell mediators which function in normal immune responses to amplify cell responses. How this system will be useful to further define aspects of immunoresponsiveness remains to be seen.

Specific Immunopotentiation

In addition to nonspecific potentiators of immune responses, there are 2 additional classes of potentiators which deserve mention: (1) transfer factor and (2) immunogenic RNAs. Our comparative understanding of specific potentiators is severely limited.

A. Transfer Factor: Transfer factor, a dialyzable extract obtained from human peripheral blood white cells, was first described 25 years ago. Since its discovery, it has largely remained a novel clinical entity despite extensive attempts to characterize its active component or mode of action and to develop an animal model. The original experiments demonstrated that a dialyzable, DNase-resistant human white blood cell extract could transfer specific skin test sensitivity (to PPD for example) from donor to recipient in the apparent absence of antigenic exposure.

Much of the subsequent research was directed toward possible clinical applications of such a preparation, but it remains to be studied in a clinical setting in a systematic way (ie, double-blind studies). In part this has had to await the development of satisfactory models to test its effects objectively. International studies are in progress to evaluate its effectiveness, particularly in immune-deficient disease states. Reports to date indicate some effectiveness in children with immunodeficiencies and possible effectiveness in cancer patients and patients with limited immunodeficiencies (the suspected situation in patients with certain fungal diseases).

This field is hampered by a lack of success in developing an animal model or in establishing a reasonable theoretical basis for the function of transfer factor in a normal immunologic setting.

B. Immunogenic RNAs: Possibly related to transfer factor are the so-called immunogenic RNAs. RNA isolated from mouse or rabbit peritoneal cells (macrophages and lymphocytes) has been reported to "transfer" the ability to respond to an antigen (in this case to a bacteriophage) to a recipient animal in the absence of antigen. This report stimulated a large research effort directed at identifying the nature of this RNA and its possible role in the control of immunoresponsiveness. A great quantity of experimental data was produced, but these results left unclear the role of these molecules in immune responses. The data suggested that a portion of this RNA might be coupled to small amounts of antigen, yielding what was called a "superantigen." While research efforts in this area have decreased, there still remains a large bulk of inexplicable data apparently showing the transfer of specific antigen reactivity not only between animals of the same species but between animals of different species. How

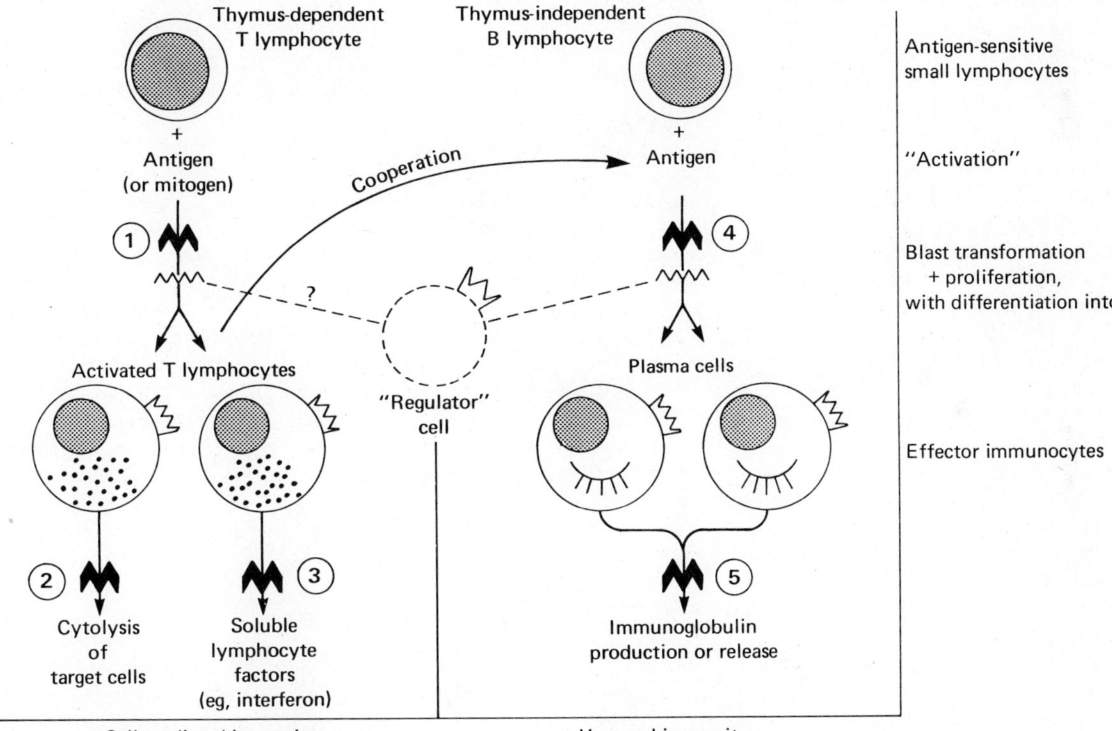

Figure 22–1. Simplified scheme illustrating sites at which immunosuppressors or immunopotentiators may act in regulating immune responses. Antigen-specific thymus-dependent (T) or thymus-independent (B) lymphocytes are thought to be "activated" by contact with antigen to produce either specific tolerance (not shown) or blast transformation, followed by proliferation of differentiated clones of effector immunocytes capable of producing antibody- or cell-mediated immunity. The sawtooth symbols on the surfaces of effector cells indicate that the appearance of hormone receptors may be one result of their differentiation. The heavy wave symbols indicate steps at which experimental evidence suggests *(1)* inhibition or stimulation of mitogen- or antigen-induced blast transformation and proliferation of T lymphocytes; *(2)* inhibition or stimulation of specific immune cytolysis of allogeneic target cells; *(3)* inhibition or stimulation of production (or release) of soluble lymphocyte products such as interferon; *(4)* reversal of antigen-induced immune suppression when lymphocytes are exposed to cAMP-active drugs during initial contact with antigen, prevention of humoral (agglutinating) antibody response to allogeneic cells by cholera enterotoxin, or inhibition of proliferation of antibody-forming cells; or *(5)* inhibition or stimulation of production (or release) of antibody to heterologous erythrocytes. A hypothetic "regulator cell" is also shown, although its relation to the other cells is not clearly defined. (Redrawn and reproduced, with permission, from Bourne HR & others: Science 184:19, 1974. Copyright © 1974 by the American Association for the Advancement of Science.)

these results will be resolved and what their potential usefulness may be remain to be determined.

CONCLUSIONS

It is clear that much remains to be done before the varied facets of immunosuppression and immunopotentiation are understood. The use of agents which enhance or suppress specific immune responses is increasingly important in our attempts at dissecting the immune system. The points at which an immune response might be altered by drugs affecting cAMP levels are outlined in Fig 22–1. This same figure may be used to generalize the known effects of both immunosuppressive and immunopotentiating agents.

The development of methods of specific immunosuppression remains a major task for the clinical immunologist, particularly in relation to graft rejection. The possible utility of potentiation may lie in its role as therapy for patients with suppressed responses, as in some forms of cancer.

• • •

References

Braun W: Pages 4–23 in: *Cyclic AMP, Cell Growth, and the Immune Response.* Braun W, Lichtenstein LM, Parker CW (editors). Springer, 1974.

Katz DH, Benacerraf B (editors): *Immunological Tolerance.* Academic Press, 1974.

Lance EM, Medawar PB, Taub RN: Antilymphocyte serum. Page 2 in: *Advances in Immunology.* Vol 17. Dixon FS, Kunkel HG (editors). Academic Press, 1973.

Lawrence HS, Landy M (editors): *Mediators of Cellular Immunity.* Academic Press, 1969.

Makinodan T, Santos GW, Quinn RP: Immunosuppressive drugs. Pharmacol Rev 22:189, 1970.

Parker CW, Sullivan TJ, Wedner HJ: Cyclic AMP and the immune response. Pages 1–79 in: *Advances in Cyclic Nucleotide Research.* Greengard P, Robinson GA (editors). Raven Press, 1974.

Parker CW, Vaura JD: Immunosuppression. Prog Hematol 6:1, 1974.

Sercarz EG, Williamson AR, Fox CF (editors): *The Immune System.* Academic Press, 1974.

Smith RT, Landy M (editors): *Immune Surveillance.* Academic Press, 1970.

Uhr JW, Landy M (editors): *Immunologic Intervention.* Academic Press, 1971.

23 . . .
Aging & the Decline of Immune Responsiveness

Marguerite M.B. Kay, MD

Aging is characterized by declining ability of the individual to adapt to environmental stress. This is exemplified physiologically by an inability to maintain homeostasis. Because more and more people are surviving to an older age, aging is potentially the most critical issue facing mankind–socially, economically, and biomedically. Enhanced interest in the diseases and disabilities associated with aging has led to the systematic investigation of many biologic systems with the hope that methods will be found for delaying the onset, lessening the severity, or perhaps preventing some of the pathologic changes of aging. The immune system is perhaps the most productive field in which to conduct studies on aging for the following reasons:

(1) The immune system is "organismal" in that it is in constant contact with most, if not all, of the cells, tissues, and organ systems within the body. Thus, any alteration of the immune system could be expected to affect all other systems. If one views aging as a perturbation of homeostasis, then a physiologically active system such as the immune system is perhaps the ideal one with which to study such perturbations and their consequences.

(2) As individuals age, certain normal immune functions can decline (Fig 23–1); associated with this decline is the emergence of diseases which can profoundly affect many tissues.

(3) Our understanding of the cellular, molecular, and genetic basis of differentiation and of ontogenetic and phylogenetic processes of the immune system is as complete as our understanding of most other systems, or even more so.

(4) The immune system is amenable to both cellular and molecular analyses and therefore offers great promise for successful experimental manipulation.

(5) Delay, reversal, or prevention of the decline in normal immune functions may delay the onset or lessen the severity of diseases associated with aging.

In this chapter, the following topics related to aging of the immune system will be discussed: (1) age-related changes in the immune system, (2) mechanisms responsible for the decline in immune function, and (3) mechanisms responsible for diseases associated with declining immune functions.

Marguerite M.B. Kay is with the Laboratory of Cellular and Comparative Physiology, Gerontology Research Center, National Institute on Aging, National Institutes of Health, PHS, United States Department of Health, Education, and Welfare, Bethesda, and Baltimore City Hospitals, Baltimore.

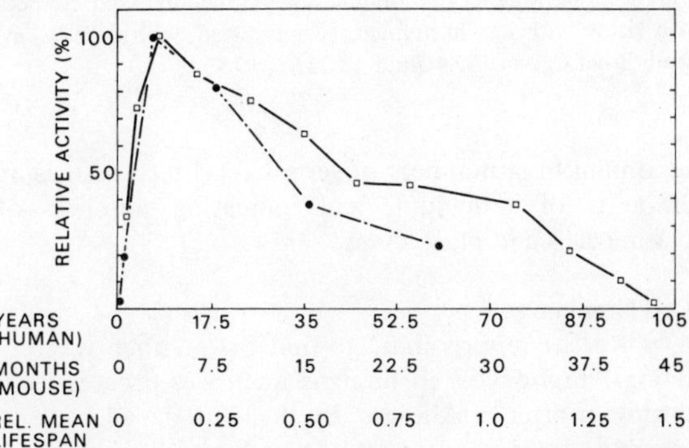

Figure 23–1. Effects of age on serum agglutinin titers in the human and the mouse. □ = Natural serum anti-A isoagglutinin titers in the human. (Thomsen O, Kettel K: Z Immunitätsforsch 63:67, 1929.) • = Peak serum agglutinin response titer to sheep red cell stimulation by intact long-lived mice. (Makinodan T, Adler W: Fed Proc 34:153, 1975.)

AGE-RELATED CHANGES IN IMMUNE FUNCTIONS

Morphology

The first suggestion that normal immune functions may decline with age came from classical morphologists who showed both in laboratory animals and in humans that the thymic lymphatic mass decreased with age. This was primarily a result of atrophy of the thymic cortex, which began at the time of sexual maturity (Fig 23–2).

The size of lymph nodes and spleen in normal individuals remains the same or decreases slightly after adulthood. In long-lived mice, the number of T and B cells in the spleen remains relatively constant until at least 2 years of age, when tumors begin to appear in lymphatic and other tissues. Probably more significant are age-related histologic changes in lymphatic tissues,

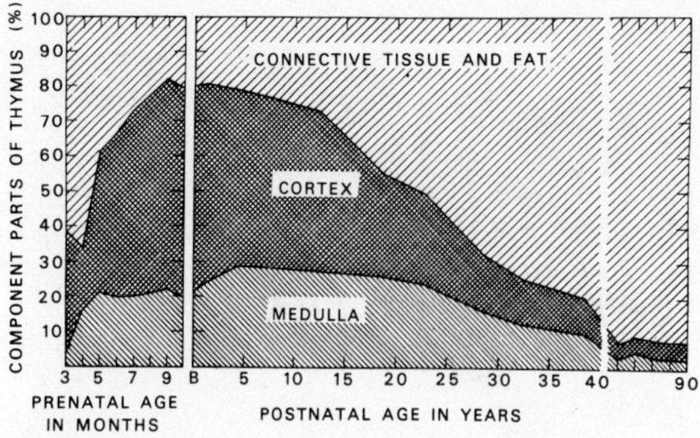

Figure 23–2. Changes in thymic cortex, medulla, and connective tissue with age in humans. (Reproduced, with permission, from Boyd E: Am J Dis Child 43:1162, 1932.)

ie, diminishing numbers of germinal centers, increasing amounts of reticulum, and increasing numbers of plasma cells and phagocytes.

Cell Number

Recent reports indicate that the number of circulating lymphocytes in humans decreases progressively during or after middle age. By the sixth decade, a level which is about 70% of that of a young adult is reached, and the decrease is due to a reduction in the absolute number of circulating T cells while the number of B cells remains essentially the same. In these reports, the number of T and B cells was calculated from estimates of their concentration and proportion as determined by sheep erythrocyte rosettes and immunofluorescence for surface immunoglobulin. In aging mice, the pattern of change in the absolute number of T cells varies with the strain, with hybrids of strains, and with the organ. In some strains, the absolute number of T cells in spleen and lymph nodes shows no change, while in others an increase or decrease is noted. Nonetheless, changes in the number or proportion of T cells both in humans and in mice are not sufficient to account for the observed decrease in immunologic functions. Furthermore, as will be discussed in a later section, a decrease in the number of cells bearing T cell membrane markers does not mean that the number of T cells has necessarily decreased; it could mean that the number of T cells in a particular stage of differentiation has decreased.

Cell-Mediated Immunity

There are conflicting reports concerning the effect of age on T cell functions. Some investigators report a decrease in delayed hypersensitivity to common skin test antigens (eg, PPD, streptokinase-streptodornase, candida, trichophyton, mumps) in previously sensitized individuals. Others report no decrease except in elderly persons with acute illness. In general, when assessed with an antigen to which the individual has *not* been sensitized previously (eg, DNCB), it appears that T cell functions decline with age. These conflicting results could be attributed to (1) utilization of only one skin test antigen to assess T cell function; (2) selection of skin test antigens (only a fraction of the population of the USA has been immunized to tuberculosis; therefore, a negative result does not imply defective immunologic memory); and (3) selection of population samples (some studies used hospitalized patients or medical clinic populations).

A battery of common skin test antigens should be used for assessing immunologic memory. For assessing the ability of an individual to become sensitized to a "new" antigen, DNCB is probably the best choice if for no other reason than that it allows comparison of results between different laboratories. It could be argued that any decrease in delayed hypersensitivity seen in elderly persons reflects aging of the skin rather than of the immune system. However, tumor cell rejection tests in aging mice gave comparable results and, since tumor cells were injected intraperitoneally in these tests, aging of the skin was not a limiting factor.

In vivo studies in mice indicate that T cell functions decline with age. Cells from old mice have a decreased ability to mount a GVH reaction even when enriched T cell populations are utilized to compensate for the possibility that old animals may have fewer T cells.

The in vitro findings show that the proliferative capacity of human or rodent T cells to plant mitogens (PHA and ConA) and to allogeneic cells declines with age. The decline is most striking in mice regardless of their life span (Fig 23–3). In contrast, the decline in cytolytic activity of T cells of long-lived mice against allogeneic tumor cells is only moderate, and the de-

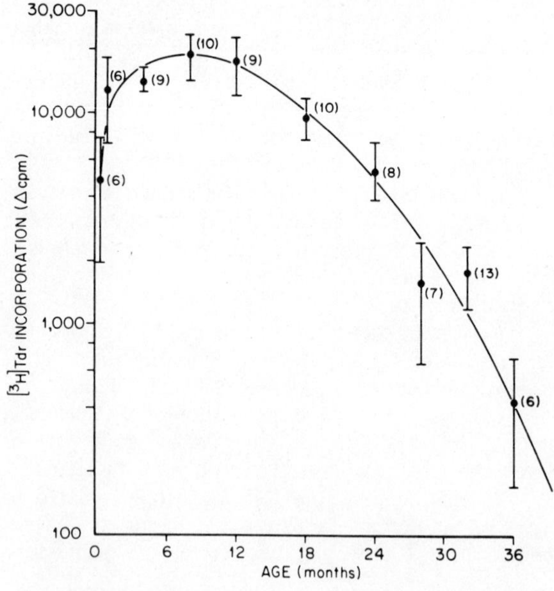

Figure 23–3. Decline with age in PHA mitogenic activity of splenic T cells of long-lived mice. (Figures in parentheses are number of mice used to obtain the data for each point on the graph.) (Reproduced, with permission, from Hori Y, Perkins E, Halsall M: Proc Soc Exp Biol Med 144:48, 1973.)

cline in activity against certain syngeneic tumor cells is not readily apparent.

There are conflicting reports on the effect of age on MLC reactions. Some investigators reported a marked decrease with age in the response of cells; others reported that cells from old mice are as efficient or more so than cells from young mice both as responding and as stimulating cells in the MLC reaction, but the same cells showed a decreased GVH activity.

The helper function of T cells declines with age. This has been demonstrated in intact animals and by means of in vivo and in vitro assays.

Humoral Immunity

Normal B cell immune functions reflective of humoral immunity have been analyzed in terms of circulating levels of natural isoantibodies and heteroantibodies and in terms of antigen-induced antibody response. Circulating levels of natural antibodies have been assessed most systematically in humans, and these levels decline with age starting shortly after the thymus begins to involute and after the serum level of thymosin, a thymic hormone, begins to decline.

Aging rodents have been used for the study of antigen-induced antibody responses, and results show that primary—but not necessarily secondary—antibody responses decrease with age. The onset of decline in antibody responses can occur as early as the period of thymus involution. This would suggest that with many types of primary antibody responses, aging is affecting regulator T cells and not necessarily B cells. This suspicion has been supported by the subsequent demonstration that antibody responses of B cells to complex antigens generally require the cooperation of T cells. Fig 23–1 relates human and murine B cell immune functions to their life span. The patterns of rise and decline in B cell functions are remarkably similar.

There have been exceptions to this general finding, however, with some reports showing no decline in primary antibody response, especially against bacterial and viral vaccines. Two explanations can be offered: (1) These individuals have been previously exposed to the antigen and are therefore, in fact, mounting a secondary response; and (2) the reactions are T-independent antibody responses to antigens which do not require the participation of T cells.

MECHANISMS FOR THE AGE-RELATED DECLINE IN NORMAL IMMUNE FUNCTIONS

The decline with age of normal immunologic functions may be secondary to changes in the cellular environment or milieu, to changes in the cells of the immune system, or to both of these changes.

Cellular Milieu

The effects of changes in the physiologic milieu on the expression of immune potential have been investigated by cell transfer experiments. Old cells have been transferred to young recipients and young cells to old recipients. Results indicate that changes both intrinsic and extrinsic to the cells affect immune responses but that only about 10% of the normal age-related decline can be attributed to changes in the cellular milieu, while 90% of the decline can be attributed to changes intrinsic to the cells.

The responsible factor or factors in the cellular milieu were then shown to be systemic and noncellular, based on the humoral responses of spleen cells of young mice when transferred to x-irradiated, syngeneic young and old recipients. Spleen cells were cultured with test antigen either in the recipient's spleen by the cell transfer method or in the recipient's peritoneal cavity by the diffusion chamber method. A 2-fold difference in response was observed between young and old recipients at both anatomic sites, indicating that the factor is systemic, and the effect was observed in cells grown in cell-impermeable diffusion chambers, indicating that a noncellular factor is involved. A comparable 2-fold difference was also observed when the colony-forming activity of bone marrow stem cells was assessed in spleens of young and old syngeneic recipients. This suggests that the factors influence both lymphocytopoiesis and hematopoiesis.

At present we do not know what these factors are. They could be deleterious substances of metabolic or viral origin, or they could be essential substances which are deficient in old mice. Factors of both types are present and change with age; moreover, several factors of each type may exist. For example, in vivo blood clearance of colloidal carbon is reduced in older mice, but their macrophages are as efficient as those from young mice in their ability both to engulf and to digest opsonized sheep red cells in vitro. Thus, the lower blood clearance index of older mice may reflect a lower level of opsonins rather than a decrease in functional ability of macrophages. Indeed, subsequently it was found that the in vitro phagocytosis of allogeneic and xenogeneic tumor cells by macrophages from young mice is greater when the tumor cells are opsonized with serum from young rather than old mice.

Cells

Three types of cellular changes in the immune system could result in a decline in normal immunologic functions with age: (1) an absolute decrease in cell numbers, (2) a relative decrease in cell numbers due to an increase in regulatory cells with suppressor activity, and (3) a decrease in the functional efficiency of cells.

A. Stem Cells: In mouse bone marrow, which contains 90% stem cells, the cell concentration generally decreases gradually with age. However, as the cell concentration decreases, the total volume of marrow increases proportionately. Therefore, the total number of stem cells remains relatively constant throughout the life span. Moreover, unlike stem cells transferred in vivo, whose self-replicating ability can be exhausted, stem cells in situ can self-replicate throughout the natural life span of the mouse. The phenomenon of limited self-replicating potential of transferred stem cells, although a fascinating problem for tissue culturists, is not crucial for the animal.

Stem cells do not lose their differentiation ability with age. However, their *rate* of generating hematopoietic colonies and B lymphocytes and the *size* of the colonies seem to decline with age, as does their ability to repair DNA damage after sublethal doses of ionizing radiation. These results indicate that aging reduces the rate at which stem cells can proliferate and differentiate. Questions to be resolved are (1) the extent to which changes extrinsic and intrinsic to stem cells are responsible for the reduction and (2) the extent to which the reduction is reversible by transplantation of old stem cells in young recipients and by chemical manipulation.

B. Accessory Cells: Accessory cells are primarily macrophages but also include reticulum cells, endothelial cells, and epithelial cells. These cells are accessory to antigen-sensitive T and B cells and participate in the immune response.

Because macrophages as well as other accessory cells may confront antigens before T and B cells, any defect in them could decrease immunologic function without appreciable change in the number or functional ability of T and B cells. It is not surprising, therefore, that some early aging studies focused on accessory cells. In one series of studies, antigen-processing ability was assessed indirectly by injection of young or old mice with doses of sheep red cells over a 10,000-fold range. The results suggested that the antigen-processing accessory cells prevented antigen-sensitive T and B cells from responding maximally to limiting doses of the antigen, as reflected in the different slopes of the regression curves for young and old mice (Fig 23–4) and in the 10-fold difference in the minimum dose of antigen needed to generate a maximum response. Associated with decreased antigen processing is a failure of antigens to localize in the follicles of antigen-stimulated old mice. Perhaps a subpopulation of antigen-destructive macrophages increases with age to become a formidable competitor of the T and B cells for limiting doses of antigen. In any event, this implies that the ability of individuals to detect low doses of antigens, especially "weak" antigens such as syngeneic tumor antigens, can decline with age without any appreciable change in the number or function of T and B cells. Such a change in accessory cells could contribute to the poor surveillance against low doses of certain syngeneic tumor cells in mice. It could also account in part for the observation that resistance to allogeneic tumor cell challenge can decline with age more than 100-fold in mice showing only a 4-fold decline in T cell-mediated cytolytic activity against the same tumor cell.

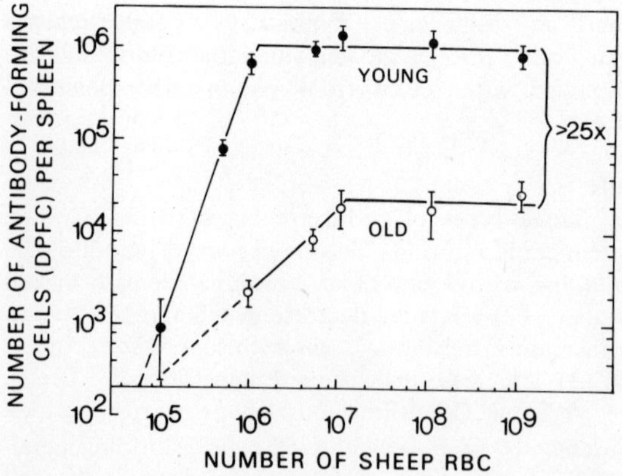

Figure 23–4. Effect of antigen dose on peak antibody response of young and old mice. Vertical bars indicate 95% confidence limits. DPFC = direct plaque-forming cells. (Reproduced, with permission, from Makinodan T, Adler W: Fed Proc 34:153, 1975; for details, see Price GB, Makinodan T: J Immunol 108: 403, 1972.)

Since the accessory cell most commonly implicated in antigen processing is the macrophage, the influence of age on its ability to phagocytose and "handle" antigens in the initiation of antibody response was determined systematically. The results revealed the following: (1) The in vitro phagocytic activity of peritoneal macrophages of old mice, as judged by their ability to engulf and digest optimally opsonized sheep red cells, is equal to if not better than that of young mice. (2) The activity of at least 3 lysosomal enzymes (cathepsin D, β-glucuronidase, and acid phosphatase) in peritoneal macrophages increases gradually with age. (3) The ability of antigen-laden peritoneal macrophages from old mice to initiate primary and secondary antibody responses in vivo is comparable to that of young mice. (4) The capacity of splenic accessory cells to cooperate with T and B cells in the initiation of antibody responses in vitro is unaffected by age. These results show that the activities of accessory cells in handling of antigens, initiation of immune responses, and phagocytosis do not seem to diminish with age.

C. B Cells: The number of B cells in the spleen and lymph nodes of mice does not seem to change appreciably with age, as judged by the number of cells with immunoglobulin receptors and of cells responsive to T cell-independent antigens and specific mitogens (Fig 23–5). At most, B cells seem to decrease slightly in certain strains, but the decrease can be overcome readily by one cell division. In humans, studies limited primarily to circulating B cells indicate that these also remain relatively stable throughout life. Unfortunately, we do not know how the number of circulating B cells corresponds to the number in the spleen and lymph nodes. The size of certain B cell subpopulations could fluctuate with age depending on their susceptibility to regulatory forces. Support for this view comes from the observation that the number of B cells responsive to a T cell-independent antigen decreases only slightly with age in a long-lived hybrid mouse as well as from human studies showing that serum IgG and IgA tend to increase with age whereas serum IgM tends to decrease.

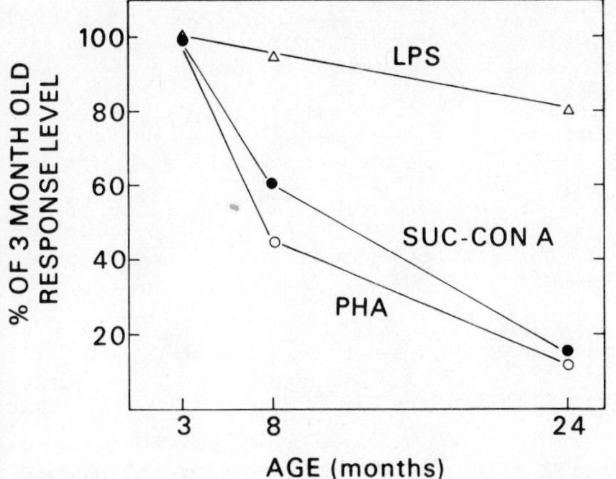

Figure 23–5. In vitro response of spleen cells from long-lived mice of different ages to stimulation with a B cell mitogen, bacterial lipopolysaccharide (LPS), and T cell mitogens, phytohemagglutinin (PHA) and succinyl-concanavalin A (Suc-ConA). Responses are based on comparative levels of tritiated thymidine incorporation during the last 18 hours of 72-hour cultures. Note that the age-related decrease in the B cell response to LPS is minimal, whereas the T cell response to PHA and Suc-Con A decreases drastically with age. (Reproduced, with permission, from Makinodan T, Adler W: Fed Proc 34:153, 1975.)

Although the number of B cells remains relatively constant with age, their responsiveness to stimulation with certain antigens decreases markedly. Limiting-dilution and dose-response analyses of the responses of young and old mice to sheep red cells have shown that the decline is due to both (1) a decrease with age in the number of antigen-sensitive immunocompetent units (which are composed of 2 or more cell types in various proportions) and (2) a decrease in immunologic burst size (the number of antibody-forming effector cells generated per immunocompetent unit). Table 23–1 summarizes the results, showing that a 50-fold decrease in the in situ antibody response per spleen between young and old mice is apparently due to a 5-fold decrease in the number of immunocompetent units per spleen and a 10-fold decrease in immunologic burst size. We do not know the underlying causes of the reduction with age in these components. Because the number of immunoglobulin-bearing B cells remains relatively constant with age and because the proliferation rate of mitogen-sensitive B cells also remains unaltered with age, the reduction could be secondary to changes in the regulatory forces which can inhibit the interaction of precursor cells. It is also conceivable that certain antigen-sensitive B cells from old mice have become less efficient in their ability to interact with other cells and to differentiate.

D. T Cells: Present evidence suggests that the decline in normal immune functions which accompanies aging is due primarily to changes in the T cell component of the immune system. Since involution of the thymus precedes the age-related functional decline, a cause and effect relationship is suspected (ie, thymus involution results in a decreased capacity of the system to generate functional T cells). In spite of the obvious importance of establishing such a relationship on more than inferences derived from temporal events, only recently has an attempt been made to provide rigorous experimental proof. Previous experiments demonstrated that adult thymectomy accelerates the decline of immune responsiveness, as evidenced by a decrease in the IgM hemagglutinin response to sheep red cells, a marked decrease in the GVH reaction, the poor general condition of the mice, and reduced antibody response to BSA. The effect on the latter response was less pronounced than the effect on the GVH reaction. Thymus lobes from mice 1 day to 33 months old were transplanted into young adult T cell-deprived recipients to assess kinetically the emergence of T cells. The ability of thymic tissue to influence the differentiation or maturation of cells into functional T cells decreased with increasing age, and different T cell indices exhibited differential susceptibility to thymus involution. Specifically, with increasing age, thymic tissue sequentially loses the capacity to influence the following functions: (1) lymphocyte repopulation of T cell-dependent areas of lymph nodes, (2) mitogenic reactivity of splenic cells to the T cell-specific mitogens PHA and ConA, (3) number of theta-positive splenic lymphocytes and helper T cell function, and (4) blastogenic response of splenic T cells to allogeneic lymphocytes. These results suggest that the control mechanism for lymph node population or repopulation resides in newborn thymus. Thymic tissue from new-

Table 23–1. Quantitative evaluation of the differentiation process of spleen cells of young and old $BC3F_1$ mice in response to sheep red cell stimulation in situ.*

DPFC = direct plaque-forming cells. IU = immunocompetent unit.
IBS = immunologic burst size. $BC3F_1$ = (C57BL × C3H)F_1 hybrid mouse.

	(A)		(B)		(C)	
Relative Age of Mice (Months)	**Response (DPFC/Spleen) (Millions)**	**Ratio of Young:Old**	**IU/Spleen (Thousands)**	**Ratio of Young:Old**	**IBS/Spleen (Col A ÷ Col B) (Thousands)**	**Ratio of Young:Old**
Young (3–4)	1.0	50:1	1.0	5:1	1.0	10:1
Old (30–35)	0.02		0.2		0.1	

*Values presented are averages. For details, see Price GB, Makinodan T: J Immunol 108:403, 413, 1972.

born mice but not from mice over 3 months of age was able to repopulate lymph node T-dependent areas. The decrease in thymus function may not be directly attributable to the extracellular milieu. Follow-up experiments have shown that when thymus tissue from old mice is implanted in normal young animals even the morphologic changes associated with age are not completely reversed.

The primary effect of aging on the T cell component of the immune system involves a differentiation pathway. On the basis of the following observations, it appears that one or more subsets of T cells do not respond to stimulation, possibly as a result of insufficiency of hormones in the milieu or alterations intrinsic to the cells: (1) The proportion of lymphocytes bearing Thy-1 antigen decreases with age, as does the amount of Thy-1 antigen on cell surfaces. There is no compensatory increase in B lymphocytes nor does the total lymphocyte number change significantly. This suggests an increase in T cells that do not carry detectable Thy-1 receptors on their surface. (2) Although PHA-induced blastogenesis of cells from old mice is significantly reduced, the same cells bind ^{125}I-labeled PHA just as well as cells from young mice. Because there seems to be no significant decrease in binding affinities or receptor sites for PHA on cells of old mice, the defect is not likely to be in their membrane receptors. (3) The concentration of cGMP which increases when T cells are stimulated by mitogens is found in relatively low concentrations in mitogen-stimulated T cells of old mice. This suggests that the age-related change in T cells is intracellular and may be hormone-dependent. (4) The life span of hypopituitary dwarf mice, which are T cell-deficient, can be extended from 4 months to 12 months by a single intraperitoneal injection of 150 × 10^6 lymph node cells, but one injection of an equal number of thymocytes or 50 × 10^6 bone marrow cells is ineffective. (Lymph nodes are rich, whereas thymus and bone marrow are deficient, in *mature* T cells.) (5) Studies of synergy between subpopulations of lymphocytes in the MLC reaction suggest that lymph node T_2 cells (amplifier cells) display a greater functional decline with age than do spleen and thymus T_1 lymphocytes (the precursors of T_2 cells). (6) Density distribution analysis using discontinuous gradients of bovine albumin and Ficoll shows that the frequency of less dense cells (sp gr 1.06–1.08) increases at the expense of the more dense cells (sp gr 1.10–1.12) (Fig 23–6). This density shift within the lymphocyte population can also be seen in young mice shortly after they are immunized with heterologous red cells or allogeneic lymphocytes and in tumor-bearing mice. In these cases, however, the spleen cell number increases, whereas in unimmunized old mice it does not. This suggests that there is a relative increase with age in immature T_1 cells at the expense of mature T_2 cells. (7) The in vitro PHA response of T cells from old mice can be significantly increased by addition of mercaptoethanol to the cultures, as can the antibody response to sheep red cells.

Fig 23–7 shows a possible model of T cell differentiation. In this model, T_1 upon antigenic stimulation produces effector cells for certain T cell functions (such as "helper" cells for T-dependent antibody responses) and upon thymic hormone stimulation (K) produces antigen-sensitive T_2 cells. T_2 upon antigenic stimulation produces other effector cells (such as cells active in GVH responses). Each effector cell proliferates in the presence of an antigen, thus producing more effector cells. Since the level of serum thymic hormones decreases with age, it would seem reasonable to assume that the effect of aging is to decrease K. This would lead to an accumulation of T_1 cells, a decrease in T_2 cells, and, subsequently, a skewed distribution in effector T cells, which obviously can profoundly decrease the immune function. This is simply a schematic diagram. The precise number of cells involved is not known at this time.

In part because of our lack of understanding of how these cells function, studies on age-related changes in T cells involved in the regulation of B cell immune responses have been minimal. We know in general that few T cells act to enhance a response, but many can suppress it. We do not know whether or not there exist 2 distinct subpopulations of regulator T cells, suppressor and promoter T cells, or one population of regulator T cells with the potential both to promote and to suppress a B cell immune response. In any event, the relative number of T cells participating in a

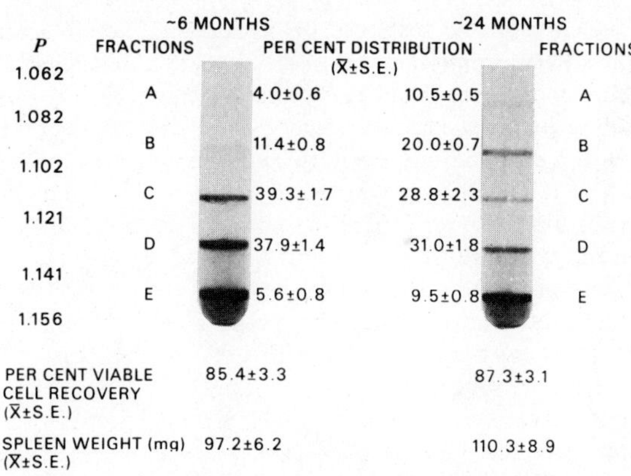

Figure 23–6. Density distribution of spleen cells of young and old long-lived mice. (Reproduced, with permission, from Makinodan T, Adler W: Fed Proc 34:153, 1975.)

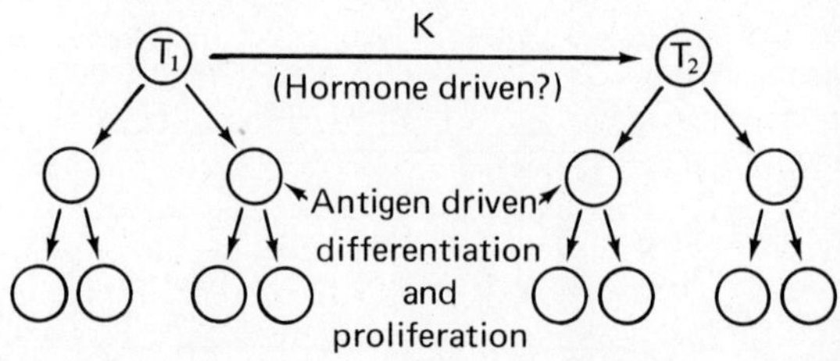

Figure 23–7. Postulated model of T cell differentiation. K = thymic hormone stimulation. (See text for details.)

B cell immune response decreases with age in short-lived, autoimmune-prone mice. This could account for the emergence of autoantibodies in these mice. On the other hand, the relative number of T cells participating in a B cell immune response increases slightly in long-lived mice. Because excessive numbers of regulator T cells tend to interfere with the B cell response to antigenic stimulation, this could account for the decline in the number of antibody-responsive immunocompetent units and immunologic burst units. The notion that the number of regulator cells with inhibitory activities increases with age was tested by assessing the anti-sheep red cell response of spleen cells from young mice in the presence and in the absence of spleen cells from old mice. The proliferative response of T cells from young mice to PHA and allogeneic target cells was assessed in a similar manner. The ratio of the observed response to that which would be expected if the response of young and old cells were additive was less than 1. These results indicate that spleens of old mice contain regulator cells which can interfere with the immunologic activities of spleen cells from young mice.

Finally, it should be noted that T cells may also regulate hematopoiesis, since hematopoiesis of parental stem cells in heavily irradiated F_1 recipients can be augmented in the presence of parental T cells.

Thymus

All the relevant studies to date indicate that the process of involution and atrophy of the thymus is the key to the aging of the immune system. It follows, then, that the search for the causes and mechanisms of aging of the immune system should be oriented around the thymus. The causes can be either extrinsic or intrinsic to the thymus. The most likely extrinsic cause is a possible regulatory breakdown in the neuroendocrine axis in its relation to the thymus. Intrinsic causes might be found at either the DNA level or the non-DNA level. (For molecular theories of aging, see, for example, the discussion by Strehler cited in the references at the end of the chapter.)

Three possible mechanisms of involution and atrophy can be proposed. One is clonal exhaustion, ie, thymus cells might have a genetically programmed clock mechanism to self-destruct and die after undergoing a fixed number of divisions, similar to the Hayflick phenomenon of human fibroblasts in vitro. This would require the thymus to count the cells leaving it or the cells themselves to count the divisions they have undergone. Another possible mechanism is alteration of the DNA of thymus cells either randomly or through viral infection, and it is known that various stable alterations of DNA can occur, including cross-linking and strand breaks. The DNA-altered or mutated cells could then disrupt the self-tolerance mechanism by destroying normal cells. The third possible mechanism is a stable molecular alteration at the non-DNA level through subtle error-accumulating mechanisms, as proposed for those occurring at the DNA level.

Evidence is mounting to indicate that only a few genes may be responsible for the aging process. If so, the 17th chromosome, which carries immune response genes, the histocompatibility system (H-2), and other immunologically important genes in the mouse, and the sixth chromosome, carrying immune response genes and the histocompatibility system (HLA) in the human, might be probable sites of genes which play an important role in the aging process.

MECHANISMS RESPONSIBLE FOR DISEASES ASSOCIATED WITH DECLINING IMMUNE FUNCTIONS

As normal immune functions decline with age, the incidence of infections, autoimmune and immune complex diseases, and cancer increases.

Infections

Elderly individuals tend to be more susceptible to infections and to have a more prolonged course, with higher morbidity and mortality rates, than young adults. During the influenza epidemic of 1957–1958, an estimated 40 million persons in the USA became ill with influenza, and the deaths due to influenza were in excess of 8000. During this period, there were 60,000 more deaths from various causes than would be expected under normal conditions. The highest mortality rate was in infants under age 1 and adults over age 60. During the subsequent influenza epidemics in 1962 and 1963, the excess deaths were mainly among the elderly. These deaths were due to many causes, including renal and cardiovascular diseases and secondary bacterial pneumonias. The higher death rate among the elderly during and following influenza epidemics and the increased risk of infections with other respiratory viruses may be attributed to the decrease in normal T cell functions. This view is supported by the following evidence: (1) acute manifestations of a viral infection often subside prior to the detection of neutralizing antibody; (2) children with hypogammaglobulinemia usually recover from respiratory infections, measles, mumps, chickenpox, and poliomyelitis in a normal manner; and (3) these children show evidence of long-lasting immunity to reinfection with the same virus although they tend to undergo repeated infections with the same bacteria. B cells may also play a role, as demonstrated by the presence of antiviral antibodies in the circulation. These can act as an effective barrier to cell-to-cell transmission of a virus and thereby limit the spread of viruses following reinfection.

Autoimmunity

The phenomenon of autoimmunity presents an extremely interesting and challenging problem. Thus, autoimmune disease is often seen in immunologically hyporesponsive individuals, yet normal healthy individuals possess autoantibodies which perform important physiologic roles—eg, by enabling macrophages to remove senescent and damaged cells. The evidence for the existence of physiologic autoantibodies is derived from experiments on human red cells aged in vitro and in situ. Red blood cells aged in vitro where phagocytosed when they were incubated in pooled, normal human IgG, allogeneic immunoglobulin, or autologous IgG, washed, and then incubated with autologous macrophages. Red blood cells treated in the same way but incubated in IgM or IgA, immunoglobulin-depleted serum, or medium alone were not phagocytosed. This indicates that immunoglobulin is required for phagocytosis and suggests that the antibody that attaches to red blood cells is IgG. When freshly drawn red blood cells were separated into young (Y) and old (O) cells according to density and incubated with autologous macrophages, less than 5% of the young cells were phagocytosed, whereas more than 30% of the old cells were phagocytosed. This was independent of whether the final incubations were performed in medium without serum or autologous immunoglobulin-depleted serum or whole serum (Fig 23–8). This indicates that (1) the immunoglobulin is attached in situ to the old red blood cells, and that (2) phagocytic recognition is not inhibited by other serum components. Scanning electron microscopy, employing labeled anti-IgG, IgM, and IgA reagents, revealed that young cells had essentially no immunoglobulin on their surfaces, whereas old cells had IgG on their surfaces (Fig 23–9). These findings suggest that IgG attaches in situ to senescent human red blood cells, making them vulnerable to phagocytosis by macrophages. These findings were confirmed by isolating the antibody from red blood cells aged in situ and showing it to be IgG. The isolated antibody specifically reattached to red blood cells aged in vitro, leading to their selective destruction by macrophages, but it did not attach to young red cells. These homeostatic or regulatory autoantibodies permit the more efficient mature cells to carry out their vital functions without hindrance from the less efficient senescent cells or from pathologic reactions which could arise as a consequence of senescent cells dying and decaying within the organism. Therefore, it would seem prudent to distinguish physiologic autoantibody, which performs regulatory functions, from pathologic autoantibody, which contributes to a destructive disease process.

Subsequent discussions will be limited to the various mechanistic theories about the pathologic component of autoimmunity because the evidence today strongly suggests that the decline in normal T cell functions with age predisposes to autoimmune disease, and there is at present no information about the effects of aging on physiologic autoantibodies.

A. Regulatory Theories: Although the existence of pathologic serum autoantibody is well documented, its causes and mechanisms of formation remain ob-

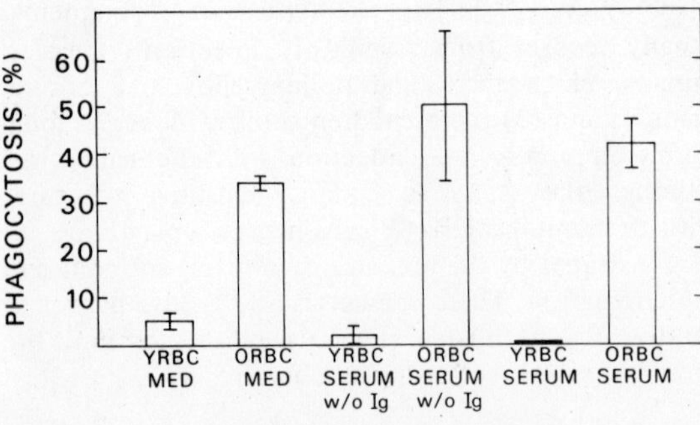

Figure 23–8. Phagocytosis of red cells (RBC) aged in situ. Freshly drawn red cells were separated by density into young (YRBC) and old (ORBC) cells, washed 3 times with Medium 199, resuspended in Medium 199 (Med), autologous hypogamma serum (serum w/o Ig), or autologous fresh, whole serum (serum), and incubated for 3 hours at 37 C with autologous macrophages. Vertical bars indicate standard error. (From Kay MMB: Proc Natl Acad Sci USA 72:3523, 1975.)

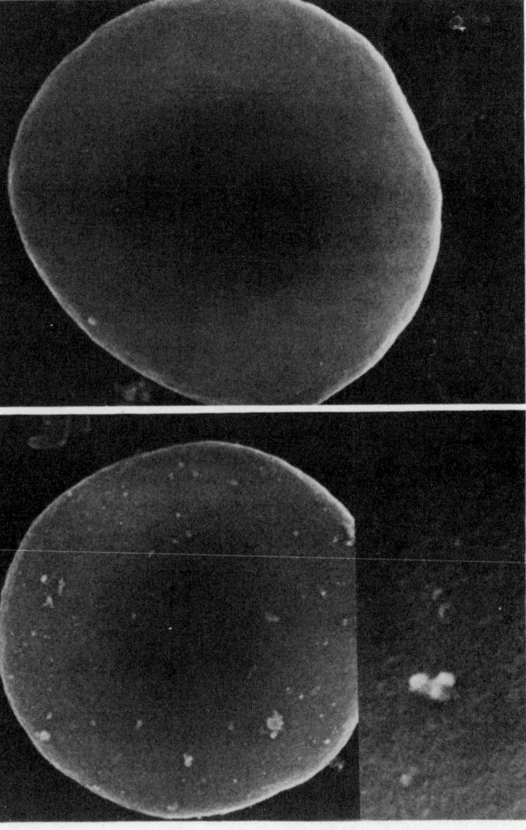

Figure 23–9. Scanning electron micrograph of red cells aged in situ which were incubated with SV40 virus-labeled antihuman IgG, T_2 virus-labeled antihuman IgA, and KLH-labeled antihuman IgM. Freshly drawn red cells were separated by density into young and old cells, washed 3 times in Medium 199, and incubated with scanning electron microscopy marker conjugates. ***Top:*** Low magnification of a young red cell demonstrating smooth surface. No marker is visible. (X 15,000.) ***Bottom:*** Low magnification of an old red cell. "Spots" on surface are scanning electron microscopy marker. (X 14,000.) Inset shows "spots" to be SV40 virus-labeled antihuman IgG on the cell surface. (X 75,000.) (From Kay MMB: Proc Natl Acad Sci USA 72:3524, 1975.)

scure. According to the clonal selection theory, self-tolerance depends on a thymic mechanism for eliminating any self-recognizing cells (forbidden clones) that may develop during fetal life or emerge later by mutation. This theory does not satisfactorily explain the following findings: (1) physiologic autoantibody circulates in normal, healthy individuals and is required for removal of senescent cells; and (2) tetraparental mouse chimeras (the product of fusion of 2 zygotes) depend for their survival on one or more serum factors which block cellular recognition. If cells of these mice are washed and put into culture, they are self-destructive. Adding autologous serum blocks this response. These findings indicate that there are B cells which produce autoantibody with regulatory functions that are fundamental to the individuals' survival. Hence, these B cell clones or their regulator cells cannot be "forbidden" but must be part of the normal immune mechanism. Other regulatory theories which maintain that forbidden clones are held in check by suppressor or regulator cells (a decrease in which leads to autoimmune disease) are inadequate for the same reasons and therefore must be revised.

B. Sequestered Antigen Theory: Another theory is that host antigens normally sequestered in tissues which are inaccessible to the immune system can be released into the circulation and provoke autoimmunity. This mechanism may explain the autoimmunity to lens protein (phacoanaphylaxis) often seen following traumatic rupture of the eye, since the lens is isolated early in embryonic development and is avascular. Nonetheless, it does not satisfactorily explain other autoimmune diseases since the immune system is in continuous contact with most tissues.

C. Innocent Bystander Theory: This theory explains some drug-induced autoimmune diseases. It states that the exogenous antigen, in this case a drug, attaches to a cell. Serum antibodies directed against the drug then lyse the cell to which it is attached. Thus, the cell is an "innocent bystander." This mechanism has been documented for Coombs-positive hemolytic anemias induced by penicillin and insulin and for cephalothin (Keflin)-induced granulocytopenia.

D. Microbial Theories: Before proceeding to discussion of the role of microbes in autoimmune disease, it would seem prudent to make a distinction between autoimmune reactions directed against self antigens (a presumably inappropriate immune response) and autoimmune reactions directed against microbial antigens expressed on infected self tissue (an appropriate response). Both processes can result in self-destruction, but the mechanisms are different.

Autoimmune reactions can be provoked by the intracellular residence of microbes. We will discuss an example of such a reaction, subacute sclerosing panencephalitis (SSPE). Other similar reactions include acute necrotizing hemorrhagic encephalitis, which generally follows a respiratory infection in adults, and the postvaccinal (vaccinia) and postinfectious (rubella, varicella, smallpox) encephalopathies. Regarding the age dependence of some central nervous system diseases, it has been observed that neural disease induced by immunization with syngeneic leukemic cells and mediated by antibody can be induced in normal old mice but not in young mice.

Subacute sclerosing panencephalitis is associated with prior measles infection and is mainly a disease of children and young adults, although it also affects people over 40 years of age. The interval between the onset of acute measles and the beginning of clinical symptoms ranges from 2–21 years, with a mean of 7.2 years. The evidence for a viral cause of subacute sclerosing panencephalitis can be summarized briefly as follows: (1) paramyxovirus has been demonstrated in and isolated from the brains of patients; (2) inclusion bodies containing RNA have been observed in ganglion cells adjacent to demyelinated "plaques" in the cerebral cortex; (3) an oligoclonal IgG, which complexes with measles virus antigens, is present in the cerebrospinal fluid of these patients; and (4) serum and cerebrospinal fluid from a patient with subacute sclerosing panencephalitis was shown to lyse cultured autologous brain cells only when measles virus antigens were expressed on the cell surface. Lysis could also be induced by sera from patients who had recovered from a normal measles virus infection and with heterologous rabbit antiserum against measles virus. Complement-binding immune complexes have been reported in sera and spinal fluid of panencephalitis patients, and immune complex deposits have been reported along renal glomerular basement membranes. The evidence strongly suggests (1) that subacute sclerosing panencephalitis results from a host response to a paramyxovirus closely related to, if not identical to, measles virus; and (2) that destruction of autologous tissue occurs only when viral antigens are expressed.

The obvious question, then, is why, in view of the high incidence of measles, only a relatively few individuals go on to develop panencephalitis. The answer may be found either in the characteristics of the virus (defective virus production), the nature of the host response (a defective immune mechanism), or both. As mentioned earlier, neutralizing antibodies can effectively limit the spread of free virus. However, cure of a viral infection often cannot be accomplished even with neutralizing antibodies of high titer. Recovery from infection probably requires a T cell-mediated immune response directed against the infected cell. The host may have subtle impairment of its T cell immune response which prevents eradication of infection but limits it to immunologically privileged sites or to tissues for which it has a tropism (eg, the brain). Viral expression on cell surfaces may be modulated by antibody. If so, this would add still another dimension to the complexity of the problem. Finally, genes of the histocompatibility region may be involved in cell-mediated cytolysis of virus-infected cells.

Evidence suggests that systemic lupus erythematosus and multiple sclerosis in man and the disease of New Zealand black (NZB) mice which closely resembles systemic lupus erythematosus may result from host responses to viral antigens. Evidence suggests that the T cell component of the immune response, at least in NZB mice, declines early, that this decline precedes autoimmune disease, and that the onset of the disease can be retarded by the injection of syngeneic young thymocytes. Although much knowledge has been gained by studies of animal models such as NZB mice, it is still uncertain whether these animals are appropriate models for immune deficiency as they occur in long-lived aging animals and humans. That is, the causes and mechanisms of the decline in normal immune functions and of immunodeficient diseases in these animal models may be different from those occurring in old people. If so, we may be observing phenotypic caricatures of old-age immune deficiency analogous to the phenotypic features of accelerated aging seen in progeria in humans.

Other microbial hypotheses include the view that microbes function as adjuvants; that microbial products (such as toxins) increase vascular permeability, thus permitting access of antibody to antigen; and that antibodies to microbial antigens cross-react with self antigens. The best example of a disease in which the latter mechanism is suspected to operate is rheumatic fever or glomerulonephritis following infection with β-hemolytic streptococci. Still another view is that viruses infect immune cells which become transformed in later life and recognize noninfected cells as foreign.

E. Microbial Enzyme/Product Theory: This theory explains autoimmunity in terms of a deficit in T cell function. The deficit could result from subtle immune deficiencies of childhood which escape clinical detection or from the slow decline in function associated with aging. The evidence that autoimmune disease follows a decline in T cell function is derived from studies of both humans and animals and includes the following: (1) An age-related decrease in T cell function as determined by T cell-dependent antibody synthesis is associated with an increase in the frequency of ANA in humans (Figs 23–10 and 23–11). (2) Neonatally thymectomized mice whose kidneys have been irradiated develop renal disease with immunoglobulin deposits indistinguishable from that of NZB mice. (3) Congenitally athymic nude mice have an increase in serum DNA-binding capacity, and both IgG and complement are deposited in their kidneys at an early age. (4) Mice thymectomized in the newborn period have a high incidence of autoimmune disease, including Coombs-positive hemolytic anemia.

The basic premise of the microbial enzyme/product theory is that the T cell component of the immune system is defective whereas the B cell component remains relatively intact. This appears to be the case with aging humans and mice. It is hypothesized that a decrease in T cell responsiveness allows microbes to establish an infection and to circulate freely. As a consequence, microbes or their products (enzymes or envelope glycoproteins) can alter membranes of host cells. For example, enzymes from these microbes will cleave molecules from cell surfaces, or viral envelope glycoproteins could fuse with cell membranes, thus exposing carbohydrate determinants to which B cells can make antibody. Inherent in this view is the assumption that it is the host response rather than the virus which determines whether complete recovery or sequelae such as autoimmune disease will follow an infection (Table 23–2).

Influenza virus infection will be discussed as an example of this mechanism, as the virus is common and the infection is not particularly serious in healthy adult individuals. Influenza virus contains hemagglutinins on its outer surface in the form of surface projections or "spikes," as well as a surface enzyme, neuraminidase, which cleaves N-acetylneuraminic acid (sialic acid) from cell surface glycoproteins. It is envisioned that the hemagglutinin enables the virus to attach to host cells while the neuraminidase releases the virus from the cell surface by cleaving the sialic

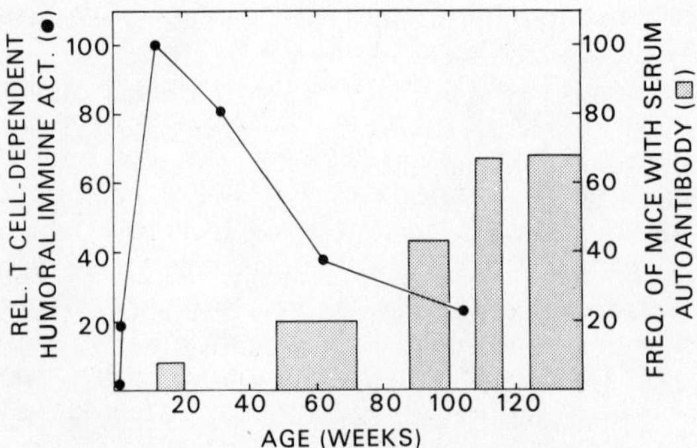

Figure 23–10. The capacity for T cell-dependent antibody response in relation to natural autoantibody formation in long-lived mice. (Reproduced, with permission, from Makinodan T, Peterson W: Dev Biol 14:96, 1966; and Peterson W, Makinodan T: Clin Exp Immunol 12:273, 1972.)

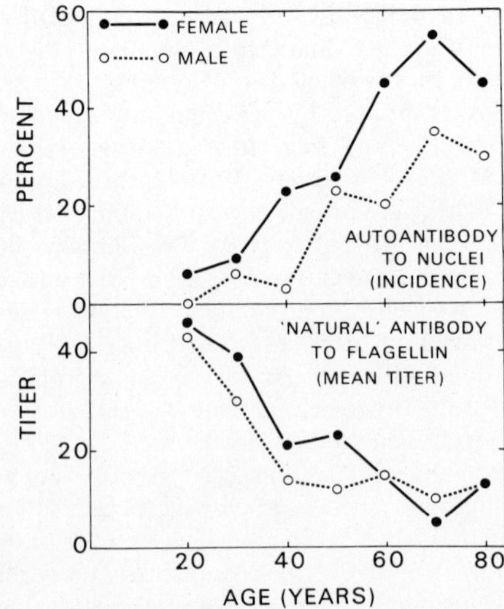

Figure 23–11. Fall in natural anti-salmonella flagellin titer with age and rise in the incidence of antinuclear factor in humans of both sexes. (Reproduced, with permission, from Rowley JJ, Buchanan H, Mackay IR: Lancet 2:24, 1968.)

Table 23–2. Initiation by parainfluenza type 2 virus of Coombs-positive autoimmune hemolytic anemia in adult and middle-aged mice rendered T cell-deficient and in old mice. Prior to infection, all mice were Coombs-negative. Following infection, TXB mice (which are deficient of all T cells save those immature precursors generated in the bone marrow) and old mice (20–24 months of age) develop Coombs-positive autoimmune hemolytic anemia whereas young and middle-aged mice which have not been rendered T cell-deficient do not. Thymectomized mice (T mice) whose peripheral cells have not been destroyed by radiation convert to Coombs positivity but do not develop anemia. Virus particles were not present on the red cells as determined by transmission and scanning electron microscopy. The T cell-mitogenic responsiveness of lymph node and spleen cells prior to the infection decreased with age, so that by 24 months it was 42% and 30%, respectively, of adult values.

Age	Time Relative to Viral Infection	Treatment*	Coombs Test	Hematocrit (%)†
Adult	Pre	None	–	ND
	Post	None	–	43
	Pre	T	–	ND
	Post	T	+	45
Middle-aged	Pre	None	–	ND
	Post	None	–	46
	Post	T	+	43
	Post	TXB	+	26
Old	Pre	None	–	ND
	Post	None	+	30

*T, thymectomized at 4 weeks of age; TXB, thymectomized at 4 weeks and irradiated and reconstituted with bone marrow at 6 weeks of age.

†ND = not determined.

acid to which the hemagglutinin has become bound. The virus thus released retains all its activity and can reattach to another uninfected host cell; however, the original host cells can no longer act as targets for the same type of virus since its hemagglutinin receptor has been altered by the loss of sialic acid. Thus, these 2 properties of the virus enable it to attach to red cells, circulate with them, detach from them, and reattach to other host cells. Removal of sialic acid from cell surfaces by neuraminidase exposes antigenic determinants to which antibodies can bind. Autoimmune disease could be perpetuated by chronic low-grade infection of dividing cells, leading to continuing viral activity. Indeed, Coombs-positive hemolytic anemias, anti-basement membrane antibodies in the lungs and kidneys, and diabetes have been associated with influenza virus infections.

Although influenza is primarily a respiratory infection, it is obvious that the viruses in the lungs have ample exposure to red cells to which they can attach and travel to all parts of the body. Virus has been isolated from heart, kidneys, and other extrapulmonary tissues in some fatal cases of human infections. In other cases, however, fatal influenzal myocarditis, hemorrhage in the adrenals, pancreas, and ovaries, and renal tubular degeneration have been found, yet the virus could not be isolated from these lesions.

Neoplasia

There is an inverse relationship between immune activity and susceptibility to neoplasia which appears to be causal in nature. The question is, does the decline in immune function precede or follow neoplasia? Evidence of several kinds suggests that neoplasia occurs more readily in individuals with compromised or deficient immune function: (1) The incidence of cancer in persons with childhood immunodeficiency diseases ranges from 1:20 to 1:10, despite the fact that these individuals have a much shorter life span in which to develop cancer. Only about one out of 300 persons in the general population has or has had cancer. (2) The incidence of cancer in adult-onset immunodeficiency is higher than normal—estimated by some to be one out of every 10 affected individuals. (3) Patients given antilymphocyte serum have a greater than normal incidence of malignancies. It has been suggested that antilymphocyte serum preferentially suppresses T cells. (4) Immunosuppression both in animals and in humans increases the incidence of spontaneous tumors. An immunosuppressed transplant patient has a 350 times greater chance of developing reticulum cell sarcoma than members of the normal population. (5) Immunosuppression enhances transplanted tumor "takes" and increases the incidence of metastases of transplanted tumors both in humans and in animals. A patient developed hepatocarcinoma 3 years after renal transplantation from a donor who died of a histologically similar disease. Cessation of immunosuppressive therapy resulted in the eventual rejection of the tumor. (6) In humans and long-lived mice, the decline in certain normal immune functions begins shortly after sexual maturity, when the thymus begins to involute and atrophy. Obviously, this is long before age-related immunodeficiency diseases are manifested. (7) The mortality rate is higher among aged humans with reduced cell-mediated immune function than among those with normal cell-mediated immune function, and death associated with cancer and cardiovascular disease is higher among those with serum ANA than among those without such antibody.

The mechanisms whereby decreased immune function permits the growth of neoplasms are as yet unknown. Various theories have been advanced. The first is that immunologic surveillance prevents the growth of neoplastic cells which presumably contain nonself antigens. The second is that decreased immunologic responsiveness permits the growth of oncogenic viruses. This is consistent with evidence derived from experimental animals which indicates that manipulation of the host immune response is often necessary for induction of tumors with oncogenic viruses. A third theory is that chronic immunostimulation leads to lymphoid hyperplasia which progresses to malignancy. This theory purports to explain the relatively high incidence of lymphoid malignancies in transplant recipients.

• • •

References

Kay MMB: Autoimmune disease: The consequence of deficient T cell function? J Am Geriatr Soc 24:253, 1976.

Kay MMB: Mechanism of removal of senescent cells by human macrophages in situ. Proc Natl Acad Sci USA 72:3521, 1975.

Kay MMB, Makinodan T: Immunobiology of aging: Evaluation of current status. Clin Immunol Immunopathol 5:(5), 1976.

Mackay IR: Ageing and immunological function in man. Gerontologia 18:285, 1972.

Price GB, Makinodan T: Aging: Alteration of DNA-protein information. Gerontologia 19:58, 1973.

Strehler BL: Cellular aging. Ann NY Acad Sci 138:661, 1967.

Walford RL: The immunologic theory of aging: Current status. Fed Proc 33:2020, 1974.

Section III

Immunologic Laboratory Tests

24 . . .

Laboratory Methods for Detection of Antigens & Antibodies

Daniel P. Stites, MD

One of the major challenges for modern medical science is the translation of basic advances in immunochemistry and immunobiology into diagnostic and therapeutic procedures that will be of use in the practice of clinical medicine. Much of this work will be done in the clinical immunology laboratory, where tests which utilize a great many of the recently elucidated principles of basic immunology can be performed on a wide variety of samples taken from patients. The results of these laboratory procedures are then utilized by practicing physicians in the diagnosis and treatment of clinical disorders. Furthermore, qualitative and quantitative analysis of several features of the immune response has led to better understanding of the pathogenesis of many clinical disorders. In turn, this understanding has stimulated further basic scientific research in immunology. In fact, observations made by clinical investigators in immunology have frequently dramatically changed the course of basic research in immunology and related fields.

In the past 2 decades, immunologic laboratory methods have gradually become increasingly more refined and simplified. Because of their inherent specificity and sensitivity, these methods have now achieved a central role in modern clinical laboratory science. The goals of laboratory medicine are to improve the availability, accuracy, and precision of a body of medically important laboratory tests, to assure correct interpretation, and to assess the significance of new tests introduced into clinical medicine. With the marked proliferation of new laboratory tests employing immunologic principles, these methods of laboratory diagnosis have often been uncritically applied to clinical situations. A better understanding of the methods used in the immunology laboratory should provide the student and practitioner of medicine with a useful guide for correct application and interpretation of this body of knowledge.

In the present chapter, tests for the detection of antigens and antibodies are discussed. Most of the technics described involve application in the clinical laboratory of the principles of immunochemistry discussed in detail in Section I. This chapter and the next one are not meant to be comprehensive laboratory manuals. Rather, the principles of the various immunologic methods and their application to clinical problems are reviewed. It is hoped that careful study of these 2 chapters in conjunction with the first 2 sections of this book will provide the reader with a solid background for an enhanced understanding of the detailed discussions of clinical immunology presented in Section IV.

The topics covered in this chapter include the following:

(1) Immunodiffusion
(2) Electrophoresis and immunoelectrophoresis
(3) Immunochemical and physicochemical methods
(4) Radioimmunoassay
(5) Immunohistochemical technics (immunofluorescence)
(6) Agglutination
(7) Complement function

IMMUNODIFFUSION

Immunoprecipitation (see Chapter 4) is the simplest and most direct means of demonstrating antigen-antibody reactions in the laboratory. The application of immunoprecipitation to the study of bacterial antigens launched the field of serology in the first part of the 20th century. In 1946, Oudin described a system of single diffusion of antigen and antibody in agar-filled tubes. This important advance was soon followed by Ouchterlony's classical description of double diffusion in agar layered on slides. This method is still in widespread use today and has many applications in the detection and analysis of precipitating antigen-antibody systems.

The purpose of all immunodiffusion technics is to detect the reaction of antigen and antibody by the precipitation reaction. Although the formation of anti-

Daniel P. Stites is Assistant Professor of Medicine and Laboratory Medicine and Director, Immunology Laboratory, University of California School of Medicine, San Francisco.

Françoise Chenais (section on Immunochemical & Physicochemical Methods) is Fellow in Immunology, Medical University of South Carolina, Charleston.

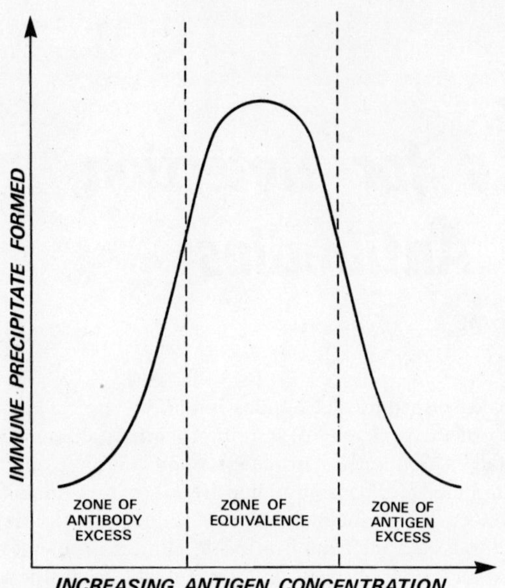

Figure 24–1. Antigen-antibody precipitin curve. Typical precipitin curve resulting from titration of increasing antigen concentration plotted against amount of immune precipitate formed. Amount of antibody is kept constant throughout.

gen-antibody complexes in a semisolid medium such as agar is dependent on buffer electrolytes, pH, and temperature, the most important determinants of the reaction are the relative concentrations of antigen and antibody. This relationship is depicted schematically in Fig 24–1. Maximal precipitation forms in the area of equivalence, with decreasing amounts in the zones of antigen excess or antibody excess. Thus, formation of precipitation lines in any immunodiffusion system is highly dependent on relative concentrations of antigen and antibody.

Immunodiffusion has its most important clinical application in the quantitation of serum immunoglobulins. In fact, virtually any serum protein (or antigen) can be accurately determined by single radial diffusion in agar as long as one has specific precipitating antibody directed against the particular serum protein in question.

METHODOLOGY & INTERPRETATION

Double Diffusion in Agar

This simple and extremely useful technic is based on the principle that antigen and antibody diffuse through a semisolid medium (eg, agar) and form stable immune complexes which then can be analyzed visually.

The test is performed by pouring molten agar onto glass slides or into Petri dishes and allowing it to harden. Small wells are punched out of the agar a few millimeters apart. Samples containing antigen and antibody are placed in opposing wells and allowed to diffuse toward one another in a moist chamber for 18–24 hours. The resultant precipitation lines that represent antigen-antibody complexes are analyzed visually in indirect light with the aid of a magnifying lens.

The 3 basic characteristic patterns of reactions are shown in Fig 24–2. In addition to these 3 basic patterns, more complex interrelationships may be seen between antigen and antibody. The formation of a single precipitation line between an antigen and its corresponding antiserum can be utilized as a rough qualitative estimation of antigen or antibody purity. However, the relative insensitivity of the test and the limitation of immunodiffusion to *precipitating* antigen-antibody reactions partly restrict the applications of this technic.

Double immunodiffusion in agar can also be used for semiquantitative analysis in human serologic systems where the specificity of the precipitation lines has already been determined. Such an analysis is per-

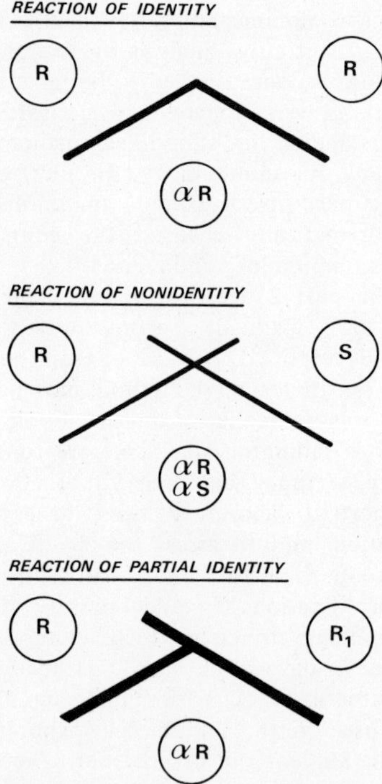

Figure 24–2. Reaction patterns in double immunodiffusion (Ouchterlony). R = antigen R, S = antigen S, R_1 = antigen R_1, αR = antibody to R, αS = antibody to S. *Reaction of identity:* Precisely similar precipitin lines have formed in the reaction of R with αR. Note that the lines intersect at a point. *Reaction of nonidentity:* Precipitin lines completely cross owing to separate interaction of αR with R and αS with S when R and S are non-cross-reacting antigens. *Reaction of partial identity:* αR reacts with both R and R_1 but forms lines that do not form a complete cross. Antigenic determinants are *partially* shared between R and R_1.

formed by placing antibody in a central well surrounded circumferentially by antigen wells (Fig 24–3). Serial dilutions of antigen are placed in the surrounding wells, and the development of precipitation lines can be taken as a rough measure of antigen concentration. Alternatively, this form of analysis is very useful in determining the approximate precipitating titer of an antiserum by simply reversing the location of antigen and antibody in the pattern (Fig 24–3).

Single Radial Diffusion

The double immunodiffusion system is only semiquantitative. In 1965, Mancini introduced a novel technic employing single diffusion for accurate quantitative determination of antigens. This technic grew out of the simple linear diffusion technic of Oudin by means of the incorporation of specific antibody into the agar plate. Radial diffusion is based on the principle that a quantitative relationship exists between the amount of antigen placed in a well cut in the agar-antibody plate and the resulting ring of precipitation. The technic is performed as diagrammed in Fig 24–4.

In the method described originally by Mancini, the *area* circumscribed by the precipitation ring was proportionate to the antigen concentration. This method requires that the precipitation rings reach the maximal possible size, which often requires 48–72 hours of diffusion. Alternatively, the single radial diffusion method of Fahey allows measurement of the rings prior to full development. In this modification, the logarithm of the antigen concentration is proportionate to the *diameter* of the ring.

A standard curve is experimentally determined with known antigen standards and the equation which describes this curve can then be used for the determination of antigen concentration corresponding to any diameter size (Fig 24–5). The sensitivity of this method is in the range of 1–3 μg/ml of antigen.

The most important clinical application of single radial diffusion is in the measurement of serum immunoglobulin concentrations. A monospecific antiserum directed only at Fc or H chain determinants of the immunoglobulin molecule must be incorporated into the agar in order to determine immunoglobulin concentrations. Owing to the relatively low concentrations of IgD and IgE in human serum, this technic is used primarily to determine the other 3 immunoglobulin classes, IgG, IgA, and IgM. However, by decreasing the amount of specific anti-immunoglobulin antiserum placed in the agar, so-called "low level" plates can be produced which have increased sensitivity for detection of reduced levels of serum immunoglobulins.

There are a number of common pitfalls in the interpretation of single radial diffusion tests for immunoglobulin quantitation: (1) Polymeric forms of immunoglobulin such as occur in multiple myeloma or Waldenström's macroglobulinemia diffuse more slowly than native monomers, resulting in underestimation of immunoglobulin concentrations in these diseases. (2) High-molecular-weight immune complexes which may circulate in cryoglobulinemia or rheumatoid arthritis will result in falsely low values by a similar mechanism. (3) Low-molecular-weight forms such as 7S IgM in sera of patients with macroglobulinemia, systemic lupus erythematosus, rheumatoid arthritis, and ataxia-telangiectasia may give falsely high values. This phe-

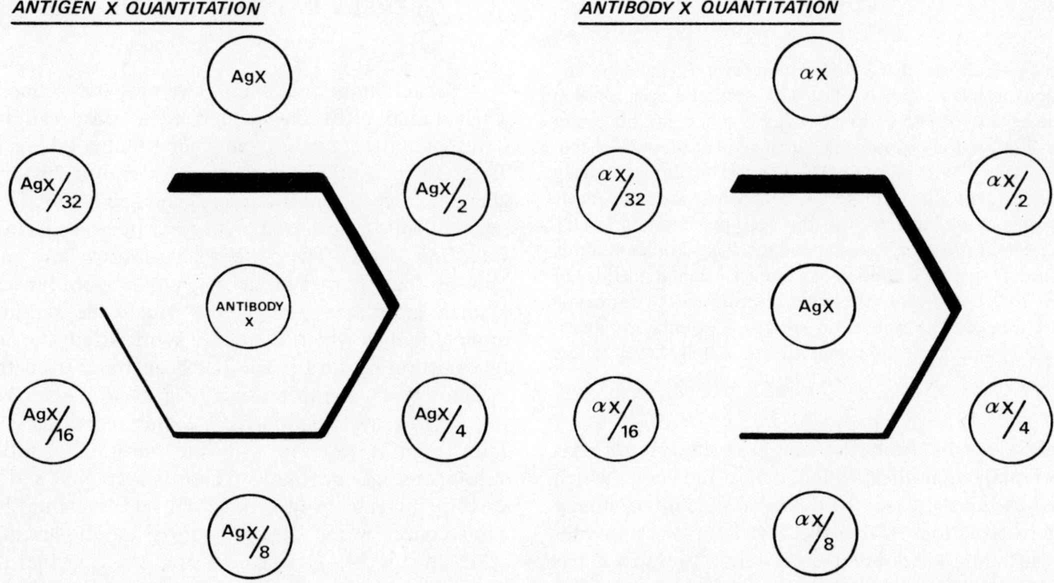

Figure 24–3. Semiquantitative analysis of antigen and antibody by double immunodiffusion. Antigen X is serially diluted and placed circumferentially in wells surrounding the central well containing antibody against antigen X. Precipitin lines form with decreasing thickness until no longer visible at dilution of 1:32 of antigen X. On the right, a similar pattern is generated but with serial 2-fold dilutions of antibody X. Formation of a single precipitin line indicates that a single antigen-antibody reaction has occurred.

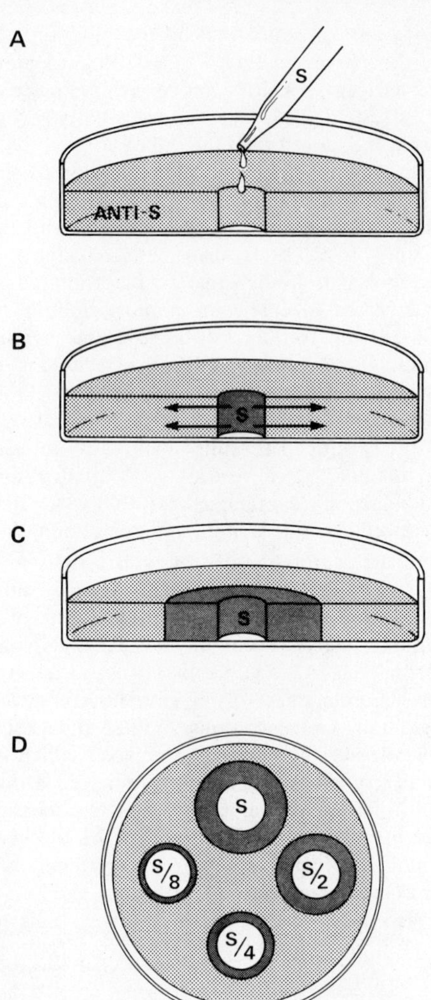

Figure 24–4. Single radial diffusion in agar (radial immunodiffusion). *A:* Petri dish is filled with semisolid agar solution containing antibody to antigen S. After agar hardens, the center well is filled with a precisely measured amount of material containing antigen S. *B:* Antigen S is allowed to diffuse radially from the center well for 24–48 hours. *C:* Where antigen S meets corresponding antibody to S in the agar, precipitation results. After reaction proceeds to completion, a sharp border or a ring is formed. *D:* By serial dilution of a known standard quantity of antigen S–S/1, S/2, S/4, S/8–rings of progressively decreasing size are formed. The amount of antigen S in unknown specimens can be calculated and compared with standard (Fig 24–5).

nomenon results from the fact that 7S IgM diffuses more rapidly than the 19S IgM parent molecule, which is used as the standard. (4) Reversed precipitation may occur in situations where the test human serum contains anti-immunoglobulin antibodies. In such a circumstance, diffusion and precipitation occur in 2 directions simultaneously and may result in falsely high values. This phenomenon has been well documented in the case of subjects with IgA deficiency who have antibodies to ruminant proteins in their serum.

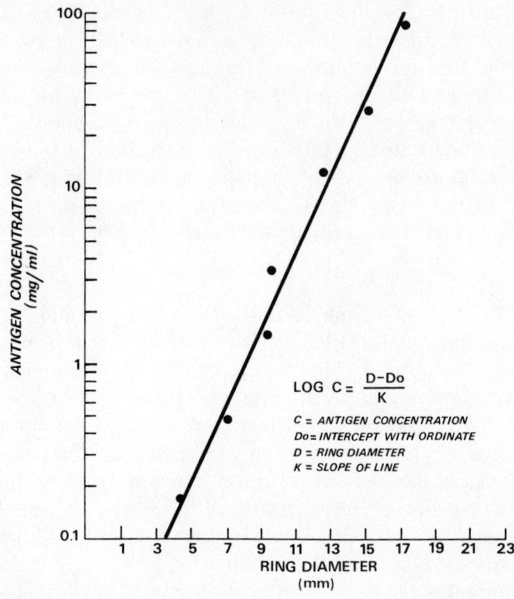

Figure 24–5. Standard curve for single radial diffusion. Relationship between ring diameter and antigen concentration is described by the line constructed from known amounts of antigen (Fig 24–4).

The problem of IgA quantitation in this circumstance can be avoided by using anti-immunoglobulin from rabbits (ie, a nonruminant species).

APPLICATIONS: SERUM IMMUNOGLOBULIN LEVELS IN HEALTH & DISEASE

Serum immunoglobulin levels as determined by single radial diffusion are dependent on a variety of developmental, genetic, and environmental factors. These include ethnic background, age, sex, history of allergies or recurrent infections, and geographic factors (eg, endemic infestation with parasites results in elevated IgE levels). The patient's age is especially important in the interpretation of immunoglobulin levels. Human infants are born with virtually no serum immunoglobulins which they have synthesized; the entire IgG portion of cord serum has been transferred transplacentally from the mother (Fig 24–6). After birth, this IgG decays, resulting in a falling serum IgG level. This trend is reversed with the onset of significant autologous IgG synthesis. There is a gradual and progressive increase in IgG, IgA, and IgM levels until late adolescence, when nearly normal adult levels are achieved (Fig 24–7). Furthermore, it is clear that there is a great deal of variability in immunoglobulin levels in the normal population (Fig 24–7 and Table 24–1).

Individual changes in serum immunoglobulins have been recorded in many diseases. A partial list of the instances of polyclonal increases in immunoglobu-

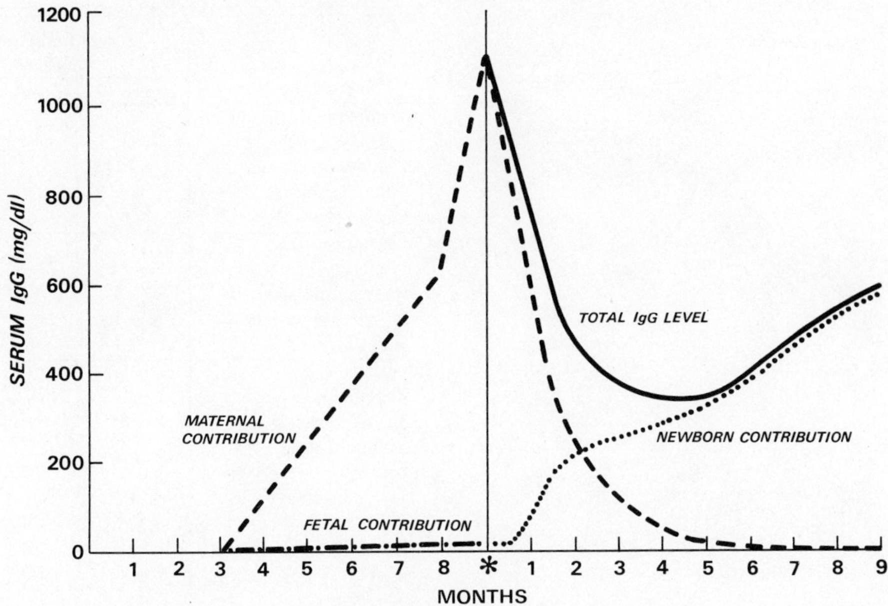

Figure 24–6. Development of IgG levels with age. Modified from Allansmith & others: J Pediatr 72:289, 1968. Relationship of development of serum levels of IgG during fetal and newborn stages and maternal contribution.

Table 24–1. Levels of immune globulins in serum of normal subjects at different ages.*

Age	Number of Subjects	Level of IgG† mg/dl (Range)	Level of IgG† % of Adult Level	Level of IgM† mg/dl (Range)	Level of IgM† % of Adult Level	Level of IgA† mg/dl (Range)	Level of IgA† % of Adult Level	Level of Total γ-Globulin† mg/dl (Range)	Level of Total γ-Globulin† % of Adult Level
Newborn	22	1031±200 (645–1244)	89±17	11±5 (5–30)	11±5	2±3 (0–11)	1±2	1044±201 (660–1439)	67±13
1–3 months	29	430±119 (272–762)	37±10	30±11 (16–67)	30±11	21±13 (6–56)	11±7	481±127 (324–699)	31±9
4–6 months	33	427±186 (206–1125)	37±16	43±17 (10–83)	43±17	28±18 (8–93)	14±9	498±204 (228–1232)	32±13
7–12 months	56	661±219 (279–1533)	58±19	54±23 (22–147)	55±23	37±18 (16–98)	19±9	752±242 (327–1687)	48±15
13–24 months	59	762±209 (258–1393)	66±18	58±23 (14–114)	59±23	50±24 (19–119)	25±12	870±258 (398–1586)	56±16
25–36 months	33	892±183 (419–1274)	77±16	61±19 (28–113)	62±19	71±37 (19–235)	36±19	1024±205 (499–1418)	65±14
3–5 years	28	929±228 (569–1597)	80±20	56±18 (22–100)	57±18	93±27 (55–152)	47±14	1078±245 (730–1771)	69±17
6–8 years	18	923±256 (559–1492)	80±22	65±25 (27–118)	66±25	124±45 (54–221)	62±23	1112±293 (640–1725)	71±20
9–11 years	9	1124±235 (779–1456)	97±20	79±33 (35–132)	80±33	131±60 (12–208)	66±30	1334±254 (966–1639)	85±17
12–16 years	9	946±124 (726–1085)	82±11	59±20 (35–72)	60±20	148±63 (70–229)	74±32	1153±169 (833–1284)	74±12
Adults	30	1158±305 (569–1919)	100±26	99±27 (47–147)	100±27	200±61 (61–330)	100±31	1457±353 (730–2365)	100±24

*Reproduced, with permission, from Stiehm ER, Fudenberg HH: Pediatrics 37:717, 1966.
†Mean ± 1 SD.

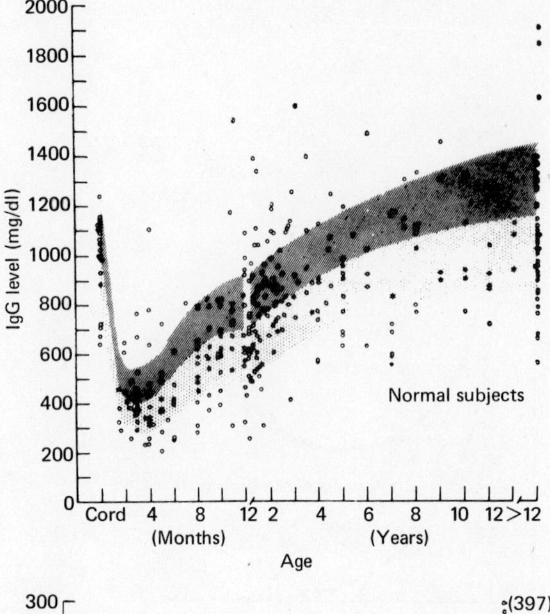

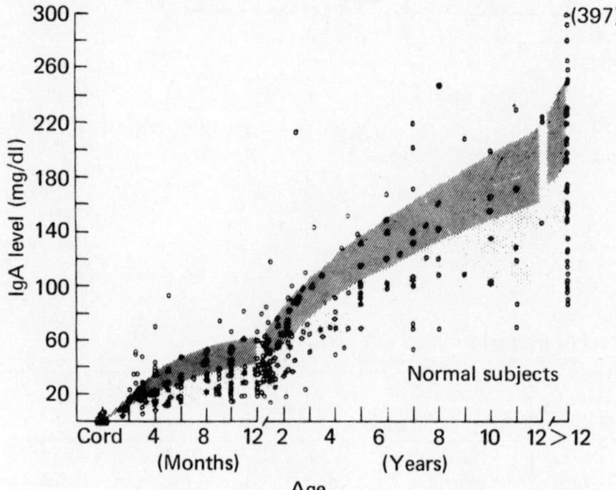

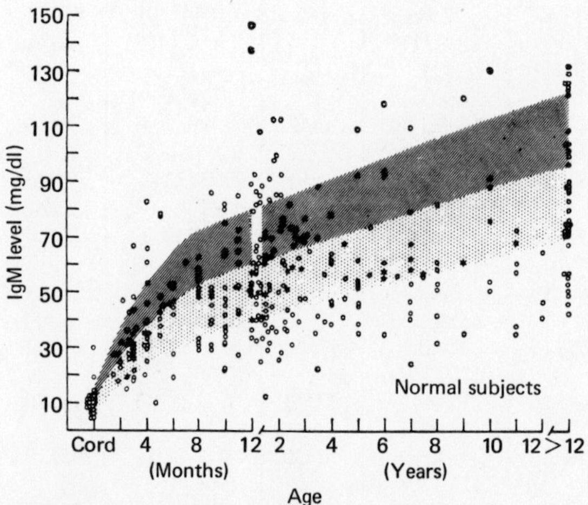

Figure 24–7. Variation of serum levels of IgG, IgA, and IgM with age. From Stiehm ER, Fudenberg HH: Pediatrics 37:718, 1966. Scattergrams of levels of IgG, IgA, and IgM in normal subjects. Shaded areas are ± 1 SD of the mean; each point represents one subject.

Table 24–2. Serum immunoglobulin concentrations in diseases associated with polyclonal gammopathies.*

	Serum Immunoglobulin Concentration		
Diseases	**IgG**	**IgA**	**IgM**
Liver diseases			
Infectious hepatitis	↑ ↔ ↑↑	N ↔ ↑	N ↔ ↑↑
Laennec's cirrhosis	↑ ↔ ↑↑↑	↑ ↔ ↑↑↑	N ↔ ↑↑
Biliary cirrhosis	N	N	↑ ↔ ↑↑
Lupoid hepatitis	↑↑↑	↑	N ↔ ↑↑
Collagen disorders			
Lupus erythematosus	↑ ↔ ↑↑	N ↔ ↑	N ↔ ↑↑
Rheumatoid arthritis	N ↔ ↑	↑ ↔ ↑↑↑	N ↔ ↑
Sjögren's syndrome	N ↔ ↑	N ↔ ↑	↓ ↔ ↑↑
Scleroderma	N ↔ ↑	N	↑
Infections			
Tuberculosis	↑ ↔ ↑↑	N ↔ ↑↑↑	↓ ↔ N
Subacute bacterial endocarditis	↑ ↔ ↑↑	↓ ↔ N	↑ ↔ ↑↑
Leprosy	↑ ↔ ↑↑	N	↑
Trypanosomiasis	N ↔ ↑	N ↔ ↑	↑↑ ↔ ↑↑↑
Malaria	↓ ↔ ↑	N	↑ ↔ ↑↑
Kala-azar	↑↑	N	N
Infectious mononucleosis	↑ ↔ ↑↑	N ↔ ↑	↑ ↔ ↑↑
Fungus diseases	N	N ↔ ↑	N
Bartonellosis	↑	↓ ↔ N	↑↑ ↔ ↑↑↑
Lymphogranuloma venereum	↑↑	N	N
Actinomycosis	↑↑↑	↑↑	↑↑↑
Sarcoidosis	N ↔ ↑↑	N ↔ ↑↑	N ↔ ↑
Miscellaneous			
Hodgkin's disease	↓ ↔ ↑↑	↓ ↔ ↑	↓ ↔ ↑↑
Monocytic leukemia	↑	↑	↑↑
Cystic fibrosis	↑ ↔ ↑↑	↑ ↔ ↑↑	N ↔ ↑↑

N = Essentially normal serum immunoglobulin levels.
↓ = Decreased immunoglobulin concentrations.
↑, ↑↑, ↑↑↑ = Slight, moderate, or marked increases in serum immunoglobulin concentrations.
↔ = Range of immunoglobulin levels.

*Reproduced, with permission, from Ritzmann & Levin: Lab Synopsis 2:17, 1967.

lins is listed (Table 24–2). For a detailed discussion of immunoglobulin deficiencies, the reader is referred to Chapter 26.

ELECTROPHORESIS

Analysis of the heterogeneity in individual proteins is most readily accomplished by electrophoresis. The separation of proteins in an electrical field was perfected in 1937 by Tiselius, who used free or moving boundary electrophoresis. However, owing to the relative complexity of this method, zone electrophoresis in a stabilizing medium such as paper or cellulose acetate has replaced free electrophoresis for clinical use.

In 1952, a two-stage method was reported which

combined electrophoresis with immunodiffusion for the detection of tetanus toxoid by antiserum. Shortly thereafter, the now classical method of immunoelectrophoresis (IEP) was introduced by Williams and Grabar. In this technic, both electrophoresis and double immunodiffusion are performed on the same agar-coated slide. During the past 20 years, immunoelectrophoresis has become the cornerstone of clinical paraprotein analysis as well as a standard method for immunochemical analysis of a wide variety of proteins. More recently, radioimmunoelectrophoresis and electroimmunodiffusion methods have been introduced. Various electrophoretic methods and examples of their uses in clinical immunodiagnosis are described in the following paragraphs.

ZONE ELECTROPHORESIS

Proteins are separated in zone electrophoresis almost exclusively on the basis of their surface charge (Fig 24–8). The supporting medium is theoretically inert and does not impede or enhance the flow of molecules in the electrical field. Generally, paper or cellulose acetate strips are employed as supporting media. However, a major advantage of cellulose acetate is the speed of completion of electrophoretic migration (ie, 60–90 minutes compared to hours for paper). Additionally, cellulose acetate is optically clear; microquantities of proteins may be applied; and it is adaptable to histochemical staining procedures. For these reasons, cellulose acetate is almost universally used as the supporting medium for clinical zone electrophoresis.

In the technic itself, serum or other biologic fluid samples are placed at the origin and separated by electrophoresis for about 90 minutes using alkaline buffer solutions. The strips are then stained and scanned. Scanning converts the band pattern into peaks and allows for quantitation of the major peaks. Normal human serum is separated into 5 major electrophoretic bands by this method, ie, albumin, α_1-globulin, α_2-globulin, β-globulin, and γ-globulin.

A

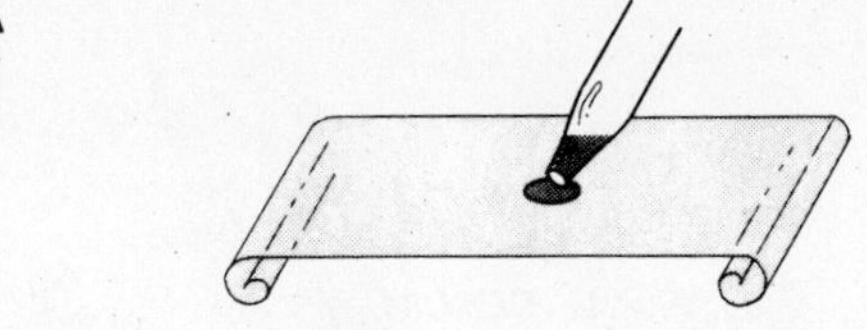

B

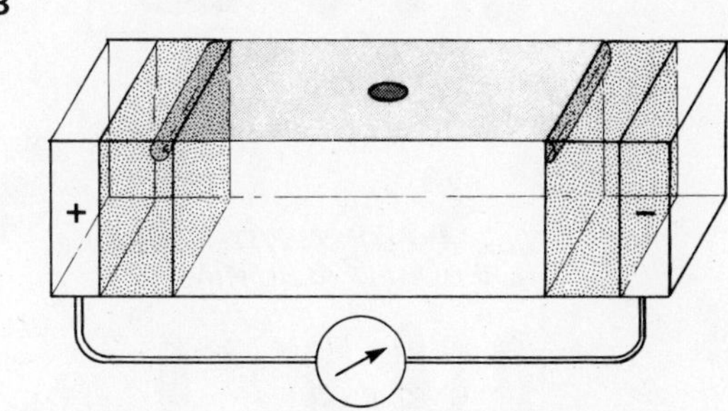

C

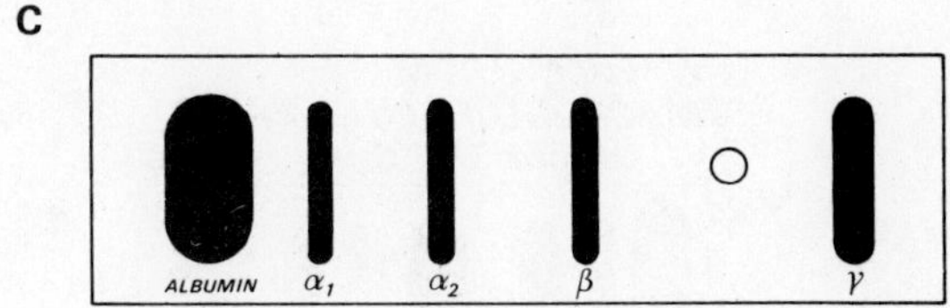

D

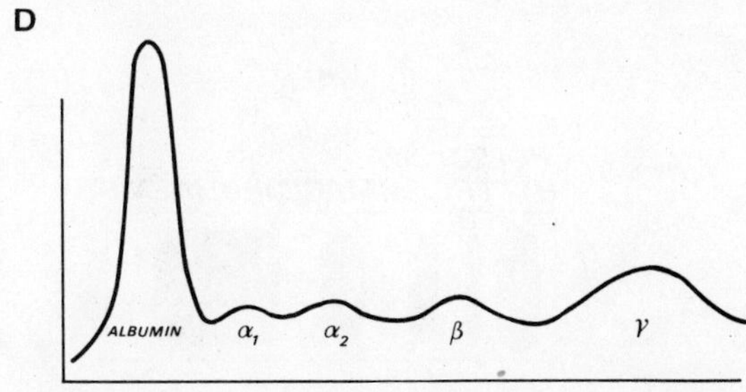

Figure 24–8. Technic of cellulose acetate zone electrophoresis. ***A:*** Small amount of serum or other fluid is applied to cellulose acetate strip. ***B:*** Electrophoresis of sample in electrolyte buffer is performed. ***C:*** Separated protein bands are visualized in characteristic position after being stained. ***D:*** Densitometer scanning from cellulose acetate strip converts bands to characteristic peaks of albumin, α_1-globulin, α_2-globulin, β-globulin and γ-globulin.

Applications

Zone electrophoresis is extremely valuable in the diagnosis of human paraprotein disorders such as multiple myeloma and Waldenström's macroglobulinemia (Fig 24–9). In these disorders, an electrophoretically restricted protein spike usually occurs in the γ-globulin region of the electrophoretogram. Since in zone electrophoresis the trailing edge of immunoglobulins extends into the β region and occasionally the α region, spikes in these regions are also consistent with paraproteinemic disorders involving immunoglobulins.

A decrease in serum γ-globulin concentration such as occurs in hypogammaglobulinemia can also be detected with this technic (Fig 24–9). Free light chains are readily detectable in urine when present in increased amounts such as in Bence Jones proteinuria of myeloma (Fig 24–10). Zone electrophoresis has also been useful in the diagnosis of certain central nervous system diseases with alterations in cerebrospinal fluid proteins (Fig 24–11).

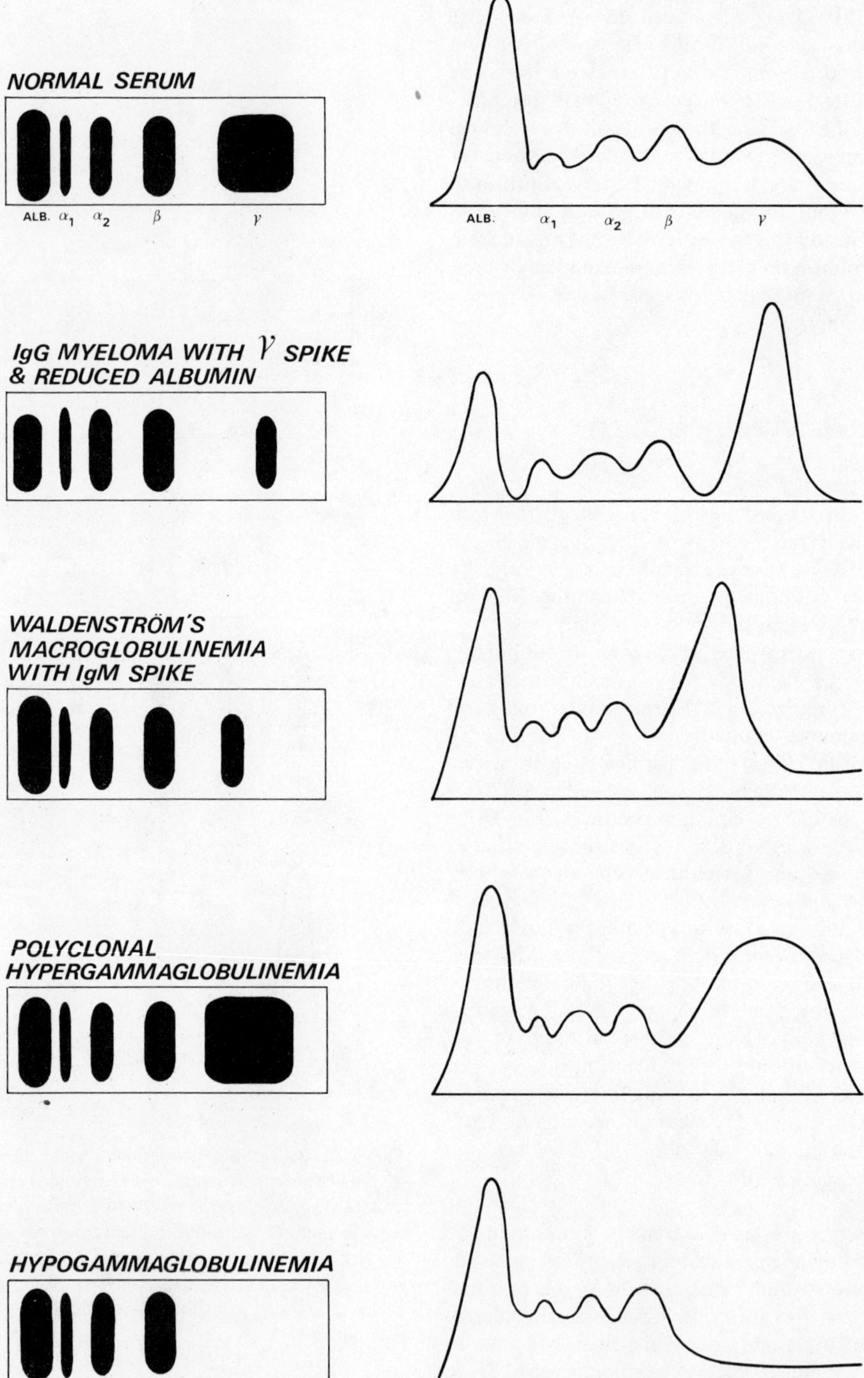

Figure 24–9. Zone electrophoresis patterns of serum abnormalities in various diseases.

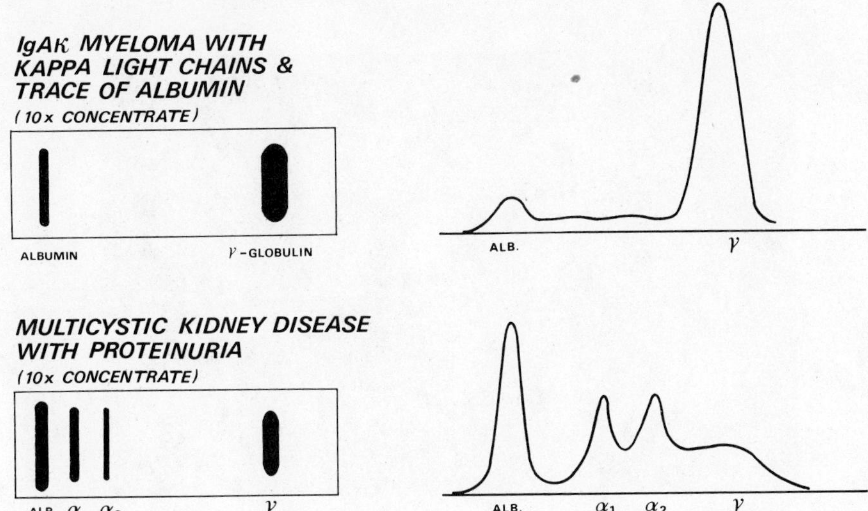

Figure 24–10. Zone electrophoresis patterns of urine abnormalities in various diseases.

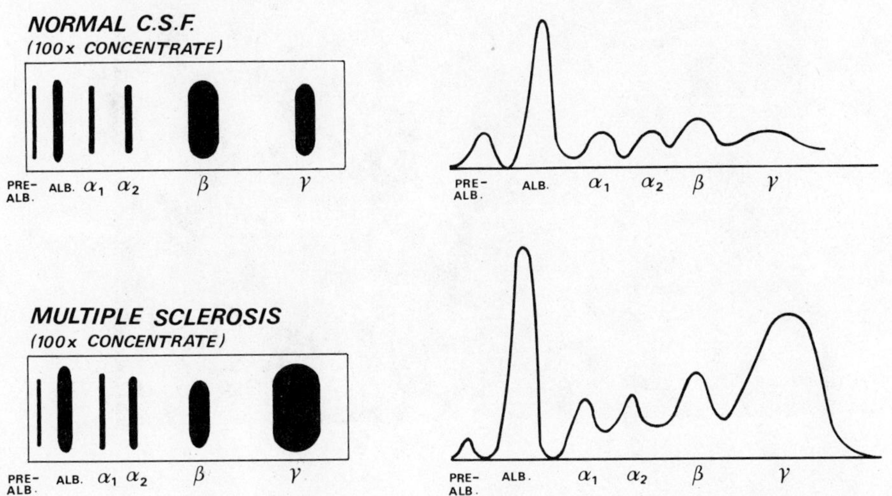

Figure 24–11. Zone electrophoresis patterns of cerebrospinal fluid from normal subject and multiple sclerosis patient.

IMMUNOELECTROPHORESIS (IEP)

Immunoelectrophoresis combines both electrophoretic separation and immune precipitation of proteins. Both identification and approximate quantitation can thereby be accomplished for individual proteins present in serum, urine, or other biologic fluid.

In this technic (Fig 24–13), a glass slide is covered with molten agar or agarose in a buffer solution (pH 8.2, ionic strength 0.025). An antigen well and antibody trough are cut with a template cutting device. The serum sample (antigen) is placed in the antigen well and is separated in an electrical field with a potential difference of 3.3 V/cm for 30–60 minutes. Antiserum is then placed in the trough and allowed to diffuse for 18–24 hours. The resulting precipitation lines may then be photographed or the slide washed, dried, and stained for a permanent record.

A comparison of the relationship of precipitation lines developed in normal serum by immunoelectrophoresis and zone electrophoresis is shown in Fig 24–14.

Applications of Immunoelectrophoresis

In the laboratory diagnosis of paraproteinemias, the results of zone electrophoresis and immunoelectrophoresis should be combined. The presence of a sharp increase or spike in the γ region on zone electrophoresis strongly suggests the presence of a monoclonal paraprotein. However, it is necessary to perform immunoelectrophoresis to determine the exact H chain class

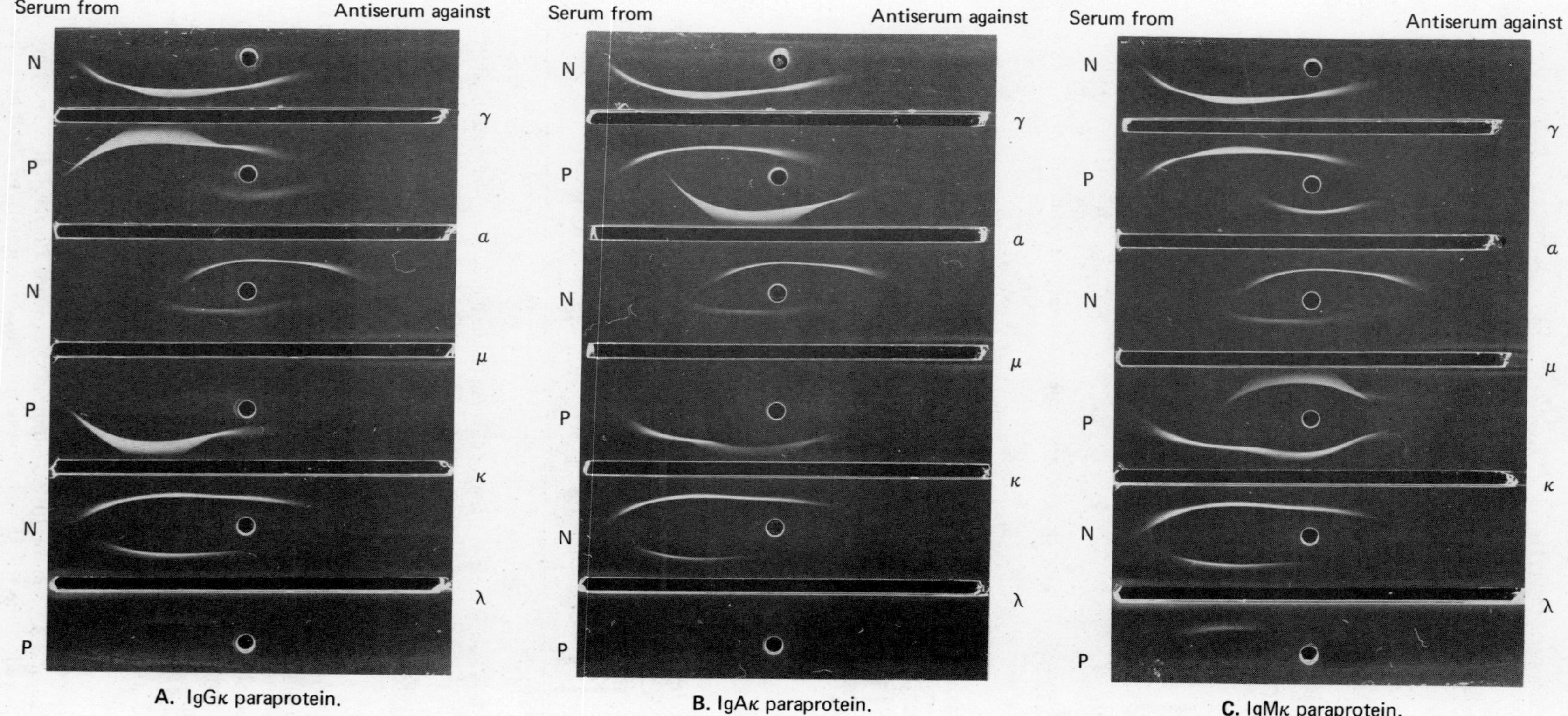

A. IgGκ paraprotein.

B. IgAκ paraprotein.

C. IgMκ paraprotein.

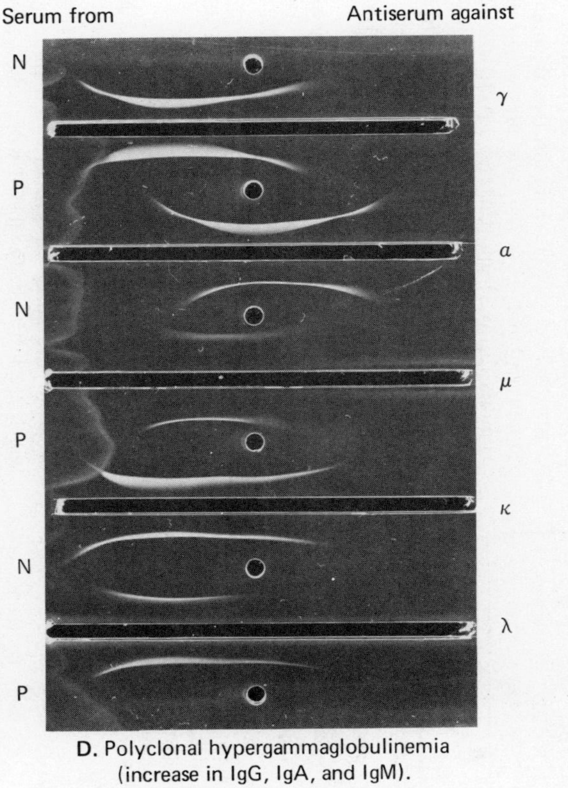

D. Polyclonal hypergammaglobulinemia (increase in IgG, IgA, and IgM).

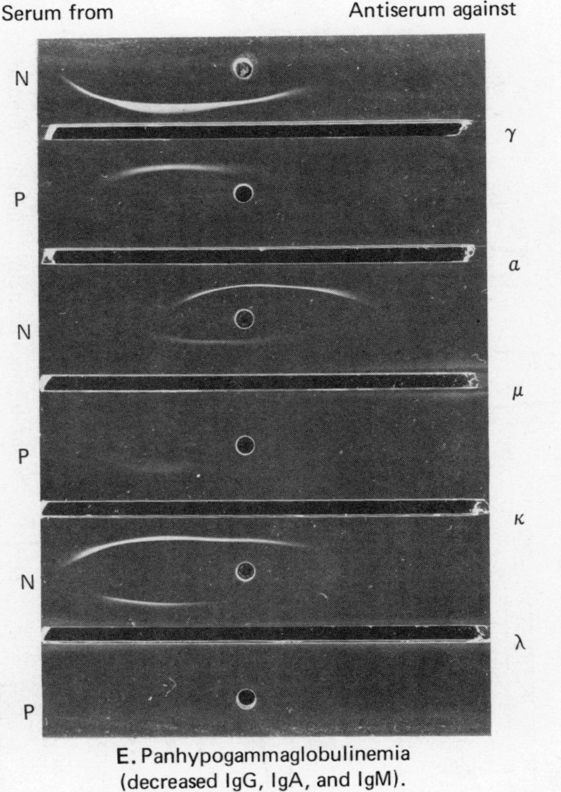

E. Panhypogammaglobulinemia (decreased IgG, IgA, and IgM).

Figure 24–12. Immunoelectrophoresis patterns of serum in various diseases. ***A:*** IgGκ paraprotein. ***B:*** IgAκ paraprotein. ***C:*** IgMκ paraprotein. ***D:*** Polyclonal hypergammaglobulinemia. ***E:*** Panhypogammaglobulinemia. Individual patterns of serum from normal (N) and patient (P) with various serum protein abnormalities. In each case, N and P sera are reacted against antisera which are monospecific for γ, α, and μ heavy chains and κ and λ light chains.

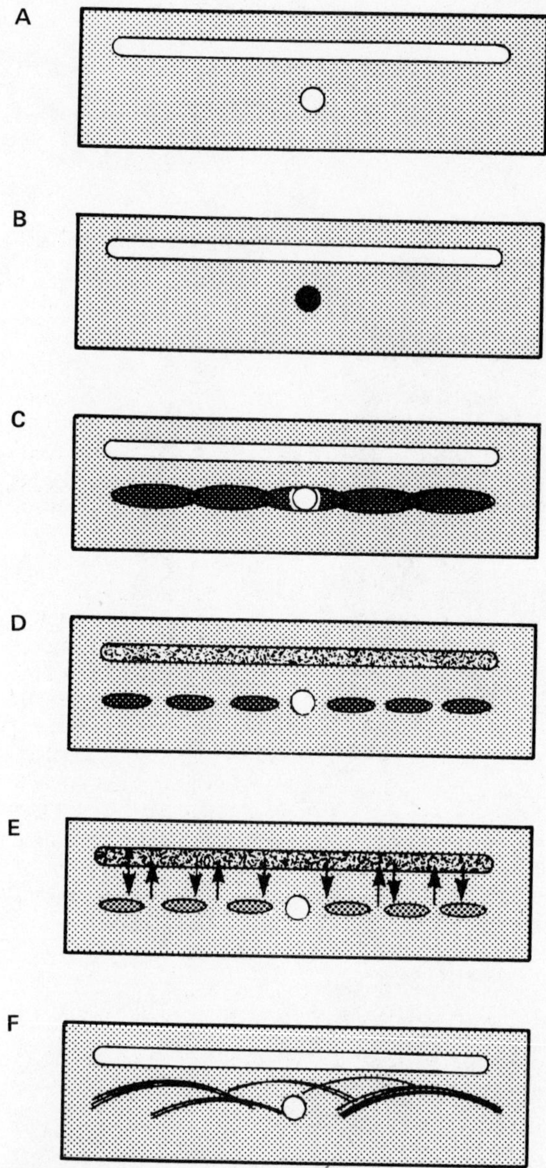

Figure 24–13. Technic of immunoelectrophoresis. *A:* Semisolid agar poured onto glass slide and antigen well and antiserum trough cut out of agar. *B:* Antigen well filled with human serum. *C:* Serum separated by electrophoresis. *D:* Antiserum trough filled with antiserum to whole human serum. *E:* Serum and antiserum diffuse into agar. *F:* Precipitin lines form for individual serum proteins.

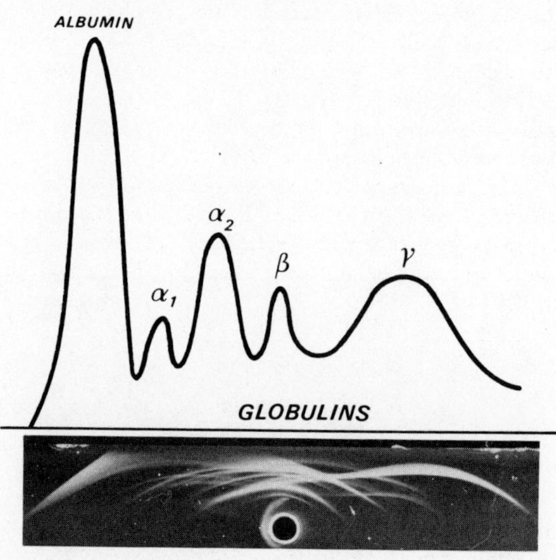

Figure 24–14. Comparison of patterns of zone and immunoelectrophoresis of normal human serum.

and L chain type of the paraprotein. Several examples of the use of immunoelectrophoresis in demonstrating the identity of human serum paraproteins are shown in Fig 24–12.

Immunoelectrophoresis can aid in distinguishing polyclonal from monoclonal increases in γ-globulin (Fig 24–12). Additionally, decreased or absent immunoglobulins seen in various immune deficiency disorders can be analyzed with this technic. However, a further quantitative analysis such as single radial diffusion or radioimmunoassay should be performed for accurate measurement of immunoglobulin levels.

Immunoelectrophoresis is also of great practical benefit in identifying L chains in the urine of patients with plasma cell dyscrasias or autoimmune disorders. Thus, with specific anti-κ and anti-λ antisera, the monoclonal nature of Bence Jones protein in myeloma can be confirmed. In H chain diseases, fragments of the immunoglobulin H chain are present in increased amounts in the serum (Chapter 28). It was by careful analysis of immunoelectrophoretic patterns that Franklin initially discovered the existence of this rare but extremely interesting group of disorders. Finally, immunoelectrophoresis is helpful in identifying increased amounts of proteins present in the cerebrospinal fluid in patients with various neurologic diseases.

RADIOIMMUNOELECTROPHORESIS

Radioimmunoelectrophoresis combines immunoelectrophoresis and radioautography for the detection of radiolabeled antigens. It has been applied most often to the study of proteins or immunoglobulins which are intrinsically labeled with radioactive ^{14}C or ^{3}H amino acids during cellular biosynthesis in tissue culture. Plasma cells or lymphoblastoid cells from continuous cell lines are grown in tissue culture with radioactive amino acids. The resultant supernatant fluid contains radioactive proteins which are actively synthesized by the cultured cells. Concentrated culture supernates are then subjected to electrophoresis in standard immunoelectrophoresis plates. The troughs are filled with antiserum to human serum as well as with specific antisera for L and H chains. After the precipitation lines have developed, the plate is dried and overlaid with high-speed x-ray film. After a period of exposure, the film is developed and the resultant pattern compared with the normal serum proteins present on the stained immunoelectrophoresis plate.

This technic can be extremely useful in the investigation of paraproteinemias. Its chief function is to confirm a specific serum protein as the biosynthetic product of a particular organ, tissue, or cell population (see Chapter 9).

Table 24–3. Clinical applications of double electroimmunodiffusion.

1. HB_sAg (viral hepatitis)
2. Cryptococcal-specific antigen in cerebrospinal fluid
3. Meningococcal-specific antigen in cerebrospinal fluid
4. Haemophilus-specific antigen in cerebrospinal fluid
5. Fibrinogen
6. Cord IgM in intrauterine infection
7. Carcinoembryonic antigen (CEA)
8. a_1-Fetoprotein

ELECTROIMMUNODIFFUSION

In immunodiffusion technics described earlier in this chapter, antigen and antibody are allowed to come into contact and to precipitate in agar purely by diffusion. However, the chance of antigen and antibody meeting—and thus the speed of development of a precipitin line—can be greatly enhanced by electrically driving the 2 together. There has recently been renewed interest in the technics of electroimmunodiffusion, especially in the serologic diagnosis of infectious diseases by serum *antigen* detection (eg, HB_sAg). Although numerous variations have been described coupling electrophoresis with diffusion, only 2 have as yet achieved any degree of clinical applicability. These are *one-dimensional double electroimmunodiffusion* (counterimmunoelectrophoresis) and *one-dimensional single electroimmunodiffusion* (Laurell's rocket electrophoresis).

One-Dimensional Double Electroimmunodiffusion

This method is also known as countercurrent immunoelectrophoresis, counterimmunoelectrophoresis, and electroprecipitation. The basic principle of the method involves electrophoresis in a gel medium of antigen and antibody in opposite directions simultaneously from separate wells with resultant precipitation at a point intermediate between their origins (Fig 24–15).

The principal disadvantages of double diffusion without electromotive force are the time required for precipitation (24 hours) and the relative lack of sensitivity. Double electroimmunodiffusion in one dimension can produce visible precipitin lines within 30 minutes and is approximately 10 times more sensitive than standard double diffusion technics. However, this technic is only semiquantitative. Some of the antigens detected by double electroimmunodiffusion are listed in Table 24–3.

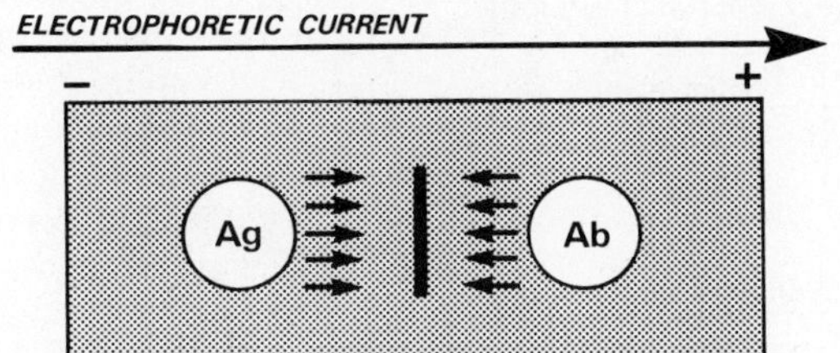

Figure 24–15. Double electroimmunodiffusion in one dimension. Antigen and antibody are placed in well and driven together with an electric current. A precipitin line forms within a few hours after beginning electrophoresis.

One-Dimensional Single Electroimmunodiffusion

This method is also known as "rocket electrophoresis" or the Laurell technic. The principal application of this technic has been to quantitate antigens other than immunoglobulins. In this technic, antiserum to the particular antigen or antigens one wishes to quantitate is incorporated into an agarose supporting medium on a glass slide. The specimen containing an unknown quantity of the antigen is placed in a small well. Electrophoresis of the antigen into the antibody-containing agarose is then performed. The resultant pattern of immunoprecipitation resembles a spike or rocket—thus the term rocket electrophoresis (Fig 24–16).

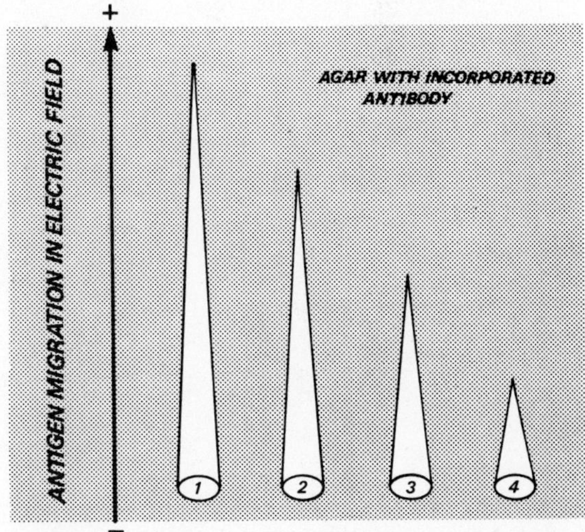

Figure 24–16. Single electroimmunodiffusion in one dimension (rocket electrophoresis, Laurell technic). Antigen is placed in wells numbered 1–4 in progressively decreasing amounts. Electrophoresis is performed and antigen is driven into antibody-containing agar. Precipitin pattern forms in the shape of a "rocket." Amount of antigen is directly proportionate to the length of the rocket.

This pattern occurs because precipitation occurs along the lateral margins of the moving boundary of antigen as the antigen is driven into the agar containing the antibody. Gradually, as antigen is lost through precipitation, its concentration at the leading edge diminishes and the lateral margins converge to form a sharp point. The total distance of antigen migration for a given antiserum concentration is proportionate to the antigen concentration. The sensitivity of this technic is approximately 0.5 μg/ml for proteins. Unfortunately, the weak negative charge of immunoglobulins prevents their electrophoretic mobility in this system unless special electrolytes and agar are employed. Recently, several commercially available systems have been introduced for quantitating serum immunoglobulins and C components with this technic.

Currently, electroimmunodiffusion tests have not fully realized their valuable potential as immunodiagnostic tools. They provide rapid and sensitive technics for quantitation of selected antigens, and further application and development of these technics is certainly expected in the future.

IMMUNOCHEMICAL & PHYSICOCHEMICAL METHODS

Françoise Chenais, MD

Evaluation of serum protein disorders can usually be effectively accomplished by immunodiffusion and electrophoretic methods. Occasionally, more detailed study of immunologically relevant serum constituents is necessary. In this section, a number of the more complex immunochemical and physicochemical technics are described which have proved to be important adjuncts in the characterization of serum protein disorders. These technics have become increasingly available in the clinical laboratory and include ultracentrifugation, column chromatography, measurement of serum viscosity, and methods to detect cryoglobulins, pyroglobulins, and immune complexes.

ULTRACENTRIFUGATION

Ultracentrifugation was the first method developed which clearly demonstrated the existence of

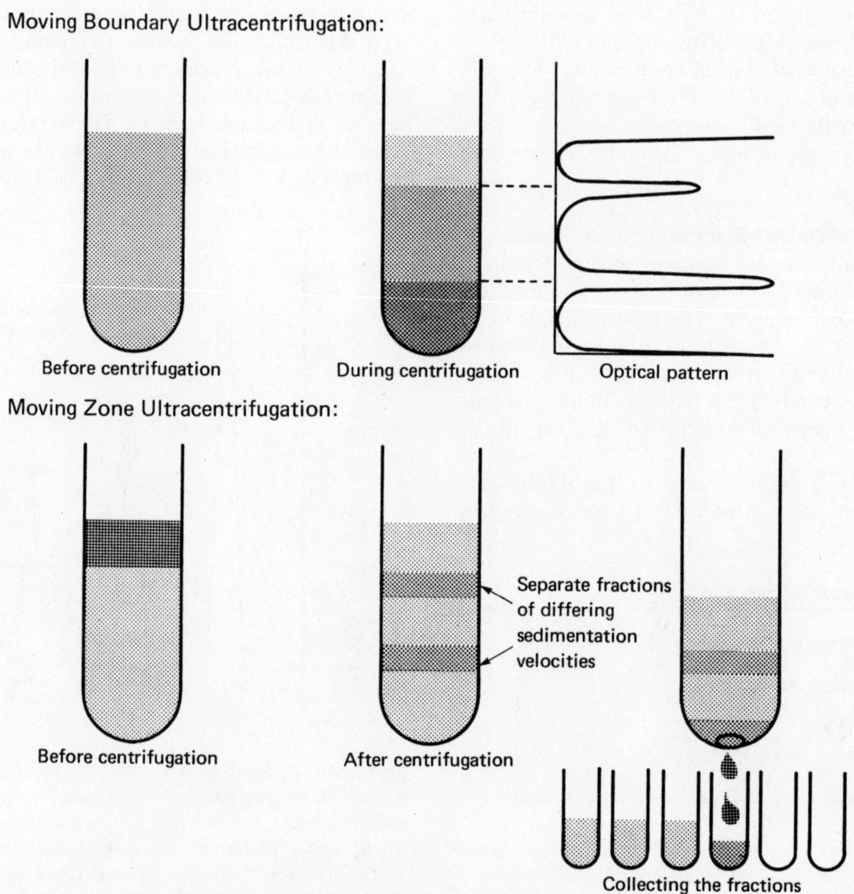

Figure 24–17. Moving boundary and moving zone ultracentrifugation.

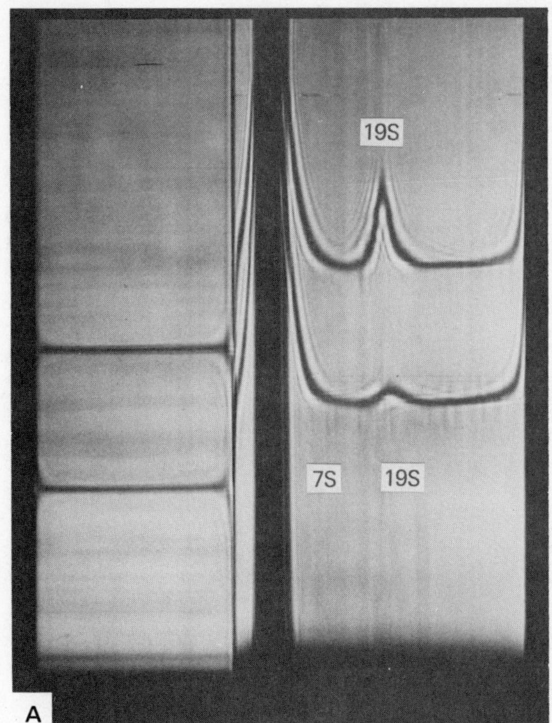

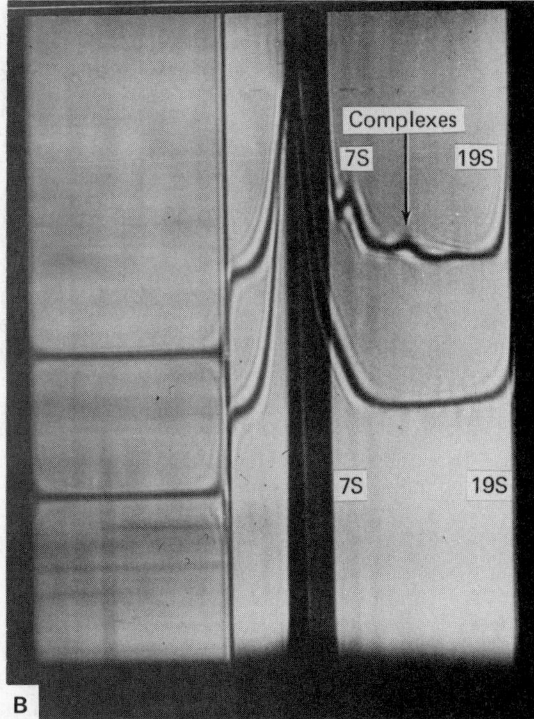

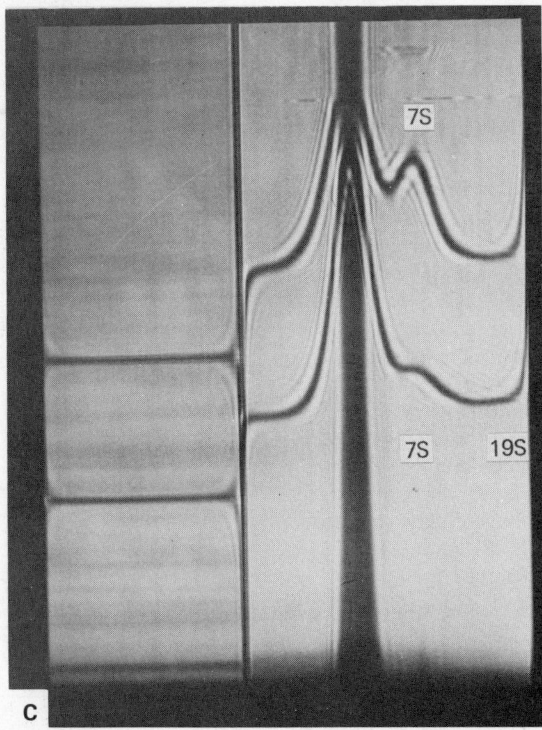

Figure 24–18. Analytic ultracentrifugation patterns of various sera. ***A (Top):*** Macroglobulinemic serum with increased 19S (IgM) component. ***A (Bottom):*** Normal serum. ***B (Top):*** Serum containing immune complexes between 7S and 19S sedimentation coefficients. ***C (Top):*** Serum with increased 7S molecules. ***C (Bottom):*** Normal serum. In each case, sedimentation is from left to right.

several classes of immunoglobulins. Human immunoglobulins were initially subdivided according to their sedimentation coefficients, ie, 7S or 19S. Although other simpler technics are now available for isolation and characterization of immunoglobulins, ultracentrifugation is still a useful technic for identification of immunoglobulins. The application of centrifugal force to molecules in solution gives them a sedimentation velocity depending on their size, mass, and density relative to the solvent.

In moving boundary ultracentrifugation, the sample is initially uniformly layered in the tube. During centrifugation, the molecules move in the solvent and a concentration boundary develops between the top and the bottom of the tube. Multiple boundaries will develop in complex solutions (Fig 24–17). Another application of analytic ultracentrifugation is the determination of the sedimentation coefficient of abnormal serum proteins (Fig 24–18).

In moving zone ultracentrifugation, the sample is layered over a density gradient. When a centrifugal force is applied to a complex mixture, moving bands of different sedimentation velocity appear (Fig 24–17). The density gradient is used to prevent radial convection currents and thus stabilize the moving zones. It is then possible to obtain a good resolution of the different components. Individual components can be obtained after separation with preparative ultracentrifugation by collecting several fractions layer by layer.

COLUMN CHROMATOGRAPHY

Chromatographic technics are currently the most widely used methods for protein fractionation and isolation of immunoglobulins. In these technics, a sample is layered on the top of a glass cylinder or column filled with a synthetic gel and is allowed to flow through the gel. The physical characteristics of protein molecules result in retention in the gel matrix to differing degrees, and subsequent elution under appropriate conditions permits protein separation.

Ion exchange chromatography separates proteins by taking advantage of differences in their electrical charges. The functional unit of the gel is a charged group absorbed on a backbone, usually cellulose. Diethylaminoethyl-cellulose (DEAE-cellulose) is used for fractionation of negatively charged molecules (Fig 24–19). Carboxymethyl-cellulose (CM-cellulose) is used for fractionation of positively charged molecules. Changing the pH of the buffer passing through the column affects the charge of the protein molecule. Increasing the molarity of the buffer provides more ions to compete with the protein for binding to the gel. By gradually increasing the molarity or decreasing the pH of the elution buffer, the proteins are eluted in order of increasing number of charged groups bound to the gel. For example, Table 24–4 gives the molarity and

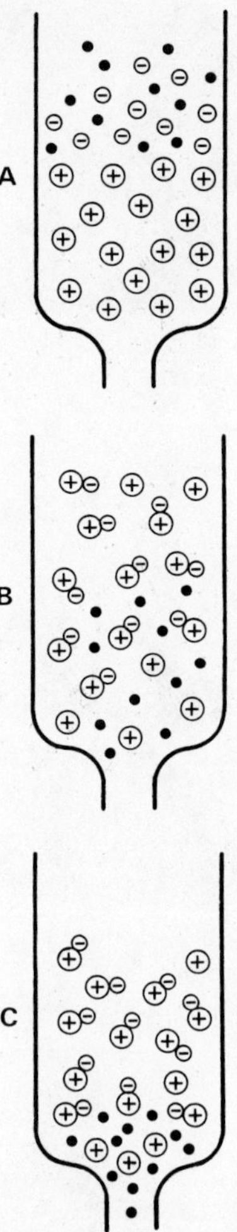

Figure 24–19. Principles of ion exchange chromatography. Three stages of protein separation by ion exchange chromatography are shown: ***A:*** The column bed is made up of a matrix of positively charged cellulose beads ⊕. ***B:*** The negatively charged molecules ⊖ in the protein mixture bind to the column and are retained. ***C:*** The neutral molecules ● pass between the charged particles and are eluted.

Table 24–4. Molarity of NaCl and pH required to elute human plasma protein from DEAE-cellulose. (Adapted from Oh & Sanders, 1966.)

NaCl Molarity	pH	Proteins Eluted
0.025	7.8	IgG
0.045	7.0	Transferrin, fibrinogen
0.050	7.0	α_2-Globulin, albumin, IgA
0.080	6.5	Albumin, α_2-globulin, β-lipoprotein
0.100	6.5	α_2-Globulin, β-globulins, haptoglobin
0.150	6.5	IgM, β-lipoprotein, β-globulin

pH required to elute serum immunoglobulins. DEAE-cellulose chromatography is an excellent technic for isolation of IgG, which can be obtained nearly free of all other serum proteins.

Gel filtration separates molecules according to their size. The gel is made of porous dextran beads. Protein molecules larger than the largest pores of the beads cannot penetrate the gel pores. Thus, they pass through the gel in the liquid phase outside the beads and are eluted first. Smaller molecules penetrate the beads to a varying extent depending on their size and shape. Solute molecules within the gel beads maintain a concentration equilibrium with solute in the liquid phase outside the beads; thus, a particular molecular species moves as a band through the column. Molecules therefore appear in the column effluent in order of decreasing size (Fig 24–20).

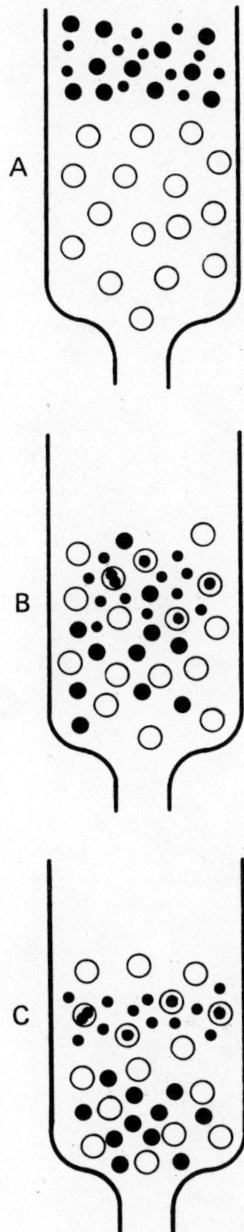

Figure 24–20. Principles of gel filtration chromatography. Three stages of protein separation by gel filtration are shown: ***A:*** Open circle ○ represents polymerized dextran beads onto which a mixture of small • and large ● protein molecules are layered. ***B:*** The molecules enter and pass through the column at different rates depending primarily on size and are separated by a simple sieving process. ***C:*** Larger molecules are eluted while smaller ones are retained.

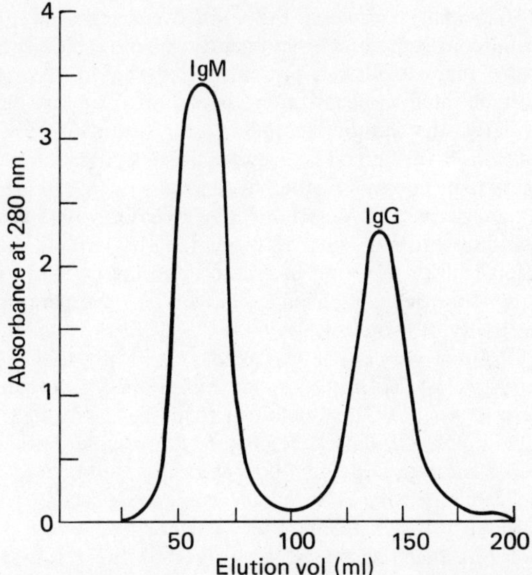

Figure 24–21. Separation of IgG-IgM mixed cryoglobulin by gel filtration. Two peaks are eluted from gel filtration column. The larger IgM molecules precede the smaller IgG molecules which were dissociated by dissolving the cryoprecipitate in an acidic buffer prior to application to the column. The absorbance at 280 nm measures relative amount of protein in various eluted fractions.

IgM can be easily separated from other serum immunoglobulins by gel filtration. Fig 24–21 shows the separation of the IgM and the IgG components of a mixed IgM-IgG cryoglobulin. Gel filtration is widely used also to separate H and L chains of immunoglobulins or to isolate pure Bence Jones proteins from the urine of patients with multiple myeloma.

Immunochromatography separates molecules by their antibody specificity. An antigen is coupled to an insoluble matrix such as Sepharose, or the antigen molecules are rendered insoluble by cross-linking them with glutaraldehyde. When a mixture of antibodies of different specificities is passed through the column, those with a specific activity against the antigen are retained by binding to the antigens complexed with the gel. These specific antibodies can be recovered by washing the column with an acidic buffer which disrupts the antigen-antibody bonds. A similar technic can be used to purify a specific antigen by coupling an antibody to the inert matrix.

SERUM VISCOSITY

The measurement of serum viscosity is a simple and valuable tool in evaluation of patients with paraproteinemia. Normally, the formed elements of the blood contribute more significantly to whole blood viscosity than do plasma proteins. However, in diseases with elevated concentrations of serum proteins, particularly the immunoglobulins, the serum viscosity may reach very high levels and result in a characteristic symptom complex—the hyperviscosity syndrome. Serum viscosity is determined by a variety of factors including protein concentration; the size, shape, and deformability of serum molecules; and the hydrostatic state (solvation), molecular charge, and temperature sensitivity of proteins.

Serum viscosity is measured in clinical practice in an Ostwald viscosimeter. A few milliliters of serum are warmed to 37 C and allowed to descend through a narrow bore capillary tube immersed in a water bath at 37 C. The rate of descent between calibrated marks on the capillary tube is recorded. The same procedure is repeated using distilled water. The relative serum viscosity is then calculated according to the following formula:

$$\text{Relative serum viscosity} = \frac{\text{Rate of descent in seconds of serum sample}}{\text{Rate of descent in seconds of distilled water}}$$

Normal values for serum viscosity range from 1.4–1.9. Similar measurements can be performed using plasma instead of serum. However, fibrinogen present in plasma is a major determinant of plasma viscosity, and variations in this protein, especially in the presence of nonspecific inflammatory states, can markedly affect the results. For this reason, measurement of serum viscosity is preferred.

Serum viscosity measurements are primarily of use in evaluating patients with Waldenström's macroglobulinemia, multiple myeloma, and cryoglobulinemia. In myeloma, aggregation or polymerization of the paraprotein in vivo often results in hyperviscosity. In general, there is a correlation between increased serum viscosity and increased plasma volume. However, the correlation between levels of relative serum viscosity and clinical symptoms is not nearly as direct. A detailed discussion of the hyperviscosity syndrome is presented in Chapter 28. Disorders with increased serum viscosity are listed in Table 24–5.

Table 24–5. Disorders with increased serum viscosity.

Waldenström's macroglobulinemia
Essential macroglobulinemia
Multiple myeloma
Cryoglobulinemia
Hypergammaglobulinemic purpura
Rheumatoid diseases associated with immune complexes or paraproteinemias
Rheumatoid arthritis
Sjögren's syndrome
Systemic lupus erythematosus

CRYOGLOBULINS

Precipitation of serum immunoglobulins in the cold was first observed in a patient with multiple myeloma. The term "cryoglobulin" was introduced to designate a group of proteins which have the common property of forming a precipitate or a gel in the cold. This phenomenon was reversible by raising the temperature. Since those initial descriptions, cryoglobulins have been found in a wide variety of clinical situations. Purification and immunochemical analysis have led to classification of this group of proteins (Table 24–6). Type I cryoglobulins consist of a single monoclonal immunoglobulin. Type II cryoglobulins are mixed cryoglobulins; they consist of a monoclonal immunoglobulin with antibody activity against a polyclonal immunoglobulin. Type III cryoglobulins are mixed polyclonal cryoglobulins, ie, one or more immunoglobulins are found, none of which are monoclonal.

Technical Procedure for Isolation & Analysis

Blood must be collected in a warm syringe and kept at 37 C until it clots. Serum is separated by centrifugation at 37 C and then stored at 4 C. When a cryoglobulin is present, a white precipitate or a gel appears in the serum after a variable period, usually 24–72 hours. However, the serum should be observed for 1 week to make certain that unusually late cryo-

Table 24–6. Classification of types of cryoglobulins and associated diseases.

Type of Cryoglobulin	Immunochemical Composition	Associated Diseases
Type I		
Monoclonal cryoglobulin	IgM IgG IgA Bence Jones protein	Myeloma Waldenström's macroglobulinemia Chronic lymphocytic leukemia
Type II		
Mixed cryoglobulin	IgM-IgG IgG-IgG IgA-IgG	Rheumatoid arthritis Sjögren's syndrome Mixed essential cryoglobulinemia
Type III		
Mixed polyclonal cryoglobulin	IgM-IgG IgM-IgG-IgA	Systemic lupus erythematosus Rheumatoid arthritis, Sjogrën's syndrome Infectious mononucleosis Cytomegalovirus infections Acute viral hepatitis Chronic active hepatitis Primary biliary cirrhosis Poststreptococcal glomerulonephritis Infective endocarditis Leprosy Kala-azar Tropical splenomegaly syndrome

precipitation does not go undetected. The reversibility of the cryoprecipitation should be tested by rewarming an aliquot of precipitated serum.

Quantitation of the cryoprecipitate can be done in several ways. Centrifugation of the whole serum in a hematocrit tube at 4 C allows determination of the relative amount of cryoglobulin (cryocrit). Alternatively, the protein concentration of the serum may be compared before and after cryoprecipitation. The precipitate formed in an aliquot of serum may be isolated and dissolved in an acidic buffer and the cryoglobulin level estimated by the absorbance at 280 nm.

After isolation and washing of the precipitate, the components of the cryoglobulin are identified by immunoelectrophoresis or by double diffusion. These analyses are performed at 37 C, using antiserum to whole human serum and antisera specific for γ, α, μ, κ, and λ chains. In this way, cryoglobulins can be classified into the 3 types described above.

Clinical Significance

Type I and type II cryoglobulins are usually present in large amounts in serum (often more than 5 mg/ml). In general, they are present in patients with monoclonal paraproteinemias, eg, they are commonly found in patients with lymphoma or multiple myeloma. However, some are found in patients lacking any evidence of lymphoid malignancy, just as are "benign" paraproteins (see Chapter 28). Type III cryoglobulins indicate the presence of circulating immune complexes and are the result of immune responses to various antigens. They are present in relatively low concentrations (usually less than 1 mg/ml) in rheumatoid diseases and chronic infections (Table 24–6).

All types of cryoglobulins may be responsible for specific symptoms that occur as a result of changes in the cryoglobulin induced by exposure to cold. The symptoms include Raynaud's phenomenon, vascular purpura, bleeding tendencies, cold-induced urticaria, and even distal arterial thrombosis with gangrene.

Since type II and type III cryoglobulins are circulating soluble immune complexes, they may be associated with a serum sickness-like syndrome characterized by polyarthritis, vasculitis, glomerulonephritis, or neurologic symptoms (see Chapter 27). In patients with mixed essential IgM-IgG cryoglobulinemia, a rather distinctive syndrome may occur that is associated with arthralgias, purpura, weakness, and frequently lymphadenopathy or hepatosplenomegaly. Glomerulonephritis is a common finding. In some instances, it occurs in a rapidly progressive form and is of ominous prognostic significance.

PYROGLOBULINS

Pyroglobulins are monoclonal immunoglobulins which precipitate irreversibly when heated to 56 C. The thermoprecipitability is not solely restricted to Bence Jones proteinemia. In fact, the entire immunoglobulin molecule or even the H chain fragment may be responsible for this phenomenon.

Pyroglobulins are usually found in patients with multiple myeloma but may be discovered incidentally when serum is heated to 56 C to inactivate complement during a routine serologic test. They are not responsible for any particular symptoms and have no known prognostic significance.

DETECTION OF IMMUNE COMPLEXES

The factors involved in the deposition of immune complexes in tissues and the production of tissue damage are discussed in Chapter 20. Subsequent chapters will deal with the clinical manifestations of diseases associated with immune complexes, including rheumatoid diseases (Chapter 27), hematologic diseases (Chapter 28), and renal diseases (Chapter 32). These clinical situations have in common the presence of detectable immune complexes in tissues or in the circulation.

Detection of Immune Complexes in Tissues

Detection of immune complexes in tissues is performed by immunohistologic technics using immunofluorescence or immunoperoxidase staining. The antisera used are specific for the immunoglobulin classes, complement components, fibrin or fibrinogen, and, in selected cases, the suspected antigen.

By analogy with animal findings, granular deposits of immunoglobulins usually accompanied by complement components are considered to represent immune complexes. The antigen moiety of the complex is rarely detected, since it is unknown in most cases.

Detection of Immune Complexes in Serum

Several indirect findings constitute presumptive evidence for the existence of circulating immune complexes. These include anticomplementary activity of serum detected during any complement fixation test and low serum complement activity measured by CH_{50} or C3 level.

Cryoglobulins of types II and III, when detected in serum, represent immune complexes which can be easily isolated and characterized. Except in this special circumstance, methods for the detection of circulating immune complexes are still controversial. The variety of the technics currently available suggests that none is completely satisfactory (Table 24–7). Two of them are considered to be relatively sensitive and applicable to clinical studies:

A. Platelet Aggregation Test: Antigen-antibody complexes interact with the surface of blood platelets and result in aggregation. The test is carried out in U-shaped microtiter plates. A platelet suspension is prepared from fresh blood, and serial dilutions of serum are mixed with the platelet suspension. Aggrega-

Table 24–7. Technics used for detection of immune complexes.

Ultracentrifugation
Gel filtration
Precipitin reaction with C1q
Monoclonal rheumatoid factor precipitation
Platelet aggregation test
Binding to surface receptors of cultured lymphoblasts (Raji cells)
Inhibition of uptake of aggregates by macrophages
Consumption of complement
C1q binding test
Inhibition of agglutination of IgG-coated latex particles

tion is read after an overnight incubation at 4 C, using dark background illumination. A smooth white button on the bottom of the well indicates a negative result; a dark even pattern indicates a positive result.

Because of variation in the sensitivity of individual preparations of platelets, the test must be done in triplicate using 3 different preparations of platelets and aggregated human IgG as a positive control.

B. Radiolabeled C1q Binding Test: This test is based on the C1q-binding properties of immune complexes and their precipitability in polyethylene glycol. The latter property is related to their large molecular size and allows separation of free and complex-bound radiolabeled C1q. 50 μl of patient's serum is mixed with an equal volume of ^{125}I-C1q containing 1 mg/ml of C1q. Polyethylene glycol is added to make a final concentration of 2.5%. The tubes are incubated for 1 hour and centrifuged at 1500 *g* for 20 minutes. The supernate is discarded, and the radioactivity is counted in the precipitates.

The results are expressed as a percentage of the total protein-bound radioactivity; 100% radioactivity is obtained by mixing 0.4 ml of normal human serum with 50 μl of ^{125}I-C1q, precipitating the proteins with trichloroacetic acid, and counting the radioactivity in the precipitate.

This test appears to be one of the most reproducible procedures for the detection of immune complexes. It can detect as little as 50 μg/ml of complexed antibody. Normal sera have been found to bind about 1.4% of radiolabeled C1q. A significant increase has been found in patients with immune complex diseases.

RADIOIMMUNOASSAY (RIA)

Radioimmunoassay (RIA) was introduced into clinical medicine in 1960 by Berson and Yalow, who first described its use as a practical method for the quantitation of plasma insulin levels. Since then, radioimmunoassay has achieved widespread use as a sensitive and specific method for the quantitation of microquantities of a large number of clinically relevant compounds. Radioimmunoassay has enjoyed a central role in clinical endocrinology and has largely supplanted the more expensive, cumbersome, and relatively imprecise bioassays of hormones. In fact, radioimmunoassay has profoundly altered clinical endocrinology since virtually all hormones can now be measured accurately. Some new hormones have been described as a result of analysis of anomalies in radioimmunoassay tests. Recently, radioimmunoassay has been applied to microdetermination of drugs, eg, digoxin, and other small molecules, eg, steroid hormones, which immunologically are classified as haptens. The burgeoning field of tumor immunology owes much of its recent growth to application of radioimmunoassay technics in measuring carcinoembryonic antigen. The radioimmunoassay of HB_sAg has provided blood banks with an excellent method for detecting hepatitis antigen in blood and thereby minimizing transmission of the disease by transfusion. In the coming decades, one can expect further applications of radioimmunoassay in the detection of levels of many drugs and the presence of other immunologically relevant molecules in virtually all tissue fluids. Through the use of automated technics and computer analysis, radioimmunoassay has become firmly established as an indispensable tool in laboratory medicine.

Radioimmunoassay methods derive their fundamental and general applicability as laboratory tools in clinical medicine from 2 separate but related properties: great sensitivity and specificity. Virtually any compound to which an antibody can be produced may be measured by radioimmunoassay down to the picogram (10^{-12} g) range. With proper manipulation, radioimmunoassay can be designed to distinguish between molecules which differ by only one amino acid or which are stereoisomers. Furthermore, the ability of molecules to be measured by radioimmunoassay is independent of their biologic activity. This fact has led to some rather surprising discoveries. For example, in classical hemophilia, a disease caused by deficiency of factor VIII, radioimmunoassay as well as hemagglutination inhibition assay has demonstrated normal levels of antigenically reactive but biologically inert procoagulant activity (see Chapter 28). Thus, radioimmunoassay has led to important insights into basic mechanisms of disease and has served as a clinically useful diagnostic tool in many areas of medicine and biology.

RADIOIMMUNOASSAY METHODOLOGY & INTERPRETATION

Summary of Radioimmunoassay Procedure

The general methodology of radioimmunoassay is, in theory, relatively simple. An outline of the steps

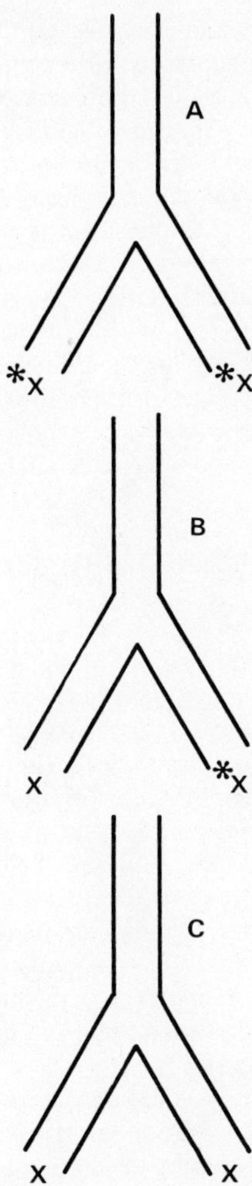

Figure 24–22. General scheme of radioimmunoassay. Schematic representation of competitive binding of antigen X or antigen *X (radioactive) to antibody against X. ***A:*** No X added and antibody binds only *X. ***B:*** Approximately equal amounts of X and *X added with equal binding to antibody. ***C:*** Excess of X compared to *X displaces radiolabeled antigen from antibody binding sites.

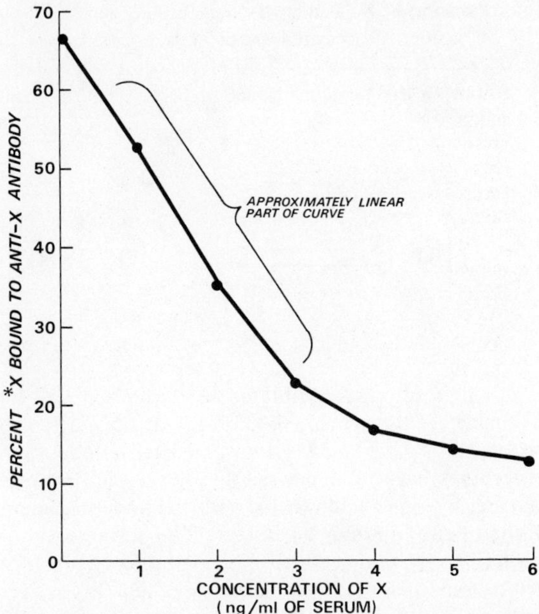

Figure 24–23. Standard curve for radioimmunoassay of hormone X. Theoretical standard curve for estimating amount of hormone X in sera with unknown concentration of X. As amount of X is increased over narrow range (1–6 ng/ml), the percentage of *X bound to anti-X diminishes. This relationship is linear over part of the range, which allows estimation of the amount of X in various serum samples.

required to establish a radioimmunoassay for a hypothetical human protein hormone "X" is as follows:

(1) Antiserum to X is raised in heterologous species, eg, rabbit or guinea pig.

(2) If the hormone X is itself nonimmunogenic, ie, a hapten, it is first coupled to a macromolecular carrier, eg, bovine γ-globulin, and the hapten and carrier complex is then used to raise an antiserum.

(3) X is then radiolabeled, usually with ^{125}I (*X).

(4) Labeled antigen *X reacts with enough antibody to bind about 70% of *X.

(5) Various known amounts of unlabeled hormone X are added to a mixture of *X and anti-X and compete for antibody combining sites.

(6) After an appropriate incubation period, labeled *X bound to antibody is separated from unbound *X.

(7) From the amount of *X bound at various X concentrations (Fig 24–22), a curve can be constructed which will allow computation of any unknown X concentration desired (Fig 24–23).

Antisera for Radioimmunoassay

In general, large protein or polypeptide hormones such as parathyroid hormone, growth hormone, and insulin are good immunogens, and suitable antisera to these hormones can be prepared in rabbits, goats, or guinea pigs. Many of these hormone antisera are now commercially available, and the cost of purchase may be justified because of the expense of maintaining animal colonies for local antiserum production. High avidity is a desirable feature of antibody, and this can be achieved by prolonged immunization schedules, beginning with the hormone emulsified in Freund's complete adjuvant followed by antigen in Freund's incomplete adjuvant. If one wishes to develop an antiserum for radioimmunoassay of a small nonimmunogenic compound, ie, a hapten such as digoxin or a corticosteroid, coupling of the hapten to a larger macromolecule carrier prior to immunization will result in a suitable antiserum directed at free hapten as well as the carrier.

Radiolabeling of X (Antigen)

A generally accepted method is iodination with ^{125}I or ^{131}I, in which the iodine molecule is covalently bound to the tyrosine group in the case of protein antigens:

$$\text{(O, ring, R)} + I_2^* \rightleftharpoons \text{(O, ring–}I^*\text{, R)} + HI^*$$

This reaction is facilitated in the presence of an oxidizing agent such as chloramine T. If the antigen to be labeled lacks tyrosine groups, alternative iodination procedures have been devised. For example, intrinsic labeling by organic synthesis with ^3H can be accomplished with steroid hormones. The advantages of iodination are that it usually does not affect the antigenic properties of the molecule and that it achieves high specific activity with relatively long isotope half-life, eg, ^{125}I with a 60-day half-life. However, radiation damage, oxidation, and changes in physicochemical structure of the antigen may be deleterious to its reactivity in radioimmunoassay.

Separation of Antibody-Bound Antigen From Free Labeled Antigen

After incubation of labeled antigen *X with specific antibody in the presence of varying amounts of unlabeled free X, separation of bound antibody from free *X must be accomplished to estimate the amount of X present in the competitive binding reaction (Fig 24–22). In general, separation can be accomplished by either physicochemical or immunologic means (Table 24–8). The double antibody method is preferred in most laboratories. It has the advantage of being applicable to any test volume. It is gentle, thus avoiding dissociation of (anti-X)-*X complex, and is relatively simple. One must confirm that the second antibody does not react with any substance in the test material other than antigenic sites on the first antibody. Possible disadvantages include the relatively high cost of the method and the large amount of second antibody required.

Table 24–8. Methods of separation of antibody-*X from free *X in radioimmunoassay.

Method	
Physicochemical	
Electrophoresis on paper or cellulose acetate	
Chromatography	
Gel diffusion	
Adsorption	
Talc	Precipitate free *X and leave antibody-*X in supernate.
Activated charcoal	
Zirconyl phosphate	
Immunologic	
Double antibody method: Addition of second antibody directed at Fc region of anti-X so that antigenic sites of first antibody are bound by second antibody.	

Standard Curve & Radioimmunoassay Procedure

After reacting *X and X with anti-X and subsequent separation of the free *X from anti-X-*X complex, a standard curve relating bound *X to free *X can be constructed (Fig 24–23). Thus, the amount of X in any tissue fluid sample can be calculated, based on the slope of the standard curve.

SOLID PHASE RADIOIMMUNOASSAY SYSTEMS

In recent modifications of the liquid or soluble phase radioimmunoassay, antibody is either adsorbed onto tubes or covalently linked to a solid matrix. In the coated method, antibody is simply adsorbed to polystyrene tubes and then free antibody is removed by washing. Unlabeled antigen is added, followed by labeled antigen. After equilibration, the tubes are washed and dried, and radioactivity is measured in a gamma spectrometer. In the covalently linked antibody method, antibody is covalently bound to cross-linked dextrans, eg, Sepharose or Sephadex, and separation of the bound labeled antigen is accomplished by centrifugation. Alternatively, the second antibody in the double antibody method can be covalently bound to Sepharose and separation of labeled complex performed by centrifugation.

IMMUNORADIOMETRY

Recently, a technic which employs radiolabeled antibody rather than antigen has been introduced. Its main advantage appears to be increased sensitivity.

APPLICATIONS OF RADIOIMMUNOASSAY

Table 24–9 lists some of the substances currently measured by radioimmunoassay. Radioimmunoassay can also be employed as a general method for a competitive binding inhibition system. Thus, in the case of cAMP, cGMP, or vitamin B_{12}, specific (nonantibody) binding proteins supplant antibody. Otherwise, the principles are identical to those described in the discussion of standard radioimmunoassay.

Table 24–9. Substances measurable by radioimmunoassay.

Steroid Hormones	**Peptide Hormones (cont'd)**
Aldosterone	α- and β-Melanocyte-stimulating hormones
Androstenedione	Oxytocin
Corticosterone	Parathyroid
Cortisol	Placental lactogen
Cortisone	Renin
Deoxycorticosterone	Secretin
Deoxycortisol	Thyroglobulin
Dehydroepiandrosterone	Thyrotropin (TSH)
Dehydrotestosterone	Thyroxine (T_4)
Estradiol-17β	Triiodothyronine (T_3)
Estriol	Vasopressin
Estrone	**Drugs**
Progesterone	Digitoxin
Testosterone	Digoxin
Peptide Hormones	Morphine
ACTH	Ouabain
Angiotensin I	**Other**
Angiotensin II	Anti-DNA antibodies
Bradykinin	Carcinoembryonic antigen (CEA)
Calcitonin	Cyclic AMP (cAMP)
Follicle-stimulating hormone (FSH)	Cyclic GMP (cGMP)
Gastrin	Fibrinopeptide A
Glucagon	Folic acid
Growth hormone	Hepatitis B antigen (HB_SAg)
Human chorionic gonadotropin (HCG)	IgE
Insulin	Intrinsic factor
Luteinizing hormone (LH)	Prostaglandins
	Vitamin B_{12}

IMMUNOHISTOCHEMICAL TECHNICS

IMMUNOFLUORESCENCE

Immunofluorescence is essentially a histochemical or cytochemical technic for detection and localization of antigens. Specific antibody is conjugated with fluorescent compounds, resulting in a sensitive tracer with unaltered immunologic reactivity. The conjugated antiserum is added to cells or tissues and becomes fixed to antigens, thereby forming a stable immune complex. Nonantibody proteins are removed by washing, and the resultant preparation is observed in a fluorescence microscope. This adaptation of a regular microscope contains a high-intensity light source, excitation filters to produce a wavelength capable of causing fluorescence activation, and barrier filters to remove interfering wavelengths of light. When observed in the fluorescence microscope against a dark background, antigens bound specifically to fluorescent antibody can be detected by virtue of the bright color of the latter.

The technic of immunofluorescence was introduced in 1941 by Coons, who employed β-anthracene, a blue fluorescing compound, coupled to pneumococcus antiserum, to detect bacterial antigens in tissue sections. Shortly thereafter, his group employed fluorescein-conjugated antisera which emitted a green light that could be differentiated from the blue autofluorescence of many tissues.

Fluorescence is the emission of light of one color, ie, wavelength, while a substance is irradiated with light of a different color. The emitted wavelength is

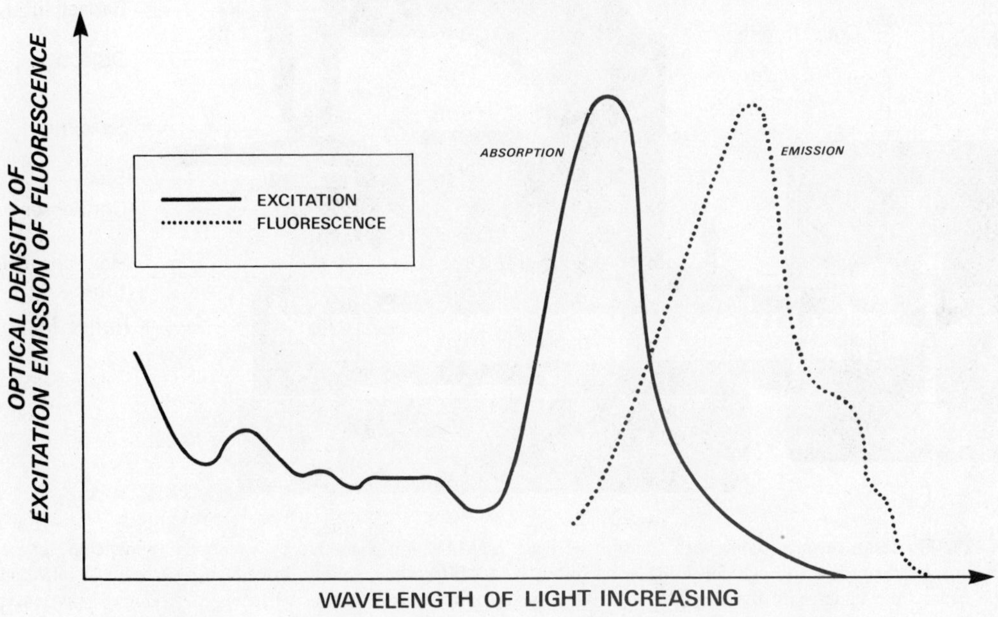

Figure 24–24. Absorption and emission spectra for a fluorescent compound.

necessarily at a lower energy level than the incident or absorbed light (Fig 24–24). Fluorochromes such as rhodamine or fluorescein used in clinical laboratories have characteristic absorption and emission spectra. Fluorescein isothiocyanate (FITC) is a chemical form of fluorescein which readily binds covalently to proteins at alkaline pH primarily through ϵ amino residues of lysine and terminal amino groups. Its absorption maximum is at 490–495 nm, and it emits its characteristic green color at 517 nm. Tetramethylrhodamine isothiocyanate, which emits red, has an absorption maximum at 550 nm and maximal emission at 580 nm (for rhodamine-protein conjugates). Consequently, different excitation and barrier filters must be employed to visualize the characteristic green or red color of these fluorescent dyes. Generally, one wants to achieve an exciting wavelength nearly equal to that of the excitation maximum of the dye. Similarly, the barrier filter should remove all but the emitted wavelength spectrum. In practice, the actual brightness of fluorescence observed by the eye depends on 3 factors: (1) the efficiency with which the dye converts incident light into fluorescent light; (2) the concentration of the dye in the tissue specimen; and (3) the intensity of the exciting (absorbed) radiation.

Microscopes used for visualizing immunofluorescent specimens are simple modifications of standard transmitted light microscopes (Fig 24–25). In 1967, Ploem introduced an epi-illuminated system which employs a vertical illuminator and a dichroic mirror. In this system (Fig 24–26), the excitation beam is focused directly on the tissue specimen through the lens objective. Fluorescent light emitted from the epi-illuminated specimen is then transmitted to the eye through the dichroic mirror. There are several distinct advantages to the Ploem system. Fluorescence may be combined with transmitted light for phase contrast examination of the tissues, thereby allowing better definition of morphology and fluorescence. Also, interchangeable filter systems permit rapid examination of the specimen at different wavelengths for double fluorochrome staining, eg, red and green (rhodamine and fluorescein, respectively). This advantage in technic has resulted in superior sensitivity for examining cell membrane fluorescence in living lymphocytes.

Methodology & Interpretation

Virtually any antigen can be detected in fixed tissue sections or in live cell suspensions by immunofluorescence. It is the combination of great sensitivity and specificity together with the use of histologic technics that make immunofluorescence so useful. The steps involved in immunofluorescence include preparation of immune antiserum or purified γ-globulin, con-

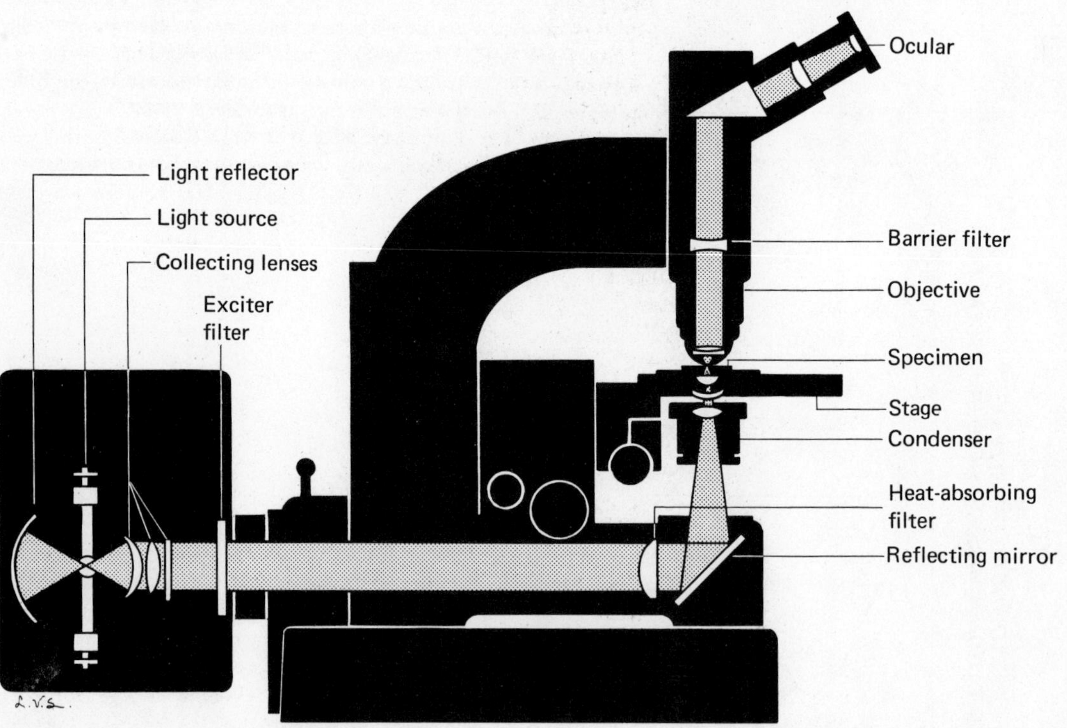

Figure 24–25. Fluorescence microscope with transmitted light. Light beam is generated by a mercury vapor lamp, reflected by a concave mirror, and projected through collecting lenses to the exciter filter which emits a fluorescent light beam. A reflecting mirror directs the beam from underneath the stage, through the condenser into the specimen. A barrier filter removes wavelengths other than those emitted from the fluorescent compound in the specimen, and the fluorescent pattern is viewed through magnification provided by the objective and ocular lenses.

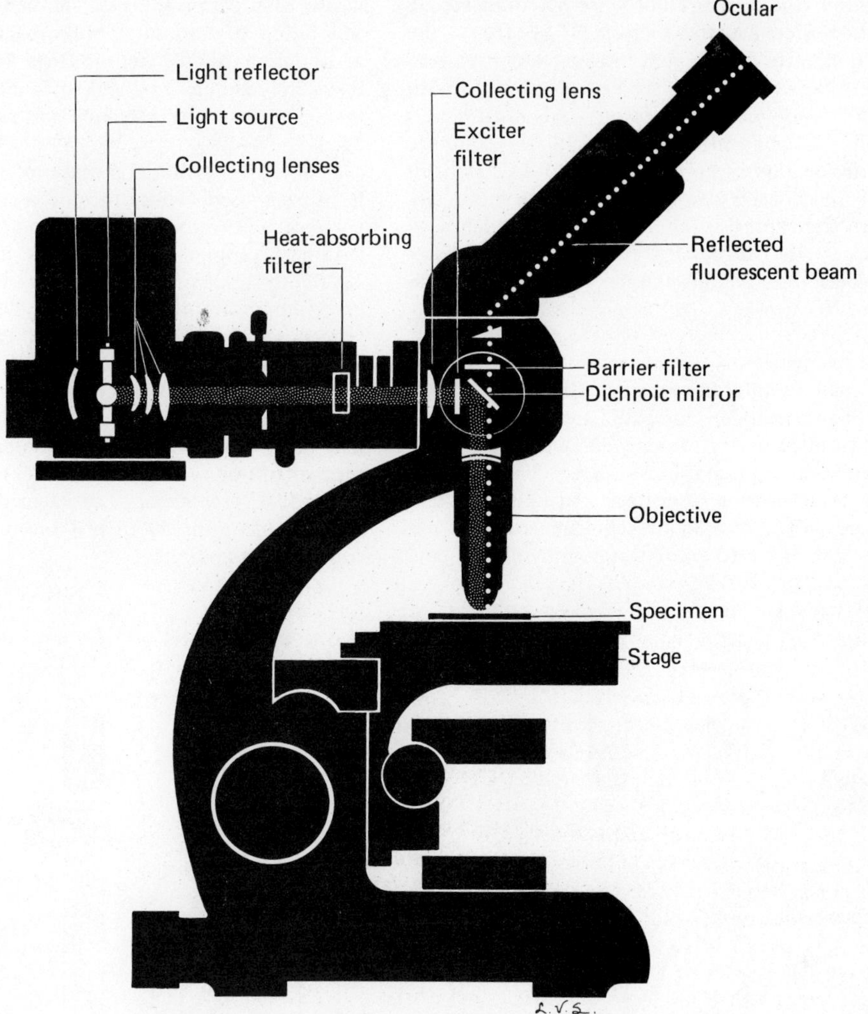

Figure 24–26. Fluorescence microscope with epi-illumination. The light beam is directed through the exciter filter and down onto the specimen. A dichroic mirror allows passage of selected wavelengths in one direction but not another. After reaching the specimen, the light is reflected through the dichroic mirror and emitted fluorescent light is visualized at the ocular.

jugation with fluorescent dye, and finally the staining procedure.

For *direct* immunofluorescence, an antiserum to the antigen one wishes to detect is raised in heterologous species, eg, goat or rabbit. Potent antisera are needed which should be prepared to contain milligram amounts of antibody per milliliter of antiserum. The potency of antisera is usually assessed by quantitative precipitation or passive hemagglutination. Specificity must be assured at a level which exceeds that detectable in ordinary double diffusion or immunoelectrophoretic technics. Several more sensitive methods are available, including hemagglutination inhibition and radioimmunoassay. Unwanted antibodies present in either direct conjugates or antiglobulin reagents for the *indirect* test can be removed with insoluble immunoabsorbents.

After one is assured of a direct antiserum of high potency and appropriate specificity, the γ-globulin fraction can be prepared by ammonium sulfate precipitation or a combination of salt precipitation and DEAE-cellulose ion exchange chromatography. It is necessary to partially purify serum immunoglobulin since subsequent conjugation should be limited to antibody as much as possible. This will increase the efficiency of staining and avoid unwanted nonspecific staining by fluorochrome-conjugated nonantibody serum proteins which can adhere to tissue components.

Conjugation of γ-globulin depends largely on the particular dye one wishes to combine with the antibody molecule. From a clinical standpoint, only fluorescein and rhodamine have been used widely. Fluorescein in the form of FITC, or rhodamine as tetramethylrhodamine isothiocyanate, is reacted either directly with γ-globulin in alkaline solution overnight at 4 C or dialyzed against γ-globulin. Unreacted dye is then removed from the protein-fluorochrome conjugate by gel filtration or exhaustive dialysis. If necessary, the resultant conjugate can be concentrated by lyophilization, pressure dialysis, or solvent extraction with water-soluble polymers. Thereafter, one must determine both the concentration of γ-globulin and the dye/protein or fluorescein/protein ratio of the compound. This is usually done spectrophotometrically with corrections for the alteration in absorbance of γ-globulin by the introduced fluorochrome. Fluorochrome-labeled compounds are best stored in the dark, frozen at −20 C.

Staining Technics

A. Direct Immunofluorescence: (Figs 24–27 and 24–28.) In this technic, conjugated antiserum is added directly to the tissue section or viable cell suspension.

B. Indirect Immunofluorescence: This technic allows for the detection of antibody in unlabeled sera and is especially useful in the clinical laboratory. It eliminates the need to purify and individually conjugate each serum sample. The method is basically an adaptation of the antiglobulin reaction (Coombs test) or double antibody technic (Figs 24–27 and 24–28). Specificity should be checked as diagrammed and further established by blocking and neutralization methods (Fig 24–29).

Several additional variations in staining technics have been used. These include a conjugated anticomplement antiserum for the detection of antigen-antibody-complement complexes and double staining with both rhodamine and fluorescein conjugates.

Immunofluorescence employing routine serologic procedures for the detection of antibody in human serum specimens has been widely accepted. Sensitivity levels are generally higher than is the case with complement fixation and lower than with hemagglutination inhibition. Methods for detecting antibody by immunofluorescence include (1) the antiglobulin method, (2) inhibition of labeled antibody-antigen reaction by antibody in test serum, and (3) the anticomplement method.

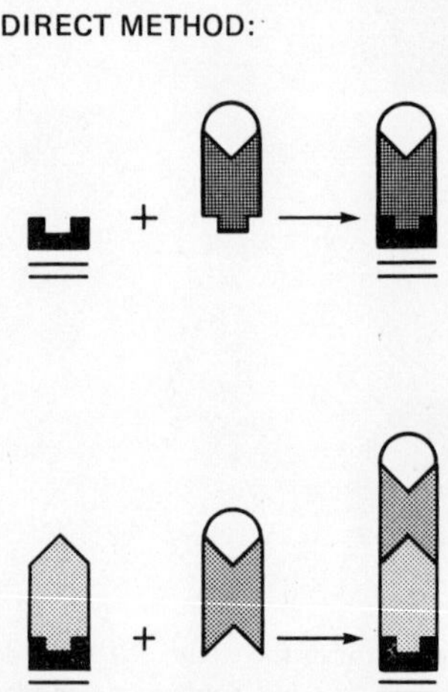

Figure 24–27. Mechanism of immunofluorescence technics. (Modified and reproduced by permission of Nordic Immunology, Tilburg, The Netherlands.) **Direct Method.** ***(Top):*** Antigen in substrate detected by direct labeling with fluorescent antibody. ***(Bottom):*** Antigen-antibody (immune) complex in substrate labeled with fluorescent antiglobulin reagent.

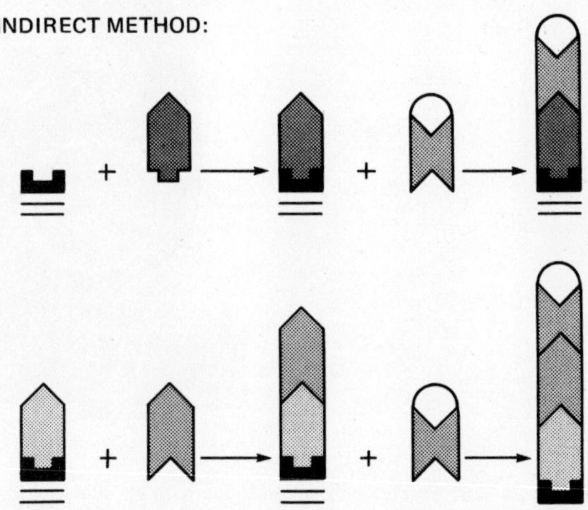

Figure 24–28. Mechanism of immunofluorescence technics. (Modified and reproduced by permission of Nordic Immunology, Tilburg, The Netherlands.) **Indirect Method.** ***(Top):*** Incubation of antigen in substrate with unlabeled antibody forms immune complex. Labeling performed with fluorescent antiglobulin reagent. ***(Bottom):*** Immune complex in substrate reacted with unlabeled antiglobulin reagent and then stained with fluorescent antiglobulin reagent directed at unlabeled antiglobulin.

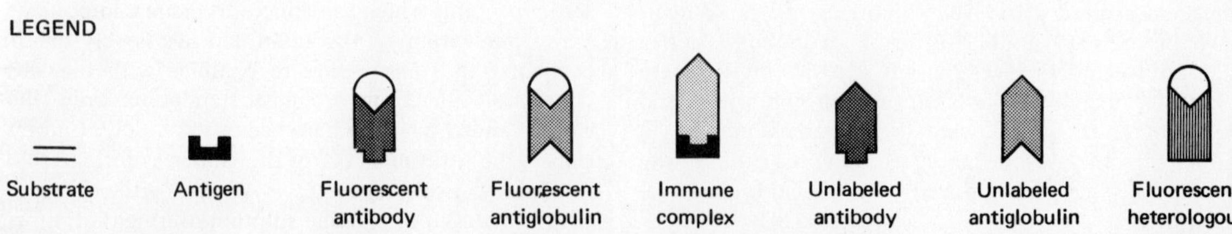

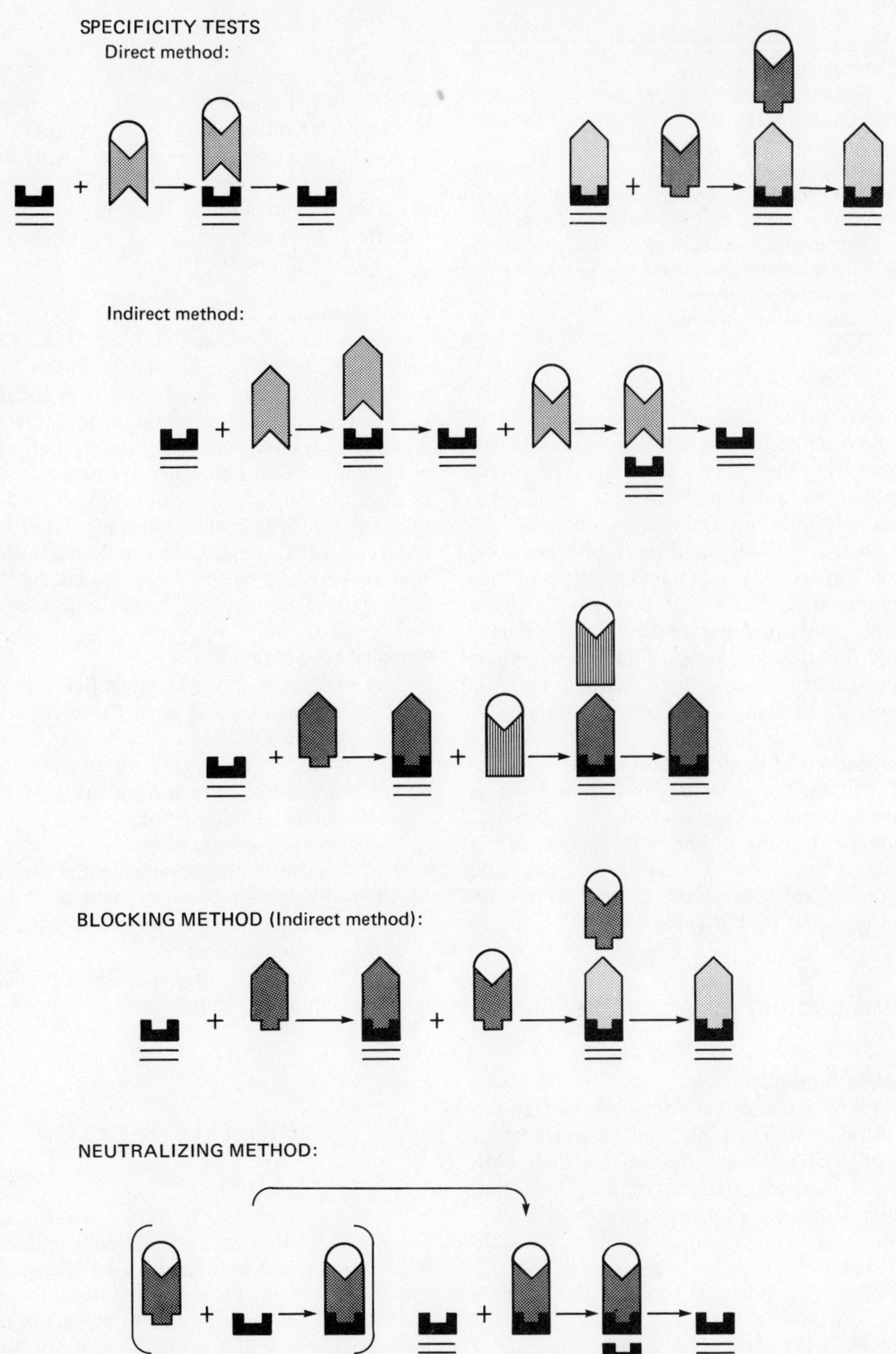

Figure 24–29. Specificity tests. **Direct method.** ***(Left):*** Substrate antigen fails to react with fluorescent antiglobulin reagent. No fluorescence results. ***(Right):*** Immune complex-substrate fails to react with fluorescent antibody directed against unrelated antigen. No fluorescence results. **Indirect method.** ***(Top):*** Unlabeled specific antiglobulin is replaced by unrelated antibody. In second step, fluorescent antiglobulin cannot react directly with antigen in substrate which has not bound specific antiglobulin. No fluorescence results. ***(Bottom):*** First step performed by reacting specific antibody with substrate antigen. In second stage, the specific conjugate is replaced by unrelated fluorescent heterologous antibody. No fluorescence results. **Blocking method.** Substrate antigen is incubated with unlabeled specific antibody prior to addition of specific fluorescent antibody. Decreased fluorescence results. **Neutralizing method.** Substrate antigen is incubated with specific fluorescent antibody after it is absorbed with specific antigen in substrate. No fluorescence results.

Table 24–10. Clinical applications of immunofluorescence.

Identification of T and B cells in blood
Detection of autoantibodies in serum, eg, ANA
Detection of immunoglobulins in tissues
Detection of complement components in tissues
Detection of specific, tissue-fixed antibody
Rapid identification of microorganisms in tissue or culture
Identification of chromosomes of specific banding patterns
Identification of tumor-specific antigens on neoplastic tissues
Identification of transplantation antigens in various organs
Localization of hormones and enzymes
Quantitation of serum proteins and antibodies

C. Quantitative Immunofluorescence: The amount of light emitted from a fluorescent specimen can be precisely measured by a microfluorometer. With the development of automated equipment and standard fluorescence units for fluorescein, observer bias may be eliminated. Recently, a novel technic involving binding of an antigen to an insoluble matrix and subsequent staining with fluorescent antibody has been developed for rapid quantitation of serum immunoglobulins by fluorometric assay. Important applications of quantitative immunofluorescence are forthcoming, especially in tissue typing and autoimmunity.

Clinical Applications of Immunofluorescence

Direct and indirect immunofluorescent staining technics have achieved widespread use in many areas of clinical medicine. In general, immunofluorescence has been of greatest usefulness as a sensitive and specific diagnostic tool. A partial list of its applications in clinical immunology is outlined in Table 24–10.

OTHER IMMUNOHISTOCHEMICAL TECHNICS

Enzyme-Linked Antibody

This method depends on conjugation of an enzyme to antibody which is directed at a cellular or tissue antigen. The resulting conjugate is then both immunologically and enzymatically active. Thereafter, the principles are entirely analogous to those underlying the direct or indirect immunofluorescence technics described above.

Horseradish peroxidase is usually the enzyme chosen for coupling to antibody. Tissues are first stained directly with antibody-enzyme conjugate or directly with enzyme-linked antiglobulin reagent following incubation with unlabeled immune serum. Thereafter, the tissue is incubated with the substrate for the enzyme. The enzyme in this case is detected visually by formation of a black color after incubation with hydrogen peroxide and diaminobenzidine. One advantage of this method is that ordinary light microscopes may be utilized for analysis of tissue sections. Furthermore, enzyme-coupled antibody can be used for ultrastructural studies in the electron microscope.

Ferritin-Coupled Antibody

Ferritin, an iron-containing protein, is highly electron-dense. When coupled to antibody, it can be used for either direct or indirect tissue staining. Localization of ferritin-coupled antibody-antigen complexes in fixed tissue can then be achieved with the electron microscope. Other electron-dense particles such as gold or uranium can also be introduced chemically into specific antitissue antibodies. These reagents have also been applied in immunoelectronmicroscopy.

Autoradiography

Radioactive isotopes such as ^{125}I which can be easily introduced into immunoglobulins by chemical means provide highly sensitive probes for localization of tissue antigens. The antigens are detected visually after tissue staining by overlaying or coating slides with photographic emulsion. The appearance of silver grains as black dots has been used for subcellular localization of antigen both at light microscopic and ultrastructural levels. Autoradiography has also been applied to detection of proteins or immunoglobulins synthesized by cells in tissue culture.

Miscellaneous Methods

A variety of other methods have been described for localization of antigens in tissues. Many have not found widespread clinical application. In most cases, these technics depend on secondary phenomena which occur as a result of the antigen-antibody interaction. These methods include the following:

(1) Complement fixation
(2) Conglutinating complement absorption test
(3) Antiglobulin consumption test
(4) Mixed hemadsorption
(5) Immune adherence
(6) Hemagglutination and coated particle reaction
(7) Immunoprecipitation

AGGLUTINATION

Agglutination and precipitation reactions are the basis of the most commonly used technics in laboratory immunology. Whereas precipitation reactions are quantifiable and simple to perform, agglutination technics are only semiquantitative and somewhat more difficult. The agglutination of either insoluble native antigens or antigen-coated particles can be simply assessed visually with or without the aid of a microscope. Important advantages of agglutination reactions are their high degree of sensitivity and enormous variety of substances detectable through use of antigen- or antibody-coated particles.

According to Coombs, the 3 main requirements in agglutination tests are the availability of a stable cell or particle suspension, the presence of one or more antigens close to the surface, and the knowledge that "incomplete" or nonagglutinating antibodies are not detectable without modifications, eg, antiglobulin reactions.

Agglutination reactions may be classified as either direct or indirect (passive). In the simple direct technic, a cell or insoluble particulate antigen is agglutinated directly by antibody. An example is the agglutination of group A red blood cells by anti-A sera. Passive agglutination refers to agglutination of antigen-coated cells or inert particles which are passive carriers of otherwise soluble antigens. Examples are latex fixation for detection of rheumatoid factor and agglutination of DNA-coated red cells for detection of anti-DNA antibody. Alternatively, *antigen* can be detected by coating latex particles or red blood cells with purified *antibody* and performing so-called reversed agglutination. Another category of agglutination involves spontaneous agglutination of red blood cells by certain viruses. This viral hemagglutination reaction can be specifically inhibited in the presence of antiviral antibody. Thus, viral hemagglutination can be used either to quantify virus itself or to determine by homologous inhibition the titer of antisera directed against hemagglutinating viruses.

Inhibition of agglutination, if carefully standardized with highly purified antigens, can be used as a sensitive indicator of the amount of antigen in various tissue fluids. Hemagglutination inhibition using passive hemagglutination reactions has recently been semi-automated in microtiter plates and is sensitive for measuring antigens in concentrations 0.2–9 μg/ml. With appropriate modification, passive hemagglutination with protein-sensitized cells can detect antibody at concentrations as low as 0.03 μg/ml.

AGGLUTINATION TECHNICS

Direct Agglutination Test

Red blood cells, bacteria, fungi, and a variety of other microbial species can be directly agglutinated by serum antibody. Tests to detect specific antibody are carried out by serially titrating antisera in 2-fold dilutions in the presence of a constant amount of antigen. Direct agglutination is relatively temperature-independent except for cold-reacting antibody, eg, cold agglutinins. After a few hours of incubation, agglutination is complete and particles are examined either directly or microscopically for evidence of clumping. The results are usually expressed as a titer of antiserum, ie, the highest dilution at which agglutination occurs. Because of intrinsic variability in the test system, a titer usually must differ by at least 2 dilutions ("2 tubes") to be considered significantly different from any given titer. Tests are carried out in small test tubes in volumes of 0.2–0.5 ml or in microtiter plates with smaller amounts of reagents, resulting in greater sensitivity.

Indirect (Passive) Agglutination

The range of soluble antigens that can be passively adsorbed or chemically coupled to red blood cells or other inert particles has dramatically extended the application of agglutination reactions. Many antigens will spontaneously couple with red blood cells and form stable reagents for antibody detection (Table 24–11). When red blood cells are used as the inert particles, serum specimens often must be absorbed with washed, uncoated red blood cells to remove heterophilic antibodies that would otherwise nonspecifically agglutinate the red blood cells. The advantages of using red blood cells for coating are their ready availability, sensitivity as indicators, and storage capabilities. Red blood cells can be treated with formalin, glutaraldehyde, or pyruvic aldehyde and stored for prolonged periods at 4 C. Although not applicable to all coating antigens, treatment with these preservatives may often be performed either before or after antigen coupling.

Coupling technics vary greatly in their applicability and success in individual laboratories. A list of general methods available for coating antigens on red blood cells is presented in Table 24–12. Perhaps the most widely used method is the tanned cell technic. Treatment of red blood cells with tannic acid increases the amount of most protein antigens subsequently adsorbed. This higher density of coated antigen greatly increases the sensitivity of the agglutination reaction. Although highly purified antigens are required for immunologic specificity, slightly denatured or aggregated antigens coat tanned red blood cells best.

Agglutination tests may be performed in tubes or microtiter plates. The prozone phenomenon can be seen in agglutination technics with antisera of very high titer. However, the use of standard serial dilution eliminates this difficulty. Since IgM antibody is about 750 times as efficient as IgG in agglutination, the presence of high amounts of IgM may markedly influence test results.

Table 24–11. Substances which spontaneously adsorb to red blood cells for hemagglutination.

Escherichia coli antigens
Yersinia antigens
Lipopolysaccharide from *Neisseria meningitidis*
Toxoplasma antigens
Purified protein derivative (PPD)
Endotoxin of Mycoplasma species
Viruses
Antibiotics, especially penicillin
Ovalbumin
Bovine serum albumin
DNA
Haptens, eg, DNCB

Table 24–12. Methods used to coat fresh and aldehyde-treated red blood cells with various antigens and antibodies for passive hemagglutination assay.

Coupling Agent	Comments on Coupling	Antigens Commonly Coated
None	Simple adsorption	Penicillin, bacterial antigens including endo- and exotoxins, viruses, and ovalbumin.
Tannic acid	Adsorption possibly caused by changes analogous to enzymes. Most popular; usually satisfactory, but often difficult and unreliable.	A wide spectrum of antigens: serum proteins, microbial and tissue extracts, homogenates, thyroglobulin, and tuberculin proteins.
Bisdiazotized benzidine (BDB)	Chemically stable covalent azo bonds.	Proteins and pollen antigens.
1,3-Difluoro-4, 6-dinitrobenzene (DFDNB)	Adsorption after modification of cell membrane.	Purified proteins and chorionic gonadotropin.
Chromic chloride ($CrCl_3$)	Proteins bound to red cells by the charge effect of trivalent cations.	Proteins.
Glutaraldehyde, cyanuric chloride, tetrazotized O-dianisidine	Cross-linking and covalent coupling.	Various proteins and certain enzymes.
Tolylene-2,4-diisocyanate	Covalently bound.	Proteins.
Water-soluble carbodiimide	Covalently bound.	Proteins.

Modified and reproduced, with permission, from Fudenberg HH: Hemagglutination inhibition: Passive hemagglutination assay for antigen-antibody reactions. In: *A Seminar on Basic Immunology*. American Association of Blood Banks, 1971.

HEMAGGLUTINATION INHIBITION

The inhibition of agglutination of antigen-coated red blood cells by homologous antigen is a highly sensitive and specific method for detecting small quantities of soluble antigen in blood or other tissue fluids. The principle of this assay is that antibody preincubated with soluble homologous or cross-reacting antigens will be "inactivated" when incubated with antigen-coated red blood cells. Thus, the test proceeds in 2 stages (Fig 24–30). Antibody in relatively low concentration is incubated with a sample of antigen of unknown quantity. After combination with soluble antigen, antigen-coated cells are added and agglutinated by uncombined or free antibody. (The degree of inhibition of agglutination reflects the amount of antigen present in the original sample.) Controls, including samples of known antigen concentration and uncoated red blood cells, must be employed. This hemagglutination inhibition method has proved very useful in the detection of HB_SAg in hepatitis and in the detection of factor VIII antigen in hemophilia and related clotting disorders.

CLINICALLY APPLICABLE TESTS WHICH EMPLOY AGGLUTINATION REACTIONS

Antiglobulin Test (Coombs Test)

The development of this simple and ingenious technic virtually revolutionized the field of immunohematology, and in various forms it has found widespread application in all fields of immunology. Antibodies frequently coat red blood cells but fail to form the necessary lattice which results in agglutination. A typical example is antibody directed at the Rh determinants on human red blood cells. However, the addition of an antiglobulin antiserum produced in a heterologous species (eg, rabbit anti-human γ-globulin) produces marked agglutination. Thus, the antiglobulin or Coombs test is used principally to detect subagglutinating or nonagglutinating amounts of antierythrocyte antibodies of any γ-globulin molecule. However, more specific Coombs reagents directed at specific immunoglobulin classes, eg, anti-IgG, anti-IgA, or anti-L chains, may also be employed to detect cellbound immunoglobulin. So-called "non-gamma Coombs" reagents which are directed against various complement components, eg, C3 or C4, may also produce red cell agglutination in the case of autoimmune hemolytic anemia. In some instances of this disorder, only complement components are bound to the red cell and the classical antiglobulin reaction is negative. The *direct Coombs test* detects γ-globulin or other serum proteins which are adherent to red blood cells taken directly from a sensitized individual. The *indirect Coombs test* is a 2-stage reaction for detection of incomplete antibodies in a patient's serum. The serum in question is first incubated with test red blood cells, and the putative antibody-coated cells are then agglutinated by a Coombs antiglobulin serum. The major applications of Coombs tests include red cell typing in blood banks, the evaluation of hemolytic disease of the newborn, and the diagnosis of autoimmune hemolytic anemia.

Bentonite Flocculation Test

Passive carriers of antigen other than red blood cells have been widely used in serology for the demonstration of agglutinating antibody. Wyoming bentonite is a form of siliceous earth which can directly adsorb most types of protein, carbohydrate, and nucleic acid. After adsorption, many antigens are stable on bentonite for 3–6 months. Simple flocculation on slides with appropriate positive and negative control sera indicates the presence of serum antibody. Bentonite flocculation has been employed to detect antibodies to trichinella, DNA, and rheumatoid factor.

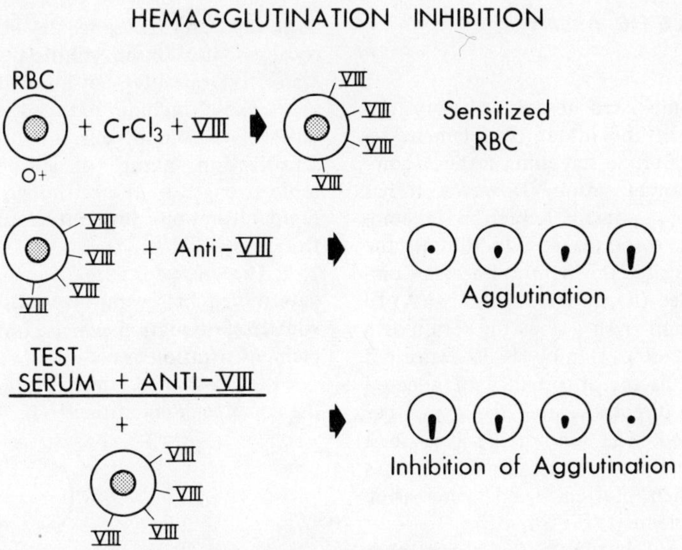

HEMAGGLUTINATION INHIBITION

Figure 24–30. Hemagglutination inhibition. Human O+ red blood cells (RBC) are conjugated with coagulation factor VIII antigen by chromic chloride. The sensitized red blood cells are reacted with specific antibody to factor VIII and are agglutinated. In the well of a V-shaped microtiter plate, agglutinated red blood cells appear as discrete dots. Nonagglutinated cells form a streak when the plate is incubated at a 45 degree angle. Agglutination of sensitized red blood cells can be inhibited by the presence of homologous factor VIII antigen present in the test serum. With decreasing amounts of serum added to the test, the specific antibody agglutinates sensitized cells and forms a dot in the microtiter well. A semiquantitative estimation of the amount or titer of antigen in a test serum can be made in this way.

Latex Fixation Test

Latex particles may also be used as passive carriers for adsorbed soluble protein and polysaccharide antigens. The most widespread application of latex agglutination (fixation) has been in the detection of rheumatoid factor. Rheumatoid factor is a 19S IgM antibody directed against 7S IgG (see Chapter 27). If 7S IgG is passively adsorbed to latex particles, specific determinants on the IgG are revealed which then react with IgM rheumatoid factors. This method is more sensitive but less specific for rheumatoid factor than the Rose-Waaler test (see below). Latex fixation has also been used to detect urine HCG in pregnancy testing.

Rose-Waaler Test

This passive hemagglutination test is also used for the detection of rheumatoid factor. Tanned red blood cells (usually sheep) are coated with subagglutinating amounts of rabbit 7S IgG antibodies specific for sheep red blood cells. Human rheumatoid factor will agglutinate these rabbit immunoglobulin-sensitized sheep red blood cells by virtue of a cross-reaction between rabbit IgG and human 7S IgG. The use of this test and latex fixation in the diagnosis of rheumatoid diseases (especially rheumatoid arthritis) is discussed in Chapter 27.

COMPLEMENT FUNCTION

Complement is one of the main humoral effector mechanisms of immune complex-induced tissue damage (see Chapters 6 and 20). Clinical disorders of complement function have been recognized for many decades, but their mechanism and eventual treatment have awaited elucidation of the complement sequence itself. The 9 major complement components (C1–C9) and various inhibitors can now be measured in human serum. Clinically useful assays of complement consist primarily of CH_{50} or total hemolytic assay and specific functional or immunochemical assays for various components. Immunochemical means are available for determining serum concentrations of selected components, but these assays do not provide data regarding the functional integrity of the various molecules.

It is worth emphasizing that the collection and storage of serum samples for functional or immunochemical complement assays present special problems as a result of the remarkable lability of some of the complement components. Rapid removal of serum from clotted specimens and storage at temperatures of −70 C or lower are required for preservation of maximal activity.

Finally, complement fixation or utilization, which occurs as a consequence of the antigen-antibody reaction, provides a sensitive and highly useful means of detecting antigens or antibodies and has been of particular use in serology.

HEMOLYTIC ASSAY

Specific antibody-mediated hemolysis of erythrocytes in the presence of the intact complement sequence can be used as a crude screening test for complement activity in human serum. However, it has limited usefulness since a drastic reduction in components is necessary to produce a reduction in the hemolytic assay. Classically, the hemolytic assay employs sheep erythrocytes (E), rabbit antibody (A) to sheep red blood cells, and fresh guinea pig serum as a source of complement (C). Hemolysis is measured spectrophotometrically as the absorbance of released hemoglobin and can be directly related to the number of red blood cells lysed. The amount of lysis in a standardized system employing E, A, and C describes an S-shaped curve when plotted against increasing amounts of added complement (Fig 24–31).

The curve is S-shaped, but in the mid region, near 50% hemolysis, a nearly linear relationship exists between the degree of hemolysis and the amount of complement present. In this range, the degree of red blood cell lysis is very sensitive to any alteration in complement concentration. For clinical purposes, measurement of total hemolytic activity of serum is taken at 50% hemolysis level. The CH_{50} is an arbitrary unit which is defined as the quantity of complement necessary for 50% lysis of red cells under rigidly standardized conditions of red blood cell sensitization with antibody (EA). These results are expressed as the reciprocal of the serum dilution giving 50% hemolysis. Many test variables can influence the degree of hemolysis. These include red cell concentration, fragility (age) of red blood cells, amount of antibody used for sensitization, nature of antibody (eg, IgG or IgM), ionic strength of the buffer system, pH, reaction time, temperature, and divalent cation (Ca^{++} or Mg^{++}) concentrations.

The value for CH_{50} units in human serum may be determined in several ways. Usually, one employs the von Krogh equation which converts the S-shaped complement titration curve into a nearly straight line.

The S-shaped curve in Fig 24–31 is described by the von Krogh equation:

$$X = K\left(\frac{Y}{1-Y}\right)^{1/n} \qquad (1)$$

where X = ml of diluted complement added,
Y = degree or percentage lysis,
K = constant,
n = 0.2 ± 10% under standard E and A conditions.

It is convenient to convert the von Krogh equation to a log form which renders the curve linear for plotting of clinical results (Fig 24–32):

$$\log X = \log K + \frac{1}{n} \log \frac{Y}{1-Y} \qquad (2)$$

The values of Y/1–Y are plotted on a log–log scale against serum dilutions. The reciprocal of the dilution of serum which intersects the curve at value of Y/1–Y = 1 is the CH_{50} unit. Values for normal CH_{50} units vary greatly depending on particular conditions of the test employed. It should again be emphasized that the CH_{50} or hemolytic assay is relatively insensitive to reduction in specific complement components and may in fact be normal or only slightly depressed in the face of significant reductions in individual components.

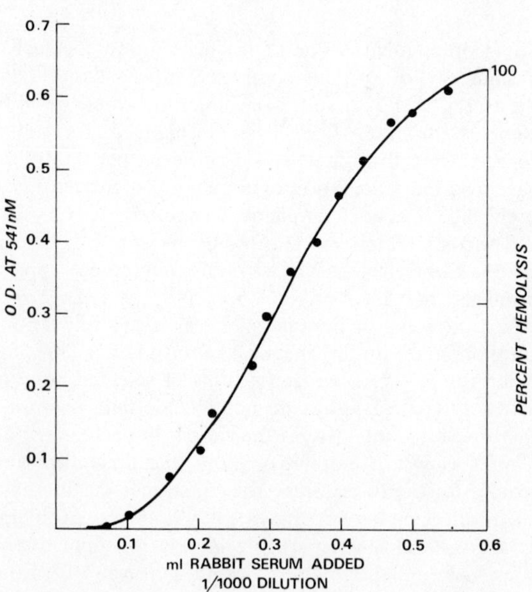

Figure 24–31. Relationship of complement concentration and red blood cells lysed. Curve relating the percentage of hemolysis that results from increasing amounts of fresh rabbit serum (diluted 1:1000) as complement source is added to sensitized sheep red blood cells (erythrocyte amboceptor [EA]). Hemolysis can be precisely determined by measuring the optical density of hemolysis supernates at 541 nm, the wavelength for maximal absorbance by hemoglobulin.

MEASUREMENT OF INDIVIDUAL COMPLEMENT COMPONENTS

Functional Assays

Activation of the entire complement sequence of C1–C9 must occur to produce lysis of antibody-coated erythrocytes (EA). Thus, a general scheme can be proposed to determine the level of activity of individual complement components. Initially, one must obtain pure preparations of each of the individual components. These pure components are then added sequentially to EA until the step is reached just prior

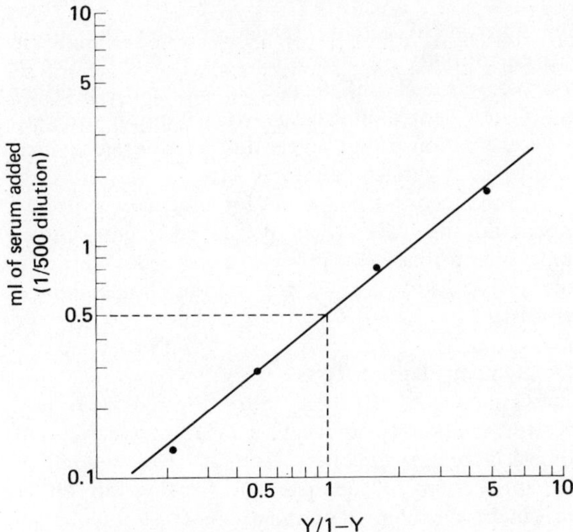

Figure 24–32. Determination of CH_{50} units from serum. Standard curve relating ml of serum 1:500 dilution to Y/1 – Y from von Krogh equation. When Y/1 – Y = 1.0, the percentage of lysis equals 50%. In the example shown, 0.5 ml of 1:500 serum dilution has produced Y/1 – Y = 1.0, or 50% lysis. The CH_{50} value for this serum equals 1000, since 1 ml of serum would have 1000 lytic units.

to the component to be measured. The test sample is added and the degree of subsequent erythrocyte lysis is then related to the presence of the later-acting components. Of course, all proximal components must be supplied in excess in order to measure more distally acting intermediates. Alternatively, the presence of genetically defined complement deficiencies has made available to the laboratory a further source of specifically deficient reagents for estimating individual component activity. A description of the technic of functional assays for complement components is found in the monograph of Rapp & Borsos (p 315).

Immunoassays for Complement Components

Antibodies can be prepared against most of the major complement components, thereby allowing for simple and precise immunochemical determinations of complement components. Technics which have been utilized for this purpose include electroimmunodiffusion (Laurell rocket electrophoresis) and single radial diffusion. Although immunologic assay of complement components is independent of their biologic function, alterations in chemical composition of complement components during storage may alter their behavior in these immunoassays. For example, in storage, C3 spontaneously converts to C3c, which has a smaller molecular size than native C3. Thus, in radial diffusion—but not in electroimmunodiffusion—stored serum will give falsely high estimates because more rapid diffusion produces a larger ring diameter. Recently, a semiautomated nephelometric technic to measure antigen-antibody reactions has been applied to large-scale screening of clinical samples for quantitative levels of complement components.

Significance of CH_{50} Units

A. Reduced Serum Complement Activity: Reduced amounts of serum complement activity have been reported in a variety of disease states (Table 24–13). The reduction in serum complement activity could be due to any one or a combination of (1) complement consumption by in vivo formation of antigen-antibody complexes, (2) decreased synthesis of complement, (3) increased catabolism of complement, or (4) formation of an inhibitor. Although complement has been demonstrated fixed to various tissues, eg, glomerular basement membrane, in association with antibody, tissue fixation of complement is apparently not an important mechanism in lowering serum complement activity. In addition, hemolytic activity (CH_{50}) may be relatively unaffected by major changes in concentration of individual complement components. Isolated reduction in human serum levels of C1, C2, C3, C6, or C7 to 50% of normal only slightly reduces hemolytic activity. For this reason, many laboratories have switched from classical hemolytic assay to a more simple immunochemical determination of C3. In general, the reduction of C3 correlates positively with CH_{50} activity reduction.

B. Elevated Complement Levels: Although complement levels are elevated in a variety of diseases (Table 24–14), the significance of this observation is not clear. The most likely mechanism is overproduction.

The development of specific functional and immunologic methods for detecting complement components has led to the discovery of a variety of genetically determined disorders of the complement system. A discussion of the specific disease states which result

Table 24–13. Diseases associated with reduced hemolytic complement activity.

Systemic lupus erythematosus with glomerulonephritis
Acute glomerulonephritis
Membranoproliferative glomerulonephritis
Acute serum sickness
Immune complex diseases
Advanced cirrhosis of the liver
Disseminated intravascular coagulation
Severe combined immunodeficiency
Infective endocarditis with glomerulonephritis
Infected ventriculoarterial shunts
Hereditary angioneurotic edema
Hereditary C2 deficiency
Paroxysmal cold hemoglobinuria
Myasthenia gravis
Infective hepatitis with arthritis
Allograft rejection
Mixed cryoglobulinemia (IgM-IgG)
Lymphosarcoma

Table 24–14. Diseases associated with elevated serum complement concentrations.

Obstructive jaundice
Thyroiditis
Acute rheumatic fever
Rheumatoid arthritis
Polyarteritis nodosa
Dermatomyositis
Acute myocardial infarction
Ulcerative colitis
Typhoid fever
Diabetes
Gout
Reiter's syndrome

from selective deficiency of the various complement components is found in Chapter 26.

COMPLEMENT FIXATION

The fixation of complement occurs during the interaction of antigen and antibodies. Thus, the consumption of complement in vitro can be used as a test to detect and measure antibodies, antigens, or both. The test depends on a 2-stage reaction system. In the initial stage, antigen and antibody react in the presence of a known amount of complement and complement is consumed (fixed). In the second stage, hemolytic complement activity is measured to determine the amount of complement fixed and thus the amount of antigen or antibody present in the initial mixture (Fig 24–33). The amount of activity remaining after the initial antigen-antibody reaction is back-titrated in the hemolytic assay (see above). Results are expressed as either the highest serum dilution showing fixation for antibody estimation or the concentration of antigen which is limiting for antigen determinations.

Extremely sensitive assays for antigen or antibody concentrations have been developed using microcomplement fixation. However, these assays are too cumbersome and complex for routine clinical laboratory use.

Complement Fixation Tests

Complement fixation tests (Fig 24–33) have received widespread application in both research and clinical laboratory practice. Table 24–15 lists some of the applications of complement fixation for either antigen or antibody determination. It should be recalled that all complement assay systems involving functional tests can be inhibited by anticomplementary action of serum. This may result from antigen-antibody complexes, heparin, chelating agents, and aggregated immunoglobulins, eg, as in multiple myeloma.

Table 24–15. Applications of complement fixation tests.

Hepatitis-associated antigen (HB_sAg)
Antiplatelet antibodies
Anti-DNA
Immunoglobulins
L chains
Wassermann test for syphilis
Coccidioides immitis antigen

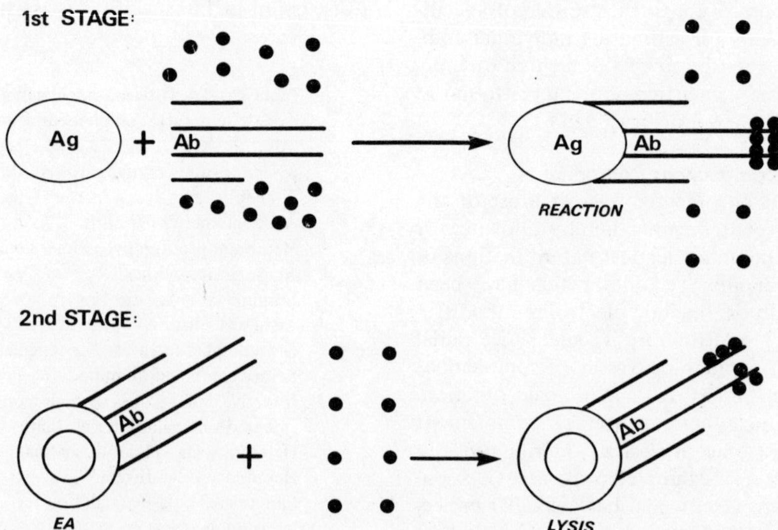

Figure 24–33. Principles of complement fixation. In the first stage, antigen (Ag) and antibody (Ab) are reacted in the presence of complement (●). The interaction of Ag and antibody fixes some but not all of the complement available. In the second stage, the residual or unfixed complement is measured by adding EA (erythrocyte amboceptor), which is lysed by residual complement. Thus, a reciprocal relationship exists between amounts of lysis in second stage and antigen present in the first stage.

• • •

References

Immunodiffusion

Crowle AJ: *Immunodiffusion,* 2nd ed. Academic Press, 1973.

Gilliland BC, Mannik M: Immunologic quantitation of proteins in serum, urine, and other body fluids. Pages 13–30 in: *Laboratory Diagnosis of Immunologic Disorders.* Vyas GN, Stites DP, Brecher G (editors). Grune & Stratton, 1975.

Ouchterlony O, Nilsson LÅ: Immunodiffusion and immunoelectrophoresis. Chap 19 in: *Handbook of Experimental Immunology.* Weir DM (editor). Blackwell, 1973.

Stiehm ER, Fudenberg HH: Serum levels of immune globulins in health and disease: A survey. Pediatrics 37:715, 1966.

Electrophoresis

Cawley LP: *Electrophoresis and Immunoelectrophoresis.* Little, Brown, 1969.

Cawley LP & others: *Basic Electrophoresis, Immunoelectrophoresis and Immunochemistry.* American Society of Clinical Pathologists Commission on Continuing Education, 1972.

Crowle AJ: *Immunodiffusion,* 2nd ed. Academic Press, 1973.

Franklin EC: Electrophoresis and immunoelectrophoresis in the diagnosis of dysproteinemias. Chap 1 in: *Laboratory Diagnosis of Immunologic Disorders.* Vyas GN, Stites DP, Brecher G (editors). Grune & Stratton, 1975.

Gilliland BC, Mannik M: Immunologic quantitation of proteins in serum, urine, and other body fluids. Chap 2 in: *Laboratory Diagnosis of Immunologic Disorders.* Vyas GN, Stites DP, Brecher G (editors). Grune & Stratton, 1975.

Ouchterlony O, Nilsson LÅ: Immunodiffusion and immunoelectrophoresis. Chap 19 in: *Handbook of Experimental Immunology.* Weir DM (editor). Blackwell, 1973.

Immunochemical & Physicochemical Methods

Broute JC & others: Biological and clinical significance of cryoglobulins: A report of 86 cases. Am J Med 57:775, 1974.

Fahey JL, Terry EW: Ion exchange chromatography and gel filtration. Chap 7 in: *Handbook of Experimental Immunology.* Weir DM (editor). Blackwell, 1973.

Grey HM, Kohler PF: Cryoimmunoglobulins. Semin Hematol 10:87, 1973.

Somer T: The viscosity of blood plasma and serum in dys- and paraproteinemias. Acta Med Scand (Suppl 456):180, 1966.

Trautman R, Cowan KM: Preparative and analytical ultracentrifugation. Pages 81–118 in: *Methods in Immunology and Immunochemistry.* Vol 2. Williams CA, Chase MW (editors). Academic Press, 1968.

Wilson CB, Dixon FJ: Diagnosis of immunopathologic renal disease. Kidney Int 5:389, 1974.

Radioimmunoassay

Berson SA, Yalow RS: Radioimmunoassay: A status report. Page 287 in: *Immunobiology.* Good RA, Fisher DW (editors). Sinauer Associates, Inc, 1971.

Hunter WM: Radioimmunoassay. Chap 17 in: *Handbook of Experimental Immunology.* Weir DM (editor). Blackwell, 1973.

Kirkham KE, Hunter WM (editors): *Radioimmunoassay Methods.* Livingstone, 1971.

Newton WT, Donati RM (editors): *Radioassay in Clinical Medicine.* Thomas, 1974.

Skelley DS, Brown LP, Besch PK: Radioimmunoassay. Clin Chem 19:146, 1973.

Yalow RS: Radioimmunoassay methodology applied to problems of heterogeneity of peptide hormones. Pharmacol Rev 25:161, 1973.

Immunohistochemical Technics

Goldman M: *Fluorescent Antibody Methods.* Academic Press, 1968.

Hijmans W, Schaeffer M (editors): Fifth International Conference on Immunofluorescence and Related Staining Techniques. Ann NY Acad Sci, vol 265, 1975. [Entire issue.]

Nairn RC: *Fluorescent Protein Tracing,* 4th ed. Longman, 1975.

Agglutination

Fudenberg HH: Hemagglutination inhibition. Pages 101–110 in: *A Seminar on Basic Immunology.* American Association of Blood Banks, 1971.

Gell PGH, Coombs RRA, Lachmann PJ (editors): *Clinical Aspects of Immunology,* 3rd ed. Blackwell, 1975.

Herbert WJ: Passive hemagglutination with special reference to the tanned cell technique. Chap 20 in: *Handbook of Experimental Immunology.* Weir DM (editor). Blackwell, 1973.

Complement Function

Alper CA, Rosen FS: Complement and clinical medicine. Chap 4 in: *Laboratory Diagnosis of Immunologic Disorders.* Vyas GN, Stites DP, Brecher G (editors). Grune & Stratton, 1975.

Mayer MM: The complement system. Sci Am 229:54, Nov 1973.

Rapp JH, Borsos T: *Molecular Basis of Complement Action.* Appleton-Century-Crofts, 1970.

Ruddy S, Gigli I, Austen KF: The complement system of man. (4 parts.) N Engl J Med 287:489, 545, 592, 642, 1972.

Schultz DR (editor): *Monographs in Allergy.* Vol 6: *The Complement System.* Karger, 1971.

Schur PH, Austen KF: Complement in human disease. Annu Rev Med 19:1, 1968.

25 . . .
Laboratory Methods of Detecting Cellular Immune Function

Daniel P. Stites, MD

INTRODUCTION

The immune system in humans can be divided into 2 major parts, one involving humoral immunity (antibody and complement) and the other immunocompetent cells. In many ways this separation is artificial, and many examples of the interdependence of cellular and humoral immunity could be cited (see Chapter 8). Nevertheless, dividing the immune system into parts in this way has provided a conceptual and practical framework for the laboratory evaluation of immunity in clinical practice.

In the preceding chapter we reviewed methods of detecting antibodies and methods that employ antibodies for antigen detection. Recently, the role of a variety of distinct cell types (Chapter 7) in immune mechanisms in normal and diseased persons has become measurable in the clinical laboratory. Immunocompetent cells, including lymphocytes, macrophages, and granulocytes, are all involved in the delayed hypersensitivity reactions that are so important in immunity to intracellular infection, tumor immunity, and transplant rejection. The clinical laboratory investigation of the number and function of these cells is still beset by difficulties in test standardization, biologic variability, the imprecise nature of many assays, and the complexity and expense of the procedures. Nevertheless, several tests that are of value in assessing cellular function are gradually becoming available for clinical use.

The present chapter reviews the tests that have medical application in the detection of cellular immune function. The intention is not to provide a comprehensive laboratory manual but to familiarize the reader with the principles, applications, and interpretation of these assays. It can be expected that our understanding of cellular immunity will continue to expand and that technologic advances in methods for its assessment will soon be forthcoming.

The subject matter of this chapter includes (1) delayed hypersensitivity skin tests, (2) lymphocyte activation, (3) assays for T and B lymphocytes, and (4) neutrophil function.

Daniel P. Stites is Assistant Professor of Medicine and Laboratory Medicine and Director, Immunology Laboratory, University of California School of Medicine, San Francisco.

DELAYED HYPERSENSITIVITY SKIN TESTS

Despite the development of a multitude of complex procedures for the assessment of cellular immunity, the relatively simple intradermal test remains a useful tool, occasionally serving to establish a diagnosis. Delayed hypersensitivity skin testing merely detects cutaneous hypersensitivity to an antigen or group of antigens and, when one is testing for an infectious disease, does not necessarily imply active infection with the agent being tested for. Delayed hypersensitivity skin tests are also of great value in the overall assessment of immunocompetence and in epidemiologic surveys. Inability to react to a battery of common skin antigens is termed *anergy,* and clinical conditions associated with this hyporeactive state are listed in Table 25–1.

Technic of Skin Testing

(1) Lyophilized antigens should be stored sterile at 4 C, protected from light, and reconstituted shortly before use. The manufacturer's expiration date should be observed.

(2) Test solutions should not be stored in syringes for prolonged periods before use.

(3) A 25 or 27 gauge needle usually assures intradermal rather than subcutaneous administration of antigen. Subcutaneous injection leads to dilution of the antigen in tissues and can lead to a resultant false-negative test.

(4) Both erythema and induration should be measured with a ruler and recorded at both 24 and 48 hours.

(5) Hyporeactivity to any given antigen or group of antigens should be confirmed by testing with higher concentrations of antigen or, in ambiguous circumstances, by a repeat test with the intermediate dose.

Contact Sensitivity

Direct application to the skin of chemically reactive compounds results in systemic sensitization to various metabolites of the sensitizing compound. The precise chemical fate of the sensitizing compounds is not known, but sensitizing agents such as dinitrochlo-

Table 25–1. Clinical conditions associated with anergy.*

I. Technical errors in skin testing
Improper dilutions
Bacterial contamination
Exposure to heat or light
Adsorption of antigen on container walls
Faulty injection (too deep, leaking)
Improper reading of reaction
II. Immunologic deficiency
Congenital
Combined deficiencies of cellular and humoral immunity
Ataxia-telangiectasia
Nezelof's syndrome
Severe combined immunodeficiency
Wiskott-Aldrich syndrome
Cellular immunodeficiency
Thymic and parathyroid aplasia (DiGeorge syndrome)
Mucocutaneous candidiasis
Acquired
Sarcoidosis
Chronic lymphocytic leukemia
Carcinoma
Immunosuppressive medication
Rheumatoid diseases
Uremia
Alcoholic cirrhosis
Biliary cirrhosis
Surgery
Hodgkin's disease and lymphomas
III. Infections
Influenza
Mumps
Measles
Viral vaccines
Typhus
Miliary and active tuberculosis
Disseminated mycotic infection
Lepromatous leprosy
Scarlet fever

*Modified from Heiss LI, Palmer DL: Am J Med 56:323, 1974.

robenzene (DNCB) probably form dinitrophenyl-protein complexes with various skin proteins. Sensitization with DNCB is often a helpful adjunct to delayed hypersensitivity skin testing in the suspected anergic patient. Following application of DNCB to the skin, a period of about 7–10 days elapses before contact sensitivity can be elicited by a challenge dose applied to the skin surface. This sensitivity persists for years. The ability of a subject to develop contact sensitivity is a measure of cellular immunity to a new antigen to which the subject has not been previously exposed. Thus, the establishment of a state of cutaneous anergy in various disease states may be confirmed and extended by testing with DNCB.

Interpretation of contact sensitivity reactions depends on development of a flare or vesicular reaction at the site of challenge. Induration rarely occurs since the test dose is not applied intradermally. In some clinical situations, a nonspecific depression in the inflammatory response can result in apparent anergy. A local irritant such as croton oil is occasionally employed to test the ability to mount a nonspecific inflammatory response.

Interpretation & Pitfalls

The inflammatory infiltrate which occurs 24–48 hours following intradermal injection of an antigen consists primarily of mononuclear cells. This cellular infiltrate and the accompanying edema result in induration of the skin, and the diameter of this reaction is an index of cutaneous hypersensitivity. A patient may also demonstrate immediate hypersensitivity to the same test antigen, ie, a coexistent area of erythema (wheal and flare) which usually fades by 12–18 hours but may occasionally persist longer (see Chapter 29). Induration 5 mm or more in diameter is the generally accepted criterion of a positive delayed skin test. Smaller but definitely indurated reactions suggest sensitivity to a closely related or cross-reacting antigen. There is no definitive evidence that repeated skin testing can result in conversion of delayed hypersensitivity skin tests from negative to positive. However, with some antigens, intradermal testing can result in elevations of serum antibody titers and confuse a serologic diagnosis. For this reason, blood for serologic study should always be obtained before skin tests are performed.

Delayed hypersensitivity skin testing is of relatively little value in establishing the diagnosis of defective cellular immunity during the first year of life. Infants may fail to react because of lack of antigen contact with resultant sensitization to various test antigens. Consequently, in vitro assay for T cell numbers and function is much more useful in the diagnosis of congenital immunodeficiency disease (see Chapter 26).

Possible Adverse Reactions to Skin Tests

Occasional patients who are highly sensitive to various antigens will have marked local reactions to skin tests. These are most likely to occur with second strength and more concentrated doses. Reactions include erythema, marked induration, and, rarely, local necrosis. Systemic side-effects such as fever or anaphylaxis are uncommon. Injection of corticosteroids locally into hyperreactive indurated areas may modify the severity of the reaction. Similarly, the painful blistering and inflammation that sometimes occur following surface application of DNCB can be reduced by topical corticosteroids.

LYMPHOCYTE ACTIVATION

Lymphocyte activation or stimulation refers to an in vitro correlate of an in vivo process which regularly occurs when antigen interacts with specifically sensitized lymphocytes in the host (see Chapters 7 and 8). Lymphocyte transformation is a nearly synonymous term first used by Nowell in 1960 and later by Hirschhorn and others to describe the morphologic changes that resulted when small, resting lymphocytes were transformed into lymphoblasts on exposure to the mitogen phytohemagglutinin (PHA). Blastogenesis refers to the process of formation of large pyroninophilic blastlike cells in cultures of lymphocytes stimulated by either nonspecific mitogens or antigens.

Lymphocyte activation is an in vitro technic commonly used to assess cellular immunity in patients with immunodeficiency, autoimmunity, infectious diseases, and cancer. A myriad of complex biochemical events occurs following incubation with mitogens. These are substances that stimulate large numbers of lymphocytes and do not require a sensitized host, as is the case with antigens. These biochemical events include early membrane-related phenomena such as increased synthesis of phospholipids, increased permeability to divalent cations, activation of adenylate cyclase, and resultant elevation of intracellular cAMP. Synthesis of protein, RNA, and finally DNA occurs shortly thereafter. It is this latter phenomenon, the increase in DNA synthesis, that eventually results in cell division and is the basis for most clinically relevant assays for lymphocyte activation. Convenience and custom have led clinical immunologists to use DNA synthesis rather than earlier events, eg, cAMP or phospholipid metabolism, as a marker for lymphocyte activation.

Although the relationship between lymphocyte activation and delayed hypersensitivity is not always absolute, the method has found widespread use in clinical immunology. The in vivo delayed hypersensitivity skin test is actually the result of a series of complex phenomena including antigen recognition, lymphocyte-macrophage interaction, release of soluble lymphocyte mediators, and changes in vascular permeability. In vitro methods such as lymphocyte activation are useful for studying cellular hypersensitivity since they permit analysis of specific stages in the immune response. In addition, they avoid challenge of the patient with potentially detrimental antigens such as drugs, transplantation antigens, or tumor antigens. Lymphocyte activation measures the *functional* capability of lymphocytes to proliferate following antigenic challenge and is therefore a more reliable test of immunocompetence than merely counting types of lymphocytes (ie, T and B cell assays).

In a number of diseases, serum factors, eg, antigen-antibody complexes, α-globulins, hormones, and α-fetoprotein, have been shown to block lymphocyte activation nonspecifically. Culture of peripheral blood lymphocytes, both in the presence and absence of autologous plasma, can shed light on the potential role of these interesting immunoregulatory factors.

METHODS & INTERPRETATIONS

Mitogen Stimulation

A number of plant lectins and other substances have been employed in assessing human lymphocyte function (Table 25–2). In contrast to studies in mice, there is no incontrovertible evidence that T or B lymphocytes are selectively activated by nonspecific mitogens. As discussed in Chapter 7, PHA and concanavalin A are predominantly T cell mitogens, whereas pokeweed mitogen stimulates principally B cells. Neither lipopolysaccharide nor anti-immunoglobulin antibody appears to be a potent B cell stimulant in humans.

Lymphocyte Culture Technic

Lymphocytes are purified from heparinized peripheral blood by density gradient centrifugation on Ficoll-Hypaque. Cultures are set up in triplicate in test tubes or microtiter trays at a cell concentration of approximately 1×10^6 lymphocytes per ml. The culture medium is supplemented with 10 to 20% serum—either autologous, heterologous, or pooled human sera. Mitogens are added in varying concentrations on a weight basis, usually over a 2–3 log range. Cultures are incubated in a mixture of 5% CO_2 in air for 72 hours, at which time most mitogens produce their maximal effect on DNA synthesis. The rate of DNA synthesis was originally estimated by morphologic assessment of the percentage of lymphoblasts present in the culture. However, this method has been largely abandoned owing to the extreme variability and subjectivity of the results. A more accurate measure of DNA synthesis is accomplished by pulse-labeling the cultures with tritiated thymidine (^{3}H-Tdr), a nucleoside precursor which is incorporated into newly synthesized DNA. The amount of ^{3}H-Tdr incorporated—and therefore the rate of DNA synthesis—is determined either by autoradiography and grain counts or by scintillation counting in a liquid scintillation spectrophotometer. The latter method is currently the generally accepted one in most clinical immunology laboratories.

Scintillation counting yields data in counts per

Table 25–2. "Nonspecific" mitogens which activate human lymphocytes.

Mitogen	Abbreviation	Biologic Source
Phytohemagglutinin	PHA	*Phaseolus vulgaris* (kidney bean)
Concanavalin A	ConA	*Canavalia ensiformis* (jack bean)
Pokeweed mitogen	PWM	*Phytolacca americana* (pokeweed)
Staphylococcal filtrate	SLF	*Staphylococcus aureus*
Streptolysin S	SLS	Group A streptococci
Antilymphocyte globulin	ALG	Heterologous antiserum

minute (cpm) or corrected for quenching to disintegrations per minute (dpm), which are then used as a standard measure of lymphocyte responsiveness. In order to express data, the cpm in control cultures are either subtracted from or divided into stimulated cpm, which yields a ratio commonly referred to as the stimulation index.

Obviously there are a multitude of technical as well as conceptual variables which can affect the results of this sensitive assay system. These include the concentration of cells, the geometry of the culture vessel, contamination of cultures with nonlymphoid cells or microorganisms, the dose of mitogen, the incubation time of cultures, and the technics of harvesting cells.

Two of these factors deserve special mention: culture time and dose-response kinetics. Since clinically important defects in cellular immunity are rarely absolute, quantitative relationships in lymphocyte activation are of crucial importance. This is especially true when comparing the reduction of responsiveness of normal control subjects with a group of patients with altered lymphocyte function. With the use of microtiter culture systems and semiautomated harvesting devices, an attempt can be made to determine both dose- and time-response kinetics of either mitogen- or antigen-stimulated cultures (Figs 25–1 and 25–2).

Altered lymphocyte function can result in shifts in either time- or dose-response curves to the left or right. These shifts determine the optimal dose and optimal time of the lymphocyte response. Without such detailed analyses, it is usually impossible to accurately observe partial or subtle defects in lymphocyte responsiveness in various disease states. Cultures assayed at a single time with a single stimulant dose period are often grossly misleading.

Confusion may result from a nonstandardized format for presentation of data. Many laboratories present results of lymphocyte stimulation as a ratio of cpm in stimulated culture to those in control cultures—the so-called stimulation index. Others report "raw" cpm or dpm as illustrated in Figs 25–1 and 25–2. Neither method is entirely satisfactory. The stimulation index is a ratio, and marked changes can therefore result from changes in background or control cpm of the denominator. It is perhaps best to report data in both ways to permit better interpretations.

Antigen Stimulation

Whereas mitogens stimulate large numbers of lymphocytes, antigens stimulate far fewer cells which are specifically sensitized to the antigen in question. In most instances, only T cells respond to antigens in this test. A wide variety of antigens have been employed in lymphocyte activation, many of them also being used for delayed hypersensitivity skin testing (Table 25–3). In general, normal subjects show agreement between the results of skin tests and antigen-induced lymphocyte activation. However, in many conditions, the in vitro technic is apparently a more sensitive index of specific antigen-mediated cellular hypersensitivity.

Table 25–3. Antigens commonly used to assess human cellular immunity in vitro.

PPD
Candida
Streptokinase/streptodornase
Coccidioidin
Tetanus toxoid
Tumor antigens
Histoincompatible cells (mixed leukocyte reaction)
Vaccinia virus
Herpes simplex viruses

Mixed lymphocyte cultures (MLC) (see Chapter 15) can also be used to assay for cellular immunocompetence in various clinical states (Chapter 26). MLC is a special case of antigen stimulation since responding cells do not require prior active sensitization. As a nonspecific indicator of T cell function, MLC may also show discordance with PHA- or antigen-induced activation. Allogeneic lymphocytes, antigens, and selected mitogens stimulate discrete and functionally unique populations of T cells.

Culture Technic

Culture methods are virtually identical to those described for mitogen stimulation. Additional factors to be considered include the possible presence in serum supplements of antibody directed against stimulating antigens. Antigen-antibody complexes may block or occasionally nonspecifically stimulate lymphocytes.

As in the case of mitogen-induced activation, time- and dose-response kinetics are of crucial importance in generating reliable data. Representative examples of such curves are shown in Figs 25–3 and 25–4. In contrast to mitogen-induced lymphocyte activation, antigen stimulation results in lower total DNA synthesis. Furthermore, the time of maximal response does not occur until the culture has been allowed to continue for 5–7 days. Fig 25–4 clearly illustrates both the usefulness and the necessity of performing careful time- and dose-response kinetics in assessing human lymphocyte function.

ASSAYS FOR HUMAN T & B LYMPHOCYTES

The era of modern cellular immunology essentially began with the discovery that lymphocytes are divided into 2 major functionally distinct populations. Evidence for the existence of T (thymus-derived) and B (bursa-derived) lymphocytes in humans consists principally of analogic reasoning from studies of other mammalian and avian species and analysis of lymphocyte populations in immunodeficiency diseases (see Chapters 7 and 26).

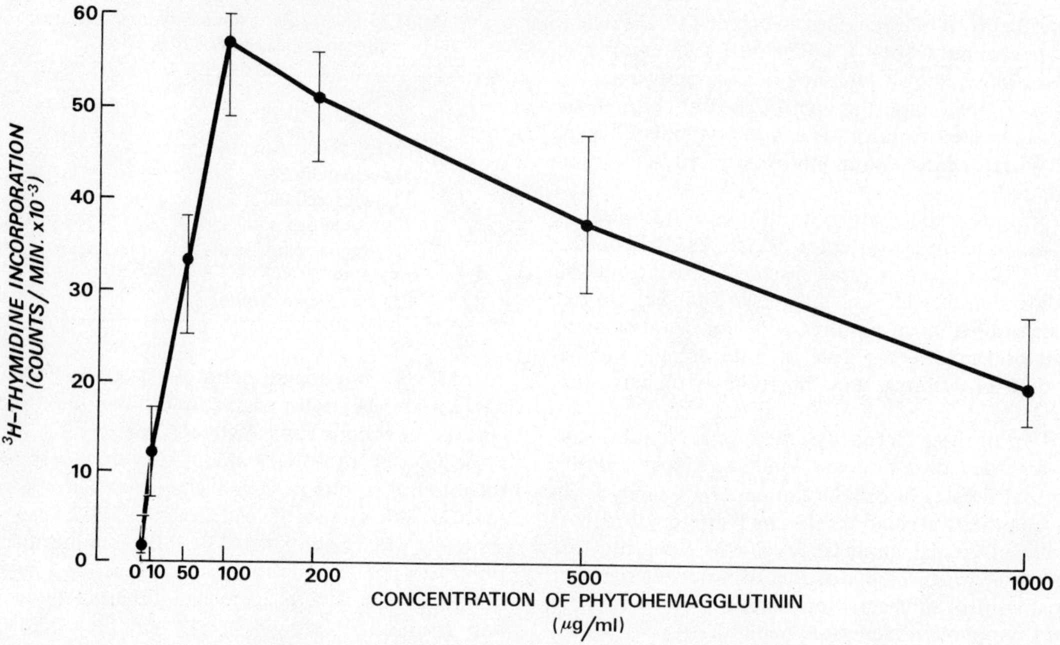

Figure 25–1. Dose-response curve for mitogen stimulation of 10^6 lymphocytes. Dose-response curve of a group of 10 normal adults whose peripheral blood lymphocytes were stimulated with varying concentrations of phytohemagglutinin for 72 hours. Lymphocytes were pulse-labeled with 2 μCi of tritiated (^{3}H) thymidine 6 hours prior to harvesting. Counts per minute of ^{3}H-thymidine incorporation were determined by liquid scintillation spectrometry and are plotted as the mean of 10 individual determinations ± the range. A maximal response occurred at approximately 100–200 μg/ml of phytohemagglutinin.

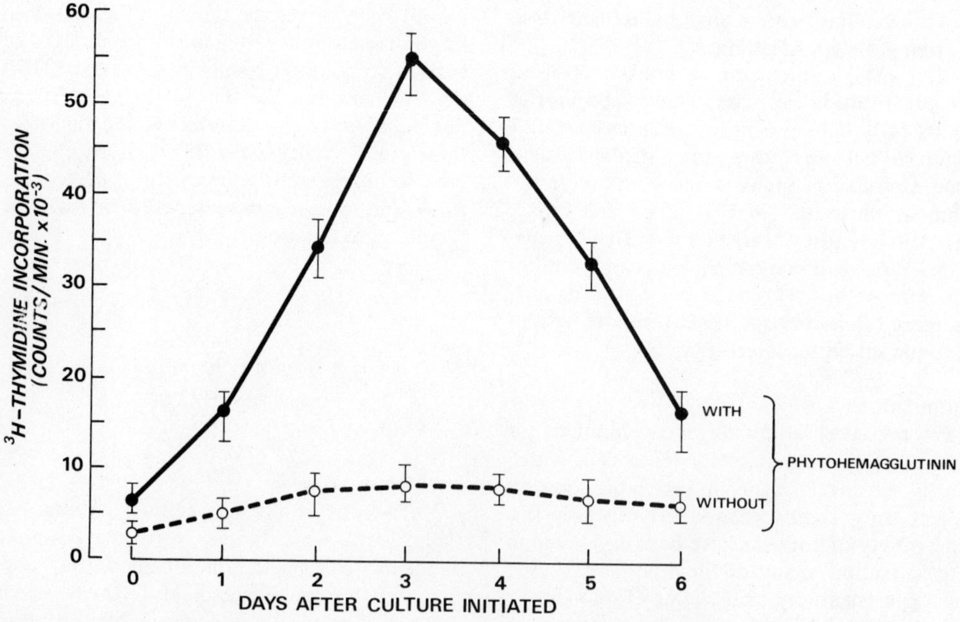

Figure 25–2. Time-response curve for mitogen stimulation of 10^6 lymphocytes. Time-response curve of peripheral blood lymphocytes from 10 normal adults stimulated in tissue culture for various lengths of time with an optimal concentration of phytohemagglutinin (100 μg/ml). Cultures were pulse-labeled with tritiated thymidine for 6 hours on the day of harvest. Maximal response occurred at 3 days after initiating the culture. Results are plotted as mean ± the range of counts per minute.

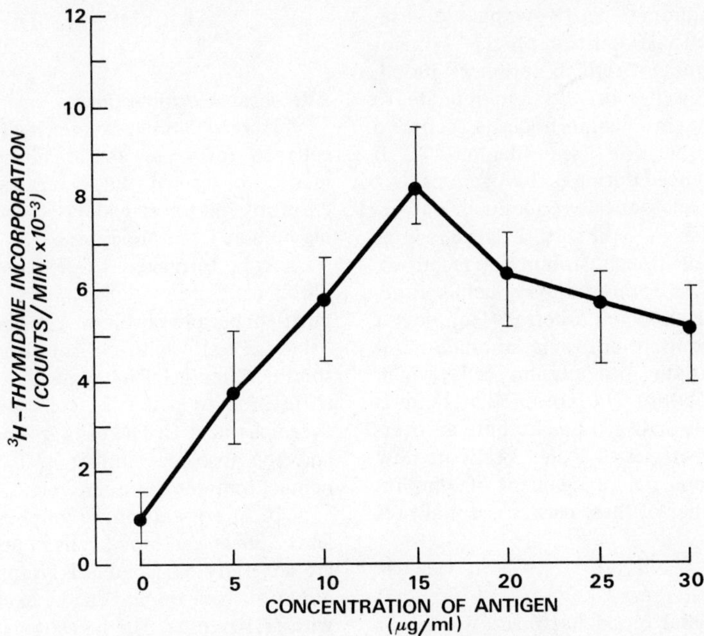

Figure 25–3. Dose-response curve for antigen stimulation of 10^6 lymphocytes. Dose-response curve of lymphocytes from 15 normal individuals with delayed hypersensitivity to the antigen. Cultures were harvested at 120 hours of culture after a 6-hour pulse with tritiated (^{3}H) thymidine. Counts per minute were determined by scintillation spectrometry. Results are plotted as mean ± the range from 15 skin test-positive subjects at various antigen concentrations. Maximum response is at 15 μg/ml of antigen.

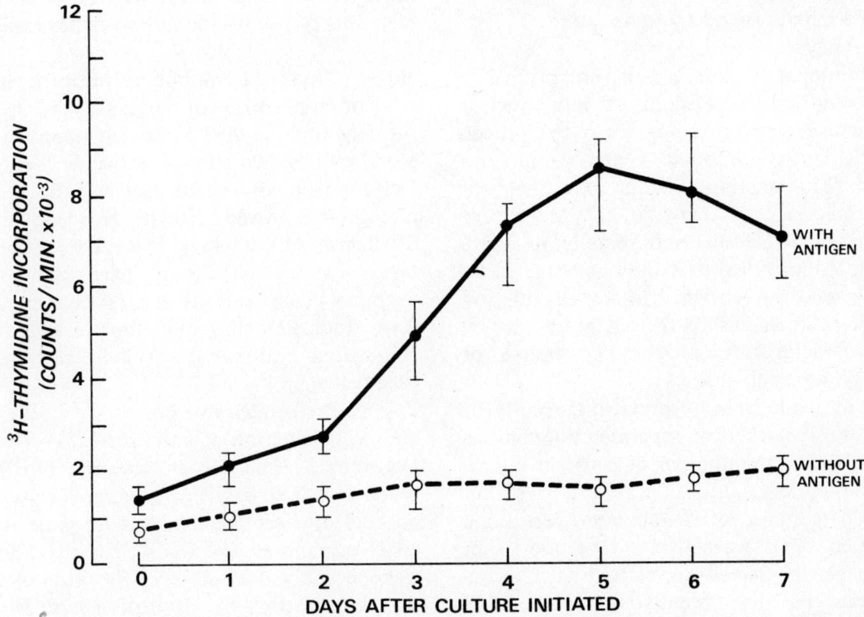

Figure 25–4. Time-response curve for antigen stimulation of 10^6 lymphocytes. Responses of peripheral blood lymphocytes from 15 normal adults with delayed hypersensitivity to the antigen. Cells were cultured as described in Fig 25–3. Antigen concentration for all cultures was 15 μg/ml. Maximal response occurred from 5–7 days of culture. Results plotted as mean ± the range for 15 individual determinations.

The terms T lymphocyte and B lymphocyte usually denote the functional entities of the 2 major classes of immunocompetent cells in peripheral blood. T lymphocytes arise in the *thymus* and migrate to peripheral lymphoid organs–lymph nodes, spleen, and blood–during embryonic life (see Chapter 7). B lymphocytes are influenced during embryogenesis by a functional–but as yet anatomically undefined–equivalent of the avian bursa of Fabricius. T lymphocytes function as effector cells in cellular immune reactions, cooperate with B cells to form antibody (helper function), and suppress certain B cell functions (suppressor function). After appropriate antigenic stimulation, B lymphocytes differentiate into plasma cells which eventually secrete antibody. The notion that there is only one type of T cell or B cell has become an oversimplification since subclasses of T and B cells are now recognized. Furthermore, rigid assignment of lymphocytes to one or the other of these classes is not always possible.

Assays for T and B cells are currently in wide use in clinical immunology. Precise counting of T and B cells in human peripheral blood has made important contributions to our understanding of (1) immunodeficiency disorders, (2) autoimmunity diseases, (3) tumor immunity, and (4) infectious disease immunity. It should be emphasized, however, that mere counting of T or B cells gives no specific information regarding the functional capacity of these cells. At best, these assays provide a nosologic classification of immunocompetent cells; further evaluation of lymphocyte function must be performed to fully assess immunologic competence in clinical practice.

Separation of Peripheral Blood Lymphocytes for T & B Cell Assays

Tests for human T and B cells are ordinarily performed on purified suspensions of mononuclear blood cells. The accepted procedure for obtaining cell suspensions is density gradient centrifugation on Ficoll-Hypaque. This method results in a yield of 70–90% mononuclear cells with a high degree of purity but may selectively eliminate some lymphocyte subpopulations. Mononuclear preparations obtained by this method are relatively enriched in *monocytes,* and these cells must be distinguished from lymphocytes by morphologic characteristics, phagocytic ability, or endogenous enzymatic activity.

In order to avoid misinterpretation, results of tests for T and B cell markers on separated populations should be expressed as the number of cells per microliter of whole blood. Many published studies have indicated only the percentages of lymphocytes carrying a particular marker. Such a result could be due to an increase in the particular cell population or, alternatively, a decrease in other populations. Thus, it is mandatory that each laboratory establish standard absolute numbers of T and B cells per microliter of whole blood from normal individuals.

T LYMPHOCYTE ASSAYS

E Rosette-Forming Cells

Human lymphocytes which bind sheep red blood cells to form rosettes are T cells (Fig 25–5). This marker is termed the E (erythrocyte) rosette and is currently the most widely accepted means of identifying human T lymphocytes.

A. Performance of E Rosette Test: Sheep red blood cells are mixed in ratios of 100:1 to 50:1 with purified peripheral blood lymphocytes suspended in a balanced salt solution supplemented with 10–25% serum. After brief incubation at 37 C and gentle centrifugation to pellet the cells, the tubes are incubated overnight at 4 C. The cells are then gently resuspended and the absolute number of E rosettes counted in a hemacytometer chamber.

B. Interpretation: Lymphocytes which bind at least 3 sheep red blood cells in normal peripheral blood are generally considered T lymphocytes. Dead cells do not form rosettes and can be excluded by vital staining with trypan blue. The percentage of E rosette-forming cells in normal blood is approximately 65–75%. Results in each laboratory test should be expressed in absolute numbers of T cells per microliter by calculation from the lymphocyte count in the original blood sample.

Recently, a modification of the E rosette test, called the "active" E rosette test, has been developed. Active E rosettes are those formed after a brief period of incubation of lymphocytes and sheep erythrocytes. Although it is claimed that the percentage of active E rosettes correlates better with in vivo cellular immunity, this contention requires further validation.

Human Thymus Lymphocyte Antigen; Hu-TLA

Immunization of animals with human T cells (usually thymocytes) can result in antisera which have specificity against surface antigenic markers of T cells. Development of potent and specific antisera by this method has proved difficult. However, the availability of such an immunologic reagent provides many advantages over E rosette assay, particularly the ability to examine tissue sections of lymphoid tissue and to perform double-labeling experiments with fluorochrome-conjugated anti-immunoglobulin antisera for B cells. (See below.)

A. Performance of Test:

1. Production of anti-Hu-TLA–T cells from various sources–especially thymocytes, purified peripheral blood T cells, T leukemia cells, or T cells from continuous culture–can be used for immunization of either goats or rabbits. The resulting antisera have both species-specific and T cell-specific antibodies. The former may be removed by absorption with B cells, liver, or kidney cells. Specificity must be shown by positive reaction with E rosette-forming cells and negative reaction with B cells.

2. Detection of T cell markers with specific antisera–Immunofluorescence of either live lymphocytes

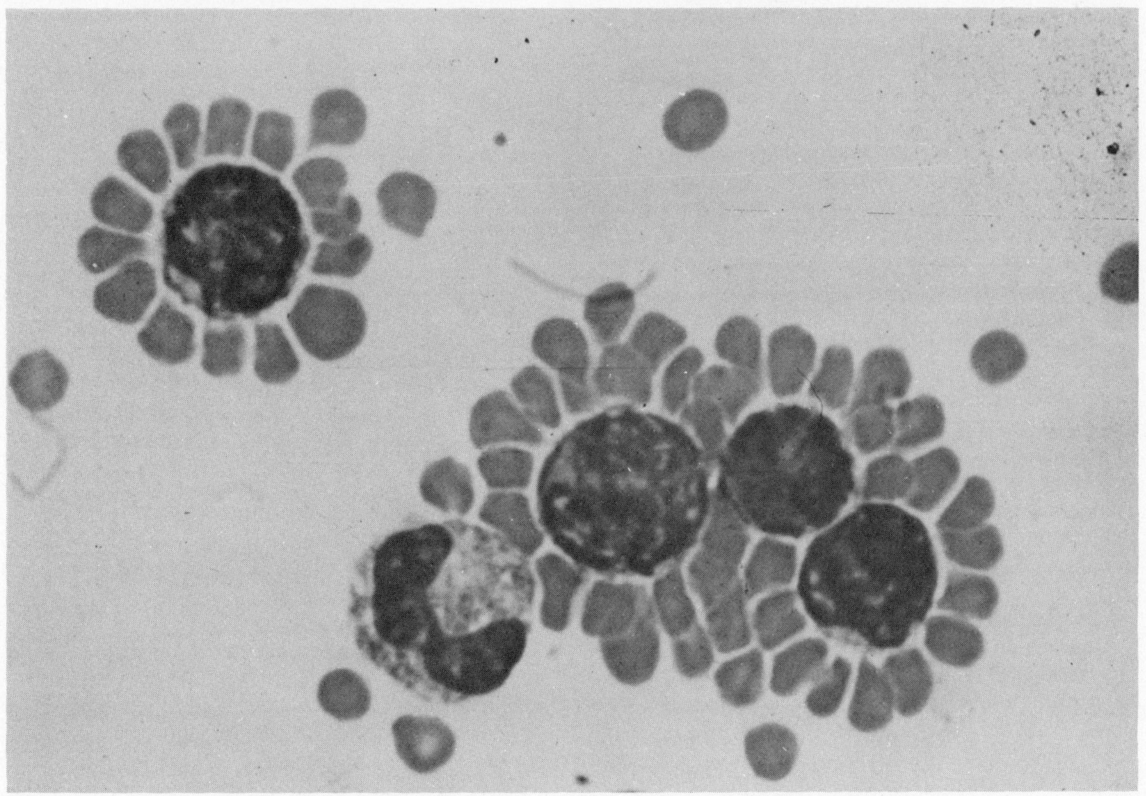

Figure 25–5. E rosette-forming cells. Lymphocytes from human peripheral blood which have formed rosettes with sheep erythocytes. Such cells are T lymphocytes. A granulocyte has failed to form a rosette. (Courtesy of M Kadin.)

or frozen tissue sections is possible. Direct immunofluorescence is performed with fluorochrome-labeled γ-globulin fractions from anti-T cell serum.

In vitro cytotoxicity of human T cells by specific antisera may also be used to estimate T cell populations. Methods for assessing T cell killing include trypan blue vital staining or ^{51}Cr release assay.

B. Interpretation: The number of T cells can be determined by their ability to bind specific anti-T cell antibody. This technic has the disadvantage of requiring a relatively expensive fluorescence microscope, whereas counting E rosette-forming cells requires only a simple light microscope. On the other hand, specific anti-T cell antisera can prove extremely valuable in identifying T cells in frozen tissue sections or inflammatory exudates. The use of a fluorescence-activated cell sorter has the potential for large-scale separation of human T cells from impure or mixed populations.

In general, the percentages and total numbers of T cells estimated by anti-Hu-TLA have been in agreement with those determined by E rosette test.

B LYMPHOCYTE ASSAYS

Surface Immunoglobulin

Lymphocytes with readily demonstrable surface immunoglobulin are B cells. This surface immunoglobulin is synthesized by the lymphocyte and under ordinary conditions does not originate from serum, ie, it is not cytophilic antibody. Lymphocytes generally bear monoclonal surface immunoglobulin, ie, immunoglobulin of a single H chain class and L chain type.

A. Performance of Test: Polyspecific antisera against all immunoglobulin classes permit detection of total numbers of B cells in a blood sample. Alternatively, a mixture of anti-κ and anti-λ antisera will detect total numbers of B cells. Monospecific antisera are developed by immunization with purified paraproteins and appropriate absorptions.

Tests for surface immunoglobulin-bearing B cells are performed by direct immunofluorescence with fluorochrome-labeled γ-globulin fractions derived from heterologous anti-immunoglobulin antisera. A major difficulty is to ensure the absence of all aggregated immunoglobulin in these test reagents (see below).

Generally, small amounts of anti-immunoglobulin antisera are mixed with purified lymphocyte suspensions for 20–30 minutes at 4 C. After removal of unbound immunoglobulin, the presence of surface immunoglobulin is determined by counting in a fluorescence microscope.

Table 25–4 summarizes data on the numbers of surface immunoglobulin-bearing B cells in normal subjects. In certain disease states, eg, systemic lupus erythematosus, antilymphocyte antibody may be bound to B or T cells in vivo. In order to prove that surface immunoglobulin is a metabolic product of that cell, enzymatic removal and resynthesis of surface immunoglobulin may be performed in vitro.

B. Interpretation: The percentages of IgG-bearing lymphocytes are in fact considerably lower than previously reported. Falsely high levels are detected owing to formation of IgG-anti-IgG complexes at the cell surface with bonding to B cells via the Fc receptor. When $F(ab')_2$ anti-IgG reagents were prepared, the percentage of IgG-bearing cells was reduced from 5% to less than 1%. Most investigators agree that IgM and IgD are the predominant surface immunoglobulins on human peripheral B lymphocytes.

EAC Rosettes (Erythrocyte-Amboceptor-Complement)

A certain percentage of lymphocytes contain surface receptors for complement. This B cell marker is most readily demonstrated by a rosetting technic similar to E rosette assay (see above). However, to avoid confusion with T cell rosettes, ox cells may be used which do not bind spontaneously to human lymphocytes. Ox red blood cells are coated with IgM antibody to red blood cells in the presence of complement which is deficient in C5 to avoid red cell lysis. These C- and antibody-coated erythrocytes are called EAC. The EAC are then incubated with separated lymphocytes, and rosetted cells surrounded by 3 or more EAC cells are considered positive.

The mean value for EAC rosette-forming cells from various laboratories is 15.4%, with a reported range of 10–19%. Since monocytes and polymorphonuclear leukocytes may also form EAC rosettes, other procedures are necessary to identify these cells. However, this test has the advantage of not requiring fluorescence microscopy.

Table 25–4. Surface immunoglobulin-bearing B lymphocytes in normal adult blood.*

Surface Immunoglobulin	Mean %	Range
Total Ig	21	16–28
IgG	7.1	4–12.7
IgA	2.2	1–4.3
IgM	8.9	6.7–13
IgD†	6.2	5.2–8.2
IgE‡	. . .	. . .
κ	13.9	10–18.6
λ	6.8	5–9.3

*From: WHO Workshop on Human T & B Cells. Scand J Immunol 3:525, 1974.

†IgD and IgM are frequently expressed on the same cell.

‡IgE B cells are extremely rare.

Table 25–5. Surface markers of human T and B cells.

Marker	Method
T cells	
E rosettes	Binding of sheep red blood cells
Anti-T cell antibody	Direct or indirect immunofluorescence or cytotoxicity study
B cells	
Surface immunoglobulin	Direct immunofluorescence
EAC rosettes (complement receptor)	Binding of complement and IgM-coated sheep or ox red blood cells
Aggregated immunoglobulin	Direct or indirect immunofluorescence
Anti-B cell antibody	Direct or indirect immunofluorescence or cytotoxicity study

Fc Receptor

B cells also have receptors for the Fc region of immunoglobulin. This receptor is capable of binding antigen-antibody complexes but not Fc regions of native immunoglobulin. Heat-aggregated immunoglobulin is also bound to the Fc receptor and forms the basis of this assay.

Human immunoglobulin is fluorochrome-labeled and then aggregated by heating at 63 C. The large aggregates are then incubated with separated lymphocytes and counted with aid of fluorescence microscopy. However, monocytes and polymorphonuclear leukocytes are also positive in this test. Normal values are 17.2%, with a range of 11–22%. Since a subpopulation of T cells also binds aggregated immunoglobulin, this test is of doubtful value as a selective B cell assay.

Anti-B Cell Antibody

Purified B cells can be used to develop heterologous antisera for B cell detection. Large numbers of homogeneous B cells can be obtained from the blood of patients with chronic lymphocytic leukemia. After appropriate absorption to remove anti-T cell and species-specific antibodies, this reagent is employed in either immunofluorescence or cytotoxicity assays as described above for anti-Hu-TLA. Tests for T and B cells are summarized in Table 25–5.

CLINICAL APPLICATION OF B & T CELL ASSAYS

Counting of B and T cells in peripheral blood and tissue specimens has widespread application in both the diagnosis and investigation of pathophysiologic mechanisms of many disease states. Current applications include the following:

(1) Diagnosis and classification of immunodeficiency diseases (Chapter 26).

(2) Determination of origin of malignant lymphocytes in lymphocytic leukemia and lymphoma (Chapter 28).

(3) Evaluation of immunocompetence and mecha-

nisms of tissue damage in autoimmune disease, eg, systemic lupus erythematosus and rheumatoid arthritis (Chapter 27).

(4) Detection of changes in cellular immune competence in cancer (Chapter 21).

NEUTROPHIL FUNCTION

Polymorphonuclear neutrophils (PMNs) are bone marrow-derived white blood cells with a finite life span which play a central role in defense of the host against infection. For many types of infections, the neutrophil plays the primary role as an effector or killer cell. However, in the bloodstream and extravascular spaces, neutrophils exert their antimicrobial effects through a complex interaction with antibody, complement, and chemotactic factors. Thus, in assessing neutrophil function, one cannot view the cell as an independent entity; its essential dependence on other immune processes, both cellular and humoral, must be taken into account.

Defects in neutrophil function can be broken down into 2 general categories: quantitative and qualitative. In quantitative disorders, the total number of normally functioning neutrophils is reduced below a critical level, allowing infection to ensue. Drug-induced or idiopathic neutropenia (see Chapter 28) with absolute circulating granulocyte counts of less than 1000/μl are examples of this sort of defect. In these situations, granulocytes are functionally normal but are present in insufficient numbers to maintain an adequate defense against infection. In qualitative neutrophilic disorders, the total number of circulating polymorphonuclear neutrophils is either normal or sometimes actually elevated, but the cells fail to exert their normal microbicidal functions. Chronic granulomatous disease is an example of this type of disorder (see Chapter 26). The cause of chronic granulomatous disease is unknown; what is known is that the normal or increased numbers of circulating neutrophils in such patients are unable to kill certain types of intracellular organisms.

Phagocytosis by polymorphonuclear neutrophils can be divided into 5 distinct and temporally sequential stages: (1) motility, (2) recognition, (3) ingestion, (4) degranulation, and (5) intracellular killing (Fig 25–6). The microbicidal activity of the neutrophil is the sum of the activity of these 5 phases. The clinical syndromes resulting from defects in many of the various stages in phagocytosis are discussed in Chapter 26. The laboratory tests used in clinical practice to evaluate phagocytic function in humans with various diseases will be discussed in terms of the 5 major steps in the process. It should be emphasized that for many neutrophil functions no standard assay exists. The following sections will include examples of useful clinical tests of neutrophil function.

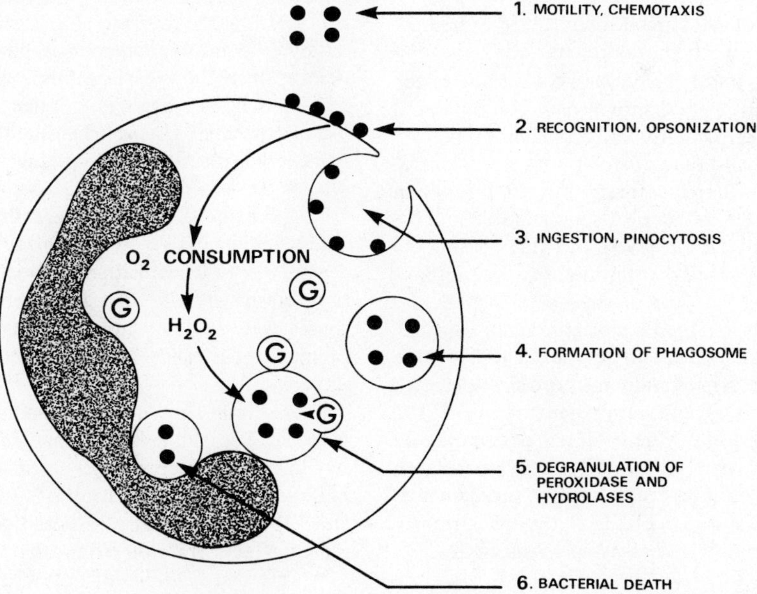

Figure 25–6. Steps in process of phagocytosis. Schematic representation of phagocytosis by a granulocyte. **1**: Bacteria attract phagocytic cells by chemotactic stimulus. **2**: Presence of opsonins (immunoglobulin and complement) facilitates recognition and surface attachment. **3**: Invagination of cell membrane with enclosed opsonized bacteria. **4**: Intracellular organelle, the phagosome, forms. **5**: Granules fuse with phagosomes and release enzymes into the phagolysosome. **6**: Bacterial death and digestion result. (Modified from Baehner: Chronic granulomatous disease. Page 175 in: *The Phagocytic Cell in Host Resistance.* Bellanti JA, Dayton DH [editors]. Raven Press, 1975.)

TESTS FOR MOTILITY

Neutrophils are constantly in motion. This movement can be either random or directed. Random or passive motion is the result of *brownian movement*. In *chemotactic movement* the cells are actively attracted to some chemotactic stimulus. Chemotaxins are produced by complement activation (C3a, C5a, $\overline{C567}$; see Chapter 6), by microorganisms themselves (endotoxins), and by other leukocytes (lymphocyte chemotactic factor). Relatively simple assays have been designed to assess leukocyte movement in vitro. Actually, an in vivo technic, the Rebuck skin window, preceded the development of in vitro assays and was one of the earliest methods developed for assessing leukocyte function.

Test for Random Motility

Random motility is tested for by the *capillary tube method*. Purified neutrophils in 0.1% human albumin solution at a concentration of 5×10^6/ml are placed in a siliconized microhematocrit tube. The tube is enclosed in a chamber specially constructed from microscope slides and embedded in adhesive clay. After being filled with immersion oil, the entire chamber is placed on the stage of a microscope. Motility is assessed by observing the leading edge of the leukocyte column in the microscope at hourly intervals. Measurements are expressed in millimeters of movement from the starting boundary of the packed leukocyte layer.

Test for Chemotaxis

Quantitation of directional locomotion of neutrophils toward various chemotactic stimuli is accomplished by use of a Boyden chamber. Cells to be tested are placed in the upper chamber and are separated from the lower chamber containing a chemotactic substance by a filter membrane of small pore size. Neutrophils can enter the filter membrane but are trapped in transit through the membrane. After a suitable incubation period, the filter is removed and stained and the underside is microscopically examined for the presence of neutrophils.

Although this method is theoretically simple, there are numerous technical difficulties. These include nonavailability of filters of standard pore size, observer bias in quantitation of migrating neutrophils in the microscope, loss of cells which fall off or completely traverse the filter, and failure of many workers to standardize cell numbers and serum supplements. Nevertheless, the Boyden chamber method is currently the most practical and useful assay of chemotaxis.

TESTS FOR RECOGNITION

As the neutrophil in an immune host approaches its target, either by random or directed motility, it recognizes microorganisms by the presence of antibody and complement fixed to the surface of the microorganisms. Enhancement of phagocytosis (opsonization) occurs under these circumstances.

Tests to detect the presence of complement and antibody Fc receptors on neutrophils are research tools and have no direct clinical applications. The need for either antibody or complement (opsonins) coating of microorganisms for phagocytosis can be determined by employing sera devoid of either or both of these factors followed by an assay for ingestion and subsequent intracellular killing. Furthermore, IgG and complement receptors on neutrophils as well as mononuclear phagocytes can be readily detected by rosette formation with IgG-coated or complement-coated erythrocytes. Such assays have not been widely applied clinically in the study of failure of host defenses against infection but have considerable promise for elucidating defects in the recognition phase of phagocytosis.

TESTS FOR INGESTION

Ingestion of microorganisms by neutrophils is an active process which requires energy production by the phagocytic cell. Internalization of antibody-coated and complement-coated microorganisms occurs rapidly following their surface contact with neutrophils. Since subsequent intracellular events–ie, degranulation and killing–depend on the success of ingestion, tests for ingestion provide a rapid and relatively simple means of assessing the overall phagocytic process. Unfortunately, the term phagocytosis has often been used to denote *only* the ingestion phase of the process. Thus, terms such as phagocytic index which refer to the average number of particles ingested really should be considered measurements of ingestion rather than of phagocytosis.

All tests to measure the ability of neutrophils to ingest either native or opsonized particles employ 2 general approaches. Either a direct estimate is made of the cellular uptake of particles by assaying the cells themselves, or the removal of particles from the fluid or medium is taken as an indirect estimate of cellular uptake.

Methods for quantitation of the ingestion of particles by cellular assays include (1) direct counting by light microscopy; (2) estimation of cell-bound radioactivity after ingestion of a radiolabeled particle; and (3) measurement of an easily stained lipid, eg, oil red O, after extraction from cells.

One disadvantage of many of these assays is that particles adherent to the neutrophil membrane are included as ingested particles. Other elements that influence results in performing ingestion assays include the presence of humoral factors (opsonins) which enhance uptake, the presence of serum containing acute phase reactants which depress uptake, the need for constant agitation or tumbling of cells and particles to maximize contact and subsequent uptake, the type or size of the test particle used, and, finally, the ratio of particles to ingesting cells. No well-standardized assay is currently available for estimating particle ingestion.

TESTS FOR DEGRANULATION

Following ingestion of particles or microorganisms, the ingested element is bound by invaginated cell surface membrane in an organelle termed the *phagosome*. Shortly thereafter, lysosomes fuse with the phagosome to form a structure called the *phagolysosome*. Degranulation is the process of fusion of lysosomes and phagosomes with the subsequent discharge of intralysosomal contents into the phagolysosome.

Degranulation is an active process and requires energy expenditure by the cell. Thus, impairment of normal metabolic pathways of the neutrophil—especially oxygen consumption and the metabolism of glucose through the hexose monophosphate shunt—interferes with degranulation and subsequent intracellular killing.

A test for degranulation called frustrated phagocytosis has recently been developed and applied to the study of some neutrophil dysfunction syndromes. The frustrated phagocytosis system (Fig 25–7) allows for examination of degranulation independently of ingestion. Heat-aggregated γ-globulin or immune complexes are fixed to the plastic surface of a Petri dish so that they cannot be ingested. Neutrophils are placed in suspension in Petri dishes with and without attached aggregated γ-globulin. The cell membranes of the neutrophils are stimulated by contact between γ-globulin and appropriate cell membrane receptors. This process results in fusion of intraleukocyte granules (lysosomes) with the cell membrane. As a result, intralysosomal contents are discharged into the suspending medium. The rate of release of lysosomal enzymes, particularly β-glucuronidase and acid phosphatase, is taken as an estimate of the rate of degranulation. Nonspecific cell death or cytolysis can be estimated by measuring the discharge of lactate dehydrogenase (a nongranule enzyme) into the medium. This assay system has been used to demonstrate retardation in the degranulation rate by neutrophils from patients with chronic granulomatous disease.

TESTS FOR INTRACELLULAR KILLING

The primary function of the neutrophil in host resistance is intracellular killing of microorganisms. This final stage of phagocytosis is dependent on the successful completion of the preceding steps: motility, recognition, ingestion, and degranulation. A variety of intraleukocytic systems make up the antimicrobial armamentarium of the neutrophil (Table 25–6). Obviously, a defect in intracellular killing could be the result of any one or a combination of these functions. However, in clinical practice only 2 assays have received widespread use, ie, the nitroblue tetrazolium dye reduction test and the intraleukocytic killing test. It is hoped that specific metabolic and antimicrobial assays for other intraleukocytic events will also become available in future.

Nitroblue Tetrazolium Dye Reduction Test

Nitroblue tetrazolium (NBT) is a clear, yellow, water-soluble compound that forms formazan, a deep blue dye, on reduction. Neutrophils can reduce the dye following ingestion of latex or other particles subsequent to the metabolic burst generated through the hexose monophosphate shunt. The reduced dye can be easily measured photometrically after extraction from neutrophils with the organic solvent pyridine. The

Table 25–6. Antimicrobial systems of neutrophils.*

Acid pH of phagolysosome
Lysozyme
Lactoferrin
Cationic proteins
Myeloperoxidase-halogenation system
Hydrogen peroxide
Superoxide radical

*For a further description of these systems, see Klebanoff SJ: Semin Hematol 12:117, 1975.

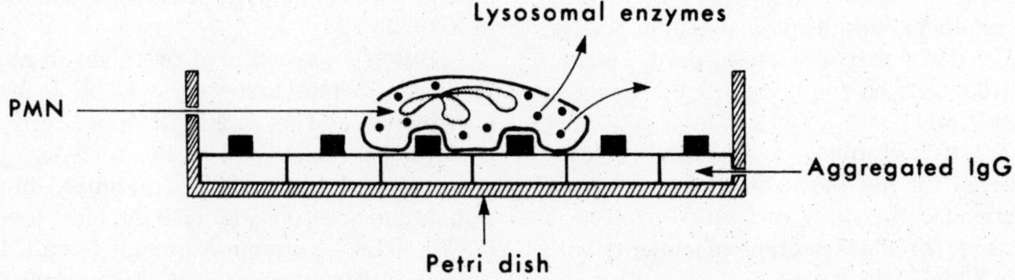

Figure 25–7. Assay of granulocyte degranulation by the "frustrated phagocytosis" method. Neutrophil is attached to aggregated IgG fixed to bottom of Petri dish. Lysosomal enzymes are discharged into supernate as the cell attempts to phagocytose the IgG but is "frustrated." (Courtesy of S Gold.)

reduction of NBT to a blue color thus forms the basis of the quantitative NBT test. The precise mechanism of NBT reduction is not known, but the phenomenon is closely allied to metabolic events in the respiratory burst following ingestion, including increased hexose monophosphate shunt activity, increased oxygen consumption, and increased hydrogen peroxide and superoxide radical formation. Since the generation of reducing activity in intact neutrophils parallels the metabolic activities following ingestion, NBT reduction is a useful means of assaying overall metabolic integrity of phagocytosing neutrophils. Failure of NBT dye reduction is a consistent and diagnostically important laboratory abnormality in chronic granulomatous disease. Neutrophils from these patients fail to kill certain intracellular microbes and fail to generate H_2O_2 or the superoxide radical.

Quantitative NBT Test

Isolated neutrophils are incubated in a balanced salt solution with latex particles and NBT. After 15 minutes of incubation at 37 C, the reduced dye (blue formazan) is extracted with pyridine and measured spectrophotometrically at 515 nm. The change in absorbance between cultures of cells that actively phagocytose latex particles and those that do not is taken as an index of neutrophil function. The test is strikingly abnormal in chronic granulomatous disease (see Chapter 26). Various modifications of the quantitative NBT test have been developed as screening tests for chronic granulomatous disease. Prominent among these are so-called slide tests in which neutrophils, latex, and NBT are placed in a drop on a glass slide and the reduction to blue formazan assayed under the microscope. It can be performed on a single drop of blood, but abnormal results should be confirmed with the more precise quantitative method described above.

NBT Tests in Diagnosis of Bacterial Infection

Since NBT dye reduction is enhanced by ingestion of latex particles, it has been reasoned that dye reduction should also be enhanced by phagocytosis of bacteria in infected humans. However, initial enthusiasm for the use of simple spontaneous NBT dye reduction assays, usually performed by the slide method, has been tempered by reports of false-positive or false-negative results in numerous diseases (Table 25–7). (The many factors responsible for these inappropriate results have been summarized by Segal in Lancet 2:1250, 1974.) It is not currently recommended that NBT tests be employed for the diagnosis of bacterial infection.

The NBT test performed by quantitative assay should be reserved for the diagnosis of chronic granulomatous disease, for the study of factors involved in phagocytosis, and for the detection of patients with intraleukocytic killing defects.

Neutrophil Microbicidal Assay

Many strains of bacteria and fungi are effectively engulfed and killed by human neutrophils in vitro. Assuming that all of the stages of the phagocytic process that precede killing within the phagolysosome are intact, microbicidal assays are extremely useful tests for neutrophil function. As an example, the bactericidal capacity of neutrophils for the common test strain 502A of *Staphylococcus aureus* will be described in some detail.

Bacteria are cultured overnight in nutrient broth to make certain that they will be in a logarithmic growth phase. They are then diluted to give about 5 bacteria per neutrophil in the final test. Neutrophils are separated from whole heparinized blood by dextran sedimentation and lysis of red blood cells with 0.84% NH_4Cl. Opsonin is provided as a 1:1 mixture of pooled frozen serum (−70 C) and serum from freshly clotted blood. Bacteria, neutrophils, and opsonin are incubated in tightly capped test tubes and tumbled end over end at 37 C. An aliquot of the entire mixture is

Table 25–7. Diseases in which false-negative and false-positive NBT tests have been reported.*

False-Negative	False-Positive
Pyogenic bacterial infection	Nonpyogenic infections
Arthritis	Fungal infection
Appendicitis	Malaria
Meningitis	Mycoplasma
Streptococcal pharyngitis	Parasitic disease
Systemic bacterial infection	Leprosy
	Toxoplasmosis
	Viral infections
Drug therapy	Drug therapy
Antibiotics	Oral contraceptives
Glucocorticoids	
Phenylbutazone	
Salicylates	
Immune deficiency diseases	Immune deficiency disease
Chronic granulomatous disease	Chédiak-Higashi syndrome
Glucose-6-phosphate dehydrogenase deficiency	
Hypogammaglobulinemia	
Lipochrome histiocytosis	
Myeloperoxidase deficiency	
Other conditions	Other conditions
Nephrosis	Behçet's syndrome
Premature infants (infected)	Hemophilia
Sickle cell disease	Inflammatory bowel disease
Systemic lupus erythematosus	Lymphoma
	Myelofibrosis
	Myocardial infarction
	Neonatal period
	Neoplasia
	Osteogenesis imperfecta
	Polycythemia vera
	Pregnancy
	Psoriasis
	Postoperative period
	Typhoid vaccination

*From Segal AW: Nitroblue tetrazolium tests. Lancet 2:1250, 1974.

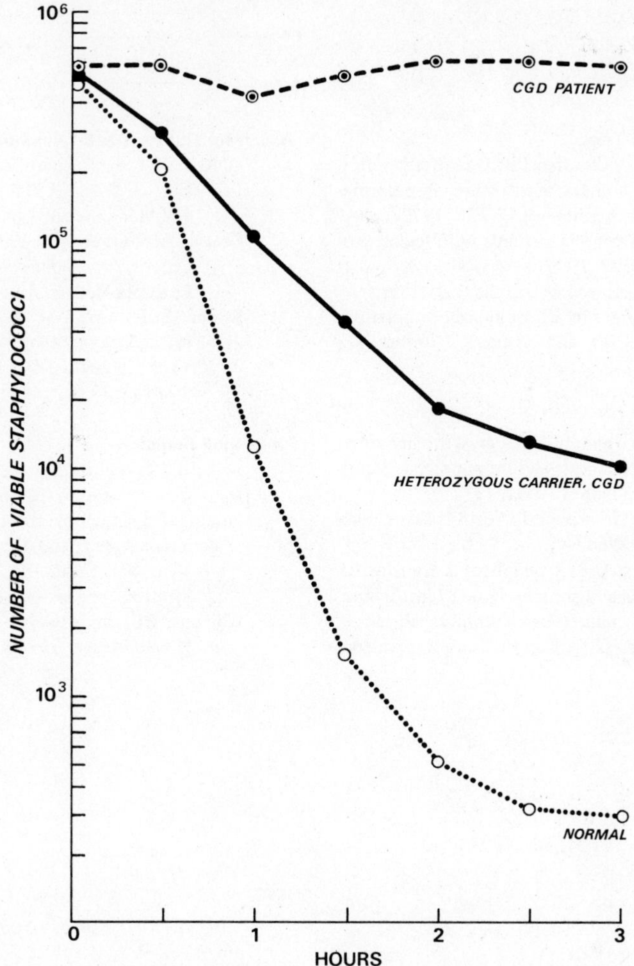

Figure 25–8. Bactericidal assay of granulocytes. Curves represent number of viable intracellular organisms which survive after being ingested by granulocytes. Note marked decline in bacterial survival in normal cells compared to reduced to absent killing by cells from patients and relatives with CGD (chronic granulomatous disease).

sampled at 0 time. After 30 minutes of incubation, antibiotics are added to kill extracellular bacteria. Aliquots of neutrophils with ingested organisms are sampled at 30, 60, and 120 minutes. Intracellular microorganisms are liberated by lysis of neutrophils by sterile water and the number of *viable* intracellular bacteria is estimated by serial dilutions and plating of lysed leukocytes. Results plotted as in Fig 25–8 show that normal neutrophils result in almost a 2-log reduction in viable intracellular *S aureus* within 1 hour after incubation. Killing is virtually absent in cells from patients with chronic granulomatous disease and intermediate in heterozygous carriers for this inherited group of diseases.

By varying the test organism or the source of opsonin, this assay can be effectively used to measure a wide range of microbicidal activities and serum-related defects. Obviously, falsely "normal" killing will be the interpretation of the results if cells fail to ingest organisms normally. Thus, an independent assay for microbial ingestion must be performed prior to the neutrophil microbicidal test.

Some diseases with defective microbicidal activity demonstrable with this assay are listed in Table 25–8. For further details, see Chapter 26.

Table 25–8. Disorders of neutrophil function.

Chronic granulomatous disease (X-linked or autosomal recessive)
Job's syndrome
Chédiak-Higashi syndrome
Myeloperoxidase deficiency
Glucose-6-phosphate dehydrogenase deficiency
Acute leukemia
Down's syndrome
Premature infants
Transient neutrophil dysfunction
Acute infections
Ataxia-telangiectasia
Cryoglobulinemia

• • •

References

Delayed Hypersensitivity Skin Tests

Catalona WJ, Taylor PT, Chretien PB: Quantitative dinitrochlorobenzene contact sensitization in a normal population. Clin Exp Immunol 12:325, 1972.

Heiss LI, Palmer DL: Anergy in patients with leukocytosis. Am J Med 56:323, 1974.

Palmer DL, Reed WP: Delayed hypersensitivity skin testing: 1. Response rates in a hospitalized population. 2. Clinical correlates and anergy. J Infect Dis 130:132, 138, 1974.

Lymphocyte Activation

Douglas SD: Human lymphocyte growth in vitro: Morphologic, biochemical, and immunologic significance. Int Rev Exp Pathol 10:41, 1971.

Ling NR: *Lymphocyte Stimulation.* North-Holland Publishing Company, 1968.

Oppenheim JJ & others: Use of lymphocyte transformation to assess clinical disorders. Page 87 in: *Laboratory Diagnosis of Immunologic Disorders.* Vyas GN, Stites DP, Brecher G (editors). Grune & Stratton, 1975.

Assays for Human T & B Lymphocytes

Aiuti F & others: Identification, enumeration and isolation of B and T lymphocytes from human peripheral blood. Scand J Immunol 3:521, 1974.

Greaves MF, Owen JJT, Raff MC: *T and B Lymphocytes: Origins, Properties and Roles in Immune Responses.* Excerpta Medica, American Elsevier, 1974.

Strober S, Bobrove AM: Assays for T and B cells. Page 71 in: *Laboratory Diagnosis of Immunologic Disorders.* Vyas GN, Stites DP, Brecher G (editors). Grune & Stratton, 1975.

Neutrophil Function

Bellanti JA, Dayton DH (editors): *The Phagocytic Cell in Host Resistance.* Raven Press, 1975.

Miller ME: Assays of phagocytic function. Page 127 in: *Laboratory Diagnosis of Immunologic Disorders.* Vyas GN, Stites DP, Brecher G (editors). Grune & Stratton, 1975.

Williams RC Jr, Fudenberg HH (editors): *Phagocytic Mechanisms in Health and Disease.* Thieme, 1972.

Section IV

Clinical Immunology

26 . . .
Immunodeficiency Diseases

Arthur J. Ammann, MD, & H. Hugh Fudenberg, MD

Four major immune systems assist the individual in the defense against a constant assault by viral, bacterial, fungal, protozoal, and nonreplicating agents which have the potential of producing infection and disease. These systems consist of antibody-mediated immunity, cell-mediated immunity, phagocytosis, and complement. Each system may act independently or in concert with one or more of the others.

Deficiency of one or more of these systems may be congenital (eg, X-linked infantile hypogammaglobulinemia) or acquired (eg, acquired hypogammaglobulinemia). Deficiencies of the immune system may be secondary to an embryologic abnormality (eg, the DiGeorge syndrome), may be due to an enzymatic defect (eg, chronic granulomatous disease), or may be of unknown cause (eg, Wiskott-Aldrich syndrome).

In general, the symptomatology of immunodeficiency is related to the degree of deficiency and the particular system which is deficient in function. General features are listed in Table 26–1 parts A and B. Features associated with specific immunodeficiency disorders are listed in Table 26–1 part C. The type of infections that occur often provide an important clue to the type of immunodeficiency disease present. Recurrent bacterial otitis media and pneumonia are common in hypogammaglobulinemia. Patients with defective cell-mediated immunity are susceptible to infection with fungal, protozoal, and viral organisms which may present as pneumonia or chronic infection of the skin and mucous membranes or other organs. Systemic infection with uncommon bacterial organisms, normally of low virulence, is characteristic of chronic granulomatous disease. Other phagocytic disorders are associated with superficial skin infections or systemic infections with pyogenic organisms. Complement deficiencies are associated with recurrent infections with pyogenic organisms.

Numerous advances have recently been made in the diagnosis of specific immunodeficiency disorders (Table 26–2). Screening tests are available for each component of the immune system (Table 26–3). These tests enable the physician to diagnose over 75% of immunodeficiency disorders. The remainder can be diagnosed by means of more complicated studies which may not be available in all hospital laboratories.

Arthur J. Ammann is Associate Professor of Pediatrics and Director of Pediatric Immunology, University of California School of Medicine, San Francisco. H. Hugh Fudenberg is Professor and Chairman of Basic and Clinical Immunology and Microbiology, Medical University of South Carolina, Charleston.

In addition to antimicrobial agents for treatment of specific infections, new forms of immunotherapy are available to assist in the control of immunodeficiency or perhaps even to cure the underlying disease. The usefulness of some of these treatment methods, such as bone marrow transplantation, may be limited by the availability of suitable donors. The discovery of enzyme deficiencies (eg, adenosine deaminase) in association with immunodeficiency offers a potential new avenue of therapy.

In the sections that follow, immunodeficiency disorders are discussed under 4 main categories: antibody or B cell deficiency, cellular or T cell immunodeficiency, phagocytic dysfunction, and complement deficiency. In general, the terminology used for specific deficiencies agrees with the classification recently

Table 26–1. Clinical features associated with immunodeficiency.*

A. Features Frequently Present and Highly Suspicious:
1. Chronic infection
2. Recurrent infection (more than expected)
3. Unusual infecting agents
4. Incomplete clearing between episodes of infection or incomplete response to treatment

B. Features Frequently Present and Moderately Suspicious:
1. Skin rash (eczema, candida, etc)
2. Diarrhea (chronic)
3. Growth failure
4. Hepatosplenomegaly
5. Recurrent abscesses
6. Recurrent osteomyelitis

C. Features Associated With Specific Immunodeficiency Disorders:
1. Ataxia
2. Telangiectasia
3. Short-limbed dwarfism
4. Cartilage-hair hypoplasia
5. Idiopathic endocrinopathy
6. Partial albinism
7. Thrombocytopenia
8. Eczema
9. Tetany

*Reproduced, with permission, from Ammann A, Wara D: Evaluation of infants and children with recurrent infections. Curr Probl Pediatr 5:11, 1975.

Table 26–2. Classification of immunodeficiency disorders.

I. Antibody (B cell) immunodeficiency diseases
- X-linked hypogammaglobulinemia (congenital hypogammaglobulinemia)
- Transient hypogammaglobulinemia of infancy
- Common, variable, unclassifiable immunodeficiency (acquired hypogammaglobulinemia)
- X-linked immunodeficiency with hyper-IgM
- Selective IgA deficiency
- Selective IgM deficiency
- Selective deficiency of IgG subclasses

II. Cellular (T cell) immunodeficiency diseases
- Congenital thymic aplasia (DiGeorge syndrome)
- Chronic mucocutaneous candidiasis (with or without endocrinopathy)

III. Combined antibody-mediated (B cell) and cell-mediated (T cell) immunodeficiency diseases
- Severe combined immunodeficiency disease (autosomal recessive, X-linked, sporadic)
- Cellular immunodeficiency with abnormal immunoglobulin synthesis (Nezelof's syndrome)
- Immunodeficiency with ataxia-telangiectasia
- Immunodeficiency with eczema and thrombocytopenia (Wiskott-Aldrich syndrome)
- Immunodeficiency with thymoma
- Immunodeficiency with short-limbed dwarfism
- Immunodeficiency with enzyme deficiency
- Episodic lymphocytopenia with lymphotoxin
- GVH disease

IV. Phagocytic dysfunction
- Chronic granulomatous disease
- Glucose-6-phosphate dehydrogenase deficiency
- Myeloperoxidase deficiency
- Chédiak-Higashi syndrome
- Job's syndrome
- Tuftsin deficiency
- "Lazy leukocyte syndrome"
- Elevated IgE, defective chemotaxis, eczema, and recurrent infections

V. Complement abnormalities and immunodeficiency diseases
- C1q, C1r, and C1s deficiency
- C2 deficiency
- C3 deficiency (type I, type II)
- C5 dysfunction

Table 26–3. Initial screening evaluation.

Antibody-mediated immunity
- Quantitative immunoglobulin levels: IgG, IgM, IgA
- Schick test: measures specific IgG antibody response
- Isohemagglutinin titer (anti-A and anti-B): measures IgM function

Cell-mediated immunity
- White blood count with differential: measures total lymphocytes
- Delayed hypersensitivity skin tests: measures specific T cell and macrophage response to antigens

Phagocytosis
- White blood count with differential: measures total neutrophil
- NBT: measures neutrophil metabolic function

Complement
- C3 and hemolytic complement quantitation (CH_{50}): quantitates complement activity
- C3 level: measures amount of important complement component

Table 26–4. Evaluation of antibody-mediated immunity.

Test	Comment
Protein electrophoresis	Use to presumptively diagnose hypogammaglobulinemia or to evaluate for paraproteins.
Radial immunodiffusion	Best procedure for quantitation of IgG, IgM, IgA, and IgD.
Radioimmunoassay	IgE quantitation.
Schick test	DTP immunization must be complete. Use to evaluate IgG function.
Isohemagglutinins	Use to evaluate IgM function. Titer > 1:4 after 1 year of age.
Specific antibody response	Use to evaluate immunoglobulin function. Tetanus, diphtheria, typhoid, etc. Do not immunize with live virus if immunodeficiency is suspected.
B cell quantitation	Measurement of the number of circulating B cells. Normal is 15–25% (total IgG-, IgM-, IgD-, and IgA-bearing cells).

proposed by a committee of the World Health Organization (Table 26–2).

ANTIBODY (B CELL) IMMUNODEFICIENCY DISORDERS

Antibody immunodeficiency disorders comprise a spectrum of diseases with decreased immunoglobulins ranging from complete absence of all classes to selective deficiency of a single immunoglobulin class. The degree of symptoms found in patients with antibody immunodeficiency disorders is chiefly dependent on the degree of antibody deficiency. Patients with hypogammaglobulinemia become symptomatic earlier and experience more severe disease than patients with selective immunoglobulin deficiency. Screening tests for the specific diagnosis of antibody deficiency disorders are readily available in most hospital laboratories (see Table 26–3 and Chapter 24) and usually afford early diagnosis with prompt institution of appropriate treatment. Newer procedures, such as counting B cells in peripheral blood, have permitted a more precise diagnosis of these disorders as well as a greater understanding of the causes (Table 26–4).

X-LINKED INFANTILE HYPOGAMMAGLOBULINEMIA

Major Immunologic Features

- Symptoms of recurrent pyogenic infections usually begin by 5–6 months of age.
- IgG less than 200 mg/dl with absence of IgM, IgA, IgD, and IgE.
- Absence of circulating B cells in peripheral blood.
- Patients respond well to treatment with γ-globulin.

General Considerations

In 1952, Bruton described a male child with hypogammaglobulinemia, and this is now recognized as the first clinical description of an immunodeficiency disorder. The disorder is easily diagnosed using standard laboratory tests which demonstrate marked deficiency or complete absence of all 5 immunoglobulin classes. Male infants with this disorder usually become symptomatic following the natural decay of transplacentally acquired maternal immunoglobulin at about 5–6 months of age. They suffer from severe chronic bacterial infections which can be controlled readily with γ-globulin and antibiotic treatment. The incidence of this disorder in the USA is not precisely known, but estimates in the United Kingdom suggest an overall incidence of one case per 100,000 population.

Immunologic Pathogenesis

Extirpation of the bursa of Fabricius in avian species results in complete hypogammaglobulinemia. The bursal equivalent in man has not been identified. Several investigators think that the bursal equivalent consists of gastrointestinal tract-associated lymphoid tissue, ie, tonsils, adenoids, Peyer's patches, and appendix. Other investigators consider that the bursal equivalent in man exists in the bone marrow, which provides a source of stem B cells. In X-linked infantile hypogammaglobulinemia, it is felt that this stem cell population is absent, resulting in complete absence of plasma cells and peripheral blood B lymphocytes.

Clinical Features

A. Symptoms and Signs: Patients with X-linked infantile hypogammaglobulinemia usually remain asymptomatic until 5–6 months of age, when passively transferred maternal IgG reaches its lowest level. The loss of maternal immunoglobulin usually coincides with the age at which these children are increasingly exposed to pathogens. Initial symptoms consist of recurrent bacterial otitis media, bronchitis, pneumonia, meningitis, and dermatitis. Many infections respond promptly to antibiotic therapy, and this response occasionally will delay the diagnosis of hypogammaglobulinemia. The most common organisms responsible for infection are pneumococci and *Haemophilus influenzae;* other organisms such as streptococci and certain gram-negative bacteria are occasionally responsible. Although patients normally have intact cell-mediated immunity and respond normally to viral infections such as varicella and measles, there have been reports of paralytic poliomyelitis and progressive encephalitis following immunization with live virus vaccines or exposure to wild virus. These observations suggest that some patients with hypogammaglobulinemia may also be unusually susceptible to some viral illnesses.

An important clue to the diagnosis of hypogammaglobulinemia is the failure of infections to respond completely or promptly to appropriate antibiotic therapy. In addition, many patients with hypogammaglobulinemia have a history of continuous illness, ie, they do not have periods of well-being between bouts of illness.

Occasionally, patients with hypogammaglobulinemia may not become symptomatic until early childhood. Some of these patients may present with other complaints, such as chronic conjunctivitis, abnormal dental decay, or malabsorption. The malabsorption may be severe and may cause retardation of both height and weight. Frequently the malabsorption is associated with infestation by *Giardia lamblia.* A disease resembling rheumatoid arthritis has been reported in association with hypogammaglobulinemia. This occurs principally in untreated infants or is an indication for more intensive therapy with γ-globulin.

Physical findings usually relate to recurrent pyogenic infections. Chronic otitis media and externa, serous otitis, conjunctivitis, abnormal dental decay, and eczematoid skin infections are frequently present. Despite the repeated infections, lymphadenopathy and splenomegaly are absent.

B. Laboratory Findings: The diagnosis of infantile X-linked hypogammaglobulinemia is based on the demonstration of absence or marked deficiency of all 5 immunoglobulin classes. Although a diagnosis can be established utilizing immunoelectrophoresis, specific quantitation of immunoglobulins is recommended, especially during early infancy. Total immunoglobulins are usually less than 250 mg/dl. IgG is usually less than 200 mg/dl, while IgM, IgA, IgD, and IgE are extremely low or absent. Rarely, patients have complete hypogammaglobulinemia except for the presence of normal amounts of IgE. It is unusual for patients with hypogammaglobulinemia to have depressed levels of IgG and normal levels of IgM or IgA. Before a diagnosis of hypogammaglobulinemia is established, there should be a demonstration of failure to make antibody following antigenic stimulation.

Isohemagglutinins which result from natural immunization are present in normal infants of the appropriate blood group by 1 year of age. Titers of anti-A and anti-B should be greater than 1:4 in normal individuals. Individuals who have received the complete series of DTP immunizations should react negatively to the Schick test. Previous γ-globulin therapy (within 1 month) may result in a nonreactive Schick test in a patient with hypogammaglobulinemia. Antibody to a specific antigen may be measured following immunization, but a patient suspected of having an immunodeficiency disorder should never be immunized with live attenuated viral vaccine. Although lymph node biopsies have been recommended in the past, with currently available diagnostic studies this would appear to be an unnecessary procedure. Rarely, in difficult cases, an intestinal biopsy may be necessary to assist in the diagnosis. In X-linked infantile hypogammaglobulinemia, there is a complete absence of plasma cells in the lamina propria of the gut. Studies of peripheral blood lymphocytes indicate a complete absence of circulating B cells with normal to increased numbers of T cells. Studies of T cell immunity indicate that this system is intact. Delayed hypersensitivity skin tests are usually positive; isolated peripheral blood lymphocytes respond normally to PHA and allogeneic cells (MLC); and there are normal numbers of circulating peripheral blood T cells.

C. Other Studies: X-ray of the lateral nasopharynx has been suggested as a method of demonstrating the lack of lymphoid tissue. It is doubtful that this information adds significantly to the findings on physical examination. X-rays of the sinuses and chest should be obtained at regular intervals to follow the course of the patient and to determine adequacy of treatment. Pulmonary function studies should also be performed on a regular basis, beginning as soon as patient cooperation can be obtained. Patients with hypogammaglobulinemia who have gastrointestinal tract symptoms should be investigated for the presence of *Giardia lamblia.*

Immunologic Diagnosis

Total immunoglobulins are less than 250 mg/dl; IgG is less than 200 mg/dl; and IgM, IgA, IgD, and IgE are markedly reduced or absent. B cells are absent in peripheral blood, and there are no plasma cells containing immunoglobulins in tissue and lymph nodes. Lymph nodes are markedly depleted in B cell-dependent areas. No antibodies are formed following specific immunization. T cell immunity is intact.

Differential Diagnosis

A diagnosis of X-linked infantile hypogammaglobulinemia may be difficult to establish in the age range of 5–9 months. By this time most infants have lost their maternal immunoglobulins and are susceptible to recurrent infections. The majority of normal infants during this time have levels of IgG less than 350 mg/dl but usually show some evidence of IgM and IgA production (usually greater than 20 mg/dl). If the diagnosis appears uncertain, several approaches may be utilized. Immunoglobulin levels may be determined again 3 months after the initial values. If there is an increase in IgG, IgM, or IgA, it is highly unlikely that the patient has hypogammaglobulinemia. Alternatively, the patient may be immunized with killed vaccines and specific antibody levels determined. The most difficult diagnostic problem is the differentiation of prolonged physiologic hypogammaglobulinemia from X-linked infantile hypogammaglobulinemia. In the former instance, the hypogammaglobulinemia may be severe enough to require treatment, and immunoglobulin levels may be identical to those of patients with congenital hypogammaglobulinemia. Normal production of immunoglobulins may not occur until as late as 18 months of age in patients with physiologic hypogammaglobulinemia. However, in most instances, these patients will begin to produce their own immunoglobulin despite concurrent γ-globulin administration. This is manifested by increasing levels of IgG as well as IgM and IgA. Since commercial γ-globulin contains less than 10% of IgM or IgA, a gradual increase in these values argues strongly against congenital hypogammaglobulinemia. The best way to avoid mistaking congenital hypogammaglobulinemia for prolonged physiologic hypogammaglobulinemia in infants is to carefully compare immunoglobulin levels with age-matched controls (see Chapter 24) and to obtain sequential measurements of immunoglobulins at 3-month intervals during the first year of diagnostic uncertainty.

Patients with severe malabsorption—particularly protein-losing enteropathy—may have severely depressed levels of immunoglobulins. In most instances, a diagnosis of protein-losing enteropathy can be established by the demonstration of a concomitant deficiency of serum albumin. Occasionally, however, patients with severe malabsorption and primary hypogammaglobulinemia may also lose albumin through the intestinal tract. Under these circumstances, a diagnosis can best be made by obtaining an intestinal biopsy. Patients with protein-losing enteropathy have normal numbers of plasma cells in the gut which contain intracellular immunoglobulins.

Polyarthritis may be a presenting feature in patients with hypogammaglobulinemia. Most patients with juvenile rheumatoid arthritis have elevated levels of immunoglobulins. Patients with arthritis and hypogammaglobulinemia usually respond promptly following institution of γ-globulin therapy.

Patients with chronic lung disease should also be suspected of having cystic fibrosis, asthma, or α_1-antitrypsin deficiency.

Treatment

Treatment schedules have varied. Commercial γ-globulin is the mainstay of therapy and is usually given in starting doses of 0.2 ml/kg as a single intramuscular dose. The final amount given and the frequency of injections should be regulated by the control of symptoms rather than a calculated amount or a particular serum level. Following the administration of an initial dose once a month, the amount given can be increased by 2–3 ml per injection. If the amount injected into a single site becomes too large, it may be divided and given in 2 sites at the same time. As amounts continue to increase, injections may be given every 2 weeks or every week. Some patients prefer weekly injections of smaller amounts rather than large monthly injections.

Anaphylactoid reactions to γ-globulin administration have been observed. These are not mediated through the classical IgE allergic pathway, since most patients with hypogammaglobulinemia entirely lack IgE. The chief causes of these reactions are aggregate formation in the γ-globulin preparation and inadvertent intravenous administration. Patients who have repeated reactions to γ-globulin should be treated with an alternative preparation obtained from a different commercial source. If patients continue to have reactions, it may be necessary to ultracentrifuge the preparation to remove aggregates prior to administration. Intravenous preparations of γ-globulin are not available in the USA but have been used in Europe. The reaction rate to these preparations is nevertheless high.

Additional therapy may be necessary in patients who fail to respond to maximum doses of γ-globulin. Because commercial γ-globulin contains primarily IgG and little IgM or IgA, some immunologists consider that there is a beneficial effect of monthly intravenous infusions of fresh-frozen plasma. To avoid the risk of hepatitis, a "buddy system" has been devised whereby the patient receives plasma from a single reliable donor. Alternatively, screening of plasma for HB_sAg should be done. γ-Globulin therapy should be continued if frozen plasma is used. Fresh-frozen plasma therapy may provide other antibacterial substances in addition to IgG, IgM, and IgA.

Continuous use of antibiotics may be necessary. Broad-spectrum antibiotics such as ampicillin in low to moderate doses may be effective in controlling recurrent infection. Physical therapy with postural drainage should be utilized in patients with chronic lung disease or bronchiectasis.

Occasionally, a patient with hypogammaglobulinemia may be discovered who has no symptoms. These patients should receive γ-globulin therapy even though they have not experienced repeated infection. Avoidance of infection with subsequent permanent complications is an important part of treatment in these patients.

Malabsorption, which is occasionally found in patients with hypogammaglobulinemia, usually responds to treatment with γ-globulin or intravenous fresh-frozen plasma (or both). If Giardia is found, it should be treated with metronidazole in doses of 35–50 mg/kg per 24 hours in 3 divided doses for 10 days in children and 750 mg orally 3 times a day for 10 days in adults.

Complications & Prognosis

Although patients with congenital hypogammaglobulinemia have survived to the second and third decades, the prognosis must be guarded. Despite what may appear to be adequate γ-globulin replacement therapy, many patients develop chronic lung disease. The presence of severe infection early in infancy may result in irreversible damage. Patients who recover from meningitis may have severe neurologic handicaps. Patients with severe pulmonary infection frequently develop bronchiectasis and chronic lung disease. Regular examinations and prompt institution of therapy are necessary to control infections and prevent complications.

TRANSIENT HYPOGAMMAGLOBULINEMIA OF INFANCY

Almost all infants go through a period of hypogammaglobulinemia at approximately 5–6 months of age. Under normal circumstances, maternal IgG is passively transferred to the infant beginning at the 16th week of gestational life. At the time of birth the serum IgG value of the infant is usually higher than that of the mother. IgA, IgM, IgD, and IgE are not placentally transferred under normal circumstances. In fact, the presence of elevated values of IgM or IgA in cord blood suggests premature antibody synthesis, usually as a result of intrauterine infection. Over the first 4–5 months of life, there is a gradual decrease in serum IgG and a gradual increase of serum IgM and IgA. The IgM usually rises more rapidly than the IgA. At 5–6 months, serum IgG reaches its lowest level (approximately 350 mg/dl). At this point, many normal infants begin to experience recurrent respiratory tract infections. Immunoglobulin values obtained at this age must be compared to those of normal infants of the same age. Occasionally, an infant may fail to produce normal amounts of IgG at this time, resulting in transient hypogammaglobulinemia or so-called physiologic hypogammaglobulinemia. The presence of normal serum levels of IgM or IgA argues strongly against a diagnosis of X-linked hypogammaglobulinemia. However, some infants with transient hypogammaglobulinemia may also fail to produce normal amounts of IgM or IgA.

Additional studies may be of no diagnostic usefulness, since many infants fail to respond to immunization at this age and isohemagglutinin titers may be low. Under these circumstances, a lymph node or intestinal biopsy may assist in establishing the diagnosis. Patients with congenital hypogammaglobulinemia lack plasma cells containing immunoglobulins in the intestinal tract and in peripheral lymph nodes. In addition, patients with congenital hypogammaglobulinemia lack circulating peripheral blood B cells. If the patient is not experiencing severe recurrent infection, it is possible to wait 3–5 months and repeat immunoglobulin measurements. In the presence of an increasing IgG, IgM, or IgA level, congenital hypogammaglobulinemia is unlikely. If the patient has been treated with γ-globulin to prevent severe or recurrent infection, then measurement of IgM and IgA assumes greater importance. Because commercial γ-globulin contains primarily IgG, the administration of γ-globulin will not affect serum levels of IgM and IgA. Increasing levels of these immunoglobulin classes indicate that the patient had transient hypogammaglobulinemia.

The cause of transient hypogammaglobulinemia is not known. In some cases, IgG anti-Gm antibodies have been demonstrated during the last trimester of pregnancy in women who have had infants with transient hypogammaglobulinemia. It is postulated that these antibodies cause suppression of endogenous immunoglobulin production in a manner similar to the suppression of normal red cell production in infants with passive transfer of antibody against Rh factors.

Occasionally, these infants become sufficiently symptomatic so that they must be treated just like those with X-linked hypogammaglobulinemia. γ-Globulin therapy may be required for as long as 18 months. Routine immunization should not be given during the period of transient hypogammaglobulinemia. Once a normal immune system has been established, the complete series of pediatric immunizations should be administered (see Chapter 39).

COMMON, VARIABLE, UNCLASSIFIABLE IMMUNODEFICIENCY (Acquired Hypogammaglobulinemia)

Major Immunologic Features

- Recurrent pyogenic infections with onset at any age.
- Total immunoglobulins less than 300 mg/dl, with IgG less than 250 mg/dl.
- B cells usually normal in number.

General Considerations

Patients with acquired hypogammaglobulinemia present clinically like patients with X-linked hypogammaglobulinemia except that they usually do not become symptomatic until 15–35 years of age. In addition to increased susceptibility to pyogenic infections, they have a high incidence of autoimmune disease. These patients also differ from patients with congenital hypogammaglobulinemia in that they have a higher than normal incidence of abnormalities in T cell immunity, which in most instances shows progressive deterioration with time. Acquired hypogammaglobulinemia affects both males and females and may occur at any age.

Immunologic Pathogenesis

The cause of acquired hypogammaglobulinemia is unknown. Recent studies have demonstrated an inhibitory effect of peripheral blood lymphocytes from patients with acquired hypogammaglobulinemia on the immunoglobulin synthesis of cells from normal patients. A suggested increase in suppressor T cells has been postulated as a cause of this disorder. Genetic studies have demonstrated an autosomal recessive mode of inheritance in certain families. In most instances, however, no clear-cut genetic transmission can be demonstrated. An increased incidence of other immunologic disorders, including autoimmune disease, has been observed in families of patients with acquired hypogammaglobulinemia. The presence of normal numbers of circulating peripheral blood B cells in most of these patients suggests that the disorder is a result of diminished synthesis or release of immunoglobulin rather than production of fewer immunoglobulin-synthesizing cells.

Clinical Features

A. Symptoms and Signs: In most instances, the initial presentation of acquired hypogammaglobulinemia consists of recurrent sinopulmonary infections. These may be chronic rather than acute and overwhelming, as in X-linked hypogammaglobulinemia. Infections may be caused by pneumococci and *H influenzae* as well as other pyogenic organisms. Chronic bacterial conjunctivitis may be an additional presenting complaint. Some patients develop severe malabsorption prior to the diagnosis of hypogammaglobulinemia. The malabsorption may be severe enough to cause protein loss with the subsequent development of edema.

Autoimmune disease has been a presenting complaint in some patients with acquired hypogammaglobulinemia. A rheumatoid arthritis-like disorder, systemic lupus erythematosus, idiopathic thrombocytopenic purpura, dermatomyositis, hemolytic anemia, and pernicious anemia have been reported in association with acquired hypogammaglobulinemia.

In contrast to patients with infantile X-linked hypogammaglobulinemia, patients with acquired hypogammaglobulinemia may have marked lymphadenopathy and splenomegaly. Intestinal lymphoid nodular hyperplasia has been described in association with malabsorption. Other abnormal physical findings relate to the presence of chronic lung disease or intestinal malabsorption.

B. Laboratory Findings: Immunoglobulin measurements may show slightly higher IgG values than are reported in infantile X-linked hypogammaglobulinemia. Total immunoglobulins are usually less than 300 mg/dl, and IgG is usually less than 250 mg/dl. IgM and IgA may be absent or may be present in significant amounts. The Schick test is useful to demonstrate lack of normal antibody response, but it should be performed following booster immunization with diphtheria antigen. Isohemagglutinins are absent or present in low titers (less than 1:10). The failure to produce antibody following specific immunization establishes the diagnosis in patients who have borderline immunoglobulin values. Live attenuated vaccines should not be utilized for immunization. Peripheral blood B lymphocytes are usually present in normal numbers in patients with acquired hypogammaglobulinemia—in contrast to patients with infantile X-linked hypogammaglobulinemia.

Although most patients with acquired hypogammaglobulinemia have intact cell-mediated immunity, a significant number demonstrate abnormalities as evidenced by absent delayed hypersensitivity skin test responses, depressed responses of isolated peripheral blood lymphocytes to PHA and allogeneic cells, and decreased numbers of T cell rosettes. Patients should be followed sequentially, as the immunodeficiency appears to progressively involve cell-mediated immunity, resulting in additional immunologic deficiencies.

Biopsy of lymphoid tissue demonstrates a lack of plasma cells. Although some lymph node biopsies demonstrate lymphoid hyperplasia, there is a striking absence of cells in the B cell-dependent areas.

C. Other Studies: Other tests which may be abnormal in these patients relate to associated disorders. The chest x-ray usually shows evidence of chronic lung disease, and sinus films show chronic sinusitis. Pulmonary function studies are abnormal. Patients with malabsorption may have abnormal gastrointestinal tract biopsies, with blunting of the villi similar to that seen in celiac disease. Studies for malabsorption may indicate a lack of normal intestinal enzymes and an abnormal D-xylose absorption test. Occasionally, autoantibodies may be found in patients who have an associated autoimmune hemolytic anemia or systemic lupus erythematosus. In pernicious anemia, autoantibodies are not found, but biopsies of the stomach demonstrate marked lymphoid cell infiltration. Associated lymphoreticular malignancies and thymomas have been described.

Immunologic Diagnosis

The total immunoglobulin level is less than 300 mg/dl, with IgG less than 250 mg/dl. IgM and IgA may be absent or present in significant amounts. The antibody response following specific immunization is absent. Isohemagglutinins are depressed, and the Schick test is nonreactive. Circulating peripheral blood B cells are usually present in normal numbers but may be depressed.

Cell-mediated immunity may be intact or may be depressed with negative delayed hypersensitivity skin tests, depressed responses of peripheral blood lymphocytes to PHA and allogeneic cells, and decreased numbers of circulating peripheral blood T cells. B cells may be normal or diminished in number in the peripheral blood. There is occasionally an increased number of null cells, ie, lymphocytes lacking surface markers for either T or B cells.

Differential Diagnosis

Occasionally the diagnosis of hypogammaglobulinemia in patients with infantile X-linked hypogammaglobulinemia may be delayed as long as 10 years. Because the treatment of infantile X-linked hypogammaglobulinemia and of acquired hypogammaglobulinemia is identical, this does not present a major clinical problem. Severe malabsorption associated with protein-losing enteropathy may be associated with hypogammaglobulinemia. These patients always have a simultaneous deficiency of serum albumin. A diagnosis of protein-losing enteropathy versus acquired hypogammaglobulinemia may be difficult under circumstances where protein-losing enteropathy is also associated with loss of lymphoid cells. In both groups of patients, depressed antibody responses and deficient cell-mediated immunity have been described. When the presenting feature of acquired hypogammaglobulinemia is an autoimmune disease, the diagnosis may be delayed to the patient's detriment. In most instances, however, patients with autoimmune disease have normal to elevated immunoglobulin values. Patients with chronic lung disease should also be suspected of having cystic fibrosis, chronic allergy, or α_1-antitrypsin deficiency.

Treatment

The treatment of acquired hypogammaglobulinemia is identical to that of infantile X-linked hypogammaglobulinemia. γ-Globulin, fresh-frozen plasma, and continuous antibiotics may be required in various combinations. Patients should be followed at regular intervals with chest x-rays and pulmonary function tests to determine adequacy of therapy. Pulmonary physical therapy is an essential part of treatment in patients with chronic lung disease.

Specific treatment of malabsorption problems may be required. Some patients respond to treatment with γ-globulin or with fresh-frozen plasma. In others, the malabsorption may be associated with secondary enzymatic deficiencies resulting in a picture similar to that of celiac disease. These patients may respond to dietary restrictions. If the malabsorption is associated with Giardia infection, metronidazole therapy should be as for infantile X-linked hypogammaglobulinemia (see p 335).

Caution should be exercised in the treatment of associated autoimmune disorders. The use of corticosteroids and immunosuppressive agents in a patient with immunodeficiency may result in markedly increased susceptibility to infection. Splenectomy has been used in the treatment of hypogammaglobulinemia and hemolytic anemia, but the mortality rate from overwhelming infection was high.

Complications & Prognosis

Patients with acquired hypogammaglobulinemia may survive to the seventh or eighth decade. Women with this disorder have had normal pregnancies and delivered normal infants (albeit hypogammaglobulinemic until 6 months of age). The major complication is chronic lung disease, which may develop despite adequate γ-globulin replacement therapy. An increased incidence of malignant disease has also been observed. Patients who develop acquired T cell deficiencies have increasing difficulty with infection characteristic of both T and B cell deficiencies. (See Table 26–1 parts A and B.)

X-LINKED IMMUNODEFICIENCY WITH HYPER-IgM

This syndrome, characterized by an increased level of IgM (ranging from 150–1000 mg/dl) associated with a deficiency of IgG and IgA, is relatively rare, and in most instances appears to be inherited in an X-linked manner. However, several cases have been reported of an acquired form which affects both sexes. The cause is not known. It has been postulated that in the normal individual there is a sequential development of immunoglobulins initiated by IgM production and subsequently resulting in the production of IgG and IgA (Chapter 11). Arrest in the development of immunoglobulin-producing cells after the formation of IgM-producing cells would be a possible cause.

Patients present with recurrent pyogenic infections, including otitis media, pneumonia, and septicemia. Some patients have recurrent neutropenia, hemolytic anemia, or aplastic anemia.

Laboratory evaluation reveals a marked increase in serum IgM with absence of IgG and IgA. Isohemagglutinin titers may be elevated, and the patient may form antibodies following specific immunization. Detailed studies of cell-mediated immunity have not been performed, but brief reports indicate that it is intact. Patients with this disorder may develop an infiltrating malignancy of IgM-producing cells.

Treatment is similar to that of infantile X-linked hypogammaglobulinemia. Because few cases have been reported, it is difficult to determine the prognosis.

SELECTIVE IgA DEFICIENCY

Major Immunologic Features

- IgA less than 5 mg/dl with other immunoglobulins normal or increased.
- Cell-mediated immunity usually normal.
- Increased association with allergies, recurrent sinopulmonary infection, and autoimmune disease.

General Considerations (See also Chapter 16.)

Selective IgA deficiency is the most common immunodeficiency disorder. The incidence in the normal population has been estimated to vary between 1:800 and 1:600. Considerable debate exists about whether individuals with selective IgA deficiency are "normal" or have significant associated diseases. Studies of individual patients and extensive studies of large numbers of patients suggest that absence of IgA predisposes to a variety of diseases. The diagnosis of selective IgA deficiency is established by finding an IgA level in serum of less than 5 mg/dl.

Immunologic Pathogenesis

The cause of selective IgA deficiency is not known. The presence of normal numbers of circulating IgA B cells suggests that this disorder is associated with decreased synthesis or release of IgA rather than absence of IgA B lymphocytes. Utilizing the concept of sequential immunoglobulin production (IgM → IgG → IgA) discussed in Chapter 11, selective IgA deficiency could result from an arrest in the development of immunoglobulin-producing cells following the normal sequential development of IgM to IgG. The variety of diseases associated with selective IgA deficiency may be the result of enhanced or prolonged exposure to a spectrum of microbial agents and nonreplicating antigens as a consequence of deficient secretory IgA. The continuous assault by these agents on a compromised immune system could result in an increased incidence of infection, autoantibody, autoimmune disease, and malignancy.

Clinical Features

A. Symptoms and Signs:

1. Recurrent sinopulmonary infection—The most frequent presenting symptoms are recurrent sinopulmonary viral or bacterial infections. Patients may occasionally present with recurrent or chronic right middle lobe pneumonia. Pulmonary hemosiderosis occurs with increased frequency in patients with selective IgA deficiency and may be confused with chronic lung disease.

2. Allergy—In surveys of atopic populations the incidence of selective IgA deficiency is 1:400–1:200, as compared to an incidence of 1:800–1:600 in the normal population. Although the reasons for this association are not known, the absence of serum IgA may result in a significant reduction in the amount of antibody competing for antigens capable of combining with IgE. It is also possible that patients who lack IgA in their secretions may absorb intact proteins with an enhanced susceptibility to the formation of allergic responses. Allergic diseases in patients with selective IgA deficiency are often more difficult to control than the same allergies in other patients. It has also been the impression of several immunologists that these patients' symptoms are "triggered" by infection as well as by other environmental agents.

An increased incidence of antibody to bovine proteins, including bovine immunoglobulin, has been found in patients with selective IgA deficiency. This has been interpreted as providing additional evidence for abnormal gastrointestinal tract absorption. However, removal of milk from the diet has not been clearly associated with amelioration of symptoms.

A unique form of allergy exists in these patients. Certain patients with selective IgA deficiency develop high titers of antibody directed against IgA. Following the infusion of blood products, many of these patients develop anaphylactic reactions. The incidence of antibodies directed against IgA in patients is much higher (30–40%) than the incidence of anaphylactoid transfusion reactions. Most patients who have anti-IgA antibodies have not had a history of γ-globulin or blood administration. Whether these antibodies are "autoantibodies" or antibodies resulting from sensitization is not certain. Possible sources of sensitization include breast milk feeding, passive transfer of maternal IgA, and cross-reaction with bovine immunoglobulin.

3. Gastrointestinal tract disease—An increased incidence of celiac disease has been noted. The disease may present at any time and is similar to celiac disease unassociated with IgA deficiency. Intestinal biopsies demonstrate an increase in IgM-producing cells. An anti-basement membrane antibody has been found with increased incidence.

Ulcerative colitis and regional enteritis have also been reported in association with selective IgA deficiency. Pernicious anemia has been reported in a significant number of patients. These patients have antibodies against both intrinsic factor and gastric parietal cells, which is not the case in hypogammaglobulinemia.

4. Autoimmune disease–A significant number of autoimmune disorders have been described in association with selective IgA deficiency. The disorders include systemic lupus erythematosus, rheumatoid arthritis, dermatomyositis, pernicious anemia, thyroiditis, Coombs-positive hemolytic anemia, Sjögren's syndrome, and chronic active hepatitis. Although the association of IgA deficiency and certain autoimmune disorders may be fortuitous, the increased incidence of IgA deficiency in systemic lupus erythematosus and rheumatoid arthritis is statistically significant (1:200–1:100).

The clinical presentation of patients with selective IgA deficiency and autoimmune disease does not appear to differ significantly from that of individuals with the identical disorder and normal or elevated levels of IgA. Because patients with selective IgA deficiency are capable of making normal amounts of antibody in the other immunoglobulin classes, they usually have characteristic autoantibodies associated with the specific autoimmune disease (antinuclear antibody, anti-DNA antibody, anti-parietal cell antibody, etc).

5. Selective IgA deficiency in apparently healthy adults–Because patients with selective IgA deficiency are capable of making normal amounts of antibody of the IgG and IgM classes, it is not surprising that many are entirely asymptomatic. However, long-term follow-up of some of these patients indicates that they may develop significant disease with time. There may be additional reasons why some patients remain asymptomatic. A small percentage of patients with selective IgA deficiency have normal amounts of secretory IgA and normal numbers of plasma cells containing IgA along the gastrointestinal tract. Some patients have increased amounts of low-molecular-weight (7S) IgM in their secretions. Finally, patients with selective IgA deficiency may have different exposures to pathogens and noxious agents in the environment.

6. Selective IgA deficiency and genetic factors–Both an autosomal recessive and an autosomal dominant mode of inheritance of IgA deficiency have been postulated. IgA deficiency appears with greater than normal frequency in families with other immunodeficiency disorders such as hypogammaglobulinemia. Partial deletion of the long or short arm of chromosome 18 (18q syndrome) or ring chromosome 18 have been described in selective IgA deficiency. However, many patients with abnormalities of chromosome 18 have normal levels of IgA in their serum.

7. Selective IgA deficiency and malignancy–Selective IgA deficiency has been reported in association with reticulum cell sarcoma, squamous cell carcinoma of the esophagus and lung, and thymoma. Several patients with IgA deficiency and malignancy also had concomitant autoimmune disease and recurrent infection.

B. Laboratory Findings: Selective IgA deficiency has been defined as a serum level of less than 5 mg/dl of IgA with normal or increased values of IgG, IgM, IgD, and IgE. Studies of B cell immunity indicate that these patients are capable of forming normal amounts of antibody following immunization. In most instances, absence of IgA in the serum is associated with absence of IgA in the secretions and with the presence of normal secretory component. Increased amounts of 7S IgM may be found in the serum and secretions. Abnormal κ/λ ratios are found. Evidence of abnormal antibody formation consists of an increased incidence of autoantibody, including antibodies directed against IgG, IgM, and IgA. The number of circulating peripheral blood B cells (including IgA-bearing B cells) is normal.

Cell-mediated immunity is normal in most patients. Delayed hypersensitivity skin tests, the response of isolated peripheral blood lymphocytes to PHA and allogeneic cells, and the number of circulating T cells are normal. In a few patients, a depressed level of T cells and diminished production of T cell interferon have been found.

Other laboratory abnormalities are those typical of the associated diseases. Individuals who have chronic sinopulmonary infection may have abnormal x-rays and abnormal pulmonary function studies. Patients with IgA deficiency and celiac disease have abnormal gastrointestinal tract biopsies, abnormal D-xylose absorption, and an increased incidence of antibody directed against basement membrane. Patients with IgA deficiency and autoimmune disease have characteristic autoantibodies–eg, anti-DNA, antinuclear, anti-parietal cell, a positive Coombs test.

Immunologic Diagnosis

Serum IgA and secretory IgA are absent in most patients. Some individuals have normal levels of secretory IgA. Other individuals have increased amounts of serum and secretory 7S IgM. The antibody response to specific antigens is normal. Studies of cell-mediated immunity, including delayed hypersensitivity skin tests, response of peripheral blood lymphocytes to PHA and allogeneic cells, and numbers of circulating T cells are usually normal.

Differential Diagnosis

Selective IgA deficiency must be distinguished from other, more severe immunodeficiency disorders associated with IgA deficiency. Forty percent of patients with ataxia-telangiectasia have selective IgA deficiency. These patients usually have cellular immunodeficiency as well. If IgA deficiency is found during the first years of life, a definitive diagnosis may not be possible because the complete ataxia-telangiectasia syndrome may not be present until the patient is 4–5 years old. Other immunodeficiency disorders which have been associated with selective IgA deficiency are chronic mucocutaneous candidiasis and cellular immunodeficiency with abnormal immunoglobulin synthesis (Nezelof's syndrome).

Treatment

Patients with selective IgA deficiency *should not* be treated with γ-globulin therapy, since they are capable of forming normal amounts of antibody of other immunoglobulin classes and may recognize injected IgA as foreign. The use of γ-globulin in these patients enhances the risk of development of anti-IgA antibodies and subsequent anaphylactoid transfusion reactions. There is as yet no means by which the deficient IgA can be safely replaced. Patients with recurrent sinopulmonary infection should be treated aggressively with broad-spectrum antibiotics to avoid permanent pulmonary complications. Patients with systemic lupus erythematosus, rheumatoid arthritis, celiac disease, etc respond to treatment (or not) in the same way as patients with the same diseases but no IgA deficiency. Transfusion reactions in patients with selective IgA deficiency may be minimized by several means. If the patient requires a blood transfusion, packed washed (3 times) red cells may be utilized. Although this does not completely eliminate the possibility of a transfusion reaction, it will decrease the risk. Alternatively, patients may be given blood from an IgA-deficient donor whose blood type matches the recipient's. Some immunologists have suggested frozen storage of the patient's own plasma and red cells for future use.

Complications & Prognosis

Patients have survived to the sixth or seventh decade without severe disease. Most individuals, however, become symptomatic during the first decade of life. Recognition of the potential complications and prompt therapy for associated diseases will increase longevity and reduce the morbidity rate. Regular follow-up examination is necessary for early detection of associated disorders and complications.

SELECTIVE IgM DEFICIENCY

Selective IgM deficiency is a rare disorder associated with the absence of IgM and normal levels of other immunoglobulin classes. Some patients are capable of normal antibody responses in the other immunoglobulin classes following specific immunization, whereas others respond poorly. Cell-mediated immunity appears to be intact, but detailed studies have not been reported in a sufficient number of cases.

The cause of selective IgM deficiency is not known. The absence of IgM with presence of IgG and IgA appears to contradict the theory of sequential immunoglobulin development (see Chapter 11). The disorder has been described in both males and females.

Patients are susceptible to autoimmune disease and to overwhelming infection with polysaccharide-containing organisms (pneumococci, *H influenzae*). Insufficient data are available to determine appropriate therapy. It would appear logical to manage these patients in a manner similar to the way an infant is managed following splenectomy, with immediate antibiotic (penicillin or ampicillin) treatment of all infections or with continuous antibiotic treatment.

SELECTIVE DEFICIENCY OF IgG SUBCLASSES

Several patients have been described with varying combinations of deficiency of the 4 IgG subclasses (IgG1, IgG2, IgG3, IgG4). Depending on the severity of the defect, the total serum IgG level may be normal or decreased. Serum levels of IgM and IgA are normal. Some patients respond with normal antibody production following immunization whereas others do not. All of the patients described suffered from repeated pyogenic sinopulmonary infections with pneumococci, *H influenzae,* and *Staphylococcus aureus.* Several patients reached the second decade of life before a diagnosis was established. All responded to treatment with intramuscular γ-globulin. The diagnosis is suggested by demonstrating an abnormal electrophoretic migration of IgG or by specific quantitation of IgG subclasses.

CELLULAR (T CELL) IMMUNODEFICIENCY DISORDERS

Immunodeficiency disorders associated with isolated defective T cell immunity are rare. In most patients, defective T cell immunity is associated with abnormalities of B cell immunity as well. This reflects the necessary collaboration between T and B cells before normal antibody formation to many antigens can occur. Almost all patients with complete T cell deficiency have some impairment of antibody formation. Some patients with T cell deficiency have normal levels of immunoglobulin but fail to produce specific antibody following immunization. These patients are considered to have a qualitative defect in antibody production.

Patients with cellular immunodeficiency disorders are susceptible to a variety of microbial agents including viral, fungal, and protozoal infections. The infections may be acute or chronic.

Screening tests utilized to evaluate T cell immunity are listed in Table 26–3. The availability of newer technics for the evaluation of T cell immunity has resulted in more precise diagnosis (Table 26–5) in many instances. (See also Chapter 25.)

Table 26–5. Evaluation of cell-mediated immunity.

Test	Comment
Total lymphocyte count	Normal at any age: >1200/μl.
Delayed hypersensitivity skin test	Used to evaluate specific immunity to antigens. Suggest candida, mumps, PPD, and streptokinase-streptodornase. (4 units per 0.1 ml.)
Lymphocyte response to mitogens (PHA), antigens, and allogeneic cells (mixed lymphocyte culture, MLC)	Used to evaluate T cell function. Results expressed as stimulated counts divided by resting counts equals stimulation index.
T cell rosettes (E-rosettes)	Used to quantitate the number of circulating T cells. Normal: > 60%.
Migration inhibitory factor (MIF)	Used to detect lymphokine released from sensitized lymphocytes, which causes inhibition of macrophage migration.

CONGENITAL THYMIC APLASIA (DiGeorge Syndrome, Immunodeficiency With Hypoparathyroidism)

Major Immunologic Features

- Congenital aplasia or hypoplasia of the thymus.
- Lymphocytopenia reflects decreased numbers of T cells.
- Absent T cell function in peripheral blood.
- Variable antibody function.
- Successfully treated with thymus graft.

General Considerations

The DiGeorge syndrome is one of the few immunodeficiency disorders associated with symptoms immediately following birth. The syndrome consists of the following features: (1) abnormal facies consisting of low-set ears, "fish-shaped" mouth, hypertelorism, notched ear pinnae, micrognathia, and an antimongoloid slant of eyes; (2) hypoparathyroidism; (3) congenital heart disease; and (4) cellular immunodeficiency. Initial symptoms are related to associated abnormalities of the parathyroids and heart which may result in hypocalcemia and congestive heart failure. If the diagnosis of the DiGeorge syndrome is suspected because of these early clinical findings, then confirmation may be obtained by demonstrating defective T cell immunity. The importance of early diagnosis is related to the complete reconstitution of T cell immunity which can be achieved following a fetal thymus transplant.

Immunologic Pathogenesis

During the sixth to eighth weeks of intrauterine life, the thymus and parathyroid glands develop from epithelial evaginations of the third and fourth pharyngeal pouches. The thymus begins to migrate caudally during the 12th week of gestation. At the same time, the philtrum of the lip and the ear tubercle become differentiated along with other aortic arch structures. It is likely that the DiGeorge syndrome is the result of interference with normal embryologic development at approximately 12 weeks of gestation. In some patients, the thymus has not been absent but is in an abnormal location or is extremely small, though the histologic appearance is normal. It is possible that such patients represent "partial" DiGeorge syndrome in which hypertrophy of the thymus may take place with subsequent development of normal immunity. The rapid reconstitution of immunity following thymic transplantation, the lack of GVH reaction, and the lack of cellular chimerism suggest that patients lack a thymic humoral factor capable of expanding their own T cell immunity.

Clinical Features

A. Symptoms and Signs: The most frequent presenting sign in patients with the DiGeorge syndrome is hypocalcemia in the first 24 hours of life which is resistant to standard therapy. Various types of congenital heart disease have been described, some of which result in early congestive heart failure. Some patients have the characteristic facial appearance described above. Patients who survive the immediate neonatal period may then develop recurrent or chronic infection with various viral, bacterial, fungal, or protozoal agents. Pneumonia, chronic infection of the mucous membranes with candida, diarrhea, and failure to thrive may be present.

Spontaneous improvement of cell-mediated immunity occasionally occurs. These patients are considered to have "partial" DiGeorge syndrome, but the reason for the spontaneous improvement in cell-mediated immunity is not known. Patients have also been suspected of having the DiGeorge syndrome on the basis of hypocalcemia and congenital heart disease with or without the abnormal facies but have been found to have normal cell-mediated immunity. Subsequently, these patients may develop severe T cell deficiency.

B. Laboratory Findings: Evaluation of T cell immunity can be performed immediately after birth in a patient suspected of having the DiGeorge syndrome. The lymphocyte count is usually low (less than 1200/μl) but may be normal. In the absence of stress during the newborn period, a lateral view of the anterior mediastinum may reveal absence of the thymic shadow. Delayed hypersensitivity skin tests are of little value during early infancy because sufficient time has not elapsed for sensitization to occur. T cell rosettes are markedly diminished in number, and the peripheral blood lymphocytes fail to respond to PHA and allogeneic cells.

Studies of antibody-mediated immunity are of little value in early infancy because immunoglobulins consist primarily of passively transferred maternal IgG. Although it is felt that some of these patients have a normal ability to produce specific antibody, the majority have some impairment of antibody formation.

Sequential studies of both T and B cell immunity are necessary, since spontaneous remissions and spontaneous deterioration of immunity with time have been described.

A diagnosis of hypoparathyroidism is established by the demonstration of low serum calcium associated with an elevated serum phosphorus and an absence of parathyroid hormone. Congenital heart disease may be diagnosed immediately following birth and includes right-sided aortic arch and tetralogy of Fallot. Other congenital abnormalities include esophageal atresia, bifid uvula, and urinary tract abnormalities.

Immunologic Diagnosis

T cell immunity is usually absent at birth as indicated by lymphocytopenia, depressed numbers of T cell rosettes, and no response of peripheral blood lymphocytes to PHA and allogeneic cells. Rarely, normal T cell immunity may develop with time, or previously normal T cell immunity may become deficient.

Some patients have normal B cell immunity as indicated by normal levels of immunoglobulins and a normal antibody response following immunization. However, some patients with the DiGeorge syndrome have abnormal immunoglobulin values and fail to make specific antibody following immunization. Live attenuated viral vaccines should be used neither to establish a diagnosis nor to attempt immunization because the infection that may result can be fatal.

Differential Diagnosis

Many infants with severe congenital heart disease and subsequent congestive heart failure develop transient hypocalcemia. These infants should be suspected of having the DiGeorge syndrome. When the characteristic facial features are found, in addition to the hypocalcemia and congenital heart disease, an even stronger suspicion is present. Studies of cell-mediated immunity will usually establish a diagnosis except in those infants with the DiGeorge syndrome who have developed effective cell-mediated immunity with time. It is essential that all infants with congenital heart disease and hypocalcemia be followed until they are at least 1 year of age. The hypocalcemia associated with the DiGeorge syndrome is permanent, in contrast to that seen in congenital heart disease with congestive heart failure. Congenital hypoparathyroidism is usually not associated with congenital heart disease. However, both in this disorder and in the DiGeorge syndrome, low to absent levels of parathyroid hormone are present and the patients are resistant to the standard treatment of hypocalcemia. Low parathyroid hormone levels may also be found in transient hypocalcemia in infancy.

Immunologic studies in a patient with the DiGeorge syndrome and in one with severe combined immunodeficiency disease may be identical in the newborn period. The presence of hypocalcemia, congenital heart disease, and an abnormal facies differentiates the DiGeorge syndrome from severe combined immunodeficiency disease.

Treatment

A fetal thymus transplant should be given as soon as possible following diagnosis. This can result in permanent reconstitution of T cell immunity. The technic of thymus transplantation varies from local implantation in the rectus abdominis muscle to implantation of a thymus in a Millipore chamber. The thymus may also be minced and injected intraperitoneally. Because patients with the DiGeorge syndrome have been observed to develop a GVH reaction following administration of viable immunocompetent lymphocytes, fetal thymus glands older than 14 weeks' gestation should not be utilized. Thymocytes from glands younger than 14 weeks' gestation may lack cells capable of GVH reaction but can provide needed stem cells for further T cell development.

The hypocalcemia is rarely controlled by calcium supplementation alone. Calcium should be administered orally in conjunction with vitamin D or parathyroid hormone.

Congenital heart disease frequently results in congestive heart failure and may require immediate surgical correction. If surgery is performed prior to the availability of a fetal thymus transplant, any blood given should be irradiated with 3000 R to prevent a GVH reaction.

Complications & Prognosis

Prolonged survivals have been reported following successful thymus transplantation or spontaneous remission of immunodeficiency. Sudden death may occur in untreated patients or in patients initially found to have normal T cell immunity. Congenital heart disease may be severe, and the infant may not survive surgical correction. Death from GVH disease following blood transfusions has been observed in patients in whom a diagnosis of the DiGeorge syndrome was not suspected.

CHRONIC MUCOCUTANEOUS CANDIDIASIS (With & Without Endocrinopathy)

Major Immunologic Features

- Onset may be either with chronic candidal infection of the skin and mucous membranes or with endocrinopathy.
- Delayed hypersensitivity skin tests to candida antigen are negative despite chronic candidal infection.

General Considerations (See also Chapter 33.)

Chronic mucocutaneous candidiasis affects both males and females. A familial occurrence has been reported, suggesting an autosomal recessive inheritance. The disorder is associated with a selective defect in cell-mediated immunity, resulting in susceptibility to chronic candidal infection. Antibody-mediated immunity is intact, resulting in a normal antibody response to candida, and, in some patients, the development of autoantibodies associated with idiopathic endocrinopathies. The disorder may appear as early as 1 year of age or may be delayed until the second decade.

Various theories have been proposed to explain the association of chronic candidal infection and the development of endocrinopathy. Initially it was felt that hypoparathyroidism predisposed to candidal infection. Subsequently it was found that many patients developed severe candidal infection without evidence of hypoparathyroidism. A basic autoimmune disorder has been postulated with the suggestion that the thymus also functions as an endocrine organ and that the thymus and other endocrine glands are involved in an autoimmune destructive process.

Clinical Features

A. Symptoms and Signs: The initial presentation of chronic mucocutaneous candidiasis may be either chronic candidal infection of mucous membranes, nails, and skin or the appearance of an idiopathic endocrinopathy. If candidal infection appears first, several years to several decades may elapse before endocrinopathy occurs. Other patients may present with the endocrinopathy first and subsequently develop candidal infection. Candidal infection may involve the mucous membranes, skin, nails, and, in older patients, the vagina. In severe forms, infection of the skin occurs in a "stocking and glove" distribution and is associated with the formation of granulomatous lesions. Patients are usually not susceptible to systemic candidal infection. Rarely, they may develop infection with other fungal agents.

Other symptoms are related to the development of a specific endocrinopathy. Hypoparathyroidism is the most common and is associated with hypocalcemia and tetany. Addison's disease is the next most common. A variety of other endocrinopathies have been reported, including hypothyroidism, diabetes, and pernicious anemia. Occasionally, there is a history of acute or chronic hepatitis preceding the onset of endocrinopathy.

B. Laboratory Findings: Studies of T cell immunity reveal a specific though variable defect in T cell immunity. Patients usually have a normal total lymphocyte count; isolated peripheral blood lymphocytes respond to PHA and to allogeneic cells and to antigens other than candida. The least severe T cell defect is an absent delayed hypersensitivity skin test response to candida antigen in the presence of documented chronic candidiasis. Other patients may have additional defects, including the inability to form migration inhibitory factor (MIF) in response to candida antigens or inability of lymphocytes to be activated by candida antigens. Antibody-mediated immunity is intact, as demonstrated by the presence of normal or elevated levels of immunoglobulins, increased amounts of antibody directed against candida, and autoantibody formation.

Other laboratory abnormalities are related to the presence of endocrinopathies. Hypoparathyroidism is associated with decreased serum calcium, elevated serum phosphorus, and low or absent parathyroid hormone. Increased skin pigmentation may herald the onset of Addison's disease prior to disturbances in serum electrolytes. An ACTH stimulation test is useful to document the presence of Addison's disease. Other abnormalities of endocrine function include hypothyroidism, abnormal vitamin B_{12} absorption, and diabetes. Abnormal liver function studies indicate chronic hepatitis. Occasionally, iron deficiency is present which, when treated, results in improvement in the candidal infection. Autoantibodies associated with specific endocrinopathy are usually present before and during the development of endocrine dysfunction. They may be absent when complete endocrine deficiency is present. Patients should be evaluated on a yearly basis for endocrine function because the endocrinopathies are progressive.

Immunologic Diagnosis

Major aspects of T cell immunity are normal, as indicated by a normal response of peripheral blood lymphocytes to PHA and allogeneic cells. Activation of lymphocytes and MIF production in response to antigens other than candida is normal. T cell rosettes are present in normal numbers. In some patients, only the delayed hypersensitivity skin test response to candida antigens is absent. Other patients have an absence of MIF production or an absence of lymphocyte activation by candida antigens. Plasma inhibitors of cellular immunity may also occur. B cell immunity is intact, with normal production of antibody to candida.

Differential Diagnosis

Children with chronic candidal infection of the mucous membranes may have a variety of immunodeficiency disorders. Detailed studies of antibody- and cell-mediated immunity differentiate between chronic mucocutaneous candidiasis, in which there is a selective deficiency of T cell immunity to candida antigens, and other disorders where cell-mediated immunity may be completely deficient. Patients with the DiGeorge syndrome (thymic aplasia and hypoparathyroidism) present early in infancy, whereas chronic mucocutaneous candidiasis with hypoparathyroidism is a disorder of later onset and progressive nature. Patients with late-onset idiopathic endocrinopathies should be considered to have chronic mucocutaneous candidiasis even though candidal infection is not present at the time of diagnosis. These patients may develop chronic candidal infection as late as 10–15 years after the onset of endocrinopathy.

Treatment

There is no treatment to prevent the development of idiopathic endocrinopathy. The physician must be alert to the gradual development of endocrine dysfunction—particularly Addison's disease, which is the major cause of death. Chronic skin and mucous membrane candidal infection is difficult to treat. Topical treatment with a variety of antifungal agents has been attempted but has usually been unsuccessful. Local miconazole therapy has provided control in some patients in recent trials. This drug has also been used intravenously on an experimental basis with some success. Courses of intravenous amphotericin B have resulted in improvement in a significant number of patients, but this form of treatment is limited by the renal toxicity of the drug. The combination of transfer factor therapy subcutaneously and amphotericin B intravenously has been successful in approximately 50% of patients. Transfer factor is obtained from normal candida skin test-positive donors and administered before or during–or both before and during–amphotericin therapy. A single patient, refractory to all other forms of therapy, was successfully treated with a fetal thymus transplantation.

Complications & Prognosis

Patients may survive to the second or third decade but usually experience extensive morbidity. Individuals with severe candidal infection of the mucous membrane and skin develop serious psychologic difficulties. Systemic infection with candida usually does not occur. Rarely, patients may develop systemic infection with other fungal agents. Hypoparathyroidism is difficult to manage, and complications are frequent. Addison's disease is the major cause of death and may develop suddenly without previous symptoms.

COMBINED ANTIBODY-MEDIATED (B CELL) & CELL-MEDIATED (T CELL) IMMUNODEFICIENCY DISEASES

Combined immunodeficiency diseases are due to various causes and are of variable severity. Defective T cell and B cell immunity may be complete, as in severe combined immunodeficiency disease, or partial, as in ataxia-telangiectasia. The association of distinct clinical features in ataxia-telangiectasia serves to further differentiate the disorder from severe combined immunodeficiency disease and also suggests that the causes of these disorders are not the same. Enzymatic deficiencies in the purine pathway have recently been described in association with combined immunodeficiency disease. This discovery has provided additional evidence for a diverse etiology of combined immunodeficiency diseases.

Studies of both T and B cell immunity are necessary to completely evaluate patients with combined immunodeficiency disorders (Tables 26–3, 26–4, and 26–5). In addition, analysis of red and white cell enzymes (adenosine deaminase and nucleoside phosphorylase) may provide additional information for appropriate classification.

The onset of symptoms in patients with combined immunodeficiency diseases is usually early in infancy. They are susceptible to a very wide spectrum of microbial agents. Immunotherapy is frequently difficult and often not available.

SEVERE COMBINED IMMUNODEFICIENCY DISEASE

Major Immunologic Features

- Onset of symptoms by 6 months of age with recurrent viral, bacterial, fungal, and protozoal infection.
- Occurs in both X-linked and autosomal forms.
- Complete absence of both T and B cell immunity.

General Considerations

The immunologic deficiency includes complete absence of T and B cell immunity, resulting in early susceptibility to infection with virtually any type of microbial agent. Patients rarely survive beyond 1 year of age before succumbing to one or more opportunistic infections. The disease is inherited in 2 forms: an X-linked recessive form (X-linked lymphocytopenic agammaglobulinemia) and an autosomal recessive form (Swiss-type lymphocytopenic agammaglobulinemia). The exact incidence of this disorder is not known, and many patients die before the diagnosis is made. Because the immune system of patients with this disorder may be made completely normal by bone marrow transplantation, early diagnosis is urgent to prevent irreversible complications.

Immunologic Pathogenesis

The basic defect is not known, but it has been postulated that severe combined immunodeficiency disease is a result of failure of differentiation of stem cells into T and B cells. The successful use of histocompatible bone marrow transplantation has provided support for the concept of a basic stem cell defect. However, some authors argue that the defect may reside in failure of the thymus and bursa equivalent to develop normally. Normal stem cells would not be processed into T and B cells under these circumstances.

Clinical Features

A. Symptoms and Signs: Patients with severe combined immunodeficiency disease usually succumb to overwhelming infection within the first year of life. Early findings include failure to thrive, chronic diarrhea, persistent thrush (oral candidiasis), pneumonia, chronic otitis media, and sepsis. The microbial agents which result in acute and chronic infection include viruses, bacteria, fungi, and protozoa. Infants with this disease are particularly susceptible to candida, cytomegalovirus, and *Pneumocystis carinii* infection. When smallpox immunization was administered routinely, many of these infants developed progressive vaccinia. Death from progressive poliomyelitis following attenuated viral immunization has been documented. During the first several months of life, patients may be partially protected from bacterial infections by the passive transfer of maternal IgG. They subsequently develop susceptibility to a wide variety of gram-positive and gram-negative organisms.

As these patients entirely lack T cell immunity, they are susceptible to GVH reactions which may develop following maternal infusion of cells during gestation or delivery, infusion of viable cells in the form of blood transfusions, or attempts at immunotherapy. (See section on GVH disease.) The presence of an acute or chronic GVH reaction may complicate the diagnosis of severe combined immunodeficiency disease. Some of these patients have been misdiagnosed as having an acute viral illness, histiocytosis X, or other chronic disorders.

Physical findings relate to the degree and type of infections present. Pneumonia, otitis media, thrush, dehydration, skin infections, and developmental retardation may be present. Lymphoid tissue and hepatosplenomegaly are absent unless the disease is complicated by a GVH reaction.

B. Laboratory Findings: All tests of T cell immunity are abnormal. The thymus shadow is absent, lymphocytopenia is usually present, T cell rosettes are markedly depressed, and the response of isolated peripheral blood lymphocytes to PHA and allogeneic cells is absent. Rarely, some patients have a proliferative response to allogeneic cells. Delayed hypersensitivity skin tests are not useful for diagnosis because in most cases insufficient time has elapsed for cellular sensitization to occur. During the first 5–6 months of life, a diagnosis of severe combined immunodeficiency disease may be difficult to establish because of the presence of maternal IgG. However, most normal infants who have had repeated infection will develop significant amounts of serum IgM or IgA (or both). If the diagnosis is doubtful, it may be necessary to specifically immunize a patient and determine specific antibody responses. Patients suspected of having immunodeficiency diseases should never be immunized with attenuated live virus vaccines. Assistance in the diagnosis may be obtained by counting peripheral blood B cells. In severe combined immunodeficiency, they are absent or markedly reduced from birth.

Biopsy of lymphoid tissue is rarely necessary to establish a diagnosis. If biopsies are obtained, they should be performed cautiously because secondary infection is frequent. Biopsy of lymph nodes (if they can be found) demonstrates lymph nodes severely depleted of lymphocytes without corticomedullary differentiation and without follicle formation. Biopsy of the intestinal tract shows a complete absence of plasma cells.

Patients who have pulmonary infiltrates that do not respond to antibiotic therapy or which are associated with rapid respiration and a low P_{O_2} should be suspected of having *P carinii* infection. Because this disorder can be treated, it is important to establish an early diagnosis. Some debate exists about whether the diagnosis is best made by means of concentrated sputum examination, bronchoscopy, needle biopsy, or open lung biopsy. In most instances, open lung biopsy provides the most complete information. Cytomegalovirus infection should be considered in all patients. Cultures of blood, mucous membranes, and stool for predominant bacterial organisms may be important in determining subsequent treatment. Individuals who have been inadvertently immunized with live poliovaccine should have stools cultured for poliovirus.

Patients frequently have anemia and lymphocytopenia. Complications such as chronic systemic infection and GVH reaction may result in multiple abnormalities including elevation of liver enzymes, jaundice, chronic diarrhea with subsequent electrolyte abnormalities and dehydration, pulmonary infiltrates, cardiac irregularities, and abnormal cerebrospinal fluid analysis.

Immunologic Diagnosis

Severe combined immunodeficiency disease is associated with complete absence of T and B cell immunity. Evaluation of T cell immunity reveals lymphocytopenia, absence of thymus shadow, depressed T cell rosettes, absence of peripheral blood lymphocyte responses to PHA, allogeneic cells, and antigens, and absence of response to delayed hypersensitivity skin tests. Evaluation of B cell immunity reveals hypogammaglobulinemia, absence of antibody response following immunization, and depressed or absent numbers of circulating B cells.

Differential Diagnosis

Severe combined immunodeficiency disease must be differentiated from other immunodeficiency disorders with defects in T and B cell immunity. The early onset of symptoms and the complete absence of both T and B cell immunity found in severe combined immunodeficiency disease usually result in a specific diagnosis. Several disorders associated with combined immunodeficiency and absence of enzymes in the purine pathway (adenosine deaminase and nucleoside phosphorylase) have been described. These disorders are usually less severe clinically and immunologically. The presence of a GVH reaction in severe combined immunodeficiency may complicate the diagnosis. If chronic dermatitis is present in association with hepatosplenomegaly and histiocytic infiltration, then a mistaken diagnosis of Letterer-Siwe syndrome may be made. Some patients may present with chronic diarrhea and pigmentary skin changes resulting in an erroneous diagnosis of acrodermatitis enteropathica. (See discussion of GVH disease.)

Treatment

Aggressive diagnostic measures are necessary to establish the cause of chronic infection before treatment can be instituted. Open lung biopsy should be performed if *P carinii* infection is suspected. The treatment of choice for pneumocystis consists of pentamidine. Specific antibiotic treatment is necessary for suspected bacterial infection. Superficial candidal infection is treated with topical antifungal agents, but systemic infection requires intravenous amphotericin B therapy.

Complications must be avoided. Live attenuated viral immunization should not be performed. Blood products containing potentially viable lymphocytes should be irradiated with 3000–6000 R prior to administration.

During the initial period of evaluation, γ-globulin may be administered in doses of 0.2–0.4 ml/kg. Definitive treatment consists of transplantation of histocompatible bone marrow. Because of the inheritance of the histocompatibility antigens, the usual donor for a bone marrow transplant is a histocompatible sibling. The bone marrow must be matched by both the HLA and MLC tests. (See Chapters 15 and 28.) Despite careful matching, a GVH reaction may develop. Several technics have been utilized in performing bone marrow transplantation, including intraperitoneal injection and intravenous infusion of filtered bone marrow. The dose of bone marrow cells administered has varied, but as few as 1000 nucleated cells per kilogram have resulted in successful immunologic reconstitution. Transplantation of unmatched marrow has always resulted in a fatal GVH reaction. Recently, some investigators have utilized HLA-nonidentical, MLC-identical bone marrow. Insufficient data exist about the efficacy of this method.

In the absence of a histocompatible bone marrow donor, other forms of therapy have been utilized. Long-term survivors of fetal liver transplants (less than 8 weeks' gestation) and of fetal thymus transplantation (less than 14 weeks' gestation) have been observed. In both of these technics, the use of older fetal liver or thymus will result in a fatal GVH reaction, probably because of the presence of mature histocompatible cells.

Complications & Prognosis

Patients with severe combined immunodeficiency disease are unusually susceptible to infection with many microbial agents and will succumb prior to 1 year of age if untreated. If the diagnosis is not made immediately, the patient may receive live attenuated viral immunization and succumb to progressive vaccinia or poliomyelitis. In other instances, patients may receive unirradiated blood products and die from complications of GVH disease. Following successful bone marrow transplantation, 10-year survivals with maintenance of normal T and B cell function have been recorded. Patients have survived as long as 1 year following fetal liver transplantation and as long as 4 years following fetal thymus transplantation. The reconstitution of immunity in patients receiving fetal organ transplantation has not been complete.

CELLULAR IMMUNODEFICIENCY WITH ABNORMAL IMMUNOGLOBULIN SYNTHESIS (Nezelof's Syndrome)

Major Immunologic Features

- Susceptibility to viral, bacterial, fungal, and protozoal infection.
- Absent to depressed T cell immunity.
- Various degrees of antibody immunodeficiency associated with various combinations of increased, normal, or decreased immunoglobulin levels.

General Considerations

The disorders included in this classification are diverse and probably do not all have the same cause. Consistent features include marked deficiency of T cell immunity and varying degrees of deficiency of B cell immunity. Disorders with specific clinical symptomatology such as ataxia-telangiectasia and Wiskott-Aldrich syndrome are excluded. Part of the difficulty in defining disorders in this category relates to recent developments in the diagnosis of T cell immunity which were not available when some of these cases were first reported. An example would be Nezelof's syndrome, which was reported before detailed studies of T cell immunity became available. Most of the cases included in this category are sporadic and do not have a definite inherited pattern.

Immunologic Pathogenesis

The cause is not known. There appears to be no specific genetic pattern, and the disease is sporadic in distribution and occurs in both males and females. The presence of moderate to severe deficiencies of T cell immunity with varying degrees of B cell immunodeficiency suggests that the primary defect is within the thymus. It is possible that this disorder is the result of thymic hypoplasia with deficient interaction of T and B cells and subsequent abnormal antibody formation.

Clinical Features

A. Symptoms and Signs: Patients are susceptible to recurrent fungal, protozoal, viral, and bacterial illnesses. The spectrum of infection is similar to that found in patients with congenital hypogammaglobulinemia and other forms of combined immunodeficiency. Patients frequently have marked lymphadenopathy and hepatosplenomegaly, in contrast to patients with congenital hypogammaglobulinemia and severe combined immunodeficiency disease.

B. Laboratory Findings: Studies of T cell immunity are abnormal, but the degree of deficiency may vary. Lymphocytopenia may be present, but occasionally a normal lymphocyte count is obtained. T cells are moderately to markedly decreased. The lymphocyte response to PHA and specific antigens may be absent or slightly depressed, and the lymphocyte response to allogeneic cells may vary from nil to normal. B cell immunity is abnormal. The 5 immunoglobulin classes may be present in varying combinations of increased, normal, or decreased amounts. Total circulating B cells are usually present in normal numbers, although the distribution among various types of surface immunoglobulin-bearing B cells may vary. Despite the presence of normal or elevated levels of immunoglobulin, there is no antibody response following specific immunization. Antibody to specific substances may be found, however, indicating that at one time some of these patients may have been able to form antibody. Isohemagglutinins may be absent or normal, and the Schick test may be reactive or nonreactive.

Biopsy of lymphoid tissue in these patients may reveal the presence of plasma cells. The lymph nodes may be large and may contain numerous histiocytes and macrophages with granuloma formation.

Immunologic Diagnosis

The principal immunologic features in this group of disorders consist of moderate to marked reductions in numbers of total lymphocytes and T cell rosettes and a diminished response of isolated peripheral blood lymphocytes to PHA, allogeneic cells, and specific antigens. There is usually no response to delayed hypersensitivity skin tests. Variable degrees of B cell deficiency are present, consisting of varying combinations of elevated, normal, or low levels of specific immunoglobulin classes. The antibody response to specific antigens is usually absent. Some evidence of prior antibody formation may be found, eg, nonreactive Schick test, isohemagglutinins. The number of total circulating B cells is usually normal.

Differential Diagnosis

Because there is a lack of uniformity in the clinical and laboratory presentation of these patients, it is necessary to rule out other disorders with definite clinical or laboratory associations. The clinical features of ataxia-telangiectasia are usually present by 3–4 years of age. Patients with Wiskott-Aldrich syndrome have thrombocytopenia from birth and can be excluded on this basis. Patients with severe combined immunodeficiency disease have complete absence of T and B cell immunity. Immunodeficiency disorders associated with enzyme deficiencies may have a similar presentation and are excluded on the basis of enzyme analysis of red or white blood cells. Patients with short-limbed dwarfism are excluded on the basis of characteristic clinical and radiologic features. Patients with cellular immunodeficiency and abnormal immunoglobulin synthesis do not develop endocrine abnormalities and are therefore easily distinguished from patients with the DiGeorge syndrome and chronic mucocutaneous candidiasis who are capable of normal antibody synthesis.

Treatment

Aggressive treatment of infection is necessary. If the patient fails to demonstrate an antibody response following immunization (even if immunoglobulin levels are normal), he should be treated with monthly γ-globulin administration. (See treatment section, congenital hypogammaglobulinemia.) Continuous broad-spectrum antibiotic coverage may be useful in specific instances. Postural drainage is important for the prevention of chronic lung disease.

Although histocompatible bone marrow transplantation would appear to be curative in these patients, few successful cases have been reported. This appears to be due to lack of histocompatible donors rather than the complications of transplantation. Transfer factor therapy has been utilized with some success. Thymus transplantation has been reported to provide reconstitution of T cell immunity and partial reconstitution of B cell immunity.

Complications & Prognosis

Patients do not develop the severe complications observed in severe combined immunodeficiency disease. GVH reaction has not been reported. Some of these patients, however, may develop progressive encephalitis following live attenuated viral immunization. Chronic lung disease, chronic fungal infection, and later development of malignancy are long-term complications. Survival until age 18 has been reported.

IMMUNODEFICIENCY WITH ATAXIA-TELANGIECTASIA

Major Immunologic Features

- Clinical onset by 2 years of age.
- Complete syndrome consists of ataxia, telangiectasia, and recurrent sinopulmonary infection.
- Selective IgA deficiency present in 40% of patients.

General Considerations

Ataxia-telangiectasia is inherited in an autosomal manner. It is associated with characteristic features, including ataxia, telangiectasis, recurrent sinopulmonary infection, and abnormalities in both T and B cell immunity. The disorder was first considered to be primarily a neurologic disease and is now known to involve the vascular, endocrine, and immune systems.

There is no unifying theory which explains the multisystem abnormalities present in ataxia-telangiectasia. A defect in the development of mesoderm has been postulated but not confirmed. The disorder is progressive, with both the neurologic abnormalities and the immunologic deficiency becoming more severe with time.

Clinical Features

A. Symptoms and Signs: Ataxia may have its onset at 9 months to 1 year of age or may be delayed as long as 4–6 years. Telangiectases are usually present by 2 years of age but have been delayed until 8–9 years of age. As patients become older, additional neurologic symptoms develop, consisting of choreoathetoid movements, dysconjugate gaze, and extrapyramidal and posterior column signs. Telangiectasia may develop first in the bulbar conjunctiva and subsequently appear on the bridge of the nose, the ears, or in the antecubital fossae. Recurrent sinopulmonary infections may begin early in life, or patients may remain relatively symptom-free for 10 years or more. Susceptibility to infection includes both viral and bacterial infections. Secondary sexual characteristics rarely develop in patients at puberty, and most patients appear to develop mental retardation with time.

B. Laboratory Findings: Varying degrees of abnormalities in T and B cell immunity have been described. Lymphocytopenia may be present, T cell rosettes may be normal or decreased, and the response of lymphocytes to PHA and allogeneic cells may be normal or decreased. There may be no response to delayed hypersensitivity skin tests. Serum IgA is absent in approximately 40% of patients. In still other patients, IgE may be absent. Antibody responses to specific antigens may be depressed. The number of circulating B cells is usually normal.

Other laboratory abnormalities relate to associated findings. Abnormalities have been shown on pneumoencephalography, electromyography, and electroencephalography. Endocrine studies have shown decreased excretion of 17-ketosteroids and FSH. An insulin-resistant form of diabetes has been described. Liver function tests are abnormal. An increased incidence of autoantibodies has been found. Increased levels of α-fetoprotein have been described.

Immunologic Diagnosis

Selective IgA deficiency is found in 40% of patients. IgE deficiency and variable deficiencies of other immunoglobulins may also be found. The antibody response to specific antigens may be depressed. Variable degrees of T cell deficiency are observed which usually become more severe with advancing age.

Differential Diagnosis

If the onset of recurrent infection occurs before the development of ataxia or telangiectasia, it may be difficult to differentiate this disorder from cellular immunodeficiency with abnormal immunoglobulin synthesis. If a patient has a gradual onset of cerebellar ataxia unassociated with telangiectasis and immunologic abnormalities, one may have to wait years before a diagnosis can be established with certainty. Usually, by age 4, the characteristic recurrent sinopulmonary infections, immunologic abnormalities, ataxia, and telangiectasia are present concomitantly. Because selective IgA deficiency is the most common immunodeficiency disorder detected and many patients with selective IgA deficiency have no associated symptomatology, one may have to wait several years before a diagnosis of ataxia-telangiectasia can be excluded.

Treatment

Early treatment of recurrent sinopulmonary infections is essential to avoid permanent complications. Some patients may benefit from continuous broad-spectrum antibiotic therapy. In patients who develop chronic lung disease, physical therapy with postural drainage is of benefit. Transfer factor has been utilized in some patients without apparent benefit. Successful bone marrow transplantation has not been performed, but this is probably related to the lack of histocompatible bone marrow donors. Fetal thymus transplantation has provided some benefit in a limited number of patients. Monthly infusions of frozen plasma have been suggested as a source of passively administered antibody.

Complications & Prognosis

Patients who survive for long periods of time develop progressive deterioration of neurologic and immunologic functions. The oldest patients have reached the fifth decade of life. The chief causes of death are overwhelming infection and the development of lymphoreticular malignancies. As these patients reach the second decade, morbidity becomes severe, with chronic lung disease, mental retardation, and physical debility the principal problems.

IMMUNODEFICIENCY WITH THROMBOCYTOPENIA, ECZEMA, & RECURRENT INFECTION (Wiskott-Aldrich Syndrome)

Major Immunologic Features

- Complete syndrome consists of eczema, recurrent pyogenic infection, and thrombocytopenia.
- Can be diagnosed at birth by demonstration of thrombocytopenia in a male infant with a positive family history.
- Serum IgM usually low with elevated serum IgA and IgE.

General Considerations

Patients may become symptomatic early in life, with bleeding secondary to thrombocytopenia. Subsequently they develop recurrent bacterial infection in the form of otitis media, pneumonia, and meningitis. Eczema usually appears by 1 year of age. The disease appears to be progressive, with increasing susceptibility to infection. It is inherited in an X-linked manner.

The earliest abnormalities found in patients are thrombocytopenia and hypercatabolism of immunoglobulin. A hypothesis linking thrombocytopenia, eczema, and recurrent infection is not available. It has been suggested that the α granules of platelets and macrophages of patients and carriers are abnormal. Another suggestion is that the inability of patients to respond to polysaccharide antigens results in immunologic attrition. This does not explain the thrombocytopenia or eczema.

Clinical Features

A. Symptoms and Signs: Recurrent infection usually does not start until after 6 months of age. Patients are susceptible to infection with polysaccharide-containing organisms (eg, pneumococcus, meningococcus, and *H influenzae*) and may develop meningitis, otitis media, pneumonia, and sepsis. As they become older, they become susceptible to infection with other types of organisms and may have recurrent viral infection.

Eczema is usually present by 1 year of age and is typical in distribution. It may be associated with other allergic manifestations. Frequently, it is secondarily infected.

Thrombocytopenia is present at birth and may result in early manifestations of bleeding. Bleeding usually increases during episodes of infection and is associated with a decrease in the platelet count. The bleeding tendency becomes less severe as the child becomes older.

B. Laboratory Findings: Thrombocytopenia is present at birth. The platelet count may range from 5–100 thousand/μl. Anemia is frequently present and may be Coombs-positive. An increased incidence of renal disease has been reported. Studies of B cell immunity demonstrate normal IgG, decreased IgM, increased IgA and IgE, low to absent isohemagglutinins, normal numbers of B cells, and an inability to respond to immunization with polysaccharide antigen. T cell immunity is usually intact early in the disease but may decline with advancing years.

Immunologic Diagnosis

The earliest detected immunologic abnormality consists of hypercatabolism of immunoglobulins. The typical pattern of low to absent isohemagglutinins, low IgM, and elevated IgA and IgE may not be present until 1 year of age. B cells are normal in number. Patients fail to form antibody following immunization with polysaccharide antigens. T cell immunity may be normal initially and show gradual attrition with advancing age.

Differential Diagnosis

When the complete syndrome is present, there is little confusion in diagnosis. Idiopathic thrombocytopenia in a male child may be difficult to differentiate from Wiskott-Aldrich syndrome. In idiopathic thrombocytopenia, the immunoglobulins, isohemagglutinins, and response to polysaccharide antigens are normal. Similarly, male patients with eczema and recurrent infection have normal immunologic studies and normal platelet counts, although they may have elevated IgA and IgE.

Treatment

Infections should be treated promptly with antibiotics (ampicillin) to cover the most common organisms. Corticosteroids should not be used to treat the thrombocytopenia as they will enhance the susceptibility to infection. Splenectomy has been fatal in virtually all patients. Treatment of immunodeficiency is difficult. Infusions of frozen plasma have been utilized on a monthly basis as a source of passive protection. γ-Globulin is not used because of the thrombocytopenia and potential bleeding at injection sites. Transfer factor has been advocated, but controlled studies have not been performed. A successful bone marrow transplant has been performed.

Complications & Prognosis

With aggressive therapy, the long-term prognosis has improved. Immediate complications are related to bleeding episodes and acute infection. As patients become older, they become susceptible to a wider spectrum of microbial agents. Chronic keratitis secondary to viral infection is frequent. Lymphoreticular malignancies, especially of the central nervous system, occur in older patients.

IMMUNODEFICIENCY WITH THYMOMA

Recurrent infection may be the presenting sign if the thymoma is associated with immunodeficiency. Infection takes the form of sinopulmonary infection, chronic diarrhea, dermatitis, septicemia, stomatitis, and urinary tract infection. Thymoma has also been associated with muscle weakness (when found in conjunction with myasthenia gravis), aregenerative anemia, thrombocytopenia, diabetes, amyloidosis, chronic hepatitis, and the development of nonthymic malignancy.

Patients with acquired hypogammaglobulinemia should be followed at regular intervals for the development of thymoma, usually detected on routine chest x-rays. Occasionally, the thymoma may be detected prior to the development of immunodeficiency. Marked hypogammaglobulinemia is usually present. The antibody response following immunization may be abnormal. Some patients have deficient T cell immunity as assayed by delayed hypersensitivity skin tests and response of peripheral blood lymphocytes to PHA. In patients who have aregenerative anemia, pure red cell aplasia is seen on marrow aspiration. Thrombocytopenia, granulocytopenia, and autoantibody formation are occasionally observed. In 75% of cases, the thymoma is of the spindle cell type. Some tumors may be malignant.

In no instance has the removal of the thymoma resulted in improvement of immunodeficiency. This is in contrast to pure red cell aplasia and myasthenia gravis, which may improve following removal of thymoma. γ-Globulin is of benefit in controlling recurrent infections and chronic diarrhea. (See treatment section under X-linked hypogammaglobulinemia.)

The overall prognosis is poor, and death secondary to infection is common. Death may also be related to associated abnormalities such as thrombocytopenia and aregenerative anemia.

IMMUNODEFICIENCY WITH SHORT-LIMBED DWARFISM

Three forms of immunodeficiency with short-limbed dwarfism exist. Type I is associated with combined immunodeficiency, type II with cellular immunodeficiency, and type III with antibody immunodeficiency.

The clinical features of each type vary with the degree of immunodeficiency. In short-limbed dwarfism associated with combined immunodeficiency, symptoms of infection are identical to those seen in severe combined immunodeficiency disease. Susceptibility to viral, bacterial, fungal, and protozoal infection is observed. Patients usually die in the first year. Patients with short-limbed dwarfism and cellular immunodeficiency are susceptible to recurrent sinopulmonary infection, fatal varicella, and progressive vaccinia, and may develop a malabsorption-like syndrome. Patients with short-limbed dwarfism and antibody immunodeficiency experience recurrent pyogenic infections in the form of pneumonia, sepsis, otitis media, and meningitis. In all patients, short-limbed dwarfism is characterized by short, pudgy hands and extremities. The head is normal in size, which distinguishes this disorder from achondroplasia. During infancy, redundant skin folds are often seen around the neck and large joints of the extremities. Patients with short-limbed dwarfism and cellular immunodeficiency may also have cartilage-hair hypoplasia manifested by light, thin, and sparse hair.

Abnormal immunologic studies vary with the degree of immunodeficiency. In short-limbed dwarfism associated with combined immunodeficiency, there is complete absence of T and B cell immunity. In short-limbed dwarfism associated with cellular immunodeficiency, T cell immunity is deficient as measured by delayed hypersensitivity skin tests and responsiveness of peripheral blood lymphocytes to PHA, allogeneic cells, and varicella antigens. B cell immunity is intact. In short-limbed dwarfism associated with antibody immunodeficiency, B cell immunity is absent and T cell immunity is intact.

Radiologic abnormalities consist of scalloping, irregular sclerosis, and cystic changes in the metaphyseal portions of long bones. Aganglionic megacolon has been reported. Patients with cartilage-hair hypoplasia have reduced hair diameters and lack the pigmented central core.

Treatment of these disorders is individualized to the associated immunodeficiency (eg, severe combined immunodeficiency, cellular immunodeficiency, and antibody immunodeficiency).

The prognosis varies with the degree of immunodeficiency. There have been no survivors with severe combined immunodeficiency. Patients with cellular immunodeficiency may survive to the fourth or fifth decade only to succumb to overwhelming varicella infection. The prognosis in patients with antibody immunodeficiency is similar to that of X-linked hypogammaglobulinemia.

IMMUNODEFICIENCY WITH ENZYME DEFICIENCY

Patients do not differ significantly from individuals with combined immunodeficiency disease and normal enzyme levels. Adenosine deaminase and nucleoside phosphorylase are enzymes necessary for the normal catabolism of the purine adenosine. Adenosine deaminase catalyzes the conversion of adenosine to inosine, and nucleoside phosphorylase catalyzes the conversion of inosine to hypoxanthine. The means by which a deficiency of these enzymes results in immunodeficiency is not known. It has been postulated that the immunodeficiency is a result of pyrimidine starvation secondary to the accumulation of adenine nucleotides. Others postulate a direct suppressive effect of accumulated adenosine or inosine on lymphocyte function.

The degree of combined immunodeficiency is variable. The spectrum of immunologic aberrations varies from complete absence of T and B cell immunity, as observed in patients with severe combined immunodeficiency disease, to mild abnormalities of T and B cell function. Patients with enzyme deficiencies should be evaluated completely to determine the extent of the immunologic deficiency. As a result of the marked variability in immunodeficiency, there is a considerable variation in the age at onset, severity of symptoms, and eventual outcome. Patients with adenosine deaminase deficiency and severe combined immunodeficiency may have characteristic radiologic abnormalities which include concavity and flaring of the anterior ribs, abnormal contour and articulation of posterior ribs and transverse processes, platyspondylisis, thick growth arrest lines, and an abnormal bony pelvis. Only a single patient with nucleoside phosphorylase deficiency and cellular immunodeficiency has been described. This patient had normal x-rays, absent T cell immunity, and normal B cell immunity. She had a history of anemia and recurrent infection.

The mode of inheritance of these enzyme defects appears to be autosomal recessive. The carrier state can be demonstrated in both sexes as evidenced by diminished adenosine deaminase or nucleoside phosphorylase activity. The enzymes are absent in red cells, white cells, tissue, and cultured fibroblasts in these patients. An intrauterine diagnosis of adenosine deaminase deficiency has been made.

Treatment of this disorder is similar to that of severe combined immunodeficiency or combined immunodeficiency. Several successful bone marrow transplants have been performed, with subsequent return of immunologic function. The patient's cells continue to have no enzyme activity following transplantation.

EPISODIC LYMPHOCYTOPENIA WITH LYMPHOTOXIN

Approximately 12 patients, both males and females, have been reported with this disorder. The major features include abnormal T and B cell immunity, recurrent viral and bacterial infections, eczema, and the presence of a circulating lymphotoxin. No specific treatment is available. Therapy should be directed toward treatment of bacterial infections. γ-Globulin may be useful. Other forms of immunotherapy have not been tried. The prognosis is uncertain. One patient survived to 11 years of age.

GRAFT-VERSUS-HOST (GVH) DISEASE

GVH disease occurs when there is an unopposed attack of histo*in*compatible cells on an individual who is unable to reject foreign cells. The requirements for the GVH reaction are (1) histocompatibility differences between the graft (donor) and host (recipient), (2) immunocompetent graft cells, and (3) immunodeficient host cells. A GVH reaction may result from the infusion of any blood product containing viable lymphocytes, as may occur in maternal-fetal blood transfusion, intrauterine transfusion, therapeutic whole blood transfusions, or transfusions of packed red cells, frozen cells, platelets, fresh plasma, or leukocyte-poor red cells; or transplantation of fetal thymus, fetal liver, or bone marrow. The GVH reaction may have its onset 7–30 days following infusion of viable lymphocytes. Once the reaction is established, little can be done to modify its course. In the majority of immunodeficient patients, a GVH reaction is fatal. The exact mechanism whereby a GVH reaction is produced is not known. All cells of the body have histocompatibility antigens with the exception of red blood cells. Biopsy of active GVH lesions usually demonstrates infiltrations by mononuclear cells as well as phagocytic and histiocytic cells. The GVH reaction may appear in 3 distinct forms: acute, hyperacute, and chronic.

In the *acute form,* the initial manifestation is a maculopapular rash which is frequently mistaken for a viral or allergic rash. Initially, it blanches with pressure and then becomes diffuse. If the rash is persistent, it will begin to scale. Diarrhea, hepatosplenomegaly, jaundice, cardiac irregularity, central nervous system irritability, and pulmonary infiltrates may occur during the height of the reaction. Enhanced susceptibility to infection is also present and may result in death from sepsis.

In the *hyperacute form* of GVH reaction, the rash may also begin as a maculopapular lesion but then rapidly progresses to a form resembling toxic epidermal necrolysis. This has not been associated with staphylococcal infection. Clinical and laboratory abnormalities similar to those found in the acute form may be observed. Death occurs shortly after the onset of the reaction.

The *chronic form* of GVH disease may be a result of maternal-fetal transfusion or attempts at immunotherapy with histocompatible bone marrow transplantation. The clinical and laboratory features may be markedly abnormal or only slightly so. Chronic desquamation of the skin is usually present. Hepatosplenomegaly may be prominent along with lymphadenopathy. Chronic diarrhea and failure to thrive are usually present. Secondary infection is a frequent complication. On biopsy of skin or lymph nodes, histiocytic infiltration may be found. This has led to an erroneous diagnosis of Letterer-Siwe disease. Patients with Letterer-Siwe disease, however, have normal immunoglobulin values and normal T cell immunity–in contrast to patients with chronic GVH disease, who have severe immunodeficiency. Chronic GVH disease has also been confused with acrodermatitis enteropathica.

The diagnosis is suggested by the diffuse clinical abnormalities present in a patient known to have cellular immunodeficiency and who has received a transfusion of potentially immunocompetent cells in the preceding 5–30 days. The diagnosis is established by the demonstration of sex chromosome or HLA chimerism.

There is no adequate treatment of GVH disease once it is established. Use of corticosteroids only enhances the susceptibility to infection. Antilymphocyte globulin also results in further suppression of immunity. The only treatment is prevention. Any infant suspected of having cellular immunodeficiency who requires the administration of a blood product should receive cells that have been subjected to 3000–6000 R of radiation to destroy viable lymphocytes and thus prevent GVH disease.

PHAGOCYTIC DYSFUNCTION DISEASES

Phagocytic disorders may be divided into extrinsic and intrinsic defects. Included in the extrinsic category are deficiencies of opsonins secondary to deficiencies of antibody and complement factors; suppression of the total number of phagocytic cells by immunosuppressive agents; interference of phagocytic function by corticosteroids; and suppression of the number of circulating neutrophils by autoantibody directed specifically against neutrophil antigens. Other extrinsic disorders may be related to abnormal neutrophil chemotaxis secondary to complement deficiency or abnormal complement components. Intrinsic phagocytic disorders are related to enzymatic deficiencies within the metabolic pathway necessary for killing of bacteria. These include chronic granulomatous disease

Table 26–6. Evaluation of phagocytosis.

Test	Comment
Quantitative nitroblue tetrazolium (NBT)	Used for diagnosis of chronic granulomatous disease and for detection of carrier state.
Quantitative intracellular killing curve	Used for diagnosis of chronic granulomatous disease. Can be performed using organisms isolated from individual.
Chemotaxis	Abnormal in a variety of disorders associated with frequent bacterial infection. Does not provide a specific diagnosis. Performed using a Boyden chamber utilizing a microscopic or radioactive technic. Rebuck skin window provides a qualitative result, in vivo.
Random migration	Abnormal in "lazy leukocyte syndrome." Tests nonchemotactic migration of leukocytes.
Cotton wool, glass wool adherence	Abnormal in several disorders associated with recurrent bacterial infection. Does not provide a specific diagnosis.

with a deficiency of NADPH or NADH oxidase, myeloperoxidase deficiency, and glucose-6-phosphate dehydrogenase deficiency.

Susceptibility to infection in phagocytic dysfunction syndromes may range from mild recurrent skin infections to severe overwhelming, fatal systemic infection. Characteristically, all of these patients are susceptible to bacterial infection and have little difficulty with viral or protozoal infections. Some of the more severe disorders may be associated with overwhelming fungal infections.

Numerous tests can now be performed to evaluate phagocytic dysfunction (see Chapter 25). Screening tests are listed in Table 26–3, and definitive studies in Table 26–6.

CHRONIC GRANULOMATOUS DISEASE

Major Immunologic Features

- Susceptibility to infection with unusual organisms normally of low virulence, eg, *Staphylococcus epidermidis, Serratia marcescens,* aspergillus.
- X-linked inheritance (female variant occurs).
- Onset of symptoms by 2 years of age: draining lymphadenitis, hepatosplenomegaly, pneumonia, osteomyelitis, abscesses.
- Diagnosis established by quantitative nitroblue tetrazolium test and quantitative killing curve.

General Considerations

Chronic granulomatous disease is inherited as an X-linked disorder with clinical manifestations appearing during the first 2 years of life. A rare female variant of the disease has been described. Patients are susceptible to infection with a variety of normally nonpathogenic and unusual organisms. Characteristic abnormal laboratory studies will detect both patients and female carriers of the disease. Female carriers are usually asymptomatic. Early diagnosis and aggressive therapy have improved the prognosis in these patients.

The enzymatic deficiency in chronic granulomatous disease is felt to be either NADH or NADPH oxidase. In the female variant, glutathione peroxidase is felt to be deficient. As a result of these enzymatic deficiencies, the intracellular metabolism of neutrophils and monocytes is abnormal, resulting in decreased oxygen consumption, decreased utilization of glucose by the hexose monophosphate shunt, decreased production of hydrogen peroxide, diminished iodination of bacteria, and decreased superoxide anion production. The net result is decreased intracellular killing of certain bacteria and fungi.

Clinical Features

A. Symptoms and Signs: In the majority of patients, the diagnosis can be established before 2 years of age. The most frequent abnormalities consist of marked lymphadenopathy, hepatosplenomegaly, chronic draining lymph nodes, and at least one episode of pneumonia. Other symptoms include rhinitis, conjunctivitis, dermatitis, ulcerative stomatitis, perianal abscess, osteomyelitis, and chronic diarrhea with intermittent abdominal pains. Chronic and acute infection occurs in lymph nodes, skin, lung, intestinal tract, liver, and bone. A major clue to early diagnosis is the finding of a normally nonpathogenic or unusual organism. Organisms responsible for infection include *S aureus, S epidermidis, S marcescens,* pseudomonas, *Escherichia coli,* candida, and aspergillus.

B. Laboratory Findings: The most readily available study for diagnosis is the quantitative nitroblue tetrazolium test. (See Chapter 25.) Patients have absent nitroblue tetrazolium dye reduction, whereas carriers may have normal or reduced nitroblue tetrazolium reduction. Patients with chronic granulomatous disease are unable to kill certain bacteria at a normal rate. The killing curves for organisms to which these individuals are susceptible usually indicate little or no killing in a period of 2 hours. Other abnormal studies include decreased oxygen uptake during phagocytosis and abnormal bacterial iodination.

The peripheral white cell count is usually elevated even if the patient does not have active infection. Hypergammaglobulinemia is present, and antibody function is normal. Cell-mediated immunity is normal, and complement factors may be elevated. During episodes of pneumonia, the chest x-ray is frequently severely abnormal. Liver function tests may be abnormal as a result of chronic infection. Pulmonary function tests are usually abnormal following episodes of pneumonia and may not return to normal for several months.

Immunologic Diagnosis

A diagnosis can be established utilizing the quantitative nitroblue tetrazolium dye reduction assay. Confirmation is obtained utilizing specific bactericidal assays. These assays may also be utilized to identify the carrier state. Both male and female variants of chronic granulomatous disease have abnormal studies. Antibody-mediated immunity, cell-mediated immunity, and complement are normal.

Differential Diagnosis

Few clinical disorders are easily confused with chronic granulomatous disease. Two other disorders with abnormal enzymatic function are associated with clinical symptoms and laboratory features similar to those of chronic granulomatous disease. One of these is the female variant of chronic granulomatous disease associated with deficient glutathione peroxidase; the other is associated with deficient glucose-6-phosphate dehydrogenase. Any child presenting with osteomyelitis, pneumonia, liver abscess, or chronic draining lymphadenopathy associated with a normally nonpathogenic or unusual organism should be suspected of having chronic granulomatous disease.

Treatment

Aggressive diagnostic measures and therapy are necessary for long-term survival and diminished morbidity. Blood cultures, aspiration of draining lymph nodes, liver biopsy, and open lung biopsy should be utilized to obtain a specific bacterial diagnosis. Therapy should be instituted immediately while results of cultures are pending. The choice of antibiotics should be one which covers the spectrum of infectious agents. An appropriate choice would be penicillin and gentamicin or penicillin and chloramphenicol. These agents cover the majority of organisms with the exception of candida and aspergillus. For these latter organisms, amphotericin is the treatment of choice. Amphotericin therapy should be given intravenously, starting with high doses in the range of 1 mg/kg/day. The ultimate survival of the patient is dependent upon early and intensive therapy. Treatment of the patient with antibiotics may be prolonged, requiring 5–6 weeks of total therapy. Additional therapy has included the use of white blood cell infusions, but experience has been extremely limited. Several investigators have utilized continuous anti-infective therapy with sulfisoxazole.

Complications & Prognosis

Chronic organ dysfunction may result from severe or chronic infection. Examples are abnormal pulmonary function, chronic liver disease, chronic osteomyelitis, and malabsorption secondary to gastrointestinal tract involvement. The mortality rate in chronic granulomatous disease has been considerably reduced by early diagnosis and aggressive therapy. Survivals into the second decade and beyond have been recorded.

GLUCOSE-6-PHOSPHATE DEHYDROGENASE DEFICIENCY

Males and females with complete absence of leukocyte glucose-6-phosphate dehydrogenase activity have been described. Some investigators have demonstrated deficient NADH and NADPH activity with decreased hexose monophosphate shunt activity and decreased hydrogen peroxide production in the white blood cells. Leukocytes are unable to kill certain organisms at a normal rate in a manner similar to that found in chronic granulomatous disease. The clinical presentation and susceptibility to microbial agents of these patients are similar to those of chronic granulomatous disease. The laboratory diagnosis is based on the demonstration of deficient white blood cell glucose-6-phosphate dehydrogenase. The nitroblue tetrazolium test may be normal in these patients, but the killing curve is abnormal. Treatment and prognosis are similar to those of chronic granulomatous disease.

MYELOPEROXIDASE DEFICIENCY

Several patients with complete deficiency of leukocyte myeloperoxidase have been described. Myeloperoxidase is one of the enzymes necessary for normal intracellular killing of certain organisms. The leukocytes of these patients have normal oxygen consumption, hexose monophosphate shunt activity, and hydrogen peroxide production. The intracellular killing of organisms is delayed but may reach normal levels with increased incubation times. Susceptibility to candidal and staphylococcal infections has been the chief problem. The diagnosis can be established utilizing a peroxidase stain of peripheral blood. No specific treatment is available other than appropriate antibiotic therapy.

CHÉDIAK-HIGASHI SYNDROME

Chédiak-Higashi syndrome is a multisystem autosomal recessive disorder. Symptoms include recurrent bacterial infections with a variety of organisms, hepatosplenomegaly, partial albinism, central nervous system abnormalities, and a high incidence of lymphoreticular malignancies.

The characteristic abnormality of giant cytoplasmic granular inclusions in white blood cells and platelets is observed on routine peripheral blood smears under ordinary light microscopy. Additional abnormalities include abnormal neutrophil chemotaxis and abnormal intracellular killing of organisms (including streptococci and pneumococci as well as those organisms found in chronic granulomatous disease). The killing defect consists of delayed killing time. Oxygen consumption, hydrogen peroxide formation, and hexose monophosphate shunt activity are normal.

There is no treatment other than specific antibiotic therapy for infecting organisms. The prognosis is poor because of increasing susceptibility to infection and progressive neurologic deterioration. Most patients die during childhood, but survivors to the second and third decade have been reported.

JOB'S SYNDROME

Job's syndrome was originally described as a disorder of recurrent "cold" staphylococcal abscesses of the skin, lymph nodes, or subcutaneous tissue. The first patients were fair-skinned, red-headed girls of Italian descent. Initial descriptions also included eczematoid skin lesions, otitis media, and chronic nasal discharge. Few signs of systemic infection or inflammatory response occurred in association with the infection. Additional reports of Job's syndrome indicated that the disorder might be a variant of chronic granulomatous disease. However, most of the patients studied do not have abnormal immunologic tests.

Treatment consists of appropriate antibiotic therapy. The prognosis is uncertain.

TUFTSIN DEFICIENCY

Tuftsin deficiency has been reported as a familial deficiency of a phagocytosis-stimulating tetrapeptide which is cleaved from a parent immunoglobulin molecule in the spleen. Two families with the deficiency have been described. Tuftsin also appears to be absent in patients who have been splenectomized. Local and severe systemic bacterial infections occur. Tuftsin levels are determined only in a few specialized laboratories.

There is no treatment, and the prognosis is uncertain. γ-Globulin therapy appeared to be beneficial in the 2 families reported.

LAZY LEUKOCYTE SYNDROME

Patients have been described who have a defective chemotactic response of neutrophils in association with neutropenia. These individuals also have an abnormal in vivo inflammatory response as determined by the "Rebuck window," and they fail to demonstrate an increased number of peripheral blood neutrophils following epinephrine or endotoxin stimulation. The random migration of peripheral leukocytes is abnormal as determined by the vertical migration of white blood cells in a capillary tube. Patients are susceptible to severe bacterial infections.

Treatment with specific antibiotics is indicated. The prognosis is unknown.

ELEVATED IgE, DEFECTIVE CHEMOTAXIS, ECZEMA, & RECURRENT INFECTION

Patients, both male and female, have an early onset of eczema and recurrent bacterial infection in the form of abscesses, secondary infection of eczema, and pneumonia. The organisms responsible for infection include *S aureus* and group A β-hemolytic streptococci. Studies of antibody- and cell-mediated immunity are normal. The serum IgE levels are markedly elevated, usually greater than 10 times normal. Chemotactic function is abnormal, but other studies of phagocytosis are within the normal range.

Antibiotic therapy is indicated for specific bacterial infections. The prognosis is unknown.

COMPLEMENT ABNORMALITIES & IMMUNODEFICIENCY DISEASES

A variety of complement deficiencies and abnormalities of complement function have been associated with increased susceptibility to infection (Table 26–7). Complement factors are necessary for normal opsonization, bacterial killing, and neutrophil chemotaxis. Despite the participation of complement components in the phagocytic process, a number of complement deficiencies are unassociated with enhanced susceptibility to infection. Many of these disorders are associated with increased susceptibility to autoimmune disease (see Chapter 27).

Table 26–7. Evaluation of complement disorders.

C1q, C1r, C1s	Deficiency initially suspected by decreased hemolytic complement (CH_{50}). Specific assays required for confirmation.
C2	Deficiency initially suspected by decreased CH_{50}. Specific assays required for confirmation.
C3	Deficiency detected using quantitative assay available in most hospital laboratories.
C5	Present in normal amounts but abnormal in function in "C5 dysfunction" syndrome.

C1q DEFICIENCY

A deficiency of C1q has been reported in patients with X-linked hypogammaglobulinemia and severe combined immunodeficiency disease. The cause of this deficiency is not certain, but it may be related to hypercatabolism as a result of enhanced susceptibility to infection in patients with primary immunodeficiency disorders. The degree to which C1q deficiency increases the susceptibility to infection in patients with other primary immunodeficiency disorders is not known. C1q deficiency has also been described in a single patient with a systemic lupus erythematosus-like syndrome and increased susceptibility to bacterial infection.

C1r & C1s DEFICIENCY

Familial deficiencies of C1r and C1s have been described in patients with susceptibility to autoimmune disease. Most of these patients had a systemic lupus erythematosus-like syndrome. In addition, these patients appeared to have an increased susceptibility to bacterial infection. No specific treatment of this disorder has been proposed. The infusion of complement components might theoretically result in enhanced immune complex disease and worsening of the lupus-like disorder.

C2 DEFICIENCY

C2 deficiency has been reported in several patients with systemic lupus erythematosus-like disorders and increased susceptibility to infection. The patients have chronic renal disease and antibody directed against DNA. An autosomal recessive mode of inheritance is suggested by familial studies. The patients are susceptible to bacterial infection. Recently, C2 deficiency has been associated with the HLA haplotype A10, B18.

Treatment is directed toward the underlying autoimmune disease with specific antibiotic therapy for infections. In one patient who received a blood transfusion, the levels of serum C3, C5, C6, and C7 decreased dramatically. This observation suggests that complement replacement therapy might result in increased activation of the complement components and increased immune complex disease.

C3 DEFICIENCY

Two forms of C3 deficiency exist. In type I, a marked decrease of C3 is present in the serum. However, C3 is probably deficient as a result of a deficiency of C3 inactivator. In the single patient reported, increased susceptibility to bacterial infection was present throughout life. The patient also had Klinefelter's syndrome. Infusion of normal plasma corrected the abnormalities in the patient and resulted in diminished susceptibility to infection.

A second form of C3 deficiency (type II) has been reported in a single patient. Partial lipodystrophy was present in association with an increased susceptibility to bacterial infection. The decreased level of C3 was found to be associated with increased destruction and decreased synthesis. The abnormalities were partially explained by the demonstration of an enzyme, C3 convertase, capable of cleaving C3 in vitro and in vivo.

FAMILIAL C5 DYSFUNCTION

C5 dysfunction has been described as a familial defect in patients presenting with failure to thrive, diarrhea, seborrheic dermatitis, and susceptibility to infection with bacterial organisms.

Laboratory studies usually demonstrate leukocytosis and hypergammaglobulinemia. The total hemolytic complement and C5 levels are normal. Despite the normal levels of C5, chemotaxis is ineffective and can be corrected by adding normal C5 to the testing procedure.

Treatment consists of appropriate antibiotic therapy for infecting organisms. Fresh plasma has been recommended as a potential source of normal C5. Fresh-frozen plasma is not believed to contain sufficient amounts for therapy. However, some of the clinical findings in patients with familial C5 dysfunction closely resemble those found in patients with cellular immunodeficiency disorders. The use of fresh irradiated plasma is recommended to prevent a GVH reaction if the diagnosis has not been established with certainty. Ideally, patients should have studies of cell-mediated immunity performed prior to the institution of treatment.

• • •

References

General References

Ammann AJ, Wara DW: Evaluation of infants and children with recurrent infections. Curr Probl Pediatr 5 (11), 1975. [Entire issue.]

Bergsma D, Good RA, Finstad J (editors): *Immunodeficiency in Man and Animals.* National Foundation-March of Dimes Original Article Series. Sinauer Associates, 1975.

Bergsma D, McKusick FA (editors): *Immunologic Deficiency Diseases in Man.* National Foundation-March of Dimes Original Article Series. Williams & Wilkins, 1968.

Fudenberg HH & others: Primary immunodeficiencies: Report of a World Health Organization committee. Pediatrics 47:927, 1971.

Stiehm ER, Fulginiti V (editors): *Immunologic Disorders in Infants and Children.* Saunders, 1973.

X-linked Hypogammaglobulinemia

Good RA, Zak SJ: Disturbances in gammaglobulin synthesis as "experiments of nature." Pediatrics 18:109, 1956.

Rosen FS, Janeway CA: The gammaglobulins. 3. The antibody deficiency syndromes. N Engl J Med 275:709, 1966.

Acquired Hypogammaglobulinemia

Geha RS & others: Heterogeneity of "acquired" or common variable agammaglobulinemia. N Engl J Med 291:1, 1974.

Good RA & others: Clinical investigations of patients with agammaglobulinemia and hypogammaglobulinemia. Pediatr Clin North Am 7:397, 1960.

X-linked Immunodeficiency With Hyper-IgM

Stiehm ER, Fudenberg HH: Clinical and immunologic features of dysgammaglobulinemia type 1. Am J Med 40:805, 1966.

Selective IgA Deficiency

Ammann AJ, Hong R: Selective IgA deficiency: Presentation of 30 cases and a review of the literature. Medicine 50:223, 1971.

Selective IgM Deficiency

Hobbs JR, Milner RDG, Watt PJ: Gamma-M deficiency predisposing to meningococcal septicaemia. Br Med J 2:583, 1967.

Selective IgG Deficiency

Schur PH & others: Selective gamma-G globulin deficiencies in patients with recurrent pyogenic infections. N Engl J Med 283:631, 1970.

Thymic Aplasia With Hypoparathyroidism

DiGeorge AM: Congenital absence of the thymus and its immunologic consequences: Concurrence with congenital hypoparathyroidism. In: *Immunologic Deficiency Diseases in Man.* Bergsma D, McKusick FA (editors). National Foundation-March of Dimes Original Article Series. Williams & Wilkins, 1968.

Chronic Mucocutaneous Candidiasis

Kirkpatrick CH, Rich RR, Bennett JE: Chronic mucocutaneous candidiasis: Model building in cellular immunity. Ann Intern Med 74:955, 1971.

Lehner T: Chronic candidiasis. Trans St Johns Hosp Dermatol Soc 50:8, 1964.

Severe Combined Immunodeficiency Disease

Hitzig WH: Congenital thymic and lymphocytic deficiency disorders. In: *Immunologic Disorders in Infants and Children.* Stiehm ER, Fulginiti V (editors). Saunders, 1973.

Cellular Immunodeficiency With Abnormal Immunoglobulin Synthesis

Lawlor GJ & others: The syndrome of cellular immunodeficiency with immunoglobulins. J Pediatr 84:183, 1974.

Ataxia-Telangiectasia

Boder E, Sedgwick RP: Ataxia-telangiectasia: A familial syndrome of progressive cerebellar ataxia, oculocutaneous telangiectasia and frequent pulmonary infection. Univ Southern Calif Med Bull 9:15, 1957.

Peterson RDA, Cooper MD, Good RA: Lymphoid tissue abnormalities associated with ataxia-telangiectasia. Am J Med 41:342, 1966.

Wiskott-Aldrich Syndrome

Blaese RM & others: The Wiskott-Aldrich syndrome: A disorder with a possible defect in antigen processing or recognition. Lancet 1:1056, 1968.

Cooper MD & others: Wiskott-Aldrich syndrome: Immunologic deficiency disease involving the afferent limb of immunity. Am J Med 44:489, 1968.

Immunodeficiency With Thymoma

Waldmann TA & others: Thymoma, hypogammaglobulinemia and absence of eosinophils. J Clin Invest 46:1127, 1967.

Immunodeficiency With Short-limbed Dwarfism

Ammann AJ, Sutliff W, Millinchick E: Antibody mediated immunodeficiency in short-limbed dwarfism. J Pediatr 84:200, 1974.

Lux SE & others: Chronic neutropenia and abnormal cellular immunity in cartilage-hair hypoplasia. N Engl J Med 282:234, 1970.

Combined Immunodeficiency With Enzyme Deficiency

Giblett ER & others: Nucleoside phosphorylase deficiency in a child with severely defective T cell immunity and normal B cell immunity. Lancet 1:1010, 1975.

Meuwissen HJ, Pollara B, Pickering RJ: Combined immunodeficiency disease associated with adenosine deaminase deficiency. J Pediatr 86:169, 1975.

Episodic Lymphocytopenia With Lymphotoxin

Kretschmer R & others: Recurrent infections, episodic lymphopenia and impaired cellular immunity. N Engl J Med 281:285, 1969.

Chronic Granulomatous Disease

Johnston RB, Baehner RL: Chronic granulomatous disease: Correlation between pathogenesis and clinical findings. Pediatrics 48:730, 1971.

Quie PG: Chronic granulomatous disease of childhood. Adv Pediatr 16:287, 1969.

Glucose-6-phosphate Dehydrogenase Deficiency

Cooper MR & others: Complete deficiency of leukocyte glucose-6-phosphate dehydrogenase with defective bactericidal activity. J Clin Invest 51:769, 1972.

Myeloperoxidase Deficiency

Lehrer RI, Cline MJ: Leukocyte myeloperoxidase deficiency and disseminated candidiasis: The role of myeloperoxidase in resistance to candida infection. J Clin Invest 48:1478, 1969.

Chédiak-Higashi Syndrome

Stossel TP, Root RK, Vaughan M: Phagocytosis in chronic granulomatous disease and the Chédiak-Higashi syndrome. N Engl J Med 286:120, 1972.

Tuftsin Deficiency

Constantopoulos A, Najjar VA, Smith JW: Tuftsin deficiency: A new syndrome with defective phagocytosis. J Pediatr 80:564, 1972.

Lazy Leukocyte Syndrome

Miller ME, Oski FA, Harris MB: Lazy-leukocyte syndrome: A new disorder of neutrophil function. Lancet 1:665, 1971.

Increased IgE, Abnormal Chemotaxis, & Recurrent Infections

Hill HR, Quie PG: Raised serum IgE levels and defective neutrophil chemotaxis in three children with eczema and recurrent bacterial infections. Lancet 1:183, 1974.

C1q,r,s Deficiency

Day NK & others: C1r deficiency: An inborn error associated with cutaneous and renal disease. J Clin Invest 51:1102, 1972.

Wara DW & others: Persistent C1q deficiency in a patient with a systemic lupus-like syndrome. J Pediatr 86:743, 1975.

C2 Deficiency

Day NK & others: C2 deficiency: Development of lupus erythematosus. J Clin Invest 52:1601, 1973.

C3 Deficiency

Alper CA, Bloch KJ, Rosen FS: Increased susceptibility to infection in a patient with type II essential hypercatabolism of C3. N Engl J Med 288:601, 1973.

Alper CA & others: Studies in vitro and in vivo on an abnormality in the metabolism of C3 in a patient with increased susceptibility to infection. J Clin Invest 49:1975, 1970.

Familial C5 Dysfunction

Miller ME, Nilsson UR: A familial deficiency of the phagocytosis-enhancing activity of serum related to a dysfunction of the fifth component of complement (C5). N Engl J Med 282:354, 1970.

27 . . .
Rheumatoid Diseases

Ken Fye, MD, Haralampos Moutsopoulos, MD, & Norman Talal, MD

Many of the major rheumatologic disorders are autoimmune in nature. Therefore, a thorough understanding of and working familiarity with mechanisms of the immune response is essential to the rheumatologist. In this chapter we shall discuss the rheumatologic diseases with proved or hypothesized immunologic pathogenesis. It might be helpful to refer to the previous chapter on autoimmunity if questions arise during the study of the rheumatoid diseases.

SYSTEMIC LUPUS ERYTHEMATOSUS (SLE)

Major Immunologic Features

- Positive LE phenomenon.
- High-titer antinuclear antibodies (diffuse or outline pattern on immunofluorescence).
- Anti-single-stranded and anti-double-stranded DNA antibodies.
- Depressed serum complement levels.
- Deposition of immunoglobulin and complement along glomerular basement membrane and at the dermal-epidermal junction.
- Numerous other autoantibodies.

General Considerations

The systemic manifestations of systemic lupus erythematosus were first described by Osler in 1895. Prior to that time, lupus was considered to be a disfiguring but nonfatal skin disease. It is now known to be a chronic systemic inflammatory disease which follows a course of alternating exacerbations and remissions. Multiple organ system involvement (eg, arthritis, nephritis, pleuritis) characteristically occurs during periods of disease activity. An erythematous rash occurs on the face or other areas exposed to sunlight. Laboratory findings include anemia, leukocytopenia, thrombocytopenia, hyperglobulinemia, increased sedimentation rate, and chronically false-positive tests for syphilis. The cause is not known. The disease affects predominantly females (4:1) of childbearing age; however, the age at onset ranges from 2–90 years. The incidence is higher among nonwhites (particularly blacks) than whites.

Ken Fye and Haralampos Moutsopoulos are Postdoctoral Fellows in Immunology, University of California School of Medicine, San Francisco. Norman Talal is Professor of Medicine, Department of Medicine, University of California School of Medicine and Veterans Administration Hospital, San Francisco.

Immunologic Pathogenesis

The discovery of the LE cell phenomenon marked the start of the modern era of research into the pathogenesis of systemic lupus erythematosus. This initial clinical observation led to the finding of antinuclear factors and antibodies to DNA in the sera of patients with systemic lupus erythematosus. Further studies of renal eluates from patients with systemic lupus erythematosus established the importance of DNA-containing immune complexes in the causation of lupus glomerulonephritis. Reduced serum complement and the presence of antibodies to ds-DNA have become routine correlates of active systemic lupus erythematosus, distinguishing this entity from other lupus variants. The cause of antibody formation to DNA is uncertain. Antibodies to ds-DNA cannot be provoked by experimental immunization and occur almost exclusively in systemic lupus erythematosus and in New Zealand black (NZB) mice, an animal model for systemic lupus erythematosus (see Chapter 14.) It is not known whether viral or host DNA is the immunogen for anti-DNA antibody formation. Several lines of evidence favor a viral role in the pathogenesis of systemic lupus erythematosus. The presence of antibodies to viral surface antigens, to ds-DNA, and to DNA:RNA hybrids is indirect evidence that immunization to viral antigens may be occurring in the disease.

Additional autoantibody activity is also intimately associated with the pathogenesis of systemic lupus erythematosus. Lymphocytotoxic antibodies (with predominant specificity for T lymphocytes) occur in many patients with systemic lupus erythematosus and in NZB mice. Such antibodies are capable of killing T lymphocytes in the presence of complement and of coating peripheral blood T cells so as to interfere with HLA typing and with certain functional activities such as proliferative response to alloantigens. These antibodies have specificity for T cell surface antigens and can be released from the lymphocyte cell surface in the form of specific antigen-antibody complexes. Such complexes may themselves attach to and block the function of other lymphocytes or may contribute to immune complex deposition, leading to vasculitis and nephritis.

The overall immune status in systemic lupus erythematosus and in NZB mice can generally be summarized as an imbalance in which T cell activity is depressed and B cell activity is enhanced. Delayed hypersensitivity responses may be impaired, in part because of the action of lymphocytotoxic antibodies. Antibody formation is both qualitatively and quantitatively excessive, with unusual and higher-titered antibody responses occurring.

Autoantibody formation is normally prevented through the action of T regulatory lymphocytes called "suppressor T cells." Although the mechanism of suppression is unknown, such suppressor T cells probably play an important role in immunologic tolerance and self/nonself discrimination (see Chapters 13 and 14). A deficiency of suppressor T cells has been demonstrated in NZB mice. This deficiency is related to a decrease in concentration of circulating thymic hormone. Administration of thymic hormone to NZB mice can prevent this loss of suppressor T cells and slightly delay the onset of autoimmunity. As NZB mice age and clinical autoimmune disease becomes apparent, there is a marked loss of other T cell effector functions. Such mice are immunologically impaired and susceptible to various infectious agents, including oncogenic viruses. Lymphomas and monoclonal macroglobulinemia commonly develop at this stage. With the use of corticosteroids and immunosuppressive drugs, the major causes of death in systemic lupus erythematosus now are infections and malignancies. These clinical observations parallel the experience with NZB mice.

Clinical Features

A. Symptoms and Signs: Systemic lupus erythematosus presents no single characteristic clinical pattern. The onset can be acute or insidious. Constitutional symptoms include fever, weight loss, malaise, and lethargy. Every organ system may become involved.

1. Skin—The most common skin lesion is a symmetric erythematous rash involving areas of the body chronically exposed to ultraviolet light. A relatively small number of patients with systemic lupus erythematosus develop the classical "butterfly" rash or the characteristic erythematous rash over the fingertips and palms. In some cases, the rash is similar in appearance to that of discoid lupus erythematosus. The rash may resolve without sequelae or may result in scar formation, atrophy, and hypo- or hyperpigmentation. In addition, bullae, patches of purpura, urticaria, angioneurotic edema, patches of vitiligo, and thickening of the skin may be seen. Vasculitic lesions are common and can lead to ischemic ulceration or pyoderma gangrenosum. Alopecia, which may be diffuse, patchy, or circumscribed, is also common. Mucosal ulcerations, involving both oral and genital mucosa, are present in about 15% of cases. Raynaud's phenomenon also occurs in about 15% of patients with systemic lupus erythematosus.

2. Joints and muscles—Polyarthralgia is the most common manifestation of systemic lupus erythematosus (90%). The arthritis of systemic lupus erythematosus is symmetric and can involve almost any joint. It may resemble rheumatoid arthritis, but bony erosions and ulnar deviation are unusual.

Tenosynovitis seldom occurs, and subcutaneous nodules are very rare. Avascular necrosis of the head of the femur or the humerus is a frequent occurrence in systemic lupus erythematosus; corticosteroids, which are a major therapeutic resource in systemic lupus erythematosus, may play a role in the pathogenesis of this complication. Myalgias, with or without frank myositis, are common.

3. Polyserositis—Pleurisy, with or without effusion, is a frequent manifestation. Although one-third of cases have bilateral pleural fluid, massive effusion is rare. Involvement of the pleura produces pleuritic chest pain and shortness of breath. Pericarditis is the commonest form of cardiac involvement and can be the first manifestation of systemic lupus erythematosus. The pericarditis is usually benign, presenting with mild chest discomfort and a pericardial friction rub. However, severe symptomatic pericarditis leading to tamponade may rarely be seen. Peritonitis alone is extremely rare, although 5–10% of patients with pleuritis and pericarditis have concomitant peritonitis. Manifestations of peritonitis include abdominal pain, anorexia, and nausea and vomiting.

4. Lungs—Lupus pneumonitis is an unusual manifestation (0.9% of patients). When a pulmonary infiltrate develops in a patient with systemic lupus erythematosus, particularly one being treated with corticosteroids or immunosuppressive drugs, infection must be the first consideration. The commonest form of lupus pulmonary involvement is interstitial lung disease, which may be asymptomatic and detectable only by pulmonary function tests, with results that are characteristic of restrictive lung disease. The chest x-ray is usually normal but may show "platelike" atelectasis or interstitial fibrosis with "honeycombing."

5. Heart—When myocarditis occurs in systemic lupus erythematosus it commonly leads to congestive heart failure, with tachycardia, gallop rhythm, and cardiomegaly. Arrhythmias are rare and considered a preterminal event. The endocarditis of systemic lupus erythematosus is very difficult to diagnose. Almost all patients have heart murmurs secondary to anemia or fever. The verrucous endocarditis of systemic lupus erythematosus, with the characteristic Libman-Sacks vegetations, is usually diagnosed only at autopsy. Thickening of the aortic valve cusps with resultant aortic insufficiency can occur.

6. Kidney—Renal involvement is a frequent and serious feature of systemic lupus erythematosus. Seventy-five percent of patients have nephritis at autopsy. With the extensive use of percutaneous renal biopsy and the study of renal tissue by light microscopy, immunofluorescence, and electron microscopy,

3 fairly distinctive histologic lesions associated with rather distinctive clinical features can be distinguished: (1) Focal proliferative glomerulonephritis presents with only mild to moderate proteinuria. This lesion responds completely to corticosteroid therapy and rarely progresses to renal failure. (2) Diffuse proliferative glomerulonephritis presents with marked proteinuria, hematuria, and cylindruria (the so-called "telescopic" urine). Untreated, this lesion can progress to renal failure within 1–3 years. It too responds to corticosteroid and immunosuppressive treatment. (3) Membranous glomerulonephritis presents as the nephrotic syndrome. It slowly progresses to renal failure and does not respond to treatment with corticosteroids. Systemic hypertension is a common finding in acute or chronic lupus renal disease.

7. Nervous system–Cerebral involvement is a life-threatening complication of systemic lupus erythematosus. Disturbances of mentation and aberrant behavior, such as psychosis or depression, are the commonest manifestations of central nervous system involvement. Convulsions, cranial nerve palsies, lethargy, and cerebrovascular accidents may also occur. Peripheral neuritis is uncommon (8% of patients).

8. Eye–Ocular involvement, both retinal and corneal, is present in 20–25% of patients. The characteristic retinal finding (the cytoid body) is a fluffy white exudative lesion in the nerve fiber layer of the retina. Corneal ulceration occurs in conjunction with Sjögren's syndrome (see below).

9. Gastrointestinal system–Gastrointestinal ulceration due to vasculitis can occur in systemic lupus erythematosus but is uncommon. Pancreatitis is not unusual. Hepatomegaly is present in 30% and mild splenomegaly in 15% of patients.

10. Hematopoietic system–See Laboratory Findings, below.

11. Sjögren's syndrome–Five to 10% of patients with systemic lupus erythematosus develop the sicca complex (keratoconjunctivitis sicca, xerostomia).

12. Drug-induced lupus-like syndrome–Certain drugs may provoke a lupus-like picture in susceptible individuals. The most commonly implicated drugs, hydralazine and procainamide, can induce arthralgias, arthritis, skin rash, and, less commonly, fever and pleurisy. Nephritis and central nervous system involvement are thought not to occur. The serologic picture is similar to that of systemic lupus erythematosus, but antibody to native double-stranded (ds) DNA has only been associated with hydralazine. The disease usually remits when the drug is discontinued. The list of agents that produce a lupus-like syndrome is increasing rapidly and includes phenytoin (diphenylhydantoin), trimethadione, mephenytoin, isoniazid, aminosalicylic acid, penicillin, tetracyclines, penicillamine, sulfonamides, streptomycin, griseofulvin, phenylbutazone, oral contraceptives, methyl- and propylthiouracil, methyldopa, and levodopa.

B. Laboratory Findings: Anemia is the commonest hematologic finding in systemic lupus erythematosus. Eighty percent of patients present with a normochromic, normocytic anemia due to marrow suppression. A few (5%) develop Coombs-positive hemolytic anemia. Leukocytopenia is common, but the white count rarely falls below 2000/μl. Thrombocytopenia is commonly seen. Urinalysis reveals hematuria, proteinuria, and red and white cell casts. The sedimentation rate is high in almost all cases. Serologic abnormalities are described in the section on immunologic diagnosis (below). The synovial fluid in systemic lupus erythematosus is yellow and clear, with a low viscosity. The white cell count does not exceed 4000/μl, most of which are lymphocytes. Complement levels are low. The pleural effusion of systemic lupus erythematosus is a transudate with a predominance of lymphocytes and a total white cell count of no more than 3000/μl. A hemorrhagic pleural effusion is very rare. In central nervous system lupus, the cerebrospinal fluid protein concentration is high, with a mild lymphocytosis.

There are numerous characteristic pathologic changes in systemic lupus erythematosus:

(1) The verrucous endocarditis of Libman-Sacks consists of ovoid vegetations, 1–4 mm in diameter, which form along the edge of the valve and, rarely, on the chordae tendineae and papillary muscles.

(2) The "wire loop" lesion of the kidney is a segmental thickening of the basement membrane of the glomerular tuft.

(3) A peculiar periarterial concentric fibrosis results in the so-called "onion skin" lesion seen in the spleen.

(4) The pathognomonic finding in systemic lupus erythematosus, the "hematoxylin body," consists of a homogeneous globular mass of nuclear material which stains bluish purple with hematoxylin. Hematoxylin bodies have been found in the heart, kidneys, lungs, spleen, lymph nodes, and serous and synovial membranes. It should be emphasized that patients with fulminant systemic lupus erythematosus involving the central nervous system, skin, muscles, joints, and kidneys may not have any distinctive pathologic abnormalities at autopsy.

C. X-Ray and Other Findings: Chest x-ray may reveal cardiomegaly (due either to pericarditis or myocarditis), pleural effusion, platelike atelectasis, or interstitial fibrosis with a "honeycomb" appearance. The EEG or brain scan is abnormal in most cases of central nervous system involvement.

Immunologic Diagnosis

A. Proteins and Complement: Most patients with systemic lupus erythematosus (80%) present with elevated α_2- and γ-globulins. Hypoalbuminemia is present in 34% of patients. The serum complement is reduced in nephritis, in extensive skin involvement, in central nervous system involvement, and in acute systemic lupus erythematosus. The reduction of serum complement may be the result of increased utilization due to immune complex formation, to reduced synthesis, or to a combination of both factors. The serum of patients with active systemic lupus erythematosus occasionally contains circulating cryoglobulin complexes of

IgM/IgG aggregates and complement that will precipitate in the cold. The concentration of free urinary light chains correlates positively with the activity of renal disease.

B. Autoantibodies:

1. LE cell phenomenon–This phenomenon was first described in the bone marrow of patients with systemic lupus erythematosus. The routine laboratory test for the LE cell phenomenon is now performed on heparinized peripheral blood which has been incubated for 30–60 minutes. The formation of the LE cell depends on the presence of a 7S IgG antibody that reacts with deoxyribonucleoprotein in the nucleus of damaged leukocytes and, in the presence of complement, leads to the destruction of the normal chromatin pattern. The DNA, immunoglobulin, and complement form a large homogeneous mass that is extruded from the damaged cell and ingested by a polymorphonuclear leukocyte. The LE cell is the leukocyte that has engulfed one or more of these homogeneous masses. The masses, which stain dark reddish-purple with Wright's stain, may form rosettes around neutrophils or may be seen free on a slide preparation. The LE cell phenomenon is observed in 75–80% of patients with systemic lupus erythematosus. Positive LE tests may also be seen in approximately 15% of patients with rheumatoid arthritis, scleroderma, or polydermatomyositis. The 7S IgG which initiates the phenomenon can be identified by complement fixation, immunofluorescent studies, hemagglutination, passive cutaneous anaphylaxis, and precipitin reactions. This antibody causes the homogeneous pattern in the fluorescent antinuclear antibody reaction. The antibody can cross the placenta but is not absorbed by intact cells. Like complement, it can be heat-inactivated.

2. Antinuclear antibodies (ANA)–Immunoglobulins of all classes may form antinuclear antibodies. There is no correlation between the immunoglobulin class of ANA and the clinical manifestations of systemic lupus erythematosus. Friou in 1957 introduced the indirect immunofluorescence technic. Six different morphologic patterns of immunofluorescent staining have been described, 4 of which have clinical significance (Fig 27–1).

a. The "homogeneous" ("diffuse" or "solid") pattern is the morphologic expression of antideoxyribonucleoprotein and is strongly associated with active systemic lupus erythematosus. In this pattern the nucleus shows diffuse and uniform staining.

b. The "outline" ("shaggy" or "peripheral") pattern is the morphologic expression of anti-ds-DNA antibodies and antibodies to soluble nucleoprotein. The outline pattern is best seen when human leukocytes are used as substrate. It is characteristic of active systemic lupus erythematosus.

c. The "speckled" pattern reflects numerous points of fluorescence scattered throughout the nucleus. It is the morphologic expression of various antigens within the nucleus. Two antigens have been characterized: (1) the Sm antigen, a macromolecule resistant to ribonuclease and slowly destroyed by trypsin; and (2) an antigen associated with ribonucleoprotein, which is sensitive to both ribonuclease and trypsin. A speckled pattern is associated with scleroderma and is less frequently seen in systemic lupus erythematosus and other connective tissue diseases.

d. The "nucleolar" pattern is caused by the homogeneous staining of the nucleolus. It has been suggested that this antigen may be the ribosomal precursor of ribonucleoprotein. It is commonly seen in progressive systemic sclerosis (54%) and less frequently in systemic lupus erythematosus (24%) and rheumatoid arthritis (9%).

All the nuclear staining patterns must be interpreted with caution for the following reasons: (1) the serum of a patient with any collagen vascular disease may contain many autoantibodies to different nuclear constituents, so that a "homogeneous" pattern may obscure a "speckled" or "nucleolar" pattern; (2) different antibodies in the serum can be present in different titers, so that by diluting the serum one can change a "homogeneous" pattern to a "speckled" pattern; (3) the stability of the different antigens is different and can be changed by fixation or denaturation; and (4) the pattern observed appears to be influenced by the types of tissues or cells used as substrate for the test.

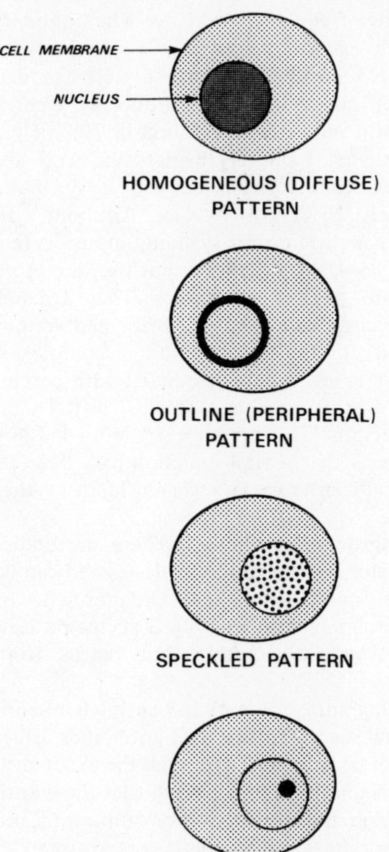

Figure 27–1. Patterns of immunofluorescent staining for antinuclear antibodies.

ANA determination is a very nonspecific test which is occasionally positive in normal individuals, in patients with various chronic diseases, and in the aged. However, the titer of ANA should be determined since high titers are most often associated with systemic lupus erythematosus. Absence of ANA is strong evidence against a diagnosis of systemic lupus erythematosus.

3. Anti-DNA antibodies–Three major types of anti-DNA antibodies can be found in the sera of lupus patients: (1) anti-single-stranded or "denatured" DNA (ss-DNA); (2) anti-double-stranded or "native" DNA (ds-DNA); and (3) antibodies which react to both ss-DNA and ds-DNA. These antibodies may be either IgG or IgM immunoglobulins. Anti-ds-DNA antibodies are seen in patients with active lupus nephritis or extensive skin involvement. In contrast, anti-ss-DNA antibodies are not specific and can be found in other autoimmune diseases, eg, rheumatoid arthritis, chronic active hepatitis, and primary biliary cirrhosis. Furthermore, antibodies to ss-DNA occur in drug-induced lupus-like syndrome and can be induced in experimental animals by the injection of DNA complexed to protein and emulsified in Freund's complete adjuvant. Antibodies to DNA can be quantitatively measured by a radioimmunoassay using labeled DNA. The amount of antibody correlates well with disease activity, and the antibody titer frequently decreases when patients enter remission.

4. Anti-RNA antibodies–Anti-double-stranded RNA (ds-RNA) antibodies and antibodies against DNA:RNA hybrid molecules are found in 70% of patients with systemic lupus erythematosus. Anti-ds-RNA antibodies react to viral as well as synthetic ds-RNA (eg, poly I · C, poly A · U). Antibodies to ds-RNA are not as specific for systemic lupus erythematosus as anti-ds-DNA antibodies, but they are more specific than anti-ss-DNA antibodies. They are not necessarily associated with lupus nephritis and are not generally found in the renal immune complexes. Because ds-RNA is commonly associated with certain types of viruses, it is possible that anti-ds-RNA reflects viral infection. The presence of anti-ds-RNA antibodies suggests that a viral infection may have an etiologically significant role in systemic lupus erythematosus.

5. Antierythrocyte antibodies–These antibodies belong to all major immunoglobulin classes and can be detected by the direct Coombs test. The prevalence of these antibodies among systemic lupus erythematosus patients is not precisely known but ranges from 10–65%.

6. Circulating anticoagulants and antiplatelet antibodies–It is now suspected that IgG antibodies affect the first stages of coagulation. Although the exact antigenic substrate is uncertain, it is known that these antibodies act only in the presence of prothrombin and that they decrease the prothrombin time. Antiplatelet antibodies are found in 75–80% of patients with systemic lupus erythematosus. These antibodies inhibit neither clot retraction nor thromboplastin generation in normal blood. They probably induce thrombocytopenia by direct effects on platelet surface membrane.

7. False-positive serologic test for syphilis–A false-positive VDRL test is seen in 10–20% of patients with systemic lupus erythematosus. The serologic test for syphilis can be considered an autoimmune reaction because the antigen is a phospholipid present in many human organs.

8. Rheumatoid factors–Almost 30% of patients with systemic lupus erythematosus have a positive latex fixation test for rheumatoid factors.

9. Organ-specific antibodies–Antibodies to thyroglobulin have been found in 20% of patients, though thyroiditis is not common in systemic lupus erythematosus (1%). Antimuscle antibodies are very rare. By testing the sera of patients with lupus against crude organ extracts, antibodies against liver, kidney, and joint tissue have been found. This phenomenon probably represents anticytoplasmic or antinuclear antibody activity.

10. Anticytoplasmic antibodies–Numerous anticytoplasmic antibodies (antimitochondrial, antiribosomal, antilysosomal) have been found in patients with systemic lupus erythematosus. These antibodies are not organ- or species-specific. The antiribosomal antibodies are found in the sera of 25–50% of patients. The major antigenic determinant is ribosomal RNA. Antimitochondrial antibodies are more common in other diseases (eg, primary biliary cirrhosis) than in systemic lupus erythematosus.

C. Tissue Immunofluorescence Studies:

1. Kidney–(See Chapter 32.) Irregular or granular accumulation of immunoglobulin and complement occurs along the glomerular basement membrane in patients with lupus nephritis. On electron microscopy, these deposits are seen to be both subepithelial and subendothelial.

2. Skin–Almost 90% of patients with systemic lupus erythematosus have immunoglobulin and complement deposition in the dermal-epidermal junction of skin which is *not* involved with an active lupus rash. Patients with discoid lupus erythematosus show deposition of immunoglobulin and complement only in involved skin (see Chapter 33).

Differential Diagnosis

The diagnosis of systemic lupus erythematosus in patients with classical multisystem involvement and a positive ANA test is not difficult. However, the onset of the disease can be vague and insidious and can therefore present a perplexing diagnostic problem. When migratory polyarthritis is the major complaint, rheumatoid arthritis and rheumatic fever have to be considered. When Raynaud's phenomenon is the predominant complaint, progressive systemic sclerosis must be considered. Systemic lupus erythematosus can present with a myositis similar to that of polymyositis-dermatomyositis.

Felty's syndrome (thrombocytopenia, leukocytopenia, splenomegaly in patients with rheumatoid arthritis) can simulate systemic lupus erythematosus. Sometimes the diagnosis of systemic lupus erythematosus can be facilitated by finding anti-ds-DNA or a high titer of ANA (outline pattern) in serum. Some patients with discoid lupus erythematosus may develop leukocytopenia, thrombocytopenia, hypergammaglobulinemia, ANA, and an elevated sedimentation rate. Ten percent of patients with discoid lupus erythematosus have LE cells and associated mild systemic symptoms. Although the exact relationship between systemic lupus erythematosus and discoid lupus erythematosus is uncertain, the frequent presence of anti-ds-RNA in discoid lupus erythematosus suggests that they are parts of a single disease spectrum.

Treatment

The efficacy of the drugs used in the treatment of systemic lupus erythematosus is difficult to evaluate, since spontaneous remissions occur in the disease. There are few controlled studies, because it is difficult to withhold therapy in the face of the life-threatening disease which can develop in fulminant systemic lupus erythematosus. Depending on the severity of the disease, no treatment, minimal treatment (aspirin, antimalarials), or intensive treatment (corticosteroids, immunosuppressive drugs) may be required.

When arthritis is the predominant symptom and other organ systems are not significantly involved, aspirin in high doses is the treatment of choice. When the skin or mucosa is predominantly involved, antimalarials (hydroxychloroquine or chloroquine) and topical corticosteroids are very beneficial. Because high-dosage antimalarial therapy may be associated with irreversible retinal toxicity, these drugs should be used judiciously and in low doses.

Systemic corticosteroids in severe systemic lupus erythematosus can suppress disease activity and prolong life. The administration of systemic corticosteroids in the absence of fulminant or life-threatening systemic lupus erythematosus is unnecessary and dangerous. The mode of action is unknown, but the immunosuppressive or anti-inflammatory properties of these agents presumably play a significant role in their therapeutic efficacy. High-dosage corticosteroid treatment (eg, prednisone, 1 mg/kg/day orally) decreases γ-globulin levels and autoantibody titers and suppresses immune responses. High-dosage corticosteroid therapy is recommended in acute fulminant lupus, acute lupus nephritis, acute central nervous system lupus, acute autoimmune hemolytic anemia, and thrombocytopenic purpura. The course of corticosteroid therapy should be monitored by the clinical response and meticulous follow-up of laboratory and immunologic parameters—complete blood count with reticulocyte and platelet counts, anti-ds-DNA titer, complement levels, etc.

If the clinical and immunologic status of the patient fails to improve, or if serious side-effects of corticosteroid therapy develop, immunosuppressive therapy with alkylating agents or antimetabolites is indicated. These agents have cytotoxic, immunosuppressive, and anti-inflammatory properties. Because of serious complications (malignancy, marrow suppression, infection, and liver and gastrointestinal toxicity), immunosuppressive agents should be used with discretion.

Complications & Prognosis

Systemic lupus erythematosus can run a very mild course confined to one or a few organs, or it can be a fulminant life-threatening disease leading to death. Renal failure and central nervous system lupus were the leading causes of death until the corticosteroids and cytotoxic agents came into widespread use. Since then, infection and malignancy have become the commonest causes of death. The 5-year survival rate of patients with systemic lupus erythematosus has markedly improved over the past decade and now approaches 80–90%.

RHEUMATOID ARTHRITIS (RA)

Major Immunologic Features

- 7S and 19S IgM and 7S IgG rheumatoid factors in serum and synovial fluid.
- Decreased complement and elevated β_2-microglobulin in synovial fluid.
- Pannus and rheumatoid nodule formation.

General Considerations

Rheumatoid arthritis is a chronic recurrent, systemic inflammatory disease primarily involving the joints. Constitutional symptoms include malaise, fever, and weight loss. The disease characteristically begins in the small joints of the hands and feet and progresses in a centripetal and symmetric fashion. Deformities are common. Extra-articular manifestations include vasculitis, atrophy of the skin and muscle, subcutaneous nodules, lymphadenopathy, splenomegaly, and leukocytopenia.

The disease affects 1–3% of Americans annually, with a female to male ratio of 3:1. Family studies have failed to reveal any direct genetic transmission of the disease.

Immunologic Pathogenesis

The antigenic stimulus that initiates the immune response and subsequent inflammation in rheumatoid arthritis is unknown. For several reasons (including decreased sensitivity of rheumatoid synovial cells to infection by Newcastle disease virus and rubella virus), it is suspected that rheumatoid arthritis may be caused by a "slow" or persistent virus infection. However, no virus particles have ever been identified. Whatever the antigenic stimulus, the sequence of immunologic events leading to subsequent rheumatoid joint disease has been well described (Fig 27–2).

Synovial lymphocytes produce IgG that is recognized as foreign and stimulates an immune response within the joint, with production of 7S IgG, 7S IgM, and 19S IgM anti-immunoglobulins, ie, rheumatoid factors. The presence of IgG aggregates or IgG-rheu-

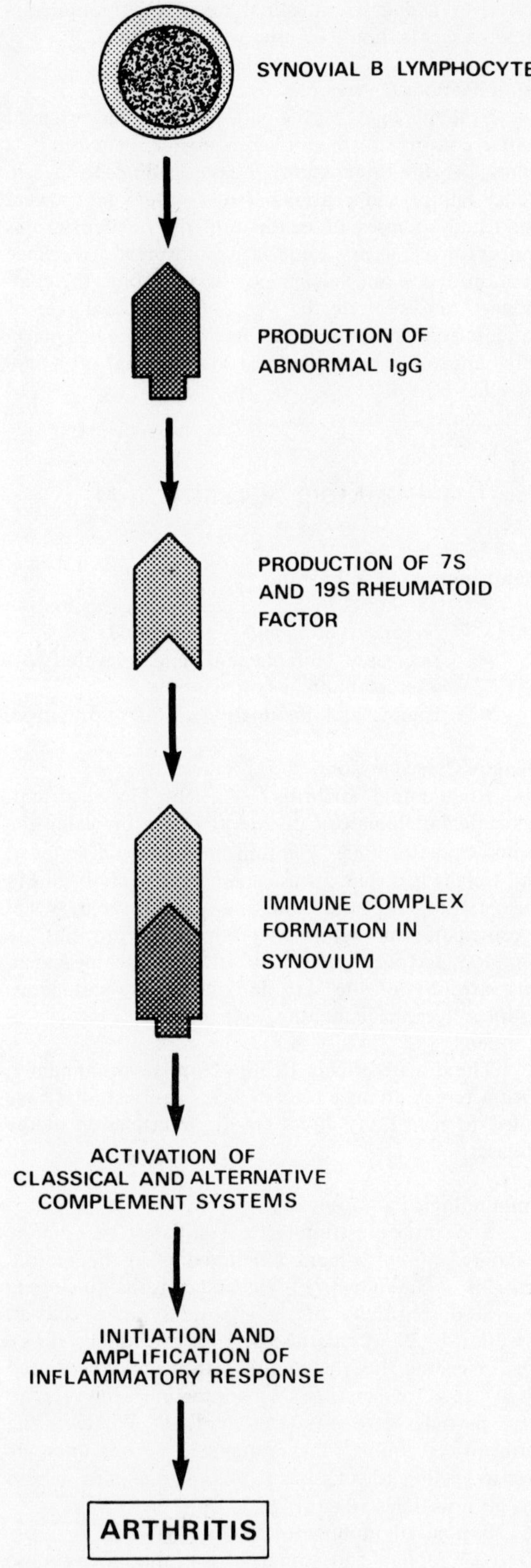

Figure 27–2. Hypothetical immunopathogenesis in rheumatoid arthritis.

matoid factor complexes results in activation of the classical complement system. Breakdown products of complement accumulate within the joint and amplify the activation of complement by stimulation of the alternative (properdin) system. Activation of the complement system results in a number of inflammatory phenomena, including histamine release, the production of factors chemotactic for polymorphonuclear leukocytes and mononuclear cells, and membrane damage with cell lysis (see Chapter 6). There is a marked influx of white cells into the synovial space. Some polymorphonuclear cells, called "RA cells" or "ragocytes," contain characteristic dense cytoplasmic inclusion bodies composed of ingested IgG aggregates, rheumatoid factor, complement, and fibrin. Activated lysosomes and enzymes released into the synovial space by leukocytes further amplify the inflammatory and proliferative response of the synovium. The mononuclear infiltrate characteristically seen within the synovium includes perivascular collections of small lymphocytes, lymphoblasts, plasma cells, and macrophages. The lymphocytic infiltrate is made up of both T and B cells. The immunologic interaction of these cells leads to the liberation of lymphokines responsible for the accumulation of macrophages within the inflammatory synovium and to continued immunoglobulin and rheumatoid factor synthesis.

Rheumatoid factor probably plays a role in the causation of extra-articular disease. Patients with rheumatoid vasculitis have high titers of 19S and 7S IgM and 7S IgG rheumatoid factors. Antigen-antibody complexes infused into experimental animals in the presence of IgM rheumatoid factor induce necrotizing vasculitis. Theoretically, immune complexes initiate vascular inflammation by the activation of complement. Pulmonary involvement is associated with the deposition of 11S and 15S protein complexes containing IgG in the walls of pulmonary vessels and alveoli. 19S IgM rheumatoid factor has also been detected in arterioles and alveolar walls adjacent to cavitary nodules. Rheumatoid factors do not initiate the inflammatory process that causes rheumatoid disease, but they probably perpetuate and amplify that process by their effects on complement activation.

A recent finding in the joint effusion of patients with active rheumatoid arthritis is an elevation of β_2-microglobulin levels. Beta$_2$-microglobulin is a small protein (MW 11,800) found on the surface of all human cells as part of the HLA antigen complex. Its amino acid sequence is similar to that of a constant region domain of the IgG heavy chain (see Chapter 2). It is normally present in low concentrations in serum and other body fluids but is elevated—probably because of increased local production—in the joint fluid of patients with rheumatoid arthritis.

Clinical Features

A. Symptoms and Signs:

1. Onset—The usual age at onset is 20–40 years. In most cases the disease presents with joint manifestations; however, some patients first develop extra-articular manifestations, including fatigue, weakness, weight loss, mild fever, and anorexia.

2. Articular manifestations–Patients experience stiffness and joint pain which are generally worse in the morning and improve throughout the day. These symptoms are accompanied by signs of articular inflammation, including swelling, warmth, erythema, and tenderness on palpation. The arthritis is symmetric, involving the small joints of the hands and feet, ie, the proximal interphalangeals, metacarpophalangeals, the wrists, and the subtalars. Large joints (knees, hips, elbows, ankles, shoulders) commonly become involved later in the course of the disease. Although the cervical spine may be involved, the thoracic and lumbosacral spine is usually spared.

Periarticular inflammation is common, with tendonitis and tenosynovitis resulting in weakening of tendons, ligaments, and supporting structures. Joint pain leads to muscle spasm, limitation of motion, and, in advanced cases, muscle contractions and ankylosis with permanent joint deformity. The most characteristic deformities in the hand are ulnar deviation of the fingers, the "boutonniere" deformity (flexed proximal interphalangeal joints are forced through the extensor hood), and the "swan neck" deformity (hyperextension of proximal interphalangeal joints and flexion of the distal interphalangeal joints).

3. Extra-articular manifestations–Twenty to 25% of patients (particularly those with severe disease) have subcutaneous or subperiosteal nodules, the so-called "rheumatoid nodules." These are usually present over bony eminences and may be difficult to distinguish clinically from gouty tophi. The most common sites of nodule formation are the olecranon bursa and the extensor surface of the forearm. Nodules are firm, nontender, round or oval masses which can be movable or fixed. They may be found in the myocardium, pericardium, heart valves, pleura, lungs, sclera, dura mater, spleen, larynx, and synovial tissues.

Lung involvement includes pleurisy (seen in up to 15% of patients) and interstitial lymphocytic pneumonitis or fibrosis (or both) (seen in less than 2% of patients). Caplan's syndrome is the development of large nodules in the lung parenchyma in patients with rheumatoid arthritis who also have pneumoconiosis. The manifestations of rheumatoid cardiac disease are myocarditis, valvular insufficiency, and conduction disturbances. Pericarditis has been found in 40% of autopsied rheumatoid patients.

Several types of vasculitis are associated with rheumatoid arthritis. The commonest form is an obliterative vasculitis due to intimal proliferation which leads to peripheral neuropathy. Less common is a subacute vasculitis associated with ischemic ulceration of the skin. The rarest form of rheumatoid vasculitis is a necrotizing vasculitis of medium and large vessels indistinguishable from polyarteritis nodosa. The major neurologic abnormalities in rheumatoid arthritis involve peripheral nerves. In addition to the peripheral neuropathy associated with vasculitis, there are a number of entrapment syndromes due to impingement of periarticular inflammatory tissue or amyloid on nerves passing through tight fascial planes that allow little room for inflammatory swelling. The carpal tunnel syndrome is a well-known complication of wrist disease; however, entrapment can also occur at the elbow, ankle, and knee.

Sjögren's syndrome (keratoconjunctivitis sicca and xerostomia) may occur in up to 30% of patients. Myositis with lymphocytic infiltration of involved muscle is rarely seen. The eye may be involved with a chronic inflammatory process leading to scleromalacia. A catastrophic but rare complication of scleromalacia is perforation of the eye with extrusion of vitreous (scleromalacia perforans).

4. Felty's syndrome–Felty's syndrome is the association of rheumatoid arthritis, splenomegaly, and leukocytopenia. The syndrome almost always develops in patients with high rheumatoid factor (RF) titers and rheumatoid nodules. Other features of hypersplenism and lymphadenopathy may also be present. Because of the leukocytopenia, these patients are at increased risk of developing bacterial infections.

B. Laboratory Findings: A normochromic, normocytic anemia is universal among patients with active disease. One-fourth of patients have lymphocytosis. The sedimentation rate is elevated, and the degree of elevation correlates roughly with disease activity.

The synovial fluid is more inflammatory than that seen in degenerative osteoarthritis or systemic lupus erythematosus but not as inflammatory as the synovial fluid in septic or crystalloid-induced arthritis. The synovial fluid protein concentration ranges from 2.5 g/dl to over 3.5 g/dl. The white cell count is 5000–20,000/μl (rarely over 50,000/μl). Two-thirds of the cells are polymorphonuclear leukocytes which discharge lysosomal enzymes into the synovial fluid, leading to depolymerization of synovial hyaluronate, decreased viscosity, and a poor mucin clot. The glucose level may be low or normal. Rheumatoid factor can be found in synovial fluid, and complement is often depressed.

The rheumatoid pleural effusion is an exudate containing less than 5000 mononuclear or polymorphonuclear leukocytes per microliter. Protein exceeds 3 g/dl, and glucose is often reduced below 20 mg/dl. Rheumatoid factors can be detected, and complement levels are usually low.

There are 3 basic pathologic findings. The first is a recurrent or chronic inflammation of the joints leading to an inflammatory thickening of the synovium, called the pannus. The pannus may erode the articular cartilage and underlying bone, causing destruction and deformity of the joint.

The second finding, the rheumatoid nodule, consists of an irregularly shaped central zone of fibrinoid necrosis surrounded by a margin of large mononuclear cells. This core is surrounded in turn by an outer zone of granulation tissue containing plasma cells and lymphocytes. The third finding, the vasculitis, has been mentioned above.

C. X-Ray Findings: The first detectable x-ray abnormalities are soft tissue swelling and juxta-articular demineralization. The destruction of articular cartilage leads to joint space narrowing. Bony erosions develop at the junction of the synovial membrane and the articular cartilage. Destruction of the cartilage and laxity of ligaments lead to maladjustment and subluxation of articular surfaces. Spondylitis is usually limited to the cervical spine with osteoporosis, joint space narrowing, erosions, destruction, and finally subluxation of the involved articulations. Atlantoaxial subluxation may lead to crush injury of the cord and result in quadriplegia.

Immunologic Diagnosis

The differential diagnosis between rheumatoid arthritis, systemic lupus erythematosus, scleroderma, and rheumatic fever is sometimes difficult. Although the clinical picture may be characteristic, the final diagnosis often depends on immunologic evaluation. In rheumatoid arthritis, serum protein electrophoresis may show an increased α_2-globulin, a polyclonal hypergammaglobulinemia, and hypoalbuminemia. Cryoprecipitates composed of immunoglobulins are often seen in rheumatoid vasculitis. Serum complement levels are usually normal but may be factitiously reported as low in the presence of cryoprecipitates. Five to 10% of patients have a false-positive VDRL; 8–27% have a positive LE cell preparation; and 20–70% have antinuclear antibodies. The most important serologic finding is the elevated rheumatoid factor titer, present in over 75% of patients. Rheumatoid factors are immunoglobulins with specificity for the Fc fragment of IgG. Most laboratory technics detect 19S IgM rheumatoid factor, but rheumatoid factor properties are also seen in 7S IgM, IgG, and IgA immunoglobulins. 19S IgM rheumatoid factor may combine with IgG molecules to form a soluble circulating 22S immunoglobulin complex in the serum.

Several tests are available in the laboratory to detect rheumatoid factor. The earliest test, now rarely used, was the streptococcal agglutination reaction. The latex fixation test is now the most commonly used method for detection of rheumatoid factor. Aggregated γ-globulin (Cohn fraction II) is adsorbed onto latex particles, which will then agglutinate in the presence of rheumatoid factor. The latex fixation test is not specific but is very sensitive, resulting in a high incidence of false-positive results. The sensitized sheep red cell test (Rose-Waaler test) depends on specific antibody binding and is the most specific test in common use. Sheep red blood cells are coated with rabbit antibody against sheep red blood cells, and the sensitized sheep cells will then agglutinate in the presence of rheumatoid factor. More complicated tests include a radioimmunoassay for IgM rheumatoid factor and an immunodiffusion assay, which provides better quantification and more precise information on the immunoglobulin classes of rheumatoid factor.

It is important to emphasize that a negative rheumatoid factor by routine laboratory procedures does not exclude the diagnosis of rheumatoid arthritis. The so-called seronegative patient may have 7S IgG or IgM rheumatoid factor or circulating IgG-anti-IgG complexes. Conversely, rheumatoid factors are not unique to rheumatoid arthritis. Rheumatoid factor is also present in patients with systemic lupus erythematosus (30%), in a high percentage (90%) of patients with Sjögren's syndrome, and less often in patients with scleroderma or polymyositis. Positive agglutination reactions with the latex or bentonite tests also occur in patients with hypergammaglobulinemia associated with liver disease, kala-azar, sarcoidosis, and syphilis. The sensitized sheep red cell test is usually negative in these conditions. In some chronic infectious diseases such as leprosy and tuberculosis, both the latex and the sensitized sheep red cell tests may be positive. In subacute bacterial endocarditis, both tests may be positive during active disease and revert to negative as patients improve. The transient appearance of rheumatoid factor has been noted following vaccinations in military recruits. Epidemiologic studies have shown that a small number of normal people also have rheumatoid factors. A large proportion of old people have a positive latex test, though the sensitized sheep red cell test is generally negative.

Differential Diagnosis

In the patient with classical articular changes, bony erosions of the small joints of the hands and feet, and rheumatoid factor in serum or synovial fluid, the diagnosis of rheumatoid arthritis is not difficult. Early in the disease, or when extra-articular manifestations dominate the clinical picture, other rheumatic diseases (including systemic lupus erythematosus, Reiter's syndrome, gout, psoriatic arthritis, degenerative osteoarthritis, and the peripheral arthritis of chronic ulcerative and inflammatory bowel disease) may mimic rheumatoid arthritis. Patients with systemic lupus erythematosus can be distinguished by their characteristic skin lesions, renal disease, and diagnostic serologic abnormalities. Reiter's syndrome occurs in young men and is associated with urethritis and conjunctivitis. Gouty arthritis is usually an acute monoarthritis with negatively birefringent sodium urate crystals present within the white cells of inflammatory synovial fluid. Psoriatic arthritis often involves distal interphalangeal joints and produces nail changes. Degenerative arthritis is characterized by Heberden's nodes, lack of symmetric joint involvement, and involvement of the distal rather than the proximal interphalangeal joints. The peripheral arthritis of bowel disease usually occurs in large weight-bearing joints and is often associated with bowel symptoms. The polyarthritis associated with rubella vaccination, HB_sAg antigenemia, or infectious mononucleosis can mimic early rheumatoid arthritis.

Treatment

A. Physical Therapy: A rational program of physical therapy is vital in the management of patients with rheumatoid arthritis. Such a program should consist of an appropriate balance of rest and exercise and the judicious use of heat therapy. The patient may require complete or intermittent bed rest on a regular basis to combat inflammation or fatigue. In addition, specific joints may have to be put at rest through the use of braces, splints, or crutches. An exercise program emphasizing active range of motion movements must be initiated to maintain strength and mobility. Heat is valuable in alleviating muscle spasm, stiffness, and pain. Many patients need a hot shower or bath to loosen up in the morning, and others cannot perform their exercises adequately without prior heat treatment. Heating pads or paraffin baths are often used to apply heat to specific joints.

B. Drug Treatment:

1. Salicylates–Salicylates are the mainstay of medical therapy of rheumatoid arthritis. Aspirin is an anti-inflammatory as well as an antipyretic and analgesic agent. Although its exact mechanism of action is uncertain, it may act in part by inhibiting the production of prostaglandins. The doses used in patients with rheumatoid arthritis range from 3.6–5.4 g (12–18 tablets) per day in divided doses. High-dosage aspirin therapy is associated with numerous side-effects. Tinnitus–with or without hearing loss–can be bothersome but is usually reversible with a minor decrease in dosage. Gastric upset is almost universal but can be partly alleviated by liberally using antacids and by encouraging patients to take their aspirin with meals. Microscopic blood loss from the gastrointestinal tract is very common and is not an indication for stopping aspirin therapy. Since aspirin does decrease platelet adhesiveness, it should be used cautiously in patients receiving coumarin anticoagulants.

2. Other nonsteroid agents–Several other nonsteroid anti-inflammatory agents have found limited use in the treatment of rheumatoid arthritis. Phenylbutazone may be used temporarily in acute flare-ups; it is not useful on a long-term basis because of its multiple severe side-effects (agranulocytosis, peptic ulceration, salt and water retention). Indomethacin appears to be of particular benefit in patients with hip disease, but it too causes serious side-effects (gastric intolerance, peptic ulceration, psychic disturbances, marrow depression). Other newer preparations (fenoprofen, ibuprofen, naproxen) may be useful in patients who cannot tolerate aspirin because of its gastrointestinal side-effects.

Many rheumatologists advocate the use of antimalarial drugs for prolonged periods in patients with severe disease. The antimalarials act slowly, often requiring 1–6 months of treatment for maximum therapeutic benefit. The preparations and dosages most often used are chloroquine, 250 mg orally daily, or hydroxychloroquine, 200–600 mg orally daily. The toxic side-effects of these agents include skin rashes, nausea and vomiting, and both corneal and retinal damage. The incidence of eye toxicity is rare at the low doses used in rheumatoid arthritis, but patients should have ophthalmologic examinations every 4–6 months while on antimalarial therapy.

3. Parenteral gold salt therapy, although associated with a high incidence of toxic side-effects, is of significant benefit to many patients. It is one of the few therapeutic agents that is believed to alter the long-term course of the disease. Gold acts as a lysosomal membrane stabilizer, but the relationship of this action to its therapeutic benefit is unclear. It is administered intramuscularly, with an initial test dose of 10 mg of gold salt, followed in 1 week by a dose of 25 mg. If no toxic reactions occur after the second dose, the patient receives 50 mg of gold salt intramuscularly every week for 10–14 weeks, every other week for 16 weeks, and then every 3–4 weeks indefinitely or until toxicity develops. Toxic side-effects occur in 40% of patients and include dermatitis, photosensitivity, stomatitis, agranulocytosis, hepatitis, aplastic anemia, peripheral neuropathy, nephritis with nephrotic syndrome, ulcerative enterocolitis, and keratitis. Before each dose, the patient should have a physical examination, a urinalysis, and a complete blood count. Liver function tests should be performed periodically. If toxic side-effects develop, the drug should be withdrawn. Corticosteroids and dimercaprol or penicillamine may be of benefit if life-threatening toxicity occurs.

4. Penicillamine–In Europe, penicillamine has been found to be useful in the treatment of rheumatoid arthritis. The mechanism of action is unknown, but it appears to lead to slow improvement, requiring up to 12 months to achieve maximum clinical benefit. The initial dose of 150 mg orally daily is increased by 150 mg every 4 weeks until improvement occurs or until the patient is receiving a maximum dose of 600 mg daily. Toxic side-effects include rash, loss of sense of taste, nausea and vomiting, anorexia, proteinuria, agranulocytosis, aplastic anemia, and thrombocytopenia. Since penicillamine is a chelating agent, it cannot be used simultaneously with gold salt therapy.

5. Corticosteroids–Corticosteroids can be used locally or systemically. Intermittent intra-articular injection of corticosteroids is useful if the patient has a limited number of symptomatic joints. Relief may last for months. However, multiple intra-articular corticosteroid injections of weight-bearing joints should be avoided, since multiple injections may lead to infection and are associated with an increased incidence of degenerative arthritis. Systemic corticosteroids may induce a dramatic clinical response but do not alter the course of the disease. Usually, no more than 5–10 mg of prednisone daily are required. Corticosteroids should be considered as an adjunct to salicylate therapy rather than a substitute. It is difficult to withdraw corticosteroids, since attempts to do so often result in clinical exacerbation of arthritis. Long-term systemic corticosteroid treatment results in hyperadrenocorticism and disruption of the pituitary-adrenal axis. Manifestations of corticosteroid toxicity include weight gain, moon facies, ecchymoses, hirsutism, diabetes mellitus, hypertension, osteoporosis, avascular necrosis of the femoral head, cataracts, myopathy, mental disturbances, activation of tuberculosis, and infections.

6. Immunosuppressive agents have been known to induce dramatic improvement in patients with severe disease and, like gold, may alter the course of the disease. Alkylating agents (eg, chlorambucil, cyclophosphamide) and purine analogues (eg, mercaptopurine, azathioprine) have been used in the treatment of rheumatoid arthritis. However, these drugs are associated with major toxic side-effects, are teratogenic, and are associated with an increased incidence of lymphoma and infection. The routine use of these agents in the treatment of rheumatoid arthritis is to be strongly discouraged.

C. Orthopedic Surgery: Surgery is an essential part of the general management of the patient with rheumatoid arthritis. Surgical procedures can correct or compensate for joint damage. Arthroplasty is employed to maintain or improve joint motion. Arthrodesis can be used to correct deformity and alleviate pain, but it results in loss of motion. Some authorities advocate early synovectomy to prevent joint damage and deformity. Synovectomy will decrease pain and inflammation in a given joint, but the synovium often grows back and symptoms return.

Complications & Prognosis

Several clinical patterns of rheumatoid arthritis are apparent. Spontaneous remission may occur, usually within 2 years after the onset of the disease. Other patients have brief episodes of acute arthritis with longer periods of low-grade activity or remission. Rare patients will have sustained progression of active disease resulting in deformity and death. The presence of active disease for more than 1 year, an age of less than 30 at onset of disease, and the presence of rheumatoid nodules and high titers of rheumatoid factor are unfavorable prognostic factors.

Follow-up of patients after 10–15 years shows that 50% are stationary or improved, 70% are capable of full-time employment, and 10% are completely incapacitated. Death from vasculitis or atlantoaxial subluxation is rare. Fatalities are more often associated with sepsis or the complications of therapy.

JUVENILE RHEUMATOID ARTHRITIS (JRA)

Major Immunologic Features

- Negative or "hidden" rheumatoid factor in the serum and synovial fluid.
- Depressed in vivo and in vitro delayed hypersensitivity.
- Elevated serum and depressed synovial complement.

General Considerations

Juvenile rheumatoid arthritis is a crippling form of arthritis of unknown cause that usually affects individuals under 16 years of age. The principal symptoms are a nonmigratory monarticular or polyarticular arthropathy with a tendency to involve large joints or proximal interphalangeal joints. Systemic manifestations include fever, erythematous rashes, nodules, and leukocytosis. Iridocyclitis, pleuritis, pericarditis, hepatitis, and nephritis occur with less frequency. Although upper respiratory infections and trauma have both been implicated as precipitating factors, the roles of infection, trauma, and heredity in the pathogenesis of the disease are unclear. The disease affects predominantly girls. Although the onset of the disease may be as early as 6 weeks of life, most children are between 2 and 5 or between 9 and 12 years of age at onset. Juvenile rheumatoid arthritis is a major cause of fever of undetermined origin in children.

Immunologic Pathogenesis

The basic immunopathogenic mechanisms in juvenile rheumatoid arthritis are unknown. However, both humoral and cellular defects occur in these patients. Diffuse hypergammaglobulinemia, involving IgG, IgA, and IgM, is present. Rheumatoid factors of all immunoglobulin classes have been detected. Approximately 20% of children with juvenile rheumatoid arthritis have a positive latex fixation test for 19S IgM rheumatoid factor. When IgM of patients with juvenile rheumatoid arthritis is isolated from serum, the percentage of latex positivity rises to 46%. Two major theories have been brought forward in an attempt to explain the presence of this "hidden" rheumatoid factor in juvenile rheumatoid arthritis. First, IgM rheumatoid factor may bind avidly to native IgG in the patient's serum and therefore may not be able to bind IgG coating the latex particles. Second, an abnormal IgG may be present which preferentially binds IgM, thereby blocking latex fixation. Cold-reacting (4 C) 19S IgM rheumatoid factors (cryoglobulins) are associated with severe disease.

A number of studies of antibody responses to various antigens have been performed in patients with juvenile rheumatoid arthritis. The primary response appears to be normal. However, the secondary response, particularly to diphtheria and tetanus toxoids, is hyperactive. Except for rheumatoid factors, no abnormal autoantibodies or isohemagglutinins have been detected in these patients.

Serum components of both the classical and alternative (properdin) complement systems are elevated, although this elevation is less in patients who have rheumatoid factors or severe disease. CH_{50}, C3, and C4 in the synovial fluid tend to be low, particularly in patients with a positive serum latex fixation or with IgG rheumatoid factor in the synovial fluid. Elevation of serum complement may reflect a secondary overcompensation in response to increased consumption, or possibly a general increase in protein synthesis. Studies of the metabolism of complement actually demonstrate hypercatabolism. The depression of complement in synovial fluid is probably secondary to complement activation by the immune complexes, similar to that seen in rheumatoid arthritis.

A defect in cellular immunity may contribute to the immunopathogenesis of juvenile rheumatoid arthritis, since decreased delayed hypersensitivity has been demonstrated in some patients. Transfer factor therapy has been used in a few patients, with improvement in their in vivo skin test responses as well as their in vitro responses to mitogens. The improvement in cellular immunity has been associated with clinical improvement, although a causal relationship is not established.

Clinical Features

A. Symptoms and Signs:

1. Onset–The disease has several clinically distinct modes of onset:

a. Twenty percent of children, usually boys, present with high, spiking fever in a severe toxic state (Still's disease). Polyarthralgias usually precede frank arthritis. These children have hepatosplenomegaly, lymphadenopathy, and a characteristic salmon-colored morbilliform rash. Pleuritis, pericarditis, and myocarditis have been described in severe cases.

b. About half of patients with juvenile rheumatoid arthritis present with an asymmetric polyarticular arthritis. The onset may be abrupt or insidious, and 4 or more joints may be involved.

c. Thirty percent of patients present with few systemic manifestations and asymmetric involvement of only one or 2 joints. Iridocyclitis is most likely to develop in this group of patients.

2. Joint manifestations–It is remarkable that children have few articular complaints even in the presence of severe arthritis. The knees, wrists, ankles, and neck are common sites of initial involvement. Older children may occasionally develop symmetric involvement in the small joints of the hands (metacarpophalangeal, proximal interphalangeal, distal interphalangeal). Involved joints are red, warm, tender, and swollen. In severe disease, children are more likely to develop radial rather than ulnar deviation. Severe involvement of the feet may lead to hallux valgus or hammer toe deformity. Achillobursitis and achillotendonitis may cause tender, swollen heels.

3. Systemic manifestations–Fever, often high and spiking, is seen in the majority of children. Anorexia, weight loss, and malaise are common. Thirty percent of children develop an evanescent, salmon-colored maculopapular rash that coincides with periods of high fever. Ten percent of patients with juvenile rheumatoid arthritis have clinically manifest cardiac involvement, with pericarditis being the most common cardiac manifestation. Even though pericarditis is present in 45% of severe cases at postmortem examination, it rarely leads to dysfunction or constriction. Myocarditis, which is an unusual manifestation of the cardiac disease, has been known to cause heart failure.

Cases of acute pneumonitis or pleuritis have been described. However, chronic rheumatoid lung disease is rarely seen in juvenile rheumatoid arthritis.

Iridocyclitis occurs in 5–15% of cases, usually those with monarticular disease. This manifestation rarely precedes articular involvement, but it often persists even when joints become quiescent. The iridocyclitis often runs an insidious course and is best monitored by frequent slitlamp examinations.

Lymphadenopathy and hepatosplenomegaly are associated with severe systemic disease and are uncommon in patients with chiefly articular manifestations. It is felt that the abdominal pain which occurs in some children is due to mesenteric lymphadenopathy.

Subcutaneous nodules occur in 6% of children with juvenile rheumatoid arthritis. They resemble the nodules of rheumatic fever and are histologically quite different from the classical rheumatoid nodule.

4. Complications–Vasculitis and encephalitis have been occasionally described in patients with juvenile rheumatoid arthritis. Secondary amyloidosis occurs in 10% of patients. The major complication, which occurs in up to 50% of patients with juvenile rheumatoid arthritis, is impairment of growth and development. The extent of the impairment is correlated with the severity and the duration of disease activity. Irreversible retardation of development is due to early epiphyseal closure. This is particularly common in the mandible, causing micrognathia, and in the metacarpals and metatarsals, leading to abnormally small digits.

B. Laboratory Findings: The synovial lesion of juvenile rheumatoid arthritis is a nonspecific synovitis with increased vascularity, synovial hypertrophy, and infiltration of synovial fluid with lymphocytes, plasma cells, and macrophages. A mild leukocytosis, between 15–25 thousand/μl, is the rule, but 15% of patients develop leukocytopenia. A normochromic microcytic anemia–in the range of 8–11 g/dl hemoglobin–is common. These patients have an elevated erythrocyte sedimentation rate and abnormal C-reactive protein. Thirty to 50% of children have elevated ASO titers, making it impossible to use this test to differentiate juvenile rheumatoid arthritis from rheumatic fever. Abnormal serologic findings include the presence of rheumatoid factor in 10–20% of patients, ANA in 13% of patients, and, occasionally, the LE cell phenomenon. Serum protein electrophoresis shows an increase in acute phase reactants (alpha globulins) and a polyclonal increase of γ-globulin. The synovial fluid in active juvenile rheumatoid arthritis is exudative, with a white count of 5–20 thousand/μl (mostly neutrophils), a poor mucin clot, and decreased glucose compared to serum glucose. Synovial fluid complement may be depressed, but not to the same degree as in adult rheumatoid arthritis.

C. X-Ray Findings: Radiographic changes which are seen early in the disease include periosteal bone accretion, premature closure of the epiphyses, cervical zygapophyseal fusion (particularly at C2–3), and osseous overgrowth of the interphalangeal joints, resembling Heberden's or Bouchard's nodes. Late findings include juxta-articular demineralization and erosion and narrowing of the joint space.

Immunologic Diagnosis

Currently, the diagnosis of juvenile rheumatoid arthritis is based on clinical criteria. Although certain abnormalities of immunoglobulins, complement, and cellular immunity are compatible with the diagnosis of juvenile rheumatoid arthritis, no specific immunologic test is available.

Differential Diagnosis

The diagnosis of juvenile rheumatoid arthritis sine arthritis is extremely difficult since the disease can present with nonspecific constitutional signs and symptoms in the absence of arthritis. Other causes of fever, particularly infections and cancer, must be considered. Leukemia can present in childhood with fever, lymphadenopathy, and joint pains. Rheumatic fever closely resembles juvenile rheumatoid arthritis, particularly early in the disease. However, the patient with juvenile rheumatoid arthritis tends to have higher spiking fevers, lymphadenopathy and hepatosplenomegaly in the absence of carditis, and a more refractory, long-lasting arthritis. Rheumatic fever patients are more likely to have evidence of recent streptococcal infection, including elevated titers of antihyaluronidase, antistreptokinase, and antistreptodornase. ASO titers are elevated in both disorders. Rheumatoid diseases that may begin in childhood, such as systemic lupus erythematosus or dermatomyositis, can be differentiated by their different clinical course, different organ system involvement, and characteristic serologic abnormalities.

When juvenile rheumatoid arthritis presents primarily with arthritis, examination of synovial fluid is of paramount importance in excluding tuberculosis and other infectious arthritides.

Treatment

The major goals of therapy are to prevent contractures and deformities and to promote normal emotional and physical development. These goals are best achieved by a comprehensive program of physical, medical, and, when necessary, surgical therapy.

A. Physical Therapy: As in the treatment of adult rheumatoid arthritis, rest is an important part of physical therapy. Complete rest is indicated during exacerbations and may be necessary for short afternoon periods on a routine basis. Specific joints can be put at rest by the use of splints, collars, and braces which support the joint and help prevent deformity. Judiciously used heat will decrease pain and muscle spasm and is particularly useful prior to exercise. Exercises tend to promote muscle strength and prevent deformity.

B. Medical Therapy:

1. Aspirin–The disease responds to aspirin at a dosage level of 90–130 mg/kg/day given in 4–6 doses. Tinnitus and salicylate levels are poor parameters of aspirin toxicity in children. Drowsiness and intermittent periods of hyperpnea are early signs. The manifestations of acute aspirin toxicity vary with the age of the child. Acidosis and ketosis may develop in infants. Respiratory alkalosis, due to primary stimulation of the respiratory center, occurs in older children.

2. Gold salts–Gold salts should only be used in children that are unresponsive to salicylates. If a test dose of 10 mg intramuscularly does not result in toxic signs, 1 mg/kg/week intramuscularly should be given. Best results are obtained when the drug is used early in the course of the disease. However, toxic effects may be more marked in children than in adults.

3. Corticosteroids–Intra-articular corticosteroid injections are useful in pauciarticular disease. Systemic corticosteroids are reserved for more severe disease with myocarditis, vasculitis, or iridocyclitis. Patients with iridocyclitis may require prolonged corticosteroid therapy. In children, the major toxic effects of corticosteroid therapy include subcapsular cataract formation, vertebral osteoporosis and collapse, infection, premature skeletal maturation with diminished growth, and pseudotumor cerebri with intracranial hypertension.

C. Surgical Treatment: The aim of surgery in juvenile rheumatoid arthritis is to correct or compensate for joint damage. Arthroplasty may maintain or increase motion. Arthrodesis can be performed for pain relief and correction of deformities but will decrease joint motion. Synovectomy is helpful in decreasing pain and inflammation in large joints. Unfortunately, surgery in children can lead to increased deformity as the child grows.

Complications & Prognosis

Seventy percent of patients experience a spontaneous and permanent remission by adulthood. Patients with Still's disease tend to have 1–10 recurrences per year. Patients presenting with oligoarthritic disease tend to remain oligoarthritic while those presenting with polyarthritis remain polyarthritic. Rarely, the disease persists into adulthood. This usually occurs in children with symmetric polyarthritis similar to that seen in adults. Sometimes a patient with juvenile rheumatoid arthritis in apparent remission develops rheumatoid arthritis as an adult. In an occasional unfortunate case, the disease becomes a prolonged crippling polyarthritis. Small joint involvement, positive serum rheumatoid factor, and onset in later childhood all portend a poor prognosis.

SJÖGREN'S SYNDROME

Major Immunologic Features

- Lymphocyte and plasma cell infiltration of involved tissues.
- Hypergammaglobulinemia, rheumatoid factor, and antinuclear antibodies.
- Autoantibodies against salivary duct antigens.
- Decreased lymphocyte responses to mitogens.
- Elevated salivary β_2-microglobulin.

General Considerations

Sjögren's syndrome is a chronic inflammatory disease of unknown cause characterized by diminished lacrimal and salivary gland secretion resulting in keratoconjunctivitis sicca and xerostomia. There is characteristic dryness of the eyes, mouth, nose, trachea, bronchi, vagina, and skin. Half of these patients have rheumatoid arthritis, and a small percentage have other connective tissue diseases. Ninety percent of patients with Sjögren's syndrome are female. Although the mean age at onset is 50 years, the disease has been detected rarely in children.

Immunologic Pathogenesis

The strong association of Sjögren's syndrome with rheumatoid arthritis and systemic lupus erythematosus suggests that immunologic processes play a role in the pathogenesis of this disease. It has been hypothesized that patients with Sjögren's syndrome respond abnormally to one or more unidentified antigens, perhaps a virus or a virus-altered autoantigen. This abnormal response is characterized by excessive B cell and plasma cell activity, manifested by polyclonal hypergammaglobulinemia and the production of rheumatoid factor, antinuclear factors, cryoglobulins, and anti-salivary duct antibodies. Immunofluorescent studies have shown both B and T lymphocytes and plasma cells infiltrating involved tissues. Large quantities of IgM and IgG are synthesized by these infiltrating lymphocytes. In patients with coexisting macroglobulinemia, monoclonal IgM may be synthesized in the salivary glands.

It has been suggested that excessive B cell activity may not be due to a primary B cell defect but rather to defective T lymphocyte regulation. A subpopulation of T lymphocytes exists whose normal physiologic role is the suppression of excessive B cell proliferation and synthesis of autoantibodies. In Sjögren's syndrome, this "suppressor" T cell population may fail to adequately control B cell responses to an antigenic challenge, leading to excessive B cell activity. New Zealand black (NZB) mice, a model for autoimmunity, develop decreased suppressor T cell activity and lymphocytic infiltrates in many organs, including salivary glands. These NZB mice eventually develop generalized lymphoproliferation and malignant lymphomas, as do patients with Sjögren's syndrome, in whom an intermediate stage of lymphoproliferation (called "pseudolymphoma"), as well as frank lymphoma may develop. About one-third of patients have decreased in vitro responsiveness to mitogens (such as PHA) and decreased numbers of peripheral blood T lymphocytes, as measured by E rosettes (see Chapter 25). Some patients are resistant to sensitization with DNCB.

Clinical Features

A. Symptoms and Signs:

1. Oral—Dryness of the mouth is usually the most distressing symptom and is often associated with burning discomfort and difficulty in chewing and swallowing dry foods. Polyuria and nocturia develop as the patient drinks increasing amounts of water in an effort to relieve these symptoms. The oral mucous membranes are dry and erythematous and the tongue becomes fissured and ulcerated. Severe dental caries is often seen. Half of these patients have intermittent parotid gland enlargement with rapid fluctuations in the size of the gland.

2. Ocular—The major ocular finding is keratoconjunctivitis sicca. Symptoms of keratoconjunctivitis sicca include burning, itching, decreased tearing, ocular accumulation of thick mucoid material during the night, photophobia, pain, and a "gritty" or "sandy" sensation in the eyes. Decreased tearing is demonstrated by an abnormal Schirmer test. Slitlamp examination reveals punctate rose bengal or fluorescein staining of the conjunctiva and cornea, strands of corneal debris, and a shortened tear film break-up time. Severe ocular involvement may lead to corneal ulceration, vascularization with opacification, or perforation.

3. Miscellaneous—The nose, posterior oropharynx, larynx, and respiratory tract may be markedly dry, which leads to epistaxis, dysphonia, recurrent otitis media, tracheobronchitis, or pneumonia. The vaginal mucosa is also dry, and women commonly complain of dyspareunia. Since half of patients with Sjögren's syndrome have rheumatoid arthritis, active synovitis is a common finding. Twenty percent of patients with Sjögren's syndrome complain of Raynaud's phenomenon.

B. Laboratory Findings: Anemia, leukocytopenia, and an elevated erythrocyte sedimentation rate are common features. Parotid salivary flow is less than the normal 5 ml/10 minutes/gland. Secretory sialography with radiopaque dye demonstrates many findings of glandular disorganization. Salivary scintigraphy with technetium-99m pertechnetate reveals decreased parotid secretory function. Histologically, a lymphocytic infiltrate involves exocrine glands of the respiratory, gastrointestinal, and vaginal tracts as well as glands of the ocular and oral mucosa. The minor salivary glands of the lower lip offer a convenient biopsy site and are infiltrated in 75% of patients.

Immunologic Diagnosis

There is no immunologic test which is specifically diagnostic for Sjögren's syndrome. However, a myriad of nonspecific immunologic abnormalities occur in these patients.

A. Humoral Abnormalities: Hypergammaglobulinemia is seen in half of patients. Although serum protein electrophoresis usually shows a polyclonal hypergammaglobulinemia, occasional patients develop monoclonal IgM paraproteinemia. Patients who develop lymphoma sometimes become severely hypogammaglobulinemic and show disappearance of autoantibodies. With latex agglutination, rheumatoid factor is present in 90% of patients. ANA in a speckled or homogeneous pattern is present in 70% of patients, and small amounts of anti-ds-DNA antibodies are occasionally found. The LE cell phenomenon occurs in up to 20% of patients with Sjögren's syndrome associated with rheumatoid arthritis but is rare in keratoconjunctivitis sicca and xerostomia alone. Autoantibodies against salivary duct antigens have been detected in 50% of patients.

B. Cellular Abnormalities: Thirty percent of patients with Sjögren's syndrome have decreased lymphocyte responses to mitogenic stimulation. A few patients also have decreased numbers of circulating T lymphocytes in the peripheral blood (see Immunologic Pathogenesis, above).

C. Beta$_2$-Microglobulin: Beta$_2$-microglobulin is a normal cell membrane component present on all human cells and linked to the HLA surface antigen complex. It is elevated in the synovial fluid of patients with active rheumatoid arthritis and in the saliva of patients with Sjögren's syndrome (as measured by radioimmunoassay). The concentration in saliva correlates directly with the content of lymphocytic infiltration as graded on lip biopsy. Elevated serum β_2-microglobulin levels may be seen in severe Sjögren's syndrome, particularly when associated with pseudolymphoma or lymphoma.

Differential Diagnosis

The diagnosis of Sjögren's syndrome can be made on the basis of 2 of the 3 classical manifestations (xerostomia, keratoconjunctivitis sicca, and rheumatoid arthritis). However, the varied and multisystemic nature of the disease may obscure the diagnosis. Certainly, any patient with a rheumatoid disease—eg, systemic lupus erythematosus, rheumatoid arthritis, or scleroderma—should be observed for Sjögren's syndrome; likewise, any patient with Sjögren's syndrome should be examined for the purpose of ruling out other rheumatoid diseases. Parotid malignancy must always be considered in a patient with unilateral parotid swelling.

Treatment

A. Symptomatic Measures:

1. Oral—Patients must be urged to maintain fastidious oral hygiene, with regular use of fluoride toothpaste, mouthwashes, and regular dental examinations. Frequent sips of water and the use of sugarless gum or candy to stimulate salivary secretion are sometimes helpful in relieving xerostomia.

2. Ocular—Methylcellulose artificial tears alleviate ocular symptoms and protect against ocular complications. Shielded glasses offer protection against the drying effects of wind.

B. Systemic Measures: Sjögren's syndrome can usually be adequately controlled with symptomatic therapy only. In severe or life-threatening disease, corticosteroids or immunosuppressive agents have been used. These drugs are indicated primarily in patients with lymphoma, Waldenström's macroglobulinemia, or massive lymphocytic infiltration of vital organs (such as the lung).

Complications & Prognosis

In the vast majority of patients, significant lymphoproliferation is confined to salivary, lacrimal, and other mucosal glandular tissue, resulting in a benign chronic course of xerostomia and xerophthalmia. Rarely, patients develop significant extraglandular lymphoid infiltration or neoplasia.

Splenomegaly, leukocytopenia, and vasculitis with leg ulcers may occur even in the absence of rheumatoid arthritis. Hypergammaglobulinemic purpura (a nonthrombocytopenic purpura), often associated with renal tubular acidosis, has been described and may be a presenting complaint. Glomerulonephritis associated with cryoglobulinemia (mixed IgM-IgG type) may occur; symptoms related to cryoglobulinemia may predominate. Five percent of patients with Sjögren's syndrome develop chronic (Hashimoto) thyroiditis. Primary biliary cirrhosis, chronic active hepatitis, gastric achlorhydria, pancreatitis, renal and pulmonary lymphocytic infiltration, and adult celiac disease have all been associated with Sjögren's syndrome. Neuromuscular complications include polymyositis, peripheral or cranial (particularly trigeminal) neuropathy, and cerebral vasculitis. Rarely, patients with Sjögren's syndrome develop lymphoid malignancy, usually histiocytic lymphoma (reticulum cell sarcoma) or Waldenström's macroglobulinemia.

PROGRESSIVE SYSTEMIC SCLEROSIS

Major Immunologic Features

- Antinuclear antibodies with a speckled or nucleolar pattern.
- Presence of immunoglobulins and complement in fibrinoid lesions in renal arterioles of patients with renal involvement.

General Considerations

Progressive systemic sclerosis (PSS) is a disease of unknown cause manifested by abnormally increased collagen deposition in almost every organ. The onset is usually insidious, with edema and then atrophy of the skin of the feet and hands, and Raynaud's phenomenon. The course is usually slowly progressive and chronically disabling, but it can be rapidly progressive and fatal. It commonly begins in the third or fourth decade of life. Children are rarely affected. The incidence of the disease is 4–12.5 cases per million population. Women are affected twice as often as men, and there is no racial predisposition.

Immunologic Pathogenesis

Progressive systemic sclerosis has many clinical features in common with other rheumatoid diseases (systemic lupus erythematosus, rheumatoid arthritis, polymyositis). The association of progressive systemic sclerosis with Sjögren's syndrome and, less often, with thyroiditis—and the serologic abnormalities seen in the majority of cases (presence of ANA, rheumatoid factor, polyclonal hypergammaglobulinemia)—are suggestive of an immunologic aberration in these patients. At present, there is scanty evidence for a humoral mechanism in the pathogenesis of the disease. Immunoglobulins have not been found at the dermal-epidermal junction in scleroderma, although examination of the fibrinoid lesions seen in the walls of renal arterioles has revealed the presence of γ-globulin and complement. The ability of lymphocytes from patients with progressive systemic sclerosis to destroy embryonic fibroblasts in tissue cultures may indicate an alteration in cellular immunity in these patients. However, in contrast to other autoimmune diseases, cellular infiltration in scleroderma is minimal or absent in all organs except the synovium, where impressive collections of lymphocytes and plasma cells can be seen. Unfortunately, research on the pathogenesis of progressive systemic sclerosis is severely hampered by the absence of an animal model.

Clinical Features

A. Symptoms and Signs:

1. Onset—In more than half of cases, Raynaud's phenomenon heralds the onset of the disease. Progressive systemic sclerosis frequently begins with skin changes, and in one-third of patients polyarthralgias and polyarthritis are the first manifestations. Initial visceral involvement without skin manifestations is very unusual.

2. Skin abnormalities—There are 3 stages in the clinical evolution of scleroderma: the edematous, sclerotic, and atrophic stages. In the edematous phase, symmetric nonpitting edema is present in the hands and, rarely, in the feet. The edema can progress to the forearms, arms, upper anterior chest, abdomen, back, and face. In the sclerotic phase the skin is tight, smooth, and waxy and seems bound down to underlying structures. Skin folds and wrinkles disappear. The hands are involved in two-thirds of patients, with painful, slowly healing ulcerations of the fingertips in half of those cases. The face appears stretched and mask-like, with thin lips and a "pinched" nose. Pigmentary changes and telangiectases are frequent findings at this stage. The skin changes may stabilize for prolonged periods and then either progress to atrophy or soften and return to normal. Subcutaneous calcifications, usually in the fingertips (calcinosis circumscripta), occur more often in women than in men. The calcifications may vary in size from tiny deposits to large masses. They usually develop over the knees, elbows, and other bony prominences.

3. Raynaud's phenomenon—Raynaud's phenomenon occurs in 30% of patients. In the so-called CRST phenomenon—*c*alcinosis, *R*aynaud's phenomenon, *s*clerodactyly, and *t*elangiectases—the disease may remain confined to the skin for prolonged periods (without progression to visceral involvement).

4. Joints and muscles—Articular complaints are very common in progressive systemic sclerosis and may begin at any time during the course of the disease. The arthralgias, stiffness, and frank arthritis seen in progressive systemic sclerosis may be difficult to distinguish from those of rheumatoid arthritis, particularly in the early stages of the disease. Involved joints include the metacarpophalangeals, proximal interphalangeals, wrists, elbows, knees, ankles, and small joints of the feet. Flexion contractures, due to changes in the skin or joints, are common. The manifestations of muscle involvement are clinically indistinguishable from those of polymyositis, with muscle weakness, tenderness, and pain of proximal muscles of the upper and lower extremities. Muscle atrophy and wasting are late manifestations of the disease.

5. Lungs—The lungs are almost always involved in progressive systemic sclerosis, either clinically or at autopsy. A low diffusion capacity is the earliest detectable abnormality, preceding alterations in ventilation or clinical and radiologic evidence of disease. Dyspnea on exertion is the most frequently reported symptom. Orthopnea and paroxysmal nocturnal dyspnea are seen in advanced cases. A chronic cough with variable production of sputum is also seen in scleroderma lung disease. Hemoptysis, fever, chest pain, and hoarseness are infrequent manifestations of pulmonary involvement. Pleurisy (with associated pleural friction rub) can also occur. Patients with diffuse pulmonary involvement have an intense bronchiolar epithelial proliferation. This cellular proliferation may be related to the high incidence of alveolar cell carcinoma in this disorder.

6. Heart—Because of the frequency of pulmonary fibrosis, cor pulmonale is the commonest cardiac finding in progressive systemic sclerosis. Myocardial fibrosis, leading to digitalis-resistant left-sided heart failure, is a poor prognostic sign. Cardiac arrhythmias and conduction disturbances are common manifestations of myocardial fibrosis. The pericarditis of progressive systemic sclerosis is usually asymptomatic and is found incidentally at autopsy. Although 40% of patients have pericardial effusion by electrocardiography, tamponade is extremely rare.

7. Kidneys—Renal involvement is an uncommon but serious and life-threatening development in progressive systemic sclerosis. It presents as rapidly progressive oliguric renal failure with or without malignant hypertension.

8. Gastrointestinal tract—The gastrointestinal tract is commonly affected in progressive systemic sclerosis. The esophagus is the most frequent site of involvement, with reflux esophagitis occurring in 80% of patients. Gastric and small bowel involvement presents with cramping, bloating, and diarrhea alternating with constipation. Hypomotility of the gastrointestinal tract with bacterial overgrowth may result in malabsorption. Colonic scleroderma is associated with chronic constipation.

9. Sjögren's syndrome—Keratoconjunctivitis sicca is seen in 5–7% of patients.

10. Uncommon clinical manifestations—Biliary cirrhosis and mononeuropathy, either cranial or peripheral, may rarely be associated with progressive systemic sclerosis.

11. Mixed connective tissue disease (MCTD)—Mixed connective tissue disease is a recently described syndrome with features of scleroderma, systemic lupus erythematosus, and polymyositis-dermatomyositis. The manifestations of the disease include nondeforming arthritis, Raynaud's phenomenon, scleroderma of the fingers, muscle weakness and tenderness, and a skin rash resembling that of dermatomyositis. These patients have a high-titer speckled pattern of ANA and antibody to an "extractable nuclear antigen" (ENA). The nuclear antigen contains both ribonuclease-resistant and ribonuclease-sensitive components. Patients with mixed connective tissue disease have antibodies to the ribonuclease-sensitive component. Renal disease is rare in these patients, and they appear to respond to corticosteroid treatment.

B. Laboratory Findings: The normochromic normocytic anemia of chronic inflammatory disease is usually seen in progressive systemic sclerosis with visceral involvement. Microangiopathic and autoimmune hemolytic anemia can occur. Eosinophilia may rarely occur. An elevated erythrocyte sedimentation rate and polyclonal hypergammaglobulinemia are common.

Skin biopsy reveals thinning of the epidermis with loss of the rete pegs, atrophy of the dermal appendages, hyalinization and fibrosis of arterioles, and a striking increase of compact collagen fibers in the reticular dermis.

Synovial tissue findings range from an acute inflammatory lymphocytic infiltration to diffuse fibrosis with relatively little inflammation.

The histologic changes seen in muscle tissue include interstitial and perivascular inflammatory infiltration followed by fibrosis and myofibrillar necrosis, atrophy, and degeneration.

On gross examination, the kidneys are pale, with numerous hemorrhagic infarctions. The microscopic picture is similar to that of malignant hypertensive nephropathy, with intimal proliferation of the interlobular arteries and fibrinoid changes in the intima and media of more distal interlobular arteries and of afferent arterioles.

There is increased collagen deposition in the lamina propria, submucosa, and muscularis of the gastrointestinal tract. With loss of normal smooth muscle, the large bowel is subject to development of the characteristic wide-mouthed diverticula and to infiltration of air into the wall of the intestine (pneumatosis intestinalis).

C. X-Ray Findings:

1. Bone x-rays–Thickening of the periarticular soft tissues and juxta-articular osteoporosis are seen in involved joints. Erosions may be seen on the distal phalangeal tufts and at the joint margins of the proximal and distal interphalangeal joints. Absorption of the terminal phalanges is often associated with soft tissue atrophy and subcutaneous calcinosis.

2. Chest x-rays–Characteristically, diffuse interstitial fibrosis is seen in the lower lung fields of patients with moderate to severe pulmonary involvement. "Honeycombing," nodular densities, and disseminated pulmonary calcifications may also be seen.

3. Gastrointestinal x-rays–Upper gastrointestinal series will often reveal decreased or absent esophageal peristaltic activity, even in patients without symptoms of dysphagia. Long-standing disease leads to marked dilatation of the lower two-thirds of the esophagus. Gastrointestinal reflux is present in the majority of cases, and ulcers or strictures of the lower esophagus due to peptic esophagitis are commonplace. With gastrointestinal involvement, barium is often retained in the second and third portions of the duodenum. Intestinal loops become dilated and atonic, with irregular flocculation and hypersegmentation.

The barium enema may reveal large, wide-mouthed diverticula along the antimesenteric border of the transverse and descending colon.

4. Renal arteriography–Marked changes are seen on renal arteriography in patients with scleroderma kidney. Irregular arterial narrowing, tortuosity of the interlobular arterioles, persistence of the arterial phase, and absence of a nephrogram phase are typical findings.

Immunologic Diagnosis

Polyclonal hypergammaglobulinemia is a frequent serologic abnormality in progressive systemic sclerosis. Rheumatoid factors are found in 25–30% of patients. The fluorescent antinuclear antibody test shows a speckled or nucleolar pattern in 70% of cases. The LE cell phenomenon is rarely seen. Antibodies to DNA or RNA are present in the sera of patients with progressive systemic sclerosis.

Differential Diagnosis

When classical skin changes and Raynaud's phenomenon are associated with characteristic visceral complaints, the diagnosis is obvious. In cases which present with visceral or arthritic complaints in the absence of skin changes, the diagnosis is difficult. In many cases only the presence or absence of antibodies to ribonuclease-sensitive extractable nuclear antigen makes it possible to differentiate scleroderma from mixed connective tissue disease.

Treatment

There is at present no effective treatment for progressive systemic sclerosis. Sympathectomy has resulted only in transient relief of vascular symptoms. Corticosteroids have no effect on the visceral progression of the disease, though they are beneficial in scleroderma with myositis and mixed connective tissue disease. Penicillamine has been used because it interferes with intermolecular cross-linking of collagen fibers, but the clinical results have been disappointing.

Patients should avoid exposure to cold and should wear gloves to protect their hands. Tobacco should be avoided. Skin ulcers require careful antiseptic care. Cor pulmonale and left-sided heart failure should be treated appropriately with diuretics and digitalization, although the response is often poor. Tetracyclines may be beneficial in decreasing intestinal bacterial overgrowth that leads to malabsorption.

Hypertensive crisis in renal disease associated with progressive systemic sclerosis is very difficult to control even with potent hypotensive agents. The arthritis can often be controlled with aspirin and other analgesics. Lotions can be used for skin lubrication to alleviate dryness and cracking.

Complications & Prognosis

Spontaneous remissions occur in progressive systemic sclerosis, but the usual course of the disease is one of relentless progression from dermal to visceral involvement. Involvement of the heart or colon is associated with a very high mortality rate, and scleroderma renal disease leads to death within a few weeks to months. Aspiration pneumonia resulting from esophageal dysfunction is a frequent complication in advanced disease.

Although the prognosis for any given patient is extremely variable, the overall 5-year survival rate for progressive systemic sclerosis is approximately 40%.

POLYMYOSITIS-DERMATOMYOSITIS

Major Immunologic Features

- Focal deposition of complement, IgG, and IgM in vessel walls of involved tissue.
- Production of cytotoxin by lymphocytes incubated with autologous muscle.
- Lymphocytic and plasma cell infiltration of involved muscle.

General Considerations

Polymyositis-dermatomyositis is an acute or chronic inflammatory disease of muscle and skin that may occur at any age. Women are affected twice as commonly as men. There is no racial preponderance. The incidence of the disease is 1 per 200,000 population.

Polymyositis-dermatomyositis can be subclassified into 5 categories: (1) idiopathic polymyositis, (2) idiopathic dermatomyositis, (3) polymyositis-dermatomyositis associated with malignancy, (4) childhood polymyositis-dermatomyositis, and (5) polymyositis-dermatomyositis associated with other rheumatoid diseases (Sjögren's syndrome, systemic lupus erythematosus, progressive systemic sclerosis, mixed connective tissue disease).

Immunologic Pathogenesis

Although the precise pathogenetic mechanisms are unknown, there is a great deal of circumstantial evidence to suggest that autoimmunity may play a role in disease causation. Experimental polymyositis has been induced in rats and guinea pigs by the injection of allogeneic muscle tissue in Freund's complete adjuvant. Polymyositis-dermatomyositis may coexist with other autoimmune diseases. An infectious cause (viral or bacterial) has been suggested, but no microorganism has ever been identified, and the only possible evidence for viral infection is the occurrence of tubular inclusion bodies within the cytoplasm and nuclei of involved skin and muscle cells.

A. Humoral Factors: Polyclonal hypergammaglobulinemia is common in patients with polymyositis-dermatomyositis, and rheumatoid factors and antinuclear antibodies occur in 20% of cases. Focal deposits of complement, IgG, and IgM have been seen in vessel walls of involved skin and muscle.

B. Cellular Factors: There is evidence that cellular immunity plays a role in the pathogenesis of polymyositis-dermatomyositis. Polymyositis has been induced in rats and guinea pigs by the transfer of sensitized lymphoid cells. Lymphocytes from patients with polymyositis-dermatomyositis, after incubation with normal autologous muscle, produce a lymphokine that is toxic to monolayers of human fetal muscle cells. The lymphocytes in the muscle infiltrate of patients with polymyositis-dermatomyositis produce this lymphotoxin upon simple incubation of involved muscle. Thus, the lymphocytes of patients with polymyositis-dermatomyositis may respond to their own muscle antigens as if they were foreign (Fig 27–3). It is not known whether this is a primary defect in antigen recognition by the lymphocytes or whether these muscle antigens are cross-reactive with an unidentified foreign antigen.

Clinical Features

A. Symptoms and Signs:

1. Onset—Although the symptoms may begin abruptly, the onset of the disease is usually insidious. Constitutional symptoms are unusual except in acute polymyositis-dermatomyositis.

2. Muscle involvement—The commonest manifestation of the disease is weakness of involved striated muscle. The proximal muscles of the extremities are most often affected, usually progressing from the lower to the upper limbs. The distal musculature is involved in only 25% of patients. Weakness of the cervical muscles with inability to raise the head and weakness of the posterior pharyngeal muscles with dysphagia and dysphonia are common manifestations of polymyositis-dermatomyositis. Facial and extraocular muscle involvement is unusual. Muscle pain, ten-

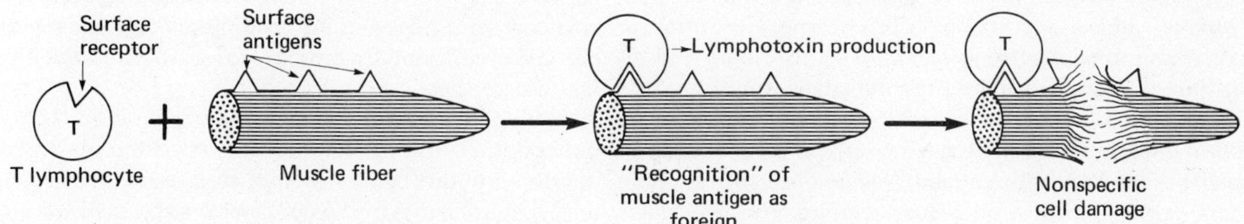

Figure 27–3. Defective "recognition" in polymyositis.

derness, and edema may be seen in acute polymyositis-dermatomyositis but are uncommon in the chronic form of the disease.

3. Skin involvement–The characteristic rash of dermatomyositis, present in approximately 40% of patients, consists of raised, smooth or scaling, dusky red plaques over the face and bony prominences of the hands, elbows, knees, and ankles. Less commonly seen is the pathognomonic "heliotrope" rash of the face (a dusky, lilac suffusion of the upper eyelids). One-fourth of patients have various dermatologic manifestations ranging from skin thickening to scaling eruptions to erythroderma. One-third have Raynaud's phenomenon.

4. Malignancy–Seventeen percent of all patients with polymyositis-dermatomyositis are found to have a concomitant malignancy, usually a carcinoma of the lung, prostate, ovary, uterus, breast, or large intestine. Malignancies of the stomach, gallbladder, and parotid gland are less commonly seen. In men over 40 years of age, the association between polymyositis-dermatomyositis and malignancy may be as high as 40–50%. Removal of the tumor may result in a dramatic improvement in the polymyositis-dermatomyositis.

5. Miscellaneous features–A mild transitory arthritis is seen in half of patients. Sjögren's syndrome occurs in 5–7% of cases. Gastrointestinal ulceration with abdominal pain, hematemesis, and melena occurs in children. Rarely, patients develop interstitial pneumonia and pulmonary fibrosis.

B. Laboratory Findings: An elevated erythrocyte sedimentation rate and a mild anemia are very common. Half of patients have elevated α_2- and γ-globulins on serum protein electrophoresis. Myoglobinemia and myoglobinuria are often seen. Up to 20% of patients with acute polymyositis have nonspecific T wave abnormalities on their electrocardiogram.

1. Muscle enzymes–When muscle cells are injured, a number of muscle enzymes, including glutamic-oxaloacetic transaminase, creatine phosphokinase, and aldolase are released into the blood. The serum enzyme elevation reflects the severity of muscle damage as well as the amount of muscle mass involved.

2. Urinary creatine–Creatine released into the blood from damaged muscle cells is quickly cleared by the kidneys. The urine creatine concentration is the most sensitive laboratory test for muscle damage and is a valuable indicator of disease activity. It is the first detectable laboratory abnormality in relapse of disease.

3. Muscle biopsy–Biopsy of involved muscles is diagnostic in only 50–80% of cases. Therefore, a normal muscle biopsy does not rule out the diagnosis of polymyositis-dermatomyositis in a patient with a characteristic clinical picture, muscle enzyme elevations, and an abnormal electromyogram. The histologic findings in acute and subacute polymyositis-dermatomyositis include (1) focal or extensive primary degeneration of muscle fibers, (2) signs of muscle regeneration (fiber basophilia, central nuclei), (3) necrosis of muscle fibers, and (4) a focal or diffuse lymphocytic infiltration. Chronic myositis leads to a marked variation in the cross-sectional diameter of muscle fibers and a variable degree of interstitial fibrosis.

4. Electromyography–When involved muscles are examined, 70–80% of patients will demonstrate myopathic changes on electromyography. These changes are nonspecific but can point to the diagnosis of myositis. They include (1) spontaneous "saw-tooth" fibrillatory potentials; (2) complex polyphasic potentials, often of short duration, indicative of involuntary fiber contraction; and (3) salvos of repetitive high-frequency action potentials (pseudomyotonia).

Immunologic Diagnosis

There is no known immunologic test that is pathognomonic for polymyositis-dermatomyositis. The diagnosis must be based on the nonimmunologic clinical and laboratory data discussed above.

Differential Diagnosis

The 5 major criteria for the diagnosis of polymyositis-dermatomyositis are (1) weakness of the shoulder or pelvic girdle, (2) biopsy evidence of myositis, (3) elevation of muscle enzymes, (4) electromyographic findings of myopathy, and (5) typical skin changes. The diagnosis is "definite" if 4 of the criteria are met and "probable" if 3 are met. A number of diseases can affect muscles and lead to clinical and laboratory abnormalities which are identical to those seen in polymyositis-dermatomyositis. The diagnostic criteria outlined above cannot be strictly applied in patients with these diseases, which include sarcoidosis, muscular dystrophy, systemic lupus erythematosus, progressive systemic sclerosis, mixed connective tissue disease, drug-induced myopathy (alcohol, clofibrate), rhabdomyolysis, and various metabolic and endocrine disorders (McArdle's syndrome, hyperthyroidism, myxedema). A diligent search for occult malignancy should be made in any patient who develops polymyositis-dermatomyositis as an adult.

Treatment

A. Supportive Therapy: Bed rest is mandatory during the acute phase of the disease. Since these patients are susceptible to thromboembolism, elastic stockings and passive and active leg exercises should be encouraged. As the patient recovers, physical therapy should be initiated to prevent muscle atrophy and to increase strength.

B. Corticosteroids: Prednisone, 60–80 mg orally daily, will usually induce a remission. The dose is tapered slowly, with clinical and laboratory monitoring. Creatinuria is the most sensitive index of disease activity and is often the first indication of relapse as corticosteroid dosage is reduced. Some patients require chronic prednisone therapy (5–20 mg daily) to control the disease.

C. Methotrexate: Methotrexate is indicated in patients that do not respond to corticosteroids or who develop life-threatening complications of high-dosage corticosteroid therapy. The usual dosage is 25–50 mg weekly intravenously.

Complications & Prognosis

Polymyositis-dermatomyositis is a chronic disease characterized by spontaneous remissions and exacerbations. Most patients respond to corticosteroid therapy. Patients with severe muscle atrophy show little response to either corticosteroid or other immunosuppressive therapy. When the disease is associated with malignancy, improvement often occurs following treatment of the neoplasm. Childhood polymyositis-dermatomyositis has a poor prognosis and is usually fatal despite corticosteroid treatment.

POLYARTERITIS NODOSA, WEGENER'S GRANULOMATOSIS, & OTHER VASCULITIDES

Major Immunologic Features

- Deposition of immunoglobulin and complement in vessel walls and glomerular basement membrane.
- Association with streptococcal and viral antigens (HB_sAg) and with various drugs.

General Considerations

There are a number of inflammatory vascular diseases with differing clinical and histologic characteristics. The vasculitides represent a spectrum of pathologic and clinical disease ranging from acute, overwhelming necrotizing vasculitis to chronic, indolent vascular inflammation. Granuloma formation is present to a greater or lesser degree in most of these entities, but the basic lesion is vascular. It is important to classify and to differentiate the vasculitides because the course, treatment, and prognosis are different for each disease.

Immunologic Pathogenesis & Diagnosis

No unifying pathogenetic mechanism has yet been defined for any of the vasculitides. Most are probably hypersensitivity disorders, but no causative antigens have been identified. Many inciting antigens which could induce specific clinical responses may exist. Alternatively, there may be relatively few causative antigens, with the type of clinical response being determined by host factors (heredity or various environmental factors).

A. Humoral Pathogenesis:

1. Polyarteritis nodosa—Several animal experiments suggest that humoral factors may play a role in the pathogenesis of polyarteritis nodosa. Repeated intravenous injections of horse serum into rabbits will induce an arteritis similar to that seen in polyarteritis nodosa. Bovine albumin serially administered intravenously into rabbits will also induce a vasculitis. (Bovine γ-globulin administration induces immune complex renal disease with only minor inflammatory vascular changes.) The intravenous injection of immune complexes, particularly in the presence of rheumatoid factor, will induce vasculitis in rats. Immunofluorescent studies in humans have demonstrated immunoglobulin and complement in vessel walls during active disease. Hepatitis B antigen (HB_sAg), either alone or with immunoglobulin and complement, has been demonstrated in the vessel walls of patients with polyarteritis nodosa who have circulating HB_sAg (Fig 27–4). However, HB_sAg-antibody complexes are responsible for only a minority of cases of polyarteritis nodosa.

2. Hypersensitivity angiitis—Vascular deposition of immunoglobulin and complement in patients with hypersensitivity angiitis has been documented by immunofluorescence studies.

3. Wegener's granulomatosis—Ultrastructural and immunofluorescent studies of renal biopsies from patients with Wegener's granulomatosis have demonstrated subepithelial basement membrane deposition of IgG and complement in a lumpy-bumpy pattern in glomerular tufts, characteristic of immune complex disease. Circulating autoantibodies against smooth muscle have been detected in a few patients, and circulating immune complexes have occasionally been detected by complement consumption technics.

4. Henoch-Schönlein purpura—Examination of renal biopsies reveals subendothelial granular and nodular deposition of IgA, IgG, and complement along the glomerular basement membrane. Adequate vascular studies in Henoch-Schönlein purpura are lacking.

5. Takayasu's disease—Patients with Takayasu's disease commonly have elevated serum IgG, IgA, and IgM levels. False-positive VDRL and rheumatoid factors are not uncommon. Rarely, patients will have the LE cell phenomenon. Circulating autoantibodies against vascular antigens have been demonstrated by sheep cell agglutination, complement fixation, and tanned red cell agglutination.

6. Giant cell arteritis—Immunofluorescent studies have revealed IgG, IgA, IgM, and complement deposition in the cytoplasm of cells and along the elastic tissue within vessel walls. Antinuclear antibodies against nuclei of vessel wall cells occur in patients with serum antinuclear antibody.

B. Cellular Pathogenesis:

1. Wegener's granulomatosis—Decreased delayed cutaneous hypersensitivity to various antigens (PPD, mumps, streptokinase-streptodornase, keyhole limpet hemocyanin), as well as decreased in vitro lymphocyte mitogenic responses, have been documented in patients with Wegener's granulomatosis. However, most studies have been done on patients being treated with corticosteroids or cytotoxic drugs.

2. Giant cell arteritis—It has recently been shown that lymphocytes from patients with polymyalgia rheumatica respond in vitro to homogenates of whole muscle. Since muscle biopsies in these patients are normal, the response may be due to vascular antigens that contaminate whole muscle preparations.

C. Antigens Associated With the Vasculitides:

1. Streptococcal antigens—Antecedent upper respiratory infections, occasionally streptococcal in origin, have been associated with Henoch-Schönlein pur-

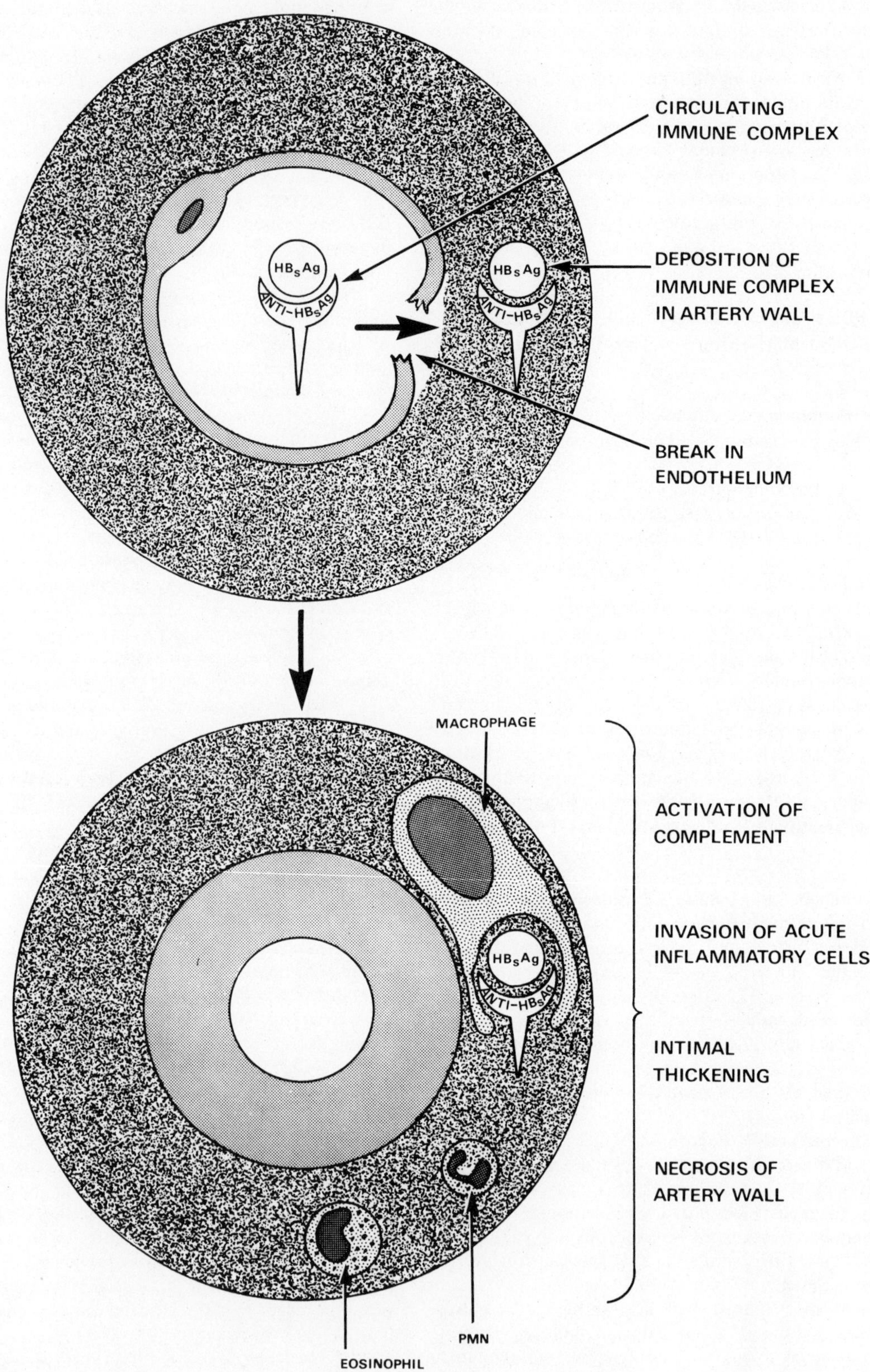

Figure 27–4. Hypothetical immunopathogenesis in HB_SAg-associated polyarteritis nodosa.

pura, hypersensitivity angiitis, and polyarteritis nodosa. A necrotizing arteritis can be induced in the coronary arteries of rats receiving repeated injections of hemolytic streptococcal antigens.

2. **Viral antigens**–Various viral infections (upper respiratory infections, influenza, influenza vaccination) are known to occasionally precede Henoch-Schönlein purpura, hypersensitivity angiitis, and polyarteritis nodosa. Serum HB_sAg and circulating HB_sAg-anti-HB_sAg complexes are present in some patients with polyarteritis nodosa. HB_sAg, IgG, IgM, and complement have also been detected in the vessel walls of patients with polyarteritis nodosa who have circulating HB_sAg.

3. **Drugs**–Drugs have been implicated in the etiology of polyarteritis nodosa, hypersensitivity angiitis, and Henoch-Schönlein purpura. Suspected agents include sulfonamides, penicillin, phenytoin (diphenylhydantoin), arsenicals, thiouracil, iodides, and thiazides. There is also a very high incidence of polyarteritis nodosa in parenteral methamphetamine abusers. Although there is still controversy over the role of HB_sAg in these patients, the association of intravenous amphetamines and polyarteritis nodosa seems valid.

4. **Autoantigens**–Anti-vessel wall antibodies have been detected in some patients with Takayasu's disease. However, such antibodies could result from the vascular inflammatory process. Lymphocyte activation by homologous muscle has been demonstrated in patients with polymyalgia rheumatica.

Clinical Features

A. Symptoms and Signs:

1. **Polyarteritis nodosa**–Polyarteritis nodosa is a necrotizing vasculitis of small muscular arteries (0.5–1 mm in diameter). Involved vessels contain a segmental perivascular inflammatory infiltrate that consists predominantly of polymorphonuclear leukocytes and eosinophils. Segmental fibrinoid necrosis of the media and adventitia and weakening of the vessel wall with aneurysm formation occur. As the lesion evolves, intimal proliferation results in luminal obliteration and ischemia of involved tissues. Finally, as inflammation subsides, the vessel is replaced by fibrous tissue. Biopsy of involved tissue from patients with classical polyarteritis nodosa will show lesions at all stages of development.

Polyarteritis nodosa usually occurs in middle-aged men who present with fever, malaise, and weight loss. The protean manifestations of polyarteritis nodosa reflect the multisystemic organ involvement of the disease.

a. **Kidney**–The kidneys are involved in 70% of patients, and renal insufficiency is the commonest cause of death. Renovascular hypertension develops in 50% of patients.

b. **Heart**–Sixty percent of patients have cardiac involvement, with congestive heart failure being the commonest manifestation. Myocardial infarction may be seen in up to 20% of patients.

c. **Gastrointestinal tract**–Half of patients develop vasculitis of the gastrointestinal tract, manifested by pancreatitis, hepatitis, cholecystitis, bowel infarction or perforation, and gastrointestinal bleeding.

d. **Lungs**–The lung is involved pathologically in 25% of cases. Typical clinical manifestations include asthma, bronchitis, and pneumonia. Pulmonary infection complicates the course of half of patients with polyarteritis nodosa.

e. **Muscles**–Twenty percent of cases show signs of myositis such as pain, weakness, and tenderness.

f. **Central nervous system**–Eight to 25% of patients have some central nervous system abnormality. The major complication is infarction.

g. **Skin**–One-fourth of patients have a variety of skin manifestations, including livedo reticularis, subcutaneous nodules, and pyoderma gangrenosum.

h. **Testis**–Although the testis is a favorite site for biopsy, only 19% of autopsy cases show testicular involvement. In the absence of signs or symptoms of testicular involvement, biopsy will probably be unproductive.

Polyarteritis nodosa was once thought to have only a 10% 5-year survival rate. With better diagnosis and therapy, most modern studies indicate a 5-year survival rate of nearly 50%.

2. **Hypersensitivity angiitis**–Hypersensitivity angiitis is usually a more fulminant disease than classical polyarteritis nodosa. It occurs with equal frequency in both sexes, at any age, and often begins after infections or drug treatment. Pathologically, hypersensitivity angiitis differs from classical polyarteritis nodosa in that smaller vessels (including capillaries) are involved and individual lesions appear to be at the same stage of development. Clinically, the lungs, spleen, and skin are commonly involved, and gastrointestinal involvement is unusual. Hypertension is uncommon. Cases associated with a known antigen may go into remission when the offending agent is removed.

3. **Henoch-Schönlein purpura (allergic purpura)**–Henoch-Schönlein purpura usually occurs in boys. The histopathologic features are virtually identical to those of hypersensitivity angiitis, with involvement of venules and capillaries as well as small arterioles. Henoch-Schönlein purpura also frequently follows antigenic exposure, eg, infection or drugs, and some patients have a history of food allergies.

Patients with Henoch-Schönlein purpura demonstrate a fairly characteristic clinical picture, with nonthrombocytopenic purpura, colicky abdominal pain, arthralgias of the knees and ankles, and glomerulonephritis. They may develop nephrotic syndrome and progress to renal failure. There is a high incidence of intestinal hemorrhage and intussusception. The disease is usually limited to a single episode lasting 4–6 weeks, but recurrences can occur up to 2 years thereafter.

4. **Wegener's granulomatosis**–Wegener's granulomatosis consists of a triad of pathologic findings including (1) generalized focal necrotizing vasculitis involving arteries and veins, (2) necrotizing granulomas in the upper and lower air passages (nose, sinuses, nasopharynx, trachea, bronchi, and bronchioles), and (3) glomerulitis with thrombosis of glomerular capillaries,

adhesions of the glomerular tuft to Bowman's capsule, necrosis, and granuloma formation. Wegener's granulomatosis is one cause of lethal midline granuloma. Men and women are affected with equal frequency. With involvement of the upper and lower respiratory tract, patients develop sinusitis, rhinitis, septal perforation, tracheobronchitis, asthma, and pneumonia. With the onset of renal involvement, the patient progresses rapidly to renal failure. As in hypersensitivity angiitis, hypertension is uncommon. Other manifestations of Wegener's granulomatosis include arthralgias, polyneuropathy, parotitis, prostatitis, pericarditis, myocarditis (occasionally with infarction), skin involvement, and ocular disease (exophthalmos, episcleritis, conjunctivitis, and corneal erosion).

Before modern methods of therapy became available, patients with Wegener's granulomatosis almost always died in renal failure, and even today a patient's renal status still determines his long-range outlook. Survival with current treatment regimens approaches 90%.

5. Takayasu's arteritis (pulseless disease, aortic arch syndrome, giant cell arteritis of the aorta)– Takayasu's disease is a disease of females, age 10–50, described most often in Japanese women. It is an indolent inflammatory process involving the thoracic aorta and large arteries. The inflammation, which can be diffuse or focal, is characterized by mononuclear cell infiltration and giant cell formation in the media and adventitia. Degeneration of the media with disruption of the elastic layer leads occasionally to aneurysm formation. Proliferation of fibrous tissue leads to narrowing and obliteration of the lumens of involved vessels. Extensive vascular calcification resembling that seen in atherosclerosis develops in patients with longstanding disease. Takayasu's disease has been described in patients with other rheumatoid diseases such as systemic lupus erythematosus or rheumatoid arthritis.

Constitutional symptoms of fever, night sweats, and weight loss are universal among patients with Takayasu's disease. Erythema nodosum and pyoderma gangrenosum may be seen. Carotid and vertebral arterial involvement leads to cerebrovascular insufficiency with transient ischemic attacks, vertigo, and intermittent visual disturbances. Takayasu's disease of the renal artery is associated with renovascular hypertension. Involvement of the femoral and iliac arteries leads to peripheral claudication. Either the coronary ostia or the coronary arteries themselves may become involved, leading to angina pectoris or infarction. The case fatality rate is 25–75% within 5 years, with a high incidence of sudden death.

6. Giant cell arteritis (temporal arteritis)–Giant cell arteritis is a disease of old people, being very unusual in patients under 55 years of age. Women are affected twice as often as men. Pathologically, the disease is characterized by nonsuppurative granulomatous inflammation (either focal or diffuse) of the aorta and large vessels. Giant cells are conspicuous on histologic examination.

Constitutional findings include fever, weight loss, and malaise. Patients characteristically complain of symmetric arthralgias, myalgias, morning stiffness, and weakness of pelvic and shoulder girdles. The characteristic morning headache, which is described as constant and "boring," may be limited to the temporal areas or radiate widely over the head. The complications of the disease depend on the vessels involved. The temporal arteries may become warm, red, and tender, with or without painful nodules. With ocular vessel involvement, visual symptoms (ranging from intermittent blurring to diplopia to blindness) may result. Without treatment, blindness may occur in up to 30% of patients with acute giant cell arteritis. The manifestations of cerebrovascular involvement include transient ischemic attacks, stroke, and cranial nerve palsies. With involvement of the aorta and other large vessels, peripheral claudication or myocardial ischemia can be seen. Giant cell arteritis is usually a self-limited disease which lasts 6 months to 5 years. Because of the high incidence of blindness, it is crucial to make the diagnosis and treat the disease. The definitive diagnostic technic is temporal artery biopsy, but a large segment of temporal artery is required because of the focal nature of the disease. The relationship of giant cell arteritis to polymyalgia rheumatica is a matter of some controversy. The 2 diseases have the same age and sex distribution, and the systemic symptoms are virtually identical. Forty percent of patients with polymyalgia rheumatica have giant cell arteritis on biopsy even in the absence of signs of temporal arteritis. At this time, polymyalgia rheumatica should be considered a clinical syndrome often, but not always, associated with giant cell arteritis.

B. Laboratory Findings: Eighty percent of patients with vasculitis have leukocytosis (20–50 thousand/μl). Eosinophilia–often up to 1500/μl–occurs most commonly in polyarteritis nodosa, particularly with lung involvement. Anemia is very common and may be due to blood loss, autoimmune hemolytic anemia (in Wegener's granulomatosis), microangiopathic damage, or chronic disease.

Proteinuria, hematuria, and granular or cellular casts may be seen with renal involvement. Azotemia is a common complication of the disseminated vasculitides. Nonspecific laboratory tests indicating inflammation, such as the erythrocyte sedimentation rate and the "acute phase reactants" (eg, C-reactive protein), are almost universally abnormal. Polyclonal hypergammaglobulinemia is a common finding. Cryoglobulinemia, macroglobulinemia, rheumatoid factor, and a false-positive VDRL may all occur.

C. X-Ray Findings: With active pulmonary involvement, the chest film may reveal multiple infiltrates with interstitial fibrosis (polyarteritis nodosa) or nodular densities with or without cavitation (Wegener's granulomatosis). Patients with Takayasu's disease may show diffuse vascular calcifications similar to those seen in atherosclerosis. On angiography, up to 70% of patients with polyarteritis nodosa will have microaneurysms in small arteries, 0.5–1 mm in diameter, throughout the visceral circulation. Angiography may show beading and irregularity of involved arteries in patients with giant cell arteritis.

Treatment

A. Corticosteroids: Corticosteroids are useful in polyarteritis nodosa and hypersensitivity angiitis. They may result in rapid clinical improvement and have been shown to increase the 12-month survival rate in these 2 diseases. Carefully controlled studies of the effects of corticosteroids on long-term survival in these diseases have not been done. The suggested therapeutic regimen is prednisone, 60–80 mg orally daily, using clinical and laboratory parameters to determine the duration of therapy. Corticosteroids are also the major mode of therapy in giant cell arteritis. In patients with polymyalgia rheumatica without temporal arteritis, the recommended treatment is prednisone, 30 mg orally daily, using the erythrocyte sedimentation rate and clinical symptoms to determine how fast to taper the drug. When temporal arteritis is suspected, the artery should be biopsied immediately and the patient begun on prednisone, 60 mg orally daily, to forestall the possibility of blindness. These patients usually respond dramatically within 4 days. Corticosteroids should be tapered to the lowest dose required to control symptoms and therapy continued for 2 years, after which attempts should be made to withdraw corticosteroids completely. The use of corticosteroids in Takayasu's disease has been shown to control acute inflammatory reactions and probably to stop the progression of the disease. Prednisone is begun in a dosage of 30 mg orally daily and, after 9 weeks, is tapered to a maintenance dose of 5–10 mg daily. The duration and the long-term effectiveness of therapy have not been determined.

Corticosteroids are of little benefit in Henoch-Schönlein purpura. Although they decrease acute inflammatory symptoms and can be used when the response to aspirin is inadequate, they have no effect on the severity or progression of the renal disease.

B. Cytotoxic Agents: Cytotoxic drugs have dramatically improved the prognosis in Wegener's granulomatosis. Cyclophosphamide or azathioprine, starting at 1–2 mg/kg daily (orally or intravenously depending on the severity of the clinical situation), has been employed most commonly. The drugs are administered until there is a clinical response or until signs of toxicity develop (marrow suppression, gastrointestinal intolerance, alopecia, hemorrhagic cystitis–depending on the agent and the dose used). The duration of therapy required is unknown. Long-term remissions have been induced, so periodic attempts should be made to withdraw these potentially dangerous drugs. Corticosteroids are used concurrently only with severe inflammatory disease. Cytotoxic agents have been used in polyarteritis nodosa patients who do not respond to corticosteroids, but there has been too little experience with these agents in polyarteritis nodosa to advocate their general use.

SERUM SICKNESS

Serum sickness is an adverse immunologic response to a foreign antigen, usually a heterologous protein. The incidence of the disease has declined with the decreasing therapeutic use of heterologous antisera; however, it still occurs following the administration of various heterologous antitoxins, including those for rabies, diphtheria, snake venom, and clostridia, and following administration of certain drugs, eg, penicillin and sulfonamides.

Signs and symptoms begin 7–15 days after exposure to the offending antigen and include fever, myalgias, arthralgias, arthritis, urticaria, lymphadenopathy, and splenomegaly. The arthritis may involve large or small joints, and although pain, swelling, and effusions are common, heat and erythema are seldom reported.

Laboratory evaluation reveals an elevated erythrocyte sedimentation rate, leukocytosis (occasionally with eosinophilia), hematuria, proteinuria, and decreased complement levels (CH_{50}). The synovial fluid white count is over 20,000/μl, mostly polymorphonuclear leukocytes, and the complement level is decreased. The disease is usually self-limited, with no residua. Rare complications include laryngeal edema, mononeuritis, glomerulonephritis, and vasculitis.

Serum sickness is the prototype immune complex disease. During the initial immune response, there is antigen excess leading to the formation of soluble antigen-antibody complexes which diffuse into involved tissues, activate complement, and initiate the inflammatory response that causes the disease. As antibody titers rise and approach equivalence, insoluble complexes are formed which are quickly cleared by the reticuloendothelial system. Precipitating antibodies that fix complement can be demonstrated in most patients with serum sickness. Hemagglutinating antibodies against sheep red blood cells can be detected in virtually 100% of patients. Titers of hemagglutinating antibody rise following the onset of clinical manifestations and peak with clinical recovery.

The urticaria responds to epinephrine and antihistamine therapy, and salicylates are effective in controlling constitutional symptoms and the arthritis. A short course of corticosteroids may be required in severely ill patients.

BEHÇET'S DISEASE

Behçet's disease is a chronic recurrent inflammatory disease affecting adults of both sexes. The major manifestations of the disease are aphthous stomatitis, iritis, and genital ulcers. Other common findings include vasculitis (particularly of the skin), arthritis, meningomyelitis, and inflammatory bowel disease. The differential diagnosis includes viral (herpes simplex) or chlamydial (inclusion conjunctivitis, lymphogranuloma venereum) infections, Reiter's syndrome, and systemic lupus erythematosus.

The cause is unknown, although there is some evidence to suspect a viral infection. Cerebrospinal fluid from patients with Behçet's disease will produce encephalitis, optic neuritis, uveitis, keratitis, and conjunctivitis in rabbits. A viral agent cultured from the eye, blood, and urine of one patient has produced encephalitis in mice. However, some authorities consider Behçet's disease to be an autoimmune phenomenon. Antibodies against various human mucosal antigens have been detected, and indirect immunofluorescence has demonstrated circulating anticytoplasmic antibodies. Furthermore, lymphocytes and plasma cells are prominent in the perivascular infiltrate of Behçet's vasculitis. Amyloidosis may develop in these patients.

Local corticosteroids are useful in the treatment of the ocular and oral lesions, and systemic corticosteroids are usually effective in the systemic disease. The use of whole blood transfusions has reportedly been helpful in patients refractory to corticosteroid therapy. It is not known whether this effect is due to the transfer of antibodies, cell-bound transfer factors, or activated lymphocytes.

ANKYLOSING SPONDYLITIS

Ankylosing spondylitis is a chronic progressive inflammatory arthritis involving the sacroiliac joints, spine, and large peripheral joints. Ninety percent of cases occur in males, with the usual age at onset being the second or third decade of life.

The disease begins with the insidious onset of low back pain and stiffness. Symptoms of the acute disease include pain and tenderness in the sacroiliac joints and spasm of the paravertebral muscles. Findings in advanced disease include ankylosis of the sacroiliac joints and spine, with loss of lumbar lordosis, marked dorsocervical kyphosis, and decreased chest expansion. Twenty-five percent of patients will also have iritis or iridocyclitis. Carditis with or without aortitis is seen in 10% of patients, with 1–4% progressing to insufficiency of the aortic valves. Rare complications include pericarditis and pulmonary fibrosis.

Patients with ankylosing spondylitis are seronegative for rheumatoid factor. Hypergammaglobulinemia and antinuclear antibodies are not seen in ankylosing spondylitis. An elevated erythrocyte sedimentation rate and a mild anemia are almost universal. Electrocardiographic abnormalities, such as atrioventricular block, left or right bundle branch block, and left ventricular hypertrophy reflect cardiac involvement. X-rays of the sacroiliac joints reveal osteoporosis and erosions early in the disease and sclerosis with fusion in advanced disease. Calcification of the anterior longitudinal ligament of the spine leads to "squaring" of the vertebrae, seen on lateral x-ray. Eventually the vertebrae become fused by bony bridges called syndesmophytes.

On pathologic examination, these patients have a chronic proliferative synovitis very similar to that of rheumatoid arthritis. The characteristic skeletal change in advanced disease is ossification of the sacroiliac joints and interspinous and capsular ligaments. Pathologic cardiac findings include focal inflammation and fibrous thickening of the aortic wall and valve cusps.

The physical findings of patients with severe osteoarthritis of the spine may resemble those of patients with end-stage ankylosing spondylitis. However, degenerative osteoarthritis begins much later in life, does not involve the sacroiliac joints, and is characterized radiographically by osteophytes rather than syndesmophytes. The differentiation of ankylosing spondylitis from those diseases associated with sacroiliitis and spondylitis, such as psoriatic arthritis, Reiter's syndrome, regional enteritis, and ulcerative colitis, depends upon the presence or absence of the clinical and radiologic characteristics of those diseases.

The basic pathogenesis of ankylosing spondylitis is unknown. Although the presence of mononuclear cells in acutely involved tissue and the histologic similarity of the synovitis to rheumatoid arthritis suggest a possible immunologic mechanism, there are no real data to support an autoimmune pathogenetic mechanism. There is a strong genetic component. Several members of the same family are often involved, and twin concordance for ankylosing spondylitis has been described. Furthermore, 90% of patients with ankylosing spondylitis have HLA-B27. The gene that determines this specific cell surface antigen may be linked to other genes that determine pathologic autoimmune phenomena or that lead to an increased susceptibility to infectious or environmental agents. There is no specific immunologic diagnostic test.

The treatment of ankylosing spondylitis consists of giving anti-inflammatory agents to decrease acute inflammation and relieve pain and of instituting physical therapy to maintain muscle strength and a position of function. The anti-inflammatory agents suggested are phenylbutazone, 300–400 mg orally daily, or indomethacin, 75–100 mg orally daily, in divided doses. Both of these agents are associated with significant toxic side-effects. Posturing exercises (lying flat for periods during the day, sleeping without a pillow, breathing exercises), braces and collars for back and neck support, and the judicious use of local heat are all part of a rational physical therapy program. Surgically, total hip replacement may offer considerable relief to patients with ankylosis of the hips.

REITER'S SYNDROME

Reiter's syndrome is a clinical triad consisting of arthritis, urethritis, and conjunctivitis. It usually affects men, though women and children have developed Reiter's syndrome following outbreaks of dysentery. The arthritis is recurrent or chronic, migratory, asymmetric, and polyarticular, involving small joints of the hands and feet as well as large weight-bearing joints. Fever, malaise, and weight loss occur commonly with acute arthritis. The urethritis is probably nonspecific and often asymptomatic. The conjunctivitis is usually bilateral. Twenty to 50% of patients develop iritis. Balanitis circinata, painless oral ulcerations, and keratoderma blennorrhagicum (thick keratotic lesions of the palms and soles) are frequent mucocutaneous manifestations. Unusual complications include spondylitis and carditis.

Most patients have a leukocytosis of 10–18 thousand/μl. The urethral discharge is purulent, but smear and culture are negative for *Neisseria gonorrhoeae.* Synovial fluid is sterile, with a white count of 2000–50,000/μl, mostly polymorphonuclear neutrophils. The classical radiographic finding is periosteal proliferation of the heels, ankles, metatarsals, phalanges, knees, and elbows.

The major diseases in the differential diagnosis include gonococcal arthritis, psoriatic arthritis, and ankylosing spondylitis. Patients with psoriatic arthritis also develop urethritis or conjunctivitis. The differentiation of psoriatic arthritis and Reiter's syndrome is difficult to make on the basis of the skin lesion, since keratoderma blennorrhagicum is histologically indistinguishable from pustular psoriasis. Reiter's syndrome can be differentiated from ankylosing spondylitis by the presence of the urethritis and conjunctivitis and by the radiologic characteristics of the spine disease.

The cause of Reiter's syndrome is not known. Some cases have been associated with sexual contact. Several infectious agents, including shigellae, gonococci, mycoplasmas, and chlamydiae, have been irregularly associated with Reiter's syndrome, but there is no consensus on the significance of these associations. Ninety percent of patients with Reiter's syndrome have HLA-B27. It is not known whether this antigenic marker implies an increased susceptibility to environmental or infectious agents or the presence of unusual autoantigens. The presence of lymphocytes and plasma cells in the inflammatory synovial fluid of patients with Reiter's syndrome suggests a persistent immune response.

Salicylates, indomethacin, or phenylbutazone may be used to control acute inflammation. Although the acute attack usually subsides in a few months, recurrences are common and some patients develop a chronic deforming arthritis.

PSORIATIC ARTHRITIS

Psoriatic arthritis is a chronic or recurrent, erosive polyarthritis seen in 5–7% of patients with psoriasis. The arthritis is usually preceded by the skin lesion, and there is a correlation between the activity (but not the severity) of the skin and joint disease. The onset of the arthritis may be acute or insidious. It characteristically involves the distal interphalangeal joints of the fingers and toes, the hips, the sacroiliac joints, and the spine. Constitutional signs and symptoms, such as fever and fatigue, are common. Severe erosive disease may lead to marked deformity of the hands and feet (arthritis mutilans), and marked vertebral involvement can result in ankylosis of the spine.

An elevated erythrocyte sedimentation rate and a mild anemia are extremely common. Hyperuricemia is occasionally seen in patients with severe skin disease. Serum immunoglobulin levels are normal, and rheumatoid factor is absent. Synovial fluid examination reveals a white cell count of 5–40 thousand/μl, mostly polymorphonuclear leukocytes. Characteristic x-ray findings include resorption of the distal phalanges and erosion and tapering of the distal end of involved bones. Sacroiliac changes, including erosions, sclerosis, and ankylosis similar to that in ankylosing spondylitis, occur in 10–30% of patients.

The major diseases that must be differentiated from psoriatic arthritis include rheumatoid arthritis, ankylosing spondylitis, and Reiter's syndrome. Psoriatic arthritis is differentiated from rheumatoid arthritis by the absence of rheumatoid factor and subcutaneous nodules, the involvement of distal interphalangeals, the characteristic x-ray findings of psoriatic arthritis, and the presence of psoriasis. The presence of the skin lesion, the involvement of distal interphalangeals, and differences in the radiologic appearance of the spine help differentiate psoriatic arthritis from ankylosing spondylitis. The differentiation of psoriatic arthritis from Reiter's syndrome is particularly difficult, since both diseases are associated with HLA-B27 and involve the sacroiliac joints and spine and since keratodermia is histologically indistinguishable from pustular psoriasis. The diagnosis of psoriatic arthritis rests on the absence of urethritis, conjunctivitis, and oral ulcers.

The cause of psoriasis and psoriatic arthritis is unknown. Genetic factors appear to play a role in disease causation. Psoriasis and rheumatic diseases are found in family members of 12–13% of patients. Furthermore, 20% of patients with psoriatic arthritis and 45% of patients with spondylitis have HLA-B27. HLA-A13, HLA-Bw16, and HLA-Bw17 are all increased in psoriasis without arthritis. The high incidence of genetic markers might be associated with an increased susceptibility to unknown infectious or environmental agents or to primary abnormal autoimmune phenomena. However, no immunologic pathogenetic mechanism has yet been demonstrated.

Skin and arthritic manifestations require therapy. Corticosteroids, coal tar and ultraviolet light, or immunosuppressive agents can be used to treat the skin disease.

RELAPSING POLYCHONDRITIS

Relapsing polychondritis is a rare disease characterized by recurrent episodes of inflammatory necrosis involving cartilaginous tissues of the ears, nose, upper respiratory tract, and peripheral joints. The disease begins abruptly with swollen, painful, erythematous lesions of the nose or ears, usually associated with fever. The inflammation destroys supporting cartilaginous tissues, and patients are left with characteristic "floppy ear" and "saddle nose" deformities. Involvement of the upper respiratory tract leads to collapse of the trachea with recurrent bronchitis and pneumonia; the commonest cause of death in these patients is airway obstruction. Recurrent episcleritis, cataract formation, auditory and vestibular defects, and arthritis are common manifestations of relapsing polychondritis. Aortic insufficiency due to destruction and dilatation of the aortic valve ring occurs rarely.

Laboratory abnormalities include an elevated erythrocyte sedimentation rate, increased serum immunoglobulins, a false-positive VDRL, and mild anemia. Pathologic examination reveals infiltration of the cartilage-connective tissue interface with lymphocytes, plasma cells, and polymorphonuclear leukocytes. As the lesion evolves, the cartilage loses its basophilic stippling and stains more acidophilic. Eventually, the cartilage becomes completely replaced by fibrous tissue.

The pathogenesis of this disease is unknown. However, there is some evidence that autoimmune phenomena play a role. Indirect immunofluorescence has revealed the presence of anticartilage antibodies in the serum of a few patients. In some patients with relapsing polychondritis, cartilage antigen will induce lymphocyte activation and lymphocyte production of MIF. These observations must be verified and expanded before definitive statements on the immunopathogenesis of relapsing polychondritis can be made.

Corticosteroids are effective in controlling acute inflammation during recurrent episodes.

RELAPSING PANNICULITIS
(Weber-Christian Disease)

Relapsing panniculitis is a rare syndrome characterized by recurrent episodes of discrete nodular inflammation and nonsuppurative necrosis of subcutaneous fat. The majority of patients are women. Painful, erythematous nodules appear over the face, trunk, and limbs, but involvement of splanchnic fatty tissue is unusual. The nodules usually progress to local atrophy and fibrosis, but they may undergo necrosis with the discharge of a fatty fluid. Constitutional signs, including fever, usually accompany an acute episode. Histologically, lesions show edema, mononuclear cell infiltration, and fat necrosis, with local vessels showing perivascular inflammatory cuffing and endothelial proliferation. The differential diagnosis includes superficial thrombophlebitis, polyarteritis nodosa, necrotizing vasculitis, erythema induratum, and erythema nodosum.

The cause of relapsing panniculitis is not known. The syndrome has been associated with a number of environmental factors, including trauma, cold, exposure to toxic chemicals, and infection. It has been seen in patients with systemic lupus erythematosus, rheumatoid arthritis, diabetes mellitus, sarcoidosis, tuberculosis, withdrawal from corticosteroid therapy, and acute and chronic pancreatitis. In some patients it appears to be a hypersensitivity phenomenon since it follows repeated injections of various drugs. An autoimmune mechanism is suggested by the association of relapsing panniculitis with several autoimmune diseases and with numerous phenomena which could conceivably expose or alter autoantigens in fatty tissue. However, the only autoantibodies demonstrated to date are circulating leukoagglutinins.

Acute episodes respond to corticosteroid therapy.

HEREDITARY COMPLEMENT DEFICIENCIES & COLLAGEN VASCULAR DISEASES

The past decade has seen the development of technics for the evaluation and characterization of complement and complement inhibitors (see Chapter 6). The use of these technics has revealed hereditary deficiencies of various components of the complement system. Complement deficiency is seen in one in a million normal adult males and is much more common in patients with various rheumatoid diseases.

Deficiencies of a number of complement components have been associated with several rheumatoid diseases. C1r deficiency has been described in a patient with a lupuslike syndrome consisting of skin rash, arthritis, and immune complex glomerulonephritis without ANA or the LE cell phenomenon. C2 deficiency has been found in several patients with a variety of rheumatoid symptoms, including lupuslike syndrome, polydermatomyositis, and synovitis of the hip. A single patient with C6 deficiency developed gonococcal arthritis, and C7 deficiency has been described in a patient with telangiectasia, acrosclerosis, and Raynaud's phenomenon.

The significance of complement deficiency in the causation of collagen vascular disease has yet to be clarified. However, it is hypothesized that complement deficiency may lead to an increased susceptibility to infectious agents, particularly viruses. Such infectious agents could stimulate the autoimmunity which results in disease.

At present there is no specific treatment for most complement deficiencies. Therapy is directed at the associated disease.

HYPOGAMMAGLOBULINEMIA & ARTHRITIS

Hypogammaglobulinemia is an acquired or congenital disorder which may involve all or any one of the specific classes of immunoglobulin (see Chapter 26). Hypogammaglobulinemia is associated with infections, chronic inflammatory bowel disease, sarcoidosis, a number of rheumatoid diseases (systemic lupus erythematosus, scleroderma, Sjögren's syndrome, polymyositis-dermatomyositis), an increased incidence of malignancy, and a seronegative rheumatoid-like arthritis. Patients with classical adult and juvenile rheumatoid arthritis may develop hypogammaglobulinemia.

Hypogammaglobulinemia patients may develop a seronegative, symmetric arthritis, with morning stiffness, occasional nodule formation, and radiographic evidence of demineralization and joint space narrowing. Bony erosions are rarely seen. Biopsy of the synovium reveals chronic inflammatory changes without plasma cells. Despite the reduction of serum immunoglobulins, immunoglobulin may be detected in the inflammatory synovial fluid. Total hemolytic complement is commonly depressed in the synovial fluid, suggesting immune complex formation.

It has been hypothesized that hypogammaglobulinemia results in an increased susceptibility to infection by unidentified viruses that may induce the autoimmune phenomena (including arthritis) seen in these patients.

Hypogammaglobulinemic arthritis may improve after the administration of gamma globulin.

• • •

References

Systemic Lupus Erythematosus

Aptekar RG, Lawless A, Decker JL: Deforming nonerosive arthritis of the hand in SLE. Clin Orthop 100: 120, 1974.

Attias MR, Sylvester RA, Talal N: Antibodies to reovirus RNA in SLE detected by a cellulose ester filter radioimmunoassay. Arthritis Rheum 15:428, 1972.

Baldwin D & others: The clinical course of the proliferative and membranous forms of lupus nephritis. Ann Intern Med 73:929, 1970.

Bennett K & others: Neuropsychiatric problems in SLE. Br Med J 4:342, 1972.

Castro O, Farber LR, Clyne LP: Circulating anticoagulants against factors IX and XI in systemic lupus erythematosus. Ann Intern Med 77:543, 1972.

Comerford FR, Cohen AS: The nephropathy of systemic lupus erythematosus. Medicine 46:425, 1967.

Dubois EL (editor): *Lupus Erythematosus,* 2nd ed. Univ Southern California Press, 1974.

Eisenberg H, Dubois EL, Sherwin RP: Diffuse interstitial lung disease in SLE. Ann Intern Med 79:37, 1973.

Keeffe EB & others: Antibody to DNA and DNA-anti-DNA complexes in cerebrospinal fluid. Ann Intern Med 80:58, 1974.

Notman DD, Kurata N, Tan EM: Profiles of antinuclear antibodies in systemic rheumatic diseases. Ann Intern Med 83:464, 1975.

Pekin TJ, Zvaifler NJ: Synovial fluid findings in SLE. Arthritis Rheum 13:777, 1970.

Petz LD & others: Serum and cerebral spinal fluid complement and serum autoantibodies in SLE. Medicine 50:259, 1971.

Reichlin M, Mattioli M: Antigens and antibodies characteristic of SLE. Bull Rheum Dis 24:756, 1973–1974 series.

Rothfield NF, Stollar BD: The relation of immunoglobulin class, pattern of antinuclear antibody and complement fixing antibodies to DNA in sera from patients with SLE. J Clin Invest 46:1785, 1967.

Shearn M: The heart in SLE. Am Heart J 58:452, 1959.

Spriggs B, Epstein W: Clinical and laboratory correlates of L-chain proteinuria in systemic lupus erythematosus. J Rheum 1:287, 1974.

Steinberg AD & others: Cytotoxic drugs in treatment of nonmalignant diseases. Ann Intern Med 76:619, 1972.

Talal N: Immunologic and viral factors in the pathogenesis of SLE. Arthritis Rheum 13:887, 1970.

Trimble RB & others: Preliminary criteria for the classification of SLE. Arthritis Rheum 17:184, 1974.

Ziff M: Viruses and the connective tissue diseases. Ann Intern Med 45:951, 1971.

Rheumatoid Arthritis

Abruzzo JL, Heimer R: IgG anti-IgG antibodies in rheumatoid arthritis and certain other conditions. Ann Rheum Dis 33:258, 1974.

Askari A, Moskowitz RW, Goldberg VM: Subcutaneous rheumatoid nodules and serum rheumatoid factors without arthritis. JAMA 229:319, 1974.

Goldman JA, Hess EV: Treatment of rheumatoid arthritis–1970. Bull Rheum Dis 21:609, 1970.

Gowans JDC, Salami M: Response of rheumatoid arthritis with leukopenia to gold salts. N Engl J Med 288:1007, 1973.

Franco AE, Schur PH: Hypocomplementemia in rheumatoid arthritis. Arthritis Rheum 14:231, 1971.

Hasselbacher P, LeRoy EC: Serum DNA binding activity in healthy subjects and in rheumatic disease. Arthritis Rheum 17:63, 1974.

Hollander JL & others: Studies on the pathogenesis of rheumatoid joint inflammation. Ann Intern Med 62:271, 1965.

Johnson JS & others: Rheumatoid arthritis–1970–1972. Ann Intern Med 78:937, 1973.

Morgan ES & others: A study of the relation of seronegative and seropositive rheumatoid arthritis to each other and to necrotizing vasculitis. Am J Med 47:23, 1969.

Pope RM, Teller DC, Mannik M: The molecular basis of self-association of antibodies to IgG (rheumatoid factors) in rheumatoid arthritis. Proc Natl Acad Sci

USA 71:517, 1974.

Schmid FR & others: Arteritis in rheumatoid arthritis. Am J Med 30:56, 1961.

Stage DE, Mannik M: 7SγM-globulin in rheumatoid arthritis: Evaluation of its clinical significance. Arthritis Rheum 14:440, 1971.

Ziff M: Relation of cellular infiltration of rheumatoid synovial membrane to its immune response. Arthritis Rheum 17:313, 1974.

Zvaifler NJ: Further speculation on the pathogenesis of joint inflammation in rheumatoid arthritis. Arthritis Rheum 13:895, 1970.

Zvaifler NJ: Rheumatoid synovitis: An extravascular immune complex disease. Arthritis Rheum 17:297, 1974.

Juvenile Rheumatoid Arthritis

Bianco NE & others: Immunologic studies of juvenile rheumatoid arthritis. Arthritis Rheum 14:685, 1971.

Bujak JG & others: Juvenile rheumatoid arthritis presenting in the adult as fever of unknown origin. Medicine 52:431, 1973.

Calabro JJ, Katz RM, Maltz BA: A critical reappraisal of juvenile rheumatoid arthritis. Clin Orthop 74:101, 1971.

Granberry WM, Brewer EJ: Results of synovectomy in children with rheumatoid arthritis. Clin Orthop 101:120, 1974.

Hollander JL, McCarty DJ (editors): *Arthritis and Allied Conditions,* 8th ed. Lea & Febiger, 1972.

Moore T, Dorner RW, Zuckner J: Hidden rheumatoid factor in seronegative juvenile rheumatoid arthritis. Ann Rheum Dis 33:255, 1974.

Rodnan GP, McEwen C, Wallace SL (editors): Primer on the rheumatic diseases. JAMA 224 (Suppl 5):661–812, 1973. [Entire issue.]

Sjögren's Syndrome

Anderson LG, Talal N: The spectrum of benign to malignant lymphoproliferation in Sjögren's syndrome. Clin Exp Immunol 9:199, 1971.

Bloch KJ & others: Sjögren's syndrome: A clinical, pathological, and serological study of sixty-two cases. Medicine 44:187, 1965.

Shearn MA: *Sjögren's Syndrome.* Saunders, 1971.

Talal N, Sokoloff L, Barth WF: Extra-salivary lymphoid abnormalities in Sjögren's syndrome (reticulum cell sarcoma, "pseudolymphoma," macroglobulinemia). Am J Med 43:50, 1967.

Talal N, Zisman E, Schur PH: Renal tubular acidosis, glomerulonephritis and immunologic factors in Sjögren's syndrome. Arthritis Rheum 11:774, 1968.

Talal N & others: T and B lymphocytes in peripheral blood and tissue lesions in Sjögren's syndrome. J Clin Invest 53:180, 1974.

Progressive Systemic Sclerosis

Cannon PJ & others: The relationship of hypertension and renal failure in scleroderma (progressive systemic sclerosis) to structural and functional abnormalities of the renal cortical circulation. Medicine 53:1, 1974.

Medscer TA & others: Skeletal muscle involvement in progressive systemic sclerosis. Arthritis Rheum 11: 554, 1968.

Rodnan GP, McEwen C, Wallace SL (editors): Primer on the rheumatic diseases. 9. Progressive systemic sclerosis. JAMA 224:711, 1973.

Rothfield NF, Rodnan GP: Serum antinuclear antibodies in progressive systemic sclerosis. Arthritis Rheum 11:607, 1968.

Sharp GC & others: Mixed connective tissue disease. Ann Intern Med 62:148, 1972.

Weaver AL, Divertie MD, Titus JL: The lung in scleroderma. Mayo Clin Proc 42:754, 1967.

Winkelmann RK: Classification and pathogenesis of scleroderma. Mayo Clin Proc 46:83, 1971.

Winkelmann RK & others: Management of scleroderma. Mayo Clin Proc 46:128, 1971.

Polymyositis-Dermatomyositis

Bohan A, Peter JB: Polymyositis-dermatomyositis. (2 parts.) N Engl J Med 292:344, 403, 1975.

Dowben RM & others: Polymyositis and other diseases resembling muscular dystrophy. Arch Intern Med 115:584, 1965.

Johnson RL, Fink CW, Ziff M: Lymphotoxin formation by lymphocytes and muscle in polymyositis. J Clin Invest 51:2435, 1972.

Pearson CM: Patterns of polymyositis and their responses to treatment. Ann Intern Med 59:827, 1963.

Vignos PJ, Goldwyn J: Evaluation of laboratory tests in diagnosis and management of polymyositis. Am J Med Sci 263:291, 1972.

Vasculitides

Bron KM, Gajara A: Demonstration of hepatic aneurysms in polyarteritis nodosa by angiography. N Engl J Med 282:1024, 1970.

Collagen Diseases and Hypersensitivity Panel: Treatment of polyarteritis nodosa with cortisone: Results after three years. Br Med J 1:1399, 1960.

Couleru O & others: Immune complexes in large particles of Australia antigen in polyarteritis. Lancet 1:455, 1972.

Fauci AS, Wolff SM, Johnson JS: Effect of cyclophosphamide upon the immune response in Wegener's granulomatosis. N Engl J Med 285:1493, 1971.

Fraga A & others: Takayasu's arteritis: Frequency of systemic manifestations (study of 22 patients) and favorable response to maintenance steroid therapy with adrenocorticosteroids (12 patients). Arthritis Rheum 15:617, 1972.

Frohnert PP, Sheps SG: Long-term follow-up study of periarteritis nodosa. Am J Med 43:8, 1967.

Hamilton CR, Shelly WM, Tumulty PA: Giant cell arteritis–Including temporal arteritis and polymyalgia rheumatica. Medicine 50:1, 1971.

Meadow SR & others: Schönlein-Henoch nephritis. Q J Med 41:241, 1972.

Shillitoe EJ & others: Immunologic features of Wegener's granulomatosis. Lancet 1:281, 1974.

Vinijchaukul K: Primary arteritis of the aorta and its main branches (Takayasu's arteriopathy): A clinicopathologic autopsy study of eight cases. Am J Med 43:15, 1967.

Serum Sickness

Dixon FJ & others: Immunology and pathogenesis of experimental serum sickness. Page 354 in: *Cellular and Humoral Aspects of Hypersensitivity States.*

Lawrence HS (editor). Hoeber, 1959.

Vaughan JH & others: Serum sickness. Ann Intern Med 57:596, 1967.

Weigle WO, Dixon FJ: Relationship of circulating antigen-antibody complexes, antigen elimination and complement fixation in serum sickness. Proc Soc Exp Biol Med 99:226, 1958.

Behçet's Disease

Haim S, Sherf K: Behçet's disease. Isr J Med Sci 2:69, 1966.

O'Duffy JD: Suggested criteria for the diagnosis of Behçet's disease. VI Pan-American Congress on Rheumatic Diseases. J Rheum (Suppl) 18, 1974.

O'Duffy JD, Carney JA, Deodhar S: Behçet's disease. Ann Intern Med 75:561, 1971.

Ankylosing Spondylitis

Calabro JJ, Maltz BA: Ankylosing spondylitis. N Engl J Med 282:606, 1970.

Dick HM & others: Inheritance of ankylosing spondylitis and HL-A antigen W27. Lancet 1:24, 1974.

McEwen C & others: Ankylosing spondylitis and spondylitis accompanying ulcerative colitis, regional enteritis, psoriasis, Reiter's disease: A comparative study. Arthritis Rheum 14:291, 1971.

Schlosstein L & others: High association of an HL-A antigen, W27, with ankylosing spondylitis. N Engl J Med 288:704, 1973.

Reiter's Syndrome

Ford DK: Reiter's syndrome. Bull Rheum Dis 20:588, 1970.

Morris R & others: HL-A W27: A clue to the diagnosis and pathogenesis of Reiter's syndrome. N Engl J Med 290:554, 1974.

Schachter J & others: Isolation of bedsoniae from the joints of patients with Reiter's syndrome. Proc Soc Exp Med 122:283, 1966.

Psoriatic Arthritis

Baker H, Golding DM, Thompson M: Psoriasis and arthritis. Ann Intern Med 58:909, 1963.

Brewerton DA & others: HL-A 27 and arthropathies associated with ulcerative colitis and psoriasis. Lancet 1:956, 1974.

McDevitt HO, Bodmer WF: HL-A, immuno-response genes, and disease. Lancet 2:1269, 1974.

Polychondritis

Herman JH, Dennis MV: Immunopathologic studies in relapsing polychondritis. J Clin Invest 52:549, 1973.

Hughes RAC & others: Relapsing polychondritis. Q J Med 41:363, 1972.

Rogers PH & others: Relapsing polychondritis with insulin resistance and antibodies to cartilage. Am J Med 55:243, 1973.

Panniculitis

Fayemi AO, Williams J, Cuttner J: Systemic Weber-Christian disease and thrombocythemia terminating in reticulum cell sarcoma. Am J Clin Pathol 62:88, 1974.

Förström L, Winkelmann RK: Factitial panniculitis. Arch Dermatol 110:747, 1974.

MacDonald A, Fiewel M: A review of the concept of Weber-Christian panniculitis with a report of five cases. Br J Dermatol 80:355, 1968.

Hereditary Complement Deficiency

Leddy JP & others: Hereditary complement C_2 deficiency with dermatomyositis. Am J Med 58:83, 1975.

Stroud RM: Genetic abnormalities of the complement system of man associated with disease. Transplant Proc 6:59, 1974.

Hypogammaglobulinemia & Arthritis

Ammann AJ, Hong R: Selective IgA deficiency: Presentation of 30 cases and a review of the literature. Medicine 50:223, 1971.

Talal N: Connective tissue disease and other immunologic disorders. Page 589 in: *Arthritis and Allied Conditions,* 8th ed. Hollander JL, McCarty DJ (editors). Lea & Febiger, 1972.

28 . . .
Hematologic Diseases

J. Vivian Wells, MD, & Curt A. Ries, MD

There are few areas in hematology that are not significantly affected by immunologic processes. A hematologic disorder may be primarily a disease of the immune system, eg, plasma cell malignancies; or immunologic processes may play a role in pathogenesis, as is the case with autoimmune hemolytic anemia; or immunologic laboratory methods may be important in diagnosis, as in hemophilia. Diseases that appear to be primarily immunologic ones will be discussed in some detail in this chapter, while those in which immunologic factors play a contributing role will be discussed solely from the point of view of those factors. The subject matter of this chapter consists of disorders of white cells, red cells, and platelets; bone marrow transplantation; disorders of hemostasis; and blood banking and transfusion with whole blood and its components.

I. WHITE BLOOD CELL DISORDERS

Since many of the cells of the lymphoid system in peripheral blood and in tissue are included in the general category of white blood cells, it is not surprising that many diseases affecting these cells involve immunologic processes. These include the leukemias, lymphoreticular disorders, and granulocytopenias. Disorders involving lymphocytes have been studied with particular interest, and it appears that in man, as in lower animals, there are several stages of differentiation of lymphocytes from a stem cell to a mature B cell (and plasma cell) or a mature T cell. The clinicopathologic correlations with the stage of differentiation in specific diseases are not yet known since technics are not yet available to characterize the stage of differentiation of the lymphoid cells in each patient with, for example, lymphoma.

J. Vivian Wells is Senior Staff Specialist in Clinical Immunology, Kolling Institute of Medical Research, Royal North Shore Hospital of Sydney, St. Leonards, N.S.W. 2065 Australia. Curt A. Ries is Associate Clinical Professor of Medicine, University of California School of Medicine, San Francisco.

LEUKEMIAS

The leukemias are characterized by lack of normal differentiation and accumulation of white blood cells. They are classified as acute or chronic on the basis of clinical and hematologic features. The main types of leukemias are acute lymphocytic leukemia, acute myelogenous leukemia (and subtypes: acute myelomonocytic, monocytic, and promyelocytic leukemia), chronic lymphocytic leukemia, and chronic myelogenous leukemia. Two rare forms of leukemia are plasma cell leukemia (discussed below with the plasma cell dyscrasias) and lymphosarcoma cell leukemia. Leukemia is classified as acute or chronic according to clinical presentation, morphologic appearance, and prognosis.

ACUTE LEUKEMIA

Acute lymphocytic leukemia affects mainly children and responds better to treatment than other types of acute leukemia. Acute myelogenous leukemia and its variants occur mainly in adults and are generally more resistant to treatment.

The cause of leukemia in man is unknown, but accumulating evidence continues to implicate viruses. Acute leukemia develops in a significant number of individuals exposed to ionizing radiation and some chemicals. Genetic factors are also involved since leukemia is more frequent in some individuals with chromosomal abnormalities. Viral leukemia has been studied in lower species, especially mice, fowl, cats, and nonhuman primates. In several instances, the virus is inherited. It may also be passed in the milk of the mother to the offspring. Animal experiments show that genetic factors are important both in susceptibility to infection with leukemia virus and its expression as clinical disease. Detection of the enzyme RNA-dependent DNA polymerase (reverse transcriptase) in cells indicates that they may possess part of the structure of RNA oncogenic virus. This enzyme has been detected in animal and human leukemia cells.

Both human and animal leukemia cells possess cell surface antigens not found in normal cells of the same type. These human leukemia-associated antigens have been isolated and partially characterized. Antibodies to leukemia-associated antigens can be detected in the blood or on the leukemia cells of many patients with acute leukemia and in the blood of some normal household contacts of leukemia patients. Antibodies to these antigens can also be prepared by immunization of laboratory animals, eg, rabbits and nonhuman primates.

Further support for a viral cause of acute leukemia comes from observations of patients who have received irradiation and chemotherapy to ablate their leukemia cells prior to transplantation of normal human bone marrow. Leukemia subsequently reappeared in a few cases in the donor cells in the bone marrow graft. C-type oncogenic RNA virus particles have been isolated from human leukemia cells, and the relationship of these structures to specific RNA viruses in lower species is being studied.

There is thus increasingly strong evidence that RNA viruses are involved in the etiology of leukemia, but their precise role is not yet known.

Several immunologic laboratory procedures aid in the diagnosis of leukemia and its accompanying immunologic abnormalities. Unfortunately, many of these tests can only be performed in specialized immunology laboratories, eg, detection of serum leukemia-associated antigens and antibodies. These can be detected by radioimmunoassay (see Chapter 24). Some laboratories have developed antisera that react with antigens common to all forms of leukemia or just acute leukemia; others have developed antisera that react with only a single type of leukemia. In some cases, the human antibodies function in cytotoxicity tests. About 15% of acute leukemia patients have serum antibodies that are cytotoxic for acute lymphocytic or acute myelogenous leukemia cells and long-term human cultured lymphoid cell lines. They are not cytotoxic for normal bone marrow cells, chronic myelogenous leukemia cells, or lymphocytes transformed by exposure to PHA.

Membrane-bound immunoglobulins have been detected on the surface of human leukemia cells. In acute myelogenous and acute lymphocytic leukemia, they may represent adsorbed serum antibodies which can be eluted and characterized. Leukemia-associated antigens can also be demonstrated on human leukemia cells by immunofluorescence technics with antisera prepared in laboratory animals, although these antisera are not yet routinely available.

Foreign antigens on leukemia cells can also be demonstrated by the ability of leukemia cells to stimulate lymphocytes from patients or normal subjects. To eliminate the problem of different histocompatibility antigens (see Chapter 15), leukemia cells from a patient are isolated at diagnosis, stored deep-frozen, and subsequently tested against lymphocytes of the same patient during the course of the disease. A patient in remission can demonstrate stimulation of his lymphocytes by his own stored leukemia cells.

Characterization of the cells in acute lymphocytic leukemia can be performed using the markers for T and B cells described in Chapter 25. Human T cells are recognized by their ability to form spontaneous rosettes with sheep red blood cells and their reactivity with antisera specific for T cells. Human B cells are recognized by the presence of readily detectable membrane immunoglobulins and the presence of membrane receptors for C3 and the Fc fragment of IgG. The leukemia cells in approximately 80% of cases of acute lymphocytic leukemia of childhood have neither T nor B lymphocyte characteristics. They are termed *null cells,* but their relationship to the null cells detected in normal human peripheral blood is unknown. The leukemia cells are T cells in approximately 20% of children with acute lymphocytic leukemia. This is an important distinction since patients with T cell acute lymphocytic leukemia have a higher median age, a higher incidence of mediastinal thymic tumors, poorer response to treatment, and a worse prognosis.

Several immunologic tests may indicate the overall prognosis in acute lymphocytic leukemia of childhood. A poorer prognosis is suggested by abnormalities in specific immunity, eg, greater amounts of antileukemia antibody and leukemia-associated antigens, and abnormalities in general immune function, eg, reduced lymphocyte activation by PHA. Patients with T cell acute lymphocytic leukemia have a high T lymphocyte blood count and a poor prognosis. However, patients with acute lymphocytic leukemia and a markedly reduced normal residual T cell count also have a poor prognosis, probably reflecting a reduction in cellular immunity. Comparable studies in acute myelogenous leukemia have not been completed.

Clinical Features

A. Symptoms and Signs: Acute leukemia is typically manifested by weakness, fatigue, fever, weight loss, petechiae, purpura or bleeding, sternal tenderness, lymphadenopathy, and splenomegaly.

B. Laboratory Findings: The principal laboratory findings are either leukocytosis or leukocytopenia (occasionally normal white blood count) with immature abnormal white cells in peripheral blood and bone marrow, anemia, and thrombocytopenia. About 25% of patients present with leukocytopenia rather than leukocytosis, but the bone marrow shows a marked increase in blast cells. Specialized staining technics are used to characterize the leukemia cell type in blood and bone marrow since there is a significant correlation between the type of leukemia and response to treatment.

Treatment

Treatment of all types of leukemia relies on chemotherapy to destroy as many of the leukemia cells as possible while temporarily supporting the patient's impaired bone marrow function with transfusions of red cells and platelets and treating infections with antibiotics and granulocyte transfusions when necessary.

More effective chemotherapeutic agents for acute

leukemia have become available during the past 2 decades. Use of multiple agents in combination with variations in drug scheduling and dosages are all designed to achieve maximal destruction of the tumor mass of approximately $10^{12}-10^{13}$ leukemia cells at the time of diagnosis. The goal of initial therapy is to reduce this to approximately 10^9 or less leukemia cells, resulting in clinical and hematologic remission. This is the stage of remission induction, and a primary remission can be achieved in over 95% of patients with childhood acute lymphocytic leukemia and 60–75% of adults with acute myelogenous leukemia. The second stage is remission consolidation, usually with a different regimen, to reduce the number of leukemia cells to 10^5-10^6. These reductions in numbers of leukemia cells are achieved by giving multiple drugs that attack leukemia cells in different phases of their cell cycle. For example, methotrexate inhibits synthesis of DNA, RNA, and protein; corticosteroids destroy lymphoblasts in the resting period and prevent their entering into DNA synthesis; vincristine stops leukemia cells in mitosis, etc. After remission consolidation, patients usually receive maintenance chemotherapy for 3 years or until relapse. Recurrence of leukemia in the central nervous system is a common mode of relapse, and most centers use cranial irradiation and intrathecal methotrexate to prevent this.

A. Acute Lymphocytic Leukemia: The most common current regimen for remission induction in childhood acute lymphocytic leukemia is vincristine and prednisone for 3–4 weeks, with remission consolidation and maintenance being achieved with a combination of methotrexate, mercaptopurine, and cyclophosphamide. High-risk patients also receive daunorubicin or asparaginase. This approach has achieved markedly prolonged survival and a much improved quality of life for these patients when combined with supportive measures such as transfusion of red cells, platelets, and treatment of infections with antibiotics.

The immune system is best equipped to deal with a tumor antigen load of 10^5-10^6 cells, and various trials have been performed with immunotherapy for acute lymphocytic leukemia. Attempts to stimulate specific antitumor immunity by parenteral administration of irradiated leukemia cells have proved disappointing. Attempts to boost nonspecific immunity with agents such as BCG (see Chapter 40) have been more effective in some situations. It remains unclear from clinical studies whether immunization of patients in remission with BCG is a useful adjunct to chemotherapy. Children treated with BCG may have a lower incidence of intercurrent infections, especially with unusual organisms such as fungi, compared to children receiving continuous maintenance chemotherapy.

B. Acute Myelogenous Leukemia: The most active single agents for treatment of acute myelogenous leukemia are cytarabine and either daunorubicin or doxorubicin (Adriamycin). Most centers are now using remission induction protocols which include cytarabine and one of the other drugs with or without vincristine, prednisone, or thioguanine.

Immunotherapy with irradiated leukemia cells, BCG, or both has been studied by several groups for remission maintenance in adults with acute myelogenous leukemia. The results are conflicting, but several studies report encouraging responses. Immunotherapy has been given as the sole treatment to maintain remission or as an adjunct to monthly courses of maintenance chemotherapy. Immunotherapy may consist of weekly injections of altered allogeneic or pooled leukemia cells, weekly vaccinations with BCG, or both. Prolongation of survival has been found in some studies but not in others.

Bone marrow transplantation has been used in treatment of both acute lymphocytic and acute myelogenous leukemia after ablation of the leukemic bone marrow (see below).

CHRONIC LEUKEMIA

The 3 diseases to be discussed are chronic myelogenous leukemia, chronic lymphocytic leukemia, and leukemic reticuloendotheliosis.

1. CHRONIC MYELOGENOUS LEUKEMIA

Chronic myelogenous leukemia is characterized by the presence of abnormal myeloid cells in the blood, bone marrow, spleen, and other organs. The clinical and hematologic manifestations are similar to those of acute leukemia, ie, weakness, weight loss, sweats, splenomegaly, abdominal discomfort, anemia, and leukocytosis with immature cells in blood and bone marrow. However, the prognosis is quite different from that of acute leukemia.

The peripheral blood contains myeloid cells of variable maturity but relatively few myeloblasts. The bone marrow shows intense myeloid hyperplasia. The immature myeloid cells characteristically contain the Philadelphia chromosome, an abnormal autosomal chromosome 22.

Leukemia-associated antigens on chronic myelogenous leukemia cells cross-react with antigens on acute myelogenous leukemia cells. This is consistent with the observation that over half of patients with chronic myelogenous leukemia undergo a "blastic" transformation indistinguishable from that of acute myelogenous leukemia. Most hematologists consider this transformation intrinsic to the disease itself, but it could represent a change in differentiation of the cells influenced by the immune response of the host against the leukemia, or possibly a mutation induced by therapy.

The initial stages of chronic myelogenous leukemia are often asymptomatic, and no therapy is indicated. Generally, however, symptoms of hypermetabolism, splenomegaly, or anemia soon develop and require chemotherapy. Splenic irradiation was also widely used in the past and may still be indicated in certain circumstances. The drug of choice is busulfan on a continuous or intermittent schedule, with careful monitoring of blood counts to avoid excessive bone marrow suppression. Immunotherapy in chronic leukemia has not been fully investigated.

2. CHRONIC LYMPHOCYTIC LEUKEMIA

Chronic lymphocytic leukemia is characterized by the progressive accumulation of small lymphocytes of abnormally long life span in blood, bone marrow, liver, spleen, lymph nodes, and other tissues. The total tumor mass may be very great. The leukemia cell in chronic lymphocytic leukemia most often appears as a small but otherwise normal lymphocyte with a low mitotic rate. Occasionally, larger cells are seen resembling those in infectious mononucleosis. Chronic lymphocytic leukemia increases in frequency with age and is often diagnosed by examination of a routine blood film. In many cases it is a relatively benign nonprogressive disease, causing no troublesome symptoms for several years. However, it may become rapidly worse, causing recurrent infections and early death.

Deficiency of serum immunoglobulins may develop with resultant recurrent infections. A reduction in the serum IgM level often occurs first, followed by reduction of serum IgG and IgA.

A serum monoclonal immunoglobulin, most frequently IgM, is a relatively common finding. Generally, however, the concentration of IgM monoclonal protein is not great, and the clinical features of Waldenström's macroglobulinemia do not occur. There may be biclonal gammopathy.

The leukemia cell is a B lymphocyte in about 98% of cases of chronic lymphocytic leukemia. In the remainder, the cell is either a T cell or a null cell. In most B cell cases there is evidence that the abnormal cells come from a single clone. Not only do some patients have a circulating serum monoclonal protein, but the surface immunoglobulin on the B cells is restricted to a single L chain type and H chain class. IgM is the most common monoclonal surface immunoglobulin. If B lymphocytes are obtained fresh from a patient with chronic lymphocytic leukemia and treated with trypsin to remove surface immunoglobulin, reexamination of the cells after a period of culture to allow autologous synthesis of surface immunoglobulin reveals that the newly synthesized surface immunoglobulin is of a single L chain type and H chain class in most cases. However, more than one H chain class may be detected on lymphocytes in approximately 15% of cases of chronic lymphocytic leukemia. IgD and IgM occur frequently on cells from these patients.

In rare cases, lymphocytes from patients with chronic lymphocytic leukemia synthesize, but do not secrete, a monoclonal immunoglobulin that may be seen as intracytoplasmic crystals or inclusions.

Hemolytic anemia develops in some patients with chronic lymphocytic leukemia and frequently is clinically severe. Over half of the patients who become anemic have autoimmune hemolytic anemia with a positive Coombs test. Some patients with chronic lymphocytic leukemia have autoimmune thrombocytopenia as well.

Patients with chronic lymphocytic leukemia have an increased tendency to develop malignancies of other types. In one series, 16% of patients with chronic lymphocytic leukemia had malignant solid tumors and 7% had other lymphoreticular malignancies.

A series of alloantigens has been discovered on B cells in patients with chronic lymphocytic leukemia. Family studies of these markers are being done in an effort to determine their relationship to the HLA system (see Chapter 15), to establish whether these alloantigens are present on normal human B lymphocytes, and to identify the biologic importance of these antigens in terms of the major histocompatibility complex and immune response genes (see Chapter 12).

Many asymptomatic patients with chronic lymphocytic leukemia do not require treatment. The onset of symptoms, a rapidly rising lymphocyte count, or a falling red cell and platelet count generally warrants treatment. Chemotherapy usually consists of intermittent or continuous administration of chlorambucil in low doses, although intermittent high doses of chlorambucil-prednisone in combination are also employed. The development of complications requires active treatment, eg, increased prednisone dosage for autoimmune hemolytic anemia or thrombocytopenia. Injections of therapeutic human γ-globulin (ISG) may be necessary in patients with secondary hypogammaglobulinemia and significant recurrent bacterial infections.

3. LEUKEMIC RETICULOENDOTHELIOSIS

This uncommon disease is also known as *reticulum cell leukemia* or *hairy cell leukemia.* It affects mainly elderly male adults who present with fatigue, malaise, infection, abdominal discomfort, pancytopenia, splenomegaly, and moderate lymphadenopathy. The main pathologic findings are in peripheral blood, bone marrow, spleen, and liver. Pancytopenia is generally found on presentation and is often due to hypersplenism. The number of abnormal cells in the peripheral blood is variable, but in most cases it is 30–60%. The characteristic cell in blood and tissue is shown in Figs 28–1 and 28–2. Routine light microscopy shows the irregular fingerlike projections of cytoplasm which give rise to the term hairy cell leukemia, and these are confirmed by transmission electron microscopy. Scanning electron microscopy further emphasizes the presence of these projections and shows the rufflelike ridges on the surface. The cell adheres to surfaces, is

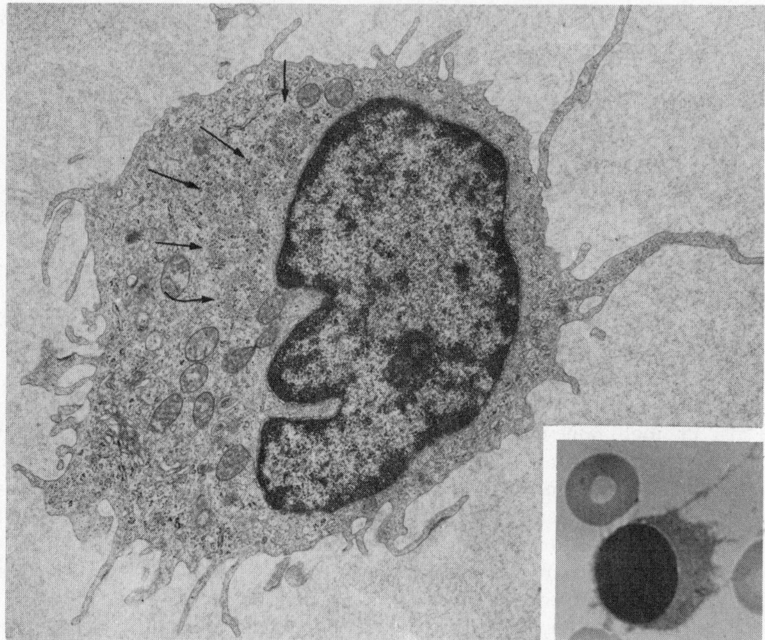

Figure 28–1. Electron micrograph of the neoplastic hairy cell in peripheral blood in leukemic reticuloendotheliosis. (Original magnification X 10,000.) Note the long cytoplasmic projections and multiple ribosome-lamella complexes in the cytoplasm (arrows). The inset is a light photomicrograph of a hairy cell from a peripheral blood smear. (Wright-Giemsa stain; original magnification X 1300.) (Reproduced, with permission, from Katayama I, Li CY, Yam LT: Ultrastructural characteristics of the "hairy cells" of leukemic reticuloendotheliosis. Am J Pathol 67:361, 1972.)

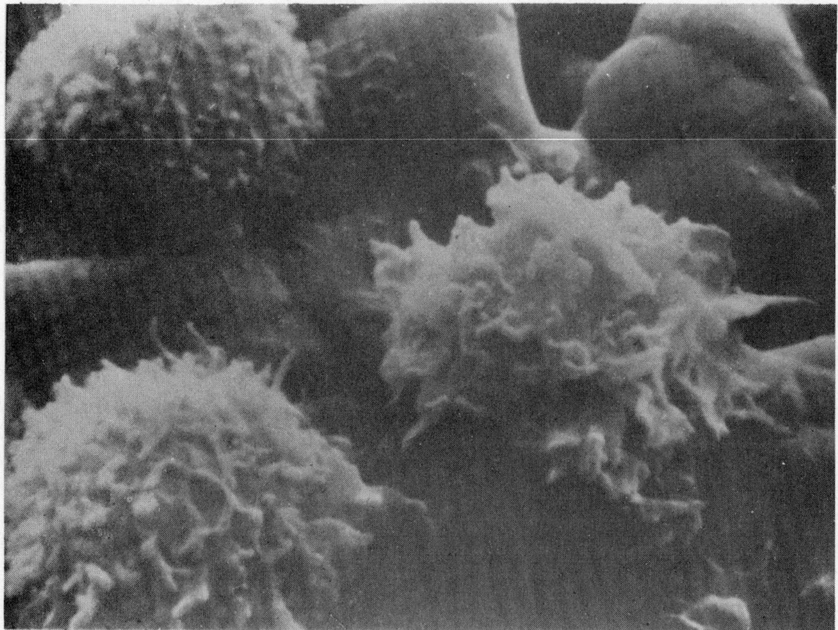

Figure 28–2. Scanning electron micrograph of 2 hairy cells in leukemic reticuloendotheliosis, demonstrating the exaggerated ruffled membranes, ridgelike profiles, and occasional microvilli, resembling monocyte-macrophage cells. A spherical lymphocyte with microvilli is seen in the upper left corner. (Original magnification X 9025.) (Reproduced, with permission, from Polliack A & De Harven E: An interpretative review. Surface features of normal and leukemic lymphocytes as seen by means of scanning electron microscopy. Clin Immunol Immunopathol 3:412, 1975.)

capable of phagocytosis, and probably belongs to the monocyte-macrophage series. In some patients with similar clinical features, the cells appear to be B cells. Just as acute lymphoblastic leukemia might be considered a null cell or T cell leukemia and chronic lymphocytic leukemia a B cell leukemia, leukemic reticuloendotheliosis might be considered a macrophage or possibly a B cell leukemia.

Despite the pathologic features of the disease and the presence of troublesome symptoms on presentation, the prognosis is not as poor as one might suspect. Splenomegaly with pancytopenia is best treated by splenectomy, often with excellent results. Chemotherapy is probably of questionable value and appears to be associated with a high mortality rate.

LYMPHORETICULAR DISORDERS

These are disorders other than the leukemias that are manifested chiefly by abnormal proliferation of cells in the lymphoid, reticulum cell, and monocyte-macrophage series. Classification apart from the leukemias is to some degree artificial since the lymphoreticular disorders may undergo transition to overt leukemia. The groups of diseases discussed include the paraproteinemias, malignant lymphomas, and infectious mononucleosis.

PARAPROTEINEMIAS

These diseases are also called the *plasma cell dyscrasias* or *monoclonal gammopathies.* They comprise a heterogeneous group of diseases characterized by the presence in serum or urine of a monoclonal immunoglobulin. This protein is also called a paraprotein, M protein (factor), or myeloma protein. It is the product of a single clone of lymphoid cells, is of restricted electrophoretic mobility, and appears in serum electrophoretograms as a narrow band or "spike" (Fig 28–3). The paraproteinemias are classified in Table 28–1.

Table 28–1. Classification of paraproteinemias.

Classification
Malignant monoclonal gammopathy
Multiple myeloma
Waldenström's macroglobulinemia
Solitary plasmacytoma
Amyloidosis
Heavy chain diseases
Malignant lymphoma
Chronic lymphocytic leukemia
Secondary monoclonal gammopathy
Cancer (nonlymphoreticular)
Monocytic leukemia
Hepatobiliary disease
Rheumatoid disorders
Chronic inflammatory states
Cold agglutinin syndrome
Papular mucinosis
Immunodeficiency
Benign monoclonal gammopathy
Transient
Persistent

Laboratory Investigation of Paraproteinemias

Serum paraproteins may be found (1) during routine screening of serum samples, (2) during investigation of a patient with an apparently unrelated complaint, and (3) when a patient has symptoms or signs suggesting malignant plasma cell dyscrasia. The laboratory investigations should include *hematologic tests,* including complete blood count with differential and reticulocyte count, erythrocyte sedimentation rate, and bone marrow examination; *routine clinical chemistry,* including serum levels of total protein, albumin, globulin, calcium, phosphate, other electrolytes, alkaline phosphatase, uric acid, blood urea nitrogen, creatinine, and cholesterol; *hemostatic profile,* including bleeding and clotting tests, platelet count, and specific factor assays if indicated; *serum viscosity* measured in an Ostwald viscosimeter; *radiologic examination,* including routine chest x-ray, skeletal bone survey, and bone scan with radiolabeled tracer if indicated; and *renal function tests,* including urinalysis, 24-hour urine protein, creatinine clearance, and measurement of renal acidification to rule out renal tubular acidosis.

The *immunologic tests* (see Chapter 24) to be performed should be serum protein electrophoresis and immunoelectrophoresis after separation of the serum at 37 C to avoid loss of a serum paraprotein as a cryoprecipitate. Fig 28–3 demonstrates the various patterns of paraproteins and the inability to predict H chain class and L chain type from zone electrophoresis alone. The amount of paraprotein is measured by densitometric tracing (see Chapter 24). Immunologic typing of an IgG paraprotein by immunoelectrophoresis is demonstrated in Fig 28–4. This is routinely performed with antisera to detect γ, α, μ, κ, and λ chains. If no abnormality is shown with these antisera and other evidence suggests a malignant paraproteinemia, immunoelectrophoresis should be performed with antisera specific for δ and ϵ chains to detect rare cases with IgD or IgE myeloma proteins. The main feature in the immunoelectrophoretic pattern which identifies a paraprotein is the change in the shape of the precipitin arc. Other changes are the reduction in amount of normal immunoglobulin of the same class as the paraprotein and localized splitting of the precipitin lines. Almost all paraproteins show an abnormal precipitin arc for either κ or λ chains which is similar in electrophoretic mobility to the H chain. The only exception is in H chain disease (see below).

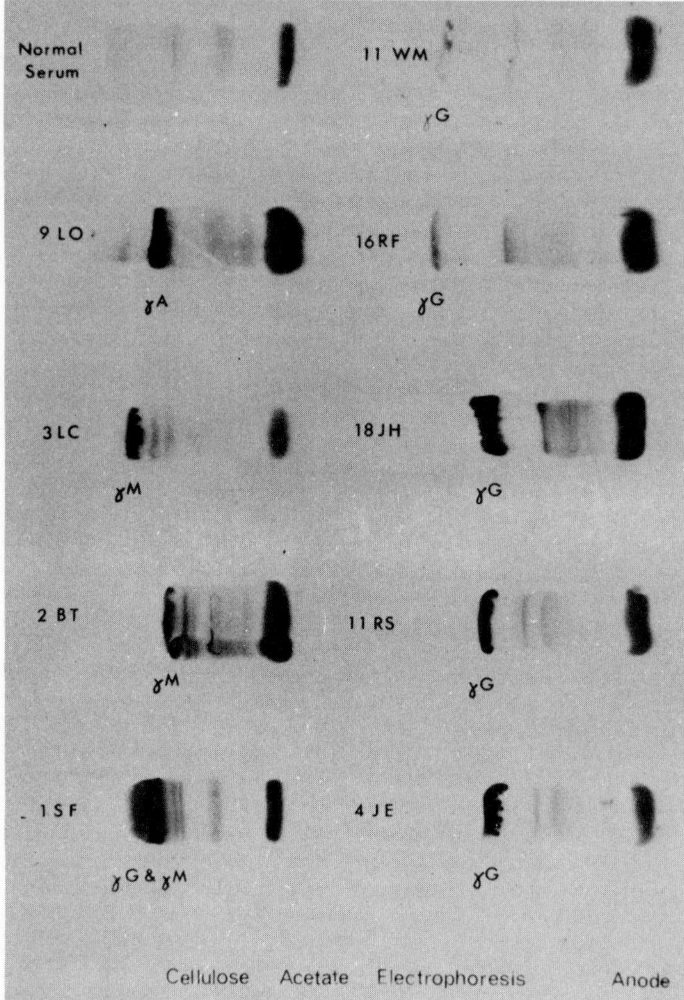

Figure 28–3. Patterns of serum electrophoretograms from 9 patients with paraproteinemia and one normal control. The anode is on the right and the H chain class, as determined by immunoelectrophoresis, is indicated below each example. Note the differences in concentration and electrophoretic mobility between paraproteins, the inability to predict immunologic type from the electrophoretogram alone, and the nonspecific sign of "scalloping" in the electrophoretogram (4 JE and 2 BT). (Reproduced, with permission, from Wells JV, Fudenberg HH: Paraproteinemia. Disease-A-Month, February 1974.)

All patients with paraproteins and suspected plasma cell dyscrasias without serum paraproteins must be tested for the presence of Bence Jones protein in the urine. Bence Jones protein consists of either monoclonal κ or λ light chains (see Chapter 2) which are excreted in significant amounts in about half of patients with multiple myeloma. They are best detected by zone electrophoresis and immunoelectrophoresis of the concentrated urine.

Immunofluorescence microscopy is now routinely performed in several centers on specimens of bone marrow with fluorescein-labeled specific antisera to various H and L chains. This is the only method that can confirm the intracellular location of a monoclonal immunoglobulin in rare cases of nonsecretory myeloma (see below).

Ancillary investigations include tests for euglobulin (protein which precipitates at low ionic strength), cryoglobulin, rheumatoid factor, and cold agglutinins. In special cases it is necessary to perform analytic ultracentrifugation of the serum to measure the molecular size of a paraprotein.

An assessment of immune function is now often performed in patients with paraproteins who present with a history of infection. This includes some of the methods described in Chapters 24 and 25 for measurement of cellular immunity (delayed hypersensitivity skin testing, PHA-induced lymphocyte activation, counting T cells), humoral immunity (antibody response to antigen), and granulocyte function. Abnormalities in granulocyte function are common in malignant paraproteinemia (see Chapter 25).

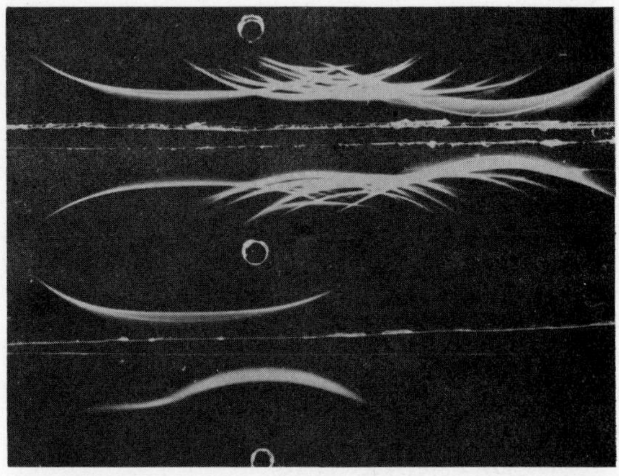

Figure 28–4. Immunoelectrophoresis of normal human serum (upper and center wells) and IgG myeloma serum (lower well). The upper trough contains antiserum to whole human serum and the lower trough antiserum specific to γ chains. Note the different shape and shorter precipitin line of myeloma IgG compared to normal IgG. (Reproduced, with permission, from Wells JV, Fudenberg HH: Paraproteinemia. Disease-A-Month, February 1974.)

Classification

The classification of paraproteinemias in Table 28–1 is intended for clinical use; the term malignant paraproteinemias is chosen to emphasize the clinically malignant nature of the diseases. Each person with a paraprotein has an abnormal or malignant clone of lymphoid cells which continues to synthesize a single immunoglobulin product. The malignant paraproteinemias comprise approximately 1.5% of all malignancies.

1. MULTIPLE MYELOMA

Major Immunologic Features

- Recurrent infections.
- Serum paraprotein (80%).
- Urinary paraprotein (50%).
- Reduced serum levels of nonmyeloma immunoglobulins.
- Presence of immature plasma cells in bone marrow.

General Considerations

Multiple myeloma is a distinct clinical syndrome consisting typically of the presence of a serum or urine paraprotein, anemia, and lytic bone lesions. It is the result of malignant transformation of a single clone of plasma cells. The diagnosis depends on the typical finding of large numbers of malignant plasma cells in the bone marrow, characteristic lytic bone lesions, and an associated serum or urine monoclonal protein.

Clinical Features

A. Symptoms and Signs: Bone pain and tenderness are a common presenting feature of multiple myeloma. Spontaneous pathologic fractures are not infrequent. Other major presenting features are anemia (weakness, pallor), recurrent infections (especially of the sinuses and respiratory tract), and occasionally renal failure.

B. Laboratory Findings: There is normocytic, normochromic anemia, with normal to slightly decreased white blood count and platelet count, and an elevated erythrocyte sedimentation rate. Azotemia and hypercalcemia are common complications. The bone marrow shows increased numbers of plasma cells with many abnormal forms which often completely replace the marrow. The plasma cells may be arranged in sheets; many are large immature cells having large or multiple nuclei and nucleoli.

C. X-Ray Findings: X-rays show characteristic punched-out lytic lesions in most patients. Generalized osteoporosis is also common.

Immunologic Diagnosis

Serum or urine paraproteins detected by zone electrophoresis (Fig 28–3) are typed by immunoelectrophoresis (see Chapter 24). Serum levels of immunoglobulins other than the myeloma class are significantly lower than normal in almost all patients. Bence Jones protein is detected in the urine in about half of these patients. About 20% of patients have only Bence Jones proteinuria. These findings have important clinical and prognostic correlations.

Of all patients with myeloma, about 50% have IgG paraproteins and 25% have IgA paraproteins. IgD myeloma comprises 2% of cases of multiple myeloma but differs from the main group in several ways. A review of 133 cases in the literature disclosed that patients with IgD myeloma had a lower mean age (56 years) than patients with other forms of multiple myeloma; that over 50% had marked lymphadenopathy, hepatomegaly, or splenomegaly; and that extraosseous lesions, amyloidosis, severe anemia, and azotemia were more common. The serum levels of total protein and monoclonal protein are usually not very high, but Bence Jones proteinemia is common and Bence Jones proteinuria almost invariable. The L chain type is λ in 90% of cases of IgD myeloma compared to approximately 30% in IgG and IgA myelomas. The survival time in IgD myeloma is short—approximately 14 months after diagnosis.

In Bence Jones or L chain myeloma, the only detectable paraprotein occurs in the patient's urine as monoclonal κ or λ chains. This group comprises approximately 20% of myeloma patients. These patients are more likely to present with severe renal failure. The absence of an obvious serum paraprotein may present diagnostic difficulty in some cases, but Bence Jones proteinemia (monoclonal light chains in the serum) occurs in 80% and hypogammaglobulinemia and lytic bone lesions in over 60% of patients. Although patients with λ type Bence Jones myeloma have more protein in the urine, this does not always correlate directly with renal function or the overall survival rate. Amyloidosis is more frequent in Bence Jones myeloma and may dominate the clinical course. Bence Jones myeloma has a poorer overall prognosis than IgG or IgA myeloma. Defects in cellular immunity and granulocyte function are also found in multiple myeloma.

Nonsecretory myeloma refers to otherwise typical multiple myeloma with no paraprotein detectable in blood or urine. Plasma cell dyscrasias without paraproteinemia account for approximately 1% of myeloma patients. The plasma cell tumor is incapable of secreting the synthesized intracellular monoclonal protein. This protein can be detected either by immunofluorescence microscopy of bone marrow or immunochemical analysis of a lysate of the tumor cells.

Differential Diagnosis

This can be considered in 3 parts: (1) paraproteinemia, (2) lytic bone lesions, and (3) overall clinical assessment.

It is necessary to confirm by means of immunoelectrophoresis that the heavily stained band in the serum electrophoretogram is an immunoglobulin rather than fibrinogen, transferrin, or another protein.

Lytic bone lesions in an anemic patient may be metastases from a tumor of the breast, prostate, thyroid, kidney, or other primary site. The main distinguishing features are confirmation of a primary tumor or a history of its removal, the histopathologic features of the lytic lesion, abnormal plasma cells in bone marrow, and paraproteinemia. However, there are many reports of coexisting paraproteinemia and primary malignant nonlymphoid tumor.

Differentiation between clinically malignant and benign monoclonal gammopathies is discussed below with the latter group.

Treatment

A. General Measures: Supportive management is essential. Control pain with analgesics, provide adequate fluid intake, and give blood transfusions for symptomatic anemia. Ambulation should be maintained whenever possible to avoid further bone loss and hypercalcemia; adequate analgesics and mechanical support with corsets and braces often allow early ambulation, especially when the vertebral column is affected.

B. Antibiotics: Recurrent bacterial infections, especially with pneumococci and sometimes with gram-negative organisms, are a problem in some patients. Prompt evaluation of fevers and other symptoms of infection, with appropriate cultures and prompt coverage with appropriate antibiotics, is essential in these patients. Gamma globulin may also be useful in the treatment of established bacterial infection. Prophylactic administration of antibiotics, γ-globulin, or both is not warranted as a routine measure.

C. Irradiation: Local radiation therapy is very useful for relief of pain and reduction of tumor mass for isolated plasmacytoma or myeloma with localized painful bony lesions. Care must be taken to avoid large-scale radiation of active bone marrow sites since this may cause severe pancytopenia and limit chemotherapy.

D. Chemotherapy: Cytotoxic chemotherapy, together with improved general management, will achieve good therapeutic responses in about 70% of patients with multiple myeloma and will produce increased median survival with improved quality of life. Response is gauged by clinical and laboratory observations such as general status and pain relief, hemoglobin concentration, serum or urine paraprotein levels, and plasma cell counts in the bone marrow.

Melphalan with or without prednisone is the drug regimen of choice for the initial treatment of myeloma. The 2 most popular schedules for the use of melphalan are (1) intermittent high-dose melphalan-prednisone for 4 days every 4–6 weeks, and (2) a loading dose of melphalan for 7–10 days followed by a continuous low maintenance dose, usually given daily. The white cell and platelet count must be checked frequently to avoid toxicity. Prednisone should probably not be used when patients present with renal failure or serious infection. Poor-risk patients, ie, patients who present with renal failure, serious infection, hypercalcemia, leukocytopenia, thrombocytopenia, extensive lytic bone disease, and very large amounts of M protein, have a significantly shorter mean survival than patients who do not have these abnormalities.

Cyclophosphamide is also a widely used alkylating agent for the treatment of myeloma. It is probably as effective as melphalan but has additional adverse side-effects (alopecia, hemorrhagic cystitis, sterility). It is sometimes useful for patients who have become refractory to melphalan.

Multiple drug regimens are currently being assessed in patients who fail to respond to an alkylating agent initially or who respond and then relapse. The drugs used include melphalan, cyclophosphamide, carmustine (BCNU), procarbazine, vincristine, doxorubicin, thioguanine, and other agents in various combinations. None of these combinations have yet been proved to be the treatment of choice for refractory myeloma.

E. Surgery: Emergency laminectomy followed by local radiation therapy is indicated for acute spinal cord compression. Internal fixation of long-bone fractures and prosthetic hip replacement may allow early return to ambulation after pathologic fractures. Occasionally, surgical cure of a solitary plasmacytoma may be successful.

F. Complications:

1. Infections–Patients with suspected infections should have cultures taken and appropriate antibiotics should be given in full dosage. Gamma globulin may be useful in established severe bacterial infection.

2. Hypercalcemia–This may present as an emergency with vomiting, dehydration, azotemia, coma, and cardiac arrhythmias. Rapid rehydration is essential. Patients usually respond to rehydration, diuretics, and high doses of corticosteroids; refractory cases may require phosphate infusion or mithramycin.

3. Renal failure–Both acute and chronic renal failure are common. Etiologic factors include precipitation of the paraprotein in tubules (especially Bence Jones protein), amyloidosis, hypercalcemia, hyperuricemia, invasion of the kidney by malignant plasma cells, precipitation of cryoimmunoglobulins, hyperviscosity syndrome, pyelonephritis, and nephrotoxic antibiotics. Renal disease appears more frequently and often is more severe in patients with light chain myeloma (Bence Jones paraproteins). Prevention of dehydration is very important in those patients. Fluid restriction should be avoided, especially fluid restriction for intravenous urography. Rapid effective treatment of complications such as hypercalcemia and hyperuricemia will help to avoid irreversible renal damage. Successful chemotherapy of multiple myeloma will prevent most of the factors leading to renal failure. Hemodialysis may be lifesaving and allow time for chemotherapy in patients with acute renal failure due to Bence Jones paraproteinemia.

4. Spinal cord compression–Acute spinal cord compression is fortunately an uncommon initial presentation of myeloma but requires emergency laminectomy when it occurs. Treatment for cord compression of gradual onset includes localized radiotherapy, chemotherapy, and supportive physiotherapy, including a brace. Despite the frequent radiologic evidence of widespread involvement of the vertebral column and frequent vertebral compression fractures, cord compression is not a frequent complication. Continued ambulation with adequate analgesia must be maintained if at all possible.

5. Hyperviscosity syndrome–This occurs occasionally in multiple myeloma and is discussed below with Waldenström's macroglobulinemia.

6. Acute leukemia–Over 30 cases of acute leukemia have been reported developing 1–10 years after a diagnosis of malignant paraproteinemia has been made, especially multiple myeloma. Almost invariably the leukemia is of the acute monocytic or myelomonocytic type. This is a serious complication; there are no reports of survivals beyond 6 months after diagnosis. It is not yet known if the leukemia is part of the natural history of multiple myeloma which only becomes obvious with prolonged survival or if it is due to chromosomal or other abnormalities induced by cytotoxic therapy. Dyserythropoietic anemia and chromosomal abnormalities may be detected prior to overt leukemia.

Prognosis

Seventy percent of patients with multiple myeloma respond to therapy and have a mean overall survival rate of more than 30 months. Patients presenting with serious infection, thrombocytopenia, leukocytopenia, or azotemia have a poorer prognosis. A large amount of paraprotein and a low serum albumin indicate a large plasma cell tumor mass and are associated with a poorer prognosis. Patients with IgG-type myeloma proteins tend to do better than those with IgA-type or Bence Jones proteins. The rate of response to chemotherapy also appears to be useful in predicting prognosis. Patients who do not respond to chemotherapy at all and those that respond very rapidly to initial chemotherapy have a poorer prognosis. The "fast responders" quickly relapse and often are resistant to further chemotherapy. The prognosis appears to be best for the "slow responders," ie, patients who show a slow but gradual and steady response to chemotherapy.

Radiologically proved bone healing occurs in approximately 30% of patients who respond to treatment, generally after a fall in serum paraprotein concentration. Serial observations of lytic lesions in the skull, ribs, and pelvis provide an index of disease activity in long-term management. However, bone healing is not a prognostic sign, since patients who respond to therapy and show bone healing do not have longer remissions or longer overall survival times than those who respond without bone healing.

2. WALDENSTRÖM'S MACROGLOBULINEMIA

The main clinical and laboratory features of Waldenström's macroglobulinemia are listed in Table 28–2 and compared to those of multiple myeloma. Most of the clinical manifestations of this disease can be directly attributed to the excess monoclonal IgM in the blood. Patients frequently present with hyperviscosity syndrome (Table 28–3). A relative serum viscosity of > 3.0 may be associated with symptoms, although severe symptoms do not usually occur until the viscosity is $> 7.0–10.0$ (see Chapter 24). Severe hyperviscosity is a medical emergency and requires

Table 28–2. Comparison of main clinical and laboratory features of Waldenström's macroglobulinemia and multiple myeloma.

	Macroglobulinemia	Multiple Myeloma
Recurrent bacterial infections		+++
Bone pain		+++
Lytic bone lesions		+++
Bleeding from mucosal areas	+++	+
Hepatosplenomegaly	+++	+
Lymphadenopathy	+++	+
Neuropathy		+
Changes in visual state	+++	+
Abnormalities in optic fundus	+++	
Anemia	++	+++
Leukocytopenia		+
Thrombocytopenia		+
Hypercalcemia		++
Serum hyperviscosity	+++	+
Renal insufficiency		++

Table 28–3. Symptoms and signs of hyperviscosity syndrome.

System	Findings
General	Weakness, fatigue, malaise, anorexia.
Cardiovascular	Congestive heart failure, hypervolemia.
Neurologic	Headache, dizziness, vertigo, nystagmus, deafness, somnolence, stupor, coma, generalized seizures, electroencephalographic abnormalities.
Hematologic	Recurrent epistaxis, bleeding from oral mucosa, hematuria, hematemesis, melena, prolonged postoperative bleeding, anemia.
Ocular	Loss of visual acuity (may be total), retinal hemorrhages, distention and tortuosity of retinal veins, papilledema.

prompt treatment. There is marked variation in the level of viscosity that causes symptoms in patients, but each patient tends to develop the same symptoms at the same viscosity level. Several factors contribute to hyperviscosity, including the serum concentration of monoclonal IgM, polymer or aggregate formation, abnormal shape of the IgM with aggregate formation, cryoprecipitation, antibody activity against serum proteins, and red cell and vascular abnormalities.

Monoclonal IgM mainly exists in the pentamer 19S form or aggregates thereof, but many patients also have monomeric 7S IgM. A biosynthetic abnormality exists in which the malignant clone is not always able to assemble all of the synthesized IgM in the pentamer form. Bence Jones proteinuria is found in approximately 10% of patients.

Plasmapheresis is the treatment of choice for most patients with Waldenström's macroglobulinemia to remove the excess IgM and restore the plasma volume to normal. It is performed either with sterile plastic bags in a closed system which permits readministration of the patient's red cells after centrifugation or with an automatic continuous flow cell separator. The latter can remove a much greater amount of paraprotein in one treatment period, but patients treated in this way usually have to be given normal plasma to prevent hypovolemia. Standard plasmapheresis using plastic bags is less efficient but still very effective. Patients with severe hyperviscosity need as many as 4–6 units per day of plasmapheresis for several days. Subsequently, plasmapheresis is given on a maintenance basis to keep the patient free of hyperviscosity symptoms with a serum viscosity preferably under 3.0. Plasmapheresis of 2 units every 2–4 weeks is often sufficient for maintenance. Chemotherapy is necessary if plasmapheresis is required more frequently than every 2 weeks. Chlorambucil is usually given in low doses on a daily basis, with frequent monitoring of blood counts to prevent bone marrow depression.

3. SOLITARY PLASMACYTOMA

Solitary plasmacytoma consists of a single bone lesion—or, rarely, extramedullary lesion—composed of abnormal malignant plasma cells. Occasionally there is a small amount of circulating monoclonal protein, but as a rule the clinical features of multiple myeloma are not present. Solitary plasmacytoma may be discovered on routine x-ray or may be diagnosed in a patient who complains of local pain or pressure on adjacent structures, eg, the spinal cord. The diagnosis must be confirmed by biopsy. Treatment consists of local radiotherapy. Some of these patients develop local recurrence after treatment; about half ultimately develop generalized multiple myeloma. Close follow-up and frequent evaluation of serum and urine protein are essential in any patient in whom a solitary plasmacytoma is found.

4. AMYLOIDOSIS

Amyloidosis has proved an enigma to clinicians and pathologists ever since the 19th century, when Rokitansky and Virchow argued about its nature and origin. Its relationship to chronic infection and prolonged antigenic stimulation are well known but still unexplained to this day.

Clinically suspected amyloid deposition must be confirmed by biopsy of appropriate tissues. Light microscopy of H&E-stained sections shows amyloid as an eosinophilic material. Typical birefringence occurs when stained sections are examined under polarized light. Electron microscopy shows characteristic nonbranching fibrils 8.5 nm wide and of varying lengths.

Solubilization of amyloid fibrils and amino acid sequence analysis show that in many cases a major component of amyloid is a fragment of an immunoglobulin L chain, especially the V region. This explains the negative results of earlier tests with antisera to detect immunoglobulins in amyloid tissue, since such antisera are made against C region and not V region determinants. Antiserum prepared against V region determinants of a Bence Jones protein from a patient with Bence Jones proteinuria and amyloidosis reacted with a component in that patient's amyloid tissue. Identical amino acid sequences in a patient's Bence Jones protein V region and a peptide component of his amyloid tissue have also been described.

Possible mechanisms which might account for the deposition of immunoglobulin components in amyloid tissue are as follows: (1) Catabolism by macrophages of deposited antigen-antibody complexes. (2) De novo synthesis in situ of whole immunoglobulins or of L chains with reduced solubility. (3) Genetic deletions in the L chain gene, producing an anomalous protein of reduced solubility. (4) Separate synthesis of discrete regions of the L chain.

The major nonimmunoglobulin component of amyloid is known as nonimmunoglobulin protein of unknown origin, amyloid of unknown origin, or protein "A." It has a molecular weight of approximately 8000 (76 amino acids), and it may be derived by proteolytic digestion of an unidentified protein precursor. Approximately 10% of amyloid tissue consists of doughnut-like structures 8–10 nm in diameter composed of 5 globular subunits surrounding a central cavity. (The "P" or plasma component may aggregate into "periodic rods" with a periodicity of 4 nm. It is a glycoprotein, unrelated to fibril protein but related antigenically to an α_1-globulin present in small amounts in normal human plasma.)

The classification of amyloidosis as primary or secondary is of little benefit etiologically or clinically. Amyloid fibrils of L chain origin can occur in both primary and secondary forms, as can the nonimmunoglobulin protein of unknown origin. A more useful classification of amyloidosis is based mainly on the pattern of distribution in the body (Table 28–4). Pattern I represents most cases of primary amyloidosis. It is the pattern most commonly associated with plasma cell dyscrasias (especially multiple myeloma), and all cases have a paraprotein, usually a Bence Jones protein.

The clinical features reflect the particular site and extent of amyloid deposition, especially in the gastrointestinal tract, nervous system, and kidneys. Renal involvement is often a poor prognostic sign. Treatment is mainly symptomatic since no chemotherapy has been shown to consistently benefit patients with established amyloidosis. Patients with pattern I amyloidosis and plasma cell dyscrasia occasionally respond to melphalan or other drugs. Current trials with colchicine are directed toward blocking the deposition of new amyloid.

Table 28–4. Classification of amyloidosis.

Pattern	Sites of Deposition	Clinical Correlations	Percentage With Paraproteins
I	Heart, tongue, skin, nerves, smooth muscles, carpal ligaments, gastrointestinal tract	Plasma cell dyscrasia (especially multiple myeloma)	100%
II	Liver, spleen, kidneys, adrenals	Chronic infections, rheumatoid arthritis, familial Mediterranean fever, Hodgkin's disease	53%
Mixed (I, II)	Combinations of patterns I and II	Plasma cell dyscrasia, chronic inflammatory disorders	87%
Localized	Single organ or tissue	Lichen amyloidosis, solitary plasmacytoma	100%

5. H CHAIN DISEASES

These diseases are characterized by a serum paraprotein composed of incomplete H chains without L chains. The 3 types are γ (over 30 known cases), μ (10 known cases), and α (approximately 50 cases). The paraprotein is generally in relatively low concentration in blood and shows broad zone electrophoretic pattern, but it is frequently excreted in urine in measurable amounts. Immunoelectrophoresis confirms the diagnosis, with demonstration of a paraprotein that reacts with antiserum to γ, μ, or α chains but not with κ or λ chains. No cases of δ or ϵ disease have been reported.

Much information on the genetic aspects of immunoglobulin biosynthesis has come from analysis of the paraproteins in H chain diseases. The abnormalities include partial deletion in the Fd portion of the H chain (with a normal amino acid sequence from residue 216), deletion in the hinge region (see Chapter 2), or a combination of the 2 findings.

Clinical Features

A. Gamma Chain Disease: The clinical features in γ chain disease vary markedly—from a malignant process with death within weeks of presentation to a course extending over 20 years. The most common presentation is a lymphoproliferative disorder with hepatosplenomegaly, lymphadenopathy, and uvular and palatal edema. Recurrent febrile episodes are not uncommon. Infection is the most common cause of death. The peripheral blood generally shows anemia, leukocytopenia, and atypical lymphocytes or plasma cells.

B. Alpha Chain Disease: The clinical features in α chain disease are those of a severe malabsorption syndrome with chronic diarrhea, steatorrhea, weight loss, hypocalcemia, and lymphadenopathy. Biopsy of bowel shows infiltration of the small bowel with plasma cells, lymphocytes, and reticulum cells. With disease progression, the plasma cells become more immature and extend beyond the lamina propria. Abdominal lymphoma and α chain disease are closely associated in the area of the Mediterranean Sea. Two reported cases of α chain disease involved the respiratory tract instead of the gastrointestinal tract.

C. Mu Chain Disease: The clinical features in 3 cases of μ chain disease were those of long-standing chronic lymphocytic leukemia with progressive hepatosplenomegaly.

6. BENIGN MONOCLONAL GAMMOPATHY

Benign monoclonal gammopathy is defined as the presence of a monoclonal serum or urine protein without any of the other manifestations of malignant paraproteinemia. Monoclonal protein spikes have been found in approximately 5% of all persons over 50 years of age and 8% of those over 70 years. Some of these people will ultimately develop multiple myeloma, but most will not.

Clinically, the problem is deciding whether a patient found to have a small monoclonal immunoglobulin spike has early multiple myeloma or benign monoclonal gammopathy. The following laboratory features tend to support a diagnosis of malignant paraproteinemia: serum paraprotein level > 2 g/dl, reduced serum levels of nonmonoclonal immunoglobulins, presence of immunoglobulin fragments in serum, increased serum or urine light chains, presence of radiographic bone lesions, presence of increased and abnormal plasma cells in the bone marrow, and, most importantly, increasing serum or urine paraprotein levels with time. Thus, the patient with a high and increasing serum paraprotein level, low serum levels of normal immunoglobulins, and significant amounts of Bence Jones protein in his serum and urine is likely to develop the full clinical picture of multiple myeloma within a relatively short period of time. Decreased total numbers of circulating B lymphocytes are present in malignant but not benign monoclonal gammopathies.

It is essential to review all patients with monoclonal gammopathies until the benign or malignant nature of the disease is established.

7. PLASMA CELL LEUKEMIA

Plasma cell leukemia is a variant of multiple myeloma where abnormal plasma cells are found not only in the bone marrow but also in the peripheral blood. Plasma cell leukemia may be acute or chronic. Acute plasma cell leukemia presents as acute leukemia, and a mistaken diagnosis of acute lymphocytic or acute myelogenous leukemia may be made. The true nature of the leukemic cell is recognized when a paraprotein is detected in blood or urine, lytic bone lesions develop, severe hypercalcemia is noted, or renal failure supervenes. The correct diagnosis can also be confirmed by electron microscopic or immunofluorescence technics. Plasma cell leukemia also occurs in patients with known multiple myeloma; such patients have a much higher incidence of hepatosplenomegaly, more severe anemia and thrombocytopenia, more renal failure, and a poorer prognosis than myeloma patients without plasma cell leukemia.

Occasionally, plasma cell leukemia occurs as a terminal event in multiple myeloma, with a rapidly rising plasma cell count and death from infection and renal failure.

The associated paraproteins are most commonly IgG type, but IgA, IgM, and κ and λ paraproteins have been described with plasma cell leukemia.

Therapy of plasma cell leukemia should be directed at the underlying multiple myeloma, although cell cycle-specific drugs, similar to those used in other acute leukemias, may be more useful than alkylating agents. The overall prognosis of plasma cell leukemia is poor, with a mean survival of 9 months in patients without myeloma and 5 months in those with previously diagnosed myeloma.

8. CRYOGLOBULINEMIA

A number of serum and plasma proteins precipitate at low temperature, including cryofibrinogen, C-reactive protein-albumin complex, heparin-precipitable protein, and immunoglobulins. The first step in evaluating a suspected cryoimmunoglobulin, therefore, is to rule out nonimmunoglobulin cryoproteins. The following points should be kept in mind when looking for a cryoglobulin: (1) Some monoclonal cryoglobulins may precipitate at temperatures as high as 33 C. Adequate precautions such as prewarming of syringes, containers, etc and centrifugation at 37 C should therefore be taken to avoid loss of the cryoprotein from the supernate on centrifugation. (2) Some cryoglobulins rapidly precipitate in the cold, while others may take days. The serum should therefore be observed at 4 C for at least 72 hours. (3) Most normal people have a small amount of polyclonal serum cryoglobulin—up to 80 μg/ml.

Cryoglobulinemias can be classified into the following 3 immunologic and clinical types:

Type I (25%) cryoglobulins are monoclonal proteins, most commonly IgM, occasionally IgG, and rarely IgA or Bence Jones protein.

Type II (25%) are mixed cryoglobulins with a monoclonal component. The monoclonal protein is usually IgM but is occasionally IgG or IgA, and it complexes with autologous normal IgG in the cryoprecipitate.

Type III (50%) are mixed polyclonal cryoglobulins, with a mixture of polyclonal IgM and IgG being by far the most frequent combination.

The clinical features in patients with cryoglobulins depend largely on the type of cryoglobulin involved. Patients with monoclonal cryoglobulins (type I) suffer primarily from the symptoms of their underlying disease process, eg, multiple myeloma or Waldenström's macroglobulinemia. Patients with "mixed cryoglobulins" (types II and III) often have "immune complex disease," with vascular purpura, arthritis, and nephritis. These immune complexes often fix complement in vivo and in vitro.

Type II and III cryoglobulinemias generally have a worse prognosis than type I. They are frequently associated with autoimmune disorders. Many of the patients with type II and III cryoglobulinemia remain in the idiopathic or essential category with no detectable underlying cause.

Treatment of cryoglobulinemias is generally directed toward treatment of the underlying disorder if it is recognized. General measures such as avoidance of cold objects or weather are often helpful. Management of the idiopathic mixed cryoglobulinemias may be difficult. Cytotoxic drugs, with or without prednisone, are generally used. Excellent remissions with reduction of serum cryoglobulin levels and control of nephritis, arthritis, and purpura can cometimes be achieved. Plasmapheresis is generally not very useful for the chronic control of patients with cryoglobulins.

BICLONAL GAMMOPATHY

More patients are being recognized whose serum contains 2 distinct paraproteins. This does not include the combination of a paraprotein and its corresponding Bence Jones protein. The most common combinations are 2 different monoclonal IgM proteins or monoclonal IgM and IgG proteins. Rarely, one may find 3 monoclonal serum proteins in one patient. Some of these patients are of great interest because their paraproteins show sharing of identical parts of their primary structure, supporting the *genetic switch hypothesis* (see Chapter 2).

The clinical features are most frequently those of macroglobulinemia or lymphoma, and IgM is generally the monoclonal protein in highest concentration.

MALIGNANT LYMPHOMAS

Lymphomas are tumors derived from reticular stem cells, their histiocytic or lymphocytic derivatives, or combinations of these cell types. They represent solid tumors of the immune system, and immunologic abnormalities are common in lymphoma patients. Despite the close relationship between the immune system and lymphomas, they have been studied traditionally by conventional clinical and histologic methods. Immunologic principles and technics have recently been applied to the study of lymphomas, and this has improved our understanding of them.

Etiology

There are several examples of viruses causing lymphomas in animals, including nonhuman primates. A viral etiology has been proposed for human lymphomas, but causative viruses have not been isolated nor infectivity confirmed. The best-studied example is Epstein-Barr virus (EBV) in Burkitt's lymphoma (discussed below with infectious mononucleosis). It may be that viruses exist in lymphomas not as infectious virions but only as part of the viral genome incorporated into the DNA of host cells.

A current hypothesis is that a lymphoma represents the result of imbalance between homeostatic control mechanisms and immune responses. Specifically, it is suggested that a suppressor lymphocyte population is absent or ineffective and the immune response to a virus or other agent is abnormal, permitting development of malignant lymphoid transformation.

Classification & Immunologic Features

A. Hodgkin's Disease: The clinical manifestations, natural history, histologic findings, and cell type in Hodgkin's lymphoma are distinct from those of other forms of lymphoma. Several conflicting histologic classifications have been proposed, based on the presence of diagnostic Reed-Sternberg cells, lymphocytes, plasma cells, histiocytes, and fibrous tissue. The currently accepted classification (Rye Conference, 1971) is as follows:

(1) Lymphocyte predominance type: (The best prognosis.) Numerous lymphocytes, plasma cells, and histiocytes; infrequent Reed-Sternberg cells; a higher incidence in young males.

(2) Nodular sclerosis type: Fibrous septa dividing the lymphoid tissue into nodules, with large numbers of Reed-Sternberg cell variants called lacunar cells. This is the most frequent type (approximately 75%). It has a higher incidence in young females and a better prognosis than types (3) and (4).

(3) Mixed cellularity types: Numerous atypical histocytes and Reed-Sternberg cells, necrosis and infiltration with eosinophils, and reduced numbers of lymphocytes. This type is found in older patients.

(4) Lymphocyte depletion type: (The worst prognosis.) Numerous Reed-Sternberg cells, extensive diffuse fibrosis, and marked reduction in lymphocytes. It occurs in older people. Abdominal and bone marrow involvement often occurs early.

This classification has both diagnostic and prognostic implications, with lymphocyte predominance and nodular sclerosis probably representing a strong host immune response to the lymphoma, and lymphocyte depletion representing failure of the immune response.

Defects in cell-mediated immunity occur in Hodgkin's disease, even in early stage I or stage II patients. The tests used include delayed hypersensitivity skin testing and in vitro lymphocyte transformation in response to mitogens, antigens, and allogeneic cells. The patients must be tested before chemotherapy or radiotherapy, which are themselves immunosuppressive. Analysis of dose-response curves for PHA stimulation in 27 patients revealed that 16 had significantly depressed responses. The depression may be more severe and occur at all PHA concentrations (5–800 μg/ml), or it may be less severe and occur only at low PHA concentrations, Anergy was found in 13 of these 27 patients.

MLC tests performed with lymphocytes from patients with Hodgkin's disease showed that 53% produced abnormally low levels of stimulation of normal leukocytes. This was due to suppressive action of some patients' lymphocytes, and the defect disappeared when the patient achieved remission. The defect in advanced Hodgkin's disease includes a disproportionate excess of suppressor lymphocytes despite overall lymphocyte depletion with frequent lymphocytopenia.

Tissue cultures from lymph nodes or spleen of Hodgkin's disease have been used to isolate an antigen and prepare antisera in rabbits. The antigen is specifically associated with Hodgkin's disease but requires an initial period of in vitro culture. However, the antiserum does not react with tumor tissue from patients with Hodgkin's disease. Measurement of in vitro IgG synthesis by splenic tissue showed increased total IgG synthesis in 91% of cases of Hodgkin's disease. The IgG synthesized showed significant binding to lymphocytes from patients with Hodgkin's disease. This suggests that in Hodgkin's disease the spleen is responding with humoral antibody to an antigen associated with lymphocytes. It is not yet known if this is identical to the antigen detected in cultures and if it is a viral component, a tumor-associated or oncofetal antigen (see Chapter 21), or a normal tissue component.

B. Non-Hodgkin's Lymphomas: This heterogeneous group of disorders with widely varying clinical and histologic features has been classified as follows: (1) undifferentiated type A (Burkitt's), (2) undifferentiated type B (pleomorphic), (3) histiocytic type, (4) mixed type (histiocytic/lymphocytic), (5) lymphocytic type, poorly differentiated, and (6) lymphocytic type, well-differentiated. In addition, lymphomas may be nodular or diffuse depending on the growth pattern seen with low-power microscopic magnification. The foregoing classification does not include the term reticulum cell sarcoma because of disagreement over its proper use.

This and earlier classifications provide no information on the immunologic nature of the cells involved. The recent availability of methods to identify circulating and tissue T and B cells led Lukes and Collins to attempt classification of lymphomas in this way (Table 28–5). It introduces the concept of the main type of cell in the lymphoma but still is based on clinical and especially histologic findings. It relies on interpretation of stages of differentiation of the B cells in the center of lymph node follicles, but space will not permit discussion of these aspects. Some comments are necessary on the classification:

1. Undefined cell type–This type consists of lymphoma due to lymphoid stem cells lacking T and B cell markers. It is not yet known if cells of this type correspond to stem cells or null cells.

2. T cell types–The cutaneous T cell lymphomas comprise a group of disorders in which the skin is infiltrated by cells identifiable in vitro as T cells. Mycosis fungoides represents the most advanced form and Sézary syndrome a less severe form.

a. Mycosis fungoides–This primary cutaneous lymphoma may spread to regional lymph nodes and may terminate in visceral involvement with lymphoma. The skin lesions progress classically through the 3 stages of eczema, plaque, and tumor and may include a mixture of eczema, exfoliative erythroderma, macules, nodules, tumors, and psoriatic dermatitis. Patients may present with any of the features, but the prognosis is worse with multiple lesions. If any one of the 3 findings of cutaneous tumors, cutaneous ulcers, or lymphadenopathy is present, 50% die within 2½ years; if all 3 are present, 50% die within 1 year. A small number of Sézary-like cells (see below) have been found in the blood of patients with mycosis fungoides. Skin biopsies in mycosis fungoides are indistinguishable from those in Sézary syndrome and classically contain diagnostic intraepidermal Pautrier microabscesses consisting of aggregates of lymphoma cells.

b. Sézary syndrome–This is primary cutaneous lymphoma associated with chronic leukemia and generalized erythroderma. The skin lesions are often exfoliative (Fig 28–5) and may develop plaques. The key symptom is extreme itching. The diagnostic feature is the Sézary cell in peripheral blood. It is a large mononuclear cell, but several varieties are now recognized. They have been identified as abnormal T cells. Skin biopsy shows a progression of changes from bandlike dermal infiltration with mature lymphocytes (Fig 28–6) to deeper infiltration with more immature cells. Similar infiltrates may be found in internal organs with systemic involvement, and lymphadenopathy is detected in approximately 60% of patients. Despite these findings in skin, blood, and occasionally elsewhere, these patients generally feel well at diagnosis. They do not have fever, malaise, weakness, weight loss, or any of the other common features of malignant lymphoma. However, the patient may subsequently develop generalized lymphoma. Some patients present initially with erythroderma as a manifestation of drug hypersensitivity.

Patients are now recognized with generalized erythroderma and exfoliation and increased numbers of lymphocytes in the dermis but normal peripheral blood differential counts. Long-term studies will determine if these patients represent the first clinical stage in the spectrum of T cell lymphomas which progress through Sézary syndrome and mycosis fungoides.

Table 28–5. Suggested classification of lymphomas by the immunologic nature of the main cell type.

(1) Undefined cell type
(2) T cell types:
    Cutaneous lymphomas: mycosis fungoides, Sézary syndrome
    Convoluted lymphocyte
(3) B cell types:
    Small lymphocyte (chronic lymphocytic leukemia, well-differentiated lymphocytic lymphoma)
    Plasmacytoid lymphocyte (Waldenström's macroglobulinemia)
    Follicular center cell (poorly differentiated lymphocytic lymphoma, nodular and diffuse)
        Small cleaved
        Large cleaved
        Small noncleaved
        Large noncleaved
    Angioimmunoblastic lymphadenopathy
    Immunoblastic sarcoma
(4) Histiocytic cell type
(5) Unclassifiable cell type

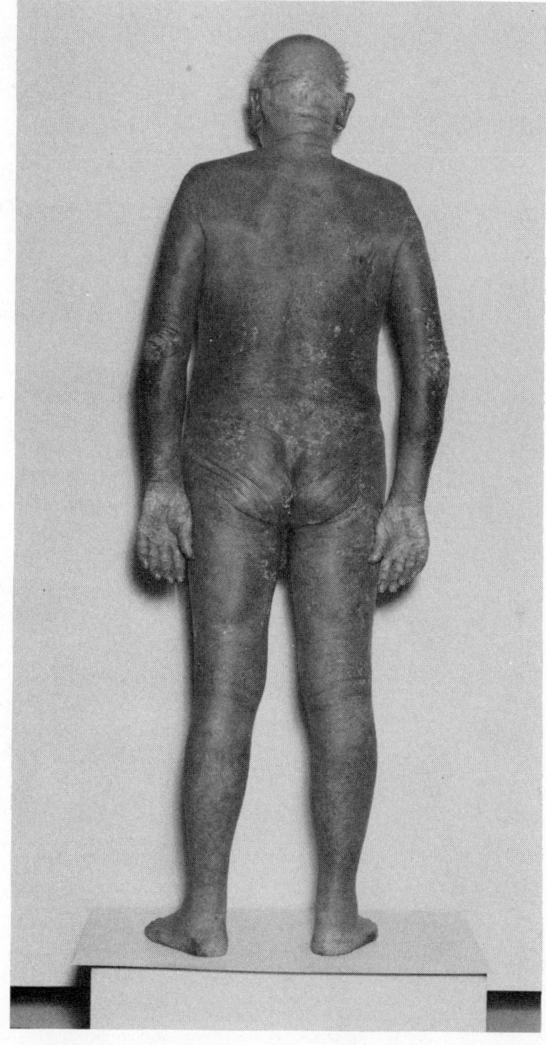

Figure 28–5. Exfoliative dermatitis and Sézary syndrome following chronic dermatitis of the legs. Note the alopecia, exfoliation, and palmar keratoderma. (Reproduced, with permission, from Winkelmann RK: Clinical studies of T cell erythroderma in the Sézary syndrome. Mayo Clin Proc 49:519, 1974.)

3. B cell types–The subtypes are at present classified according to the microscopic features of the cells, especially the nuclei. These are thought to represent different stages of differentiation of B cells between stem cells and plasma cells, but there are no other markers available to confirm this interpretation. Some malignant diseases of certain stages of B cell differentiation have already been discussed, ie, chronic lymphocytic leukemia and the monoclonal gammopathies, especially multiple myeloma and Waldenström's macroglobulinemia.

a. Burkitt's lymphoma–This B cell lymphoma not infrequently presents with facial or jaw tumors, occurs in tropical areas of malarial endemicity, has a constant association with EBV, and is extremely sensitive to

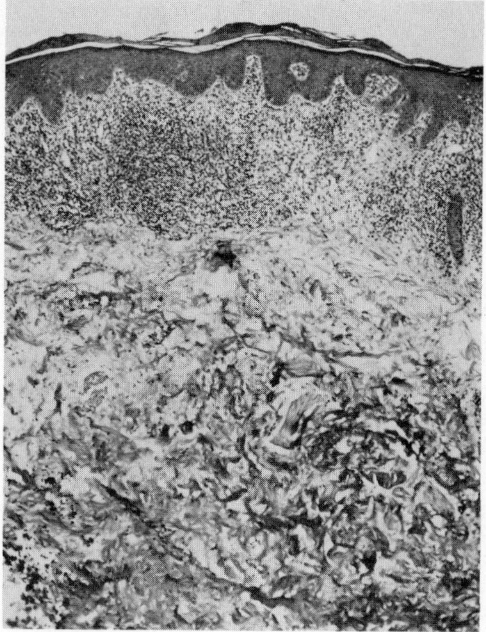

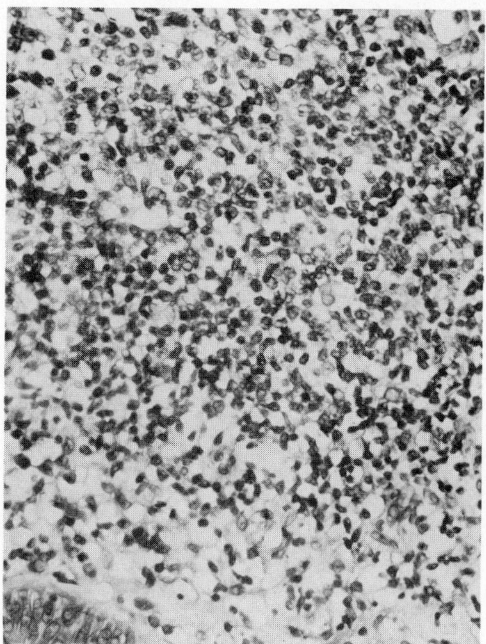

Figure 28–6. Dermal lymphocytic reticulosis is the most frequent finding in skin biopsies from Sézary syndrome. (***Top:*** H&E stain, original magnification × 64. ***Bottom:*** H&E stain, original magnification × 400.) It shows the bandlike infiltration of monomorphous mature lymphocytes in papillary and reticular layers of the dermis, with hyperkeratosis, parakeratosis, and irregular acanthosis. (Reproduced, with permission, from Holdaway DR, Winkelmann RK: Histopathology of Sézary syndrome. Mayo Clin Proc 49:541, 1974.)

radiotherapy or methotrexate. It is a lymphoma of small noncleaved type, with cells of uniform size and small inconspicuous nucleoli. A variant of Burkitt's lymphoma has been described in America with similar histologic findings but with a high incidence of abdominal and bone marrow involvement and a very poor prognosis.

b. Angioimmunoblastic lymphadenopathy–This recently recognized disorder presents clinically with fever, sweats, weight loss, and often rash, lymphadenopathy, and hepatosplenomegaly. There is consistent polyclonal hypergammaglobulinemia and a high incidence of autoimmune hemolytic anemia. The histologic diagnosis is based on the triad of proliferation of arborizing small blood vessels, proliferation of immunoblasts, and amorphous acidophilic interstitial material (Fig 28–7). It is thought to represent an abnormal hyperimmune response of B cells rather than a true lymphoma, but it usually has a progressive course with a median survival of 15 months. Moreover, it may terminate as immunoblastic sarcoma.

c. Immunoblastic sarcoma–This disease may arise de novo or secondary to a previously diagnosed immunologic disorder, eg, angioimmunoblastic lymphadenopathy, Sjögren's syndrome, α chain disease, congenital immunodeficiency, or chronic allograft rejection. The main cell is now termed an *immunoblast* (Fig 28–8). It is similar to the large noncleaved follicular center cell or transformed lymphocyte. Lymphomas with this appearance are generally clinically aggressive.

Immunologic Pathogenesis

Some specific examples of abnormalities in immune function were given above with individual diseases.

A. Serum Immunoglobulins: The presence of monoclonal proteins is of course one of the diagnostic requirements in multiple myeloma and Waldenström's macroglobulinemia. However, serum monoclonal proteins are also found in chronic lymphocytic leukemia and in various forms of lymphoma. Monoclonal IgM peaks were found in 5% of lymphomas with a diffuse infiltration of lymph nodes. In some cases the monoclonal protein is a cryoglobulin.

Polyclonal hypergammaglobulinemia is a feature of angioimmunoblastic lymphadenopathy but may occur occasionally in other subjects as a response to infection.

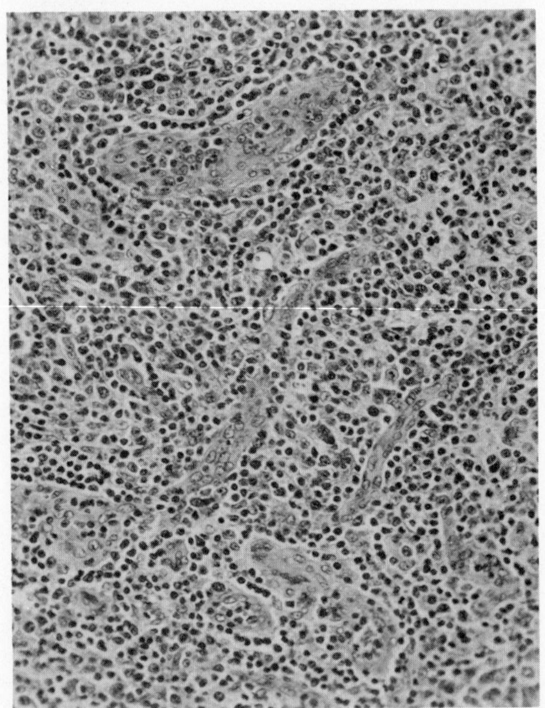

Figure 28–7. Histologic findings in lymph node biopsy of angioimmunoblastic lymphadenopathy. (Giemsa stain, original magnification × 250.) Note the arborizing thick-walled small blood vessels, the amorphous interstitial material, and the mixed cell population, including immunoblasts, plasmacytoid cells, mature plasma cells, and lymphocytes with different intermediate forms. (Reproduced, with permission, from Lukes RJ, Tindle BH: Immunoblastic lymphadenopathy. N Engl J Med 292:1, 1975.)

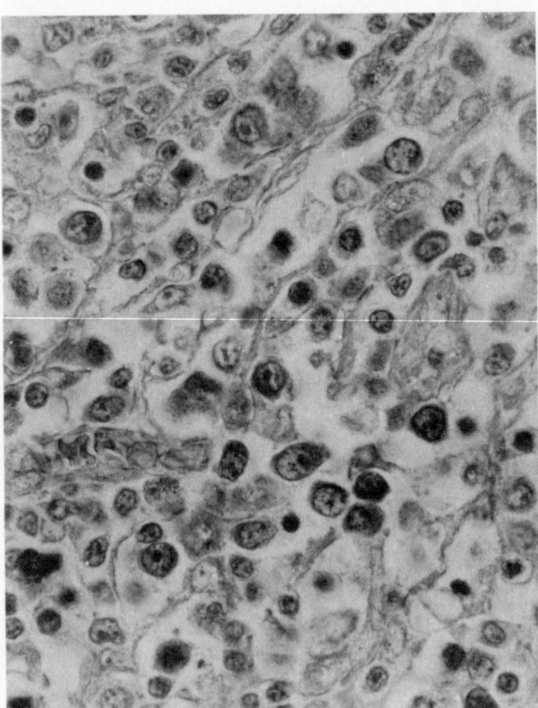

Figure 28–8. Histologic findings in lymph node biopsy of angioimmunoblastic lymphadenopathy which transformed to immunoblastic sarcoma. (Giemsa stain, original magnification × 1000.) Note the cells and numerous immunoblasts. The latter are 15–25 μm in diameter and have large oval nuclei with freely dispersed, pale, basophilic fine chromatin, with one large or 2–3 smaller nucleoli close to the nuclear membrane. (Reproduced, with permission, from Lukes RJ, Tindle BH: Immunoblastic lymphadenopathy. N Engl J Med 292:1, 1975.)

Hypogammaglobulinemia implies a poor prognosis in chronic lymphocytic leukemia or lymphoma, generally indicating advanced disease. It not infrequently leads to death from infection.

B. Cellular Immunity: Anergy is a common finding in Hodgkin's disease, but it can occur with any type of lymphoma at an advanced stage. It is more frequent in later than earlier stages but does not always correlate positively with the stage of disease. Other tests such as lymphocyte activation also commonly indicate defects in cellular immunity. This is expressed clinically as infection with fungi, viruses, or uncommon organisms such as *Pneumocystis carinii.*

C. Autoimmunity: Lymphoma is recognized as a late complication in patients with autoimmune manifestations, eg, systemic lupus erythematosus or Sjögren's syndrome. Moreover, some patients with lymphoma may subsequently develop autoimmune abnormalities, eg, autoimmune hemolytic anemia in chronic lymphocytic leukemia or angioimmunoblastic lymphadenopathy, immune thrombocytopenic purpura, or other rheumatoid diseases such as dermatomyositis.

Treatment

The patient with Hodgkin's disease or non-Hodgkin's lymphoma must be fully evaluated before treatment can be logically planned. This evaluation, called staging, is used to determine the extent of involvement by lymphoma. Since radiation therapy is often curative when disease is limited to lymph nodes, it is particularly important to evaluate nonnodal tissues such as bone marrow, liver, spleen, etc for possible involvement. This often requires a "staging laparotomy" with resection of multiple lymph nodes from various intra-abdominal and retroperitoneal areas, splenectomy, open liver biopsy, and open bone marrow biopsy. If after such a full evaluation no tumor can be found outside of lymph nodes (stages I, II, and III), the patient most often is treated with "extended field" or "total nodal" radiation to 4000–4500 R with curative intent. If tumor is found in bone marrow, liver, lung, etc (stage IV), the patient is not a candidate for radiation therapy and should be treated with chemotherapy. Patients with unfavorable histologic types are often treated with chemotherapy in addition to radiation therapy even when their disease appears to be confined to lymph nodes, since they often have undetected microscopic extranodal disease.

Extended field or total nodal radiation therapy is curative for 90% of patients with stage I and II Hodgkin's disease with favorable histologic types. Stage III patients also may be cured, but these patients often must receive "prophylactic" chemotherapy as well. Patients with non-Hodgkin's lymphomas more frequently have involvement of extranodal tissues and therefore are less likely to be candidates for radiation. However, selected patients have been cured with local or extended field radiation therapy.

Advanced Hodgkin's disease responds very well to multiple drug combination chemotherapy. The best-known regimen is "MOPP" therapy, which includes mechlorethamine, vincristine (Oncovin), procarbazine, and prednisone, given in monthly cycles. Complete remission rates of over 80% can be achieved with current multiple drug therapy in Hodgkin's disease. Well-differentiated and nodular lymphocytic lymphomas also respond very well to chemotherapy; diffuse histiocytic and poorly differentiated lymphocytic lymphomas are much more refractory to chemotherapy.

The future typing of lymphomas as T or B cell lymphomas may have therapeutic applications, with the possible development of cytotoxic agents or antisera specific for these different types of cells.

INFECTIOUS MONONUCLEOSIS

Major Immunologic Features

- Lymphadenopathy and splenomegaly.
- Proliferation of atypical lymphocytes.
- Absolute T cell and B cell lymphocytosis.
- Sheep cell agglutinin > 1:100.
- Antibodies to EBV antigens.
- Antibodies to other viruses and autoantigens.

General Considerations

Infectious mononucleosis is a common acute, usually self-limited disease caused by a virus identical or closely similar to EBV. It may occur at any age, though the highest incidence is in teenagers and young adults. It is usually spread by respiratory droplet infection in epidemic or sporadic epidemiologic distribution.

Immunologic Pathogenesis

Infectious mononucleosis has been considered to be a lymphoproliferative disease distinguished from lymphoma only by its tendency to spontaneous regression. Several observations testify to the intense lymphoproliferation. The peripheral blood contains atypical cells with a high rate of turnover and DNA synthesis. Histologic examination shows marked lymphoproliferation in almost all lymphoid tissues. Lymph nodes show marked hyperplasia, especially in the T-dependent paracortical areas. Distortion of normal architecture by lymphoproliferation and the presence of occasional Reed-Sternberg cells rarely leads to an incorrect diagnosis of lymphoma. Lymphocytes taken during the acute phase proliferate in continuous in vitro cultures and will produce lymphomalike lesions if injected into immunosuppressed animals. These lesions can also be produced by fresh noncultured lymphocytes, and human immunoglobulins may be synthesized.

The lymphoproliferation in infectious mononucleosis is secondary to the entry of EBV into B cells. This induces a small and short-lived increase in B cells, which is followed by a marked, prolonged T cell response. This accounts for the variable findings of T and B cell typing of the atypical lymphocytes at different stages of the disease. These responses produce detectable changes in both cellular and humoral immunity. Decreased delayed skin hypersensitivity to antigens is found during the acute phase. Humoral changes include a polyclonal increase in IgG and synthesis of several antibodies (Table 28–6).

A. Antibodies: The heterophil antibody is the IgM antibody in the diagnostic Paul-Bunnell test. It agglutinates sheep red blood cells and can be absorbed by preincubation with beef red blood cells but not guinea pig kidney. A slide spot test is now used for screening purposes, and positive reactions are confirmed by means of the Paul-Bunnell test. The antibody titer generally rises after day 3 of the illness, reaches a maximum at 2 weeks, and remains high for approximately 6 weeks.

Low-titer IgM antibodies to i blood group antigen are present in 20–90% of patients. Occasionally, a high-titer response to i is associated with autoimmune hemolytic anemia as a complication.

Serum antibodies to EBV capsid antigen appear de novo within 7 days of clinical disease, increase in titer, fall gradually, and then remain positive at a low level indefinitely. Antibodies to other EBV antigens appear later and are more transient.

B. Epstein-Barr Virus (EBV): The association of this herpesvirus with Burkitt's lymphoma was reported in 1964, and intensive study has provided compelling but not fully confirmatory evidence for the oncogenicity of EBV.

There is a high incidence of antibodies to EBV antigens, especially the early antigen, in Burkitt's lymphoma. High titers of antibodies to early antigen are found in all patients. However, up to 30% of patients with American Burkitt's lymphoma do not have EBV antibodies. Furthermore, antibodies to EBV capsid antigen have been detected in some patients with sarcoidosis, systemic lupus erythematosus, and Guillain-Barré syndrome. Efforts to demonstrate enveloped viral particles, nucleocapsids, or early antigens in Burkitt's lymphoma biopsies are generally negative. The continued production of EBV antibodies might be a general indication of B cell overactivity, somehow induced nonspecifically by the lymphoma, or might indicate that viral replication is continuing elsewhere in the body, as happens with Marek's lymphoma in chickens. Fluorescence studies have now demonstrated EBV membrane antigen on tumor cells.

Table 28–6. List of antibodies produced in infectious mononucleosis.

Heterophil antibody
Antibodies to i antigen on red blood cells
EBV-associated antibodies:
Early antigen
Membrane antigen
Viral capsid (cytoplasmic) antigen
Nuclear antigen
Virus-neutralizing antibody
Antibodies to Newcastle disease virus
Rheumatoid factor
Antinuclear antibody (ANA)
Syphilis reagins

The application of RNA-DNA hybridization technics to tumor cells, long-term human lymphoblastoid cell lines, and tissues from animals with lymphomas has demonstrated the wide distribution of the EBV genome. The genome may be detected in cells which do not produce infectious virions, and the relevance of this fact to EBV oncogenicity has yet to be explained. Another major paradox is the association of EBV with at least 3 distinct entities, ie, a lymphoid malignancy (Burkitt's lymphoma), a self-limited lymphoproliferative disease (infectious mononucleosis), and an epithelial malignancy (nasopharyngeal carcinoma). These differences may be due to other etiologic agents in these 3 diseases.

Recent reports of 3 families clearly demonstrate the role of genetic factors in determining the outcome of exposure of an individual to EBV. In one family several male members were affected by successive, progressive, combined variable X-linked immunodeficiency (Duncan's disease). A fatal lymphoproliferative disease occurred in 6 of the 18 boys in the kindred, and laboratory evidence confirmed infectious mononucleosis in at least 3 cases. A second family was characterized by fulminant infectious mononucleosis in previously normal male children, with replacement of T cells by atypical B cells. Normal or increased serum immunoglobulins were observed, but antibodies to EBV were not produced. The third family also showed a predilection for fulminant infectious mononucleosis in male children; in 2 cases the children survived, but with severe acquired hypogammaglobulinemia.

Clinical Features

A. Symptoms and Signs: The most frequent presentation is with fever and sore throat, tender lymphadenopathy, anorexia, malaise, headache, and myalgia. There is discrete, moderately tender lymphadenopathy which often is generalized but may be limited to the neck. Splenomegaly occurs in most patients. A macular, maculopapular, or petechial rash occurs in half of cases, but such rashes occur in almost all patients with infectious mononucleosis who have been given ampicillin.

Symptoms may be referable to specifically involved organ systems: myocarditis, manifested by arrhythmias and congestive heart failure; hepatitis, manifested by hepatomegaly and jaundice; central nervous system involvement, manifested by headache, photophobia, neck stiffness, or, rarely, transverse myelitis; and respiratory involvement, manifested by cough, pain, and dyspnea.

B. Laboratory Findings: There is initial granulocytopenia followed by an absolute lymphocytosis. The lymphocytes include many atypical forms which are often larger, with abundant cytoplasm, and show nuclear and cytoplasmic vacuolization. The atypical lymphocytes are not specific for infectious mononucleosis and occasionally are confused with lymphoblasts of acute lymphocytic leukemia.

Liver function tests usually show evidence of mild hepatocellular dysfunction.

The cerebrospinal fluid may show increased pressure and protein and atypical lymphocytes.

The sheep cell agglutination test is discussed above.

Differential Diagnosis

Viral and streptococcal tonsillitis must be excluded as causes of the exudative tonsillitis. Rubella, toxoplasmosis, and infection with cytomegalovirus may resemble some of the manifestations of infectious mononucleosis.

Treatment

There is no specific treatment. Short-term corticosteroids may be useful for acutely ill patients who are very toxic and for the complications of hepatitis, myocarditis, and central nervous system involvement.

Complications & Prognosis

The complications of infectious mononucleosis include secondary bacterial pharyngitis, rupture of the spleen, autoimmune hemolytic anemia, autoimmune thrombocytopenia, myocarditis, hepatitis, and central nervous system involvement with meningoencephalitis or transverse myelitis. Rarely, one may see fatal fulminant infectious mononucleosis or acquired hypogammaglobulinemia.

Fever generally subsides within 10 days and the lymphadenopathy and splenomegaly within 4 weeks. Occasionally, symptoms may last for up to 3 months, and lethargy and malaise may persist for 6–12 months. The mortality rate is negligible.

LEUKOCYTOPENIA

Leukocytopenia is defined as a reduction in the number of circulating leukocytes below 4000/μl. Granulocytopenia occurs more commonly than lymphocytopenia. Granulocytopenia may be caused either by decreased granulocyte production by the bone marrow or by increased granulocyte utilization or destruction. Decreased granulocyte production occurs in aplastic anemia, leukemia, and other diseases characterized by bone marrow infiltration; many drugs also cause leukocytopenia by this mechanism. Increased granulocyte utilization or destruction occurs in hypersplenism, autoimmune neutropenia, and possibly in some forms of drug-induced leukocytopenia.

Many drugs can cause neutropenia; cytotoxic drugs are particularly likely to lower the white count. Certain drugs cause very severe acute granulocytopenia; agranulocytosis may be produced by either a toxic or an immunologic mechanism.

CHRONIC AUTOIMMUNE NEUTROPENIA

This rare disease occurs in children with recurrent fever and infection, though the infections are often not severe. These children are found to have serum antibodies to neutrophils with no other evidence of autoimmune disease. Prednisone therapy has benefited some of these children. This antineutrophil antibody may be of maternal origin.

DRUG-INDUCED AUTOIMMUNE NEUTROPENIA

Although most drugs produce neutropenia by bone marrow suppression, some may cause neutropenia by the attachment of drug-antibody immune complexes to the surface of the granulocytes, with subsequent removal from the circulation. This is the so-called "innocent bystander" mechanism which is known to occur in drug-induced immune hemolytic anemia and thrombocytopenia. Cephalothin produces granulocytopenia in approximately 0.1% of patients, and anticephalothin antibodies may be responsible for this.

II. RED CELL DISORDERS

The red cell disorders in which immune processes play an important role are the immune hemolytic anemias, including autoimmune hemolytic anemia and drug-induced immune hemolytic anemia, paroxysmal nocturnal hemoglobinuria, and pure red cell aplasia.

IMMUNE HEMOLYTIC ANEMIAS

The immune hemolytic disorders are classified in Table 28–7. The classification is based on the type of antibodies involved and whether there is a demonstrable underlying disease or not. Since correct identification of the type of antibody is essential to correct diagnosis in patients with suspected immune hemolytic anemia, the immunologic laboratory investigation of such patients will be discussed before the individual diseases.

Table 28–7. Classification of immune hemolytic anemias.

Autoimmune hemolytic anemias
Warm antibody types:
Idiopathic: No underlying disease
Secondary:
Chronic lymphocytic leukemia
Lymphomas
Systemic lupus erythematosus and other rheumatoid diseases
Hepatitis
Infections: Other viruses
Cold antibody types:
Cold agglutinin syndromes
Idiopathic: No underlying disease
Secondary:
Infections: *Mycoplasma pneumoniae*, infectious mononucleosis
Lymphoma
Paroxysmal cold hemoglobinuria
Idiopathic
Secondary: Syphilis, viral infections
Drug-induced immune hemolytic anemias
Methyldopa
Penicillin
Aminosalicylic acid
Cephalothin
Chlorpromazine
Quinidine
Quinine
Stibophen
Alloantibody-induced immune hemolytic anemias
Hemolytic transfusion reactions
Hemolytic disease of the newborn

Immunologic Laboratory Investigations

There are 2 basic groups of immunologic tests necessary to properly investigate patients with suspected immune hemolytic anemias: (1) tests to detect and characterize antibodies involved in the hemolytic process, and (2) tests to aid in diagnosis of possible underlying disease processes. Tests which define underlying disorders include detection of anti-DNA antibodies and ANA in systemic lupus erythematosus, rheumatoid factors in rheumatoid arthritis, and monoclonal B cells in chronic lymphocytic leukemia.

The serologic tests used to characterize antibodies in serum and on red cells are basic blood-banking procedures, with the addition of monospecific antisera to identify specific proteins on red cells and titration technics to precisely quantitate antibody activity. Laboratory evaluation of such patients can be considered as a series of questions: (1) Are the red cells of the patient coated with IgG, complement components, or both? (2) How heavily are the red cells sensitized? (3) What antibodies are eluted from the red cells of the patient? (4) What antibodies are present in the serum?

Routine screening is performed by means of the direct antiglobulin (Coombs) test by tube or slide agglutination (see Chapter 24) using antisera with broad specificity. Subsequent evaluation requires testing the red cells with dilutions of monospecific antisera, especially antisera to IgG and C3. The activity of the antibody is examined at different temperatures to see if the temperature of maximal activity identifies it as a "warm" or "cold" antibody. Direct antiglobulin tests in warm antibody autoimmune hemolytic anemia demonstrated IgG and C3 on the red cells of 50% of cases, IgG alone in 30%, and C3 alone in 20%.

False-negative and false-positive results can be obtained in direct antiglobulin tests. Approximately 20% of all patients with immune hemolytic anemias will have a negative or only weakly positive direct antiglobulin test unless the antiserum contains adequate titer of antibodies to complement components, especially C3. This inability to detect complement on red cells was probably the cause of many early reported cases of Coombs-negative autoimmune hemolytic anemia. A positive direct antiglobulin test may be seen in situations other than autoantibodies on red cells and does not necessarily mean autoimmune hemolytic anemia. Causes of such reactions include the following: (1) antibody formation against drugs rather than intrinsic red cell antigens (see below); (2) damage to the red cell membrane due to infection or cephalosporins, leading to nonimmunologic binding of proteins; (3) in vitro complement sensitization of red blood cells by low-titer cold antibodies (present in many normal individuals) in clotted blood samples stored at 4 C prior to separation; (4) delayed transfusion reactions; and (5) unknown mechanisms. The above reactions are generally weak and can be differentiated by clinical and detailed serologic studies.

Serologic investigations of the patient's serum and red cell eluates should then answer another series of questions: (1) Are antibodies present? (2) Do they act as agglutinins, hemolysins, or incomplete antibodies? (3) What is their thermal range of activity? (4) What is their specificity?

The patient's serum is tested both undiluted and with fresh added complement against untreated and enzyme-treated pools of red cells. Enzyme treatment enhances the sensitivity of the system. The tests are run at 37 C and 20 C and examined at 1 hour for agglutination and lysis. Cold agglutinin titration at 4 C is also performed. Red cell eluate is similarly tested.

Specialized tests may be performed to detect antibodies to drugs in cases of drug-induced immune hemolytic anemia.

The specificity of the antibodies is tested at different temperatures with a panel of red cells of different genotypes and with cells of different types in the Ii blood group system (see below).

The results of the serologic investigations are then correlated with clinical and other laboratory investigations to establish a definitive diagnosis.

1. AUTOIMMUNE HEMOLYTIC ANEMIA

Major Immunologic Features

- Positive direct antiglobulin (Coombs) test.
- Preceding lymphoreticular malignancy or autoimmune disease may be present.
- Splenomegaly common.

General Considerations

Warm antibody autoimmune hemolytic anemia is the most common type of immune hemolytic anemia. It may be either idiopathic or secondary to chronic lymphocytic leukemia, lymphomas, systemic lupus erythematosus, or other autoimmune disorders or infections (Table 28–7). The idiopathic form may follow overt or subclinical viral infection.

Clinical Features

A. Symptoms and Signs: Patients usually present with symptoms of anemia (weakness, fatigue), congestive heart failure (dyspnea), angina pectoris, and hemolysis (fever, jaundice, splenomegaly). There may also be manifestations of an underlying disease, eg, lymphadenopathy, hepatosplenomegaly, or manifestations of autoimmune disease.

B. Laboratory Findings: Normochromic normocytic or slightly macrocytic anemia is usually present; spherocytosis is common, and nucleated red cells may occasionally be found in the peripheral blood. Leukocytosis and thrombocytosis are often present, but occasionally (especially in systemic lupus erythematosus) leukocytopenia and thrombocytopenia are seen. There is usually a moderate to marked reticulocytosis. The bone marrow shows marked erythroid hyperplasia with plentiful iron stores. There is an increase in the serum level of indirect (unconjugated) bilirubin. Stool and urinary urobilinogen may be greatly increased. Transfused blood has a short survival time.

Immunologic Diagnosis

The results of the serologic tests discussed above are summarized in Table 28–8. The most common pattern is IgG and complement on red cells, with IgG in the eluate. The eluate generally has no activity if the red cells are sensitized only with complement.

Warm hemolysins active against enzyme-treated red cells occur in 24% of sera, but warm serum agglutinins or hemolysins against untreated red cells are rare. The indirect antiglobulin test (Chapter 24) is positive in approximately 40% of patients' sera tested with untreated red cells but in 80% of serum samples tested with enzyme-treated red cells. This warm antibody is usually IgG but may be IgM, IgA, or both.

The specificity of antibodies in warm antibody autoimmune hemolytic anemia is very complex, but the main specificity is directed against determinants in the Rh complex (see below). Identification is generally performed by blood banks or hematology laboratories with reference panels of red cells of rare types.

Differential Diagnosis

Congenital nonspherocytic hemolytic anemia, hereditary spherocytosis, and hemoglobinopathies can

Table 28–8. Summary of serologic findings in patients with autoimmune hemolytic anemia.*

	Red Cells		Serum		
Disease Group	Direct Antiglobulin Test	Eluate	Immunoglobulin Type	Serologic Characteristics	Specificity
Warm antibody type	IgG 30% IgG + complement 50% Complement 20%	IgG IgG No activity	IgG (rarely also IgA or IgM)	Positive indirect antiglobulin test 40% Agglutination enzyme-treated red cells 80% Hemolysis enzyme-treated red cells 24% Agglutination of untreated red cells (20 C) 20% Agglutination or hemolysis of untreated red cells (37 C) Very rare	Rh system (often with a "nonspecific" component)
Cold agglutinin syndrome	Complement	No activity	IgM (rarely IgA)	High-titer cold agglutinin (usually 1:1000 at 4 C) up to 32 C; monoclonal IgM-κ in chronic disease.	Anti-I usually (can be anti-i or anti-Pr)
Paroxysmal cold hemoglobinuria (very rare)	Complement	No activity	IgG	Potent hemolysin also agglutinates normal cells. Biphasic (usually sensitizes cells in cold up to 15 C and hemolyzes them at 37 C).	Anti-P blood group

*Modified from Petz LD, Garratty G: Laboratory correlations in immune hemolytic anemias. Page 139 in: *Laboratory Diagnosis of Immunologic Disorders.* Vyas GN, Stites DP, Brecher G (editors). Grune & Stratton, 1975.

usually be differentiated by the family history, routine hematologic tests, hemoglobin electrophoresis, and a negative direct antiglobulin test.

Treatment

A. General Measures: Treatment of the underlying disease is necessary when autoimmune hemolytic anemia is secondary to an underlying disease process. Blood transfusions may be necessary for life-threatening anemia but should be avoided when possible since the transfused cells are rapidly destroyed. Careful serologic studies are needed to minimize the risks of serious hemolytic transfusion reactions, and cross-matching can be difficult or impossible in this situation.

B. Specific Measures: Hemolysis can be controlled with relatively high doses of corticosteroids (prednisone, 60–120 mg/day) in most patients. The dose is fairly rapidly tapered to 20 mg/day and then slowly reduced until the clinical state, hemoglobin level, and reticulocyte count indicate the appropriate maintenance dose. Occasionally it is possible to gradually withdraw steroids completely. Regular monitoring is necessary since acute relapses may occur in patients in remission.

Monitoring generally includes serologic studies, eg, direct and indirect antiglobulin tests, and these may show improvement with reduced amounts of IgG and complement on red cells and lower antibody titers or a negative test. However, there is no consistent correlation between clinical response and serologic tests; prednisone often induces clinical remissions in patients with warm antibody autoimmune hemolytic anemia in spite of persistently positive direct antiglobulin tests.

If prednisone therapy fails or if unacceptable side-effects occur, splenectomy is usually performed. Since splenectomy often produces long-term remissions in patients with idiopathic autoimmune hemolytic anemia, splenectomy is the treatment of choice if hemolysis persists after 2–3 months of corticosteroids. High doses of steroids should not be given for more than 2 or 3 months unless the patient has failed to respond to splenectomy. ^{51}Cr-labeled red cell survival studies can be used to identify abnormal splenic red cell sequestration prior to splenectomy; however, clinical remissions may occur after splenectomy even when abnormal splenic sequestration cannot be documented. Continued significant hemolysis or late relapse occurs in some patients after splenectomy and requires further therapy with steroids with or without other immunosuppressive agents.

Prognosis

In many instances the prognosis is that of the underlying disease, eg, systemic lupus erythematosus or lymphoma. The prognosis of idiopathic warm antibody autoimmune hemolytic anemia is fairly good; however, there are occasional fatal cases, and relapses are not infrequent.

2. COLD AGGLUTININ SYNDROMES

These diseases may also be primary or may be secondary to infections or the lymphomas (Table 28–7). The infections include mycoplasmal pneumonia and infectious mononucleosis and other viral infections.

The clinical features are often those of the underlying disease. Cold-reactive symptoms such as Raynaud's phenomenon or vascular purpura are seen in some patients. Hemolysis is generally mild but may occasionally be severe, especially in cases secondary to lymphoreticular malignancy. The onset may be acute in cases secondary to infection. The idiopathic form is generally slow in onset and runs a chronic course in older patients.

These diseases are characterized by very high serum titers of agglutinating IgM antibodies which react optimally in the cold. Some, however, may have a thermal range reacting up to 37 C. These patients have cold agglutinin titers in the thousands or millions, while normal individuals may have low-titer IgM cold agglutinins, and patients with chronic parasitic infections and most patients with Ancylostoma infection have titers up to 1:500. The specificity of the IgM is generally anti-I in the Ii system, but occasionally it is anti-i or anti-Pr (Table 28–8). In chronic idiopathic cases or cases associated with lymphoreticular malignancy, the cold agglutinin is generally a monoclonal IgM-κ paraprotein. The direct antiglobulin test is frequently positive using antiserum to C3.

Treatment consists of keeping the patient warm and waiting for spontaneous resolution in acute cases. Chronic cases sometimes respond to chlorambucil in low doses. Corticosteroids and splenectomy are probably not helpful.

The prognosis is generally good except for patients with severe underlying disease such as malignant lymphoma.

3. DRUG-INDUCED IMMUNE HEMOLYTIC ANEMIA

Many cases of immune hemolytic anemia have been reported in association with drug administration; the most common examples are included in Table 28–7. There are 3 stages in the investigation of a patient with suspected drug-induced hemolytic anemia: a history of intake of the drug, confirmation of hemolysis, and serologic tests. Detailed serologic tests are necessary to confirm the diagnosis since different drugs produce hemolysis by different mechanisms. The immunopathologic mechanisms and clinical and laboratory features are summarized in Table 28–9. The mechanisms are classified as *immune complex formation, hapten adsorption, nonspecific adsorption,* and *other unknown mechanisms.*

Table 28–9. Summary of immunopathologic mechanisms and clinical and laboratory features in drug-induced immune hemolytic disorders.*

Mechanism	Drugs	Clinical Findings	Serologic Evaluation: Direct Antiglobulin Test	Serologic Evaluation: Antibody Characterization
Immune complex formation (drug + antidrug antibody)	Quinine, quinidine, phenacetin	History of small doses of drugs. Acute intravascular hemolysis and renal failure. Thrombocytopenia occasionally found.	Complement (IgG occasionally also present).	Drug + patient's serum + enzyme-treated red cells → Hemolysis, agglutination, or sensitization. Antibody often complement-fixing IgM. Eluate generally nonreactive.
Drug adsorption to red cell membrane (combination with high-titer serum antibodies to drug)	Penicillins, cephalosporins	History of large doses of drugs. Other allergic features may be absent. Usually subacute extravascular hemolysis.	IgG (strongly positive if hemolysis occurs). Rarely, weak complement sensitization also present.	Drug-coated red cells + serum → Agglutination or sensitization (rarely hemolysis). High-titer antibody. Eluate reacts only with antibiotic-coated red cells.
Membrane modification (nonimmunologic adsorption of proteins to red cells)	Cephalosporins	Hemolytic anemia rare.	Positive with reagents with antibodies to a variety of serum proteins.	Drug-coated red cells + serum → Sensitization to antiglobulin antisera in low titer.
Unknown	Methyldopa	Gradual onset of hemolytic anemia. Common.	IgG (strongly positive if hemolysis occurs).	Antibody sensitizes normal red cells without drug. Antibody in serum and eluate identical to warm antibody. No in vitro tests demonstrate relationship to drug.

*Adapted from Garratty G, Petz LD: Drug-induced immune hemolytic anemia. Am J Med 58:398, 1975.

(1) Immune complex formation: Circulating preformed immune complexes between the drug and antibody to the drug sensitize the red cell ("innocent bystander" phenomenon). Quinine in low doses is a typical example. There is great variability in clinical features and serologic findings.

(2) Drug (hapten) adsorption: The drug acts as a hapten in that it is bound to the red cell membrane and stimulates the production of a high titer of antidrug antibodies.

(3) Nonspecific adsorption: The drug affects the red cells so that various nonimmunologic proteins are adsorbed onto red cells and give a positive Coombs test. This does not result generally in marked hemolysis.

(4) Unknown mechanisms: This type is exemplified by the positive Coombs test that develops within 3 months in 20% of patients treated with methyldopa. The IgG that coats red cells in these patients does not have antibody activity against the drug, and the drug is not required in in vitro tests.

The hemolysis may be acute and severe, but only rarely is blood transfusion required. The main treatment is to stop the offending drug and monitor the patient to be sure the hemolysis disappears. The prognosis is therefore excellent.

4. PAROXYSMAL COLD HEMOGLOBINURIA

This rare disease may be transient or chronic. It may occur as a primary idiopathic disease or secondary to syphilis or viral infection. It is characterized clinically by signs of hemolysis and hemoglobinuria following local or general exposure to cold. Symptoms may include combinations of fatigue, pallor, aching and pain in the back, legs, or abdomen, chills and fever, and the passing of dark-brown urine. The symptoms may appear from within a few minutes to a few hours after exposure to cold.

The disease is characterized by the presence of the classic biphasic Donath-Landsteiner antibody. This IgG antibody sensitizes red cells in the cold (usually below 15 C), so that complement components are detected on the red cells by the direct antiglobulin test after rewarming. Heavily sensitized cells are hemolyzed when warmed to 37 C.

Acute attacks are treated symptomatically, and postinfectious cases generally resolve spontaneously.

PAROXYSMAL NOCTURNAL HEMOGLOBINURIA

This rare disease occurs in adults as a chronic hemolytic anemia with acute exacerbations. It may follow other hematologic disorders such as idiopathic or drug-induced bone marrow aplasia and may terminate in acute myelogenous leukemia. The intravascular hemolysis causes intermittent hemoglobinemia and hemoglobinuria. This activity fluctuates throughout the day; the classical timing with nocturnal hemoglobinuria is seen in only 25% of cases.

The diagnosis is suggested by the findings of intermittent or chronic intravascular hemolysis, a low leukocyte alkaline phosphatase value, and frequently pancytopenia. The diagnosis of paroxysmal nocturnal hemoglobinuria is confirmed by any of the following tests: the acid hemolysis (Ham) test, the sugar water test, and the inulin test. These tests are presumably expressions of the 2 presently known abnormalities in paroxysmal nocturnal hemoglobinuria, ie, the exquisite sensitivity of paroxysmal nocturnal hemoglobinuria red cells to complement lysis and the abnormally low acetylcholinesterase activity in the red cell membrane. Patients' cells are lysed by approximately 4% of the amount of complement required to lyse normal red cells. These tests demonstrate the sensitivity to complement lysis of paroxysmal nocturnal hemoglobinuria red cells but do not elucidate the fundamental underlying cause of paroxysmal nocturnal hemoglobinuria. The alternative complement pathway may well be involved in this disease, as suggested by the inulin test, since inulin activates this pathway. However, serum complement studies are normal, no antibody has been identified either in the serum or on red cells, and no abnormalities have been defined in membrane lipids and phospholipids. Electron microscopy shows a pitted surface on red cells, but this has not been correlated with the functional complement abnormalities.

Treatment is mainly symptomatic. Transfusions are often required. Androgens may be useful if there is underlying bone marrow hypoplasia. Corticosteroids and splenectomy are probably not useful.

PURE RED CELL APLASIA

This rare form of anemia is characterized by a marked reduction or absence of bone marrow erythroblasts and blood reticulocytes, with normal leukocytopoiesis and thrombocytopoiesis. It may occur in children as the congenital Diamond-Blackfan syndrome, but most cases occur as an acquired disorder in adults, either in an idiopathic form, or associated with thymoma, lymphoma, drugs, or underlying severe infection, or preceding hemolysis. Patients usually present with an insidious onset of anemia; bone marrow examination confirms the diagnosis.

Thymoma is present in a small number of adults with pure red cell aplasia. Other immunologic abnormalities include hypogammaglobulinemia, paraproteinemia, the presence of ANA, and autoimmune hemolytic anemia. Some of these patients, as well as patients without thymoma, have serum IgG antibodies that react with erythroblasts. These IgG antibodies are demonstrated by immunofluorescence in a pattern of fluorescence showing staining nuclei of bone marrow erythroblasts. Some of these antibodies have been shown to fix complement and to be specifically cytotoxic for erythroblasts.

Studies of in vitro erythropoiesis and ^{59}Fe incorporation in some of these patients have shown that a patient's bone marrow will show normal stimulation by erythropoietin if cultured in normal plasma but depressed or absent stimulation in autologous plasma. IgG isolated from such a patient's plasma can inhibit erythropoiesis of normal bone marrow.

Treatment of patients with thymoma consists of surgical removal, and this induces a remission in 30% of patients with pure red cell aplasia. Patients who do not respond to thymectomy and who have idiopathic pure red cell aplasia are treated with immunosuppressive drugs. Corticosteroids are usually used first, but if this does not induce a remission, cytotoxic drugs are added, usually cyclophosphamide, mercaptopurine, or azathioprine. Some patients may require a trial of androgen therapy. It is not known if children with Diamond-Blackfan syndrome have similar immunologic abnormalities; these children usually respond to corticosteroid therapy.

III. PLATELET DISORDERS

Thrombocytopenia—a reduced number of circulating platelets—may arise from one or more of these major mechanisms: (1) increased platelet destruction, (2) deficient platelet production, and (3) abnormal platelet distribution.

Immunologic factors are primarily associated with thrombocytopenia due to increased platelet destruction. These disorders are classified in Table 28–10. Thrombocytopenias due to deficient platelet production, or abnormal distribution, such as pooling in an enlarged spleen, are not usually associated with immunologic abnormalities.

Immunologic Mechanisms of Platelet Damage

There are several immunologic mechanisms that can cause platelet damage and lead to thrombocytopenia.

A. Antiplatelet Antibodies: Platelet autoantibodies usually develop spontaneously in previously healthy individuals who develop idiopathic thrombo-

Table 28–10. Classification of thrombocytopenia due to increased platelet destruction by immunologic mechanisms.

(1) Idiopathic (immune) thrombocytopenic purpura	
(2) Secondary immune thrombocytopenic purpura:	
Systemic lupus erythematosus and other autoimmune diseases	
Lymphoma and chronic lymphocytic leukemia	
Infections	
(3) Drug-induced immune thrombocytopenic purpura:	
Acetazolamide	Hydroxychloroquine
Aminosalicylic acid	Methyldopa
Antazoline	Phenytoin
Apronalide (Sedormid)	Quinidine
Arsenicals	Quinine
Carbamazepine	Rifampin
Chlorothiazides	Stibophen
Chlorpropamide	Sulfamethazine
Desipramine	Sulfathiazole
Digitoxin	
(4) Alloantibodies:	
Multiple blood product transfusions	
Fetomaternal incompatibility	
Maternal thrombocytopenic purpura	

cytopenic purpura; occasionally they develop following viral or other infections or in the setting of other autoimmune disease. Platelet alloantibodies may develop after multiple transfusions. This is becoming a serious problem in the long-term platelet support of patients with leukemia and aplastic anemia. Patients refractory to platelet transfusions often have IgG complement-dependent cytotoxic antiplatelet antibodies. Some patients also have cell-dependent cytotoxic antibodies requiring the presence of normal lymphocytes to lyse the platelets. Sensitive methods are needed to detect antiplatelet antibodies, especially autoantibodies; standard agglutination and complement fixation technics are too insensitive to detect most antiplatelet antibodies. The best tests available at present appear to be the radioactive serotonin release test, platelet factor 3 release test, lymphocyte transformation by platelet-antiplatelet antibody immune complexes, and phagocytosis of platelet-antiplatelet antibody immune complexes by neutrophils.

B. Antibodies to Adsorbed Antigens: Antibodies may be produced against antigenic components, eg, drugs, adsorbed to platelet surfaces. These antibodies may cause platelet agglutination and, with complement, platelet lysis. This mechanism is frequently involved in drug-associated thrombocytopenia.

C. Antigen-Antibody Complexes: Antigen-antibody complexes which form in the circulation may bind to platelets and cause thrombocytopenia. This may occur in infections, with drugs, or in autoimmune diseases such as systemic lupus erythematosus.

D. Cell-Mediated Immunity: Lymphocyte activation occurs in vitro in the presence of autologous platelets in some patients with idiopathic thrombocytopenic purpura. It also occurs when normal platelets are incubated with idiopathic thrombocytopenic purpura serum and then exposed to normal lymphocytes from the platelet donor. This latter finding suggests that the lymphocytes are reacting to platelet-antiplatelet antibody immune complexes. However, it is possible that cellular immunity, especially of the lymphocytes in the spleen, may play some role in platelet destruction in idiopathic thrombocytopenic purpura.

E. Endotoxins: Endotoxins are lipopolysaccharide components of bacterial cell walls which can cause platelet destruction in vivo. Complement activation generally occurs in the reaction, with the involvement of specific or cross-reacting antibody. Nonantibody mechanisms may also contribute to the reaction. Pathologic changes other than platelet destruction occur with the generation of the biologically active complement components and the release of vasoactive amines from platelets (see Chapter 20).

IDIOPATHIC THROMBOCYTOPENIC PURPURA

Major Immunologic Features

- Antiplatelet antibodies demonstrable on platelets and in serum.
- Shortened platelet survival.
- Cellular immunity to autologous platelets often demonstrable.
- Preceding viral infection common.
- Therapeutic response to prednisone and splenectomy.

General Considerations

Idiopathic thrombocytopenic purpura is the most common cause of thrombocytopenic purpura in previously healthy individuals. It may be either acute or chronic, but these are different forms on a spectrum of the same disease, not different diseases. Idiopathic thrombocytopenic purpura affects all age groups. In all cases, the thrombocytopenia is due to increased platelet destruction. Normally, platelets survive 8–10 days, but in idiopathic thrombocytopenic purpura their survival is usually less than 1 day and may be less than 1 hour.

Childhood idiopathic thrombocytopenic purpura occurs with equal frequency in both sexes. Eighty-five percent of patients are under 8 years old, and at least half give a history of infection 1–6 weeks before the purpura. The history is usually of viral infections of the upper respiratory tract, but rubella, measles, measles immunization, chickenpox, mumps, smallpox vaccination, infectious mononucleosis, and cytomegalovirus infection may also precede this disorder. Idiopathic thrombocytopenic purpura in adults tends to be most common in young women but can occur in either sex and at any age.

Clinical Features

A. Symptoms and Signs: The onset may be acute, with sudden development of petechiae, ecchymoses, epistaxis, bleeding gums, gastrointestinal bleeding, hematuria, and vaginal bleeding. Alternatively, the disease may be gradual in onset and chronic in course. Often, however, chronic idiopathic thrombocytopenic purpura is slowly progressive or suddenly becomes acute.

B. Laboratory Findings: In acute idiopathic thrombocytopenic purpura the platelet count is usually under 20–30 thousand/μl; in chronic idiopathic thrombocytopenic purpura, the platelet count is usually 30–100 thousand/μl. There may be moderate anemia due to blood loss. The white cells are normal or slightly increased. Platelets are larger than usual on blood smear.

The bone marrow shows normal or increased numbers of megakaryocytes. They may be normal or immature in appearance. Sometimes they are larger than normal with an increased number of nuclear lobes.

Differential Diagnosis

Acute leukemia and aplastic anemia are excluded by examination of the peripheral blood and bone marrow. Thrombotic thrombocytopenic purpura and hemolytic-uremic syndrome are associated with microangiopathic hemolytic anemia, renal abnormalities, and possibly central nervous system abnormalities in addition to thrombocytopenia. These patients are much more acutely ill than patients with idiopathic thrombocytopenic purpura. This is also true for patients with disseminated intravascular coagulation, who have coagulation disturbances as well as thrombocytopenia.

Other causes of thrombocytopenic purpura must be excluded. Patients with hypersplenism almost always have easily palpable spleens; patients with idiopathic thrombocytopenic purpura do not. Secondary causes of immune thrombocytopenia such as systemic lupus erythematosus, lymphomas, and chronic lymphocytic leukemia must be excluded by appropriate tests. Drug-induced immune thrombocytopenia must also be excluded by history and serologic investigations.

Serum IgG antibodies specific for platelets are detected in most adult patients with idiopathic thrombocytopenic purpura provided that the newer, more sensitive tests for autoantibody are used. Children with idiopathic thrombocytopenic purpura often do not demonstrate platelet autoantibody. This appears to be an important difference between childhood and adult idiopathic thrombocytopenic purpura. The spleen is the major site of platelet destruction in most patients with idiopathic thrombocytopenic purpura. Hepatic destruction may also occur in some patients. The spleen has also been shown to produce some of the platelet autoantibody in idiopathic thrombocytopenic purpura patients. However, the spleen's major role appears to be removal of antibody-coated platelets from the circulation.

Treatment

Children with mild or moderate thrombocytopenia should be observed without therapy. When severe thrombocytopenia and bleeding occur, corticosteroids are usually given. Childhood idiopathic thrombocytopenic purpura does not respond as consistently as adult idiopathic thrombocytopenic purpura to steroids. Splenectomy should only be considered in children if severe thrombocytopenia persists for more than 3–6 months since most children will have spontaneous remissions by this time.

Adults with idiopathic thrombocytopenic purpura with platelet counts of less than 50,000/μl are usually treated with corticosteroids. For severe thrombocytopenia (platelet count less than 20,000/μl), prednisone is usually given in a dosage of 60–120 mg daily for adults until the platelet count rises to normal. The prednisone is then tapered to a maintenance dose (10–20 mg/day) for 1–3 months and then withdrawn. Patients who fail to respond to steroids or who relapse when the dosage of steroids is tapered require splenectomy. Splenectomy produces long-term remissions in 70–90% of adult patients with idiopathic thrombocytopenic purpura and is the treatment of choice for this disease.

Complications & Prognosis

Hemorrhage from the nose, mouth, bowel, or uterus may be severe but is seldom fatal. Fatal central nervous system hemorrhage occurs in less than 1% of patients.

Childhood idiopathic thrombocytopenic purpura is usually self-limited, and spontaneous remission occurs in most patients in a few weeks or a few months regardless of whether corticosteroids are used or not. Adults with idiopathic thrombocytopenic purpura rarely have spontaneous remissions, and although steroids temporarily correct the platelet count in most patients, lasting remissions do not usually occur until after splenectomy. These prognostic considerations are obviously essential when planning therapy.

DRUG-ASSOCIATED THROMBOCYTOPENIC PURPURA

The principal drugs that may cause thrombocytopenic purpura are listed in Table 28–10. The best-studied example is the sedative apronalide (Sedormid) (no longer in use); the drugs most commonly used in clinical practice that can produce thrombocytopenic purpura are sulfonamides, chlorothiazide derivatives, chlorpropamide, quinidine, and gold.

There is a variable period of sensitization after initial exposure to the drug, but subsequent drug exposure is rapidly followed by thrombocytopenia. Patients therefore give a history of having taken the drug in the past or for at least several weeks if this is their first exposure. A very small plasma concentration of drug and very small amounts of antibody may induce thrombocytopenia. The drug itself generally shows only weak and reversible binding to the platelet; the thrombocytopenia in most cases is apparently caused by adsorption of the drug-antibody complexes to the platelet membrane with complement activation.

Treatment consists mainly of withdrawal of the offending drug (and all drugs) and monitoring for return of normal blood platelet counts, generally within 10–14 days. Thrombocytopenia may persist if the drug is slowly excreted. Often when a patient who is taking a number of suspicious drugs is first seen it is impossible to tell whether he has drug-induced immune thrombocytopenia or idiopathic thrombocytopenic purpura. In vitro tests can now be used to confirm drug-antibody reactions involving platelets. In vivo drug challenges of sensitized patients for confirmation should be avoided as they are too hazardous.

ISOIMMUNE THROMBOCYTOPENIC PURPURA

Isoimmune thrombocytopenic purpura is a rare but interesting disorder in which purpura is caused by antiplatelet antibodies. It may arise from fetomaternal incompatibility for platelet isoantigen when antibodies from a sensitized mother cross the placenta into the fetus. Antiplatelet IgG antibody may also cross the placenta from a mother with idiopathic thrombocytopenic purpura and induce transient neonatal thrombocytopenia.

Isoantibodies may also develop in patients who receive repeated transfusions of blood products and lead to very short survival times for subsequently transfused platelets. This problem is now being approached by transfusion of refractory patients with HLA-matched platelets with considerable success.

IV. BONE MARROW TRANSPLANTATION

Extensive studies with different species over a period of 25 years provided the experimental background for bone marrow transplantation in humans; however, the great majority of the initial human bone marrow transplants failed. Failure was due in many cases to the often moribund condition of the recipient before grafting, but the main reason was histoincompatibility. More recently, these problems have been partly overcome, and improved results have been obtained in selected patients undergoing bone marrow transplantation.

The diseases for which bone marrow transplantation has been performed are aplastic anemia, acute leukemia, immunodeficiency, and occasionally miscellaneous disorders, including radiation accidents, solid malignant tumors sensitive to chemotherapy and radiotherapy, genetic disorders such as sickle cell disease and thalassemia, and malignant histiocytosis.

DONOR SELECTION FOR BONE MARROW TRANSPLANTATION

The initial factor in selection of an appropriate donor is histocompatibility. Syngeneic transplantation from an identical donor may be performed with either autologous bone marrow obtained from the patient before radiation or chemotherapy or with bone marrow from a genetically identical twin. The great majority of bone marrow transplants are obtained from allogeneic donors, which implies 2 possible major problems of histoincompatibility: graft rejection and GVH disease. Rejection of the graft by the recipient is also known as failure of engraftment. By GVH disease is meant reaction against host tissues by immunocompetent lymphoid cells in the graft. The donor is chosen after HLA typing and MLC tests to reduce the likelihood of these complications of histoincompatibility. HLA typing is performed on various members of the patient's family, and HLA-identical members are tested in MLC to determine whether reactions occur between their cells and the patient's cells. Unfortunately, many patients who might be candidates for bone marrow transplants have no suitable donor. The chances are 25% that a full-blooded sibling will be HLA-identical. MLC tests are particularly important since there are rare examples of successful bone marrow transplantation between donors and recipients who were HLA-nonidentical but MLC-nonreactive.

TECHNICS OF BONE MARROW TRANSPLANTATION

Bone marrow transplantation does not involve complicated surgery. The marrow is obtained by multiple aspirations from the iliac crests of the donor under sterile conditions using spinal or general anesthesia. Up to 800 ml of bone marrow diluted with blood may be obtained during the procedure, and it is advisable to store 1 unit of blood from the donor during the preceding week for infusion during the procedure. Multiple bone marrow sites are aspirated, with 1–3 ml of bone marrow being taken from each site, to reduce contamination of the marrow by peripheral blood. The bone marrow is transferred into tissue culture medium in containers without heparin or preservative, passed through stainless steel mesh screens (0.3 mm pore size), and examined microscopically to exclude potentially lethal marrow fat emboli. Within 1 hour at room temperature, $5–30 \times 10^9$ nucleated marrow cells are injected intravenously into the recipient.

CLINICAL MANAGEMENT

Preparation of Patient

This includes correction of severe anemia and thrombocytopenia by transfusion of packed red blood cells and platelets and vigorous treatment of infection if present. Management of the patient with significant leukocytopenia depends on the underlying disease. Seriously infected patients with aplastic anemia and acute leukemia with significant granulocytopenia may benefit from granulocyte transfusions, but patients with immunodeficiency and marked lymphocytopenia are best treated by marrow transplantation. Patients with severe combined immunodeficiency disease or immunosuppression may develop GVH disease from viable immunocompetent stem cells in transfused blood or plasma; it is therefore necessary to irradiate all blood products with 1500 rads in vitro before administration to the patient. The donors of the blood products should be HLA-matched with the recipient before the bone marrow transplantation to avoid sensitization to transplantation antigens. The marrow donor should never be used prior to transplantation as a blood donor in order to avoid sensitization of the recipient. These patients should be cared for in special units with protection against exogenous infections and should have 24-hour attention from an experienced bone marrow transplantation team.

Recipients with immunocompetent cells must be treated to suppress those cells and prevent rejection of the graft. This is not necessary for syngeneic grafts between identical twins. Total body irradiation may be used, but the dose must be large (1000 rads), and many previously unsuccessful grafts were probably due partly to inadequate pregrafting irradiation. Current regimens use cyclophosphamide with or without total body irradiation immediately prior to engraftment. Failure of a bone marrow graft after pretreatment with cyclophosphamide alone may be followed by successful engraftment if the recipient is reprepared with cyclophosphamide, procarbazine, and antithymocyte globulin for 4 days prior to transplantation.

Supportive Care

It is essential to support the patient with platelet, red cell, and granulocyte transfusions and antibiotics as indicated pending evidence of engraftment and maintenance of satisfactory blood counts. Attempts have been made to prevent infection by gut sterilization using broad-spectrum antibiotics, but most patients present with established infection requiring multiple antibiotics.

Engraftment

Successful engraftment is shown by the recovery of hematopoietic and lymphocytopoietic functions. Hematopoietic function is indicated by rising platelet, granulocyte, red cell, and reticulocyte counts. This occurs in many cases of immunodeficiency before evidence of establishment of immunocompetence. Assessment of immunologic status must be based on several tests since various aspects of cellular and humoral immunity may become functional at variable periods after engraftment.

SPECIFIC DISEASES IN WHICH BONE MARROW TRANSPLANTATION MAY BE INDICATED

Aplastic Anemia

Severe aplastic anemia carries a grave prognosis with a mortality rate of about 90% despite efforts at management with corticosteroids, androgens, supportive therapy, and antimicrobial agents. Survival is significantly improved in 25–60% of patients transplanted with bone marrow from HLA-identical siblings. Within 3 weeks after diagnosis it should be possible to fully evaluate any signs of spontaneous recovery. Continuing severe aplastic anemia after this interval increases the likelihood of potentially fatal complications and decreases the chances for successful engraftment. Some patients with aplastic anemia have successfully accepted grafts from a normal identical twin. These patients have experienced complete recovery of marrow function and survive normally. For allogeneic grafting, the recipient is given large doses of cyclophosphamide, for 4 days prior to the bone marrow infusion. GVH disease occurs in about 75% of engrafted patients surviving 50 days after transplantation. It is life-threatening in about 25%. Since successful engraftment is less likely in terminal patients with severe infection, sensitization to transplantation antigens, etc, the family members should all be tissue-typed as soon as possible (see Chapter 15), and transfusions from family members should be avoided.

Leukemia

The abnormal population of leukemic bone marrow cells must first be eradicated by intensive chemotherapy and whole body irradiation. Failure of bone marrow transplantation in acute leukemia is often due to the advanced state of the disease after failure of conventional antileukemic therapy. Regimens tested include the administration of cyclophosphamide prior to whole body irradiation and the use of multiple chemotherapeutic agents such as cytarabine, daunorubicin, and thioguanine.

Despite these measures, there is a high risk of recurrence of leukemia. A recent review of 70 cases of allogeneic bone marrow transplantation for acute leukemia reported GVH disease in 73% and relapse of leukemia in 30%. The overall survival at 1 year is 30%. The leukemia recurrence rate may be 50% in patients surviving more than 100 days. More careful patient selection and earlier engraftment appear to be necessary to improve the results of bone marrow transplantation in acute leukemia. Most patients with acute myelogenous leukemia should probably be transplanted after the first relapse–or perhaps even during the first remission–if a suitable donor is available.

Immunodeficiency

The principal indication for early bone marrow transplantation is severe combined immunodeficiency disease (see Chapter 26). Data from the NIH Organ Transplant Registry in January 1975 showed that 95 bone marrow transplants had been performed in 52 patients with immunodeficiency and that 22 patients had survived with functioning grafts in 18. Most survivors had received grafts from HLA-identical, MLC-nonreactive siblings. The causes of failure included lack of engraftment and death from infection.

COMPLICATIONS OF BONE MARROW TRANSPLANTATION

Failure of Engraftment

The graft fails to "take" in approximately 10–20% of recipients. Factors that may contribute to failure of engraftment include infusion of insufficient numbers of nucleated stem cells; reduced viability of the cells due to the handling procedures; inadequate bone marrow "space" because of residual tumor or leukemic cells; and rejection by functioning immunocompetent host cells possibly sensitized by prior transfusion and not destroyed by preparatory immunosuppressive therapy. Finally, a potentially successful graft may fail because the recipient is in a terminal stage and dies from preexisting infection before the graft becomes established. Careful selection of donors for histocompatibility, attention to the technics of transplantation, and the clinical status of the recipient should reduce the incidence of failure of engraftment.

GVH Disease

This denotes the clinical and pathologic sequelae of the reactions of immunocompetent cells in the graft against the histoincompatible cells of the recipient (see Chapter 15). Fatal GVH reactions occur in approximately 25% of grafted patients. In one study significant GVH disease was found in 19 of 40 patients given an allogeneic bone marrow graft from an HLA-identical, MLC-nonreactive donor. Thus, there are biologically important genetically determined antigenic determinants on lymphoid cells, and current studies are analyzing their role in transplantation.

The clinical and pathologic findings of GVH disease occur mainly in the skin, gut, liver, and lymphoid system. The skin shows a fine maculopapular erythematous rash resembling measles, with maximal localization on the trunk. It has a fine "sandpaper" feel and may become confluent, hemorrhagic, and grossly exfoliative. The main gastrointestinal symptom is diarrhea. Severe diarrhea may be associated with abdominal cramps and melena. Abnormalities in liver function include increases in serum bilirubin, alkaline phosphatase, and glutamic-oxaloacetic transaminase. The effects on the lymphoid system are defects in cellular immunity with infection. A grading system for the severity of GVH disease is presented in Table 28–11.

Management of GVH disease has proved difficult, and several regimens have been tested. Most centers now give methotrexate routinely after marrow grafting to attempt suppression of immunocompetent cells in the graft, thereby preventing GVH reactions. Life-threatening exacerbations of GVH disease are usually treated with antithymocyte globulin.

Experimental approaches have been tried as well as pregrafting immunosuppression. The cells in donor bone marrow responsible for GVH disease may be

Table 28–11. Clinicopathologic grading of the severity of human GVH disease.*

Parameter	Grade I	Grade II	Grade III	Grade IV
Skin rash	Mild	Moderately severe	Moderately severe	Severe
Gastrointestinal tract abnormalities	Nil	Mild	Moderately severe	Severe
Liver dysfunction	Nil	Mild	Moderately severe	Severe
Overall clinical status	Unchanged	Unchanged	Significant impairment	Marked impairment
Microscopic findings				
Skin	Focal or diffuse vacuolar degeneration of epidermal basal cells and acanthocytes.	Basal vacuolar degeneration; spongiosis; dyskeratosis and degeneration of epidermal cells.	Spaces from necrosis of basal cells and acanthocytes; separation at dermal-epidermal junction.	Loss of entire epidermal layer
Gut	Focal dilatation and degeneration of the mucosal glands.	Changes in mucosal and intestinal glands.	Focal mucosal denudation.	Diffuse mucosal denudation.
Liver	Degeneration and necrosis of parenchyma and epithelium of small bile ducts (< 25% bile ducts affected).	25–49% bile ducts affected.	50–74% bile ducts affected.	> 75% bile ducts affected.

*Compiled from data in Storb R & others: Treatment of established human graft-versus-host disease by antithymocyte globulin. Blood 44:47, 1974.

partly separated by fractionation on discontinuous albumin gradients before transplantation or eliminated by exposing them to foreign cells in vitro and inducing them to "commit suicide" by incorporating highly radioactive DNA precursors into their nuclei during blast transformation. Donors may be treated with soluble HLA antigens, or children with immunodeficiency disorders may be treated with alloantibodies of maternal origin.

Infection

Infection is the most common fatal complication of aplastic anemia, acute leukemia, and immunodeficiency disorders; infection after bone marrow transplantation also remains a common cause of death. The organisms may come from endogenous or exogenous sources. This increased susceptibility is partly due to the cytotoxic and immunosuppressive therapy given before and after transplantation. It is also due, however, to immunosuppression due to GVH reactions and inadequate immunologic reconstitution.

Infections due to staphylococci and gram-negative bacilli are most frequent during the marked leukocytopenia that occurs just before and after transplantation. Infections with gram-negative bacilli such as pseudomonas may occur after antibiotic therapy when the organisms have developed resistance. The patient may survive these initial infections, but, if engraftment is not successful or if GVH disease progresses, infection with fungi (eg, candida, aspergillus) and other opportunistic organisms is more likely. Mixed or bacterial and fungal infections are not uncommon.

Significant interstitial pneumonitis occurs in about half of patients in the first 5 months after transplantation, with cytomegalovirus found in 50% and *Pneumocystis carinii* in 10% of these patients with pneumonitis. Approximately half of the cases run a fatal course. Active cytomegalovirus infection occurs in at least 30% of patients in whom engraftment is successful and represents a major problem since safe and effective therapy is not available.

Relapse of Malignancy

Recurrent acute leukemia in transplanted patients is an increasingly common problem now that patients are surviving longer. Cytogenetic analysis in a few cases has shown that recurrence of the leukemia has occurred in donor cells, consistent with a viral etiology of leukemia and also other possible interpretations. This complication may restrict the role of bone marrow transplantation in malignancy unless pretransplantation therapy can achieve total tumor eradication.

It will also be necessary to monitor long-term bone marrow transplantation survivors for the development of other malignancies, especially lymphoreticular ones. Both human and experimental subjects with chronic allograft rejection and long-term immunosuppression show an increased incidence of malignancy. Total body irradiation and cyclophosphamide in high doses might also predispose to the development of malignancy.

CONCLUSION

Bone marrow transplantation is a highly specialized investigational procedure which should be performed only in referral centers with facilities for the necessary investigatory work and full patient support. At present, the 3 main indications for allogeneic bone marrow transplantation are aplastic anemia, acute leukemia, and severe immunodeficiency. Successful long-term uncomplicated engraftment is much more likely with a syngeneic identical twin. Significant GVH disease and infection remain major factors in determining both patient and graft survival, even in those who appear compatible by present methods of HLA and MLC testing. Recurrent leukemia also limits survival in patients transplanted for leukemia. Effective methods to circumvent or treat these complications are necessary before bone marrow transplantation can be used more widely as a therapeutic procedure.

V. HEMOSTATIC DISORDERS

Hemostasis refers to the complex sequence of events which occurs when blood vessels are damaged, resulting in cessation of bleeding. Abnormalities of the hemostatic system may present as abnormal bleeding or bruising, or diffuse or localized intravascular clotting. Hemostasis will be discussed in terms of the vascular, platelet, and coagulation phases.

VASCULAR PHASE

Normal blood vessels, with intact endothelium and normal perivascular tissues, are necessary for normal hemostasis. Immunologic factors that might act on the vessel to produce abnormalities include antibodies to vascular endothelium, circulating preformed antigen-antibody complexes, monoclonal proteins such as IgM or IgG polymers or aggregates, cryoglobulins, vasoactive amines, and complement components. The patient may present clinically with spontaneous or cold-induced vascular purpura. The nature of the hemostatic abnormalities in patients with vascular purpura can be established by demonstration of any of the above immunologic abnormalities or an underlying disease such as systemic lupus erythematosus.

Treatment is directed at the underlying disease. Patients with immunologically mediated vasculitis are frequently treated with prednisone in the acute phase.

PLATELET PHASE

Adequate numbers of normally functioning platelets are necessary for normal hemostasis. Immunologic aspects of abnormalities involving platelets have already been described.

COAGULATION PHASE

Coagulation is the process that converts fluid blood into an insoluble fibrin clot. A series of interconnected enzyme-substrate steps involving plasma coagulation factors produces the final fibrin clot. The coagulation mechanism resembles the complement cascade in some respects (see Chapter 6). Blood coagulation may be initiated by either an extrinsic pathway as a result of the action of tissue thromboplastic factors or an intrinsic pathway following contact activation of Hageman factor (factor XII). Hageman factor is also involved in initiation of the kinin-forming and fibrinolytic systems (see Chapter 20). The final stages of coagulation involve the conversion of plasma fibrinogen through intermediate stages to an insoluble fibrin clot. Localized deposition of fibrin may occur in vivo during immunologic reactions, eg, a severe Arthus reaction.

Plasma levels of fibrinopeptides and plasminogen can be measured by radial immunodiffusion in commercial antibody-agar plates (see Chapter 24). The normal plasma fibrinogen level is 200–400 mg/dl. Bleeding from congenital or acquired hypofibrinogenemia usually does not occur until the plasma fibrinogen level is less than 100 mg/dl. Acquired deficiency is usually due to disseminated intravascular clotting, a result of severe liver disease; overactive fibrinolysis may also rarely occur.

Disseminated intravascular coagulation (defibrination syndrome) is seen with greater frequency as physicians become more aware of the disorder. Disseminated intravascular coagulation is a bleeding disorder resulting from excessive intravascular clotting with depletion of platelets, fibrinogen, and other procoagulants. It may occur following incompatible blood transfusion, major surgery (especially thoracic or prostatic), bacterial sepsis, premature separation of the placenta and other complications of pregnancy, disseminated malignancy, snakebite, and numerous other disorders. Fibrin degradation products (fibrin split products) are formed as a result of proteolytic digestion of the fibrinogen and fibrin and can be detected in serum by radial immunodiffusion, passive hemagglutination inhibition, or counterelectrophoresis (see Chapter 24). The presence of elevated blood levels of fibrin split products is an important diagnostic criterion for the diagnosis of disseminated intravascular coagulation.

Circulating Inhibitors of Coagulation

Abnormal bleeding is occasionally due to a circulating inhibitor blocking one or more plasma coagulation factors. Inhibitors may occur in normal subjects, pregnant women, or patients with hemophilia, systemic lupus erythematosus, disseminated malignancy, monoclonal gammopathy, and malignant lymphoma. Inhibitors may appear abruptly and be associated with life-threatening hemorrhage or may be chronic and associated with little or no bleeding.

The inhibitors interfere most frequently with factor VIII (antihemophilic factor), but some block multiple factors. Rarely, the paraprotein in a monoclonal gammopathy has inhibitor activity against a coagulation factor, eg, factor VIII. Many inhibitors are IgG antibodies capable of crossing the placenta. Immunosuppressive therapy is often used, with variable success, in patients who have bleeding due to circulating inhibitors.

Hemophilia & Von Willebrand's Disease

Hemophilia is a congenital X-linked recessive disorder characterized by a low level of factor VIII procoagulant activity in clotting assays. Von Willebrand's disease is an autosomally inherited bleeding disorder; these patients have low factor VIII levels, long bleeding times, and reduced platelet adhesiveness. Factor VIII activity in normal subjects may vary between 50 and 150% of normal with exercise, stress, infection, etc. Factor VIII levels in hemophilia vary, but a level below 1% almost always means severe bleeding both spontaneously and after minor injury. Symptoms are milder in the 5–20% range. Because of the wide normal range of factor VIII activity, attempts to identify carriers by clotting assays alone are unsuccessful.

Factor VIII is an α_2-globulin glycoprotein of disputed molecular weight. Several laboratories suggest it contains a high-molecular-weight material (> 1 million) and a subunit in the range of 100–200 thousand. Tests with antisera to purified factor VIII reveal that nearly all patients with hemophilia have normal blood levels of a substance that cross-reacts antigenically with factor VIII. This cross-reacting substance is thought to represent antigenic determinants on the factor VIII molecule distinct from the functional site detected in conventional clotting assays. The smaller subunit probably represents this molecule. Rarely, a patient with hemophilia has no cross-reacting substance. Carriers of the abnormal hemophilia gene may be detected with 75–95% confidence by combining conventional factor VIII clotting assays with immunologic assays for cross-reacting substance (eg, hemagglutination or electroimmunodiffusion). Factor VIII antigenic activity is always greater than factor VIII clotting activity in hemophilia carriers.

By comparison, nearly all patients with von Willebrand's disease have a true deficiency of factor VIII, lacking both the cross-reacting and functional procoagulant substances. The large factor VIII subunit appears to be necessary for normal platelet adhesiveness and ristocetin aggregation.

Human antibodies to factor VIII have been compared to rabbit antibodies in neutralization, immunodiffusion, and hemagglutination tests. Some human antibodies are specific for the functional site of the factor VIII molecule. However, patients with clinically severe hemophilia appear to lack the determinants associated with the functional site and detected by these human antibodies. Other human antibodies are specific for determinants on the part of the molecule also detected by rabbit antisera. Further immunologic differences between the 2 diseases were shown by studies in which factor VIII concentrates stimulated lymphocytes from some hemophiliacs and nontransfused normal donors but not lymphocytes from patients with von Willebrand's disease. Further clinical, immunologic, genetic, and functional studies will probably reveal distinct forms of both hemophilia and von Willebrand's disease. It is not known whether these findings will alter management of these patients with factor VIII replacement preparations. Routine monitoring of treatment is performed with factor VIII clotting assays and bleeding time tests and not immunologic tests. Patients who develop reactions or resistance to these replacement preparations can often be shown to have developed antibodies, and immunosuppressive therapy may be necessary to permit continued replacement therapy.

VI. BLOOD REPLACEMENT THERAPY

A wide range of blood products may be administered therapeutically, including whole blood, packed red cells, plasma, specific plasma protein fractions, leukocytes, and platelets. Blood transfusion is now a routine procedure, but correct matching of blood is necessary. This matching by blood bank procedures is based on immunologic principles.

BLOOD GROUPS

The existence of blood groups was discovered by Landsteiner in 1900. Blood groups are systems of inherited antigenic determinants on the surfaces of red cells. The more important blood group systems include those designated ABO, Rh, Lewis, MN, P, Kell, Duffy, and Kidd. In routine blood bank practice, only the ABO and Rh types are determined unless antibodies are detected in donor or recipient. The ABO and Lewis antigens are also found in water-soluble form in tissue fluids and secretions. Blood group substances are glycolipids on red cells but appear as glycoproteins in the secretory form. Recent work has provided detailed chemical characterization of some blood group antigens.

ABO & Lewis Systems

The A and B antigens are the products of 2 co-

Table 28–12. ABO blood group system.

Blood Group Phenotype	Genotype	Antigens on Red Cells	Antibodies In Serum
O	*OO*	Nil	Anti-A Anti-B
A	*AA* *AO*	A	Anti-B
B	*BB* *BO*	B	Anti-A
AB	*AB*	A and B	Nil

dominant allelic genes (*A* and *B*). A key feature of the ABO system is that subjects who have A antigen on red cells have anti-B antibodies in their plasma and vice versa (Table 28–12). Group O subjects with neither A nor B on their red cells have both anti-A and anti-B antibodies in plasma. They also have antibodies to H substance on their red cells. Group O subjects are therefore really group H, but the term O is retained for historical reasons. Subjects of the *Bombay phenotype* lack A, B, and H antigens on their red cells and in their secretions.

The secretor status is under the genetic control of 2 genes, *Se* and *se*. The genotypes are *SeSe* and *Sese* (secretors) and *sese* (nonsecretors).

The Lewis system is controlled by 2 allelic genes, Le and le, and the main antigens are Le^a and Le^b. They are acquired from plasma and are not integral parts of the red cell membrane. The ABO, Lewis, and secretor systems are related but under separate genetic control.

The different A, B, H, and Le substances are produced as the result of sequential enzymatic changes of a glycoprotein precursor. Blood group substances obtained from body fluids are glycoproteins composed of 80–85% carbohydrate and 15–20% amino acids. They vary in size but have an average molecular weight of approximately 300,000. They consist of a peptide backbone with multiple oligosaccharide chains attached to the backbone by alkali-labile glycosidic bonds to the hydroxyl group of the amino acids serine or threonine (Fig 28–9). Most are attached by an N-acetyl-D-galactosamine residue. There are 2 types of backbone structure. Type 1 chains have the galactose linked $\beta(1\rightarrow3)$ to N-acetyl-D-glucosamine and type 2 chains linked $\beta(1\rightarrow4)$. Type 1 chains can acquire Le^a activity, but type 2 chains cannot. Antigenic blood group specificity is determined by the final sugars at the terminal nonreducing end of the carbohydrate chains. When it is N-acetyl-D-galactosamine, the molecule has A specificity; when it is D-galactose, it has B specificity.

Ii System

The I antigen is present on the red cells of normal adults. The red cells of adults also have a small amount of i antigen. Greater amounts of i antigen are seen in adults with bone marrow stress, eg, hemolytic anemia, and on the red cells of neonates. Cold agglutinins gen-

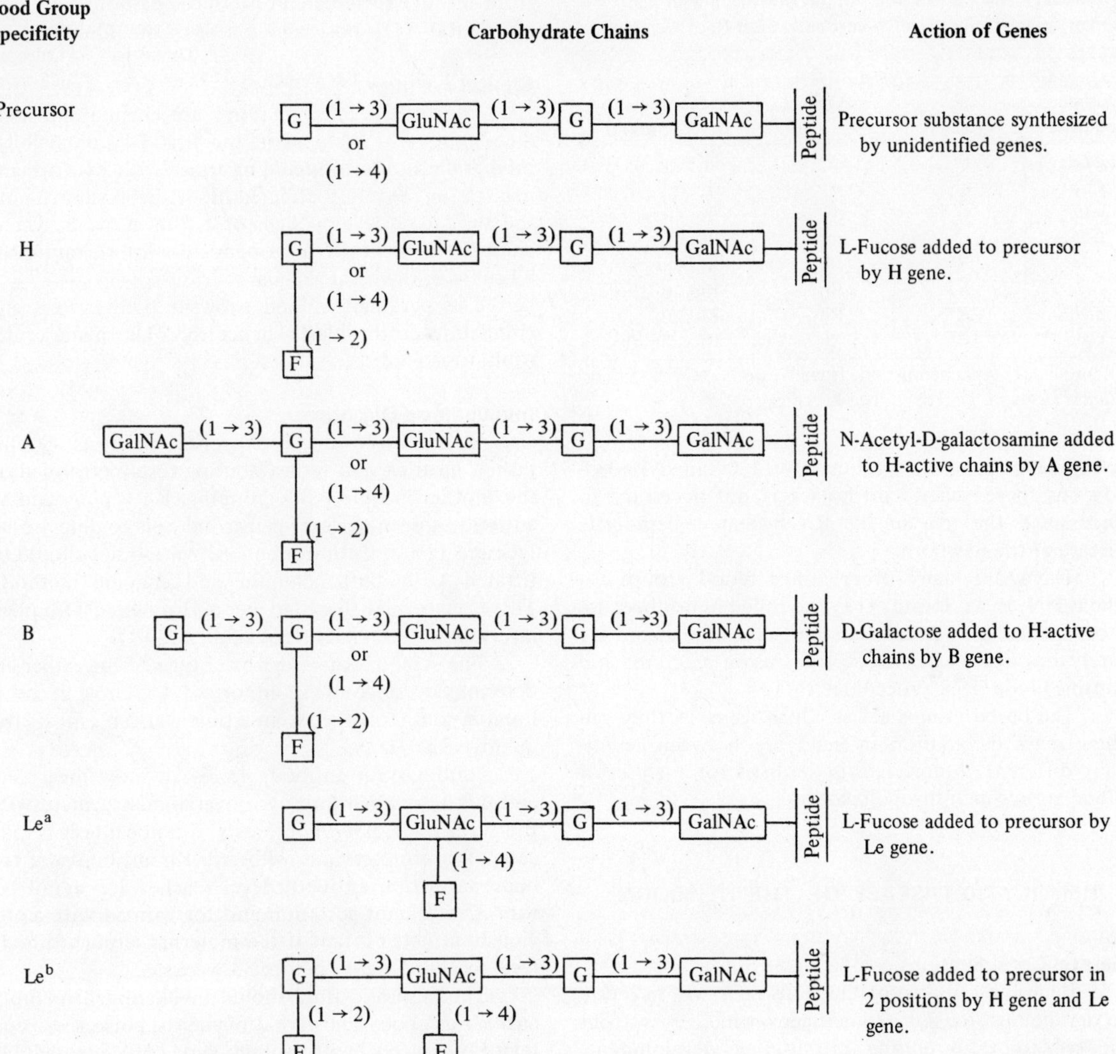

Figure 28–9. Diagrams of proposed structure of carbohydrate side chains of A, B, H, Le^a, and Le^b glycoproteins. The attachment of the side chains is via serine or threonine residues in the peptide backbone. GalNAc, N-acetyl-D-galactosamine; G, D-galactose; GluNAc, N-acetyl-D-glucosamine; F, L-fucose. The numerical notations (1 → 2, 1 → 3, and 1 → 4) refer to the specific carbon atom positions at which bonds are formed.

erally have a specificity in the Ii system, and several specificities have been defined. The primary structure of these glycoproteins has not been defined, but they appear to be located close to the stage of precursor substance.

Rh System

The discovery of this system in 1940 led to a very complex system of at least 30 red cell antigens and antibodies. It is called the Rhesus system since initial studies showed that antisera to rhesus monkey red cells also agglutinated human red cells. Persons who possess these determinants are called "rhesus-positive" (approximately 85% of Caucasians).

Considerable confusion still unfortunately exists in the field since there are 2 conflicting terminologies.

The linked gene theory of Fisher and Race postulated 3 pairs of closely linked allelic genes: Cc, Dd, and Ee. Each parent contributes 3 genes, and the genotype appears, for example, as *CDe/cde*.

The multiple allele theory of Wiener postulates that a single gene locus is responsible for an antigen complex or *agglutinogen.* This is identified by its blood factors and appropriate antibodies (Table 28–13). Most workers have adopted the suggestion of Wiener that italics be used for genes or genotypes, medium Roman type for agglutinogens and phenotypes, and boldface Roman type for blood factors and corre-

Table 28–13. Summary of the Rh system with the terminologies of Wiener and Fisher-Race.*

Genes			
Fisher and Race	**Wiener**	**Agglutinogens**	**Blood Factors Expressed**
cde	r	rh	hr′, hr″, hr
Cde	r'	rh′	rh′, hr″
cdE	r''	rh″	rh″, hr′
CdE	r^y	rh^y	rh′, rh″
cDe	R^0	Rh_0	Rh_0, hr′, hr″, hr
CDe	R^1	Rh_1	Rh_0, rh′, hr″
cDE	R^2	Rh_2	Rh_0, rh″, hr′
CDE	R^z	Rh_z	Rh_0, rh′, rh″

*Reproduced, with permission, from Wintrobe MM & others: *Clinical Hematology,* 7th ed. Lea & Febiger, 1975.

sponding antibodies. Fortunately, a detailed knowledge of these genetic intricacies is not necessary to understand the role of the Rh system in hemolytic disease of the newborn.

There are many other minor blood group systems—MN, P, Ss, U, etc. They are called minor because most of them are weakly immunogenic in man and are rarely involved in hemolytic transfusion reactions and routine blood bank procedures.

The blood groups act as alloantigens, ie, they can show marked variation in incidence between genetically different groups. This is the basis for analyses of blood groups in anthropologic studies.

HEMOLYTIC DISEASE OF THE NEWBORN

General Considerations

Hemolytic disease of the fetus or newborn is due to antibodies to red cell antigens which pass from mother to fetus during intrauterine development. Although different antibodies have been described, approximately 95% of cases are due to IgG antibody to the Rh_0 (D) antigen. This formerly caused disease in one out of 180 newborn Caucasian infants.

Immunologic Pathogenesis

Most cases are due to IgG anti-Rh_0 (D) produced by an Rh_0 (D)-negative mother in response to sensitization to the Rh_0 (D) antigen. This sensitization may result from earlier blood transfusion or injection of blood products or from earlier pregnancy, including miscarriages. There is a general tendency for hemolytic disease to miss the first child but to become more severe with successively affected infants. Obviously, Rh-negative children will not be affected. The actual Rh phenotype of the infant partly determines the severity of the disease, eg, Rh_0 (D) infants with E are more severely affected than Rh_0 (D) infants with C. It has been suggested but not confirmed that genetic factors also influence the response of the mother to the Rh_0 (D) antigen.

The specific IgG antibody crosses the placenta from mother to fetus and produces pathologic effects on the RH_0 (D)-positive red cells of the infant.

Clinical Features

The usual clinical features are anemia and jaundice present at birth or in the first 24 hours. Some infants die in utero, including those with hydrops and maceration. Severely affected infants who survive until the third day develop signs of central nervous system damage *(kernicterus)* from deposition of unconjugated bilirubin in the basal ganglia.

The peripheral blood shows reticulocytosis and circulating erythroblasts—hence the older name erythroblastosis fetalis.

Immunologic Diagnosis

Immunologic diagnosis relies on tests of the father, mother, and fetus. Routine tests performed on the mother include ABO grouping, Rh typing, and an antibody screening test against red cells to detect both IgG and IgM anti-Rh antibodies. Antibodies should be titrated with both albumin and enzyme methods. These tests may have to be performed at frequent intervals in mothers at risk (Table 28–14).

The ABO group and Rh subtype of the father are determined, since it is important to know if he is homozygous for the stimulating antigen, most frequently Rh_0 (D).

Maternal Rh antibody levels are now measured, and this has further improved overall management with the availability of *amniocentesis.* Amniocentesis is indicated for primigravidas with anti-Rh antibodies if the maternal serum antibody level reaches 1.5 μg/ml before 35 weeks of gestation and for women with a previously affected infant if the maternal serum antibody level reaches 1 μg/ml before 35 weeks.

The amniotic fluid should be examined for both anti-Rh antibody and blood pigments, since these correlate positively with subsequent cord hemoglobin values, clinical severity, and survival. An amniotic fluid antibody level below 0.2 μg/ml was associated with a cord hemoglobin level over 110 g/l and mild to moderate disease. An amniotic fluid antibody level above 0.6 μg/ml was associated with a cord hemoglobin level below 80 g/l and severe clinical disease.

Full serologic testing is required on the infant's red cells and cord serum. A positive direct antiglobulin (Coombs) test indicates antibody on the red cells, but the strength of the reaction is not a direct indication of clinicopathologic severity nor an automatic indication for treatment. No treatment is required in approximately 40% of infants with a positive direct antiglobulin test. The cord hemoglobin level is the best guide to clinical severity, with low levels (< 80 g/l) indicating severe disease.

Differential Diagnosis

The main distinction that must be made is from physiologic jaundice of the newborn, which does not develop within the first 24 hours after delivery and has no associated serologic abnormalities.

Table 28–14. Serologic investigations in pregnancy.*

Rh Typing of Mother	History	Abnormal Maternal Antibodies	Serologic Investigations
Rh_0(D)-positive	Normal	Nil	A: No further tests.
	Suggestive of hemolytic disease	Nil	B: Tests as in D.
	Normal or suggestive of hemolytic disease	Present	C: Tests as in F.
Rh_0(D)-negative	Normal	Nil	D: Antibody tests: At 34 weeks of gestation. At delivery. 10 days postpartum. 12 weeks postpartum (if baby Rh_0 [D]-positive).
	Suggestive of hemolytic disease	Nil	E: Antibody tests: Monthly from 28 weeks to delivery. 10 days postpartum. 12 weeks postpartum (if baby Rh_0 [D]-positive).
	Normal or suggestive of hemolytic disease	Present	F: Titration of antibody: At 1-month intervals. At delivery. 10 days postpartum. Father and baby tested.

*Adapted from Dodd BE, Lincoln PJ: *Blood Group Topics.* Vol 3. *Current Topics in Immunology Series.* Turk JL (editor). Arnold, 1975.

Treatment

Transfusion is the treatment of choice in severely affected infants, using blood compatible with the maternal antibody causing the disease. With severe cases confirmed by amniocentesis that have not progressed beyond 34 weeks of gestation, intrauterine transfusion is performed by introducing the transfused red cells into the fetal peritoneal cavity. This should only be considered in specialized centers. After 34 weeks, severely affected infants are treated by premature induction and delivery to avoid further damage from the greater amounts of maternal IgG normally transferred to infants in the last weeks of pregnancy. Exchange transfusion is performed after delivery with compatible blood to replace 90% of the infant's blood. Exchange transfusion suppresses the production of autologous IgG and IgA but stimulates IgM synthesis.

Prevention is now possible in Rh-negative women with a success rate of over 95%. It relies on the observation that passive anti-D IgG antibody administered within 72 hours after exposure to Rh_0 (D)-positive red cells prevents sensitization and antibody production. Rh-negative mothers are given 100 μg anti-D (2 ml) by intramuscular injection within 60 hours of delivery. Therapeutic anti-D is human Rh_0 (D) immune globulin (RhoGAM). This biologic agent is best given within 24 hours of delivery, and it may be worthwhile to give it as late as 1–2 weeks if earlier administration is not possible. Rh-negative women should receive 50 μg anti-D IgG after therapeutic or spontaneous abortion.

The therapeutic anti-D IgG is prepared from the plasma of previously immunized mothers with a persistently high titer, men with spontaneous anti-Rh antibody, or volunteer male donors immunized against Rh_0 (D)-positive red cells.

BLOOD TRANSFUSION

The only indication for whole blood transfusion is hemorrhage, either posttraumatic, during surgery, or associated with massive gastrointestinal bleeding or other bleeding. Routine blood grouping and cross-matching between donor and recipient are performed before administration of any blood product containing red cells.

Packed red cells are given to restore the red cell mass in patients with chronic anemias without hypovolemia. Advantages of giving packed red cells instead of whole blood include the following: more oxygen-carrying capacity with less volume, ability to fractionate blood into multiple blood components, and reduced administration of sodium, potassium, lactic acid, and donor antibodies. Blood transfusions should not be given as a substitute for full investigation of a patient with anemia and correction of specific abnormalities, eg, vitamin B_{12} deficiency or iron deficiency.

Special indications for blood transfusion are the requirement for fresh blood in some patients with severe hepatic disease or disseminated intravascular coagulation and intractable hemorrhage, intrauterine transfusion and exchange transfusion in hemolytic disease of the newborn, and autologous transfusion in patients with very rare blood groups or antibodies undergoing major elective surgery.

BLOOD TRANSFUSION REACTIONS

These are classified as those due to nonimmune mechanisms and those due to immune mechanisms.

Nonimmune reactions include hemodynamic abnormalities from fluid overload, hemostatic disturbances from massive transfusions, infectious organisms in donor blood (especially HB_SAg-positive hepatitis), and other complications including embolism and thrombophlebitis.

The immune reactions include allergic reactions, red cell incompatibility, incompatibilities associated with leukocytes and platelets, and alloantibody reactions.

The most serious reactions with intravascular hemolysis are usually due to ABO incompatibility. The patient develops fever, malaise, chills, and backache soon after the transfusion starts and may go into shock. Acute renal failure is the greatest risk.

The most common cause of extravascular hemolysis is Rh incompatibility with anti-Rh_0 (D). The clinical features are less severe, and their onset may be delayed for an hour. Acute renal failure is less common. Delayed transfusion reactions from Rh incompatibility may not be obvious for 4–14 days after transfusion.

Reactions to white cells and platelets involve antibodies to HLA and other cell membrane alloantigens. These reactions produce fever and chills but usually do not cause other serious complications. Specially prepared blood such as leukocyte-poor or frozen washed red cells must be used when transfusing patients who are sensitized to these antigens.

Antibodies to human serum immunoglobulins are found in some patients, and antibodies to IgA are of clinical importance. Patients with selective IgA deficiency or (rarely) hypogammaglobulinemia may develop antibodies to IgA (see Chapter 26). These antibodies include various specificities which react with the IgA class, IgA subclasses, and IgA allotypes. Subsequent exposure of such a sensitized patient to blood or blood products containing IgA may produce an urticarial reaction or even a possibly fatal anaphylactic one.

The various laboratory tests to be considered in the investigation of a suspected transfusion reaction are listed in Table 28–15.

Prevention of blood transfusion reactions depends upon adequate blood bank procedures. However, despite all precautions, nonhemolytic reactions occur in an average of 4% of transfused patients.

The first step in management of a suspected reaction is to stop the transfusion, assess the patient, and, if the reaction is very severe, administer antihistamine, corticosteroid, or pressor agents depending on the type of reaction. Every effort should be made to maintain effective circulatory volume and urine flow. Hemodialysis may be required for severe renal failure.

Table 28–15. Laboratory investigations to be considered in a patient with a suspected immune transfusion reaction.

Tests to detect hemolysis:
- Plasma hemoglobin level increased.
- Hemoglobinuria.
- Plasma haptoglobin level reduced.
- Methemalbuminemia.
- Hyperbilirubinemia.

Tests for intravascular coagulation:
- Platelet count reduced.
- Fibrinogen level low.
- Fibrin degradation products present.

Serologic studies:
- Red cells:
  - Retyping of patient's and donor's blood.
  - Direct antiglobulin test on patient's cells.
  - Indirect antiglobulin test:
    - Patient's cells plus donor plasma.
    - Donor cells plus patient's plasma.
- White cells and platelets:
  - HLA typing of patient and donor.
  - Cytotoxic antibodies (HLA-specific and HLA-nonspecific).
- Anti-immunoglobulin antibodies:
  - Antibodies to IgA and IgG.

Miscellaneous:
- Measurement of renal function.
- Complement studies.
- Blood culture (aerobic and anaerobic).

BLOOD FRACTIONATION PRODUCTS

There is increasing use of specific blood fractions rather than whole blood or packed cell transfusions in the treatment of specific diseases. Many of the complications of blood transfusion can still occur.

Plasma

Plasma and plasma products are useful for emergency treatment of hypovolemia while whole blood is being cross-matched. Fresh-frozen plasma was formerly used for the treatment of hemophilia and still may be used for other hemostatic abnormalities. It is used in patients having acute attacks of angioneurotic edema due to C1 esterase inhibitor deficiency. It is also used to provide immunoglobulins and other nonspecific factors in selected patients with humoral immunodeficiency.

Cryoprecipitate

Cryoprecipitate is formed from plasma by freezing and contains high concentrations of factor VIII. It is the most widely used preparation in the management of patients with hemophilia.

Plasma Protein Fractions

A. Immune Serum Globulin: Therapeutic human γ-globulin contains antibodies present in plasma from normal human donors and is given to patients with hypogammaglobulinemia (see Chapter 26) or patients exposed to certain infectious diseases (see Chapter 39).

B. Hyperimmune Globulins: Immune serum globulins with high titers of antibodies against specific diseases have now been prepared from convalescent donors or specifically immunized donors. They include anti-Rh_0 (D), antirubella, antivaccinia, antitetanus, antirabies, and antihepatitis immune serum globulins.

White Cell Transfusions

Increasing numbers of patients with severe leukocytopenia and infection now receive white cell (granulocyte) transfusions. These include patients with drug-induced agranulocytosis, aplastic anemia, and functional granulocyte abnormalities, as well as those with leukemia, lymphoma, or other malignancies undergoing intensive chemotherapy or radiotherapy. Preliminary studies in patients with acute leukemia, severe leukocytopenia, and bacterial sepsis show improved survival in those patients given daily granulocyte transfusions.

Granulocytes can be obtained from a donor by means of simple single unit leukapheresis, but adequate numbers for transfusion can only be obtained by either continuous flow centrifugation in a cell separator or by continuous flow filtration leukapheresis. The cell separator achieves a yield of $5-15 \times 10^9$ granulocytes from normal donors or $1-2 \times 10^{11}$ from patients with chronic myelogenous leukemia. Agents such as etiocholanolone or corticosteroids in the donor or hydroxyethyl starch in the extracorporeal circuit may double the yield. Continuous flow filtration leukapheresis is based on the fact that granulocytes adhere selectively to nylon fiber filters and subsequently can be eluted off the fibers with minimal damage.

HLA-matched donors should be used for granulocyte transfusions whenever possible, since reactions may develop in sensitized recipients.

Platelet Transfusions

Platelet transfusions are indicated for treatment or prevention of bleeding due to thrombocytopenia. They are most often used in acute leukemia and aplastic anemia. They have limited usefulness in ITP, DIC, and other thrombocytopenias due to increased platelet destruction. Sensitization often occurs in patients receiving multiple platelet transfusions from nonmatched random donors. This sensitization may be due to HLA or non-HLA antigens. Improved platelet responses may be obtained by giving sensitized patients HLA-matched platelets.

• • •

References

Leukemia

Belpomme D & others: T and B lymphocyte markers on the neoplastic cell of 20 patients with acute and 10 patients with chronic lymphoid leukemia. Biomedicine 20:109, 1974.

Foadi MD, Pegrum GD: The acute leukemias. Page 375 in: *Medical Oncology*. Bagshawe KD (editor). Blackwell, 1975.

Gunz FW, Baikie AG: *Leukemia,* 3rd ed. Grune & Stratton, 1974.

Hansen MM: Chronic lymphocytic leukemia. Scand J Haematol [Suppl] 18, 1973.

Immunotherapy for acute myeloid leukaemia. (Editorial.) Lancet 1:846, 1974.

Levin AS & others: Hematologic malignancies and other marrow failure states: Progress in the management of complicating infections. Semin Hematol 11:141, 1974.

Mann DL & others: Studies on the immunologic reactivity of sera from acute leukemia patients. Prog Exp Tumor Res 19:102, 1974.

Metzgar RS, Mohanakumar T, Miller DS: Membrane-bound immunoglobulins on human leukemic cells: Evidence for humoral immune responses of patients to leukemia-associated antigens. J Clin Invest 56:331, 1975.

Seligmann M, Preud'homme J-L, Brouet J-C: B and T cell markers in human proliferative blood diseases and primary immunodeficiencies, with special reference to membrane bound immunoglobulins. Transplant Rev 16:85, 1973.

Sen L, Borella L: Clinical importance of lymphoblasts with T markers in childhood acute leukemia. N Engl J Med 292:828, 1975.

Williams RC Jr, Messner RP: Alterations in T- and B-cells in human disease states. Annu Rev Med 26:181, 1975.

Paraproteinemias

Bloch KJ, Maki DG: Hyperviscosity syndromes associated with immunoglobulin abnormalities. Semin Hematol 10:113, 1973.

Brouet J-C & others: Biologic and clinical significance of cryoglobulins. Am J Med 57:775, 1974.

Defronzo RA & others: Acute renal failure in multiple myeloma. Medicine 54:209, 1975.

Farhangi M, Osserman EF: The treatment of multiple myeloma. Semin Hematol 10:149, 1973.

Glenner GG, Terry WD, Isersky C: Amyloidosis: Its nature and pathogenesis. Semin Hematol 10:65, 1973.

Gordon DA & others: Amyloid arthritis simulating rheumatoid disease in five patients with multiple myeloma. Am J Med 55:142, 1973.

Grey HM, Kohler PF: Cryoimmunoglobulins. Semin Hematol 10:87, 1973.

Hansen OP, Jessen B, Videbaek A: Prognosis of myelomatosis on treatment with prednisone and cytostatics. Scand J Haematol 10:282, 1973.

Isobe T, Osserman EF: Patterns of amyloidosis and their association with plasma cell dyscrasia, monoclonal immunoglobulins and Bence Jones proteins. N Engl J Med 290:474, 1974.

Jancelewicz Z & others: IgD multiple myeloma: Review of 133 cases. Arch Intern Med 135:87, 1975.

Kyle RA, Maldonado JE, Bayrd ED: Plasma cell leukemia: Report on 17 cases. Arch Intern Med 133:813, 1974.

Kyle RA, Pierre RV, Bayrd ED: Multiple myeloma and acute leukemia associated with alkylating agents. Arch Intern Med 135:185, 1975.

Lackner H: Hemostatic abnormalities associated with dysproteinemias. Semin Hematol 10:125, 1973.

Mackenzie MR, Fudenberg HH: Macroglobulinemia: An analysis of 40 patients. Blood 39:874, 1972.

Ritzmann SE & others: Idiopathic (asymptomatic) monoclonal gammopathies. Arch Intern Med 135:95, 1975.

Rodriguez LH & others: Bone healing in multiple myeloma with melphalan chemotherapy. Ann Intern Med 76:551, 1972.

Stone MJ, Frenkel EP: The clinical spectrum of light chain myeloma. Am J Med 58:601, 1975.

Wells JV, Fudenberg HH: Paraproteinemias. Disease-a-Month. February 1974.

Zawadzki ZA, Edwards GA: Nonmyelomatous monoclonal immunoglobulinemia. Prog Clin Immunol 1:105, 1972.

Malignant Lymphomas

Aisenberg AC, Long JC: Lymphocyte surface characteristics in malignant lymphoma. Am J Med 58:300, 1975.

Arseneau JC & others: American Burkitt's lymphoma: A clinicopathologic study of 30 cases. (2 parts.) Am J Med 58:314, 322, 1975.

Bodey GP: Infections in cancer patients. Cancer Treat Rev 2:89, 1975.

Davis S: Hypothesis: Differentiation of the human lymphoid system based on cell surface markers. Blood 45:871, 1975.

Epstein EH Jr & others: Mycosis fungoides. Medicine 51:61, 1972.

Long JC, Aisenberg AC, Zamecnick PC: An antigen in Hodgkin's disease tissue cultures: Radioiodine-labeled antibody studies. Proc Natl Acad Sci USA 71:2605, 1974.

Longmire RL & others: In vitro splenic IgG synthesis in Hodgkin's disease. N Engl J Med 289:763, 1973.

Lukes RJ, Collins RD: Immunologic characterization of human malignant lymphomas. Cancer 34:1488, 1974.

Lutzner M & others: Cutaneous T-cell lymphomas: The Sézary syndrome, mycosis fungoides, and related disorders. Ann Intern Med 83:534, 1975.

Nilsson K, Ponten J: Classification and biological nature of established human hematopoietic cell lines. Int J Cancer 15:321, 1975.

Stein H, Lennert K, Parwaresch MR: Malignant lymphomas of B-cell type. Lancet 2:855, 1972.

Twomey JJ & others: Hodgkin's disease: An immunodepleting and immunosuppressive disorder. J Clin Invest 56:467, 1975.

Walden PAM: The lymphomas. Page 419 in: *Medical Oncology*. Bagshawe KD (editor). Blackwell, 1975.

Winkelmann RK: Clinical studies of T-cell erythroderma in the Sézary syndrome. Mayo Clin Proc 49:519, 1974.

Ziegler JB, Hansen P, Penny R: Intrinsic lymphocyte defect in Hodgkin's disease: Analysis of the phytohemagglutinin dose-response. Clin Immunol Immunopathol 3:451, 1975.

Infectious Mononucleosis

Bar RS & others: Fatal infectious mononucleosis in a family. N Engl J Med 290:363, 1974.

Carter RL: Infectious mononucleosis: Model for self-limiting lymphoproliferation. Lancet 1:846, 1975.

Fernbach DJ, Starling KA: Infectious mononucleosis. Pediatr Clin North Am 19:957, 1972.

Henle W & others: Antibodies to early antigens induced by Epstein-Barr virus in infectious mononucleosis. J Infect Dis 124:58, 1971.

Mackinney AA, Cline WS: Infectious mononucleosis. Br J Haematol 27:367, 1974.

Miller G: The oncogenicity of Epstein-Barr virus. J Infect Dis 130:187, 1974.

Pagano JS: Diseases and mechanisms of persistent DNA virus infection: Latency and cellular transformation. J Infect Dis 132:209, 1975.

Provisor AJ & others: Acquired agammaglobulinemia after a life-threatening illness with clinical and laboratory features of infectious mononucleosis in three related male children. N Engl J Med 293:62, 1975.

Purtilo DT & others: X-linked recessive progressive combined variable immunodeficiency (Duncan's disease). Lancet 1:935, 1975.

Smith RT, Bausher JC: Epstein-Barr virus infection in relation to infectious mononucleosis and Burkitt's lymphoma. Annu Rev Med 23:39, 1972.

Stites DP, Leikola J: Infectious mononucleosis. Semin Hematol 8:243, 1971.

Leukocytopenia

Boxer LA, Yokoyama M, Lalezari P: Isoimmune neonatal neutropenia. J Pediatr 80:783, 1972.

Levin AS & others: Granulocytopenia induced by anti-cephalothin antibodies. Clin Res 19:424, 1971.

Nepo AG & others: Autoimmune neutropenia in an infant. J Pediatr 87:251, 1975.

Red Cell Disorders

Abramson N, Lee DP: Immune hemolytic anemias. Disease-a-Month. April 1974.

Atkinson JP, Frank MM: Complement-independent clearance of IgG-sensitized erythrocytes: Inhibition by cortisone. Blood 44:629, 1974.

Garratty G, Petz LD: Drug-induced immune hemolytic anemia. Am J Med 58:398, 1975.

Krantz SB: Pure red cell aplasia. Br J Haematol 25:1, 1973.

Petz LD, Garratty G: Laboratory correlations in immune hemolytic anemias. Page 139 in: *Laboratory Diagnosis of Immunologic Disorders.* Vyas GN, Stites DP, Brecher G (editors). Grune & Stratton, 1975.

Shulman NR: Analyses of drug antibodies with autoimmune implications. Page 31 in: *Laboratory Diagnosis of Immunologic Disorders.* Vyas GN, Stites DP, Brecher G (editors). Grune & Stratton, 1975.

Platelet Disorders

Clancy R: Cellular immunity to autologous platelets and serum-blocking factors in idiopathic thrombocytopenic purpura. Lancet 1:6, 1972.

Finch SC & others: Immunosuppressive therapy of chronic idiopathic thrombocytopenic purpura. Am J Med 56: 4, 1974.

Gardner FH: Idiopathic thrombocytopenic purpura. Page 1111 in: *Immunological Diseases,* 2nd ed. Samter M (editor). Little, Brown, 1971.

MacDonald JS & others: Complement-dependent and cell-dependent antiplatelet humoral antibody in sera from multi-transfused patients. Clin Exp Immunol 21:259, 1975.

McClure PD: Idiopathic thrombocytopenic purpura in children: Diagnosis and management. Pediatrics 55:68, 1975.

Osler AG, Siraganian RP: Immunologic mechanisms of platelet damage. Prog Allergy 16:450, 1972.

Wybran J, Fudenberg HH: Cellular immunity to platelets in idiopathic thrombocytopenic purpura. Blood 40:856, 1972.

Bone Marrow Transplantation

Camitta BM & others: Selection of patients for bone marrow transplantation in severe aplastic anemia. Blood 45:355, 1975.

Cline MJ & others: Bone marrow transplantation in man. Ann Intern Med 83:691, 1975.

Good RA, Bach FH: Bone marrow and thymus transplants: Cellular engineering to correct primary immunodeficiency. Clin Immunobiol 2:63, 1974.

Mathé G & others: Bone marrow transplantation for aplasias and leukemias. Clin Immunobiol 2:33, 1974.

Pagano JS: Infections with cytomegalovirus in bone marrow transplantation: Report of a workshop. J Infect Dis 132:114, 1975.

Storb R & others: Treatment of established human graft-versus-host disease by antithymocyte globulin. Blood 44:57, 1974.

Thomas ED: Bone marrow transplantation. Clin Immunobiol 2:1, 1974.

Thomas ED & others: Bone-marrow transplantation. (2 parts.) N Engl J Med 292:832, 895, 1975.

Hemostatic Disorders

Barrow EM, Graham JB: Blood coagulation factor VIII (antihemophilic factor)–with comments on von Willebrand's disease and Christmas disease. Physiol Rev 54:23, 1974.

Koutts J & others: Heterogeneity in biological activity of human factor VIII antibodies. Br J Haematol 29:99, 1975.

Rizza CR & others: Detection of carriers of haemophilia: A blind study. Br J Haematol 30:447, 1975.

Sarji KE & others: Nature of von Willebrand factor: A new assay and a specific inhibitor. Proc Natl Acad Sci USA 71:2937, 1974.

Zimmerman TS, Edgington TS: Molecular immunology of factor VIII. Annu Rev Med 25:303, 1974.

Blood Replacement Therapy

Cline MJ & others: Granulocytes in human disease. Ann Intern Med 81:801, 1974.

Dodd BE, Lincoln PJ: *Blood Group Topics.* Vol 3. *Current Topics in Immunology Series.* Turk JL (editor). Arnold, 1975.

Foerster J, Wintrobe MM: Blood groups and blood transfusion. Page 1631 in: *Harrison's Principles of Internal Medicine,* 7th ed. Wintrobe MM & others (editors). McGraw-Hill, 1974.

Gardner FH: Use of platelet transfusions. Br J Haematol 27:537, 1974.

Goldman JM: Leucocyte separation and transfusion. Br J Haematol 28:271, 1974.

Herzig RH & others: Correction of poor platelet transfusion responses with leukocyte-poor HL-A matched platelet concentrates. Blood 46:743, 1975.

Mantalenaki-Asfi K & others: Influence of exchange transfusion on the development of serum immunoglobulins. J Pediatr 87:396, 1975.

Marcus DM: The ABO and Lewis blood-group system. N Engl J Med 280:994, 1969.

Morgan WTJ, Watkins WM: Genetic and biochemical aspects of human blood group A-, B-, H-, Le^a- and Le^b-specificity. Br Med Bull 25:30, 1969.

Perkins HA: Immunologic investigation of transfusion reactions. Page 201 in: *Laboratory Diagnosis of Immunologic Disorders.* Vyas GN, Stites DP, Brecher G (editors). Grune & Stratton, 1975.

Schiffer CA & others: Clinical experience with transfusion of granulocytes obtained by continuous flow filtration leukapheresis. Am J Med 58:373, 1975.

29 . . .
Allergic Diseases

Abba I. Terr, MD

Immunologic defense against infectious microorganisms, toxins, neoplasms, and tissue grafts involves recognition of the foreign nature of antigens and the resultant activation of cellular and humoral mediators of inflammation. Allergy results from the same immunologically mediated mechanism of inflammation, but it usually involves environmental antigens that are not intrinsically harmful. Allergic diseases have been classified by Gell and Coombs into 4 types based on the nature of the immunologic reaction:

Type I: IgE antibodies fixed to mast cells react with antigen, triggering release of histamine and activation of slow-reacting substance (SRS-A) and eosinophil chemotactic factor (ECF-A). This is the mechanism responsible for atopy, anaphylaxis, urticaria, and angioedema (Chapter 19).

Type II: IgG or IgM antibodies react with antigen on target cells and activate complement, causing cell lysis. This occurs in certain types of drug reactions.

Type III: IgG or IgM antibodies form complexes with antigen and complement, generating neutrophil chemotactic factors with resultant local tissue inflammation and destruction. Serum sickness involves this mechanism.

Type IV: Sensitized T lymphocytes react directly with antigen, producing inflammation through the action of lymphokines. The principal example is allergic contact dermatitis.

Certain allergic diseases may be expressions of 2 or more types. This chapter will deal primarily with type I allergy, whereas the remaining types are discussed throughout the clinical immunology chapters.

ATOPY

About one out of every 10 persons in the USA suffers from symptomatic atopic disease. The most common is allergic rhinitis, usually seasonal pollen allergy (hay fever). Less frequently, atopic disease is expressed as bronchial asthma or atopic dermatitis, and rarely as gastrointestinal food allergy. The patient may have 2 or more manifestations of the atopic state, but not always at the same time.

Atopic allergy is a type I hypersensitivity reaction to environmental antigens (allergens) in genetically susceptible individuals who produce IgE antibodies to allergens such as pollens, molds, house dust, animal danders, or foods. Exposure to the offending allergen results in the release of mediators, including histamine, SRS-A, and ECF-A, in the target organ. The action of these mediators on blood vessels, smooth muscle, and secretory glands with its associated inflammatory reaction is responsible for the clinical manifestations and pathologic features of the disease. Individual allergic sensitivities can usually be identified accurately, but the clinical manifestations are modified and influenced by many nonimmunologic factors such as infections, emotions, and drugs.

Genetic factors have long been suspected in atopy, and there is a strong familial clustering of cases. IgE antibody responses are present in normal persons and are not unique to atopic patients, so the genetic control in atopy is probably in the absorption or processing of antigen prior to its exposure to IgE antibody-forming cells. IgE antibody to ragweed in hay fever patients has recently been shown to be determined by an immune response (Ir) gene closely linked to the histocompatibility gene complex. The IgE response to inhaled antigens could also be caused by enhanced absorption of antigens through respiratory mucous membranes.

Atopic Allergens

The patient with atopic disease may be sensitive to one or many allergens, and the success of treatment may depend on their identification.

A. Inhalants: Plant pollens, fungal spores, animal danders, and certain airborne particles in the home are the most common inhalant allergens.

Wind-pollinated (anemophilous) plants discharge large numbers of light-weight pollen grains into the air. These pollens are buoyant and can be dispersed by wind currents over a wide area. Within each geographic location, the common allergenic trees, grasses, and weeds pollinate each year during a specific and predictable season. For example, in midwestern USA the important allergenic trees—maple, elm, oak, and birch—pollinate for 6 or 8 weeks beginning with the

Abba I. Terr is Clinical Associate Professor of Medicine, Stanford University School of Medicine, Stanford.

spring thaw; grass pollen appears principally during June and July; and the weeds pollinate from the middle of August until the first frost. Pollinating seasons in the Far West are long and overlapping. In the San Francisco Bay Area, for example, there are about 12 important allergenic trees with pollen seasons covering the period from December through September; this overlaps with the grass and weed pollen season, which begins in April and continues through October. Allergists must be familiar with the allergenic plants and pollinating seasons in their area. Air-sampling devices for identifying and quantitating pollen are available, and their use requires a person trained in pollen morphology.

Plants with attractive flowers are generally insect-pollinated and therefore not important in allergy because they produce small amounts of heavy pollen which does not become airborne and thus is not inhaled.

Spores of fungi in soil and on decaying vegetation are important aeroallergens and are found in air samples in significant quantities throughout the year except when there is snow cover on the ground. Although sensitivity to fungi is less common than pollen allergy, the spores of *Alternaria, Hormodendrum, Helminthosporium, Aspergillus, Pullularia, Mucor, Rhizopus, Penicillium,* and others are important allergens for some patients. Rusts and smuts that infect certain crops and grasses also produce allergenic spores.

In certain localities, insect debris has been identified as the cause of allergic symptoms in some patients.

House dust is the most common indoor allergen. For many dust-sensitive patients, the allergen is a house dust mite, *Dermatophagoides farinae* or *D pteronyssinus.* These mites flourish on human skin scales and are found especially in dust from pillows and mattresses. Feathers in down pillows, quilts, comforters, sleeping bags, or jackets may be allergenic. Animal danders from household pets (cats, dogs, hamsters, guinea pigs) or from horses, farm stock, or zoo animals also cause allergy.

The patient's occupation can sometimes be responsible for allergy. A prominent example of this is baker's asthma. The repeated inhalation of wheat flour by bakers results in allergic rhinitis or asthma in about 25% of bakers. Sensitization to toluene diisocyanate in some workers in the plastics industry and to platinum salts in some chemists has been described.

B. Ingestants: Absorption of allergens from the alimentary tract can lead to IgE antibody production with subsequent allergic symptoms to foods, food additives, and drugs.

C. Contactants: Direct skin contact with a pollen or food can cause localized urticaria or systemic allergic symptoms in a patient highly sensitive to the allergen.

SKIN TESTING FOR IMMEDIATE HYPERSENSITIVITY

Skin tests are used to determine specific immediate sensitivity in patients with atopic disease or anaphylaxis. Within minutes after introduction of the allergen, histamine released from skin mast cells causes vasodilatation (erythema), localized edema from increased vascular permeability (wheal), and pruritus. The skin reacts to allergen in almost all patients with type I allergy, even though their symptoms occur in other target organs, such as the nose, conjunctiva, lungs, or gastrointestinal tract. Many tests with different allergens can be performed simultaneously. Skin testing is convenient, safe, and reliable, and experience over many years has shown it to be useful for diagnosis in most patients with suspected allergic disease if care is taken to correlate the findings with the history and other clinical information.

Antihistaminic drugs inhibit or diminish skin test responses and so must be discontinued 24 hours or more before testing. Hydroxyzine is inhibitory for as long as 1 week. Xanthines, sympathomimetic drugs, corticosteroids, and cromolyn sodium do not inhibit immediate skin test reactions and need not be withdrawn prior to testing.

Best results are obtained by using a combination of cutaneous and intracutaneous methods, and each test series should include the diluent as a control. Some allergists also include histamine or a nonspecific histamine liberator (or both) as positive controls, although these are not necessary for routine use.

Cutaneous Tests

Cutaneous tests should always be done first. Either prick or scratch testing can be used. The tests are applied to the back or the volar surfaces of the forearms, depending upon the number of tests. The skin is cleansed with a sterile alcohol pledget and then wiped dry. In prick testing, a drop of concentrated extract is applied and a needle prick of the skin is made through the drop. After 20 minutes, the drop is wiped off and the reaction is quantitated and recorded as indicated in Table 29–1. When properly done, the control is negative, and a result 2+ or greater is significant. Allergens giving a negative or 1+ prick test should be retested intracutaneously.

Scratch tests are done by making a short linear scratch in the skin to which the allergen is then applied. This method is more likely to produce nonspecific irritant reactions, causes more discomfort to the patient, and occasionally leaves scars.

Intracutaneous Tests

Negative or questionable prick tests must always be followed by the more definitive intracutaneous test. This is a more sensitive technic but has the disadvantage of being more likely to produce a systemic reaction in a highly sensitive subject. Intracutaneous tests should always be done on the extremities. The

Table 29–1. Wheal and erythema skin tests.

	Reaction	Appearances
Prick	Neg	No wheal or erythema.
	1+	No wheal; erythema <20 mm in diameter.
	2+	No wheal; erythema >20 mm in diameter.
	3+	Wheal and erythema.
	4+	Wheal with pseudopods; erythema.
Intracutaneous	Neg	Same as control.
	1+	Wheal twice that of control; erythema < 20 mm in diameter.
	2+	Wheal twice that of control; erythema > 20 mm in diameter.
	3+	Wheal 3 times that of control; erythema.
	4+	Wheal with pseudopods; erythema.

Table 29–2. Allergenic plant pollens and mold spores in the San Francisco Bay Area.*

Trees and Shrubs	Weeds	Grasses	Fungi
Acacia	Beach sandbur	Bermuda	Alternaria
Alder	Cocklebur	Bluegrass	Aspergillus
Ash	English plantain	Brome	Cephalothecium
Birch	Lamb's quarters	Orchard	Fusarium
Box elder	Mugwort	Perennial rye	Helminthosporium
Cottonwood	Pickleweed	Sweet vernal	Hormodendrum
Cypress	Pigweed	Velvet	Mucor
Elm	Ragweed, false	Wild oat	Penicillium
Juniper	Ragweed, western		Rhizopus
Live oak	Russian thistle		
Mulberry	Sheep sorrel		
Olive	Wingscale		
Privet			
Sycamore			
Walnut			

*Example of one area's allergenic pollens. For further details regarding other geographical areas see Samter M, Durham OC: *Regional Allergy of the US, Canada, Mexico and Cuba.* Thomas, 1955.

lateral aspect of the upper arm is preferred, but the volar aspect of the forearm may be used. The number of intracutaneous tests should be limited to about 12 at one sitting even though the allergens have been shown to be prick test-negative for that patient.

The skin is wiped with a sterile alcohol pledget as for any injection. No more than 0.01 ml (preferably 0.005 ml) of sterile extract is injected intracutaneously and the reaction read in 20 minutes as indicated in Table 29–1. A 2+ or greater reaction is considered a positive test. Many allergens give false-positive irritant reactions if a high concentration is injected even in nonallergic individuals, so the proper concentration is important and must be determined for each allergen. A 1:500 (w/v) dilution of pollens and fungi is generally satisfactory for routine use. Some allergists use serial dilution titrations for each allergen, but this is time-consuming and rarely provides more diagnostic information than a single properly selected dilution.

Selection of Tests

The specific allergens to be tested should be determined by the history. Table 29–2 lists the important pollen and mold allergens for patients living in the San Francisco Bay Area. Extracts of house dust, feathers, danders from various animals, and other common inhalant allergens are readily available, but occasionally it is necessary to test materials directly from the patient's home or place of work.

Skin testing in patients with suspected food allergy is discussed elsewhere.

The intensity of the skin test reaction is also influenced by a number of factors not directly related to the patient's symptoms, such as the potency of the extract and reactivity of the skin. The size of the skin test response therefore should not be used to indicate how "allergic" the patient is to that particular allergen, although it should be considered in assessing the possible risk of a systemic reaction in immunotherapy.

For patch testing, see Chapter 33.

IMMUNOTHERAPY (Hyposensitization)

Treatment of allergic disease requires long-term use of a variety of measures, including avoidance of allergens, drug therapy, and immunotherapy. It must be individualized and periodically reassessed.

The offending allergen should be avoided if possible. In food or drug allergy, this can be accomplished once the offending allergen is identified. Elimination of inhalant allergens is generally more difficult. Removal of the animal pet from the household, dust control measures, synthetic materials in pillow stuffing, and a dehumidifier to inhibit molds are all helpful when indicated, but there is no way to avoid airborne pollens or mold spores from outdoor sources. Avoidance of pollens and molds from outdoor sources is possible only if the patient can remain indoors in an air-conditioned environment. Immunotherapy is effective in reducing symptoms of allergic rhinitis in patients with seasonal pollen allergy and is probably effective also in mold or dust allergy.

Several immunologic changes occur during the course of immunotherapy in atopic patients. Circulating IgE antibody increases slightly during the initial months of treatment and then gradually falls below pretreatment levels over a period of several years. However, it is rarely eliminated completely, ie, a true state of desensitization is seldom achieved. Blocking antibody, which is an IgG antibody with specificity for the injected allergen that binds circulating allergen without initiating a type I reaction, appears in the serum of most treated patients. The normal postseasonal rise in IgE antibody to pollens is abolished by immunotherapy, suggesting that treatment may induce a form of partial immunologic tolerance.

Clinical improvement during immunotherapy correlates better with blocking antibody response than with other immunologic changes, but a combination of several mechanisms might be required for optimal results. This treatment is effective but empirical, and a better understanding of the mechanism of immunotherapy should lead to improvements in methods of treatment.

Methods of Treatment

Several types of injection schedules have been devised, but only 2 are in current general use: perennial and preseasonal. In the perennial method, the patient receives injections containing a mixture of the relevant allergens throughout the year. Treatment is begun at a dosage low enough to avoid any local or systemic reactions, and frequent injections, usually once or twice a week, are administered at increasing dosages until the highest dose the patient can tolerate without excessive local or systemic reactions is reached. This is the maintenance dose, which is then continued at less frequent intervals, usually every 1–6 weeks depending upon the patient's response. If treatment is begun during a pollen season, the starting dose must be quite low to avoid reactions.

In the preseasonal method, frequent injections of increasing dosages are administered beginning 3–6 months before the anticipated start of the pollen season, and the treatment is stopped just before the season begins. The same procedure is repeated each year. This is a more cumbersome method to use in patients with multiple seasonal allergies.

Because of the large number of injections required in immunotherapy of atopic disease, several attempts have been made to use immunologic adjuvants to reduce the number of injections to as few as one for each season. Freund's incomplete adjuvant, an emulsion of aqueous allergen extract suspended in mineral oil and administered intramuscularly, was given extensive trials in the 1960s but is rarely used today because of concern about possible adverse effects of mineral oil in tissues. Alum-adsorbed allergen extracts are available commercially, but studies have not yet shown that they are superior to aqueous allergens. Formalin treatment of allergens to render them nonallergenic while retaining immunogenicity ("allergoids") is an approach currently under study with the aim of achieving good blocking antibody levels in all patients without risk of allergic reactions.

Technic of Administering Allergy Injections

The success of immunotherapy using conventional aqueous extracts requires proper technic. Injections are given subcutaneously using a tuberculin syringe for accurate measurement of the dose and a 26 or 27 gauge needle. The preferred site is the lateral or dorsal aspect of the upper arm, about midway between the shoulder and elbow. Excess allergen on the needle should be wiped away and the injection given slowly. The patient should be observed for 20 minutes afterwards so that a systemic reaction can be treated immediately if it occurs. In the event of a systemic reaction, the next dose should be decreased. Swelling up to 3 or 4 cm in diameter lasting less than 24 hours and accompanied by erythema and itching is to be expected at the maintenance dose level. Local reactions greater than this indicate the need to reduce the dose.

Duration of Treatment

The optimum length of treatment differs for each patient. When injections are continued for several years, most patients report that symptoms lessen with each succeeding year. After 2 full years with little or no allergic symptoms, it is probably desirable to discontinue the injections, although many patients want to continue on a maintenance dose even longer.

Adverse Effects of Immunotherapy

Immunotherapy of atopic disease is effective, and the risk of discomfort or serious reaction is relatively low if treatment is done properly. The principal danger is the immediate systemic reaction, an anaphylactic response to an excessively high dose or inadvertent administration into a blood vessel. The symptoms and treatment of anaphylaxis are discussed below. Reactions to allergy injections can be minimized by scrupulous record-keeping, questioning the patient each time about local reactions from the previous dose, and proper technic of administration. Anaphylactic deaths have occurred from allergy injections, but in most cases this has been attributed to an incorrect dose or improper procedure.

There is no evidence that repeated administration of allergens to atopic patients induces other forms of immunologic disease.

ALLERGIC RHINITIS
(Hay Fever)

Major Immunologic Features

- Allergic rhinitis is the most common clinical expression of atopic hypersensitivity.
- Allergic rhinitis is type I allergy localized in the nasal mucosa and conjunctiva.
- Pollens, fungal spores, dust, and animal danders are the usual atmospheric allergens.

General Considerations

Allergic rhinitis is the most common manifestation of an atopic reaction to inhaled allergens. At least 20 million persons in the USA suffer from this disease. The disease can begin at any age, but the onset is usually during childhood or adolescence.

The immunologic pathogenesis of allergic rhinitis is discussed above along with the discussion of atopy.

Clinical Features

A. Symptoms and Signs: A typical attack consists

of symptoms of profuse watery rhinorrhea, paroxysmal sneezing, and nasal obstruction. Itching of the nose and palate is common. There is frequently an accompanying allergic blepharoconjunctivitis, with intense itching of the conjunctiva and eyelids. In some patients, conjunctivitis may occur in the absence of nasal symptoms. The disease occurs seasonally in patients with pollen allergy, year-round if the sensitivity is to a perennial allergen such as house dust, or there may be perennial symptoms with seasonal exacerbations in patients with multiple allergies. Severe attacks are often accompanied by systemic symptoms of malaise and sometimes muscle soreness after intense periods of sneezing. Fever is absent. Swelling of the nasal mucosa may lead to headache because of obstruction of the ostia of the paranasal sinuses.

Physical examination shows a pale, swollen nasal mucosa with watery secretions. The conjunctiva is suffused or injected, and the lids are frequently swollen. These changes revert to normal when there is no allergen exposure and the patient is asymptomatic.

B. Laboratory Findings: Eosinophils are numerous in the nasal secretions, but blood eosinophilia is slight. IgE levels in serum are normal or slightly elevated.

Immunologic Diagnosis

The diagnosis of allergic rhinitis is based on the history, physical findings during a symptomatic phase, and nasal eosinophilia. Wheal-and-erythema skin tests will detect the specific sensitivities.

Differential Diagnosis

Chronic vasomotor rhinitis is a common disorder of unknown cause in which the primary complaint is nasal congestion, usually associated with postnasal drainage. It differs from allergic rhinitis by the absence of sneezing paroxysms, minimal rhinorrhea, and lack of eye symptoms. The congestion may be unilateral or bilateral and often shifts with position. Symptoms occur year-round and are generally worse in cold weather or in dry climates. The nasal mucosa is unusually sensitive to irritants such as tobacco smoke, fumes, and smog. Symptoms usually begin in adult life, and the disease is more common among women. It may begin during pregnancy. Examination shows swollen, erythematous nasal mucosa and strands of thick mucoid postnasal discharge in the pharynx. Allergy skin tests are negative or unrelated to the symptoms. There is a good response to decongestants and humidification, but antihistamines are usually not effective.

Rhinitis medicamentosa denotes the severe congestion that occurs from the rebound effect of sympathomimetic nasal sprays or nose drops used excessively. In this disease the mucosa is often bright red and swollen, but these changes are reversible with complete avoidance of nose drops or sprays even if they have been used excessively for many years.

Infectious rhinitis is almost always due to a virus, and most patients with allergic rhinitis can distinguish their allergic symptoms from those of a common cold, which usually produces fever, an erythematous nasal mucosa, and polymorphonuclear rather than eosinophilic exudate in the nasal secretions. Primary bacterial or fungal infections of the nasal passages are rare.

Treatment

Treatment consists of environmental measures to avoid allergen exposure, drugs, and immunotherapy.

A. Avoidance of Allergen: In any allergic disease, avoidance of the allergen is the ideal method of treatment. Elimination of household pets, control of house dust exposure by frequent cleaning and avoidance of dust-collecting toys or other objects in the bedroom, and dehumidification and repair of leaking pipes or roofs to prevent mold growth are indicated where these are appropriate to the patient's allergy. Avoidance of pollen and outdoor molds is not possible unless the patient is able to stay in an air-conditioned home or office. In some cases the patient might arrange his vacation trip to a pollen-free area during the peak pollen season.

B. Drug Treatment: Antihistaminics are the most useful drugs in allergic rhinitis, although they have drawbacks. They act as competitive inhibitors of histamine and so must be used repeatedly and regularly to be effective, and their usefulness is restricted by their sedative property. Antihistaminics also have anticholinergic activity, producing dryness of the mouth which may be unacceptable to some patients, and they occasionally cause nausea, dizziness, or blurred vision. Nasal decongestants may be helpful, either alone or in combination with antihistaminics. Sympathomimetic eye drops are useful for allergic conjunctivitis.

Corticosteroids can be extremely effective in relieving symptoms of allergic rhinitis, but since the disease is a chronic, recurrent, benign condition, these drugs should be used with extreme care. An occasional patient with very severe symptoms lasting for only a few days or several weeks each year who does not respond to antihistaminics can be given oral prednisone or nasal dexamethasone spray for 1 or 2 weeks in a dosage low enough to repress symptoms for that patient. Dexamethasone spray is readily absorbed and can lead to systemic effects and adrenocortical suppression.

C. Immunotherapy: Immunotherapy has been shown to be effective in allergic rhinitis. Because of the length of treatment required and the potential danger of serious systemic reactions, injection treatment is used in patients whose symptoms are uncontrolled in spite of appropriate environmental measures and symptomatic medications. This is discussed in detail above.

Complications & Prognosis

Bronchial asthma may develop in patients with allergic rhinitis, but this is another atopic manifestation rather than a complication per se. Secondary purulent sinusitis and otitis media can result from obstruction of the sinus ostia or auditory tubes, respectively. The development of nasal polyps is not directly related to the severity of the allergic disease.

Although no definitive studies have been done on the course of untreated allergic rhinitis, symptoms can be expected to recur or persist for many years, if not for life, although the severity of the symptoms is dependent upon the degree of exposure to the allergen. A patient with pollen allergy who moves to an area devoid of that particular plant will no longer be symptomatic.

ASTHMA

Major Immunologic Features

- Allergic asthma is a manifestation of type I allergy localized in the bronchus.
- Immunologically released or activated mediators are histamine, SRS-A, and ECF-A.
- Hyperirritability of bronchial mucosa amplifies the bronchoconstricting effects of mediators.

General Considerations

Bronchial asthma is a chronic disease characterized by hyperirritability of the bronchial mucosa and eosinophilia. It may begin at any age and results in attacks of wheezing and dyspnea which can range in severity from mild discomfort to life-threatening respiratory failure. Some patients are symptom-free between attacks, whereas others are never entirely free of airway obstruction.

Extrinsic asthma (allergic, atopic, or immunologic asthma). About 50% of asthmatics have evidence of atopic allergy. As a group they generally develop the disease early in life, usually in infancy or childhood. Other manifestations of atopy—eczema or allergic rhinitis—often coexist. A family history of atopic disease is common. Attacks of asthma occur during pollen seasons, in the presence of animals, or on exposure to house dust, feather pillows, or other allergens, depending upon that patient's particular allergic sensitivities. Skin tests give positive wheal and flare reactions to the suspected allergens. Total serum IgE concentration is frequently elevated but is sometimes normal.

Intrinsic asthma (nonallergic or idiopathic asthma). It is characteristic of this type of asthma to appear first during adult life, usually after an apparent respiratory infection, so that the term "adult-onset asthma" is sometimes applied to this disorder. This term should be discarded because in some cases the disease first appears during childhood, and some allergic asthmatics become symptomatic for the first time as adults because they have not previously been exposed to the relevant allergen. Intrinsic asthma pursues a relentless course with chronic or recurrent bronchial obstruction unrelated to pollen seasons or exposure to other allergens. Skin tests are negative to the usual atopic allergens. Serum IgE concentration is normal. The personal and family histories are usually negative for other atopic diseases.

Immunologic Pathogenesis

The cause of asthma is unknown. There is evidence that bronchoconstriction is mediated by an autonomic reflex mechanism involving (1) afferent receptors in the bronchial mucosa or submucosa which respond to irritants or chemical mediators and (2) efferent cholinergic (vagal) impulses causing bronchial muscle contraction. In the asthmatic patient, these receptors appear to be sensitized to respond to a low threshold of stimulation. It has been proposed that the hyperirritable state of the bronchial mucosa results from defective functioning or blockade of the beta-adrenergic receptor, preventing a homeostatic bronchodilating response from endogenous catecholamines.

The abnormality is presumably the same in all asthmatics, differing only in degree. In allergic asthma, allergen-induced attacks can be initiated by direct reaction between inhaled allergen and IgE antibody on bronchial mast cells, releasing histamine and SRS-A to stimulate local bronchial receptors, or indirectly by allergen or mediators reaching the site via the circulation if the allergen is ingested or injected.

Clinical Features

A. Symptoms and Signs: The asthmatic attack causes shortness of breath, wheezing, and tightness in the chest, with difficulty in moving air during both inspiration and expiration. Coughing is usually present, and with prolonged asthma the cough may produce thick, tenacious sputum which may be either clear or yellow. Physical examination during the attack shows tachypnea, audible wheezing, and use of the accessory muscles of respiration. The pulse is usually rapid, and blood pressure may be elevated. Pulsus paradoxus indicates severe asthma. The lung fields are hyperresonant, and auscultation reveals diminished breath sounds, wheezes, and rhonchi but no rales.

B. Laboratory Findings: Blood and sputum eosinophilia are characteristic of asthma, whether or not allergy is present. The chest x-ray may be normal during the attack or may show signs of hyperinflation, and there may be transient scattered parenchymal densities indicating focal atelectasis caused by mucous plugging in scattered portions of the airway.

Pulmonary function tests show the abnormalities of airway obstructive disease. Flow rates and FEV_1* are decreased, vital capacity is normal or decreased, and total lung capacity and functional residual capacity are increased over normal values. Diffusing capacity is usually normal or slightly increased but may be decreased with extreme bronchospasm. Following administration of a bronchodilator, such as isoproterenol in aerosol form, ventilation improves, with significant increase in flow rates and FEV_1, indicating the reversible

*FEV_1 = forced expiratory volume in 1 second, the greatest amount of air that can be expelled in that time beginning with full inspiration.

nature of the bronchial obstruction. The lack of response to isoproterenol in a patient already receiving large doses of sympathomimetic drugs does not rule out reversibility, and the test should be repeated at a later date after additional treatment such as hydration, corticosteroids, and chest physical therapy.

Repeated tests of ventilatory function are helpful in the long-term management of the asthmatic patient. Serial determinations of FEV_1, maximal expiratory flow rate (MEFR), or peak flow rates are easily done with inexpensive equipment in the office or clinic, and they will often detect degrees of airway obstruction not apparent to the patient or on auscultation of the chest.

Increased total eosinophil count in the peripheral blood is almost invariably present unless suppressed by corticosteroids or sympathomimetic drugs. Sputum examination reveals eosinophils, Charcot-Leyden crystals, and Curschmann's spirals.

Immunologic Diagnosis

The diagnosis of bronchial asthma is based on the history, physical examination, and pulmonary function tests. The history is the primary diagnostic tool for evaluating the presence of allergy and identifying the relevant allergens. In general, those inhalant allergens that are important in allergic rhinitis are also implicated in allergic asthma: pollens, fungi, animal danders, house dust, and other household and occupational airborne allergens. In young children and infants, allergy to foods may also cause asthma. If atopic allergy is suggested by the history, skin testing for wheal and flare reactions will verify the specific sensitivities to inhalant allergens but is unreliable for detection of food allergens.

Bronchial inhalation challenge testing with allergenic extracts has been proposed as more definitive than skin tests, but this procedure has a number of inherent drawbacks. Aqueous allergen extract in aerosol form is not deposited in the same portion of the airway as are naturally inhaled pollen grains, mold spores, or other allergenic particles. Some extracts may be irritating and therefore may give nonspecific irritant responses. The testing procedure is cumbersome and time-consuming compared to skin testing. A positive bronchial challenge may provoke severe bronchospasm, causing discomfort and danger to the patient, so the procedure must be done in a hospital with appropriate measures for immediate control of the severe asthmatic reaction. It should not be used for routine evaluation.

Differential Diagnosis

Chronic bronchitis and emphysema (chronic obstructive lung disease) produce airway obstruction that does not respond to sympathomimetic bronchodilators or corticosteroids, and there is no associated eosinophilia in the blood or sputum. In children, acute bronchiolitis, cystic fibrosis, aspiration of a foreign body, and airway obstruction caused by a congenital vascular anomaly must be considered. Benign or malignant bronchial tumors or external compression from an enlarged substernal thyroid, thymus enlargement, aneurysm, or mediastinal tumor may cause wheezing. Acute viral bronchitis may produce enough bronchial inflammation with symptoms of obstruction and wheezing to be called asthmatic bronchitis. Cardiac asthma is mild, intermittent dyspnea (resembling allergic asthma) caused by left ventricular failure. Carcinoid tumors may occasionally cause attacks of wheezing because of release of serotonin or activation of kinins by the neoplasm.

Treatment

Since the cause of asthma is unknown, correction of the basic defect, the hyperirritable bronchial mucosa, is not possible. The aim of treatment is symptomatic control with drugs, environmental measures, and immunotherapy.

A. Drug Treatment:

1. Sympathomimetics–Adrenergic bronchodilator drugs are the mainstay of treatment and are used in the acute attack or for long-term management. Epinephrine, 0.2–0.5 ml of 1:1000 aqueous solution given subcutaneously, acts rapidly and is the first drug to be used for the acute attack. Its duration of action is short, so that if repeated injections are required, long-acting epinephrine 1:200 (Sus-Phrine) or epinephrine in oil (2 mg/ml) can be used. Epinephrine can also be given by inhalation as an aerosol, but isoproterenol is preferable because of its predominant β-adrenergic activity. It is available as a solution to be administered by a hand-held nebulizer or in an intermittent positive pressure breathing (IPPB) device. It is also dispensed in convenient metered-dose pressurized inhalers, but these may be dangerously overused. Patients must be cautioned that overuse can lead to paradoxic bronchial constriction and worsening of the asthma. Deaths from isoproterenol aerosol abuse have been reported.

The most widely used oral sympathomimetic bronchodilator is ephedrine sulfate. The dose is 25 mg 4 times daily, often combined in a fixed combination with a xanthine and a sedative. Recently, 2 oral β-adrenergic drugs—terbutaline and metaproterenol—have become available, but their clinical superiority over ephedrine has yet to be established. Side-effects of nervousness, muscle twitching, palpitations, tachycardia, and insomnia can occur with all sympathomimetic drugs.

2. Xanthines–Aminophylline and related compounds are bronchodilators especially effective when used in combination with sympathomimetic drugs. Intravenous aminophylline, 250–500 mg, can be administered fairly rapidly in the acute asthmatic attack, and various oral forms of theophylline are available for long-term oral use. Absorption of the drug when given orally may be erratic, so determination of blood theophylline levels may be helpful in adjusting the dose in individual cases. Rectal administration of aminophylline by enema or suppository results in excellent absorption and may obviate the need for intravenous use if the attack is not too critical.

3. Corticosteroids–Glucocorticoids are remarkably effective in the treatment of asthma. Even when all other forms of treatment have failed, the response to adequate steroid treatment is so dependable that failure of response might be considered grounds for questioning the diagnosis of asthma. The mechanism of action is unknown, and these drugs are just as effective in reversing asthma in nonallergic patients as in patients suffering allergen-induced attacks.

In spite of their effectiveness, however, corticosteroids should not be considered primary agents in the treatment of asthma, and in actual practice their use is often reserved for situations in which other forms of treatment prove inadequate. The dangers of long-term steroid usage must be kept in mind by any physician using these drugs.

Treatment is started in high dosage and continued until the obstruction is alleviated, with return of physical findings and flow rates to normal. The dose necessary to achieve this varies with the individual patient, but 30–60 mg of prednisone daily are usually sufficient. An occasional steroid-resistant patient may require a much higher dose because of abnormally accelerated rate of drug catabolism. After complete clearing of the attack, the daily dose is reduced by slow tapering over many days or weeks to avoid a flare-up. Long-term maintenance therapy is required by some patients, using a dose as low as possible to maintain symptomatic control, usually at a level of 10–15 mg of prednisone daily. Single-dose alternate-day maintenance therapy minimizes adrenocortical suppression, but not all steroid-dependent asthmatic patients can be controlled in this fashion.

4. Cromolyn sodium—This drug is a powder administered in 20 mg doses by inhalation using a specially designed inhaler. It is not a bronchodilator but is believed to inhibit release of mediators of immediate hypersensitivity in the lung. It is administered as long-term prophylactic treatment and is more effective in younger patients with allergic asthma than in adults. Cromolyn has no effect in the acute attack.

5. Other drugs—Antibiotics are used if secondary bacterial bronchitis or pneumonia occurs. Expectorants and hydration are helpful for thick, tenacious sputum.

B. Environmental Control: Irritants such as smoke, fumes, dust, and aerosols should be avoided. If the diagnostic evaluation indicates allergy to animal danders, feathers, molds, or house dust, these should be eliminated from the house.

C. Immunotherapy: The effectiveness of injection treatment in pollen hay fever has been shown in several controlled studies, and most allergists feel that allergic asthma responds just as well. (See section on immunotherapy, above.)

D. Treatment of Status Asthmaticus and Respiratory Failure: A severe attack of asthma unresponsive to repeated injections of epinephrine or other sympathomimetic drugs is termed status asthmaticus, a medical emergency requiring immediate hospitalization and prompt treatment. Factors leading to this condition include respiratory infection, excessive use of respiratory depressant drugs such as sedatives or opiates, overuse of aerosolized bronchodilators, rapid withdrawal of corticosteroids, and ingestion of aspirin in an aspirin-sensitive asthmatic patient.

Immediate determination of arterial blood gases and pH with repeated measurements until the patient responds satisfactorily is necessary for optimal treatment. Injections of epinephrine, Sus-Phrine, or epinephrine in oil are continued. Aminophylline, 250–500 mg, is given intravenously over a period of 10–30 minutes initially, in some cases followed by slow intravenous drip, but careful attention must be paid to toxic symptoms of nausea, vomiting, or headache. Serum theophylline determinations, if available, are useful in maintaining the optimal therapeutic level of 10–20 μg/ml of serum. Intravenous corticosteroids are indicated if the patient has previously received steroids, if the attack was caused by aspirin, if excessive aerosolized isoproterenol was a factor in the attack, or if significant CO_2 retention exists. Hydrocortisone, 400–600 mg/24 hours intravenously, should be given until the patient can switch to oral prednisone, 60–80 mg daily in divided doses.

Dehydration usually accompanies status asthmaticus and may give rise to inspissated mucous plugs which further impair ventilation. During the first 24 hours, up to 3–4 liters of intravenous fluid may be necessary for rehydration. Oxygen should be supplied by tent, face mask, or nasal catheter to maintain arterial P_{O_2} at about 90–100 mg Hg. Expectorants and chest physical therapy are helpful adjuncts to eliminate mucous plugs. Sedatives should be avoided even in the anxious patient because of the danger of respiratory depression. Antibiotics are used only if bacterial infection is documented.

Respiratory failure, indicated by an arterial P_{CO_2} level of 65 mm Hg or more and arterial blood pH below 7.25, may require mechanical assistance of ventilation in addition to all the measures listed above. This should be performed by a team of physicians, nurses, and technicians experienced in respiration therapy.

Complications & Prognosis

The disease is chronic, and its severity may change in an unpredictable fashion. Some children apparently "outgrow" asthma in the sense of becoming asymptomatic, but they will continue to show evidence of bronchial lability, and symptoms can reappear later in life. The acute attack can be complicated by pneumothorax, subcutaneous emphysema, rib fractures, atelectasis, or pneumonitis. There is no evidence that emphysema, bronchiectasis, pulmonary hypertension, or cor pulmonale results from long-standing asthma.

ATOPIC DERMATITIS

Major Immunologic Features

- Often accompanies atopic respiratory allergy.
- Clinical course often independent of allergen exposure.
- There may be an accompanying partial T cell defect.

General Considerations

Atopic dermatitis is associated with allergic rhinitis and asthma in families and frequently in the same patient, suggesting that it is a cutaneous form of atopic hypersensitivity. However, it is often difficult to prove that allergy plays a role, because the dermatitis often does not appear in relation to exposure to known allergens, does not correlate positively with skin tests, or does not respond to immunotherapy. There is evidence for an underlying target organ (skin) abnormality which might be a metabolic or biochemical defect, possibly determined genetically. Recent studies suggest a partial deficiency in cell-mediated immunity.

Atopic dermatitis may begin at any age. Onset at 3–6 months is typical, but it may appear later during childhood or adolescence and occasionally during adult life.

Immunologic Pathogenesis

A. The Role of Allergy in Atopic Dermatitis: Atopic respiratory diseases with hypersensitivity to environmental allergens, eosinophilia, elevated serum IgE levels, and a family history of allergy are frequently associated with atopic dermatitis. Nevertheless, it is often difficult to attribute the dermatitis to allergy. The skin lesions rarely flare during pollen seasons, although in some patients there is an association with exposure to house dust, animals, or other environmental allergens. More commonly, food allergy in children can be demonstrated. Milk, corn, soybeans, fish, nuts, and cereal grains are frequently implicated, but other foods may occasionally be important.

B. Association With Systemic Disorders: Eczema indistinguishable from atopic dermatitis is found in children with phenylketonuria. The skin lesions of Letterer-Siwe disease are also very similar. Atopic dermatitis without allergy is a feature of several immunologic deficiency disorders, especially Wiskott-Aldrich syndrome, ataxia-telangiectasia, and X-linked hypogammaglobulinemia.

Clinical Features

In infancy the forehead, cheeks, and extensor surfaces of the extremities are usually involved, but later the lesions show a characteristic flexural pattern of distribution with predilection for the antecubital and popliteal areas and the neck. The face, especially around the eyes and ears, is often affected when distribution is more widespread. The skin is excessively dry. Active lesions are initially erythematous and pruritic. This leads to scratching, which results in excoriations, papules, and scaling. If treated promptly, these changes revert to normal; but with prolonged scratching the skin becomes lichenified and pigmentation is altered. The disease often improves spontaneously during the summer months.

Differential Diagnosis

Generalized neurodermatitis, localized neurodermatitis (lichen simplex chronicus), and contact dermatitis result in similar eczematous changes of the skin. Seborrhea and dermatophytoses are occasionally confused with atopic dermatitis.

Treatment

Atopic dermatitis is a chronic disease requiring constant attention to proper skin care, environmental control, drugs, and avoidance of allergens when indicated. Dry skin enhances the tendency to itch, so frequent application of nonirritating topical lubricants is the most important preventive measure. Areas involved with active eczema respond well to topical corticosteroids, but acute involvement of large areas of skin may warrant a brief course of systemic corticosteroids beginning with a high dose initially and tapering slowly after the skin clears. Oral antihistaminics help to control itching. Even if their sedative effect precludes use during the daytime, a bedtime dose will help to control involuntary scratching during sleep. Frequent bathing or washing, irritating fabrics such as wool, and harsh detergents should be avoided. The hands and fingernails must be kept clean to prevent secondary infection, and if infection does occur an appropriate antibiotic should be prescribed.

Complications & Prognosis

Atopic dermatitis has an unpredictable tendency to remit spontaneously, even after years of involvement, and this is not related to the severity of involvement, the presence or absence of allergy, or treatment. Allergic rhinitis and asthma are not complications but rather additional manifestations of the underlying atopic disease.

The most frequent complication is secondary infection from scratching. The most serious complication is eczema vaccinatum from exposure to vaccinia virus by inadvertent vaccination or contact with a recently vaccinated person in the family or classroom. Eczema herpeticum is a similar condition caused by the virus of herpes simplex. Topical antibiotics or antihistaminics may cause secondary contact dermatitis. Cataracts occur in a small proportion of patients, but the cause is unknown.

ANAPHYLAXIS

Major Immunologic Features

- Systemic anaphylaxis is the simultaneous occurrence of a type I reaction in multiple organs.
- The usual causative allergen is a drug, insect venom, or food.
- The reaction can be evoked by a minute quantity of allergen and is potentially fatal.

General Considerations

Anaphylaxis is a systemic form of immediate hypersensitivity affecting several organ systems simultaneously. The reaction occurs rapidly and may cause death through respiratory obstruction or irreversible vascular collapse. Systemic anaphylaxis is usually mediated by IgE antibodies with release of histamine and SRS-A, but IgG- or IgM-mediated complement-dependent mechanisms generating anaphylatoxins or kinins may account for some anaphylactic reactions.

In most cases, anaphylaxis is a systemic effect of type I allergy. The allergen combines with IgE antibodies on mast cells, releasing histamine from its stores within mast cell granules and generating SRS from unknown precursor sites. The vasodilating, permeability-increasing, and smooth muscle-constricting properties of these chemical mediators account for most of the pathophysiologic changes in anaphylaxis. Histamine release may also occur in the absence of IgE antibody. IgG or IgM antibodies which activate the complement system can generate anaphylatoxins, C3a and C5a, which are cleavage products of C3 and C5 capable of stimulating mast cell release of histamine. In cases of profound vascular collapse, it is likely that kinins—oligopeptides with vasodilating activity—are activated from the complement cascade.

The allergen-IgE antibody-mast cell-mediator pathogenesis of anaphylaxis is the same mechanism responsible for atopy, but the allergens and route of exposure differ, and genetic factors and target organ hyperresponsiveness are not present in anaphylaxis.

The most common sources of allergens causing anaphylaxis are drugs, diagnostic reagents, foods, and insect stings (Table 29–3).

Table 29–3. Common causes of anaphylaxis.

Drugs
Proteins (presumably complete antigens)
Foreign serum
Vaccines
Allergen extracts
Enzymes
Nonprotein drugs (presumably haptens)
Penicillin and other antibiotics
Sulfonamides
Local anesthetics
Salicylates
Diagnostic compounds
Sulfobromophthalein
Sodium dehydrocholate
Radiographic contrast media
Foods
Legumes (especially peanuts)
Nuts
Berries
Seafoods
Egg albumin
Stinging insects
Honeybees
Wasps
Hornets
Yellow jackets
Fire ants

Clinical Features

The reaction begins within seconds or minutes after exposure to the allergen. There may be an initial fright or sense of impending doom, followed rapidly by symptoms in one or more target organs: cardiovascular, respiratory, cutaneous, and gastrointestinal.

The cardiovascular response may be peripheral or central. Hypotension and shock are symptoms of generalized arteriolar vasodilatation and increased vascular permeability producing decreased peripheral resistance and leakage of plasma from the circulation to extravascular tissues, thereby lowering blood volume. In some patients without previous heart disease, cardiac arrhythmias may occur. Death can result from blood volume depletion and irreversible shock or from a cardiac arrhythmia.

The respiratory tract from the nasal mucosa to the bronchioles may be involved. Nasal congestion from swelling and hyperemia of the nasal mucosa and profuse watery rhinorrhea with itching of the nose and palate simulate an acute hay fever reaction. The hypopharynx and larynx are especially susceptible, and obstruction of this critical portion of the airway by edema is responsible for some of the respiratory deaths. Bronchial obstruction from bronchospasm, mucosal edema, and hypersecretion of mucus results in an asthma-like paroxysm of wheezing dyspnea. Obstruction of the smaller airways by mucus may lead to respiratory failure.

The skin is a frequent target organ in anaphylaxis with generalized pruritus, erythema, urticaria, and angioedema. Occasionally, urticaria may persist for many weeks or months after all other symptoms have subsided.

Gastrointestinal involvement occurs because of contraction of intestinal smooth muscle, resulting in crampy abdominal pain and sometimes nausea or diarrhea. Similarly, uterine muscle contraction may cause pelvic pain.

Immunologic Diagnosis

A history of symptoms and signs of anaphylaxis immediately after an insect sting, after parenteral administration of a drug, diagnostic agent, or vaccine, or following the ingestion of a drug or food likely to cause anaphylaxis is sufficient to make the diagnosis.

Occasionally, a reaction occurs after injection of 2 agents with high anaphylactic potential (eg, penicillin and horse serum) or after a meal which included suspicious foods such as fish, legumes, nuts, or berries. A positive immediate skin test to the suspected drug or food is probably diagnostic, but a negative test to these allergens never excludes sensitivity. Prick testing should always be done first, followed by serial-dilution intradermal tests if the prick test is negative. If the cause of the reaction is obvious from the history, skin testing should not be done.

Differential Diagnosis

Cardiogenic, hypovolemic, septic, and neurogenic causes of shock must be considered. Acute respiratory obstruction may occur in asthma, pulmonary edema, mechanical obstruction by foreign body or tumor, or adult respiratory distress syndrome. Some patients experience vasovagal syncope after injections, particularly local anesthetics.

Prevention

Once an episode of anaphylaxis has occurred, every effort should be made to identify the allergen so that the patient can avoid further exposure. Any physician or nurse who administers drugs by injection should be prepared to treat a possible anaphylactic reaction by having appropriate drugs available, and patients should remain under observation for 15–20 minutes after any injection.

Treatment

Speed is essential, but treatment must be individualized according to organ involvement. Always give epinephrine as soon as anaphylaxis is suspected, then examine carefully to determine what further measures are needed. The severity of the reaction is inversely related to the interval between exposure to the allergen and the onset of symptoms.

A. Immediate Treatment: Give epinephrine, 1:1000 aqueous solution, 0.2–0.5 ml intramuscularly into the deltoid muscles. Repeat every 30–60 minutes as necessary, or use a long-acting preparation, such as Sus-Phrine (1:200) or epinephrine in oil, 2 mg/ml. If the reaction was caused by an injected drug or insect sting, give 1:1000 aqueous epinephrine, 0.1–0.2 ml subcutaneously at the injection site, to slow down absorption. If the injection was into an extremity, apply a tourniquet proximally.

B. Hypotension and Shock: Restoration of circulating fluid volume is definitive, but initial vasopressors such as levarterenol bitartrate or metaraminol bitartrate given intravenously may be used. Monitor blood pressure. Give 1000–2000 ml physiologic saline or 5% glucose in saline rapidly intravenously. If there is no response, use plasma or other plasma expanders. If the patient is in profound shock, give whole blood while monitoring central venous pressure.

C. Laryngeal Edema: Maintain the airway. Passage of an endotracheal tube may be difficult because of the swelling, in which case tracheostomy should be performed. Continue epinephrine and give diphenhydramine, 50–100 mg intravenously.

D. Bronchospasm: Treat as for status asthmaticus. Aminophylline, 250–500 mg intravenously, should be administered over a 10-minute period while observing carefully for signs of gastrointestinal or CNS toxicity. Isoproterenol, 1:200 as aerosol, can be administered by hand nebulizer or intermittent positive pressure breathing.

E. Urticaria, Angioedema, and Gastrointestinal, Genitourinary, or Uterine Symptoms: These respond well to antihistaminic drugs. If severe, inject diphenhydramine, 50–100 mg intravenously or intramuscularly. For milder symptoms, oral antihistaminics are satisfactory.

F. Other Measures: Oxygen therapy must be given to correct hypoxia caused by respiratory obstruction or shock. Cardiopulmonary resuscitation should be administered in case of cardiac arrest. Corticosteroids have no known "antianaphylactic" property, and there is no rationale for their use in the critical initial stages of treatment. However, they may be helpful in refractory shock, persistent urticaria or angioedema after subsidence of the acute reaction, and bronchospasm in the asthmatic patient previously treated with corticosteroids.

Complications & Prognosis

Death from laryngeal edema, respiratory failure, shock, or cardiac arrythmia usually occurs within minutes after onset of the reaction, but in occasional cases irreversible shock persists for hours. Permanent brain damage may result from the hypoxia of respiratory or cardiovascular failure. Urticaria or angioedema may recur for months after penicillin anaphylaxis.

STINGING INSECT HYPERSENSITIVITY

Anaphylactic sensitivity to hymenoptera venom can be easily identified, and the patient can be protected from future potentially fatal reactions by desensitization and simple protective measures. The venom of hymenoptera insects—honeybees, wasps, hornets, fire ants, and yellow jackets—contains several protein antigens, some of which are species-specific and others common to all insects in the order.

The sting of a single insect is sufficient to produce a severe, even fatal anaphylactic reaction in a sensitive patient. Sensitization occurs from prior stings, and if the patient is allergic to a common or cross-reacting antigen he may have an anaphylactic reaction should he be stung by any species of hymenoptera insect. There is no evidence that other allergic disease, including atopy and drug anaphylaxis, predisposes to hymenoptera anaphylaxis.

The normal response of erythema, itching, and localized swelling from a hymenoptera sting is caused by vasoactive and irritant chemical substances in the venom. In some patients, this localized reaction is unusually large and persistent, possibly indicating type III (immune complex) or type IV (cellular) hypersensitivity. Such reactions are not related to anaphylactic sensitivity.

The diagnosis must rest solely on a history of anaphylactic symptoms immediately after an insect sting, although mild reactions may not begin until several hours after the sting. Precise insect identification is possible only if the insect is caught and saved for study by an expert, but identification is not necessary for treatment since a mixture of antigens from all hymenoptera insects is used.

Commercially available insect extracts prepared from whole insect bodies are too crude for diagnostic skin testing, since many nonsensitive persons react positively to testing. Venom is probably more reliable, but it is not readily available.

Treatment

The management of anaphylaxis from a hymenoptera sting is the same as for any anaphylactic reaction (see above). In the case of honeybee sting, the venom sac and stinger usually remain in the skin and should be removed promptly by scraping with a knife or fingernail.

Local reactions require only cold compresses to ease pain and reduce swelling.

A. Hyposensitization: All patients anaphylactically sensitive to insect stings should receive hyposensitization treatment. Although skin testing is not diagnostic, serial-dilution skin test titration can be used to determine a suitable starting dose, and repeated injections with increasing dosage are given subcutaneously until a maintenance dose is determined by the appearance of a local reaction to 0.5 ml of 1:10 dilution of whole body extracts. Since accurate identification of the insect is often difficult, all patients should receive a mixed extract of hymenoptera insects. The injections are continued at the maintenance level every 2–6 weeks for the rest of the patient's life. Hyposensitization significantly reduces the risk of anaphylaxis, and fatal reactions in patients treated in this fashion are extremely rare.

B. Anaphylaxis Kit: The patient should carry on his person at all times a small kit containing an antihistamine tablet and a preloaded syringe of epinephrine. Epinephrine or isoproterenol in a pressurized-aerosol hand nebulizer is not reliable protection for anaphylactic shock.

C. Protective Measures: Avoid using strong scents such as perfumes and hair sprays when outdoors. Wear shoes outdoors. Avoid garbage cans. Do not tamper with beehives or with wasp or hornet nests.

URTICARIA & ANGIOEDEMA

Major Immunologic Features

- These are cutaneous forms of anaphylaxis.
- Allergens causing acute urticaria are usually foods or drugs.
- Chronic urticaria is usually related to nonimmunologic causes or is idiopathic.

General Considerations

Urticaria affects a large portion of the population at some time, usually as an acute self-limited episode but occasionally in a chronic or recurrent form. The lesion—a localized area of increased vascular permeability—appears as multiple areas of swelling of the skin usually accompanied by pruritus. It can result from a variety of causes, some of which are immunologic. Angioedema is a similar condition in which the affected blood vessels are deeper, resulting in diffuse swelling, usually without pruritus. Urticaria and angioedema may appear together in the same patient. When an allergic cause can be found, the disease is actually a localized cutaneous form of anaphylaxis since the immunologic mechanism and the causative allergens are similar.

Causes of urticaria and angioedema. Allergy, infections, physical factors, certain systemic diseases, and emotional stress have all been associated with urticaria.

Ingestant allergens are much more frequent causes of urticaria than inhalants. Any food or drug can cause hives. Occult sources of drugs such as penicillin in milk and proprietary medications such as laxatives, headache remedies, and vitamin preparations must be considered. Food and drug additives are occasionally responsible.

A localized or systemic infection may provoke urticaria, usually as an incidental feature of the host's immune response to the infecting organism. This is particularly true with parasitic diseases, which are often associated with eosinophilia and a prominent IgE immune response. Urticaria may appear during the prodromal phases of certain viral infections, especially HB_SAg-associated hepatitis and infectious mononucleosis. Bacterial infections are much less likely to cause urticaria.

"Physical allergy" refers to a type of urticaria in which external physical stimuli cause hives or swelling. The most frequent type is cold urticaria, in which exposure to cold temperature results in hives and angioedema, either during the cold exposure or after rewarming. In some cases the sensitivity to cold can be passively transferred by serum to normal skin, suggesting an antibody mechanism, but the nature of the antigen is unknown. It is assumed that cold alters a normal skin protein in such a way as to make it antigenic. Occasional patients have been described with urticaria or angioedema on exposure to heat, sunlight ("actinic"), water ("aquagenic"), and vibratory stimulation of the skin. The localization of urticaria to areas of the skin subjected to mild pressure or trauma is characteristic of urticaria in general.

Cholinergic urticaria is a condition in which small wheals with a large area of surrounding flare appear after exercise, being overheated, or emotional stress. These patients usually show a prominent urticarial response to intradermal methacholine.

Urticaria occasionally is a sign of an underlying systemic disease. Neoplasms–especially Hodgkin's disease and lymphomas–and connective tissue disorders–particularly systemic lupus erythematosus–have been reported to cause hives.

Emotional trauma can precipitate acute urticaria or angioedema or aggravate the chronic form of the disease.

Multiple pathogenetic mechanisms are probably capable of final expression as urticaria. Allergic hives appearing acutely after exposure to an allergenic food, drug, or insect venom is a type I reaction, with histamine release producing cutaneous vasodilatation, increased permeability, and pruritus. The pathogenetic mechanisms of other forms of urticaria are uncertain. Physical agents or trauma may release histamine from cutaneous mast cells by mechanical stimulation.

Immunologic Diagnosis

Food allergy is diagnosed by careful dietary history, use of elimination diets, and appropriate food challenges. Drug allergy requires close scrutiny of the patient's recent drug history, elimination of suspected drugs, and occasionally deliberate challenge, although skin testing is helpful for certain drugs such as penicillin. The diagnosis of cold urticaria is made by application of an ice cube to the forearm for 5 minutes and the appearance of localized urticaria after the skin has been rewarmed. Similar tests with heat, ultraviolet light, or water to a test area of skin are appropriate if the history suggests these causes.

In cholinergic urticaria, intradermal injection of 0.01 mg of methacholine produces small satellite wheals and erythema at the injection site.

Differential Diagnosis

In all patients, a thorough medical history and complete physical examination are necessary, and additional studies as indicated to rule out parasitic infestations, hepatitis, neoplasm, or other systemic diseases. In most cases of chronic urticaria, no cause will be found initially, but follow-up examination may be rewarding. Hereditary angioedema is a rare cause of this syndrome (see below).

Treatment

Urticaria caused by foods or drugs is treated by avoidance of the offending agents, although hyposensitization to a drug might be necessary in rare instances in which no alternative drug is available. Urticaria associated with infection is self-limited if the infection is adequately treated. In cases of physical allergy, protective measures to avoid heat, sunlight, or cold must be advised. Drug treatment is a useful adjunct in the management of all patients whether or not the cause has been found, but a good response to symptomatic treatment should not deter the physician from efforts to find an underlying cause.

Antihistaminic drugs are the principal method of treatment, but they must be given in adequate dosage. Epinephrine injections may relieve hives transiently and should be used in treating angioedema involving the pharynx or larynx. Corticosteroids are usually ineffective and should not be used to treat urticaria of unknown cause.

HEREDITARY ANGIOEDEMA
(Hereditary Angioneurotic Edema)

This rare form of angioedema is caused by an inherited deficiency of C1 inactivator (C1 esterase inhibitor), resulting in uncontrolled activation of the early components of the complement system with generation of a kininlike substance causing recurrent episodes of angioedema involving the skin, gastrointestinal tract, and larynx. Patients with this disease often give a family history of the same disorder and have recurrent attacks of swelling beginning during childhood. Death may occur from laryngeal swelling. The disease is unusual but not rare. There are 2 forms of the disease: in about 85% of kindreds, the C1 inactivator is absent from the serum, and in the remaining 15% it is present in normal amount but is functionally inactive. The disease is not associated with urticaria, and the history alone is usually sufficient to suggest the diagnosis, which can then be confirmed by laboratory tests. Measurement of serum C4 by functional or immunologic assay is the best screening test because C4 levels are markedly diminished in almost all patients, even during symptom-free intervals. The diagnosis can be confirmed by measurement of C1 inactivator protein by immunoassay and its functional activity by hemolytic assay. There is no specific treatment, although plasmin inhibitors such as aminocaproic acid (EACA, Amicar) in high doses orally have been helpful in some patients. Administration of fresh plasma to supply the missing inactivator can help to prevent attacks that are precipitated by trauma such as dental surgery. Any attack of laryngeal edema in this disease requires close observation–even hospitalization if necessary–in case tracheostomy is required.

DRUG ALLERGY

Major Immunologic Features

- Any of the 4 types of hypersensitivity can cause an allergic drug reaction.
- An immunogenic response to a drug usually requires covalent binding of haptenic drug determinant to host carrier protein.
- The allergenic determinant may be a drug metabolite.

General Considerations

Drugs cause allergic reactions by virtue of their ability to evoke an immune response. Most drugs function immunologically as haptens and must couple in vivo to a host carrier protein before they become immunogenic. Proteins such as sera, vaccines, biologicals, and allergen extracts are intrinsically antigenic and carry a high risk of allergic sensitization.

Many factors influence the allergic potential of a drug. Topical administration is more likely to induce sensitization than the oral or parenteral routes. Infection may increase the risk of drug allergy, but atopy and other immunologic diseases do not. Certain patients are multiple drug reactors, possibly on a genetic basis. Children are much less susceptible than adults. Allergy to a particular drug is independent of its pharmacologic properties but highly dependent upon the ease with which the drug or its metabolite couples to carrier protein.

Type I allergic reactions to drugs include anaphylaxis, urticaria, and angioedema. These can occur with any drug, but systemic anaphylaxis is most likely to result if the drug is given by injection, although severe reactions and even death have occurred from oral administration of penicillin.

Type II allergic reactions are complement-dependent and therefore involve IgG or IgM antibodies. The drug-antibody-complement complex is fixed to a cell, usually a circulating blood cell, resulting in complement-dependent cell lysis. Such reactions may involve erythrocytes, leukocytes, or platelets.

There are 4 mechanisms by which drugs can induce immunologic damage to cells: (1) The drug first fixes to the cell membrane, followed by reaction of the antibody to the cell-fixed drug antigen, resulting in a cell-antigen-antibody complex. The complex then activates the complement sequence with lysis of the cell. Immunohemolytic anemia from penicillin is an example of this mechanism. (2) The drug-antibody-complement complex is formed first in the plasma, and the complex secondarily fixes to the cell, after which lysis occurs. In these reactions the direct antiglobulin (Coombs) test is positive. Autoimmune hemolytic anemia, leukocytopenia, and thrombocytopenia from quinidine, sulfonamides, and stibophen are examples of this type of drug reaction. (3) The membrane of red blood cells may be modified by drugs so that the cells adsorb proteins nonspecifically and give positive antiglobulin tests. However, disease from this mechanism is rare. (4) Methyldopa causes hemolytic anemia by inducing autoantibody formation. The drug damages normal red cells to expose erythrocyte autoantigens which induce an autoimmune hemolytic anemia that can persist even after the drug has been withdrawn. It is possible that some drugs may produce type II reactions by more than one of these 4 mechanisms.

Type III drug reactions are exemplified by serum sickness, a term applicable to the reaction whether caused by heterologous serum or by a haptenic drug such as penicillin. The disease is a multi-system complement-dependent vasculitis in which immune complexes are deposited along the endothelial surfaces of blood vessels, stimulating inflammation and vascular wall damage. There is a latent period of several days after administration of the drug before sufficient antibody is produced to generate immune complexes capable of activating the complement system. The classical symptoms of serum sickness are fever, arthralgias, lymphadenopathy, and a skin eruption which is often urticarial. The serum sickness caused by penicillin is generally mild, although the urticaria may persist for many weeks.

Type IV (cell-mediated) allergy is the mechanism of allergic contact dermatitis from topically applied drugs. Topical antibiotics, antihistamines, local anesthetics, and certain additives found in topical medications, including parabens and lanolin, are frequent causes of this type of allergy.

In many adverse drug reactions, allergy is strongly suspected but the immunologic mechanism is difficult to prove. Allergy is suggested by (1) a reaction occurring in a small proportion of persons exposed to the drug, (2) a latent period between exposure to the drug and the appearance of a reaction which is of shorter duration with succeeding exposures to the drug, (3) elicitation of the reaction by very small doses, and (4) an association with other signs suggesting allergic disease, such as eosinophilia. Erythematous, morbilliform, or other skin eruptions, drug fever, and cholestatic liver disease induced by certain drugs belong to the category of suspected allergic reactions.

Certain drug reactions can be caused by allergic or nonallergic means. Urticaria and angioedema may be produced either by type I allergy to a drug or by nonspecific liberation of mast cell histamine by drugs such as morphine.

Clinical Features

An allergic reaction to a drug occurs after sufficient exposure to induce an immune response, so some patients may react even though the drug had been used frequently in the past without incident. A reaction on first exposure suggests prior sensitization by a cross-reacting drug or antigen. Once a reaction occurs, any subsequent use of the drug, sometimes even in trace amounts, can cause a recurrence of symptoms.

All 4 types of allergy have occurred from drugs, and these can produce a variety of clinical manifestations (Table 29–4).

Immunologic Diagnosis

A high index of suspicion and a careful history to uncover all sources of drugs the patient might have taken are the most important means of diagnosis. In addition to prescribed drugs, the patient must be asked about the use of proprietary medications such as aspirin, cold tablets, headache remedies, laxatives, vitamins, and nose drops.

Laboratory tests for identification of allergy to a specific drug are available only in certain situations. Protein drugs causing type I allergy will give an immediate wheal and flare skin test reaction, but a proper

Table 29–4. Clinical manifestations of drug allergy.

Systemic anaphylaxis
Serum sickness
Fever
Cutaneous eruptions
Urticaria
Angioedema
Erythema multiforme, Stevens-Johnson syndrome
Pruritus
Allergic contact dermatitis, photoallergic dermatitis
Purpura
Morbilliform, erythematous, exfoliative rash
Fixed drug eruption
Hematologic abnormalities
Hemolytic anemia
Leukocytopenia
Thrombocytopenia
Eosinophilia
Hepatic cholestasis
Acute interstitial nephritis

dilution of the drug must be used to avoid a nonspecific irritant reaction. Haptenic drugs will usually not give a positive test, but penicillin is an important exception. For suspected type II allergy, an appropriate in vitro test can be devised for each particular reaction. Agglutination tests using normal red cells, white cells, or platelets incubated with the patient's serum and drug will detect the antibody, but such tests require a specialized laboratory staffed by personnel with experience in these technics. In type III reactions, antibodies may be found by gel precipitation tests if the antigen is a protein, by passive hemagglutination, or by Arthus-type skin tests, in which the response to intradermal injection of antigen is a localized swelling and inflammation maximal at 5–8 hours. Patch testing is the appropriate procedure in allergic contact dermatitis.

Many other in vitro tests have been proposed for diagnostic use in drug allergy, including the basophil degranulation test, lymphocyte activation test, radioallergosorbent test, and others, but at present their usefulness is questionable. In each case, the selection of the test must be appropriate to the drug and to the type of immune response suspected from the clinical picture. Furthermore, the fact that the patient has an antibody to a particular drug is not proof that the antibody is the cause of his allergic reaction.

In vivo testing by readministration of a small test dose of the drug after the initial reaction has subsided may prove that the reaction is drug-associated. This should not be attempted with serious reactions such as anaphylaxis or exfoliative dermatitis.

Differential Diagnosis

Nonallergic drug reactions are adverse pharmacologic, chemical, and physical effects of the drug which are not immunologically mediated. These include toxicity, idiosyncrasy, intolerance, and side-effects.

Treatment

Proved or even suspected drug reactions require withdrawal of the drug. If a substitute drug is given, it should be one which is unlikely to cross-react antigenically. Symptomatic treatment is used where indicated. The patient must be advised to avoid use of the same drug in the future, but there are instances in which desensitization may be attempted.

PENICILLIN ALLERGY

The haptenic determinants of type I penicillin allergy are metabolic degradation products. Penicilloic acid is the major determinant and is responsible for late urticarial reactions and probably other skin eruptions. Anaphylaxis and immediate urticaria or angioedema are caused by other minor determinants that have not yet been fully characterized. The source of the protein carrier is unknown. The nature of the antigenic determinant in type II, III, and IV reactions has not been studied.

The antibodies, cell types, mediators, and tissue responses in each type of allergic drug reaction have been described in the preceding sections.

Clinical Features

Penicillin can cause almost every known type of allergic reaction. Anaphylaxis occurs about once in every 10,000 patient courses of the drug and accounts for about 300 deaths in the USA each year. Urticaria or angioedema appearing within an hour after administration of the drug is a form of anaphylaxis. Urticaria which begins days to weeks after the drug is administered has less serious implications and in some cases may disappear even if penicillin treatment is continued. The most common manifestation of penicillin allergy is a diffuse erythematous or morbilliform skin eruption. Serum sickness occurs occasionally, and immunohemolytic anemia may complicate high-dosage intravenous therapy. Allergic contact dermatitis is common after topical penicillin. It is estimated that some type of adverse reaction to penicillin occurs in 3% of patient courses of the drug.

Immunologic Diagnosis

IgE antibodies to major and minor penicillin allergy determinants are detected by wheal and flare skin tests. Penicilloyl-polylysine 6×10^{-5} M solution elicits a positive skin test in most patients with a history of late urticaria and many of those with exanthematous reactions. A "minor determinant mixture" for testing suspected anaphylactically sensitive patients is not presently marketed, but a skin test using penicillin G, 1000 units/ml, is usually positive in persons with documented anaphylaxis. The tests are performed by injecting 0.005 ml intradermally and reading for wheal and erythema at 20 minutes.

Skin testing with these 2 reagents has predictive value if used in relation to the patient's history. If there is a history of penicillin anaphylaxis, the diagnosis is certain, and no tests should be done since anaphylaxis can be produced by the test. If late urticaria or other skin eruptions are suspected on the basis of the history, negative reactions to both determinants strongly suggest that the patient is not allergic to penicillin and the drug can be administered with no greater risk of reaction than in those patients who had not received penicillin before. If the minor determinant test is positive, the risk of anaphylaxis is almost certain, and if the major determinant test is positive the chance of a skin eruption is very high. However, the appearance of late-onset urticaria does not always signify that the drug must be withdrawn or withheld, since continued treatments may result in the appearance of IgG blocking antibody, causing the urticaria to disappear without interfering with the therapeutic effect of the drug. Hemagglutination tests may be used to detect serum IgG or IgM antibody. The former can function as a blocking antibody, but either might produce type II hemolytic anemia if the drug is given in high dosage intravenously.

Differential Diagnosis

Penicillin toxicity is exceedingly low, so the appearance of an adverse reaction during therapy almost always indicates allergy to the drug. Exanthematous eruptions, however, frequently complicate those infections for which penicillin is prescribed and may be erroneously diagnosed as penicillin allergy. This is particularly true in children given penicillin for viral or streptococcal respiratory infections.

Treatment

As with any drug allergy, the reaction will subside when penicillin is discontinued. In some cases, hives persist for many months afterward, occasionally traceable to small amounts of penicillin in dietary milk. Avoidance of milk products may be helpful.

Patients with a history of late urticaria and major (but not minor) determinant skin test reactivity may be given penicillin if no alternative antibiotic is available. The drug will stimulate IgG blocking antibody and should be started at a low dose subcutaneously, followed by increasing dosage at frequent intervals until a therapeutic level is achieved. This is not "desensitization" but rather an immunization procedure to stimulate blocking antibody. Immunization should not be attempted in any other type of penicillin allergy. Semisynthetic penicillins, eg, methicillin, nafcillin, oxacillin, and cloxacillin, all cross-react with the parent compound and should be used with the same precautions discussed for penicillin itself.

Symptomatic treatment of anaphylaxis, urticaria, and angioedema is discussed above.

Penicillinase to eliminate residual drug in tissues is rarely effective and frequently causes allergic reactions.

FOOD ALLERGY

Major Immunologic Features

- Type I reactions to foods include systemic anaphylaxis, urticaria, and exacerbation of atopic symptoms.
- Prevalence is inversely proportionate to age because of maturation of gastrointestinal digestion of food allergens.
- Current diagnostic technics, including skin testing, are not generally useful.

General Considerations

Food allergy is too often used to explain subjective complaints without proper documentation. The diagnosis should be reserved for patients whose symptoms occur reproducibly after ingestion of a certain food and in whom an immunologic basis is proved or suspected. This will prevent needless elimination of foods and delay in making a correct diagnosis of a different disorder responsible for the symptoms.

Allergic reactions to foods occur more commonly in children than in adults, are usually type I, and frequently accompany other manifestations of atopic disease.

Immunologic Pathogenesis

These are type I reactions in which the allergen is a food protein or a partially digested product. Carbohydrates, fats, additives such as preservatives or flavoring and coloring agents, and contaminating drugs are other potential allergens in foodstuffs. Closely related foods may contain common or cross-reacting allergens; for example, some patients react to all legumes, including beans, peas, and peanuts. Some food allergens are heat-labile, so that sufficient cooking may render the food nonallergenic.

In gastrointestinal allergy, the allergen reacts locally with IgE antibodies in the intestinal mucosa with subsequent mediator release. The respiratory and cutaneous manifestations are initiated by absorbed allergen which reaches the target organs via the bloodstream.

Clinical Features

Systemic anaphylaxis, urticaria, angioedema, eczema, and respiratory and gastrointestinal symptoms are the usual manifestations of food allergy.

A. Anaphylaxis: The reaction typically appears promptly after the food is ingested, so the patient is generally aware of the causative food. Peanuts and other legumes, nuts, seafoods (especially shellfish), and berries are frequent offenders. However, any food can potentially sensitize a person and then cause anaphylaxis. In most cases the diagnosis is apparent; if there is doubt or confusion about which of several foods might have been responsible, skin testing for wheal and flare reaction is appropriate since the test would generally be positive in this disease. Skin tests to highly potent allergens such as peanuts or cottonseed protein should be avoided if the diagnosis is certain on the basis of the history.

B. Urticaria and Angioedema: Food allergy is a common cause of acute urticaria. In chronic or recurrent urticaria, a food or food additive is occasionally responsible.

C. Eczema: Food allergies are prominent in infantile and childhood eczema but unusual in adults. Milk, wheat, eggs, corn, fish, and soybeans are some of the more frequent offenders, but other foods must also be considered.

Immunologic Diagnosis

Diagnosis begins with a careful dietary history to note the association of symptoms with specific foods. If necessary, this is supplemented with a diet-symptom record. Careful examination of the record may reveal previously unsuspected food allergens or eliminate previously suspected ones. Where the record is inconclusive, trial elimination diets are used.

Elimination diets are for short-term diagnostic use only. They are frequently deficient in essential nutrients or vitamins, so that their prolonged use may cause nutritional problems. While on the diet, the patient keeps a diet-symptom record and avoids medications that might suppress symptoms.

Several types of diets are suitable. If the list of suspect allergens is short, these foods alone can be eliminated and then reintroduced separately if the symptoms disappear. If there are no strong suspicions, an arbitrary group of "highly allergenic foods" such as wheat, milk, eggs, corn, legumes, fish, and nuts can be eliminated. In extreme cases, a synthetic diet can be used. In any case, the elimination period should be continued no longer than 7 days. If symptoms clear completely, the avoided foods are then reintroduced one at a time, usually every other day, to determine which one actually precipitates symptoms. Successful challenge will provoke an allergic reaction within minutes or several hours but rarely more than 24 hours if the reaction is a type I allergic response. Once a positive response occurs, the food is again eliminated and later rechallenged. The diagnosis can be made if symptoms occur on several such challenges.

Skin testing in food allergy. Wheal and erythema skin tests rarely have any clinical significance. Type I food allergy may be associated with negative skin tests because the testing material is unstable or because the allergen is a digested breakdown product rather than the native food. Significant positive tests are usually obtained in cases of anaphylaxis from a food, but testing is usually unnecessary and may be dangerous. False-positive skin tests to foods are frequent in atopic individuals, either because of nonspecific histamine liberators in the food or because cooking or the digestive process effectively destroys potential allergens. For these reasons, skin tests are unnecessary and misleading in most cases of suspected food allergy. The radioallergosorbent test (RAST), which detects IgE antibodies in serum, has not been shown to be reliable in the diagnosis of food allergy.

Differential Diagnosis

Gastrointestinal milk allergy may be confused with intestinal lactase deficiency, which can be ruled out by lactose tolerance testing or enzyme assay from a jejunal biopsy specimen.

Treatment

The treatment of food allergy is avoidance. This is usually not difficult, since patients are rarely allergic to more than one or at most a small number of foods, permitting them to eat an adequate diet without difficulty. In the case of anaphylactic sensitivity, avoidance must be complete and scrupulous, since severe reactions can occur from minute amounts of the allergen.

An antihistamine tablet taken before a meal may occasionally prevent an attack. Recent preliminary reports suggest that oral cromolyn sodium can inhibit symptoms of food allergy in some patients, but use of the drug for this purpose is still experimental in the USA.

Complications & Prognosis

Allergy to foods tends to diminish with age. Infants and children with bona fide food sensitivities frequently tolerate these foods without difficulty later in life. It is not known whether this is acquired immunologic tolerance or physiologic maturation of the digestive process, preventing absorption of intact food proteins.

Anaphylactic sensitivity does not remit and is potentially lethal throughout life.

• • •

References

General

Brostoff J: *Clinical Immunology–Allergy in Paediatric Medicine.* Blackwell, 1973.

Gell PGH, Coombs RRA, Lachmann PJ (editors): *Clinical Aspects of Immunology,* 3rd ed. Lippincott, 1975.

Patterson R (editor): *Allergic Diseases: Diagnosis and Management.* Lippincott, 1972.

Samter M (editor): *Immunological Diseases,* 2nd ed. Little, Brown, 1971.

Sheldon JM, Mathews KP, Lovell RG: *Manual of Clinical Allergy,* 2nd ed. Saunders, 1967.

Atopy

Brocklehurst WE: Slow reacting substance and related compounds. Prog Allergy 6:539, 1962.

Broder I, Barlow PP, Horton RJ: The epidemiology of asthma and hay fever in a total community, Tecumseh, Michigan. 2. The relationship between asthma and hay fever. J Allergy Clin Immunol 33:524, 1962.

Butcher BT, Salvaggio JE, Leslie GA: Secretory and humoral immunologic response of atopic and non-atopic individuals to intranasally administered antigen. Clin Allergy 5:33, 1975.

Ishizaka K, Ishizaka T: Mechanisms of reaginic hypersensitivity: A review. Clin Allergy 1:9, 1971.

Levine BB, Stember RH, Fotino M: Ragweed hay fever: Genetic control and linkage to HL-A haplotypes. Science 178:1201, 1972.

Marsh DG & others: Association of the HL-A7 cross-reacting group with a specific reaginic antibody response in allergic man. Science 179:691, 1973.

Skin Testing for Immediate Hypersensitivity

Bruce CA & others: Diagnostic tests in ragweed-allergic asthma. A comparison of direct skin tests, leukocyte histamine release, and quantitative bronchial challenge. J Allergy Clin Immunol 53:230, 1974.

Curran WS, Goldman G: The incidence of immediately reacting allergy skin tests in a "normal" adult population. Ann Intern Med 55:777, 1961.

Fineman AH: Studies on hypersensitiveness. 23. A comparative study of the intradermal, scratch, and conjunctival tests in determining the degree of pollen sensitivity. J Immunol 11:465, 1926.

Immunotherapy (Hyposensitization)

Franklin W, Lowell FC: Comparison of two dosages of ragweed extract in the treatment of pollenosis. JAMA 201:915, 1967.

Johnstone DE, Dutton A: The value of hyposensitization therapy for bronchial asthma in children: A 14-year study. Pediatrics 42:793, 1968.

Lichtenstein LM, Norman PS, Winkenwerder WL: Clinical and in vitro studies on the role of immunotherapy in ragweed hay fever. Am J Med 44:514, 1968.

Lowell FC, Franklin W: A double-blind study of the effectiveness and specificity of injection therapy in ragweed hay fever. N Engl J Med 273:675, 1965.

Norman PS: Specific therapy in allergy. Med Clin North Am 58:111, 1974.

Sherman WB, Connell JT: Changes in skin-sensitizing antibody titer (SSAT) following two to four years of injection (aqueous) therapy. J Allergy Clin Immunol 37:123, 1966.

Terr AI: Immunologic basis for injection therapy of allergic diseases. Med Clin North Am 53:1257, 1969.

Allergic Rhinitis (Hay Fever)

Chan JCM, Logan GN, McBean JB: Serous otitis media and allergy: Relation to allergy and other causes. Am J Dis Child 114:684, 1967.

Connell JT: Quantitative intranasal pollen challenges. 3. The priming effect in allergic rhinitis. J Allergy Clin Immunol 43:33, 1969.

Patterson R: Rhinitis. Med Clin North Am 58:43, 1974.

Solomon WR: Comparative effects of transient body surface cooling, recumbency, and induced obstruction in allergic rhinitis and control subjects. J Allergy Clin Immunol 37:216, 1966.

Asthma

Beall GN (moderator): Asthma: New ideas about an old disease. Ann Intern Med 78:405, 1973.

Falliers CJ: Interpretation of consecutive lung function tests for asthma. Ann Allergy 30:443, 1972.

Franklin W: Current concepts: Treatment of severe asthma. N Engl J Med 290:1469, 1974.

Middleton E: Autonomic imbalance in asthma with special reference to beta adrenergic blockade. Adv Intern Med 18:177, 1972.

Nadel JA: Mechanisms of airway response to inhaled substances. Arch Environ Health 16:171, 1968.

Rebuck AS, Pengelly LD: Development of pulsus paradoxus in airways obstruction. N Engl J Med 288:66, 1973.

Reed CW: Abnormal autonomic mechanisms in asthma. J Allergy Clin Immunol 53:34, 1974.

Samter M, Beers RF: Intolerance to aspirin. Ann Intern Med 68:975, 1968.

Spector S, Farr RS: Bronchial inhalational procedures in asthmatics. Med Clin North Am 58:71, 1974.

Szentivanyi A: The beta adrenergic theory of the atopic abnormality in bronchial asthma. J Allergy Clin Immunol 47:23, 1971.

Terr AI: Bronchial asthma. Page 421 in: *Textbook of Pulmonary Diseases.* Baum G (editor). Little, Brown, 1974.

Atopic Dermatitis

Baer RL: *Atopic Dermatitis.* New York Univ Press, 1955.

Brunsting LA, Reed WB, Baer HL: Occurrence of cataracts and keratoconus with atopic dermatitis. Arch Dermatol 85:17, 1962.

Conference on infantile eczema. J Pediatr 66:163, 1965.

Copeman PW, Wallace HS: Eczema vaccinatum. Br Med J 2:906, 1964.

Lobitz WC, Honeyman SF, Winkler NW: Suppressed cell-mediated immunity in two adults with atopic dermatitis. Br J Dermatol 86:317, 1972.

Norins AL: Atopic dermatitis. Pediatr Clin North Am 18:801, 1971.

Peterson RDA: Immunologic responses in infantile eczema. J Pediatr 66:24, 1965.

Sedlis E: Natural history of infantile eczema: Its incidence and course. J Pediatr 66:161, 1965.

Anaphylaxis

Austen KF: Systemic anaphylaxis in the human being. N Engl J Med 291:661, 1974.

James LP, Austen KF: Fatal systemic anaphylaxis in man. N Engl J Med 270:597, 1964.

Kelly JF, Patterson R: Anaphylaxis: Course, mechanisms and treatment. JAMA 227:1431, 1974.

Stinging Insect Hypersensitivity

Insect Allergy Committee of the American Academy of Allergy: Insect sting allergy: Questionnaire study of 2606 cases. JAMA 193:115, 1965.

Lichtenstein LM, Valentine MD, Sobotka AK: A case for venom treatment in anaphylactic sensitivity to hymenoptera sting. N Engl J Med 290:1223, 1974.

Mueller JL: Further experiences with severe allergic reactions to insect stings. N Engl J Med 261:374, 1959.

Parrish HM: Analysis of 460 fatalities from venomous animals in the United States. Am J Med Sci 245:35, 1963.

Urticaria & Angioedema

Beall GN: Urticaria: A review of laboratory and clinical observations. Medicine 43:131, 1964.

Beck P & others: Hereditary angioneurotic edema. Q J Med 42:317, 1973.

Donaldson VH, Rosen FS: Action of complement in hereditary angioneurotic edema: Role of C'1-esterase. J Clin Invest 43:2204, 1964.

Matthews KP: A current view of urticaria. Med Clin North Am 58:185, 1974.

Tas J: Chronic urticaria: A survey of one hundred hospitalized cases. Dermatologica 135:90, 1967.

Drug Allergy

Dash CH, Jones HEH: *Mechanisms in Drug Allergy.* Williams & Wilkins, 1972.

Gralnick HR & others: Hemolytic anemia associated with cephalothin. JAMA 217:1193, 1971.

Levine BB, Redmond AP: Immune mechanisms of penicillin-induced Coombs positivity in man. J Clin Invest 46:1085, 1967.

LoBuglio AF, Jandl JH: The nature of the alpha-methyldopa red-cell antibody. N Engl J Med 276:658, 1967.

Neely CL, Kraus AP: Mechanisms of drug-induced hemolytic anemia. Adv Intern Med 18:59, 1972.

Parker CW: Drug allergy. (3 parts.) N Engl J Med 292:511, 732, 957, 1975.

Weinstein L, Weinstein AJ: The pathophysiology and pathoanatomy of reactions to antimicrobial agents. Adv Intern Med 19:109, 1974.

Penicillin Allergy

Ackroyd JF: The immunological basis of purpura due to drug hypersensitivity. Proc R Soc Med 55:30, 1962.

Adkinson NF Jr & others: Routine use of penicillin skin testing on an inpatient service. N Engl J Med 285:222, 1971.

Bierman CW, Van Arsdel PP Jr: Penicillin allergy in children: The role of immunological tests in its diagnosis. J Allergy Clin Immunol 43:267, 1969.

Fellner MJ & others: Mechanisms of clinical desensitization in urticarial hypersensitivity to penicillin. J Allergy Clin Immunol 45:55, 1970.

Levine BB: Immunologic mechanisms of penicillin allergy. A haptenic model system for the study of allergic diseases of man. N Engl J Med 275:1115, 1966.

Levine BB, Zolov DM: Prediction of penicillin allergy by immunologic tests. J Allergy Clin Immunol 43:231, 1969.

Van Dellen RG & others: Differing patterns of wheal and flare skin reactivity in patients allergic to penicillins. J Allergy Clin Immunol 47:230, 1971.

Food Allergy

Goldman AS & others: Milk allergy. 1. Oral challenge with milk and isolated milk proteins in allergic children. Pediatrics 32:425, 1963.

Goldstein GB, Heiner DC: Clinical and immunological perspectives in food sensitivity. J Allergy Clin Immunol 46:270, 1970.

Walker WA, Hong R: Immunology of the gastrointestinal tract. (2 parts.) J Pediatr 83:517, 711, 1973.

30. . .
Gastrointestinal & Liver Diseases

Keith B. Taylor, MD

The mammalian gastrointestinal system, including the liver, contributes to the total immune responsiveness of the body. In both qualitative and quantitative terms, this contribution is no better defined than that of other organs, including the thymus, which is itself derived from the foregut. Knowledge of what and how the digestive system contributes to total immune activity is incomplete, as is our understanding of how the immune functions of the digestive organs and of the body as a whole serve to maintain homeostasis of the gastrointestinal tract. Transient or chronic failure of any of these functions may underlie or contribute to human gastroenterologic diseases. The pathogenesis of almost all such diseases except those associated with infection by recognized pathogenic microorganisms is unknown. Immunologic phenomena are associated with many of them.

STRUCTURAL & FUNCTIONAL COMPONENTS OF THE IMMUNE SYSTEM PECULIAR TO THE GASTROINTESTINAL TRACT

The lymphoreticular components of the mature gastrointestinal tract consist of plasma cells, Peyer's patches, and intraepithelial lymphocytes (theliolymphocytes).

Plasma Cells

The plasma cells are distributed rather homogeneously throughout the lamina propria of the small gut. They are not present before birth, and their appearance coincides with population of the alimentary tract with microorganisms. It has been shown experimentally that sterile fetal small bowel implanted under the skin or renal capsule will also become populated with plasma cells, demonstrating that exogenous antigens may not be necessary for this phenomenon to occur. Plasma cells are derived from large B lymphocytes. They contain immunoglobulins of classes A, G, M, E, and D. IgA-containing cells predominate (A, 80%; M, 15%; G, $< 5\%$; D and E, $\sim 2\%$) and elaborate a major part of total body 7S IgA.

Keith B. Taylor is George DeForest Barnett Professor of Medicine, Stanford University School of Medicine, Stanford.

Peyer's Patches

Peyer's patches are groups of subepithelial lymphoid follicles located in the mucosa of the small intestine, being more numerous in the ileum than the jejunum. They are recognizable in man by the 24th week of gestation, becoming larger and more numerous by puberty. Each patch is only one follicle thick, and the overlying epithelium is devoid of villi and consists of a single layer of cells. These cells in man have the appearance of transporting cells and have been called microfold or M cells. Serial studies in animals have shown that Peyer's patches are initially populated predominantly by thymus-derived cells but that numbers of marrow-derived B cells later accumulate, so that in adult animals the population is approximately 70% T cells and 30% B cells.

The function of Peyer's patches is not known. It has been suggested that they are the mammalian analogue of the avian bursa of Fabricius, the central lymphoid organ responsible for the generation of B cells in birds. However, repopulation of irradiated Peyer's patches by peripheral lymphocytes has been observed—in contrast to the absence of repopulation of the irradiated mammalian thymus, which is unequivocally a central lymphoid organ. It has also been observed that the rate of cell proliferation in Peyer's patches in young animals is not sufficiently high to account for the appearance of B cells in other organs.

Peyer's patches are not capable of mounting a primary immune response in vivo. This appears to be due to lack of an antigen-trapping mechanism. Experiments using cells from mouse Peyer's patches in vitro have shown that antigen-sensitive T and B cells are present but that exogenous accessory adherent cells are required for generation of a primary immune response. There is a paucity of IgA plasma cells as well as those of other immunoglobulin classes in Peyer's patches. However, cells from Peyer's patches in the rabbit repopulate the irradiation-depleted lamina propria with predominantly IgA plasma cells, a few IgG and IgM cells being found as well.

One theory holds that Peyer's patches are a source of large lymphocytes found in thoracic duct lymph which circulate and populate the intestinal mucosa with immunoglobulin-containing plasma cells, of which the great majority are IgA.

Intraepithelial Lymphocytes or Theliolymphocytes

These are small lymphocytes whose function and fate are unknown. They are contiguous with intestinal epithelial cells. The isolation, characterization, and quantification of lymphoid cells from the intestinal wall of the rabbit have unexpectedly revealed that of the whole population of lymphoid cells, excluding those of Peyer's patches, immunoglobulin-containing cells (plasma cells) constitute only 1% and the theliolymphocytes more than one-third of the total population. Although theliolymphocytes have not been found either in the blood or in thoracic duct lymph, experimental studies have shown that the majority do not persist more than 3–4 days in the epithelium.

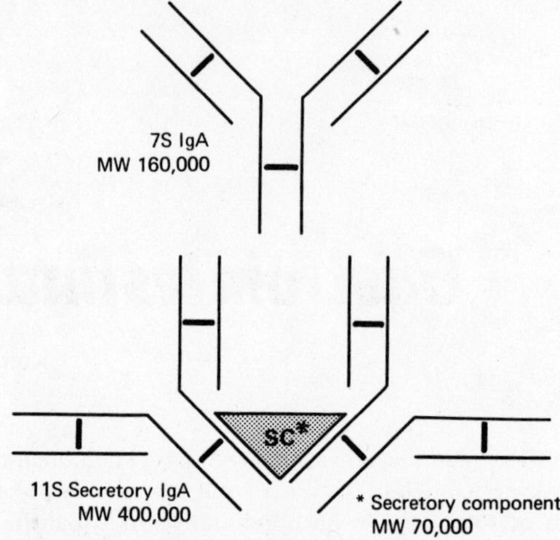

Figure 30–1. The secretory component (MW 70,000) is probably added at the stage of passage of the IgA molecule through the intestinal epithelial cell. ***Top:*** Properties of IgA: Specific antibody activity. Antigen-antibody reactions activate complement by alternative (C3) pathway and therefore are not involved in Arthus-type reactions. ***Bottom:*** Properties of secretory IgA: Reactions similar to those with IgA but also more resistant to proteolysis.

IMMUNOGLOBULINS IN THE INTESTINAL TRACT

(See Chapter 16.)

All classes of immunoglobulin are found in gastric and intestinal secretions, but IgA predominates. Similarly, immunofluorescence studies reveal all classes of immunoglobulins in the intercellular spaces of the lamina propria.

The IgA in gastrointestinal (and other) secretions is a dimer, designated secretory IgA, different from that found in the serum by virtue of the addition of a protein so-called secretory component (SC) (11S) (Fig 30–1). It contains 4 types of polypeptide chains: four L, four H, one J, and one SC.

Secretory IgA constitutes the major part of the coproantibodies found in the feces of man and animals following natural, therapeutic, or experimental infection, including immunization. Similar antibody production in response to ingested antigens unrelated to microorganisms and to autoantigens of the gastrointestinal tract itself has been demonstrated. Immunoglobulin-containing plasma cells in the lamina propria of stomach or gut have been shown to contain specific antibodies to such antigens, and IgA predominates. It is therefore clear that the gut is capable of mounting a local primary immune response. Such a response could be (1) protective, (2) regulatory of the gut flora, or (3) pathogenic.

In man and other species, it has been shown that oral administration of antigen also results in the production of *circulating* antibodies. The class of serum antibodies formed as a consequence of oral administration of antigen varies. In mice fed ferritin, it is predominantly IgA, whereas in man administration of live attenuated poliovirus is followed by a response initially of IgM followed by IgG, similar to that seen after parenteral inoculation. Systemic lymphoid tissue acquires the capacity to produce antibodies to ingested antigens. Thus, antigen must reach this lymphoid tissue across the mucosal and vascular structures, or lymphoid cells which are committed to specific antibody production migrate to systemic lymphoid tissue from the gut.

THE GASTROINTESTINAL TRACT AS A SITE OF IMMUNOLOGIC REACTIONS

The gut possesses the capacity to mount a primary immunologic response, a rich vascular supply, and mast cells and other cells capable of releasing substances associated with immediate allergic reactions and contraction of smooth muscle. Theoretically, it could be involved in any type of allergic reaction:

Type I: Anaphylactic reactions involving specific IgE and allergen. The IgE (reagin) is bound to mast cells and other cell surfaces through a specialized part of the Fc fragment. The allergen-reagin reaction damages cell membranes, releasing pharmacologically active amines such as histamine.

Type II: Cytotoxic reactions. Interaction of IgG and IgM antibodies with antigens attached to cell surfaces, causing phagocytosis of the cells or death by K (killer) cells or lysis by activation of the complement system.

Type III: Reaction of antigen with antibody in antigen excess to form soluble complexes which activate the complement system. Cells are damaged by direct toxic effect or secondarily as a consequence of damage to vascular endothelium.

Type IV: Delayed reactions involving interaction of allergen and sensitized T lymphocytes to release lymphokines. The result is a subacute or chronic inflammatory response, with cell damage or destruction.

The primary antigen may be extrinsic (microorganism, dietary constituent) but may share antigenic determinants with autoallergens of the gastrointestinal tissues; or a disturbance of immune responsiveness may allow primary autoimmunization to occur. These potential reactions are expressed schematically in Fig 30–2.

ACUTE GASTROINTESTINAL ALLERGY

Major Immunologic Features

- Acute reactions of type I.
- Involves reaction of specific IgE antibody and alimentary antigens.
- Subsequent release of histamine and other mediators of immediate hypersensitivity.

General Considerations

Acute and subacute allergic reactions occurring in the gastrointestinal tract as a consequence of ingestion of allergens are well documented. It has been estimated that in the USA 0.3–0.7% of infants are sensitive to cow's milk protein. The β-lactoglobulin component is an important allergen. It is absent from human milk, which usually does not evoke a reaction in an infant intolerant to cow's milk. Tolerance develops with maturity in most subjects. Hypersensitivity to other dietary proteins occurs less frequently. What may be interpreted as allergy to milk is sometimes an expression of intestinal lactase deficiency and lactose intolerance. This may be primary, or secondary to intestinal damage associated with an allergic response. Reactions to small amounts of milk or to lactose-free milk products such as cheeses are not due to alactasia and are probably allergic.

Immunologic Pathogenesis

The reason why some individuals are atopic is unknown. The atopic child appears to have the same exposure to ingested antigens as the normal child. Some data suggest that hypersensitivity occurs significantly more often in subjects who are deficient in IgA. Absence of secretory IgA in the intestinal mucosa or lumen may impair the physiologic mechanisms responsible for excluding potential allergens from the body without involvement of tissue-damaging or exciting reactions. The consequence might be the recruitment of more vigorous immune reactions involving other classes of antibody. Stimulation of normally responsive precommitted IgE plasma cells during a transient IgA-deficient period at the age of about 3 months has been proposed as a cause of the development of subsequent type I allergy or atopy to dietary proteins. An apparently—though not necessarily—conflicting view is that acute allergic disease occurs as a consequence of early contact with allergens and a genetically favored IgE pathway of antibody formation.

The sequence of events following presentation of an allergen to the intestinal tract of a hypersensitive subject has been studied by serial mucosal biopsy in infants sensitive to cow's milk. At 6 hours after challenge, edema and a small excess of plasma cells are noted in the jejunal lamina propria. By 12 hours, the numbers of mast cells and plasma cells, eosinophils, and neutrophils have greatly increased. The increase of plasma cells consists mainly of those containing IgE and IgM.

Experimental studies of passive anaphylaxis in intestine and skin have shown that the magnitude and timing of responses at both sites are the same whether the antigen is administered orally, intravenously, or locally. This suggests that allergen does not reach mast cells in the mucosa directly from the lumen but via the bloodstream. Thus, inhaled or injected allergens may produce reactions in the intestinal tract.

Clinical Features

A. Symptoms and Signs: Abdominal discomfort, nausea and vomiting, watery and sometimes bloody diarrhea, and, in severe cases, prostration and fever may occur. Extraintestinal responses such as bronchospasm, skin eruptions, and migrainous headaches may complicate the clinical picture. Much more frequent than acute, severe gastrointestinal allergy to cow's milk is a more insidious subacute reaction occurring in infants 2–3 months old typically 1 month after introduction of cow's milk into the diet and characterized by vomiting, prolonged diarrhea, failure to thrive, and sometimes atopic asthma and recurrent respiratory infection.

B. Laboratory Findings: A transient eosinophilia may be the only objective finding, but it may be short-lived and is often missed. Thus, in clinical practice, the diagnosis often depends solely on the history, and objective evidence is rarely obtained. Lacking such evidence, many clinicians regard the whole subject skeptically.

Immunologic Diagnosis

The results of skin tests with suspected allergens correlate poorly with the clinical history. The presence of IgG and IgM serum antibodies to dietary proteins detected by standard technics such as gel diffusion and passive hemagglutination does not correlate positively with clinical sensitivity.

Studies by Ishizaka and others have established that reagins are immunoglobulins of the class designated IgE. IgE-containing plasma cells are found in relatively small numbers in the mucosa of the small intestine, which may be the site of sensitization to dietary allergens. Increased numbers of IgE plasma

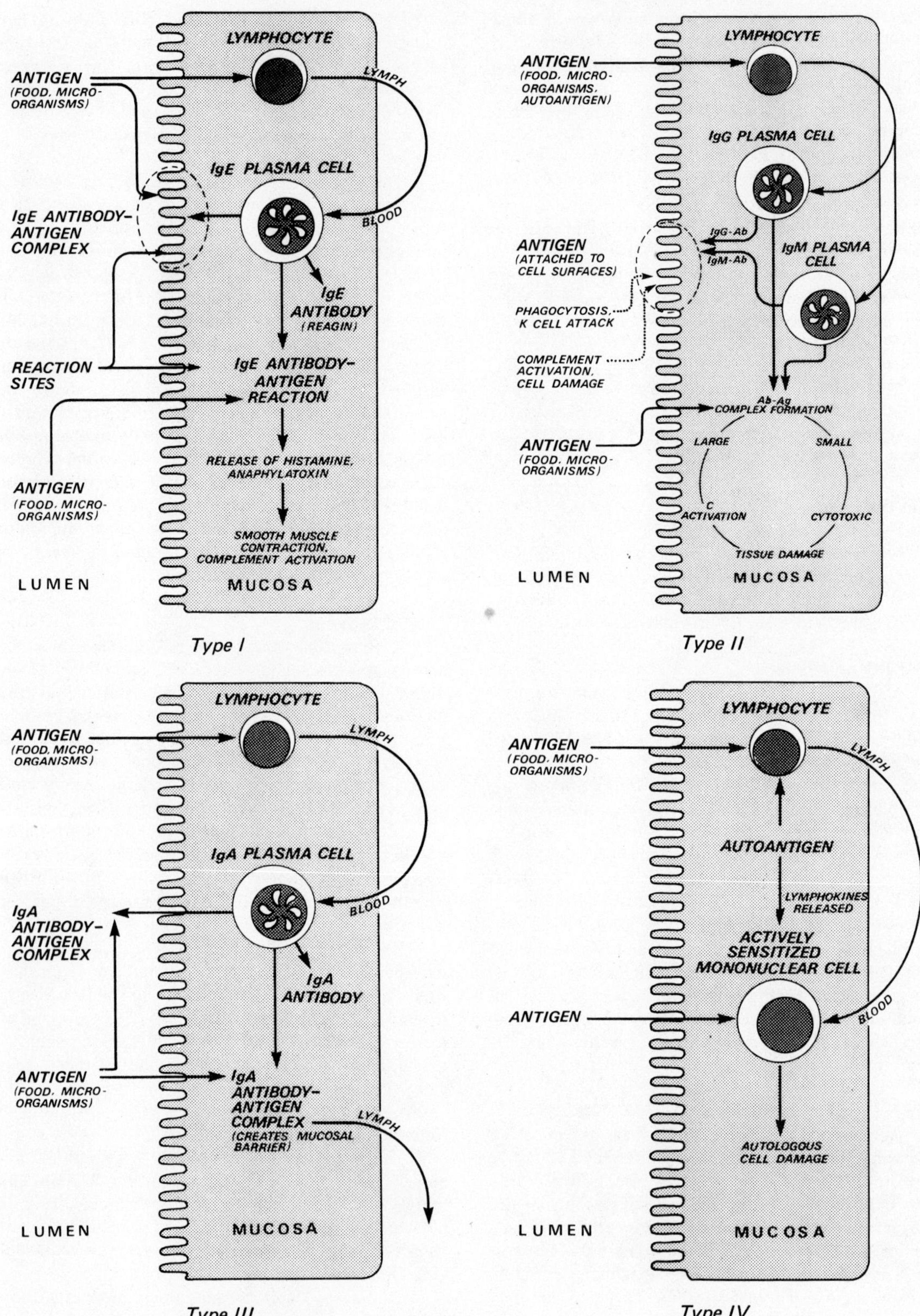

Figure 30–2. Immune events in the small intestinal mucosa in health and in expressions of various types of allergy. For simplicity, helper and suppressor T cells have not been included. Antigens probably reach mast cells in the gut via the bloodstream and not directly from the lumen. For explanation of specific types I–IV, see p 450.

cells have been reported in the jejunum of children with food allergy. Elevated serum IgE concentrations are found in some but not all subjects with gastrointestinal allergy.

The Prausnitz-Küstner (PK) test, which requires intradermal injection of the possibly allergic subject's serum into a healthy human recipient followed by injection of the suspected antigen at the same site, provides good evidence of specific circulating IgE antibodies, but the test is positive in only two-thirds of subjects with unequivocal acute gastrointestinal and alimentary allergy. The risk of transmitting viral hepatitis has eliminated the use of this test in man. The response can be elicited in other primates.

Confident diagnosis of gastrointestinal allergy is difficult. Tests other than the PK are required. Human skin from cadavers has been used successfully in vitro as a site for the anaphylactic reaction. It is unlikely to be more discriminating than the PK test. Radioallergosorbent technics may provide sensitive methods for detecting specific reagins with high concordance with provocative tests. At present, tests involving dietary exclusion and challenge, sometimes combined with jejunal biopsy, are the diagnostic tools most often employed. Valid blind tests have not been reported. There is often a psychogenic component to the complaints of sufferers from gastrointestinal allergy.

Differential Diagnosis

Acute gastrointestinal allergy may be mistaken at first for lactase deficiency, infectious gastroenteritis, or the onset of chronic nonspecific ulcerative colitis. Persistence of symptoms despite exclusion of cow's milk or other protein component of the diet prior to the clinical attack points to some other cause of the symptoms and requires thorough fecal examination and proctosigmoidoscopy.

Treatment

Treatment usually consists of identifying the allergen and excluding it from the diet. If it is an important item nutritionally, a substitute must be found.

Recent trials of cromolyn sodium, administered orally to atopic children, have been encouraging.

Complications & Prognosis

Complications of an acute attack are vomiting and diarrhea, resulting sometimes in serious dehydration and circulatory collapse. Bronchospasm may rarely be fatal, as may acute laryngeal edema.

Malabsorption and failure to thrive, atopic eczema, and recurrent respiratory infections are seen in less severely affected children until the specific allergen is excluded from their diet. Available data suggest that the hypersensitivity abates with age in most affected children and that in some cases full recovery is possible.

CHRONIC OR RELAPSING INFLAMMATORY DISEASES OF THE GASTROINTESTINAL TRACT

1. APHTHOUS ULCERATION OF THE BUCCAL CAVITY

This distressing condition is often dismissed by nonsufferers as trivial. The lesions consist of painful, recurrent ulcers on the tongue and buccal mucosa, lasting several days. About one in 10 otherwise healthy subjects suffers from the condition. In some, exposure to chocolate, nuts, or other foodstuffs is the precipitating cause. The lesions begin as tender red swellings and on histologic examination show acute inflammatory change with some mononuclear cell infiltration. The surface sloughs and becomes secondarily infected; healing with fibroblast activity occurs over days or weeks, usually leaving no scar.

The pathogenesis is unknown. The disease is not associated with herpes simplex. In some patients, a specific allergen can be identified. Serum antibodies to crude extracts of buccal mucosa have been demonstrated by complement fixation in subjects suffering from recurrent aphthous ulceration, although their significance is uncertain.

In sprue, Crohn's disease, ulcerative colitis, and intestinal lymphoma, more severe aphthous ulceration may occur, causing anorexia and providing a site for candidal and other infection. It is not known whether this more severe type of lesion is an expression of poor nutrition or of an abnormal immune response, possibly of an immune complex disease, as has been suggested in the case of pyoderma gangrenosum associated with inflammatory bowel disease. The lesions respond when the bowel disease is treated successfully.

2. SJÖGREN'S SYNDROME

(See Chapter 26.)

The complete Sjögren syndrome consists of conjunctival and buccal dryness, recurrent swelling of lacrimal and salivary glands, rheumatoid arthritis, and a higher incidence of malignant lymphoma than in the normal population. Salivary glands show plasma cell and lymphocyte infiltration.

Humoral antibodies to salivary tissue occur; in a large proportion of patients, antibodies to thyroid and nuclear antigens may also be found (Table 30–1).

3. CHRONIC ATROPHIC GASTRITIS & PERNICIOUS ANEMIA

Major Immunologic Features

- Evidence for both humoral and cellular immunity to gastric mucosal antigens.
- High incidence of anti-parietal cell antibodies—one to canaliculi and the other to intrinsic factor.
- Autoantibodies found in gastric mucosal plasma cells and in secretions (IgA).

General Considerations

The primary pathologic feature of pernicious anemia is progressive destruction of the normal glands of the body of the stomach. This is associated with partial or complete loss of acid, pepsinogen, and intrinsic factor secretion. When the last is complete, failure of vitamin B_{12} absorption occurs. In an undetermined number of subjects, this loss of intrinsic factor secretion may require many years or may never occur. The gastric mucosa is infiltrated, homogeneously or in patchy distribution, with variable numbers of polymorphonuclear and mononuclear leukocytes—predominantly the latter. Atrophy of the mucosa is a consequence of destruction and failure of regeneration of gastric parietal and chief cells. Often the gastric body mucosa is partly or wholly replaced by antral or small intestinal mucosa, a phenomenon called metaplasia.

Immunologic Pathogenesis

The evidence of immunologic pathogenesis in pernicious anemia is indirect. Experimentally, chronic inflammatory lesions of the gastric mucosa, glandular atrophy, and loss of gastric secretory function have been produced in dogs by immunization using gastric mucosal material and Freund's complete adjuvant. Other species, such as rabbits, rats, mice and guinea pigs, are resistant to these procedures. In dogs, the appearance of gastric lesions is associated more closely with the development of cell-mediated immunity than with humoral antibodies. However, repeated injection of human gastric antibodies into rats has resulted in loss of gastric secretory cells after several weeks.

Humoral antibodies are found in pernicious anemia to 2 antigens of the gastric parietal cell. One is a glycoprotein, Castle's intrinsic factor, and the other a lipoprotein of the microvilli of the parietal cell canalicular system. Neither antigen is species-specific; both are completely cell-specific. Serum parietal cell canalicular antibody is present, as determined by immunofluorescence, in about 90% of patients with pernicious anemia, and intrinsic factor antibody in 60–70%, with the exception of an Asian Indian population with pernicious anemia in which no intrinsic factor antibodies were found though parietal cell canalicular antibody was present with the expected frequency.

There are 2 types of intrinsic factor antibody: type I blocks the attachment of vitamin B_{12} to the intrinsic factor molecule and type II attaches to intrinsic factor or the intrinsic factor-B_{12} complex (Fig 30–3). Type II intrinsic factor antibody occurs with about half the frequency of type I and only rarely occurs in the absence of type I. Experimentally, the immunogenicity of the intrinsic factor antigenic site for type I antibody is greater than that for type II. Evidence suggests that antibodies to intrinsic factor are capable of inhibiting intrinsic factor-mediated vitamin B_{12} absorption in vivo.

Gastric antibodies in serum are mainly of the IgG class, with some IgA and rarely IgM. In chronic atrophic gastritis of the body of the stomach without the lesion of pernicious anemia, serum parietal cell canalicular antibody occurs less frequently than in pernicious anemia, and intrinsic factor antibodies are found so rarely that their presence requires further diagnostic work-up which almost always reveals pernicious anemia. They do not occur in the absence of severe gastritis, but a group of patients with thyroid disease has

Table 30–1. Autoantibodies in gastrointestinal and hepatic disease.

Disease	Antigen	Detection of Antibody
Aphthous ulceration	Buccal mucosa	Complement fixation
Sjögren's syndrome	Salivary ducts	Immunofluorescence
	Nuclei	Immunofluorescence and complement fixation
	Thyroid	Immunofluorescence and complement fixation
Pernicious anemia	Parietal cell canalicular lipoprotein	Immunofluorescence on gastric mucosa Complement fixation
	Thyroid	Immunofluorescence and complement fixation
	Intrinsic factor	Inhibition of biologic activity Blocking B_{12} binding Coprecipitation
Gluten-sensitive enteropathy	Reticulin	Immunofluorescence
Chronic inflammatory bowel disease	Colonic epithelial lipopolysaccharide	Immunofluorescence Passive hemagglutination
Chronic active hepatitis	Smooth muscle ("actomyosin")	Immunofluorescence
Primary biliary cirrhosis	Nuclei	Immunofluorescence
	Mitochondria	Immunofluorescence and complement fixation (kidney or other tissue)

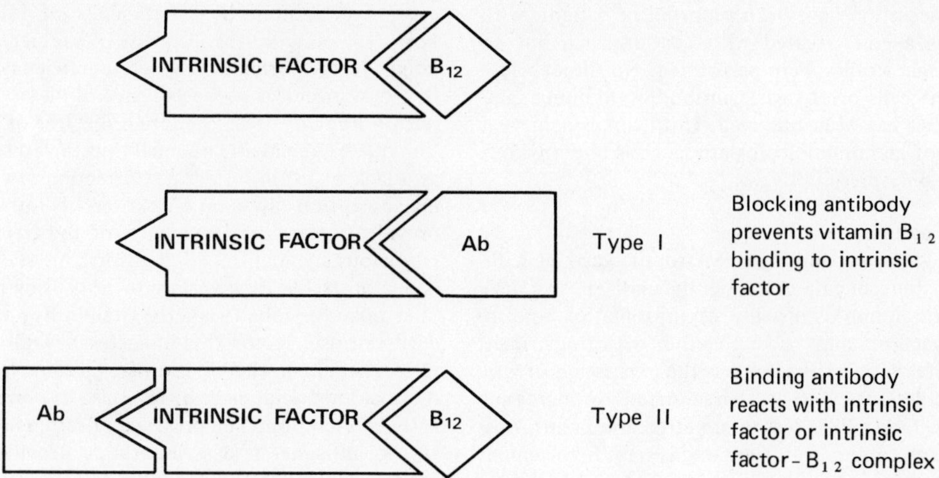

Figure 30–3. The 2 types of intrinsic factor antibody.

been described in which humoral intrinsic factor antibodies were present despite some acid and intrinsic factor secretion which persisted during many years of follow-up. Such subjects are rare.

Parietal cell canalicular antibodies—but not intrinsic factor antibodies—are found in first-order relatives of patients with pernicious anemia. They are also present with significantly increased frequency in iron deficiency anemia, thyroid disease, idiopathic Addison's disease, diabetes mellitus, and vitiligo in association with chronic gastritis (Table 30–2). The frequency of parietal cell canalicular antibody increases in apparently healthy subjects with age. This antibody is rarely or never found unless chronic gastritis is present, and the prevalence of this condition increases with age.

Thyroid microsomal and thyroglobulin antibodies are also found in some pernicious anemia subjects, though in lower frequency than in subjects with thyroid diseases.

Gastric autoantibodies are not detectable in patients with chronic gastritis associated with gastric and duodenal ulcer disease or following partial gastrectomy for ulcer disease, nor in gastric carcinoma. The gastritic lesions in these conditions are histologically indistinguishable from those in pernicious anemia, but gastric functional changes are usually less severe.

Table 30–2. Frequency of circulating parietal cell canalicular antibody in pernicious anemia and other diseases.

Patient Group	Approximate Positive Parietal Cell Canalicular Antibody (%)
Pernicious anemia	86
Normal population*	11
Vitiligo	20
Thyroiditis	30
Thyrotoxicosis	25
Addison's disease	24
Diabetes mellitus	21
Iron deficiency anemia	20

*Chronic gastritis not excluded.

Gastric antibodies in gastric secretions. Both parietal cell canalicular antibody and intrinsic factor antibody are present in the gastric juice of the majority of pernicious anemia patients. Intrinsic factor antibodies may form complexes with any residual intrinsic factor secreted. The antibodies are IgG and IgA, and some activity is present in 11S (secretory) IgA. This, together with demonstration of the presence of both parietal cell canalicular antibody and intrinsic factor antibody in plasma cells in the inflamed mucosa and the absence of thyroid antibodies from gastric juice in subjects with thyroid antibodies in their sera, attests to gastric antibody formation in the diseased gastric mucosa.

Cell-mediated immunity in pernicious anemia. Cellular immunity to intrinsic factor and gastric parietal cell canalicular antigen was measured by lymphocyte activation and MIF production. Positive responses were detected in patients with pernicious anemia, in patients with pernicious anemia and immunoglobulin deficiency, and in a few normal individuals.

Response of the gastric lesion of pernicious anemia to corticosteroids and immunosuppressive drugs. Improved vitamin B_{12} absorption, enhanced intrinsic factor secretion, some regeneration of gastric parietal cells, and decreased titers of circulating gastric antibodies have been reported in pernicious anemia subjects treated with corticosteroids. Achlorhydria usually persists. However, there is a lack of correlation in treated individuals between improved vitamin B_{12} absorption, improved gastric structure and function, and changes of intrinsic factor antibody titers in either serum or gastric juice, and the mode of action of corticosteroids remains uncertain.

Parietal cell regeneration and restoration of gastric acid secretion have been reported in patients with pernicious anemia treated with azathioprine, but no immunologic studies were performed. No direct effect of immune cells or of gastric antibodies on human gastric mucosa has been observed. Until this is achieved, evidence of an immunologic pathogenesis in pernicious anemia is only presumptive.

Clinical Features

A. Symptoms and Signs: Atrophic gastritis without pernicious anemia is frequently undiagnosed since the gastric lesion is usually asymptomatic. Mild to severe dyspepsia may occur together with impairment of appetite. Pernicious anemia is the expression of vitamin B_{12} deficiency. It is characterized by increasing weakness, fatigability, loss of appetite, and pallor. Loss of weight is common, but wasting is rare. Involvement of the nervous system, which is quite variable, may include peripheral neuropathy, damage to pyramidal tract and posterior column neurons, and disturbance of higher cortical functions.

Pernicious anemia displays a strong familial association, but how much is environmentally and how much genetically determined is still unknown. No specific HLA genotype has been unequivocally associated with the disease. There is an association between pernicious anemia and thyroid disease, especially thyrotoxicosis, which occurs frequently in close relatives of pernicious anemia patients. Less strong associations have been claimed with diabetes mellitus and idiopathic Addison's disease. Pernicious anemia also occurs in acquired immunoglobulin deficiency, most commonly of IgA but sometimes of IgG or IgM also.

B. Laboratory Findings: Macrocytic anemia and hypersegmentation of the nuclei of the neutrophil granulocytes are the morphologic findings in the peripheral blood. Bone marrow aspirates show megaloblastosis. Serum vitamin B_{12} values below 120 pg/ml are found (normal: 200–1500 pg/ml). Serum lactate dehydrogenase activity is markedly elevated owing to excessive intramedullary destruction of red blood cells. The excretion of methylmalonate in the urine is increased. Vitamin B_{12} therapy corrects all of these abnormalities except that some damage to the central nervous system may be irreversible.

Immunologic Diagnosis

The finding of circulating parietal canalicular antibodies by complement fixation or immunofluorescence almost certainly indicates chronic gastritic disease, though negative serologic findings do not exclude this diagnosis. Antibodies to intrinsic factor indicate the lesion of pernicious anemia with the rare exceptions of a few patients with thyroid disease. Cell-mediated immune tests are not yet generally available.

Differential Diagnosis

Clincially, other anemias and untreated myxedema and pituitary hypofunction may be confused with pernicious anemia. The finding of megaloblastic anemia reduces the possibilities to three—namely, deficiency of vitamin B_{12}, deficiency of folic acid, or both. Unequivocal involvement of the nervous system points to the former. However, a deficiency of vitamin B_{12} may occur as a consequence of dietary deficiency (an unsupplemented vegetarian diet) or of malabsorption due to pancreatic or small intestinal disease as well as a lack of intrinsic factor. Correction of vitamin B_{12} malabsorption by administration of intrinsic factor provides unequivocal evidence of the basic lesion of pernicious anemia. Impaired absorption of vitamin B_{12} is demonstrable by a variety of tests using tracer doses of radioactive cobalt-labeled vitamin B_{12} without and with intrinsic factor (Schilling test). Aspirated gastric juice contains negligible intrinsic factor activity and no hydrochloric acid, even in response to powerful stimulants of secretion. The presence of serum antibodies to gastric antigens, as described, may provide confirmatory evidence.

Treatment

Intramuscular injections of vitamin B_{12} will maintain remissions in pernicious anemia. Corticosteroids and immunosuppressive agents have only been used experimentally. There is no practicable means at present of recognizing the gastric lesion sufficiently early to offer any hope of instituting therapy at a reversible stage of the disease.

Complications & Prognosis

The only important complication is gastric carcinoma, which is probably 3 times more common in patients with pernicious anemia than in the population at large. No immunologic or other test has yet been devised which reliably identifies subjects prone to develop gastric carcinoma or provides early recognition of such a lesion.

GLUTEN-SENSITIVE ENTEROPATHY; CELIAC SPRUE

Major Immunologic Features

- Genetic association with HLA-A1 and HLA-B8.
- Infiltration of jejunal lamina propria with lymphocytes and plasma cells when untreated.
- Possible local IgA deficiency with production of IgM antigluten antibodies.

General Considerations

This disease, also termed nontropical sprue and, in adults, idiopathic steatorrhea, is a disease of the small intestine characterized by functional disturbances causing malabsorption of food and nutrients and structural changes of partial or complete villous atrophy. The normally columnar jejunal epithelial cells become stunted and cuboid, and distortion of their microvilli occurs. The lamina propria becomes infiltrated with inflammatory cells, of which the majority are mononuclear in type. In contrast, the ileal mucosa is relatively or completely normal.

Dicke showed more than 25 years ago that ingestion of wheat gluten was the causative factor, and the term gluten-sensitive enteropathy has now been adopted.

Immunologic Pathogenesis

Two theories have been advanced to explain the damaging effect of wheat protein in this condition and the improvement in jejunal structure and function that follows dietary gluten exclusion. The enzymatic hypothesis holds that the intestinal mucosa in gluten-sensitive enteropathy congenitally lacks a peptidase necessary for hydrolysis of a toxic partial breakdown product of wheat gluten and that accumulation of this material, apparently of low molecular weight (1000), produces damage to the intestinal mucosa. However, in gluten-sensitive enteropathy in remission, jejunal mucosal biopsies have revealed no peptidase deficiency.

The second, immunologic theory is supported by the following observations:

(1) In a small number of gluten-sensitive enteropathy patients maintained on gluten-exclusion diets, ingestion of small amounts of wheat gluten results in what clinically appears to be an acute (type I) allergic reaction. This has been termed gluten shock.

(2) In untreated gluten-sensitive enteropathy, the jejunal lamina propria is heavily infiltrated with lymphocytes and plasma cells and an increase of theliolymphocytes which have the ultrastructure of immunoblasts, which are not seen in healthy mucosa. In treated gluten-sensitive enteropathy, the histologic appearances are partially or wholly restored to normal. The events in the jejunal mucosa following oral challenge with wheat gluten are as follows: (a) eosinophilic infiltration within 4–5 hours; (b) polymorphonuclear infiltration and vascular endothelial swelling at 10–16 hours; and (c) plasma cell increase of predominantly IgM-containing cells, this IgM being largely antibody-specific for gluten. IgA and IgM immune complexes appear in the basement membrane region, with variable complement fixation.

(3) Anti-inflammatory doses of corticosteroids correct the clinical and histologic abnormalities of gluten-sensitive enteropathy and effectively suppress gluten shock. Of itself, this clearly does not imply an immune basis for gluten-sensitive enteropathy.

(4) Humoral and secretory antibodies to gluten are present in many patients with untreated gluten-sensitive enteropathy. However, antibodies to other dietary antigens also occur in excess in such patients, suggesting an enhanced immune responsiveness, probably at the mucosal level, due either to increased access of antigens in the lumen as a result of mucosal damage or a quantitative increase in immune-responsive tissue. The latter seems more likely.

(5) Immunoglobulin disturbances occur in untreated gluten-sensitive enteropathy, including elevated or depressed levels of serum IgA, depressed serum IgM, and a significantly more frequent absence of IgD than in normal subjects. Following successful treatment, the IgA levels return to normal limits. A subgroup of subjects have the lesion of gluten-sensitive enteropathy and a persistent IgA deficiency. The jejunal lesion responds to gluten exclusion. An isolated IgA deficiency is found in approximately one in 700 normal individuals and in one in 70 subjects with gluten-sensitive enteropathy. The reason for this discrepancy is unknown.

In the jejunal mucosa, the most constant finding in untreated gluten-sensitive enteropathy is an increased number of IgM plasma cells, though IgA cells still predominate. There is a corresponding increase in IgM in jejunal secretions. In IgA-deficient subjects, IgM and IgG plasma cells are found in the lamina propria, compensating to a variable degree for absence of IgA cells. A relative failure of jejunal IgA antibody response might be pathogenetically significant, since an IgM and IgG compensatory antibody response might result in tissue-damaging immune reactions.

(6) Reticulin antibodies are found in the sera of 60% of untreated gluten-sensitive enteropathic children, 30% of gluten-sensitive enteropathic adults, and 25% of patients with dermatitis herpetiformis. Following treatment by gluten exclusion, the antibody titer may fall or disappear. There is no validated explanation for this phenomenon. The occurrence of similar reticulin antibodies in subjects with small bowel inflammation due to other causes (eg, Crohn's disease) suggests a nonspecific response. Others have claimed that gluten and reticulin share antigenic determinants. The problem has still to be resolved.

(7) Circulating antigen-antibody complexes occur. A relatively simple method of demonstrating the presence of circulating immune complexes depends on the property of a component of the complement system, C1q, to precipitate soluble complexes in agar gel (see Chapter 24). This technic has revealed circulating antigen-antibody complexes in untreated gluten-sensitive enteropathy. That the antigen involved is gluten or a derivative is still speculative.

In summary, it is possible that the intestinal damage of gluten-sensitive enteropathy is a consequence of an Arthus-like immune reaction and that it occurs because of a tendency for local production in the jejunum of IgM rather than IgA antibodies in response to a gluten challenge. This might result from abnormal handling of the antigen by the intestinal epithelium or other structures or an inherent immune abnormality. The fact that only a minority of IgA-deficient subjects have gluten-sensitive enteropathy is unexplained.

Clinical Features

A. Symptoms and Signs: Malabsorption is associated with stunting of growth in the child, loss of weight in the adult, various deficiency states, and greasy, bulky stools of high fat content. The disease expresses itself at any age, but most frequently in childhood.

B. Laboratory Findings: In the untreated subject

there may be electrolyte depletion, reflected in abnormally low serum potassium and calcium values. Hypoalbuminemia may reflect protein depletion. Anemia is often present and may be due to iron deficiency, folic acid deficiency, or both. Analysis of the stools reveals increased excretion of fat and nitrogen, and tests of absorption of glucose and xylose reveal malabsorption. The diagnosis is established on the basis of an abnormal jejunal biopsy and response to gluten exclusion.

Recent studies have revealed an association of the disease with the HLA-A1 and HLA-B8 histocompatibility antigens, suggesting a genetic basis for the previously noted familial association of the disease. The frequency of HLA-B8 in celiac disease is 80% compared with 20–25% in the population at large. (HLA-A1 is also much more frequent, but this gene is associated with HLA-B8 as a consequence of linkage disequilibrium.) It has also been noted that a skin disease, dermatitis herpetiformis, is associated with small bowel malabsorption and that the latter responds like uncomplicated gluten-sensitive enteropathy to a gluten-exclusion diet though the skin disease is not affected. HLA-B8 occurs in dermatitis herpetiformis in an abnormal frequency similar to that in gluten-sensitive enteropathy. Thus, as in the case of ankylosing spondylitis, tissue histocompatibility typing may have diagnostic value in the future.

Immunologic Diagnosis

There are no clinically useful immunologic tests. The finding of circulating gluten antibodies has not as yet been applied diagnostically. Quantitative serum immunoglobulin levels may reveal an underlying immunoglobulin deficiency.

Differential Diagnosis

The list of causes of small intestinal malabsorption in both children and adults is very large. In infants and children, sensitivity to cow's milk or dietary proteins other than gluten, lactase deficiency, cystic fibrosis of the pancreas, parasitic infestations, Crohn's disease, and congenital anatomic abnormalities of the gastrointestinal tract must be considered. In the adult, the consequences of upper gastrointestinal surgery, chronic pancreatitis, intestinal lymphoma, Crohn's disease, and Whipple's disease may present in a manner that makes these disorders indistinguishable from gluten-sensitive enteropathy.

Treatment

Exclusion of even traces of wheat gluten from the diet almost always results in restoration of small bowel structure and function to normal. This may take weeks or months, and until it is accomplished, dietary supplements and even parenteral administration of some essential nutrients are required. In initially refractory patients, corticosteroids may sometimes induce significant improvement.

Complications & Prognosis

Failure to recognize and treat the disease may result in severe malnutrition, the most important expression of which is irreversible stunting of growth. Delays in initiating treatment may result in a refractory state of malnutrition which does not respond to gluten exclusion and standard oral supplementation. Parenteral nutritional technics may have to be used.

There is an increased risk of developing intestinal lymphoma (6–10% after a mean duration of the disease of 21 years). Malignancies of the foregut also occur in significantly higher incidence in subjects with celiac disease. A variable degree of splenic atrophy and immune deficiency may occur when the disease is of long duration. Otherwise it appears that rigorous dietary control can achieve a prognosis of normal health and longevity.

CROHN'S DISEASE
(Intestinal Granulomatous Disease)

Major Immunologic Features

- Granulomatous response in intestinal lesions and regional lymph nodes.
- No consistently demonstrable alterations in humoral immunity.
- Abnormalities in cellular immunity may be secondary to malnutrition.

General Considerations

This condition may affect any part of the gastrointestinal tract, most frequently the terminal ileum. The inflammatory lesion is primarily submucosal but ultimately involves the whole thickness of the gut wall. Ulceration of the mucosa occurs and may extend deeply to reach the serosa and cause local perforation and the development of fistulas. Obstructive lymphedema and lymphadenoid hyperplasia occur. In 50–70% of such lesions, noncaseating granulomas are found.

Granulomas are also frequently present in regional mesenteric lymph nodes. The affected bowel becomes thickened and rigid. Two or more diseased segments may be separated by relatively normal bowel (skip lesions).

Immunologic Pathogenesis

The cause of Crohn's disease is not known. Granulomatous lesions can be transmitted to the bowel and footpads of experimental and usually immunologically depressed animals using cell-free and ultrafiltered extracts of Crohn's lesions, which would seem to suggest that an infectious agent may be responsible. However, there is contrary evidence in reported failures to reproduce these results, the nonspecific nature of granulomas, failure of the disease to respond to any antibiotic, and absence of epidemiologic evidence of infectivity. The disease displays some familial tendency but not within a pattern suggesting a genetic determinant. No satisfactory experimental analogue has been produced. Immune phenomena are not well substantiated in Crohn's disease. Experimentally, granulomatous response appears to be a delayed hypersensitivity reaction, but there are many inciting agents, inorganic or organic, living or dead, which produce the same lesions. Immunosuppressive agents inhibit the production of experimental granulomas but have not been shown to be of substantial therapeutic value in Crohn's disease.

A. Humoral Factors: There is no consistent alteration of any class of circulating immunoglobulin in Crohn's disease. Low plasma protein concentrations occasionally occur as a consequence of protein-losing enteropathy.

Antibodies to a colonic epithelial lipopolysaccharide and to a similar antigen derived from *E coli* O14 but not to any small intestinal antigen are demonstrable in the blood of some patients with Crohn's disease.

Antigen-antibody complexes have been demonstrated by at least 2 technics in the sera of some patients with Crohn's disease. The nature of the antigen or antigens involved and the significance of these findings are unknown. Some of the extraintestinal diseases might be due to immune complex deposition. The cytotoxic effect on colonic epithelial cells of normal lymphocytes incubated with the sera of some patients with Crohn's disease might be due to the presence of circulating colonic antibodies. Serum complement activity is not abnormal in active Crohn's disease. Recently, lymphocytotoxicity has been demonstrated in some Crohn's sera, the effect being more marked on lymphocytes from healthy subjects than Crohn's subjects. This is not HLA-associated.

B. Delayed Hypersensitivity:

1. Skin tests—No consistent pattern of response to standard antigens such as PPD or DNCB is evident to suggest either anergy or hypersensitivity.

Some discrepant results may be a consequence of nutritional deficiencies secondary to severe Crohn's disease or to quantitative differences in peripheral lymphocyte populations. Reports of positive Kveim tests in patients with Crohn's disease suggest a link with sarcoidosis (as do the successful attempts to transmit granulomatous changes experimentally). Other reports are negative, and variations in Kveim reagents are currently being examined.

2. Tests of lymphocyte activation and MIF production using lymphocytes of patients with Crohn's disease in vitro and antigens of adult and fetal human and rat small and large intestine reveal no abnormal responses.

3. Peripheral lymphocytes of some patients with Crohn's disease exert a cytotoxic effect on human rectal epithelial cells but not on the mucosa of small intestine. There is a relative deficiency of circulating T cells in Crohn's disease, possibly as a consequence of selective lymphocytotoxic factor present in Crohn's sera.

In summary, there is no evidence of primary immunologic pathogenesis in Crohn's disease. The factors involved in the formation of the typical granulomatous lesions remain obscure. At present, conclusive evidence for or against involvement of a transmissible agent of the size of a mycoplasma or smaller is awaited. An unexplained observation of healing of the granulomatous lesion following surgical diversion of the fecal stream may favor the theory that some dietary constituent plays a role in causing or perpetuating the disease.

Clinical Features

A. Symptoms and Signs: The disease is clinically manifested by fever, abdominal colic, diarrhea, malabsorption with loss of weight, and consequences of specific nutritional deficiencies of iron, folic acid, and vitamin B_{12}. Frank intestinal bleeding is rare, but the presence of fecal occult blood is common. The lesion may present as a palpable and often tender mass, most commonly in the right lower quadrant of the abdomen. Surgery may be required to resect or bypass stenosed segments of bowel, fistulous involvement of the body wall and skin, or other viscera such as the urinary bladder; occasionally, surgery is needed to resect bleeding ulceration.

Extraintestinal disease. The skin, eyes, liver, and joints may be involved in Crohn's disease, but the reason is not known. There is little or no correlation with the apparent severity of the bowel disease. (1) Lesions of skin and buccal mucosa: erythema nodosum, pyoderma gangrenosum, and aphthous ulceration. (2) Lesions of the eye: uveitis (including iritis) and episcleritis. (3) Liver: fatty infiltration and portal triaditis (pericholangitis); possibly cirrhosis and biliary tract carcinoma. (4) Ankylosing spondylitis. (5) Episodic polysynovitis.

There is a strong association between ankylosing spondylitis in Crohn's disease (and nonspecific ulcerative colitis; see p 460) and HLA-B27, and the same is true in uncomplicated ankylosing spondylitis, whereas neither Crohn's disease nor ulcerative colitis has been associated with any HLA genotype.

B. Laboratory Findings: Some degree of anemia, usually due to chronic blood loss and iron deficiency, is common. There may be hematologic evidence of vitamin B_{12} deficiency.

An elevated erythrocyte sedimentation rate is often a valuable indication of active Crohn's disease.

Immunologic Diagnosis

No reliable methods are available.

Differential Diagnosis

Nonspecific ulcerative colitis, lymphoma of the small intestine, Whipple's disease, giardiasis, gluten-sensitive enteropathy, tuberculous enteritis, and small bowel neoplasms are some of the conditions which may clinically resemble Crohn's disease.

Treatment

Treatment of this disease remains quite unsatisfactory. No controlled therapeutic trials have established clear superiority of any regimen. Corticosteroids, sulfasalazine (salicylazosulfapyridine), and azathioprine are used in various combinations. Surgery is never curative but may be required to relieve the complications of obstruction and fistula formation.

Complications & Prognosis

The major complications have been described as part of the clinical features. The prognosis can only be characterized as extremely uncertain. The disease varies in its activity. In some patients the course is relentless and may lead to death as a consequence of repeated resections of bowel and ultimate uncorrectable malnutrition. In others the disease is self-limiting or may require a single surgical resection, with no recurrence over a period of many years.

Another complication, recently recognized, is a high incidence of malignant change in both affected large and small bowel.

NONSPECIFIC CHRONIC ULCERATIVE COLITIS

Major Immunologic Features

- Lymphocytes are cytotoxic for colonic epithelial cells.
- Antibodies detected against intestinal epithelial antigens do not seem pathogenic.
- Antibody to intestinal lipopolysaccharide cross-reacts with *E coli* O14.

General Considerations

Ulcerative colitis is a chronic inflammatory disease of the colonic mucosa. The early changes are confined to the mucosa, which is diffusely inflamed and ulcerated to a variable degree. Inflammatory changes in the submucosa are seen only in long-standing chronic disease. Infiltration of the lamina propria with mononuclear inflammatory cells is an invariable feature. Eosinophilic infiltration is at times marked, and in severe disease polymorphonuclear leukocytes abound. The mucosal vessels are dilated. The crypt abscess, a focal collection of polymorphonuclear leukocytes in the deepest part of the lamina propria, contiguous with dilated crypts of Lieberkühn, is found in more severe disease. Ulcers may be superficial or may involve the entire thickness of mucosa, which may then be lost and replaced by granulation tissue. Granuloma formation rarely occurs.

Immunologic Pathogenesis

The cause of ulcerative colitis is unknown. Specific infections and psychologic, nutritional, and immunologic theories have been entertained without solid evidence. The immunologic theory of causation received limited support from studies of the disease, including convincing evidence in some patients of beneficial effects of dietary exclusion of cow's milk or other proteins and of immediate and severe relapse following oral challenge with the same protein. There is also a higher than normal frequency of atopic eczema, asthma, and hay fever in persons with chronic ulcerative colitis.

A. Humoral Immunity: No consistent differences in circulating immunoglobulins are found. The presence and titer of circulating antibodies to cow's milk and other dietary proteins do not correlate positively with the severity or extent of chronic ulcerative colitis, though there may be some correlation with its chronicity and tendency to relapse. Responses to dietary exclusion of cow's milk do not correlate positively with milk antibody titers. No reaginic activity to suspected allergens has been convincingly demonstrated in chronic ulcerative colitis.

Antibodies of IgG, IgA, or IgM classes against an intestinal epithelial lipopolysaccharide are found in the sera of patients with chronic ulcerative colitis with variable frequency and more often in children than in adults with the disease. They have been reported in some healthy relatives of patients with chronic ulcerative colitis. Other immunologic features can be summarized as follows: (1) Antibody titers are independent of duration, extent, severity, or complications of chronic ulcerative colitis. (2) Antibodies persist following colectomy. (3) Antibodies are not cytotoxic to colonic epithelial cells even in the presence of complement. (4) Attempts to demonstrate antibody bound to colonic epithelial cells in chronic ulcerative colitis have been unsuccessful. (5) Antibodies cross-react with lipopolysaccharide antigen of *E coli* O14. It has been concluded that coliform antigens may break tolerance to intestinal epithelial antigen. A pathogenetic role cannot be substantiated. Chronic ulcerative colitis has been described in patients with hypogammaglobulinemia.

B. Immune Complexes in Chronic Ulcerative Colitis: These have been demonstrated in the sera of some patients by different technics. The antigen or antigens have not been identified, but the antibody is IgG. Theoretically, their presence might be responsible for extracolonic complications of chronic ulcerative colitis, some of which strongly resemble those seen in serum sickness, but no association has been demonstrated. They might also serve to "arm" K cells, rendering them cytotoxic (see below).

C. Cellular Immunity:

1. Skin tests–Patterns of response in chronic ulcerative colitis to standard tests do not differ from those of healthy controls. Delayed cutaneous hypersensitivity to DNA is reported in one-third of chronic ulcerative colitis patients. This may explain observed reactions to intradermal autologous leukocytes.

2. Tests of lymphocyte activation and MIF production using lymphocytes from patients with chronic ulcerative colitis have given inconclusive results. PHA, PPD, colonic antigen, and *E coli* O14 antigen resulted in no differences in these 2 tests using chronic ulcerative colitis lymphocytes and normal lymphocytes in many studies. One study showed some depression using cells from patients with chronic ulcerative colitis during attacks.

There is a single report of leukocyte migration inhibition using lymphocytes from patients with chronic ulcerative colitis in the presence of extracts of human fetal colon. Colectomy abolished this abnormal response.

3. **Cytotoxicity**–Lymphocytes from patients with chronic ulcerative colitis and with Crohn's disease are specifically cytotoxic to allogeneic colonic epithelial cells in vitro, gastric and ileal cells being unaffected. This phenomenon persists in remissions of chronic ulcerative colitis but not following colectomy; is specific for chronic ulcerative colitis and Crohn's disease; is inhibited by preincubation of lymphocytes with horse anti-human thymus serum; is inhibited by preincubation of lymphocytes with serum from other patients with chronic ulcerative colitis and Crohn's disease but not by autologous serum; is inhibited by preincubation with *E coli* O119:B14 lipopolysaccharide; and does not require the presence of complement.

Furthermore, cytotoxicity is conferred on lymphocytes of healthy subjects by preincubation with *E coli* O119:B14 lipopolysaccharide (but not with PHA) and by preincubation with serum from patients with chronic ulcerative colitis or Crohn's disease. This effect is due to IgM in the sera.

These findings suggest the possible involvement of either sensitized T cells binding to epithelial cells through specific surface receptors or K cells coated with immune complex recognizing target epithelial cells through free antibody valencies in the complex.

Clinical Features

A. Symptoms and Signs: Patients have symptoms which range from mild diarrhea without systemic upset to a severe illness, with sustained fever, prostration associated with dehydration, and passage of more than 8–10 bloody stools daily, which may be life-threatening. The complications may be local or remote. Local ones occur around the large bowel and anus; perforation is the most dangerous. Fistula formation is less common than in Crohn's disease. The remote complications are similar to those of Crohn's disease, involving predominantly the skin, eyes, liver, and joints.

B. Laboratory Findings: Disease of abrupt onset is distinguished from shigella and amebic dysentery by the absence of specific pathogens in the stool and negative serologic findings for these organisms. The peripheral blood may exhibit eosinophilia and neutrophilia. There may be variable anemia due to acute or chronic blood loss. The erythrocyte sedimentation rate may be elevated. The stool contains no pathogens.

Immunologic Diagnosis

At present no immunologic tests have demonstrated diagnostic value.

Differential Diagnosis

Nonspecific ulcerative colitis of acute onset must be distinguished from shigella and amebic dysentery by the history of potential infection and fecal and serologic examinations. In older subjects, abrupt infarction of the colon or small bowel may present a diagnostic problem. Occasionally, sigmoid diverticulitis and even a colonic carcinoma may present with bloody diarrhea and lower abdominal pain. Crohn's disease when it involves the colon may be almost indistinguishable from ulcerative colitis.

Treatment

As in Crohn's disease, treatment of the first attack or relapse of chronic ulcerative colitis includes general supportive measures. Glucocorticoids and sulfasalazine (salicylazosulfapyridine) have been shown to be effective in controlled trials. Azathioprine may be useful in allowing reduction of corticosteroid dosage.

Complications & Prognosis

One complication of the acute attack is colonic perforation. Anal fissures and fistulas may occur. The extraintestinal complications may rarely be so severe as to warrant colectomy when the severity of the colonic disease would not do so. The gravest problem is the indisputable association of chronic ulcerative colitis with cancer of the colon occurring 10 years or more after the onset of colitis.

HEPATITIS

Role of the Liver in Immune Responses

The adult liver has an extensive reticuloendothelial system and receives a major part of its blood supply from the intestinal tract and the spleen. There is evidence of a heavy load of antigens of microorganisms and their products and of dietary components in portal blood. Macrophages in the liver (Kupffer cells) have the property of sequestering such material, possibly for periods up to months after exposure. These Kupffer cells may process antigenic material which then stimulates immune responses elsewhere in the body. Thus, the healthy liver may exercise a modulating effect on immune responsiveness. Damage to the liver leading to antigenic bypassing of Kupffer cells is associated with polyclonal hypergammaglobulinemia. Chronic liver diseases are also associated with depressed cell-mediated immunity. The hyperglobulinemia and the tendency to increased humoral antibody production in these diseases may thus be an expression of both Kupffer cell bypassing and release of inhibition of B lymphocytes as a consequence of lack of suppressor T cells.

1. ACUTE VIRAL HEPATITIS

Major Immunologic Features

- HB_SAg in serum diagnostic for hepatitis B.
- Lifelong immunity conferred after infection with hepatitis A.
- High incidence of nonpathogenic smooth muscle antibodies in viral hepatitis.

General Considerations

Immune responses to infection with hepatitis viruses A and B are poorly characterized at present. Evidence for virus A is epidemiologic and circumstantial, and knowledge of specificity resides in lifelong immunity following a single attack of acute, short incubation period hepatitis. Infections with B virus (homologous serum jaundice) display a longer incubation period and a strong association with a lipoprotein antigen found in sera and tissues of affected subjects and designated HB_sAg. The virus itself is believed to be the Dane particle, 40 nm in diameter. Its coat or envelope (HB_sAg) is viral material, probably derived partially from the cytoplasm of host cells, which becomes detached and is found in body fluids as a 20 nm sphere or in elongated tubular form. The 27 nm core (HB_cAg) has been identified in the nuclei of hepatocytes. The coat and core are immunologically distinct. The coat antigens vary, all sharing a common *a* antigen but also having either *y* or *d* and *w* or *r* antigen so that 4 subtypes are possible. The severity of the liver damage does not correlate with these subtypes. They are useful in epidemiologic studies. An *e* antigen distinct from HB_sAg has recently been described in the sera of patients with B virus hepatitis.

In acute viral hepatitis the liver parenchyma is infiltrated with macrophages and lymphocytes. It is postulated, but not proved, that antibodies may be formed in the liver in acute hepatitis, and, since HB_sAg is host-derived, autoantibodies may thus be formed.

Immunologic Pathogenesis

A. Humoral Changes in Acute Viral Hepatitis: Polyclonal hypergammaglobulinemia occurs in acute viral hepatitis. IgG is elevated in both HB_sAg-negative and HB_sAg-positive acute hepatitis, but only in the former is there a frequent occurrence of marked serum IgM elevation. The reason for this is not known.

Antibodies (usually IgM) to a component of mammalian smooth muscle are found in up to 80% of both HB_sAg-positive and HB_sAg-negative acute hepatitis sera. The antigen is related to actomyosin and appears to be present also in hepatic cell membranes, suggesting that virus-induced autoantigenicity may occur. Other agents such as cytomegalovirus and EB virus may stimulate formation of the same antibody. There is no evidence that this antibody contributes to hepatic parenchymal damage.

Extrahepatic disturbances of polyarteritis nodosa, arthralgia of the sort seen in serum sickness, skin lesions, and glomerulonephritis occur in association with viral hepatitis B more so than in A and in chronic active hepatitis. They may precede the onset of overt hepatitis and may be associated with low serum complement levels. Demonstrations of HB_sAg and complement in target tissues have suggested that HB_sAg-containing immune complexes are involved.

B. Cell-Mediated Immunity: HB_sAg-containing serum induces specific activation of lymphocytes of subjects who have had HB_sAg-positive hepatitis. Leukocyte migration inhibition has similarly been observed. With either test, positive results are obtained using cells from subjects who no longer have HB_sAg in their sera. Those with persistent antigen are negative. It has been suggested that subjects who exhibit the most severe defect in cell-mediated immunity and depression of T cell function early in the disease are most likely to suffer liver damage and become carriers of HB_sAg.

Clinical Features

A. Symptoms and Signs: Malaise, anorexia, mild pyrexia, dull pain in the hepatic region, a palpable tender liver, and jaundice are the major clinical features. Edema, ascites, and coma occur in the most ill patients.

The course may be a few days in duration or may last 2–3 weeks, followed by complete clinical recovery in most patients. Some may show mild fluctuations of serum bilirubin and enzyme activities for months or years following an attack without evidence of progressive disease (chronic persisting hepatitis).

A few patients develop an active progressive hepatitis which leads eventually to cirrhosis and liver failure. This is termed chronic aggressive or chronic active hepatitis and is discussed in the next section. It is not known whether most cases fitting this category do or do not represent a consequence of virus A or B infection. One subset of such patients is HB_sAg-associated.

B. Laboratory Findings: Leukocytopenia, lymphocytopenia, and neutropenia occur in the preicteric phase. The serum bilirubin concentration is elevated, and damage to liver parenchyma results in increased activity of hepatocyte-derived enzymes, such as transaminases, in the blood. Hyperglobulinemia and hypoalbuminemia also occur. Bilirubin appears early in the urine, before the serum level is elevated, and disappears while the serum level is still elevated.

Immunologic Diagnosis

Detection of HB_sAg in a patient with clinical and laboratory evidence of hepatitis is considered diagnostic of hepatitis B infection. The most commonly used technics for detection of HB_sAg are counterelectrophoresis and radioimmunoassay (see Chapter 24).

A radioimmunoassay for detection of hepatitis A antigens has recently been described, and current studies are assessing its use in clinical diagnosis.

Differential Diagnosis

In the preicteric phase, infectious mononucleosis, acute gastroenteritis, and acute surgical abdomen, including appendicitis and cholecystitis, may be confused with viral hepatitis.

In the icteric phase, obstructive and drug-induced jaundice present the major differential possibilities.

Treatment

There is no specific treatment. Active immunization to prevent HB_sAg-associated hepatitis may soon be achieved. Gamma globulin injections may confer some passive protection and prevent or modify the disease.

Complications & Prognosis

The great majority of patients with acute viral hepatitis make a complete clinical recovery with full return of liver function. The mortality rate is 1–2 per 1000, and the deaths that do occur are usually associated with acute fulminant hepatitis and extensive liver necrosis.

A variable number of patients go on to a benign chronic persistent hepatitis in which clinical well-being is associated with nonprogressive abnormalities of liver function expressed as minor elevations of bilirubin and enzymes. Another group proceeds to subacute massive hepatic necrosis, often terminating in liver failure in 3–12 weeks or in chronic active hepatitis with cirrhosis, sometimes complicated by primary carcinoma of the liver after many years.

2. CHRONIC HEPATITIS

Major Immunologic Features

- Autoantibodies to smooth muscle and nuclei are nonspecific.
- Polyclonal hypergammaglobulinemia. Hyperglobulinemia is common.
- Immunologic disturbances in chronic hepatitis may not be pathogenic.

General Considerations

Chronic active hepatitis is a form of progressive liver disease with a variable frequency of multisystem involvement and evidence of immunologic disturbance. On the basis of the clinical picture and serum findings, a number of names have been applied, such as lupoid hepatitis, autoimmune hepatitis, plasma cell hepatitis, and juvenile cirrhosis.

Because of our present ignorance of the pathogenesis, it seems appropriate to regard rather arbitrarily classified groups of patients as belonging in the same clinical, pathologic, and immunologic spectrum. At one end lies a group of predominantly young and middle-aged women in whom the disease has an insidious onset and in whom extrahepatic involvement, including arthralgias, rheumatoid arthritis, membranous glomerulonephritis, positive lupus erythematosus (LE) cell tests, and ANA occurs frequently. At the other end of the spectrum is a group, mainly male, in whom the onset is more likely to be acute (about 45–50%) and in whom extrahepatic disease is uncommon and HB_sAg is found in the serum. Many cases occupy the middle regions of the spectrum.

Immunologic Pathogenesis

This is uncertain. The observation that a human liver-specific lipoprotein will induce release of a leukocyte inhibition factor by lymphocytes of 70% of patients with chronic aggressive hepatitis is regarded by some as supporting the concept that an autoimmune process is involved in pathogenesis of the hepatic lesion.

Serum antibodies to a smooth muscle component occur in many patients with the disease but are not specific. They cross-react with a component of hepatic cells resembling smooth muscle actomyosin. It has been suggested that viral infection of the hepatocyte may render this actomyosin autoantigenic.

Some of the extrahepatic complications may be an expression of immune complex formation involving HB_sAg, antibodies, and complement. Depositions of such complexes have been observed in the vessel walls of patients with polyarteritis nodosa and glomerulonephritis.

Clinical Features

A. Symptoms and Signs: The onset may be insidious or acute. Malaise, easy fatigability, discomfort in the right upper quadrant, intermittent fever, and mild, rarely severe jaundice characterize the insidious type of onset. Amenorrhea may occur in young women, and arthralgias and other extrahepatic complications are common. The liver is tender to percussion or palpation. The spleen may be palpable. The acute onset may be similar to that of acute viral hepatitis and is commoner in males. Extrahepatic symptoms are unusual.

B. Laboratory Findings: There are no constant abnormalities in the peripheral leukocytes. The erythrocyte sedimentation rate is usually greatly accelerated. Gross abnormalities of liver function tests occur, often displaying considerable fluctuations. Serum transaminases and bilirubin are moderately elevated, the alkaline phosphatase less so. The prothrombin time is prolonged and fails to respond to vitamin K. The serum albumin concentration is often low; when it is very low, dependent edema results. Polyclonal hypergammaglobulinemia occurs in about 75% of cases.

In about 25% of cases of chronic aggressive hepatitis of the acute onset type, HB_sAg is found in the serum, and evidence suggests that the incidence might be higher if the antigen were sought earlier in the course of the disease.

Liver biopsy, when not contraindicated by prolonged prothrombin time or evidence of an abnormal bleeding tendency, reveals necrosis of hepatocytes (often in patchy distribution), loss of the limiting plate of the hepatic lobe, infiltration of the periportal spaces and parenchyma with plasma cells and lymphocytes, and a variable degree of collagen bridging. An established active cirrhosis may be present, with evidence of hepatocyte regeneration, including rosette formation.

Immunologic Diagnosis

Polyclonal hypergammaglobulinemia is common. Serum IgG and, to a lesser extent, IgM and IgA are elevated in at least 75% of patients. Nuclear antibodies are found in as many as 50% of cases. These give the smooth or homogeneous immunofluorescence pattern. Some sera give a positive LE cell test. Antibodies to smooth muscle are present in most patients. These are not specific for chronic active hepatitis, occurring also in acute viral hepatitis and some cases of drug-induced hepatitis. High-titer IgG smooth muscle antibodies appear to be present only in HB_sAg-negative patients. Low serum complement activity may be found. It is believed to be due to depressed hepatic synthesis of these proteins.

Few studies of cell-mediated immune reactions have been reported, and the results are inconclusive. Nonspecific lymphocyte activation by PHA is impaired in chronic active hepatitis. Some antigen-mediated lymphocyte activation has been observed with liver tissue. Both stimulatory and inhibitory factors of leukocyte migration have been detected. A human liver lipoprotein has been reported to induce production of MIF by lymphocytes from two-thirds of patients with chronic active hepatitis.

Differential Diagnosis

Hepatitis of insidious onset may mimic chronic infections, primary biliary cirrhosis, and even psychiatric disease. Abnormal liver function tests and a characteristic liver biopsy will usually serve to establish the diagnosis.

Treatment

Controlled therapeutic trials have shown that corticosteroids and azathioprine may have a beneficial effect on the course of the disease. This is particularly true in those patients in whom immunologic disturbances are manifest.

Complications & Prognosis

Permanent arrest of the pathologic process may occur, or liver destruction may be progressive and lead to death. Portal hypertension is a major complication carrying the added risk of bleeding from esophageal varices.

Portal hypertension with splenomegaly and esophageal varices occurs frequently in the later stages. The portal hypertension and reduced oncotic pressure due to hypoalbuminemia result in ascites. Bleeding from esophageal varices is a major cause of death.

The prognosis in general is poor, the disease running a fluctuating but inexorable course to death usually within 5 years as a result of hepatic failure, infection, or gastrointestinal bleeding. However, recognition of less florid cases and a favorable response to treatment are changing our concept of the course of this group of diseases.

3. PRIMARY BILIARY CIRRHOSIS

Major Immunologic Features

- Very high incidence (90%) of antimitochondrial antibodies.
- Granulomas adjacent to bile ducts and plasma cells in region of lysing biliary ductules suggest delayed immune response.

General Considerations

The disease is rare and affects predominantly middle-aged women. The essential lesion is intrahepatic cholestasis, the course is inexorable, and the mean life expectancy is 5 years from the onset of symptoms.

Immunologic Pathogenesis

This is at best presumptive. The pathogenetic factors involved are unknown. As in other diseases in which an autoimmune cause has been invoked, the appearance in hepatic biopsies of biliary ductules apparently lysing in the neighborhood of collections of plasma cells and in some cases the appearance of granulomas adjacent to ductular walls have been cited to support an immunologic basis for the disease. The discovery of circulating mitochondrial antibodies has reinforced this claim.

Clinical Features

A. Symptoms and Signs: The onset is insidious, and liver biopsy studies suggest that the disease may progress for years before the patient becomes symptomatic. Fatigue or pruritus may be the first evidence of disease, or minimal jaundice may occur, with dark urine and pale stools. Cutaneous xanthomas, especially in the skin flexures of the hands, are a later manifestation. Retention of bile salts causes sometimes intractable generalized pruritus. As the disease progresses, pigmentation of the skin becomes deeper, the liver becomes enlarged and firm, and the spleen is often palpable. Weight loss and diarrhea occur as a consequence of intestinal malabsorption due to cholestasis, and bleeding may occur as a result of hypoprothrombinemia. Pathologic fractures and compression of vertebrae result from malabsorption of calcium and vitamin D. The disease progresses to cirrhosis with portal hypertension.

B. Laboratory Findings: The serum contains increased amounts of mainly conjugated bilirubin. Hepatocellular function is good in the early stages so that plasma albumin levels are normal and transaminases are normal or minimally elevated. The serum alkaline phosphatase is markedly increased, and serum cholesterol gradually increases to very high levels.

In later stages of the disease, liver failure occurs, cholesterol levels fall, the patient becomes hypoalbuminemic, and ascites and peripheral edema appear.

On histologic examination, the liver shows bile stasis and patchy inflammation, with plasma cells and lymphocytes infiltrating the portal triads. Eosinophilia may be a striking feature. The bile ductules appear usually to be the primary target and undergo lysis. Granulomas may occur in the region of damaged ducts. Later in the course of the disease, the appearances merge into those of postnecrotic cirrhosis.

Immunologic Diagnosis

Elevations of serum immunoglobulins, particularly IgM, are often present, but the most interesting and diagnostically important finding is of mitochondrial antibodies. These are not present in chronic obstructive jaundice due to other causes. Some samples of sera from patients with chronic aggressive hepatitis are also positive. The best source of mitochondrial antigen for the immunofluorescence test is the distal renal tubule. Rat kidney is most commonly used in routine testing—although human kidney is preferable—and the antibody is also detectable by complement fixation.

The antigen is a lipoprotein of the inner mitochondrial membrane. However, it is likely that antibodies to other components of cell organelles may occur as well, particularly to a membrane antigen of rough endoplasmic reticulum and to the outer nuclear membrane. Using the distal renal tubule in immunofluorescence tests as the site of strongest reaction for the primary biliary cirrhosis, mitochondrial antibody gives reasonably clear-cut results.

Cell-mediated immune reactions. Although both impaired skin tests and nonspecific lymphocyte activation have been reported in primary biliary cirrhosis, complicating factors such as abnormal biochemical factors in vivo and nutritional deficiencies may have effects which have not been quantified. Consequently, the significance of these findings as expressions of a primary immune disturbance is unclear.

Similarly, MIF production using specific human hepatic lipoprotein cannot be construed as proof that cell-mediated immune reactions have pathogenetic importance.

Differential Diagnosis

Obstructive jaundice due to extrahepatic disease such as calculus or carcinoma of the pancreas, primary biliary carcinoma, and sclerosing cholangitis may simulate primary biliary cirrhosis, as may drug-induced cholestatic jaundice. The serologic finding of mitochondrial antibodies strongly reinforces a diagnosis of primary biliary cirrhosis since positive serology is extremely uncommon in obstructive jaundice due to any other cause. When serologic tests and liver biopsy both support the diagnosis, exploration by laparotomy to establish a diagnosis may be unnecessary.

Treatment

Primary biliary cirrhosis does not respond to corticosteroids. Azathioprine and other immunosuppressive agents have not been given systematic clinical trials. At present, treatment is directed at maintaining adequate nutritional status and reducing bile salt retention by use of the orally administered exchange resin cholestyramine.

Complications & Prognosis

The major complications have been mentioned. The prognosis is uniformly bad, patients with primary biliary cirrhosis dying on average about 5 years after symptoms first appear. The cause of death may be liver failure, gastrointestinal bleeding, or infection.

• • •

References

General

Crabbé PA, Heremans JF: The distribution of immunoglobulin-containing cells along the human gastrointestinal tract. Gastroenterology 51:305, 1966.

Tomasi TB: Secretory immunoglobulins. N Engl J Med 287:500, 1972.

Allergic Reactions

Coombs RRA, Gell PGH: Classification of allergic reactions responsible for clinical hypersensitivity and disease. Pages 761–781 in: *Clinical Aspects of Immunology,* 3rd ed. Gell PGH, Coombs RRA, Lachmann PJ (editors). Blackwell, 1975.

Sjögren's Syndrome

Whaley K & others: Sjögren's syndrome. 2. Clinical associations and immunological phenomena. Q J Med 42:513, 1973.

Chronic Atrophic Gastritis & Pernicious Anemia

Goldberg LE & others: Human autoimmunity, with pernicious anemia as a model. Ann Intern Med 81:372, 1974.

Strickland RG: Gastritis. Front Gastrointest Res 1:12, 1975.

Gluten-Sensitive Enteropathy; Celiac Sprue

Crabbé PA, Heremans JF: Selective IgA deficiency with steatorrhea: A new syndrome. Am J Med 42:319, 1967.

Douglas AP: The immunological basis of coeliac disease. Front Gastrointest Res 1:49, 1975.

Shiner M: Ultrastructural changes suggestive of immune reactions in the jejunal mucosa of coeliac children following gluten challenge. Gut 14:1, 1973.

Crohn's Disease

Thayer WR Jr: The immunopathology of intestinal granulomatous disease. Front Gastrointest Res 1:74, 1975.

Ulcerative Colitis

Hammarström S & others: Immunological studies in ulcerative colitis. J Exp Med 122:1075, 1965.

Kirsner JB, Shorter RG: *Inflammatory Bowel Disease.* Lea & Febiger, 1975.

Shorter RG & others: Inflammatory bowel disease: Cytophilic antibody and the cytotoxicity of lymphocytes for colonic cells in vitro. Am J Dig Dis 16:673, 1971.

Hepatitis

Doniach D: Autoimmune aspects of liver disease. Br Med Bull 28:145, 1972.

Hepatitis viruses. Chap 32, pages 381–391, in: *Review of Medical Microbiology*, 12th ed. Jawetz E, Melnick JL, Adelberg EA. Lange, 1976.

Javitt N: Chronic active hepatitis. Am J Med 55:733, 1973.

Klatskin G, Kantor FS: Mitochondrial antibody in primary biliary cirrhosis and other diseases. Ann Intern Med 77:533, 1972.

Nielsen JO & others: Incidence and meaning of persistence of Australia antigen in patients with acute viral hepatitis: Development of chronic hepatitis. N Engl J Med 285:1157, 1971.

Popper H, Mackay IR: Relation between Australia antigen and autoimmune hepatitis. Lancet 1:1161, 1972.

Sherlock S, Scheuer P: The presentation and diagnosis of 100 patients with primary biliary cirrhosis. N Engl J Med 289:674, 1973.

31 . . .
Cardiac & Pulmonary Diseases

Joseph L. Caldwell, MD

The heart and lungs are the sites of pathologic alterations in a great number of diseases. Most of these disorders are infections, neoplasms, or diseases that are degenerative in origin, and few well-defined cardiac and pulmonary diseases can be classified as primary immunologic disorders. Immune responses associated with infectious diseases are discussed in Chapter 34. Allergic asthma is discussed in Chapter 29.

Our knowledge of humoral and cellular immune phenomena which affect the heart and lungs is rather limited. This is due in part to the relative inaccessibility of these organs, and repeated laboratory examination of biopsy material during the course of diseases has not been feasible. With the recent development of safer and more efficient methods for securing cardiac and lung tissues for examination, a better understanding of immune pathophysiologic mechanisms should develop. In addition, progress in understanding cardiac and pulmonary immune disorders has been limited by the lack of well-defined animal models for many clinically prevalent human diseases. Again, with the adaptation of animal laboratory models, the future should see considerable progress in this area of immunology.

POSTPERICARDIOTOMY SYNDROME (Postmyocardial Infarction Syndrome; Dressler's Syndrome)

Major Immunologic Features

- Circulating anticardiac antibodies.
- Possible activation of classical complement pathway.
- Circulating immune complexes.

General Considerations

Damage to myocardial and pericardial tissues can result from trauma, from surgical procedures, or from myocardial infarctions. Several days to several months after the initial injury, about 10% of postthoracotomy patients and 1% of postmyocardial infarction patients will develop a syndrome of recurrent fever, pericarditis, and effusions. The cause of this syndrome is unknown, but the temporal relationship to cardiac damage, the high frequency of anticardiac antibodies, and prompt clinical response to corticosteroid therapy suggest that this syndrome may result from autoimmune responses to antigens released from damaged cardiac tissue.

Immunologic Pathogenesis

Circulating antibodies against cardiac antigens can frequently be demonstrated following traumatic, surgical, or vascular injury to cardiac or pericardial tissue. Hemagglutination, immunofluorescence, and complement fixation assays have detected circulating antibodies in up to 80–90% of patients who have had cardiac surgery. The immunofluorescence studies demonstrated 3 main patterns of staining of cardiac muscle fibers: (1) diffuse sarcoplasmic, (2) sarcolemmal-subsarcolemmal, and (3) intermyofibrillar. The sarcolemmal-subsarcolemmal pattern of staining was present in both cardiac and skeletal muscle but not in other organs.

Hemagglutination and complement fixation assays have employed saline and alcoholic extracts of cardiac tissue as the antigen, and results have been variable. These antigen extracts are complex preparations and have been incompletely defined in terms of antigen specificity. In patients known by immunofluorescence studies to be positive for circulating anticardiac antibodies, hemagglutination or complement fixation studies have given only a 10–45% frequency of positive responses.

The relationship between circulating anticardiac antibody and the development of clinical symptoms is poorly defined. The lack of clear correlation may be partly the result of the particular antigen preparation or assay system used in clinical studies. Many patients develop anticardiac antibodies without demonstrating any symptoms of Dressler's syndrome, and the quantitative levels of antibody do not appear to correlate well with either the onset or severity of symptoms.

More recently, total hemolytic complement levels and C3 and C4 inactivation products were studied in a group of patients several weeks after myocardial infarction. Although serum complement levels normally rise slightly after myocardial infarction, rarely is there evi-

Joseph L. Caldwell is Assistant Research Immunologist, University of California School of Medicine and Veterans Administration Hospital, San Francisco. The section on rheumatic fever is contributed by Ken Fye, MD, Haralampos Moutsopoulos, MD, and Norman Talal, MD. (See p 151 for academic affiliations of these authors.)

dence for activation of complement via the classical pathway. Some of these patients developed symptoms suggestive of Dressler's syndrome, and, although the evidence is limited, this suggests that Dressler's syndrome (and similar clinical disorders) might result from circulating immune complexes of cardiac antigen and anticardiac antibody.

Clinical studies measuring only the serum antibody response to cardiac antigens frequently ignore the contribution to clinical symptoms resulting from cell-mediated immune reactions to heart tissue. Studies of cardiac transplantation in man and other animals clearly show that cardiac cells are sensitive to the cytolytic effect of activated lymphocytes, and myocardial injury may produce sufficient alterations in the tissue to induce autoimmune pathologic changes. However, no clinical studies have been performed to assess the importance of cell-mediated cardiac damage in such patients. Clearly, much additional work will be required to define the manner in which immune reactions contribute to the pathogenesis of these postinjury disorders.

Clinical Features

A. Symptoms and Signs: The disease is characterized by intermittent fever and episodes of mild to severe chest pain. The chest pain is usually mild to moderate in intensity, made worse by deep inspiration, and persists for days to weeks. Sometimes, however, the pain can be very severe and resemble the crushing pain of myocardial ischemia. Pericardial or pleural effusions may be present, and a pericardial friction rub may be heard.

B. Laboratory Findings: The laboratory findings are nonspecific and are usually of little help in diagnosis of the syndrome. There may be leukocytosis, an increased red cell sedimentation rate, and a positive test for C-reactive protein. The ECG can show changes of pericarditis as well as the findings associated with the underlying cardiac disease, such as myocardial infarction, which preceded the onset of the syndrome. Circulating immune complexes and anticardiac antibodies have been demonstrated in a high percentage of patients (see above), but their relationship to the clinical onset of symptoms remains unclear.

Differential Diagnosis

If the chest pain is severe and abrupt in onset, it must be differentiated from additional ischemia or infarction of myocardial tissue. Interval changes in the ECG or changes in serum levels of cardiac muscle enzymes may be helpful. The presence of chest pain and pleural effusions may suggest pulmonary emboli, and a distinction between emboli and this syndrome is important. Anticoagulant therapy is not recommended in Dressler's syndrome due to the risk of hemopericardium.

Treatment & Prognosis

Most patients with this disease require no treatment beyond a simple analgesic. Normally, the symptoms and fever can be controlled and will clear spontaneously over several weeks. At times, however, the patient will become sufficiently ill to require corticosteroid therapy for symptomatic relief. The clinical response to corticosteroids is usually prompt, but the symptoms may reappear after cessation of therapy. The ultimate outcome is related to the underlying cardiac disease and not to the development of Dressler's syndrome. Tamponade from pericardial effusions is rare.

ACUTE RHEUMATIC FEVER

Major Immunologic Features

- Occurs after group A streptococcal infection, with antibodies against various group A streptococcal antigens.
- Presence of circulating autoantibodies directed at cardiac tissues and group A streptococcal antigens.
- Deposition of immunoglobulin and complement in myocardial and valvular tissues.

General Considerations

Rheumatic fever is a multisystemic inflammatory disease associated with a recent history of group A streptococcal infection. The disease usually occurs in children between 5–15 years of age. It only develops after repeated oropharyngeal streptococcal infections and is usually not associated with streptococcal skin infections. The incidence, which varies from 0.4% to 2–3% of patients with streptococcal oropharyngitis, is falling, probably as a result of an increased standard of living in the industrialized world. Genetic factors may play a role in the development of the disease since many patients have a family history of rheumatic fever.

The Jones criteria (revised) for the diagnosis of rheumatic fever are often helpful (Table 31–1). The presence of 2 major or one major and 2 minor criteria, along with clinical or laboratory evidence of recent streptococcal infection, is highly suggestive of rheumatic fever. Sydenham's chorea is diagnostic of rheumatic fever even in the absence of any other criteria.

Table 31–1. Jones criteria (revised) for the diagnosis of rheumatic fever.

Major Criteria	Minor Criteria
Carditis	Fever
Polyarthritis	Arthralgia
Erythema marginatum	Previous rheumatic fever
Subcutaneous nodules	Prolonged P–R interval on ECG
Sydenham's chorea	Elevated erythrocyte sedimentation rate; elevated C-reactive protein; leukocytosis (any of these)

Immunologic Pathogenesis

Several theories on the pathogenesis of rheumatic fever have been proposed.

A. Infection Theory: It has been suggested that the disease is caused by the direct invasion of involved tissue either by group A streptococci or their "L" forms. However, neither of these has been isolated from involved tissues.

B. Streptococcal Toxin Theory: It has been hypothesized that the manifestations of rheumatic fever are secondary to the action of streptococcal toxins. Group A streptococci produce a number of potent toxins which could, either singly or in combination, cause some manifestations of rheumatic fever.

1. Streptolysin S (SS)–Streptolysin S is a nonantigenic hemolysin which is responsible for the hemolytic zones characteristically produced by group A streptococcal cultures on blood agar. The action of streptolysin S is inhibited by a nonspecific serum lipoprotein, the "serum inhibitor of streptolysin S." Since serum inhibitor of streptolysin S is decreased in patients with rheumatic fever, such patients may have an increased susceptibility to the action of streptolysin S. However, serum inhibitor of streptolysin S is also depressed in juvenile and adult rheumatoid arthritis and several other rheumatoid diseases. Streptolysin S may cause the arthritis of rheumatic fever by disrupting the lysosomal membranes of polymorphonuclear leukocytes infiltrating the joint. The resultant discharge of active enzymes into synovium and joint space leads to increased inflammation and arthritis. Streptolysin S has been shown to stimulate an intense inflammatory response when injected into the joints of rabbits.

2. Streptolysin O (SO)–Streptolysin O is an antigenic protein found in low or moderate titer in most human sera. Although streptolysin O is not as effective a hemolysin as streptolysin S, it is known that streptococcal strains associated with rheumatic fever produce more streptolysin O than non-rheumatic fever-associated strains. It has been postulated that serum complexes of streptolysin O-antistreptolysin O circulate in rheumatic fever patients and that specific myocardial substrates compete with the immunoglobulin for the toxin, which is then deposited in the heart, where it leads to rheumatic carditis.

3. Streptococcal proteinase (SP)–Streptococcal proteinase is an antigenic enzyme produced by streptococci of low virulence. When injected into rabbits, streptococcal proteinase produces myocardial lesions similar to those seen in acute rheumatic carditis. Streptococcal proteinase, like streptolysin O, is antigenic, and one would have to invoke the presence of streptococcal proteinase-antiproteinase circulating complexes with a cardiac binding site competing for the enzyme to implicate streptococcal proteinase in the pathogenesis of rheumatic carditis.

4. C-polysaccharide and protein complexes–High-molecular-weight preparations of fragmented streptococci injected into animals induce chronic inflammatory changes in various organs, including the heart. This reaction is not a typical immune response since it begins within 3 hours of administration and is not affected by repeated injections.

C. Allergic Theory: Because of the clinical similarity of rheumatic fever to serum sickness, it has been suggested that rheumatic fever is an allergic reaction to components of products of group A streptococci. There are several arguments against this hypothesis. First, recurrent allergic reactions manifest a progressively shorter latent period, which does not occur in rheumatic fever. Second, patients with serum sickness have decreased serum complement owing to increased consumption by immune complexes. In rheumatic fever, serum complement is often elevated. Third, it is difficult to explain the characteristic Aschoff body on the basis of an allergic reaction.

D. Autoimmune Theory: (Fig 31–1.) At present this is the most widely accepted theory of the pathogenesis of rheumatic fever.

1. Humoral mechanism–Autoantibodies against cardiac tissue have been demonstrated in up to 80% of patients with acute rheumatic fever. Those with acute carditis or recurrences tend to have the highest titers of autoantibody, but 60% of patients with inactive rheumatic heart disease also have significant titers. Technics used to demonstrate anticardiac autoantibodies include complement fixation, collodion particle agglutination, tanned red cell agglutination, antiglobulin consumption, and precipitin reactions. Immunofluorescent staining demonstrates that serum from rheumatic fever patients contains autoantibodies against cardiac myofibrils, smooth muscle of cardiac vessels, and endocardium. These autoantibodies cross-react with group A streptococcal antigens, many of which are closely associated with M protein. Cross-reactivity between group A streptococcal carbohydrate and cardiac glycoprotein has also been demonstrated, as has cross-reactivity between streptococcal hyaluronate and protein-polysaccharide complexes in mammalian cartilage. Half of patients with rheumatic fever or inactive rheumatic heart disease have anticardiac autoantibodies that cross-react with streptococcal cell wall or cell membrane preparations. Immunofluorescence technics reveal that 18% of patients with inactive rheumatic heart disease have focal deposits of immunoglobulin throughout the myocardium. Patients with active rheumatic carditis have diffuse myocardial deposition of γ-globulin and complement as well as valvular deposition of IgG, but not IgA, IgM, nor complement. It is not known whether the immunoglobulin deposited in the myocardium cross-reacts with streptococcal antigens. In summary, it appears that antibodies against streptococcal antigens cross-react with autologous myocardial antigens and thereby mediate myocardial damage, either in the presence or absence of complement (Fig 31–1).

2. Cellular mechanism–Streptococcal cell wall antigens present in streptolysin S preparations are lymphocyte mitogens. Patients with rheumatic fever show a decreased mitogenic response during the first attack, but mitogenic response is normal during subsequent attacks. Streptococcal M protein can induce

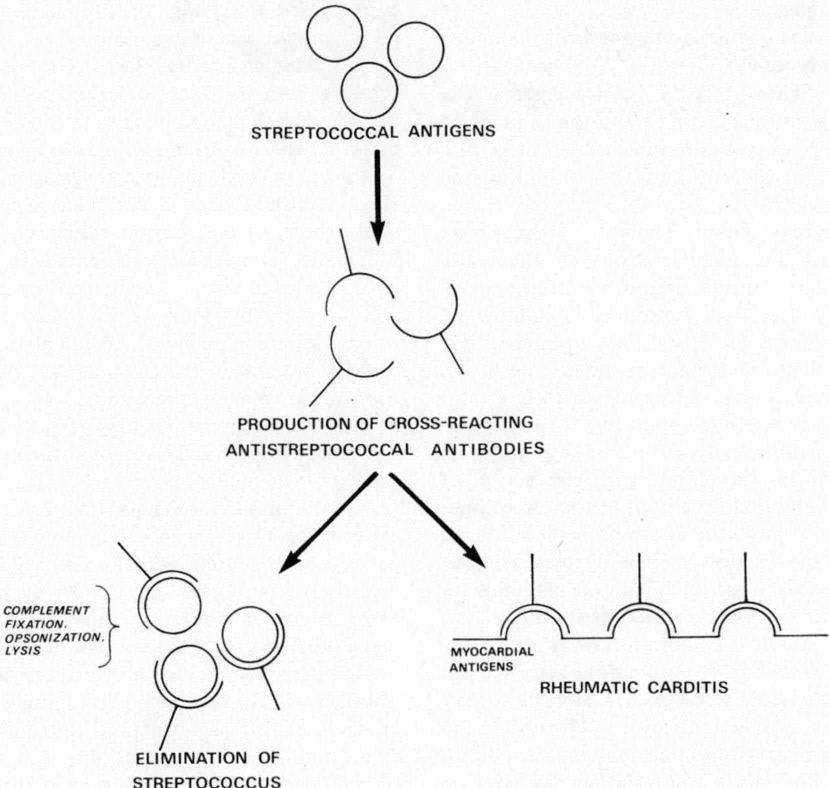

Figure 31–1. Autoantibodies as mediators of carditis in rheumatic fever.

delayed hypersensitivity in humans or animals, as measured by in vivo skin testing and in vitro lymphocyte activation and MIF production. However, lymphocytes of normal children, as well as of patients with rheumatic fever, are stimulated by streptococcal cell wall antigens. This suggests that cellular hypersensitivity to these antigens is not a major immunologic determinant of disease.

Clinical Findings

A. Symptoms and Signs:

1. Preceding streptococcal infection–Almost half of patients recall having had a sore throat prior to their first attack of rheumatic fever, whereas only 30% of recurrences are preceded by symptomatic infections. The latent period between the infection and the onset of rheumatic fever is approximately 18 days.

2. Arthritis–The arthritis of rheumatic fever is an acute migratory polyarthritis, with only transient involvement of each joint. The large joints of the legs and arms are usually involved. Soft tissue swelling without bony erosions is seen radiographically.

3. Carditis–One-third of patients develop carditis with the first attack, and the incidence of cardiac involvement increases with each recurrence. Carditis, which is often asymptomatic, involves the myocardium, endocardium, and pericardium. Myocarditis may be present with or without overt congestive heart failure. Mitral valve regurgitation with a resultant pansystolic murmur is the commonest manifestation of endocardial involvement. In some patients with mitral regurgitation, the increased diastolic flow across the mitral valve results in a "relative" mitral stenosis and a transient diastolic rumbling murmur (Carey Coombs murmur). Aortic valvulitis with regurgitation is less common. Pericarditis is commonly associated with pain and transitory friction rubs but rarely leads to pericardial effusion or tamponade.

4. Chorea (Sydenham's chorea, St. Vitus' dance)–Chorea is a neurologic disorder characterized by purposeless, nonrepetitive, spasmodic movements of any voluntary muscle. It occurs in only 5% of patients with rheumatic fever, most commonly in females. Chorea may last for up to 14 weeks; recovery without residual neurologic deficit is the invariable rule.

5. Subcutaneous nodules–The subcutaneous nodules of rheumatic fever are firm, painless, transient, "pea-sized" nodules that develop over bony prominences. When present, there are usually only 3 or 4 of these nodules. They occur in 5% of rheumatic fever patients and are often associated with severe carditis.

6. Erythema marginatum–Patients with rheumatic fever may have an evanescent, painless, nonpruritic, nodular or raised rash over the trunk or proximal limbs. Erythema marginatum occurs in 5% of patients and is usually associated with carditis. This characteristic recurrent skin eruption may appear, migrate, and then disappear over the course of a few hours.

7. **Nonspecific manifestations**—Fever, anorexia, and nausea and vomiting are almost universal. A vague periumbilical pain of unknown cause may occur. Epistaxis, previously present in up to 48% of patients, now occurs in only 4–9%. Erythema nodosum, pleurisy, and rheumatic pneumonitis are rare manifestations of rheumatic fever.

B. Laboratory Findings: Elevations in acute phase reactants, including erythrocyte sedimentation rate, C-reactive protein, complement, mucoproteins, α- and γ-globulins, and fibrinogen, are almost universal. Leukocytosis and mild anemia are common. A transient microscopic hematuria rarely occurs.

The subcutaneous nodules of rheumatic fever are composed largely of edema fluid and strands of fibrinoid material. The cellular infiltrate consists of fibroblasts, histiocytes, lymphocytes, and a few polymorphonuclear leukocytes.

Histologic findings in acute myocarditis include swelling and necrosis of muscle cells and fibrinoid degeneration of collagen tissue. The classical myocardial lesion in rheumatic fever is the Aschoff body, which consists of a central focus of degeneration and necrosis surrounded by mononuclear cells and by large, multinuclear cells (Anitschkow cells) with a "banded" or serrated appearance of their nuclear chromatin and with a clear area adjacent to the nuclear membrane. Acute rheumatic fever valvulitis is characterized by the development of translucent verrucae on the valve cusps. In chronic rheumatic heart disease, the valves become retracted, thickened, and deformed.

Biopsy of involved joints reveals only a mild nonspecific synovitis.

C. Electrocardiographic Findings: The electrocardiogram shows prolongation of the P–R interval in 25% of all cases. T wave inversions may also be seen. However, electrocardiographic changes correlate poorly with clinical carditis.

Immunologic Diagnosis

There is no specific immunologic test for the diagnosis of rheumatic fever. Evidence of prior streptococcal infection can be obtained serologically. Virtually all rheumatic fever patients have antibodies to streptococcal antigens, although the height of the antibody titer bears no relationship to the severity of the disease. Most normal individuals also have low titers of antistreptococcal antibodies. Therefore, decisive evidence of recent infection rests on showing a rise in antibody titers. There are 2 basic classes of streptococcal antigens that stimulate the production of antibodies used in the diagnosis of rheumatic fever.

A. Typing Antigens:

1. The C-carbohydrate component of the cell wall forms the basis of the Lancefield classification of streptococcal groups A–O.

2. M protein is a cell wall component that inhibits phagocytosis and therefore increases virulence. It forms the basis of the precipitin test used for specific typing within the major Lancefield groups. M protein stimulates both a cellular and a humoral response.

3. T substance is an antigen that stimulates the production of an agglutinin useful in typing streptococcal strains.

B. Antigenic Streptococcal Products:

1. **Streptokinase (fibrinolysin)**—Streptokinase is a streptococcal enzyme that converts plasminogen to plasmin. Its activity is inhibited by a nonspecific serum factor as well as by the specific antibody (antistreptokinase) that is helpful in the diagnosis of prior infection.

2. **Streptodornase (deoxyribonuclease)**—Streptodornase depolymerizes deoxyribonucleoprotein and deoxyribonucleotide. Antistreptodornase remains elevated longer than other antibodies and is very useful in the diagnosis of chorea. Streptodornase, which consists of 4 antigenically distinct proteins with the same enzymatic activity, is also capable of lymphocyte transformation in previously immunized patients.

3. **Hyaluronidase (spreading factor)**—Hyaluronidase splits the hyaluronic acid of ground substance and aids in the spread of microorganisms through infected tissues. Antihyaluronidase is most useful in the diagnosis of acute infection.

4. **Erythrogenic factor**, which causes the rash of scarlet fever, is produced only by streptococci infected with a temperate phage. Antibodies to erythrogenic factor prevent the erythrogenic effect of this factor but do not protect from infection by streptococci.

5. **Hemolysins**—Two hemolysins are produced by streptococci. Streptolysin O is an antigenic hemolysin whose antibody, antistreptolysin O (ASO), blocks the hemolytic activity and forms the basis for the most commonly used serologic test for the diagnosis of rheumatic fever. High antistreptolysin O titers may represent either recent infection or persistence of antibody from an earlier infection. Eighty percent of patients with rheumatic fever have a significant antistreptolysin O titer rise within 2 months after an attack. Since antistreptolysin O is so common among the normal population, only high titers—250 Todd units in adults and 333 units in children—constitute evidence of recent infection.

Differential Diagnosis

The clinical manifestations of fever, arthralgia or arthritis, and a heart murmur, in association with mild leukocytosis and anemia, are compatible with infective endocarditis, juvenile rheumatoid arthritis, systemic lupus erythematosus, and acute leukemia. In many instances the differentiation between these diseases rests entirely on laboratory data. Patients with rheumatic fever have negative blood cultures, no erosive joint disease, no ANA in their sera, a negative LE cell test, and nonleukemic bone marrow. Sometimes the diagnosis remains in doubt despite intensive laboratory evaluation. The diagnosis of rheumatic fever cannot be made in the absence of evidence of streptococcal infection; however, its presence obviously does not exclude other diseases.

Treatment

A. General Measures: The aim of therapy is to decrease morbidity and mortality rates. Despite the dictates of traditional therapy, no specific benefit is achieved by prescribing bed rest. Patients with carditis and chorea will limit their activities voluntarily. More than anything else, patients with chorea need reassurance and the understanding of family and friends. It must be emphasized that the course is self-limited and that there are no neurologic residuals. Barbiturates and tranquilizers are of benefit in patients with severe chorea. Congestive heart failure should be treated with salt restriction, diuretics, and digitalis preparations as appropriate.

B. Specific Measures:

1. Antibiotics–Even though throat cultures are negative, antibiotics should be administered. Organisms may be present in areas inaccessible to culture, and the persistence of organisms presumably means the continued presence of streptococcal antigens cross-reactive to the myocardium. Either a single intramuscular injection of 1.2 million units of benzathine penicillin G or 600,000 units for procaine penicillin G intramuscularly daily for 10 days is adequate.

2. Anti-inflammatory agents–Patients often show a dramatic symptomatic response to salicylates. Aspirin, 0.1 g/kg orally daily, is the drug of choice. If no improvement is seen with salicylate therapy or if the patient has severe carditis, corticosteroids–usually prednisone, 10–15 mg orally every 6 hours or its equivalent–may be used. The duration of therapy depends on the severity of the inflammatory process and the course of the disease.

Course & Prognosis

If no exacerbations occur within 2 months following an attack of rheumatic fever, the disease is considered to have resolved. If carditis is absent, full recovery without residuals results in 95% of patients. Patients with carditis should limit their activity for 6 months after an attack. In patients with a residual murmur, the dynamics of cardiac function will determine the level of activity.

The most important sequelae are those involving the heart. The incidence of residual heart disease is directly correlated with the severity of the acute attack. Half of patients with a pathologic murmur during an attack of rheumatic fever develop residual heart disease. Seventy percent of patients with rheumatic fever who develop pericarditis or congestive heart failure will have a murmur 5 years later. Of the total number of patients with rheumatic fever, 1.4% have mitral stenosis at 5 years and 5% have mitral stenosis 10 years later. A chronic post-rheumatic fever arthritis (Jaccoud's arthritis) has been frequently described in Europe but is seen only rarely in the USA. It is characterized by ulnar deviation without bone destruction and is essentially asymptomatic. The mortality rate of rheumatic fever is related to the severity of the heart disease. The overall mortality rate for first attacks is less than 1%; for subsequent attacks, 3%.

Recurrences are a major problem in rheumatic fever since anyone who has had one attack has an increased susceptibility to subsequent attacks. Because the incidence of cardiac involvement increases with each recurrence, it is important to prevent recurrent rheumatic fever. This is accomplished by preventing streptococcal infections by the use of prophylactic antibiotics. Acceptable prophylactic regimens include 1.2 million units of benzathine penicillin G intramuscularly every month; sulfadiazine, 1 g orally daily; or potassium penicillin, 200,000 units orally twice daily. There is some controversy over the duration of prophylactic therapy. One view is that prophylaxis should be continued for at least 5 years after the last attack of rheumatic fever and until the patient is 25 years of age. The other major view is that anyone under 18 who develops rheumatic fever or anyone with rheumatic heart disease should be continued on prophylaxis indefinitely.

HYPERSENSITIVITY PNEUMONITIS
(Extrinsic Allergic Alveolitis)

Major Immunologic Features

- Frequent presence of precipitating serum antibodies against specific extrinsic antigens.
- Onset of symptoms 5–6 hours after exposure to antigen.
- Specific IgE antibodies in some patients.

General Considerations

Ambient air contains a wide variety of particulate dusts and organic substances which can act as allergens. In most people these inhaled antigens produce little or no respiratory discomfort. In sensitized individuals, exposure to air containing the appropriate antigen can result in an acute illness characterized by cough, fever, dyspnea, and even cyanosis. Chronic exposure to the offending antigen can progress to a disease marked by weight loss, chronic dyspnea, severe coughing, and pulmonary fibrosis.

Immunologic Pathogenesis

The prototype disease of this group of disorders was first recognized in 1932 in farmers exposed to silage hay. Several hours after exposure to the hay, some of the farmers complained of respiratory symptoms. Investigation revealed that the silage hay was moldy, and the important antigens in this disease were associated with spores produced by thermophilic actinomycetes. Since this initial work, an increasing number of antigens have been shown to be specific causes of hypersensitivity pneumonitis.

It is unfortunate that many of the early cases of this disorder were classified by offending antigenic material and given a variety of exotic names–maple bark stripper's disease, sequoiosis, mushroom grower's disease, thatched roof disease, etc. Although these

Table 31–2. Selected causes of hypersensitivity pneumonitis.

Disease	Antigen	Antigen Source
Farmer's lung	Thermophilic actinomycetes	Moldy hay
Mushroom grower's lung	*Trichophyton vulgaris* and *Micropolyspora faeni*	Mushroom beds
Thatched roof disease	Thatch proteins, fungi (?)	Thatched roof
Malt worker's disease	*Aspergillus clavatus* and *A fumigatus*	Moldy barley and malt dust
Maple bark stripper's disease	*Cryptostroma corticale* spores	Tree bark
Bagassosis	*T vulgaris* and *T sacchare*	Sugarcane stalks
Sequoiosis	*Pullularia pullulans* spores	Redwood trees
Cheese washer's disease	*Penicillium casei* spores	Cheese casings
Bird fancier's disease	Avian serum and gut proteins (?)	Bird excreta
Fish meal lung	Fish proteins	Fish meal in pet food
Furrier lung	Animal protein (?)	Fox fur
Air conditioning lung	Thermophilic and aspergillus organisms	Fungi present in water in air conditioning system

names adequately describe epidemiologic features of the illnesses in question, they have given the impression that these disorders are rare and esoteric. Although any one physician is unlikely to ever see a case of mushroom grower's disease, the list of known extrinsic antigens related to this group of disorders is growing (Table 31–2). Therefore, these disorders should be considered as a diagnostic possibility in patients with unexplained episodic pneumonitis or chronic pulmonary fibrosis.

The normal immunologic response to these inhaled antigens is production of IgG-precipitating antibody. With reexposure to the antigen, this antibody reacts and precipitates within pulmonary tissues to produce an immune complex inflammatory response. This explains the delay of several hours in the onset of symptoms after antigen exposure. In some cases of aspergillus pneumonitis, there is a specific IgE as well as an IgG antibody response. This modifies the clinical presentation to include an acute response to inhaled antigen followed in several hours by the expected delayed response. Particularly in the initial stages, the serum of patients with hypersensitivity pneumonitis frequently contains precipitating antibodies which are useful in diagnosis.

Two families (19 members) have recently been described who presented modifications of the usual clinical pattern of these disorders. Seven patients had characteristic symptoms and radiographic findings of hypersensitivity pneumonitis. Some members had no symptoms but possessed circulating antifungal antibodies. However, cell-mediated immune reactions, as measured by the migration inhibition assay, were performed using saline extracts of fungi as the stimulating antigen. There were specific members of the families who gave positive responses in this test without other evidence of the classical disease. These families present preliminary evidence to suggest that subtle pulmonary changes may occur in patients who have cellular sensitization to fungal antigens without the overt clinical picture.

Clinical Features

A. Symptoms and Signs: The clinical features of these disorders are similar no matter what the implicated antigen. Following inhalation of the antigen, there is a period of 5–6 hours without symptoms. Fever, a dry cough, malaise, and dyspnea then occur. Radiographic studies of the chest demonstrate interstitial edema that can progress to patchy infiltration. Pulmonary function studies suggest decreased respiratory reserve, decreased gas exchange across the alveolar membrane, and normal expiratory function. Lung biopsies performed during acute episodes demonstrate a mixed granulocytic and lymphocytic infiltration. The acute attack normally clears in 3–4 days without sequelae. Recurrent acute attacks can lead to interstitial fibrosis with noncaseating interstitial granulomatous changes.

Chronic exposure to the offending antigens may result in a number of different clinical presentations. The clinical manifestations are dependent on the degree of hypersensitivity of the patient and the quantitative level of antigen exposure. Continuous antigen exposure can produce a low-grade disease marked by chronic cough, marked weight loss, chest pain, intermittent low-grade fever, profound malaise, and pulmonary fibrosis. A patient with these symptoms can present a difficult diagnostic problem.

Hypersensitivity to antigens related to Aspergillus species appears to be the most commonly diagnosed of these disorders, and the clinical presentation of aspergillus hypersensitivity can vary from the typical history just presented. The disease is normally chronic, with prolonged periods of low-grade illness marked by acute episodes of fever, cough, and eosinophilia. The fungi can frequently be isolated from cultures of bronchial mucus, and these viable organisms probably result in continuous exposure to the sensitizing antigens.

B. Laboratory Findings: Other than the immunologic tests to be described below, routine laboratory tests offer little assistance in the diagnostic evaluation of patients with hypersensitivity pneumonitis. There may be episodic leukocytosis with eosinophilia and an increased red cell sedimentation rate. In the absence of recent antigen exposure, all laboratory tests may be normal. Chest x-rays are usually normal, but chronic pneumonitis may lead to a pattern of diffuse interstitial fibrosis.

Immunologic Diagnosis

In addition to the routine history, physical examination, and initial laboratory studies, the clinical history must be meticulously searched for temporal and geographic clues suggesting specific antigen exposure.

Remembering that clinical symptoms normally follow antigen exposure by several hours, it is important to inquire carefully about exposures to organic materials, dusts, hobby materials, birds, pets, certain areas of work or home, etc. Serum precipitation tests against a panel of common fungal and organic antigens are helpful, but the presence or absence of precipitating antibody does not restrict the diagnosis. Patients may have a strong precipitating antibody early in their disease and then lose the antibody. In addition, the presence of precipitating antibody merely indicates that the person has been exposed to that antigen, not necessarily that the antibody is implicated in the disease process. If no precipitating antibody can be demonstrated by testing against routine antigen preparations, the patient's serum should be tested against an extract of his own suspected antigen source.

Pulmonary function studies and chest x-rays are useful in following the clinical course of the patient during treatment but are of limited diagnostic assistance. Lung biopsies or provocative exposure to suspected antigens can be helpful in diagnosis, but their use should be limited to carefully selected patients after completion of other studies.

Differential Diagnosis

In the absence of a strong clinical suspicion of hypersensitivity pneumonitis, patients early in their disease may be diagnosed as having intermittent pulmonary edema or asthma, depending on the age and general health of the patient. The chronic form of the disease frequently presents as a fever of unknown origin, and a great variety of neoplastic and infectious diseases are considered in the differential diagnosis.

Treatment & Prognosis

The primary treatment is removal of the patient from additional antigen exposure. Most patients will remain free of symptoms and have no long-term adverse effects. It may not be possible to identify the offending antigen source, however, and the patient may have progressive disease leading to pulmonary fibrosis, cardiac dysfunction, and severe physical disability. Acute episodes may be considerably relieved by the administration of corticosteroids, but the influence of this treatment on pulmonary fibrosis resulting from continued antigen exposure is not clear. The patient may suffer severe social restrictions and economic loss in his attempts to avoid antigen exposure, and the physician should feel secure in the diagnosis before suggesting major changes in a patient's vocation or environment.

SARCOIDOSIS

Major Immunologic Features

- Depression of cell-mediated immune responses.
- Granuloma formation characteristic but not diagnostic of sarcoid.
- Positive Kveim test in 80% of cases.
- Polyclonal hypergammaglobulinemia.

General Considerations

Sarcoidosis is a chronic systemic granulomatous disorder that is fatal in about 5% of cases. Many causes have been suspected (viruses, organic dusts, pine pollen, fungi, beryllium, mycobacteria, etc), but the cause remains unknown. Most of the agents suggested as the cause of this disease were later found to be associated with other disorders clinically similar to sarcoidosis or to have no role in the etiology of sarcoidosis. The disease appears in 2 clinical forms, and both are currently considered to have the same etiology. The acute form of the disease is marked by prominent hilar lymphadenopathy, erythema nodosum, and slow resolution over a 2-year period. The chronic form is characterized by lung parenchymal involvement and cutaneous granulomas and has a poorer prognosis.

Sarcoidosis is more often diagnosed in the temperate zones, but it has a worldwide distribution and affects all ethnic groups. The disease rate varies widely; the USA has approximately 31–36 cases per 100,000 population, Sweden has 64 cases per 100,000 population, and Irishwomen in London have up to 200 cases per 100,000. The incidence rates and the severity of the disorder vary among different populations and geographic regions, but in the USA black persons appear to have both a higher incidence and a more severe clinical course than people with lighter skin pigmentation. Since the diagnosis is one of exclusion and the cause is unknown, the statistics offered above may be much lower than the actual prevalence in less well developed countries.

Immunologic Pathogenesis

Multiple abnormalities of the immune system are present in this disorder, but their relationship to either the pathogenesis or the clinical severity of the disease has not been elucidated. Alterations in immunoglobulin production and in cellular immunity are present in 3 main areas: (1) depression of delayed hypersensitivity, (2) lymphoproliferation with increased serum gamma globulins, and (3) granulomatous reactions characteristic but not pathognomonic of sarcoidosis.

Delayed hypersensitivity skin test reactions to various antigens (mumps, tuberculosis, DNCB, pertussis, KLH, etc) are greatly reduced or absent. As a whole, the delayed skin test reactivity of patients with sarcoidosis is not as depressed as the responses of patients with malignant lymphoproliferative disorders. The tuberculin skin test is negative in two-thirds of patients with sarcoidosis upon initial testing. With clinical improvement, the tuberculin skin test can revert to positive (confusing the diagnostic evaluation in a complex patient), but other workers have not seen any significant degree of return of skin test responses with clinical improvement. Immunization with mumps virus antigens can produce circulating antibody though at the same time it fails to elicit a positive delayed hypersensitive response. This suggests that a selective defect in cellular function with affected subpopulations of T cells is present in sarcoidosis.

Phytohemagglutinin (PHA) is a mitogen which nonspecifically stimulates lymphocytes (see Chapter 25). Lymphocytes from patients with sarcoidosis fail to respond (or respond with diminished vigor) to stimulation with PHA. This decreased responsiveness is reported to be most profound in severely ill patients, and the response improves as the patient improves. Some patients continue to have a depressed lymphocyte response to PHA even after clinical improvement. A positive correlation is apparent between the skin test responses of a particular patient to a variety of antigens and the responses of his lymphocytes to PHA.

The correlation between skin test and PHA responsiveness has resulted in several attempts to elicit in vitro responses to antigens extracted from tissues from sarcoid patients. These responses have been variable in the laboratories of different investigators, and no in vitro assay is currently of proved value in the diagnosis or follow-up of sarcoid patients. The failure to respond to PHA in vitro has been associated with the failure to become sensitized to DNCB, a contact sensitizer (see Chapter 25). Although 76% of a control population responded to both PHA and DNCB, only 2% of patients with sarcoidosis so responded. In addition, no control patient was unresponsive to both PHA and the sensitizing compound, but 71% of sarcoid patients showed greatly reduced responses or no responses to both of these tests. Other disorders of the immune system can produce analogous depression of these responses, so they are not diagnostic of the disease; but they can be helpful indicators of the immune status of the patient at the time of diagnosis or useful as an indicator of return of response with clinical improvement.

Attempts to produce lymphocyte migration inhibition factors by the incubation of Kveim antigens in the presence of lymphocytes from sarcoid and control patients have produced mixed results. Some investigators have obtained results that correlated positively with the known skin test reactions, whereas others have found the test to be of no value for the diagnostic evaluation of sarcoid patients. There are apparently a great many false-positive and false-negative assay results. These difficulties may be partially related to differences in antigen preparations employed in the assays, and considerable effort is currently being expended toward the preparation of a standard pool of antigen.

Counting the T and B lymphocyte populations by various assays (see Chapter 25) has demonstrated alterations in the numbers of these cells in sarcoid patients. T cell rosette formation with sheep red cells is lower in sarcoid patients than in controls. The number of B cells, defined as circulating lymphocytes with easily detectable surface immunoglobulin, is increased. One problem with these assays, however, is that circulating immune complexes, considered responsible for some of the clinical symptoms of sarcoid patients, may nonspecifically attach to lymphocytes via their Fc receptor. Lymphocytes bearing complement receptors (B cells) are also increased in sarcoid patients.

A general nonspecific activation of B cells present in sarcoid patients results in a general increase in the levels of serum immunoglobulins. Elevations of IgG, IgA, and IgM have been described, and clinical improvement may decrease the IgG and IgM, but the IgA usually remains elevated. There is no clinical correlation between the radiographic findings present in the chest, the clinical activity of the disease, and the serum immunoglobulin levels (other than the small quantitative association just mentioned). Immunoglobulin levels in bronchial washings of patients with sarcoidosis are increased, but similar increases can occur in diseases unrelated to sarcoid.

As previously mentioned, there is evidence for circulating immune complexes in this disorder. Some workers have noted an increase in clinical severity with an increase in the presence of circulating complexes. Administration of corticosteroid therapy will decrease the symptoms and the amount of immune complexes. Early reports suggested that total hemolytic complement was also increased in the acute form of sarcoidosis, but later studies have not supported this finding. Several autoantibodies have been sought and found in sarcoid patients, but the incidence of autoantibodies is not greater than that found in patients with many other diseases. The presence or absence of antimitochrondrial antibodies can be useful in discriminating between sarcoidosis and granulomatous disorders of the liver (biliary disorders).

Clinical Features

A. Symptoms and Signs: The clinical presentation of sarcoidosis has been compared in several worldwide series and is remarkably similar in all cases. The disease most often presents before age 40 and affects both sexes equally. The principal symptoms are respiratory, dermatologic, or ocular in origin, and dyspnea, erythema nodosum, acute iritis, splenomegaly, peripheral lymphadenopathy, or cardiac arrhythmias may be present at the time of initial examination. Most patients have asymptomatic sarcoidosis, however, and the disease is first noticed on a routine chest x-ray. Radiographic findings vary from prominent bilateral hilar lymphadenopathy to extensive pulmonary infiltrates with fibrosis. Skin nodules are present in about one-fifth, peripheral lymphadenopathy in about one-third, and splenomegaly in slightly over one-tenth of patients. It should be emphasized, however, that sarcoidosis is a protean disease which can present with symptomatic involvement of almost any organ system.

B. Laboratory Findings: Radiographic findings vary from prominent hilar lymphadenopathy to extensive pulmonary infiltrates with fibrosis (Table 31–3). The routine blood count is usually normal. Polyclonal hypergammaglobulinemia may be present and usually represents increased IgG, but IgM and IgA may also be increased. Hypercalcemia is present in about 15% of

Table 31–3. International convention for staging chest roentgenograms of patients with sarcoidosis.

Stage 0:	Clear chest roentgenogram.
Stage 1:	Bilateral hilar lymphadenopathy.
Stage 2:	Bilateral hilar lymphadenopathy plus parenchymal pulmonary infiltration.
Stage 3:	Advanced parenchymal pulmonary infiltration with nodular densities.

Table 31–4. Prognosis and treatment of sarcoidosis.

Chest X-Ray	Prognosis	Corticosteroid Therapy
Stage 1	Resolves in 60% of cases.	No corticosteroid therapy.
Stage 2	Resolves in 46% of cases	Corticosteroids to decrease pulmonary fibrosis and relieve symptoms.
Stage 3	Resolves in 12% of cases.	Same as stage 2.

patients, but this percentage has varied considerably in different clinical series. The Kveim test (see below) is positive in about 80% of patients.

Immunologic Diagnosis

The best assay for the differential diagnosis of sarcoidosis is the skin test assay performed with known potent antigenic extracts of sarcoid tissue. This test—the Kveim skin test—is positive in 80% of patients with sarcoidosis and has only a 2% false-positive rate. These figures are dependent to some extent on the diagnostic experience of the pathologist interpreting the assay. The test antigen is not commercially available and must be secured from clinical investigators active in the field. Early in the clinical trials of the Kveim test, several lots of inactive antigen were used and the interpretation of the data suggested that the test was not as useful as had been reported. The preparation of highly standardized antigen lots, however, has supported the initial enthusiasm for this diagnostic test.

The test antigen is prepared by extracting human spleen tissue obtained from a patient with active sarcoidosis. A small quantity (0.15 ml) of the preparation is injected intradermally in a manner similar to a PPD skin test, but the site is observed for 6 weeks to note the development of a nodule. Any nodule which forms is biopsied, and the test is considered positive if the nodule contains a sarcoid granulomatous reaction.

Differential Diagnosis

The ability of sarcoidosis to involve multiple organ systems can result in considerable difficulty in establishing the diagnosis when the disorder has an atypical presentation. Pulmonary symptoms may suggest tuberculosis or hypersensitivity pneumonitis. Extrathoracic sarcoidosis should be distinguished from Hodgkin's disease or biliary cirrhosis.

Treatment & Prognosis

The prognosis in sarcoidosis associated with bilateral hilar lymphadenopathy and erythema nodosum is uniformly favorable. In other stages of sarcoidosis, the prognosis is dependent on the extent of lung involvement and the presence of extrathoracic lesions. Corticosteroid therapy is given to decrease clinical symptoms and prevent extensive pulmonary fibrosis. (See Table 31–4.) Renal involvement, extensive skin lesions, bone lesions, central nervous system lesions, etc frequently require intensive corticosteroid therapy and have a poorer prognosis. The disease is fatal in about 5% of cases.

IDIOPATHIC INTERSTITIAL PULMONARY FIBROSIS (Hamman-Rich Syndrome)

The original description of this syndrome included patients with the slowly progressive onset of dyspnea which progressed to respiratory insufficiency and death. However, application of the diagnosis has been broadened considerably in recent years and now includes a variety of patients with chronic or progressive pulmonary fibrosis of uncertain cause.

No immunologic test can be used to confirm the diagnosis of this syndrome, but several immunologic tests are abnormal as compared to patients with other lung diseases. Serum immunoglobulin levels are increased, and ANA, rheumatoid factor, or antithyroid antibodies can be present. Specific antilung antibodies have not been documented, but increased amounts of IgM can be demonstrated in some lung tissue sections if circulating IgM antinuclear antibodies are present.

Circulating immune complexes have been demonstrated in several diseases (eg, rheumatoid arthritis, systemic lupus erythematosus) which also can present with progressive pulmonary fibrosis. An experimental model of diffuse lung fibrosis has been produced in the rabbit by producing continuous serum levels of BSA-anti-BSA complexes. Such data suggest that any disease which results in circulating immune complexes predisposes to interstitial lung fibrosis.

Clinical Features

A. Symptoms and Signs: The syndrome may occur at any age in either sex, but most patients are in their sixth decade. The illness begins with dyspnea on exertion, but otherwise there are few symptoms. As the disease progresses and respiratory insufficiency occurs, weight loss, clubbing of the fingers, cough, and cyanosis may become prominent. The lung fibrosis may lead to right ventricular hypertrophy or failure.

B. Laboratory Findings: The chest x-ray shows a fine reticular pattern, more common in the lower portions of the lung. With advancement of the disease, the fibrosis produces a honeycomb appearance of the chest x-ray, but bullae are uncommon. Most laboratory values are normal, but pulmonary function studies demonstrate decreased diffusing capacity and lung volume. Lung compliance is also decreased. Several autoantibodies have been described in the sera of patients with this syndrome (see below), but their relationship to the clinical onset or progression of the disease is not clear.

Treatment & Prognosis

Corticosteroid therapy has been useful in some patients in decreasing symptoms and producing improvement of pulmonary findings. Thus, a trial of corticosteroids is appropriate in the rapidly progressive case. Most patients are not helped by therapy, however, and about half of newly diagnosed patients will grow progressively worse and die within 2–3 years. However, some patients stabilize their lung function and live up to 10 years or longer.

GOODPASTURE'S SYNDROME

Goodpasture's syndrome (see Chapter 32) is an uncommon disease of unknown cause that occurs principally in children and young adults. The disease normally presents with hemoptysis and is associated with fever, recurrent episodes of glomerulonephritis, cough, dyspnea, recurrent pulmonary hemorrhages, and iron deficiency anemia. Histologic examinations of renal biopsy specimens show linear deposits of IgG and complement components along the glomerular basement membrane. Immunoglobulin deposition can also be demonstrated in lung tissue, but some workers have obtained varied results in relating the lung and renal immunoglobulin. It seems clear that IgG and IgA antibodies reactive to the renal basement membrane have been documented. When these antibodies were eluted from the renal tissue, they reacted with normal human kidney tissue but not with normal human lung tissue. Other workers have eluted lung immunoglobulins and demonstrated their reaction with renal tissue.

The cause of the syndrome is unclear, but some investigators have postulated a mechanism by which viral modification of cell surface proteins common to renal and pulmonary tissue leads to production of an autoantibody. This could help explain some of the disparate results obtained with antibodies eluted from both tissues.

Chest x-ray shows pulmonary infiltrates in various stages of resolution as the hemoptysis waxes and wanes. Pulmonary tissue is packed with hemosiderin-filled macrophages, and, since this iron is not available for hematopoiesis, an iron deficiency anemia may develop.

Goodpasture's syndrome can be confused with acute bacterial pneumonias and with uremic pneumonitis accompanying more common forms of nephritis.

This disease has a poor prognosis and frequently progresses to death within a few months from uremia or pulmonary hemorrhage. Treatment with corticosteroids and cytotoxic drugs may give some relief of pulmonary symptoms but does not appear to prolong survival. Exchange transfusion or plasmapheresis has been used to decrease circulatory anti-glomerular basement membrane antibodies. When the procedure was combined with cytotoxic drugs, a remission of pulmonary symptoms resulted. Removal of all renal tissue by nephrectomy, hemodialysis, and subsequent renal transplantation have been used in a few cases with promising results.

PULMONARY REACTIONS TO LEUKOAGGLUTININS

The infusion of blood which is incompatible with white cell antigens and contains leukoagglutinating antibodies can result in fever, chills, cough, transient pulmonary infiltrates, and normovolemic pulmonary edema. These reactions have an immunologic basis and are associated with leukoagglutinins in either the transfused blood or the recipient's serum. The reactions may be grossly divided into 2 types depending on whether the incompatible white blood cells or the leukoagglutinin is infused. Acute febrile reactions are common when whole blood containing incompatible leukocytes is infused into a recipient having preformed circulating leukoagglutinins. These reactions are most common in patients with a history of multiple transfusions, and the febrile reactions can be prevented by carefully separating the white cells from the blood prior to transfusion. No pulmonary manifestations have been noted when only incompatible leukocytes were infused.

On the other hand, when blood containing leukoagglutinins is infused, the donor serum contains an antibody that reacts with recipient white cells and produces an acute clinical syndrome of fever, dyspnea, cough, and pulmonary infiltrates. These are not anti-HLA antibodies. In the more severe cases, cyanosis and hypertensive episodes have also been described. Although the onset and symptoms suggest acute pulmonary edema, the presence of hypervolemia has been excluded in most of the reported cases either by appropriate measurements or by inference from the clinical presentation. Corticosteroids appear to relieve some of the symptoms, but several days may be required for clearing of the chest x-ray. Laboratory studies may demonstrate the presence of the agglutinating antibody in the donor serum.

• • •

References

Postpericardiotomy Syndrome

Carlisle R: A classification for the cardiomyopathies. Am J Cardiol 28:242, 1971.

Kaplan MH: Autoimmunity to heart and its relationship to heart disease: A review. Prog Allergy 13:408, 1969.

Robbins S: Cardiac pathology: A look at the last five years. Part 1. Hum Pathol 5:9, 1974.

Shaper AG & others: Immunological studies in endomyocardial fibrosis and other forms of heart-disease in the tropics. Lancet 1:598, 1967.

Rheumatic Fever

Hess EV & others: Heart muscle antibodies in rheumatic fever and other diseases. J Clin Invest 43:886, 1964.

Hollander JL, McCarty DJ Jr (editors): *Arthritis and Allied Conditions,* 8th ed. Lea & Febiger, 1972.

Kaplan MH, Frengley JD: Autoimmunity to the heart in cardiac disease: Current concepts of the relation of autoimmunity to rheumatic fever, postcardiotomy and postinfarction syndromes and cardiomyopathies. Am J Cardiol 24:459, 1969.

McLaughlin JF & others: Rheumatic carditis: In vitro responses of peripheral blood leukocytes to heart and streptococcal antigens. Arthritis Rheum 15:600, 1972.

Read SE & others: Cellular reactivity studies to streptococcal antigens: Migration inhibition studies in patients with streptococcal infections and rheumatic fever. J Clin Invest 54:439, 1974.

Rodnan GP, McEwen C, Wallace SL (editors): Primer on the rheumatic diseases. JAMA 224 (Suppl 5):661, 1973.

Spagnulo M, Pasternack B, Taranta A: Risk of rheumatic fever recurrences after streptococcal infections: Prospective study of clinical and social factors. N Engl J Med 285:641, 1971.

Hypersensitivity Pneumonitis

Goldstein GB, Yokoyama M: Studies of the dual antibody response in allergic bronchopulmonary aspergillosis. J Allergy 46:340, 1970.

Schlueter DP: Response of the lung to inhaled antigens. Am J Med 57:476, 1974.

Sarcoidosis

James DG, Neville E, Walker A: Immunology of sarcoidosis. Am J Med 59:388, 1975.

Siltzbach LE & others: Course and prognosis of sarcoidosis around the world. Am J Med 57:847, 1974.

Idiopathic Interstitial Fibrosis

Hinson KFW: Diffuse pulmonary fibrosis. Hum Pathol 1:275, 1970.

Goodpasture's Syndrome

Donald KJ, Edwards RL, McEvoy JDS: Alveolar capillary basement membrane lesions in Goodpasture's syndrome and idiopathic pulmonary hemosiderosis. Am J Med 59:642, 1975.

Leukoagglutinins

Thompson JS & others: Pulmonary "hypersensitivity" reactions induced by transfusion of non-HL-A leukoagglutinins. N Engl J Med 284:1120, 1971.

32 . . .
Renal Diseases

Curtis B. Wilson, MD, Wayne A. Border, MD, & David H. Lehman, MD

GLOMERULONEPHRITIS

Over the past 75 years, 2 major antibody-associated mechanisms of glomerular injury have been identified. In one, antibodies react with antigens present in the glomerular basement membrane. In the other, antibodies react with nonglomerular antigens in the circulation to form immune complexes which are deposited in the glomerulus. The accumulated immune complexes or anti-glomerular basement membrane antibodies can cause glomerular damage either directly or by involving mediators of immunologic injury such as the complement (C), kinin-forming, and coagulation systems. The precise individual contribution of these mediator systems in the production of human glomerulonephritis is not known. We do know that most antigen-antibody interactions directly activate the complement system, which is a primary link between the initial immunologic events and the ensuing inflammatory response and tissue damage.

The general conclusion drawn from studies of experimental nephritis is that the main immunopathogenic effect of complement is to attract neutrophils to sites of antibody deposition. Complement can attract neutrophils through the chemotactic activity of the cleavage fragments of C3 and C5, which are C3a and C5a, and the trimolecular complex $C\overline{576}$ and retains the neutrophils through immune adherence membrane receptor sites specific for other C3 cleavage fragments.

In theory, there are other ways by which complement activation could damage the glomerulus. In addition to being chemotactic, C3a and C5a also are anaphylatoxins, ie, they cause the release of histamine from mast cells, thereby increasing capillary permeability. Capillary permeability is thought to be an important factor in determining whether or not circulating immune complexes can be deposited in arterial and glomerular capillary walls.

Curtis B. Wilson is Associate Member, Department of Immunopathology, Scripps Clinic and Research Foundation, La Jolla, California. Wayne A. Border is Fellow in Nephrology, Harbor General Hospital, Torrance, California. David H. Lehman is Fellow in Nephrology, University of California School of Medicine, San Francisco.

Complement activation also affects platelets by means of a poorly understood mechanism, possibly involving platelet binding of complement fragments and platelet release of enzymes, vasoactive amines, and platelet factor III. Like anaphylatoxin-induced histamine release, vasoactive amines released by platelets are known to increase capillary permeability. By releasing platelet factor III or other substances, the affected platelets generate a coagulant activity capable of initiating systemic coagulation, thrombosis, and fibrinolysis. Fibrin deposition is thought to contribute to development of glomerular crescents and irreversible glomerular scarring. Hageman factor, one of the early-acting proteins of the clotting system, plays a key role in linking the complement, coagulation, and kinin-forming systems. Once activated, Hageman factor can recruit the kinin-forming system by converting prekallikrein to kallikrein. Hageman factor also interacts with plasminogen to produce plasmin, which, in addition to having fibrinolytic properties, can also activate the classical complement pathway.

Possibly, then, some or all of the pathobiologic effects of complement, kinin-forming, and coagulation systems play a role in the pathogenesis of human glomerulonephritis. However, our present understanding of these mediators is based largely upon in vitro observations. These mediator systems may be common to both the immune complex and anti-glomerular basement membrane antibody mechanisms of renal injury, making their clinical and pathologic presentations indistinguishable from each other unless studied by immunopathologic means. There is currently little evidence for a direct role of immune cells in the production of glomerular injury, although cellular sensitivity can occasionally be identified.

Recently, a possible third mechanism of glomerular injury involving "nonimmune" complement activation has been postulated to explain the pathogenesis of a membranoproliferative form of glomerular injury in children with persistent hypocomplementemia. Some of these patients have circulating nonimmunologic activators of the alternative complement pathway called nephritic factor (NF, C3NeF). These factors are discussed in the section on hypocomplementemic glomerulonephritis.

1. ANTI-GLOMERULAR BASEMENT MEMBRANE ANTIBODY-INDUCED GLOMERULONEPHRITIS

Major Immunologic Features

- Anti-glomerular basement membrane antibodies usually detectable in serum by indirect immunofluorescence or radioimmunoassay.
- Linear deposition of immunoglobulin and complement along glomerular basement membrane.

General Considerations

The nephritogenicity of antikidney antisera was noted in 1900 by Lindemann. Subsequent studies by Masugi and others amplified these early observations, and in the 1950s Krakower and Greenspon convincingly demonstrated that the major nephritogenic antigens of the kidney were in the glomerular basement membrane. The old term nephrotoxic antisera has now been largely replaced by the more specific term anti-glomerular basement membrane antibody.

Immunologic Pathogenesis

Two forms of experimental anti-glomerular basement membrane antibody-induced glomerulonephritis have been demonstrated. First, anti-glomerular basement membrane antibodies can be induced by immunizing animals with glomerular basement membrane in adjuvant. The antibody can then be used to induce anti-glomerular basement membrane nephritis in normal recipients. For example, rabbit, sheep, or duck anti-rat-glomerular basement membrane antibodies are often used to induce anti-glomerular basement membrane glomerulonephritis in rats. The resulting glomerular injury occurs in 2 phases. If sufficient quantities of anti-glomerular basement membrane antibodies are given (75 μg of kidney-fixing antibody per gram of kidney in the rat), immediate injury and proteinuria occur. If insufficient antibody is given to cause immediate injury, overt glomerulonephritis does not develop until the recipient has produced antibody reactive with the foreign immunoglobulin already bound to its glomerular basement membrane. Quantitative differences in the numbers of antibody molecules required to induce immediate glomerular injury as well as the severity of the resultant glomerulonephritis have been equated with the antibody's ability to activate complement and involve polymorphonuclear leukocytes. This has led to designation of the antibody as dependent on or independent of complement and polymorphonuclear leukocytes and indicates that separate mediators of immunologic injury must be utilized by the complement-independent antibodies. Similarly, about one-fourth of human patients with anti-glomerular basement membrane antibodies have no detectable complement fixed in the glomeruli, suggesting complement-independent processes.

In the second form of experimental anti-glomerular basement membrane nephritis, some animals immunized with glomerular basement membrane in adjuvant (sheep are particularly susceptible) develop anti-glomerular basement membrane antibodies which cross-react with their own glomerular basement membrane. Severe glomerulonephritis follows which can prove fatal to the sheep within 2–3 months. This lesion is similar in many ways to that of spontaneous anti-glomerular basement membrane glomerulonephritis in man. Circulating anti-glomerular basement membrane antibodies are clearly pathogenic because they can be used to transfer glomerular injury to normal lambs.

In the mid 1960s, immunofluorescence of kidney sections from occasional patients with glomerulonephritis showed anti-glomerular basement membrane antibodies bound along the glomerular basement membrane in a smooth linear pattern. In 1967, Lerner and others demonstrated anti-glomerular basement membrane antibodies in the circulations of such patients. These investigators also isolated anti-glomerular basement membrane antibodies from the circulations or eluted them from the kidneys of these patients and showed the antibodies' pathogenicity by using them to transfer anti-glomerular basement membrane glomerulonephritis to subhuman primates. The most convincing evidence of similar pathogenicity in man came when glomerulonephritis was accidentally transferred to a renal transplant placed in a patient who had circulating anti-glomerular basement membrane antibodies.

In patients with Goodpasture's syndrome, anti-basement membrane antibodies can be found bound to the alveolar basement membranes, and antibodies cross-reactive with the glomerular basement membrane can be eluted from the involved lung tissue. Antilung antibodies produced experimentally induce glomerulonephritis in rats. Sheep immunized with human lung develop glomerulonephritis much as sheep immunized with glomerular basement membrane do. The evidence then suggests that anti-basement membrane antibodies are responsible for both pulmonary and renal injury in associated Goodpasture's syndrome.

Little is known about the events responsible for the induction of spontaneous anti-glomerular basement membrane responses. Materials cross-reactive with the glomerular basement membrane have been identified in the urine of animals and humans. These materials accumulate in the circulation after nephrectomy, suggesting that they represent basement membrane fragments detached during basement membrane metabolism throughout the body and normally excreted in the urine. Immunization of rabbits with basement membrane antigens from their own urine can induce anti-glomerular basement membrane glomerulonephritis, suggesting the same potential in man. In addition, noxious environmental or infectious insults to basement membranes (eg, in the lung) could induce anti-basement membrane antibody responses. Indeed, both hydrocarbon solvent inhalation and influenza A2 infections have been related to anti-glomerular basement membrane antibody-associated Goodpasture's syndrome. The lung damaged in this way might also react more easily with anti-glomerular basement membrane antibodies formed for unrelated reasons. In virtually all instances, the production of anti-glomerular basement membrane antibodies is short-lived, lasting only weeks to 1 or 2 years, and suggesting that the immunologic stimulus is also transient.

Clinical Features

About 5% of cases of glomerulonephritis in humans appear to be caused by anti-glomerular basement membrane antibodies which most commonly induce proliferative crescent-forming histologic types of glomerular injury with rapidly progressive clinical courses. About half of these patients with glomerulonephritis also have pulmonary hemorrhage and respiratory failure, a condition referred to as Goodpasture's syndrome. Males in the second to fourth decade of life are most commonly affected. The first symptoms may be either renal or pulmonary or both, with onset occurring simultaneously or separated by as much as a year. In over 75% of cases, renal failure necessitating dialysis develops rapidly. Occasionally—in about 10% of cases—chronic forms of anti-glomerular basement membrane glomerulonephritis may be observed. As experience with the disease has increased and better diagnostic methods have become available, it has become evident that a milder self-remitting form does occur. This milder form, however, probably accounts for fewer than 15% of cases. In a few patients, the pulmonary features of the disease predominate or are the sole clinical manifestation. Anti-basement membrane antibodies may then be responsible for an as yet undetermined percentage of cases of so-called pulmonary hemosiderosis. Nephrotic syndrome is unusual in anti-glomerular basement membrane glomerulonephritis, probably because renal failure supervenes before sufficient urinary protein spillage, leading to nephrosis, has occurred.

Immunologic Diagnosis

Patients with rapidly progressive glomerulonephritis or Goodpasture's syndrome should be suspected of having anti-glomerular basement membrane antibodies. A diagnosis of anti-glomerular basement membrane glomerulonephritis is based on identifying anti-glomerular basement membrane antibodies by at least 2 of the 3 following means: (1) linear deposits of immunoglobulin along the glomerular basement membrane seen by immunofluorescence, (2) elution of anti-glomerular basement membrane antibodies from renal tissue, and (3) detection of circulating anti-glomerular basement membrane antibodies.

By immunofluorescence, anti-glomerular basement membrane antibodies appear as linear deposits of IgG and infrequently IgA or IgM along the glomerular basement membrane (Fig 32–1). Irregular IgM deposits along the glomerular basement membrane are pres-

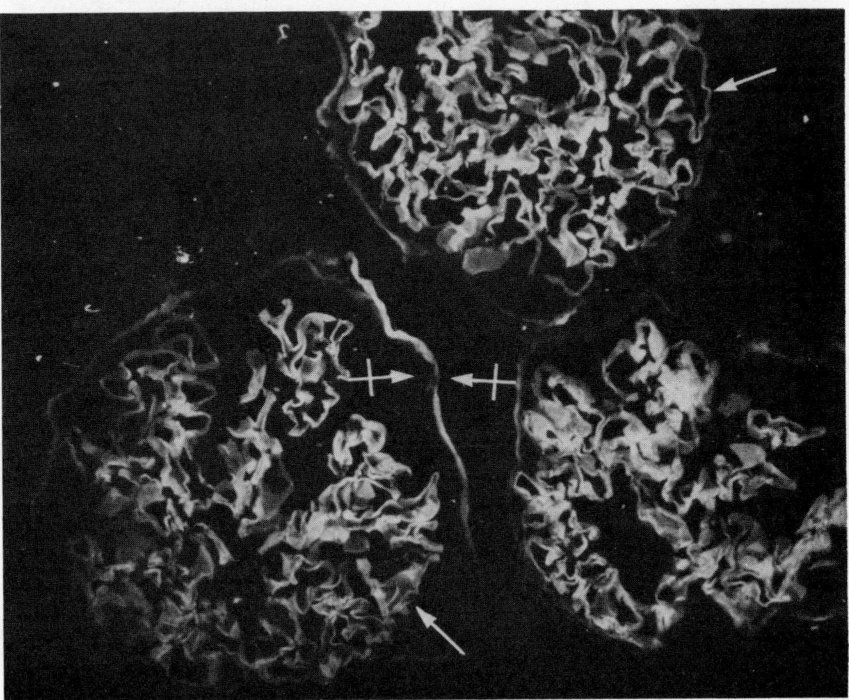

Figure 32–1. Smooth linear deposits of IgG (arrows) representing anti-glomerular basement membrane antibodies are seen outlining the glomerular basement membrane of 3 glomeruli from a young man with Goodpasture's syndrome. The antibody also had reactivity with Bowman's capsule (opposed hatched arrows). (Original magnification × 160.)

ent in less than half of the kidneys studied. Linear deposits of immunoglobulin are also frequently present along the tubular basement membranes (see later section). The linear deposits of immunoglobulin are accompanied by linear or irregular deposits of C3 in about two-thirds of these kidneys. Fibrin-related antigens may be striking in areas of extracapillary proliferation and crescent formation. When C3 is present, it is usually accompanied by deposits of other components of the classical complement pathway. Nonimmunologic accumulations of IgG are sometimes observed in a linear pattern along the glomerular basement membrane, particularly in kidneys from patients with diabetes mellitus, in kidneys obtained at autopsy, and in kidneys perfused in preparation for transplantation. These occasional "false-positive" kidneys indicate the need for confirming diagnoses by eluting anti-glomerular basement membrane antibodies or detecting them in the circulation.

Anti-glomerular basement membrane antibodies can be dissociated from renal tissue by elution in acid buffers or buffers containing chaotropic ions (KI, KSCN, etc), which can dissociate hydrophobic and ionic bonds. The eluted immunoglobulin can then be concentrated and tested for anti-glomerular basement membrane reactivity in vitro by indirect immunofluorescence or radioimmunoassay, or in vivo by injection into subhuman primates. The ability to elute glomerular basement membrane-reactive antibodies from renal tissue confirms the specificity of immunofluorescence observations and establishes a clear-cut diagnosis.

Anti-glomerular basement membrane antibodies can be sought in the circulation by using indirect immunofluorescence, hemagglutination, or, more recently, radioimmunoassay. About 80% of patients with Goodpasture's syndrome and 60% of patients with anti-glomerular basement membrane antibody-associated glomerulonephritis alone have anti-glomerular basement membrane antibodies detectable by indirect immunofluorescence. By radioimmunoassay, almost all patients with anti-glomerular basement membrane antibody-associated Goodpasture's syndrome and 80% of patients with anti-glomerular basement membrane antibody-associated glomerulonephritis alone are positive. Nephrectomy has no immediate effect on the levels of circulating anti-glomerular basement membrane antibodies, suggesting that damaged kidneys have little or no immunoabsorptive properties. The quantitative radioimmunoassay offers the advantage of monitoring the activity of the disease and giving an immediate assessment of the effect of therapy.

Treatment

No specific treatment is yet available. Immunosuppression with a variety of drugs has been tested in uncontrolled series, usually with little success. Corticosteroids are thought to be helpful in the management of acute pulmonary hemorrhage in patients with anti-glomerular basement membrane antibody-associated Goodpasture's syndrome. The variable duration and intensity of the transient anti-glomerular basement membrane response must be considered in evaluating any therapeutic regimen, and occasional patients have recovered adequate renal function "spontaneously" even after being on dialysis for short periods of time. Recently, repeated plasmapheresis has been used in conjunction with immunosuppression to reduce the levels of circulating anti-glomerular basement membrane antibodies until antibody production declines and ceases. Initial results are promising if the combined therapy is instituted before irreversible renal damage has taken place; however, insufficient data are currently available to fully assess this therapeutic approach.

Nephrectomy has been advocated by some as being helpful—even lifesaving—in the management of severe pulmonary hemorrhage in Goodpasture's syndrome. The results of nephrectomy are by no means clear-cut, and several nephrectomized patients have continued to manifest pulmonary hemorrhage, sometimes leading to death. Nephrectomy is also not essential to terminate production of anti-glomerular basement membrane antibody. Nephrectomy precludes the occasional spontaneous recovery and should be considered only as a last resort.

Circulating anti-glomerular basement membrane antibodies can transfer glomerulonephritis to a transplanted kidney. It is therefore advisable to postpone transplantation in patients with anti-glomerular basement membrane antibody-associated glomerulonephritis until circulating anti-glomerular basement membrane antibodies have been undetectable for 2–3 months. The mean duration of the anti-glomerular basement membrane antibody response is about 8 months (range: a few weeks to 2 years). It is not known whether immunosuppression, plasmapheresis, or nephrectomy influences the overall duration of the anti-glomerular basement membrane antibody response.

2. IMMUNE COMPLEX GLOMERULONEPHRITIS

Major Immunologic Features

- Circulating immune complexes are occasionally detectable.
- Granular deposition of immunoglobulins and complement along the glomerular basement membrane.

General Considerations

In 1911, von Pirquet recognized the relationship between the immune response and the symptoms of serum sickness. During the 1950s, Dixon and others demonstrated that immune complexes composed of antigen and antibody were the toxic products responsible for the tissue injury of serum sickness. The principles of immune complex-induced renal injury are best understood by examining the events that accompany acute and chronic serum sickness in rabbits. To induce acute serum sickness, rabbits are given large amounts of foreign proteins such as BSA (250 mg/kg). The BSA rapidly equilibrates with the intra- and extravascular fluids and then disappears at a rate governed by its catabolic half-life. Antibody production is initiated, and, after 4–5 days, sufficient antibody is present to combine with the circulating antigen and to be detected in circulating immune complexes. Since antigen is present in great excess, the complexes remain small and continue to circulate. As antibody production increases, the complexes enlarge and after 10–12 days are eliminated by the mononuclear phagocytic system (formerly termed the phagocytic reticuloendothelial system). During the process of elimination of the immune complexes, small amounts (mean: 18 μg) of BSA in immune complex form are deposited in the kidney, inducing a severe but transient proliferative glomerulonephritis manifested clinically by heavy proteinuria. Immune complexes are also deposited in other vascular beds, inducing conditions such as arteritis and synovitis. Depletion of complement and of polymorphonuclear leukocytes prevents arteritis, a feature of experimental acute serum sickness, but does not prevent glomerular injury—again indicating that mediator systems other than complement, although poorly understood, are important in the production of glomerular injury. After antigen has been eliminated from the circulation, free antibody appears and can combine with the antigen complexed within the glomerulus. This demonstrates that tissue-bound immune complexes are in equilibrium with antibody and with antigen from the circulation; the composition of the glomerular-bound immune complexes is then determined at any point in time by the relative concentrations of antigen or antibody in the circulation.

If the rabbits are given BSA repeatedly in amounts to balance antibody production, chronic serum sickness glomerulonephritis, which resembles most forms of human glomerulonephritis, can be induced. During the 6–8 weeks of daily intravenous BSA injection required for the development of chronic serum sickness glomerulonephritis, only small amounts of immune-complexed BSA are deposited in the kidney. When viewed by immunofluorescence, the deposition is confined largely to the mesangium, where it induces mesangial proliferation. After this time, the deposition increases to about 0.5% of the daily injected dose (10–200 mg) and the localization of deposition changes from the mesangium to the peripheral glomerular basement membrane, with occasional deposits observed in extraglomerular renal structures (tubular basement membrane and peritubular capillaries) as well. A wide variety of histologic changes are induced by the immune complex deposition, apparently governed in part by the quantity and rate of this deposition. Rabbits which produce antibody poorly are given small amounts of antigen and form small amounts of immune complexes. Such rabbits tend to have membranous glomerulonephritis. In contrast, active antibody producers given large amounts of antigen form large amounts of circulating immune complexes and have more proliferative (often rapidly progressive) histologic changes.

The half-life for disappearance of the bound antigen from the kidneys of rabbits with chronic serum sickness glomerulonephritis is about 5 days. It has been possible to hasten the disappearance of the renal-bound immune complexes by deliberately creating huge antigen excess in the rabbit's circulation. This treatment dissolves the glomerular-bound immune complexes as detected by immunofluorescence and electron microscopy, and recovery follows if excess antigen is given before irreversible glomerular changes develop. Administration of a huge antigen excess also terminates the antibody response, preventing formation of additional immune complexes. The multiple therapeutic benefits of this treatment may eventually be useful in man.

Although still incompletely understood, several factors which may influence the tissue localization of immune complexes have been identified. The glomerulus seems to be a uniquely susceptible site of immune complex deposition, probably related in part to its function as an arterial capillary filter with a fenestrated endothelial lining. Vascular bifurcations, aortic coarctation, and hypertension have been shown to predispose to immune complex deposition. Vasoactive substances released as part of the immune response—in particular that involving mast cell-bound or basophil-bound IgE—can enhance vascular permeability and potential immune complex localization. Indeed, antihistamines and antiserotonins have been shown to decrease immune complex deposition in rabbits with acute serum sickness. Immune complex size is also an important determinant of immune complex deposition, with complexes around 19S being most nephritogenic. Immune complex size is influenced by the relative antigen-antibody ratio, with either antigen or antibody excess causing immune complexes either too small to lodge in the kidney or so large that the complexes are handled harmlessly by the mononuclear phagocytic system. The avidity of the antibody may also influence the stability of the immune complex; however, this phenomenon is poorly understood. There is also a suggestion that uptake by the glomerular mesangium may reduce the phlogogenic potential of otherwise nephritogenic immune complexes. Certainly, with greater knowledge of events influencing immune complex deposition, methods of treatment could be designed to prevent the injurious sequelae.

Numerous models of glomerulonephritis have been developed and studied in experimental animals. Most persisting infectious processes provide sufficient exogenous antigens to eventually provoke circulating and potentially nephritogenic immune complex formation. Viral infections are the most frequently studied, and responses to chronic lymphocytic choriomeningitis virus by mice are considered the prototype of the viral immune complex mechanisms. Mice infected with lymphocytic choriomeningitis virus maintain lifelong infection and produce antibodies reactive with these circulating viral antigens. The antibody is completely complexed with the antigen and is undetectable by the most commonly employed immunologic technics. The complexes lodge in the glomeruli, beginning shortly after birth in mice infected in utero, possibly simulating congenital nephrosis in man. Viral antigens from murine leukemia virus, Aleutian mink disease virus, and infectious equine anemia virus lead to immune complex glomerulonephritis in mice, mink, and horses, respectively.

Endogenous or self antigens involved in autoimmune antibody production may also cause immune complex diseases. New Zealand mice, particularly the New Zealand black and the New Zealand black-white hybrid, develop antibodies reactive with nuclear materials such as DNA. These antibody responses are associated with the development of a systemic lupus erythematosus-like immune complex disease. The immune complex deposits are not confined to the glomeruli but may involve extraglomerular renal sites (tubular basement membrane and interstitium) and structures such as the choroid plexus as well. Recent studies have linked this complicated immune complex disease with C-type murine leukemia viruses harbored by New Zealand mice. It is not known how the autoimmune responses are related to the persistent viral infection; however, other mouse strains with little spontaneous antinuclear antibody form antinuclear antibodies when purposely infected with the New Zealand C-type virus. The C-type virus also contributes antigens to which antibodies form, producing nephritogenic immune complexes. The association of autoimmune disease and viral infection in the New Zealand mice suggests a similar association in human systemic lupus erythematosus. Other endogenous antigens such as renal tubular brush border, thyroglobulin, and erythrocyte surface antigens can cause immune complex glomerulonephritis in rats, rabbits, and mice, respectively.

An ever-increasing number of antigen-antibody systems are being identified in immune complex glomerulonephritis in man (Table 32–1). As in animals, the antigens in humans can be divided into exogenous or foreign and endogenous or self antigens. Administration of foreign proteins in the form of immune serum used for passive antibody transfers, inoculations, and drugs can result in serum sickness-like immune complex diseases. Infectious agents provide the largest number of antigens identified to date in man. Streptococcal antigen was identified in poststreptococcal glomerulonephritis. Staphylococcal antigen was found in children with infected atrioventricular shunts used to treat hydrocephalus. Enterococcal antigen was evident in glomerular immune complex deposits of a patient with subacute bacterial endocarditis, and salmonella antigen was found in glomerulonephritis associated with typhoid fever. *Treponema pallidum* antigens were recently identified in a patient with syphilis-associated glomerulonephritis. Chronic parasitic infections also provide antigens for immune complex formation. Both *Plasmodium malariae* and *P falciparum* antigens were found in patients with malaria and glomerulonephritis. Patients with congenital toxoplasmosis and glomerulonephritis had immune complexes containing *Toxoplasma gondii* antigens. Filariasis and schistosomiasis were also associated with immune complex glomerulonephritis—again presumably related to antigens from these parasitic infections. Hepatitis B, measles, and EB viral antigens in patients with hepatitis, subacute sclerosing panencephalitis, and Burkitt's lymphoma, respectively, also can contribute to nephritogenic immune complex formation. Oncornaviral antigens related to feline leukemia virus were identified in glomerular immune complex deposits in leukemia as well.

Table 32–1. Antigen-antibody systems known to cause or strongly suspected of causing immune complex glomerulonephritis in man.

Antigens	Clinical Condition
Exogenous or foreign antigens	
Iatrogenic agents	
Drugs, toxoids, foreign serum	Serum sickness, heroin nephropathy (?), gold nephropathy (?), etc
Infectious agents	
Bacterial: Nephritogenic streptococci, *Staphylococcus albus, Corynebacterium bovis,* enterococcus, *Streptococcus pneumoniae, Treponema pallidum, Salmonella typhi*	Poststreptococcal glomerulonephritis, infected ventriculoatrial shunts, endocarditis, pneumonia, syphilis, typhoid fever
Parasitic: *Plasmodium malariae, P falciparum, Schistosoma mansoni, Toxoplasma gondii, Filaria loa*	Malaria, schistosomiasis, toxoplasmosis
Viral: Hepatitis B, oncornavirus-related antigen, measles, Epstein-Barr virus	Hepatitis, leukemia, subacute sclerosing panencephalitis, Burkitt's lymphoma
Perhaps others as yet undetermined	Endocarditis, leprosy, kala-azar, filarial loiasis, dengue fever, mumps, varicella, infectious mononucleosis
Endogenous or self antigens	
Nuclear antigens	Systemic lupus erythematosus
Immunoglobulin	Cryoglobulinemia
Tumor antigens, CEA	Neoplasms
Thyroglobulin	Thyroiditis
Renal tubular antigen	Membranous glomerulonephritis in Japan, sickle cell anemia

Endogenous antigens leading to immune complex formation are best exemplified in the glomerulonephritis of patients with systemic lupus erythematosus, who form antibodies reactive with a variety of nuclear materials. Their immune responses can lead to nephritogenic immune complex formation, and their disease activity most clearly relates to native DNA antigen-antibody complexes. Rheumatoid factors and cryoglobulins may also contribute to the phlogogenic glomerular accumulations in systemic lupus erythematosus. Immunoglobulin aggregates or complexes may also cause glomerular injury and essential cryoglobulinemia. Thyroglobulin-antithyroglobulin immune complexes have been identified in glomeruli of patients with thyroiditis. Care may need to be taken when treating a patient with thyroiditis and circulating antithyroglobulin antibodies. Radiation-induced thyroid damage can release sufficient thyroglobulin to shift the ratio of circulating antigen and antibody so that nephritogenic immune complexes form. Recently, a renal tubular brush border antigen was identified in a few patients in Japan who had membranous glomerulonephritis and in patients in the USA with sickle cell anemia or renal carcinoma and glomerulonephritis. Renal tubular antigen immune complex glomerulonephritis is similar to that induced years ago by Heymann, who repeatedly immunized rats with rat kidney homogenized in Freund's complete adjuvant. In our experience, however, the tubular antigen-antibody system does not appear frequently in man. Antigens associated with neoplasms, such as CEA, have also been identified in glomerular immune complex deposits of patients with neoplasia.

Other immune complex systems should soon be identifiable in immune complex glomerulonephritis, particularly in glomerulonephritis associated with infectious disease such as leprosy, subacute bacterial endocarditis, infectious mononucleosis, or varicella. Identification of the antigenic makeup of presumed immune complex deposits occasionally found in glomeruli of patients with conditions such as sarcoidosis or neoplasia or amyotrophic lateral sclerosis may clarify the etiology of these conditions.

Immune complex deposits also appear to be responsible for glomerular injury in glomerulonephritis associated with systemic illnesses other than systemic lupus erythematosus. For example, Henoch-Schönlein purpura may be complicated by immune complex glomerulonephritis. The antigenic nature of the presumed immune complex has not been identified; however, when Henoch-Schönlein purpura can be associated with specific hypersensitivity or infection, the offending antigen would be suspect. The mesangial location of these patients' deposits suggests that their immune complexes are relatively large and perhaps originate during antibody excess. This disease is typified by unusual amounts of IgA in the presumed immune complex deposits. In addition, fibrin-related antigen deposits may be striking. Similar deposits of IgA and fibrin-related antigen may be identified in the cutaneous capillaries of these patients.

Clinical Features

Immune complex deposits both in the glomerular basement membrane and in the mesangium appear to be responsible for over 75% of cases of human glomerulonephritis. Virtually all histologic and clinical forms of human glomerulonephritis (Table 32–2) can be caused by immune complex deposition, including diffuse, focal, and crescent-forming proliferative types of glomerulonephritis, membranous glomerulonephritis, membranoproliferative (mesangioproliferative) glomerulonephritis, focal glomerulosclerosis, and chronic glomerulonephritis. At times, mesangial hypertrophy and focal endothelial and epithelial cell proliferation accompanied by hematuria and proteinuria are the first indications of immune complex glomerulonephritis, and the involvement never progresses further. More often, diffuse proliferative changes occur, particularly in glomerulonephritis associated with infections like poststreptococcal glomerulonephritis. Proliferative glomerulonephritis is also frequently observed in association with systemic diseases such as systemic lupus erythematosus. When particularly fulminant, the proliferative changes may involve parietal epithelial cells with crescent formation leading to rapidly progressive glomerular alterations indistinguishable from those induced by anti-glomerular basement membrane antibodies. Immune complex deposits may cause membranous thickening of the glomerular basement membrane (membranous glomerulonephritis) without accompanying proliferative changes. Proliferation and interposition of mesangial cell cytoplasm between the endothelium and glomerular basement membrane give rise to membranoproliferative glomerulonephritis. Chronic glomerulonephritis may follow any of these histologic forms of glomerular injury. Nephrotic syndrome occurs in immune complex glomerulonephritis when urinary protein loss exceeds the body's capacity for protein replacement. Goodpasture's syndrome, most commonly caused by anti-glomerular basement membrane antibodies, may also occasionally be observed in patients with immune complex glomerulonephritis; in these patients, the pulmonary injury is presumably secondary to immune complex deposition.

Immunologic Diagnosis

The diagnosis of immune complex glomerulonephritis is based on finding granular deposits of immunoglobulin, usually accompanied by complement, in the glomeruli. This is, of course, only presumptive evidence until the antigens can be identified. The immunoglobulin most commonly found in these deposits is IgG, with IgA or IgM occasionally predominating (Table 32–3). The glomerular immune complex deposition may involve the entire glomerular basement membrane in membranous or diffuse proliferative glomerulonephritis (Fig 32–2A). In focal glomerulonephritis, the deposits tend to involve only segments of the glomerular basement membrane but may be more widespread than expected from the focal nature of the histologic change. In some patients, the immune complex deposition appears to be confined to the mesangium, usually with only mild histologic and clinical evidence of glomerular damage (Fig 32–2B).

There has been recent interest in the predominant IgA (almost always associated with IgG) deposits of patients with focal glomerulonephritis and recurrent benign hematuria. The association has been so striking in some series that the term *IgG-IgA nephropathy* has been coined to denote the condition. In the authors' experience, IgM may be the predominant immunoglobulin in patients with similar, rather benign clinical

Table 32–2. Generalizations regarding morphologic and clinical features of presumed immune complex-induced glomerulonephritis in man.

Morphology	Clinical Features
Proliferative glomerulonephritis	
Diffuse proliferative glomerulonephritis; diffuse proliferation of endothelial, epithelial, or mesangial cells (or all 3 types); electron-dense glomerular basement membrane deposits	Proteinuria, hematuria; nephrotic syndrome may be present. Onset and course variable but often progressive to renal failure.
Poststreptococcal glomerulonephritis; as above with subepithelial electron-dense "humps"	Proteinuria, hematuria, active urinary sediment, edema, hypertension. Acute onset. Usually resolves in children.
Diffuse proliferative, crescent-forming glomerulonephritis; diffuse proliferation with extracapillary proliferation and crescent formation; electron-dense glomerular basement membrane deposits	Proteinuria, hematuria, active urinary sediment. Often rapidly progressive renal failure, nephrotic syndrome unusual.
Focal or segmental proliferative glomerulonephritis; focal and segmental proliferation; often confined to the mesangium; electron-dense deposits in the glomerular basement membrane or mesangium (or both)	Proteinuria or hematuria frequent; otherwise may be asymptomatic. Progresses slowly if at all. Nephrotic syndrome may occur.
Membranous glomerulonephritis	
Thickening of the glomerular basement membrane with little or no proliferative changes; subepithelial "spikes" with silver stains; diffuse subepithelial electron-dense deposits	Proteinuria, nephrotic syndrome frequent. Slow progression to renal failure with remission in 30%.
Membranoproliferative glomerulonephritis	
Mesangial proliferation and hypertrophy with interposition between endothelium and thickened glomerular basement membrane; 2 electron microscopic variants on basis of dense deposits: subendothelial and intramembranous	Proteinuria, often with nephrotic syndrome. Frequent hypocomplementemia. Most common in children. Usually progressive to renal failure.
Focal sclerosing glomerulonephritis	
Segmental glomerular sclerosis progressing to hyalinization; most severe in juxtamedullary glomeruli	Proteinuria, corticosteroid-unresponsive nephrotic syndrome common. Frequently progresses to renal failure.
Chronic glomerulonephritis	
End stage renal architecture, hyalinized glomeruli, extensive tubulo-interstitial damage; electron-dense glomerular basement membrane deposits may be present	Proteinuria, hypertension frequent. Renal failure progressing to uremia. End stage of other morphologic and clinical forms of glomerulonephritis.

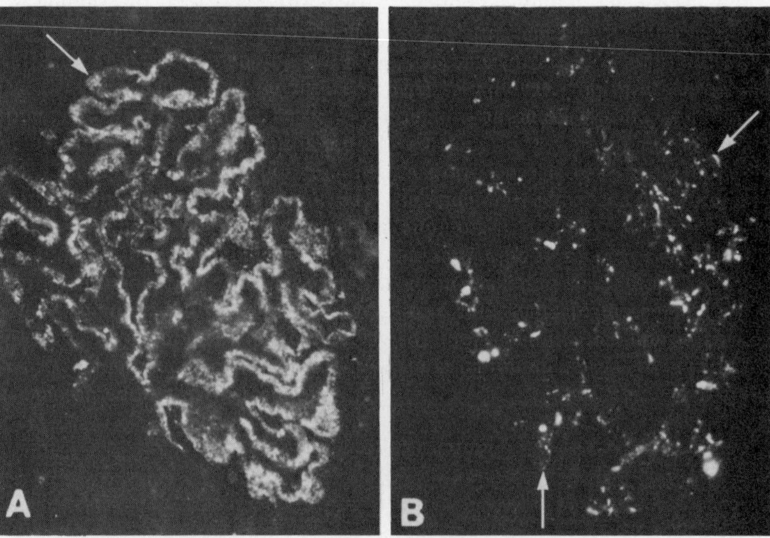

Figure 32–2. Granular deposits of IgG are seen in the glomeruli of patients with immune complex-induced glomerulonephritis. ***A:*** Heavy diffuse deposits (arrow) are present in a patient with membranous glomerulonephritis and nephrotic syndrome. ***B:*** Focal granular deposits (arrows), largely confined to the mesangium, are present in a patient with focal proliferative glomerulonephritis and mild proteinuria. (Original magnification X 250.)

Table 32–3. Generalizations regarding immunofluorescence findings in immune complex glomerulonephritis in man.

Morphologic Type of Glomerulonephritis	Immunofluorescence Findings		
	Granular Immunoglobulin	**Granular C3**	**Fibrinogen-Related Antigen**
Proliferative glomerulonephritis			
Diffuse proliferative glomerulonephritis, including poststreptococcal glomerulonephritis	IgG, variable IgA and IgM diffusely along glomerular basement membrane	Similar to immunoglobulin (may be seen when immunoglobulin minimal or absent in poststreptococcal glomerulonephritis)	Usually minimal
Diffuse proliferative, crescent-forming glomerulonephritis	IgG, variable IgA and IgM diffusely along glomerular basement membrane	Similar to immunoglobulin (may be seen when immunoglobulin minimal or absent in poststreptococcal glomerulonephritis)	Heavy in areas of crescents
Focal or segmental proliferative glomerulonephritis	IgG, often prominent IgA or IgM in segmental or mesangial pattern	Similar to immunoglobulin	Usually minimal
Membranous glomerulonephritis	IgG, variable IgA and IgM diffusely along glomerular basement membrane	Similar to immunoglobulin	Usually minimal
Membranoproliferative glomerulonephritis	IgG, variable IgA and IgM	Prominent, present without immunoglobulin in one-third of patients	Variable
Focal sclerosing glomerulonephritis	Minimal IgG and IgM in areas of sclerosis	Similar to immunoglobulin	Usually minimal
Chronic glomerulonephritis	Variable IgG, IgA, and IgM, usually most prominent in least damaged glomeruli	Similar to immunoglobulin, may also be present in absence of immunoglobulin	Usually minimal
Systemic diseases with glomerulonephritis			
Systemic lupus erythematosus	IgG, IgA, and IgM distributed segmentally to diffusely along glomerular basement membrane and in mesangium	Similar to immunoglobulin	Variable, heavy when crescents present
Henoch-Schönlein purpura	IgG, sometimes prominent IgA, variable IgM often confined to the mesangium	Similar to immunoglobulin	Frequently prominent

courses, often manifested by recurrent hematuria. Since the deposits tend to be confined to the mesangium, the immune complexes are probably large. The rapidity with which hematuria follows an infectious episode suggests that the immune complexes may be forming during antibody excess, possibly with preformed antibody to a common infectious agent of the oropharynx.

In systemic lupus erythematosus, the immune complex deposits may be widespread, involving glomeruli and, in 70% of instances, extraglomerular renal tissues as well. Indeed, granular deposits of immunoglobulin and complement in tubular basement membranes or peritubular capillaries should suggest the diagnosis of systemic lupus erythematosus. IgA and C1q deposits are prominent in kidneys of patients with systemic lupus erythematosus—particularly when present diffusely along the glomerular basement membrane—and also suggest this diagnosis.

The antigenic makeup of glomerular immune complex deposits can be sought either by detection of the antigen with fluoresceinated specific antisera or by elution of antibody from the kidney with subsequent detection of its reactivity. For the latter method, it is important to show that antibody has been specifically concentrated in the glomerular eluate in an amount greater than that expected from serum contamination alone. Large amounts of renal tissue must usually be available for elution; however, the small amounts of antibody present in tissue sections of frozen renal biopsies have recently been eluted and antibody reactivity identified in some instances. One must remember that when immune complexes are eluted from renal tissue, they recombine in part upon return of the eluate to physiologic conditions, which may mean that antigen and antibody are lost for subsequent study. Attempts have also been made to isolate infectious virus from renal biopsies as a way of gaining insight into possible virus antigens in glomerular immune complexes; however, this has been largely unsuccessful. Even if such a virus were found, it would be difficult to relate any viral isolate to the immune complex as such.

The patient's physician plays an important part in helping the immunopathologist to identify antigen-antibody systems in individuals with immune complex glomerulonephritis. Careful environmental histories may narrow the field of possible antigenic exposures to a few testable systems with emphasis placed upon detection of chronic, possibly subclinical infective processes.

Successful identification and quantitation of circulating immune complexes would add a new dimension to the diagnosis and management of patients with immune complex-induced glomerulonephritis. Clinically applicable methods of detecting immune complexes are just beginning to emerge with the advent of such technics as radioactive C1q binding, platelet aggregation, complement consumption, and utilization of cell surface complement receptors to detect complement fixation. One or more of these technics, when fully explored, should replace the relatively insensitive research methods now used, including analytic and sucrose density gradient ultracentrifugation, gel filtration, and C1q or monoclonal rheumatoid factor precipitation in gel. Surface receptors for complement on the Raji lymphoblastoid cell line and radioactive C1q binding both seem to detect on the order of 10–50 μg of immune complex per milliliter of serum. A greater incidence and quantity of circulating immune complexes are detected in immune complex glomerulonephritis when it occurs in systemic disease than when it occurs alone.

Treatment

Nonspecific antiphlogistic and immunosuppressive types of treatment employing corticosteroids, cyclophosphamide, azathioprine, and occasionally mechlorethamine (nitrogen mustard), singly or combined, have been widely used, mostly in uncontrolled trials, for patients with immune complex-induced glomerulonephritis. The results of these trials are difficult to interpret because of problems with classification, variable treatment regimens, and lack of controls to establish the natural courses (untreated) of the specific immune complex glomerulonephritis under consideration. In general, membranous and membranoproliferative forms of immune complex glomerulonephritis resist immunosuppressive treatment, although some investigators believe that corticosteroids are beneficial for the latter condition in children. Proliferative forms of immune complex glomerulonephritis are usually also unresponsive to immunosuppressive therapy, but occasional apparent success continues to spur its usage. The presumed immune complex glomerulonephritis of Wegener's granulomatosis seems to respond favorably to immunosuppression. Some studies have shown similar benefits in patients with systemic lupus erythematosus, although the long-term effects of immunosuppression on maintenance of renal function in this condition are not yet clear.

Attempts have also been made to modify the effects of mediators of immune complex-induced glomerulonephritis. The observation that vasoactive amines may influence vascular and glomerular immune complex deposition has prompted trials (in progress) of antihistamines and antiserotonins. There has also been some degree of enthusiasm for anticoagulation and antiplatelet drugs in the management of immune complex glomerulonephritis, but one must await carefully controlled trials to judge their true value. Nonspecific anti-inflammatory drugs such as indomethacin are useful in decreasing proteinuria, but their effects on long-term renal function are unknown.

The ideal management of immune complex-induced glomerulonephritis would be either to eradicate the source of the antigen or to inhibit production of the involved antibody. These approaches stress the need for identification of the antigen-antibody systems in each case. Acute infections, such as streptococcal pharyngitis, should be treated. Removal of antigen by treatment of an infectious agent, such as *T pallidum*, has been beneficial in syphilitic immune complex glomerulonephritis, as has removal of malignant tissue in immune complex glomerulonephritis associated with neoplasia. The use of immunoadsorbents, perhaps in the form of antigen- or antibody-coated hemodialysis membranes, is being considered to remove circulating antibody, antigen, or immune complexes. It may also be possible to develop adsorbents which would remove immune complexes by utilizing C1q or cell surface complement receptors fixed to a solid matrix.

Many forms of immune complex nephritis progress to renal failure, necessitating renal transplantation. As with anti-glomerular basement membrane antibody-induced glomerulonephritis, immune complex-induced glomerulonephritis may recur in the transplanted kidney. Until sensitive methods are available to detect circulating immune complexes, no definite program of management can be arranged to circumvent the possibility of this recurrent injury. It seems prudent, however, to delay renal transplantation in patients whose renal failure is from rapidly progressive immune complex glomerulonephritis until the production of nephritogenic immune complexes has decreased. When methods are available to quantitate circulating immune complexes precisely, such judgments can be made.

3. HYPOCOMPLEMENTEMIA & GLOMERULONEPHRITIS

Major Immunologic Features

- CH_{50} and other complement components may be reduced.
- Complement components detectable on glomerular basement membrane depending on nature of glomerulonephritis.
- Nephritic factor detectable in serum of some patients with membranoproliferative glomerulonephritis.

General Considerations

There are 2 modes of complement activation, the classical and alternative pathways (Chapter 6). The classical pathway consists of multiple components divided functionally into the recognition unit (C1q,

C1r, C1s), the activation unit (C4, C2, C3), and the membrane attack mechanism (C5, C6, C7, C8, C9). These components react, in the presence of calcium ions (Ca^{++}) and magnesium ions (Mg^{++}), in the order listed. C1 can be activated by immune complexes, aggregated immunoglobulins, various biologic substances such as endotoxins and DNA, and possibly by damaged glomerular basement membrane. Upon interaction with activated C1, C4 and C2 are sequentially cleaved. Their membrane-bound fragments (C4b and C2a) possess enzymatic activity specific for cleaving C3 into C3b, which, together with C4b and C2a, forms a membrane-bound trimolecular complex capable of cleaving C5, the last enzymatic step in the sequence of complement activation. The absorption of C6, C7, C8, and C9 onto C5b results in the formation of a multimolecular complex capable of damaging cellular membranes.

The recently defined alternative complement pathway (or properdin system) requires Mg^{++} but not Ca^{++} to activate C3, bypassing C1, C4, and C2. The C5 through C9 activation steps are similar in both pathways. The alternative pathway can be activated by properdin, nephritic factor, IgA aggregates (and possibly IgA immune complexes), polysaccharides such as inulin and zymosan, and endotoxins. How properdin is activated in normal human serum is unknown, but, once activated, properdin cleaves C3 using as cofactors native C3, proactivator (C3PA), proactivator convertase (C3PAse), and Mg^{++}. Nephritic factor (NF, C3NeF), found in sera of some hypocomplementemic patients with membranoproliferative glomerulonephritis, cleaves C3 independently of properdin but utilizes the same cofactors. Whether or not nephritic factor has an analogue in normal human serum is under investigation. C3b generated by either the classical or alternative pathways can initiate further C3 cleavage via C3b feedback, which requires Mg^{++}, proactivator, and proactivator convertase as cofactors. Most of the C3b generated in normal human serum is rapidly degraded by the C3b inactivator.

As noted earlier, glomerulonephritis associated with systemic lupus erythematosus is an immune complex disease in which granular deposits of immunoglobulin with antinuclear antigen specificity are present. C1q is present in over 75% of systemic lupus erythematosus kidneys, C3 and C4 in 100%, and properdin in about 40%, but proactivator is rarely found. The serum complement profile usually shows reduced levels of C1q, C4, C2, C3, and C5 and normal or reduced levels of properdin and proactivator. The presence of both early and late complement components in glomerular deposits and the reduction of the serum levels of these components indicate immune complex activation of the classical pathway.

Although acute poststreptococcal glomerulonephritis is thought to be an immune complex disease involving the glomerular deposition of antibody and streptococcal antigens, the evidence for an immune complex basis is less clear than in systemic lupus erythematosus. Roughly 60% of acute poststreptococcal glomerulonephritis patients have immunoglobulin in their kidneys, and in only a few have streptococcal antigens been convincingly demonstrated. However, nearly all these kidneys contain C3, often with C4, C1q, and properdin. Serum levels of C4, C2, C3, C5, and properdin are reduced; C1q and proactivator are usually normal. The time of taking the biopsy or serum sample in poststreptococcal glomerulonephritis is critical. Immunoglobulin and streptococcal antigen deposits disappear rapidly, and serum C4 and C2 levels return to normal shortly after the onset of the disease. Serum C3 and properdin levels can remain low for up to 2 months. The presence of properdin in kidneys of patients with glomerulonephritis associated with systemic lupus erythematosus and acute poststreptococcal glomerulonephritis does not necessarily indicate involvement of the alternative pathway, since recent work has shown that properdin attaches to membrane-bound C3b.

The mechanism of the hypocomplementemia in membranoproliferative glomerulonephritis is currently an area of interest and speculation. By immunofluorescence, about 70% of patients have detectable immunoglobulin, almost all have C3 and properdin, about half have some C1q and C4, and only a few patients have proactivator. Although most of the data from immunofluorescence testing in membranoproliferative glomerulonephritis are reminiscent of those from acute poststreptococcal glomerulonephritis, in some patients the serum complement profile is unique. The serum levels of the early components C1, C4, and C2 are normal or slightly reduced, and the levels of C3, C5, and properdin are quite low. The complement profile in these patients with membranoproliferative glomerulonephritis is similar to that produced by inulin or to that achieved by the reaction of normal human serum with zymosan. Both inulin and zymosan are known activators of the alternative pathway. Sera from nearly 50% of young adults with membranoproliferative glomerulonephritis contain nephritic factor, which forms an enzyme capable of cleaving C3. Nephritic factor isolated from patients with membranoproliferative glomerulonephritis is a 7S γ-globulin distinct from immunoglobulin (MW 150,000) and is heat-stable at 56 C for 30 minutes. Nephritic factor-like activity has been reported in a few patients with acute poststreptococcal glomerulonephritis; however, one substance was found to be heat-labile, suggesting that it differs from the nephritic factor in membranoproliferative glomerulonephritis. Nephritic factor-like activity was also isolated from a patient with glomerulonephritis associated with systemic lupus erythematosus. Preliminary results using a sensitive assay for nephritic factor done on sera from patients with membranoproliferative glomerulonephritis suggest that, in general, the presence of nephritic factor correlates positively with a low serum C3 level. Although hypocomplementemia may be produced when either immune complexes or nephritic factor activates complement, one must be aware that hyposynthesis or hypercatabolism of complement components can also lead to hypocomplementemia. As a result of electron microscopic studies, membranoproliferative glomerulonephritis is now subdivided into a subendothelial dense deposit form, which has many similarities to immune complex-induced glomerulonephritis, and an intramembranous dense deposit form, which has many features suggesting alternative complement pathway activation.

The rather characteristic clinical, histologic, and immunofluorescence picture in some patients with membranoproliferative glomerulonephritis, coupled with their changes in complement levels, suggests that the alternative complement pathway may be activated "nonimmunologically," which could represent an additional pathogenic mechanism of glomerular injury. However, this complement activation may merely perpetuate glomerular injury induced originally by immune complex deposits. It is currently unknown if nephritic factor-associated activation of complement is ever involved in the initiation of glomerulonephritis or if complement abnormalities predispose to immune complex types of glomerular injury. It is of interest that patients with partial lipodystrophy sometimes have nephritic factor and complement abnormalities that precede the development of overt membranoproliferative glomerulonephritis.

Clinical Features

Hypocomplementemia can be found in many types of glomerulonephritis; however, it is most commonly found in glomerular nephritis associated with systemic lupus erythematosus, poststreptococcal glomerulonephritis, and membranoproliferative glomerulonephritis. The hypocomplementemia itself produces no unique signs or symptoms not attributable to the basic nephritic process. Glomerulonephritis associated with systemic lupus erythematosus usually begins silently in a patient, most often a woman under 30 years of age, already affected with systemic lupus erythematosus. The nephritic involvement may simply be manifested as proteinuria and hematuria or may progress to the nephrotic syndrome or renal failure. Poststreptococcal glomerulonephritis and membranoproliferative glomerulonephritis are predominantly diseases of children and young adults. Poststreptococcal glomerulonephritis usually begins as an acute illness with edema, hypertension, proteinuria, and hematuria. The majority of these patients recover, but a few ultimately develop chronic renal failure. Thirty-five percent of patients with membranoproliferative glomerulonephritis present with acute nephritis, 40% with nephrotic syndrome, and 25% with proteinuria only. The prognosis of membranoproliferative glomerulonephritis is much worse than that of acute poststreptococcal glomerulonephritis, with the majority of patients slowly progressing toward eventual renal failure. Membranoproliferative glomerulonephritis also has been reported to recur in allografted kidneys.

Immunologic Diagnosis

Measurements of complement components in serum are important in establishing the presence of hypocomplementemia. The levels of C1, C4, C3, C5, proactivator, and properdin give a rather complete complement profile and insight into the major pathway of complement activation in each patient. When all of these studies are unavailable, a simple C3 titer or even a CH_{50} value can be helpful. The presence of immunoglobulin and the pattern of glomerular complement component deposition should be established by immunofluorescence study of renal biopsy tissue.

An assay for nephritic factor is indicated for all patients with membranoproliferative glomerulonephritis and probably any with hypocomplementemic glomerulonephritis. At present, the most sensitive and rapid assay involves measuring the consumption of C3 and C5 in normal human serum in the presence of Mg^{++} but not Ca^{++}, which renders only the alternative pathway operational.

Treatment

Corticosteroid therapy may lower nephritic factor levels and increase serum C3 levels in patients with membranoproliferative glomerulonephritis. However, these effects are transient and are not necessarily associated with clinical improvement. Therapies for glomerulonephritis associated with systemic lupus erythematosus and poststreptococcal glomerulonephritis are described in the prior section on immune complex glomerulonephritis. (See also Chapter 27.)

TUBULO-INTERSTITIAL NEPHRITIS

Tubulo-interstitial renal damage can occur with glomerulonephritis or as a primary event. Both mechanisms of antibody-induced glomerular injury—immune complexes and anti-basement membrane antibodies—can directly induce tubular damage. Primary interstitial nephritis can result from a variety of causes, including urinary tract obstruction, hyperuricemia, nephrocalcinosis, analgesic abuse, irradiation, and bacterial infection. An immunologic role is most evident in drug-induced interstitial nephritis and hyperglobulinemic renal tubular acidosis.

1. TUBULO-INTERSTITIAL INJURY IN GLOMERULONEPHRITIS

Major Immunologic Features

- Frequently, circulating anti-tubular basement membrane antibodies are detected in patients with anti-glomerular basement membrane glomerulonephritis.
- Immunoglobulins and complement are present in either linear or granular pattern on tubular basement membrane.

General Considerations

Interstitial deposition of either immune complexes (in association with immune complex glomerulonephritis) or anti-tubular basement membrane antibodies (in association with glomerular basement membrane glomerulonephritis) can lead to tubulo-interstitial injury (Fig 32–3A and B). Interstitial immune complex deposits are seen with particular frequency in patients with glomerulonephritis associated with systemic lupus erythematosus. In fact, 70% of such patients have immune complex deposits along the tubular basement membrane or in peritubular capillaries (or both) and occasionally in arteries or arterioles as well. Similar interstitial deposition may occur with cryoglobulinemic glomerulonephritis. As a rule, interstitial deposits are not seen in membranous glomerulonephritis or membranoproliferative glomerulonephritis.

About 80% of patients with anti-glomerular basement membrane glomerulonephritis have anti-tubular basement membrane antibodies as well. Anti-tubular basement membrane antibody deposits are more common in patients with Goodpasture's syndrome than in patients with anti-glomerular basement membrane nephritis alone (without pulmonary hemorrhage).

The role of interstitial immune complex deposition in inducing tubulo-interstitial injury has been determined by studying chronic serum sickness in rabbits. Rabbits having active immune responses and forming large amounts of immune complexes accumulate these complexes on tubular basement membrane, in peritubular capillaries, and in interstitial spaces in addition to the glomerular basement membrane. Along with such deposits, these rabbits have prominent tubulo-interstitial histopathologic injury that is much more severe than in rabbits with glomerular immune complex deposition alone. Extraglomerular renal deposits of immune complexes and consequent interstitial damage are frequent in systemic lupus erythematosus. In patients with systemic lupus erythematosus (as in rabbits), the circulating immune complexes may be unique in quantity—or quality—which may allow these complexes to become deposited in the renal interstitium in addition to the glomerulus.

The pathogenic effect of anti-tubular basement membrane antibodies has been well demonstrated in animal models. Rats or guinea pigs immunized with homologous or heterologous tubular basement membrane develop complement-fixing anti-tubular basement membrane antibodies which bind to their own tubular basement membrane (primarily of proximal tubules), thereby inducing interstitial nephritis. The disease can be transferred to normal animals by passive administration of antibody from diseased animals. This nephritis is associated with tubular dysfunction, eg, glycosuria or lysozymuria, and is sometimes fatal.

It is of interest that the tubular basement membrane antigen against which these antibodies react is strain-specific in rats, ie, some inbred strains possess the antigen and others do not. Rats with tubular basement membrane antigen-negative kidneys form anti-tubular basement membrane antibodies which react with the tubular basement membrane antigen-positive kidneys that they have received as transplants. Such antibodies may contribute to transplant failure in these rats. In humans, similar variability in the occurrence of tubular basement membrane antigens possibly accounts for the development of anti-tubular base-

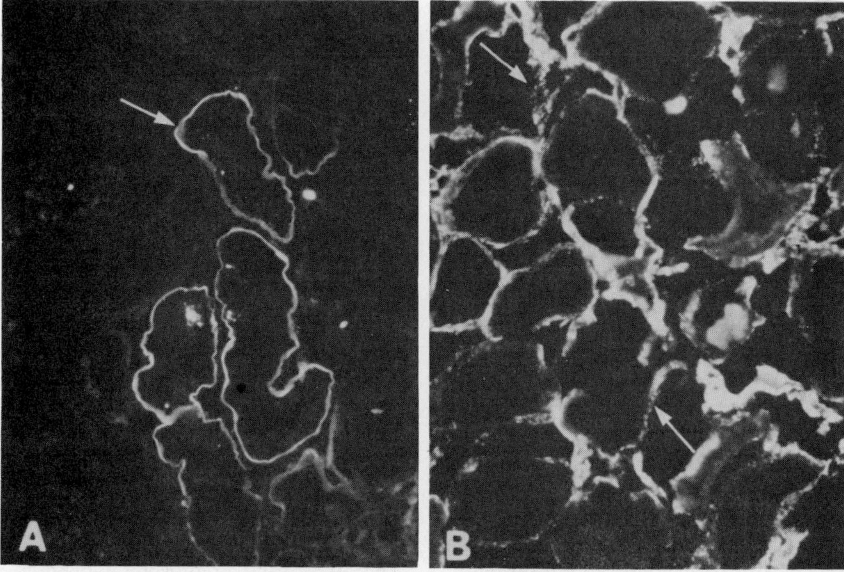

Figure 32–3. *A:* Linear deposits of IgG (arrow) are present along the tubular basement membrane of focal renal tubules in the renal biopsy of a patient with anti-glomerular basement membrane glomerulonephritis. *B:* Diffuse granular deposits of IgG (arrows) are seen along the tubular basement membrane of most renal tubules in the renal biopsy of a patient with systemic lupus erythematosus and immune complex glomerulonephritis. (Original magnification × 250.)

ment membrane antibodies in some renal allograft recipients.

Anti-tubular basement membrane antibodies may develop infrequently in the course of immune complex-induced glomerulonephritis. This suggests that immunologic damage to the kidney may very occasionally lead to autoantibody formation.

Clinical Features

The clinical course is that of the underlying glomerulonephritis (see earlier sections). There have been reports of abnormalities of tubular function in patients with nephritis associated with systemic lupus erythematosus, particularly increased urinary light chain excretion, which may have diagnostic implications but little clinical significance.

Immunologic Diagnosis

When examining renal biopsy specimens by immunofluorescence, one should give particular attention to the renal interstitium. Interstitial deposits of immunoglobulin and complement are almost always focal and less intense than glomerular deposits and therefore are easily overlooked.

Treatment

The associated glomerulonephritis is treated as outlined in previous sections.

2. DRUG-INDUCED INTERSTITIAL NEPHRITIS

Major Immunologic Features

- Immunoglobulins, complement, and drugs may occasionally be found in linear pattern along tubular and occasionally glomerular basement membranes.
- Anti-drug or anti-tubular basement membrane antibodies may be present in the blood.

General Considerations

Methicillin has been shown to induce acute interstitial nephritis, and other penicillin analogues, including ampicillin and oxacillin, as well as penicillin itself, have been reported to induce acute renal failure as well. Recently, the cephalosporins, which are structurally similar to penicillin, have also been incriminated in the pathogenesis of acute interstitial nephritis. In all of these reports, large doses of antibiotics had been given for at least 1 week.

Immunologic Pathogenesis

Penicillin derivatives are secreted by the proximal tubules and are thus highly concentrated in the renal interstitium. They tend to form stable conjugates with proteins, and it has now been amply demonstrated that such derivatives can bind to tubular basement membrane. It is not known whether conjugation of penicillin derivatives to tubular basement membrane occurs in all, most, or only a few patients receiving high doses of penicillin or its analogues. Some patients may develop an antibody (or cellular sensitivity) to the penicillin-tubular basement membrane conjugate, with the kidney merely injured as an innocent bystander. On the other hand, the drug might alter the tubular basement membrane enough to make it immunogenic to the host. (It is well known from experimental studies that native proteins can be made immunogenic to a host animal by conjugating them with a foreign hapten.) Thus, antibodies (or cells) directed against the tubular basement membrane itself might be induced, resulting in interstitial nephritis. Indeed, anti-tubular basement membrane antibodies have been detected in 2 patients with methicillin-induced interstitial nephritis. Further study will (1) elucidate the frequency of binding of antibiotic derivatives to tubular basement membrane in patients receiving penicillin analogues and (2) further dissect and quantitate the roles of anti-tubular basement membrane antibodies and cell-mediated immunity in these patients.

Clinical Features

The sudden onset of oliguric renal failure in a patient receiving penicillin analogues, particularly methicillin, should always suggest drug-induced nephropathy. Differential diagnosis should include examination for septic emboli and, in patients with endocarditis, acute immune complex glomerulonephritis. Fever, rash, and often flank pain herald drug-induced nephritis. The blood count reveals eosinophilia, and urinalysis shows white cells and white cell or granular casts. Proteinuria is minimal to absent.

Immunologic Diagnosis

Immunologic study of serum, peripheral blood lymphocytes, and renal biopsy are useful in patients with a drug-induced nephropathy. Serum should be assayed for antibodies to tubular basement membrane by indirect immunofluorescence (Chapter 24), using normal human kidney tissue as a target, and by hemagglutination assay for antibodies to antibiotic derivatives. Blood lymphocytes should be tested for sensitivity to both basement membrane and the drug, using one of the standard in vitro technics for assaying cell sensitivity (Chapter 25). The renal biopsy specimen should be tested for drug deposition along basement membranes by using specific fluoresceinated antiserum to the drug. In addition, the specimen should be examined for deposition of immunoglobulin and complement.

Treatment

The offending antibiotic should be discontinued immediately in all patients with drug-induced nephropathy and replaced by a suitable structurally unrelated alternative drug. Prednisone appears to diminish fever and rash and perhaps the degree and the duration of renal failure, although these effects of prednisone have not been subjected to disciplined study. Some patients require a short course of hemodialysis until recovery.

Recovery of renal function appears to be complete in most cases; however, incomplete though life-sustaining recovery of renal function has been reported in several cases.

3. HYPERGAMMAGLOBULINEMIC RENAL TUBULAR ACIDOSIS

Major Immunologic Features

- Polyclonal increase in serum immunoglobulins.
- Circulating antibodies to renal tubular cell cytoplasm may occasionally be detectable.

General Considerations

Over 50 case reports have now associated renal tubular acidosis with hypergammaglobulinemic states. Most of these patients have Sjögren's syndrome (Chapter 27); in fact, over half of patients with Sjögren's syndrome are said to have renal tubular acidosis, either latent or clinically overt. In addition, a variety of other hypergammaglobulinemic patients have renal tubular acidosis, including patients with hyperglobulinemic purpura, cryoglobulinemia, Waldenström's macroglobulinemia, chronic active hepatitis, idiopathic hypergammaglobulinemia, etc.

It is now felt that hypergammaglobulinemia per se does not induce renal tubular acidosis since many patients with marked hypergammaglobulinemia do not have even latent renal tubular acidosis and some patients with Sjögren's syndrome and normal γ-globulin levels have renal tubular acidosis. Rather, it is believed that at least in some patients, renal tubular acidosis is an autoimmune phenomenon. Most of these patients have Sjögren's syndrome and a wide variety of autoimmune antibodies including antibodies against nucleoprotein, salivary duct epithelium, and immunoglobulin (Chapter 27). Antibodies to the cytoplasm of renal distal tubular epithelial cells have also been demonstrated in either sera or renal biopsy specimens from these patients. Renal biopsies have revealed a peritubular interstitial lymphocytic infiltrate. It is known that another form of "autoimmunity," renal allograft rejection, can cause acute renal tubular acidosis. It is therefore likely that autoimmunity to renal tubular cells is the cause of renal tubular acidosis in at least some patients.

Clinical Features

In most individuals with hypergammaglobulinemia, renal tubular acidosis is latent, ie, they have no clinical symptoms but do not respond to an exogenous acid load with normal acidification of the urine. In some asymptomatic individuals, abdominal x-ray examination reveals nephrocalcinosis. Individuals with renal tubular acidosis may have symptoms of muscle weakness or periodic paralysis (due to hypokalemia), bone pain (due to osteomalacia secondary to hypercalciuria), or renal colic (due to passage of a calcium phosphate stone).

Immunologic Diagnosis

Hypergammaglobulinemic sera should be studied for autoantibodies, including rheumatoid factor, antinuclear antibody, and antisalivary duct antibody. Antibody to renal tubular cells should be assayed by indirect immunofluorescence. Renal biopsy should be performed only after careful consideration in asymptomatic individuals, but, once taken, tubular interstitial cells and tubular basement membrane should be examined for the presence of immunoglobulin and complement. In addition, it would be of interest to examine peripheral blood lymphocytes for sensitivity to tubular antigens.

Treatment

In most patients, renal tubular acidosis is not clinically apparent, so that treatment is required only for the underlying disease. When treatment is necessary, correction of acidosis with bicarbonate or citrate salts and of hypokalemia with potassium supplements should be undertaken.

RENAL DISEASES OF UNPROVED IMMUNOPATHOGENESIS

In addition to those nephritides already discussed, which clearly are due to immunologic disorders, there is a group of renal diseases in which immune mechanisms may play an as yet unproved role. These diseases include lipoid nephrosis, vasculitides, diabetes mellitus, coagulopathies, amyloidosis, and dysproteinemias. With the exception of lipoid nephrosis and diabetes mellitus, these disorders account for only a small segment of the nephritic population.

Lipoid Nephrosis

Lipoid nephrosis or "nil" disease is the most common cause of nephrotic syndrome in childhood and occurs occasionally in adults as well. Interestingly, in adults it is sometimes associated with Hodgkin's disease. Patients usually develop edema insidiously. The diagnosis of lipoid nephrosis is suggested by finding selective proteinuria and confirmed by performing renal biopsy. Examination with the light microscope shows only minimal changes (thus, the term "nil" disease), but the electron microscope reveals fusion of the epithelial foot processes. Despite the clear-cut clinical response to corticosteroids or cyclophosphamide, there is no clear-cut immunopathologic basis for this disease, and glomerular deposits of IgE, in the absence of other immunoreactants reported earlier, have not been confirmed in recent investigations. Thymus cell dysfunction and serum IgM elevations in patients with lipoid nephrosis as well as possible immune complex glomerular injury without detectable immune deposits in animals are recent observations which will continue to spark interest in finding an immune pathogenesis for nil disease. The disease remits frequently, either spontaneously or following administration of corticosteroid drugs; and, though relapses are frequent, renal failure is unusual.

Vasculitides

Three major vascular inflammatory syndromes are associated with glomerulonephritis: Henoch-Schönlein purpura (discussed in the section on immune complex glomerulonephritis), polyarteritis nodosa, and Wegener's granulomatosis. Each has its own characteristic clinical and laboratory features, though all are probably immune complex diseases (Chapter 27).

Polyarteritis nodosa most commonly affects adult males. It is frequently preceded by drug ingestion or upper respiratory infections. In a few patients, viral hepatitis B antigen is responsible for the immune complex reaction, although in most cases the responsible antigen is not known. The clinical manifestations are protean and can include fever, pneumonitis, weakness, weight loss, neuropathy, arthralgia, myalgia, abdominal pain, and renal failure. Eosinophilia is often present. Renal arteriography may demonstrate small aneurysmal dilatations of the larger renal arteries. This syndrome probably represents an immune complex arteritis and glomerulonephritis. Granular deposits of IgG and C3 can often be detected in arteries and glomeruli. Both corticosteroids and cytotoxic drugs may be beneficial. Nevertheless, death due to renal failure occurs in 25–50% of these patients.

Wegener's granulomatosis represents a triad of necrotizing granulomatous lesions of arteries and veins in the upper and lower respiratory tracts and in the glomeruli. It occurs in middle-aged men and women. Onset is frequently insidious, and patients often develop chronic rhinitis, sinusitis, or otitis progressing to bronchitis, pneumonitis, and glomerulonephritis. Sometimes, however, this disease is acute and explosive in onset, causing rapid deterioration of multiple organ systems. Diagnosis is made by biopsy of nasal structures, lung, or kidney. Glomerular electron-dense deposits and granular IgG and C3 deposits suggestive of immune complexes have been detected only irregularly. In the past, average survival after onset was only 6 months, but cytotoxic drugs, particularly cyclophosphamide, have greatly improved the outlook for these patients.

Diabetes Mellitus

Although the renal involvement in diabetes is variable, a large number of patients develop proteinuria within 20 years after the onset of diabetes and frequently die from renal failure within 5 years. It is still controversial whether good control of blood sugar levels can prevent this progression. The primary renal insult is microangiopathic, but several pieces of evidence suggest that immunologic mechanisms might contribute to renal impairment of persons with diabetes. First, glomerular immunoglobulin deposits in patients receiving beef insulin have been infrequently observed, suggesting the possible entrapment of circulating beef insulin antigen-antibody immune complexes. However, diabetic nephropathy occurs in the absence of exogenous insulin, so that although this mechanism might contribute to diabetic renal disease, it is not the primary event. Second, during experimentally induced diabetes, rats (not given exogenous insulin) accumulate IgG and C3 in their renal mesangia, suggesting impairment of mesangial function. Whether such deposits contribute to renal dysfunction in man is only conjectural at this time. The striking linear accumulations of IgG, albumin, and other major plasma proteins that occur in diabetic basement membranes (both glomerular and tubular) are not thought to have immunologic specificity. (See earlier section.)

Coagulopathies

Several systemic coagulation syndromes can cause acute renal failure, including the hemolytic-uremic syndrome, thrombotic thrombocytopenic purpura, and postpartum renal failure. All 3 syndromes consist of a microangiopathic hemolytic anemia, thrombocytopenia, neurologic deficits, and renal failure and appear to have a similar pathogenesis. The hemolytic-uremic syndrome usually occurs shortly after an upper respiratory infection or gastroenteritis. This is primarily a syndrome of infants and children but sometimes afflicts adults. Thrombotic thrombocytopenic purpura usually occurs in adults without signs of previous infection. In postpartum renal failure there is diffuse vascular deposition of fibrin thrombi without evidence of vasculitis.

Disseminated intravascular coagulation occurs as a secondary if not primary event. Infectious agents (or a retained product of conception) may act, perhaps through immunologic mechanisms, to cause intravascular platelet aggregation as the triggering event. Immunoreactants other than fibrin are not generally seen in the kidney, and the exact role of immunologic mechanisms in these syndromes is undefined. Despite anticoagulation therapy, the mortality is high.

A "localized" coagulopathy, renal vein thrombosis, can also affect the kidney. This diagnosis is suggested when back pain is associated with the nephrotic syndrome and can be confirmed by renal angiography. Renal vein thrombosis is often associated with a classical membranous glomerulonephritis, including thickening of the glomerular basement membrane (margination of polymorphonuclear leukocytes may be observed) and granular deposition of IgG and C3. The causal relationship between the membranous nephropathy and renal vein thrombosis is not clear. The membranous lesion probably somehow predisposes to local thrombosis by a local alteration either in blood flow or in the coagulation system. Less likely, renal vein thrombosis might induce renal injury, releasing renal antigens and thereby causing an endogenous immune complex nephritis. Unfortunately, neither immunosuppression nor anticoagulation is effective in treating this syndrome.

Amyloidosis

Prior to the advent of antibiotic therapy, renal amyloidosis was most frequently associated with chronic infectious diseases, particularly tuberculosis. Amyloidosis now most frequently occurs secondary to plasma cell dyscrasia and multiple myeloma, usually in old people (see Chapter 28). Amyloidosis also is seen in conditions such as rheumatoid arthritis and familial Mediterranean fever. Clinical features include tubular dysfunction, proteinuria, the nephrotic syndrome, and renal failure. Diagnosis is made by renal biopsy, although renal amyloidosis may increase the risk of hemorrhage from this procedure. Underlying systemic disease, particularly multiple myeloma, should be sought. It has recently been shown that some amyloid deposits contain portions of immunoglobulin light chains, and immunofluorescence reagents reacting with light chains should be employed in the study of suspected amyloid kidneys. Amyloidosis is usually progressive, and treatment is primarily that of the underlying disease.

Dysproteinemias

Several gammopathies, including mixed IgG-IgM cryoglobulinemia and Waldenström's macroglobulinemia, can occasionally cause renal failure. Mixed IgG-IgM cryoglobulins are sometimes present in rheumatoid arthritis or systemic lupus erythematosus, but they are also seen in the absence of these diseases in a syndrome characterized by purpura, arthralgia, and anemia. Patients with cryoglobulinemia sometimes develop chronic glomerulonephritis or membranoproliferative glomerulonephritis, with renal failure, and have hypocomplementemia and granular deposits of IgG, IgM, and C3 in their glomeruli. The IgM in cryoglobulins often has rheumatoid factor activity, so that the renal disease is thought to be induced by glomerular deposition of IgM-anti-IgG immune complexes. However, rheumatoid factor activity is sometimes not detectable, suggesting that IgG and IgM directed against an as yet unknown antigen are bound in immune complexes. Immunosuppressive drugs may be of benefit.

Waldenström's macroglobulinemia, a monoclonal increase of IgM of either κ or λ type, is seen in the elderly. It causes anemia, a lymphoma/leukemia picture with hepatosplenomegaly and lymphadenopathy, and symptoms of cryoglobulinemia and hyperviscosity. Proteinuria is sometimes seen, but renal failure is rare. (Similarly, heavy chain disease, also causing a lymphomatous syndrome, can be associated with proteinuria.) In Waldenström's macroglobulinemia there is glomerular deposition of IgM of a single light chain type, corresponding to the circulating monoclonal IgM but with little glomerular proliferative response. This local deposition of IgM is thought to result from physical trapping rather than from immunologic mechanisms. Treatment, consisting of plasmapheresis and chemotherapeutic drugs, can be of substantial benefit.

• • •

References

Andres GA, McCluskey RT: Tubular and interstitial renal disease due to immunologic mechanisms. Kidney Int 7:271, 1975.

Churg J, Grishman E: Ultrastructure of glomerular disease: A review. Kidney Int 7:254, 1975.

Cochrane CG, Janoff A: The Arthus reaction: A model of neutrophil and complement mediated injury. Page 85 in: *The Inflammation Process.* Zweifach BW, Grant L, McClusky RT (editors). Academic Press, 1974.

Cochrane CG, Koffler D: Immune complex disease in experimental animals and man. Adv Immunol 16:185, 1973.

Germuth FG Jr, Rodriguez E: *Immunopathology of the Renal Glomerulus: Immune Complex Deposit and Antibasement Membrane Disease.* Little, Brown, 1973.

Glassock RJ, Bennett CM: The glomerulopathies. In: *The Kidney.* Brenner BM, Rector FC Jr (editors). Saunders, 1976.

Habib R: Classification of glomerulonephritis based on morphology. Page 17 in: *Glomerulonephritis: Morphology, Natural History, and Treatment.* Kincaid-Smith P, Mathew TH, Becker EL (editors). Wiley, 1973.

Koffler D: Immunopathogenesis of systemic lupus erythematosus. Annu Rev Med 25:149, 1974.

Lehman DH, Wilson CB, Dixon FJ: Extraglomerular immunoglobulin deposits in human nephritis. Am J Med 58:765, 1975.

McIntosh RM & others: Cryoglobulins. 3. Further studies on the nature, incidence, clinical diagnostic, prognostic, and immunopathologic significance of cryoproteins in renal disease. Q J Med 174:285, 1975.

McLean RH, Michael AF: Activation of the complement system in renal conditions in animals and man. Prog Immunol 5:69, 1974.

Morel-Maroger L, Leathem A, Richet G: Glomerular abnormalities in nonsystemic diseases: Relationship between findings by light microscopy and immunofluorescence in 433 renal biopsy specimens. Am J Med 53:170, 1972.

Müller-Eberhard HJ: The complement system and nephritis. Adv Nephrol 4:3, 1974.

Peters DK: The immunological basis of glomerulonephritis. Proc R Soc Med 67:557, 1974.

Schreiber RD & others: Properdin- and nephritis factor-dependent C3 convertases: Requirement of native C3 for enzyme formation and the function of bound C3b as properdin receptor. J Exp Med 142:621, 1975.

Unanue ER, Dixon FJ: Experimental glomerulonephritis: Immunologic events and pathogenetic mechanisms. Adv Immunol 6:1, 1967.

West CD & others: Mechanisms of hypocomplementemia in glomerulonephritis. Kidney Int 3:116, 1973.

Wilson CB, Dixon FJ: Anti-glomerular basement membrane antibody induced glomerulonephritis. Kidney Int 3:74, 1973.

Wilson CB, Dixon FJ: Diagnosis of immunopathologic renal disease. (Editorial.) Kidney Int 5:389, 1974.

Wilson CB, Dixon FJ: Immunopathology and glomerulonephritis. Annu Rev Med 25:83, 1974.

Wilson CB, Dixon FJ: Renal response to immunological injury. Page 838 in: *The Kidney*. Brenner BM, Rector FC Jr (editors). Saunders, 1976.

33 . . .
Dermatologic Diseases

Thomas T. Provost, MD

Advances in immunologic laboratory methods and a better understanding of the basic immunologic mechanisms of tissue injury, including autoantibody formation and cell-mediated immunity, are making valuable contributions to research in the pathogenesis of skin disease. Specifically, during the past few years, immunofluorescent technics have demonstrated the deposition of various immunoglobulins, complement components, and alternative pathway components of complement activation at the site of lesions in various bullous diseases, including pemphigus and bullous pemphigoid. In addition, direct immunofluorescent technics have demonstrated the presence of immunoglobulins and complement, presumably in the form of immune complexes, in the blood vessel walls of patients with various forms of vasculitis. At present, immunologic data also indicate an important immunopathologic role of cell-mediated immunity in allergic contact dermatitis and photoallergic contact dermatitis. Preliminary data suggest an important role of normal host cell-mediated immunity in the defense against cutaneous fungi. Absence of this cell-mediated immunity may result in widespread cutaneous fungal diseases as well as mucocutaneous candidiasis.

ALLERGIC CONTACT DERMATITIS

Major Immunologic Features

- T cell-mediated eczematous disease.
- Characterized by a 48-hour delayed eczematous response to the epicutaneous application of the allergen.

General Considerations

Allergic contact dermatitis is probably an example of a disease involving cell-mediated immunity. Although the exact incidence of allergic contact dermatitis in the general population is unknown, it is certainly the most common immunologic disease encountered by dermatologists. In fact, about 3–5% of patients seen by dermatologists are evaluated for possible allergic contact dermatitis. The potential contact sensitizing antigens to which humans are exposed are multitudinous and include drugs, dyes, plant oleoresins, preservatives, and metals. The 5 most common contact sensitizing antigens encountered in clinical practice are Rhus species of plants (poison ivy, oak, or sumac), paraphenylenediamine, nickel compounds, rubber compounds, and the dichromates.

Thomas T. Provost is Associate Professor, Department of Dermatology, State University of New York at Buffalo, Buffalo.

Immunologic Pathogenesis

The exact underlying immunologic basis of allergic contact dermatitis is unknown. Much has been learned by experimental application of simple chemicals such as dinitrochlorobenzene (DNCB) to the skin of guinea pigs. It is hypothesized that these chemicals react with skin components to form hapten-carrier molecules. The precise identification of the hapten-carrier molecule responsible for sensitization has been difficult since DNCB is a highly reactive substance which can form dinitrophenyl-protein bonds with a variety of tissue substances. Early experiments showed that induction of sensitization to a topically applied antigen required an intact local lymphatic system and regional lymph node. Severing the local lymphatics or excising the regional lymph node prevented active cutaneous sensitization but did not interfere with a secondary response once sensitization was established. The participation of regional lymph nodes was demonstrated by the observation of their proliferation (predominantly in the thymus-dependent paracortical area) following the experimental induction of allergic contact dermatitis in animals.

The primary role of the regional lymph node and lymphatic system has been made doubtful by the suggestion that the "training ground" for actively sensitizing the lymphocytes occurs at the site of antigen deposition. When radiolabeled antigen was injected intradermally, much of this antigen rapidly disappeared from the injection site. Subsequently, the antigen could not be identified in the local lymphatic system or regional lymph node. However, a small quantity of antigen remained at the site of injection, and the intensity of the cell-mediated response could be directly correlated with the persistence of this local antigen depot. These data suggest that peripheral sensitization at the site of antigen deposition can occur and that regional lymph node proliferation may occur as sensitized lymphocytes recruit other lymphocytes. It is not known whether these 2 sets of experiments, one demonstrating peripheral sensitization and the other the need for an intact regional lymph node and lymphatic system in the development of allergic contact dermatitis, are contradictory or represent a difference in experimental design.

The central role of the lymphocyte in the pathogenesis of allergic contact dermatitis was first reported in the classical experiment of Landsteiner and Chase in 1942. These investigators specifically transferred allergic contact dermatitis from a sensitized guinea pig to an unsensitized one by the intraperitoneal injection of peritoneal exudate cells. Similar experiments substituting serum for peritoneal exudate cells failed. Furthermore, lymph node lymphocytes from sensitized animals, placed in tissue culture with the appropriate sensitizing antigen, underwent a proliferative response measured by increased DNA synthesis. In mice, the proliferative response of sensitized lymphocytes to the antigen could be abolished by pretreatment of the lymphocytes with anti-Thy-1 (θ) serum, which suggested that T lymphocytes are involved in the sensitization process.

In addition to these animal studies, in vitro studies in humans have demonstrated that peripheral lymphocytes from some patients with allergic contact dermatitis, cultured with the sensitizing antigen, undergo a proliferative response. In fact, peripheral lymphocytes from a patient suffering from nickel contact dermatitis produced migration inhibitory factor (MIF) on exposure to nickel in tissue culture.

Several years ago, Polak and others presented some evidence to indicate that the spontaneous flare of chromium dermatitis may involve plasma cells. Their experiments in animals failed to detect circulating antibody to chromium. Furthermore, it was possible to specifically transfer this "flare-up" reaction by the intradermal injection of peritoneal exudate cells from sensitized donors to normal recipients followed by the intravenous injection of chromium. However, peritoneal cells from animals permanently desensitized (tolerant) to contact hypersensitivity to chromium continued to produce "flare reactions" when injected into normal animals. These data suggest that small quantities of chromium may be absorbed from a site of inadvertent contact and could be systemically transported to sites of previous eczematous disease. There, the antigen would activate previously sensitized B cells, producing reexacerbation of the eczematous disease.

Clinical Features

Allergic contact dermatitis is an eczematous reaction. Eczema is characterized in the acute form by erythema, edema, and vesiculation and in the chronic form by scaling. Histologically, eczematous lesions are characterized by a perivascular mononuclear infiltrate and varying degrees of dermal and epidermal edema (spongiosis).

The site of allergic contact dermatitis is often a clue to diagnosis. For example, nickel contact sensitization may be manifested by an eczematous reaction on the ear lobes, around the neck, the upper mid back, the wrists, and the upper thighs. These sites correspond to points of contact with earrings, necklaces, brassiere clasps, bracelets or wrist bands, and girdle clasps, respectively.

Immunologic Diagnosis

The diagnosis of allergic contact dermatitis is based on the distribution of the lesions, an exhaustive history, and examination of the patient's home and place of work for possible sensitizing compounds. The diagnosis is confirmed by patch testing, a procedure introduced in 1896 by Jadassohn. Patch testing consists of applying a nonirritating (low) concentration of the suspected contact antigen to the patient's skin, usually the back, and covering with an occlusive dressing. The dressing is removed after 48 hours. An eczematous reaction at the site of the patch test constitutes a positive response.

Differential Diagnosis

An eczematous reaction is not pathognomonic of allergic contact dermatitis. Similar skin reactions occur with bacterial and fungal diseases (infectious eczematoid dermatitis). Eczema also occurs when the skin is repeatedly traumatized by scratching (neurodermatitis) or following the cutaneous application of harsh chemicals and solvents (primary irritant dermatitis). Eczematous lesions are characteristic features of certain inherited diseases such as atopic dermatitis, X-linked hypogammaglobulinemia (see Chapter 26), and Wiskott-Aldrich syndrome (thrombocytopenia, recurrent infections, and eczema). These conditions can be differentiated from allergic contact dermatitis on the basis of the history and clinical features and by immunologic patch testing (see below).

Treatment

Avoidance of exposure to an identified allergen is theoretically curative, but avoiding known allergens may prove difficult. For example, common sensitizers such as benzocaine are employed in a variety of topical medications such as sunburn preparations and antiseptic creams. If individuals with sensitivity to benzocaine fail to read the labels on these preparations, they may inadvertently reexpose themselves to the offending agent. Another example of unwitting exposure to a known allergen such as poison ivy is contact with the smoke from burning leaves. If poison ivy is present in the leaves, the pentadecacatechols, the allergen in poison ivy, will vaporize and can be transmitted to a sensitized individual as an aerosol without direct contact with the plant.

In addition, the patient may exacerbate an allergic contact dermatitis by exposure to cross-reacting chemical compounds that are quite similar to the allergen to which he was originally sensitized. The most common example of a cross-reacting chemical is the para-aminobenzoic acid group (PABA). Para-aminobenzoic acid is used in sunscreens and will cross-react with sulfonamides, sulfonylurea diuretics (eg, chlorothiazides), azo dyes, and topical analgesics (eg, benzocaine).

One valuable clinical tool in the management of persistent allergic contact dermatitis is to have the patient bring in the contents of his medicine cabinet. This simple procedure will often lead to prompt identification of the offending agent.

Symptomatic treatment consists of the application of wet dressings employing Burow's solution and a 1% hydrocortisone cream or lotion. Oral or parenteral corticosteroids (eg, triamcinolone, 40 mg intramuscularly per week, or prednisone, 40 mg orally daily) may be needed temporarily in severe cases.

Oral desensitization with poison ivy extracts has been employed with some claims of success. Although data are now available that indicate that one can produce tolerance to DNCB by oral administration, the clinical feasibility of oral desensitization remains unproved.

Prognosis

Most patients with allergic contact dermatitis respond to the procedures mentioned above. In some cases—particularly chromium contact dermatitis—the course is chronic with frequent spontaneous exacerbations.

PHOTOALLERGIC CONTACT DERMATITIS

Major Immunologic Features

- T cell-mediated eczematous disease.
- Ultraviolet light plays an essential role in generating the allergen.

General Considerations

Photoallergic contact dermatitis is characterized by a chronic eczematous reaction in areas of skin exposed to light (the backs of the hands, the face, the V of the neck). Unexposed areas of skin are usually not affected.

This disorder became a prominent dermatologic problem following the introduction of germicidal soaps in the late 1950s and early 1960s. Several chemicals, particularly halogenated salicylanilides and bithionol, were found to be prime offenders in producing sensitization. However, other drugs and chemicals such as chlorpromazine and sulfonamides have also been found to produce photoallergic contact dermatitis when applied topically, either intentionally or accidentally.

The role of ultraviolet light in the production of photoallergic contact dermatitis is controversial. Evidence has been presented that ultraviolet light causes photodecomposition of topically applied chemicals and in the process generates a potent sensitizing contact antigen which, when applied to the skin of a sensitized individual in the absence of ultraviolet light, produces an eczematoid reaction. An alternative hypothesis is that ultraviolet light forms free radicals which generate a strong covalent bond between the chemical contactant and host skin structures and that binding of the chemical to the skin results in formation of the contact antigen.

Although the exact role of ultraviolet light is still unclear, there is little doubt about the immunologic nature of this eczematous disease. Photoallergic contact dermatitis has been passively transferred employing the intraperitoneal injection of mononuclear cells from a sensitized to an unsensitized guinea pig.

Clinically, the diagnosis is made by observation of the characteristic eczematous involvement in areas of skin exposed to light and by a history of exposure to photocontactants. A special form of patch testing is employed to confirm the diagnosis. This procedure consists of applying the suspected agent to the patient's skin and then later—usually within 24 hours—exposing the patch test site to ultraviolet light. A second covered patch test serves as a control. An eczematous eruption at 48 hours at the patch test site represents a positive response. The reaction duplicates the clinical lesion.

Topical and systemic corticosteroids, avoidance of the offending agent, and avoidance of sunlight have all been used with some success, but persistence or recurrence of the eczema is common. There is evidence that persistence of the disease is due to prolonged retention of the offending agent in the skin, but this is controversial. Thus, despite lack of recent exposure to the antigen, patients can develop eczematous disease upon exposure to ultraviolet light.

ATOPIC DERMATITIS

Major Immunologic Features

- Characterized by increased incidence of reagin-mediated positive skin tests.
- High serum IgE levels.
- Partial defect in T cell function.
- Impaired neutrophil chemotaxis.

General Considerations

The term atopy was coined to denote a constellation of heritable disorders including asthma, hay fever, allergic rhinitis, and eczema (atopic dermatitis). Atopic dermatitis occurs predominantly in flexor areas (antecubital and popliteal fossae). Dry skin (xerosis) and pruritus commonly accompany atopic dermatitis, and pyoderma is an occasional complication. Other complications include disseminated herpes simplex and disseminated vaccinia (Kaposi's varicelliform eruption).

The association of atopic dermatitis with allergic rhinitis, hay fever, and asthma has provided a strong incentive to investigate the possible role of the immune system in the pathogenesis of the skin disease. Indeed, atopic dermatitis patients readily form reagins (IgE skin-sensitizing antibodies), as evidenced by the high incidence of positive immediate wheal and flare reactions to the intradermal injection of a battery of common food and inhalant antigens. The serum IgE is elevated 5- to 10-fold in approximately 80% of these patients. Increased tissue levels of IgE have also been reported in atopic dermatitis. It is not known, however, whether the high IgE levels fluctuate with skin disease activity or whether these levels are more closely correlated with the presence of allergic rhinitis. It must also be emphasized that elevated IgE levels are not specific for atopic dermatitis. Elevated IgE levels have been found in the sera of patients with bullous pemphigoid, parasitic infections, Wiskott-Aldrich syndrome, and pulmonary aspergillosis. However, the strongest argument against a significant role for IgE in the pathogenesis of the skin disease is the fact that an IgE-mediated cutaneous response is characterized by urticaria and not by eczema.

In addition to elevated IgE levels, an impairment in cell-mediated immunity may occur in some patients with atopic dermatitis. Defects in cell-mediated immunity are manifested both by absence of a delayed cutaneous hypersensitivity to a battery of intradermal antigens and by the inability to be sensitized by DNCB. In vitro studies in some patients have demonstrated a poor proliferative response of peripheral leukocytes to phytohemagglutinin (PHA) and other mitogens. More recent evidence indicates that some patients suffering from atopic dermatitis have decreased numbers of T lymphocytes in their peripheral blood as measured by sheep red blood cell rosette formation.

Another abnormality recently described in some patients with atopic dermatitis is chemotactic and phagocytic dysfunction of neutrophils.

Whether any of these immunologic abnormalities in atopic dermatitis results in lowered resistance to cutaneous bacterial and viral infections is unknown.

Treatment

Treatment of atopic dermatitis in the acute stage involves the use of wet dressings employing 1% Burow's solution. One percent hydrocortisone lotion and cream are also used. The subacute and chronic phases of atopic eczema respond to the frequent application (6–8 times a day) of 1% hydrocortisone cream or ointment. The vehicle for the hydrocortisone is very important since chronic eczematous disease is characterized by marked dryness of the skin; one must add an emollient such as petrolatum in order to prevent the rapid evaporation of moisture brought to the surface by the systemic circulation. Treatment of chronic eczema must be continued for at least a month after clinical evidence of the disease has disappeared. Stopping treatment before this time may result in rapid drying of the skin with recurrence of the eczematous disease.

These patients suffer from severe pruritus, which can usually be relieved by various antihistamines, eg, hydroxyzine, 25 mg orally 3–4 times a day. Intense pruritus may require the use of a tranquilizer such as thioridazine (Mellaril), 25 mg orally twice daily, or chlorpromazine (Thorazine), 25 mg orally 3 times daily. Only rarely are oral corticosteroids such as prednisone, 40 mg daily, justified to temporarily treat atopic dermatitis.

Prognosis

Atopic dermatitis is characterized by exacerbations and remissions. Some children, as they grow older, become relatively free of the manifestations of atopic dermatitis. In others, the problem may persist into adult life, resulting in chronic eczema of the flexural areas of the body. At times an acute exacerbation may lead to widespread eczematous involvement, resulting in exfoliative erythroderma. Still other patients may have eczematous disease involving only the hands.

Atopic dermatitis patients are also susceptible to generalized cutaneous herpes simplex infections. In addition, the patient's disease may be complicated by the presence of severe recurrent staphylococcal pyodermas.

Because patients with atopic dermatitis may develop eczema vaccinatum following smallpox inoculation, they should not be vaccinated.

DERMATOPHYTOSIS

Dermatophytes are saprophytic fungi capable of evoking an eczematous response on infecting the skin. They commonly produce infection in the groin (jock itch), on the fingernails and toenails, and between the toes (athlete's foot). Preliminary studies by Jones and others indicate that an intact cell-mediated immune response may play an important role in the normal host's response to dermatophyte infections. These authors have demonstrated that the experimental inoculation of dermatophytes in the skin of an unsensitized individual results in propagation of the fungal disease (an eczematous lesion). However, within 48 hours the cutaneous fungal infection resolves. This resolution corresponds to the development of delayed hypersensitivity to the fungus. Subsequent infection of the arm of a sensitized individual results in a more intense transient initial eczematous response with persistent failure of the fungal infection to spread.

Fungal infections of the feet can be readily treated by the use of various topical preparations, including undecylenic acid powder, 2% miconazole cream, and tolnaftate solution or cream. Severe cases require the use of microsize griseofulvin, 0.5–1 g orally daily for approximately 3 weeks.

Fungal infections are usually self-limited, involving only the moist areas of the body. However, generalized fungal infections involving large areas of the body have been reported in patients with defective cell-mediated immunity, especially Hodgkin's disease.

MUCOCUTANEOUS CANDIDIASIS

Major Immunologic Features

- Syndrome of cutaneous candidiasis generally found in the presence of T cell dysfunction.
- T cell defects include lymphocytopenia, the presence of lymphocytotoxin, serum factors inhibiting lymphocyte activation, absence of a 48-hour delayed skin test response to a variety of antigens, and impaired lymphocyte transformation or MIF production.
- Neutrophil chemotactic defects may be present.

General Considerations

Mucocutaneous candidiasis is a rare syndrome associated with skin and mucous membrane infection with *Candida albicans* that occurs most commonly—though not exclusively—in patients with defective cell-mediated immunity. It has been found in patients suffering from Hodgkin's disease and thymomas, in children born with severe combined immune deficiency, and in the DiGeorge and Nezelof syndromes. This form of candidal infection has also been found in children born with ill-defined and subtle profound defects in function of the T lymphocyte system.

C albicans, a saprophytic yeast, is a common inhabitant in the human gastrointestinal tract. Exposure begins in early infancy. During pregnancy, approximately 25% of women have significant yeast vaginitis. Approximately 5% of newborn infants develop oral candidiasis (thrush of mouth). Oral candidiasis generally disappears during the neonatal period. By the end of the first year of life, almost all children have been exposed to *C albicans* as indicated by the presence of serum candida-agglutinating antibodies. One study also indicates that approximately 60% of children over 1 year of age can mount a 48-hour delayed response to the intradermal injection of *C albicans* skin test antigen.

Children with mucocutaneous candidiasis may also have other fungal infections. However, *C albicans,* by virtue of its colonization of the gut in infancy, is the first potentially pathogenic fungus to challenge children with defective cell-mediated immunity.

Immunologic Pathogenesis (See Chapter 26.)

Extensive immunologic studies of patients with mucocutaneous candidiasis have demonstrated a variety of abnormalities of the cell-mediated immune mechanism. Most patients are unable to respond with a 48-hour delayed skin reaction to a battery of skin tests. This cutaneous "anergy" appears on infrequent occasions to be limited to the candida antigen. These patients also have delayed homograft rejection and an inability to become sensitized with DNCB. Some in vitro studies have demonstrated lymphocyte failure to respond to an antigenic challenge with increased DNA synthesis and migration inhibitory factor (MIF) production. Other patients' lymphocytes appear to have normal MIF production, but lymphocyte proliferation does not occur in response to antigenic challenges. On the other hand, some patients have a normal lymphocyte proliferative response but fail to produce additional MIF.

Mucocutaneous candidiasis has also been reported in association with a serum inhibitory factor that prevents lymphocytes from proliferating in response to antigenic challenge in vitro. One report describes clearance of the inhibitory factor and return of cell-mediated immunity following successful eradication of the *C albicans* infection with amphotericin B. This suggests that this serum inhibitory factor may be secondary to the candida infection.

Recent studies also suggest that some of these patients may have defective neutrophil and mononuclear chemotaxis in addition to a defective cell-mediated immunity.

Clinical Findings

Mucocutaneous candidiasis generally develops during the first 2 years of life. It commonly presents as persistent oral candidiasis beyond the neonatal period. The candidiasis may spread to involve large areas of skin. Granulomatous lesions may or may not form. The esophagus and nails may be involved. Multiple endocrinopathies and, at times, iron deficiency anemia may also be present.

Immunologic Diagnosis

The diagnosis of mucocutaneous candidiasis is made by culturing *C albicans* from the cutaneous lesions. For information regarding in vitro lymphocyte testing to evaluate the suspected underlying cell-mediated defect, see Chapter 24.

Differential Diagnosis

The granulomatous lesions of mucocutaneous candidiasis must be differentiated from pyodermas, cutaneous coccidioidomycosis, histoplasmosis, blastomycosis, and leishmaniasis.

Treatment

Some children with mucocutaneous candidiasis have been successfully treated by immunologic reconstitution with transfusions of normal homologous leukocytes. Thymic transplantation and amphotericin B, followed by transfer factor therapy, have also been successfully employed. Topically, 2% miconazole cream and clotrimazole have both been successfully employed.

Prognosis

The prognosis is guarded. Theoretically, defective T cell function makes these individuals susceptible to viral, fungal, and protozoal infections as well as autoimmune disorders.

BULLOUS DISEASES

The bullous diseases can only be properly understood if the distinctive anatomic features of the skin are clearly visualized. The epidermis is composed of layers of epidermal cells. These cells originate in the basal layer of the epidermis and then migrate toward the stratum corneum. During this migration, the cells undergo a process of keratinization. Upon reaching the skin surface, these compacted keratinized epidermal cells form the *stratum corneum* or *horny layer* of the skin.

Individual epidermal cells, during their upward migration, are held together by cytoplasmic projections ending on desmosomes ("intercellular bridges"). These epidermal cells also interdigitate with one another, and in the intercellular spaces there is an amorphous material called intercellular "cement." Destruction of the intercellular spaces interferes with the cohesion of the epidermis, leading to blister formation.

The epidermis is anatomically anchored to the dermis by a lamellar structure termed *basement membrane.* Extending from the basal layer of the epidermis to this structure are "anchoring" structures termed *half desmosomes.* Destruction of the integrity of the basement membrane and surrounding structures results in separation of epidermis from the dermis and blister formation (Table 33–1).

Table 33–1. Immunofluorescent studies in bullous skin diseases.

Disease	Site of Blister Formation	Location of Ig and C Deposits	Auto-antibodies
Pemphigus	Intraepidermal	Epidermal, intercellular	Yes
Bullous pemphigoid	Subepidermal	Basement membrane	Yes
Benign mucous membrane pemphigoid	Subepidermal	Basement membrane	Yes
Herpes gestationis	Subepidermal	Basement membrane	Yes
Dermatitis herpetiformis	Subepidermal	Granular pattern, beneath basement membrane	No
Erythema multiforme	Subepidermal	None	No

PEMPHIGUS VULGARIS

Major Immunologic Features

- Immunoglobulin and complement deposition found in the squamous intercellular spaces.
- Serum antibody directed against intercellular substance of stratified squamous epithelium.

General Considerations

Pemphigus vulgaris is a chronic bullous disease which formerly was reported almost exclusively in Jews. It has now been documented in all races and ethnic groups. Pemphigus vulgaris has been reported in association with bullous pemphigoid, thymoma, myasthenia gravis, and systemic lupus erythematosus. Before the corticosteroid and antibiotic drugs became available, pemphigus vulgaris was fatal in a large percentage of cases. Patients died of fluid and electrolyte abnormalities, cachexia, and sepsis secondary to the denudation of large areas of skin.

Immunologic Pathogenesis

Direct immunofluorescence of the skin lesions in pemphigus vulgaris has demonstrated the deposition of immunoglobulins (predominantly IgG), complement components (C1, C4, C3), properdin factor B (C3 proactivator), and, to a lesser extent, properdin at the site of involvement, the epidermal intercellular spaces. In addition to evidence of complement deposition at the disease site, complement levels in the blister fluid—in contrast to serum complement levels—are markedly decreased. These studies have been interpreted as suggesting local activation and consumption of complement at the site of blister formation.

Most (not all) specimens of serum from pemphigus patients contain a circulating IgG antibody (Fig 33–1) directed against a substance in the intercellular spaces of squamous epithelia. Several groups of investigators have attempted to induce pemphigus lesions in animals by the passive transfer of high-titer human pemphigus serum, and one group has claimed success.

Clinical Features

Pemphigus vulgaris is characterized by the development of thin flaccid bullae on normal-appearing skin. The mucous membranes are commonly involved. In fact, the disease commonly begins with extensive oral erosions. Shearing force applied to normal-appearing skin or direct pressure applied to the blister will cause further denudation of the skin and extension of the blister (Nikolsky's sign). The ruptured blisters display little tendency to heal.

Histologic examination of the blister reveals intraepidermal blister formation (the epidermis forms both the roof and base of blisters). In the blister fluid one can see single, unattached, rounded epidermal cells (Tzanck cells). At the margin of the blister, intercellular clefts may be seen between the individual epidermal cells (acantholysis).

Electron microscopic studies have demonstrated that destruction of the intercellular "cement" substance is the earliest finding in pemphigus vulgaris.

Immunologic Diagnosis

The diagnosis is made by the clinical features and histologic demonstration of acantholytic intraepidermal bulla formation. The diagnosis of pemphigus can also be made by the direct immunofluorescent demonstration of immunoglobulin deposition in the intercellular spaces of diseased or "normal"-appearing skin of the patients. This can also be confirmed by demonstrating the typical pemphigus antibody in the patient's serum using indirect immunofluorescent technics that employ heterologous tissue as a substrate. Rarely, pemphigus-like antibodies (Fig 33–1) may be seen in the sera of patients with penicillin hypersensitivity skin rashes, cutaneous fungus infections, or thermal burns. However, pemphigus antibody titers in these sera are usually low, and the clinical and histologic features of these conditions are distinct from those of pemphigus vulgaris.

Differential Diagnosis

This disease must be differentiated from other blistering diseases such as bullous pemphigoid, erythema multiforme, and benign mucous membrane pemphigoid.

Treatment

This disease can be successfully controlled with high doses of corticosteroids. In the past, prednisone in doses as large as 300–500 mg/day was required to control the lesions. In recent years, either azathioprine, 100–150 mg orally daily, methotrexate, 25–50 mg intramuscularly once weekly, or cyclophosphamide, 50–100 mg orally daily, usually in conjunction with corticosteroids, 40–60 mg orally daily, have been employed to treat these patients. The combined use of corticosteroids with immunosuppressive therapy allows one to employ much smaller doses of the former, thus avoiding the objectionable complications of corticosteroid therapy.

Prognosis

The prognosis of this disease has changed radically in the last 2 decades. Death during the first or second year after onset occurred in approximately 50% of patients in the preantibiotic and precorticosteroid era. The mortality rate is now being reported as 8% in several studies. However, morbidity (gastrointestinal bleeding, osteoporosis, diabetes) associated with large doses of corticosteroids is high. The addition of an immunosuppressive agent (azathioprine, methotrexate, and cyclophosphamide) to small doses of corticosteroids promises to minimize the corticosteroid side-effects while still controlling the disease.

BULLOUS PEMPHIGOID

Major Immunologic Features

- Immunoglobulin and complement deposition on the skin basement membrane.
- Serum anti-skin basement membrane antibody found in approximately 80% of patients.

General Considerations

This is a chronic bullous disease occurring mostly in middle-aged and older people. Like pemphigus vulgaris, this blistering skin disease had a significant mortality rate prior to the advent of corticosteroids and antibiotics.

Bullous pemphigoid is a blistering disease characterized by formation of tense bullae on an erythematous base. The flexor areas of the body (axillary, inguinal, and sides of the neck) are the common sites of involvement. The blister forms subepidermally (the roof is formed by the epidermis, and the base of the blister is the dermis). The individual bullae are difficult to rupture. Mucous membrane lesions are not a common feature.

Immunologic Pathogenesis

Direct immunofluorescent studies have demonstrated the deposition of IgG, IgA, IgM, IgD, IgE, C1q, C4, C3, C5, properdin, properdin factor B, and fibrin along the skin basement membrane (the site of bullous formation).

Complement component levels in the blister fluid are markedly decreased, whereas the total serum complement in these patients is normal. As in pemphigus vulgaris, these studies have been interpreted as suggesting local activation of complement at the site of blister formation.

In addition to these studies, indirect immunofluorescent technics (Fig 33–1) have demonstrated, in the sera of approximately 80% of these patients, a complement-fixing IgG antibody to skin basement membrane. However, attempts to passively transfer this disease to animals by the infusion of high-titer human pemphigoid serum have thus far failed.

Immunologic Diagnosis

The diagnosis is made clinically by observing the typical clinical features and by demonstrating a subepidermal bulla on a histologic preparation. The diagnosis may also be established by demonstrating, by direct immunofluorescence, the deposition of immunoglobulins or complement (C3) along the skin basement membrane (Fig 33–2). The serum may also be employed in indirect fluorescent technics to demonstrate IgG skin basement membrane antibodies.

Differential Diagnosis

This bullous disease must be differentiated from pemphigus vulgaris and especially erythema multiforme.

Treatment

Like pemphigus vulgaris, bullous pemphigoid responds to high doses of corticosteroids (eg, prednisone, 40–60 mg orally daily). Azathioprine, 100–150 mg orally daily, and methotrexate, 25–50 mg intramuscularly once weekly, have also been successfully employed, along with corticosteroids, in the treatment of bullous pemphigoid. As in pemphigus vulgaris, the combined use of corticosteroids and immunosuppres-

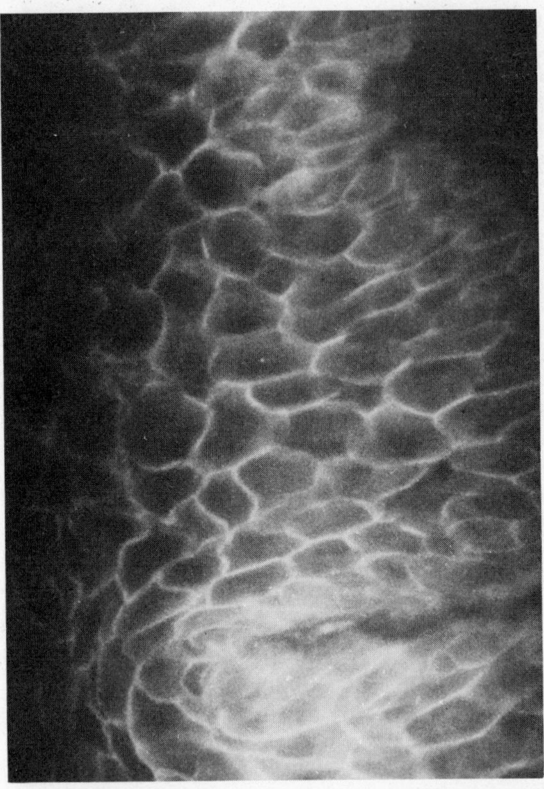

Figure 33–1. Indirect immunofluorescent examination of pemphigus serum, demonstrating the presence of IgG antibody to intercellular substance. The substrate is monkey esophagus.

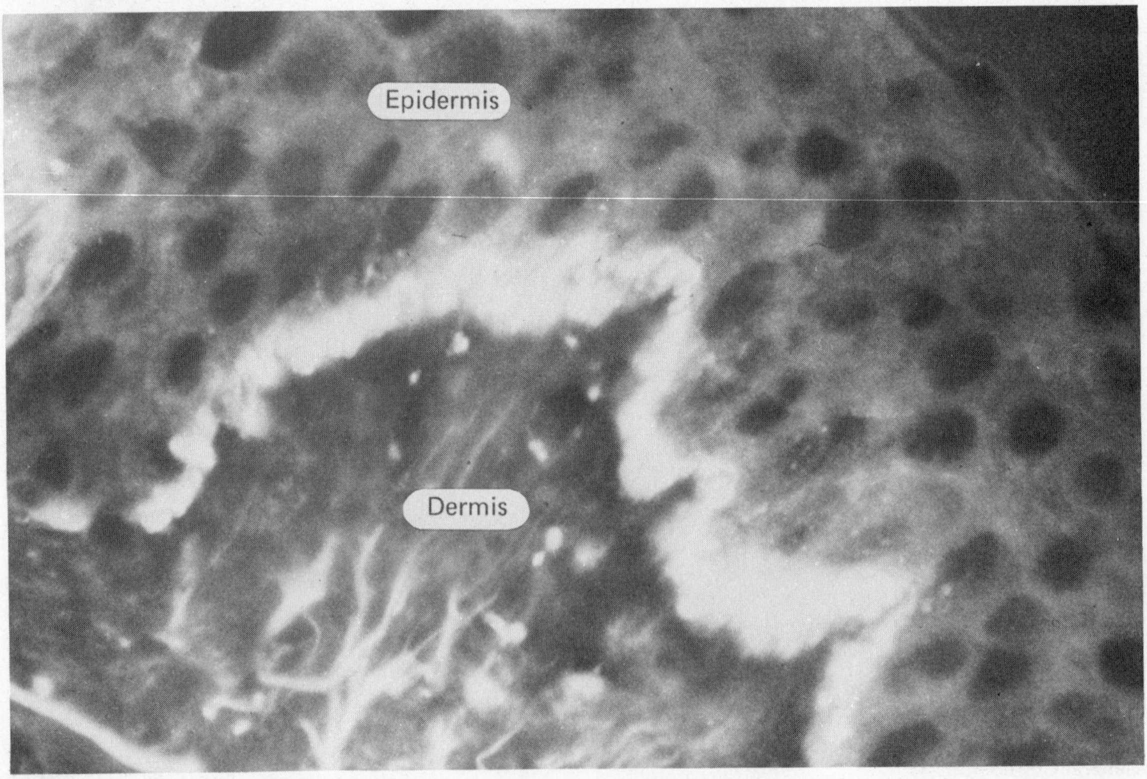

Epidermis

Dermis

Figure 33–2. Direct immunofluorescent examination of the skin of a patient with bullous pemphigoid. Note heavy IgG deposition along the basement membrane.

sive agents has allowed one to employ low doses of corticosteroids, thereby reducing the incidence of severe corticosteroid complications.

Prognosis

The prognosis for life is much improved, although, as in pemphigus vulgaris, large doses of corticosteroids in elderly people involve great risks that can only be undertaken if the probable benefits outweigh the possible hazards.

BENIGN MUCOUS MEMBRANE PEMPHIGOID

This is a subepidermal blistering disease involving the mucous membranes of the eyes, mouth, and vagina. Scar formation may occur. Few or no blisters appear on the skin. Recent investigations have now firmly established the presence of immunoglobulins and complement components along the basement membrane of the mucous membrane (the site of blister formation). In addition, several authors have now demonstrated circulating IgG antibody to skin basement membrane in the sera of some of these patients. These observations suggest a possible relationship between this disease and bullous pemphigoid.

Treatment of this disease is difficult. Local forms of therapy with corticosteroid eyedrops and surgical procedures do not produce lasting benefits. There is some evidence that these lesions respond partially to systemic corticosteroid therapy (eg, prednisone, 40–60 mg orally daily). The benefits of corticosteroid therapy must be weighed against the possible serious side-effects of corticosteroids in elderly persons. Immunosuppressive therapy (azathioprine, 100–150 mg orally) has been used in some of these patients, although its efficacy remains to be proved.

Prognosis

Benign mucous membrane pemphigoid is a chronic scarring disease of mucous membranes. Conjunctival scarring leads to failure to close the eye. Severe dryness and infection follow, and ultimately blindness.

HERPES GESTATIONIS

Major Immunologic Features

- Complement and, at times, immunoglobulin deposition on skin basement membrane.
- Avid complement-fixing serum autoantibody.

General Considerations

Herpes gestationis is a rare subepidermal bullous disease of pregnancy, occurring in one out of every 10–30 thousand pregnancies. The term herpes in this disease does not refer to herpesviruses but to the serpentine appearance of the lesions. It is characterized by an intense burning pruritus and subepidermal blister formation on erythematous papules. Histologically, the blister formation is indistinguishable from that of bullous pemphigoid.

Herpes gestationis may occur at any time during pregnancy but most commonly in the late second or early third trimester. It disappears following the termination of pregnancy, but persistence into the postpartum period and episodic flares with menses have been reported. The disease has also been reported following the use of estrogen-containing birth control pills. It may recur in succeeding pregnancies and may have an earlier and more severe onset. Infants born of affected mothers are generally without evidence of skin disease, but on rare occasions a transient bullous skin disease has been reported.

Direct immunofluorescent studies of the skin of patients with herpes gestationis have demonstrated IgG, IgE, C1, C4, C3, C5, and properdin deposition along the basement membrane. In many cases biopsy shows only heavy C3 deposition. The serum may or may not contain a factor capable of depositing complement components C1, C4, or C3 on the skin basement membrane. While some technical difficulty has been encountered in demonstrating a serum anti-basement membrane autoantibody in some of these patients, it appears likely that this basement membrane complement-fixing serum factor is an immunoglobulin.

Direct immunofluorescent studies of the skin of infants afflicted with the disease have thus far revealed the deposition of only C4 and C3 on the basement membrane.

These studies suggest a role for immunoglobulin and complement in the pathogenesis of the bullous disease of the mother and infant. The relationship between this disease and bullous pemphigoid is unknown, although immunofluorescent staining of specimens of basement membrane gives quite similar results.

Treatment

Treatment of herpes gestationis is difficult. These patients, in addition to the blistering skin disease, complain of an intense pruritus. The disease can be controlled during pregnancy with low to moderate doses of prednisone (15–30 mg orally daily). The aim is to control the disease and make the patient comfortable until she delivers. One possible complication is that the prednisone may suppress the fetus' adrenals. At birth, the neonatologist should be warned of the possibility of adrenal insufficiency in the infant.

Prognosis

Generally, the bullous disease disappears within a few months after termination of pregnancy. Exacerbations may occur with subsequent menses or with the use of birth control pills. The mechanism of induction by birth control pills is completely unknown. Subsequent pregnancies may result in a more acute and earlier onset of the bullous disease.

DERMATITIS HERPETIFORMIS

Major Immunologic Features

- Deposition of IgA at the dermal-epidermal junction.
- Increased incidence of HLA-B8 antigen.

General Considerations

Dermatitis herpetiformis is a chronic bullous disease that may occur at any age. Unlike pemphigus and, to a lesser extent, bullous pemphigoid, untreated dermatitis herpetiformis is not fatal.

Immunologic Pathogenesis

Direct immunofluorescent studies show that granular deposition of IgA is almost always present at the dermal-epidermal junction and IgG and IgM deposition much less commonly so. C3 is often found at sites corresponding to IgA deposition, especially in areas of blister formation. C1q and C4 are only occasionally found. These studies have been interpreted as suggesting activation of complement, predominantly via the alternative pathway, at the site of blister formation. No serum autoantibodies have been demonstrated, and serum complement levels are normal.

Immunologic studies of the gut have demonstrated increased levels of IgA and IgM in the gastrointestinal fluid. Gluten has been found in vitro to induce increased IgA synthesis in the gut tissues of these patients. Serum IgA levels are increased.

Genetic studies have demonstrated that approximately 90% of patients with dermatitis herpetiformis have HLA-B8 antigen compared to a frequency of $<30\%$ in the general population. Approximately 90% of patients suffering from adult celiac disease have this same HLA-B8 antigen.

The relationship between the gut disease and the skin disease is unknown. This may be a hypersensitivity disease in genetically predisposed individuals. Conceivably, antigen–perhaps gluten–is presented to the host via the gastrointestinal tract, preferentially stimulating the secretory immune system (IgA). Combining the antigen with IgA in the gut could produce the patchy duodenal or jejunal atrophy. The damaged mucosa may then permit IgA immune complexes to diffuse into the systemic circulation. For unknown reasons, these IgA complexes may be deposited in the skin, where they activate the complement system via the alternative pathway and produce the skin disease. Another hypothesis is that the inciting antigen and a normal skin structure–perhaps reticulin fibers–may bear antigenic similarities to each other. The IgA directed against the inciting antigen may then cross-react with the skin structure.

Admittedly, all of this is speculative, and much more investigation must be done to explore association of the skin and gut forms of dermatitis herpetiformis.

Clinical Features

Dermatitis herpetiformis is characterized by small groups of tense vesicles on an erythematous base. Symmetrical distribution over the extensor surfaces is common, and the buttocks, lower back, and shoulders are most severely affected. An intense burning pruritus accompanies this disease.

Histologically, the lesions demonstrate a subepidermal bullous formation. Eosinophilic microabscesses are seen in the dermal papillae.

In addition to the cutaneous manifestations, dermatitis herpetiformis has recently been shown to be a systemic disease. Biopsies of the small intestine have revealed a patchy duodenal or jejunal atrophy indistinguishable from adult celiac disease. Signs and symptoms of a malabsorption syndrome, however, are only occasionally seen (probably because of the patchy involvement of the gut disease).

Immunologic Diagnosis

In addition to the characteristic clinical and histologic features of this disease, the direct immunofluorescent demonstration of granular IgA deposition in the upper dermis of these patients is considered diagnostic of dermatitis herpetiformis.

Differential Diagnosis

Dermatitis herpetiformis must be differentiated from other intensely pruritic diseases such as scabies, pediculosis, and neurodermatitis and the blistering disease bullous pemphigoid.

Treatment

Dapsone (diaminodiphenylsulfone) (100 mg daily) and sulfapyridine (1–3 g daily) are effective in controlling the cutaneous features of this disease. They have no effect on the gastrointestinal lesions. The mechanisms of action of these drugs are unknown. The gut lesions respond to a gluten-free diet, and in one recent report it was claimed that a prolonged gluten-free diet resulted in clearance of the skin lesions.

Prognosis

The prognosis is excellent. Unlike bullous pemphigoid and pemphigus vulgaris, no deaths occur as a result of this disease. Untreated, it persists for years and is characterized by chronic low-grade activity with acute exacerbations. Patients treated with dapsone and free of disease for years, upon discontinuation of the dapsone, may have recurrence of their disease within 72–96 hours.

VASCULITIDES

Major Immunologic Features

- Deposition of immunoglobulin and complement in blood vessel walls.
- Serum complement levels may be decreased.
- Cryoglobulins and rheumatoid factor may be present in serum.

General Considerations

A partial list of vasculitic diseases includes leukocytoclastic angiitis, allergic granulomatosis, polyarteritis nodosa, giant cell arteritis, and Wegener's granulomatosis.

All forms of vasculitis may have significant cutaneous features. The size of the vessel, its anatomic location, and the intensity of the inflammatory insult determine what the cutaneous manifestations will be. Vasculitis may therefore present as petechial, urticarial, nodular, or ulcerative lesions. Recent studies have demonstrated deposits of various immunoglobulins, complement, and alternative pathway components in the diseased blood vessel walls of patients suffering from various forms of leukocytoclastic angiitis. Electron microscopic studies of blood vessel walls of early lesions of leukocytoclastic angiitis have demonstrated electron-dense deposits (presumably immune complexes). Immunoglobulin and complement are deposited in the temporal arteries of some patients suffering from temporal arteritis. Some patients with polyarteritis nodosa have deposits of HB_sAg, immunoglobulins, and complement in the diseased blood vessel walls. In addition, circulating HB_sAg antigen has been found in the serum of some of these patients.

These studies suggest that the deposition of immune complex in the blood vessel walls may play a role in the pathogenesis of several forms of necrotizing vasculitis. Evidence also suggests that circulating immune complexes and complement activation may play a role in the pathogenesis of urticarial and angioneurotic edema-like lesions frequently seen in the prodromal stage of acute viral hepatitis. See Chapter 27 for further clinical discussions of these disorders.

DISCOID LUPUS ERYTHEMATOSUS

Major Immunologic Features

- Lesions may or may not be associated with systemic lupus erythematosus.
- Immunoglobulins and complement components generally found in the dermal-epidermal junction in old discoid lesions.

General Considerations

The cutaneous lesions of discoid lupus erythematosus may be characterized as sharply demarcated atrophic plaques. Telangiectasia, follicular plugging, and a hyperkeratotic scale are often prominent. These lesions can involve any part of the body but are usually in light-exposed areas, especially the face and scalp. Histologically, the lesions are characterized by a patchy lymphocytic infiltrate at the dermal-epidermal junction. Liquefaction degeneration of the basal layer of the epidermis and epidermal atrophy are common features. These discoid lesions may be seen in the absence of any systemic disease or as part of the clinical picture of systemic lupus erythematosus.

Direct immunofluorescent study of these lesions has revealed the deposition in a granular pattern of immunoglobulins, complement, and alternative pathway components at the dermal-epidermal junction. DNA is also found in the deposits. Elution studies have demonstrated that these immunoglobulins have antinuclear specificity. Antibodies to skin basement membrane have also been eluted from the granular deposits, which are found in about 90% of the discoid skin lesions. However, the role of these granular deposits in the pathogenesis of discoid lesions is doubtful for 2 reasons: (1) Similar immunoglobulin and complement deposits are found in normal-appearing light-exposed skin in approximately 60% of patients with systemic lupus erythematosus. These deposits have been found in patients who have never had any skin lesions. (2) Ultraviolet light is capable of inducing classical discoid lesions in patients with systemic lupus erythematosus. Direct immunofluorescent studies of these experimental ultraviolet light-induced lesions have failed to consistently demonstrate immunoglobulin or complement deposition. If deposition does occur, it is found only after the lesions are several months old.

Despite the lack of evidence that immune complexes play a role in the pathogenesis of the cutaneous lesions, their presence in the skin of patients with

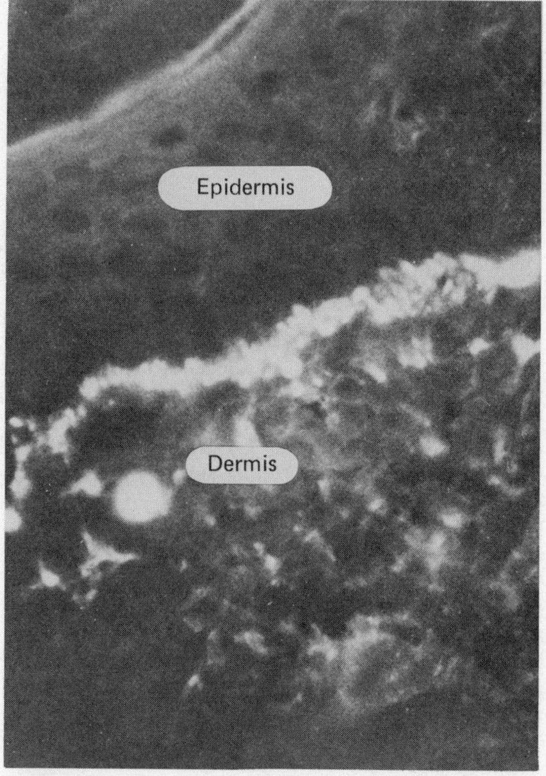

Figure 33–3. Direct immunofluorescent examination of the skin, not exposed to light, of a patient with systemic lupus erythematosus and severe nephritis. Note heavy granular deposition of IgM.

systemic lupus erythematosus that has not been exposed to light appears to be a reflection of the systemic immune complex disease. The presence of these cutaneous deposits is very often associated with severe lupus nephritis (Fig 33–3). Several studies have shown that about 70% of patients with clinical and laboratory evidence of lupus nephritis have these cutaneous deposits. Because of this association, the routine examination of the noninvolved and nonexposed skin of patients with systemic lupus erythematosus may provide valuable information regarding the presence or absence of immune complex nephritis.

Treatment

Without treatment, the discoid lesions of lupus erythematosus may produce severe scarring. Discoid lesions may be treated by the frequent application of a fluorinated corticosteroid, eg, triamcinolone, 0.1%, applied 4–8 times daily; intralesional injection of corticosteroids, eg, triamcinolone, 0.5 mg/ml; or the application of corticosteroid-impregnated occlusive tape. If the discoid lesions are widespread, oral corticosteroids (10–20 mg of prednisone daily) may be temporarily needed to prevent additional scarring.

Prognosis

Without treatment, the discoid lesions result in scarring.

CUTANEOUS MANIFESTATIONS OF COMPLEMENT DEFICIENCIES

(See also Chapter 22.)

In recent years, individual deficiencies of the complement components have been described for all but one of the 9 complement components; C9 is the only complement component that has not yet been observed as an isolated deficiency. Absence of C1q, C1r, C1s, C2, C4, and C5 has been associated with the presence of systemic lupus erythematosus. Some of these patients have had the classical discoid lesions of lupus erythematosus. There are now 2 reports of selective deficiency of C2 and anaphylactoid purpura. The occurrence of these 2 unusual diseases–lupus erythematosus and anaphylactoid purpura–together with the rare selective deficiencies of early complement components, suggests that this occurrence is not fortuitous.

Isolated deficiencies of the late complement components, ie, C3–C9, have also been associated with prominent skin manifestations. A partial lipodystrophy has been described in a patient with low C3 concentrations, ascribed to both hyposynthesis and hypercatabolism of this complement component. Infants born with a dysfunction of C5 have been found to have severe seborrheic dermatitis (Leiner's disease). In addition, they have increased susceptibility to bacterial and fungal cutaneous infections. Infusion of fresh plasma containing normal quantities of functional C5 results in marked improvement of the severe seborrheic dermatitis. An isolated patient with a defect of C7 has been described. This individual appears to have the cutaneous and systemic findings of a mixed connective tissue syndrome.

Defects in the regulatory proteins of the complement system may be associated with prominent cutaneous manifestations. Patients born with an absence or dysfunction of C1 inactivator have hereditary angioneurotic edema. These patients may initially present to the dermatologist with an explosive onset of painless edema of the eyes and lips. Recently, several patients with hereditary angioneurotic edema have also developed systemic lupus erythematosus. At least one of the patients had the classical butterfly rash.

CONCLUSIONS

Many of the immunologic technics employed in the investigation of these diseases (immunofluorescence, immunoglobulin quantitation, skin testing, etc) are now becoming routine diagnostic procedures in the clinical practice of dermatology. The advances in our understanding of these diseases have been considerable. With the widespread application of immunologic technics to the study of other skin diseases, the prospect seems favorable for the development of additional information that will be useful in understanding the pathogenesis and in facilitating the diagnosis and treatment of dermatologic disorders.

• • •

References

Allergic Contact Dermatitis

Fisher AA: *Contact Dermatitis.* Lea & Febiger, 1974.

Landsteiner K, Chase MW: Experiments on transfer of cutaneous sensitivity to simple compounds. Proc Soc Exp Biol Med 49:688, 1942.

Macher E, Chase MW: Studies on the sensitization of animals with simple chemical compounds. 11. The fate of labeled picryl chloride and dinitrochlorobenzene after sensitizing injections. 12. The influence of excision of allergenic depots on onset of delayed hypersensitivity and tolerance. J Exp Med 129:81, 103, 1969.

Milner JE: In vitro lymphocyte responses in contact hypersensitivity IV. J Invest Dermatol 62:591, 1974.

Photoallergic Contact Dermatitis

Willis I, Kligman AM: The mechanism of the persistent light reactor. J Invest Dermatol 51:385, 1968.

Willis I, Kligman AM: The mechanism of photoallergic contact dermatitis. J Invest Dermatol 51:378, 1968.

Atopic Dermatitis

Buckley RH, Wray BB, Belmaker EZ: Extreme hyperimmunoglobulinemia E and undue susceptibility to infection. Pediatrics 49:59, 1972.

Chenowith BR, Lobitz WC, Dobson RL: Atopic dermatitis. Section 13–2 in: *Clinical Dermatology.* Vol 3. Demis DJ & others (editors). Harper & Row, 1975.

Hill HR, Quie PG: Raised serum-IgE levels and defective neutrophil chemotaxis in three children with eczema and recurrent bacterial infections. Lancet 1:183, 1974.

Lobitz WC Jr, Honeyman JF, Winkler NW: Suppressed cell-mediated immunity in two adults with atopic dermatitis. Br J Dermatol 86:317, 1972.

Dermatophytosis

Jones HE, Reinhardt JH, Renaldi MG: Acquired immunity to dermatophytes. Arch Dermatol 109:840, 1974.

Mucocutaneous Candidiasis

Kirkpatrick CH, Rich RR, Bennett JE: Chronic mucocutaneous candidiasis: Model-building in cellular immunity. Ann Intern Med 74:955, 1971.

Levy RL & others: Thymic transplantation in a case of chronic mucocutaneous candidiasis. Lancet 2:898, 1971.

Patterson PY & others: Mucocutaneous candidiasis, anergy and a plasma inhibitor of cellular immunity: Reversal after amphotericin B therapy. Clin Exp Immunol 9:595, 1971.

Snyderman R & others: Defective mononuclear leukocyte chemotaxis: A previously unrecognized immune dysfunction: Studies in a patient with chronic mucocutaneous candidiasis. Ann Intern Med 78:509, 1973.

Pemphigus Vulgaris

Beutner EH & others: *Immunopathology of the Skin: Labeled Antibody Studies.* Dowden, Hutchinson & Ross, 1973.

Jordon RE & others: Classical and alternate pathway activation of complement in pemphigus vulgaris lesions. J Invest Dermatol 63:256, 1974.

Jordon RE & others: Complement activation in pemphigus vulgaris blister fluid. Clin Exp Immunol 15:53, 1973.

Van Joost T, Cormane RH, Pondman KW: Direct immunofluorescent study of the skin on occurrence of complement in pemphigus. Br J Dermatol 87:466, 1972.

Bullous Pemphigoid

Provost TT, Tomasi TB Jr: Evidence for complement activation via the alternate pathway in skin diseases. 1. Herpes gestationis, systemic lupus erythematosus, and bullous pemphigoid. J Clin Invest 52:1779, 1973.

Benign Mucous Membrane Pemphigoid

Bean SF & others: Cicatricial pemphigoid: Immunofluorescent studies. Arch Dermatol 106:195, 1972.

Herpes Gestationis

Bushkell LL, Jordon RE, Goltz RW: Herpes gestationis: New immunologic findings. Arch Dermatol 110:65, 1974.

Kolodny RC: Herpes gestationis: A new assessment of incidence, diagnosis, and fetal prognosis. Am J Obstet Gynecol 104:39, 1969.

Provost TT, Tomasi TB Jr: Evidence for complement activation via the alternate pathway in skin diseases. 1. Herpes gestationis, systemic lupus erythematosus, and bullous pemphigoid. J Clin Invest 52:1779, 1973.

Dermatitis Herpetiformis

Brow JR & others: The small intestinal mucosa in dermatitis herpetiformis. 1. Severity and distribution of the small intestinal lesions and associated malabsorption. Gastroenterology 60:355, 1971.

Gebhard RL & others: Dermatitis herpetiformis: Immunologic concomitants of small intestinal disease and relationship to histocompatibility antigen HLA-8. J Clin Invest 54:98, 1974.

Provost TT, Tomasi TB Jr: Evidence for the activation of complement via the alternate pathway in skin diseases. 2. Dermatitis herpetiformis. Clin Immunol Immunopathol 3:178, 1974.

Seah PP & others: Alternate-pathway complement fixation by IgA in the skin in dermatitis herpetiformis. Lancet 2:175, 1973.

Vasculitides

Braverman IM, Yen A: Demonstration of immune complexes in spontaneous and histamine-induced lesions and in normal skin of patients with leukocytoclastic angiitis. J Invest Dermatol 64:105, 1975.

Gocke DJ & others: Vasculitis in association with Australia antigen. J Exp Med 134 (Suppl):330s, 1971.

Schroeter AL & others: Immunofluorescence of cutaneous vasculitis associated with systemic disease. Arch Dermatol 104:254, 1971.

Lupus Erythematosus

Cripps DJ, Rankin J: Action spectra of lupus erythematosus and experimental immunofluorescence. Arch Dermatol 107:563, 1973.

Gilliam JN & others: Immunoglobulin in clinically uninvolved skin in systemic lupus erythematosus: Association with renal disease. J Clin Invest 53:1434, 1974.

Landry M, Sams WM Jr: Systemic lupus erythematosus: Studies of the antibodies bound to skin. J Clin Invest 52:1871, 1973.

Tan EM, Kunkel HG: An immunofluorescent study of the skin lesions in systemic lupus erythematosus. Arthritis Rheum 9:37, 1966.

Complement Deficiencies

Alper CA, Block KJ, Rosen FS: Increased susceptibility to infection in a patient with type II essential hypercatabolism of C3. N Engl J Med 288:601, 1973.

Gelfand EW, Clarkson JE, Minta JO: Selective deficiency of the second component of complement in a patient with anaphylactoid purpura. Clin Immunol Immunopathol 4:269, 1975.

34 . . .
Infectious Diseases

David J. Drutz, MD, & John Richard Graybill, MD

Infectious diseases are associated so intimately with the functions of the immune system that it is possible to classify every human infection on the basis of local/systemic, specific/nonspecific, and cellular/humoral immune mechanisms. In essence, any infectious disease implies that the immune defense system has been successfully breached. It was the search for knowledge about protection against infection that turned up much of the basic information underlying the science of immunology today.

In this chapter, representative infectious diseases have been separated into categories based upon broad patterns of interaction between pathogenic microorganisms and the components of the immune system (Table 34–1). Such a classification is by nature arbitrary; clearly, such categories are not mutually exclusive. However, we hope this approach will emphasize the common immunologic features of diverse infective processes. Such an approach is not intended to serve as a substitute for the traditional study of specific pathogens and clinical syndromes.

EXTRACELLULAR INFECTIONS IN WHICH OPSONINS & POLYMORPHONUCLEAR NEUTROPHILS ARE DECISIVE IN RECOVERY

Major Immunologic Features

- Microorganisms possess antiphagocytic surface factors.
- Serum opsonins promote phagocytosis.
- Phagocytosis by polymorphonuclear neutrophils (PMNs) is followed by microbial death.
- Infection may progress because of qualitative or quantitative defects of opsonins or PMNs.
- Lymphocytes and macrophages apparently play no decisive role.

David J. Drutz is Associate Professor of Medicine and Chief, Division of Infectious Diseases, Department of Medicine, The University of Texas Health Science Center at San Antonio and Audie L. Murphy Memorial Veterans Hospital, San Antonio, Texas. John Richard Graybill is Assistant Professor of Medicine, Division of Infectious Diseases, Department of Medicine, The University of Texas Health Science Center at San Antonio and Clinical Investigator, Audie L. Murphy Memorial Veterans Hospital, San Antonio, Texas.

General Considerations

Many microorganisms are characterized by the presence of surface factors which retard phagocytosis. Since their presence in tissues stimulates an outpouring of PMNs, they are known as *pyogenic microorganisms.* Because they are highly susceptible to being killed by PMNs, they rely upon evasion of phagocytosis for their survival. Hence, they are also known as *extracellular pathogens.* Opsonins are humoral factors which promote phagocytosis and are needed to overcome antiphagocytic surface factors so that PMNs can ingest these microorganisms. Examples of microorganisms which must evade phagocytosis in order to survive (and the nature of the antiphagocytic surface factors) include *Streptococcus pneumoniae, Neisseria meningitidis, Haemophilus influenzae, Klebsiella pneumoniae,* and *Pseudomonas aeruginosa* (capsular polysaccharide), *Streptococcus pyogenes* (hyaluronic acid and M protein), *Staphylococcus aureus* (protein A), *Neisseria gonorrhoeae* (pili composed of protein), *Yersinia pestis* (Fl and VW antigens), and *Bacillus anthracis* (capsular polypeptide).

1. PNEUMOCOCCAL INFECTION

Streptococcus pneumoniae (pneumococcus) is a gram-positive, lancet-shaped diplococcus which is soluble in bile, sensitive to optochin (ethylhydrocupreine), a quinine derivative, and highly susceptible to autolytic enzymes. It possesses a series of 82 antigenically specific capsular polysaccharides which confer type-specific immunity in mice. Capsules are most easily demonstrated by examining the microorganisms in India ink.

Pneumococci are found normally in the pharynx in 40–70% of adults. Infection is unusual by comparison, generally occurring when there is a breach of host defenses such as aspiration, inhalation of irritants, viral upper respiratory infection, or pulmonary edema. Pneumonia is the most common clinical manifestation of pneumococcal disease. An estimated 420,000 cases of pneumococcal pneumonia occur yearly in the USA. Hematogenous spread may result in endocarditis, meningitis, arthritis, or other localized suppurative complications. Otitis media, sinusitis, and mastoiditis presumably reflect direct extension from the pharynx.

The capsules of pneumococci are composed of

Table 34–1. Infectious diseases classified by mechanisms of immunity, associated diseases, or causative agents.

Extracellular infections in which opsonins and PMNs are decisive in recovery:
- Pneumococcal infection
- Meningococcal infection
- *Haemophilus influenzae* infection
- Gonorrhea
- *Streptococcus pyogenes* infection
- *Klebsiella pneumoniae* infection
- *Pseudomonas aeruginosa* infection
- Plague
- Anthrax

Infections in which antibody may be decisive in prevention or in recovery through a mechanism other than opsonization: Diseases in which antibody—
- Neutralizes exotoxins
- Blocks epithelial attachment
- Participates in complement-mediated bacteriolysis
- Neutralizes viruses

Infections in which humoral and cellular immunity collaborate in host defense:
- Cryptococcosis
- Syphilis
- Salmonellosis
- Candidiasis
- Listeriosis

Intracellular infections in which lymphocytes and macrophages are decisive in recovery and humoral mechanisms play no protective role:
- Measurement of antibody not useful in diagnosis and prognosis
  - Tuberculosis
  - Leprosy
  - Infections with atypical mycobacteria
- Measurement of antibody useful in diagnosis and prognosis
  - Histoplasmosis
  - Coccidioidomycosis
  - Brucellosis
  - Tularemia

Infections characterized by unique host-parasite relationships:
- *Mycoplasma pneumoniae* infection
- *Bordetella pertussis* infection
- Chlamydial infection
- Rickettsial infection

Infections complicated by deposition of circulating immune complexes:
- Infective endocarditis
- Viral hepatitis
- Poststreptococcal glomerulonephritis
- Quartan malaria
- Syphilis
- Typhoid fever
- Leprosy

The spectrum of host-virus immunologic relationships:
- Viral diseases (acute, chronic, latent, slow)

Opportunistic infections: Infections associated with—
- Hypogammaglobulinemia
- Granulocytopenia
- Depressed cellular immunity
- Hemolytic anemia
- Splenectomy
- Foreign bodies
- Gastrectomy

large polysaccharides which are hydrophilic gels. The complete structures of only a few capsular types (types 3, 6, and 8) are known. Type 3, for example, has a capsule composed of repeating cellobiuronic acid units joined by $\beta(1\rightarrow3)$ glucosidic bonds. Capsular polysaccharide subserves an antiphagocytic function, but the precise manner in which capsules inhibit phagocytosis is unclear.

In general, the amount of capsular material is directly proportionate to the degree of virulence. Types 1, 2, 3, 5, 7, and 8 are all considered highly virulent. Type 3 pneumococci generally have the largest capsules and are the most difficult to phagocytose; infections with these microorganisms are associated with a poor prognosis. Type 3 pneumococci may result in pulmonary abscesses, which are extremely rare in infection with other types. There is some evidence that type 14 pneumococci share antigenic determinants with blood group substances. Such infections would theoretically be harder to control since the host might have difficulty discerning "nonself" from "self."

Pneumococcal polysaccharide dissociates from the surface of microorganisms and is detectable in the tissues, blood, and urine for some time after recovery from pneumococcal infection. There is some evidence that this material may be endocytosed and later extruded from macrophages. Pneumococcal polysaccharide antigenemia is associated with a poorer prognosis for recovery from pneumococcal pneumonia.

Aside from the capsular antigens of pneumococci, other immunogenic constituents of the microorganisms (C substance, M protein, etc) do not appear to play an important role in virulence or host response. However, C substance, a polysaccharide antigen probably equivalent to the group-specific C substances of *Streptococcus pyogenes,* does have the peculiar ability to precipitate a β-globulin (C-reactive protein) found in the sera of patients with diverse inflammatory diseases.

Clinical Features

Pneumococcal pneumonia begins classically with a single hard shaking chill, pleuritic chest pain, and cough productive of bloody (rusty) sputum. Bacteremia is a regular early feature of infection, generally occurring in close temporal relationship to the chill. The bacteremia may be self-limited or may result in metastatic infection of heart valves, meninges, or joints. Patients with ascites due to cirrhosis or the nephrotic syndrome seem particularly prone to pneumococcal peritonitis, often in the absence of any obvious respiratory infection. Prior to the advent of antimicrobial therapy, about two-thirds of patients with pneumococcal pneumonia would spontaneously recover by "crisis,' the change in clinical course reflecting the synthesis of specific anticapsular antibody and the resultant enhancement of the phagocytic process after several days of acute illness.

Immunologic Diagnosis

Individual capsular types of pneumococci can be identified by the quellung phenomenon (*Quellung,* swelling). In the presence of type-specific antiserum, polysaccharide capsules undergo refractive changes and swelling which can be detected by light microscopy, especially if the preparation is examined in the presence of India ink. In the era preceding the use of antimicrobial agents, precise identification of capsular type was very important; antisera used in treatment were often selected on the basis of the capsular type of the infecting strain. The capsular types most often associated with infection may vary from time to time and from community to community. In adults they generally include types 1, 3, 4, 7, 8, and 12; in children, types 1, 3, 6, 14, 19, and 23. Effective therapy with penicillin and other antibiotics has done away with the need for identifying individual capsular types except for epidemiologic purposes.

Some investigators employ a polyvalent omniserum to assist in rapid identification of pneumococci in clinical specimens. This reagent consists of a mixture of antisera to capsules of the common pneumococcal types. Since pneumococci are often transiently present among the normal throat flora, their presence in a sputum specimen is not significant unless they are the only microorganisms present. Transtracheal aspirations are often far more helpful in determining the true cause of pneumonia by avoiding the heavily colonized pharynx in the collection of a specimen from the respiratory tree. An omniserum-produced quellung phenomenon with gram-positive microorganisms recovered from a transtracheal aspirate would confirm a suspected diagnosis of pneumococcal pneumonia.

The presence of antibody to a given pneumococcal capsular type can be detected by the Francis skin test. Here, capsular polysaccharide injected into the skin produces a wheal and flare response if antibody is present. This test is rarely if ever employed today; antibody is detected by more conventional technics, including quantitative precipitation, hemagglutination, and radioimmunoassay.

Pneumococcal capsular polysaccharide antigen can be detected in blood and other body fluids by counterelectrophoretic, rocket electrophoretic, or radioimmunoassay technics. Although blood cultures are generally positive when pneumococcal polysaccharide is detectable in the blood, the advantage of immunologic detection of this antigen is the rapidity with which diagnosis may be established (around 30 minutes) so that definitive treatment can be started. A full day may be required before blood cultures show evidence of growth (see Chapter 24).

Differential Diagnosis

Pneumococcal pneumonia must be differentiated from other bacterial and viral pneumonias, from fungal and mycobacterial infections, and from noninfective processes such as pulmonary embolization. The diagnosis is established by isolation and cultivation of the infecting pathogen.

Prevention

Persons 50 years of age and older, patients with underlying immune defects (splenectomy; sickle cell anemia), and those with debilitating illnesses may be unusually susceptible to pneumococcal infection. These persons can be protected by active immunization with specific capsular types of pneumococci. Dodecavalent pneumococcal vaccine containing purified capsular polysaccharide from types 1, 3, 4, 6, 7, 8, 9, 12, 14, 18, 19, and 23 is currently under study. If one assumes that 70% of the approximately 420,000 cases of pneumococcal pneumonia occurring in this country are caused by pneumococcal types contained in this vaccine, that the vaccine is 80% effective, and that 25% of such infections are demonstrably bacteremic with an overall fatality rate of 17%, then there should be an annual saving of 17,000 lives if the vaccines were widely employed. Furthermore, the economic impact of disease in younger patients not at risk of dying of pneumonia would also be greatly reduced. Antibody response to pneumococcal vaccine in infants and very young children is not as reliable as in older persons.

Treatment

Penicillin is the drug of choice in the treatment of pneumococcal pneumonia and its hematogenous complications as well as in pneumococcal sinusitis, otitis media, mastoiditis, and peritonitis. The dosage and duration of treatment depend upon the exact form of the infection. For example, pneumonia generally responds to a low dose given for a short time (600,000 units of procaine penicillin G intramuscularly twice daily for 1 week), whereas endocarditis demands a higher dose for a longer time (10–20 million units of aqueous penicillin intravenously daily for 4 weeks).

Pneumococci have shown no significant propensity to develop penicillin resistance, whereas tetracycline and erythromycin-resistant strains have been encountered.

Complications & Prognosis

A small percentage of patients with bacteremic pneumococcal pneumonia die regardless of the rapidity with which a diagnosis is established and specific bactericidal antibiotic therapy is begun. The factors responsible for this presently "irreducible minimum" of deaths are uncertain. The mortality rate is higher in patients at the extremes of age; in alcoholics; in those with multilobar pulmonary involvement, meningitis, or endocarditis; in those infected with type 3 pneumococci; in those with profound leukocytopenia; and in patients who have been previously splenectomized. Splenectomy often portends a fulminating clinical course, with death in less than a day. There may be associated disseminated intravascular coagulation.

2. MENINGOCOCCAL INFECTION

Neisseria meningitidis (meningococcus) is a gram-negative biscuit-shaped diplococcus (flat sides adjacent) with fastidious growth requirements; it multiplies best in an atmosphere of 5–10% CO_2 in air, and is highly subject to autolysis. Meningococci possess group-specific capsular polysaccharides with antiphagocytic capacity and a lipopolysaccharide-endotoxin complex which is thought to play an important role in the fulminating clinical course of acute meningococcemia.

Meningococcal disease is unique to man. A variable proportion of normal persons carry meningococci in the nasopharynx either asymptomatically or with symptoms of mild upper respiratory infection. Carriage persists for days to months and is an apparently important stimulus to production of protective serum antibodies (which do not themselves affect the nasopharyngeal carrier state). Under conditions of stress and crowding, such as might occur in a military recruit population, the carrier rate climbs rapidly. This is a common setting for epidemics, although there is no direct relationship between the nasopharyngeal carrier rate in a given population and the incidence of clinical infection.

The factors that lead to benign nasopharyngeal carriage for the majority of meningococcal contacts—and progressive infection for an unfortunate minority—are uncertain. However, the presence of circulating meningococcal antibody (specifically, antibody that participates with complement in direct meningococcal bacteriolysis in vitro) appears to be an important indicator of protection. Whether actual bacteriolysis occurs in vivo or whether opsonic antibody alone is important in protection under clinical circumstances is uncertain. Although meningococcal bloodstream invasion and its sequelae do not occur in everyone who lacks serum bactericidal activity, the patients who do develop fulminating meningococcal disease appear to be recruited from this population. Infection in such patients develops very rapidly following the nasopharyngeal acquisition of meningococci.

Meningococci can be divided into 9 groups on the basis of agglutination reactions. Three groups are considered major (A, B, and C); the remainder are minor (D, X, Y, Z, 29E, and 135). Group A antigen consists of N-acetyl-O-acetylmannosamine phosphate. The B and C antigens both consist of N-acetylneuraminic acid (sialic acid), which is partially O-acetylated in the C antigen. Groups A and C meningococci differ from the others in that capsular swelling (quellung phenomenon) can be demonstrated with specific antisera.

Historically, group A meningococci have been responsible for cyclic worldwide epidemics of meningitis, whereas types B and C have been considered interepidemic strains. Major fluctuations in this pattern have occurred since 1963. Group B meningococci predominated from 1964–1968 and have done so since 1972. Group C strains were predominant from 1969–1971. Group Y disease appears to be on the upswing in some military populations.

Groups A and C capsular polysaccharides induce specific IgG or IgM antibody formation, whereas group B polysaccharide is relatively nonimmunogenic. It has been postulated that group B meningococcal neuraminic acid is so similar to that present on host cell membranes that the microorganism fails to be recognized as "nonself." Alternatively, host neuraminidase might break down group B capsular polysaccharide too rapidly to allow potent immunity to develop.

As noted above, the meningococcal lipopolysaccharide-endotoxin complex may be responsible for the fulminating nature of meningococcemia and the production of disseminated intravascular coagulation, peripheral vascular collapse, and shock. Meningococci "shed" endotoxin in vitro in the form of blebs from their surfaces.

Clinical Features

Meningococcal infection arising from the nasopharynx (or possibly from meningococci aspirated into the lungs) may produce a spectrum of clinical manifestations ranging from transient, asymptomatic bacteremia to fulminating and rapidly fatal septicemia characterized by disseminated intravascular coagulation; or Waterhouse-Friderichsen syndrome. Metastatic infection may involve joints, heart valves, and a wide variety of other loci, but the most common targets are the skin (infective vasculitis) and the meninges.

The rash of meningococcemia is typically widespread and purpuric. *Chronic meningococcemia* is a rare manifestation of meningococcal infection characterized by episodes of fever of a few days' duration which recur at daily, weekly, or monthly intervals. Rash is uncommon, but the occurrence of erythema nodosum-like lesions around the joints suggests that this disease may be partially due to the deposition of circulating immune complexes.

Immunologic Diagnosis

The measurement of antibodies to meningococci is not of practical diagnostic importance. However, the measurement of free capsular polysaccharide antigen by counterelectrophoresis and other technics may have practical significance in rapidly establishing the diagnosis and prognosis of patients with meningococcal disease. In recent studies of group C meningococcal infection, the presence of meningococcal antigen in serum portended a more severe clinical course; pretreatment levels were directly related to the degree of subsequent leukocytopenia, thrombocytopenia, and hypofibrinogenemia. High levels of antigen in the cerebrospinal fluid were associated with prolonged coma and elevated intracranial pressure.

Differential Diagnosis

A variety of pyogenic microorganisms (particularly pneumococci and *Haemophilus influenzae*) can produce purulent meningitis. Skin rash and the occurrence of disseminated intravascular coagulation are suggestive but not diagnostic of meningococcal infection. The diagnosis is established by isolating *N meningitidis* on appropriate bacteriologic media.

Prevention

Outbreaks of meningococcal infection are sporadic, and secondary cases are actually relatively rare. Thus, the intense emotionalism engendered by the occurrence of a case of meningococcal disease in a community is seldom justified. When a secondary case does occur, it is generally in a person who has been in prolonged intimate contact with the patient.

Until 10 years ago, the danger of meningococcal spread could be minimized by the simple expedient of treating close personal contacts of patients and carriers with prophylactic sulfonamides. The advent of sulfonamide-resistant meningococci prompted a search for alternative chemoprophylactic agents none of which has been fully satisfactory. Minocycline, a tetracycline drug, is capable of preventing nasopharyngeal acquisition of meningococci. It is the only tetracycline derivative possessing this capability. Unfortunately, minocycline so often produces vertigo in the dosage range required for meningococcal prophylaxis that its use is no longer recommended. Rifampin, an excellent bactericidal drug for the treatment of tuberculosis and leprosy, is also capable of preventing nasopharyngeal acquisition of meningococci. Unfortunately, rifampin-resistant meningococcal strains are known to occur, so that the usefulness of this drug may be limited. At present, however, rifampin is the drug of choice for meningococcal prophylaxis. Although penicillin is the treatment of choice for established meningococcal infection, *it is not useful prophylactically* because it apparently cannot prevent nasopharyngeal acquisition of the meningococcus. At present, it appears that sulfonamide-sensitive group B meningococci are becoming more common; perhaps it will some day be possible to return to sulfonamide prophylaxis.

Within the past year, 3 meningococcal vaccines composed of purified meningococcal polysaccharide (monovalent A, monovalent C, and bivalent A and C vaccine) have been released for limited use, predominantly in military populations. These vaccines are highly effective in preventing meningococcal infection except in children under 2 years of age. Side-effects are negligible. It has been suggested that vaccination should be considered an adjunct to antibiotic chemoprophylaxis for household contacts of patients with meningococcal disease since half of the secondary family cases occur more than 5 days after the onset of the primary case; this is considered long enough to yield potential benefit from vaccination in case antibiotic prophylaxis is not successful.

There remain a number of problems with meningococcal vaccines. Of major concern is the apparent lack of immunogenicity of group B polysaccharides and the poor antibody responses of infants and young children to group A and C polysaccharides.

Treatment

Meningococcal meningitis and other complications of meningococcemia are best treated with penicillin. Chloramphenicol is the drug of choice in patients with life-threatening penicillin allergy. Because disseminated intravascular coagulation often complicates meningococcemia, anticoagulation with heparin has been suggested as a therapeutic adjunct. This cannot currently be considered of definite benefit.

Complications & Prognosis

Acute meningococcemia carries a high mortality rate, and meningococcal meningitis may be followed by neurologic defects and impaired learning. Speed in establishing the diagnosis and initiating specific therapy are essential. There is virtually no other acute infectious disease that can kill with the rapidity of meningococcemia. The occurrence of meningitis is paradoxically a good prognostic sign, for it indicates that the patient has survived the initial bacteremia long enough to develop symptomatic secondary metastatic infection.

The occurrence of bilateral adrenal hemorrhage during acute meningococcemia (as a part of the Waterhouse-Friderichsen syndrome) has often prompted the use of corticosteroid therapy on the grounds that death occurs from acute adrenal insufficiency. In fact, direct measurements of adrenal corticosteroids in the blood indicate no such deficiency. Adrenal hemorrhage presumably reflects the general occurrence of vasculitis and disseminated intravascular coagulation.

3. *HAEMOPHILUS INFLUENZAE* INFECTION

Haemophilus influenzae is a small pleomorphic gram-negative rod with fastidious growth requirements, including dependence upon 2 factors derived from blood: X factor (hematin) and V factor (the function of which is subserved by NAD, NADH, or adenine nucleoside). Six types of *H influenzae* (a–f) have been identified on the basis of capsular polysaccharides. Invasive infection with *H influenzae* (meningitis, arthritis, cellulitis, epiglottitis) is virtually always due to type b strains. However, otitis media generally results from nontypable strains.

H influenzae is far more important as a pathogen of children than of adults. Protective antibody acquired as a result of experience with this microorganism may account for the relative age-specificity of the infection. *H influenzae* is the most common cause of bacterial meningitis in the first years of life and is responsible for many deaths as well as mental retardation.

The nasopharynx is considered to be the principal site for carriage and dissemination of *H influenzae* strains. Most strains are nontypable, but up to 38% of children have had nasopharyngeal carriage experience with type b strains by 5 years of age.

The capsular polysaccharides of *H influenzae* are considered to subserve an antiphagocytic function. The specific carbohydrates of types a, b, and c are polysugarphosphates; capsular polysaccharide of the clinically important type b strain is composed of polyribophosphate. Individual *H influenzae* types are readily identified with agglutination, precipitation, and quellung tests performed with specific antisera.

There has been much debate about the relative importance of opsonization and phagocytosis versus antibody- and complement-mediated bacteriolysis of *H influenzae* in protection against type b disease. In 1933, Fothergill and Wright noted an inverse relationship between the bactericidal activity of blood for *H influenzae* and susceptibility to meningeal infection. The period of peak susceptibility between 6 months and 3 years of age was considered to represent the gap reflecting loss of transplacental bactericidal antibody on the one hand and acquisition of active immunity on the other. There is now serious question about whether direct bactericidal activity of blood (ie, antibody- and complement-mediated bacteriolysis) plays any real role in protection or whether it is more important as an in vitro indicator of immunity. The preponderance of data suggests that opsonic antibody, directed principally against polyribophosphate of type b strains (and to some extent against somatic antigens), is the principal protective system.

Because not all persons become nasopharyngeal carriers of type b *H influenzae,* it is not clear why hematogenous infection (meningitis, etc) is so rarely encountered beyond 4 or 5 years of age in the absence of an immunizing event. It has been suggested that immunity may take place through colonization of body surfaces with microorganisms possessing cross-reactive surface antigens. For example, certain strains of *Escherichia coli* and *S pneumoniae* stimulate production of antibody which cross-reacts with type b *H influenzae* strains.

Clinical Features

The principal clinical manifestations of *H influenzae* infection in children are meningitis and otitis media. This microorganism is also found in the respiratory secretions of adults with chronic obstructive pulmonary disease and may be responsible for intermittent infective exacerbations of chronic bronchitis.

Immunologic Diagnosis

The measurement of antibodies to *H influenzae* is not of practical diagnostic importance. Circulating type b polyribophosphate capsular antigen can be detected by a variety of technics including counterelectrophoresis and latex particle agglutination. Rapid diagnosis of *H influenzae* meningitis has been made possible by examination of cerebrospinal fluid using counterelectrophoresis.

Differential Diagnosis

H influenzae must be considered in the differential diagnosis of a variety of pyogenic infective processes but may usually be suspected on clinical grounds as a cause of otitis, meningitis, or epiglottitis in children of susceptible age.

Prevention

Despite the availability of potent antibiotics, *H influenzae* meningitis remains an important source of morbidity and mortality in children. There are an estimated 10,000 cases of *H influenzae* meningitis yearly, with 400–500 deaths and 3000–5000 survivors who have residual central nervous system damage. Recent studies have concentrated upon development of a vaccine against type b *H influenzae* based upon immunization with purified polyribophosphate. Adults respond to such a vaccine with long-lived bactericidal and opsonic antibody production. Side-effects are minimal. Unfortunately, children under age 2 years (and especially under age 6 months)—the population at risk—respond poorly to polyribophosphate vaccination in terms of antibody response.

Treatment

The drug of first choice for treatment of *H influenzae* infection is ampicillin. Recent detection of ampicillin-resistant strains of type b meningococci is an alarming development which has prompted many physicians to include or substitute chloramphenicol in any treatment regimen directed against *H influenzae.* Ampicillin resistance is mediated by a plasmid coding for penicillinase production.

4. GONORRHEA

Neisseria gonorrhoeae (gonococcus) is a gram-negative bean-shaped diplococcus (concave sides adjacent) with fastidious growth requirements. It grows best in the presence of 5–10% CO_2 in air and is highly susceptible to autolysis. Gonococci are not normal constituents of the body flora but may infect any mucosal surface (urethra, cervix, rectum, pharynx, conjunctiva, and prepubertal vagina). Asymptomatic carriage may occur in any of these loci. In a small proportion of patients, symptomatic bloodstream infection occurs with production of arthritis, tenosynovitis, and metastatic skin lesions.

Gonorrhea is currently epidemic throughout the world, with an estimated 100 million new cases occurring yearly. Factors predisposing to this epidemic include a short incubation period, high infectivity, widespread asymptomatic carriage (at least 80% of uterine cervical infections, up to 40% of male urethral infections, and perhaps the majority of pharyngeal and rectal infections in both sexes are asymptomatic), transmissibility of infection from asymptomatic carriage sites, absence of a reliable serologic test for infection, relaxed sexual mores, and greater resistance of current strains of gonococci to antimicrobial agents.

The current upsurge in gonorrhea has rekindled interest in the immunologic pathogenesis of this disease since it is now apparent that bactericidal antibiotics have not been the key to control.

The first step in the production of a gonococcal infection is attachment of the microorganism to a susceptible mucosal surface. Adherence appears to be mediated by pili (fimbriae), hairlike proteinaceous appendages found on virulent gonococci. Pili cannot be the only determinant of local invasiveness, however, because many nonpathogenic Neisseria species (such as *N flavescens*) are also piliated. Local immune response to the gonococcus is manifested by the prompt appearance of secretory IgA antibody in genital secretions. Unfortunately, there are no direct in vitro studies to indicate whether secretory IgA can prevent attachment of gonococci to urethral mucosal cells. Clinical observations suggest that local IgA antibody is not protective against reinfection. Once gonococci have become attached to epithelial cells, they are endocytosed. Intracellular and extracellular gonococcal multiplication results in spread to contiguous cells and to the subepithelial tissues.

It is widely accepted that either the pili of gonococci or another surface component ("leukocyte association factor") subserves an antiphagocytic function. In their ability to mediate epithelial cell attachment while simultaneously retarding phagocytosis by polymorphonuclear leukocytes, pili appear to behave similarly to the M protein of streptococci. If gonococci truly possess antiphagocytic surface factors, then the question arises why gonococci in urethral exudates generally appear to be intracellular. One possible explanation is "surface phagocytosis," the process whereby phagocytosis is enhanced by crowding together of microorganisms and phagocytic leukocytes, bypassing the need for opsonic antibody.

Except for its opsonic capacity, serum antibody against *N gonorrhoeae* is probably not directly protective against infection. This was not always considered to be the case; gonococci have been shown to be susceptible to antibody- and complement-mediated bacteriolysis. However, recent studies suggest that antibody and complement susceptibility is an attribute of gonococci passaged in vitro. Freshly isolated gonococci possess a surface factor which renders them resistant to lysis. Resistance can be reconferred upon passaged strains by culturing them on agar containing an extract of human prostate. It is uncertain whether prostatic extract provides an additional virulence factor that is lost on subculture or merely allows synthesis of a hardier cell wall by virtue of its nutritional value.

Clinical Features

A. Local Infection: The particular mucous membranes which become infected depend upon the sexual proclivities of the patient. Gonococcal urethritis in the male is generally characterized by dysuria and a purulent penile discharge. If untreated, infection may progress posteriorly, resulting in prostatitis, seminal vesiculitis, and epididymitis. These complications are rare today because medical attention is generally sought as soon as symptoms appear. Infection of the uterine cervix is generally asymptomatic; sometimes there is a purulent vaginal discharge. Infections of Bartholin's and Skene's glands may occur. The adult vagina is resistant to infection, but prepubertal girls, lacking the protective effect of estrogen on the vaginal mucosa, may suffer from severe gonococcal vaginitis. Oropharyngeal and rectal infections are probably asymptomatic in most patients, but frank pharyngitis and purulent proctitis have been reported. Gonococcal conjunctivitis (ophthalmia neonatorum) is usually a disease of newborns acquired during passage through an infected birth canal. Other mucosal surfaces (pharynx, rectum) may be similarly infected in newborns. Severe conjunctivitis may occur in sexually active patients who inadvertently transfer infected secretions to their eyes with their fingers.

B. Systemic Infection: In approximately 1% of patients, gonococci gain access to the bloodstream and produce the syndrome of disseminated gonococcal infection. Disseminated gonococcal infection is characterized by suppurative arthritis (often monoarticular), tenosynovitis, and metastatic skin lesions reflecting a frank infective vasculitis. Disseminated gonococcal infection may arise from asymptomatic or symptomatic loci of mucosal infection. Cultures of blood and joint fluid are positive in under 25% of cases; accurate diagnosis rests upon clinical acumen and recovery of gonococci from infected mucosal surfaces.

Gonococcal bloodstream invasion sometimes leads to endocarditis or meningitis; direct peritoneal extension of infection from the cervix and uterine tubes may result in gonococcal perihepatitis (Fitz-Hugh and Curtis syndrome).

Immunologic Diagnosis

There currently is no reliable serologic test for gonorrhea. Attempts to develop such tests have been frustrated by the use of impure antigens and by unreproducible tests based on detection of small differences in antibody levels between patients and controls. The gonococcal complement fixation test, used extensively in the past, lacks apparent specificity and sensitivity. The recent development of technics for detecting antibody to gonococcal pili holds promise that a means may be available for the detection of asymptomatic carriers, especially women, in whom antibody titers tend to be relatively high.

Differential Diagnosis

Gonococcal urethritis is easily diagnosed in males by the presence of typical gonococci in gram-stained smears of urethral exudate. Nongonococcal urethritis (or nonspecific urethritis) also produces purulent urethral discharge but there is no stainable or easily cultivable etiologic agent. About half of these infections may be due to *Chlamydia trachomatis* subtypes. "Gonococcal" salpingitis (pelvic inflammatory disease) is probably more often due to a mixed anaerobic infection with genital flora than to gonococci per se. It is crucial to bear in mind the great frequency with which gonococcal infection is asymptomatic.

Prevention

Since there is currently no evidence that specific immunity occurs as a result of gonococcal infection, the basis for the development of a gonococcal vaccine is lacking. Infection may be prevented in gonococcal contacts by treatment with full therapeutic doses of probenecid and penicillin.

Treatment

The treatment of choice for both men and women with genital gonorrhea is 1 g of probenecid orally followed in 30 minutes by aqueous procaine penicillin G, 2.4 million units intramuscularly into each hip. Treatment of patients with penicillin allergy and nongenital or hematogenous infection is beyond the scope of this discussion, and other sources should be consulted.

Complications & Prognosis

Infective complications of gonorrhea are beyond the scope of this discussion. Immunity to gonococcal infection is apparently not sustained; sexually active patients may be repeatedly infected. An alternative possibility is that subsequent infections reflect acquisition of different gonococcal serotypes. There is at present no reliable means for serotyping gonococci, and the number of immunologically discernible subtypes of this microorganism is unknown.

5. *STREPTOCOCCUS PYOGENES* INFECTION

The genus Streptococcus comprises a heterogeneous group of microorganisms with a broad range of animal hosts. They can be divided into a number of immunologically specific groups (A through O) based upon the presence of group-specific carbohydrate (C) antigens in their cell walls. The group-specific carbohydrate in group A streptococci is N-acetylglucosamine. Group A streptococci (with *S pyogenes* as the prototype species) are the most common streptococcal pathogens of man, accounting for more (and more clinically distinct) disease than group B or group D (enterococcal) strains, which are also common human pathogens. Group A strains produce complete (beta) hemolysis when streaked on sheep blood agar. Group B and D strains are usually nonhemolytic but sometimes produce beta or alpha (incomplete or "green") hemolysis. Careless usage has resulted in substitution of the phrase hemolytic streptococci for group A streptococci. The fallacy should be obvious.

Group A streptococci can be divided into 60 or more immunologic types based upon the presence of specific M proteins in the cell wall. Immunity to group A streptococci is type-specific. Two other protein antigens (T and R) are not directly related to virulence.

Group A streptococci possess 2 antiphagocytic surface components: *hyaluronic acid* (which is not immunogenic, presumably because of its close structural relationship to the ground substance of human connective tissue) and *M protein.* The M protein is a readily accessible surface antigen, not blocked by the hyaluronic acid envelope of encapsulated strains, and is displayed as surface fimbriae. In addition to its antiphagocytic properties, M protein augments the attachment of streptococci to host epithelial cells.

Group A streptococci may produce a diversity of clinical syndromes ranging from invasive infection (pharyngitis, lymphangitis-lymphadenitis, erysipelas, pneumonia), to immune complex disease (poststreptococcal glomerulonephritis), to "hypersensitivity disease" (acute rheumatic fever), to toxin production (scarlet fever). Notwithstanding the rich immunogenic potential of this microorganism, it is possible that none of the diverse sequelae of streptococcal infection would be encountered if prompt phagocytosis and killing were to take place. Attempts to stimulate opsonic antibody with purified M protein vaccines have produced severe hypersensitivity reactions at the inoculation sites. A fear related to the use of these vaccines is that rheumatic fever might be precipitated.

6. *STAPHYLOCOCCUS AUREUS* INFECTION

S aureus is a gram-positive coccal microorganism that grows in grapelike clusters. Our present knowledge of the immunopathology of this common microorganism is sufficiently incomplete that it can be classified as a minor infectious disease for immunologic purposes.

There is probably no other human pathogen that produces as many candidate virulence factors ("aggressins") as *S aureus.* Among the best characterized are alpha toxin (one of 4 known hemolysins), coagulase, lipase, leukocidin, enterotoxin, exfoliatin, and protein A. Coagulase production and virulence are so closely (although probably coincidentally) linked that coagulase positivity is often considered to be synonymous with staphylococcal virulence. Enterotoxin and exfoliatin will be considered elsewhere in this chapter. Protein A has the unique ability to bind to the Fc portion of opsonic IgG, thus acting, in essence, as an antiphagocytic surface factor. Although some special staphylococcal strains will demonstrate capsule formation under highly defined in vitro conditions, staphylococci are not generally considered to possess antiphagocytic capsules.

Staphylococcal infection is highly destructive and produces prominent abscess formation. Most staphylococci appear to be killed once they are ingested by PMNs, although a few may survive under experimental conditions. Whether escape from PMN bactericidal activity is an important virulence mechanism in staphylococcal disease is presently uncertain. There is evidence that cell-mediated immunity may play a role in host defense against staphylococcal infection, although granuloma formation is distinctly unusual in this disease.

7. *KLEBSIELLA PNEUMONIAE* INFECTION

K pneumoniae is an encapsulated gram-negative rod found in the respiratory tracts and feces of 5–10% of healthy subjects and a higher percentage of hospitalized patients regardless of their underlying illness. *K pneumoniae* is an unusual cause of primary pneumonia except in debilitated patients, particularly alcoholics. It is a common nosocomial invader in hospitalized patients.

The invasive properties of *K pneumoniae* depend upon the antiphagocytic properties of its capsule; unencapsulated (rough) strains are avirulent. Seventy-seven capsular (K) polysaccharide antigens of *K pneumoniae* have been identified. Unlike the situation with *S pneumoniae* and *H influenzae,* all capsular types appear to be equally virulent. Type-specific antisera are useful in epidemiologic studies of nosocomial infection; the quellung phenomenon is readily demonstrable in vitro.

Presumably, Klebsiella species are killed when ingested by phagocytic cells. However, the propensity of this microorganism to produce tissue destruction and abscess formation (unlike, for example, *S pneumoniae*), its occurrence in debilitated patients, and the relatively limited number of antimicrobial agents to which it is susceptible (cephalosporins; many aminoglycosides) combine to result in a poor prognosis.

8. *PSEUDOMONAS AERUGINOSA* INFECTION

Ps aeruginosa is a gram-negative rod found widespread in nature (soil, water) and in the feces of less than 10% of normal persons. Infection with *Ps aeruginosa* is uncommon in otherwise healthy individuals. However, patients with granulocytopenia (often induced by cytotoxic therapy) and severe burns may be unusually prone to progressive infection with this microorganism. Furthermore, respiratory colonization of cystic fibrosis patients is extremely common. In the latter circumstance, *Ps aeruginosa* takes on mucoid characteristics owing to the development of encapsulation. Encapsulated *Ps aeruginosa* strains are rarely encountered in patients without cystic fibrosis.

Most clinical strains of *Ps aeruginosa* are highly resistant to the bactericidal activity of serum; the principal role of antibodies appears to be opsonization. In nonencapsulated strains, the opsonins are directed toward heat-stable lipopolysaccharide. Once ingested by phagocytes, *Ps aeruginosa* appears to be killed. Granulocytopenic patients with *Ps aeruginosa* may not respond to even synergistic combinations of specific, bactericidal antimicrobial agents. Granulocyte transfusions are often the critical determinant in recovery of infected leukopenic patients.

9. PLAGUE

Yersinia (Pasteurella) pestis is a gram-negative nonmotile coccobacillus with a tendency to stain in a bipolar (safety pin) fashion. Freshly isolated strains contain a capsular envelope antigen (fraction 1; Fl) and the VW antigen system consisting of a protein (V) and a lipoprotein (W). These antigens all act to retard phagocytosis.

Plague is a natural disease of rodents and is transmitted by the bites of fleas. In the fleas, bacilli proliferate in the intestinal tract and produce obstruction. When the fleas next bite, they regurgitate bacilli and aspirated blood into the new host. If rodents are not available as hosts, man may become involved by default. Bacilli enter dermal lymphatics and produce severe regional lymphadenitis (buboes; *bubonic* plague). Infection may disseminate hematogenously. When metastatic pneumonia occurs, infection may be spread by airborne droplets (*pneumonic* plague). This is a particularly contagious and malignant form of infection.

Bacilli contained in the gut of the flea are neither encapsulated nor endowed with VW antigen. Consequently, they are promptly ingested and destroyed by polymorphonuclear leukocytes. When taken up by mononuclear phagocytes, however, they survive, multiply, and emerge containing both Fl and VW antigens. Apparently the low body temperature of fleas (25 C) masks development of the virulence factors. The ability to survive and multiply in mononuclear phagocytes is a key factor in virulence of *Y pestis.* Nevertheless, specific antibodies do promote phagocytosis and killing by PMNs. Effective plague vaccines must include both antiphagocytic antigens (Fl and VW).

10. ANTHRAX

Bacillus anthracis is a large gram-positive, spore-forming microorganism possessing an antiphagocytic capsule composed of a gamma polypeptide of D-glutamic acid. Although important in the initiation of infection, evasion of phagocytosis is a less critical pathogenetic factor than toxin production once disease becomes established. Hence, virulence of the anthrax bacillus is due to both capsule formation and toxin production. Anticapsular antibody alone is not sufficient to prevent anthrax; vaccines must stimulate antitoxin immunity as well.

Table 34–2. Diseases resulting from exotoxin production.

Bacterial Species	Occurrence in Nature	Disease Produced	Tissue Invasion	Toxin and Mechanisms of Action	Role of Antibody and Vaccines	Comments
Vibrio cholerae (gram-negative bacillus)	Human cases and carriers	Cholera	No	Enterotoxin (choleragen), a chromosomal (ie, intrinsic) toxin. Activates gut epithelial adenylate cyclase → production of cyclic AMP → hypersecretion of chloride, HCO_3^-, and water → severe diarrhea.	Presently unclear. Vaccines: (1) Parenteral killed bacterial vaccine: limited protection. (2) Parenteral toxoid: very limited protection. (3) Living attenuated oral vaccine still a research goal; should stimulate secretory IgA to block *V cholerae* attachment to bowel as well as stimulate local antitoxic activity in gut.	Noncholera vibrios (nonagglutinating [NAG] vibrios) have also been described which secrete enterotoxin and produce a similar clinical syndrome.
Escherichia coli (gram-negative bacillus)	Human cases and carriers; animals	Diarrhea (enterotoxigenic *E coli* diarrhea)	No	Enterotoxin (transmitted by an extrachromosomal plasmid). Mechanism of action similar to that of cholera toxin. Since toxin production is plasmid-related, production of enterotoxin is not unique to specific *E coli* serotypes.	Presently unclear. No available vaccines.	Must be differentiated from invasive *E coli* syndrome which reflects actual epithelial invasion by *E coli* (enteropathogenic *E coli*).
Shigella dysenteriae type I (Shiga's bacillus) (gram-negative bacillus)	Human cases and carriers	Dysentery	Epithelial cells of gastrointestinal tract; rarely beyond submucosa	Neurotoxin (producing motor ataxia in rabbits and meningismus in humans). May be identical to enterotoxin (produces diarrhea). Common mechanism of action seems to be capillary endothelial cell damage.	Presently unclear. No available vaccines.	Epithelial cell invasion may be more important than toxin production.
Clostridium botulinum (gram-positive sporulating bacillus)	Soil	Botulism	No	Neurotoxin (released by cellular autolysis, ie, an intracellular toxin). Eight type-specific toxins known (A, B, C_1, C_2, D, E, F, G); only A, B, E, and F common in humans. Spores germinate in foods → ingestion of preformed toxin. Spores may rarely germinate in wounds. Toxin binds at neuromuscular junction; blocks presynaptic release of acetylcholine, resulting in impaired breathing and swallowing, diplopia, and flaccid paralysis.	No immunity conferred by infection; enough botulinus toxin to immunize is enough to kill. Active immunization: toxoid. Passive immunization: antitoxin (polyvalent A, B, E; equine); critical in treatment of botulism.	Botulism is less an infection than an intoxication.
Clostridium tetani (gram-positive sporulating bacillus)	Soil and gastrointestinal tract of man and animals	Tetanus	No	Tetanospasmin (released by cellular autolysis, ie, an intracellular toxin). Acts pre- or postsynaptically to block inhibition mediated by internuncial neurons in the spinal cord → spasmodic muscle contractions (spastic paralysis). May also interfere with muscle relaxation.	No immunity conferred by infection. The lethal dose is insufficient to immunize. Active immunization: toxoid. Passive immunization: tetanus antitoxin (human).	Tetanolysin (a hemolysin) is also produced but plays no apparent role in neuromuscular problems.

Clostridium perfringens (gram-positive sporulating bacillus)	Soil and gastro-intestinal tract of man and animals	Gas gangrene (clostridial myonecrosis)	Minimal	Eleven soluble toxins produced that may be active in various aspects of disease (including phospholipase C, collagenase, hemolysin, proteinase, and DNase). The chief lethal component is *α* toxin (phospholipase C; lecithinase). In some cases (especially clostridial myonecrosis of the uterus), sufficient *α* toxin may be liberated to produce massive intravascular hemolysis.	Highly questionable (although polyvalent equine antitoxin is often used in gas gangrene, even in the absence of the massive hemolysis syndrome). Commercially available antisera neutralize only a small portion of the spectrum of toxins.	*Cl novyi* and *Cl septicum* may also produce gas gangrene. Mainstays of treatment are surgical excision, antibiotics, and, probably, hyperbaric oxygen.
		Clostridial entero-toxin – mediated diarrhea	No	Enterotoxin: released by sporulating microorganisms in gastrointestinal tract which lyse to → toxin → diarrhea.	Systemic vaccination in animals without effect on toxin production in gut. No information in humans.	Perhaps due to ingestion of pre-formed toxin as well.
Corynebacterium diphtheriae (gram-positive bacillus)	Human cases and carriers	Diphtheria	No	Diphtheritic toxin (produced only by corynebacteria which are themselves infected by a tox + temperate phage). Blocks protein synthesis by depleting elongation factor 2 (EF-2), an enzyme necessary for peptide chain elongation in protein synthesis. Toxin has diffuse effects but is principally manifested by cardiotoxicity (cardiomyopathy) and neurotoxicity (motor paralysis; cranial nerves generally first).	Antibody to toxin prevents toxin-related death but has no effect on epithelial cell attachment or production of pseudomembrane by *C diphtheriae*. Active immunization: toxoid. Passive immunization: equine antitoxin; critical in management of suspected diphtheria.	Can measure presence of circulating antitoxin by intradermal injection of diphtheria toxin (Schick test). Lack of response demonstrates immunity. Possibility of nonspecific reactivity requires multiple controls.
Streptococcus pyogenes (gram-positive coccus)	Human cases and carriers	Scarlet fever	Yes	Erythrogenic toxin (produced by *S pyogenes* strains infected by tox + temperate phage). Any *S pyogenes* can be converted to toxigenicity. Mechanism of action may be direct skin toxicity or hypersensitivity reaction.	Antibody can prevent rash but has no effect on streptococcal infection.	An incidental complication of *S pyogenes* infection; clinically dramatic, but with no real pathogenic significance. Historically an important illness; not common in USA today. Can measure presence of circulating antitoxin by intradermal injection of erythrogenic toxin (Dick test). Lack of response demonstrates immunity. Can also use a skin test to establish diagnosis (Schultz-Charlton reaction). Here a scarlet fever rash is blanched by locally injected serum from a convalescent patient. Large numbers of other toxins are also produced by *S pyogenes* but without clear clinical effect.

Table 34–2 (cont'd). Diseases resulting from exotoxin production.

Bacterial Species	Occurrence in Nature	Disease Produced	Tissue Invasion	Toxin and Mechanisms of Action	Role of Antibody and Vaccines	Comments
Staphylococcus aureus (gram-positive coccus)	Human cases and carriers	Scalded skin syndrome (Ritter's disease; toxic epidermal necrolysis; generalized exfoliative dermatitis; pemphigus neonatorum)	No	Exfoliatin (often due to phage group 2 *S aureus*) produces disruption of desmosomes between granular cells of epidermis → epidermal cleavage plane. Intense erythema about mouth and nose spreads to neck, trunk, and extremities. Followed by loosening of epidermis, bulla formation, and peeling. Bullous impetigo and scarlatiniform rash (erythema without exfoliation) may be variants. More common in young children. Often no clear site of infection apparent.	Unclear. Immunization with exfoliatin will prevent its effects in mice.	Exfoliatin-positive strains appear unique in their ability to → subcutaneous infection in mice without the intervention of a foreign body. Since experimental skin infection with *S aureus* is ordinarily difficult to establish using bacteria alone, exfoliatin may be an important virulence factor.
		Staphylococcal food poisoning	No	Preformed enterotoxin (6 types) → vomiting and diarrhea (toxin absorbed → stimulation of vomiting center).	Unclear.	Ingestion of preformed toxin.

INFECTIONS IN WHICH ANTIBODY MAY BE DECISIVE IN PREVENTION OR IN RECOVERY THROUGH A MECHANISM OTHER THAN OPSONIZATION

1. DISEASES RESULTING FROM EXOTOXIN PRODUCTION
(Table 34–2)

Major Immunologic Features

- Microorganisms are generally poorly invasive.
- Important disease manifestations are based predominantly upon toxin-related effects.
- Antitoxins may prevent the disease or ameliorate its course.

General Considerations

The diffusible toxins produced by certain gram-positive and gram-negative microorganisms are referred to as *exotoxins* because they are by-products of living bacteria and are not intrinsic to the bacterial cell walls (as are *endotoxins*). Exotoxins may be actively excreted by growing microorganisms in which no appreciable autolysis has occurred, or they may be released by microbial autolysis (intracellular toxins). All characterized exotoxins are proteins and thus are capable of stimulating antibody formation. In many of the diseases to be discussed, active immunization against exotoxins is carried out by preparing *toxoids* through the introduction of substituent groups such as formaldehyde or iodine. Toxoids are antigenic but essentially nontoxic.

Many of the diseases in Table 34–2 rely solely upon toxin production for their clinical manifestations (eg, tetanus). In others, production of toxin is coincidental and not essential to disease production (eg, erythrogenic toxin elaborated by *Streptococcus pyogenes*). In some diseases (eg, anthrax, pertussis, plague, *Ps aeruginosa* infection), exotoxins are suspected of playing important pathogenetic roles but data are not sufficient to permit their inclusion in the table. Many fungi produce poisonous substances (mycotoxins). For example, aflatoxin from *Aspergillus flavus* may be important in hepatic neoplasia and may also impair antibody formation, complement activation, phagocytosis, and blastogenesis under diverse experimental circumstances. A discussion of mycotoxins is beyond the scope of this chapter.

2. INFECTIONS IN WHICH EPITHELIAL CELL ATTACHMENT IS THE CRITICAL FIRST STEP IN ESTABLISHMENT OF INFECTION

Secretory IgA antibody may be critical in preventing the attachment to epithelial cells of potential pathogens (*Vibrio cholerae,* Shigella species, Salmonella species, etc). The physiologic role of secretory antibody is discussed elsewhere in this book (see Chapter 16).

3. COMPLEMENT-MEDIATED BACTERIOLYSIS

Many gram-negative microorganisms are lysed by complement in the presence of specific antibody. As already noted, measurement of such bactericidal antibody in meningococcal infections is an important means for assessing immunity to infection. There is serious question whether this mechanism is ever operative under clinical conditions since microorganisms passaged in vitro are often used in these tests. Such microorganisms may be more susceptible to membrane damage than microorganisms encountered in vivo, during actual infections. Further, patients with granulocytopenia do not appear to be protected from sepsis with antibody- and complement-susceptible gram-negative rods even when their humoral immune mechanisms are apparently intact.

Antibody- and complement-mediated bacteriolysis may be augmented by lysozyme. The practical significance of this interaction remains uncertain.

4. VIRAL NEUTRALIZATION

As noted elsewhere, direct inhibition of viral infectivity by interaction of antibody with viral surface antigens is a critically important host defense mechanism. Antibody prevents attachment and host cell penetration by susceptible viruses. Not all viruses are susceptible to the effects of antibody.

INFECTIONS IN WHICH HUMORAL & CELLULAR IMMUNITY COLLABORATE IN HOST DEFENSE

Major Immunologic Features

- An etiologically heterogeneous group.
- Infecting microorganisms may be extracellular or facultatively intracellular pathogens.
- The dominant protective immune mechanism varies with each pathogen.

General Considerations

The microorganisms in this group are extremely diverse. The justification for grouping them together at all is partially negative; they do not fit easily into the other groups. None of these microorganisms is considered to be either strictly extracellular (and under the control of opsonins and PMNs) or strictly intracellular (and under the sole control of lymphocytes and macrophages). Some of them are characterized by an apparent immunologic paradox: *Cryptococcus neoformans* possesses an antiphagocytic capsule, and yet PMNs do not appear to be the critical host defense; *Treponema pallidum* appears to function as an extracellular pathogen, and yet cell-mediated immunity is unquestionably important in its control.

1. CRYPTOCOCCOSIS

Cryptococcus neoformans is a yeastlike fungus which reproduces by budding; abortive pseudomycelia are occasionally formed. Parent and daughter cells are surrounded by a thick polysaccharide capsule, and a characteristic "halo" is produced by the capsule when India ink is added to an infected body fluid. *C neoformans* can be distinguished biochemically, metabolically, biologically, and immunologically from other cryptococcal species. Unlike its nonpathogenic relatives, *C neoformans* can grow at both 20 and 37 C; it is the only member of the genus which can cause meningitis and hydrocephalus in the mouse.

Cryptococci occur widely in nature. The most frequent source of human infection may be avian droppings, especially from pigeons and starlings. The birds are not ill, but their feces contain extremely high numbers of cryptococci. Pigeon breeders and handlers are usually skin test-positive to extracts of *C neoformans.*

Man is thought to acquire cryptococcosis from inhalation of fungi. Man-to-man transmission has not been documented. It is likely that many are exposed to *C neoformans,* but few develop the disease. There are an estimated 300 new cases of symptomatic cryptococcosis per year in the USA.

Among the major systemic mycoses, the interaction between the host and *C neoformans* is perhaps the least well understood. One problem in dissecting the immune response has been the absence of potent and specific antigens to use as immunologic tools. Poor antigenicity of *C neoformans* may also be a practical problem for the host during natural infection.

Once established in the tissues, cryptococci evoke 2 principal histopathologic patterns. In the first, fungi proliferate largely unchecked, forming large gelatinous masses which reflect the presence of abundant capsular polysaccharide surrounding clumps of yeasts. There is little tissue reaction, and no necrosis occurs. In the second, there is granuloma formation with macrophages, lymphocytes, and plasma cells. Cryptococci may be found in centrally located giant cells. Again, there is no necrosis. Reactive lymphadenopathy is not common in lymph nodes draining cryptococcal pulmonary lesions. Healing is not associated with the intense scarring and calcification which characterize histoplasmosis, tuberculosis, and other infections evoking an intense delayed hypersensitivity reaction (ie, there is no "bystander" tissue injury).

The most important pathogenic cryptococcal constituent identified thus far is capsular polysaccharide. Capsular polysaccharide contains substantial amounts of hexose and pentose, but its exact composition is not yet defined. There are 4 serotypes of *C neoformans;* all are equally virulent. Capsular polysaccharide is poorly immunogenic, a problem which is reflected in the difficulties in immunizing laboratory animals and the low antibody titers in patients with cryptococcosis.

Capsular polysaccharide subserves an antiphagocytic function. Nonencapsulated cryptococcal mutant strains which are easily phagocytosed are avirulent for mice; the encapsulated parent strains are highly lethal. Addition of capsular polysaccharide to in vitro systems impairs phagocytosis by PMNs. In vivo inoculation of capsular polysaccharide shortens survival of mice when they are later challenged with encapsulated cryptococci.

Both antibody and complement appear to be important in potentiating phagocytosis of cryptococci. Guinea pigs which are decomplemented in vivo have enhanced susceptibility to cryptococcosis. Complement activation appears to follow the alternative pathway.

It has been postulated that antibody- and complement-dependent opsonization may be the crucial factor in limiting cryptococcal infection in most tissues and that the prominence of central nervous system infection may represent an "escape" of fungi to a milieu in which complement components penetrate in low titer or not at all. However, this is speculative and deemphasizes the unquestionably important role of cell-mediated immune mechanisms in cryptococcosis. Without invoking an important role for lymphocytes and macrophages, it would be difficult to explain (1) the virtual absence of PMNs from nonneurologic lesions; (2) the classical granulomatous response which is present in many tissues; (3) the apparent lack of undue susceptibility of hypogammaglobulinemic patients to cryptococcosis; and (4) the susceptibility to cryptococcosis of patients with Hodgkin's disease.

There is now evidence that certain polysaccharide- or protein-containing cryptococcal extracts prepared from culture filtrates or from the "cell sap" of disrupted cryptococci are able to elicit cell-mediated immune responses. The skin test response in sensitized humans and nonprimates is of the delayed type. Lymphocyte activation and MIF have been demonstrated in lymphocyte cultures from healthy subjects exposed to *C neoformans.* These responses appear to be defective in patients with active and even resolved cryptococcosis. Immunization of mice with cryptococcal extracts elicits a delayed cutaneous hypersensitivity response that correlates with increased protection on challenge. Finally, activated macrophages have increased killing capacities against *C neoformans* and may be able to do so by some mechanism other than phagocytosis.

From these bits of information, we are gradually

gaining insight into the pathogenesis of cryptococcosis. Development of disease in exposed persons depends on many factors, some of which are still unrecognized. Resolution of the relative importance of each component awaits further studies.

Clinical Features

The clinical manifestations of cryptococcosis depend largely upon the state of host immune defenses. The first encounter between man and fungus is probably in the lung. In persons with intact immune defenses, cryptococci may reside saprophytically in the upper respiratory tract; approximately half of subjects with respiratory isolates of *C neoformans* show absolutely no evidence of disease. About 10% of clinical cryptococcosis is represented by obvious pulmonary infection, especially pulmonary nodules and infiltrates. In patients with sufficient immunity to develop symptomatic pulmonary cryptococcosis, clinically apparent dissemination to other sites is not common. However, pulmonary surgery may be followed by postoperative cryptococcal meningitis in up to 10% of cases.

Spontaneous extrapulmonary dissemination accounts for 90% of all cases of cryptococcosis and is characteristically (although not exclusively) seen in patients with underlying immune deficiency. Half of these patients either have primary lymphoreticular disease or are receiving immunosuppressive medications for other disorders. Clinical manifestations are seldom acute. Asymptomatic hematogenous dissemination may result in metastatic foci of infection in the skin, mucous membranes, bones, adrenals, prostate, kidney, spleen, lymph nodes, liver, and other viscera. However, by far the most common site of disease is the central nervous system. Almost all patients with meningeal invasion develop headache, which may be indolent and intermittent. Irritability and subtle changes in personality may occur. About one-third of patients have papilledema, and one-fifth have cranial nerve involvement. This is reflected in blurred vision, diplopia, facial numbness or weakness, and hearing loss. Long tract signs are less frequent.

Without treatment, cryptococcal meningitis runs an irregular course of months to years, ending with seizures, hydrocephalus, dementia, coma, and death.

Immunologic Diagnosis

The diagnosis of cryptococcosis generally depends upon the demonstration of microorganisms in cerebrospinal fluid by India ink staining, together with their isolation on appropriate artificial media. Animal inoculation studies may be useful but are seldom practical. Attempts to establish a diagnosis of cryptococcosis on the basis of elevated antibody titers have been frustrated by the absence of reliable tests, reflecting perhaps the poor antigenicity of *C neoformans* and the fact that many infected patients have underlying immune disorders that might compromise antibody synthesis.

Unfortunately, some patients with cryptococcal meningitis have negative India ink preparations of the spinal fluid, negative cultures, and an absence of demonstrable antibody. In many of these patients, a diagnosis can be made using a recently developed test for free cryptococcal polysaccharide antigen. The test uses high-titer rabbit anticryptococcal antibody adsorbed onto latex beads. In the presence of even minute amounts of cryptococcal antigen, a suspension of the latex beads agglutinates. Nonspecific reactions which formerly occurred in persons with rheumatoid factors have been eliminated, and the test is pathognomonic in any detectable titer in serum or cerebrospinal fluid. In addition to its diagnostic value, the latex cryptococcal agglutination test has prognostic value. Falling titers are associated with improvement, and many physicians use an end-titer of 1:4 or less to terminate therapy.

Tests for cell-mediated immunity are presently of little help, as many patients are "anergic" to skin test antigens during active disease. Some convert skin tests as they improve, but others do not.

Differential Diagnosis

The clinical constellation of prolonged headache, low-grade fever, and impaired mentation is also seen in meningitis due to tuberculosis, coccidioidomycosis, histoplasmosis, and in patients with meningeal neoplasm. Cerebrospinal fluid findings of lymphocytosis, elevated protein, and depressed glucose may be seen in any of these disorders.

Confirmation of the diagnosis of cryptococcosis rests upon microbial or immunologic demonstration of a specific pathogen.

Prevention

There is no commercially available cryptococcal vaccine. Experimental models have failed to show a benefit from passive immunization with "immune" serum. On the other hand, prior infection of mice with low numbers of cryptococci appears to confer immunity against later challenge with high numbers of the same strain. Immunization of mice with cryptococcal extracts or intact cells in complete Freund's adjuvant also protects mice. However, use of live vaccines would be hazardous to immunosuppressed humans, and complete Freund's adjuvant cannot be used in man.

Treatment

The mainstay of treatment is amphotericin B, given over a long course. Flucytosine (5-fluorocytosine) may be of adjunctive use in some cases.

A few patients who have failed to respond to chemotherapy have been treated with transfer factor. Some have improved immunologically and clinically while others have not. The value of transfer factor in this situation remains controversial at present.

Complications & Prognosis

Complications of cryptococcosis include obstructive hydrocephalus from cryptococcal meningitis and arachnoiditis from the intrathecal instillation of amphotericin B. Diverting ventriculoatrial or ventriculoperitoneal shunts may cause dissemination of cryptococci to extraneurologic sites.

2. SYPHILIS

Treponema pallidum is a noncultivable, motile, highly infectious spirochete which appears to function predominantly as an extracellular pathogen. It is extremely susceptible to heat and drying, so that direct transfer by intimate contact, preferably in the presence of moisture, is essential for its survival. Sexual contact is therefore an ideal mode of transmission of syphilis. Syphilis occurs naturally only in man.

Three clinically identifiable stages of syphilis are traditionally described. The first 2 (*primary* and *secondary* syphilis) both occur early in the infectious, spirochetemic stage of disease. The third stage (*tertiary* syphilis) occurs much later, following a period of prolonged latency, and reflects a tissue–damaging immunologic response to previously deposited microorganisms (bystander cell injury).

Immunity in syphilis develops as a result of a complex interaction between humoral and cellular immune factors. Evidence for the participation of humoral immunity in syphilis is as follows:

(1) A variety of nonspecific ("reaginic") and specific antibodies are regularly present in the serum of patients who have syphilis.
(2) *Treponema pallidum* immobilizing antibodies (TPIA) are regularly present in the serum of patients who have syphilis.
(3) The frequency with which TPIA are found increases as syphilis progresses to latent and tertiary infection.
(4) Partial immunity can be conferred in rabbits by passive transfer of serum from syphilis-immune animals.

Recent investigations in animal models have increasingly implicated cell-mediated immunity as the more critical element in host response to *T pallidum.* Evidence for the participation of cell-mediated immunity in syphilis is as follows:

(1) Passive transfer of syphilis immune serum is only partially protective and does not follow classical models of humoral immunity.
(2) Syphilis progresses through primary and secondary stages despite the presence of antibodies that immobilize the infecting organism.
(3) Delayed hypersensitivity to treponemal antigens is absent in primary and early secondary syphilis but develops late in secondary infection and is regularly present in latent and tertiary syphilis.
(4) Granulomatous lesions characterize tertiary syphilis.
(5) Immunization with killed microorganisms is usually unsuccessful, whereas immunization with live attenuated organisms has produced immunity.
(6) In vitro lymphocyte reactivity to treponemal and nontreponemal antigens is suppressed during primary and secondary syphilis.
(7) Infecting rabbits with *T pallidum* stimulates acquired cellular resistance to listeria; this reaction is mediated by T lymphocytes.

It is puzzling why so much time is required for patients to develop humoral and cellular immunity to syphilis. One theory holds that the mucoid envelope of *T pallidum* renders it highly resistant to phagocytosis; only after the treponemes have remained in the host for some time is the mucoid coat broken down enough for phagocytosis to occur. As a result, treponemal proliferation outstrips the rate of antigenic processing for stimulation of humoral and cellular immune mechanisms and a condition of "antigen overload" occurs with the production of secondary immunosuppression. An alternative explanation is that sensitization with treponemal antigen leads primarily to generation of antibodies that then "block" antigenic sites, thereby inhibiting an appropriate cell-mediated immune response.

These proposed immunologic mechanisms are highly speculative. At present there is not even agreement that *T pallidum* possesses an antiphagocytic surface factor.

Clinical Features

The first clinically apparent manifestation of syphilis (*primary* syphilis) is an indurated, circumscribed, relatively avascular and painless ulcer *(chancre)* at the site of treponemal inoculation. Solitary lesions may appear at more than one site. Depending upon its location (lip, pharynx; perirectal tissues, rectal mucosa; external genitalia, cervix), a primary lesion may or may not be detectable. The chancre generally appears within 5 days to 3 months (average, 2–3 weeks) following acquisition of infection. Treponemal spread to the regional lymph nodes is prompt, with resulting local adenopathy. Spirochetemia with secondary metastatic distribution of microorganisms occurs within a few days after onset of local infection, but clinically apparent secondary lesions may not be observed for 2–4 weeks. The chancre lasts 10–14 days before healing spontaneously.

The presence of metastatic infection (*secondary* syphilis) is manifested by highly infectious mucocutaneous lesions of extraordinarily diverse description. The palms and soles are characteristically involved. Other manifestations include headache, low-grade fever, diffuse lymphadenopathy, and a variety of more sporadic phenomena ranging from alopecia areata to iritis, ocular neuritis, retinitis, hepatitis, and nephrotic syndrome. Secondary syphilis is remarkable because it ordinarily produces very few manifestations of acute systemic disease despite the presence of spirochetemia and widespread metastatic lesions. As a result, the occurrence of a cutaneous eruption of hematogenous distribution in a basically asymptomatic patient is highly suggestive of infectious syphilis. The lesions of secondary syphilis ordinarily go on to apparent spontaneous resolution in the absence of treatment. However, until solid immunity develops, a matter of some 4 years, 25% of untreated syphilitic patients may be susceptible to repeated episodes of spirochetemia and metastatic infection.

Following the resolution of secondary syphilis, the disease enters a period of *latency,* with only abnormal serologic tests to indicate the presence of infection. The term *early latent syphilis* refers to the first 4 years of latency, during which time relapses of spirochetemia may be observed. Beyond 4 years, *late latent syphilis* ensues. During the period of latency, persistent or progressive focal infection is presumably taking place, but the precise site remains unknown in the absence of specific symptoms and signs. One site of potential latency, the central nervous system, can be easily evaluated by examining the cerebrospinal fluid. Cerebrospinal fluid pleocytosis and elevated protein in the presence of a positive serologic test for syphilis are indicative of asymptomatic neurosyphilis.

Only about 15% of patients with untreated latent syphilis go on to develop symptomatic *tertiary* syphilis, but this form of the disease may be devastating (depending upon the tissues involved). Unfortunately, some patients with tertiary syphilis fail to go through clinically distinct primary and secondary phases of infection, so that the disease is never suspected.

Although any tissue in the body may be the site of a tertiary syphilitic lesion, serious or fatal syphilis in adults is virtually limited to disease of the aorta (aortitis with aneurysm formation and secondary aortic valve insufficiency), the central nervous system (tabes dorsalis, general paresis), or the eye (interstitial keratitis). Less frequently, the disease becomes apparent as localized single or multiple granulomas known as *gummas.* These lesions are typically found in skin, bones, liver, testes, or larynx. The histopathologic features of the gumma resemble those of earlier syphilitic lesions except that the vasculitis is associated with increased tissue necrosis and often frank caseation.

Immunologic Diagnosis

In its primary and secondary stages, syphilis is best diagnosed by darkfield microscopic examination of material from suspected lesions. Diagnostic serologic changes do not begin to occur until 14–21 days following acquisition of infection. Serologic tests provide important confirmatory evidence for secondary syphilis but are the only means of diagnosing latent infection. Many forms of tertiary syphilis can be suspected on clinical grounds, but serologic tests are important in confirming the diagnosis. Spirochetes are notoriously difficult to demonstrate in the late stages of syphilis.

Two main categories of serologic tests for syphilis (STS) are available: tests for reaginic antibody and tests for treponemal antibody.

A. Tests for Reaginic Antibody: (This is an unfortunate and confusing designation. There is no relationship between this antibody and IgE reaginic antibody.)

Patients with syphilis develop an antibody response to a tissue-derived substance (from beef heart) which is thought to be a component of mitochondrial membranes and has been called *cardiolipin.* Antibody to cardiolipin antigen is known as Wassermann or reaginic antibody. Numerous variations (and names) are associated with tests for this antigen. The simplest and most practical of these is the VDRL test (Venereal Disease Research Laboratory of USPHS), which employs a slide microflocculation technic and can provide qualitative and quantitative data. Positive tests are considered to be diagnostic of syphilis when there is a high or increasing titer or when the medical history is compatible with primary or secondary syphilis. The test may also be of prognostic aid in following response to therapy since the antibody titer will often fall over a 6- to 8-month period after adequate treatment.

Biologic false-positive tests. Since cardiolipin antigen is found in the mitochondrial membranes of many mammalian tissues as well as in diverse microorganisms, it is not surprising that antibody to this antigen should appear in other diseases. A positive VDRL test may be encountered, for example, in infectious mononucleosis, leprosy, hepatitis, and systemic lupus erythematosus. Although the VDRL test lacks specificity for syphilis, its great sensitivity makes it extremely useful nonetheless.

B. Tests for Treponemal Antibody: The first test employed for detecting specific antitreponemal antibody was the *Treponema pallidum* immobilization test (TPI). Although highly reliable, it proved to be too cumbersome for routine use. The major test employed today is the fluorescent *T pallidum* antibody test (FTA). If virulent *T pallidum* from an infected rabbit testicle is placed on a slide and overlaid with serum from a patient with antibody to treponemes, an antigen-antibody reaction will occur. The bound antibody can then be detected by means of a fluoresceinated antihuman γ-globulin antibody. Specificity of the test for *T pallidum* is enhanced by first absorbing the serum with nonpathogenic treponemal strains. This modification is referred to as the FTA-ABS test. (If specific anti-IgM antibody to human γ-globulin is employed, the acuteness of the infection or the occurrence of congenital syphilis can be assessed. In the latter case, IgM antibody in a newborn is necessarily of fetal origin since IgM does not cross the placenta.)

The FTA-ABS test is reactive in approximately 80% of patients with primary syphilis (versus 50% for the VDRL). Both tests are positive in virtually 100% of patients with secondary syphilis. Whereas the VDRL test shows a tendency to decline in titer with successful treatment, the FTA-ABS test may remain positive for years. The FTA-ABS test is especially useful in confirming or ruling out a diagnosis of syphilis in patients with suspected biologic false-positive reactions to the VDRL test. However, even the FTA-ABS test may be susceptible to false positives, especially in the presence of lupus erythematosus.

The interpretation of serologic data in syphilis may be extremely complex in some cases. For example, a prozone phenomenon may be encountered in secondary syphilis; serofastness may characterize late syphilis; and the VDRL test may be negative in up to one-third of patients with late latent syphilis. Specialized information on the serologic diagnosis of syphilis is beyond the scope or intent of this book.

Differential Diagnosis

Syphilis produces sufficiently diverse clinical manifestations that a discussion of its differential diagnosis should be sought in a textbook of general internal medicine. It suffices to quote the medical aphorism that "he who knows syphilis knows disease."

Prevention

Early treatment with antibiotics is the only way known to prevent the later ravages of syphilis.

Treatment

Penicillin is the drug of choice for syphilis in all its stages. Since the lesions of tertiary syphilis may be irreversible, it is crucial to identify and treat the disease before tertiary lesions begin. *T pallidum* is exquisitely sensitive to penicillin; the emphasis in treatment is upon duration of therapy rather than obtaining high peak serum levels.

Complications & Prognosis

The most frequent complication of treatment is the *Jarisch-Herxheimer reaction,* which occurs in up to half of patients with early syphilis and is manifested by fever, headache, myalgias, and exacerbation of cutaneous lesions. The intensity of a Jarisch-Herxheimer reaction reflects the intensity of local inflammation prior to treatment and is thought to result from the release of antigenic material from dying microorganisms. The reaction is of short duration (2–4 hours) and generally not harmful, although shock and death have been attributed to this reaction in tertiary forms of the disease. (The Jarisch-Herxheimer reaction has also been described in the treatment of louse-borne borreliosis, brucellosis, and typhoid fever.)

Other immunologic complications of syphilis include paroxysmal cold hemoglobinuria and nephrotic syndrome.

In patients who fail to receive any treatment for syphilis, it is estimated that one in 13 will develop cardiovascular disease; one in 25 will become crippled or incapacitated; one in 44 will develop irreversible damage to the central nervous system; and one in 200 will become blind.

3. SALMONELLOSIS

Salmonellae are gram-negative, aerobic, non-spore-forming rods that are found in the gastrointestinal tracts of man and animals. The microorganisms may survive for variable periods of time in the environment. There are 3 principal Salmonella species: *S enteritidis* (man and animals); *S choleraesuis* (animal; swine); and *S typhi* (man). More than 1800 serotypes of *S enteritidis* have been described (eg, *S enteritidis* var *typhimurium; S enteritidis* var *derby*). *S choleraesuis* and *S typhi* have only one serotype each.

Three principal syndromes result from Salmonella infection in man: (1) gastroenteritis, the most common form of salmonellosis (characteristic of *S enteritidis* serotypes); (2) enteric fever (characteristic of *S typhi* but also seen with some serotypes of *S enteritidis*); and (3) extraintestinal focal infections such as osteomyelitis, infected aortic aneurysms, etc (usually reflecting bacteremia with *S enteritidis* serotypes).

In the gastroenteritis syndrome, PMNs appear to play at least some role in the host response. PMNs can not only kill many Salmonella species in vitro but are also prominent in the intestinal lesions and stools of patients with gastroenteritis. Salmonella gastroenteritis is generally self-limited.

In enteric fever (generally due to *S typhi*), the host-parasite relationship is dramatically different. After ingestion, the microorganisms multiply asymptomatically in the gastrointestinal tract and result in a transient bacteremia, with seeding of fixed macrophages of the reticuloendothelial system. The subsequent intracellular multiplication of *S typhi* with production of a secondary sustained bacteremia constitutes an essential pathophysiologic feature of enteric fever. Invasion of the biliary system results in the reentry of microorganisms into the gastrointestinal tract in massive numbers. Involvement of lymphoid tissue in the intestinal tract, principally Peyer's patches in the terminal ileum, leads to necrosis and ulceration. Typical clinical manifestations of typhoid fever include fever, headache, apathy, cough, prostration, splenomegaly, skin rash ("rose spots"), and leukocytopenia. The course of the disease is prolonged; relapses are common.

Factors which suggest the involvement of cell-mediated immune mechanisms in salmonella enteric fever include:

(1) The occurrence of intracellular parasitism.

(2) The demonstrated ability, in animal models of systemic salmonellosis, to transfer immunity to normal animals adoptively, with lymphocytes.

(3) The absence of significant participation by PMNs in the infective process. (In fact, the presence of monocytes in a diarrheal stool is considered very suggestive of typhoid fever.)

(4) When killed salmonellae or their extracts are administered to animals in complete Freund's adjuvant, solid immunity is established which is comparable to the immunity achieved by infection with attenuated microorganisms. This is a pattern characteristic of cell-mediated immunity. Conversely, administration of killed vaccines alone will generate high-titer

antibodies and delay (but not prevent) infection. Passive immunization with immune serum is of no benefit.

(5) Delayed hypersensitivity skin tests with protein extracts of salmonellae convert to positive after animals are immunized with salmonellae in complete Freund's adjuvant.

Immunologic Diagnosis

The diagnosis of Salmonella infection should be made on the basis of recovery of the infecting microorganism in culture. An increase in titer of agglutinins against the somatic (O) and flagellar (H) antigens of *S typhi* (Widal test) usually occurs during the course of typhoid fever, reaching a peak during the third week of illness. A 4-fold titer increase is held to be significant. Unfortunately, the test is far less specific than is generally appreciated, and titers may be elevated in many hyperglobulinemic states (chronic liver disease is one example). Furthermore, progressive increases in titer occur in association with so many diseases not due to salmonella that, used alone, the test is of no value in either confirming or refuting a diagnosis of typhoid fever or other salmonella infection. The use of the agglutination reaction as a diagnostic test should always be subordinated to direct cultural demonstration of the infecting microorganism. There are no commercial tests for cell-mediated immune responses to salmonella extracts.

Prevention

Commercial typhoid vaccines consist of acetone-killed *S typhi;* they appear capable only of raising the minimum infecting dose of *S typhi* in vaccinated subjects. New vaccines made from Vi antigens (surface antigens) or from salmonella ribosomes are controversial and of uncertain clinical benefit. From the preceding discussion, it would appear that a live attenuated vaccine should offer the best chance of protection. An ideal vaccine has not yet been developed.

Treatment

Chloramphenicol and ampicillin are the major agents used to treat enteric fever or bacteremic salmonellosis; trimethoprim-sulfamethoxazole (co-trimoxazole) may be a useful alternative. Prolonged therapy is required since microorganisms are sequestered in macrophages and presumably protected from the entry of antibiotics. Salmonella gastroenteritis should not be treated with antibiotics. For details pertaining to treatment—and particularly management of the gallbladder carrier state in typhoid fever—the reader is referred to textbooks on infectious diseases.

4. CANDIDIASIS

(See also Chapters 26 and 33.)

Candida albicans is the prototype for the candida group of fungi and is responsible for the overwhelming majority of infections with this genus. It grows readily on most microbiologic media as a yeast and forms pseudomycelia in certain media. *C albicans* produces several distinctive syndromes that reflect the immune capacities of the host. Chronic mucocutaneous candidiasis (see Chapter 26) is a superficially invasive, nondisseminating infection which is associated with selective congenital defects in cell-mediated immunity.

C albicans has the capacity to penetrate intact mucosal surfaces of even the healthy host. This was clearly demonstrated years ago by a physician who, in order to prove the point, drank large numbers of viable yeasts and suffered subsequent transient symptomatic fungemia. Normally, the skin and mucosa are not exposed to high concentrations of candida, and one function of an intact host defense is to keep these numbers low. Factors considered to have a regulatory effect upon the presence of candida in external secretions include local glucose concentration and pH, the availability of iron, and the presence of other microorganisms.

It has long been known that Candida species grow well in high concentrations of glucose, and this has been considered one factor in the susceptibility of diabetic individuals to vaginal candidiasis and thrush. Candida species have specific requirements for iron and grow poorly in serum with a low iron transferrin saturation since there is competition for available iron. Addition of iron to the serum increases candidal growth; lowering the pH causes transferrin to release its iron, making it available to candida. Transferrin has a counterpart, lactoferrin, in body secretions. Unsaturated lactoferrin also competes with candida for available iron; the organism grows readily after iron is added. Broad-spectrum antibiotics do not directly affect candida but eliminate bacterial flora which have been shown to compete with candida for nutrients such as glucose. The combination of these factors is probably responsible for overgrowth of candida on mucosal surfaces, including the mouth, esophagus, lower gastrointestinal tract, vagina, and respiratory tract. With a high candida burden, it is not surprising that some of the organisms penetrate into the circulation.

Once in the bloodstream, candida are not free to proliferate unchecked. Serum anticandida "clumping factors" cause candida agglutination and may facilitate uptake of candida by phagocytic cells. PMNs, monocytes, and macrophages are capable of killing *C albicans.* Oxidative fungicidal mechanisms involving myeloperoxidase, hydrogen peroxide, and superoxide have been described in the PMN. Nonoxidative PMN mechanisms are also active against candida. Unlike the situation in chronic mucocutaneous candidiasis, the PMN is a critical cell in defense against hematogenous dissemination of candida.

The syndrome of disseminated candidiasis usually develops in patients who are "preconditioned." Preconditioning includes factors such as elevated blood glucose, corticosteroid therapy (which impairs PMN chemotaxis and contributes to high blood glucose), broad-spectrum antibiotics, and disruption of the integument with either open wounds or indwelling vascular catheters. These factors permit candida to overgrow superficially and also afford ready access to the bloodstream. Once in the bloodstream, fungi disseminate to certain preferred target tissues, including the eyes, kidneys, meninges, skin, and myocardium. Characteristic chorioretinal lesions may be of great aid in establishing the diagnosis of disseminated candidiasis. The renal tubule is an immunologically protected focus for *C albicans* replication. By budding into the renal tubules, fungi are able to transiently escape phagocytosis by PMNs, permitting them a temporal advantage in the course of infection. Mycelial mats enter the interstitial tissues and reseed the blood in a self-perpetuating mechanism. Renal papillary necrosis and obstructing bezoars of candidal mycelia in the urinary collecting system are common. Surprisingly, blood cultures for candida are often negative despite renal "saturation" with fungi. As PMN defense is overwhelmed, secondary lesions appear as maculonodules or pustules in the skin and other tissues. The final picture may be quite like that of gram-negative sepsis. The susceptibility of a patient and the speed with which candida disseminates are dramatically increased by the presence of leukocytopenia. The most fulminating forms of candidiasis occur in patients with myelotoxic cancer chemotherapy. Therefore, when candidiasis develops in these patients, antifungal chemotherapy is often supplemented with granulocyte transfusions.

Despite the dramatic clinical picture, the diagnosis of disseminated candidiasis is often quite difficult. This is caused by the difficulty in distinguishing common superficial from less common deep infection. A number of serologic tests have been devised to detect either circulating candidal antibody or candidal antigen. Desperately ill patients may not make antibody well. When they do, it may be complexed to candidal antigens and thus not be detectable as free antibody. The same problem holds for circulating antigen, which may be bound in immune complexes. Therefore, the use of agglutinin, precipitin, gel diffusion, and hemagglutination assays to document candidiasis requires further development before broad application of these tests. An alternative method has been direct nonimmunologic demonstration of candidal cell constituents by gas-liquid chromatography. Although this is promising, further work is required to be sure that the fungus constituents, which are mannose complexes, may not be mimicked by elevated blood glucose or other artifacts.

5. LISTERIOSIS

Listeria monocytogenes is a small, pleomorphic, gram-positive rod that may be confused with nonpathogenic "diphtheroids" or with beta-hemolytic streptococci. It produces sporadic infections in man, usually in the form of bacteremia and meningitis. Two features have elevated listeriosis to a position of prominence in the fields of infectious disease and immunology. First, it is clear that patients with depressed cell-mediated immunity resulting from lymphoreticular malignancy or the use of immunosuppressive drugs have an increased susceptibility to listeriosis. Second, infection with *L monocytogenes* has become an important model for studies of cell-mediated immune mechanisms in experimental animals. An important observation made with *L monocytogenes*—since confirmed with other intracellular pathogens—is that immunity can be "adoptively" transferred to noninfected animals by means of lymphocytes from animals that have recovered from listeriosis.

L monocytogenes possesses no known antiphagocytic surface factor and appears to be killed when ingested by PMNs under experimental conditions. In humans, the disease appears to be self-limited and usually does not produce prolonged granulomatous disease. Indeed, listeriosis often presents as an acute purulent meningitis with a predominance of PMNs and a low cerebrospinal fluid glucose concentration. Nevertheless, there appears to be no question that cell-mediated immune mechanisms are critically important in control of this infection. The precise factors that dictate the virulence of this pathogen are unknown.

INTRACELLULAR INFECTIONS IN WHICH LYMPHOCYTES & MACROPHAGES ARE DECISIVE IN RECOVERY & HUMORAL IMMUNE MECHANISMS PLAY NO PROTECTIVE ROLE

Major Immunologic Features

- Facultative or obligate intramacrophagic parasitism.
- Lymphocyte-macrophage interaction regulates immunity but may simultaneously mediate destruction of host tissues (bystander cell injury).
- Granulomas and giant cells characteristic of immune response.
- PMNs and opsonins inconsequential in protection.

General Considerations

Most kinds of microorganisms which fulfill these criteria are mycobacteria, of which the prototypes are *Mycobacterium tuberculosis* and *M leprae.* Although there may be considerable antibody synthesis in many mycobacterial infections (to the point of marked hypergammaglobulinemia in lepromatous leprosy), the antibody is broadly cross-reactive. Hence, its measurement is not of practical significance. Mycobacteria are easily phagocytosed in the absence of specific opsonins, perhaps because of an affinity between their lipid-rich cell walls and the lipids of macrophage cell membranes.

The second group of diseases in this section—histoplasmosis, coccidioidomycosis, brucellosis, and tularemia—are distinguished from the diseases due to mycobacteria in that measurement of antibody is useful (rather than not useful) in diagnosis, prognosis, or both.

Diseases in Which Measurement of Antibodies Is Not Useful in Diagnosis or Prognosis

1. TUBERCULOSIS

Mycobacterium tuberculosis is a facultatively intracellular, aerobic, acid-fast bacillus which is naturally pathogenic only for man. It produces no known toxins, and its virulence relates to its ability to survive and proliferate in mononuclear phagocytes. Recent studies suggest that *M tuberculosis* may evade the bactericidal activity of macrophages by preventing the fusion of enzyme-containing lysosomes with phagosomes containing the bacilli. Dead tubercle bacilli do not demonstrate this phenomenon, but its applicability in vivo remains to be demonstrated.

Several microbial constituents appear to influence the pattern of host response: (1) *Cord factor* (trehalose-6,6′-dimycolic acid), the material responsible for the in vitro serpentine cordlike growth of *M tuberculosis,* inhibits migration of leukocytes and stimulates granuloma formation. (2) High-molecular-weight *lipids* and *waxes* are probably responsible for much of the tissue reaction to this microorganism. Up to 60% of the dry weight of the cell wall of *M tuberculosis* is composed of lipid—which may account for the relative impermeability to stains, acid-fastness, unusual resistance to killing by acid and alkali, resistance to the bactericidal activity of complement, and resistance to intracellular macrophage digestion of this microorganism. (3) *Wax D* and *tuberculoproteins* may be largely responsible for the production of tuberculin hypersensitivity and skin test positivity.

The clinical manifestations of tuberculosis are clearly a function of the immune status of the host. The development of a sensitized T lymphocyte population is a double-edged sword. On the one hand, macrophages are stimulated (activated) to enhanced antimicrobial activity with limitation of mycobacterial growth. On the other hand, normal (bystander) tissues are seriously damaged by the violence of the immune (hypersensitivity) response to the infective agent. Tissue damage may reflect the discharge of hydrolytic enzymes from dying macrophages as well as direct inflammatory effects of lymphocyte mediators such as lymphotoxin, MIF, and others.

Some investigators believe that immunity and tuberculin hypersensitivity are not inextricably linked. For example, animals can be rendered tuberculin-sensitive by injecting them with wax D and tuberculoprotein; such animals are still entirely susceptible to infection with *M tuberculosis.* Conversely, certain RNA-protein complexes can be isolated from mycobacterial cells which will induce high degrees of increased resistance to tuberculous infection without inducing tuberculin hypersensitivity. Finally, animals immunized against tuberculosis with a mycobacterial-RNA protein complex do not show increased resistance to infection with other intracellular parasites. These data suggest that the general phenomenon of macrophage activation with enhanced nonspecific killing of any intracellular microorganism may not be as important as specific, lymphocyte-mediated immunity, however that specificity is mediated.

Clinical Features

Tuberculosis is predominantly a pulmonary disease which is transmitted by aerosol. Hematogenous dissemination may allow secondary infection to develop in virtually any organ system. Major sections of standard textbooks are devoted to the clinical features of this fascinating disease. This discussion will be limited to the immunologic perspective.

Pulmonary tuberculosis in the nonimmune patient is characterized initially by relatively unrestricted bacillary multiplication, with the development of infiltrative disease of the lower lobes or lower segments of the upper lobes. The inflammatory response is "exudative," being composed mainly of PMNs and monocytes. Tissue destruction and cavitation are not seen, and there may be remarkably few symptoms of infection, particularly in children. Bacilli spread via the lymphatics to regional lymph nodes and often reach the bloodstream. Infection is well tolerated for several weeks, during which time active immunity develops with resultant enhanced macrophage antimicrobial activity, curtailment of bacillary multiplication, resolution of the pneumonic process, and healing of extrapulmonary lesions. Simultaneously, a positive tuberculin skin test develops, reflecting the presence of specifically sensitized T lymphocytes. A hallmark of healed primary pulmonary tuberculosis is the *Ghon complex,* which generally consists of a calcified node in the lung parenchyma and enlarged, often calcified hilar nodes. It is crucial to realize that virulent tubercle bacilli may persist for years, or even a lifetime, in such "healed" lesions. In some cases primary tuberculosis does not heal but goes on to produce cavitation (especially in adults). Patients may also develop fulminating disseminated (miliary) tuberculosis, typically associated with meningitis.

The pattern of infection in the immune (tuberculin skin test-positive) patient results in a totally distinct disease process in which there is extensive tissue destruction. *Postprimary* or *reinfection tuberculosis* may occur as a result of exogenous reinfection but more often reflects a recrudescence of old infection *(endogenous reinfection)* in response to intercurrent debilitating illness, advanced age, or immunosuppression. Lesions are located typically in apical or subapical pulmonary segments. Regional lymph node involvement is not conspicuous; disease is far more localized. Lesions are more likely to excavate and spread by bronchogenic dissemination within the lung rather than by lymphohematogenous spread beyond the lung. The inflammatory response is characterized by granuloma formation with giant cells and *caseation necrosis* (in which the necrotic tissue remains semisolid, with the consistency of cheese). Tissue destruction is profound; pulmonary fibrosis is common, and calcification may occur.

Reinfection tuberculosis may occur at any of the sites of original hematogenous dissemination resulting from primary tuberculosis. Renal, meningeal, genitourinary, and skeletal tuberculosis are beyond the scope of this discussion.

Immunologic Diagnosis

The diagnosis of tuberculosis is established by isolating and identifying the infective etiologic agent on bacteriologic media and not by immunologic means.

Tuberculin skin test. (See Chapter 25.) The tuberculin skin test provides no diagnostic information relative to a given acute illness unless it can be established that the skin test has converted from negative to positive in temporal relation to that illness. Otherwise, a positive skin test indicates only that the patient has experienced tuberculosis or a closely related mycobacterial infection sometime in the past and that sufficient tuberculoprotein to maintain skin test reactivity remains sequestered in the body. A positive tuberculin skin test indicates the presence of specifically sensitized T lymphocytes. A strongly positive skin test is thought to represent greater liability to active infection since a larger mass of latent tuberculous disease would theoretically have to be present to maintain strong tuberculin hypersensitivity.

There are 2 principal tuberculin skin test preparations: *old tuberculin* (OT) and *purified protein derivative* (PPD). The former is prepared from a crude culture filtrate of *M tuberculosis,* whereas PPD is prepared by ammonium sulfate precipitation of culture filtrate. PPD is purer, easier to standardize, gives fewer nonspecific reactions, and is in wide use today. Irregular skin test responses resulting from adherence of PPD to the walls of syringes have been avoided by addition of stabilizers such as polysorbate 80 (Tween 80) to PPD preparations. Both OT and PPD are standardized in terms of their biologic reactivity as "tuberculin units" (TU). One TU is the activity contained in a specific weight of Seibert's PPD lot No. 49608 in a specified buffer (PPD-S). First strength tuberculin has 1 TU, intermediate strength 5 TU, and second strength 250 TU of activity.

Tuberculin may be administered intradermally (0.1 ml; Mantoux test); by patch test (gauze taped to skin; Vollmer test); or by multiple punctures (tuberculin dried on the points of several small tines [tine test]). The Mantoux procedure is the most reliable and reproducible. First strength tuberculin is reserved for use in the occasional patient suspected of being highly sensitive to tuberculin. Presumably its use might prevent an overly violent skin test response. Second strength tuberculin is frequently cross-reactive with mycobacteria other than *M tuberculosis* (atypical mycobacteria; see below) and thus lacks specificity. Intermediate strength tuberculin is the material used for most skin testing procedures. A positive response consists of 10 mm or more of erythema and induration and should be read between 48 and 72 hours after the skin test is applied. A negative skin test signifies either no tuberculosis infection or else the presence of anergy due to overwhelming infection or associated immunosuppressive illness (sarcoidosis; Hodgkin's disease). (See Chapter 25.)

Differential Diagnosis

Infiltrative and cavitary pulmonary tuberculosis must be considered in the differential diagnosis of a plethora of pulmonary diseases. Weight loss, night sweats, and hemoptysis are common clues to reinfection tuberculosis. Discussion of the differential diagnosis of pulmonary and extrapulmonary tuberculosis should be sought in standard medical textbooks.

Prevention

Living avirulent tubercle bacilli—especially BCG, an attenuated strain of *Mycobacterium bovis*—have been used to stimulate resistance to infection in persons at greater than normal risk of exposure to tuberculosis. Such immunization may provide many years of protection from tuberculosis infection, the principal disadvantage being conversion of the tuberculin skin test and hence unavailability of the test as a clue to exposure to *M tuberculosis.* BCG vaccine has never achieved popularity in the USA.

An alternative method of providing protection against tuberculosis is to treat all patients with recent skin test conversions with isoniazid for 1 year. The numbers of infecting microorganisms are low; thus, multiple drug regimens are not required. Recent data indicating the hepatotoxicity of isoniazid have resulted in greater care being taken to select patients for isoniazid prophylaxis who definitely require the drug. It is no longer suggested, for example, that anyone with a positive skin test, regardless of his age or the duration of the reaction, receive isoniazid as a matter of course.

Treatment

Cavitary pulmonary tuberculosis and disseminated forms of tuberculosis require treatment with combinations of drugs (isoniazid plus ethambutol or other combinations) to retard the ascendency of naturally occurring drug-resistant mutants which are found in small numbers in any large population of *M tuberculosis.* Other texts should be consulted for more detailed discussions of the complicated problem of the treatment of tuberculosis.

Complications & Prognosis

Some of the complications of tuberculosis have already been mentioned. Meningitis, renal infection, etc are discussed in other texts. Rarely—but especially in Scandinavian countries—tuberculosis may be complicated by the occurrence of erythema nodosum. This presumably reflects the presence of circulating immune complexes. Amyloidosis is another immunologic complication which may be seen in patients with long-standing infection.

2. LEPROSY

Mycobacterium leprae is an obligate intracellular acid-fast bacillus which has a unique ability to invade nerves and a preference for growth in cool areas of the body. *M leprae* has never been cultivated successfully in vitro but will multiply to a limited extent in the footpads of mice. More widespread infection occurs in animals thymectomized at birth, indicating the crucial role of thymus-mediated immunity in this infection. Armadillos may be susceptible to disseminated infection without the necessity for prior immunosuppression.

M leprae produces a remarkably broad spectrum of clinical disease ranging from *tuberculoid leprosy* at one extreme to *lepromatous leprosy* at the other. The pattern of infection is intimately related to the underlying degree of cell-mediated immunity. Like *M tuberculosis,* the leprosy bacillus elaborates no destructive enzymes or toxins; disease production is related directly to the ability to survive macrophage residence. Recent electron microscopic studies suggest that *M leprae* may evade macrophage antimicrobial activity by escaping from phagolysosomes to lie free in macrophage cytoplasm. The significance of these observations remains to be established.

Lepromatous leprosy is characterized by the virtual absence of a specific cellular immune response to *M leprae.* Hence, bacillary infiltration of tissues is extensive, and tissue destruction is minimal until very late in the disease. In tuberculoid leprosy the converse is true; the immune response is severe enough to damage or destroy bacilli and the nerves they infect at the outset. Borderline leprosy refers to the broad sweep of intervening disease between the lepromatous and tuberculoid "poles" and accounts for most clinical infections. Borderline leprosy is characterized by clinical and immunologic instability.

M leprae is traditionally regarded as a feeble pathogen, requiring intimate and prolonged contact for transmission. However, there are so many exceptions that leprosy has also been considered an easily transmissible infection in populations where only a few persons are sufficiently susceptible to permit development of clinically apparent disease. Unfortunately, there is no diagnostic skin test to assist in identifying persons who have experienced asymptomatic infection. Recent studies based upon examination of *M leprae*-specific lymphocyte activation in asymptomatic leprosy contacts suggest that acquisition of infection (sensitization) is relatively common despite the rarity of symptomatic disease.

The factors that dictate susceptibility to clinical infection remain uncertain. However, it is clear that inability to respond to the lepromin skin test (see below) is characteristic of patients with lepromatous leprosy and that lepromin anergy often persists despite apparent cure of disease. Thus, in a patient susceptible to lepromatous leprosy, an immune defect related to impaired recognition of *M leprae* is present. Whether the defect is predominantly one of macrophages or of lymphocytes remains hotly contested, although the preponderance of evidence suggests a highly specific lymphocyte defect.

Clinical Features

A. Lepromatous Leprosy: Lepromatous leprosy is manifested by widespread bacillary invasion of the integument (except in warm skin folds) and the cooler mucous membranes (especially the nose, which may be a source of infective aerosols). Diffuse bacillary invasion of the facial tissues results in the characteristic leonine facies of advanced disease. There is continuous heavy bacteremia (10^5-10^6 bacilli/ml), which is well tolerated; liver, spleen, and bone marrow are loaded with microorganisms. Although peripheral nerves are heavily invaded by *M leprae,* nerve destruction does not occur until late in the illness, reflecting the poor immunologic response to infection. Histologic findings reflect the lack of immune response. Macrophages are packed with acid-fast bacilli; neither lymphocytes nor giant cells are present; there is no granuloma formation.

B. Tuberculoid Leprosy: This form of the disease is characterized by the presence of no more than one or 2 extremely well-demarcated skin lesions with anesthetic atrophic centers and erythematous, raised edges. A palpable nerve trunk can often be found in the vicinity of the skin lesion. Histologic findings resemble those of sarcoidosis (epithelioid cell foci surrounded by well-defined zones of lymphocytes); however, the cutaneous nerves are destroyed by the tuberculoid leprosy granuloma, whereas nerves are spared in sarcoidosis. Rare acid-fast bacilli may be found in nerve remnants by careful serial sectioning of skin lesions. Caseation necrosis occurs very rarely in leprosy but may be seen in the nerves of patients with tuberculoid leprosy when there is a particularly vigorous immune response.

C. Borderline Leprosy: So-called borderline leprosy accounts for a broad spectrum of clinical disease. The more nearly lepromatous a case of borderline leprosy, the more plentiful the bacilli; the more numerous the skin lesions, the less well defined their edges and the less pronounced the anesthesia. The more nearly tuberculoid a case of borderline leprosy, the fewer the number of lesions (and bacilli), the sharper their edges, the more pronounced the degree of anesthesia, the greater the chances for finding enlarged peripheral nerves, and the more lymphocytes on histologic examination.

Immunologic Diagnosis

There is no immunologic test for leprosy.

Lepromin skin test. Lepromin has no diagnostic usefulness; lepromin skin test reactivity is common in normal persons by virtue of sensitivity to cross-reacting mycobacterial antigens and foreign skin proteins.

Lepromin is prepared from a homogenate of lepromatous skin nodules; the extracted leprosy bacilli are variably purified. In a person who is *known* to have leprosy, lepromin reactivity is diagnostic of tuberculoid or near-tuberculoid disease, whereas lepromin anergy carries the prognosis for progression to lepromatous leprosy in the absence of treatment. Treated patients who fail to recover lepromin reactivity are at risk of relapse and should receive antileprosy chemotherapy for life.

Differential Diagnosis

Leprosy should be suspected whenever an anesthetic skin lesion is found. Skin biopsies with stains for mycobacteria should be used to seek histologic proof of diagnosis since even apparently full-blown lepromatous leprosy may be confused with post-kala azar dermal leishmaniasis. (The striking immunologic similarities between leishmaniasis [see Chapter 38] and leprosy are noteworthy as well.) The essential histologic criterion for a diagnosis of leprosy is the presence of acid-fast bacilli in nerves. More specialized sources should be sought for details of the diagnosis of leprosy.

Prevention

Guidelines for chemoprophylaxis in highly susceptible contacts (children living with lepromatous parents) have not been clearly established. Active immunization with BCG has been shown to protect against leprosy in some (but not all) studies. This issue is currently unresolved.

Treatment

The mainstay of leprosy treatment is dapsone (diaminodiphenyl sulfone; DDS). Rifampin is bactericidal for *M leprae* and promises to be very useful in treatment; its principal problem is one of expense. Clofazimine (B663), a phenazine dye, has direct anti-*M leprae* activity, but also appears capable of stimulating macrophage bactericidal activity (at least for *Listeria monocytogenes*). In high dosages, clofazimine also suppresses erythema nodosum leprosum activity (see below).

Immunologic Complications

There are 5 principal immunologic complications of leprosy:

A. "Antigen Overload": In patients with lepromatous leprosy, lepromin anergy permits the accumulation of astounding numbers of *M leprae* (10^9/g of skin; 10^5-10^6/ml of blood; 10^7/ml of nasal secretions; 10^{11}/total body). Associated with the massive accumulation of foreign antigen are a variety of immunologic aberrations. Humoral abnormalities include polyclonal hypergammaglobulinemia, cryoglobulinemia, rheumatoid factor, biologic false-positive syphilis serology, and hyperglobulinemia-related latent distal renal tubular acidosis. Cellular abnormalities include depletion of paracortical (T) lymphocytes from lymph nodes, anergy to batteries of skin test antigens, impaired skin graft rejection, and impaired lymphocyte activation. All abnormalities are reversible with treatment except (with some exceptions) lepromin anergy.

B. Erythema Nodosum Leprosum: Erythema nodosum leprosum is a complication of lepromatous leprosy and results from an Arthus-type immune reaction in the skin and from the deposition of circulating immune complexes in the joints and kidneys. Nearly 50% of lepromatous patients will acquire erythema nodosum leprosum; it may occur spontaneously but more often follows initiation of chemotherapy. Erythema nodosum leprosum is characterized histologically by vasculitis and panniculitis and clinically by recurrent crops of up to hundreds of red, hot, tender skin lesions occurring all over the body. This complication is associated with severe systemic symptoms. The recent discovery that erythema nodosum leprosum is rapidly eradicated by thalidomide has revolutionized the therapeutic approach to this difficult problem.

C. Lucio Phenomenon (Erythema Necroticans): The Lucio phenomenon is probably a variant of erythema nodosum leprosum in which necrotizing vasculitis produces crops of large polygonal lesions characterized by ulceration and sloughing of large areas of skin. It may be peculiar to specific ethnic groups.

D. Reversal and Downgrading Reactions: These "reactions" are characteristic of borderline forms of leprosy and represent abrupt shifts in cell-mediated immunity, often with striking nerve damage. Preexisting quiescent skin lesions become abruptly red, hot, and tender. Granulomas may break up and lymphocytes become sparse (downgrading reaction), or skin lesions may show evidence of acquisition of immunologic activity with influx of lymphocytes (reversal reaction). These immunologic complications may be very severe, necessitating treatment with corticosteroids. Thalidomide is not effective.

E. Amyloidosis: Secondary amyloidosis is an important cause of renal failure and death in patients with advanced leprosy. Curiously, this complication appears to be far more common in Caucasians than other ethnic groups.

3. "ATYPICAL MYCOBACTERIA"

There are, widely distributed in nature, a group of bacteriologically and immunologically diverse mycobacteria which are responsible for sporadic pulmonary and other infections in man. Included are *M kansasii* and *M intracellulare* (Battey bacillus), which cause pulmonary disease; *M marinum* and *M ulcerans,* which cause skin disease; and *M scrofulaceum,* a cause of scrofula-like infection of cervical lymph nodes. Discussion of these pathogens, their bacteriologic classification, and the diseases they produce is beyond the scope of this chapter.

Diseases in Which Measurement of Antibody Is Useful in Diagnosis or Prognosis

The diseases in this group share many of the immunopathologic features of the mycobacterial infections, particularly tuberculosis; a major difference is that antibodies, although subserving no protective function, may assist in establishing a diagnosis or prognosis.

The fungi responsible for endemic systemic mycoses (and several bacteria) are important members of this group. Of the endemic mycoses, we have chosen to discuss only histoplasmosis and coccidioidomycosis. However, the immunopathologic basis of these diseases is representative of a much wider group of fungal diseases including North and South American blastomycosis, African histoplasmosis *(H capsulatum* var *duboisii),* sporotrichosis, phycomycosis, and possibly the actinomycete-related diseases actinomycosis and nocardiosis.* As noted previously, candidiasis and cryptococcosis fit less precisely into this category since a protective role for humoral immunity or PMN function is quite likely.

Youmans has pointed out that certain generalizations may be applicable to all of the endemic systemic mycoses:

> First, whether the portal of entry of the parasite is by way of the lung, skin, or gastrointestinal tract, the sequence of events is the same. Since these parasites are all facultative intracellular microorganisms, they are initially phagocytosed. They grow within the phagocytic cells and are then disseminated readily to other parts of the body by way of the lymphatics and blood. This initial primary infection is usually rather mild and in many cases may not even give rise to symptoms. The host responds to this primary infection by rapidly developing delayed hypersensitivity to proteins of the parasite and a cellular type of immunity to infection. The forces responsible for cellular immunity to infection usually prevail, and the multiplication of the parasites at the site of initial invasion and at those areas to which they metastasized will be controlled; eventually, the parasites may be killed. In a certain number of patients, chronic progressive disease may develop, even in the face of cellular immunity to infection, and this disease may be localized or generalized in character. When progressive disease develops, delayed hypersensitivity usually plays a large role in the genesis of the intlammatory and necrotic lesions which occur. (Page 401 of the Youmans, Paterson, & Sommers reference cited on p 551.)

Progressive systemic mycotic disease, whether local or disseminated, may occur only in the person who has some other disease or abnormality which lowers host resistance or in the person whose capacity to develop cellular immunity to infection is low or has been reduced by any one of a number of factors. In other words, progressive fungal disease, in a manner similar to progressive lepromatous leprosy, will probably occur only in the abnormal host. The nature of that abnormality is not clear. In leprosy it seems to relate to an intrinsic lymphocyte abnormality manifested most directly by absence of lepromin responsiveness; in coccidioidomycosis there is a relationship with ethnic background.

4. HISTOPLASMOSIS

Histoplasma capsulatum is a dimorphic fungus which exists in mycelial form in nature and as an intracellular yeast in man and susceptible animals. Despite its name, this fungus is not encapsulated. The mycelial form grows slowly on artificial laboratory media at room temperature, producing characteristic and highly infective spores (microconidia and tuberculate chlamydospores). Yeast phase histoplasma can also be maintained on artificial media at 35 C but requires extra nutrients such as cytosine for optimal growth.

H capsulatum grows luxuriantly in avian droppings, and disturbance of the roosting sites of chickens, starlings, etc is a common source of both primary and reinfection histoplasmosis. In the USA, the midwestern portion of the country, especially the Mississippi and Missouri River valleys, is the area of highest endemicity.

Under conditions of natural exposure, fungal spores are readily inhaled and shortly thereafter undergo conversion to the yeast phase, presumably in alveolar macrophages. *H capsulatum* produces no known toxins, and its virulence relates directly to its ability to survive and proliferate within mononuclear phagocytes. Clinical manifestations of histoplasmosis are a direct reflection of the degree of host cell-mediated immune response to infection.

Cell-mediated immunity is the critical component of host defense in histoplasmosis. Neither the phagocytosis nor the subsequent intracellular growth of *H capsulatum* appears to be affected by antibody. PMNs are unable to kill the fungi. Both mycelial and yeast phase histoplasma vaccines are able to protect mice from otherwise lethal challenge with virulent *H capsulatum.* The immunizing constituent appears to be a glycoprotein complex, and its substituent components are capable of conferring delayed histoplasmin skin

*Actinomyces and Nocardia are actually bacteria rather than fungi but are commonly discussed along with fungi in accordance with long convention.

test reactivity as well as specific lymphocyte MIF activity upon recipient guinea pigs. These findings indicate that animals develop cell-mediated immunologic reactivity following immunization with *H capsulatum* extracts.

Healthy subjects from histoplasmosis-endemic areas not only show positive delayed skin test reactivity to histoplasmin but also have strong positive reactions to histoplasmin antigens when tested by lymphocyte activation technics. Intact cell-mediated immune functions develop and are maintained in patients with self-limited acute histoplasmosis and in chronic pulmonary histoplasmosis. Granuloma formation is common and typical. Much of the intense tissue destruction in histoplasmosis is attributable to the vigor of the cell-mediated immune response to infection. An excellent example is the histoplasmoma, a chronic, sometimes enlarging pulmonary nodule which is composed of layers of cicatrix, often calcified, about a small necrotic center which may contain a few stainable fungi.

The lesions of acute and chronic disseminated histoplasmosis stand in sharp contrast to what is described above. There is little destruction of tissue. Macrophages are stuffed with yeasts, and there is little or no evidence of granuloma formation. The infection is not contained, and multiple organs are involved. Although the reticuloendothelial system is most heavily infected, the disease spreads to the skin and other organs. Parameters of cell-mediated immunity are often negative, implying a failure of macrophage activation. Humoral immune responses are intact. Histoplasma complement-fixing antibody is frequently (though not invariably) elevated. High titers imply progressing disease rather than improvement.

Clinical Features

Several distinctive syndromes of histoplasmosis are recognized:

A. Primary Histoplasmosis: Primary histoplasmosis occurs typically in children who reside in hyperendemic areas of the country. Mild exposures are generally asymptomatic or attributed to an episode of "flu"; they are recognized in retrospect only by the acquisition of histoplasmin skin test reactivity. In heavier exposures, patients are more likely to manifest cough, malaise, and fever. In most cases the disease is self-limited.

During the early phase of primary illness, fungi proliferate in the lung and are seeded hematogenously to many organs, especially those of the reticuloendothelial system. Subsequent resolution of primary and metastatic lesions occurs simultaneously over several weeks, coincident with the development of cell-mediated immunity to the infecting fungus. Pulmonary infiltrates may shrink to fibrous bands containing calcific deposits or granulomas, and metastatic lesions may also calcify, particularly in the spleen. These leave characteristic (but not pathognomonic) "buckshot" calcifications visible on x-ray.

Despite many similarities, primary histoplasmosis and primary tuberculosis differ in several respects:

1. There are often multiple simultaneous primary pulmonary lesions in histoplasmosis which give rise, in essence, to multiple Ghon complexes. There may also be more enlargement and calcification of hilar lymph nodes.

2. The vigor of the fibrotic healing response may lead to calcified obstructive broncholiths or to the development of severe mediastinal fibrosis with superior vena caval obstruction.

3. Pulmonary nodules may persist or may gradually and asymptomatically enlarge to produce "histoplasmomas."

B. Acute Disseminated Histoplasmosis: In the patient who fails to contain histoplasma dissemination at the outset, the result may be *acute disseminated histoplasmosis.* This complication occurs typically, but by no means exclusively, in children. It is characterized by fever, hepatosplenomegaly, anemia, and leukopenia. Untreated, it is a highly lethal illness, fatal in days to weeks.

C. Acute Reactivation Histoplasmosis: Patients who have recovered from primary histoplasmosis possess delayed hypersensitivity to histoplasmin. As with tuberculosis, skin test reactivity does not guarantee lifelong immunity to reinfection.

The patient with histoplasmin sensitivity who continues to reside in a histoplasmosis-endemic area is subject to reexposure to the fungus. Mild reexposures may be asymptomatic, serving only as "boosters" to maintenance of histoplasmin skin test reactivity. More massive exposures may precipitate an acute pulmonary disease the properties of which are directly related to underlying hypersensitivity to the fungus. In patients possessing cell-mediated immunity to *H capsulatum,* the course of illness resulting from a subsequent intense reexposure is characterized by a severe pulmonary inflammatory response. The heavier the exposure, the worse the pneumonia, which can be characterized by diffuse fine nodulation, or a frank "whiteout" with hypoxia, high fever, and toxicity. Since acute reinfection pulmonary histoplasmosis is related more closely to host hypersensitivity than to fungal invasiveness, anti-inflammatory drugs may be at least as important as amphotericin B in management. This form of the disease is usually, but not always, self-limited.

There is no event comparable to massive exogenous histoplasmosis reexposure in patients with tuberculosis, since neither environment nor infected patient contacts harbor mycobacteria in the concentrations necessary to produce this intense immunologic reaction. The role of endogenous reinfection in histoplasmosis is extremely difficult to assess since these patients tend to reside in geographically endemic areas where reexposure to the fungus is possible.

D. Chronic Pulmonary Histoplasmosis: Chronic pulmonary histoplasmosis bears a striking resemblance to pulmonary tuberculosis (with which it was historically confused, and may coexist). This disease occurs predominantly in middle-aged white cigarette smokers, especially those with chronic obstructive pulmonary disease. At the outset, one or more areas of infiltration usually develop in the peripheral apical-posterior segments of the lungs. Fever, chest pain, or cough may be present. The lesions may go on slowly to heal, contracting into a scarred band, or they may cavitate, with progressive cavitary enlargement and attendant pulmonary destruction. New lesions often appear as old ones are resolving, leading to the suggestion that breakdown of old lesions may lead to antigenic spillover into new sites with development of secondary inflammatory processes.

Chronic pulmonary histoplasmosis is not associated with extrapulmonary dissemination, as cellular immunity is basically intact. The disease appears to persist because of the presence of underlying abnormal pulmonary anatomy. Untreated disease pursues an irregularly destructive course with death from respiratory insufficiency or secondary bacterial infection in approximately 30% of patients.

E. Chronic Disseminated Histoplasmosis: Chronic disseminated histoplasmosis is considered to occur in patients with defective cell-mediated immunity which is either extrinsic and obvious (eg, Hodgkin's disease) or intrinsic and subtle (and poorly understood). Although interstitial pulmonary infiltrates may occasionally be present, pulmonary manifestations are not an important or characteristic part of this syndrome which reflects generalized histoplasma invasion of the reticuloendothelial system. Clinical findings include fever, anemia, leukocytopenia, hepatosplenomegaly, lymphadenopathy, and wasting. Ulcerating mucous membrane lesions are common. Diarrhea, endocarditis, and meningitis are reflections of multisystem involvement. The most serious (and surprisingly common) complication of this form of histoplasmosis is adrenal gland invasion and destruction. Adrenal destruction may continue even after treatment is begun, as a consequence of destructive fibrosis related to healing. *H capsulatum* may be recovered from cultures of bone marrow, liver, blood, urine, and mucous membrane lesions. If no treatment is given, the mortality rate is over 80%.

Differential Diagnosis

The differential diagnosis of pulmonary histoplasmosis includes a variety of respiratory infective processes, particularly tuberculosis, other endemic mycoses, and a variety of bacterial infections. Such patients are often referred to medical centers with a diagnosis of "penicillin-resistant pneumonia." The differential diagnosis of disseminated forms of histoplasmosis includes tuberculosis, other granulomatous infectious diseases, and even some lymphomas.

Immunologic Diagnosis

Despite the close correlation of immunologic and clinical status, immunologic tools are of little help in establishing a clinical diagnosis. There are several reasons for this: (1) The histoplasmin skin test is so frequently positive in endemic areas that a positive skin test is meaningless in an individual patient and merely reflects a prior infective encounter with the fungus. (2) The serologic titers are often boosted artifactually by a previous skin test. The elevation may last for months. Therefore, an elevated complement fixation titer to histoplasmin may reflect either histoplasmosis or simply an antecedent positive histoplasmin skin test. This does not happen if the skin test is negative. Because of this, the histoplasmin skin test should *never* be used in trying to make a diagnosis of histoplasmosis. Some efforts have been made to circumvent this problem by measuring complement fixation titers against yeast phase antigen (since histoplasmin is prepared from mycelial phase microorganisms). This is done in the hope that the yeast phase titer will rise only in worsening disease, in contrast to the false mycelial phase elevation from skin testing. This works better in theory than in practice, since both titers often rise after skin testing. Even a coccidioidin skin test may produce an elevation of histoplasma yeast phase complement fixing antibody titers. (3) Other serologic assays, such as precipitins and agar gel diffusion, have been used in an attempt to identify the patient with active histoplasmosis. None of these is thoroughly reliable. (4) The histoplasmin complement fixation antibody is elevated in only about half of the patients with disseminated histoplasmosis. Many are therefore missed by this test. (5) There is definite evidence of serologic cross-reaction with blastomycin antigens. Because blastomycosis occurs in the histoplasmosis-endemic areas, this could lead to misdiagnosis.

One might ask whether there is any value at all in immunologic testing. The response is a qualified yes for serology and a very limited yes for the skin test. The serologic titer might conceivably be helpful in a very ill patient with clinical findings suggesting histoplasmosis, one in whom it may be inappropriate to withhold treatment for up to 4 weeks pending culture results. If strongly elevated, and if not complicated by a preceding skin test, the high titer may be grounds for a presumptive diagnosis of histoplasmosis pending cultures.

The uses of histoplasmin skin tests are 3-fold. The first is in epidemiologic surveys. The second is in evaluating a patient for skin test anergy as part of a general immunologic evaluation *for a reason unrelated to histoplasmosis.* The third is to assess cell-mediated immunity in a *mycologically confirmed* histoplasmosis patient. This is rarely necessary and should be done for prognostic purposes, not for diagnosis. One example would be to follow the immune status in a patient to be treated with transfer factor or other immunotherapy.

In summary, many physicians use immunologic methods to diagnose histoplasmosis. Because of the pitfalls outlined above, many of these diagnoses are incorrect. The best and most absolute method is to culture *H capsulatum* from tissue of the infected patient.

Prevention

Animals can be immunized with histoplasma extracts in Freund's adjuvant, or by sublethal infections with virulent *H capsulatum.* There are, however, no suitably attenuated strains for human use. Furthermore, it is conceivable that immunization could have adverse consequences in patients in whom hypersensitivity may play the major role in disease.

Treatment

Prolonged amphotericin B is the mainstay of medical therapy. Other chemotherapeutic agents, such as miconazole or a combination of amphotericin B and rifampin, have been tried in a few cases, but no conclusions are possible yet. Several patients with histoplasmosis, both pulmonary and disseminated, have been treated with transfer factor. Negative skin test, lymphocyte activation, and MIF responses to histoplasmin converted from negative to positive in some patients, and clinical improvement ensued in a few. A causal relationship has not been proved in these instances, and further studies will be required to assess the importance of immune reconstitution in histoplasmosis. Because histoplasmosis usually responds to amphotericin B, such studies may not be forthcoming for some years.

Destructive histoplasma pulmonary lesions are often surgically resected, usually in combination with perioperative coverage with amphotericin B.

Complications & Prognosis

These may include bronchial obstruction by calcified histoplasma granulomas which become broncholiths. Destruction of lung by chronic pulmonary histoplasmosis may lead to secondary bacterial infection and respiratory insufficiency as a late complication, and even treated patients should be followed chronically for this problem.

The prognosis for spontaneous recovery from acute pulmonary histoplasmosis is excellent, whereas patients with chronic cavitary pulmonary histoplasmosis are prone to relapse even after treatment with amphotericin B. Disseminated forms of histoplasmosis are fatal in more than 80% of instances in the absence of treatment with amphotericin B.

5. COCCIDIOIDOMYCOSIS

Whereas histoplasmosis is an endemic mycosis in the midwestern USA, coccidioidomycosis is its counterpart in the southwestern United States. Coccidioidomycosis occurs throughout the Lower Sonoran Life Zone, a region of arid or semi-arid desert with hot summers and few winter freezes. This encompasses parts of a belt ranging from Texas through southern California and southward into Mexico. Foci are also present in Central and South America. The disease was first described in Argentina.

Like *H capsulatum,* the fungus *Coccidioides immitis* is dimorphic, with separate forms existing in nature and in man. However, *C immitis* is particularly well adapted for desert existence. It grows as an extremely fragile mycelium made up of tiny "barrel-shaped" arthrospores interspersed with "ghost cells." At the slightest disturbance, the mycelium disintegrates into a cloud composed of myriads of arthrospores which can be carried long distances on gentle breezes. Any wildlife in the path of these spores may inhale them and develop coccidioidomycosis. Rodents and cattle from endemic areas frequently have positive skin test reactions to coccidioidin, indicating prior exposure. Progressive disease from natural infection occurs in dogs and wild animals.

Not only do the spores travel long distances, but they survive for long periods of time. A series of meticulously conducted studies confirmed that when infected mice or dogs are buried in *C immitis*-free desert, subsequent soil samples contain the fungi for up to 5 years. Clinical outbreaks of coccidioidomycosis have occurred during archaeologic excavations in "non-endemic areas" such as northern California. Coccidioidomycosis also turns up more frequently after a rainy period, suggesting that mycelial growth occurs at this time. Human-to-human spread of *C immitis* does not occur because the parasitic spherule form of the fungus is not easily transmitted to other persons.

Shortly following inhalation, coccidioidal arthrospores convert to spherules, presumably within alveolar macrophages. Over the next 4–7 days, the spherules enlarge progressively to reach a total diameter of up to 30 μm and an outer wall thickness of 1.5 to 2 μm. The outer wall of *C immitis* spherules contains chitin, a polymer of $\beta(1\rightarrow4)$-linked N-acetylglucosamine. At maturity, the spherule contains a number of endospores. The outer wall undergoes spontaneous thinning and ruptures, releasing the endospores.

Endospores are chemotactic for PMNs, which attempt to ingest and destroy them. However, the PMNs are unsuccessful and are themselves destroyed, leaving a mass of necrotic cell debris. If not interrupted, endospores grow into successive generations of spherules and the cycle repeats itself. Primary coccidioidomycosis thus produces a process of focal pulmonary consolidation. Alveoli are filled with spherules and contain many PMNs and few mononuclear cells; regional lymph nodes are invaded. If the progress of the disease is not checked, a frank necrotizing pneumonia occurs which more closely resembles pyogenic than granulomatous infection. Primary infection, when successfully handled, permits only a limited number of growth cycles for *C immitis* spherules. The infiltrate never gets beyond a stage of focal accumulation of spherules, PMNs, and mononuclear cells. Over the course of several weeks, the host develops both a positive delayed skin test reaction to coccidioidin (mycelial antigen) or spherulin (spherule antigen) and cell-mediated immunity to infection. Several serologic parameters convert from negative to positive. The spherules are encased in granulomas, and the clinical findings, if any, subside. The host retains a positive delayed skin test response and is relatively protected against future encounters with *C immitis* arthrospores.

A critical element of host defense appears to be prevention of spherule maturation. In an active "healthy" immune response, spherules are ingested by macrophages and giant cells and surrounded by the lymphoid cells of a granuloma. The granulomas slowly decrease in size with variable amounts of fibrosis. It is not clear how the cells of a granuloma are able to destroy *C immitis* spherules in vivo. The enzyme chitinase can rapidly thin spherule walls in vitro, but liberated endospores are fully viable. In contrast, when chitin is hydrolyzed by lysozyme, over 99% of spherules and endospores are killed.

Primary infection is not always successfully handled. In the absence of effective immune defense, progressive primary disease results in the necrotizing pneumonia picture described above, together with widespread dissemination. A more subtle form of inadequate host response produces the chronic coccidioidal granuloma. This may occur in the lungs or at another site, frequently the skin. The formation of a granuloma, while suggesting strong cell-mediated immunity, does not in itself indicate spherule killing. Chronic granulomas may contain viable spherules for many years and intermittently increase or decrease in size. The skin test and lymphocyte activation response to coccidioidin are usually positive in patients with coccidioidal granuloma. MIF activity, perhaps a more subtle in vitro indicator of cell-mediated immunity, is usually absent. This suggests that the host with chronic coccidioidal granuloma has a partial defect in cell-mediated immunity which is associated with an inability to completely rid the body of active coccidioidal lesions. The greatest danger of coccidioidal granuloma is that host defenses will more seriously fail. This may be reflected in the development of more granulomas locally or at distant sites, or, more seriously, by conversion of the granuloma to an abscesslike lesion. Such lesions break down and discharge pus containing spherules, endospores, and PMNs.

Cell-mediated immune responses in coccidioidomycosis are complex and represent a dynamic balance between parasite and host. In patients with minimal immunologic defects, perhaps only a single parameter of the cell-mediated immune response will be abnormal. In patients with broader defects, all tests of the immune response will be abnormal. Three tests are used commonly to test host immunologic response to coccidioidin: (1) delayed hypersensitivity skin test (at 1:100 and 1:10 dilutions), (2) lymphocyte activation, and (3) MIF activity.

Most healthy subjects develop a positive (over 5 mm induration) skin test to 1:100 coccidioidin following exposure to *C immitis.* Many patients with pulmonary or minimally active disseminated disease will also have a positive reaction. Patients with more extensive disease will either react only to concentrated 1:10 coccidioidin or not at all. This "anergy" may be specific to coccidioidin, with the same subject having normal skin test responses to candida, mumps, or other antigens. Interpretation of the skin test has recently become even more difficult with the introduction of the spherule-derived antigen spherulin. Spherulin detects almost all persons who are skin test reactive to coccidioidin. Spherulin also detects additional healthy subjects (who have been exposed to *C immitis*) and coccidioidomycosis patients who react only to this antigen. This raises the question of whether a coccidioidin skin test-unreactive patient is immunologically depressed or simply one who reacts only to spherulin. More extensive disease is more often associated with coccidioidin and spherulin skin test anergy.

The lymphocyte activation reaction does not provide many clues to host response. This test has been considered to reflect immune recognition. It is now apparent that a number of healthy coccidioidin skin test-positive subjects have negative lymphocyte activation reactions. The significance of this finding is that it limits interpretation of a negative activation response in any given patient.

MIF is perhaps the most sensitive barometer of cell-mediated immunity. Coccidioidin skin test-positive healthy subjects almost always have a positive MIF response to coccidioidin. Those with inactive disease are also usually positive. However, even patients with low-grade clinical disease tend to have negative MIF responses. Like the skin test, this assay may indicate either a selective defect to coccidioidin or broad defect to all antigens.

The interplay of the indices of cell-mediated immunity is not well understood. Positive tests revert to negative with exacerbation of disease, and negative ones turn positive with improvement. However, all tests do not necessarily change together.

Expressions of cell-mediated immunity are also related to serologic changes. In at least one instance, a serum blocking factor has been described which is capable of depressing lymphocyte activation reactivity. More conventional antibodies, particularly complement-fixing antibodies, also relate to indices of cell-mediated immunity. In one study, 80% of patients with a coccidioidin complement fixation titer of 1:32 or less had a positive coccidioidin skin test, compared to 41% of those with higher serologic titers. Furthermore, DNCB sensitization, another index of cell-mediated immune function, was markedly depressed in those with high complement-fixation titers.

Serologic changes are not only positively correlated with cell-mediated immune function but also serve as an excellent immunologic barometer of clinical disease activity.

Both the duration and the extent of coccidioidomycosis are reflected by the complement fixation titer; as illness from recent infection persists beyond the first month, 65% of patients will have a positive complement fixation titer. This rises to 80% with illness of even longer duration.

Extrapulmonary dissemination is also reflected in a positive complement fixation test. Here the titer is roughly proportionate to the fungal burden. Only one-sixth of patients with a single extrapulmonary lesion will have a titer of 1:16 or greater, whereas over 80% of patients with extensive dissemination achieve a titer of 1:16 or more. Decline of the complement fixation antibody titer is an excellent guide to improvement.

Clinical Features

A. Primary Coccidioidomycosis: Certain clinical manifestations of primary coccidioidomycosis resemble histoplasmosis, while others are quite dissimilar. Approximately 60% of patients who experience coccidioidomycosis are totally asymptomatic and are identifiable only in retrospect by coccidioidin skin test reactivity. Most of the remainder develop transient cough, chest pain, shortness of breath, fever, headache, and chills. Pulmonary infiltrates and hilar adenopathy are frequent.

Up to 50% of symptomatic persons develop a variety of rashes which are thought to be allergic manifestations of infection. Most prominent among these are erythema nodosum and erythema multiforme. These reactions follow initial infection by 2–3 weeks, may be accompanied by eosinophilia, and are almost always associated with a positive delayed hypersensitivity skin test response to coccidioidin. "Hypersensitivity rashes" not only indicate an active immune response but usually connote an excellent prognosis. The arthralgias and arthritis of "desert rheumatism" are also thought to be hypersensitivity phenomena. Either or both of these manifestations of coccidioidomycosis occur in up to 25% of women with the disease but in only 10% of men. Women are also less likely than men to develop invasive pulmonary or disseminated disease (except during pregnancy, when the advantage of being female is totally lost and coccidioidomycosis can occur in its most fulminating forms). As noted elsewhere in this chapter, it is possible that these "hypersensitivity" phenomena may represent the response of skin and joints to antigen-antibody complex deposition.

B. Progressive Primary Coccidioidomycosis: The usual outcome of primary coccidioidomycosis is complete recovery. However, in some patients, pulmonary infiltrates may resolve only slowly or may form cavities. Characteristic thin-walled cavities may persist for years, gradually enlarging or shrinking. (Interestingly, *C immitis* may revert to a saprophytic mycelial form in large chronic cavities.) Nodular granulomas may persist from the initial infection or appear some years later, in a manner perhaps analogous to the formation of histoplasmomas. A small percentage of patients will develop progressive pulmonary disease, which may be manifested in the extreme case by fulminating miliary infiltrates. In some patients, progressive pulmonary disease is characterized by a smouldering course with chronic infiltrates and thicker walled cavities that are indistinguishable from tuberculosis. In fact, *C immitis* infection often coexists with active tuberculosis.

C. Disseminated Coccidioidomycosis: Patients who develop disseminated coccidioidomycosis usually do so within a few months of their primary pulmonary infection. A surprising number appear without any history of primary disease. *C immitis* can disseminate via the bloodstream to virtually any organ, especially the central nervous system, bones, skin, lymph nodes, soft tissues, and liver. Even transplacental infection of the fetus may occur. In general, the more extensive the metastatic lesions, the worse the prognosis.

There is a striking ethnic predilection to dissemination of coccidioidomycosis. For unexplained reasons, Filipinos are extraordinarily susceptible to fulminating disease. Up to 10% of blacks with symptomatic coccidioidomycosis will develop evidence of dissemination. Less than 1% of Caucasians will do so. Even after dissemination, the lesions in Caucasians tend to be less generalized. They appear as isolated meningitis or cutaneous granulomas rather than generalized multisystem involvement. The reasons for these strong ethnic associations are unknown.

Cutaneous coccidioidomycosis may take the form of chronic coccidioidal granuloma, often occurring as only a single demonstrable lesion. It may go on for decades, unchanging or intermittently increasing or decreasing in size. This lesion is associated with a low risk of spread to other sites. It is to be distinguished from the coccidioidal abscess. The latter is not a granuloma but a focus of necrotic tissue containing many PMNs and spherules. Coccidioidal abscesses may be entirely subcutaneous or may reflect the ultimate extension of a long sinus tract from deep viscera. There are usually multiple lesions and often multisystem disease. The patient with isolated coccidioidal granuloma is likely to have a positive coccidioidin skin test, but the person with multiple abscesses is likely to have a negative skin test.

Meningitis is a particularly important form of disease and may occur in up to one-fifth of patients with dissemination. The patient may be entirely free of neurologic manifestations at first and only later develop headache and personality changes. Examination of cerebrospinal fluid shows low glucose, high protein, and lymphocytosis. Coccidioidal meningitis is a waxing and waning disease but is ultimately fatal in all cases if untreated. Even with vigorous therapy, the mortality rate approaches 50%.

Immunologic Diagnosis

The value of testing either cell-mediated or serologic response is dependent upon the source of antigen and the test procedure used. There are 2 general sources for *C immitis* antigens: (1) mycelium (coccidioidin) and (2) spherules (spherulin). These 2 sources are important to distinguish because their antigens are not entirely identical. A variety of mycelial and spherule antigens have been prepared. They are made from ground cells, autolyzed cells, purified polysaccharides, and culture filtrates. Purified endospore antigens have also been made.

Coccidioidin prepared from autolyzed mycelia has been traditionally used for skin testing and more recently for in vitro tests of cell-mediated immunity. The precise composition of coccidioidin is not known. Immunologically active purified polysaccharides contain mannose, galactose, glucose, and monomethyl mannose. The antigen is standardized by biologic rather than biochemical activity; quantity is frequently expressed in terms of micrograms of "solids." The 1:100 dilution commonly used for skin testing is much more specific than the 1:10 concentrate. The latter cross-reacts with other fungi, most notably *H capsulatum.*

Spherulin has been introduced recently as an alternative to coccidioidin. In the skin test, spherulin appears to be as specific as 1:100 coccidioidin and is considerably more sensitive. One survey in a coccidioidomycosis-endemic area yielded 41% skin test reactions to coccidioidin and 64% to spherulin. Spherulin is also potent in in vitro assays of cell-mediated immunity.

Both coccidioidin and spherulin are now being used in serologic assays. Spherulin appears to be suitably potent but has a problem qualitatively similar to the problem presented by coccidioidin in that there is some cross-reactivity to histoplasmin.

Both coccidioidin and spherulin are useful skin test antigens. Sequential tests are of prognostic value, and the skin test does not appear to affect serologic titers. However, repeated skin testing may exert depressant or stimulant effects on results of skin tests themselves or on in vitro studies of cell-mediated immunity. The magnitude and duration of such effects vary, and their importance is unknown. Positive indices for cell-mediated immunity suggest present or prior infection with *C immitis.* They are thus useful epidemiologically but not diagnostically.

Antibody responses play no known role in host defense but can be helpful in diagnosing acute coccidioidal infection and in distinguishing acute from chronic infection. Four serologic methods are generally used: (1) tube precipitin, (2) complement fixation, (3) immunodiffusion, and (4) latex agglutination tests.

Primary coccidioidomycosis is detected by the precipitin and latex agglutination tests. In 80% of infections, the precipitin test is positive within 2 weeks of the onset of symptoms. Over 90% of positive reactions revert to negative within 6 months. The test is highly specific. A few patients with disseminated disease will have persistent or late positive precipitins. The latex agglutination test may become positive even before the tube precipitin test, but false-positive reactions occur in 10% of cases.

The complement fixation test is positive in only 10% of patients by the second week of symptoms. A positive precipitin test coupled with a negative complement fixation test therefore indicates early primary disease. As the precipitin antibody titer falls, the complement fixation titer rises, especially in the presence of long-active disease. Therefore, a positive complement fixation test, with or without a precipitin titer, indicates chronic disease. A titer of 1:2 or more is significant. As mentioned before, the complement fixation titer also correlates positively with severity of illness. The immunodiffusion test is technically simpler than the complement fixation test. It becomes positive at about the same time as the latter but can only be used for screening purposes since it is not quantitative.

Serologic assays are particularly important in diagnosing coccidioidal meningitis. *C immitis* is difficult to recover from cerebrospinal fluid, and there may be no other identifiable foci of disease. Unfortunately, up to one-fourth of patients with coccidioidal meningitis have a negative complement fixation test in the cerebrospinal fluid, and accurate diagnosis may require insight and persistence.

Differential Diagnosis

The differential diagnosis of acute pulmonary coccidioidomycosis includes tuberculosis and a broad variety of infective pneumonias. Disseminated coccidioidomycosis must be differentiated from other metastatic infectious diseases such as tuberculosis, melioidosis, and other mycoses. The differential diagnosis of coccidioidal meningitis includes cryptococcosis, tuberculosis, and other causes of the "hypoglycorrhachia" (ie, low cerebrospinal fluid glucose) syndrome.

Prevention

A number of efforts have been made to develop vaccines against *C immitis.* Inactivated vaccines have been prepared from mycelia or spherule extracts or from whole cells. These have usually been administered to mice in oil-based adjuvants and have been effective in eliciting delayed hypersensitivity skin test responses. Vaccination with formalin-killed spherules increases the LD_{50} for mice from 50 to 3000 arthrospores. It was thought that this particular vaccine provided a slow release of antigen necessary to effect protection. Killed vaccines prepared from mycelia or spherules apparently do not prevent infection, although they do minimize dissemination and fungal replication and prolong survival of challenged animals. Vaccination of humans with inactivated fractions of *C immitis* has been less successful. In general, minimal delayed hypersensitivity is elicited. The discrepancy between human and animal studies is explained at least in part by the lack of acceptable adjuvants for human vaccines.

Attenuated strains have also been used as live vaccines. These have been protective in animal studies. However, attenuated strains are not eliminated rapidly by the host and persist for long periods in granulomas. Also, attenuation has proved somewhat unstable, with gradual reversion to virulent forms. Therefore, live vaccines are still considered unacceptable for use in man.

Treatment

Amphotericin B is the only drug currently available for the treatment of coccidioidomycosis. It must be given intravenously for long periods, and intrathecally in the presence of meningitis. In many respects, amphotericin B is ameliorative rather than curative, for relapses are common. Duration of therapy is variable and is guided by complement fixation titers. Miconazole may become a useful alternative drug, but experience with it is limited.

Because many patients with severe disease are refractory to amphotericin B and have defective cell-mediated immune responses to coccidioidin, a number of investigators have attempted immune reconstitution with transfer factor. Approximately 60 patients with a variety of lesions (including 11 with meningitis) have been treated. Immune conversions were dramatic, especially for MIF activity. Many occurred within days of transfer factor; some within hours. Skin tests converted to positive frequently, and lymphocyte activation responses less often. Conversions were transient, requiring administration of more transfer factor to be sustained. Clinical improvement followed transfer factor administration in 60% of patients and was most impressive for the most desperately ill patients. Improvement occurred in at least 5 patients with meningitis, an infection located in a site allegedly "sequestered" from immune response. These changes cannot be attributed to transfer factor with confidence at present (1) because coccidioidomycosis is a variable illness characterized by spontaneous remissions and relapses; (2) because most patients were receiving concurrent amphotericin B; and (3) because it is often difficult to distinguish subjective from objective improvement in this disease. Experience with transfer factor must therefore be regarded as inconclusive until suitably controlled trials provide a definitive assessment.

Complications & Prognosis

Complications relate to tissue damage by the fungus and by amphotericin B. Specific problems include hydrocephalus from scarring at the basilar meninges, collapse of weight-bearing bones as a result of lytic lesions, and hemorrhage from erosion of blood vessels. This is a particularly serious problem in large coccidioidal cavities. Cavities may also become secondarily infected by bacteria or with another fungus, aspergillus.

The prognosis for spontaneous recovery from acute pulmonary coccidioidomycosis is excellent unless the patient is Filipino, Chinese, Japanese, Vietnamese, or black or is a pregnant woman. The prognosis is guarded, even with vigorous amphotericin B therapy, in patients with disseminated forms of infection.

6. BRUCELLOSIS

This is an acute febrile illness manifested by fever, chills, and weakness. Occasionally, chronic recurrent fevers and weakness produce the syndrome of *undulant fever.* The illness is caused by small gram-negative bacilli, including *Brucella abortus, B suis, B melitensis,* and, rarely, *B canis.* Man is an incidental host and is most commonly infected by ingesting contaminated dairy products or by inoculation through abrasions. Veterinarians and abattoir workers are particularly susceptible to infection. Once ingested, brucellae are rapidly taken up by PMNs and transported to the fixed reticuloendothelial system of the liver and spleen, where they are secondarily phagocytosed by Kupffer cells and other histiocytes and enter a period of prolonged intracellular residence. This is consistent with the incubation period of up to several weeks or, rarely, months. During this time, phagocytes containing brucellae congregate to form noncaseating granulomas. Clinical symptoms may be produced when viable or dead organisms are released from the reticuloendothelial cells. Metastatic foci may develop in bones, joints, or soft tissues.

During experimental infection, delayed hypersensitivity develops to brucella extracts. These reactions are not entirely specific, and intensity of response is variable. The brucella skin test underwent a period of popular use in the USA but has recently been discontinued because of its lack of diagnostic value. Despite this, a number of animal studies have confirmed that immunity to brucella depends on cell-mediated mechanisms.

Antibody to brucellae is not protective. However, serologic responses can be used to assist in diagnosis. Brucella agglutinating and complement-fixing antibodies have been measured. A blocking factor has been demonstrated in some chronic cases. This results from the presence of an IgA antibody which produces spuriously negative agglutinins at low dilutions and, when added to high titer serum, depresses agglutinin levels. The prozone phenomenon can be avoided by carrying agglutinin titers out to a 1:320 dilution. Another way to serologically diagnose brucellosis is to mix the brucellae and the serum to be tested, wash the brucellae, and then add antihuman globulin. This form of Coombs test will cause brucellae to agglutinate even if a prozone phenomenon is present. Serologic titers are very important in the diagnosis of brucellosis because the organisms are fastidious and require Castaneda's medium and CO_2 enrichment for optimal recovery from blood. However, there is some cross-reaction with tularemia agglutinins, and titers may rise following cholera immunization. Treatment is with tetracycline for long periods. This is often coupled with streptomycin to minimize the chance of relapse. An attenuated strain is used to immunize cattle. It does produce infection and transient bacteremia and is not used in humans.

7. TULAREMIA

Francisella (Pasteurella) tularensis is a small gram-negative coccobacillus which requires special culture media for isolation. The more virulent type A can infect man in as small a dose as 50 organisms. Type B produces milder disease. Infection occurs by inhalation or by invasion through abrasions in the skin. The organism is spread through rodent hosts—especially rabbits—by insect vectors such as ticks. Accordingly, tularemia is an occupational hazard of trappers, sheepherders, mink ranchers, hunters, and butchers, all of whom are at increased risk of handling infected tissues.

Tularemia presents as 4 relatively distinct syndromes. The most common form of infection is *ulceroglandular tularemia,* with papule and then ulcer formation at the inoculation site. Fever and tender regional lymphadenopathy develop later. In untreated patients the lymph nodes may become caseous and form suppurating buboes. The most serious form of the disease is *pneumonic tularemia.* Here, both aerosolized and hematogenously disseminated bacteria produce pulmonary infiltrates and pleural effusions. Hematogenous dissemination may also produce an illness indistinguishable from enteric fever *(typhoidal tularemia).* Inoculation of the organisms into the conjunctival sac produces *oculoglandular tularemia,* a purulent conjunctivitis teeming with organisms.

Host defense mechanisms are not fully understood. However, immunity is associated with appearance of delayed hypersensitivity skin test response to tularemia skin test antigen. Also, in vitro responses of cell-mediated immunity can develop to the skin test antigen in sensitized persons. Immunity is associated with increased ability of rabbit macrophages to kill *F tularensis.* Inactivated vaccines are of no benefit, but a live attenuated strain has been successfully used to vaccinate man and lower animals. This provides further evidence supporting the protective role of cell-mediated immunity. Finally, because the organisms are fastidious and highly infectious, serologic responses are generally used to confirm the diagnosis. Tularemia agglutinins usually rise after the first 2 weeks of illness but may take much longer. The test is relatively specific, with some cross-reactions with brucellae. As in brucellosis, there is no evidence that antibody formation is protective. Treatment is with streptomycin. Gentamicin is also effective.

INFECTIOUS DISEASES CHARACTERIZED BY UNIQUE HOST-PARASITE RELATIONSHIPS

A number of infectious diseases do not fit easily into the preceding categories because of particularly unique aspects of their relationship to the host. Among these are syndromes resulting from infection with Mycoplasma, Chlamydia, and Rickettsia species and *Bordetella pertussis.*

Mycoplasma pneumoniae

Mycoplasmas are the smallest known free-living microorganisms and differ from bacteria in lacking cell walls. They have been recognized as etiologic agents of disease in man, animals, insects, and plants. Mycoplasma species have unique morphologic, growth, and metabolic characteristics which are beyond the scope of this chapter.

The only Mycoplasma species with an unquestioned ability to regularly produce human infection is *Mycoplasma pneumoniae.* This microorganism, like *Bordetella pertussis,* appears to produce its major disease manifestations at the surface of epithelial cells. Unlike *Corynebacterium diphtheriae* and *Vibrio cholerae,* which also occupy an extraepithelial position, *M pneumoniae* produces no definite exotoxins. Unlike Shigella and Salmonella species, *M pneumoniae* does not penetrate into epithelial cells.

Presumably, *M pneumoniae* is phagocytosed and killed by leukocytes, although inhibition of macrophage function has been observed in vitro. The details of mycoplasma-host interaction are outlined in Table 34–3.

Bordetella pertussis

B pertussis is a short, ovoid, encapsulated, gram-negative rod which produces the clinical syndrome known as pertussis (whooping cough). Apparently other Bordetella species, as well as some viruses (especially adenoviruses), can also produce this syndrome. However, *B pertussis* infection is epidemic, whereas the others are sporadic. *B pertussis* acquisition is associated with a very high clinical attack rate; asymptomatic carriage is not common.

The pertussis syndrome is unique to humans and is characterized by a 1–2 week "catarrhal" phase (with symptoms of an upper respiratory infection) followed by a phase of cough paroxysms which may last 1–4 weeks. Cough paroxysms are episodic and completely unanticipated by the patient; following a series of paroxysms, the patient inspires against a partially closed glottis, producing the characteristic "whoop." Vomiting frequently follows. Complications of pertussis include hemorrhages (due to rupture of small and large blood vessels); events related to increased intrathoracic pressure (hernias, subcutaneous emphysema, etc); bacterial pulmonary infections; and encephalopathy (due to apnea? hypoglycemia?).

B pertussis possesses pili-like surface factors and 4 "phases" of in vitro growth (phases I and II are smooth and virulent; phases III and IV are rough and avirulent). In these and other respects, there is a striking resemblance to *N gonorrhoeae. B pertussis* multiplies only in association with the ciliated epithelium of the respiratory tract and does not invade epithelial cells. The microorganism is presumed to be killed by PMNs; its surface capsule is apparently not antiphagocytic. Many of the pathophysiologic manifestations of *B pertussis* infection have been attributed to a toxin (or toxins) which produce a necrotizing inflammatory response of the tracheobronchial mucous membrane and ciliary paralysis.

B pertussis is rich in a variety of potentially pathogenic factors (surface components; endotoxin; histamine-sensitizing factor; lymphocytosis-producing factor) the importance of which is unsettled in human infections. One of the most striking clinical accompaniments of pertussis is leukocytosis with an absolute lymphocytosis. This is accompanied by depletion of small lymphocytes in the thymus, spleen, and lymph nodes and reflects a failure of lymphocyte traffic back to the lymph nodes. Increased lymphocyte production is not considered to play a role. In vitro and animal

Table 34–3. Host-parasite relationships in mycoplasmal, chlamydial, and rickettsial infections.

Microorganism	Disease	Principal Manifestations	Host Relationship	Immune Pattern	Protective Mechanisms*				Serologic Test	Other
					SIgA	Opsonins	PMN	CMI		
Mycoplasmas										
M pneumoniae	"Primary atypical pneumonia"	Pneumonia. (Central nervous system and hepatic complications have been reported, but *M pneumoniae* has not been recovered regularly from these sites. Bullous myringitis has been observed in pharyngeally inoculated volunteers). Stevens-Johnson syndrome occasionally reported.	Extracellular. Attaches to and damages epithelial cells; does not penetrate. Able to prevent ameboid macrophage movement and may prevent process of phagocytosis when attached to macrophage membrane.	Acute infection. Clinical disease may not occur until after several preceding asymptomatic infections. Thus, clinical illness may reflect the development of cellular hypersensitivity to the microorganism.	(+)	(–)	(–)	(+)	CF (the most practical test). Cold agglutinins for human type O erythrocytes. Many others are available (eg, indirect hemagglutination test) but are less practical.	*M pneumoniae* infection stimulates antibodies cross-reactive with red cell membrane and can cause an acute hemolytic response. Another cross-reactive antibody is able to agglutinate streptococci of species MG. Disease usually self-limited, but antibiotics (tetracycline, erythromycin) may shorten course without eliminating organisms. Inactivated vaccine may accentuate subsequent infection.
Chlamydiae (Bedsoniae)										
C psittaci	Psittacosis (ornithosis)	Pneumonia. Occasionally hepatitis, myocarditis, encephalitis, skin rash.	Obligate intracellular pathogen (epithelial cells). *C psittaci* can prevent fusion of phagosomes with lysosomes in mouse L cells. Infects a wide variety of animals and birds.	Broad spectrum of disease ranging from acute infection to latency. Immunity may be incomplete following infection; prolonged shedding of microorganisms sometimes occurs (especially in birds).	?	(–)	(–)	(+)	CF	No skin test. Antibody titer elevation assists in establishing diagnosis. No available vaccine.
C trachomatis group	Trachoma	Chronic follicular conjunctivitis; pannus; scarring.	Obligate intracellular pathogen (predominantly epithelial cells). Infections limited to humans.	Characterized by chronicity, latency, and relapse. Hypersensitivity response due to repeated exposure may play an important pathogenic role. Scarring may reflect "bystander" cell injury due to a vigorous immune response.	?	(–)	(–)	(+)	No routine test available. Characteristic inclusion bodies in conjunctival scrapings.	The single greatest cause of blindness in the world. No skin test. No available vaccine (inactivated vaccine may accentuate subsequent infection).

	Inclusion conjunctivitis	Acute purulent conjunctivitis.	Obligate intracellular pathogen (epithelial cells). Natural habitat is genitourinary tract.	Acute illness common.	?	(–)	(–)	?	None	May be an aberrant form of trachoma. Few immunologic data available.
	Urethritis (nonspecific urethritis; NSU syndrome)	Purulent urethral discharge.	Obligate intracellular pathogen (epithelial cells).	Broad range: asymptomatic to acute urethritis.	?	(–)	(–)	?	None	A common cause of nongonococcal urethritis. Probably identical to the inclusion conjunctivitis agent.
	Lymphogranuloma venereum (LGV)	Anogenital infection; lymphadenitis (buboes). Infection initially generalized.	Intracellular (epithelial cells and beyond; invasive).	Acute or chronic illness. May be considerable mucosal scarring. Latency common.	?	(–)	(–)	(+)	CF	Transmitted by sexual intercourse. Frei skin test (and CF antibody test) can cross-react with psittacosis. Frei test becomes positive well beyond changes in serologic tests. This skin test detects a common chlamydial group antigen and is not specific for LGV. However, it is more often positive in LGV because this infection is so persistent (rarely positive in trachoma).
Rickettsiae										
R prowazekii	Epidemic typhus	Headache, fever, rash.	Intracellular pathogen (epithelial cells). Naturally pathogenic for arthropods. Bites → endothelial cell invasion → acute vasculitis → thrombosis (and DIC). Rickettsiae may actively enter macrophages but escape phagolysosomal fusion. If opsonic antibody is present, macrophages actively ingest rickettsiae → phagolysosomal formation → rickettsial death.	Acute illness. Mild to severe, depending on specific microorganism. Immunity is usually long-lasting, with some exceptions: (1) Epidemic typhus may relapse 10–20 years after apparent recovery (Brill-Zinsser disease). Clinically milder. (No rash. No OX19 antibody titer rise.) (2) Trench fever is characterized by relapses.	(–)	+	(–)	(+)	CF, Weil-Felix.	*All* can be diagnosed by CF test using yolk sac antigen. *Many* can be diagnosed by their ability to stimulate formation of antibodies which are cross-reactive with strains of *Proteus vulgaris* (Weil-Felix reaction). ***Examples:*** Epidemic and endemic typhus stimulate OX19 antibody. Scrub typhus stimulates OXK antibody. Rocky Mountain spotted fever stimulates antibody to OX19 and OX2. (Must eliminate any possibility of a concurrent Proteus infection.) No skin test.
R typhi	Endemic typhus									
R rickettsii	Rocky Mountain spotted fever									
R tsutsugamushi	Scrub typhus									
R quintana	Trench fever									
R akari	Rickettsialpox									
C burnetii	Q fever	Headache, fever, pneumonia, hepatitis.	Intracellular. Can be acquired by inhalation.	Acute or subacute illness.	?	?	?	(+)	CF	Vaccination effective but not practical.

*Symbols in parentheses: uncertain data.
Abbreviations used: CMI, cell-mediated immunity; CF, complement fixation test; DIC, disseminated intravascular coagulation; PMN, polymorphonuclear neutrophil; SIgA, secretory IgA. A question mark means that no data are available.

studies indicate a variety of contradictory alterations of cell-mediated immune responses in pertussis (immune enhancement with increased or decreased tumor growth, increased or decreased infection susceptibility, etc). The precise role of cell-mediated immune mechanisms in pertussis is unclear. However, it is important to note that successful immunization with a killed vaccine has reduced the threat of pertussis enormously in this country. Presumably, this indicates that humoral immune mechanisms may be more important in protection. The role of secretory IgA in protection is unsettled, as is the role of cell-mediated immunity in recovery from established infection.

Chlamydiae (Bedsoniae)

These microorganisms are obligate intracellular parasites which possess a unique reproductive cycle. The infectious particle is a 0.3 μm structure termed the "elementary body"; it is specialized for extracellular survival. Following endocytosis, a "reticulate body" is formed which multiplies intracellularly by binary fission. Innumerable elementary bodies are secondarily formed which are then released by rupture of the host cell. Within leukocytes, chlamydiae are apparently able to avoid lysosomal enzyme activity.

In addition to a unique developmental cycle, chlamydiae possess common morphologic characteristics and a common protoplasmic family antigen. Type-specific antigens are found in the cell wall.

Chlamydial diseases often run a protracted and relapsing course (especially trachoma). Chronicity of infection has led to the suggestion that chlamydial infection does not evoke an effective immune response. On the other hand, the host ordinarily restrains and localizes chlamydial disease without serious sequelae. Cell-mediated immune mechanisms appear to be important in chlamydial immunity. However, antibodies that combine with cell wall antigens of the parasite appear to prevent penetration of susceptible host cells, thus limiting the spread of infection.

Details of chlamydia-host interaction are outlined in Table 34–3.

Rickettsiae

Rickettsial species are small pleomorphic coccobacilli which function as obligate intracellular parasites. With the exception of *Coxiella burnetii,* the etiologic agent of Q fever, members of this group share a number of important characteristics: (1) failure to survive in the environment, (2) dependence upon arthropods as vectors and reservoirs, (3) transmission by arthropod bites, and (4) multiplication in the endothelial cells of blood vessels, with production of vasculitis, thrombosis, hematogenous dissemination, and rash.

C burnetii is more often transmitted by the respiratory route, seldom involves biting arthropods, produces no rash, and is manifested principally by pneumonia.

The details of rickettsia-host interaction are outlined in Table 34–3.

INFECTIONS COMPLICATED BY DEPOSITION OF CIRCULATING IMMUNE COMPLEXES

Major Immunologic Features

- Infections often characterized by persistence or chronicity.
- Complications include glomerulonephritis, arthritis, or skin lesions.
- Immunologic manifestations may include hypergammaglobulinemia, cryoglobulinemia, hypocomplementemia.
- Immune complex deposition in target tissues triggers vasculitis.

General Considerations

The production of antigen-antibody complexes is probably quite common in a majority of infectious diseases, but symptoms rarely result from their presence. Ordinarily, they possess physicochemical characteristics which permit their asymptomatic clearance from the bloodstream by the reticuloendothelial system. In some circumstances, however, antigens and antibodies combine under conditions which predispose to their deposition in the walls of blood vessels. As a result of such deposition, complement is activated locally and results in the establishment of an inflammatory response through the release of soluble mediators, including chemotactic factors. The result of the inflammatory response is dependent upon the site of immune complex deposition; glomerulonephritis, arthritis, and skin lesions are common clinical manifestations of this process.

Table 34–4 deals with infectious diseases which are known to be complicated by immune complex deposition. There seems to be little question that more examples will be found in the near future:

The familiar "proteinuria of fever" is very likely a manifestation of subclinical glomerulonephritis in a broad variety of infectious diseases. Acute nephritis has been described in infectious mononucleosis, mumps, variola, varicella, adenovirus (type 7) and echovirus (type 9) infection, and following vaccination.

Erythema nodosum complicates many infectious diseases (leprosy, coccidioidomycosis, histoplasmosis, tuberculosis, and streptococcal infection, to name but a few). It is likely that the cause of this complication will prove to be immune complex deposition (as does seem to be the case in leprosy) when appropriate studies are performed (see Chapter 33).

The natural history of many virus infections is biphasic, and the development of gross clinical phenomena is often preceded by a nonspecific febrile illness. Whereas the nonspecific illness is often the direct result of the virus infection, the more specific manifestations of the disease such as the exanthems are probably due to the presence of immune complexes formed by virus and antibody in the circulation. The mechanism of development of the rash may be similar to that in serum sickness.

Table 34–4. Immune complex complications of infectious diseases.

Disease	Etiologic Agent	Immunologic Predisposition	Immunologic Complications	Comments
Infective endocarditis	Bacteria (*S viridans; S aureus,* enterococci; many others). Fungi (*C albicans* and others). Miscellaneous (*Coxiella burnetii* and others; rare).	Continuous discharge of microorganisms or their antigens into the bloodstream. Infecting microorganisms protected from phagocytes by overlying fibrin network and by the avascular nature of cardiac valve tissue. High levels of rheumatoid factor may impair opsonic capacity of IgG which is specifically bound to microorganisms. Immunologic complications are directly proportionate to duration of infection (ie, more common in "subacute" than acute endocarditis).	Immune complex glomerulonephritis characterized by proteinuria, microscopic hematuria, and red cell casts in urine. Antibody, complement, and specific bacterial antigen present in renal vasculature. Nephritis may be focal or diffuse. Focal nephritis may occur in 50–90% with few sequelae. Diffuse nephritis occurs in $< 10\%$; may produce uremia. Osler's nodes (painful nodular lesions in fingertips and elsewhere), Roth spots in ocular fundi (white center with surrounding hemorrhagic zone), petechiae, splinter hemorrhages beneath nails–all may reflect hypersensitivity angiitis characterized by intimal proliferation. "Embolic" complications (especially central nervous system) may often represent hypersensitivity angiitis. Splenomegaly and presence of circulating histiocytes (especially in earlobe blood) reflect chronic stimulation of reticuloendothelial system. Other immunologic accompaniments include hyperglobulinemia, rheumatoid factor, cryoproteinemia, and, perhaps, myocarditis and anemia.	Endocarditis is a disease of heart valves; valves may be destroyed by infection. Similar immunologic sequelae may be encountered in infected arteriovenous shunts, infective endarteritis, and infected central nervous system ventriculoatrial shunt devices (usually due to *S epidermidis*). Common feature to all is continuous discharge of microorganisms into blood. Treatment consists of antibiotics. Immunologic complications currently handled expectantly; corticosteroids may exacerbate infection and are usually contraindicated.
Viral hepatitis	Hepatitis B	Persistent antigenemia due to HB_SAg stimulates production of anti-HB_S; results in circulating immune complexes. If HB_SAg is eliminated, resultant illness is similar to "one shot serum sickness" with only transient clinical manifestations. If there is continual production of HB_SAg, HB_SAg-Ab complexes are continually present, resulting in an illness resembling chronic serum sickness in animals and expressed as a generalized necrotizing vasculitis. Why most patients who acquire HB_SAg do not develop these syndromes, but only subclinical or clinical hepatitis probably relates to poorly understood "host immune factors."	The syndrome equivalent to "one shot serum sickness" is characterized by migratory, additive, or simultaneous polyarthralgias and arthritis together with skin rash which is often urticarial. Hepatitis may be subclinical or associated with jaundice. Serum and joint complement may be decreased; cryoglobulins composed of HB_SAg, anti-HB_S, and complement may be found. Occasionally associated with glomerulonephritis. The syndrome equivalent to "chronic serum sickness" is characterized by multisystem disease with a prolonged course. Manifested by arthritis, renal disease, heart disease, etc, with the features of polyarteritis or hypersensitivity angiitis. Only by finding HB_SAg can viral etiology be established. Otherwise, will be considered a "collagen vascular disease of unknown etiology." May need to test repeatedly for these viral factors. No apparent relationship between appearance of vasculitis and liver disease (if present).	"One shot" syndrome often self-limited; usually preicteric. Hepatitis A may produce a similar transient syndrome. Necrotizing vasculitis syndrome is potentially life-threatening but may evolve as a chronic debilitating disorder requiring immunosuppressive therapy.
Poststreptococcal acute glomerulonephritis	*Streptococcus pyogenes*	May follow either pharyngeal or skin infection. Related to specific M types of *S pyogenes:* pharyngeal (types 1, 4, 12, and 18; perhaps 3, 6, and 25); skin (types 2, 31, 49, 52–55, 57, 60). Seven to 14-day latent period between infection and onset of glomerulonephritis (similar to interval in experimental serum sickness).	Immune complex glomerulonephritis characterized by proteinuria, hematuria. May progress to hypertension, renal functional impairment, and edema of face and legs. All glomeruli diffusely involved. Antibody, complement deposited in renal vasculature. Hypocomplementemia during first 2 to 6 weeks of illness.	Usually heals; especially in children.

Table 34–4 (cont'd). Immune complex complications of infectious diseases.

Disease	Etiologic Agent	Immunologic Predisposition	Immunologic Complications	Comments
Quartan malaria	*Plasmodium malariae*	High level of parasitemia. High malaria antibody titers.	Immunoglobulins and complement in glomerular capillary walls. Nephrotic syndrome.	Poor response to corticosteroids. Most common in children 4–8 years of age.
Syphilis	*Treponema pallidum*	Congenital or secondary syphilis.	Nephrotic syndrome. "Hemorrhagic glomerulonephritis" has also been described.	Responds to penicillin.
Typhoid fever	*Salmonella typhi*	Persistent infection with prolonged bacteremia.	Antibody, complement, and Salmonella "Vi" antigen in glomerular capillary walls → glomerulonephritis.	Probably a common complication of typhoid fever but rarely appreciated because renal biopsies are seldom done (or justified).
Leprosy	*Mycobacterium leprae*	Erythema nodosum leprosum (see description elsewhere in chapter).		

In a simple exanthematous disease such as rubella, other signs due to circulating immune complexes such as arthritis may be seen occasionally.

THE SPECTRUM OF HOST-VIRUS IMMUNOLOGIC RELATIONSHIPS

Major Immunologic Features

- Disease may be acute, latent, chronic, or delayed ("slow virus") in onset.
- Altered disease presentation may result from prior immunization with inactivated virus.

General Considerations

Viral diseases can be divided into 2 main categories with respect to the ultimate fate of the virus in the tissues:

(1) **Virus may be eliminated from the body**: This is the pattern which is encountered in the vast majority of human viral infections, ranging from smallpox to influenza to poliomyelitis. Appropriate secretory and systemic, cellular and humoral immune defenses are garnered and the virus is dealt with appropriately. Subsequent immunity is solid and generally persists for a lifetime. (Some investigators regard the firm persistence of immunity as evidence that the virus may continue to be sequestered in the tissues for life, serving to chronically boost the host immunologic response. Even if this is the case, the viruses in this group never manifest themselves clinically beyond the initial acute illness.)

(2) **Virus may persist in the body and produce disease**: An uneasy immunologic balance between virus and host may obtain in certain viral infections, giving rise to patterns of latency, chronicity, or extremely delayed ("slow") onset. Examples of acute and persistent host-virus relationships are outlined in Table 34–5.

A third category of viral illness may be encountered in patients who have previously received certain inactivated vaccines. Here, vaccine-modified host defenses accentuate to a greater or lesser degree the characteristics of subsequent natural infection, while failing to provide adequate protection.

Measles

Recipients of formaldehyde-inactivated measles vaccine, upon subsequent natural exposure to measles, may develop a hyperacute "atypical measles" syndrome characterized by an inordinate febrile response, pneumonia with pleural effusion, and a severe hemorrhagic rash which is atypically distributed. Severe local skin reactions may also occur when previous recipients of inactivated measles vaccine receive an inoculation with the live vaccine.

It has been suggested that the prior vaccination results in an augmentation of delayed hypersensitivity to the measles virus. Alternatively, there is also evidence to suggest that "atypical measles" may reflect the presence of immune complex deposition. According to the latter explanation, inactivated vaccine produces serum IgG antibody titers, which then wane. Upon subsequent exposure to the live virus, a marked anamnestic IgG response occurs, producing antibody which complexes with viral antigen and precipitates a subsequent Arthus response in respiratory tract and skin.

Respiratory Syncytial Virus

Recipients of formaldehyde-treated, alum-precipitated respiratory syncytial virus (RSV) vaccine may develop clinically typical but much more severe illness upon subsequent natural exposure to the virus. Bronchiolitis and pneumonia, in particular, are accentuated. Again, augmented delayed hypersensitivity or Arthus-type immune complex deposition in the bronchiolar walls has been held responsible.

Immunologic exacerbation of infection by prior

Table 34–5. The spectrum of host-virus immunologic relationships.*

Fate of Virus in Tissues	Type of Infection	Characteristic Host-Virus Relationships	Specific Examples	Comments
Eliminated	Acute	Short incubation periods (2 days to 2 or 3 weeks). Virus recoverable before, but not after onset of disease. Recovery common. Recovered host is immune to same or closely related viruses.	Smallpox (high clinical attack rate; usually results in disease). Poliomyelitis (rarely results in clinical disease). Innumerable others.	The vast majority of the acute viral infections of man fall into this immunologic category. Immunity is solid and persistent.
Not eliminated; persists in host tissues for months, years, or a lifetime	Latent	Acute primary infection followed by recovery and subsequent relapses and remissions. Virus recoverable during primary and relapsing phases of infection; not recoverable from target tissues during remissions. Host immune response demonstrable but ineffective in preventing relapse.	Herpes simplex ("fever blisters"). Varicella-zoster ("shingles").	These viruses apparently persist in nerve ganglions during periods between attacks. Humoral antibody is demonstrable but not protective. Cell-mediated immunity is critical but not sufficient to prevent relapses. Immunosuppressive diseases or drugs may permit dissemination of these otherwise well-localized recurrent illnesses.
	Chronic	Variable incubation period, outcome, and course. Virus persists and is regularly recoverable. Host immune response demonstrable but does not influence pattern of disease.	Congenital rubella syndrome.	Infection of fetus occurs during second or third months of gestation. Persistent viral infection produces congenital abnormalities and vasculitis. Brisk IgM antibody response; depressed cell-mediated immunity.
			Cytomegalovirus infection.	May produce mental retardation, hepatitis when acquired in utero. Hepatitis, rash, and "mononucleosis-like" syndrome in older persons. Commonly asymptomatic but becomes apparent (variably symptomatic) in the presence of immunosuppression. High antibody titers are not protective.
			Hepatitis B infection.	Eighty-five percent of patients with acute hepatitis show HB_sAg for 1–13 weeks; 5% for up to 6 months; some carry HB_sAg chronically. Persistence of carriage is associated with suppression of T cell function.
	Slow	Incubation period of months to years. Relentless progress and lethal course of disease.	Kuru; Creutzfeldt-Jakob disease (humans); scrapie (sheep); transmissible mink encephalopathy (mink).	Progressive demyelinating syndromes characterized by "subacute spongiform encephalopathy." Kuru and Creutzfeldt-Jakob disease are transmissible to chimpanzees. Virus (or viroid) not identified.
			Progressive multifocal leukoencephalopathy.	Due to a conventional virus (SV40 or similar DNA virus) which may constitute part of the "normal brain flora." Disease emerges under immunosuppression. Virus recoverable throughout course of disease. Minimal inflammation or other evidence of host immune response.
			Subacute sclerosing panencephalitis (SSPE) (Dawson's inclusion body encephalitis).	Due to a conventional virus (measles virus) which produces persistent infection. Abnormally high titers of measles antibody present (depressed cell-mediated immunity). High IgG levels. Epidemiologic evidence suggests very early measles infection (< 2–3 years of age) with manifestations of SSPE in early teens (= "slow"). Might be classified with the "chronic" group.

*Adapted from Youmans GP, Paterson PY, Sommers HM (editors): *The Biological and Clinical Basis of Infectious Diseases.* Saunders, 1975.

vaccination is not unique to viral diseases. Local ocular immunization with *Chlamydia trachomatis* vaccine has been shown to predispose to more intense ocular infection upon subsequent challenge with a wild-type heterologous trachoma strain. Immunity to the homologous strain, in contrast, is intact. Delayed hypersensitivity is an important immune mechanism in trachoma and is presumably intensified by prior immunization. Similarly, *M pneumoniae* infection is intensified by prior immunization, but only in those patients who fail to develop growth-inhibitory mycoplasma antibody. These patients appear to be sensitized by the prior vaccination. This phenomenon is of particular interest because the occurrence of *M pneumoniae* pneumonia (typically in young adults) is considered to reflect an immune response to an agent which is encountered frequently (and asymptomatically) throughout early childhood.

OPPORTUNISTIC INFECTIONS

Major Immunologic Features

- Defective functioning of the normal immune system predisposes to infections which are characteristic for the compromised immune function.
- Infecting pathogen may be either common or rare (emerging only under circumstances of defective immunity).
- Restoration of normal immune status may be of greater importance in recovery than antimicrobial drug therapy.

General Considerations

Nothing is more revealing of the normal functional capacity of the immune system than the infec-

Table 34–6. Opportunistic infections.

Immunologic Setting	Commonly Associated Pathogens	Comments
Hypogammaglobulinemia (congenital or acquired)	Pyogenic extracellular bacteria. Some viruses.	Loss of opsonic or neutralizing antibody. (*S pneumoniae* infection is especially common in multiple myeloma.)
Granulocytopenia (< 1000 circulating granulocytes/μl; often due to cancer chemotherapy; bone marrow failure)	Pyogenic extracellular bacteria. Gram-negative enteric bacteria (*E coli*, etc). Environmental gram-negative bacteria (*Ps aeruginosa; S marcescens*). *Candida albicans.*	Inadequate circulating phagocytic cells (qualitative granulocyte defects give rise to similar infections).
Depressed cell-mediated immunity due to basic illness (Hodgkin's disease) or drug therapy (cancer chemotherapy; organ transplantation)	Intracellular pathogens (*M tuberculosis; H capsulatum*, etc.) Rare "unusual" pathogens (*N asteroides; L monocytogenes; Pneumocystis carinii; Toxoplasma gondii*). DNA-type viruses (varicella-zoster; cytomegalovirus; wart virus; progressive multifocal leukoencephalopathy).	Defective lymphocyte function. (*T gondii* is actually a very common pathogen; immunosuppression permits reactivation of quiescent cysts, especially in the brain). (*P carinii* is a protozoan parasite of the pulmonary alveolar space, where it replicates in a proteinaceous coagulum. There are no useful immunologic tests for its presence. It produces an alveolar capillary block [arterial shunt] syndrome.)
Hemolysis (chronic, severe) (especially with sickle cell disease, malaria, bartonellosis)	Salmonellosis with bacteremia and secondary local abscess formation.	Salmonella species may compete with red cell breakdown products for macrophage membrane receptor sites, resulting in impaired phagocytosis. In sickle cell disease, salmonella may infect bone infarcts, leading to high incidence of salmonella osteomyelitis.
Splenectomy	Pyogenic encapsulated extracellular bacteria (especially *S pneumoniae*). Rarely, malaria, piroplasmosis (babesiosis).	Fulminating and rapidly fatal bacterial infection, often complicated by disseminated intravascular coagulation. Risk of infection far greater when there is an underlying disease of the reticuloendothelial system or when the patient is very young (ie, adolescent splenectomy for trauma carries less risk than childhood splenectomy for thalassemia). Spleen is critically important in the early control of bacteremia, prior to the synthesis of specific opsonic antibody. Impaired synthesis of IgM, tuftsin, and complement shunt pathway components may follow splenectomy. Loss of "pitting" function for malaria and similar protozoa.
Foreign bodies (intravascular, intra-articular, etc)	Pyogenic extracellular bacteria (especially *S aureus* and *S epidermidis*). *Candida albicans* (especially during total parenteral nutrition; hyperalimentation).	Direct vascular portal from the skin (intravascular catheters). High candida incidence in hyperalimentation may reflect glucose-rich material infused. Arteriovenous shunts (as from dialysis) may predispose to infective endocarditis by changing flow characteristics across heart valves, leading to predisposition to incidental infection).
Gastrectomy	Pulmonary tuberculosis. Salmonella gastroenteritis. Cholera.	Malnutrition due to excessive stomach removal (tuberculosis reactivation). Loss of gastric acidity barrier (salmonellosis and cholera).

tious diseases which result when immunity is suppressed. In a sense, every infectious disease represents an opportunistic infection (for example, pneumococcal pneumonia occurs because of the opportunity afforded by aspiration of secretions and the absence of circulating type-specific opsonic antibody).

The diseases summarized in Table 34–6, however, result when there is a more flagrant disruption of the functional capacity of the immune system. There is no attempt to list every potential opportunistic pathogen; major relationships are stressed.

• • •

References

General

Beeson PB, McDermott W (editors): *Textbook of Medicine.* Saunders, 1975.

Davis BD & others (editors): *Microbiology,* 2nd ed. Harper & Row, 1973.

Hoeprich PD (editor): *Infectious Diseases: A Guide to the Understanding and Management of Infectious Processes.* Harper & Row, 1972.

Schlessinger D (editor): *Microbiology–1975.* American Society for Microbiology, 1975.

Wilson GA, Miles A (editors): *Topley and Wilson's Principles of Bacteriology and Immunity.* Vols 1 & 2. Williams & Wilkins, 1975.

Youmans GP, Paterson PY, Sommers HM (editors): *The Biological and Clinical Basis of Infectious Diseases.* Saunders, 1975.

Pneumococcal Infection

Austrian R: Random gleanings from a life with the pneumococcus. J Infect Dis 131:474, 1975.

Austrian R, Gold J: Pneumococcal bacteremia with especial reference to bacteremic pneumococcal pneumonia. Ann Intern Med 60:759, 1964.

Coonrod JD, Drennan DP: Pneumococcal pneumonia: Capsular polysaccharide antigenemia and antibody responses. Ann Intern Med 84:254, 1976.

Mufson MA & others: Capsular types and outcome of bacteremic pneumococcal disease in the antibiotic era. Arch Intern Med 134:505, 1974.

Meningococcal Infection

Edwards EA: Immunologic investigations of meningococcal disease. 1. Group-specific *Neisseria meningitidis* antigens present in the serum of patients with fulminant meningococcemia. J Immunol 106:314, 1971.

Edwards EA: Immunologic investigations of meningococcal disease. 2. Some characteristics of group C antigen of *Neisseria meningitidis* in the sera of patients with fulminant meningococcemia. J Infect Dis 129:538, 1974.

Hoffman TA, Edwards EA: Group-specific polysaccharide antigen and humoral antibody response in disease due to *Neisseria meningitidis.* J Infect Dis 126:636, 1972.

Meningococcal polysaccharide vaccines: Recommendation of the Public Health Service Advisory Committee on Immunization Practices. Center for Disease Control, United States Department of Health, Education, & Welfare, Atlanta, Ga. Ann Intern Med 84:179, 1976.

***Haemophilus influenzae* Infection**

Anderson P & others: Immunization of humans with polyribophosphate, the capsular antigen of *Haemophilus influenzae,* type b. J Clin Invest 51:39, 1972.

Bradshaw M & others: Bacterial antigens cross-reactive with the capsular polysaccharide of *Haemophilus influenzae,* type b. Lancet 1:1095, 1971.

Robbins JB & others: *Hemophilus influenzae* type b: Disease and immunity in humans. Ann Intern Med 78:259, 1973.

Sell SH, Karzon DT (editors): *Hemophilus influenzae: Proceedings of a Conference on Antigen-Antibody Systems, Epidemiology, and Immunoprophylaxis.* Vanderbilt Univ Press, 1973.

Smith DH & others: Responses of children immunized with the capsular polysaccharide of *Hemophilus influenzae,* type b. Pediatrics 52:637, 1973.

Gonorrhea

Buchanan TM & others: Quantitative determination of antibody to gonococcal pili: Changes in antibody levels with gonococcal infection. J Clin Invest 52:2896, 1973.

Gonorrhea: Recommended treatment schedules. Center for Disease Control. Ann Intern Med 82:230, 1975.

Grossman M, Drutz D: Venereal disease in children. Adv Pediatr 21:97, 1974.

Holmes KK & others: Disseminated gonococcal infection. Ann Intern Med 74:979, 1971.

Kearns DH & others: Paradox of the immune response to uncomplicated gonococcal urethritis. N Engl J Med 289:1170, 1973.

Ward ME, Watt PJ: Adherence of *Neisseria gonorrhoeae* to urethral mucosal cells: An electron-microscopic study of human gonorrhea. J Infect Dis 126:601, 1972.

***Streptococcus pyogenes* Infection**

Wannamaker LW: Streptococcal infections of the throat and of the skin. (2 parts.) N Engl J Med 282:23, 78, 1970.

***Staphylococcus aureus* Infection**

Cohen JO (editor): *The Staphylococci.* Wiley, 1972.

Tuazon CU, Sheagren JN: Teichoic acid antibodies in the diagnosis of serious infections with *Staphylococcus aureus.* Ann Intern Med 84:543, 1976.

***Klebsiella pneumoniae* Infection**

Edmondson EB, Stanford JP: The Klebsiella-Enterobacter (Aerobacter)-Serratia group: A clinical and bacteriological evaluation. Medicine 46:323, 1967.

***Pseudomonas aeruginosa* Infection**

Reynolds HY & others: *Pseudomonas aeruginosa* infections: Persisting problems and current research to find new therapies. Ann Intern Med 82:819, 1975.

Plague

Reed W & others: Bubonic plague in the southwestern United States: A review of recent experience. Medicine 49:465, 1970.

Anthrax

Brachman PS: Anthrax. Ann NY Acad Sci 174:577, 1970.

Exotoxin Production & Disease

Exotoxins. Pages 236–301 in: *Microbiology–1975.* Schlessinger D (editor). American Society for Microbiology, 1975.

Host-parasite relations in bacterial diseases. Chap 22, pages 629–665 in: *Microbiology,* 2nd ed. Davis BD & others (editors). Harper & Row, 1973.

Epithelial Cell Attachment & Disease

Interactions at body surfaces. Pages 106–157 in: *Microbiology–1975.* Schlessinger D (editor). American Society for Microbiology, 1975.

Penetration. Pages 158–199 in: *Microbiology–1975.* Schlessinger D (editor). American Society for Microbiology, 1975.

Viral Neutralization

Johnson TC: Host-virus interaction: General properties of animal viruses. Chap 4 in: *The Biological and Clinical Basis of Infectious Diseases.* Youmans GP, Paterson PY, Sommers HM (editors). Saunders, 1975.

Cryptococcosis

Diamond RD, Bennett JE: Prognostic factors in cryptococcal meningitis: A study in 111 cases. Ann Intern Med 80:176, 1974.

Goodman JS & others: Diagnosis of cryptococcal meningitis: Value of immunologic detection of cryptococcal antigen. N Engl J Med 285:434, 1971.

Hammerman KJ & others: Pulmonary cryptococcosis: Clinical forms and treatment. Am Rev Respir Dis 108:1116, 1973.

Mitchell TG, Friedman L: In vitro phagocytosis and intracellular fate of variously encapsulated strains of *Cryptococcus neoformans.* Infect Immun 5:491, 1972.

Schimpff SC, Bennett JE: Abnormalities in cell-mediated immunity in patients with *Cryptococcus neoformans* infection. J Allergy Clin Immunol 55:430, 1975.

Syphilis

Kaufman RE & others: The FTA:ABS (IgM) test for neonatal congenital syphilis: A critical review. J Am Vener Dis Assoc 1:79, 1975.

Musher DM, Schell RF: The immunology of syphilis. Hosp Prac 10:45, Dec 1975.

Olansky S, Norins LC: Current serodiagnosis and treatment of syphilis. JAMA 198:165, 1966.

Rockwell DH & others: The Tuskegee study of untreated syphilis: The 30th year of observation. Arch Intern Med 114:792, 1964.

Salmonellosis

Collins FM, Carter PB: Cellular immunity in enteric disease. Am J Clin Nutr 27:1424, 1974.

Grady GF, Keusch GT: Pathogenesis of bacterial diarrheas. (2 parts.) N Engl J Med 285:831, 891, 1971.

Harris JC & others: Fecal leukocytes in diarrheal illness. Ann Intern Med 76:697, 1972.

Hornick RB & others: Typhoid fever: Pathogenesis and immunologic control. (2 parts.) N Engl J Med 283:686, 739, 1970.

Candidiasis

Elin RJ, Wolff SM: Effect of pH and iron concentration on growth of *Candida albicans* in human serum. J Infect Dis 127:705, 1973.

Knight L, Fletcher J: Growth of *Candida albicans* in saliva: Stimulation by glucose associated with antibiotics, corticosteroids, and diabetes mellitus. J Infect Dis 123:371, 1971.

Kozinn PJ & others: Problems in the diagnosis and treatment of systemic candidiasis. (Correspondence.) J Infect Dis 126:548, 1972.

Miller GG & others: Rapid identification of *Candida albicans* septicemia in man by gas-liquid chromatography. J Clin Invest 54:1235, 1974.

Listeriosis

Medoff G & others: Listeriosis in humans: An evaluation. J Infect Dis 123:247, 1971.

Tuberculosis

Mackaness GB: Resistance to intracellular infection. J Infect Dis 123:439, 1971.

Wolinsky E: New antituberculosis drugs and concepts of prophylaxis. Med Clin North Am 58:697, 1974.

Youmans GP, Youmans AS: Recent studies on acquired immunity in tuberculosis. Curr Top Microbiol Immunol 48:129, 1969.

Leprosy

Abe M & others: Immunological problems in leprosy research. (2 parts.) Bull WHO 48:345, 482, 1973.

Bryceson A, Pfaltzgraff RE: *Leprosy for Students of Medicine.* Churchill Livingstone, 1973.

Bullock WE Jr: Leprosy. Pages 630–643 in: *Immunological Diseases,* 2nd ed. Samter M (editor). Little, Brown, 1971.

Drutz DJ & others: The continuous bacteremia of lepromatous leprosy. N Engl J Med 287:159, 1972.

Measurement of Antibody & Disease

Histoplasmosis, coccidioidomycosis, blastomycosis. Chap 26, pages 375–405 in: *The Biological and Clinical Basis of Infectious Diseases.* Youmans GP, Paterson PY, Sommers HM (editors). Saunders, 1975.

Histoplasmosis

Anderson KL, Marcus S: Immunity to histoplasmosis induced in mice by components of *Histoplasma capsulatum.* Am Rev Respir Dis 102:614, 1970.

Buechner HA & others: The current status of serologic, immunologic, and skin tests in the diagnosis of pulmonary mycoses. Dis Chest 63:259, 1973.

Goodwin RA, Des Pres RM: Pathogenesis and clinical spectrum of histoplasmosis. South Med J 66:13, 1973.

Howard DH: Intracellular growth of *Histoplasma capsulatum.* J Immunol 89:518, 1965.

Levin S: The fungal skin test as a diagnostic hindrance. (Editorial.) J Infect Dis 122:343, 1970.

US Public Health Service Cooperative Mycoses Study: Course and prognosis of untreated histoplasmosis. JAMA 177:292, 1961.

Coccidioidomycosis

Ajello L (editor): *Coccidioidomycosis.* Univ of Arizona Press, 1967.

Catanzaro T, Spitler L: Transfer factor therapy of coccidioidomycosis. In: *Proceedings of the Second International Conference on Transfer Factor.* Academic Press, 1976.

Fiese MJ: *Coccidioidomycosis.* Thomas, 1958.

Kobayashi GS, Pappagianis D: Preparation and standardization of antigens of *Histoplasma capsulatum* and *Coccidioides immitis.* Mycopathol Mycol Appl 41:139, 1970.

Levine HB, Gonzalez-Ochoa A, Ten Eyck DR: Dermal sensitivity to *Coccidioides immitis:* A comparison of responses elicited in man by spherulin and coccidioidin. Am Rev Respir Dis 107:379, 1973.

Smith CE & others: Pattern of 39,500 serologic tests in coccidioidomycosis. JAMA 160:546, 1956.

Brucellosis

Bradstreet CM & others: Intradermal test and serological tests in suspected brucella infection in man. Lancet 2:653, 1970.

Buchanan TM & others: Brucellosis in the United States, 1960–1972: An abattoir-associated disease. 1. Clinical features and therapy. 2. Diagnostic aspects. 3. Epidemiology and evidence for acquired immunity. Medicine 53:403, 415, 427, 1974.

Reddin JL & others: Significance of 7S and macroglobulin Brucella agglutinins in human brucellosis. N Engl J Med 272:1263, 1965.

Tularemia

Hornick RB: Tularemia. Pages 1105–1112 in: *Infectious Diseases: A Guide to the Understanding and Management of Infectious Processes.* Hoeprich PD (editor). Harper & Row, 1972.

Mycoplasma

Clyde WA Jr: Pathogenic mechanisms in mycoplasma diseases. Pages 143–146 in: *Microbiology–1975.* Schlessinger D (editor). American Society for Microbiology, 1975.

Mycoplasmas and L forms. Chap 40, pages 930–944 in: *Microbiology,* 2nd ed. Davis BD & others (editors). Harper & Row, 1973.

Chlamydiae

Grayston JT, Wang S-P: New knowledge of chlamydiae and the diseases they cause. J Infect Dis 132:87, 1975.

Rickettsiae

Hazard GW & others: Rocky Mountain spotted fever in the eastern United States: Thirteen cases from the Cape Cod area of Massachusetts. N Engl J Med 280:57, 1969.

Murray ES & others: Brill's disease: 1. Clinical and laboratory diagnosis. JAMA 142:1059, 1950.

Zdrodowskii PF, Golinevich HM: *The Rickettsial Diseases.* Pergamon Press, 1960.

Bordetella pertussis

Olson LC: Pertussis. Medicine 54:427, 1975.

Circulating Immune Complexes & Disease

Duffy J & others: Polyarthritis, polyarteritis and hepatitis B. Medicine 55:19, 1976.

Gutman RA & others: The immune complex glomerulonephritis of bacterial endocarditis. Medicine 51:1, 1972.

Heptinstall RH (editor): *Pathology of the Kidney,* 2nd ed. Vol 1. Little, Brown, 1972.

Kaye D (editor): *Infective Endocarditis.* Univ Park Press, 1976.

Sergent JS & others: Vasculitis with hepatitis B antigenemia: Long-term observations in nine patients. Medicine 55:1, 1976.

Sitprija V & others: Glomerulonephritis in typhoid fever. Ann Intern Med 81:21, 1974.

Host-Virus Relationships

Craighead JE: Report of a workshop: Disease accentuation after immunization with inactivated microbial vaccines. J Infect Dis 131:749, 1975.

Opportunistic Infections

Barrett-Connor E: Bacterial infection and sickle cell anemia: An analysis of 250 infections in 166 patients and a review of the literature. Medicine 50:97, 1971.

Bisno AL, Freeman JC: The syndrome of asplenia, pneumococcal sepsis and disseminated intravascular coagulation. Ann Intern Med 72:389, 1970.

Dilworth JA, Mandell GL: Infections in patients with cancer. Semin Oncol 2:349, 1975.

Drutz DJ: Antibiotic therapy in compromised hosts. Calif Med 119:49, July 1973.

Merigan TC, Stevens DA: Viral infections in man associated with acquired immunological deficiency states. Fed Proc 30:1858, 1971.

35 . . .
Endocrine Diseases

Noel R. Rose, MD, PhD

Some of the best-studied examples of organ-specific autoimmune disease are endocrine disorders. Organ-specific disorders affect a single organ of the body either primarily or exclusively. The target antigen of the immunologic response is unique for the affected organ, ie, it is an organ-specific antigen. Such antigens arise during embryonic differentiation and are often associated with the unique function of the organ. Organs of internal secretion, with their highly specialized physiologic functions, possess distinctive organ-specific antigens.

The regulatory factors that normally restrain immunity to self have not yet been clearly identified. Excessive amounts of antigen may eliminate progenitors of self-reactive lymphocyte clones during embryonic development or paralyze them throughout later life. Active suppressive factors, such as a special type of thymus-derived lymphocyte (suppressor T cells), may arrest autoimmune responses. In spite of such controlling measures, however, stimulation of an immunologic response by autoantigens is relatively common, especially if the antigen is anatomically isolated or found in only a limited cell population. Thus, organs with distinctive, specific antigens, like the endocrine glands, frequently induce autoimmune responses (see Table 35–1).

CHRONIC THYROIDITIS

Major Immunologic Features

- Produced experimentally by injection of thyroglobulin in adjuvants.
- Thyroid function tests may be elevated, depressed, or normal.
- Autoantibodies to thyroglobulin or thyroid microsomes (or both) present.
- Self-limited or responsive to thyroid hormone treatment.

General Considerations

The thyroid gland has certain unusual structural and functional properties that seem to predispose to the development of autoimmune responses. It is made up of a series of saclike follicles lined with cuboid epithelium. Within the follicles is found the homogeneously stained colloid, the principal constituent of which is a glycoprotein, thyroglobulin. This high-molecular-weight protein (about MW 650,000) contains iodinated amino acids, ie, mono- and diiodotyrosine, triiodothyronine (T_3), and thyroxine (T_4). The latter 2 amino acids are the active thyroid hormones. Most of the circulating thyroxine is bound to protein, whereas triiodothyronine is weakly attached to plasma proteins and diffuses freely into cells. The synthesis of thyroglobulin in the follicle-lining cells is usually balanced by its resorption and splitting by thyroid proteolytic enzymes or cathepsins. Thyroglobulin is essentially a molecular storage form of the thyroid hormones. Thyroglobulin breakdown is enhanced by one of the peptides secreted by the anterior pituitary, termed thyroid-stimulating hormone (TSH) or thyrotropin, and decreased by iodide.

Physiologically, the thyroid hormones affect the rate of cellular oxidation throughout the body. The hormones (particularly T_3) also reduce the formation or liberation of thyrotropin, providing a typical example of endocrinologic feedback inhibition. In addition to thyroxine and triiodothyronine, the thyroid gland secretes another hormone, calcitonin. This hormone has not as yet been implicated in autoimmune responses.

As might be expected of a large glycoprotein, thyroglobulin is a good antigen. Injection into foreign species readily elicits antibody formation. A large proportion of the antibodies produced to thyroglobulin are organ-specific. They react with thyroglobulin and not with other antigens of the body, such as glycoproteins isolated from other organs. In addition, antibodies to thyroglobulin of one species partially cross-react with thyroglobulins of other mammals. This lack of strict species-specificity is a characteristic of some of the most potent organ-specific antigens.

It was formerly believed that thyroglobulin is anatomically sequestered from the vascular and lymphatic pathways. More recent information indicates that low levels of thyroglobulin are found in the lymphatics draining the thyroid and in the bloodstream. By itself, thyroglobulin does not evoke formation of antibodies in the same species or same animal.

Noel R. Rose is Professor and Chairman, Department of Immunology and Microbiology, Wayne State University School of Medicine, Detroit.

Table 35–1. Endocrine diseases with autoimmune phenomena.

Disease	Antigen(s)	Methods for Detection of Antibody
Chronic thyroiditis and primary hypothyroidism	Thyroglobulin	Precipitation Tanned cell hemagglutination Chromic chloride hemagglutination Latex fixation Bentonite agglutination Immunofluorescence
	Microsomes of thyroid epithelium	Complement fixation Immunofluorescence Antiglobulin consumption Hemagglutination
	Second colloid antigen	Immunofluorescence
	Membranes	Cytotoxicity Mixed agglutination
Hyperthyroidism (Graves' disease)	Microsomes of thyroid epithelium	Bioassay (LATS)
Adrenal insufficiency (Addison's disease)	Microsomes of adrenal cortex Soluble antigen of adrenal cortex Steroid-producing cells of adrenal, ovary, testis, and placenta	Immunofluorescence Complement fixation Precipitation
Primary hypoparathyroidism	Oxyphil cells Chief cells	Immunofluorescence
Diabetes mellitus	α, β, γ cells of pancreatic islets	Immunofluorescence
Ovarian failure	Cells of theca interna of corpus luteum	Immunofluorescence
Male infertility	Germinal epithelium Spermatozoa	Agglutination Immobilization Immunofluorescence Complement fixation

However, injection of an animal's own thyroglobulin, combined with certain adjuvants, elicits production of specific autoantibodies. If given with Freund's complete adjuvant (an emulsion with mineral oil, acid-fast microorganisms, and an emulsifying agent), thyroglobulin injections elicit lymphocytic infiltration of the thyroid gland of the immunized animal. This process of chronic inflammation is referred to as thyroiditis.

Injection of foreign thyroglobulins also elicits thyroid-specific autoantibodies. Extensive immunization with these cross-reacting thyroglobulins sometimes causes thyroiditis. Thyroglobulin molecules of the same species can be rendered antigenic (without the need for adjuvants) by inserting foreign chemical determinants such as arsanilic or sulfanilic groups. These apparently provide immunologic handles similar to those supplied by the foreign determinants of cross-reacting thyroglobulins. It is also possible to make thyroglobulin antigenic by incomplete proteolytic digestion. Perhaps this procedure exposes unfamiliar sites of the molecule that act like foreign determinants.

In addition to antibody, immunization with thyroglobulin gives rise to delayed hypersensitivity. In some animals, such as the guinea pig, the skin test reaction seems to correlate more closely with thyroid lesions than does antibody. In the rabbit, on the other hand, delayed hypersensitivity appears rather late, after the onset of the disease.

The immunologic reaction to thyroglobulin is determined in part by the innate, genetically determined responsiveness of the injected animal. For example, among mice, some inbred strains are excellent responders to their own thyroglobulin while other strains are very poor responders. It is probable that several genes are involved in determining the response. The ability to produce circulating antibody to thyroglobulin can sometimes be separated from the ability to develop autoimmune lesions in the thyroid. One of the main genes controlling recognition is linked to the major histocompatibility (H-2) complex of the mouse and is probably an Ir gene coding response to a particular determinant or small number of determinants on the thyroglobulin molecule.

Some animals have a strong tendency to develop thyroiditis spontaneously, such as certain strains of beagle dogs and of rats. A closed colony of chickens has been established by selective breeding, and these birds have severe thyroid inflammation with typical clinical and biochemical evidence of thyroid failure. Study of these spontaneous models of thyroiditis provides valuable clues about the cause, pathogenesis, and genetic predisposition to autoimmune disease of the thyroid in humans.

Immunologic Pathogenesis

The similarity of chronic thyroiditis in the human to experimentally induced or hereditary thyroiditis is striking. The principal antigen is thyroglobulin. Under experimental conditions, this purified protein can be shown to be autoantigenic. Immunization results in production of autoantibodies reactive with antigen from the immunized animal itself. Lesions arise simultaneously in the thyroid gland of the animal, and these lesions are quite similar to those of the human disease. Human chronic thyroiditis fulfills these minimal criteria for diseases of autoimmune origin (Table 35–2).

Defining the precise pathogenic mechanisms of thyroiditis has proved to be difficult. In some species, such as the rabbit and mouse, it has been possible to transfer the disease from immunized to normal animals by injecting antibody-containing serum. The mechanism by which antibodies induce lymphocytic inflammation of the thyroid is uncertain. Antibodies may interact with thyroglobulin in the follicles or along the basement membrane of the thyroid gland. A localized immune complex tissue injury would result. On the other hand, the antibodies may cooperate with normal lymphocytes to produce tissue damage.

In other species, such as the guinea pig or rat, thyroiditis has thus far been transferred only with living, histocompatible lymph node cells. The histologic features of thyroiditis are more suggestive of cell-mediated than of antibody-mediated immunologic reactions. It is possible to demonstrate delayed hypersensitivity by skin tests in immunized guinea pigs and rats. In vitro indicators of cell-mediated immunity such as production of macrophage migration inhibitory factor (MIF) and lymphocyte transformation have also been shown in some species.

Thyroid lesions are produced by adoptive transfer of lymph node cells in the rabbit, guinea pig, and rat. The functions of the transferred, sensitized lymphocytes are unknown, but most of them do not localize specifically in the thyroid. They may secrete autoantibody, although such antibody cannot be found in the bloodstream at the time lesions become evident. They may interact with thyroid antigen to release active products, the lymphokines. It is possible that sensitized lymphocytes specifically destroy living target thyroid cells by direct interaction.

In the test tube, it can be shown that normal lymphocytes of the human can cooperate with thyroid antibody to damage thyroid cells or lyse carrier cells coated with thyroglobulin or thyroid microsomes. These findings support the view that antibody-dependent cell-mediated lymphotoxicity is responsible for the induction of pathologic changes in the thyroid. Circulating immune complexes have also been found in human thyroiditis sera. Complexes of appropriate size may adhere to the stroma of the thyroid gland, activate complement, and provoke inflammation. Macrophages may be attracted nonspecifically by products released from sensitized lymphocytes and specifically activated by macrophage-arming factor. Obviously, more work must be done to define the pathogenetic mechanisms in thyroiditis both in humans and in experimental animals.

Table 35–2. Criteria for establishing the autoimmune etiology of an organ-specific human disease.*

(1) Autoantibodies reactive at body temperature, or evidence of cell-mediated immunity
(2) Isolation and purification of the organ-specific antigens
(3) Production of autoantibodies to analogous antigen in experimental animals
(4) Development of similar lesions in autosensitized animals

*Modified from Witebsky E & others: Chronic thyroiditis and autoimmunization. JAMA 164:1439, 1957.

Clinical Features

Chronic lymphocytic thyroiditis is most common in the age group from 30–60 years, although juvenile thyroiditis may cause sporadic goiter in children and adolescents. The female-to-male ratio is about 5:1, an indication that sex hormones may influence expression of the disease. The incidence of thyroiditis in monozygotic twins is about 6 times greater than in dizygotic twins of the same sex, suggesting a strong genetic predisposition. A number of studies have pointed to a relationship of thyroiditis and chromosomal aberrations, especially Down's syndrome. Although unpredictable in its occurrence, the disease is found more frequently in persons who have relatives with a thyroid disorder, such as thyroiditis, hyperthyroidism, or myxedema. The relatives may have thyroid antibodies without overt disease or may have autoimmune disease of another endocrine gland, pernicious anemia, or atrophic gastritis. This immunologic overlap among the organ-specific autoimmune disorders has been taken as tentative evidence that there is some genetic fault in the immunologic regulatory mechanisms that normally control self-reactive lymphocytes.

The subacute form of thyroiditis sometimes occurs in small outbreaks following viral infections. Mumps has been reported to predispose to thyroiditis. It may be that respiratory tract infections can trigger autoimmunity to thyroid, but this relationship has not been clearly demonstrated in cases of chronic thyroiditis.

The clinical features of chronic thyroiditis in man are relatively mild. The thyroid gland may be diffusely enlarged to produce a goiter. It is usually firm to hard in consistency, only rarely tender, and smooth or scalloped without distinct nodules. Severe symptoms of neck pain with upward radiation may be present. In most thyroiditis patients, the level of circulating iodoproteins is elevated. However, caution is necessary in interpreting the biochemical findings in thyroiditis. Although the level of total protein-bound iodine (PBI) may be high, the amount of serum thyroxine or triiodothyronine may be low. This disparity seems to be due to the presence in the bloodstream of abnormal circulating iodoproteins. Thyroiditis patients may also show an abnormality in the organification of iodine. Iodide initially concentrated in the thyroid may be discharged if the patient is given potassium perchlorate, which inhibits iodide transport by the thyroid cell.

Most chronic thyroiditis patients are clinically euthyroid even though uptake of radioactive iodine by the thyroid is high. About 20% are hypothyroid when first seen, and occasionally hyperthyroidism is present initially in the disease. During the later phases of chronic thyroiditis, patients may develop signs of diminished thyroid function, suggesting failure of regeneration of the epithelial cells. The skin is dry and the hair coarse, and myxedema is sometimes present. These patients show lowered values of circulating thyroid hormones, decreased thyroidal radioiodine uptake, high serum TSH levels, and high serum cholesterol levels. Their basal metabolic rates are low.

During the active stages of thyroiditis, many patients have systemic evidence of an inflammatory process. The erythrocyte sedimentation rate may be increased. A false-positive serologic test for syphilis can occur. In some patients, increased levels of circulating γ-globulin can be demonstrated. This globulin elevation was one of the first signs which suggested an immunologic origin of thyroiditis.

Immunologic Diagnosis

The cornerstone of immunologic diagnosis of human thyroiditis is the demonstration of autoantibodies to thyroid-specific antigens. In humans, as in animals, thyroglobulin is the major autoantigen of the thyroid (Table 35–1). This protein can be readily extracted from thyroid glands with neutralized saline solution and prepared in relatively pure form by simple methods. If the concentration of antibody in the patient's serum is sufficient, direct precipitation can be produced. However, use of more sensitive technics is advisable. A suitable procedure is to coat erythrocytes with human thyroglobulin. This can be accomplished by pretreating the erythrocytes with tannic acid or chromic chloride. After washing, the erythrocytes are added to dilutions of patient's serum and the titer of antibody to thyroglobulin is measured. Most normal individuals have no detectable antibody to thyroglobulin. Approximately 60–75% of patients with various forms of chronic thyroiditis (depending upon the histologic type) show positive reactions in an indirect hemagglutination test (Tables 35–3 and 35–4). About a third of these patients have elevated hemagglutination titers of 600–1000 or more. Titers in this elevated range are strongly indicative of autoimmune thyroiditis or a related autoimmune process. Patients with primary adult myxedema may also demonstrate high titers of antibody to thyroglobulin in the same high incidence as thyroiditis (Table 35–3). About a third of patients with hyperthyroidism due to Graves' disease and one-fourth of patients with carcinoma of the thyroid (especially papillary adenocarcinoma) have antibodies to thyroglobulin, usually with titers of less than 600 (Table 35–3). In many cases of hyperthyroidism or of thyroid cancer, localized lymphocytic infiltrates are found. The presence of antibodies in these 2 diseases may be indicative of a secondary process of autoimmunization. Therefore, positive antibody findings are of limited value in the differential diagnosis of chronic thyroiditis unless markedly elevated titers are obtained.

Autoantibodies to thyroglobulin may be found in a few other diseases. Patients with pernicious anemia or atrophic gastritis frequently have antibodies to thyroid antigens. Patients with idiopathic adrenal insufficiency or parathyroid failure sometimes have autoantibodies to thyroid. In Sjögren's syndrome, autoantibodies to thyroglobulin are sometimes found in the same high titers characteristic of thyroiditis and hypothyroidism.

Table 35–3. Incidence of thyroglobulin autoantibodies in various thyroid diseases and controls (tanned cell hemagglutination method).

Histologic Diagnosis	Approximate Percentage of Positive Reactions
Thyroiditis	
Acute	10%
Subacute (granulomatous or de Quervain's)	35%
Fibrotic (Riedel's)	50%
Chronic	
Lymphocytic	60%
Fibrous	75%
Mixed (nonspecific)	75%
Primary hypothyroidism (adult myxedema)	75%
Hyperthyroidism (thyrotoxicosis or Graves' disease)	40%
Carcinoma	25%
Control hospital population	5%

Hemagglutinating autoantibodies to thyroglobulin are reported in about 3–18% of individuals with no clinical evidence of thyroid disease. This figure depends to a great extent upon the age and sex of the group being sampled. For example, the normal reactor group is much higher if made up of female subjects 40–60 years of age. It is quite plausible that the appearance of autoantibodies in these individuals actually signifies a subclinical focal thyroiditis, which has been frequently reported in middle-aged women.

The autoantibodies to thyroglobulin found in human thyroiditis provide the usual reactions in precipitation and agglutination technics. By immunofluorescence, they localize in the colloid of methanol-fixed sections, producing a floccular appearance (Fig 35–1). The antibodies may be found in any of the major immunoglobulin classes, IgG, IgM, or IgA. However, they do not fix complement.

Thyroiditis sera sometimes produce complement fixation when mixed with crude extracts or suspen-

Table 35–4. Incidence of autoantibodies to thyroglobulin and thyroid microsomes in 546 patients with various forms of thyroiditis.

Antibodies to Thyroglobulin (Tanned Cell Hemagglutination)	Antibodies to Thyroid Microsomes (Complement Fixation)	Percentage Positive
+	+	37
+	-	27
-	+	33
-	-	3

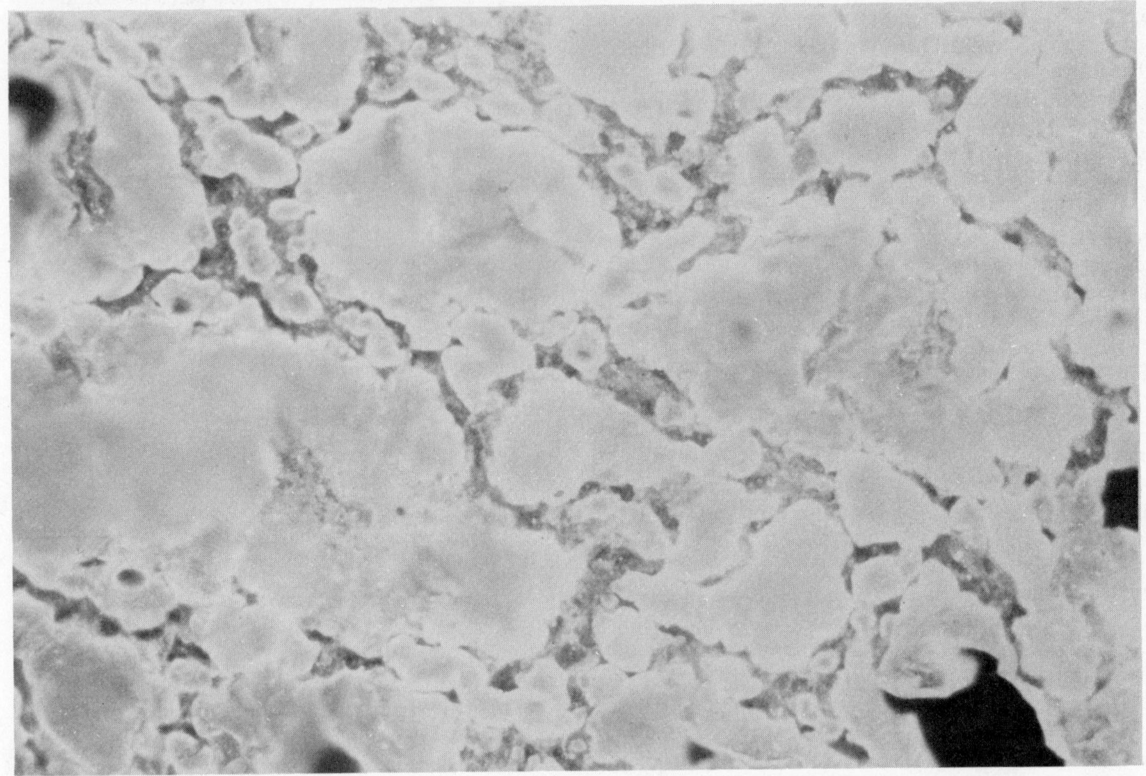

Figure 35–1. Immunofluorescent staining of thyroglobulin. Monkey thyroid tissue was frozen rapidly, thin-sectioned with a cryostat (4 μm), and fixed in methanol at 56 C for 10 minutes. It was covered with serum from a patient with chronic thyroiditis (diluted 1:10), washed, covered with fluorescein-labeled anti–human globulin goat serum, washed, and examined with the ultraviolet microscope. A floccular pattern of fluorescence is seen within the thyroid follicles, indicating staining of the colloid. (Original magnification, × 180.)

sions of thyroid. The antigen involved, however, is not thyroglobulin. It has been localized in the apical cytoplasm of the thyroid epithelial cell. More precisely, the antigen seems to be associated with a lipoprotein of the microsomal membrane. The reaction is thyroid-specific. A diagnostic titer is considered to be 8 or greater. In one series, about 70% of thyroiditis patients demonstrated this antibody.

The complement fixation test for autoantibodies to thyroid microsomes is difficult to perform because most normal thyroid extracts have relatively few microsomes. It is advantageous to use antigens prepared from thyrotoxic glands, which are richer in microsomes. Control microsomes from other tissues should be negative.

Since the group of patients with antibodies to thyroid microsomes does not correspond precisely with the group that has thyroglobulin antibodies, the total of patients in whom complement-fixing or hemagglutinating antibodies can be measured is about 97% (Table 35–4). Thus, the immunologic diagnosis of chronic thyroiditis using these 2 independent tests is more successful than with either test alone. Like hemagglutinating antibodies, the incidence of complement-fixing antibodies differs in the different forms of thyroiditis, being greatest in the mixed and fibrous varieties of chronic thyroiditis and least in the lymphocytic form of thyroiditis. About 2% of healthy male blood donors and 6% of female donors have autoantibodies to thyroid microsomes by the complement fixation method.

Because of the intrinsic difficulties of performing complement fixation with tissue suspensions, an indirect immunofluorescence test provides a convenient method for demonstrating antibodies to the microsomal antigen. It is more sensitive than complement fixation but is not readily quantitated. Fixed tissues cannot be used because the antigen is easily destroyed. Fresh frozen human or monkey thyroids are sectioned, flooded with patient's serum, washed, and treated with a fluorescent antiglobulin reagent. In the ultraviolet microscope, fluorescence is found in the apical cytoplasm of the thyroid epithelial cells (Fig 35–2). Nuclei are unstained. During the procedure, most of the thyroglobulin is washed out of the follicles, so that no reaction occurs that can be attributed to thyroglobulin antibodies. A test for antibodies to thyroid microsomes has recently been devised using the tanned cell hemagglutination technic.

Antibodies will occasionally be found that react

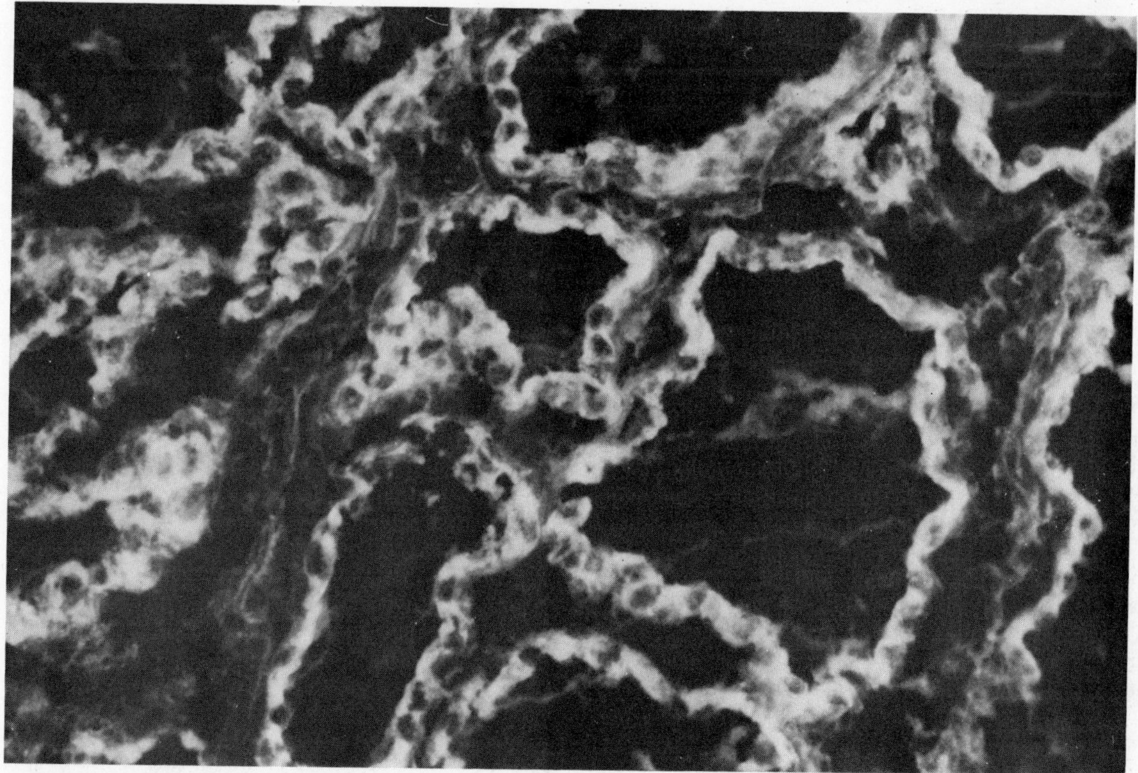

Figure 35–2. Immunofluorescent staining of thyroid microsomal antigen. Monkey thyroid tissue was prepared in the same manner as that described for Fig 35–1 except that it was not fixed in methanol. Immunofluorescent staining is seen in the cytoplasm of the thyroid epithelial cells lining the follicles. Note that the nuclei of the epithelial cells and the interstitial cells are unstained. (Original magnification, × 180.)

with the colloid in a homogeneous pattern. They are not absorbed with thyroglobulin. The reaction is attributed to a second colloid antigen. The antigen, which is not well characterized, is a noniodinated colloid protein (Table 35–1).

Suspensions of viable thyroid cells can be prepared from human or monkey thyroid glands by treating them with trypsin and collagenase. When serum of certain thyroiditis patients is mixed with these thyroid cell suspensions in the presence of complement, it will prevent the thyroid cells from attaching to the surface of the glass vessel and generating a monolayer. Control sera do not have this cytotoxic action. These cytotoxic antibodies are the only ones to have an injurious effect on thyroid cells in vitro. The antigen is a component of the thyroid epithelial cell membrane. Its presence also seems to be demonstrated on the surface of the thyroid cell by means of a mixed agglutination reaction using thyroglobulin-coated erythrocytes and a bridging antibody. The cytotoxic antigen is distinct from microsomal antigen. Many patients with positive complement fixation tests have no evidence of a cytotoxic reaction and are negative in mixed agglutination and vice versa. Cytotoxic antibodies can be found in a large proportion of patients with thyrotoxicosis and the juvenile form of thyroiditis.

Cell-mediated immunity to thyroid antigens has also been described. Some thyroiditis patients develop typical delayed hypersensitivity reactions when injected intradermally with thyroid extracts. Positive leukocyte migration inhibition and lymphocyte transformation have been obtained using crude thyroid extract, thyroglobulin, thyroid microsomes, and thyroid mitochondria. The clinical significance of these assays has not yet been established.

Differential Diagnosis

Chronic lymphocytic thyroiditis must be distinguished from nontoxic goiter, from subacute thyroiditis, from Graves' disease, and from several types of cancer of the thyroid. The first distinction can be difficult, but nontoxic goiter is usually less firm than thyroiditis, and the presence of distinct nodularity favors the diagnosis of nontoxic goiter. In adults, high titers of thyroid autoantibodies will favor a diagnosis of thyroiditis. In adolescents, however, thyroiditis may be present in the absence of high antibody titers. Evidence of hypothyroidism favors a diagnosis of thyroiditis over that of either nontoxic goiter or thyroid cancer. Thyroid cancer would be suggested by the finding of very firm or hard nodules, adherence to skin or underlying structures, hoarseness due to invasion of the recurrent laryngeal nerve, and regional lymphadenopathy, all of which are unusual signs in thyroiditis and nontoxic goiter. A thyroid scintiscan is of critical importance in the evaluation of the nodular thyroid. Areas of nonfunction are unusual in thyroiditis as compared to nontoxic goiter and cancer. A needle biopsy can be done if thyroiditis is suspected but should not be relied upon if cancer is more likely. In this instance, if a tissue diagnosis is desired, excisional biopsy is necessary.

Patients with subacute thyroiditis may complain of sore throat occurring coincident with or before the onset of thyroiditis. Perhaps the most significant statement a patient with subacute thyroiditis makes is that the throat is "sore on the outside rather than the inside." In contrast to chronic thyroiditis, the goiter of subacute thyroiditis may be accompanied by early elevations of protein-bound iodine and serum thyroxine, but these values usually return to normal later.

Acute thyroiditis is usually due to infection with pyogenic or mycobacteria strains. It is rarely associated with autoantibody production.

Histologically, several forms of thyroiditis can be differentiated (Table 35–2). Some thyroids show granulomas containing typical giant cells and epithelioid cells. This form of thyroiditis, referred to as de Quervain's type, corresponds to the subacute disease, the most common type following viral infection. The patients show systemic evidence of inflammation, such as fever, a rapid pulse, and an elevated sedimentation rate. Radioiodine uptake may be low even though circulating thyroid hormone is high.

Sometimes the gland is largely replaced by dense hyaline connective tissue with extension of the fibrotic process beyond the thyroid capsule. In this invasive form of fibrotic thyroiditis (Riedel's struma), the thyroid gland is woody hard and fixed. Esophageal constriction and dysphagia may be major complications of fibrotic thyroiditis.

The most common form of chronic thyroiditis is associated with enlargement of the gland and infiltration by lymphocytes. Lymphoid nodules with germinal centers are sometimes found. Often one sees a mixed process of inflammation. There are many small and large lymphocytes, plasma cells, and macrophages which are prominent especially within the colloid. The colloid appears thin and foamy. Phagocytosis of the colloid can sometimes be demonstrated by proper staining. Eosinophils may be seen with special stains. Fibrosis may be evident in some portions of the gland. The follicular basement membrane may appear fragmented when viewed in the electron microscope. The thyroid is usually moderately enlarged but may be small in size and weight. If inflammation is extensive, it may invade the surrounding capsular tissue.

In the fibrous variant of chronic lymphocytic thyroiditis, the gland contains prominent strands of fibrous connective tissue. In contrast to Riedel's struma, this form of fibrosis does not invade the surrounding muscle. Between the bands of fibrous tissue, the thyroid parenchyma shows changes of epithelial degeneration and chronic inflammation with infiltration of lymphocytes and plasma cells. These cases are the ones most often associated with depressed thyroid function.

In chronic thyroiditis, thyroid epithelial cells show evidence of regeneration and proliferation, appearing as oxyphilic or eosinophilic (Askenazy or Hürthle) cells. The inflammatory process is commonly multifocal, so that some portions of the gland appear relatively normal while other areas are intensely infiltrated, with consequent degeneration of the epithelium. Often one can find neighboring sections in which there is evidence of an active process of regeneration. The follicular epithelium may be hypercellular, suggesting an effort to respond to thyroid-stimulating hormone.

Although the term Hashimoto's disease or *struma lymphomatosa* is often given to all the goitrous forms of the disease, the simple designation chronic thyroiditis describes the broad spectrum of pathologic and clinical variants. In all forms of the disease, evidence of an immunologic response is found, but frequencies of antibodies may vary greatly (Table 35–2).

Treatment, Complications, & Prognosis

In most instances, the thyroid enlargement may persist if active treatment is not given. Desiccated thyroid or another form of thyroid hormone usually relieves the distressing symptoms and reduces the size of the gland, probably by suppressing pituitary thyrotropin production. Antibody titers are gradually reduced by thyroid hormone treatment. The neck pain may require treatment with analgesics such as aspirin. Corticosteroids reduce local inflammation and often produce a rapid decrease in titers of thyroid antibodies. In the cases that progress to hypothyroidism, chronic replacement therapy with desiccated thyroid or some other preparation of thyroid hormone is necessary. In theory, immunosuppressive drugs should be effective, as demonstrated in experimental animals. However, their use is rarely warranted in this disease.

Surgery of the thyroid and use of radioactive iodine are not generally indicated in chronic thyroiditis. Therefore, the differentiation of thyroiditis from thyroid carcinoma and hyperthyroidism, respectively, is a matter of great practical importance. As a matter of fact, therapeutic doses of radioactive iodine may intensify thyroiditis. Patients with preexisting antibody seem to develop more autoantibody following radioiodine treatment. An elevation in antibody to the thyroid microsomes is especially prominent.

The patient with subacute thyroiditis generally recovers complete thyroid function, and any thyroid enlargement which may obtain during the course of the disease generally disappears. The antibodies fall to undetectable levels when the inflammation has subsided. The hyperthyroidism that may accompany subacute thyroiditis does not require treatment. In fact, it is not likely that antithyroid drugs will have any beneficial effect because the hyperthyroidism is probably due to leakage of thyroglobulin into the circulation and its hydrolysis at peripheral sites with subsequent release of thyroxine.

PRIMARY HYPOTHYROIDISM
(Adult Myxedema)

Insufficiency of circulating thyroid hormones leads to hypothyroidism. The signs and symptoms depend greatly on the age at onset. Cretinism results from thyroid deficiency during fetal life and is characterized by irreversible arrest in development of the musculoskeletal and central nervous systems. There is no evidence that this disease is immunologic in origin. It occurs no more frequently in children of mothers with thyroid autoantibodies than in children of normal mothers, which means that thyroid antibody alone does not damage a normal thyroid gland.

Primary adult myxedema occurs without known cause, though it is reasonable to assume that immunologic processes play a role in the development of the disease. Patients typically have cold, dry skin, dry, coarse hair, constipation, intolerance to cold, and loss of vigor. The face is puffy and the complexion yellow as a result of carotenemia. Speech is slowed and thought processes retarded. In some cases the heart rate is slowed and the heart is enlarged, with pericardial effusion. Deep tendon reflexes are characteristically slowed, with delayed recovery return. Firm myxedema is apparent under the skin. Laboratory findings usually include a decreased radioiodine uptake and low thyroxine (T_4) and triiodothyronine (T_3) levels. Serum cholesterol is high.

Primary hypothyroidism must be differentiated from thyroid failure due to pituitary insufficiency. The thyroid in pituitary insufficiency usually responds well to administration of thyrotropic hormone.

In severe primary hypothyroidism, the thyroid gland is usually atrophic, with fibrosis and only a few isolated islets of acinar tissue. The appearance is quite different from the fibrous variant of chronic thyroiditis.

Immunologically, hypothyroidism closely resembles chronic thyroiditis. Circulating antibodies and cell-mediated immunity to thyroid antigen are present. Antibodies are found in the same high titers characteristic of thyroiditis (Table 35–3).

HYPERTHYROIDISM

Major Immunologic Features

- Presence of LATS in about 45% of patients.
- LATS is present in γ-globulin and may be an immune complex with thyroid antigen.
- Cellular immunity to thyroid microsomes.
- Autoantibodies to thyroid can be identified in most patients by a combination of hemagglutination, cytotoxicity, complement fixation, or immunofluorescence tests.

General Considerations

In older individuals, hyperfunction of the thyroid is often insidious in onset and therefore difficult to recognize clinically. Hyperthyroidism may be due to diffuse hyperplasia (diffuse toxic goiter or Graves' disease), nodular goiter, or localized autonomous adenoma. It is linked to thyroiditis by familial clustering, ie, patients with thyroiditis often have family members with hyperthyroidism and vice versa.

Because of the difficulty in recognizing mild forms of the disease, the prevalence of hyperthyroidism is not definitely known. It is clear, however, that women develop the disease 4–5 times as often as men and that the greatest incidence is in the fourth and fifth decades. In these respects also, hyperthyroidism resembles thyroiditis.

Study of the involvement of autoimmunity in hyperthyroidism is hampered by the lack of a well-defined experimental model. In the human disease, a relative increase of lymphocytes has been reported, but this may be attributed to a decrease in neutrophils. The thymus may be larger than normal. As mentioned previously, about one-third of patients with hyperthyroidism have autoantibody to one or another thyroid antigen. However, these antibodies might signify the simultaneous occurrence of thyroiditis and hyperthyroidism in the same patient rather than an immunologic cause of hyperthyroidism itself.

The strongest indication of an immunologic basis for hyperthyroidism comes from studies of long-acting thyroid stimulator (LATS). The serum of patients with diffuse hyperplasia of the thyroid produces a prolonged stimulation of guinea pig or mouse thyroids measured as an increase in radioiodine uptake. In contrast, thyrotropin causes only a brief increase in iodine uptake. The detailed study of LATS has been hampered by the fact that a bioassay is still necessary for its demonstration. The usual procedure is to measure release of radioactive iodine from the thyroid gland following injection of mice with patient's serum or concentrated γ-globulin fractions. This slow release distinguishes LATS from the rapidly acting thyroxine.

Following standard fractionation technics, LATS can be isolated from human serum in the γ-globulin fraction. It is also precipitated by anti-IgG. After cleavage of IgG with papain, LATS activity appears in the Fab fragment. Moreover, antisera to human IgG neutralize the biologic action of LATS. Crude extracts of normal human thyroid tissue also inhibit or neutralize LATS activity. The active fraction has been localized at the cell surface on the plasma membrane. It is destroyed by treatment with proteolytic enzymes but not by lipases or deoxycholate. Purified human thyroglobulin does not neutralize LATS, which seems to stimulate cells through adenylate cyclase activation.

It has not yet been possible to induce LATS production by experimental immunization. Injection of rabbits with thyroid particles sometimes results in the production of thyroid-stimulating antibodies. However, there are no concurrent changes in thyroid function to suggest that these antibodies have biologic activity. Some investigators have suggested that LATS represents a soluble complex of thyrotropin and its antibody. Slow release of thyroid-stimulating hormone from this immune complex might account for its prolonged activity as well as its migration in the IgG fraction.

Immunologic Pathogenesis

One theory of an immunologic origin of hyperthyroidism rests on the demonstration of LATS. The evidence that this factor represents a stimulating autoantibody has been outlined above. However, lack of an experimental model has hampered the definition of stimulatory antibodies. It is possible that other thyroid autoantibodies may have a stimulatory effect. For example, complement-fixing antibodies to thyroid microsomes are relatively prominent in hyperthyroidism. In small amounts, these antibodies may increase the function of thyroid cells. Immune complexes formed in certain ratios of thyroglobulin to its respective antibody may also exert stimulatory effects. Cell-mediated immunity to thyroid microsomes has been demonstrated in most hyperthyroid patients by use of the leukocyte migration inhibition (LIF) test. T lymphocytes within the thyroid gland may directly stimulate thyroid cells. Finally, there is the possibility—mentioned above—that LATS represents a complex of thyrotropin which, slowly released, induces long-standing thyroid stimulation.

The exophthalmos and pretibial myxedema of hyperthyroidism may represent a distinct pathologic process. Some investigators have suggested that it results directly from the action of LATS. Others have reported evidence of delayed hypersensitivity to retro-orbital components underlying the chronic inflammation and local infiltration. The orbital antigen involved in this possible sensitization phenomenon has not yet been defined.

Clinical Features

A. Symptoms and Signs: Hyperthyroidism (Graves' disease) results from overproduction of thyroid hormone. It is marked by an increased rate of tissue metabolism in most systems of the body. It may occur in all grades of severity. Occasionally the onset is sudden, but more commonly the symptoms develop so slowly that the patient is unaware of the disease. Symptoms may be aggravated and brought to his attention by physical or emotional trauma. The most common symptoms are restlessness, heat intolerance, weight loss, and palpitations. The principal signs include smooth, warm, and moist skin resulting from vasodilatation and excessive sweating, a diffuse goiter, tachycardia, a wide pulse pressure, fine tremor of the hands, and proximal muscle weakness. The heart rate in hyperthyroidism is typically rapid, with an elevated systolic pressure and wide pulse pressure. In other individuals, tachycardia, arrhythmia, or evidence of congestive heart failure may first bring the patient to the physician. A striking feature of many cases of hyperthyroidism is bilateral ophthalmopathy (also called exophthalmos) consisting of widened palpebral fissures, retro-orbital edema, proptosis, conjunctivitis, and sometimes loss of vision due to optic nerve ischemia.

B. Laboratory Findings: Histologically, hyperthyroidism may be associated with a diffusely hyperplastic gland, with multiple overactive nodules, or with a solitary adenoma.

Laboratory studies of patients with hyperthyroidism usually show that blood levels of protein-bound iodine, thyroxine, and triiodothyronine are high, and uptake of radioactive iodine by the thyroid gland is increased. Serum cholesterol may be low.

Immunologic Diagnosis

The demonstration of LATS requires a complex bioassay based on the release of radioiodine from the thyroid of a mouse following administration of patient's serum. About 45% of patients with diffuse hyperplasia of the thyroid have detectable amounts of LATS in their serum. Even more positive reactions are found if the concentrated γ-globulin fraction is employed. LATS is not usually found in patients with autonomous adenoma or multinodular goiter. Some individuals with normal thyroid function have LATS in their serum. It has been found that their thyroids do not respond normally to thyrotropin, suggesting that the gland is insensitive to thyroid stimulation.

Instead of LATS, patients with hyperthyroidism may have another immunoglobulin in their circulation known as LATS protector. This substance has the property of blocking the binding of LATS to the human thyroid microsomal fraction which absorbs LATS activity. It seems to be an antibody, perhaps one that combines only with human thyroid cells. LATS and LATS protector may both be found in the serum of a few patients with hyperthyroidism.

A certain proportion of patients with hyperthyroidism associated with either diffuse or nodular goiters have antibodies in their sera to thyroid microsomal antigen, thyroid surface antigen, and thyroglobulin. These antibodies can be demonstrated by complement fixation, cytotoxicity, or hemagglutination (Table 35–5). Hemagglutination and complement fixation

Table 35–5. Incidence of thyroid autoantibodies in patients with hyperthyroidism.*

Histologic Diagnosis	Percentage of Sera Positive By: Hemagglutination	Complement Fixation	Cytotoxicity
Diffuse hyperplastic goiter	38	25	61
Nodular toxic goiter	57	14	71
Chronic thyroiditis	75	67	75

*Modified from Kite JH Jr & others: Ann NY Acad Sci 124:626, 1965.

reactions are less frequently positive in hyperthyroidism than in thyroiditis, and the antibodies are found in lower titers. These antibodies are sometimes accentuated after radioiodine therapy, but after a short time they decrease in titer.

Differential Diagnosis

If symptoms are prominent, the diagnosis of hyperthyroidism usually presents no difficulty. Often, however—particularly in the early stages—the disease is mild. It may be confused with emotional anxiety states or tachycardia associated with infection or other causes. The tremor may resemble that of chronic alcoholism or parkinsonism. The diagnosis is usually based on appropriate laboratory tests. Unfortunately, the results of serum hormone determinations may be invalidated by the use of drugs such as iodides, radiopaque contrast media, or estrogens unless the clinical situation is fairly obvious.

Treatment

The treatment of hyperthyroidism includes surgical removal of the thyroid, administration of radioactive iodine, or therapy with antithyroid drugs with adjunctive use of iodide or adrenergic blocking agents. Iodide is rarely used alone for the treatment of hyperthyroidism. It is useful in reducing the size of the gland in preparation for surgery or for promoting prompt cessation of thyroid hormone release before administration of the slower-acting antithyroid drugs. Although the reduction in size and vascularity of the thyroid gland following iodide treatment is remarkable, it is generally temporary. Antithyroid drugs such as methimazole or propylthiouracil do not prevent release of preformed hormone, so their effectiveness is slower than that of iodide. After several weeks, however, they can be quite effective in alleviating the major symptoms of hyperthyroidism. The drugs may be given continuously for control of the disease or as preparation for surgical removal of the gland.

Radioiodine (^{131}I) is widely used for the treatment of hyperthyroidism. It can be employed for both diffuse and nodular goiters. The effectiveness of the isotope depends upon its preferential localization in the thyroid and emission of beta rays which damage the thyroid cells. The main problem in its use is to determine a dose that will alleviate symptoms without producing hypothyroidism. Part of the difficulty in determining the proper dose of radioiodine may reside in its tendency to increase sensitization. After ^{131}I treatment, patients show a transient elevation in the titer of thyroid microsomal and cytotoxic antibodies. Patients with autonomous toxic nodules rarely develop hypothyroidism or thyroid autoantibodies after radioiodine treatment. This observation suggests that in the absence of some predisposing condition, injury to the thyroid is not sufficient to induce autosensitization.

Subtotal thyroidectomy is an effective way of treating hyperthyroidism in a properly prepared patient. Without adequate preparation, the complications of surgery are significant. In addition, removal of a hyperfunctioning gland can lead to thyroid crisis. Following surgery, it is often necessary to provide some measure of replacement with thyroid hormone. If exophthalmos is severe, treatment with anti-inflammatory corticosteroids or surgical decompression may be necessary. Radiation has also been found to be useful in treating exophthalmos.

Complications & Prognosis

Untreated hyperthyroidism can produce irreversible problems in several organ systems. There may be gradual deterioration of the cardiovascular system leading to congestive heart failure. Stressful situations, including infection, may precipitate thyrotoxic crisis or "storm." Generally, infections are not well handled by thyrotoxic patients. Infectious hepatitis may be a serious hazard. The exophthalmos may lead to keratitis and corneal scarring or, worse, optic neuritis and blindness. Although the course of the disease may be irregular, untreated patients are always subject to recurrence and complications.

THYROGASTRIC DISEASE

The autoimmune response to thyroid antigens of patients with thyroiditis is strikingly analogous to the response to gastric mucosal antigens that occurs in patients with pernicious anemia. Antibodies that bind with or block the action of intrinsic factor are found in many adult patients with pernicious anemia (see Chapter 30). By immunofluorescence, antibodies to a cytoplasmic antigen of the gastric parietal cell can be demonstrated in pernicious anemia sera. These reactions are comparable to the reactions of thyroiditis patients with soluble thyroglobulin or thyroid microsomal antigen.

In addition, there is considerable overlap in the occurrence of circulating gastric and thyroid antibodies. One-fourth of patients with chronic thyroiditis were found in one study to have antibodies to the gastric parietal cell. One-third of myxedema patients were also positive. Conversely, about 30% of patients with pernicious anemia have antibody to one or another thyroid antigen in their serum. Equally interesting relationships emerge when the asymptomatic relatives of patients are studied. Forty-seven percent of relatives of patients with thyroiditis have antibody to thyroid antigens, and 18% have antibody to parietal cells. Of the relatives of patients with pernicious anemia, 45% showed antibody to the gastric parietal cells and 67% to thyroid antigens. When proper allowance is made for age and sex, patients with these organ-specific autoimmune disorders show little or no increase in the anticipated occurrence of the autoimmune disease systemic lupus erythematosus or of antinuclear antibodies.

The basis of this overlap is far from clear at this time. There is no special antigenic relationship between thyroid and gastric cells. More basic research is necessary before we can understand why patients should develop 2 apparently unrelated autoimmune responses. The possibility of a genetic defect in the suppression of autoimmune clones of lymphocytes is suggested by the data described.

CHRONIC ADRENOCORTICAL INSUFFICIENCY

Adrenal antibodies have been produced in experimental animals following injection of adrenal homogenate plus Freund's complete adjuvant. However, the reports with regard to the development of lesions have been variable in different species. Guinea pigs were found to develop lymphocytic and histiocytic infiltration and necrosis of the adrenal cortex following immunization with guinea pig adrenal extract. Cell-mediated immune reactions to adrenal microsomes were also present. Rabbits developed adrenalitis after injection of foreign but not rabbit adrenal homogenate. In inbred rats, disease could be induced by injection of syngeneic adrenal extract with Freund's complete adjuvant and pertussis vaccine. Adrenalitis was transferred from actively immunized donors to normal recipients by means of living lymph node cells. Lesions could be seen as early as 5 days after transfer. They seemed to be initiated by the arrival in the adrenal of a few specially sensitized lymphocytes which migrated by chance from the bloodstream. Their local stimulation by adrenal antigen may have caused the lymphocytes to produce mediators that attracted and activated macrophages and trapped additional nonsensitized lymphocytes at the site.

Patients with adrenocortical failure (Addison's disease) are recognized by typical symptoms of postural hypotension, weight loss, anorexia, weakness, and hyperpigmentation of folds of the skin. Acute adrenal failure sometimes leads to hypovolemic shock. It is necessary to distinguish secondary adrenal insufficiency caused by anterior pituitary failure from the primary form of the disease. In the latter instance, circulating corticotropin (ACTH) levels are usually high. Confirmatory diagnosis depends upon demonstrating low serum and urinary levels of cortisol unresponsive to ACTH stimulation. High plasma ACTH levels and low plasma and urinary cortisol levels are also indications of primary disease. Functional tests of the adrenal medulla are usually normal.

Two etiologic forms of primary Addison's disease are distinguished: exogenous and idiopathic. Tuberculous adrenal failure is now rare in countries where tuberculosis is well controlled. Systemic mycoses, metastatic tumors, irradiation, infarction, or amyloidosis may produce similar adrenocortical insufficiency. More common in Western countries is idiopathic adrenocortical failure. It occurs at any age, with a peak incidence in the fourth and fifth decades. It is seen more often in females in a ratio of approximately 2:1 or 3:1.

Histologically, in adrenocortical insufficiency, the adrenal cortex loses its normal 3-layered structure so that the cortical cells are reduced to disorganized islets. Lymphocytic and monocytic infiltration and fibrosis are prominent. The medulla is usually normal in appearance.

There is considerable overlap of idiopathic adrenocortical insufficiency with other diseases believed to be autoimmune in nature, including primary myxedema, chronic thyroiditis (Schmidt's syndrome), thyrotoxicosis, pernicious anemia, primary hypoparathyroidism, and diabetes mellitus. In addition to antibodies to adrenal tissue, patients with idiopathic Addison's disease frequently show antibodies to gastric parietal cells, thyroid epithelial cells, thyroglobulin, and intrinsic factor. On the other hand, the occurrence of antinuclear antibody is not unusually high in this group of patients when one takes into account their age and sex.

Antibodies to adrenal microsomes can be demonstrated by means of immunofluorescence or complement fixation (Table 35–1). A relatively small proportion of patients have precipitating antibodies to a different soluble, organ-specific adrenal antigen. Indirect immunofluorescence can be applied using frozen sections of human or monkey adrenal tissue. By this method, antibodies can be found in approximately 50% of patients (38–64% in various series) with idiopathic adrenal insufficiency. The number of positive reactions reported in sera of patients with the tuberculous form of insufficiency varies from none to 18% in different series. Antibodies persist for many years despite replacement therapy in which adrenal hormones are used.

Complement fixation tests are usually performed with saline extracts of adrenals taken from patients undergoing adrenalectomy for Cushing's adrenal hyperplasia. Glands taken from experimental animals are rarely suitable. The antigen is sedimented in the smaller particles of the cytoplasm and seems similar in cellular location to the microsomal membranes involved in thyroid and gastric disorders.

In indirect immunofluorescence microscopy, localization is usually found in the secretory cells of the zona glomerulosa, zona fasciculata, and zona reticularis. Some sera stain only one or 2 layers of the adrenal (Fig 35–3). A relatively small proportion of patients show antibodies specific for the zona fasciculata that cross-react with steroid hormone-secreting cells of the theca interna of the corpus luteum of the ovary as well as interstitial cells of the testes and placental trophoblasts. There is said to be a correlation between the presence of these antibodies to steroid-producing cells and a clinical history of ovarian failure in addisonian patients. In young women, delayed menarche or unexplained amenorrhea has been associated with these antibodies to steroid-secreting cells. The observations support the hypothesis that ovarian disorders are related by an autoimmune pathogenetic mechanism involving antigens shared by the adrenals and ovary.

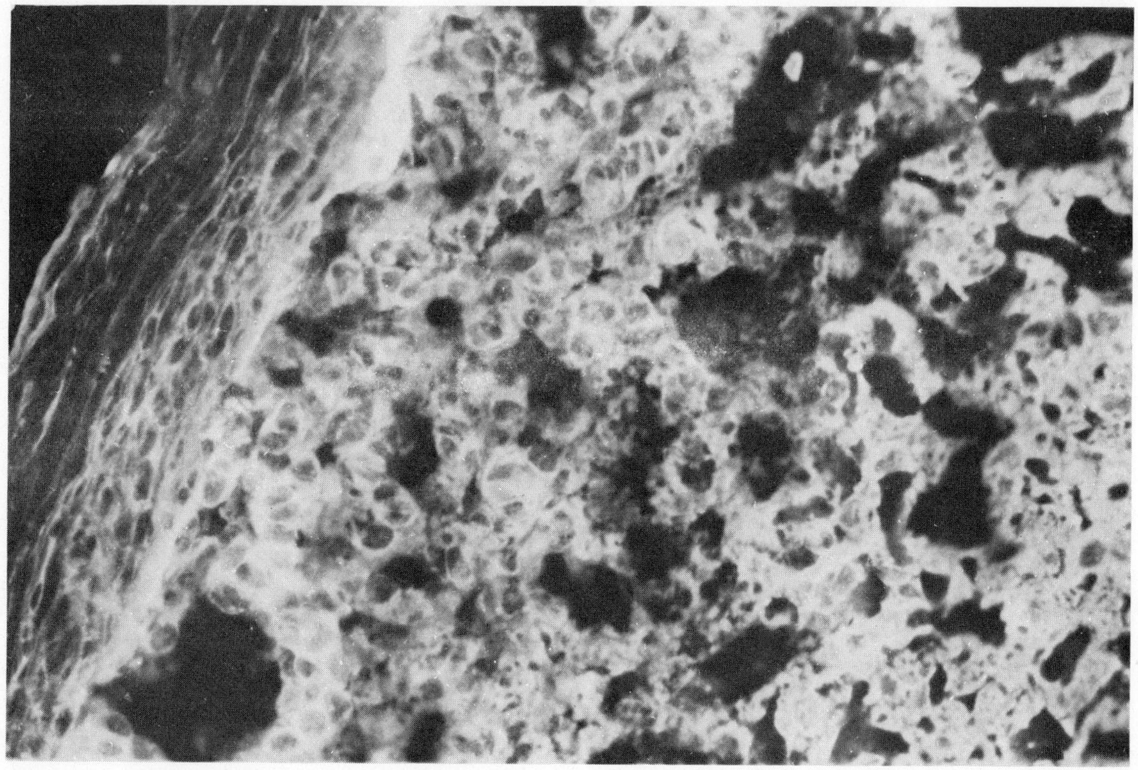

Figure 35–3. Immunofluorescent staining in adrenal insufficiency. Monkey adrenal tissue was prepared in the same manner as the thyroid tissue described in Figs 35–1 and 35–2. The tissue was not fixed and was tested with serum from a patient with adrenocortical insufficiency (diluted 1:5). Fluorescent staining of cells in the glomerulosa and fasciculata layers can be seen. (Original magnification, × 180.)

OVARIAN FAILURE

Ovarian failure is often associated clinically with multiple features of endocrinopathy such as adrenal insufficiency, thyroiditis or thyrotoxicosis, hypoparathyroidism, and diabetes mellitus, as well as chronic candidiasis. The patients have symptoms of primary or secondary amenorrhea or premature menopause, with elevation of serum and urinary pituitary gonadotropins. A high proportion of ovarian failure patients with associated autoimmune endocrinopathy have antibodies that are reactive with human ovarian tissue. Fluorescence is seen mainly on the cells of the theca interna, a pattern similar to that seen with antibodies to steroid-producing cells of the adrenal (Table 35–1). Antibodies are rare in patients with premature ovarian failure due to a genetic or developmental defect not associated with adrenal or other endocrine autoantibodies.

DIABETES MELLITUS

There is a clinical association between diabetes and diseases of putative autoimmune origin, including chronic thyroiditis, hyperthyroidism, primary hypothyroidism, pernicious anemia, idiopathic adrenal insufficiency, idiopathic hypoparathyroidism, and myasthenia gravis. The incidence of thyroid and gastric microsomal antibodies is about 3 times higher in patients with "juvenile" diabetes than in age- and sex-matched controls. Antibodies to gastric intrinsic factor are at least 4 times more common in diabetics than in control populations. Adrenal antibodies, which are rare in the absence of idiopathic Addison's disease, are more frequent in diabetic than in comparable nondiabetic groups. This elevated incidence of organ-specific autoantibodies is associated mainly with the more severe forms of early-onset diabetes, particularly in female patients (Table 35–1).

Histologically, lymphocytic and histiocytic infiltration of the pancreatic islets (insulitis) has been reported in a number of juvenile diabetics—even those not yet receiving insulin treatment. Similar inflammatory changes in the islets can be induced in experimental animals by repeated injections of heterologous insulin or inoculation of homologous islet homogenates with Freund's complete adjuvant. Transient impairment of glucose tolerance has been reported in mice following immunization with mouse pancreatic extract. Immunized animals show delayed hypersensitivity skin test reactions and inhibition of macrophage migration with crude pancreatic islet antigen.

More direct evidence for an autoimmune component of diabetes has come from studies of diabetic patients showing an immunologic response to pancreas extract, whole insulin, or the isolated beta chain of insulin. Antibodies that bind insulin can be found in the sera of nearly all patients regularly treated with foreign insulin. Untreated diabetics only rarely have insulin-binding antibodies. Approximately 30% of diabetics (not treated with insulin) show blastogenic transformation of lymphocytes or impaired leukocyte migration with human pancreas extract. These results suggest that some patients have cell-mediated immunity to an islet antigen. By means of the indirect immunofluorescence technic, circulating antibodies to pancreatic islet cells were found in the sera of about 5% of untreated diabetics. These patients all had early-onset disease, and most had a variety of other organ-specific autoantibodies in their sera. Almost all of the serologically positive patients were females. Most had clinical evidence of some other endocrinopathy. The immunofluorescent reaction was found with alpha and beta cells of the islet tissue, but there was no localization in the secretory portions of the pancreas.

These studies make it likely that some forms of diabetes mellitus are associated with autoimmunity. Reactions are most likely to be positive in juvenile or early-onset diabetes complicated by another autoimmune disease of the endocrine organs. The antibody seems to be specific for islet cells. Since both alpha and beta cells are involved, it is possible that glucagon as well as insulin may be subject to an immunologic reaction.

Diabetes is a complex disease in which both insulin and glucagon seem to be involved. It cannot be determined at present how important autoimmunity is in the development of diabetes. Recent investigations have implicated coxsackie B4 viral infection as well as heredity and obesity as etiologic factors. Further investigations are necessary to ascertain whether some forms of juvenile diabetes are primarily autoimmune in origin or whether autoimmunity represents a secondary event following infection or metabolic disturbance.

Regardless of etiologic importance, the immunologic response to insulin found in most insulin-treated diabetics may be a complicating factor. Evidence of insulin-anti-insulin complexes has been found in the vascular tissues of many treated diabetics. The immune complexes may provoke renal disease.

IDIOPATHIC HYPOPARATHYROIDISM

Parathyroid failure is predominantly a disease of childhood and adolescence. Idiopathic hypoparathyroidism in association with adrenocortical failure is found most often in younger individuals. Histologically, idiopathic hypoparathyroidism is characterized by lymphocytic infiltration of the parathyroid glands and atrophy of glandular secretory cells. Antibodies specific for parathyroid have been demonstrated by indirect immunofluorescence in about a third of patients with idiopathic hypoparathyroidism (Table 35–1). Many of these patients also had antibodies to adrenal or thyroid tissues. An unexpected feature of many cases of primary hypoparathyroidism is the occurrence of refractory mucocutaneous candidiasis. The basis of this association has not been explained.

Experimentally, it has been demonstrated that repeated injection of homologous parathyroid tissue into dogs may induce the characteristic biochemical changes of hypoparathyroidism. Histologic damage to the gland can be demonstrated, and parathyroid autoantibodies are found in low titer in dog serum by complement fixation.

INFERTILITY

In a variety of animals, testicular tissues have been found to be antigenic. Sperm suspensions from the same species, when given with Freund's complete adjuvant, will elicit antibodies that agglutinate and immobilize sperm or fix complement with testicular tissue suspensions. Since the antibodies generally react only with spermatozoa, it can be concluded that spermatozoa possess organ-specific autoantigens. Positive skin tests can also be demonstrated. Immunofluorescence studies have shown that a major antigen is found in the sperm acrosome. Since it is present only in mature sperm, testicles of young guinea pigs do not elicit this immunologic response. Other antigens are found on the head, the tail, and the tip of the tail. The testicles of immunized guinea pigs develop patchy lesions characterized by edema, atrophy of the germinal epithelium, and lymphocytic infiltration. Orchitis and aspermatogenesis have been transferred passively with humoral antibody, lymph node cells, and peritoneal exudate cells. Systemic transfer of antiserum from immunized animals to normal recipients produces little or no tissue damage unless the recipients were treated with Freund's complete adjuvant. Apparently this treatment increases tissue permeability. Lymphoid cells and macrophages can induce severe lesions if injected into the testis. The interplay of cell-mediated and humoral immunity in producing testicular damage has not yet been defined, but evidence suggests that both responses are involved.

Studies of autoantibodies to sperm have been

complicated by the fact that other organs of the reproductive tract may contribute antigens. Sperm have the tendency to take up antigens from seminal fluid, so that some of the immunologic reactions are determined by sperm-coating antigens rather than by spermatic antigens themselves. Blood group A, B, and H antigens may also be acquired from the seminal fluid. These antigens may arise from the prostate, seminal vesicles, and other adnexal glands. Histocompatibility antigens have also been demonstrated on human spermatozoa.

In some cases of male infertility, an autoimmune reaction is suggested by the demonstration of sperm agglutinins in the serum. Three to 10% of infertile males have agglutinating antibody in their serum or seminal fluid, while control samples from fertile males do not show these agglutinins. The proportion of reactive patients seems to be somewhat higher if those with traumatic, obstructive, or inflammatory disease of the genital tract are considered. In a hemagglutination test with the supernate of freeze-thawed spermatozoa, the proportion of positive reactions was even greater. Some sera show complement fixation and a few produce precipitation with sperm extract or seminal plasma (Table 35–1).

About half of vasectomized men develop antibodies to sperm as demonstrated by agglutination or immobilization technics. The immunologic response is presumably due to continuous absorption of sperm, especially through the epididymis, and indicates that extravasated sperm or their fragments are antigenic. The normal way of removing excess sperm is phagocytosis within the lumen of the epididymis, which does not induce an immunologic response.

A variable portion of infertile women have been shown to have antibodies to sperm. In some cases they react with all human sperm, but in others the sperm of only certain males seems to react. These reactions do not appear to be related to the blood group of the sperm donor. The titer of antibodies in the female patient may diminish if she refrains from sexual intercourse or if a condom is used by her partner. It is uncertain whether the sperm antibodies diffuse from the bloodstream or are produced locally in the female genital tract. The pathogenetic role of antisperm antibodies in sterile male or female patients is still not clarified.

• • •

References

Chronic Thyroiditis & Primary Hypothyroidism

Beall GN, Solomon DH: Hashimoto's disease and Graves' disease. Pages 1198–1213 in: *Immunological Diseases,* 2nd ed. Vol 2. Samter M (editor). Little, Brown, 1971.

Bigazzi PE, Rose NR: Spontaneous autoimmune thyroiditis in animals as a model for human diseases. Prog Allergy 19:245, 1975.

Doniach D, Roitt IM: Thyroid auto-allergic disease. Chap 47, pages 1355–1386, in: *Clinical Aspects of Immunology,* 3rd ed. Gell PGH, Coombs RRA, Lachmann PJ (editors). Blackwell, 1975.

Rose NR: Autoimmune diseases. Chap 8, pages 347–499, in: *The Inflammatory Process,* 2nd ed. Vol 3. Zweifach B, Grant L, McCluskey R (editors). Academic Press, 1974.

Rose NR: The autoimmune diseases. Chap 28, pages 439–451, in: *Principles of Immunology.* Rose N, Milgrom F, van Oss C (editors). Macmillan, 1973.

Rose NR, Bigazzi P: The autoimmune diseases. Pages 765–794 in: *Handbook of Microbiology.* Vol 4. Laskin AI, Lechvalier HA (editors). CRC Press, Inc., 1974.

Rose NR, Witebsky E: Thyroid autoantibodies in thyroid disease. Pages 231–277 in: *Advances in Metabolic Disorders.* Levine R, Luft R (editors). Academic Press, 1968.

Hyperthyroidism

Bonnyns M & others: Lymphocytic thyroiditis and thyrotoxicosis. Page 171 in: *Thyroiditis and Thyroid Function.* Bastenie PA, Ermans AM (editors). Pergamon Press, 1972.

Kriss JP: Inactivation of LATS by anti-kappa and anti-lambda antisera. J Clin Endocrinol Metab 28:1140, 1968.

McKenzie JM: *Current Concepts of the Etiology of Graves' Disease: The Hahnemann Conference on Advances in Disease, Philadelphia.* Grune & Stratton, 1973.

Volpé R & others: The pathogenesis of Graves' disease and Hashimoto's thyroiditis. Clin Endocrinol 3:239, 1974.

Thyrogastric Disease

Chanarin I: The stomach in allergic diseases. Chap 49, pages 1429–1440, in: *Clinical Aspects of Immunology,* 3rd ed. Gell PGH, Coombs RRA, Lachmann PJ (editors). Blackwell, 1975.

Doniach D, Roitt IM: Thyroid auto-allergic disease. Chap 47, pages 1355–1386, in: *Clinical Aspects of Immunology,* 3rd ed. Gell PGH, Coombs RRA, Lachmann PJ (editors). Blackwell, 1975.

Irvine WJ: The association of atrophic gastritis with autoimmune thyroid disease. Clin Endocrinol Metabol 4:351, 1975.

Chronic Adrenocortical Insufficiency

Irvine WJ, Barnes EW: Addison's disease and associated conditions. Chap 46, pages 1301–1354, in: *Clinical Aspects of Immunology,* 3rd ed. Gell PGH, Coombs RRA, Lachmann PJ (editors). Blackwell, 1975.

Irvine WJ, Barnes EW: Addison's disease, ovarian failure and hypoparathyroidism. Clin Endocrinol Metabol 4:379, 1975.

Ovarian Failure

Irvine WJ, Barnes EW: Addison's disease and associated conditions. Chap 46, pages 1301–1354, in: *Clinical Aspects of Immunology,* 3rd ed. Gell PGH, Coombs RRA, Lachmann PJ (editors). Blackwell, 1975.

Irvine WJ: Adrenalitis, hypoparathyroidism and associated diseases. Pages 1214–1277, in: *Immunological Diseases,* 2nd ed. Vol 2. Samter M (editor). Little, Brown, 1971.

Diabetes Mellitus

Fialkow PJ, Zavala C, Nielsen R: Thyroid autoimmunity: Increased frequency in relatives of insulin-dependent diabetes patients. Ann Intern Med 83:170, 1975.

Lendrum R, Walker G, Gamble DR: Islet-cell antibodies in juvenile diabetes mellitus of recent onset. Lancet 1:880, 1975.

Nerup J & others: Anti-pancreatic, cellular hypersensitivity in diabetes mellitus: Antigenic activity of fetal calf pancreas and correlation with clinical type of diabetes. Acta Allergol 28:223, 1973.

Idiopathic Hypoparathyroidism

Irvine WJ, Barnes EW: Addison's disease and associated conditions. Chap 46, pages 1301–1354, in: *Clinical Aspects of Immunology,* 3rd ed. Gell PGH, Coombs RRA, Lachmann PJ (editors). Blackwell, 1975.

Infertility

Johnson MH, Hekman A, Rumke PH: The male and female genital tracts in allergic disease. Chap 52, pages 1509–1544, in: *Clinical Aspects of Immunology,* 3rd ed. Gell PGH, Coombs RRA, Lachmann PJ (editors). Blackwell, 1975.

Jones WR: The use of antibodies developed by infertile women to identify relevant antigens. Pages 376–404 in: *Immunological Approaches to Fertility Control.* Diczfalusy E (editor). Bogtrykkeriet Forum, 1974.

Lipsett MB: Endocrinology of the testis. Pages 54–62 in: *Control of Male Fertility.* Sciarra JJ, Markland C, Speidel JJ (editors). Harper & Row, 1975.

Metz CB: Role of specific sperm antigens in fertilization. Fed Proc 32:2057, 1973.

Rumke PH, Hekman A: Auto- and iso-immunity to sperm in infertility. Clin Endocrinol Metabol 4:473, 1975.

Shulman S: Antigenicity and autoimmunity in sexual reproduction: A review. Clin Exp Immunol 9:267, 1971.

36 . . .
Neurologic Diseases

Paul M. Hoffman, MD

The role of immunologic mechanisms in diseases of the nervous system has recently become the focus of increased interest and investigation. In diseases such as acute idiopathic polyneuropathy (Guillain-Barré syndrome) and postinfectious encephalomyelitis, the host response to an infectious agent may trigger the immune system to make a direct assault on the nervous system. The role of immune mechanisms in the pathogenesis of multiple sclerosis is much less clear, but evidence from immunogenetic studies, the response to viral antigens, and the nature of the immunoglobulin production in cerebrospinal fluid strongly suggest that an immune response, either normal or abnormal, to one or more viruses may lead to this disease. In other diseases such as subacute sclerosing panencephalitis (SSPE), myasthenia gravis, myotonic dystrophy, and some chronic neuropathies, abnormal immune responses are known to occur, but their pathogenetic role is unclear. In the subacute spongioform encephalopathies—a group of diseases of the nervous system in which a transmissible agent or agents different from known human and animal viruses have been found—immune responses have been normal. However, since understanding the host response to these agents may be very important in establishing the pathogenesis, treatment, and prevention of these illnesses, new developments can be expected from research on the immune response in these conditions.

DEMYELINATING DISEASES

The demyelinating diseases of the central and peripheral nervous systems have unique pathologic, epidemiologic, and clinical features which suggest that immunologic mechanisms may play a role in the etiology and pathogenesis of some of these disorders. The commonly accepted pathologic criteria for a demyelinating disease are destruction of myelin sheaths of nerve fibers and relative sparing of axis cylinders and other elements of the nervous system. These lesions are frequently perivenous in location and are accompanied, at least in the acute phase, by an inflammatory infiltrate that is primarily of a mononuclear cell type. Two diseases of the central nervous system—acute disseminated encephalomyelitis and multiple sclerosis—and one disease of the peripheral nervous system—idiopathic polyneuritis (Guillain-Barré syndrome)—meet these criteria.

Paul M. Hoffman is Medical Officer in Charge, NINCDS Research Center, Tamuning, Guam, and Research Associate, Laboratory of Central Nervous System Studies, NINCDS Bethesda.

ACUTE DISSEMINATED ENCEPHALOMYELITIS (ADEM)

Major Immunologic Features

- Follows infectious diseases or immunization against them.
- Animal counterpart is experimental allergic encephalomyelitis.
- Cellular but not humoral immunity to basic protein of myelin is present during the illness.

General Considerations

Although acute disseminated encephalomyelitis is a relatively uncommon disease of the nervous system, it has become important because of the widespread practice of vaccination for prevention of infectious diseases throughout the world. The incidence is not related to race, age group, or sex. The onset of clinical illness can be several days to weeks following vaccination, or, in the case of natural infection with viruses such as measles, rubella, varicella, mumps, and influenza, it can occur concomitantly with the illness (parainfectious) or following the acute phase of the illness (postinfectious). The lesions of acute disseminated encephalomyelitis are markedly inflamed; polymorphonuclear leukocytes and hemorrhage as well as mononuclear cell infiltrates are frequently seen in perivascular areas of white matter throughout the brain. As the lesions age, they tend to become less inflamed and more sclerotic, with proliferation of astrocytes and formation of gliotic scars in the center. The lesions of acute disseminated encephalomyelitis are pathologically all of the same age, which reflects the monophasic clinical character of the illness.

Immunologic Pathogenesis

The major arguments favoring an immunologic explanation of this disorder are that multiple infectious agents produce a single stereotyped lesion in the central nervous system and the fact that this same lesion can be produced in several animal species by inoculation of brain material. Experimental allergic encephalomyelitis (EAE) is a reproducible autoimmune disease in which an animal is immunized with homologous or heterologous extracts of whole brain, the basic protein of myelin, or certain polypeptide sequences within the basic protein together with Freund's complete adjuvant. Ten to 21 days following immunization, an illness will ensue characterized by lethargy, weight loss, tremor, hind limb paresis, loss of sphincter control, and (frequently) death. The lesions are all of the same age and consist of perivascular mononuclear cell infiltrates in white matter with varying degrees of demyelination. As early as 9 days following immunization, cellular immunity to the immunizing antigens can be demonstrated by skin testing as well as by in vitro tests of cellular immunity such as inhibition of leukocyte and macrophage migration and lymphocyte activation (see Chapter 25). Antibodies to basic protein and to myelin can be demonstrated but do not correlate positively with disease production. The disease can be transferred by adoptive transfer of lymphocytes but not with serum.

Cellular immunity to basic protein has been demonstrated in acute disseminated encephalomyelitis using the lymphocyte activation assay (see Chapter 25). The response tends to be highest during the acute phase of the illness and decreases as the disease progresses. No antibodies to basic protein or myelin can be demonstrated. Cerebrospinal fluid may be abnormal in acute disseminated encephalomyelitis with mild to moderate pleocytosis and mildly elevated total protein. The proportion of γ-globulin in the cerebrospinal fluid may also be increased, but there is no evidence that this represents local immunoglobulin production in the central nervous system as occurs in multiple sclerosis.

Clinical Features

Systemic symptoms such as fever, malaise, headache, myalgia, nausea, and vomiting generally precede neurologic symptoms by 24–48 hours. Neurologic symptoms develop rapidly thereafter and include pain, numbness, paresthesias, motor weakness, incoordination, and bulbar symptoms such as dysarthria, dysphagia, pooling of pharyngeal secretions, and respiratory distress. Spasticity, extrapyramidal signs, and pathologic reflexes are commonly seen. Visual defects can occur if the optic nerve is involved, and widespread lesions in the brain can lead to stupor and coma. Seizures are common, though not early in the illness.

Differential Diagnosis

Acute disseminated encephalomyelitis must be differentiated from other diseases that can acutely and diffusely affect the central nervous system. Acute multiple sclerosis with no history of neurologic dysfunction can be difficult to differentiate from acute disseminated encephalomyelitis. The presence of fever and a preceding viral illness or vaccination favors the latter diagnosis. Allergic vasculitis such as occurs in systemic lupus erythematosus and polyarteritis nodosa can affect the nervous system primarily, although neurologic symptoms generally tend to occur during the course of the systemic illness and tend to be more focal than in acute disseminated encephalomyelitis. Evidence of vasculitis in other organs is helpful in distinguishing these diseases from acute disseminated encephalomyelitis. Primary infections of the nervous system with measles, mumps, and rubella viruses as well as with the arboviruses tend to involve gray matter as well as white and produce more evidence of neuronal dysfunction such as seizures, stupor, coma, and extrapyramidal signs early in the illness. Direct isolation of viruses from cerebrospinal fluid as well as a rise in serum antibody titer is helpful in differentiating viral encephalitides from acute disseminated encephalomyelitis. Toxoplasmosis can also directly infect the central nervous system and present as an acute disseminated encephalitis. A positive Feldman toxoplasmosis dye test or other serologic tests for toxoplasma will differentiate it from acute disseminated encephalomyelitis.

Treatment

Although the cause of acute disseminated encephalomyelitis is unpredictable, it appears that corticosteroids are of value in treatment. The successful suppression of experimental allergic encephalomyelitis and clinical recovery of animals after receiving injections of basic protein, encephalitogenic peptides, or even some basic copolymers offer hope that by manipulating the immune system a state of immune paralysis or tolerance can be produced, resulting in cessation of the attack of sensitized lymphocytes on the nervous system.

Complications & Prognosis

The mortality rate from acute disseminated encephalomyelitis varies from 1–27%, with a higher rate reported in cases associated with measles. Major and minor neurologic sequelae persist in 25–40% of survivors.

MULTIPLE SCLEROSIS

Major Immunologic Features

- Increase in frequency of HLA-A3 and HLA-B7.
- Inflammatory demyelination in central nervous system.
- Increased cerebrospinal fluid γ-globulin and measles antibody titers.

General Considerations

Multiple sclerosis is a relapsing disease in which there are signs and symptoms of multiple areas of central nervous system involvement both in time and in space. It is one of the most prevalent diseases of the central nervous system, and, because young adults are frequently affected with debilitating symptoms lasting many years, it represents a serious public health problem. Epidemiologic studies have uncovered important clues about multiple sclerosis, but the cause remains unknown. Low-risk areas of the world have a prevalence of 5–10 cases per 100,000 population; high-risk areas have a prevalence of 50–100 per 100,000 population. Populations migrating from the areas of their birth have the same risk of acquiring the disease as others born in the same region who remain there—particularly if they move after age 15. These studies, in addition to the age at onset curve, in which there is a peak onset at age 30 with few cases before age 15 or after age 55, have suggested to many that some critical event in determining the risk of acquiring multiple sclerosis occurs in adolescence. Familial cases are not uncommon, and the risk of a first-degree living relative having the disease is 10–15 times higher than the risk in the rest of the population. The disease is rare among Orientals and Africans. A consistent finding in several large studies of multiple sclerosis patients has been slightly but persistently elevated serum and cerebrospinal fluid antibody titers to measles and, less commonly, to other viruses such as vaccinia, mumps, herpes simplex, and parainfluenza viruses. These findings have suggested the possibility that a latent viral infection may play a role in the etiology of multiple sclerosis. At this time, however, only one virus—a parainfluenza virus—has been isolated from the brain of a multiple sclerosis patient. Several recent studies of histocompatibility antigens in multiple sclerosis patients have indicated a statistically significant increase in the frequency of HLA-A3 and HLA-B7. It is possible that an altered immune response, linked to the HLA antigens in man and affecting reactivity to viral antigens, may be involved in the pathogenesis of multiple sclerosis.

Immunologic Pathogenesis

The lesions of multiple sclerosis are confined to the central nervous system and involve primarily the white matter in the paraventricular areas of the cerebrum, cerebellum, brain stem, and spinal cord. In early active disease the lesions consist of inflammatory demyelination with mononuclear exudates; older lesions consist of plasma cells, mature lymphocytes, and astrocytes. Unlike the lesions of acute disseminated encephalomyelitis, these lesions appear to be of different ages and correlate positively with the appearance of clinical signs and symptoms at different times during the illness. The lesions of multiple sclerosis, termed plaques, contain increased proportions of immunoglobulin, suggesting local production. This finding is reflected in the cerebrospinal fluid, where increased concentration of γ-globulin can be found in 60–80% of multiple sclerosis patients, depending upon the method used. This is the most helpful test for the diagnosis of multiple sclerosis but is not pathognomonic, since elevated spinal fluid γ-globulin occurs in many inflammatory central nervous system processes. There is no specific immunodiagnostic test for multiple sclerosis at this time. The immunoglobulin present in the cerebrospinal fluid of multiple sclerosis patients has an abnormal kappa to lambda chain ratio. The ratio of cerebrospinal fluid to serum immunoglobulin is reduced, which suggests that the immunoglobulin is being made locally in the central nervous system. The immunoglobulin is oligoclonal on electrophoresis, and at least part of it is antibody directed against measles antigens. This may account for the consistent finding of increased serum and cerebrospinal fluid titer to measles antigens in multiple sclerosis patients.

The immunopathogenic nature of multiple sclerosis is controversial. Although there are several similarities to experimental allergic encephalomyelitis, there are enough differences between multiple sclerosis and experimental allergic encephalomyelitis that many investigators feel that the 2 conditions are not comparable. A comparison of their immunologic features is given in Table 36–1. Although the course of experimental allergic encephalomyelitis is generally a monophasic acute illness, a chronic form has been produced in guinea pigs and a relapsing form has been described in rats. The encephalitogen is known in animals, and the most encephalitogenic areas of the basic protein molecule differ from species to species. No encephalitogen related to multiple sclerosis has been identified in man. Differences in susceptibility to experimental allergic encephalomyelitis are clearly present in specific genetic strains of rats and guinea pigs. Strain 13 guinea pigs show a heightened immune response to basic protein and develop much more severe experimental allergic encephalomyelitis than do strain 2 guinea pigs, who are poor responders to this antigen. In multiple sclerosis, there is a significant increase in the frequency of HLA-A3 and HLA-B7. Preliminary evidence suggests that people with these HLA antigens, whether they have multiple sclerosis or not, have elevated antibody titers to several viruses. There are differences in the humoral responses in experimental allergic encephalomyelitis and multiple sclerosis. While antibodies against basic protein have been demonstrated in experimental allergic encephalomyelitis, no such antibodies can be demonstrated in multiple sclerosis. However, neurotoxic factors in sera with antibodylike characteristics are present both in active multiple sclerosis patients and in experimental allergic encephalomyelitis animals. These factors can be demonstrated by demyelination and inhibition of myelination as well as by suppression of polysynaptic impulse transmission in tissue culture. Delayed hypersensitivity to basic protein and crude brain antigens can be demonstrated by several in vitro tests in experimental allergic encephalomyelitis, whereas in multiple sclerosis the results are equivocal. Many studies of cellular immunity using crude and purified brain antigens in multiple sclerosis have usually shown

Table 36–1. Comparison of experimental allergic encephalomyelitis and multiple sclerosis.

	Experimental Allergic Encephalomyelitis	Multiple Sclerosis
Course	Monophasic in most species; chronic and relapsing forms rare	Chronic and relapsing
Pathology	Inflammatory demyelination	Inflammatory demyelination
Encephalitogen	Identified in several species	Unknown
Histocompatibility antigens	Differences in immune response and susceptibility in inbred rat and guinea pig strains	Increased incidence of HLA-A3 and HLA-B7
Spinal fluid immunoglobulin	Increased	Increased
Circulating antimyelin antibody	Present	Not present
Neurotoxic sera	Demyelinating and synapse-blocking activity in tissue culture	Demyelinating and synapse-blocking activity in tissue culture
Cellular immunity to brain antigens	Present	Present but nonspecific for multiple sclerosis
Disease suppression with antigens	Present	Not present
Disease suppression with immunosuppressants	Present	Not present

negative results. Positive results have occurred in multiple sclerosis and in other diseases of the nervous system in which there is extreme nerve tissue destruction. This similarity of lymphocyte responses to brain antigens suggests that the response is nonspecific.

Clinical Features

Since the lesions of multiple sclerosis tend to involve many areas of the central nervous system white matter, the symptoms of the disease are extremely varied. The most common manifestations are the development of motor weakness, paresthesias, impairment of visual acuity, and diplopia. These symptoms usually occur gradually—though rapid onset has been reported—and, following an initial attack, the patient may return to a normal functional status. Subsequent exacerbations occur at widely varying intervals and tend to subside with less complete recovery of function and more chronic disability as the disease progresses. Ataxia of gait, urinary bladder dysfunction, impotence, spasticity, mental aberrations (particularly euphoria), and seizures are common.

Differential Diagnosis

Acute episodes of multiple sclerosis must be differentiated from other structural lesions of the central nervous system. Spinal cord compression due to tumors or spondylosis usually presents with evidence of partial or complete intraspinal subarachnoid block, and the cerebrospinal fluid protein is elevated to much higher levels than in multiple sclerosis. Central nervous system tumors, both primary and metastatic, can mimic multiple sclerosis and must be ruled out with appropriate neurodiagnostic procedures such as brain scans, electroencephalograms, skull x-rays, lumbar punctures, and more extensive neuroradiologic procedures. The symptoms of neurosyphilis, particularly tabes dorsalis, may mimic multiple sclerosis. The presence of Argyll Robertson pupils, hypotonic limbs, and areflexia in the lower extremities in tabes dorsalis as well as a history of syphilitic infection or the presence of a positive serologic test for syphilis are helpful in differentiating syphilis from multiple sclerosis. Vasculitides such as systemic lupus erythematosus and polyarteritis nodosa have been mentioned previously in the discussion of acute disseminated encephalomyelitis. Finally, degenerative spinal and cerebellar disorders such as Friedreich's ataxia, parenchymatous cerebellar degeneration, and olivopontocerebellar degeneration can all mimic multiple sclerosis. These disorders tend to be familial, chronically progressive, and not associated with the elevation of spinal fluid γ-globulin that occurs in the majority of cases of multiple sclerosis.

Treatment

While experimental allergic encephalomyelitis can be successfully suppressed with specific, nonspecific, and related antigens as well as with immunosuppressive agents such as corticosteroids and cytotoxic drugs, patients with multiple sclerosis have shown less clear benefit from such treatment. The administration of basic protein to patients raises ethical questions since basic protein is a potential disease-producing agent itself. In fact, no beneficial effects have been demonstrated in limited trials. While corticosteroids tend to shorten the duration of acute exacerbations, particularly when optic neuritis is present, the long-term benefits of corticosteroid therapy are not striking. Cytotoxic agents have not been of long-term benefit in this illness.

Complications & Prognosis

The prognosis of multiple sclerosis is difficult to predict because of the extremely variable nature of the disease. Benign cases in which patients have functioned normally or with little deficit after initial episodes are not uncommon. At the other extreme, fulminant cases of acute multiple sclerosis have resulted in death during the initial episode. Most patients fall between these extremes and continue to have exacerbations and remissions for many years. The average duration of life after onset of symptoms is at least 25 years and was said to be more than 35 years in a recent follow-up study of multiple sclerosis among a Veterans Administration Hospital population.

The late complications of multiple sclerosis include recurrent urinary tract infections and respiratory infections and decubiti in debilitated and bedridden patients.

ACUTE IDIOPATHIC POLYNEURITIS (Guillain-Barré Syndrome)

Major Immunologic Features

- Commonly follows viral infections.
- Inflammatory demyelination of peripheral nerves.
- Marked similarity to experimental allergic neuritis in animals.
- Cellular immunity to nerve proteins present.

General Considerations

Acute idiopathic polyneuritis (AIP), like acute disseminated encephalomyelitis, frequently occurs following an infectious illness. Upper respiratory infections, exanthems, vaccinations, and specific viral illnesses such as measles, infectious mononucleosis, and hepatitis commonly precede acute idiopathic polyneuritis by 1–3 weeks. Fever therapy and surgery have also preceded episodes of acute idiopathic polyneuritis in some patients. The disease affects all age groups, and incidence is not related to sex or race.

Immunologic Pathogenesis

Acute idiopathic polyneuritis is a demyelinating disease of the peripheral nervous system characterized by a perivascular mononuclear cell infiltrate with segmental demyelination of peripheral nerves in the areas of inflammation. The inflammatory response is present even in the earliest stages. In areas of most severe involvement there is some axonal destruction and Wallerian degeneration. These areas often show infiltration of polymorphonuclear leukocytes as well as mononuclear cells early in the course of the disease. Later, the lesions frequently have plasma cells in the exudate. Experimentally, an identical clinical and pathologic entity can be produced in many animal species by the injection of extracts of peripheral nerve or a purified protein of peripheral nerve together with Freund's complete adjuvant. This illness, experimental allergic neuritis (EAN), begins as weakness and later leads to paralysis 10–24 days after immunization. The immunopathologic nature of the illness can be demonstrated by the fact that lymphocytes from animals with experimental allergic neuritis are sensitive to extracts of peripheral nerve and purified peripheral nerve protein and undergo activation or produce lymphokines in the presence of these antigens. Sensitivity to the immunizing antigen parallels the course of the illness. The disease can be passively transferred with sensitized cells but not with serum. Antinerve antibodies are present but are not considered pathogenic since their appearance does not parallel the appearance of clinical signs or histopathology. Lymphocytes from animals with experimental allergic neuritis have the capacity to produce demyelination in tissue culture; serum from such animals does not.

Immunologic abnormalities have also been described in acute idiopathic polyneuritis. An increased number of spontaneously transformed circulating lymphocytes has been described, as well as lymphocytes that show sensitivity to extracts of peripheral nerve and peripheral nerve proteins by activation or lymphokine production. This sensitivity appears to be specific, since there is no sensitivity to central nervous system antigens in these patients. Antinerve antibodies have been described in acute idiopathic polyneuritis and in several other types of neuropathy and may reflect immune reactions to nerve tissue destruction. There is no specific immunologic test that is diagnostic of acute idiopathic polyneuritis.

Clinical Features

The onset of acute idiopathic polyneuritis is generally characterized by a rapidly progressing weakness first of the lower extremities, then the upper extremities, and then the respiratory musculature over a period of 3–7 days. Weakness and paralysis are frequently preceded by paresthesias and numbness of the limbs, but objective sensory loss is generally mild and transient. Cranial nerves, most commonly the facial nerve, can be involved. The tendon reflexes are decreased or lost early in the course of the illness, and nerve conduction velocities in affected limbs are moderately to markedly slowed, consistent with a demyelinating peripheral neuropathy. Cerebrospinal fluid protein is increased in all cases, but frequently not during the first few days of the illness. Cerebrospinal fluid white cell counts are commonly normal or slightly elevated. The most common clinical course is one of rapid evolution of symptoms over a period of 1–3 weeks with improvement thereafter and return to normal function over a period of 6–9 months. However, other patterns such as a more gradual onset, a more prolonged period of complete paralysis, recovery with severe residual deficits, and a relapsing course have also been described. Whether these latter patterns represent different illnesses has been a topic of debate for many years, but, in the absence of clearly different causes and pathologic features, it seems more likely that they represent different clinical variants of the same underlying process.

Differential Diagnosis

Acute idiopathic polyneuritis can be differentiated from porphyric polyneuropathy by the demonstration of porphyrins in the urine of such patients. Heavy metal intoxication with lead, thallium, and arsenic can all be ruled out by appropriate blood or urine tests. Acute transverse myelitis in the early stages may resemble acute idiopathic polyneuritis, but pathologically increased reflexes and spasticity occur several days to weeks after initial flaccidity, and hyporeflexia and bowel and urinary bladder involvement are more common in transverse myelitis. Vasculitides such as systemic lupus erythematosus and polyarteritis nodosa can produce peripheral neuropathies, but these tend to present as asymmetric involvement of one or more nerves. The weakness of skeletal muscles involved in myasthenia gravis may resemble acute idiopathic polyneuritis, but the former is more likely to be associated with ocular muscle involvement and will generally respond to anticholinesterase drugs.

Treatment

The use of anti-inflammatory agents in treating acute idiopathic polyneuritis is controversial. Some patients show no beneficial effects from corticosteroids; others respond favorably and tend to relapse when these drugs are discontinued. A third group will respond to cytotoxic drugs such as cyclophosphamide or azathioprine after failing to respond to corticosteroids. In general, a short course of corticosteroid therapy should be tried early in the course of the illness, particularly if there are rapidly progressing symptoms. If there is no response after 7–10 days, the drug therapy regimen should be reassessed.

Complications & Prognosis

The widespread availability of modern methods for assisting and maintaining respiration has resulted in a marked decrease in the number of fatalities from acute idiopathic polyneuritis. However, the incidence of residual neurologic deficits is higher than previously recognized and may occur in as many as 50% of cases. Persistent deficits such as weakness and loss of reflexes are understandable, since irreversible axonal disruption and Wallerian degeneration occur in severely affected nerves. The mechanical problems of clearing respiratory secretions in patients with respiratory muscle and pharyngeal weakness favor the development of respiratory infections, which are the most severe threat to life in hospitalized patients.

• • •

MYASTHENIA GRAVIS

Major Immunologic Features

- Commonly associated with thymoma or thymic hyperplasia.
- Autoantibodies to striated muscle and thymic epithelium.
- Often associated with other autoimmune diseases.
- Antibodies against acetylcholine neural receptors may be pathogenic.

General Considerations

Myasthenia gravis is a disease of unknown cause in which there is motor weakness due to a disorder of neuromuscular transmission. The disease tends to affect young adults, more commonly women, but onset in childhood as well as onset beyond age 40 is not uncommon. Familial cases are known, but there is no racial predilection. The occurrence of myasthenia gravis with thymomas, thymic hyperplasia, autoantibodies, and certain autoimmune diseases strongly suggests that an abnormality of the immune system may be involved in the pathogenesis of this disorder.

Immunologic Pathogenesis

Immunologic abnormalities are common in myasthenia gravis. Antibodies to striated muscle that cross-react with epithelial cells in the thymus have been described, as have antinuclear and antithyroid antibodies. Cellular immunity to crude muscle antigen and purified muscle protein, measured by inhibition of leukocyte migration, has been demonstrated. These abnormalities, as well as the association of myasthenia gravis with systemic lupus erythematosus, rheumatoid arthritis, Sjögren's syndrome, and thyroiditis (more commonly than would be expected by chance alone), have focused attention on the immune system. At the level of the neuromuscular junction, however, there is no microscopic evidence of pathologic change. The binding of antimuscle antibody is to striated muscle, not to the neuromuscular junction, and what little inflammatory reaction can be seen in myasthenia gravis consists of a mononuclear cell perivascular infiltrate in areas of necrotic muscle tissue. Abnormalities are present in the thymus in 80% of myasthenics, either as true thymomas (10%) or in the form of thymic hyperplasia with increased numbers of germinal centers (70%). Recently, it has been shown that these hyperplastic thymuses contain increased numbers of B lymphocytes. The fact that two-thirds of all myasthenics who undergo thymectomy show complete or partial remission also suggests that the thymus may be the site of production of a neuromuscular blocking agent. The nature of the agent is still unclear. A proposal that this agent is the normal thymic hormone thymin (thymopoietin) has been made by Goldstein, who has been able to produce a syndrome resembling myasthenia gravis in guinea pigs by the injection of a crude muscle antigen together with Freund's complete adjuvant (Chapter 11). This syndrome cannot be produced in thymectomized animals. Another experimental myasthenic syndrome in the rabbit has been produced by the injection of purified acetylcholine receptor protein from the electric eel. Antibodies binding to receptor protein appear concomitantly with the development of myasthenia in these animals. Antibodies cross-reactive with acetylcholine receptor protein from rat muscle have also been demonstrated in the sera of myasthenic patients and suggest the possibility that a steric hindrance of the postsynaptic acetylcholine receptor by antibody may be responsible for the defect in neuromuscular transmission.

Clinical Features

Myasthenia gravis is an abnormality of muscles. The muscles may be weak or normal at rest but become increasingly weaker with repetitive use. The weakness is often first noted in the extraocular muscles and manifested as diplopia or ptosis. Pharyngeal and facial muscle weakness, resulting in dysphagia, dysarthria, and difficulty in chewing, commonly occurs. Skeletal muscle weakness is more often proximal than distal, and difficulty in climbing stairs, rising from chairs, combing the hair, or even holding up the head results. All of these symptoms show fluctuations in intensity and are more severe late in the day. The neurologic examination is normal except for the muscle weakness. The disease is said to remit spontaneously in 25% of cases within the first 2 years. Serious exacerbations of the illness, including respiratory impairment—especially in elderly patients who have other complicating diseases—account for the majority of the deaths from myasthenia gravis. Modern methods of assisted respiration and constant monitoring of cardiac and respiratory function have greatly reduced the mortality rate in myasthenia gravis, which previously was about 20–30%.

The abnormality in neuromuscular transmission in myasthenia gravis, which includes a decrease in the amplitude of the miniature end-plate potential, can usually be overcome by anticholinesterase drugs such as edrophonium (Tensilon) and neostigmine. The improvement in myasthenic weakness after injection of these drugs is helpful both in diagnosis and treatment.

Immunologic Diagnosis

Although antimuscle, antinuclear, and antithyroid antibodies as well as cellular immunity to muscle antigens can be demonstrated in myasthenia gravis, these phenomena can occur in other muscle and rheumatoid diseases and therefore are not diagnostic of myasthenia gravis.

Differential Diagnosis

Myasthenia gravis can usually be differentiated from other myopathies on the basis of its response to anticholinesterase drugs. The various forms of periodic paralysis do not show the ocular muscle involvement seen in myasthenia. The myasthenic syndrome (Eaton-Lambert syndrome) is seen in association with a remote cancer and can be differentiated by electrodiagnostic studies as well as by its response to guanidine.

Treatment

Anticholinesterase drugs such as pyridostigmine (Mestinon) and neostigmine in combination with atropine are the most commonly used form of long-term therapy. Beneficial effects from thymectomy are seen in the majority of cases, and all patients with myasthenia gravis except those with ocular myasthenia or very mild nondisabling symptoms are candidates for thymectomy. In keeping with the hypothesis that myasthenia gravis has an immune basis, the response of patients to ACTH and corticosteroids has been very encouraging. The best results have been reported using alternate-day therapy with large doses of corticosteroids.

Complications & Prognosis

The course of myasthenia gravis prior to the widespread practice of thymectomy and the use of corticosteroids was one of remission in 25% of cases during the first 2 years and a course of chronic, persistent weakness with a 20–30% mortality rate in the remainder. Improvement and remission within 5 years can now be anticipated in up to 90% of patients undergoing thymectomy, and further improvement with reduction of the dosage of anticholinesterase drugs can be expected with the use of corticosteroids. Cholinergic crisis with weakness resulting from overdosage of anticholinesterase drugs, pulmonary infections resulting from pooling of pharyngeal secretions, and lowered resistance to invading organisms resulting from corticosteroid therapy are persistent hazards for the myasthenic patient.

IMMUNOLOGIC ABNORMALITIES IN SOME UNCOMMON NEUROLOGIC DISEASES

In addition to the decreased levels of IgA noted in ataxia-telangiectasia (Chapter 26), abnormalities of the major immunoglobulin classes and abnormal immunoglobulins have been described in several seemingly unrelated neurologic diseases. The relationships of the immunoglobulin abnormalities and the neurologic deficits are still unclear, and there is no evidence of a causal relationship in any of these conditions.

MYOTONIA DYSTROPHICA

Myotonia dystrophica is an autosomal dominant disease in which there are dystrophic changes in muscle tissue leading to a syndrome of muscle weakness and atrophy in addition to the characteristic "myotonia," which is a delayed relaxation of the muscle after contraction. In addition to the changes in muscle, abnormalities in several other organ systems have been described, including testicular atrophy, early frontal balding and skull abnormalities, cataracts in adults, low basal metabolic rates, and impaired tolerance to glucose with excessive release of insulin. Serum levels of IgG are low in this disease because of increased catabolism of IgG. Poor antibody responses to bacterial antigens have also been described in several patients who had normal immunoglobulin levels. The basic immunologic defect in this disease remains to be defined.

CHRONIC POLYNEUROPATHIES & MOTOR NEURON DISEASES

In addition to the neuropathies that have been described with amyloidosis, Waldenström's macroglobulinemia, multiple myeloma, and benign monoclonal gammopathy, a large group of sporadic and familial chronic polyneuropathies and motor neuron diseases have immunologic abnormalities. Elevated levels of serum IgM occur in several patients with progressive muscular atrophy, a form of motor neuron disease. The majority of the serum IgM elevations were due to increased levels of circulating monomeric 7S IgM, an abnormality also described in infections and in neoplastic, rheumatoid, and immunodeficiency diseases. A third group of patients clinically classifiable as having hereditary sensory neuropathy were found to have increased levels of serum IgA as well as increased production of IgA in jejunal biopsy specimens. A persistent occult gastrointestinal infection might play a role in the pathogenesis of this neuropathy.

SLOW, CHRONIC, & LATENT VIRAL INFECTIONS OF THE NERVOUS SYSTEM

Several subacute and chronic degenerative diseases of human and animal nervous systems have been shown to be related to persistent or chronic infection of the nervous system with viruses and other less well defined transmissible agents. Subacute sclerosing panencephalitis in man and a similar disorder produced experimentally in hamsters are related to persistent infection of the central nervous system with measles virus. Progressive multifocal leukoencephalopathy in man has been associated with the recovery of 2 different papovaviruses previously thought not to be pathogenic for man. A third group of diseases referred to as the subacute spongioform encephalopathies, including kuru and Jakob-Creutzfeldt disease in man and scrapie and mink encephalopathy in animals, have been shown to be caused by small transmissible agents which are present in affected brain material and will produce an identical disease when inoculated into susceptible primate or nonprimate hosts after a relatively long disease-free latent period. Although the role of the host immune response is unclear in most of these disorders, the infectious nature of these diseases has directed research toward understanding the host response both in the treatment and possible prevention of these diseases.

Subacute Sclerosing Panencephalitis (SSPE)

Subacute sclerosing panencephalitis is a subacute degenerative central nervous system disease which affects mainly school-age children. Personality changes, dementia, seizures, and myoclonus are all common symptoms which progress rapidly to death over a period of 12–18 months in most cases. Pathologically, intranuclear and intracytoplasmic inclusion bodies had been noted for many years before electron microscopic studies revealed paramyxoviruslike structures in infected brain material. Later, measles virus antigen was demonstrated by fluorescent antibody staining and measles virus was recovered from infected brain material by co-cultivation technics.

The role of the host immune response is not clearly understood in this disease. There is evidence of persistent central nervous system infection with measles virus by the production of large quantities of antibody to measles. As in multiple sclerosis, this antibody is produced locally and is oligoclonal by electrophoretic studies. These antibodies to measles virus account for a large portion of the cerebrospinal fluid immunoglobulin which is present in greatly elevated quantities in this disease. The fact that there is persistent infection in spite of large amounts of antibody has suggested that these patients may have some defect in cellular immunity. Several studies using migration inhibition as an in vitro test of cellular immunity suggested a specific lack of responsiveness in subacute sclerosing panencephalitis patients to measles virus. However, more recent cytotoxicity studies using lymphocytes from subacute sclerosing panencephalitis patients against measles-infected cell lines have shown no such defects. The presence of a "blocking factor"—possibly antibody—in the cerebrospinal fluid and blood of subacute sclerosing panencephalitis patients has been found in some studies but not in others.

Some observations on the behavior of measles virus in tissue culture may be pertinent to this problem. Measles can produce several different effects in tissue culture varying from complete lysis of cells to persistence of virus in the form of incomplete viral particles detectable only as measles antigen in the nucleus of infected cells. When cellular immunity plays a role in eradicating a viral infection, lymphocytes respond to the presence of viral antigens on the surface of infected cells. It is possible that the lack of such viral antigen expression in some stages of subacute sclerosing panencephalitis is the mechanism that allows the virus to persist and escape attack by the immune system. The expression of viral surface antigens at other times may result in nerve tissue destruction by the immune system and represents a form of virus-induced immunopathologic disease.

Progressive Multifocal Leukoencephalopathy (PML)

Progressive multifocal leukoencephalopathy is a disease of adults which presents as a widespread disease of the nervous system with ataxia, spasticity, visual disturbances, difficulty with speech and swallowing, and rapid progression to coma and death over a period of 1 year. The disease occurs most frequently in patients with debilitating illnesses, most of which produce some form of immunosuppression. These include lymphomas, leukemia, sarcoidosis, systemic lupus erythematosus, and exogenous immunosuppression for renal transplantation. Papovaviruses of 2 types, JC virus and SV40 virus, have been isolated and identified immunologically by the reaction of these viruses with specific antisera produced in rabbits. How these viruses are introduced into humans is unknown, but there was definite inadvertent introduction of SV40 virus by contaminated killed poliovirus vaccines in a large number of people inoculated subcutaneously between 1955 and 1961, and some evidence of antibodies to SV40 virus in USA residents with no history of receiving contaminated poliovirus vaccine. Nothing is known about patients' immune responsiveness to these agents during the rapidly progressive course of progressive multifocal leukoencephalopathy.

Subacute Spongioform Encephalopathies

The neuropathologic similarities of kuru and Jakob-Creutzfeldt disease in man and scrapie and mink encephalopathy in animals, as well as the fact that all are transmissible to other animals, have led to the suggestion by Gajdusek and Gibbs that these diseases should be considered similar types of subacute viral encephalopathies. They are chronic illnesses which proceed relentlessly to death after a long illness-free latent period. None of the signs of acute viral encephalopathy are present. Clinically, there is no elevation of cerebrospinal fluid protein or γ-globulin and no detectable cellular response. Pathologically, there is no inflammatory reaction in the central nervous system. The pathologic changes consist of severe gliosis, loss of neurons in affected areas, and vacuolization within neuroglia. These changes are similar in naturally occurring illness and in experimentally transmitted disease.

Kuru was first described in 1957 by Gajdusek and Zigas in the Fore linguistic group of the New Guinea highlands. The disease presented as a subacute degenerative disorder characterized by progressive ataxia, tremor, dysphagia, and death within 3–18 months following the onset of symptoms. It had been noted that cannibalism was extensively practiced in this area, but its significance in terms of this disease was not appreciated until 1966 when it was demonstrated that kuru could be transmitted to chimpanzees by intracerebral inoculation of brain tissue from affected patients. It was later demonstrated that transmission could also occur by inoculation via the intradermal, intravenous, and oral routes not only with brain material but occasionally by inoculation of kidney, spleen, and lymph node material from affected patients. Since cannibalism was suppressed in this area in the 1950s, the incidence of kuru has decreased.

Jakob-Creutzfeldt disease has been known clinically and pathologically for many years. The striking neuropathologic similarity to kuru and the rapid clinical course led to the attempted transmission of the disease to monkeys, which was successful after an incubation period of 13 months. Since the original transmission experiment, Gibbs and Gajdusek have successfully transmitted the disease to several subhuman primates.

Scrapie, a naturally occurring disease of sheep and occasionally of goats, has been known since 1732. It was first described as transmissible in 1896, and this was confirmed in 1936. Later, the disease was transmitted to mice as well as monkeys after prolonged latent periods. The fact that the disease can be transmitted to mice makes it readily accessible to experimental study.

The natural course of scrapie in the mouse has been well characterized. The agent multiplies and reaches a relatively high titer in the spleen and lymphoid tissue 3–4 weeks after intracerebral and intravenous inoculation. The titer begins to fall thereafter in these organs but increases in the brain, where it reaches its peak at 6 months. The animals succumb to the disease 6–10 months following inoculation. There are no pathologic changes in the spleen or lymph nodes, but the nervous system does show spongioform changes prior to the onset of clinical symptoms.

The role of the host immune response to these agents is completely unknown. No evidence of alteration of immune function has ever been observed in any of these disorders. Specifically, no antibodies to the infecting agents, no evidence of immune paralysis using a number of tests of humoral and cellular immune function, and no alteration of the immune system have resulted in any significant changes in the course of these disorders. The fact that there is some difference in the susceptibility of different strains of mice to scrapie and of monkeys to kuru, scrapie, and Jakob-Creutzfeldt disease suggests that certain genes may enhance the expression of the disease, but this has not yet been clearly linked to specific immune response genes. Understanding the way in which a transmissible disease-producing agent can infect the nervous system without producing a significant host response may be the key to understanding not only the subacute spongioform encephalopathies but also such poorly understood "degenerative" disorders as amyotrophic lateral sclerosis, Parkinson's disease, and the presenile dementias.

• • •

References

Acute Disseminated Encephalomyelitis (ADEM)

Adams RD, Kubik CS: The morbid anatomy of the demyelinative diseases. Am J Med 12:510, 1952.

Driscoll BF, Kies MW, Alvord EC: Successful treatment of experimental encephalomyelitis in guinea pigs with homologous myelin basic protein. J Immunol 112:392, 1974.

Lisak RP & others: Cell mediated immunity to myelin basic protein in acute disseminated encephalomyelitis. Neurology 24:560, 1974.

Multiple Sclerosis

Kurtzke JF & others: Studies on the natural history of multiple sclerosis: Long-term survival in young men. Arch Neurol 22:215, 1970.

Mackay IR, Carnegie PR, Coates AS: Immunopathologic comparison between experimental autoimmune encephalomyelitis and multiple sclerosis. Clin Exp Immunol 15:471, 1973.

McAlpine D, Lumsden C, Acheson ED: *Multiple Sclerosis: A Reappraisal.* Williams & Wilkins, 1965.

McDevitt HO, Bodmer WF: HL-A, immune-response genes, and disease. Lancet 1:1269, 1974.

Olsson JE, Link H: Immunoglobulin abnormalities in multiple sclerosis. Arch Neurol 28:392, 1973.

Acute Idiopathic Polyneuritis (Guillain-Barré Syndrome)

Asbury AK, Arnason BG, Adams RD: The inflammatory lesion in idiopathic polyneuritis. Medicine 48:173, 1969.

Osler LD, Sidell AD: The Guillain-Barré syndrome: The need for exact diagnostic criteria. N Engl J Med 262:964, 1960.

Pleasure DE, Lovelace RE, Duvoisin RC: The prognosis of acute polyradiculoneuritis. Neurology 18:1143, 1968.

Rocklin RE & others: The Guillain-Barré syndrome and multiple sclerosis. N Engl J Med 284:803, 1971.

Waksman BH, Adams RD: Allergic neuritis: An experimental disease of rabbits induced by the injection of peripheral nervous tissue and adjuvant. J Exp Med 102:213, 1955.

Myasthenia Gravis

Almon RR, Andrew CG, Appel SH: Serum globulin in myasthenia gravis: Inhibition of α-bungarotoxin binding to acetylcholine receptors. Science 186:55, 1974.

Alpert LI & others: Studies in myasthenia gravis: Cellular hypersensitivity to skeletal muscle. Am J Clin Pathol 58:647, 1972.

Goldstein G, Whittingham S: Experimental autoimmune thymitis: A clinical model of human myasthenia gravis. Lancet 2:315, 1966.

McFarlin DE, Johnson JS, Seymour WFK: Antimuscle factor and antinuclear factor in patients with myasthenia gravis. 1. Heavy chain determinants. J Immunol 101:104, 1968.

Papatestas AE & others: Studies in myasthenia gravis: Effect of thymectomy. Am J Med 50:465, 1971.

Patrick J, Lindstrom J: Autoimmune response to acetylcholine receptors. Science 180:871, 1973.

Rowland LP, Layzer RB: Muscular dystrophies, atrophies, and related diseases. Chap 37, pages 1–100, in: *Clinical Neurology.* Vol 3. Baker AB, Baker LH (editors). Harper & Row, 1973.

Immunoglobulin Abnormalities

Grove DI & others: Immunological function in dystrophia myotonica. Br Med J 3:81, 1973.

Whitaker JN & others: Hereditary sensory neuropathy: Association with increased synthesis of immunoglobulin A. Arch Neurol 30:359, 1974.

Whitaker JN & others: Serum immunoglobulin and complement (C3) levels in adults with idiopathic chronic polyneuropathies and motor neuron diseases. Neurology 23:1164, 1973.

Wochner RD & others: Accelerated breakdown of immunoglobulin G in myotonic dystrophy: A hereditary error of immunoglobulin catabolism. J Clin Invest 45:321, 1966.

Slow, Chronic, & Latent Viral Infections of the Nervous System

Ahmed A & others: Demonstration of a blocking factor in the plasma and spinal fluid of patients with subacute sclerosing panencephalitis. 1. Partial characterization. J Exp Med 139:902, 1974.

Gajdusek DC, Gibbs CJ, Alpers M: Experimental transmission of a Kuru-like syndrome to chimpanzees. Nature 209:794, 1966.

Gajdusek DC, Zigas V: Degenerative disease of the central nervous system in New Guinea: The endemic occurrence of "Kuru" in the native population. N Engl J Med 257:974, 1957.

Gibbs CJ, Gajdusek DC: Isolation and characterization of the subacute spongioform encephalopathies of man: Kuru and Creutzfeldt-Jakob disease. J Clin Pathol 25 (Suppl 6):84, 1972.

Gibbs CJ & others: Jakob-Creutzfeldt disease (spongioform encephalopathy): Transmission to chimpanzees. Science 161:381, 1968.

Kreth WH, Käckell MY, ter Meulen V: Demonstration of in vitro lymphocyte-mediated cytoxicity against measles virus in SSPE. J Immunol 114:1042, 1975.

Sell KW & others: Plasma and spinal-fluid blocking factor in SSPE. N Engl J Med 288:215, 1973.

Thurman GB & others: Lymphocyte activation in subacute sclerosing panencephalitis virus and cytomegalovirus infections: In vitro stimulation in response to viral-infected cell lines. J Exp Med 138:839, 1973.

Weiner LP & others: Isolation of virus related to SV40 from patients with progressive multifocal leukoencephalopathy. N Engl J Med 286:385, 1972.

37 . . .
Eye Diseases

G. Richard O'Connor, MD

The eye is frequently considered to be a special target of immunologic disease processes, but proof of the causative role of these processes is lacking in all but a few disorders. In this sense, the immunopathology of the eye is much less clearly delineated than that of the kidney, the testis, or the thyroid gland. Because the eye is a highly vascularized organ and because the rather labile vessels of the conjunctiva are embedded in a nearly transparent medium, inflammatory eye disorders are more obvious (and often more painful) than those of other organs such as the thyroid or the kidney. The iris, ciliary body, and choroid—referred to collectively as the uvea—are the most highly vascularized tissues of the eye. The similarity of the vascular supply of the uvea to that of the kidney and the choroid plexus of the brain has given rise to justified speculation concerning the selection of these 3 tissues, among others, as targets of immune complex diseases (eg, serum sickness).

Immunologic diseases of the eye can be grossly divided into 2 major categories: antibody-mediated and cell-mediated diseases. As is the case in other organs also, there is ample opportunity for the interaction of these 2 systems in the eye.

ANTIBODY-MEDIATED DISEASES

Before it can be concluded that a disease of the eye is antibody-dependent, the following criteria must be satisfied: (1) There must be evidence of specific antibody in the patient's serum or plasma cells. (2) The antigen must be identified and, if feasible, characterized. (3) The same antigen must be shown to produce an immunologic response in the eye of an experimental animal, and the pathologic changes produced in the experimental animal must be similar to those observed in the human disease. (4) It must be possible to produce similar lesions in animals passively sensitized with serum from an affected animal upon challenge with the specific antigen.

Unless all of the above criteria are satisfied, the disease may be thought of as *possibly* antibody-dependent. In such circumstances, the disease can be regarded as antibody-mediated if only one of the following criteria is met: (1) if antibody to an antigen is present in higher quantities in the ocular fluids than in the serum (after adjustments have been made for the total amounts of immunoglobulins in each fluid); (2) if abnormal accumulations of plasma cells are present in the ocular lesion; (3) if abnormal accumulations of immunoglobulins are present at the site of the disease; (4) if complement is fixed by immunoglobulins at the site of the disease; (5) if an accumulation of eosinophils is present at the site of the disease; or (6) if the ocular disease is associated with an inflammatory disease elsewhere in the body for which antibody dependency has been proved or strongly suggested.

HAY FEVER CONJUNCTIVITIS

Major Immunologic Features

- Atopic disorder mediated by IgE antibody to pollens in conjunctiva.
- Responds to antihistamines and possibly to hyposensitization.

General Considerations & Clinical Features

This disease is characterized by edema and hyperemia of the conjunctiva and lids (Fig 37–1) and by itching and watering of the eyes. There is often an associated itching sensation in the nose and rhinorrhea. The conjunctiva appears pale and boggy because of the intense edema, which is often rapid in onset. There is a distinct seasonal incidence, some patients being able to establish the onset of their symptoms at precisely the same time each year. These times usually correspond with the release of pollens by specific grasses, trees, or weeds.

Immunologic Pathogenesis

Hay fever conjunctivitis is one of the few inflam-

G. Richard O'Connor is Director of the Proctor Foundation and Professor of Ophthalmology, University of California School of Medicine, San Francisco.

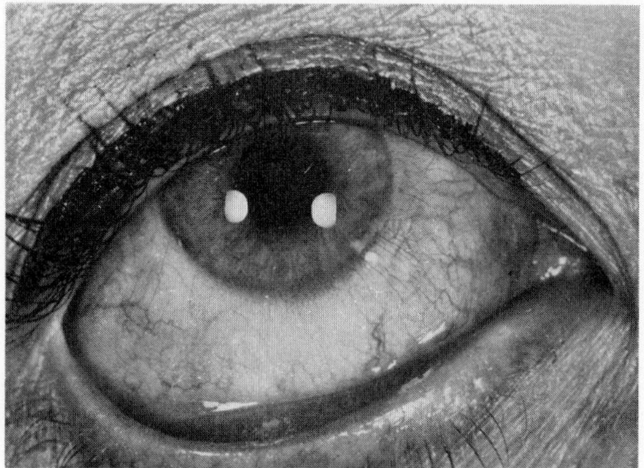

Figure 37–1. Hay fever conjunctivitis. Note edema and hyperemia of the conjunctiva. (Courtesy of M Allansmith and B McClellan.)

matory eye disorders for which antibody dependence has been definitely established. It is recognized as a form of atopic disease with an implied hereditary susceptibility. IgE (reaginic antibody) in its dimeric form is believed to be attached to mast cells lying beneath the conjunctival epithelium. Contact of the offending antigen with IgE triggers the release of vasoactive amines, principally histamine, in this area, and this in turn results in vasodilatation and chemosis.

The role of circulating antibody to ragweed pollen in the pathogenesis of hay fever conjunctivitis has been demonstrated by passively transferring serum from a hypersensitive person to a nonsensitive one. When exposed to the offending pollen, the previously nonsensitive individual reacted with the typical signs of hay fever conjunctivitis.

Immunologic Diagnosis

Victims of hay fever conjunctivitis show many eosinophils in Giemsa-stained scrapings of conjunctival epithelium. They show the *immediate* type of response, with wheal and flare, when tested intradermally with extracts of pollens or other offending antigens. Biopsies of the skin test sites have occasionally shown the full-blown picture of an *Arthus reaction,* with deposition of immune complexes in the walls of the dermal vessels. Passive cutaneous anaphylaxis can also be used to demonstrate the presence of circulating antibody.

Treatment

Systemically administered antihistaminics such as diphenhydramine or tripelennamine are effective, particularly when given prophylactically during the season of greatest exposure. Sustained release capsules of antihistaminics such as Ornade (chlorpheniramine maleate) are preferred by some. Locally applied antihistaminics such as Prefrin-A drops contain both an antihistaminic agent (pyrilamine) and a vasoconstrictor (phenylephrine). Where conjunctival edema is severe and of sudden onset, epinephrine drops (1:100,000) instilled into the conjunctival sac may help to reduce the edema quickly. Corticosteroids applied locally offer little relief. Topical use of cromolyn (disodium cromoglycate; Aarane, Intal), a stabilizer of the mast cell, is still being evaluated in clinical experiments but appears to be a promising method of treatment.

Hyposensitization with gradually increasing doses of subcutaneously injected pollen extracts and other suspected allergens appears to reduce the severity of the disease in some individuals if started well in advance of the season. The mechanism is presumed to be production of blocking antibodies in response to the injection of small, graded doses of the antigen. This procedure cannot be recommended routinely, however, in view of the generally good results and relatively few complications of antihistamine therapy. Acute anaphylactoid reactions have occasionally resulted from overzealous hyposensitization therapy.

VERNAL CONJUNCTIVITIS & ATOPIC KERATOCONJUNCTIVITIS

Major Immunologic Features

- Probably antibody-mediated disorders of immediate hypersensitivity.
- Multiple allergens responsible for ocular sensitization

General Considerations & Clinical Features

These 2 diseases also belong to the group of atopic disorders. Both are characterized by itching and lacrimation of the eyes but are more chronic than hay fever conjunctivitis. Furthermore, both ultimately result in structural modifications of the lids and conjunctiva.

Vernal conjunctivitis characteristically affects children and adolescents; the incidence decreases sharply after the second decade of life. Like hay fever conjunctivitis, vernal conjunctivitis occurs only in the warm months of the year. Most of its victims live in hot, dry climates. The disease characteristically produces giant ("cobblestone") papillae of the tarsal conjunctiva (Fig 37–2). The keratinized epithelium from these papillae may abrade the underlying cornea, giving rise to complaints of foreign body sensations.

Atopic keratoconjunctivitis affects individuals of all ages and has no specific seasonal incidence. The skin of the lids has a characteristic dry, scaly appearance. The conjunctiva is pale and boggy. Both the conjunctiva and the cornea may develop scarring in the later stages of the disease. Atopic cataract has also been described. Staphylococcal blepharitis, manifested by scales and crusts on the lids, commonly complicates this disease.

Immunologic Pathogenesis

Reaginic antibody (IgE) is fixed to subepithelial

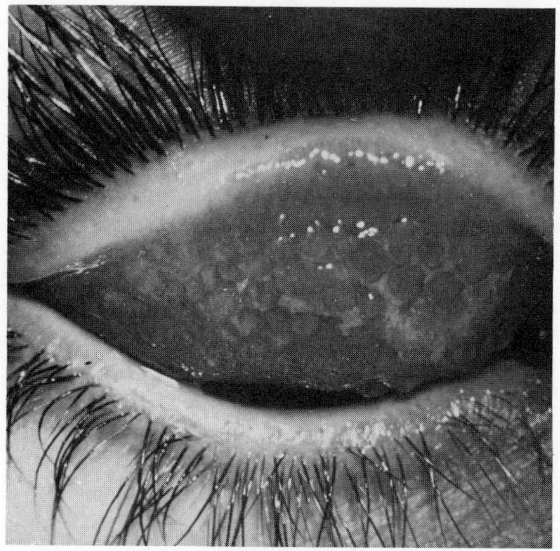

Figure 37–2. Giant papillae ("cobblestones") in the tarsal conjunctiva of a patient with vernal conjunctivitis.

mast cells in both of these conditions. Contact between the offending antigen and IgE is thought to trigger degranulation of the mast cell, which in turn provokes the release of vasoactive amines in the tissues. It is unlikely, however, that antibody action alone is responsible, since—at least in the case of the papillae of vernal conjunctivitis—there is heavy papillary infiltration by mononuclear cells. Hay fever and asthma occur much more frequently in patients with vernal conjunctivitis and atopic keratoconjunctivitis than in the general population. Of the criteria outlined above for demonstration of *possibly* antibody-mediated diseases, (2), (5), and (6) have been met by atopic keratoconjunctivitis.

Immunologic Diagnosis

As in hay fever conjunctivitis, patients with atopic keratoconjunctivitis and vernal conjunctivitis regularly show large numbers of eosinophils in conjunctival scrapings. Skin testing with food extracts, pollens, and various other antigens reveals a wheal-and-flare type of reaction within 1 hour of testing, but the significance of these reactions is not reliably established.

Treatment

Local instillations of corticosteroid drops or ointment relieve the symptoms. However, caution must be observed in the long-term use of these agents because of the possibility of steroid-induced glaucoma and cataract. Corticosteroids produce less dramatic relief in vernal conjunctivitis than in atopic keratoconjunctivitis, and the same can be said of the antihistamines. Cromolyn is currently being investigated for its usefulness in both vernal conjunctivitis and atopic disease. The initial results of clinical testing are encouraging.

Avoidance of known allergens is helpful; such objects as duck feathers, animal danders, and certain food proteins (egg albumin and others) are common offenders. Specific allergens have been much more difficult to demonstrate in the case of vernal disease, although some workers feel that such substances as rye grass pollens may play a causative role. Installation of air conditioning in the home or relocation in a cool, moist climate is useful in vernal conjunctivitis if economically feasible.

RHEUMATOID DISEASES AFFECTING THE EYE

Major Immunologic Features

- Uveitis and scleritis main manifestations of rheumatoid diseases affecting the eye.
- Underlying pathogenesis is vasculitis.
- May respond favorably to local corticosteroid treatment.

General Considerations & Clinical Features

(See also Chapter 27.)

The diseases in this category vary greatly in their clinical manifestations depending upon the specific disease entity and the age of the patient. Uveitis and scleritis are the principal ocular manifestations of the rheumatoid diseases. *Juvenile rheumatoid arthritis* affects females more frequently than males and is commonly accompanied by iridocyclitis of one or both eyes. The onset is often insidious, the patient having few or no complaints and the eye remaining white. Extensive synechia formation, cataract, and secondary glaucoma may be far-advanced before the parents notice that anything is wrong. The arthritis generally affects only one joint—usually a knee—in cases with ocular involvement.

Ankylosing spondylitis affects males more frequently than females, and the onset is in the second to sixth decades. It may be accompanied by iridocyclitis of acute onset, often with fibrin in the anterior chamber (Fig 37–3). Pain, redness, and photophobia are the initial complaints, and synechia formation is common.

Rheumatoid arthritis of adult onset may be accompanied by acute scleritis or episcleritis (Fig 37–4). The ciliary body and choroid, lying adjacent to the sclera, are often involved secondarily with the inflammation. Rarely, serous detachment of the retina results. The onset is usually in the third to fifth decade, and women are affected more frequently than men.

Reiter's disease affects men more frequently than women. The first attack of ocular inflammation usually consists of a self-limited papillary conjunctivitis. It follows, at a highly variable interval, the onset of nonspecific urethritis and the appearance of inflammation in one or more of the weight-bearing joints. Subsequent attacks of ocular inflammation may consist of acute iridocyclitis of one or both eyes, occasionally with hypopyon (Fig 37–5).

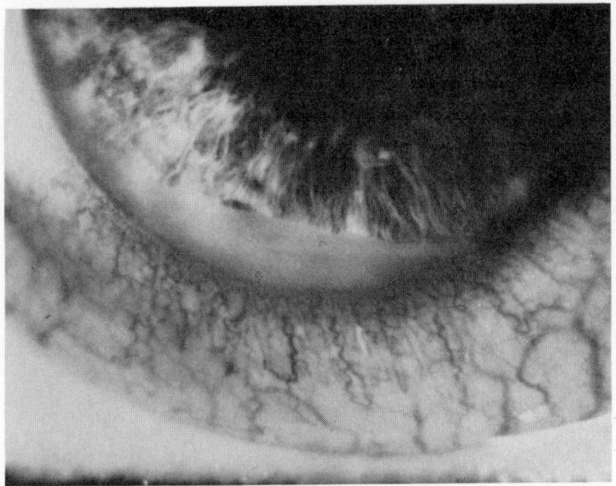

Figure 37–3. Acute iridocyclitis in a patient with ankylosing spondylitis. Note fibrin clot in anterior chamber.

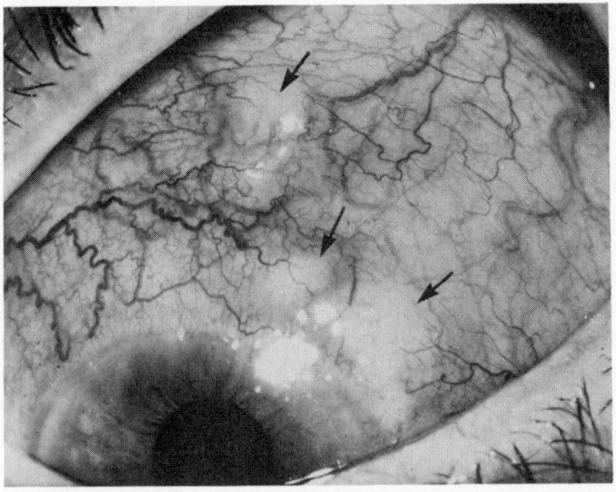

Figure 37–4. Scleral nodules in a patient with rheumatoid arthritis. (Courtesy of S Kimura.)

Immunologic Pathogenesis

Rheumatoid factor, an IgM autoantibody directed against the patient's own IgG, may play a major role in the pathogenesis of rheumatoid arthritis. The union of IgM antibody with IgG is followed by fixation of complement at the tissue site and the attraction of leukocytes and platelets to this area. An occlusive vasculitis, resulting from this train of events, is thought to be the cause of rheumatoid nodule formation in the sclera as well as elsewhere in the body. The occlusion of vessels supplying nutriments to the sclera is thought to be responsible for the "melting away" of the scleral collagen that is so characteristic of rheumatoid arthritis (Fig 37–6).

While this explanation may suffice for rheumatoid arthritis, patients with the ocular complications of juvenile rheumatoid arthritis, ankylosing spondylitis, and Reiter's syndrome usually have negative tests for rheumatoid factor, so other explanations must be sought.

Outside the eyeball itself, the lacrimal gland has been shown to be under attack by circulating antibodies. Destruction of acinar cells within the gland and invasion of the lacrimal gland (as well as the salivary glands) by mononuclear cells result in decreased tear secretion. The combination of dry eyes (keratoconjunctivitis sicca), dry mouth (xerostomia), and rheumatoid arthritis is known as Sjögren's syndrome (see Chapter 27).

A growing body of evidence indicates that the immunogenetic background of certain patients accounts for the expression of their ocular inflammatory disease in specific ways. Analysis of the HLA antigen system shows that the incidence of HLA-B27 is significantly greater in patients with juvenile rheumatoid arthritis, ankylosing spondylitis, and Reiter's syndrome than could be expected by chance alone. It is not known how this antigen controls specific inflammatory responses.

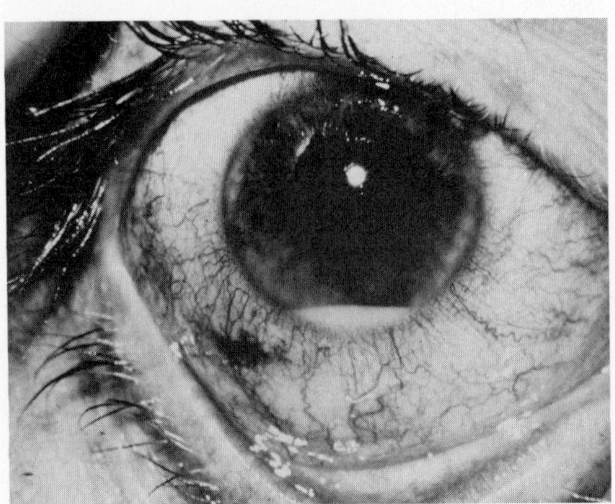

Figure 37–5. Acute iridocyclitis with hypopyon in a patient with Reiter's disease.

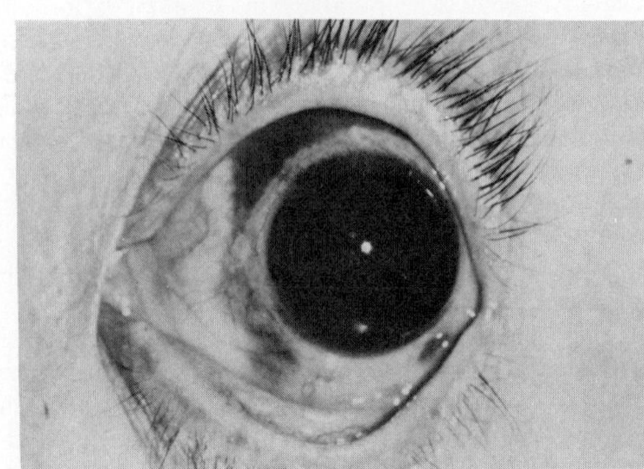

Figure 37–6. Scleral thinning in a patient with rheumatoid arthritis. Note dark color of the underlying uvea.

Immunologic Diagnosis

Rheumatoid factor can be detected in the serum by a number of standard tests involving the agglutination of IgG-coated erythrocytes or latex particles. Unfortunately, the test is not positive in the majority of isolated rheumatoid afflictions of the eye.

The HLA types of individuals suspected of having ankylosing spondylitis and related diseases can be determined by standard cytotoxicity tests using highly specific antisera. This is generally done in tissue typing centers where work on organ transplantation necessitates such studies. X-ray of the sacroiliac area is a valuable screening procedure which may show evidence of spondylitis prior to the onset of low back pain in patients with the characteristic form of iridocyclitis.

Treatment

Patients with uveitis associated with rheumatoid disease respond well to local instillations of corticosteroid drops (eg, dexamethasone 0.1%) or ointments. Orally administered corticosteroids must occasionally be resorted to for brief periods. Salicylates given orally in divided doses with meals are thought to reduce the frequency and blunt the severity of recurrent attacks. Atropine drops (1%) are useful for the relief of photophobia during the acute attacks. Shorter-acting mydriatics such as phenylephrine 10% should be used in the subacute stages to prevent synechia formation. Corticosteroid-resistant cases, especially those causing progressive erosion of the sclera, have been treated successfully with immunosuppressive agents such as chlorambucil.

OTHER ANTIBODY-MEDIATED EYE DISEASES

The following antibody-mediated diseases are infrequently encountered by the practicing ophthalmologist.

Serum sickness uveitis may result from the parenteral administration of heterologous serum proteins. It is assumed that the uvea, like the synovial membranes and the kidney, is subject to attack by immune complexes and that these in turn have the power to bind complement and attract inflammatory cells. Bilateral iritis has been described in a patient who developed generalized serum sickness on 2 occasions 9 days and 30 days after having been given a series of injections of horse antipneumococcal serum for pneumococcal pneumonia. A similar type of uveitis has been produced experimentally in the rabbit.

Systemic lupus erythematosus, associated with the presence of circulating antibodies to DNA, produces an occlusive vasculitis of the ganglion cell layer of the retina. Such infarcts result in cytoid bodies or "cotton wool" spots in the retina (Fig 37–7).

Pemphigus vulgaris produces painful intraepithelial bullae of the conjunctiva. It is associated with the presence of circulating antibodies to an intercellular antigen located between the deeper cells of the conjunctival epithelium.

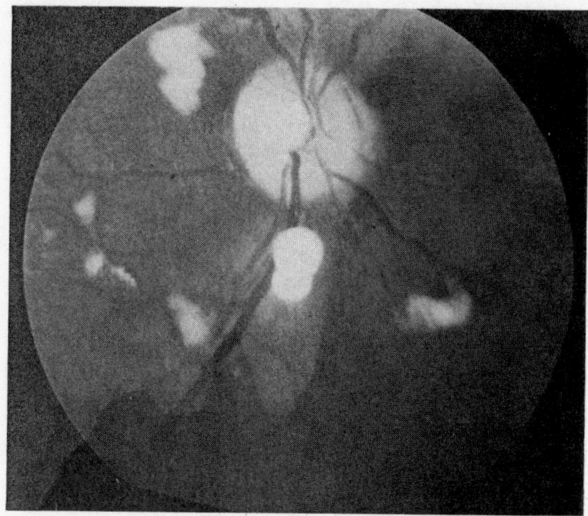

Figure 37–7. "Cotton wool" spots (cytoid bodies) in the retina of a patient with lupus erythematosus.

Benign mucous membrane pemphigoid is characterized by subepithelial bullae of the conjunctiva. It is "benign" only in the sense that it does not kill the patient. In the chronic stages of this disease, cicatricial contraction of the conjunctiva may result in severe scarring of the cornea, dryness of the eyes, and ultimate blindness. Pemphigoid is associated with circulating antibodies directed against one or more antigens located in the basement membrane of the epithelium.

Lens-induced uveitis is a rare condition that may be associated with circulating antibodies to lens proteins. It is seen in individuals whose lens capsules have become permeable to these proteins as a result of trauma or other disease. Interest in this field dates back to Uhlenhuth (1903), who first demonstrated the organ-specific nature of antibodies to the lens. Witmer showed in 1962 that antibody to lens tissue may be produced by lymphoid cells of the ciliary body.

CELL-MEDIATED DISEASES

This group of diseases appears to be associated with cell-mediated immunity or delayed hypersensitivity. Various structures of the eye are invaded by mononuclear cells, principally lymphocytes and macrophages, in response to one or more chronic antigenic stimuli. In the case of chronic infections such as tuberculosis, leprosy, toxoplasmosis, and herpes simplex, the antigenic stimulus has clearly been identified as an infectious agent in the ocular tissue. Such infections are often accompanied by delayed skin test reactivity following the intradermal injection of an extract of the organism.

More intriguing but less well understood are the granulomatous diseases of the eye for which no infectious cause has been found. Such diseases are thought to represent cell-mediated, possibly autoimmune processes, but their origin remains obscure.

OCULAR SARCOIDOSIS

Major Immunologic Features

- Panuveitis with occasional involvement of the optic nerve and retina.
- Associated with cutaneous anergy and occult granulomas.

General Considerations & Clinical Features

Ocular sarcoidosis is characterized by a panuveitis with occasional inflammatory involvement of the optic nerve and retinal blood vessels. It often presents as iridocyclitis of insidious onset. Less frequently, it occurs as acute iridocyclitis, with pain, photophobia, and redness of the eye. Large precipitates resembling drops of solidified "mutton fat" are seen on the corneal endothelium. The anterior chamber contains a good deal of protein and numerous cells, mostly lymphocytes. Nodules are often seen on the iris, both at the pupillary margin and in the substance of the iris stroma. The latter are often vascularized. Synechias are commonly encountered, particularly in patients with dark skin. Severe cases ultimately involve the posterior segment of the eye. Coarse clumps of cells ("snowballs") are seen in the vitreous, and exudates resembling candle drippings may be seen along the course of the retinal vessels. Patchy infiltrations of the choroid or optic nerve may also be seen.

Infiltrations of the lacrimal gland and of the conjunctiva have been noted on occasion. When the latter are present, the diagnosis can easily be confirmed by biopsy of the small opaque nodules.

Immunologic Pathogenesis

Although many infectious or allergic causes of sarcoidosis have been suggested, none has been confirmed (see Chapter 31). Noncaseating granulomas are seen in the uvea, optic nerve, and adnexal structures of the eye as well as elsewhere in the body. The presence of macrophages and giant cells suggests that particulate matter is being phagocytosed, but this material has not been identified.

Patients with sarcoidosis are usually anergic to extracts of the common microbial antigens such as those of mumps, trichophyton, candida, and *Mycobacterium tuberculosis.* As in other lymphoproliferative disorders such as Hodgkin's disease and chronic lymphocytic leukemia, this may represent suppression of T cell activity such that the normal delayed hypersensitivity responses to common antigens cannot take place. Meanwhile, circulating immunoglobulins are usually detectable in the serum at higher than normal levels.

Immunologic Diagnosis

The diagnosis is largely inferential. Negative skin tests to a battery of antigens to which the patient is known to have been exposed are highly suggestive, and the same is true of the elevation of serum immunoglobulins. Biopsy of a conjunctival nodule or scalene lymph node may provide positive histologic evidence of the disease. X-rays of the chest reveal hilar adenopathy in many cases.

Treatment

Sarcoid lesions of the eye respond well to corticosteroid therapy. Frequent instillations of dexamethasone 0.1% eyedrops generally bring the anterior uveitis under control. Atropine drops should be prescribed in the acute phase of the disease for the relief of pain and photophobia; short-acting pupillary dilators such as phenylephrine should be given later to prevent synechia formation. Systemic corticosteroids are sometimes necessary to control severe attacks of anterior uveitis and are always necessary for the control of retinal vasculitis and optic neuritis. The latter condition often accompanies cerebral involvement and carries a grave prognosis.

SYMPATHETIC OPHTHALMIA & VOGT-KOYANAGI-HARADA SYNDROME

Major Immunologic Features

- Represent probable autoimmune phenomena affecting pigmented structures in the eye.
- May be related to delayed hypersensitivity to melanin or to other components of pigment-bearing cells.

General Considerations

These 2 disorders are discussed together because they have certain common clinical features. Both are thought to represent autoimmune phenomena affecting pigmented structures of the eye and skin, and both may give rise to meningeal symptoms.

Clinical Features

Sympathetic ophthalmia is an inflammation in the second eye after the other has been damaged by penetrating injury. In most cases some portion of the uvea of the injured eye has been exposed to the atmosphere for at least 1 hour. The uninjured or "sympathizing" eye develops minor signs of anterior uveitis after a period ranging from 2 weeks to several years. Floating spots and loss of the power of accommodation are among the earliest symptoms. The disease may progress to severe iridocyclitis with pain and photophobia. Usually, however, the eye remains relatively quiet and painless while the inflammatory disease spreads around the entire uvea. Despite the presence of panuveitis, the retina usually remains uninvolved except for perivascular cuffing of the retinal vessels with inflammatory cells. Papilledema and secondary glaucoma may occur. The disease may be accompanied by vitiligo (patchy depigmentation of the skin) and poliosis (whitening) of the eyelashes.

Vogt-Koyanagi-Harada syndrome consists of inflammation of the uvea of one or both eyes characterized by acute iridocyclitis, patchy choroiditis, and serous detachment of the retina. It usually begins with an acute febrile episode with headache, dysacusis, and occasionally vertigo. Patchy loss or whitening of the scalp hair is described in the first few weeks of the disease. Vitiligo and poliosis are commonly present but are not essential for the diagnosis. Although the initial iridocyclitis may subside quickly, the course of the posterior disease is often indolent, with long-standing serous detachment of the retina and significant visual impairment.

Immunologic Pathogenesis

In both sympathetic ophthalmia and Vogt-Koyanagi-Harada syndrome, delayed hypersensitivity to melanin-containing structures is thought to occur. Although a viral cause has been suggested for both disorders, there is no convincing evidence of an infectious origin. It is postulated that some insult, infectious or otherwise, alters the pigmented structures of the eye, skin, and hair in such a way as to provoke delayed hypersensitivity responses to them. Soluble materials from the outer segments of the photoreceptor layer of the retina have recently been incriminated as possible autoantigens. Patients with Vogt-Koyanagi-Harada syndrome are usually of Oriental racial background, suggesting an immunogenetic predisposition to this disease.

Histologic sections of the traumatized eye from a patient with sympathetic ophthalmia may show uniform infiltration of most of the uvea by lymphocytes, epithelioid cells, and giant cells. The overlying retina is characteristically intact, but nests of epithelioid cells may protrude through the pigment epithelium of the retina, giving rise to *Dalen-Fuchs* nodules. The inflammation in its progressive form may destroy the architecture of the entire uvea, leaving an atrophic, shrunken globe.

Immunologic Diagnosis

Skin tests with soluble extracts of human or bovine uveal tissue are said to elicit delayed hypersensitivity responses in these patients. Several investigators have recently shown that cultured lymphocytes from patients with these 2 diseases undergo transformation to lymphoblasts in vitro when extracts of uvea or rod outer segments are added to the culture medium. Circulating antibodies to uveal antigens have been found in patients with these diseases, but such antibodies are to be found in any patient with long-standing uveitis, including those suffering from several infectious entities. The spinal fluid of patients with Vogt-Koyanagi-Harada syndrome may show increased numbers of mononuclear cells and elevated protein in the early stages.

Treatment

Mild cases of sympathetic ophthalmia may be treated satisfactorily with locally applied corticosteroid drops and pupillary dilators. The more severe or progressive cases require systemic corticosteroids, often in high doses, for months or years. An alternate-day regimen of oral corticosteroids is recommended for such patients in order to avoid adrenal suppression. The same applies to the treatment of patients with Vogt-Koyanagi-Harada disease. Occasionally, patients with long-standing progressive disease become resistant to corticosteroids or cannot take additional corticosteroid medication because of pathologic fractures, mental changes, or other reasons. Such patients may become candidates for immunosuppressive therapy. Chlorambucil has been used successfully for both conditions.

OTHER DISEASES OF CELL-MEDIATED IMMUNITY

Giant cell arteritis (temporal arteritis) (see Chapter 27) may have disastrous effects on the eye, particularly in elderly individuals. The condition is manifested by pain in the temples and orbit, blurred vision, and scotomas. Examination of the fundus may reveal extensive occlusive retinal vasculitis and choroidal infarcts. Atrophy of the optic nerve head is a frequent complication. Such patients have an elevated sedimentation rate. Biopsy of the temporal artery reveals extensive infiltration of the vessel wall with giant cells and mononuclear cells.

Polyarteritis nodosa (see Chapter 27) can affect both the anterior and posterior segments of the eye. The corneas of such patients may show peripheral thinning and cellular infiltration. The retinal vessels reveal extensive necrotizing inflammation characterized by eosinophil, plasma cell, and lymphocyte infiltration.

Behçet's disease (see Chapter 27) has an uncertain place in the classification of immunologic disorders. It is characterized by recurrent iridocyclitis with hypopyon and occlusive vasculitis of the retinal vessels. Although it has many of the features of a delayed hypersensitivity disease, dramatic alterations of serum complement levels at the very beginning of an attack suggest an immune complex disorder.

Contact dermatitis (see Chapter 33) of the eyelids represents a significant though minor disease caused by delayed hypersensitivity. Atropine, perfumed cosmetics, materials contained in plastic spectacle frames, and other locally applied agents may act as the sensitizing hapten. The lower lid is more extensively involved than the upper lid when the sensitizing agent is applied in drop form. Periorbital involvement with erythematous, vesicular, pruritic lesions of the skin is characteristic.

Phlyctenular keratoconjunctivitis (Fig 37–8) represents a delayed hypersensitivity response to cer-

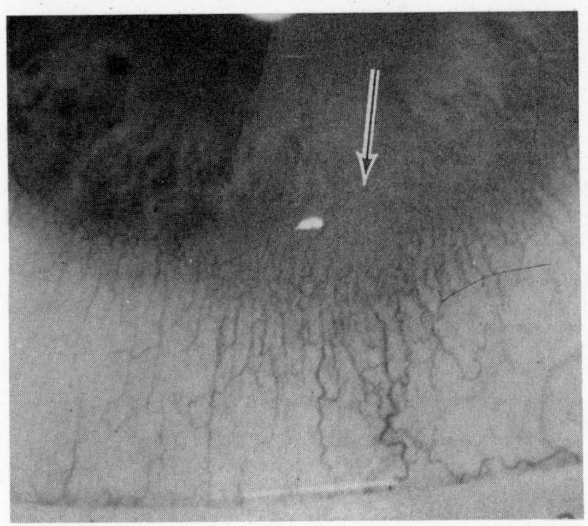

Figure 37–8. Phlyctenule (arrow) at the margin of the cornea. (Courtesy of P Thygeson.)

tain microbial antigens, principally those of *Mycobacterium tuberculosis.* It is characterized by acute pain and photophobia in the affected eye, and perforation of the peripheral cornea has been known to result from it. The disease responds rapidly to locally applied corticosteroids. Since the advent of chemotherapy for pulmonary tuberculosis, phlyctenulosis is much less of a problem than it was 30 years ago. It is still encountered occasionally, however, particularly among American Indians and Alaskan Eskimos. Rarely, other microbial pathogens such as *Staphylococcus aureus* and *Coccidioides immitis* have been implicated in phlyctenular disease.

• • •

References

Allansmith MR, O'Connor GR: Immunoglobulins: Structure, function, and relation to the eye. Surv Ophthalmol 14:367, 1970.

Godfrey WA & others: The use of chlorambucil in intractable idiopathic uveitis. Am J Ophthalmol 78:415, 1974.

Maumenee AE, Silverstein AM (editors): *Immunopathology of Uveitis.* Williams & Wilkins, 1964.

Sherman H, Feldman L, Walzer M: Studies in atopic hypersensitiveness of the ophthalmic mucous membranes. J Allergy 4:437, 1933.

Theodore FH, Lewson AC: Bilateral iritis complicating serum sickness. Arch Ophthalmol 21:828, 1939.

Theodore FH, Schlossman A: *Ocular Allergy.* Williams & Wilkins, 1958.

Witmer R: Phaco-antigenic uveitis. Doc Ophthalmol 16:271, 1962.

Wong VG, Anderson RR, McMaster PRB: Endogenous immune uveitis. Arch Ophthalmol 85:93, 1971.

38 . . .
Parasitic Diseases

Theodosia M. Welch, PhD

Parasitic diseases such as malaria, schistosomiasis, and trypanosomiasis are among the most important causes of morbidity and mortality in developing countries. Because vector control and chemotherapy have failed to completely eradicate these diseases, WHO plans a 10-year program to develop immunization procedures for humans that will reduce or eliminate the debilitating effects of many parasitic diseases. Rapid and frequent travel to all parts of the globe now makes the solution to the problem of parasitic disease imperative. However, better understanding of the immune response to parasites must precede any new program intended to develop more effective immunization procedures.

Immune responses to the complex antigenic structures of parasites have diverse manifestations. For example, immunity with complete protection to reinfection occurs after primary infection with cutaneous leishmaniasis; in babesiasis, partial protection against recurrent infection results from persistent low levels of parasitemia, which stimulate production of protective antibody. Disease can result from the immune response itself, as in the cellular response which produces hepatic granulomas in schistosomiasis or in the antibody-mediated anaphylactic shock of a ruptured hydatid cyst. Alternatively, protection can be subverted by the ability of a parasite to disguise itself as "self" with host antigens, as occurs in schistosomiasis. The ability of parasites to adapt to the host environment is the essence of successful parasitism, but it increases immeasurably the difficulty of developing immunization procedures against parasitic infection.

These varied host responses require that the host-parasite relationship be elucidated in order to detect when in the life cycle of the parasite the immune responses of the host may be exploited in the host's favor. Some progress in this area has already been made as a consequence of the increased interest of immunologists in parasitic disease and of parasitologists in immune phenomena. However, parasite antigens are exceedingly complex, and the immune responses to them form complicated mosaics. When animals respond to the multiple determinants present in these antigens, it is difficult to distinguish which determinants induce humoral or cellular responses, which produce protection, which cause disease in the host, and which possess little or no clinical significance but are of importance in diagnosis.

Theodosia M. Welch is Chief of Leprosy Research Unit, USPHS Hospital, San Francisco.

THE IMMUNE RESPONSE TO PROTOZOA

Protozoa are especially important to both clinicians and immunologists, and the immune responses they induce are as diverse as the protozoa themselves. In developing countries, particularly in Africa, malaria and trypanosomiasis take enormous tolls of life, and asymptomatic amebiasis and toxoplasmosis are widespread even in highly developed countries. The use of immunosuppressive drugs to control malignancies and to prevent rejection of transplanted organs has resulted in activation of otherwise subclinical infections with protozoa such as *Toxoplasma.* In some instances, deaths have been caused by this infection rather than by the underlying illness for which treatment was being given.

MALARIA

Major Immunologic Features

- Specific protective IgG antibody produced against merozoites.
- High serum immunoglobulin levels in endemic areas.
- Immunosuppression of other antigens during course of disease.

Human malaria is caused by species of the genus *Plasmodium.* It is transmitted by female anopheline mosquitoes which ingest the sexual forms of the parasite in blood meals. The infective sporozoites develop in the mosquito and are injected into the definitive host when he is bitten by the insect. In the definitive host, the parasites first develop in an exoerythrocytic form; the resulting merozoites invade host erythrocytes and cause the clinical syndrome of malaria. The exoerythrocytic forms apparently induce little or no immune response because *P vivax* and other relapsing forms exist for extended periods in the exoerythrocytic phase if no blood forms appear. The parasites in the blood induce an array of humoral responses in the host as demonstrated by complement fixation, precipitation, agglutination, and fluorescent antibody reactions.

The immune response that leads to protection is generally thought to be production of complement-independent antibody which inhibits entry of the merozoite into the host erythrocyte. It has been shown that people residing in endemic areas become increasingly less parasitemic with age and that children born in these areas appear to be protected during their first year of life by IgG which crosses the placenta from the immune mother during gestation. Although all immunoglobulin classes are elevated in the serum of malaria patients, it is serum IgG levels that appear to correlate best with protection.

Studies in monkeys and mice have helped to elucidate certain immune mechanisms operating during infection. When sporozoite antigens, soluble parasite material, or merozoites are injected along with Freund's complete adjuvant, they produce either partial or complete protection of monkeys infected with *P knowlesi.* Because Freund's complete adjuvant is unsuitable for use in human subjects, tests with human volunteers use irradiated sporozoite antigens that elicit an immune response but do not cause disease in man. Protection by these vaccines is fairly species-specific; nonetheless, these trials provide a basis for further work on an effective multivalent vaccine.

In malarial infection, the reticuloendothelial system is hyperactive, resulting in removal of effete red cells, parasites, parasitized red cells, and parasite metabolic by-products. An intact spleen may be needed in addition to antibody for protection, because increased reticuloendothelial system clearance appears to be nonspecific. Such enhanced clearance may augment the immune response but not be directly caused by it.

Rhesus monkeys immunized with *P knowlesi* or their extracts develop cell-mediated immunity as evidenced by delayed hypersensitivity when the immunization material is combined with Freund's complete adjuvant. These facts suggest that cell-mediated immunity is important in the protection afforded by such immunization. However, it is doubtful whether similar immune mechanisms operate in naturally acquired infections. Although depressed immune responses to other antigens can be shown during malarial infections, the mechanism of immunosuppression is unclear. It may result from antigenic competition caused by preoccupation of macrophages with the massive antigen load produced by the malarial parasites, from some specific product produced during the infection that acts on macrophages, or from a product acting on T lymphocytes of infected animals.

In summary, it appears that non-complement-dependent IgG antibodies to merozoite antigens are the main source of protection in malarial infection in the adult human, although the diverse antigens produced during infection result in other types of immunity not yet fully understood.

AMEBIASIS

Major Immunologic Features

- Specific antibody detectable following infection.
- Skin tests for immediate and delayed hypersensitivity indicate past or present disease.
- Delayed hypersensitivity depressed with liver abscess.

Many do not feel that the immune response to *Entamoeba histolytica* infection is relevant to the disease. However, *E histolytica* regularly invades human tissue and does cause immune responses. Antibodies of the IgG and IgM classes can be demonstrated by passive hemagglutination, precipitation, and fluorescent antibody technics. These antibodies can be used for diagnosis. However, the presence of specific antibody does not necessarily indicate active infection but rather an exposure to the organism at some time. Skin tests give immediate responses in many patients, indicating IgE production, and Arthus reactions can also be demonstrated. To date there is little direct evidence that immunoglobulin is protective.

Cell-mediated immunity to *E histolytica* antigens can be demonstrated by delayed hypersensitivity skin tests in many patients who do not have clinically evident disease, and recent evidence indicates that patients with amebic abscess of the liver have depressed cell-mediated immunity to amebic antigens while retaining their ability to respond to other skin test antigens such as streptokinase-streptodornase.

LEISHMANIASIS

Leishmania is a genus of obligate intracellular parasites that infect macrophages of the skin and viscera to produce disease in both animals and man. Sandflies, the principal vector, introduce the parasites into the host while taking blood meals.

1. CUTANEOUS LEISHMANIASIS

Major Immunologic Features

- Delayed hypersensitivity present.
- Little or no specific antibody.

Cutaneous leishmaniasis, which is caused by *L tropica,* results in an immune response characterized by little antibody but strong cell-mediated immunity. In cutaneous leishmaniasis it is the patient's immune response to the infection that primarily determines the form taken by the clinical disease. If the patient mounts an adequate but not excessive cell-mediated immune response to the parasite, healing of the lesions and solid protection result. However, if cell-mediated immunity to the parasite is inadequate, the result may be diffuse cutaneous leishmaniasis, a disseminated disease in which there is little chance of spontaneous cure. On the other hand, an excessive cell-mediated immune response produces lupoid leishmaniasis, in which nonulcerated lymphoid nodules form at the edge of the primary lesion; these lesions persist indefinitely, although parasites are not easily demonstrated.

Delayed hypersensitivity ordinarily occurs early during the course of cutaneous leishmaniasis; nevertheless, new lesions can develop for several months. Secondary lesions quickly assume the histologic picture of the early lesions (the isophasic reaction) and usually heal at the same time as the primary lesion or shortly thereafter. Protection appears to be permanent after a primary infection has terminated naturally, although immunosuppressive treatment of patients residing in endemic areas has resulted in reinfection in previously protected individuals. If excision is used to terminate the primary infection before spontaneous healing has taken place, protection to reinfection may not occur. Animal experiments indicate that sensitized lymphocytes are widely distributed when the lesion heals. Thereafter, new disease cannot occur, presumably because immune lymphocytes are generally distributed in lymph nodes and spleen. Reinfection is usually manifested by a prolonged delayed hypersensitivity response at the site of the sandfly bite, but ulceration does not follow. In endemic areas, vaccination with virulent strains of the parasite derived from culture is a common practice undertaken for the purpose of making certain that disfiguring lesions do not occur.

2. VISCERAL LEISHMANIASIS

Major Immunologic Features

- Delayed hypersensitivity only after spontaneous recovery or chemotherapy.
- Increased nonspecific immunoglobulin levels.

The immune response to visceral leishmaniasis (kala-azar) is remarkably different from that of cutaneous leishmaniasis, although the parasites are morphologically indistinguishable. Massive polyclonal hypergammaglobulinemia with little or no evidence of cell-mediated immunity is the rule in visceral leishmaniasis. There is no quantitative relationship between the elevated serum immunoglobulin and antiparasite antibodies which are, moreover, not species-specific. The elevated immunoglobulin diminishes rapidly when treatment begins. Delayed cutaneous hypersensitivity to parasite antigens becomes demonstrable only after spontaneous recovery or treatment, which suggests that cell-mediated mechanisms play a role in the resolution of the infectious process. Under certain circumstances, post-kala-azar dermal "leishmanoid" occurs. Nodules containing many parasites form papules as a result of incomplete or defective cell-mediated immunity. Insufficient data are available at this time to establish exact correlation between delayed hypersensitivity and protection.

3. AMERICAN LEISHMANIASIS

Major Immunologic Features

- Positive delayed hypersensitivity.
- Increased immunoglobulin levels.

Mucocutaneous leishmaniasis (espundia) may occur after infection with *L braziliensis.* In espundia, both delayed hypersensitivity and elevated immunoglobulins are detected. A primary healed lesion of *L braziliensis* gives protection to cutaneous reinfection, although parasites derived from the primary infection may persist and multiply freely in the cartilage of the mouth or nose. Espundia may result from the lack of a cell-mediated response sufficient to terminate the primary infection, and a genetic predisposition to the development of mucocutaneous lesions may exist.

TOXOPLASMOSIS

Major Immunologic Features

- Sabin-Feldman dye test positive.
- Specific antibody present.
- Nonspecific increase in serum immunoglobulins.

Toxoplasma infection in humans is generally asymptomatic; it has been estimated that as much as 40% of the adult population in the world is infected. Clinical disease, which develops in only a small fraction of those infected, ranges from benign lymphadenopathy to an acute and often fatal infection of the central nervous system. Many potential sources of infection have been proposed, including partially cooked infected meat or oocysts shed from infected cats, but these cannot account for such large numbers of infections. The major reservoirs of infection are as yet unknown.

Toxoplasma infection results in production of IgG and IgM antibodies, which can readily be demonstrated by hemagglutination, complement fixation, indirect fluorescent antibody technics, and the Sabin-Feldman dye test. The mere presence of antibody is not sufficient for protection, as shown by the ability of the parasite to persist in the presence of high antibody titers and by the fact that passive transfer of antibody is not protective.

Recent work has shown that the ability of macrophages to kill infective trophozoites is greatly increased if the parasites are first exposed to antibody and complement. This mechanism may be one way that parasite numbers are reduced in the infected host. It has been shown that the parasite can multiply only to a certain number within macrophages before the host cells are destroyed, and that when this occurs, extracellular trophozoites come into contact with antibody and may be more efficiently killed by macrophages than before.

Cell-mediated immunity is also involved in protection against *Toxoplasma* because delayed hypersensitivity and its in vitro correlates such as production of migration inhibitory factor (MIF) develop early in toxoplasmosis, and protection results only from infection with living organisms. Interferon is also produced, and activated macrophages can be demonstrated that inhibit the multiplication of the parasite. Inhibiting the multiplication of organisms would effectively reduce the parasite burden. In such cellular immunity, macrophage activation is probably effected by the action of antigen upon specifically sensitized T lymphocytes which in turn produce lymphokines that activate the macrophages (see Chapter 10). The nonspecificity of activated macrophages in toxoplasmosis has been questioned; it now appears that the macrophages inhibit multiplication of *Toxoplasma* both specifically and nonspecifically, depending upon which strain of parasite is used and when following infection the macrophages are studied.

An intact immune system is necessary for protection against *Toxoplasma* because immunosuppression to control transplant rejection or malignancies may result in active toxoplasmosis. This phenomenon may result either from the elimination of sensitized lymphocytes previously limiting an inapparent infection or from the inability of the immunosuppressed host to mount an adequate protective response to new infection.

Vaccination of the population with strains of low virulence would probably be effective in establishing protection to *Toxoplasma;* but, because most persons develop adequate protection after natural infection, this procedure is probably not worthwhile except in previously uninfected women of childbearing age in order to prevent intrauterine transmission.

TRYPANOSOMIASIS

1. AFRICAN TRYPANOSOMIASIS

Major Immunologic Features

- Increase in nonspecific IgM.
- Antigenic variation produces specific antibody sequentially.

The tsetse fly is the most important vector in the spread of African trypanosomes. In the tsetse fly the parasite undergoes cyclic development to the infective stage and is transmitted when the fly takes a blood meal. The parasite may also be spread by insects in which cyclic development does not take place. In this case, host infection occurs by contamination of the bite wound by the feces of the insect.

This group of trypanosomes characteristically multiplies in the lumens of blood vessels and in the capillaries of the internal organs and tissue spaces of the host.

Greatly increased levels of immunoglobulins, especially of the IgM class, are regularly present in infected animals. The increased immunoglobulin levels, which do not correlate positively with protection, may result from mitogenic agents produced by the trypanosomes themselves. The validity of this suggestion is supported by the observation that a large proportion of the immunoglobulin in infected hosts is nonspecific in nature.

Specific antibodies do arise in trypanosomal infections. In experimental animals, the *T brucei* group of trypanosomes produces an interesting immunologic phenomenon. Antigenic variants of the parasite that arise in the infected host elicit specific antibody to themselves and are in turn eliminated by the antibodies they generate. More than 20 variants have been shown to develop sequentially in experimental animals. It is debatable whether these variants arise from surface mutations that are unaffected by antibody to the preceding variant. The fact that a predictable series of variants can be initiated if the trypanosome is again introduced into the host after vector passage is an argument for the view that variant expression is under genetic control. In any case, antigenic variation seems to be a property of the surface coat of the trypanosome, which can be shed into the ambient medium. Organisms taken from culture or from vectors do not possess this coat. The ability of the host to respond to multiple antigenic variants with such specificity could account in part for the increased immunoglobulin levels reported during infections. However, no evidence has been presented that such antigenic variation occurs in human trypanosomiasis.

The specific antibodies can either lyse the parasites or clump them. Clumping allows for more efficient removal of the parasites by the reticuloendothelial system. Effective reduction of parasite numbers would protect the host. It is controversial whether humans or domestic animals living in endemic areas develop resistance to infection, although epidemiologic observations suggest that resistance does arise and that wild animals act as reservoirs of the parasite without displaying frank disease. For example, the fact that there are healthy human carriers of *T rhodesiense*—which usually produces a fatal infection—implies that some protective mechanism must exist. However, the precise immunologic nature of this protection is at present obscure.

Suppression of immune responses to other unrelated antigens may be observed during trypanosomal infections. It is not known whether the suppression results from suppressor T cells, lack of helper T cells, or from a smaller number of T cells available to interact with new antigens. Depletion of the T cell-dependent areas of the lymph nodes during active trypanosomiasis suggests the latter hypothesis.

Vaccines specific for antigenic variants can be developed although few common antigens have been demonstrated. The multiplicity of antigenic variants observed during field studies in bovines makes vaccination an unlikely solution to trypanosomiasis unless common antigens can be found.

2. AMERICAN TRYPANOSOMIASIS

Major Immunologic Features

- Specific antibody not necessarily indicative of active infection.
- Delayed hypersensitivity present.

An estimated 7 million people in Central and South America are infected with *T cruzi*, and 30 million more are at risk. Chagas' disease *(T cruzi)* is spread by bloodsucking reduviid bugs in whose hind gut the parasite develops and becomes infective. The disease is transmitted to man when fecal contamination from the bug occurs in fresh bites, mucous membranes, or abraded skin. The parasites actively penetrate host cells and multiply intracellularly. The acute form of the disease is characterized by myocardiopathy, lymphadenopathy, hepatosplenomegaly, parasitemia, fever, malaise, and colonies of intracellular amastigotes in the striated muscles, smooth muscles, and reticuloendothelial system. The disease is often fatal in infants or children, but in adults, a chronic form of the disease usually follows the initial infection. Chronic infection is characterized by cardiac enlargement, megacolon, megaesophagus, and degeneration of the peripheral and central nervous systems. In chronic disease, nests of parasites can be found, but parasitemia accompanied by fever is infrequent.

Antibody that can be detected by complement fixation is produced during disease. This can be a guide to diagnosis, although the antibody cross-reacts with other flagellates such as leishmaniae. Antibody may persist after infection and therefore does not indicate active disease. High titers of antibody do not appear to limit the infection in man; however, complement-dependent lysis of the parasites can be demonstrated in vitro with sera from experimentally infected hosts. This lysis may be an important mechanism for parasite control in vivo. However, lytic antibody does not afford complete protection against reinfection because passive transfer of hyperimmune serum is not always effective. Animals can be protected against virulent strains of the organism by infection with avirulent or partially virulent strains or by passive transfer of sensitized lymphocytes. Acquired resistance to virulent strains is probably the result of previous inapparent infection with strains of low virulence.

Activated macrophages can be demonstrated in *T cruzi* infections, although their role in protection has yet to be fully explored. Delayed hypersensitivity, lymphocyte activation, and MIF production can be documented during infection, but the role of cell-mediated immunity has not been fully elucidated. New work implies that cardiac damage in infected rabbits can be the result of an immune response to cross-reacting antigens of *T cruzi* and rabbit cardiac muscle because *T cruzi*-sensitized lymphocytes are cytotoxic for unparasitized cardiac muscle cells in vitro as well as for parasitized cells. Attempts to vaccinate against disease might do more harm than good if such sensitized lymphocytes against shared antigens should develop.

THE IMMUNE RESPONSE TO HELMINTHS

From the foregoing it is obvious that the immune response to unicellular parasites is complex. Multicellular animals also produce complicated immune responses in which the protective mechanisms are difficult to differentiate from deleterious or irrelevant responses. Immune responses to multicellular parasites are in fact more complicated than are those to the protozoa because in these multicellular organisms there are highly differentiated organs and structures that cause additional immune responses. In general, the primary antigens of helminths are metabolic by-products, enzymes, or other secretory products rather than structural components. For example, the eggs of *Schistosoma mansoni* have been shown to secrete unique antigens that induce granuloma formation; the various stages of developing nematodes have stage-specific antigens, often molting fluids, to which the host responds in various ways; and the granules in the stichocytes, special cells located in the "neck" of *Trichinella spiralis,* elicit specific antibody.

Nematodes, cestodes, and trematodes all share common antigens. The 2 most frequent responses to helminths—eosinophilia and reaginic antibody (IgE)—

are both T cell-dependent (see Chapters 8 and 19). In addition, certain helminths have been shown to potentiate the immune response to other antigens, perhaps by common metabolic by-products acting as nonspecific adjuvants.

TREMATODES

Trematodes are important pathogens of man and domestic animals. Fascioliasis debilitates and kills domestic animals in large numbers, and schistosomiasis is a major disease of man. The lung flukes of the genus *Paragonimus* cause central nervous system complications in man if they encyst in the brain rather than in the lung, where considerable mechanical damage results.

1. SCHISTOSOMIASIS

Major Immunologic Features

- Immediate and delayed hypersensitivity are present.
- Diagnostic antibody formed.
- Antigenic mimicry with host tissues.

Schistosomiasis in man is caused by *Schistosoma mansoni, S japonicum,* and *S haematobium.* The advent of new high dams in many areas of the world, especially Africa, has increased the incidence of schistosomiasis because the additional irrigation made possible by the dams has vastly enlarged the habitat of the freshwater snail that serves as intermediate host to the parasite. The life cycle of this parasite depends upon skin penetration of the definitive host by infective forms produced in the snail. Because attempts to reduce snail populations have largely failed, infection has become rampant in these areas.

In brief, the life cycle of the schistosomes which infect man is as follows: Infected humans and animals excrete eggs that hatch in water, releasing miracidia; these actively penetrate snails that shed a second intermediate stage, cercariae, into the water around them. The cercariae penetrate the skin of the definitive host and become schistosomula. Schistosomula penetrate the systemic circulation, are carried to the lungs, and may eventually reach the small branches of the mesenteric veins adjacent to the bowel or bladder mucosa, where they develop into egg-laying adults. Eggs laid by the mature female parasites are the principal cause of the lesions characteristic of the disease.

It is generally agreed that the protective immune response to schistosomes is mediated by antibody. However, newer evidence indicates that in this disease, as in other helminth infections, humoral and cellular protective mechanisms are interrelated. It is known that people residing in endemic areas become resistant to reinfection with schistosomes, and it has been assumed that this results from continuing exposure to small numbers of cercariae of zoophilic species.

In experimental hosts, *S mansoni* is able to coat itself with host materials such as blood group substances and can consequently exist in a host disguised as "self," whereas newly invading schistosomula are rapidly killed or immobilized by the action of antibody. This *concomitant immunity* has been established as an important way in which host protection to reinfection may be achieved while allowing the original parasites to persist.

IgG antibodies that immobilize or kill schistosomula have been demonstrated in vitro, but these same antibodies do not protect against reinfection after passive transfer. On the other hand, certain antisera have successfully produced protection, which raises the possibility that antibody of another class is protective. In fact, recent work shows that specific IgE antibody from schistosome-infected rats can enable macrophages from normal rats to kill schistosomula in vitro. Schistosomula killing can also be induced by hyperimmune human serum and peripheral blood mononuclear cells. Because titers of reaginic antibody are generally high in schistosome-infected humans, IgE production may be one of the mechanisms by which protection is achieved. Varying levels of IgE in immune sera might account for variable results in passive transfer experiments. However, more information is clearly needed to make certain that antibody alone gives protection in schistosomiasis. In fact, in a controlled study in Uganda, more than 30% of people infected with *S mansoni* displayed delayed as well as immediate hypersensitivity to *S mansoni* antigens. Although these results do not establish a role for cell-mediated immunity in protection, these findings (together with the presence of massive mononuclear infiltrations characteristic of cercarial dermatitis—see section following) do indicate that other cell-mediated events such as lymphokine-induced macrophage activation might also have some role in protection against schistosomes.

Cell-mediated immune responses mounted by the host against the parasites produce many of the lesions of schistosomiasis. In *S mansoni* and *S japonicum* infections, fibrosis of the liver is the main cause of death. This fibrosis may be the result of delayed hypersensitivity reactions to antigens produced by secretions from the eggs. Extensive work has shown conclusively that granulomas induced by *S mansoni* eggs in the lungs of mice are delayed hypersensitivity reactions, and evidence in man would not contradict the hypothesis that fibrosis results from intense granuloma formation.

In *S haematobium* infections, a florid granulomatous reaction early in the disease may spontaneously subside. It has been suggested that this abatement results from desensitization by blocking antibody or antigen-antibody complexes produced within the granuloma itself. Diminishing egg production by the worms has not been shown to be a factor in the remission because the worms live and continue egg production for long periods in the absence of reinfection.

Four to 6 weeks after infection with certain schistosomes, man may develop Katayama fever, thought to be an immunologic response that occurs at the onset of egg production by the worms. Whether this is an anaphylactic response (IgE) or a type of serum sickness (IgG) is still a subject of debate, but it is generally agreed that antibodies formed to the developing worms produce the reaction. As might be expected, hypersensitivity and protective and irrelevant antibodies are all produced to the complex worm antigens.

Immunodiagnosis of schistosome infection in the absence of egg excretion by the host can be accomplished in various ways, both humoral and and cellular. Stage-specific humoral responses can be used to produce circumoval precipitation; schistosomula growth inhibition or death; and complement fixation, hemagglutination, and various precipitation reactions. It should be emphasized that none of these reactions can be positively correlated with protection. Immediate and delayed cutaneous hypersensitivity develop in most individuals during the course of the disease; however, the specificity of these reactions is often suspect because of cross-reaction with other worms.

2. CERCARIAL DERMATITIS (Swimmer's Itch)

The invasion of a previously sensitized host by the cercariae of schistosomes, particularly those of avian origin, can cause severe 2-stage reactions in the skin. The first stage begins within minutes of contact and consists of a wheal-and-flare reaction. The second stage becomes evident 16–24 hours after contact, with development of papules which are essentially delayed hypersensitivity reactions. These reactions have been shown to be very specific in that persons infected with *S mansoni* did not react to cercariae of an avian schistosome known to cause violent reactions in persons with swimmer's itch.

CESTODES

The immune response to cestodes has been inadequately studied because it was assumed for many years that the host response to these parasites was minimal. It is now established that the larval forms of the parasites, which are tissue penetrators, evoke a humoral response that protects the hyperimmunized host against new infections. Infection with cestodes is usually life-threatening to man only when he acts as an unnatural intermediate host. *Taenia solium* from swine can develop extraintestinally in man and can be found in any organ of the body. When encysted parasites die in the brain, severe tissue reactions with resultant central nervous system disorders and even death can occur.

1. ECHINOCOCCOSIS

Major Immunologic Features

- IgE elevated.
- Anaphylaxis due to ruptured cyst fluids.
- Casoni skin test of questionable use.
- Diagnostic antibody present.

The most serious human cestode infection is that caused by *Echinococcus.* These tiny tapeworms do not produce pathologic lesions in the definitive host, the dog, but severe complications occur when their eggs are ingested by humans and other animals. The larval form of the tapeworm hatches from the egg in the intestine of the intermediate host; the larva then claws its way through the intestinal mucosa and is transported through the lymphatic and blood vessels to sites in which it is rapidly encapsulated. A heavy cyst wall is laid down both by the host and by the parasite. In man, *Echinococcus* normally forms fluid-filled cysts in the liver, but these can also occur in the lungs and other parts of the body. These hydatid cysts are highly immunogenic and result in production of high titers of reaginic antibody (IgE) and other immunoglobulins. If a cyst is ruptured, anaphylactic response to the cyst fluid can cause death. Little or no protection seems to be elicited by this highly immunogenic cestode because the hydatid cysts remain alive for years and in animals can be shown to increase in number as the host ages. Man is usually a dead-end host for this parasite because the cysts must be eaten by a canid to become sexually mature.

The Casoni skin test indicates past or present echinococcosis. The test consists of intradermal injection of hydatid cyst fluid, resulting in both immediate and delayed hypersensitivity. The specificity of this test is in doubt because of cross-reactions with other helminths. Diagnosis can be made by hemagglutination, complement fixation, and flocculation tests using serum of the patient.

NEMATODES

Nematodes are ubiquitous and parasitize not only man and his domestic animals but also the plants he cultivates. *Nippostrongylus braziliensis* in the rat has been systematically studied, as has *Trichinella spiralis* in the mouse, *Trichostrongylus colubriformis* in the guinea pig, and *Ascaris suum* in the pig. Neither *N braziliensis* nor *T colubriformis* infects man, but ascaris infection has interesting immunologic features in man and *T spiralis* is an important human pathogen.

1. TRICHINOSIS

Major Immunologic Features

- Positive skin tests for immediate and delayed hypersensitivity.
- Diagnostic antibody present.

Trichinosis is acquired by ingestion of the infective larvae of *T spiralis* in uncooked or partially cooked meat. Pork is the primary source of infection in man. The larvae are released from their cysts in the meat during digestion and rapidly develop into adults in the host's intestine. After copulation, the males die and the females migrate into the intestinal mucosa, where for about 5–6 weeks they produce larvae which migrate through the lymphatic system to the blood. These larvae travel in the blood to all parts of the body and develop in voluntary muscles, especially in the diaphragm, tongue, masticatory and intercostal muscles, larynx, and the eye. Within the sarcolemma of striated muscle fibers, the larvae coil up into a cyst which is rapidly laid down by host histiocytes. Larvae may remain viable and infective for as long as 24 years even though the cysts calcify.

Trichinella infection sometimes presents characteristic clinical symptoms such as edema of the eyelids and face but often presents less specific clinical signs such as eosinophilia, which can be suggestive of several other parasitic infections. Specific immunodiagnostic tests may thus be of great importance. The bentonite flocculation test for human trichinosis is of great value because of its high degree of specificity. In addition, there are many other immunodiagnostic tests, including complement fixation, hemagglutination, flocculation, and skin tests. Skin tests produce both immediate and delayed responses.

In man, infection with *Trichinella* initially elicits IgM antibody followed by an IgG response. IgA antibody has not been reported, which is surprising because the female worms are in the intestinal mucosa, a major site of IgA production. The immediate hypersensitivity response shows that IgE is also produced.

Even though almost all animals can be infected with this parasite, the mechanisms whereby humoral and cell-mediated immune responses afford protection are still being studied. In experimental animals, experiments have yielded equivocal results. Some species, such as the rat, can be passively protected by antibody, whereas others, such as the mouse, seem to depend mainly on cell-mediated immunity for protection. Man develops both immediate and delayed hypersensitivity to *Trichinella* antigens, which suggests that IgE alone or in combination with mononuclear cells may mediate protection. Indeed, recent work with purified antigens obtained from dead *T spiralis* larvae indicates that in rats, protection is related to reaginic antibody production. Larvae contained in implanted Millipore chambers can also induce an immune response, showing that structural antigens are not the only antigens capable of antibody induction.

Although *Trichinella* is extremely immunogenic in its hosts, it can also exert an immunosuppressive action. Certain viral infections are more severe during infection with this parasite, and skin grafts show delayed rejection. On the other hand, cellular immunity to BCG seems to be potentiated when *T spiralis* is present, and *T spiralis*-infected mice are less susceptible to *Listeria* infections. These seeming contradictions may be explained by recalling that metazoan parasites contain a large complement of antigens, some of which may produce immunosuppression and others potentiation.

2. ASCARIASIS

Major Immunologic Features

- Specific antibody detectable.
- Elevated IgE.
- Responses to unrelated antigens potentiated during infection.

Ascaris, the giant roundworm of man, is a lumen-dwelling parasite as an adult and causes little inconvenience to the host except in the heaviest infections. Ingestion of eggs results in larvae that migrate through the intestinal wall to eventually reach the lung via the bloodstream. In a previously infected host, hypersensitivity reactions in the lung resulting from high levels of IgE can cause serious pneumonitis. The most important immunologic response to this parasite in man may be potentiation of responses to other antigens during infection with *Ascaris* or when *Ascaris* antigens are given along with these antigens. *Ascaris* "potentiators" putatively augment asthma development in children infected with this nematode. Additionally, the possibility of potentiating responses to weak antigens may be of use for vaccines. At this time, however, potentiation mechanisms by nematodes are poorly understood. Acute hypersensitivity to *Ascaris* antigens often develops in laboratory workers and makes it virtually impossible for them to continue working with the nematode.

3. TOXOCARA INFECTIONS

Toxocara canis, the dog ascarid, is now known to infect small children who ingest its eggs in dirt. *Toxocara* eggs produce a population of migrating larvae that are immobilized in the tissues of man and consequently never produce worms in the intestinal tract. The syndrome caused by the immobilized larvae is called *visceral larva migrans.* Visceral larva migrans is characterized by high peripheral eosinophilia and chronic granulomatous lesions associated with the migrating larvae; such larvae in the eyes of infected children have been confused with retinoblastoma and diagnosed only after enucleation of the affected eyeball. Immunodiagnostic tests for visceral larva migrans have therefore been eagerly sought. Initially, lack of specificity for *T canis* was a great problem, but specific immunodiagnostic methods have recently been developed that should allow prompt diagnosis. Visceral larva migrans can also be caused by larvae of other nematodes such as the genus *Capillaria,* which migrate in human tissue but do not develop further.

• • •

References

General

Brent L, Holborow J (editors): *Progress in Immunology II.* North-Holland Publishing Co, 1974.

Ciba Foundation Symposium 25: *Parasites in the Immunized Host: Mechanisms of Survival.* Associated Scientific Publishers, 1974.

Goldsmith RS: Infectious diseases: Metazoal. Chap 26, pages 863–882 in: *Current Medical Diagnosis & Treatment 1976.* Krupp MA, Chatton MJ (editors). Lange, 1976.

Goldsmith RS: Infectious diseases: Protozoal. Chap 25, pages 850–862 in: *Current Medical Diagnosis & Treatment 1976.* Krupp MA, Chatton MJ (editors). Lange, 1976.

Heyneman D, Dunn FL: Medical parasitology. Appendix in: *Review of Medical Microbiology,* 12th ed. Jawetz E, Melnik JL, Adelberg EA. Lange, 1976.

Jackson GJ, Herman R, Singer I (editors): *Immunity to Parasitic Animals.* Vols 1 and 2. Appleton-Century-Crofts, 1969, 1970.

Soulsby EJL: *Helminths, Arthropods, and Protozoa of Domestic Animals,* 6th ed. Williams & Wilkins, 1968.

Soulsby EJL (editor): *Immunity to Animal Parasites.* Academic Press, 1972.

Protozoa

Alarcon-Segovia & others: Immunology of Chagas' disease. Bull WHO 50:459, 1974.

Ciba Foundation Symposium 20: *Trypanosomiasis and Leishmaniasis with Special Reference to Chagas' Disease.* Associated Scientific Publishers, 1974.

Feldman HA: Toxoplasmosis: An overview. Bull NY Acad Med 50:110, 1974.

Hoff RL, Frenkel JK: Cell mediated immunity against *Besnoitia* and *Toxoplasma* in specifically and cross-immunized hamsters and in cultures. J Exp Med 139:560, 1974.

Jacobs L: *Toxoplasma gondii:* Parasitology and transmission. Bull NY Acad Med 50:128, 1974.

Kagan IG: The immunology of amebiasis. Arch Invest Med (Mex), vol 4, suppl 1, 1973.

Mauel J, Behin R: Cell mediated and humoral immunity to protozoan infections. Transplant Rev 19:121, 1974.

McGregor IA: Mechanisms of acquired immunity and epidemiological patterns of antibody responses in malaria in man. (2 parts.) Bull WHO 50:259, 266, 1974.

Trematodes

Hang LM, Warren KS, Boros DL: *Schistosoma mansoni:* Antigenic secretions and the etiology of egg granulomas in mice. Exp Parasitol 35:288, 1974.

Lewert RM: Schistosomes. Page 981 in: *Immunity to Parasitic Animals.* Jackson GJ, Herman R, Singer I (editors). Appleton-Century-Crofts, 1970.

Smithers SR, Terry RJ, Hockley DJ: Host antigens in schistosomiasis. Proc R Soc Lond [Biol] 171:483, 1969.

Weiderman G & others: Skin tests with *Schistosoma mansoni* antigen in cases of swimmers itch. Zentralbl Bakteriol [Orig A] 224:128, 1973.

Cestodes

Gemmel MA, MacNamara RN: Immune response to tissue parasites II: Cestodes. Page 235 in: *Immunity to Animal Parasites.* Soulsby EJL (editor). Academic Press, 1972.

Weinmann CJ: Cestodes and acanthocephala. Page 1021 in: *Immunity to Parasitic Animals.* Vol 2. Jackson GJ, Herman R, Singer I (editors). Appleton-Century-Crofts, 1970.

Nematodes

Larsh JE Jr, Weatherly NF: Cell-mediated immunity against certain parasitic worms. Page 183 in: *Advances in Parasitology.* Vol 13. Dawes B (editor). Academic Press, 1975.

Ogilvie BM, Jones VE: Immunity in the parasitic relationship between helminths and hosts. Prog Allergy 17:93, 1973.

39 . . .
Immunization

Stephen N. Cohen, MD

IMMUNIZATION AGAINST INFECTIOUS DISEASES

It has been recognized for centuries that individuals who recover from certain diseases are protected from recurrences. The moderately successful but hazardous introduction of small quantities of fluid from the pustules of smallpox into the skin of uninfected persons (variolation), at a time when neither the nature of the agent, its mode of transmission, nor anything at all about the immune response was understood, was an effort to imitate this natural phenomenon.

Jenner's introduction of vaccination with cowpox (1796) to protect against smallpox was the first documented use of a live attenuated viral vaccine and the beginning of modern immunization. The term *vaccination* is properly reserved for Jennerian inoculation.

Koch demonstrated the specific bacterial cause of anthrax in 1876, and the etiologic agents of several common illnesses were rapidly identified thereafter. Attempts to develop effective immunizing agents followed. Table 39–1 lists some historical milestones in these efforts.

Table 39–1. Historical milestones in immunization.

Variolation	1721
Vaccination	1796
Rabies vaccine	1885
Diphtheria toxoid	1925
Tetanus toxoid	1925
Pertussis vaccine	1925
Viral culture in chick embryo	1931
Yellow fever vaccine	1937
Influenza vaccine	1943
Viral tissue culture	1949
Poliovaccine, inactivated (Salk)	1954
Poliovaccine, live, attenuated (Sabin)	1956
Measles vaccine	1960
Tetanus immune globulin (human)	1962
Rubella vaccine	1966
Mumps vaccine	1967
Hepatitis B vaccine (experimental)	1975

Types of Immune Response

Immunization results in the production of antibodies directed against the infecting agent or its toxic products; it may also initiate cellular responses mediated by lymphocytes and macrophages. The most important protective antibodies include those which inactivate soluble toxic protein products of bacteria (antitoxins), facilitate phagocytosis and intracellular digestion of bacteria (opsonins), interact with the components of serum complement to damage the bacterial membrane with resultant bacteriolysis (lysins), or prevent proliferation of usually infective quantities of infectious virus (neutralizing antibodies).

Antigens react with antibody in the bloodstream and extracellular fluid and at mucosal surfaces. Antibodies cannot readily reach intracellular sites of infection as are found with viral replication. However, they are effective against many viral diseases in 2 ways: (1) by interacting with virus before initial intracellular penetration occurs and (2) by preventing locally replicating virus from disseminating from the site of entry to an important target organ, as in the spread of poliovirus from the gut to the central nervous system or of rabies from a puncture wound to peripheral neural tissue. Antibodies and lymphocytes may also recognize surface changes in virus-infected cells and destroy these infected "foreign" cells.

Stephen N. Cohen is Associate Professor of Laboratory Medicine, Medicine, and Microbiology, University of California, San Francisco.

Passive Immunization

Immunization may be accomplished passively by administering either preformed immunoreactive serum or cells, or actively by presenting a suitable antigenic stimulus to the host's own immune system.

Antibody–either as whole serum or as fractionated, concentrated immune (gamma) globulin which is predominantly IgG–may be obtained from donors who have recovered from an infectious disease or have been immunized. These antibodies may provide immediate protection to an antibody-free individual. Passive immunization is thus useful for individuals who cannot form antibodies or for the normal host who might develop disease before active immunization could stimulate antibody production, which usually requires at least 7–10 days.

Antibody may be obtained from humans or animals, but animal sera are always less desirable since nonhuman proteins themselves give rise to an immune response which leads to rapid clearance of the protective molecules from the circulation of the recipient and may even result in clinical illness (serum sickness; see Hazards of Passive Immunization, below). Thus, to obtain a similar protective effect, a much greater quantity of animal antiserum must be injected compared to human antiserum, eg, 3000 units of equine tetanus antitoxin versus 300 units of human tetanus immune globulin.

No antiserum of animal origin should be given without carefully inquiring about prior exposure or allergic response to any product of the specific animal source. Patients with an unrelated allergy are probably more prone to develop serum reactions. Whenever a foreign antiserum is administered, a syringe containing aqueous epinephrine 1:1000 should be available, and eye or scratch testing (see Chapter 29) should be followed by intracutaneous testing for hypersensitivity. If allergy is present by history or test, and no alternative to serum therapy is possible, a patient may sometimes be given an essential medication to tolerance in repeated fractional doses of progressively increasing size. Simultaneous administration of antihistamines, corticosteroids, and even epinephrine may be necessary during this procedure of "desensitization," which may simply limit the allergic reactions to an acceptably small magnitude.

Persistence of certain human antibodies, eg, to varicella-zoster, is short-lived, and zoster immune globulin (ZIG) must therefore be prepared from the sera of convalescent zoster patients. By contrast, antibody to measles and hepatitis A is so ubiquitous in the population at large that normal serum globulin (ISG) will usually prevent or modify clinical illness with these infections if given early in the incubation period. Table 39–2 lists antisera generally available for passive immunization at present.

In the preantibiotic era, passive immunization was administered with some success as therapy for pneumococcal or haemophilus infection. The need to identify the infecting serotype and obtain the appropriate type-specific antiserum, the illness caused by injection of the foreign proteins, and the relatively poor therapeutic response led to the prompt abandonment of this unsatisfactory method of treatment as soon as effective antimicrobial chemotherapy became available. Today, serum therapy for established illness is largely limited to the administration of antivenins and of botulinus, tetanus, and diphtheria antitoxins to block attachment of yet unbound toxin.

In the absence of demonstrably low serum IgG or (rarely) specific antibody deficiencies, the administration of normal immune serum globulin (ISG) is of no value in the prevention of recurrent infections.

Passive Transfer of Cellular Immunity

Antibodies produced following some infections, particularly those due to mycobacteria, fungi, and many viruses, fail to protect against infection. Rather, interaction of immune lymphocytes and macrophages largely determines recovery from these illnesses. Attempts have been made to transmit this cell-mediated immunity to vaccinia virus in the progressively infected, immunologically incompetent host, to *Coccidioides immitis* in the patient with disseminated coccidioidomycosis, and to *Mycobacterium leprae* in lepromatous leprosy (see Chapter 34). Whole blood, leukocyte-rich buffy coat, and leukocyte-derived "transfer factor" (TF) have been utilized. The value of this type of therapy is uncertain, and these procedures are still experimental (see Chapter 40).

Hazards of Passive Immunization

Illness may arise from a single injection of foreign serum but more commonly occurs in patients who have previously been injected with proteins from the same or a related species. Reactions range in severity from acute anaphylaxis with hives, back pain, dyspnea, cardiovascular collapse, and even death to serum sickness arising hours to weeks following treatment. Typical manifestations of serum sickness include adenopathy, urticaria, arthritis, and fever. Rarely, the administration of human γ-globulin is attended by similar allergic reactions, particularly in patients who are congenitally deficient in one or more immunoglobulins but still capable of mounting an immune response. Hepatitis A or B may be transmitted by whole human plasma or serum, but purified immune (gamma) globulin is free of hepatitis.

Note: Great care must be exercised in administering gamma globulin to avoid accidental intravenous injection. Currently, nearly all human and animal γ-globulin preparations are given by the intramuscular route. They all contain high-molecular-weight aggregated IgG, intravenous administration of which will frequently result in moderate to severe anaphylactic reactions with possible vasomotor collapse and death.

The administration of intact lymphocytes to promote cell-mediated immunity is also hazardous if the recipient is too immunologically depressed to prevent implantation of incompatible donor cells. The engrafted donor cells may "reject" the recipient by a GVH reaction, producing rash, pancytopenia, fever, diarrhea, hepatosplenomegaly, and death (see Chapter 28).

Active Immunization

Primary active immunity develops more slowly than the incubation period of most infections and must therefore be induced prior to exposure to the etiologic agent. One exception is vaccinia-induced immunity to smallpox, which takes only 10 days as opposed to the 14-day incubation period of the virulent infection. By contrast, "booster" reimmunization in the previously immune individual provides a rapid secondary (anamnestic) increase in serum antibody which outpaces the development—to give one example—of tetanus from a contaminated wound.

Active immunization may be achieved with either living or dead materials. Nonviable antigens usually are either structural components of the infecting organism which induce antibodies that prevent infection, or de-

Table 39–2. Materials available for passive immunization.

Disease	Product	Dosage	Comments
Black widow spider bite	Black widow spider antivenin, equine	1 vial IM or IV	A second dose may be given if symptoms do not subside in 3 hours.
Botulism	ABE polyvalent antitoxin, equine	1 vial IV and 1 vial IM; repeat after 2–4 hours if symptoms persist.	Available from CDC.* 20% incidence of serum reactions. Commercial AB antitoxin is also available but should only be used if trivalent is unavailable or toxin type is known to be A or B. Only Type E antitoxin has been shown to affect outcome of illness. Prophylaxis is not routinely recommended but may be given to asymptomatic exposed persons.
Diphtheria	Diphtheria antitoxin, equine	20,000–120,000 U IM depending on severity and duration of illness	
Gas gangrene	Gas gangrene antitoxin, polyvalent, equine		Clinically ineffective. May not be available.
Hepatitis A ("infectious")	Immune serum globulin, human	0.02 ml/kg IM as soon as possible after exposure up to 6 weeks. A protective effect lasts about 2 months.	Modifies but does not prevent infection. Recommended for household contacts and other contacts of similar intensity, not office or school contacts unless an epidemic appears to be in progress. Also recommended for travel to endemic areas.
		For chronic exposure, a dose of 0.10 ml/kg is recommended every 6 months.	Personnel of mental institutions, facilities for retarded children, and prisons appear to be at chronic risk of acquiring hepatitis A, as are those who work with nonhuman primates.
Hepatitis B ("serum")	Immune serum globulin, human	0.15 ml/kg IM as soon as possible after exposure, up to 5 ml.	ISG was ineffective in early trials, but more recent lots made from HB_SAg-negative plasma have higher titers of antibody and may be effective. An experimental killed virus vaccine is under evaluation.
Hypogammaglobulinemia	Immune serum globulin, human	0.6 ml/kg IM every 3–4 weeks	Give double dose at onset of therapy. ISG is of no value in the prevention of frequent respiratory infections in the absence of demonstrable hypogammaglobulinemia.
Measles	Immune serum globulin, human	0.25 ml/kg IM as soon as possible after exposure. This dose may be ineffective in immunoincompetent patients, who should receive 20–30 ml.	Live measles vaccine will usually prevent natural infection if given within 48 hours following exposure. If ISG is administered, delay immunization with live virus for 3 months. Do not vaccinate infants under age 1 year.
Mumps	Mumps immune globulin, human		Efficacy doubtful. Possibly useful in nonimmune boys to prevent orchitis, which occurs in up to 20% of cases. Larger doses may be more effective if prophylaxis is delayed.
Pertussis	Pertussis immune globulin, human	1.5 ml IM	Efficacy doubtful. May also be given for treatment, 1.25 ml IM, with repeat dose 24–48 hours later.
Rabies	Rabies immune globulin, human. (Equine antirabies serum may be available but is much less desirable.)	20 IU/kg, 50% of which is infiltrated locally at the wound site, and the remainder given IM. (See also rabies vaccine in Table 39–3.)	Give as soon as possible after exposure. Recommended for all bite or scratch exposures to carnivores, especially bat, skunk, fox, coyote, or raccoon, despite animal's apparent health, if the brain cannot be immediately examined and found rabies-free. Give also even for abrasion exposure to known rabid animals as well as for bite (skin penetration by teeth) of escaped dogs and cats whose health cannot be determined. Not recommended for individuals with demonstrated antibody response from preexposure prophylaxis.
Rh isoimmunization (erythroblastosis fetalis)	Rh_0 (D) immune globulin, human	1 dose IM within 72 hours of abortion, obstetric delivery of an Rh-positive infant, or transfusion of Rh-positive blood in an Rh_0(D)-negative female	For nonimmune females only. May be effective at much greater postexposure interval. Give even if more than 72 hours have elapsed.

Table 39–2 (cont'd). Materials available for passive immunization.

Disease	Product	Dosage	Comments
Snakebite	Coral snake antivenin, equine		Available from CDC.*
	Crotalid antivenin, polyvalent, equine	Up to 10 vials IV	Dose depends on severity of bite. When swelling of bitten area ceases, an adequate dose has been given.
Tetanus	Tetanus immune globulin, human. (Bovine and equine antitoxins may be available but are not recommended. They are used at 10 times the dose of tetanus immune globulin.)	Prophylaxis: 250–500 U IM Therapy: 3000–6000 U IM	Give in separate syringe at separate site from simultaneously administered toxoid. Recommended only for major or contaminated wounds in individuals who have had fewer than 2 doses of toxoid at any time in the past (fewer than 3 doses if wound is more than 24 hours old). (See tetanus toxoid in Table 39–3.)
Vaccinia	Vaccinia immune globulin (VIG), human. (May be obtained commercially from Hyland Laboratories or from CDC*.)	Prophylaxis: 0.3 ml/kg IM Therapy: 0.6 ml/kg IM	Give at a different site if used to prevent dissemination in a patient with skin disease who must undergo vaccination. May prevent or modify smallpox if given within 24 hours of exposure. May be useful in treatment of vaccinia of the eye, eczema vaccinatum, generalized vaccinia and vaccinia necrosum, and in the prevention of such complications in exposed patients with skin disease such as eczema, burns, or impetigo. VIG in prophylactic dosage is also recommended for the pregnant woman who must be vaccinated to prevent fetal vaccinia.
Varicella	Zoster immune globulin (ZIG), human	3–5 ml IM within 72 hours of exposure	Available from CDC* for nonimmune leukemic, lymphomatous, immunosuppressed, or other immunoincompetent children and for neonates whose mother has developed varicella within 4 days of delivery. ZIG modifies natural disease but may not prevent the development of immunity. Convalescent plasma collected 1–5 weeks after onset of varicella or zoster is also effective at 10 ml/kg IV. If neither ZIG nor convalescent plasma is available, normal immune serum globulin, 0.6–1.2 ml/kg IM, may modify the illness.

*Center for Disease Control–Telephone: 404-633-3311 (day) or 404-633-2176 (night).

Note: Passive immunotherapy or immunoprophylaxis should always be administered as soon as possible after exposure to the offending agent. Immune antisera and globulin are always given intramuscularly unless otherwise noted. Always question carefully and test for hypersensitivity before administering animal sera.

toxified bacterial products (toxoids) which stimulate antitoxins that prevent illness without directly inhibiting the pathogen. Although tetanus toxoid provides a particularly long-lasting immunity of at least 10 years' duration, most nonliving vaccines provide protection for only a limited time. Repeated injections are needed to maintain even a moderate level of protection against plague, cholera, and typhoid fever.

Active immunization with living agents is generally preferable to immunization with killed vaccines because of a superior and long-lived immune response. A single dose of a live, attenuated virus vaccine often suffices for reliable immunization. Multiple immunizations are recommended for polio in case intercurrent enteroviral infection or interference among the 3 simultaneously administered virus types in the trivalent vaccine prevents completely successful primary immunization. The duration of immunity to many viral infections is unexplained and may include repeated natural reexposure to new cases in the community, the unusually large antigenic stimulus which infection with a living agent provides, or other mechanisms such as the persistence of latent virus.

All immunizing materials—but live agents particularly—must be properly stored to retain effectiveness. Serious failures of smallpox and measles immunization have resulted from inadequate refrigeration prior to use. Agents presently licensed for active immunization are listed in Table 39–3.

Hazards of Active Immunization

Active immunization may cause fever, malaise, and soreness at injection sites. Some reactions are relatively specific for the immunizing agent, such as arthralgia/arthritis following rubella vaccine or convulsions following pertussis vaccine, but are much less frequent and less severe than those accompanying unmodified natural illness. Reactions known to be associated with a particular product are described in the manufacturer's package insert, the *Physicians' Desk Reference,* and standard texts.

Repeated immunization, particularly with diphtheria and tetanus toxoids, may result in increasingly severe local reactions. Diphtheria antigen in adult-type combined diphtheria-tetanus toxoid (Td) is therefore 5- to 10- fold less than in childhood DTP, and a lower

Table 39–3. Materials available for active immunization.*

Disease	Product (Source)	Type of Agent	Route of Administration	Primary Immunization	Duration of Effect	Comments
Cholera	Cholera vaccine	Killed bacteria	Subcut, IM	2 doses 1 week or more apart	6 months†	50% protective; International Certificate may be required for travel.
Diphtheria	DTP, DT (adsorbed) for child under 6; Td (adsorbed) for all others	Toxoid	IM	3 doses 4 weeks or more apart	10 years‡	Use DT if convulsions follow use of DTP. Give school children and adults third dose 6–12 months after second.
Influenza	Influenza virus vaccine, monovalent or bivalent (chick embryo). Composition of the vaccine is varied depending upon epidemiologic circumstances.	Killed viruses A and/or B	IM	1 dose	1 year‡	Give immunization by November. Recommended for patients with cardiorespiratory disease, diabetes, other chronic diseases, and the elderly.
Measles§	Measles virus vaccine, live attenuated (chick embryo)	Live virus	Subcut	1 dose	Permanent	Reimmunize if given before 1 year of age; may prevent natural disease if given less than 48 hours after exposure.
Meningococcus	Meningococcal polysaccharide vaccine, group A or group C	Polysaccharide	Subcut	1 dose	?Permanent	Recommended in epidemic situations, for use by the military to prevent outbreaks in recruits, and possibly as an adjunct to antibiotic prophylaxis in preventing secondary cases in family contacts. Probably effective in infants if maternal antibody levels are low. A combination A-C vaccine is also available.
Mumps§	Mumps virus vaccine, live	Live virus	Subcut	1 dose	Permanent	Reimmunize if given before 1 year of age.
Pertussis	DTP	Killed bacteria	IM	As for DTP	See‡	Not generally recommended after age 6.
Plague	Plague vaccine	Killed bacteria	IM	3 doses 4 weeks or more apart	6 months‡	Recommended only for occupational exposure and not for residents of endemic area in the southwest USA.
Poliomyelitis	Poliovirus vaccine, live, oral, trivalent (monkey kidney, human diploid)	Live virus types I, II, III	Oral	3 doses 6–8 weeks or more apart, the last preferably 8–12 months later	Permanent	Recommended for adults only if at increased risk by travel to epidemic area or occupational contact. Killed virus vaccines are no longer recommended and are generally unavailable.
Rabies	Rabies vaccine (duck embryo). (Vaccine derived from rabbit neural tissue may still be available but is not preferred because of the higher rate of neurologic side-reactions.)	Killed virus	Subcut	**Preexposure:** 2 doses 1 month apart followed by a third dose 6–7 months later **or** 3 doses 1 week apart, followed by a fourth dose 3 months later	2–3 years‡	Preexposure immunization only for occupational or avocational risk or residence in hyperendemic area. Antibody response should be measured 3–4 weeks after last injection to ensure successful immunization, and repeat injection should be given if no response.
				Postexposure: If not previously immunized and no serum therapy given: 14 daily doses (21 daily		For animal bite, consider antitetanus measures as well. Wounds should be copiously

				doses and 2 boosters on days 31 and 41 if serum or immune globulin given). **If previously immunized *and an antibody response demonstrated,*** do not give serum therapy. For nonbite exposure, give 1 booster dose. For the bite of a rabid animal, give 5 daily boosters followed by 1 dose on day 25. If an antibody response was not previously demonstrated, treat as unimmunized.		flushed with soap and water and, after all traces of soap are removed, should be irrigated with benzalkonium chloride. (See Table 39–2 regarding use of hyperimmune serum or immune globulin.)
Rocky Mountain spotted fever	RMSF vaccine (chick embryo)	Killed bacteria	Subcut	3 doses at 7–10 day intervals	1 year‡	Recommended only for occupational exposure. Not highly protective. Experimental vaccines under study.
Rubella§	Rubella virus vaccine, live (duck embryo, rabbit kidney)	Live virus	Subcut	1 dose	Permanent	Give after 1 year of age. Do not give during pregnancy. Women must prevent pregnancy for 2 months after immunization.
Smallpox	Smallpox vaccine (calf lymph, chick embryo)	Live vaccinia virus	Intradermal	1 dose	3 years†	Certificate may be required for travel. Revaccinate if no jennerian vesicle at 6–8 days postvaccination. Do not vaccinate if child or his contacts have eczema or acute or chronic skin disease. If patients with skin disease must be vaccinated or exposed to a vaccinated household contact, they should receive vaccinia immune globulin. (See Table 39–2.)
Tetanus	DTP, DT (adsorbed) for children under age 6; Td, T (adsorbed) for all others	Toxoid	IM	3 doses 4 weeks or more apart	10 years‡**	Give schoolchildren and adults a third dose 6–12 months after second. (See Table 39–2 regarding use of hyperimmune globulin.)
Tuberculosis	BCG vaccine	Live attenuated *Mycobacterium bovis*	Intradermal, subcut	1 dose	?Permanent††	Recommended in USA only for PPD-negative contacts of ineffectively treated or persistently untreated cases and for other unusually high-risk groups.
Typhoid	Typhoid vaccine	Killed bacteria	Subcut	2 doses 4 weeks or more apart or 3 doses 1 week apart (less desirable)	3 years‡	70% protective. Recommended only for exposure from travel, epidemic, or household carrier.
Typhus	Typhus vaccine (chick embryo)	Killed bacteria	Subcut	2 doses 4 weeks or more apart	6–12 months‡	Recommended only for occupational exposure.
Yellow fever	Yellow fever vaccine (chick embryo)	Live virus	Subcut	1 dose	10 years†	Certificate may be required for travel. Recommended for residence in or travel to endemic areas of Africa and South America.

*Dosages for the specific product including variations for age are best obtained from the manufacturer's package insert. Immunizations should be given by the route suggested for the product.
†Revaccination interval required by international regulations.
‡A single dose is a sufficient booster at any time after the effective duration of primary immunization has passed.
§Combination vaccines available.
**For contaminated or severe wounds, give booster if more than 5 years have elapsed since full immunization or last booster.
††Test for PPD conversion 2 months later and reimmunize if there is no conversion.

frequency of booster immunization for tetanus is now recommended than in the past. Although experimentally hyperimmunized animals display a variety of adverse effects, including amyloidosis and malignancy, and despite the fact that immunization has been suspected of precipitating systemic lupus erythematosus in humans, careful follow-up of intensively immunized individuals over a 15-year period has not shown any clinical sequelae.

Allergic reactions may occur on exposure to egg protein or antibiotics in viral vaccine cell cultures. The quantity of irrelevant antigen in a vaccine is usually insufficient to elicit a response in the allergic individual, but a patient with intense allergy to a vaccine component may be given vaccine from a different source, eg, rubella vaccine grown in rabbit kidney instead of duck embryo for a patient with egg hypersensitivity. Improvements in antigenicity and better purification procedures in vaccine production decrease the amount and number of foreign substances injected and result in fewer side-effects.

Unique Hazards of Live Vaccines

Live vaccines should *not* be given to a pregnant woman because of their potential effect upon the fetus. Live vaccines, furthermore, can cause serious or even fatal illness in an immunologically incompetent host. They should not be given to patients receiving corticosteroids, alkylating drugs, and other immunosuppressive agents, nor to individuals who exhibit congenital or acquired defects in cell-mediated immunity, as seen in severe combined immunodeficiency disease or Hodgkin's disease.

Even if not administered to immunoincompetent hosts, live vaccines may result in mild and, rarely, severe disease. The early measles vaccines caused high fever and rash in a significant proportion of recipients. Subacute sclerosing panencephalitis, a rare complication of natural infection, has occurred following administration of live attenuated measles vaccine (see Chapter 36). Passage through the human intestinal tract occasionally results in reversion of oral attenuated poliovirus vaccine (particularly type III) to neurovirulence, and paralytic illness has occurred in recipients or their nonimmune contacts, especially adults. Vaccinia is not virulent for normal humans at its usual site of administration in the skin but may cause severe local illness if accidentally administered to a child with eczema or if rubbed into the eye.

Live vaccines may contain undetected and undesirable passengers. Epidemic hepatitis has resulted from vaccinia and yellow fever vaccines containing human serum. More recently, millions of people received SV40, a simian papovavirus not known to be harmful to humans, along with oral poliovirus vaccine prepared in monkey kidney tissue culture. SV40 can now be detected and excluded from human viral vaccines, but it is possible that presently undetected agents might be transmitted to humans with uncertain consequences, particularly by vaccines grown in nonhuman cell lines. Bacteriophages and, probably, bacterial endotoxins have also been definitely shown to contaminate live virus vaccines, although without known hazard thus far.

Live viral vaccines probably do not interfere with tuberculin skin testing, although they depress some measurements of lymphocyte function.

Nonspecific Active Immunization

Immunization with vaccinia has been employed in attempts to nonspecifically improve the immune response and thereby decrease the frequency of recurrences of herpes labialis (cold sores). Careful evaluation has shown that this practice is ineffective—and indeed has occasionally resulted in severe illness due to uncontrolled spread of vaccinia in a patient with unsuspected immunoincompetence.

Under some circumstances, however, it does appear that specific activation of cell-mediated immunity may lead to enhanced nonspecific ability of "activated" macrophages to deal with other antigens. Such an interaction has been demonstrated experimentally for tuberculosis, salmonella, brucella, listeria, and toxoplasma infection of animals. The apparent effectiveness of BCG immunization in the prevention of leprosy may be related to this phenomenon as well as to the antigenic similarity between *M tuberculosis* and *M leprae.* The possibility that nonspecific stimulation of the immune system with BCG, *Bordetella pertussis,* or *Corynebacterium parvum (Propionibacterium acnes)* can enhance the ability of the body to reject tumor cells is now being studied (see Chapters 21 and 40).

Combined Passive-Active Immunization

Passive immunization has been combined with active immunization to minimize untoward effects of certain active immunizing agents. Low-dose gamma globulin decreased the side-effects of the early attenuated measles vaccines, leading to greater patient acceptance. (Newer "further attenuated" vaccine strains no longer require the modifying effects of gamma globulin.) Similarly, vaccinia immune globulin decreases the likelihood of eczema vaccinatum if an eczematous patient must be vaccinated for travel to the (vanishing) smallpox-endemic area. Passive and active immunization are often simultaneously undertaken to provide both immediate but transient and slowly developing, durable protection against rabies or tetanus. The immune response to the active agent may or may not be impaired by gamma globulin if the injections are given at separate sites. Tetanus toxoid plus tetanus immune globulin may give a response superior to that generated by the toxoid alone, but if antiserum has been given for rabies, the course of immunization is usually extended to ensure an adequate response.

Anomalously Severe Disease in the Immunized Host

Immunization may not succeed in its intended objective of limiting the spread of infection and may sometimes contribute to the pathogenesis of the disease. A child who has received killed measles virus vaccine (no longer recommended) may attain only a poorly protective level of serum antibody combined with a delayed hypersensitivity which results in atypical and unusually severe rubeola when he is exposed to wild virus, or to an erythematous painful injection site if reimmunized with live vaccine. The presence in the serum of transplacentally transmitted antibody to respiratory syncytial (RS) virus may be responsible for the severe bronchiolitis that develops in infants first infected before 6 months of age, in contrast to the milder illness characteristic of primary infection occurring later in life when maternal gamma globulins are no longer present. A poorly antigenic experimental RS virus vaccine increased the intensity of subsequent natural illness in infant recipients. Mice congenitally infected with lymphocytic choriomeningitis (LCM) virus are clinically well until they begin to produce antibody to the virus; they then develop a fatal disorder resulting from the deposition of antigen-antibody complexes in the central nervous system and kidney. Similar problems of intensified disease in immunized subjects have been noted with experimental trachoma and *Mycoplasma pneumoniae* vaccines.

The Decision to Immunize an Individual

Immunizing procedures are among the most effective and economical measures available for preservation and protection of health.

The decision to immunize a specific person against a specific pathogen is a complex judgment based upon an assessment of the risk of infection, the consequences of natural unmodified illness, the availability of a safe and effective immunogen, and the duration of its effect.

The organisms that cause diphtheria and tetanus are ubiquitous and the vaccines have few side-effects and are highly effective, but only the immunized individual is protected. Thus, immunization must be universal. Nearly 80% of all individuals were found to be so protected by age 1–4 years in the US Immunization Survey conducted in 1969.

By contrast, a nonimmune individual who resides in a community which has been well immunized against poliovirus and who does not travel has little opportunity to encounter wild (virulent) virus. Here the immunity of the "herd" protects the unimmunized person since the intestinal tracts of recipients of oral poliovaccine fail to become colonized by or transmit wild virus. If, however, a substantial portion of the community is not immune to poliomyelitis, introduced wild virus can circulate and cause disease among the nonimmune group.

Smallpox vaccine is effective and usually safe, but the immunity it confers is of relatively short duration, declining after about 3 years. The risk of introduction of smallpox into the USA is now so small that in the opinion of expert advisers to USPHS the total illness (approximately 150 cases of all types per year) from even the low rate of complications significantly exceeds the benefits of vaccination. Childhood vaccination is being abandoned, and vaccination is no longer even suggested for health and transportation personnel likely to encounter foreign travelers, since the few remaining foci, chiefly in Ethiopia and Bangladesh, are rapidly disappearing.

Currently available rabies vaccines do rarely give rise to severe reactions. The risk of exposure is low, and preexposure immunization is thus reserved for travelers to hyperendemic areas or to persons with occupational hazard.

Immunization offers only short-term and incomplete protection against cholera, placing enormous logistic demands upon those societies most frequently afflicted but least able to mount repeated expensive immunization campaigns. It is therefore little used except by travelers or the military for short-term exposure.

Each immunologically distinct viral subtype requires a specific antigenic stimulus for effective protection. Immunization against adenovirus infection has not benefited civilian populations subject to many differing types of virus—in contrast to the demonstrated value of vaccine directed against a few epidemic adenovirus types in military recruits. Similarly, immunity to type A influenza virus is transient because of major mutations in surface chemistry of the virus every few years (antigenic shifts). These changes render previously developed vaccines obsolete and may prevent sufficient production, distribution, and utilization of new antigen in time to prevent epidemic spread of the altered strain.

Age at Immunization

The natural history of a disease determines the age at which immunization is best undertaken. Pertussis, polio, and diphtheria often strike in infancy; immunization against these diseases is therefore begun shortly after birth. Serious consequences of pertussis are uncommon beyond early childhood, and pertussis vaccination is not usually recommended after 6 years of age.

There may be an age-dependent incidence of vaccine side-effects. Serious complications of smallpox vaccination are slightly more common below age 1 year and in older children and adults; if vaccination is employed at all, it is usually performed between the first and second years of life.

The efficacy of immunization may also be age-related. Failure may occur because of the presence of interfering antibodies or an undeveloped responsiveness of the immune system. Infants cannot be reliably protected with live measles, mumps, or rubella vaccines before the age of 1 year, by which time the last vestiges of maternally derived antibody have disappeared. Infants frequently develop severe infections with *Haemophilus influenzae* type b, but injecting them with purified capsular polysaccharide has failed to reliably yield a good antibody response despite the excellent activity of the same antigen in older children and adults. Indeed, one study has shown that several children with early severe disease due to *H influenzae* did not develop active immunity and also failed to show a good antibody response to vaccine administered after 2 years of age. This failure to respond raises the question of a possible immune defect in the patients most in need of protection.

Simultaneous Immunization With Multiple Antigens

Simultaneous immunization with several antigenic stimuli might be expected to result in interference by the immune response to one antigen with the development of immunity to other antigens. Actually, the simultaneous inoculation of the nonliving antigens of diphtheria, tetanus, and pertussis gives a response equal to that seen with their separate injection; the endotoxic components of *Bordetella pertussis* may even act as an adjuvant providing a superior immune response against the additional antigens.

Similarly, the single injection of a mixture of live, attenuated measles, rubella, and mumps viruses or the simultaneous administration of live measles, smallpox, and yellow fever vaccines gives good responses to each component of the mixture. However, between 2 and 14 days following the administration of one live virus vaccine, there is a period of suboptimal response to a *subsequently injected* live virus vaccine. It is best to administer multiple immunizing agents according to a schedule which has been demonstrated to yield an effective response.

Recommendations for Childhood Immunization

A rational program of immunization against infectious diseases begins in childhood, when many of the most damaging and most preventable infections normally appear. Table 39–4 summarizes the current guidelines for immunization in childhood as compiled by the Expert Committee on Infectious Diseases of the American Academy of Pediatrics.

Immunization of Adults for Foreign Travel

National health authorities may require an International Certificate of Vaccination against smallpox, cholera, or yellow fever from travelers, usually depending upon the presence of these diseases in countries on their itinerary. Smallpox and cholera vaccinations may be given by any licensed physician. The certificate must be completed in all details and then validated with an approved stamp. Yellow fever vaccination may only be administered and the certificate validated at an officially designated center (these may be located by contacting the state or local health department). In addition to these legal requirements, all adults are advised to be adequately immunized against tetanus and diphtheria and to undergo additional immunizations (polio, typhoid, hepatitis A, plague, typhus) if visiting areas where the frequency of illness in the population or the level of sanitation increases the risk of infection. (Travelers to malaria-endemic areas should also be advised regarding chemoprophylaxis.) Information regarding individual agents may be found in Tables 39–2 and 39–3.

No special immunizations are generally recommended for persons traveling from the USA to Western Europe, Canada, or Australia. Detailed suggestions of the USPHS are given country-by-country in its Health Information for International Travel Supplement (see references).

Vaccines of Restricted Availability & Experimental Vaccines

A number of vaccines have been developed that are available for individuals at greatly increased occupational risk but not for the general public. Only a partial listing will be given here.

A. Adenovirus: Live attenuated oral vaccines have been developed for military use. These are directed against the 2 types of virus–types 4 and 7–that commonly cause severe epidemic disease in recruits. Experimental vaccines have been formulated against additional (civilian) serotypes.

B. Anthrax: A protein antigen extracted from culture filtrates can protect those who work with imported animal hides and hair and others with occupational exposure.

C. Arbovirus (Various): Vaccines against certain agents causing equine encephalitis are available for persons working with the viruses.

D. *Haemophilus influenzae* Type B: The major antigen, capsular polyribophosphate, does not induce protective antibody in infants. Oral immunization with cross-reactive *Escherichia coli* appears promising.

E. Hepatitis B: Formalinized virus is antigenic and protective in chimpanzees and is undergoing testing in humans.

F. Influenza: Live attenuated vaccines, including mutant strains that replicate poorly at deep body temperature, are being examined as potentially superior immunizing agents compared to currently licensed killed vaccines.

G. Meningococcus Group B: An adequate immunogen is being developed for this last of the major meningococcal groups. The protection-inducing antigen may be a protein, not a polysaccharide, as in groups A and C.

Table 39–4. Guidelines for routine immunization of normal infants and children.

Disease	Vaccine	Schedule of Doses				
		First	Second	Third	Fourth	Fifth
Diphtheria-tetanus-pertussis	DTP, adsorbed	2 months	4 months	6 months	1½ years	4–6 years*
Poliovirus I, II, and III	Oral trivalent	2 months	4 months	6 months	1½ years	4–6 years
Measles-mumps-rubella	MMR or singly	1 year	. . .	. . .	. . .	. . .

*Adult-type combined tetanus-diphtheria toxoid (Td) is recommended at 10-year intervals thereafter.

H. ***Mycoplasma pneumoniae:*** Early killed vaccine may have caused more severe disease in the immunized host. Live, temperature-sensitive mutants which cannot multiply at the temperature of the lower respiratory tract induce protection against experimental challenge with more virulent strains.

I. Pneumococcus: Capsular polysaccharides are antigenic and anticapsular antibodies are protective. Several serotypes commonly cause human disease, and a polyvalent vaccine is currently undergoing field trials in high-risk populations. Clinical effectiveness will require that currently uncommon serotypes do not emerge to replace the vaccine strains.

J. ***Pseudomonas aeruginosa:*** Polyvalent vaccines can stimulate the development of protective opsonizing antibodies, but clinical usefulness in immunosuppressed, neutropenic patients most at risk from this organism has not been demonstrated. Vaccination may protect the patient with normal humoral immunity and normal white cell count against bacteremia from infected burns. Side reactions to immunization are frequent.

K. Respiratory Syncytial Virus (RS virus): Recipients of killed vaccines developed more serious illness than unimmunized infants. Live attenuated virus and temperature-sensitive virus vaccines are being evaluated.

L. Rhinovirus: Live and inactivated vaccines have been produced. Their use does not appear promising at the present because of the multiplicity of serotypes which would be needed and because even natural immunity offers only partial protection.

M. Varicella: A live attenuated virus is probably effective in inducing antibody and preventing or modifying illness. However, the safety of a live virus vaccine remains to be demonstrated in the immunoincompetent patients most likely to develop life-threatening complications of wild virus infection.

IMMUNIZATION AGAINST NONINFECTIOUS DISEASES

Prevention of Rh Isoimmunization

Rh-negative females who have not already developed anti-Rh antibodies should receive Rh immune globulin within 72 hours after obstetric delivery, abortion, or accidental transfusion with Rh-positive blood. This passive immunization suppresses the mother's normal immune response to any Rh-positive fetal cells that may enter her circulation, thus avoiding erythroblastosis fetalis in future Rh-positive fetuses. Even if more than 72 hours has elapsed after exposure, the globulin should be administered since it will be effective in at least some cases. Three of 6 subjects were protected from the immunogenic effect of 1 ml of Rh-positive red cells given intravenously by 100 μg of anti-Rh globulin given 13 *days* later. Some workers have also suggested the administration of anti-Rh globulin to Rh-negative newborn female offspring of Rh-positive mothers to prevent possible sensitization from maternal-fetal transfusion (see Chapter 28).

Serum Therapy of Poisonous Bites

The toxicity of the bite of the black widow spider, the coral snake, and of crotalid snakes (rattlesnakes and other pit vipers) may be lessened by the administration of commercially available antivenins. Antisera for scorpion stings and rarer poisonous bites, especially of species foreign to North America, may be available through zoos and museums.

• • •

References

Benenson AS (editor): *Control of Communicable Diseases in Man,* 12th ed. American Public Health Association, 1975.

Collected Recommendations of the Public Health Service Advisory Committee on Immunization Practices. Morbid Mortal Wkly Rep 21(Suppl):25, June 24, 1972.

Craighead JE: Report of a workshop: Disease accentuation after immunization with inactivated microbial vaccines. J Infect Dis 131:749, 1975.

Health information for international travel. Morbid Mortal Wkly Rep 24(Suppl), Dec 1975.

Immunization Against Infectious Diseases. Brit M Bull 25:2, 1969.

A Manual for the Control of Communicable Diseases in California. California State Department of Health, 1971.

Report of the Committee on Infectious Diseases, 17th ed. American Academy of Pediatrics, 1974.

40 . . .
Experimental Aspects of Immunotherapy

Joseph Wybran, MD

Experimental approaches to immunotherapy have developed along several important lines in recent years. Many adjuvants, immunostimulants, and drugs with either specific or nonspecific effects are now under intensive clinical investigation. Although most are still restricted to a few medical centers, others have already become widely used in immunologic practice.

The immunostimulants—BCG, MER (methanol extraction residue of BCG), PPD, DNCB, *Corynebacterium parvum,* levamisole, thymus extracts, immune RNA, and transfer factor—have both nonspecific and specific actions, probably at different levels of the immune system, although in almost all of these instances the precise target cell is not known. The present indications for the use of the immunostimulants include the immunodeficiency diseases, various chronic infectious diseases, and cancer.

BACILLUS CALMETTE-GUÉRIN (BCG)

BCG is a viable attenuated strain of *Mycobacterium bovis* obtained by progressive reduction of virulence in a culture medium enriched with beef bile.

Mechanisms of Action

The first successful application of BCG was immunization against tuberculosis. Almost 4 decades elapsed between the isolation of BCG and its application in the field of cancer chemotherapy.

It is thought that BCG acts mainly by stimulating the reticuloendothelial system. It is not clear whether this is a primary effect or a secondary one mediated by T cell activation. Since experimental stimulation of the reticuloendothelial system has also been postulated as a mechanism of tumor control, it appeared logical to try BCG in various animal tumor systems. It was found that, under various circumstances, BCG can delay the appearance, decrease the incidence, inhibit the development, and induce the regression of malignant tumors caused by chemicals and viruses. Interestingly enough, it has recently been shown that BCG immunologically cross-reacts with hepatoma, melanoma, and leukemic cells—a finding that may explain some specific effects of BCG in these tumors.

The precise mode of action of BCG is not known. It may be that macrophages activated by BCG are more active killer cells, are more efficient in clearing antigens or antigen-antibody complexes, or are capable of inducing active participation of other cells of the immune system in the struggle against proliferating tumor cells. The formation of granulomas after administration of BCG may reflect this sort of defense. BCG might also affect tumor cells in nonimmunologic ways; it can increase the intracellular content of some enzymes acting on some carcinogens. In some conditions, activation of the immune system after BCG injection appears to be both nonspecific and specific in tumor-bearing animals. Finally, it has been suggested that close contact between BCG and tumor cells is required to achieve an optimal effect.

The use of BCG is not without danger since in some circumstances it enhances tumor growth. This phenomenon has been linked to the presence of serum factors (antigen-antibody complexes) that block the in vitro cytotoxicity of previously immune lymphocytes. The active component of BCG is not known. In fact, nonviable extracts of BCG as well as viable BCG have been shown to be immunostimulatory and to inhibit tumor growth.

BCG in Prevention of Human Cancer

Claims have been made that children immunized against tuberculosis have a lower incidence of acute leukemia. Unfortunately, the statistical methods used in these studies are subject to criticism, and better technics are required to produce convincing evidence. If further reports continue to be favorable, prospective trials should be undertaken to confirm the efficiency of BCG vaccination in preventing the development of acute leukemia.

BCG in Treatment of Human Cancer

It is the general impression that BCG can be helpful in the treatment of some types of cancer in humans. However, to date the number of cases reported has been small, and the optimal treatment regimen has not been clearly defined and may vary depending upon the tumor type and the immunologic

Joseph Wybran is Head, Section of Cellular Immuno-hematology, Saint-Pierre University Hospital, Brussels.

status of the patient. The best form of BCG—viable or nonviable, or BCG extracts—remains to be determined. The possibility of enhancing tumor spread also exists, and some observations are consistent with this danger.

Routes of Administration

A. Intralesional Injection: BCG can be injected into skin lesions, but this mode of administration is associated with many side-effects.

B. Intradermal Injection: BCG, often mixed with lymphoid or tumor cells (enzyme-treated or untreated), can be given intradermally, but this causes intense localized reactions.

C. By Scarification: The scarification technic is the most popular way of administering BCG. A standard technic of scarification is to make 20 scratches 5 cm long with an 18-gauge needle on a 5 × 5 cm area of the upper arm or upper thigh. The scratches should be deep enough to produce some bleeding. BCG (usually containing about 10^8 viable organisms) is then applied to the site. Except for the scars, very few complications occur. The Heaf gun makes precise incisions 2 mm deep and is now preferred by many immunologists. Usually, BCG is administered once a week. However, when the patient develops confluent papulae or other signs of hypersensitization like pustules and vesicles or induration zones, it is recommended to reduce the dose of BCG by half and to administer it only once a month. Finally, it is also advised to give the BCG in a rotating fashion on the four upper parts of the limbs close to the draining lymph nodes.

D. Oral Administration: The efficacy of oral administration is unknown. Only minor side-effects such as intestinal spasms have been noted.

E. Intravenous Injection: Intravenous administration has been tried only in animals.

Complications

Complications have been reported mainly with the intralesional or intradermal route of administration. Chills, fever, and malaise have been observed. The fever appears a few hours after the injection and may last for several days. Recurrent fever with an influenza-like syndrome can appear 3 weeks after intralesional injection but may subside spontaneously within a few weeks. Intradermal injection produces localized ulcerations associated in some cases with regional lymphadenopathy. These local reactions tend to occur more rapidly (within 24 hours) after 3–6 local injections. In immunodepressed patients, persistent BCG infection at the vaccination site and in the lymph nodes and pleura has been observed in a few instances. Patients who show evidence of progressive infection respond to antituberculosis therapy. Temporary reversible hepatic dysfunction is common. Granulomatous hepatitis that responds to antituberculosis therapy has been observed; no organisms, however, were recovered from these biopsy specimens. The most dangerous side-effect of BCG therapy is a severe hypersensitivity reaction and shock. Rarely, patients have died after intralesional therapy.

Complications of BCG therapy administered by scarification or with the Heaf gun are mild, and no fatalities have been reported. Oral BCG may be associated with temporary intestinal dysfunction.

BCG has been given to patients with various kinds of human cancer. Because the reported series are almost all on a limited number of cases and because only one type of BCG administration has been used, definitive recommendations about dosage and route cannot be offered. The optimal dosage, frequency of administration, and type of BCG are still under investigation. Viable organisms are apparently more effective than nonviable ones. Only intralesional BCG has been shown to produce regression of intradermal lesions. BCG has usually been given after reduction of the malignant mass (by surgery, chemotherapy, or radiation therapy). It can be given alone or in combination with lymphoid or tumor-cultured cells. It is also sometimes given in association with chemotherapy.

Clinical Applications

A. Malignant Melanoma: It is in this disease that BCG, when injected intralesionally, has shown its effectiveness most dramatically. The injected skin lesions regress in approximately 50% of cases, and skin lesions remote from the injection site disappear completely in about 20% of cases. It is not known, however, whether this treatment significantly increases survival rates. Intralesional administration of BCG has also been used in combination with neuraminidase treatment of tumor cells, irradiation of tumor cells, and stimulation of lymphocytes. Intralesional BCG usually has no effect on visceral metastases, and the same is true of other routes of BCG administration.

BCG has been given by scarification after surgery to patients with stage II, III, or IV melanoma. Preliminary results have been encouraging. In further studies, patients in stage IV received either chemotherapy alone—dimethyl triazeno imidazole carboxamide (DTIC)—or BCG and DTIC. Patients who received chemoimmunotherapy had more remissions, longer remissions, and longer survival than those who received only chemotherapy. In this series, it was also felt that the use of viable organisms and the presence of a soluble antigen in the BCG preparation contributed to maximal efficiency.

B. Acute Lymphocytic Leukemia: BCG was first tried by French workers in patients with acute lymphocytic leukemia. The attempt was based on the experimental observation that drugs were unable to kill all tumor cells and that other means such as immunotherapy were therefore necessary to kill the residual leukemic cells. BCG was found to be effective in animals if the number of residual malignant cells did not exceed 10^5.

In a clinical trial, a limited group of patients have received chemotherapy (induction and consolidation) and irradiation (of the central nervous system). After complete remission, the results in various groups receiving or not receiving some form of immunotherapy were compared. Patients receiving weekly doses of

BCG by scarification with or without irradiated allogeneic tumor cells appear to have responded best since 7 patients out of 20 are still in remission 8 years after initiation of treatment. This study could not be confirmed by English or American investigators using slightly different therapeutic regimens (and different sources of BCG). Recently, however, a Belgian cooperative group has shown that a type of immunotherapy similar to that used in the French trial yields the same good results as maintenance chemotherapy. The follow-up after complete remission for these two groups is two years. Finally, recent data suggest that acute lymphocytic leukemia can now be divided into subgroups according to the histologic appearance of the leukemic cells. Only some histologic forms respond well to immunotherapy. If immunotherapy is indeed of value in acute lymphocytic leukemia, it remains to be proved that it is more effective than intense chemotherapy and irradiation, which now offers a 50% chance of 5-year leukemia-free survival.

C. Acute Myelogenous Leukemia: In this disease, chemotherapy has not been successful in providing prolonged leukemia-free survival. Although few data are available on the effect of BCG, immunotherapy appeared very promising in 2 English and American studies. The patients received chemotherapy and chemotherapy plus BCG with or without allogeneic irradiated leukemic cells. Preliminary data have indicated that the group receiving immunotherapy had prolonged remissions and lived twice as long as those who received chemotherapy alone. Furthermore, it appeared in the English study that longer remissions were obtained by immunotherapy when the chemotherapy induced incomplete rather than complete remissions.

D. Chronic Myelogenous Leukemia: One study indicates that patients receiving a mixture of BCG and cultured allogeneic lymphoid cells intradermally seem to have longer survivals than selected controls. Some patients in the immunized group have survived more than 7 years.

E. Lymphomas: In a relatively well controlled study, 2 groups of patients with stage IA and IIA lymphomas were compared after radiotherapy. Immunotherapy given in one group consisted of intradermal BCG (approximately 10^6 viable bacilli) given when the tuberculin response was not positive or when a positive test reverted to negative (median time to revaccination was 11 months). The immunized group showed a lower incidence of relapses and longer remission. All of these data are impressive, but further confirmation is required, especially since irradiation with or without chemotherapy is highly effective in these diseases.

F. Other Solid Tumors: Claims have been made of longer remissions following administration of intradermal BCG in patients with squamous cell cancer of the head and neck and bronchial carcinoma. This appears to be exceptional, since patients with large tumor burdens do not usually respond to systemic BCG. However, preliminary results using chemotherapy and BCG by scarification in advanced breast cancer or in operated colon carcinoma indicate that the patients in the immunochemotherapy group survive longer than with chemotherapy alone.

SUBFRACTIONS OF BCG

MER

MER (methanol extraction residue of phenol-treated BCG) has been given in various animal solid tumors, especially mouse mammary tumors. It appears to decrease the incidence and size of the tumors and sometimes prolongs survival. Preliminary data in humans are available from a few centers, and the results appear promising in solid tumors and acute leukemias.

BCG Cell Walls

Very limited studies are available on this form of immunotherapy. Only hepatomas in guinea pigs have been investigated. It appears that BCG cell walls attached to oil droplets can produce regression of these hepatomas. The active fractions contained in these cell walls are currently being investigated.

PURIFIED PROTEIN DERIVATIVE (PPD)

Repeated intralesional injections or topical applications of PPD have produced some degree of regression in a wide variety of primary or metastatic human cutaneous malignant neoplasms. The mechanism of action is not known.

DINITROCHLOROBENZENE (DNCB)

DNCB has been applied to primary or metastatic skin tumors as a topical chemical sensitizer. Challenging doses caused more intense reaction in the cutaneous neoplasms than in adjacent normal skin and induced complete regressions. This immunotherapeutic approach for cutaneous tumors is highly interesting and appears promising in primary or secondary skin cancers and in melanoma.

CORYNEBACTERIUM PARVUM

Corynebacterium parvum belongs to the group of gram-positive corynebacteria. It is used as a heat-killed and formaldehyde-treated suspension. It is given orally or injected parenterally. It can prevent the growth of tumors in animals. It also inhibits tumor spread by preventing the development of metastases. It appears that *C parvum* acts both nonspecifically, by activating macrophages, and also specifically on T cells. Nonimmunologic mechanisms can also participate in the antitumor action. It has also been injected intralesionally and produces regression of the tumor. Preliminary reports in patients with melanoma receiving intralesional *C parvum* have been encouraging. Many clinical trials are under way, and claims of prolonged survival in breast and lung cancer in association with multiple chemotherapy have been made.

LEVAMISOLE

Levamisole is an established veterinary anthelmintic drug. It has recently been found that levamisole can increase host resistance to tumor cells in some animal systems. This has occurred under very restricted conditions, especially when used with some type of chemo- or immunotherapy which reduces tumor load. The mechanism of action is not known, but an action on macrophages and T lymphocytes has been proposed.

In man, levamisole restores and increases delayed skin hypersensitivity to various antigens in healthy people and in patients with malignant and nonmalignant diseases. Its clinical applications are very preliminary, and all reported results need confirmation. It has been given with claimed clinical improvement in aphthous stomatitis, herpes labialis and genitalis, warts, chronic staphylococcal infections, rheumatoid arthritis, and Crohn's disease. Preliminary results suggest that levamisole may have some beneficial adjuvant action in patients with lung carcinoma and in breast cancer. A proposed dosage schedule is 2.5 mg/kg/day orally for 3 consecutive days, repeated every other week. In fact, daily administration of the drug may even be immunosuppressive, and all investigators insist upon intermittent administration. No serious side-effects, except transient reversible granulocytopenia, have been reported.

THYMUS FACTORS
(See Chapter 11.)

The epithelium of the thymus synthesizes many factors which act as hormones and probably play a major role in the regulation and differentiation of T cells. Multiple factors with thymic activity have already been isolated and described (thymosin, thymus factor, thymopoietins). It is still unclear whether all of these factors are distinct or belong to a common molecule. Their reported molecular weights vary between 1000 and 12,000. They have been extracted from calf and human thymuses and from pig serum. Assays to measure the activities of these factors are quite complex and are based on the induction of specific T cell markers on stem cells. Blood levels of thymosin in humans are high throughout childhood and early adulthood, begin to fall in the third or fourth decade, and are low in elderly people. The levels are low in the DiGeorge syndrome, a classical example of T cell deficiency. Because thymosin promotes T cell differentiation and because it is possible to isolate such extracts on a large scale, much attention has recently been given to characterization of these factors and their mechanisms of action. Animal experiments have not disclosed any degree of toxicity; therefore, it is anticipated that thymus factors will be given in many clinical instances where a congenital or acquired T cell defect is suspected. Such has recently been the case in a patient with congenital T cell defect. The clinical and immunologic status of this patient has been dramatically improved after repeated injections of thymosin (see Chapter 26).

IMMUNE RIBONUCLEIC ACID

RNA extracted from lymphocytes has recently been proposed for immunotherapy. Normal human lymphocytes can be converted into "killer cells," specifically cytotoxic to human tumor cells, by xenogeneic "immune" RNA extracted from the lymphoid organs of animals immunized with the particular human tumor being studied. In vivo animal and human studies with immune RNA are currently being conducted.

DIALYZABLE TRANSFER FACTOR (TFd)

Transfer factor (TFd) is a dialyzable extract of immune leukocytes that is capable of transferring cellular immunity from a skin test-positive donor to a skin test-negative recipient. The recipient, upon retesting with antigen to which he was previously insensitive, will exhibit a specific delayed skin reaction to this antigen.

In normal subjects, transfer factor transfers not only delayed skin reactivity but also lymphocyte stimulation and production of mediators of cellular immunity such as macrophage migration inhibitory factor (MIF) in the presence of the same antigen to which the donor of transfer factor responded. There is great doubt regarding the exact chemical nature of transfer factor; indeed, there is evidence that the dialysate contains several different moieties which may act on a different subpopulation of T cells.

Mode of Action

The mode of action of transfer factor remains

undetermined. It has been proposed that transfer factor acts on a stem cell which may have specificity for an antigen or a group of antigens. It may assist in recruiting specific antigen-sensitive cells. However, recent observations suggest that transfer factor may also have a nonspecific effect. In other words, it may act as an adjuvant by enhancing the reactivity of lymphocytes.

Chemistry

Chemically, transfer factor is a small moiety with a molecular weight of about 5000–10,000. Its chemical nature is still undetermined, but it may be a small nucleopeptide. It does not appear to be homogeneous. Indeed, transfer factor can be separated on column chromatography in multiple fractions. Some of them have the biologic activities of transfer factor depending on the assay used.

Advantages

Transfer factor is a readily available nonantigenic substance which can be lyophilized and stored for long periods without loss of potency. It does not transmit infectious virus disease, and, if properly prepared and tested, appears to cause no serious side-effects. It does not produce a GVH reaction, a common and often fatal complication of the transplantation of competent lymphocytes (eg, from bone marrow grafts) into immunoincompetent patients, and it does not transfer humoral immunity. This latter advantage could be important in anticancer therapy since antitumor antibodies are among the blocking factors.

Problematic Aspects of Transfer Factor

A. Experimental Models: These have been developed only during the past year. An in vitro test, based on lymphocyte stimulation, has recently been proposed as an assay for transfer factor.

B. Selection of Donors: The selection of donors for production of transfer factor remains a difficult problem. Prior to donating lymphocytes, the donor must be tested for specific delayed sensitivity. This is an important matter since the rationale for giving transfer factor rests on the transfer of known immunologic specificity. For example, it is essential to use a donor with strongly positive candida immunity when transfer factor is given to patients with chronic mucocutaneous candidiasis. This problem is more difficult in therapeutic trials with cancer patients. Which specificity should be transferred, and how should it be tested? Common sense suggests the use of lymphocytes from a donor who is immune to the type of tumor being treated. Unfortunately, in vitro tests are not completely reliable in establishing the state of antitumor immunity. In the case of osteosarcoma, an in vitro assay for cellular cytotoxicity has been used for this purpose. In other studies, lymphocyte stimulation or production of lymphokines in the presence of soluble tumor extracts has been used. If there is a quantitative reduction of immunity in cancer patients, injections of specific transfer factor may increase this immunity. However, there is no convincing evidence that the tests used actually reflect specific immunity capable of controlling the growth of the tumor.

Furthermore, the selection of donors in the case of malignancies raises an important ethical problem. Specific immunity can be found in patients who are in remission or cured of their disease. The possibility thus exists that removal of immune lymphocytes in these patients will be associated with some recurrence of the disease. An interesting recent observation could provide a practical approach to this problem. Approximately one-fourth of patients' close contacts have specific immune lymphocytes against the type of tumor borne by the patient. These healthy individuals may be more appropriate transfer factor donors for cancer treatment. However, after repeated leukapheresis of these subjects, their antitumor immunity disappears and one must wait for several months without removing leukocytes for reappearance of immunity. The susceptibility of these cancer-free contacts to the development of tumors currently remains a theoretical possibility.

C. Immunologic Monitoring of Recipients: If specificity is the required criterion, then the recipients must be examined to determine if they have acquired donor immunity and how long this immunity lasts. Skin tests with tumor antigens remain the most widely used test for this purpose. Other tests such as lymphocyte stimulation, production of lymphokines, and cellular cytotoxicity are also used. The counting of T and B lymphocytes and particularly active T cell rosettes (see Chapter 25) appears to be useful for this evaluation. A decrease in T cells indicates the need for a new injection of transfer factor.

Preparation & Administration

One unit of transfer factor is usually defined as the dialysate of 5×10^8 leukocytes. Transfer factor is prepared from isolated leukocytes of peripheral blood, usually obtained by leukapheresis. The dialysate is checked for pyrogens after lyophilization. Prior to use, it is diluted in 1 ml of saline and injected subcutaneously.

Side-Effects & Complications

The injection of transfer factor is slightly painful and usually associated, for 1 or 2 days, with slight fever and fatigue. There are reports of immune reactions (eg, hemolytic anemia) after transfer factor therapy. This complication occurred in patients in whom such autoimmune phenomena were part of the underlying disease.

A potential cause of reaction to transfer factor arises from the initiation of a vigorous inflammatory response at the site of antigen load (microbes, tumor cells). These reactions can induce pain at the site of the malignant lesion. Potentially dangerous systemic tuberculinlike reactions could occur. No such dramatic complications have yet been reported, and the flare-up reactions can be treated with small doses of corticosteroids.

Current Applications

Transfer factor has received widespread use owing to its ready availability, its apparent safety, and the need for an immunotherapeutic tool which can reliably alter cellular immunity. Unfortunately, studies of its efficacy have usually been uncontrolled, and much further careful clinical investigation with transfer factor is needed.

A. Immunologic Deficiency Diseases:

1. Wiskott-Aldrich syndrome—Transfer factor therapy was first applied in this disease. It has resulted in improvement of the clinical status, including eradication of chronic infections and eczema, as well as amelioration in some instances of the splenomegaly, thrombocytopenia, and bleeding. About half of the patients respond to the therapy. The remissions last about 6 months. Monitoring can be done by skin testing and by determining a reduction in various cell-mediated immune parameters.

2. Severe combined immunodeficiency disease—In a very limited series, some patients have shown clinical and immunologic improvements. This unexpected response is of great interest since it would have been considered impossible on theoretical grounds inasmuch as the defect in severe combined immunodeficiency disease has been considered to be a lack of primordial lymphoid stem cells. These data suggest that at least some patients with this syndrome have normal stem cells.

3. Miscellaneous—Some immunologic and clinical response has been reported in ataxia-telangiectasia and rheumatoid arthritis.

B. Infectious Diseases:

1. Viral infections—Claims of improvement have been made in disseminated vaccinia, measles pneumonia, neonatal herpes, and subacute sclerosing panencephalitis. Confirmation is awaited in all of these diseases.

2. Fungal infections—Clinical improvement especially after reduction of antigenic load, has been reported in disseminated mucocutaneous candidiasis and disseminated coccidioidomycosis.

3. Mycobacterial diseases—One case of miliary tuberculosis has responded clinically to transfer factor. In lepromatous leprosy, skin test conversion has been reported. Clinical trials are under current study.

C. Cancer: The problems of selection of donors have been discussed. It is currently not possible to come to a conclusion about the efficacy of transfer factor in cancer patients since too few patients have been studied.

1. Osteosarcoma—This tumor has been most extensively studied, with encouraging results. Patients treated only with specific transfer factor after surgical removal of their tumor have stayed in remission for more than 2 years even if the disease was already metastatic when treatment was started. This is the only tumor in which both lasting clinical and immunologic improvements have been reported after transfer factor injections.

2. Other tumors—Transfer factor has been given in breast carcinoma, melanoma, alveolar cell carcinoma, and nasopharyngeal carcinoma. (In the latter instance, transfer factor was prepared from healthy young individuals recovering from infectious mononucleosis, a disease that is also thought to be due to the EB virus.) Some temporary tumor regression and conversion of immunologic tests have been reported in these tumors.

• • •

References

Bast RC Jr & others: BCG and cancer. (2 parts.) N Engl J Med 290:1413, 1458, 1974.

Fudenberg HH & others: The therapeutic uses of transfer factor. Hosp Practice 9:95, Jan 1974.

Klein E: Hypersensitivity reactions at tumor sites. Cancer Res 29:2351, 1969.

Levamisole. (Editorial.) Lancet 1:151, 1975.

Levin AS & others: Osteogenic sarcoma: Immunologic parameters before and during immunotherapy with tumor-specific transfer factor. J Clin Invest 55:487, 1975.

Pilch YH, Ramming KP, Deckers PJ: Induction of anti-cancer immunity with RNA. Ann NY Acad Sci 207:409, 1973.

Trainin N: Thymic hormones and the immune response. Physiol Rev 54:272, 1974.

Wara DW & others: Thymosin activity in patients with cellular immunodeficiency. N Engl J Med 292:70, 1975.

Wybran J, Staquet MJ: *Clinical Tumor Immunology*. Pergamon Press, 1976.

Wybran J & others: Rosette-forming cells, immunological disease and transfer factor. N Engl J Med 288:710, 1973.

Appendix

Glossary of Terms Commonly Used in Immunology

Abrin A potent toxin which is derived from the seeds of the jequirity plant and which agglutinates red cells (a lectin).

Absolute catabolic rate The mass of protein catabolized per day, which is determined by multiplying the fractional turnover rate by the volume of the plasma pool.

Accessory cells Lymphoid cells of the monocyte and macrophage lineage which cooperate with T and B lymphocytes in the formation of antibody and in other immune reactions.

Activated lymphocytes Lymphocytes which have been stimulated by specific antigen or nonspecific mitogen.

Activation A process in which the members of the complement sequence are altered enzymatically to become functionally active.

Adenosine deaminase An enzyme which catalyzes the conversion of adenosine to inosine and is deficient in some patients with combined immunodeficiency syndrome.

Adjuvant A compound capable of potentiating an immune response.

Adoptive transfer Transfer of immunity by immunocompetent cells from one animal to another.

Adrenergic receptors Receptors for various adrenergic agents of either the α or the β class which are present on a variety of cells and from which the action of various adrenergic drugs can be predicted.

Agammaglobulinemia See Hypogammaglobulinemia.

Agglutination An antigen-antibody reaction in which a solid or particulate antigen forms a lattice with a soluble antibody. In reverse agglutination, the antibody is attached to a solid particle and is agglutinated by insoluble antigen.

Alexin (also **alexine**) Term coined by Pfeiffer to denote a thermolabile and nonspecific factor which, in concert with sensitizer, causes bacteriolysis.

Allele One of 2 genes controlling a particular characteristic present at a locus.

Allelic exclusion The phenotypic expression of a single allele in cells containing 2 different alleles for that genetic locus.

Allergens Antigens which give rise to allergic sensitization by IgE antibody.

Allergoids Chemically modified allergens which give rise to antibody of the IgG but not IgE class, thereby reducing allergic symptoms.

Allergy An altered state of immune reactivity, usually denoting hypersensitivity.

Allogeneic Denotes the relationship which exists between genetically dissimilar members of the same species.

Allogeneic effect A form of general immunopotentiation in which specific stimulation of T cells results in the release of factors active in the immune response.

Allograft (also called **homograft**) A tissue or organ graft between 2 genetically dissimilar members of the same species.

Allotype The genetically determined antigenic difference on serum proteins, varying in different members of the same species.

Alpha-fetoprotein (AFP) An embryonic α-globulin with immunosuppressive properties which is structurally similar to albumin.

Alternative complement pathway (also known as the **properdin pathway**) The system of activation of the complement pathway through involvement of properdin factor D, properdin factor B, and C3b, finally activating C3 and then progressing as in the classical pathway.

Amboceptor Term coined by Ehrlich to denote a bacteriolytic substance in serum which acts together with complement or alexin, ie, antibody.

Am marker Allotypic determinant on the heavy chain of human IgA.

Anamnesis (also called **immunologic memory**) A heightened responsiveness to the second or subsequent administration of antigen to an immune animal.

Anaphylatoxin A substance produced by complement activation which results in increased vascular permeability through the release of pharmacologically active mediators from mast cells.

Anaphylatoxin inactivator An α-globulin with a molecular weight of 300,000 which destroys the biologic activity of C3a and C5a.

Anaphylaxis A reaction of immediate hypersensitivity present in nearly all vertebrates which results from sensitization of tissue-fixed mast cells by cytotropic antibodies following exposure to antigen.

Anergy The inability to react to a battery of common skin test antigens.

Antibody A protein that is produced as a result of the introduction of an antigen and which has the ability to combine with the antigen that stimulated its production.

Antibody combining site That configuration present on an antibody molecule which links with a corresponding antigenic determinant.

Antibody-dependent cell-mediated cytotoxicity (ADCC) A form of lymphocyte-mediated cytotoxicity in which an effector cell kills an antibody-coated target cell, presumably by recognition of the Fc region of the cell-bound antibody through an Fc receptor present on the effector lymphocyte.

Antigen A substance which can induce a detectable immune response when introduced into an animal.

Antigen-binding site The part of an immunoglobulin which binds antigen.

Antigenic competition Suppression of the immune response to 2 closely related antigens when they are injected simultaneously.

Antigenic determinant (also called **epitope**) That area of an antigen which determines the specificity of the antigen-antibody reaction.

Antigenic modulation The spatial alteration of the arrangement of antigenic sites present on a cell surface brought about by the presence of bound antibody.

Antigen processing The series of events which occurs following antigen administration and antibody production.

Antiglobulin test (Coombs test) A technic for detecting cell-bound immunoglobulin. In the direct Coombs test, red blood cells taken directly from a sensitized individual are agglutinated by antigammaglobulin antibodies. In the indirect Coombs test, a patient's serum is incubated with test red blood cells and the sensitized cells are then agglutinated with an anti-immunoglobulin or with Coombs reagent.

Antilymphocyte serum Antibodies that are directed against lymphocytes and which usually cause immunosuppression.

Antinuclear antibodies (ANA) Antibodies that are directed against nuclear constituents, usually in nucleoprotein, and which are present in various rheumatoid diseases, particularly systemic lupus erythematosus.

Antitoxins Protective antibodies which inactivate soluble toxic protein products of bacteria.

Armed macrophages Macrophages capable of antigen-specific cytotoxicity as a result of cytophilic antibodies or arming factors from T cells.

Arthus phenomenon A local necrotic lesion resulting from a local antigen-antibody reaction and produced by injecting antigen into a previously immunized animal.

Association constant (K value) The mathematical representation of the affinity of binding between antigen and antibody.

Atopy A genetically determined abnormal state of hypersensitivity as distinguished from hypersensitivity responses in normal individuals, which are not genetically determined.

Attenuated Rendered less virulent.

Autoantibody Antibody to self antigens.

Autoantigens Self antigens.

Autograft A tissue graft between genetically identical members of the same species.

Autoimmunity Immunity to self antigens (autoantigens).

Autoradiography A technic for detecting radioactive isotopes in which a tissue section containing radioactivity is overlaid with x-ray or photographic film on which the emissions are recorded.

Bacteriolysin An antibody or other substance capable of lysing bacteria.

Bacteriolysis The disintegration of bacteria induced by antibody and complement in the absence of cells.

Baseline cellular phagocytosis Digestion by phagocytic cells and effector mechanisms which have developed for dealing with potential invading pathogens.

B cell (also known as **B lymphocyte**) Strictly a bursa-derived cell in avian species and, by analogy, bursa-equivalent derived cells in nonavian species. B cells are the precursors of plasma cells that produce antibody.

BCG (bacillus Calmette-Guérin) A viable attenuated strain of *Mycobacterium bovis* which has been obtained by progressive reduction of virulence and which confers immunity to mycobacterial infection and possibly possesses anticancer activity in selected diseases.

Bence Jones proteins Monoclonal light chains present in the urine of patients with paraproteinemic disorders.

Beta-lysin A highly reactive heat-stable cationic protein which is bactericidal for gram-positive organisms.

Biosynthesis The production of molecules by viable cells in culture.

Blocking antibody See Blocking factors.

Blocking factors Substances that are present in the serum of tumor-bearing animals and are capable of blocking the ability of immune lymphocytes to kill tumor cells.

Bradykinin A 9-amino-acid peptide that is split by the enzyme kallikrein from serum α_2-globulin precursor and which causes a slow, sustained contraction of the smooth muscles.

Bursa of Fabricius The hindgut organ located in the cloaca of birds which controls the ontogeny of B lymphocytes.

Capping The movement of cell surface antigens toward one pole of a cell after the antigens are cross-linked by specific antibody.

Carcinoembryonic antigen (CEA) An antigen that is present on fetal endodermal tissue and is reexpressed on the surface of neoplastic cells, particularly in carcinoma of the colon.

Cardiolipin A substance derived from beef heart, probably a component of mitochondrial membranes, which serves as an antigenic substrate for reagin or antitreponemal antibody.

Carrier An immunogenic substance which, when coupled to a hapten, renders the hapten immunogenic.

Cationic proteins Antimicrobial substances present within granules of phagocytic cells.

Cell-mediated immunity Immunity in which the participation of lymphocytes and macrophages is predominant.

Cell-mediated lymphocytolysis An in vitro assay for cellular immunity in which a standard mixed lymphocyte reaction is followed by destruction of target cells which are used to sensitize allogeneic cells during the MLC.

Central lymphoid organs Lymphoid organs that are essential to the development of the immune response, ie, the thymus and the bursa of Fabricius.

CH_{50} unit The quantity or dilution of serum required to lyse 50% of the red blood cells in a standard hemolytic complement assay.

Chemotaxis A process whereby phagocytic cells are attracted to the vicinity of invading pathogens.

Chromatography A variety of technics useful for the separation of proteins.

Classical complement pathway A series of enzyme-substrate and protein-protein interactions which ultimately leads to biologically active complement enzymes. It proceeds sequentially C1, 423 567 89.

Clonal selection theory The theory of antibody synthesis proposed by Burnet which predicts that the individual carries a complement of clones of lymphoid cells which are capable of reacting with all possible antigenic determinants. During fetal life, clones reacted against self antigens are eliminated on contact with antigen.

Clone A group of cells all of which are the progeny of a single cell.

Coelomocyte A wandering ameboid phagocyte found in all animal invertebrates containing a coelom.

Cohn fraction II Primarily γ-globulin which is produced as the result of ethanol fractionation of serum according to the Cohn method.

Cold agglutinins Antibodies which agglutinate bacteria or erythrocytes more efficiently at temperatures below 37 C than at 37 C.

Complement A system of serum proteins which is the primary humoral mediator of antigen-antibody reactions.

Complement fixation A standard serologic assay used for the detection of an antigen-antibody reaction in which complement is fixed as a result of the formation of an immune complex. The subsequent failure of lysis of sensitized red blood cells by complement which has been fixed indicates the degree of antigen-antibody reaction.

Concanavalin A (ConA) A lectin which is derived from the jack bean and which stimulates predominantly T lymphocytes.

Concentration catabolism effect The direct effect exerted by the serum concentration of a plasma protein on its catabolic rate.

Concomitant immunity The ability of a tumor-bearing animal to reject a test inoculum of its tumor at a site different from the primary site of tumor growth.

Congenic (originally called **congenic resistant**) Denotes a line of mice identical or nearly identical with other inbred strains except for the substitution at one histocompatibility locus of a foreign allele introduced by appropriate crosses with a second inbred strain.

Contact sensitivity A type of delayed hypersensitivity reaction in which sensitivity to simple chemical compounds is manifested by skin reactivity.

Coproantibody Antibody present in the lumen of the gastrointestinal tract.

Counterimmunoelectrophoresis See Electroimmunodiffusion.

C-reactive protein (CRP) A β-globulin found in the serum of patients with diverse inflammatory diseases.

C region (constant region) The carboxyl terminal portion of the H or L chain which is identical in immunoglobulin molecules of a given class and subclass apart from genetic polymorphisms.

Cross-reacting antigen A type of tumor antigen present on all tumors induced by the same or a similar carcinogen.

Cross-reaction The reaction of an antibody with an antigen other than the one which induced its formation.

CRST phenomenon Consists of *c*alcinosis, *R*aynaud's phenomenon, *s*clerodactyly, and *t*elangiectasis and occurs in patients with progressive systemic sclerosis.

Cryoglobulin A protein which has the property of forming a precipitate or gel in the cold.

C-terminal The carboxyl terminal end of a protein molecule.

Cytotropic antibodies Antibodies of the IgG and IgE classes which sensitize cells for subsequent anaphylaxis.

Deblocking factor An antibody which, when mixed with blocking factors, neutralizes their activity.

Degranulation A process whereby cytoplasmic granules of phagocytic cells fuse with phagosomes and discharge their contents into the phagolysosome thus formed.

Delayed hypersensitivity A cell-mediated immune reaction which can be elicited by subcutaneous injection of antigen, with a subsequent cellular infiltrate and edema which are maximal between 24 and 48 hours after antigen challenge.

Dextrans Polysaccharides composed of a single sugar.

Diapedesis The outward passage of cells through intact vessel walls.

Direct agglutination Agglutination of red cells, microorganisms, or other substances directly by serum antibody.

Direct immunofluorescence The detection of antigens by fluorescently labeled antibody.

Distribution ratio Fraction of total body protein located in plasma.

Disulfide bonds Chemical S–S bonds between sulfhydryl-containing amino acids which bind together H and L chains as well as portions of H–H and L–L chains.

Domains (also called **homology regions**) Segments of H or L chains that are folded 3-dimensionally and stabilized with disulfide bonds.

Dysgammaglobulinemia Term not in common use which refers to a selective immunoglobulin deficiency.

EAC rosette Formation of a cluster of red cells (*e*rythrocytes) sensitized with *a*mboceptor (*a*ntibody) and *c*omplement around human B lymphocytes.

EAE (experimental allergic encephalomyelitis) An autoimmune disease in which an animal is immunized with homologous or heterologous extracts of whole brain, the basic protein of myelin, or certain polypeptide sequences within the basic protein, emulsified with Freund's complete adjuvant.

ECF-A An acidic peptide, MW 500, which, when released, causes influx of eosinophils.

Effector cells Usually denotes T cells capable of mediating cytotoxicity suppression or helper function.

Electroimmunodiffusion (counterimmunoelectrophoresis) An immunodiffusion technic in which antigen and antibody are driven toward each other in an electrical field and then precipitate.

Electrophoresis Separation of molecules in an electrical field.

Encapsulation A quasi-immunologic phenomenon in which foreign material is walled off within the tissues of invertebrates.

Endocytosis The process whereby material external to a cell is internalized within a particular cell. It consists of pinocytosis and phagocytosis.

Endotoxins Lipopolysaccharides which are derived from the cell walls of gram-negative microorganisms and have toxic and pyrogenic effects when injected in vivo.

Enhancement Improved survival of tumor cells in animals which have been previously immunized to the antigens of a given tumor.

Epitope The simplest form of an antigenic determinant present on a complex antigenic molecule.

Equilibrium dialysis A technic for measuring the strength or affinity with which antibody binds to antigen.

Equivalence A ratio of antigen-antibody concentration where maximal precipitation occurs.

E rosette Formation of a cluster (rosette) of cells consisting of sheep erythrocytes and human T lymphocytes.

Euglobulin A class of globulin proteins which are insoluble in water but soluble in salt solutions.

Exotoxins Diffusible toxins produced by certain gram-positive and gram-negative microorganisms.

Fab Antigen-binding fragment produced by enzymatic digestion of an IgG molecule with papain.

$F(ab')_2$ Fragment obtained by pepsin digestion of immunoglobulin molecules containing the 2 H and 2 L chains linked by disulfide bonds. It contains antigen-binding activity. An $F(ab')_2$ fragment and an Fc fragment comprise an entire monomeric immunoglobulin molecule.

Fc fragment Crystallizable fragment obtained by papain digestion of IgG molecules. Fc fragment consists of the C-terminal half of 2 H chains linked by disulfide bonds. Contains no antigen-binding capability but determines important biologic characteristics of the intact molecule.

Fc receptor A receptor present on various subclasses of lymphocytes for the Fc fragment of immunoglobulins.

Felton phenomenon Immunologic unresponsiveness or tolerance induced in mice by the injection of large quantities of pneumococcal polysaccharide.

Fetal antigen A type of tumor-associated antigen that is normally present on embryonic but not adult tissues and which is reexpressed during the neoplastic process.

F_1 generation The first generation of offspring after a designated mating.

F_2 generation The second generation of offspring after a designated mating.

Fluorescence The emission of light of one color while a substance is irradiated with a light of a different color.

Forbidden clone theory The theory proposed to explain autoimmunity which postulates that lymphocytes capable of self-sensitization and effector function are present in tolerant animals, since they were not eliminated during embryogenesis.

Four locus (4 locus) The second human histocompatibility locus to be described, now called locus B.

Fractional turnover rate Percentage of plasma pool catabolized and cleared into the urine per day.

Francis skin test An immediate hypersensitivity test for the presence of antibody on pneumococci in which pneumococcal capsular polysaccharide is injected into the skin and produces a wheal-and-flare response.

Freund's complete adjuvant An oil-water emulsion which contains killed mycobacteria and enhances immune responses when mixed in an emulsion with antigen.

Freund's incomplete adjuvant Contains all of the elements of Freund's complete adjuvant with the exception of killed mycobacteria.

Gamma globulins Serum proteins with gamma mobility in electrophoresis which comprise the majority of immunoglobulins and antibodies.

Gammopathy Paraprotein disorder involving abnormalities of immunoglobulins.

Generalized anaphylaxis A shocklike state that occurs within minutes following an appropriate antigen-antibody reaction resulting from the systemic release of vasoactive amines.

Genetic switch hypothesis A hypothesis which postulates that there is a switch in the gene controlling heavy chain synthesis in plasma cells during the development of an immune response.

Genetic theory of antibody synthesis Predicts that information for synthesis of all types of antibody exists in the genome and that specific receptors are preformed on immunocompetent cells.

Germinal centers A collection of metabolically active lymphoblasts, macrophages, and plasma cells which appears within the primary follicle of lymphoid tissues following antigenic stimulation.

Gm marker Allotypic determinant on the heavy chain of human IgG.

Graft-versus-host (GVH) reaction The clinical and pathologic sequelae of the reactions of immunocompetent cells in a graft against the cells of the histoincompatible and immunodeficient recipient.

H-2 locus The major genetic histocompatibility region in the mouse.

Halogenation A combination of a halogen molecule with a microbial cell wall which results in microbial damage.

Haplotype That portion of the phenotype determined by closely linked genes of a single chromosome.

Hapten A substance which is not immunogenic but can react with an antibody of appropriate specificity.

Hassall's corpuscles (also called **Leber's corpuscles** or **thymic corpuscles**) Whorls of thymic epithelial cells whose function is unknown.

HB_cAg (also known as **core antigen**) The 27 nm core of hepatitis B virus which has been identified in the nuclei of hepatocytes.

HB_sAg The coat or envelope of hepatitis B virus.

H chain (heavy chain) One pair of identical polypeptide chains making up an immunoglobulin molecule. The heavy chain contains approximately twice the number of amino acids and is twice the molecular weight of the light chain.

Heavy chain diseases A heterogeneous group of paraprotein disorders characterized by the presence of monoclonal but incomplete heavy chains without light chains in serum or urine.

Helper T cells A subtype of T lymphocytes which cooperate with B cells in antibody formation.

Hemagglutination inhibition A technic for detecting small amounts of antigen in which homologous antigen inhibits the agglutination of red cells or other particles coated with antigen by specific antibody.

Hematopoietic system All tissues responsible for production of the cellular elements of peripheral blood. This term usually excludes strictly lymphocytopoietic tissue such as lymph nodes.

Hemolysin Antibody or other substance capable of lysing red blood cells.

Heterocytotropic antibodies Antibody which can passively sensitize tissues of species other than those in which the antibody is present.

Heterologous antigen An antigen which participates in a cross-reaction.

High dose (high zone) tolerance Classical immunologic unresponsiveness produced by repeated injections of large amounts of antigen.

Hinge region The area of the H chains in the C region between the first and second C region domains. It is the site of enzymatic cleavage into $F(ab')_2$ and Fc fragments.

Histamine A bioactive amine of MW 111 which causes smooth muscle contraction of human bronchioles and small blood vessels, increased permeability of capillaries, and increased secretion by nasal and bronchial mucous glands.

Histocompatible Sharing transplantation antigens.

HLA (human leukocyte antigen) The major histocompatibility genetic region in man.

Homocytotropic antibody Antibody which attaches to cells of animals of the same species.

Homologous antigen An antigen which induces an antibody and reacts specifically with it.

Homopolymer Molecule consisting of repeating units of a single amino acid.

Horror autotoxicus Concept introduced by Ehrlich, proposing that an individual is protected against autoimmunity or immunization against self antigens even though these antigens are immunogenic in other animals.

Hot antigen suicide A technic in which an antigen is labeled with high-specific-activity radioisotope (^{131}I). Used either in vivo or in vitro to inhibit specific lymphocyte function by attachment to an antigen-binding lymphocyte, subsequently killing it by radiolysis.

Humoral Pertaining to molecules in solution in a body fluid, particularly antibody and complement.

Hyperacute rejection Accelerated form of graft rejection that is associated with circulating antibody in the serum of the recipient and which can react with donor cells.

Hypervariable regions At least 4 regions of extreme variability which occur throughout the V region of H and L chains and which determine the antibody combining site of an antibody molecule.

Hypogammaglobulinemia Deficiency of all major classes of serum immunoglobulins.

Ia antigens (I region-associated antigens) Antigens which are controlled by Ir genes and are present on various tissues.

Idiotype A unique antigenic determinant present on homogeneous antibody or myeloma protein. The idiotype appears to represent the antigenicity of the antigen-binding site of an antibody and is therefore located in the V region.

IgA Predominant immunoglobulin class present in secretions.

IgD Predominant immunoglobulin class present on human B lymphocytes.

IgE Reaginic antibody involved in immediate hypersensitivity reactions.

IgG Predominant immunoglobulin class present in human serum.

IgM A pentameric immunoglobulin comprising approximately 10% of normal human serum immunoglobulins, with a molecular weight of 900,000 and a sedimentation coefficient of 19S.

7S IgM A monomeric IgM consisting of one monomer of 5 tetrameric subunits.

IgT An immunoglobulin theoretically present on the surface of T cells which serves as an antigen receptor.

Immediate hypersensitivity An unusual immunologic sensitivity to antigens that manifests itself by tissue reactions occurring within minutes after the antigen combines with its appropriate antibody.

Immune adherence An agglutination reaction between a cell bearing $C\overline{423}$ and an indicator cell, usually a human red blood cell, which has a receptor for C3b.

Immune complexes Antigen-antibody complexes.

Immune elimination The enhanced clearance of an injected antigen from the circulation as a result of immunity to that antigen brought about by enhanced phagocytosis of the reticuloendothelial system.

Immune response genes (Ir genes) Genes which control immune responses to specific antigens.

Immune surveillance A theory which holds that the immune system destroys tumor cells, which are constantly arising during the life of the individual.

Immunocytoadherence A technic for identifying immunoglobulin-bearing cells by formation of rosettes consisting of these cells and red cells or other particles containing a homologous antigen.

Immunodominant That part of an antigenic determinant which is dominant in binding with antibody.

Immunoelectrophoresis A technic combining an initial electrophoretic separation of proteins followed by immunodiffusion with resultant precipitation arcs.

Immunofluorescence A histo- or cytochemical technic for the detection and localization of antigens in which specific antibody is conjugated with fluorescent compounds, resulting in a sensitive tracer which can be detected by fluorometric measurements.

Immunogen A substance which, when introduced into an animal, stimulates the immune response. The term immunogen may also denote a substance which is capable of stimulating an immune response, in contrast to a substance which can only combine with antibody, ie, an antigen.

Immunogenicity Property of a substance making it capable of inducing a detectable immune response.

Immunoglobulin A glycoprotein composed of H and L chains which functions as antibody. All antibodies are immunoglobulins, but it is not certain that all immunoglobulins have antibody function.

Immunoglobulin class A subdivision of immunoglobulin molecules based on unique antigenic determinants in the Fc region of the H chains. In man there are 5 classes of immunoglobulins designated IgG, IgA, IgM, IgD, and IgE.

Immunoglobulin subclass A subdivision of the classes of immunoglobulins based on structural and antigenic differences in the H chains. For human IgG there are 4 subclasses: IgG1, IgG2, IgG3, and IgG4.

Immunopotency Capacity of a region of an antigen molecule to serve as an antigenic determinant and thereby induce the formation of specific antibody.

Immunoradiometry A technic of radioimmunoassay which employs radiolabeled antibody rather than antigen.

Indirect immunofluorescence (also known as **double antibody immunofluorescence**) A technic whereby unlabeled antibody is incubated with substrate and then overlaid with fluorescently conjugated anti-immunoglobulin to form a sandwich.

Indirect or passive agglutination The agglutination of particles or red blood cells to which antigens have been coupled chemically.

Information theory of antibody synthesis A theory which predicts that antigen dictates the specific structure of the antibody molecule.

Inoculation The introduction of an antigen or antiserum into an animal in order to confer immunity.

Interferon A heterogeneous group of low-molecular-weight proteins elaborated by infected host cells which protect noninfected cells from viral infection.

Inv marker See Km marker.

I region That portion of the major histocompatibility complex which contains genes that control immune responses.

Ir genes See Immune response genes.

Isoagglutinin An agglutinating antibody capable of agglutinating cells of other individuals of the same species in which it is found.

Isoallotypic determinants Genetic markers which act as allotypic determinants within a specific immunoglobulin subclass and also appear on all members of at least one other subclass of IgG.

Isoantibody An antibody which is capable of reacting with an antigen derived from a member of the same species as that in which it is raised.

Isohemagglutinins Antibodies to major red cell antigens present in members of a given species and directed against antigenic determinants on red cells from other members of the species.

Jarisch-Herxheimer reaction A local or occasionally generalized inflammatory reaction that occurs following treatment of syphilis and other intracellular infections; it is presumably caused by the release of large amounts of antigenic material into the circulation.

J chain A polypeptide chain which is normally found in polymeric immunoglobulins, particularly IgA and IgM.

Kallikrein system See Kinin system.

Kappa (κ) chains One of 2 major types of L chains (qv).

K cell Killer cell responsible for antibody-dependent cell-mediated cytotoxicity (probably identical with null cells).

K and D regions Genetic loci in the major histocompatibility complex of the mouse, coding for H-2 antigens which are detectable serologically.

Kinin A peptide formed by the action of esterases on kallikreins, which then act as vasodilators.

Kinin system (also known as the **kallikrein system**) A humoral amplification system initiated by the activation of coagulation factor XII, eventually leading to the formation of kallikrein, which acts on an α-globulin substrate, kininogen, to form a bradykinin.

Km marker (also called **Inv**) Allotypic marker on the κ L chain of human immunoglobulins.

Kupffer cells Fixed mononuclear phagocytes of the reticuloendothelial system that are present within the sinusoids of the liver.

Kveim test A delayed hypersensitivity test for sarcoidosis in which potent antigenic extracts of sarcoid tissue are injected intradermally and biopsied 6 weeks later in order to observe the presence of a granuloma, indicating a positive test.

Lactoferrin An iron-containing compound which exerts a slight antimicrobial action by binding iron necessary for microbial growth.

LA locus The first human histocompatibility locus to be described, now called locus A.

Lambda (λ) chain One of 2 major types of L chains (qv).

Latex fixation test An agglutination reaction in which latex particles are used to passively adsorb soluble protein and polysaccharide antigens.

LATS (long-acting thyroid stimulator) A γ-globulin that is present in about 45% of patients with hyperthyroidism and that causes delayed uptake of iodine in an animal assay system.

LATS protector An immunoglobulin that is present in the circulation of patients with hyperthyroidism and has the property of blocking the binding of LATS to human thyroid microsomes.

L chain See Light chain.

LE cell phenomenon Phagocytic leukocytes that have engulfed DNA, immunoglobulin, and complement and are present as a large homogeneous mass which is extruded from a damaged lymphocyte in systemic lupus erythematosus and other rheumatoid diseases.

Lectin A substance that is derived from a plant and has panagglutinating activity for red blood cells. Lectins are commonly mitogens as well.

Leukocyte inhibitory factor (LIF) A lymphokine which inhibits the migration of polymorphonuclear leukocytes.

Leukocyte mitogenic factor (LMF) A lymphokine that will induce normal lymphocytes to undergo blast transformation and DNA synthesis.

Levamisole An anthelmintic drug with possible immunostimulatory capabilities.

Light chain (L chain) Polypeptide chain present in all immunoglobulin molecules. Two types exist in most species and are termed kappa (κ) and lambda (λ).

Linkage disequilibrium An unexpected association of linked genes in a population.

Lipopolysaccharide (also called **endotoxin**) A compound derived from a variety of gram-negative enteric bacteria which have various biologic functions including mitogenic activity for B lymphocytes.

Local anaphylaxis An immediate hypersensitivity reaction which occurs in a specific target organ such as the gastrointestinal tract, nasal mucosa, or skin.

Locus The specific site of a gene on a chromosome.

Low dose (low zone) tolerance A transient and incomplete state of tolerance induced with small subimmunogenic doses of soluble antigen.

Lucio phenomenon (erythema necroticans) A variant of erythema nodosum leprosum in which necrotizing vasculitis produces crops of large polygonal lesions characterized by ulceration and sloughing of large areas of skin.

Ly antigens Differentiation antigens present on thymocytes and peripheral T cells.

Lymphocyte A mononuclear cell 7–12 μm in diameter containing a nucleus with densely packed chromatin and a small rim of cytoplasm.

Lymphocyte activation (also known as **lymphocyte stimulation, lymphocyte transformation,** or **blastogenesis**) An in vitro technic in which lymphocytes are stimulated to become metabolically active by antigen or mitogen.

Lymphocyte defined (LD) antigens A series of histocompatibility antigens that are present on the majority of mammalian cells and detectable primarily by reactivity in the mixed lymphocyte reaction (MLR).

Lymphokines (also called **mediators of cellular immunity**) Soluble products of lymphocytes which are responsible for the multiple effects of a cellular immune reaction.

Lymphotoxin (LT) A lymphokine which results in direct cytolysis following its release from stimulated lymphocytes.

Lysosomes Granules that contain hydrolytic enzymes and are present in the cytoplasm of many cells.

Lysozyme (also known as **muramidase**) The cationic low-molecular-weight enzyme present in tears, saliva, and nasal secretions which reduces the local concentration of susceptible bacteria by attacking the mucopeptides of their cell walls.

Macrophage activation factor (MAF) A lymphokine which will activate macrophages to become avid phagocytic cells.

Macrophage chemotactic factor A lymphokine which selectively attracts monocytes or macrophages to the area of its release.

Macrophages Phagocytic mononuclear cells that derive from bone marrow monocytes and subserve accessory roles in cellular immunity.

Major histocompatibility complex (MHC) An as yet undetermined number of genes located in close proximity which determine histocompatibility antigens of members of a species.

Mast cell A tissue cell which resembles a peripheral blood basophil and contains granules with serotonin and histamine present.

Matthews' mamillary models A series of mathematical models which have 3 and 4 compartments and are used to predict the rates of protein metabolism.

β_2 Microglobulin A protein (MW 11,600) that is associated with the outer membrane of many cells, including lymphocytes, and which may function as a structural part of the histocompatibility antigens on cells.

Migration inhibitory factor (MIF) A lymphokine which is capable of inhibiting the migration of macrophages.

Mithridatism (after Mithridates, king of Pontus) Immunity induced against poisons by the administration of gradually increasing doses of the poison.

Mitogens (also called **phytomitogens**) Substances which cause DNA synthesis, blast transformation, and ultimately division of lymphocytes.

Mixed lymphocyte culture (mixed leukocyte culture) (MLC) An in vitro test for cellular immunity in which lymphocytes or leukocytes from genetically dissimilar individuals are mixed and mutually stimulate DNA synthesis.

Mixed lymphocyte reaction (MLR) See Mixed lymphocyte culture.

Monoclonal hypergammaglobulinemia An increase in immunoglobulins produced by a single clone of cells containing one H chain class and one L chain type.

Monoclonal immunoglobulin molecules Identical copies of antibody which consist of one H chain class and one L chain type.

Monoclonal protein A protein produced from the progeny of a single cell called a clone.

Monomer The basic unit of an immunoglobulin molecule which is comprised of 4 polypeptide chains: 2 H and 2 L.

Multiple myeloma A paraproteinemic disorder consisting typically of the presence of serum paraprotein, anemia, and lytic bone lesions.

Myeloma protein Either an intact monoclonal immunoglobulin molecule or a portion of one produced by malignant plasma cells.

Myeloperoxidase An enzyme that is present within granules of phagocytic cells and catalyzes peroxidation of a variety of microorganisms.

Natural antibody Antibody present in the serum in the absence of apparent specific antigenic contact.

NBT test A metabolic assay involving the reduction of nitroblue tetrazolium dye during activation of the hexose monophosphate shunt in phagocytic cells.

Neoantigens Nonself antigens that arise spontaneously on cell surfaces, usually during neoplasia.

Neutrophil microbicidal assay A test for the ability of neutrophils to kill intracellular bacteria.

Nonresponder An animal unable to respond to an antigen, usually because of genetic factors.

N-terminal The amino terminal end of a protein molecule.

Nucleoside phosphorylase An enzyme that catalyzes the conversion of inosine to hypoxanthine and is rarely deficient in patients with immunodeficiency disorders.

Nude mouse A hairless mouse which congenitally lacks a thymus and has a marked deficiency of thymus-derived lymphocytes.

Null cells Cells lacking the specific identifying surface markers for either T or B lymphocytes.

NZB mouse A genetically inbred strain of mice in which autoimmune disease resembling systemic lupus erythematosus develops spontaneously.

Oncogenesis The process of producing neoplasia or malignancy.

Ontogeny The developmental history of an individual organism within a group of animals.

Opsonin A substance capable of enhancing phagocytosis. Antibodies and complement are the 2 main opsonins.

Osteoclast activating factor (OAF) A lymphokine which promotes the resorption of bone.

Ouchterlony double diffusion An immunoprecipitation technic in which antigen and antibody are allowed to diffuse toward each other and form immune complexes in agar.

Paralysis The pseudotolerant condition in which an ongoing immune response is masked by the presence of overwhelming amounts of antigen.

Paraproteinemia A heterogeneous group of diseases characterized by the presence in serum or urine of a monoclonal immunoglobulin.

Passive cutaneous anaphylaxis (PCA) An in vivo passive transfer test for recognizing cytotropic antibody responsible for immediate hypersensitivity reactions.

Peripheral lymphoid organs Lymphoid organs not essential to the ontogeny of immune responses, ie, the spleen, lymph nodes, tonsils, and Peyer's patches.

Peritoneal exudate cells (PEC) Inflammatory cells present in the peritoneum of animals injected with an inflammatory agent.

Peyer's patches Collections of lymphoid tissue in the submucosa of the small intestine which contain lymphocytes, plasma cells, germinal centers, and T cell-dependent areas.

Pfeiffer phenomenon Demonstration that cholera vibrios introduced into the peritoneal cavity of an immune guinea pig lose their mobility and are lysed regardless of the presence of cells.

Phagocytes Cells which are capable of ingesting particulate matter.

Phagocytosis The engulfment of microorganisms or other particles by leukocytes.

Phagolysosome A cellular organelle which is the product of the fusion of a phagosome and a lysosome.

Phagosome A phagocytic vesicle bounded by inverted plasma membrane.

Phylogeny The developmental and evolutionary history of a group of animals.

Phytohemagglutinin (PHA) A lectin which is derived from the red kidney bean *(Phaseolus vulgaris)* and which stimulates predominantly T lymphocytes.

Phytomitogens Glycoproteins that are derived from plants and stimulate DNA synthesis and blast transformation in lymphocytes.

Pinocytosis The ingestion of soluble materials by cells.

Plaque-forming cells Antibody-producing cells capable of forming a hemolytic plaque in the presence of complement and antigenic erythrocytes.

Plasma cells Fully differentiated antibody-synthesizing cells which are derived from B lymphocytes.

Plasma half-life (half time, T½) The time necessary for 50% of a passively infused protein to disappear from serum.

Plasmin A fibrinolytic enzyme capable of proteolytically digesting C1.

Pokeweed mitogen A lectin that is derived from pokeweed *(Phytolacca americana)* and stimulates both B and T lymphocytes.

Polyclonal hypergammaglobulinemia An increase in γ-globulin of various classes containing different H and L chains.

Polyclonal mitogens Mitogens which activate large subpopulations of lymphocytes.

Polyclonal proteins A group of molecules derived from multiple clones of cells.

Polymers Immunoglobulins composed of more than a single basic monomeric unit, eg, an IgA dimer consists of 2 units.

Precipitation A reaction between a soluble antigen and soluble antibody in which a complex lattice of interlocking aggregates forms.

Primary follicles Tightly packed aggregates of lymphocytes found in the cortex of the lymph node or in the white pulp of the spleen after antigenic stimulation. Primary follicles develop into germinal centers.

Private antigen A type of tumor antigen which is expressed on a particular type of chemically induced tumor.

Properdin system A group of proteins involved in resistance to infection. The 2 main constituents consist of factor A and factor B. Properdin factor A is identical with C3, a β-globulin of MW 180,000. Properdin factor B is a β_2-globulin of MW 95,000. It is also called C3 proactivator, glycine-rich β-glycoprotein (GBG), or β_2-glycoprotein II. Properdin factor D is an α-globulin of MW 25,000, also called C3 proactivator convertase or glycine-rich β-glycoproteinase (GBGase).

Prostaglandins A variety of naturally occurring aliphatic acids with various biologic activities, including increased vascular permeability, smooth muscle contraction, bronchial constriction, and alteration in the pain threshold.

Prothymocytes Immature precursors of mature thymocytes which develop within the thymus gland.

Pyogenic microorganisms Microorganisms whose presence in tissues stimulates an outpouring of polymorphonuclear leukocytes.

Pyrogens Substances released either endogenously from leukocytes or administered exogenously, usually from bacteria, and which produce fever in susceptible hosts.

Pyroglobulins Monoclonal immunoglobulins which precipitate irreversibly when heated to 56 C.

Qp_t Percentage of protein-bound plasma activity at time t, compared to plasma activity at time 0.

Quellung The swelling of the capsules of pneumococci when the organisms are exposed to pneumococcal antibodies.

Radioallergosorbent test (RAST) A radioimmunoassay capable of detecting IgE antibody directed at specific allergens.

Radioimmunoassay A variety of immunologic technics in which a radioactive isotope is used to detect antigens or antibodies in some form of immunoassay.

Radioimmunodiffusion (Rowe's method) A modification of immunodiffusion in which a radioactive antibody is incorporated in order to increase the sensitivity by means of autoradiography.

Radioimmunosorbent test (RIST) A solid phase radioimmunoassay which can detect approximately 1 ng of IgE.

Ragocytes (RA cells) Polymorphonuclear leukocytes which have ingested characteristic dense IgG aggregates, rheumatoid factor, complement, and fibrin. Found in the joints of patients with rheumatoid arthritis.

Reagin Synonymous with IgE antibody. Also denotes a complement-fixing antibody which reacts in the Wassermann reaction with cardiolipin.

Recombinant An animal which has experienced a recombinational event during meiosis, consisting of cross-over and recombination of parts of 2 chromosomes.

Rejection response Immune response with both humoral and cellular components directed against transplanted tissue.

Reticuloendothelial system A mononuclear phagocytic system located primarily in the reticular connective tissue framework of the spleen, liver, and lymphoid tissues.

Rheumatoid factor (RF) An anti-immunoglobulin antibody directed against denatured IgG present in the serum of patients with rheumatoid arthritis and other rheumatoid diseases.

Ricin A poisonous substance which derives from the seed of the castor oil plant and agglutinates red blood cells (a lectin).

Rocket electrophoresis (Laurell technic) An electroimmunodiffusion technic in which antigen is electrophoresed into agar containing specific antibody and precipitates in a tapered rocket-shaped pattern. This technic is used for quantitation of antigens.

Rose-Waaler test A type of passive hemagglutination test for the detection of rheumatoid factor which employs tanned red blood cells coated with rabbit 7S IgG antibodies specific for sheep red blood cells.

Schultz-Dale test An in vitro assay for immediate hypersensitivity in which smooth muscle is passively sensitized by cytotropic antibody and contracts after the addition of an antigen.

Second set graft rejection Immunologic rejection of a graft in a host which is immune to antigens contained in that graft.

Secretory IgA A dimer of IgA molecules with a sedimentation coefficient of 11S, linked by J chain and secretory component.

Secretory immune system A distinct immune system that is common to external secretions and consists predominantly of IgA.

Secretory piece (T piece) A molecule of MW 70,000 produced in epithelial cells and associated with secretory immunoglobulins, particularly IgA and IgM.

Sensitizer Term introduced by Pfeiffer to denote a specific thermostable factor capable of bacterial lysis when combined with alexin.

Sequential determinants Determinants whose specificity is dictated by the sequence of subunits within the determinant rather than by the molecular structure of the antigen molecule.

Serologically defined (SD) antigens Antigens that are present on membranes of nearly all mammalian cells and are controlled by genes present in the major histocompatibility complex. They can be easily detected with antibodies.

Serotonin (5-hydroxytryptamine) A catecholamine of MW 176 which is stored in murine mast cells and human platelets and has a pharmacologic role in anaphylaxis in most species except man.

Serum sickness An adverse immunologic response to a foreign antigen, usually a heterologous protein.

Shwartzman phenomenon A nonimmunologic phenomenon which results in tissue damage both at the site of injection and at widespread sites following the second of 2 injections of endotoxin.

Side chain theory Theory of antibody synthesis proposed by Ehrlich in 1896 suggesting that specific side chains which form antigen receptors are present on the surface membranes of antibody-producing cells.

Single radial diffusion (radioimmunodiffusion) A technic for quantitating antigens by immunodiffusion in which antigen is allowed to diffuse radially into agar containing antibody. The resultant precipitation ring reflects the concentration of the antigen.

Skin-reactive factor (SRF) A lymphokine which is responsible for vasodilatation and increased vascular permeability.

Slow virus A virus which produces disease with a greatly delayed onset and protracted course.

Solid phase radioimmunoassay A modification of radioimmunoassay in which antibody is adsorbed onto solid particles or tubes.

Spermine A polyamine present in prostatic secretions which is a pH-dependent inhibitor of gram-positive microorganisms.

Spherulin A spherule-derived antigen from *Coccidioides immitis* used in delayed hypersensitivity skin testing for coccidioidomycosis.

S region The chromosomal region in the H-2 complex containing the gene for a serum β-globulin.

SRS-A An acidic lipoprotein, MW about 400, which has a prolonged constrictive effect on smooth muscle.

Suppressor T cells A subset of T lymphocytes which suppress antibody synthesis by B cells or inhibit other cellular immune reactions by effector T cells.

Surface phagocytosis Enhancement of phagocytosis by entrapment of organisms on surfaces such as leukocytes, fibrin clots, or other tissue surfaces.

S value Svedberg unit. Denotes the sedimentation coefficient of a protein, determined usually by analytic ultracentrifugation.

Syngeneic Denotes the relationship which exists between genetically identical members of the same species.

T antigens Tumor antigens, probably protein products of the viral genome present only on infected neoplastic cells.

T cell or **T lymphocyte** A thymus-derived cell which participates in a variety of cell-mediated immune reactions.

T cell rosette See E rosette.

Theliolymphocytes Small lymphocytes which are found in contiguity with intestinal epithelial cells and whose function is unknown.

Theta antigen An alloantigen present on the surface of most thymocytes and peripheral T lymphocytes.

Thymopoietin (originally termed **thymin**) A protein of MW 7000 that is derived originally from the thymus of animals with autoimmune thymitis and myasthenia gravis and which can impair neuromuscular transmission.

Thymosin A thymic hormone protein of MW 12,000 which can restore T cell immunity in thymectomized animals.

Thymus The central lymphoid organ which is present in the thorax and controls the ontogeny of T lymphocytes.

Thymus-dependent antigen Antigen which depends on T cell interaction with B cells for antibody synthesis, eg, erythrocytes, serum proteins, and hapten-carrier complexes.

Thymus-independent antigen Antigen which can induce an immune response without the apparent participation of T lymphocytes.

TL antigen A membrane antigen that is present on prothymocytes in mice with a TL+ gene, but which is lost during thymic maturation.

Tolerance Traditionally denotes that condition in which responsive cell clones have been eliminated or inactivated by prior contact with antigen, with the result that no immune response occurs on administration of antigen.

Toxoids Antigenic but nontoxic derivatives of toxins.

T piece See Secretory piece.

Transfer factor A dialyzable extract of immune lymphocytes that is capable of transferring cell-mediated immunity in humans and possibly in other animal species.

Transplantation antigens Those antigens which are expressed on the surface of virtually all cells and which induce rejection of tissues transplanted from one individual to a genetically disparate individual.

Tryptic peptides Peptides produced as a result of tryptic digestion of a protein molecule.

Tuftsin A γ-globulin which is capable of stimulating endocytosis by neutrophils.

Ultracentrifugation High-speed centrifugation technic which can be used for the analytic identification of proteins of various sedimentation coefficients or as a preparative technic for separating proteins of different shapes and densities.

Vaccination Immunization with antigens administered for the prevention of infectious diseases (term originally coined to denote immunization against vaccinia or cowpox virus).

V antigens Virally induced antigens which are expressed on viruses and virus-infected cells.

Variolation Inoculation with a virus of unmodified smallpox (variola).

Viscosity Physical property of serum which is determined by the size, shape, and deformability of serum molecules. The hydrostatic state, molecular charge, and temperature sensitivity of proteins.

Von Krogh equation An equation which relates complement to the degree of lysis of red blood cells coated with anti-red blood cell antibodies under standard conditions. Used to determine hemolytic complement titers in serum.

V (variable) region The amino terminal portion of the H or L chain of an immunoglobulin molecule, containing considerable heterogeneity in the amino acid residues compared to the constant region.

Wasting disease (also known as **runt disease**) A chronic, ultimately fatal illness associated with lymphoid atrophy in mice who are neonatally thymectomized.

Xenogeneic Denotes the relationship which exists between members of genetically different species.

Xenograft A tissue or organ graft between members of 2 distinct or different species.

Zone electrophoresis Electrophoresis performed on paper or cellulose acetate in which proteins are separated almost exclusively on the basis of charge.

Acronyms & Abbreviations Commonly Used in Immunology

ACTH adrenocorticotropic hormone
ADA adenosine deaminase
ADCC antibody-dependent cell-mediated cytotoxicity
AFC antibody-forming cells
AFP alpha-fetoprotein
AGN acute glomerulonephritis
AHA autoimmune hemolytic anemia
AHG antihemophilic globulin
AIHA autoimmune hemolytic anemia
ALG antilymphocyte globulin
ALS antilymphocyte serum
AMA antimitochondrial antibodies
AMP adenosine monophosphate
ANA antinuclear antibody
ANF antinuclear factor
APSGN acute poststreptococcal glomerulonephritis
ASO antistreptolysin O
AuAg Australia antigen

BAL dimercaprol (British anti-Lewisite)
Balb/c inbred strain of mice
BCG bacillus Calmette-Guérin
BFP biologic false-positive (tests for syphilis)
BJ Bence Jones
BPO benzyl penicilloyl
BRBC burro red blood cells
BSA bovine serum albumin
BUDR, BUdR 5-bromodeoxyuridine

CAH chronic active hepatitis
cAMP cyclic adenosine monophosphate
CEA carcinoembryonic antigen
CF complement fixation
CGD chronic granulomatous disease
cGMP cyclic guanosine monophosphate
CHS Chédiak-Higashi syndrome
CI cellular immunity
CMC chronic mucocutaneous candidiasis
CMI cell-mediated immunity
CMPGN chronic membranoproliferative glomerulonephritis
C3NeF C3 nephritic factor
CPGN chronic proliferative glomerulonephritis
ConA concanavalin A
CMV cytomegalovirus(es)
C3PA C3 proactivator
CRP C-reactive protein

DDS dapsone (diaminodiphenylsulfone)
DEAE diethylaminoethyl
DIC disseminated intravascular coagulation
DNCB 2,4-dinitrochlorobenzene
D-L Donath-Landsteiner
DLE disseminated lupus erythematosus
DNFB dinitrofluorobenzene
DNP dinitrophenyl
DPO dimethoxyphenylpenicilloyl
DSCG disodium cromoglycate
DT diphtheria and tetanus toxoids (containing a larger amount of diphtheria antigens)
DTH delayed-type hypersensitivity
DTP diphtheria and tetanus toxoid combined with pertussis vaccine

EA erythrocyte amboceptor (sensitized erythrocytes)
EAC erythrocyte amboceptor complement
EAE experimental allergic encephalitis or encephalomyelitis
EB Epstein-Barr
EBV Epstein-Barr virus
ECF eosinophil chemotactic factor
ECF-A eosinophil chemotactic factor of anaphylaxis
EDTA ethylenediaminetetraacetate
ENA extractable nuclear antigen
ER endoplasmic reticulum
ESR erythrocyte sedimentation rate

F_1 first generation
F_2 second generation
FA fluorescent antibody
Fab antigen-binding fragment
Fc crystallizable fragment
FCR fractional catabolic rate
FEV forced expiratory volume in 1 second
FSH follicle-stimulating hormone
FTA-ABS fluorescent treponemal antibody absorption test
FUDR, FUdR fluorodeoxyuridine

GALT gut-associated lymphatic (lymphoid) tissue
GBG glycine-rich beta-glycoprotein
GBM glomerular basement membrane
GFR glomerular filtration rate
GGG glycine-rich gamma-glycoprotein
Gm allotypic marker on human IgG
GMP guanosine monophosphate
GPA guinea pig albumin
GPC gastric parietal cell
G6PD glucose 6-phosphate dehydrogenase
GVH graft-versus-host (disease)
GVHR graft-versus-host reaction

HAA hepatitis-associated antigen
HAE, HANE hereditary angioneurotic edema
HbA adult hemoglobin
HB_cAg hepatitis B core antigen
HbF fetal hemoglobin
HB_sAg hepatitis B surface antigen

This list includes many abbreviations and acronyms that are not used in this book either because they have fallen into disuse or because the editors have felt that the modern tendency toward overuse of acronyms—particularly for disease names (SLE, MS, SCID, etc)—should be resisted. The attempt to make the list an extensive one is intended to assist the reader in using other books and journal articles and the older literature.

HCG human chorionic gonadotropin
HCD heavy chain disease
HDN hemolytic disease of newborn
H&E hemotoxylin and eosin (stain)
HI hemagglutination inhibition
HLA human leukocyte antigen
HMP hexose monophosphate (shunt)
HSA human serum albumin
HSF histamine-sensitizing factor
5-HT 5-hydroxytryptamine (serotonin)

IDU idoxuridine
IEP immunoelectrophoresis
IF intrinsic factor
IFA indirect fluorescent antibody
ISG immune serum globulin
ITP idiopathic thrombocytopenic purpura
INH isoniazid (isonicotinic acid hydrazide)
Inv allotypic marker on human kappa chain (κm)

JRA juvenile rheumatoid arthritis

K (cells) killer (cells)
KAF bovine conglutinin; conglutinin-activating factor
KLH keyhole limpet hemocyanin

LATS long-acting thyroid stimulator
LCM lymphocytic choriomeningitis
LD lymphocyte defined
LDH lactate dehydrogenase
LE lupus erythematosus
Lf limit flocculation (unit). (1/1000 Lf = 0.0000003 mg.)
LH luteinizing hormone
LIF leukocyte inhibitory factor
LPS lipopolysaccharide
LT lymphotoxin or lymphocytotoxin
LyNeF lytic nephritic factor

MAF macrophage activating (arming) factor
MCA methylcholanthrene
MCF macrophage chemotactic factor
MCGN mesangiocapillary (membranoproliferative) glomerulonephritis
MeBSA methylated bovine serum albumin
MER methanol extraction residue (of phenol-treated BCG)
MF mitogenic factor
MHC major histocompatibility complex
MHD minimum hemolytic dilution or dose
MIF migration inhibitory factor
MLC mixed lymphocyte (leukocyte) culture
MLD minimum lethal dose
MLR mixed lymphocyte (or leukocyte) response or reaction
6-MP mercaptopurine
MPG methyl green pyronin
MPO myeloperoxidase
MS multiple sclerosis
MTX methotrexate
MW molecular weight

NBT nitroblue tetrazolium
NeF nephritic factor
NZB New Zealand black (mice)
NZW New Zealand white (mice or rabbits)

OAF osteoclast activating factor
OPV oral poliovirus
OT old tuberculin

PA pernicious anemia
PAS *p*-aminosalicylic acid; periodic acid - Schiff (reaction)
PBC primary biliary cirrhosis
PBI protein-bound iodine
PCA passive cutaneous anaphylaxis
PCM protein-calorie malnutrition
PEC peritoneal exudate cells
PF/dil permeability factor dilute
PFC plaque-forming cells
PGE prostaglandin E (PGE_1, PGE_2, $PGE_{2\alpha}$)
PGN proliferative glomerulonephritis
PHA phytohemagglutinin
PIE pulmonary infiltration with eosinophilia
PK (P-K) Prausnitz-Küstner (reaction)
PLL poly-L-lysine
PML progressive multifocal leukodystrophy
PMN polymorphonuclear neutrophils
PNH paroxysmal nocturnal hemoglobulinuria
PPD purified protein derivative (tuberculin)
PVP polyvinylpyrrolidone
PWM pokeweed mitogen

RA rheumatoid arthritis
Ragg rheumatoid agglutinin
RAST radioallergosorbent test
RBC red blood count
RE reticuloendothelial
RES reticuloendothelial system
RF rheumatic fever; rheumatoid factor
RIST radioimmunosorbent test
RSV respiratory syncytial virus

SBE subacute bacterial endocarditis
SC secretory component
SCID severe combined immunodeficiency disease
SD serologically defined
SIDS sudden infant death syndrome
SK-SD, SKSD streptokinase-streptodornase
SLE systemic lupus erythematosus
SMA smooth muscle antibody
SMAF specific macrophage arming factor
SNagg serum normal agglutinator
SRBC sheep red blood cells
SRF skin-reactive factor
SRS-A slow-reacting substance of anaphylaxis
SS systemic sclerosis
SSPE subacute sclerosing panencephalitis
STS serologic test for syphilis

TA transplantation antigens
TD thymus-dependent
Td combined tetanus and diphtheria toxoid (adult type)
TF transfer factor
TFd dialyzable transfer factor
TI thymus-independent
TL thymic lymphocyte (antigen)
TPI *Treponema pallidum* immobilization
TSA tumor-specific antigen
TSH thyroid-stimulating hormone
TSTA tumor-specific transplantation antigens

VDRL Venereal Disease Research Laboratory
VIG vaccinia immune globulin

WBC white blood count

ZIG zoster immune globulin

Index

V

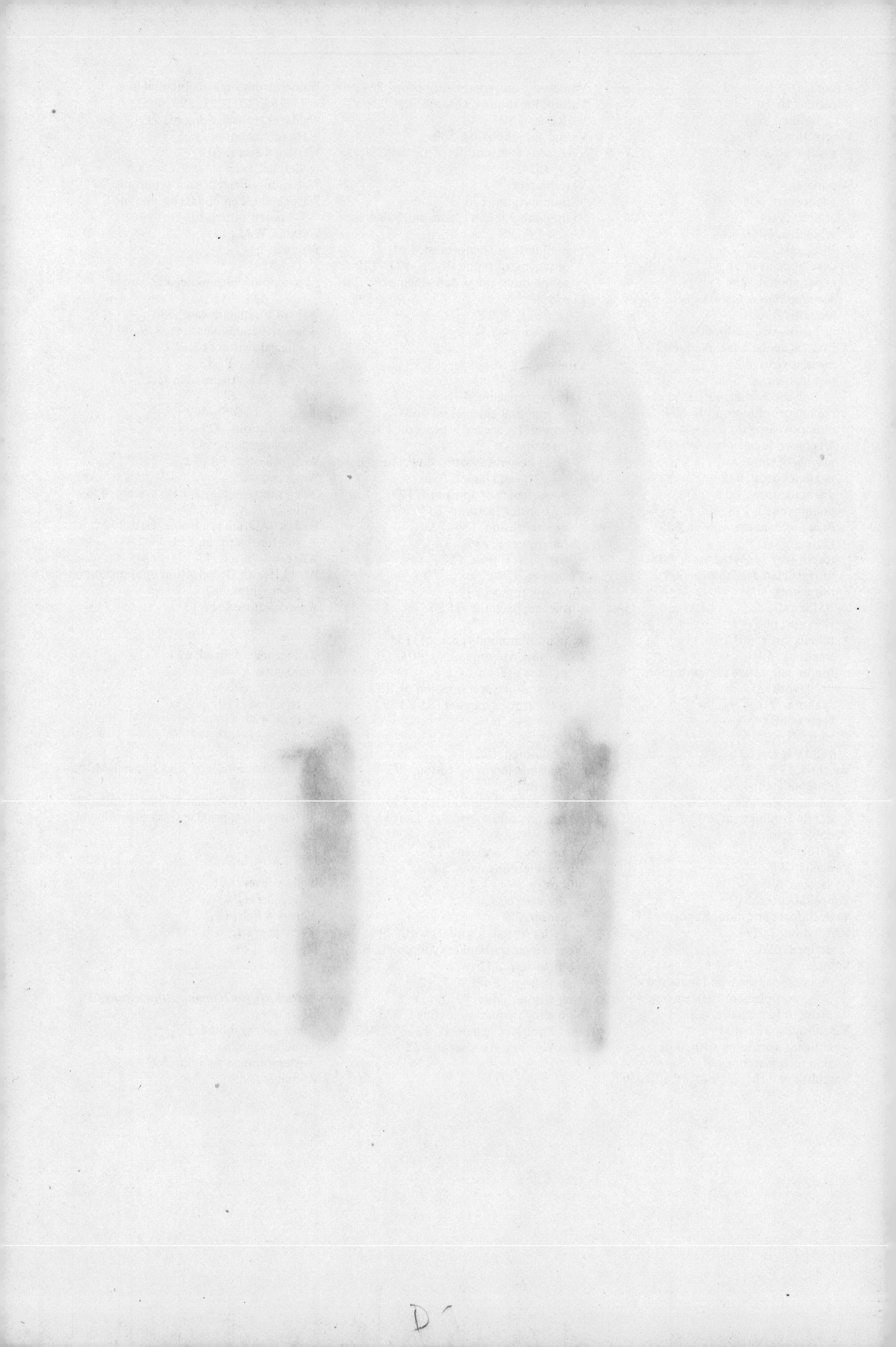